VISION IN MAN AND MACHINE

McGraw-Hill Series in Electrical Engineering

Consulting Editor
Stephen W. Director, Carnegie-Mellon University

Networks and Systems
Communications and Information Theory
Control Theory
Electronics and Electronic Circuits
Power and Energy
Electromagnetics
Computer Engineering
Introductory and Survey
Radio, Television, Radar, and Antennas

Previous Consulting Editors

Ronald M. Bracewell, Colin Cherry, James F. Gibbons, Willis W. Harman, Hubert Heffner, Edward W. Herold, John G. Linvill, Simon Ramo, Ronald A. Rohrer, Anthony E. Siegman, Charles Susskind, Frederick E. Terman, John G. Truxal, Ernst Weber, and John R. Whinnery

Computer Engineering

Consulting Editor
Stephen W. Director, Carnegie-Mellon University

Bell and Newell: *Computer Structures: Readings and Examples*
Garland: *Introduction to Microprocessor System Design*
Gault and Pimmel: *Introduction to Microcomputer-Based Digital Systems*
Givone: *Introduction to Switching Circuit Theory*
Givone and Roesser: *Microprocessors/Microcomputers: An Introduction*
Hamacher, Vranesic, and Zaky: *Computer Organization*
Hayes: *Computer Organization and Architecture*
Kohavi: *Switching and Finite Automata Theory*
Levine: *Vision in Man and Machine*
Peatman: *Design of Digital Systems*
Peatman: *Digital Hardware Design*
Peatman: *Microcomputer Based Design*
Sandige: *Digital Concepts Using Standard Integrated Circuits*
Taub: *Digital Circuits and Microprocessors*
Wiatrowski and House: *Logic Circuits and Microcomputer Systems*

VISION IN MAN AND MACHINE

Martin D. Levine

Professor of Electrical Engineering
McGill University, Montreal

Senior Fellow
The Canadian Institute for Advanced Research

McGraw-Hill Book Company

New York St. Louis San Francisco Auckland Bogotá Hamburg
Johannesburg London Madrid Mexico Montreal New Delhi
Panama Paris São Paulo Singapore Sydney Tokyo Toronto

This book was set in Times Roman.
The editors were Sanjeev Rao and James W. Bradley;
the production supervisor was Marietta Breitwieser.
The cover was designed by Joan E. O'Connor.
The drawings were done by J & R Services, Inc.
Halliday Lithograph Corporation was printer and binder.

VISION IN MAN AND MACHINE

234567890 HALHAL 898765

ISBN 0-07-037446-5

Library of Congress Cataloging in Publication Data

Levine, Martin D., date
Vision in man and machine.

(McGraw-Hill series in electrical engineering. Computer Engineering)
Includes bibliographies and index.
1. Image processing—Digital techniques. I. Title.
II. Series.
TA1632.L48 1985 001.53'4 84-21827
ISBN 0-07-037446-5

This book is dedicated
to Debbie, Jonathan, and Barbara

. . . it is marvellous in our eyes . . .

Psalm 118, Verse 23

CONTENTS

PREFACE

My interest in computer vision began about 1967, being particularly attracted by the possibility of applying these techniques to biomedical imagery. Indeed the first project I worked on involved the automated quantification of human alveolar structure in histological sections. I later spent the 1972–1973 academic year with the Image Analysis Group at the Jet Propulsion Laboratory in Pasadena, California, working on the vision system for a Martian robot. Since then I have been teaching a course on digital picture processing in the Electrical Engineering Department of McGill University in Montreal, Canada. Although this course was at the undergraduate/graduate level, the majority of the students were in fact undergraduates. The two basic prerequisites are introductory courses in computers and linear systems.

The course is the first of a two-stage sequence, in which the initial semester deals with the introductory aspects of the subject and the second follows with the more advanced and research-related topics. One way of characterizing this dichotomization is to say that the first course considers low-level vision while the second concerns itself with high-level vision. In fact, one of the goals of this book is to attempt to delineate these two processes. I suggest that low-level vision essentially deals with the measurement of the attributes of a picture, their organization into a data structure, and possibly some simple aggregative feature descriptions of this data structure. High-level vision is concerned with the interpretation of these data.

Two possible approaches may be taken to using this book as a text in a course on picture processing. The first does not place great emphasis on human and animal vision. It uses this material only for additional reading or project assignments. A typical course might cover the following: Chapter 1; Chapter 2; Sections 5.1, 5.3, 5.4, 5.5; Sections 6.1, 6.4, 6.5, 6.6; Sections 7.1, 7.3, 7.4, 7.5; Sections 8.1, 8.3, 8.4; Chapter 9; Chapter 10. An alternative treatment is to cover Chapters 1 to 7 in detail, and assign reading or projects from Chapters 8, 9, and 10. The Appendix contains an extensive set of both library and computer projects. In addition, throughout the book I have included references and bibliographies to assist both the student and the researcher.

Everyone agrees that the problem of programming a computer to analyze and, what is more, to understand the content of pictures is extremely difficult. My view is that if we are expected to write algorithms to achieve these goals, it is incumbent upon us to know how humans and animals achieve this same function. Therefore one of the major objectives of this book is to show the relevance of biological models to the design of engineering systems. They can give us hints about the trade-offs required and point out potentially interesting technical problems. Obviously the human visual system acts in the role of an "existence proof" by specifying to us at least those problems that we know can be solved. It also indicates the operative constraints, thereby challenging the designer of computer systems to overcome them. Recently, there has been a growing tendency for scientists who work with computer and human visual systems to read and study each other's literature. In my opinion, this interdisciplinary trend warrants encouragement.

The study of "living" visual systems may be considered from the point of view of either neurophysiology or psychology. Neurophysiologists are generally concerned with the behavior of single cells or small groups of cells. Psychologists who are concerned with visual perception generally treat visual processing as if it were achieved by the proverbial engineering "black box." By this is meant that the "hardware" details of the response of a human or animal to visual inputs is generally not of great concern. Perhaps this is not always the case, but we do realize that realistically it is very difficult for us to provide a linkage between a given perceptual event and its neurophysiological correlate.

If we agree that the computer scientist or engineer who will write programs for computer vision should be aware of the current research and results in these two fields, we may then ask which material should one emphasize. Throughout the period I have been teaching this course I have naturally selected certain subjects and details which I thought were both interesting and relevant. During the 1979–1980 academic year I had the opportunity to go on sabbatical at the Computer Science Department of the Hebrew University in Jerusalem, Israel. I took the time to reread some of the literature and also to rethink my ideas about what material was or was not important. One thing is absolutely clear—the amount of literature on the subject in both these areas is overwhelming! I have therefore decided to consider the complete process of computer vision in the biological sense from the point of view of systems modeling. That is, suppose for example that the human visual system were a hardware or computer system made up of elemental electronic components. Also suppose that I were able to make "input-output" measurements on this system. The obvious analogy to neurophysiological experimentation with cells and the psychophysical experimental paradigm can be seen. Then in order for the material to be considered for inclusion in this book, there should exist what I have called "correlative models" in the two fields. Thus I expect that since the psychophysical measurement is in the final analysis the result of the behavior of networks of cells, I should be able to corroborate the activity of the former by measurements related to the latter. How difficult this is to accomplish will immediately become evident to the reader if one contemplates pursuing this same type of analysis with the original computer analogy. Where such models exist, my task has been easy or relatively easy. This approach provides a very broad filter, which tends to exclude a large percentage of the literature in both fields. However, I have not been able to maintain such an uncompromising attitude throughout. In certain cases I have selected material which I thought had the best probability of being corroborated in one field by the other.

Readers may find it presumptuous on my part to be writing about psychology and neurophysiology, two subject areas in which I am admittedly a neophyte. I beg their forgiveness. My only excuse is that this book is primarily intended for computer scientists and engineers and is meant to provide them with some introductory background material about the biological process of vision. These individuals understand and love block diagrams, and I have therefore tried to present the subject using such a systems approach. This is generally not the conventional method of presentation found in most psychology and neurophysiology sources.

Throughout the book I have attempted to maintain a parallelism between vision in man and machine. This is not to suggest that the mechanisms in both cases are similar. I have generally left it to the readers to reach their own conclusions about the similarities and differences since usually these are quite obvious. Given the two primary themes, the book may be conceptually divided into three major parts. The first one involves transforming a given scene or image into a representation internal to the biological or computer system. The second is concerned with measuring the features of this stimulus input. In particular I discuss the attributes of edge content and color. The third section, the most hypothetical in nature from the point of view of living systems, deals with the organization and description of the low-level feature data.

In a certain sense the human visual system acts as an upper bound on our ambitions with regard to writing computer algorithms for picture processing. The more I have studied vision by man, the more fascinating both its intricacy and functionality have become to me. Each new scientific discovery which provides a corroborative model is exciting because generally it also seems to make sense from the point of view of information processing by computer. I hope that I have conveyed some of this enthusiasm to the reader.

Many people have assisted me in writing and preparing this book. At the outset I would like to thank George Nagy for introducing me to the subject of picture processing in the late sixties. He was very instrumental in influencing me to change my research orientation from the field of control theory. More recently, my colleague Steve Zucker, who has a zealous interest in animal vision and human perception, has intensified my own concern for the relationship between human and computer vision.

Several students have helped me by writing programs, preparing data and picture output, and carrying out library research. In this regard, I would like to thank Christian De Keresztes, Margaret Dalziel, Andreas Dill, Cem Eskenazi,

Frank Ferrie, Wade Hong, Harold Hubschman, Benjie Kimia, John Lloyd, Gail McCartney, Ahmed Nazif, Samir Shaheen, and Youssry Youssef. Without their assistance this book would not have been possible.

Various versions of the manuscript have been read and criticized, a rather odious task to request of a colleague. Thanks are due Masayoshi Aoki, Jake Aggarwal, Paul Mermelstein, Naftali Minsky, Peter Sander, Dov Rosenfeld, Herbert Freeman, K. S. Fu, R. Rajesy, Azriel Rosenfeld, Arthur Sanderson, and Harry Wechjlek. A special appreciation is also due Peter Sander, who painstakingly obtained the permissions for each of the cited figures and arranged to have them photographed. Apropos of the latter, I would like to thank Rolf Selbach of the Instructional Communications Centre at McGill for taking the many pictures I needed for the figures.

I would also like to acknowledge the aid of Fran Lew, Prema Menon, and Heather Roberts in typing and preparing the manuscript.

Finally, it is my pleasure to give particular credit to Cem Eskenazi and Fran Lew, the former my graduate student and the latter my secretary. Without their intense physical effort, their dedication, and their encouragement I would not have been able to complete the manuscript on schedule. I am truly grateful for their involvement with this book.

Martin D. Levine

VISION IN MAN AND MACHINE

CHAPTER
ONE
INTRODUCTION

1.1 VISION IN MAN AND MACHINE

Man has always had difficulty understanding the role played by his eyes in perceiving the world around him. It was not until the early part of the seventeenth century that Kepler was able to theorize the correct geometric analysis of image formation in the eye. He stated that [7]:

> Vision is brought about by a picture of the thing being formed on the white concave surface of the retina. That which is to the right outside is depicted on the left on the retina, that to the left, on the right, that above, below, and that below, above .... Green is depicted green, and in general things are depicted by whatever color they have.

Realizing that this was not yet the complete story, he nevertheless preferred to set aside the study of what happens next to this picture for the "natural philosophers." Later in the century, however, Descartes suggested that this image was in fact processed further and in an altogether different manner [7]:

> While this picture, in thus passing into our head, always retains some degree of resemblance to the objects from which it proceeds, yet we need not think ... that the picture makes us perceive the objects .... Rather we must hold that the movements that go to form the picture, acting immediately on our soul, in as much as it is united to our body, are so ordained by nature as to give it such sensations.

Thus there appear to be two processes functioning, one providing a representative picture and the other responsible for analyzing it to create our visual perceptions. Is this perhaps a distinction between the eye and the brain? We shall be investigating this important topic in later chapters.

The centrality of vision to human comprehension and understanding has been accepted for a long time. The prophet Isaiah is quoted as saying:

> They know not, neither do they understand; for their eyes are bedaubed, that they cannot see . . . .

Its power and versatility are also appreciated, as vividly stated by Barlow [5]:

> We know that the eye can detect a quantum or two, resolve down to one or two λ/D's, discriminate a few nanometers of wavelength, judge vertical to within a degree, navigate us through a crowded intersection, and tell a Matisse from a Picasso.

Note that Barlow uses the word "eye" when in fact he obviously means the eye-brain system. It would thus appear that different visual tasks involve

Figure 1.1 Chairs. [*From P. A. Kolers, "The Role of Shape and Geometry in Picture Recognition," in B. S. Lipkin and A. Rosenfeld (eds.), "Picture Processing and Psychopictorics," Academic, New York, 1970.*]

different "biological computational processes." For example, in Figure 1.1 the detection of the black areas in the picture would obviously require a different mechanism from the one used for the recognition of the names of the objects. In the second case there is strong evidence that the symbolic interpretation is considerably influenced by learned experience and knowledge [11]. Indeed it would appear that human vision is characterized by a hierarchy of processes. Experiments indicate that the detection of the black areas is most likely a low-level task. Recognition of objects does involve low-level computations, but additional tasks are also invoked.

The goal of scientific exploration is to clarify and characterize the details of this hierarchy. This is done by experimentation, which we hope will then lead to the definition of explanatory models. In this book we are interested in the two categories of perceptual and neurophysiological experiments and how they have influenced the design of computer algorithms for picture processing. The first category, that of psychophysical studies, must necessarily deal mainly—but, curiously, not exclusively—with humans, the second category with animals. Although phylogenetic considerations may be invoked to relate the two, for example monkeys and humans, this does not always prove to be fruitful. Thus the reader should be cautioned that often we are forced to make comparisons of different species in order to bolster our arguments for or against a certain phenomenon.

Uttal [24] has related the anatomical hierarchy of receptor, retina, occipital cortex, and association cortex to a hierarchy of biological computational processes. At the lowest level, the receptor is concerned with signal detection involving intensity, color, and temporal effects. We note that already at this stage the coding is nonlinear. The retinal level involves simple spatial interaction between signals and leads to an enhancement of the edge contours in a picture. The occipital cortex is characterized by pattern-dependent processes and is the first location where some organization of the data on the basis of two-dimensional geometry takes place. With regard to both biological and computer vision, this book deals exclusively with these first three levels; readers are referred to the bibliography at the end of this chapter for material in the computer literature about the highest level, which in the human takes place in the association cortex. According to Uttal [24], it is here that feature encoding, object classification, and finally perception take place. This is apparently the site for symbolic processing and for relation of perceptual experiences to specific physiological phenomena. If we consider the latter as a mechanism for coding signals at the cellular level, our objective is to associate these codes with those describing the perceived sensory experience. For a true association, "we must demonstrate that it is both necessary and sufficient for the concomitant variation of some behavioral (psychophysical) experience" [23]. Our knowledge of these relationships is indeed quite limited.

Although human vision has been a subject of interest and study from time immemorial, digital picture processing has largely evolved in the last 30 years. The first digital pictures were created and transmitted by the Bartlane method only in 1921 [14]. Nearly always, a general-purpose digital computer has been used, although the current revolution in integrated-circuit technology is beginning to make special-purpose machines more attractive. A fascinating example of this is the artificial electronic "human eye" which is being developed as a visual prosthesis [20]. In terms of the ultimate objective of these studies, we may make a simple comparison between man and machine, as given in Figure 1.2. What we are attempting to achieve by means of digital processing of images is at least an equality of result. That is, it is desirable to have the machine perform at a level no worse than that of man on a specific perceptual task. Potentially, the machine could even surpass human perceptual capabilities. The majority of computer scientists make no claim about the pertinence or adequacy of the digital models as embodied by computer algorithms to proper models of perception. Nevertheless, one would be hard put to deny the fact that a number of scientists in the three fields of computer vision, human perception, and the brain sciences do influence each other by their research. The author of this book feels that there clearly is, and should be, a strong relationship among these three.

Only the first two levels in Figure 1.2 are the concern of this book. It turns out that at present it is at the output of these two levels that it is easiest to achieve equality of objective. Most research with computer algorithms has been restricted to this level of difficulty, although a complete understanding of the issues and problems concerned is by no means available. What is generally

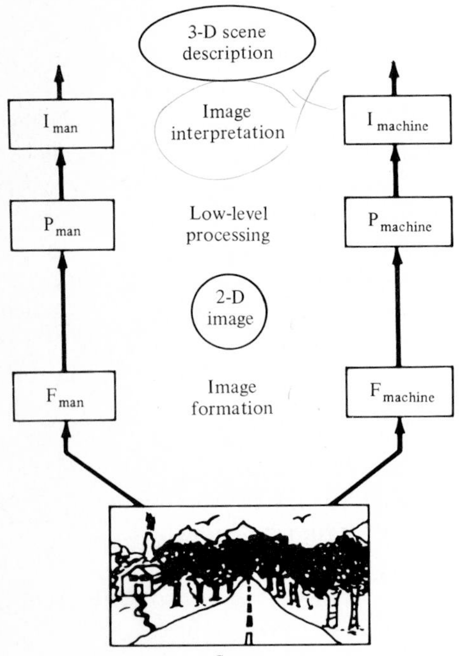

Figure 1.2 A comparison of the objectives of vision processing in man and machine. The ultimate goal of computer vision is to achieve a symbolic interpretation similar to that of man for the same input pattern. On the left side, dealing with biological vision, we really do not know how these conceptual stages map into actual physical configurations.

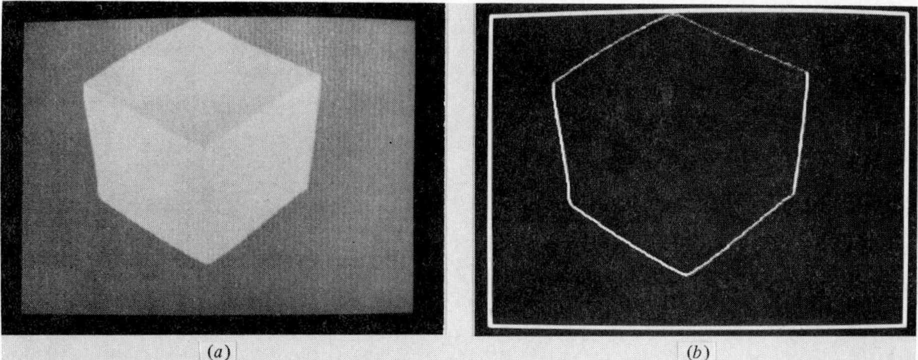

Figure 1.3 The result of processing a picture of a box with a simple edge detector. It is a straightforward task for us to sketch a correct abstraction in terms of a line drawing. However, the computational process, which is sensitive to local light variations, obviously fails. (*a*) Original image. (*b*) Machine-detected edges.

accepted now is the failure of low-level image processing alone to provide the complete basis for complex recognition and description capabilities. For example, edge detectors based on local operators are incapable of giving a complete description of the data [3, 16, 18]. Figure 1.3 clearly demonstrates this issue; we recognize the object as a simple box but observe that a local edge detector does not yield a "clean" line drawing of it. Because of poor contrast and illumination effects, the frontal surface intersection is not detected. However, it can easily be visually recognized in the original image.

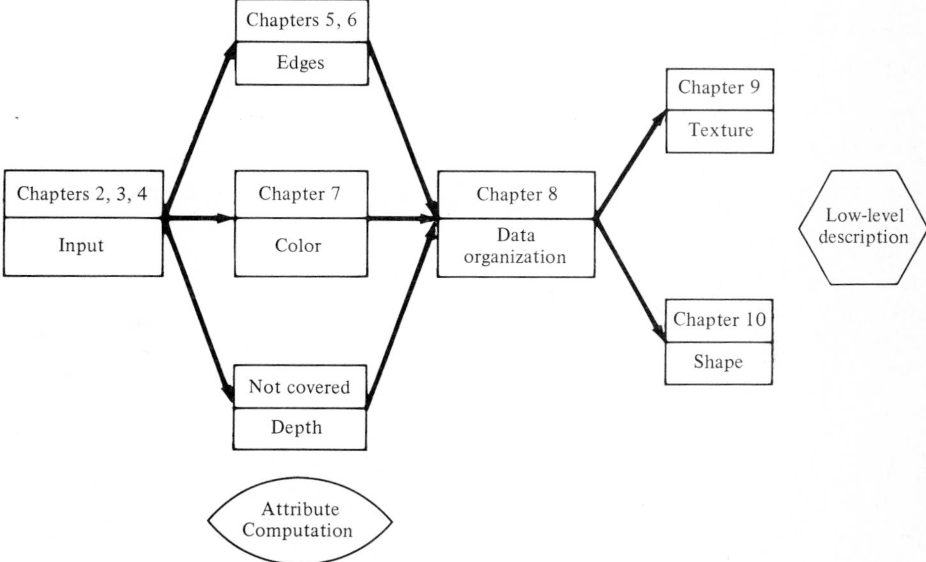

Figure 1.4 Organization of the chapters in the book.

The organization of this book is shown in Figure 1.4 and is correlated with the visual processing hierarchy implied in the previous discussions. After the signal input has been described, the basic attributes related to edge content and color are covered. The issue of depth and three-dimensional description is not discussed. This is followed by Chapter 8, in which the data organization and aggregation of the basic features are presented. Last, we deal with the description of texture (Chapter 9) and shape in two dimensions (Chapter 10). In addition to the basic features, these comprise the output of the two-dimensional low-level processing stage, just before the symbolic processing level.

The primary emphasis of this book is on computer vision. To appreciate the full complexity of this genre of computation, it is incumbent on scientists and engineers to be aware of the analogous biological phenomena. It is for this reason that pertinent psychophysical and neurophysiological studies and results are discussed.

1.2 PSYCHOPHYSICS AND NEUROPHYSIOLOGY

The distinction between psychology and neurophysiology is made by Uttal [23]:

> . . . the objects of attention of psychology are thought, perceptions, sensations, and other aspects of conscious experience.
>
> The objects of concern to . . . (neurophysiology) . . . are the processes that are performed by the specialized tissues and cells of the nervous system.

Scientists have mapped the approximate physical distribution of various sensory and cognitive functions in the brain. A modern estimate of the number of cortical areas is between 50 and 100. Thus we know more or less *where* a given psychophysical event is processed by the cellular structure. The problem is that we do not know *how* it is processed except in certain special cases. It is one of the objectives of this book to isolate those instances in the two realms mentioned where there exists strong evidence for correlative models.

One application of the human models of vision is the design of computer algorithms. Often, however, precise models are not easily obtainable and we must be content with a partial representation. Nevertheless, even if the goal of computer image processing, as we have stated earlier (see Figure 1.2), is only equivalence of result for similar input stimulus, we still remain with a significant problem. The study of computer algorithms for analyzing pictures arose out of the need to be able to automate complex vision tasks such as those found in biomedical imaging, industrial automation, and remote sensing. In most cases the data used are at least as complex as those employed by humans engaged in the same vision function. However, the scientific results emanating from neurophysiology and psychology usually do not address themselves directly to the issues arising out of the analysis of so-called real and natural scenes. In the former, the input stimulus signals generally used are rectangular on-off pulse trains of light, simple periodic sinusoidal variations, or moving versions of these. Such inputs present a very confused picture to anyone wishing to specify a computer model for perception. Here the emphasis is on monochromatic stimuli such as small objects (for example, circles or squares) against a uniform background, lights, characters, and line drawings. Rarely is an actual picture of a real environment, such as, for example, an office scene or suburban street scene, ever employed.

In Section 1.1 we suggested that vision is the result of processing first by the eye and then by the brain. Using these simple input patterns for experimentation has in fact provided us with quite a respectable, although by no means complete, model of the first level. It turns out that the eye may be likened to a photographic camera in many ways [25], but it is much more complicated. For some animals it is also involved in signal processing, albeit of a relatively simple nature. Generally speaking, it is the brain that is responsible for our perceptual and interpretational capabilities, and it is indeed a complex mechanism to study. For example, it is capable of a dual interpretation for the same input stimulus pattern viewed under the same conditions [4]. Figure 1.5 is a striking example of this multistable condition. Some people take the position that until we can explain such phenomena, we will not truly have a proper or adequate model of vision. It might also be creditably argued that more complex experimental inputs will be required to unravel the secrets of human vision and its interaction with the environment (see Figure 1.6).

Let us attempt to clarify the distinction between psychophysical and neurophysiological experiments by considering a hierarchy of conceptual levels, starting from the most general. The research to link the two fields is termed "psychobiology" by Uttal [23]. This is the attempt to isolate and model those situations in which there is an identifiable correspondence between the neural structure and the behavioral function. Figure 1.7 shows the relationship be-

Figure 1.5 An ambiguous figure which can be viewed in two stable states. It may be perceived as either a "mother-in-law" or the left profile of a young woman. It was originally drawn by the cartoonist W. E. Hill and appeared in the November 6, 1915, issue of the magazine *Puck* under the title "My Wife and My Mother-in-law." (*From E. G. Boring, "A New Ambiguous Figure," American Journal of Psychology, vol. 42, 1930, pp. 444–445.*)

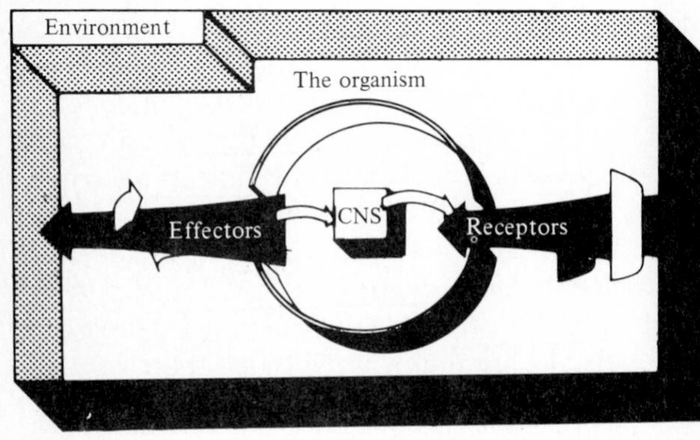

Figure 1.6 The organism in interaction with its environment: receptor responses to environmental energies and feedback signals from the effectors modify activity in the CNS (central nervous system, comprising the brain and the spinal cord), which, among other things, controls the effectors that express the activity of the organism. A considerable amount of knowledge is available concerning the receptors at the input and the output effectors at the output. An example of the sensory system is the eyes. These are ultimately connected to motor neurons which terminate on muscle cells. The intervening cell connections and interactions are less well understood. Thus, much remains to be learned regarding how visual sensory signals are processed. (*From M. A. Arbib, "The Metaphorical Brain," Wiley-Interscience, New York, 1972.*)

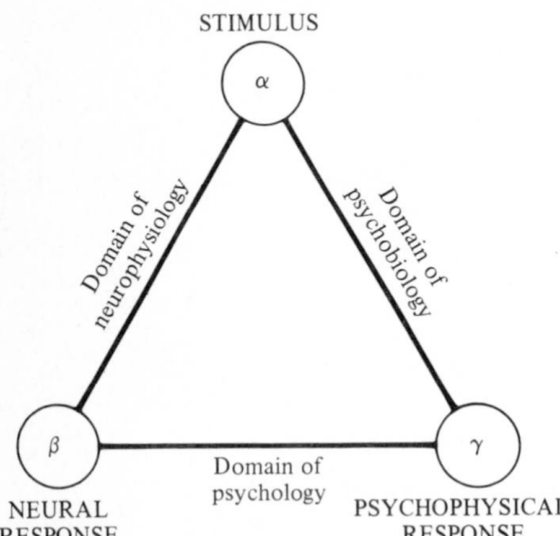

Figure 1.7 Associations between the three concepts of psychophysics, neurophysiology, and psychobiology. (*Adapted from W. R. Uttal, "The Psychobiology of Sensory Coding," Harper & Row, New York, 1973.*)

tween the three concepts and how psychobiology serves as a link between the two more traditional areas of research.

The transformation α-β deals with the coding of input sensory patterns by cells in the eye and brain. This may be conceived as existing at two distinct conceptual levels, as shown in Figure 1.8. The first is the single-cell response, in which a study is made of the behavior patterns of cells when subjected to specific inputs. Most neurophysiology is concerned with this type of analysis,

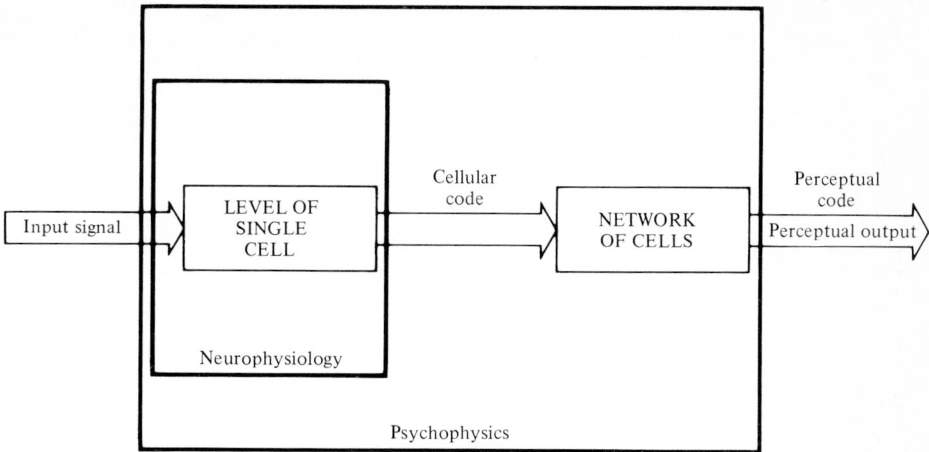

Figure 1.8 Levels of scientific study of the biological visual system.

where actual neural codes are measured. These may include the spatial location, frequency of activation, response amplitude, and so on. We are, of course, cognizant of the fact that the cells function together, especially at the higher levels of analysis, to produce an output. However, at this time it has proved to be extremely difficult to investigate the interaction of these networks of cells. The second conceptual level, the result of such complex processing, is restricted to proposing models solely on the basis of correlations of the input signals with the perceptual output. This is a classical black box experiment, in which the response is usually verbal or a specific motor action, such as the movement of a lever. No direct measurement of the system's characteristics can usually be made. The variables chosen for the study of this transformation α-γ in Figure 1.7 are normally perceived magnitude or color, dynamic relationships, and spatial discriminations.

It is the association β-γ in Figure 1.7 that is of particular interest to anyone wishing to understand the function of the eye-brain system [17]. This link relates the neural mechanisms to the psychophysical variables. We shall also see that "...similar patterns of behavior in a neurophysiological net and a behavioral trait need not necessarily lead us to the conclusion that the two are identical in their underlying neural mechanism ..." [23, p. 229]. For example, if we can observe that certain animals tend to enhance signals at the neurophysiological level in Figure 1.8 and we understand how the cells achieve this, it does not necessarily follow that perceptual enhancement of signals by man are accomplished in the same way.

1.3 COMPUTER VISION

Computer vision largely deals with the analysis of pictures in order to achieve results similar to those obtained by man. A simplified machine paradigm is

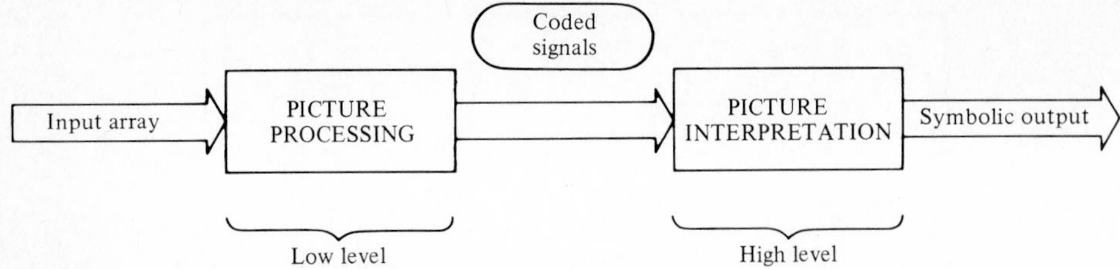

Figure 1.9 A machine paradigm for computer vision which ignores the feedback paths that probably exist from the high levels to the low levels.

shown in Figure 1.9. It consists of two computational stages, which are not analogous to those given in Figure 1.8. The first, which is concerned with low-level techniques, is the subject of this book, and is referred to as "picture processing." The second is termed "picture interpretation" and provides a symbolic output which describes the contents of the array data [12]. A more accurate depiction of Figure 1.9 would probably include a feedback path from the high-level stage to the lower levels. Our knowledge of this interaction, as well as of the high-level stage in particular, is less advanced than that of the low-level processes and in many ways deals with the more difficult and hence more interesting problems. Figure 1.9 may be thought of as a transformation from image array space into another image, or perhaps a decision, abstraction, parameterization, or symbolic description. This we observe to be analysis. The complementary process of synthesis is more commonly referred to as "computer graphics." This is the study of the transformation of abstract descriptions of pictures into image arrays, whether in black and white or in color.

Figure 1.10 is a finer specification of the different levels of analysis. This book deals with levels 0 to 3, the transformation from the scene to a coded version of it. At level 1 are the issues of image sampling, quantization, and coding, that is, how we represent a picture in a machine. Level 2 involves noise removal, restoration, and enhancement and is thus a preprocessing stage. The major emphasis however, is on level 3, the coding of the data in the picture. The features that are considered are edge content, color, texture, and shape. Many more levels are seen in the figure, and it is these that we have assumed to be characteristic of the high level. Level 4 is sometimes referred to as "pattern recognition" and there is a considerable literature on this subject [1, 2]. The reader is cautioned that this processing classification and this terminology are by no means final or universally accepted, especially at levels greater than 3.

There are many applications of picture processing. This is the case even if the techniques used are generally of a complexity related to at most levels up to 3 or 4. The three most active areas are biomedical image processing, remote sensing, and industrial automation. An example of the first is the automatic classification of the white blood cells in cervical smears for the detection and identification of cancer. Another is computerized tomography, in which three-

	LEVEL	DESCRIPTION
	M + 3	3-D scene interpretation
	M + 2	3-D scene description
	M + 1	2-D image description
	6 to M	Higher level aggregation and model matching
	5	Discovery of structural relationships
	4	Feature classification
Picture processing	3	Image segmentation and feature detection
Picture processing	2	Preprocessing and restoration
Picture processing	1	Sensor representation
Picture processing	0	Scene

Figure 1.10 Levels of analysis.

dimensional models of various organs of the body, such as the brain, are built up from a series of two-dimensional sections. Remote sensing is the process by which earth-orbiting satellites or aerial sensors collect information about the spectral reflection from the objects and areas below [6]. These multispectral data may be considered to represent a "picture" not of the visible spectrum but of many important properties of the earth. For example, by using both the Landsat satellite to estimate the wheat acreage and another satellite for meteorological data collection, it is possible to develop a model which will predict wheat yields in each country of the world [15, 27]. The third area might involve quality control or object selection and manipulation. For example, a robotic hand-eye system having a television camera (for the eye) and a computer-controlled mechanical arm working in coordination can be used for object assembly, let us say the construction of automobile water pumps. There are many other applications, such as hand-printed character recognition [21], traffic control, analysis of bubble chamber photographs, high-energy physics and face recognition [19]. The latter is extremely interesting since it brings into play many of the important issues not only in computer vision but in the human variety as well. A recent general discussion of this problem by a layman can be found in [9].

Finally we come full circle to the issue of proposing a computer system as a model of human visual perception. A simple analogy is not justified except in very broad terms. Whenever there seemed to be adequate corroboration for any particular visual phenomenon, such a submodel has been included in the book. However, it appears that it will be a long time before we will have a complete model capable of dealing with the full complexity of human vision, for example, one that can take into account optical illusions and contextual cues. The interaction of the areas of study discussed in this chapter should only tend to hasten the advent of such a model.

1.4 AN EXAMPLE OF COMPUTER IMAGE PROCESSING

A simple but important computation in image processing is the determination of the feature histogram. This is true for the machine and probably for man as well. For example, in this section, we shall employ it as a means of introducing to the reader the potential of computer analysis of pictures. We shall see in later chapters that it plays a very significant role in the segmentation of pictures into regions. It is also a curious phenomenon that histogram analysis does not readily fit into the categorization adopted in this book for biological phenomena, but it is nevertheless a very important technique. The single example of its use in a neurophysiological or psychophysical model is in the still speculative multichannel analyzer formulation of human vision, to be discussed in Section 6.3. However, the "biological computer" does require some type of mechanism for accumulating evidence. As we become more knowledgeable about the human visual system, we might find that the simple and "natural" histogram is how it accomplishes this.

Many typical industrial applications employ computer vision as a basis for decision and control. Such an arrangement may be viewed in terms of a traditional digital control system in which the feedback signal is an image of the scene. An example is an integrated-circuit (IC) chip inspection and assembly station in which picture processing is used to position the chip and to identify defects. Another example is a die-bonding machine which employs vision to isolate the bonding pads. The die-bonder head subsequently establishes a wire conducting path between certain pairs of these pads. A typical industrial application is parts selection using a hand-eye robotic system [8]. The parts to be grasped pass by on a conveyor belt and are viewed by the computer-controlled camera. The computer also directs a mechanical arm and end effector (hand) to grasp the objects after having identified them. Such a system may be used for both parts selection and assembly.

Let us consider the black-and-white image seen by the computer "eye." The sampling and quantification process in these applications results in an array of numbers, each of which represents how gray the image is in the small sampled area. This degree of grayness can vary from white to black as specified by an appropriate intensity value assigned according to, let us say, a linear scale. Consider a hypothetical example in which the camera views an image $I(x, y)$ containing an object of uniform intensity I_o and dimension 5×5 superimposed against a uniform background I_b, as shown in Figure 1.11*a*. The histogram for this array is defined as a plot or bar graph of the number of

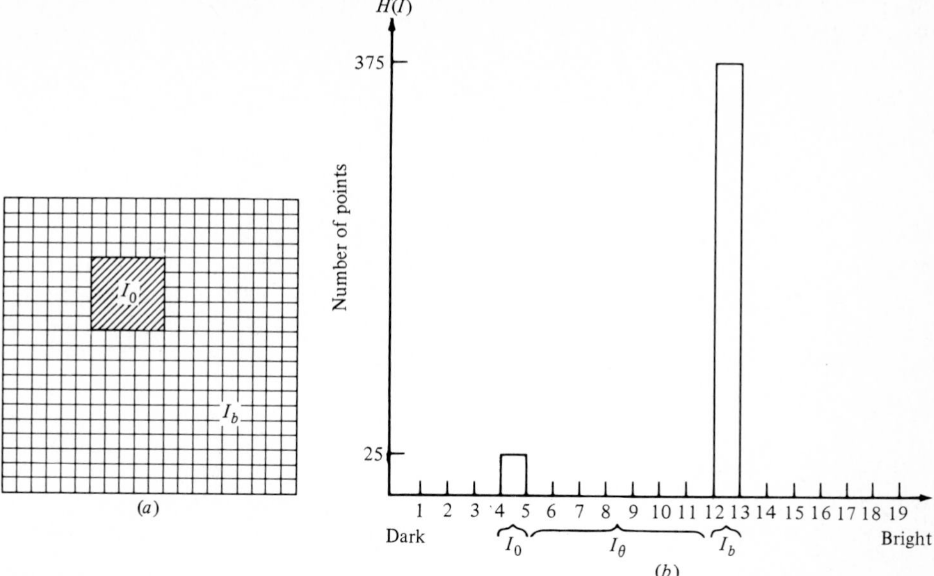

Figure 1.11 Selecting a threshold for a binary image. (*a*) An example of an image $I(x, y)$ containing a uniform object on a uniform background, sampled on a grid of 20×20. (*b*) The histogram for $I(x, y)$.

samples at a given intensity value versus the intensity value. Figure 1.11*b* shows a histogram $H(I)$ of the image in view, which is observed to be characterized by rectangular pulses (approximating impulses in the continuous domain) at intensities I_o and I_b.

We may consider the histogram $H(I)$ to be a probability density function if it is assumed that the elements of the image $I(x, y)$ are randomly selected. Certain kinds of important information are contained in this graph. Suppose that the sampled array size is $M \times N$ and that the intensity variable I can be divided into i levels. Then

$$\sum_{I=1}^{i} H(I) = MN \tag{1.1}$$

or, more generally, the summation of $H(I)$ between any two intensity levels represents the total height of points lying between the two intensity levels. Thus, for the dark object superimposed on the light background, depicted in Figure 1.11

$$\sum_{I=1}^{I_o} H(I) = 25$$

and in fact

$$\sum_{I=1}^{I_\theta} H(I) = 25$$

where $I_o < I_\theta < I_b$. We refer to I_θ as the threshold intensity since it can be used to unambiguously categorize or segment the array into two classes, one the object and the other the background. If we know I_θ, then we may convert any picture $I(x, y)$ to an equivalent binary image array $B(x, y)$ where

$$B(x, y) = 1 \qquad \text{for } I(x, y) \leq I_\theta$$

and

$$B(x, y) = 0 \qquad \text{for } I(x, y) > I_\theta \tag{1.2}$$

This is done for the picture array of Figure 1.11 in Figure 1.12. By writing a simple computer program that scans the array, line by line, until a binary 1 is found and then follows the border between the 1s and 0s until the starting point is reached again, the outline (or contour) of the square object can be obtained. Its area may be computed from the summation

$$\sum_{I=1}^{I_\theta} H(I) = \text{area of object} \tag{1.3}$$

or by counting the number of 1s in any contiguous region. A related property is the so-called integrated optical density (IOD):

$$\text{IOD} = \sum_{I=1}^{I_\theta} IH(I) \tag{1.4}$$

From the outline we may compute the coordinates needed for the arm to grasp the object. The area might be used to compute the weight and force required. Note that in order to maintain continuous feedback as the object moves along the conveyor belt or is carried by the arm, it is necessary to recompute $H(I)$

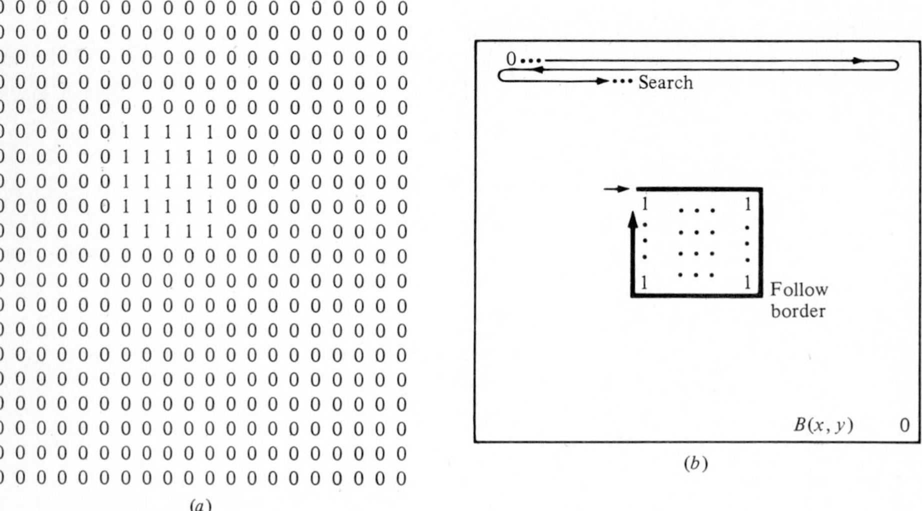

Figure 1.12 Border following. (*a*) The associated binary array $B(x, y)$ for the image $I(x, y)$ after performing a thresholding operation with I_θ.

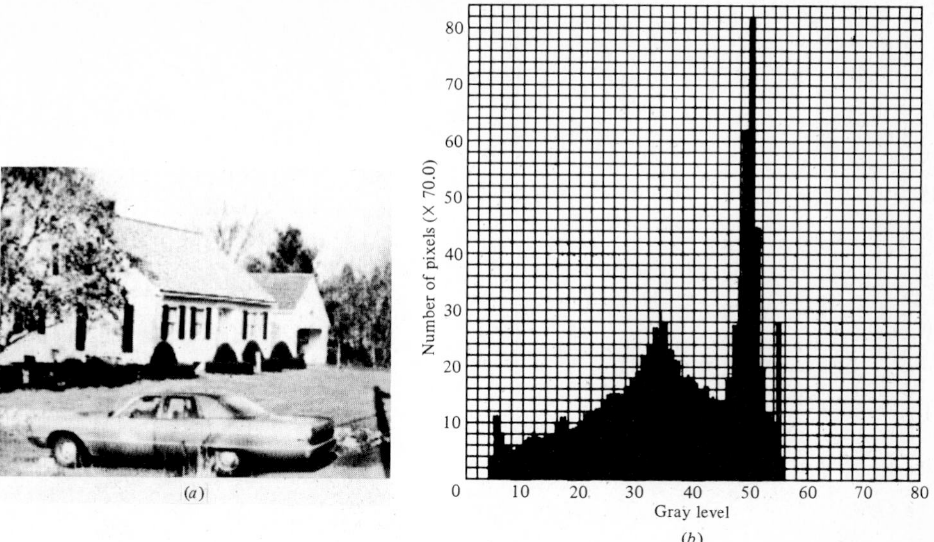

Figure 1.13 A typical outdoor scene and its multimodal histogram. (*a*) Outdoor scene. (*b*) Histogram.

and from this the boundary and area. Another important issue we have purposely ignored is how we come to know I_θ in the first place. This computation is known under the general rubric of "image segmentation," which we will be discussing in detail in Chapter 8.

The histogram of a complex scene such as the one shown in Figure 1.13 is not as simple. In this case we shall see that separating the objects from the background, itself not unambiguously defined, is a difficult task indeed. The problems involved hit at the heart of the theoretical issues we have discussed in this chapter regarding high- and low-level computational processes. Thus, we observe that the situation in Figure 1.11 is a simplified abstraction. For example, Figure 1.14 is a picture of a metal disk lying on a clear background. As in the hand-eye problem, we again have two categories of objects in the image, except that now both the disk and the background exhibit a whole range of intensities instead of being uniform. We observe that the histogram may be modeled as a mixture of two Gaussians, the natural extension of the two rectangular pulse functions shown in Figure 1.11. Segmentation requires that there exist a threshold such that points $I > I_\theta$ belong to one category, $I < I_\theta$ belong to another. Note that the I_θ in this figure, although it may be considered as the optimal segmentation level, cannot clearly separate the points which belong to either Gaussian. I_θ may also be chosen to minimize a suitable information measure of $H(I)$ [13]. Other models for histograms have also been proposed [26].

Instead of computing the global histogram we may also determine it along a particular coordinate direction. Define the horizontal signature (or projection) as

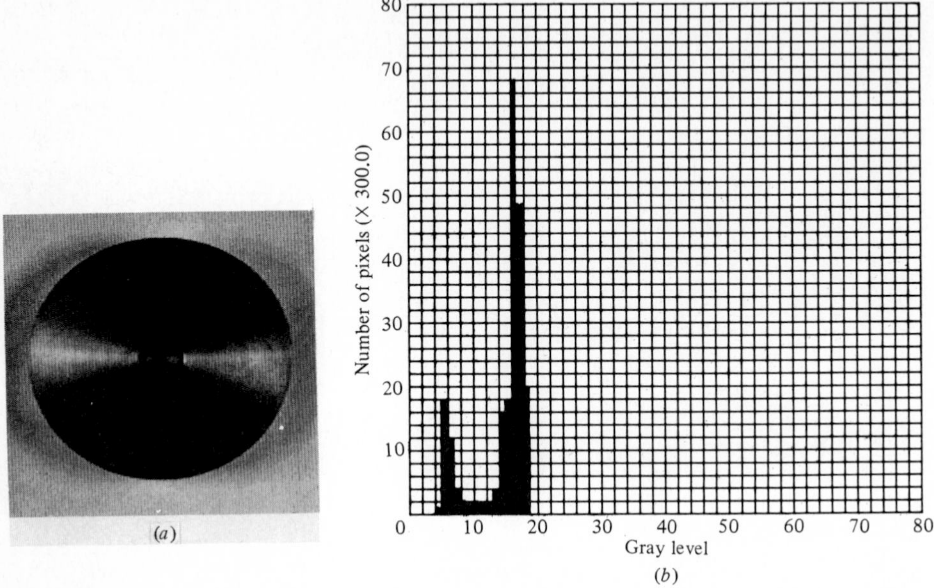

Figure 1.14 A picture of a metal disk lying on a conveyor belt and the associated bimodal histogram. I_θ may be selected as a suitable threshold for creating a binary array. (*a*) Metal disk. (*b*) Histogram.

$$h(x) = \sum_{y=1}^{M} I(x, y) \tag{1.5}$$

and the vertical signature (or projection) as

$$v(y) = \sum_{x=0}^{N} I(x, y) \tag{1.6}$$

Figure 1.15 gives an example of $h(x)$ and $v(y)$ for an industrial part which might be found on the conveyor belt. We observe that significant geometrical

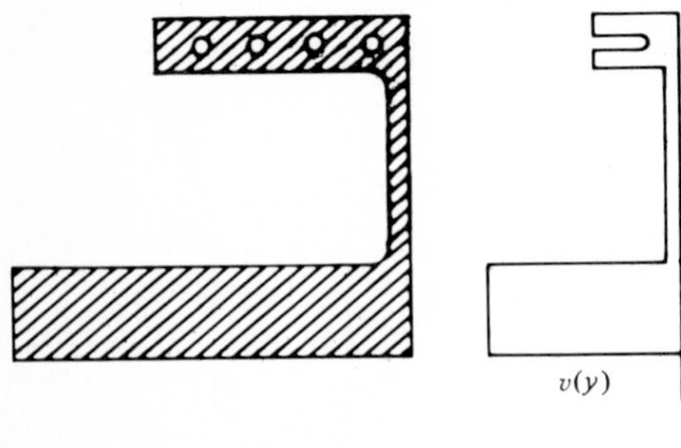

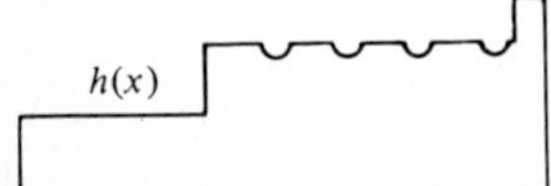

Figure 1.15 The vertical and horizontal signatures for an industrial part. Note that certain shape characteristics are evident from these graphs.

features are indicated by these curves. The computation can also be applied to selective areas of the image. For example, given the image of the disk in Figure 1.14, the peaks of the two signatures provide us with a good indication of the disk's center of gravity. A hardware projection processor for a real-time video tracking system is described in [10]. Projections are used to accurately determine the target position and orientation, as well as to provide features which model the shape of the object.

Curiously, it was once thought that the eight-armed sea creature, the octopus, possessed mechanisms for measuring $h(x)$ and $v(y)$ [22]. Octopus or not, the histogram is an extremely useful function in computer vision—so much so that special IC chips to implement its computation are being developed.

REFERENCES

1. Aggarwal, J. K. (ed.), "Machine Recognition of Patterns," IEEE Press, New York, 1977.
2. Aggarwal, J. K., Duda, R., and Rosenfeld, A. (eds.), "Computer Methods in Image Analysis," IEEE Press, New York, 1977.
3. Albano, A., Representation of Digitized Contours in Terms of Conic Arcs and Straight-Line Segments," *Computer Graphics and Image Processing*, vol. 3, no. 1, March 1974, pp. 23–33.
4. Attneave, F., "Multistability in Perception," *Scientific American*, vol. 225, no. 6, December 1971, pp. 62–71.
5. Barlow, H. B., "Performance, Perception, Dark-Light, and Grain Boxes," *Neurosciences Research Progress Bulletin*, vol. 15, no. 3, 1977, pp. 394–397.
6. Bernstein, R. (ed.), "Digital Image Processing for Remote Sensing," IEEE Press, New York, 1978.
7. Crombie, A. C., "Early Concepts of the Senses and the Mind," *Scientific American*, vol. 210, no. 5, May 1964, pp. 108–124.
8. Dodd, G. G., and Rossol, L. (eds.), "Computer Vision and Sensor-Based Robots," Plenum, New York, 1979.
9. Garfield, E., "I Never Forget a Face!," *Current Contents, Engineering, Technology and Applied Sciences*, vol. 10, no. 7, Feb. 12, 1979, pp. 5–13.
10. Gilbert, A. L., Giles, M. K., Flachs, G. M., Rogers, R. B., and You, Y. H., "A Real-Time Video Tracking System," *IEEE Transactions on Pattern Analysis and Machine Intelligence*, vol. PAMI-2, no. 1, January 1980, pp. 47–56.
11. Gombrich, E. H., "The Visual Image," *Scientific American*, vol. 227, no. 3, September 1972, pp. 82–96.
12. Hanson, A. R., and Riseman, E. M. (eds.), "Computer Vision Systems," Academic, New York, 1978.
13. Johannsen, G., and Bille, J., "A Threshold Selection Method Using Information Measures," *Proceedings 6th International Conference on Pattern Recognition*, Munich, Oct. 19–22, 1982, pp. 140–142.
14. McFarlane, M. D., "Digital Pictures Fifty Years Ago," *Proceedings IEEE*, vol. 60, no. 7, July 1972, pp. 768–770.
15. Misra, P. N., and Wheeler, S. G., "Crop Classification with Landsat Multispectral Scanner Data," *Pattern Recognition*, vol. 10, no. 1, 1978, pp. 1–13.
16. O'Callaghan, J. F., "Computing the Perceptual Boundaries of Dot Patterns," *Computer Graphics and Image Processing*, vol. 3, no. 2, June 1974, pp. 141–162.
17. Poppel, E., Held, R., and Dowling, J. E., "Neuronal Mechanisms in Visual Perception," *Neurosciences Research Progress Bulletin*, vol. 15, no. 3, October 1977, pp. 313–319.

18. Ramer, U., "Extraction of Line Structures from Photographs of Curved Objects," *Computer Graphics and Image Processing*, vol. 4, no. 2, June 1975, pp. 81–103.
19. Rosenfeld, A. (ed.), "Digital Picture Analysis," Topics in Applied Physics, vol. 11, Springer-Verlag, Berlin, 1976.
20. Schackil, A. F., "An Electronic 'Human Eye'," *IEEE Spectrum*, vol. 17, no. 9, September 1980, pp. 89–91.
21. Suen, C. Y., Berthod, M., and Mori, S., "Automatic Recognition of Handprinted Characters—The State of the Art," *Proceedings IEEE*, vol. 68, no. 4, April 1980, pp. 469–487.
22. Sutherland, N. S., "Theories of Shape Description in Octopus," *Nature*, vol. 186, no. 4728, 1960, pp. 840–844.
23. Uttal, W. R., "The Psychobiology of Sensory Coding," Harper & Row, New York, 1973.
24. Uttal, W. R., "An Autocorrelation Theory of Form Detection," Lawrence Erlbaum Associates, Hillsdale, N.J., 1975.
25. Wald, G., "Eye and Camera," *Scientific American*, vol. 183, no. 2, August 1950, pp. 32–41.
26. Wall, R. J., Klinger, A., and Castleman, K. R., "Analysis of Image Histograms," *Proceedings 2d International Joint Conference on Pattern Recognition*, Copenhagen, Aug. 13–15, 1974, pp. 341–344.
27. Wheeler, S. G., and Misra, P. N., "Crop Classification with Landsat Multispectral Scanner Data II," *Pattern Recognition*, vol. 12, no. 4, 1980, pp. 219–228.

BIBLIOGRAPHY

The four main journals that contain material on picture processing are *Computer Vision, Graphics and Image Processing*, *Pattern Recognition*, the *IEEE Transactions on Pattern Analysis and Machine Intelligence*, and *Pattern Recognition Letters*. Other IEEE transactions such as *Systems, Man, and Cybernetics*, *Computers*, *Biomedical Engineering*, *Communications*, and *Information Theory* publish pertinent articles from time to time. The showcase International Conference on Pattern Recognition takes place every second year and results in very lengthy proceedings. The IEEE Computer Society also sponsors several related conferences. In addition, there are many specialized conferences, which are usually not held on a yearly basis but which publish detailed proceedings. A relatively new phenomenon is the local national conference, which also produces a published record.

Le Grand [11] has published an excellent short history on seeing. He even refers to work done in the second century and references documents published in the sixteenth. A good intermediate introduction to the psychology of vision is that by Kaufman [9]. Other more advanced sources are by Cornsweet [1], Gregory [8], Gibson [3, 4, 5], and Dodwell [2]. A thorough review of the visual perception literature, containing over 60 pages of bibliography, has been published by Uttal [25]. The Cognitive Science Series published by Lawrence Erlbaum Associates also addresses current research in this field. Articles on both the psychology and the neurophysiology of vision by prominent researchers in the field often appear in *Scientific American*. These provide an excellent summary and introduction to various aspects of human and animal vision. An excellent introductory book on neurophysiological information processing is that by Stevens [24]. The review article by Gose [6] is an attempt to bridge the two fields of biological and machine picture processing.

A good reference pertaining to image processing by computer is that by Haralick [7]. This indexed paper is a glossary of terms used in the field and provides simple definitions of them. An excellent source of categorized bibliographic material are the yearly reviews published by Rosenfeld [12, 13, 14, 15, 16, 17, 18, 19, 20, 21, 22]. The basic stages in image processing and the current state of the art are presented in [23].

Many books which are relevant to computer picture processing have been published, and a short bibliography is presented below. A bibliography of survey articles is also included.

1. Cornsweet, T. N., "Visual Perception," Academic, New York, 1970.
2. Dodwell, P. C., "Visual Pattern Recognition," Holt, New York, 1970.
3. Gibson, J. J., "The Perception of the Visual World," Houghton-Mifflin, Boston, 1950.
4. Gibson, J. J., "The Senses Considered as Perceptual Systems," Houghton-Mifflin, Boston, 1966.
5. Gibson, J. J., "Principles of Perceptual Learning and Development," Appleton, New York, 1969.
6. Gose, E. E., "Introduction to Biological and Mechanical Pattern Recognition," in Watanabe S. (ed.), "Methodologies of Pattern Recognition," Academic, New York, 1969, pp. 203–252.
7. Haralick, R. M., "Glossary and Index to Remotely Sensed Image Pattern Recognition Concepts," *Pattern Recognition*, vol. 5, no. 4, 1973, pp. 391–403.
8. Gregory, R. L., "Eye and Brain, The Psychology of Seeing," World University Library, McGraw-Hill, New York, 1966.
9. Kaufman, L., "Sight and Mind, An Introduction to Visual Perception," Oxford University Press, Oxford, 1974.
10. Kolers, P. A., "The Role of Shape and Geometry in Picture Recognition," in Lipkin B. S., and Rosenfeld, A. (eds.), "Picture Processing and Psychopictorics," Academic, New York, 1970.
11. Le Grand, Y., "History of Research on Seeing," in Carterette, E. C., and Friedman, M. P. (eds.), "Handbook of Perception," vol. V, "Seeing," Academic, New York, 1975, pp. 3–23.
12. Rosenfeld, A., "Picture Processing by Computer," Computing Surveys, vol. 1, no. 3, 1969, pp. 147–176.
13. Rosenfeld, A., "Picture Processing: 1972," *Computer Graphics and Image Processing*, vol. 1, no. 4, December 1972, pp. 394–416.
14. Rosenfeld, A., "Progress in Picture Processing: 1969–71," *Computing Surveys*, vol. 5, no. 12, 1973, pp. 81–108.
15. Rosenfeld, A., "Picture Processing: 1973," *Computer Graphics and Image Processing*, vol. 3, no. 2, June 1974, pp. 178–194.
16. Rosenfeld, A., "Picture Processing: 1974," *Computer Graphics and Image Processing*, vol. 4, no. 2, June 1975, pp. 133–155.
17. Rosenfeld, A., "Picture Processing: 1975," *Computer Graphics and Image Processing*, vol. 5, no. 2, June 1976, pp. 215–237.
18. Rosenfeld, A., "Picture Processing: 1976," *Computer Graphics and Image Processing*, vol. 6, no. 2, June 1977, pp. 157–183.
19. Rosenfeld, A., "Picture Processing: 1977," *Computer Graphics and Image Processing*, vol. 7, no. 2, June 1978, pp. 211–242.
20. Rosenfeld, A., "Picture Processing: 1978," *Computer Graphics and Image Processing*, vol. 9, no. 4, April 1979, pp. 354–393.
21. Rosenfeld, A., "Picture Processing: 1979," *Computer Graphics and Image Processing*, vol. 13, no. 1, May 1980, pp. 46–79.
22. Rosenfeld, A., "Picture Processing: 1981," *Computer Graphics and Image Processing*, vol. 19, no. 1, May 1982, pp. 35–75.
23. Rosenfeld, A., "Image Analysis: Progress, Problems, and Prospects," *Proceedings 6th International Conference on Pattern Recognition*, Munich, Oct. 19–22, 1982, pp. 7–15.

24. Stevens, C. F., "Neurophysiology: A Primer," Wiley, New York, 1966.
25. Uttal, W. R., "A Taxonomy of Visual Processes," Lawrence Erlbaum Associates, Hillsdale, N.J., 1981.

Books Relevant to Computer Vision

1. Aggarwal, A. K. (ed.), "Machine Recognition of Patterns," IEEE Press, New York, 1977.
2. Aggarwal, J. K., Duda, R., and Rosenfeld, A. (eds.), "Computer Methods in Image Analysis," IEEE Press, New York, 1977.
3. Andrews, H. C., "Computer Techniques in Image Processing," Academic, New York, 1970.
4. Andrews, H. C., "Tutorial and Selected Papers in Digital Image Processing," IEEE Computer Society, Long Beach, Calif., 1978.
5. Andrews, H. C., and Hunt, B. R., "Digital Image Restoration," Prentice-Hall, Englewood Cliffs, N.J., 1977.
6. Ballard, D. H., and Brown, C. M., "Computer Vision," Prentice-Hall, Englewood Cliffs, N.J., 1982.
7. Batchelor, B. G. (ed.), "Pattern Recognition—Ideas in Practice," Plenum, New York, 1978.
8. Bezdek, J. C., "Pattern Recognition With Fuzzy Objective Function Algorithms," Plenum, New York, 1981.
9. Brodatz, P., "Textures," Dover, New York, 1966.
10. Casasent, D. (ed.), "Optical Data Processing, Applications," Springer-Verlag, Berlin, 1978.
11. Castleman, K. R., "Digital Image Processing," Prentice-Hall, Englewood Cliffs, N.J., 1979.
12. Chen, C. H. (ed.), "Pattern Recognition and Artificial Intelligence," Academic, New York, 1976.
13. Chen, C. H. (ed.), "Digital Waveform Processing and Recognition," CRC Press, Boca Raton, Fla., 1982.
14. Cheng, G. C., Ledley, R. S., Pollock, D. K., and Rosenfeld, A. (eds.), "Pictorial Pattern Recognition," Thomson, Washington, 1968.
15. Dainty, J. C., and Shaw, R., "Image Science," Academic, New York, 1974.
16. Devijver, P. A., and Kittler, J., "Pattern Recognition: A Statistical Approach," Prentice-Hall, International, Englewood Cliffs, N.J., 1982.
17. Dodd, G. G., and Rossol, L., "Computer Vision and Sensor-Based Robots," Plenum, New York, 1979.
18. Duda, R. O., and Hart, P. E., "Pattern Classification and Scene Analysis," Wiley, New York, 1973.
19. Duff, M. J. B., and Levialdi, S., "Languages and Architectures for Image Processing," Academic, New York, 1981.
20. Feigenbaum, E. A., and Feldman, J., "Computers and Thought," McGraw-Hill, New York, 1963.
21. Fu, K. S., "Syntactic Methods in Pattern Recognition," Academic, New York, 1974.
22. Fu, K. S. (ed.), "Syntactic Pattern Recognition: Applications," Springer-Verlag, Berlin, New York, 1977.
23. Fu, K. S. (ed.), "Applications of Pattern Recognition," CRC Press, Boca Raton, Fla., 1982.
24. Fu, K. S., and Ichikawa, T. (eds.), "Special Computer Architectures for Pattern Processing," CRC Press, Boca Raton, Fla., 1982.
25. Fukunaga, K., "Introduction to Statistical Pattern Recognition," Academic, New York, 1972.
26. Gonzalez, R. C., and Wintz, P. A., "Digital Image Processing," Addison-Wesley, Reading, Mass., 1977.
27. Goodman, J. W., "Introduction to Fourier-Optics," McGraw-Hill, New York, 1968.
28. Grasselli, A. (ed.), "Automatic Interpretation and Classification of Images," Academic, New York, 1969.
29. Hall, E. L., "Computer Image Processing and Recognition," Academic, New York, 1979.

30. Hanson, A. R., and Riseman, E. M. (eds.), "Computer Vision Systems," Academic, New York, 1978.
31. Hawkes, P. W. (ed.), "Computer Processing of Electron Microscope Images," in Lotsch, H. K. V. (gen. ed.), Topics in Current Physics, vol. 13, Springer-Verlag, Berlin, New York, 1980.
32. Herman, G. T. (ed.), "Image Reconstruction From Projections," Topics in Applied Physics, vol. 32, Springer-Verlag, Berlin, 1979.
33. Höhne, K. H. (ed.), "Digital Image Processing in Medicine," in Linberg, D. A. B., and Reichertz, P. L. (eds.), "Lecture Notes in Medical Informatics," Proceedings, Hamburg, Germany, Springer-Verlag, Berlin, New York, October 1981.
34. Huang, T. S. (ed.), "Picture Processing and Digital Filtering," Springer-Verlag, Berlin, 1975.
35. Huang, T. S., and Tretiak, O. J. (eds.), "Picture Bandwidth Compression," Gordon and Breach, New York, 1972.
36. Kaneff, S. (ed.), "Picture Language Machines," Proceedings of the Conference at the Australian National University, Canberra, Feb. 24–28, 1969, Academic, New York.
37. Klatzky, R. L., "Human Memory Structures and Processes," Freeman, San Francisco, 1975.
38. Klinger, A., Fu, K. S., and Kunii, L. (eds.), "Data Structures, Computer Graphics, and Pattern Recognition," Academic, New York, 1977.
39. Kovalevsky, V. A., "Image Pattern Recognition," Brown, A. (trans.), Springer-Verlag, Berlin, 1980.
40. Lindsay, T. H., and Norman, D. A., "Human Information Processing," Academic, New York, 1972.
41. Lintz, J. Jr., and Simonett, D. S. (eds.), "Remote Sensing of Environment," Addison-Wesley, Reading, Mass., 1976.
42. Lipkin, B. S., and Rosenfeld, A. (eds.), "Picture Processing and Psychopictorics," Academic, New York, 1970.
43. Marr, D., "Vision," Freeman, San Francisco, 1982.
44. Nagao, M., and Matsuyama, T., "A Structural Analysis of Complex Aerial Photographs," Plenum, New York, 1980.
45. Neisser, U., "Cognitive Psychology," Appleton, New York, 1967.
46. Niemann, H., "Pattern Analysis," Springer-Verlag, Berlin, 1981.
47. Nilsson, N. J., "Problem-Solving Methods in Artificial Intelligence," McGraw-Hill, New York, 1971.
48. Nudelman, S., and Patton, D. D. (eds.), "Imaging for Medicine," vol. 1, "Nuclear Medicine, Ultrasonics, and Thermography," Plenum, New York, 1980.
49. Pao, Y. H., and Ernst, G. W., "Tutorial: Context-Directed Pattern Recognition and Machine Intelligence Techniques for Information Processing," IEEE Computer Society Press, Long Beach, Calif., February 1982.
50. Pavlidis, T., "Structural Pattern Recognition," Springer-Verlag, Berlin, 1977.
51. Pavlidis, T., "Algorithms for Graphics and Image Processing," Computer Science Press, Rockville, Md., 1982.
52. Pratt, W. K., "Digital Image Processing," Wiley, New York, 1978.
53. Preston, J. K., Johnson, S. A., and Ayers, W. R. (eds.), "Medical Imaging Techniques, A Comparison," Plenum, New York, 1979.
54. Reed, S. K., "Psychological Processes in Pattern Recognition," Academic, New York, 1973.
55. Rosenfeld, A., "Picture Processing by Computer," Academic, New York, 1969.
56. Rosenfeld, A., "Digital Picture Analysis," Springer-Verlag, Berlin, 1976.
57. Rosenfeld, A., and Kak, A. C., "Digital Picture Processing," 1st ed., Academic, New York, 1976.
58. Rosenfeld, A., and Kak, A. C., "Digital Picture Processing," 2d ed., vols. 1 and 2, Academic, New York, 1982.
59. Serra, J., "Image Analysis and Mathematical Morphology," Academic, London, 1982.
60. Slagle, J. R., "Artificial Intelligence," McGraw-Hill, New York, 1971.
61. Swain, P. H., and Davis, S. M. (eds.), "Remote Sensing: The Quantitative Approach," McGraw-Hill, New York, 1978.

62. Tippelt, J. T. (ed.), "Optical and Electro-Optical Information Processing," MIT Press, Cambridge, Mass., 1965.
63. Tou, J. T., and Gonzalez, R. C., "Pattern Recognition Principles," Addison-Wesley, Reading, Mass., 1974.
64. Winston, P. H., "The Psychology of Computer Vision," McGraw-Hill, New York, 1975.

Survey and Tutorial Articles

1. Anderson, R. H., "An Introduction to Linguistic Pattern Recognition," Rand Corporation Report P-4669, July 1971.
2. Andrews, H. C., "Digital Image Processing," *IEEE Spectrum*, vol. 16, no. 4, April 1979, pp. 38–49.
3. Ball, G. H., "Data Analysis in the Social Sciences: What About the Details?" *Proceedings of* the *Fall Joint Computer Conference*, 1965, Spartan Books, Washington, 1965, pp. 553–559.
4. Barrow, H. G., and Tenenbaum, J. M., "Computational Vision," *Proceedings of the IEEE*, vol. 69, no. 5, May 1981, pp. 572–595.
5. Bartels, P. H., and Weed, G. L., "Computer Analysis and Biomedical Interpretation of Microscopic Image: Current Problems and Future Directions," *Proceedings of the IEEE*, vol. 65, no. 2, February 1977, pp. 252–262.
6. Baumeister, W., "Biological Horizons in Molecular Microscopy," *Cytobiologie*, vol. 17, 1978, pp. 246–297.
7. Billingsley, F. C., "Applications of Digital Image Processing," *Journal of Applied Optics*, vol. 9, no. 2, February 1970, pp. 289–299.
8. Burge, R. E., Dainty, J. C., and Scott, R. F., "Optical and Digital Image Processing in High Resolution Electron Microscopy," *Ultramicroscopy*, vol. 2, 1977, pp. 169–178.
9. Cannon, T. M., and Hunt, B. R., "Image Processing by Computer," *Scientific American*, vol. 245, no. 10, 1981, pp. 214–225.
10. Casasent, D., "Pattern Recognition: A Review," *IEEE Spectrum*, vol. 18, no. 3, March 1981, pp. 28–33.
11. Chin, R. T., "Machine Vision for Discrete Part Handling in Industry: A Survey," *Conference Record, 1982 Workshop on Industrial Applications of Machine Vision*, Research Triangle Park, N.C., May 3–5, 1982, pp. 26–32.
12. Chin, R. T., "Automated Visual Inspection Techniques and Applications: A Bibliography," *Pattern Recognition*, vol. 15, no. 4, 1982, pp. 343–357.
13. Cormack, R. M., "A Review of Classification," *Journal of the Royal Statistical Society*, ser. A (General), vol. 134, no. 3, 1971, pp. 321–367.
14. Davis, L. S., and Rosenfeld, A., "Cooperating Processors for Low-Level Vision: A Survey," *Artificial Intelligence*, vol. 17, no. 1–3, August 1981, pp. 245–263.
15. Duff, M. B., "Pattern Recognition," *Scientific Progress* (*Oxford*), vol. 64, 1977, pp. 423–445.
16. Fu, K. S., and Mui, J. K., "A Survey of Image Segmentation," *Pattern Recognition*, vol. 13, no. 1, 1981, pp. 3–16.
17. Gose, E. E., "Introduction to Biological and Mechanical Pattern Recognition," in Watanabe, S. (ed.), "Methodologies of Pattern Recognition," Academic, New York, 1969, pp. 203–252.
18. Harmon, L. D., "Automatic Recognition of Print and Script," *Proceedings of the IEEE*, vol. 60, no. 10, October 1972, pp. 1165–1176.
19. Harmon, L. D., and Knowlton, K. C., "Picture Processing by Computer," *Science*, vol. 164, no. 3875, April 1969, pp. 19–28.
20. Hartigan, J. A., "Clustering," *Annual Review of Biophysics and Bioengineering*, vol. 2, 1973, pp. 81–101.
21. Hawkes, P. W., "Electron Image Processing: A Survey," *Computer Graphics and Image Processing*, vol. 8, 1978, pp. 406–446.
22. Hawkes, P. W., Electron Image Processing: 1978–1980, *Computer Graphics and Image Processing*, vol. 18, no. 1, January 1982, pp. 58–96.

23. Huang, T. S., Schreiber, W. F., and Tretiak, O. J., "Image Processing," *Proceedings of the IEEE*, vol. 59, no. 11, November 1971, pp. 1586–1609.
24. Jain, R., and Aggarwal, J. K., "Computer Analysis of Scenes with Curved Objects," *Proceedings of the IEEE*, vol. 67, no. 5, May 1979, pp. 805–812.
25. Kanal, L., "Patterns in Pattern Recognition: 1968–1974," *IEEE Transactions on Information Theory*, vol. IT-20, no. 6, November 1974, pp. 697–722.
26. Kazmierczak, H., "Image Processing and Pattern Recognition," *Fourth International Congress of the IFIP*, Edinburgh, Aug. 5–10, 1968, North-Holland, Amsterdam, 1968, pp. 158–173.
27. Kittler, J. "Mathematical Methods of Feature Selection in Pattern Recognition," *International Journal of Man-Machine Studies*, vol. 7, no. 5, 1975, pp. 609–637.
28. Klug, A., "Image Analysis and Reconstruction in the Electron Microscopy of Biological Macromolecules," *Chemical Scripta*, vol. 14, 1978–1979, pp. 245–246.
29. Kübler, O., "Image Processing in Electron Microscopy: Non-periodic Objects," in Schlenker, M., Fink, M., Goedgebuer, J. P., Malgrange, C., Vienot, J. C., and Wade, R. H. (eds.), "Image Processes and Coherence in Physics," Springer-Verlag, Berlin, New York, 1980, pp. 545–554.
30. Kübler, O., "Unified Processing for Periodic and Non-periodic Specimens," *Journal of Microscopy, Spectroscopy, Electronics*, vol. 5, 1980, pp. 565–579.
31. Levine, M. D., "Feature Extraction: A Survey," *Proceedings of the IEEE*, vol. 57, no. 8, August 1969, pp. 1391–1407.
32. Martin, W. N., and Aggarwal, J. K., "Dynamic Scene Analysis: A Survey," *Computer Graphics and Image Processing*, vol. 7, no. 3, 1978, pp. 356–374.
33. Miller, W. F., and Shaw, A. C., "Linguistic Methods in Picture Processing: A Survey," *AFIPS Conference Proceedings, Fall Joint Computer Conference, part* 1, vol. 33, 1968, pp. 279–290.
34. Misell, D. L., "Image Analysis, Enhancement and Interpretation," vol. 7, in Glauert, A. M. (gen. ed.), "Practical Methods in Electron Microscopy," North-Holland, Amsterdam 1978.
35. Mori, K., and Masuda, I., "Advances in Recognition of Chinese Characters," *Proceedings 5th International Conference on Pattern Recognition*, Miami Beach, Dec. 1–4, 1980, pp. 692–702.
36. Montanari, U., "Recent Progress in Picture Processing and Scene Analysis," *2d International Joint Conference on Pattern Recognition*, Lynby-Copenhagen, Aug. 13–15, 1974, IEEE, 1974, pp. 513–516.
37. Nagao, M., "A Survey of Pattern Recognition and Picture Processing," in Latombe, J. C. (ed.), "Artificial Intelligence and Pattern Recognition in Computer Aided Design," North-Holland, Amsterdam, 1978, pp. 35–64.
38. Nagel, H. H., "Image Sequence Analysis: What Can We Learn From Applications?," in Huang, T. S. (ed.), "Image Sequence Analysis," Springer-Verlag, Berlin, 1981.
39. Nagel, H. H., "Recent Advances in Motion Interpretation Based on Image Sequences," *1982 International Conference on Acoustics, Speech and Signal Processing*, Paris, May 3–5, 1982, pp. 1179–1186.
40. Nagy, G., "State of the Art in Pattern Recognition," *Proceedings of the IEEE*, vol. 56, no. 5, May 1968, pp. 836–862.
41. Pavlidis, T., "Algorithms for Graphics and Image Processing," Computer Science Press, Rockville, Md., 1982.
42. Pooch, U. W., "Computer Graphics, Interactive Techniques, and Image Processing, 1970–1975: A Bibliography," *Computer*, vol. 9, no. 8, August 1976, pp. 46–64.
43. Preston, K., Jr., "A Comparison of Analogue and Digital Techniques for Pattern Recognition," *Proceedings of the IEEE*, vol. 60, no. 10, October 1972, pp. 1216–1231.
44. Preston, K., Jr., "Computer Processing of Biomedical Images," *Computer*, vol. 9, no. 5, May 1976, pp. 54–68.
45. Prewitt, J. M. S., "Object Enhancement and Extraction," in Lipkin, B. S., and Rosenfeld, A. (eds.), "Picture Processing and Psychopictorics," *Proceedings of the Symposium on Psychopictorics*, Apr. 14–16, 1969, Arlington, Va., Academic, New York, 1970, pp. 75–149.
46. Riseman, E. M., and Arbib, M. A., "Computational Techniques in the Visual Segmentation of Static Scenes," *Computer Graphics and Image Processing*, vol. 6, no. 2, 1977, pp. 221–276.

47. Rosenfeld, A., "Picture Processing by Computer," *Computing Surveys*, vol. 1, no. 3, September 1969, pp. 147–176.
48. Rosenfeld, A., "Visual Pattern Analysis in Machines and Animals," *Science*, vol. 177, no. 4049, Aug. 18, 1972, pp. 567–575.
49. Saxton, W. O., "Correction of Artefacts in Linear and Non-linear High Resolution Electron Micrographs," *Journal of Microscopy, Spectroscopy, Electronics*, vol. 5, 1980, pp. 665–674.
50. Saxton, W. O., "Digital Processing of Electron Images: A Survey of Motivations and Methods," in Brederoo, P., and Boom, G. (eds.), "Electron Microscopy 1980," *Proceedings of the 7th European Congress on Electron Microscopy, Physics*, vol. 1, Leiden, 1980, pp. 486–493.
51. Shirai, Y., "Recent Advances in 3-D Scene Analysis," *Proceedings of the 4th International Joint Conference on Pattern Recognition*, Kyoto, Japan, Nov. 7–10, 1978, pp. 86–94.
52. Sparkes, J. J., "Pattern Recognition," *Physics in Technology*, vol. 8, no. 5, September 1977, pp. 184–189.
53. Ting, D., and Prasada, B., "Digital Processing Techniques for Encoding of Graphics," Proceedings IEEE, vol. 68, no. 7, July 1980, pp. 757–769.
54. Thomas, A. J., and Binford, T. O., "Information Processing Analysis of Visual Perception, A Review," Stanford Artificial Intelligence Laboratory, MEMO-AIM-227, June 1974.
55. Toussaint, G. T., "Bibliography on Estimation of Misclassification," *IEEE Transactions on Information Theory*, vol. IT-20, no. 4, July 1974, pp. 472–479.
56. Toussaint, G. T., "Recent Progress in Statistical Methods Applied to Pattern Recognition," in "*Proceedings 2d International Joint Conference on Pattern Recognition*, Lynby-Copenhagen, Aug. 13–15, 1974, IEEE, New York, pp. 479–488.
57. Ullman, J. R., "A Review of Optical Pattern Recognition Techniques," *Opto-Electronics*, vol. 6, no. 4, 1974, pp. 319–332.
58. Verhagen, C. J. D. M., Duin, R. P. W., Groen, F. C. A., Joosten, J. C., and Verbek, P. W., "Progress Report on Pattern Recognition," *Report on Progress in Physics*, vol. 43, 1980, pp. 785–831.
59. Yasuda, Y., and Takagi, M., "Bibliography on Digital Facsimile Data Compression in Japan," Multi-dimensional Image Processing Center Report 77-2, Institute of Industrial Science, University of Tokyo, August 1977.
60. Welton, T. A., "A Computational Critique of an Algorithm for Image Enhancement in Bright Field Electron Microscopy," *Advances in Electronics and Electron Physics*, vol. 48, 1979, pp. 37–101.
61. Zucker, S. W., "Region Growing: Childhood and Adolescence," *Computer Graphics and Image Processing*, vol. 5, no. 3, 1976, pp. 382–399.

CHAPTER

TWO

COMPUTER VISION SYSTEMS

2.1 INTRODUCTION

Although the hardware for picture input and analysis is complex, it is a subject usually ignored by most writers, and it will only be treated relatively briefly here. This chapter and the next one deal with picture processing "hardware" in machine and man, respectively. There are many similarities and differences, and they will become evident in Chapter 3 when the anatomy of the human visual system is discussed.

A general block diagram of a computer image-processing system is depicted in Figure 2.1. There are four major components shown: image formation, image input, image computation, and output. Books can be, and have been, written on the subject of how to physically create an image. After all, there are

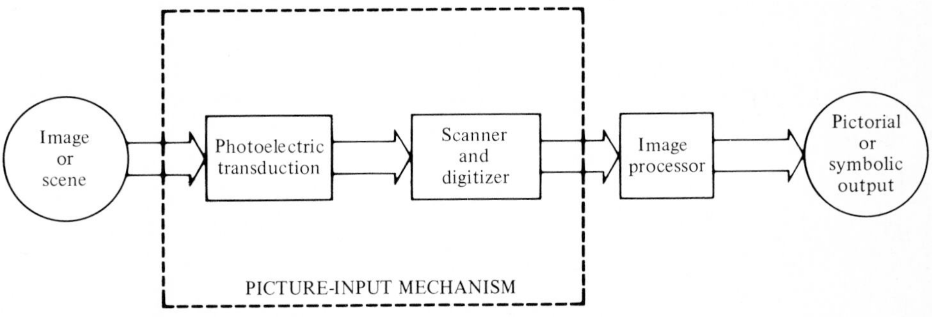

Figure 2.1 A block diagram of a computer vision system.

many different types of input data available, such as photographic transparencies and pictures, video tape, live scenes, microscope images, cine films, multispectral images, histologic slides, among many others. Each of these is indicative of a different science and a characteristic technology, and it is obviously not possible to present a detailed discussion here. We shall therefore only relate certain restrictive, albeit significant, aspects of the process.

Common to all picture inputs, even those for man and animal, are the two considerations of source illumination of the scene and the particular geometric configuration of the objects. The latter will not be covered and readers may consult the references provided on this subject. The former is discussed in Section 2.2.1 and is essentially presented as a sequence of mathematical definitions, which are by now classical. They are rarely given or referred to in the digital picture processing literature, although both psychology and neurophysiology sources usually do provide some indication of their existence. Generally practitioners of these two fields pay much more attention to the sources and characteristics of picture input than do computer scientists dealing with digital pictures.

Section 2.2.2 is concerned with the formation of a picture, still analog in nature but representative of the two major types of input data of interest to date. One is obtained from a real three-dimensional scene containing various objects, perhaps an indoor office scene or an outdoor suburban street scene. Another example of this type of data occurs in real-time automation of industrial processes, where a computer-controlled mechanical arm might be used in conjunction with a television camera in order to achieve visual feedback. All three of these examples might be considered as being characteristic of the so-called robotic vision problem. If indeed we were to construct such a robot, it would necessarily have to deal with a dynamically changing environment, and hence the term "real-time." Readers interested in the computer study of time-varying images should consult the proceedings of the first conference on this subject [1] and the comprehensive review article by Nagel [45]. The industrial robot possessing computer vision is now again a serious subject of study after a relative lull of nearly 10 years (see [38, 65] for recent discussions of the prospects in this area).

The second type of input data currently in use is the two-dimensional photographic slide. We shall discuss how it represents a real three-dimensional scene and how the two are related.

The picture input mechanism in Figure 2.1, which is discussed in Section 2.3, is seen to consist of two consecutive stages. The first involves the transduction of light energy into an electrical signal, while the second is concerned with the scanning and digitization of the still-analog resulting signal. "Scanning" refers to the two-dimensional path of the digital sampling of the image. "Digitization" is the process of converting the analog signal at each sample into a quantized digital signal. There are many such types of systems, and we restrict ourselves to the description and discussion of the two most popular ones, namely, the standard television camera and the mechanical densitometer.

Naturally, the mechanism involved is highly dependent on the system employed.

The term "image processor" refers, of course, to the computer, but from an algorithmic point of view. Section 2.4 briefly discusses the kind of vision algorithms considered to be within the scope of this book and presents a formalism which will be used to describe them. This approach is commonly referred to as "template matching" and is paradigmatic of a class of techniques in which a model of a subimage is passed over the complete image in search of a match. General-purpose processors are now being developed which make such computations very efficient. Further, we shall see later that the process of feature extraction from an image by humans and animals has been found to be performed in this same way.

The fourth stage in Figure 2.1 is the output or result of the computation. For humans this is usually embodied in a verbal response or a physical action. Selection of alternatives is the technique mostly used with animals. A computer processor may respond in two significant ways. One is by the computation and display of another picture on a graphics monitor. In this case, Figure 2.1 may be considered as a transformation from a picture input to a picture output. The second response corresponds to the human verbal mode in that the computer is also capable of providing a symbolic output. Typically both are employed, and it is a long-term goal of computer vision research, especially at the higher analysis levels, to provide the major interaction with the computer vision system in symbolic form. Perhaps it will eventually be possible to train and teach the computer system in the same way that children are trained and taught [22].

2.2 CREATING THE PICTORIAL INFORMATION SOURCE

Before an image is formed and projected onto the face of a sensor, three aspects are of concern. First, of course, are the properties of the three-dimensional scene whose two-dimensional projection is being sought. In this category might be placed such object attributes as spectral reflectivity and emissivity characteristics, physical shape, and topological relationships between the objects. The second aspect concerns the attributes of the source of illumination of the scene, which may be described in terms of both its spatial and spectral features. This illumination impinging on a scene then results in an image which is further influenced by the third aspect, that is, the nature of the projection and the prevailing physical arrangement. In image processing all three aspects are usually present. For example, in industrial hand-eye robotic systems with visual feedback, the sensor observes the scene directly. In other situations, the intermediate stage of creating a photographic transparency of the scene is involved, so that in effect this illuminated two-dimensional image now becomes the scene. Psychophysical and neurophysiological experiments, however, often combine the scene and the illumination into one by using uniformly lit surfaces or lights as input. We see that in either of these two cases it is important to be able to characterize the illumination. This physical measurement of light is referred to as "radiometry" and is defined in Section 2.2.1. How the image is formed, both when a transparency is used and when it is viewed directly, is discussed in Section 2.2.2.

Thus, Section 2.2 is concerned with the data path up to the point at which the image impinges on the electromagnetic energy conversion mechanism.

2.2.1 Radiant Sources

Biological retinal photoreceptors and hardware image sensors are both sensitive to light, a narrow band of electromagnetic radiation which travels at the speed c in a vacuum, where $c = 2.9979246 \times 10^8$ m/s. The frequency and wavelength of this radiation input are governed by the relationship

$$\lambda = \frac{c}{f} \tag{2.1}$$

where λ is the wavelength measured in nanometers (nm) and f is the frequency in hertz (Hz). When light passes through a medium other than a vacuum, the speed is divided by γ, the refractive index of the medium. Since $\gamma = 1.0003$ for visible light in air, it may be ignored for our purposes. Generally, we are concerned with visible light, which is assumed to lie in the range of approximately 380 nm (ultraviolet) to 700 nm (infrared), although young adults have been known to see beyond 1000 nm and below 300 nm (see Figure 2.2). Of course, in the case of photoelectric receptors the range may be made larger, as, for example, satellite remote sensing using multispectral scanners [8]. In either situation, detection of the electromagnetic radiation is achieved by absorbing energy. Some classical definitions involving the measurement and characterization of illumination sources are given below.

Suppose we consider a point source, that is, one in which the size of the source is small with respect to its distance from the observer. A point source radiates energy equally in all directions. If it were possible to place a spherical measuring device around such a source, we would then be able to measure the total amount of spectral radiant flux $\phi_e(\lambda)$ emitted at a wavelength λ. The units of $\phi_e(\lambda)$ are given in energy per unit time, or watts (W). The total radiant flux over all wavelengths, therefore, is defined as

$$\Phi_e = \int \phi_e(\lambda)\, d\lambda \tag{2.2}$$

Now obviously it is not simple to arrange for such spherical measurement of radiant energy, so that if we have a uniformly radiating source, we must measure the amount of radiant energy emanating per unit area. We define the spectral radiant intensity $I_e(\lambda)$ of the emitter as

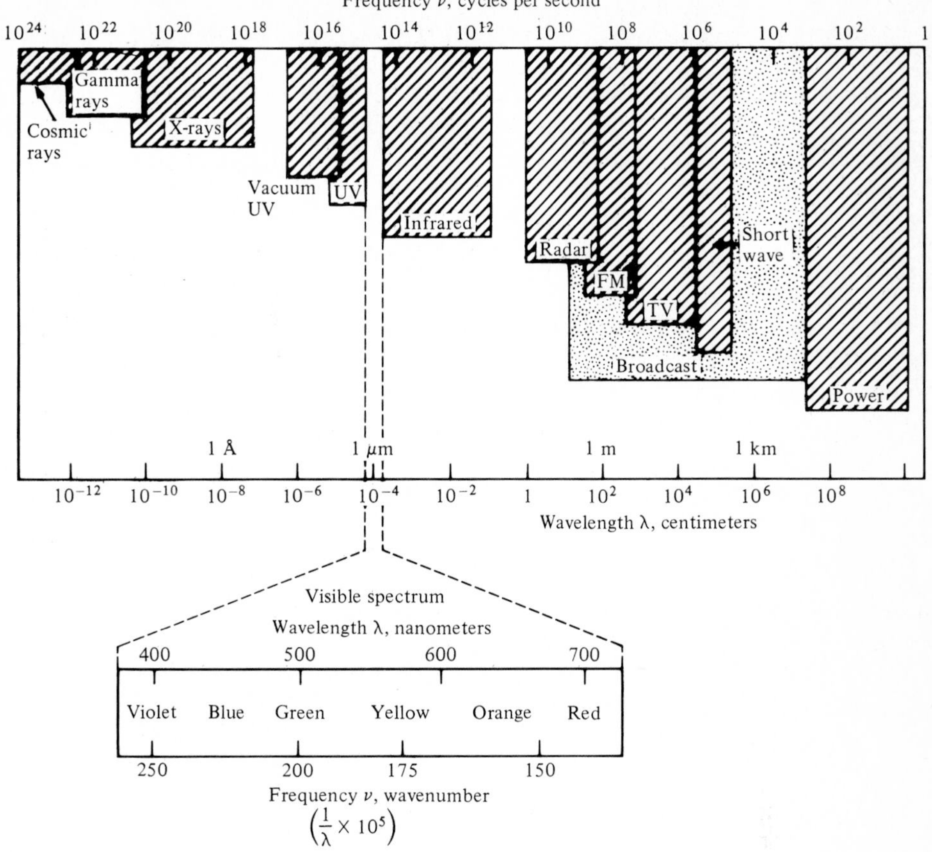

Figure 2.2 The electromagnetic spectrum.

$$I_e(\lambda) = \frac{d\phi_e(\lambda)}{d\omega_e} \tag{2.3}$$

where $\phi_e(\lambda)$ is given above, ω_e is the solid angle subtended, and $I_e(\lambda)$ is measured in watts per steradian (W/sr). A steradian (sr) is a unit solid angle subtended at the center of a sphere of one meter radius by an area of one meter squared of spherical surface. In other words, it defines a cone centered at the origin of the sphere and subtending an area of one meter squared on its surface. For an isotropic source we may therefore compute $\phi_e(\lambda)$ instead of measuring it:

$$\phi_e(\lambda) = 4\pi I_e(\lambda) \tag{2.4}$$

The total radiant intensity over the entire range of wavelengths is given by an integral equation similar to Equation (2.2):

$$\mathcal{I}_e = \int I_e(\lambda)\, d\lambda \tag{2.5}$$

Usually, instead of a point source we have what is termed an "extended source," that is, an area which radiates energy in all directions. In this case, we define the emittance $M_e(\lambda)$ such that

$$M_e(\lambda) = \frac{d\phi_e(\lambda)}{dA_e} \tag{2.6}$$

measured in watts per square meter (W/m^2) where dA_e is the area of the extended source surface. We must, of course, correct for the particular angle of view and seek to define a quantity which actually measures the intensity of the elementary area dA_e orthogonally projected onto a plane perpendicular to the direction of observation θ_e. Thus, the spectral radiance $L_e(\lambda)$, measured in W/sr · m^2, is given by

$$L_e(\lambda) = \frac{dI_e(\lambda)}{\cos\theta_e\, dA_e} = \frac{d^2\phi_e(\lambda)}{\cos\theta_e\, dA_e\, d\omega_e} \tag{2.7}$$

A simplification can be made if the source is Lambertian, that is, if it is a uniformly diffusing surface which appears equally bright from any viewing direction. Then, it can be shown that

$$L_e(\lambda) = \frac{1}{\pi} M_e(\lambda) \tag{2.8}$$

Note that the overall radiance is given by

$$\mathcal{L}_e = \int L_e(\lambda)\, d\lambda \tag{2.9}$$

In this book we are mostly concerned with the amount of light falling on a particular surface, for example, the light transmitted through a transparency or projected onto the eye. Thus, for the latter we may characterize the emitter (or source illumination) by the amount of light received at the cornea, or front of the eye (see Figure 3.2). This situation is depicted with greatest generality in Figure 2.3. The radiation is assumed to be emitted in all directions, and the amount of radiant flux falling per unit area on the extended surface is given by the spectral irradiance $E_e(\lambda)$, measured in W/m^2. Let dA_e and dA_r be the surface area of the emitter and receiver, respectively; similarly $d\theta_e$ and $d\theta_r$ are elements of solid angle at their respective surfaces. Then, we have the spectral irradiance

$$E_e(\lambda) = \frac{d\phi_e}{dA_r} \tag{2.10}$$

The solid angle $d\omega_e$ is a portion of the spherical surface, such that

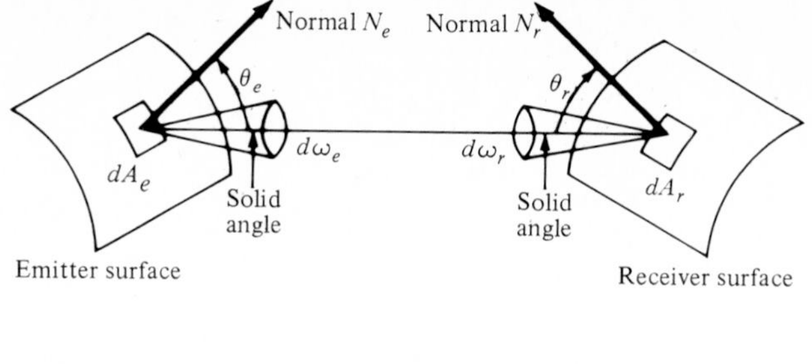

Figure 2.3 Geometry of the two surfaces required for defining the radiometric terms. (*After G. Wyszecki and W. S. Stiles, "Color Science," Wiley, New York, 1967.*)

$$R^2 = \frac{\cos\theta_e \, dA_e}{d\omega_r} = \frac{\cos\theta_r \, dA_r}{d\omega_e} \tag{2.11}$$

where R is the distance between the two surfaces. Substituting Equations (2.3) [for $d\phi_e(\lambda)$] and (2.11) [for $d\omega_e$] into Equation (2.10), we obtain

$$E_e(\lambda) = \frac{I_e(\lambda)\cos\theta_r}{R^2} \tag{2.12}$$

which is the classical inverse square law relating emitted (I_e) to received (E_e) radiation for a point source. Again, we have

$$\xi_e = \int E_e(\lambda)\, d\lambda \tag{2.13}$$

For a Lambertian surface we may use Equations (2.7), (2.11), and (2.12) to relate the spectral radiance $L_e(\lambda)$ of the emitter to the spectral irradiance $E_e(\lambda)$ of the receiver:

$$L_e(\lambda) = \frac{dE_e(\lambda)}{d\omega_r} \tag{2.14}$$

E_e in Equation (2.13) is a measure of the amount of light energy falling on a unit area per unit time. It will be of interest, when we characterize the amount of light falling on the retina, to relate this quantity to an equivalent number of photons. The energy in one photon is given by hc/λ, where h is Planck's constant and equals 6.62517×10^{-34} W/s^2. Therefore, the total spectral radiant flux $N_e(\lambda)$ can be determined by

$$N_e(\lambda) = \frac{\lambda \phi_e(\lambda)}{hc} \tag{2.15}$$

where $\phi_e(\lambda)$ is the associated amount of spectral flux emanating from the source. Also,

$$\mathcal{N}_e = \int N_e(\lambda)\, d\lambda \tag{2.16}$$

is the total number of photons passing through a surface per unit time at all wavelengths.

Many different types of sources of radiant energy and measuring devices are available and are discussed in [39, 40, 77]. Spectroradiometers are used to measure the spectral energy distribution $\phi_e(\lambda)$ of a source of radiant energy. Spectrophotometers measure the spectral transmittance and reflectance of objects in a scene. Readers who would like an elaboration on these subjects are referred to [40] and [77]. For our purposes, however, the definitions and concepts presented here are sufficient to describe image formation.

2.2.2 Image Formation

In this section we shall be concerned with two types of image formation, one the result of the reflectance of light from objects in a scene, the other arising out of the transmittance of light through a photographic transparency. These are the most common computer picture inputs, although others such as the radiant sources observed in remote sensing are also possible [8, 47]. We shall only consider very simple geometric configurations and the reader is referred to [21, 30, 50, 68, 74] for further elaboration on appropriate projective transformations. A review of the perspective transformations governing the two-dimensional images of the three-dimensional visual world can be found in [28]. Some of the work on hidden-line algorithms in computer graphics might also be of interest [48].

Let us first consider Figure 2.4, in which a source of illumination results in a spectral irradiance $E_e(x, y)$ (W/m^2) falling on a unit area perpendicular to the incident ray. The amount of light that actually falls on the surface is therefore given by the projection $E_e(x, y) \cos \theta_r \, dA_r$. The image $L_1(x, y)$ that is formed is

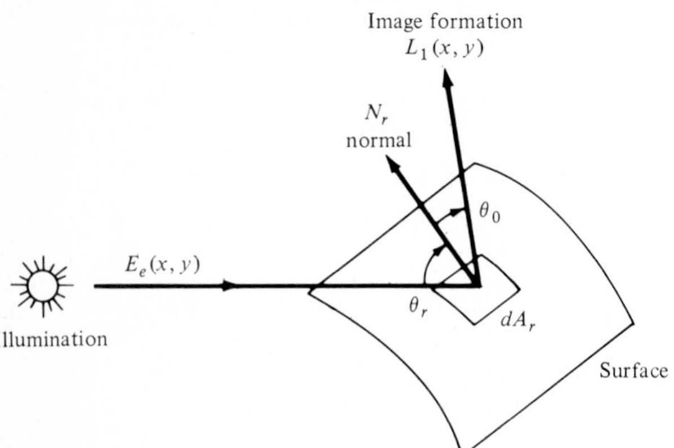

Figure 2.4 Image formation in the context of the reflection of light from a surface.

then the radiance observed at an angle of θ_0 degrees to the normal N_r. It is given in the units of $\mathrm{W/sr \cdot m^2}$, that is, per unit solid angle of the spherical viewing surface per unit area on the projected reflecting surface. The intensity of light (W/sr) intercepted by the latter is thus given by $L_1(x, y) \cos \theta_o \, dA_r$. The reflectivity function $r(x, y)$ of the surface (wavelength dependence has been suppressed) can be defined as

$$r(x, y) = \frac{L_1(x, y) \cos \theta_0}{E_e(x, y) \cos \theta_r}, \tag{2.17}$$

where

$$\infty > L_1(x, y) > 0$$

$$\infty > E_e(x, y) > 0$$

$$1 > r(x, y) > r_{\min} = 0.005$$

since we are assuming that the respective input and output images must be positive and nonzero.

A simplifying assumption that is often made is that the surface behaves as an ideal diffuser of light. In this case Equation (2.17) reduces to

$$L_1(x, y) = r(x, y) E_e(x, y) \cos \theta_r \tag{2.18}$$

since it is no longer of importance at which angle the scene is observed. Thus the radiance varies with the angle between the incident ray of light and the normal to the surface, the input irradiance, and the reflectivity of the surface. This characteristic shading pattern $L_1(x, y)$ can be used to compute the mathematical shape of a smooth geometric body with a uniform surface for the special case in which $r(x, y)$ and the position of the light sources are previously known [29, 76]. Horn and his colleagues at MIT have also shown that both the shape and the reflectance may be obtained by using multiple images where the sensor is fixed in space but the lighting conditions are altered [32]. This might be of practical application in the case of automatic inspection or manipulation of industrial parts when the latter may be viewed from several directions, either simultaneously or in sequence.

We observe from Equations (2.17) and (2.18) that there exists a unique reflectance value $r(x, y)$ for every point on a surface, which then results in a unique value of $L_1(x, y)$. With this in mind, Horn has characterized object geometry by plotting the so-called reflectance map of a surface [30, 31]. The map is defined by the contours of reflectance, plotted for every possible orientation of the object-surface normal. As such, it associates surface intensities with their orientation. Horn points out that different maps exist for different surfaces and distributions of light sources. It appears then that under certain restrictive assumptions the inverse transformation is possible and object shape may be computed from $L_1(x, y)$ alone. Similar considerations are used in computer graphics for generating shaded pictures of solid objects by using a shading function model where the effect of nonuniform illumination is included [51, 75]. A reflectance model for colored images is given in [13].

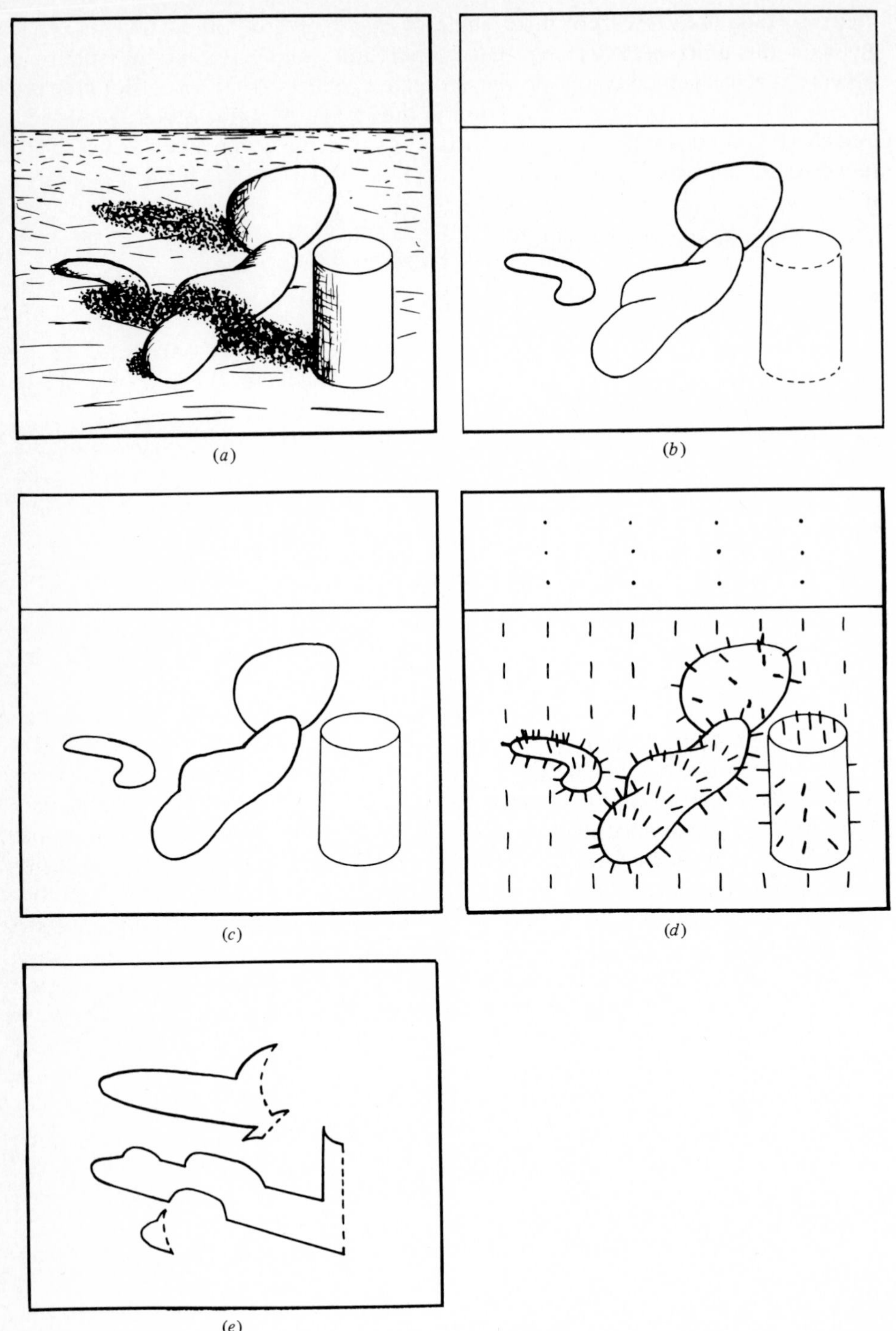
(a)
(b)
(c)
(d)
(e)

In general, for more complex objects and groups of objects, the image $L_1(x, y)$ that is formed in this way exhibits a spatial contrast variation of different gray levels, which is then used by observers to segment the different objects and to perceive the details on their surface. The surface pattern variations are referred to as "texture" and are discussed in Chapter 9. It is not obvious that a mathematical formulation exists in this case to map the data into the appropriate shape descriptions. In a sense, this would be the solution to the general computer vision problem.

From the point of view of humans, the original scene can be represented as a transformation to a family of registered images, each of which is a measure of an intrinsic characteristic such as the reflectance $r(x, y)$ but also includes the distance from the observer, surface orientation, and illumination. These are referred to as "intrinsic images" by Barrow and Tenenbaum [6]. Although we seem to be able to recognize and establish these properties within a wide range of viewing conditions without any apparent previous familiarity with the particular scene, it is not clear at present that the intrinsic images can be computed unambiguously from $L_1(x, y)$. Indeed, it is quite true that a given scene may be "new" in a certain sense, but most likely the viewer has seen many others exhibiting similar characteristics. His experiences with these, the results of which have been learned and stored away in memory in some organized and concise fashion, tend to weaken the assumption of the scene being viewed for the first time. Barrow and Tenenbaum [6] propose the use of knowledge about the constraints which are imposed by the physical world on objects to help recover the intrinsic images and thereby assign three-dimensional interpretations to edges and regions in the scene. That such information would be extremely useful is evident from Figure 2.5, where the problem of segmenting the objects in three-dimensional space has been greatly simplified. The independence of the intrinsic images leads to an unambiguous definition of the objects in the two-dimensional projection. The task still remains to develop the details of this one-to-many mapping.

We now turn to the representation of scenes on photographic slides, a very common input to image digitizers. A typical arrangement is shown in Figure 2.6, where the opaque surface in Figure 2.4 has been replaced by a transparent surface, which transmits light through it. The amount of light will be seen to

---

Figure 2.5 A set of intrinsic images derived from a single monochrome intensity image. The images are depicted as line drawings but in fact would contain values at every point. The solid lines in the intrinsic images represent discontinuities in the scene characteristic, the dashed lines represent discontinuities in its derivative. In the input image, intensities correspond to the reflected light flux received from the visible points in the scene. The distance image gives the range along the line of sight from the center of projection to each visible point in the scene. The orientation image gives a vector representing the direction of the surface normal at each point. The reflectance image gives the albedo (the ratio of total reflected to total incident illumination) at each point. (*a*) Original scene. (*b*) Distance. (*c*) Reflectance. (*d*) Orientation (vector). (*e*) Illumination [*From H. G. Barrow and J. M. Tenenbaum, "Recovering Intrinsic Scene Characteristics from Images," in A. R. Hanson and E. M. Riseman (eds.), "Computer Vision Systems," Academic, New York, 1978, pp. 3–26.*]

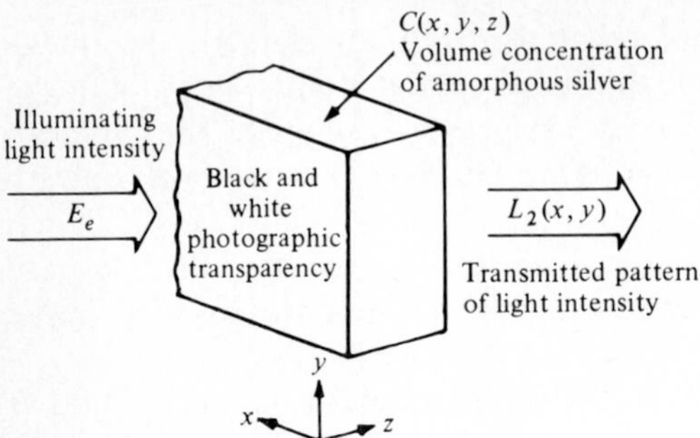

Figure 2.6 Transmission of light through a photographic transparency.

depend on the volume concentration of the amorphous silver $C(x, y, z)$ in a manner to be discussed below. Because of the physical arrangement, Equation (2.18) becomes

$$L_2(x, y) = t(x, y)E_e(x, y) \tag{2.19}$$

where $L_2(x, y)$ is the image formed by light transmission through a transparency and $t(x, y)$ is now the transmittance rather than the reflectance. The local concentration of silver, which is suspended in a gelatinous emulsion, represents the stored image and controls the amount of light transmitted.

Assume a uniform illumination E_e of the transparency. Then the intensity of light $e(x, y, z)$ at any point in the transmitting material is given by [62]

$$\frac{de}{dz} = -kC(x, y, z)e \tag{2.20}$$

where k is a constant related to the attenuation per unit concentration of amorphous silver. Integrating, we obtain

$$\int_{E_e}^{L_2(x, y)} \frac{de}{e} = -k \int_0^{z_t} C(x, y, z)\, dz \tag{2.21}$$

where z_t is the thickness of the emulsion. Note that the right-hand integral represents the total quantity of silver per unit area of the transparency, regardless of how the silver is distributed in the z dimension of a unit volumetric element. Thus let

$$\int_{E_e}^{L_2(x, y)} \frac{de}{e} = -kd(x, y) \tag{2.22}$$

where $d(x, y)$ is the quantity of amorphous silver per unit image area at point (x, y) and is the actual physical representation of the image. Integrating, we obtain

$$\ln\left[\frac{L_2(x, y)}{E_e}\right] = -kd(x, y) \tag{2.23}$$

or

$$L_2(x, y) = E_e[e^{-kd(x, y)}] \tag{2.24}$$

Comparing Equation (2.24) with Equation (2.19), we observe that the transmittance $t(x, y)$ of light through the transparency results in an exponentiation of the physical representation. Thus if $L_2(x, y)$ is to be a reproduction of the original scene from which $d(x, y)$ was formed, then the photographic process must be logarithmically proportional to the light energy in the original scene. This is indeed the case [59].

Suppose that $d(x, y)$ has resulted from a photographic process in which $L_1(x, y)$ in Equation (2.18) was exposed to film specifically used for preparing transparencies. This physical process is classically described by the so-called characteristic curve (alternately Hurter-Driffield or D–log E curve) [18], so that in our notation

$$d(x, y) = d_0 + \gamma \log_{10} L_1(x, y) \tag{2.25}$$

where d_0 is a "fog" level included to take into account the minimum residual density even with no exposure, and γ is a measure of the image contrast. Note that for transparencies $\gamma < 1$, while for hard-copy photography, which produces a negative, $\gamma > 1$. Substituting for $d(x, y)$ in Equation (2.24), we obtain

$$L_2(x, y) \propto L_1(x, y) \tag{2.26}$$

That is, the image formed by illuminating the transparency is linearly related to the original image exposed on the film, which is as it should be.

In photography, it is common to define a variable, referred to as the "density," such that

$$D(x, y) = \log_{10} L_1(x, y) \tag{2.27}$$

where $D(x, y)$ is the photographic density, which is proportional to $d(x, y)$, and $L_1(x, y)$ is the exposed image. It has been the practice in digital image processing to refer to any logarithmic representation of an image as the density, defined as

$$D(x, y) = \ln I(x, y) \tag{2.28}$$

$$I(x, y) = \exp D(x, y) \tag{2.29}$$

where $I(x, y)$ is the image intensity and is essentially an energy representation. Whether obtained by reflection or transmission, the image intensity $I(x, y)$ (L_1 for the first, L_2 for the second) is a product of an input illumination and a spatial property [$r(x, y)$ or $t(x, y)$] of a material. Therefore according to Equation (2.28), $D(x, y)$ must be an additive rather than a multiplicative process. Thus the density representation of images makes them compatible with linear processing in the subsequent analysis stages. In fact this has the result of separating the effect of the illumination component from the reflection or transmission component. If the human vision system were to perform the same computation, this might have considerable implication for the independent processing of each of these factors.

2.3 SENSORS AND DIGITIZERS

We have discussed two basic sources of image formation, of which one provides a "live" signal from a real scene and the other is observed by recreating the original scene which had been recorded on a physical medium. Typical of such media are slide transparencies, cine film, videotape, and hard-copy representations (photographs or plain paper). As observed in Figure 2.7, an optical stage which forms the image $I(x, y)$ usually precedes scanning and digitization, the process of entering pictorial data into the computer. This complete transformation from an analog image $L_1(x, y)$ or $L_2(x, y)$ to a digital image $I(i, j)$ is sometimes loosely referred to as the "computer retina." We shall see that this is a misnomer in the next chapter, where human and animal retinal capabilities will be discussed. This section will deal briefly with the hardware necessary for pictorial input to a computer. We define a digital image $I(i, j)$ as a function of two real, discrete variables i and j whose value is referred to as a gray shade, tone, or level. The latter is a nonnegative number or value assigned to an element of the array, which is proportional to either $L_1(x, y)$ or $L_2(x, y)$ in a small area centered around (x, y). These areas are the discrete resolution cells of the analog image and are called "pixels" (or sometimes "pels"). The hardware, therefore, achieves the dual operations of spatial sampling of the image into pixels and quantization of the gray levels into the integer set $I = \{I_1, I_2, I_3, \ldots, I_n\}$ where n is the total number of gray levels. Typical array sizes used are 128×128, 256×256, and 512×512, but much larger arrays of the order of 2048×2048 are not uncommon in remote sensing applications. With regard to the signal magnitude range, $n = 64$ (6 bits) gray levels are generally perfectly adequate, although in some instances as many as 256 have been used. We shall see in a later chapter how the number of levels can be chosen according to man's ability to discriminate them (generally thought to be about 30). Readers who are interested in a mathematical treatment of image sampling and quantization are referred to the excellent discussion by Rosenfeld and Kak [56, chap. 4].

The three important parameters which must be considered in designing or evaluating a scanner are the spatial resolution, dynamic range, and digitization plus read-in time. All these, of course, interact and depend on the particular hardware selected. Suppose for example, we consider a standard television camera as the input device, which is often the case in robotic hand-eye systems used in industrial automation. The camera may serve as the scanner and

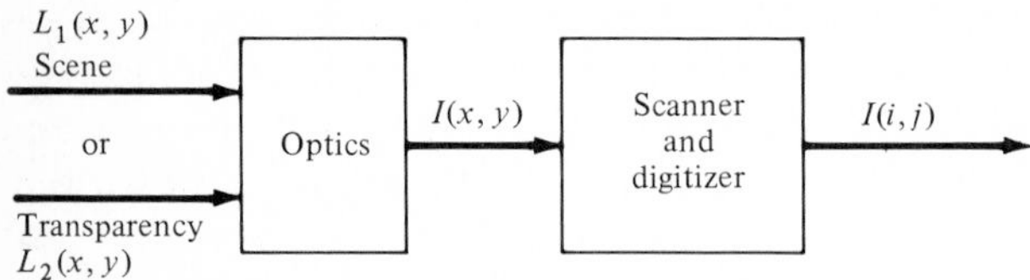

Figure 2.7 Scanning and digitization of the input.

digitizer for a computer with a 1 μs memory cycle time and 36-bit word length. Each horizontal line of video in the camera scan pattern is available for about 52 μs, which implies that a maximum of 52 read-ins are available to the computer. If the dynamic range required is 64 gray levels or 6 bits, then the maximum spatial resolution will be $52 \times (36/6) = 312$ pixels per scan line. If we are prepared to accept a smaller dynamic range, for example only 4 bits, then we have $468 = 52 \times (36/4)$ pixels per horizontal scan. Note that a maximum of 1872 bits per line is achievable no matter what is done. But what happens if our computer is a 32-bit machine? The 6-bit quantization can still be achieved in the same amount of time as previously, but more memory is required and some bits would remain unused. If a higher spatial resolution were required, let us say 512×512 with a 6-bit quantization, we would either need a new, faster computer or have to slow down the sampling. For a standard television camera with a fixed scanning pattern this presents serious consequences indeed.

The mapping from $L_1(x, y)$ or $L_2(x, y)$ to $I(i, j)$ in Figure 2.7 involves the sequential stages of photooptical energy transduction and analog to digital (A/D) conversion. The resulting digitally coded signal is stored in a separate array memory or in computer memory [70]. A general discussion of the design considerations underlying the construction of picture input systems is found in [10]. Input devices suitable for an industrial environment are discussed in [49]. We shall examine two of the most frequently used energy conversion systems: standard electronic television cameras and mechanical densitometers. The first is useful where high speed or real-time input is paramount, the second where high accuracy is a consideration. At present no single device combines both these properties into one system which allows users to select the relative emphasis they wish to place on each factor. In the past, image dissectors and flying-spot scanners were popular [27], and readers are referred to the tutorial article by Chien and Snyder [11] for a short description. A brief introduction to A/D converters can also be found there.

Figure 2.8 shows a schematic of a typical laboratory configuration using a standard television camera [16]. The light source is provided by a light box, usually consisting of a number of fluorescent bulbs covered with a thick piece of translucent plastic to diffuse the light as much as possible. It is generally assumed to be uniform, so that $E_e(x, y) = E_e$, but it is not difficult to compensate for existing variations by storing a prescan, obtained without photographic input. Alternative inputs are a light box–film transport configuration, where one frame at a time is presented under computer control to the view of the camera; a microscope with the image on the (possibly computer-controlled) stage focused through the optics onto the face of the camera; and, of course, the reflected light $L_1(x, y)$ from a real scene. In all these cases, an image to be digitized is projected by the camera optics onto the photoelectric transducing unit of the camera.

There are many types of transducers in use today. The most common is the vidicon tube, in which the incoming light falls on a photoconductive surface after having passed through a transparent metal film acting as a signal plate.

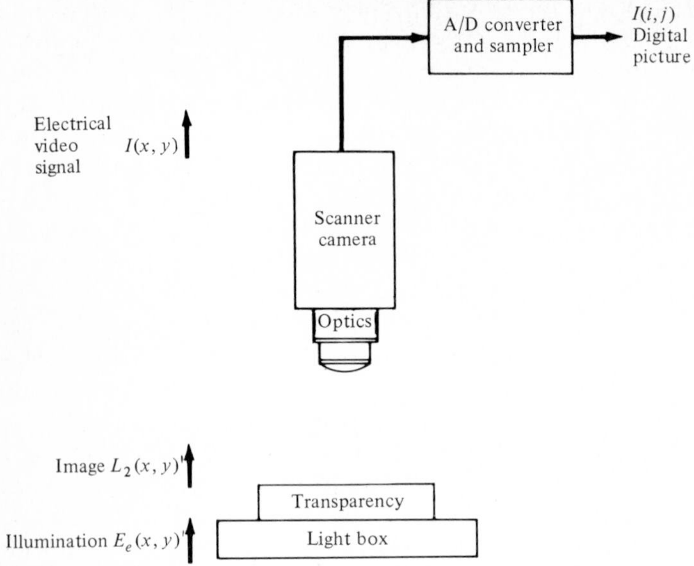

Figure 2.8 The physical arrangement for digitizing a photographic transparency with use of a standard television camera.

The input changes the resistance of the photoconductive mosaic according to the amount of light locally incident in any given neighborhood. An electron gun, supplemented by a magnetic or electrostatic deflection system for fine focusing, scans the image by passing a current through the surface to the signal plate. Obviously the local current will be inversely related to the local resistance and hence to the incoming light. A silicon vidicon is more sensitive and has a wider spectral response than the standard vidicon tube. It operates in much the same fashion, except that the photoconductive target is now a small array of diodes. The newest technology replaces the standard tubes with complete self-scanning arrays of solid-state photosensitive elements.

These systems generally consist of a mosaic of sensing elements, another array for storage, and a scanning network. There are several competing approaches, including charge injection devices (CID) [12], charge coupled devices (CCD) [42, 7, 54, 35, 36], and a combination of self-scanned photodiode arrays for sensing and CCD arrays for storage [60]. In each case the energy sampling is actually achieved by the use of independent, discrete units so that an electron beam is not required for focusing. Cameras may be purchased in which the scan is digital or analog, as in the standard vidicon. These units are very compact and lightweight, thereby providing great advantages for industrial applications. The array of discrete elements is analogous to the situation in human vision, where, as we shall see in the next chapter, the retina consists of a configuration of independent photoreceptors. However, this array is not linear in that the element's size varies with distance from the center of the gaze. Such an image digitization system for an industrial robot with visual feedback is described in [57].

Color input may be obtained by using a standard color television camera [33], a CCD array camera [24], or the more common color filter wheel. The latter consists of a wheel with four openings, each containing a different color separation filter which can be interspersed between the image and the camera face. The four filters are transparent, red, green, and blue. The last three filters must be used sequentially in three separate scans in order to input a color picture. We shall discuss this in more detail in Chapter 7. A color camera has also been constructed of a mosaic of sensing elements deposited on a single chip [34, 20]. We are quickly approaching the point at which the Dick Tracy radio wristwatch will be replaced by the James Bond color television camera tie clip!

Figure 2.9 shows a television scanning pattern which is universally fixed by the standard design. It consists of an even field, followed by an odd field, each requiring $\frac{1}{60}$ s to scan. The fields are interlaced, so that the $\frac{1}{30}$-s frame rate is effectively doubled for images that are not changing too fast. The sampling of the image is from left to right along a horizontal scan, from the top of the image to the bottom. A given horizontal scan is slightly tilted because of the finite time the scanner deflection system takes to sweep across the tube. Note that the sampling is suppressed during the periods of horizontal and vertical retrace.

The number of discrete, visible horizontal lines is fixed at 480 in standard U.S. broadcast systems. In addition, the vertical retrace time requires the equivalent of 45 (= 22 + 23) lines, totaling 525 in all. Since the image is swept 30 times each second, we have a total of 15,750 horizontal lines per second, or 63.5 μs for each line. The right-to-left retrace signal requires 12.3 μs. Therefore the number of columns in the array is fixed only by the total available time of 51.2 μs when the signal is visible along the row and the speed of the A/D converter sampling the video signal. A typical array might have 640 columns, thereby leaving only 8 nanoseconds (ns) for each sample conversion.

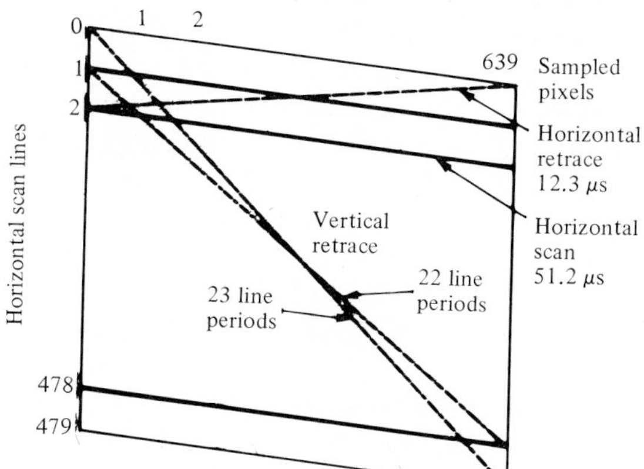

Figure 2.9 Standard television scan pattern with 640 samples along the horizontal scan.

A system which is able to function at this rate and store a complete image within one frame time ($\frac{1}{30}$s) in a special picture frame memory is called a "frame grabber" [17]. Obviously, the major drawbacks of such a camera are the fixed scan pattern and limited resolution, which cannot be altered. We may, however, slow down the scan by, for example, only sampling one column in each frame. Although it cannot be used with dynamically changing images, this so-called column digitizer may be required in order to match the image sampling rate to the maximum computer read-in rate. Nevertheless, a major advantage of the standard television camera is its high speed and relatively low cost. In addition, many image processing computations can be performed at the video rate of 10 MHz [69].

The output video signal $I(x, y)$ in Figure 2.8 is related to the input image by the equation

$$I(x, y) = kL_2(x, y)^\gamma \tag{2.30}$$

where k is a constant and γ is, again [see Equation (2.25)], a parameter of the particular photosensitive transducer chosen. Typically, $I(x, y)$ will be quantized into somewhere between 6 and 8 bits, the former usually being adequate for most purposes. For the silicon diode vidicon, γ is nearly equal to 1 ($0.95 < \gamma < 1.0$), so that the electrical response $I(x, y)$ is essentially a linear function of the pictorial input. On the other hand, $\gamma = 0.65$ for a vidicon tube, so that a nonlinear relationship obtains between input and output. Is this a problem or not? Such a nonlinearity has the effect of compressing the contrast of the input signal, a property, as we shall see in Chapter 4, that is also exhibited by the human transducing system. The dynamic range, or minimum detectable contrast, is defined as the ratio of the maximum signal output to the existing electronic noise signal, that is, the signal-to-noise ratio (SNR). Typically, a silicon diode tube will have a dynamic range of 30:1, an ordinary vidicon perhaps 200:1. In order to take into account the particular picture quality, many camera systems allow the user to operate in either a linear or logarithmic mode according to choice.

In the previous section we indicated the importance of the wavelength of the light when determining the response. Thus in addition to the sensitivity curve of the lamps in the light box, the camera tubes will also vary in their sensitivity to the wavelength of the input. This is easily seen in Figure 2.10, which compares the two types of tubes with human vision and a standard tungsten lamp. We note immediately that they do not all "see" the same image, and in fact the silicon diode has vision in the infrared region which is quite invisible to man. This sensitivity makes it useful for detection of thermal radiation. However, when used with most color separation filters, which are also sensitive to these wavelengths, it is necessary to employ an infrared blocking filter to compensate for the effect.

Another property of the digitizer is its time response, or lag, with respect to the accommodation to a change in input. This is only important if either the scene or the camera is not stationary, as might be the case in industrial

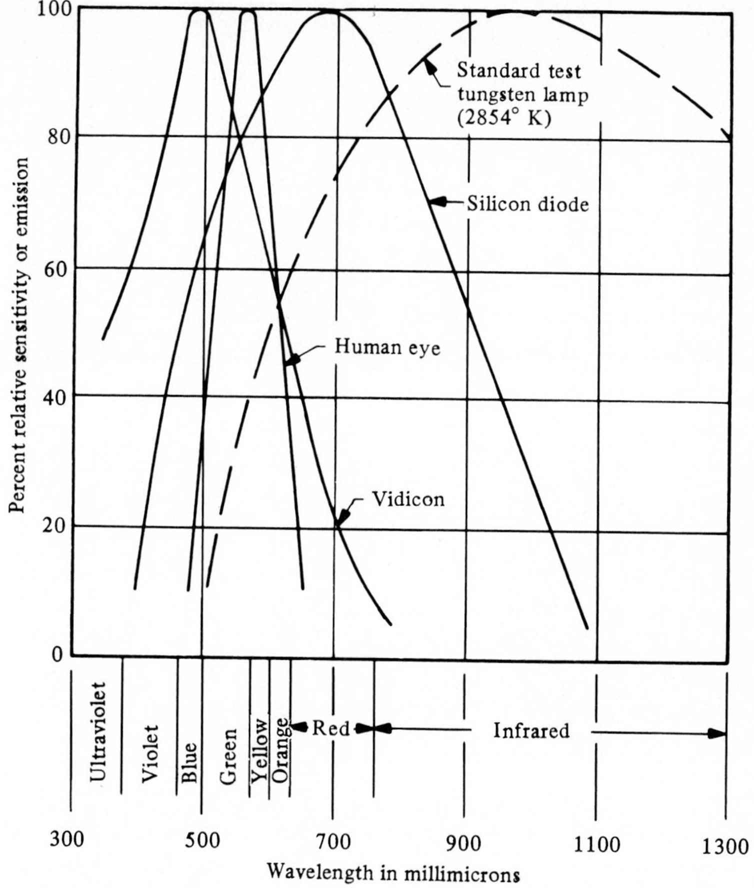

Figure 2.10 Spectral response curves. (*From "EyeCom Handbook," Spatial Data Systems Inc., Goleta, Calif., 1977, p. 15.*)

inspection, and will result in a visible trailing edge for rapid movements. Typically, a silicon diode array tube will have a lag of less than 100 ms, which is perhaps 10 times faster than an ordinary vidicon.

There are several sources of noise which degrade performance [9]. One is the so-called blooming effect, which occurs when viewing a very bright light; the spot size will be logarithmically proportional to the input intensity, causing a distortion in which the region is unnecessarily enlarged. This effect can be compensated for to some extent. Another is parabolic distortion, or shading, which results in a nonuniform response at the outer edges of the tube. This is caused by secondary emission effects of the scanning electron beam used to read out the signal. Sometimes as much as 10 percent of the outer edge of the surface is unacceptable. Figure 2.11 shows the effect of this noise nonuniformity. This may be corrected either by software or by hardware using a

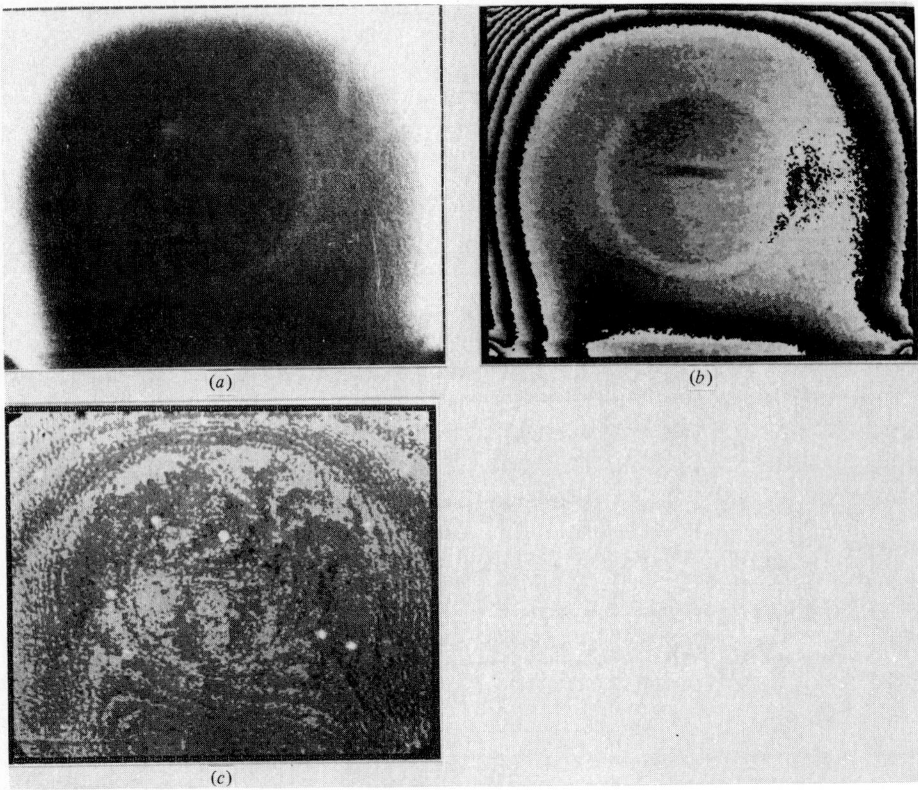

Figure 2.11 The radiometric characteristics of the vidicon cameras used in the *Mariner 10* mission to Mercury. This nonlinear response must be compensated for in order to produce acceptable images for scientific purposes. The result is shown in (*c*). (*a*) A contrast-enhanced version of a *Mariner 10* B camera flat-field calibration frame. (*b*) The same flat-field calibration frame contoured to show more effectively the small brightness differences. Each black to white cycle indicates a change of eight intensity levels. (*c*) After radiometric decalibration, a contoured version of the image reveals that it is now virtually flat, with most of the picture consisting of only two intensity levels. The residual contours in this picture are the combined effect of calibration frame smoothing and integer roundoff. (*From J. M. Soha, D. J. Lynn, J. J. Lorre, J. A. Mosher, N. N. Thayer, D. A. Elliott, W. D. Benton, and R. E. Dewar, "IPL Processing of the Mariner 10 Images of Mercury," Journal of Geophysical Research, vol. 80, no. 7, June 10, 1975, pp. 2394–2414.*)

parabolic shading generator, an amplifier whose gain varies with beam deflection and which operates on the output video signal.

Electronic scanners are generally used in applications where size, cost, and/or speed are factors. They exhibit a relatively poor signal-to-noise ratio and have generally low geometric accuracy (except for array cameras), a fixed array size with a small image input, and a limited dynamic range. Devices which eliminate all these imperfections are electromechanical instruments such as the scanning microdensitometer. These systems take advantage of the already existing high-precision mechanical techniques for locating position using a mechanical stage, a galvanometric assembly, or a cylinder (a machinist's lathe). Examples are flat-bed densitometers, rotating-mirror laser scanners, and drum scanners, a schematic of which is shown in Figure 2.12. These precision positioning systems are used to arrange for the transmission (reflection) of light through (off) an image by means of a fixed illuminating source and photodetector assembly. Because of this, it is obvious that $I(x, y)$ can be easily made to be a linear function of $L_2(x, y)$ by carefully designing the single discrete detector employed.

Areas as large as 14 in × 17 in (standard radiographic size) can be scanned and a minimum spot size as low as 0.3 μm achieved with 1024 gray levels. Color wheels and microscopes can also be used with these systems. Their primary disadvantages are long image digitization times and relatively high cost. Mechanical systems cannot scan as fast as the electronic ones and therefore we have the classic trade-off between speed and accuracy. Readers interested in the details of the design of one such system are referred to [44].

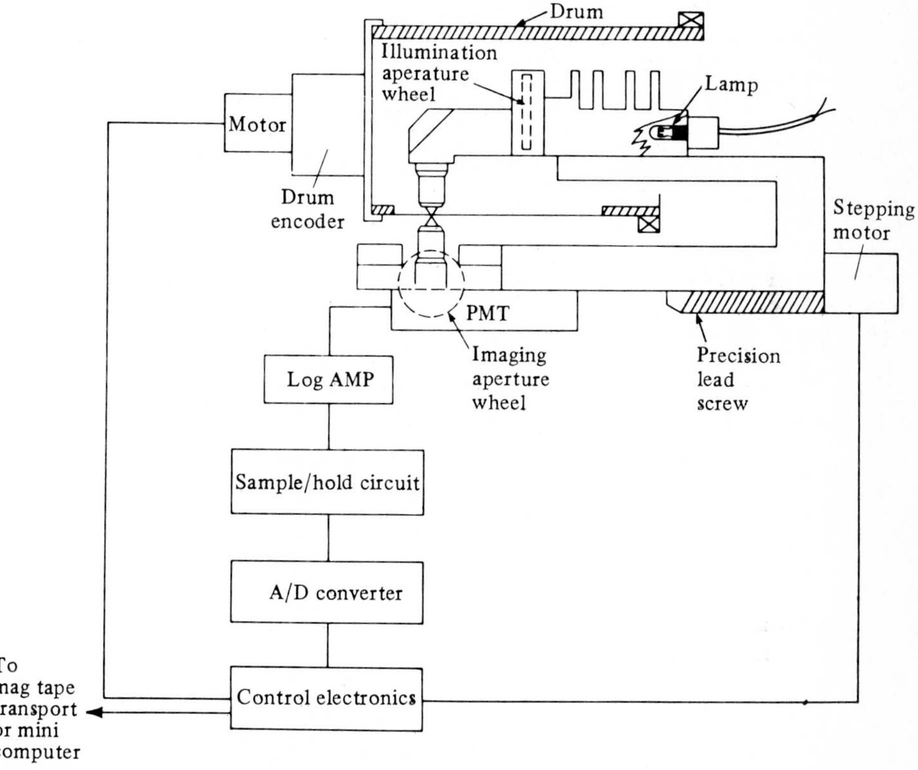

Figure 2.12 A sketch of a typical rotating-drum scanning microdensitometer. (*From G. S. Marcil, "Microdensitometric Data Acquisition," Proceedings of the Society of Photo-Optical Instrumentation Engineers, vol. 48, "Acquisition and Analysis of Pictorial Data, the Modern Science of Imagery," Conference San Diego, Aug. 19–20, 1974, pp. 23–33.*)

Recently image digitizers consisting of a single linear photosensitive array combined with mechanical scanning to produce a two-dimensional image have been constructed. This design can be viewed as a compromise between electronic and mechanical systems.

Methods for quantifying distortion in image digitization systems are discussed in [14]. Such characteristics as spot size and shape, geometric fidelity, photometric response and uniformity, and signal-to-noise ratio are considered.

2.4 THE IMAGE PROCESSOR

Image formation and input to a computation system having been described, the next obvious stage is the actual method of analysis. Most of the low-level image processing techniques discussed in this book are concerned with either point or neighborhood operations. We shall attempt to maintain this as a formalism for describing algorithms, sometimes even in the face of mathematical inconvenience, for three reasons. First, in most cases it is indeed the simplest of all descriptive mechanisms. A large number of picture operations can be described by using neighborhood operators [43]. Second, such a formalism lends itself easily to an implementation using special-purpose parallel-processing hardware [25, 61]. This is increasingly becoming a possible practical means for speeding up what are usually very time-consuming computations. Third, there is strong support for the hypothesis that the "biological image processor" uses such neighborhood operators as well. This will immediately become evident when we begin our discussion of how humans and animals look at pictures. Of course, it is not too clear what happens with the output data of these transformations, and it may not therefore be very meaningful to make comparisons between computers and brains at other levels in the analysis.

It is still a controversial question as to what constitutes low-level processing. In this book we maintain the attitude that the feature computation (at the lowest level) of intensity, color, and edges is definitely in this category. A similar case is provided by the next stage, which most would agree involves some degree of aggregation of pixels into regions and/or lines. This should not be taken to imply that either complete or consistent regions or lines are produced or exist at this point. However, we do assume that a certain level of organization of data, perhaps an elementary one, does follow the feature analysis. These simply organized data are then thought to be incorporated into the computation of texture and shape descriptors, again possibly incomplete ones. We refer to all three of these successive stages as low-level picture processing and have assumed them as the subject of this book. However the reader should be cautioned that this is not necessarily a universally held opinion.

The first stage of low-level analysis can usually be conveniently described in terms of neighborhood operations. Sometimes so can the grouping and, rarely, the shape calculation. We shall attempt as much as possible to adhere to this convention, but we will find it necessary in the later chapters to employ a more general mathematical formalism. The technique, variously referred to as "windowing," "masking," or "template matching," simply involves the comparison of a standard representative pictorial pattern with the existing data image. Such an approach has been used for a long time in connection with optical pattern recognition techniques [15, 67]. An early digital application to the calculation of edges in a picture was published in 1953 [37].

Figure 2.13 shows schematically the concept of passing a window $W(p, q)$ containing a specific pattern over an arbitrary pictorial shape in an image $I(i, j)$. We may consider these mask weights as attempting to fit a surface locally, in this case an edge segment. The window may be moved over the image in a prespecified scan pattern, often rectangular and referred to as a "raster." Another approach is to select the next position of the window based on the previous computation. This nondeterministic path, since it is data-dependent, might be more efficient and will often more easily lend itself to complex computations. We have observed that the window being used here is searching for short vertical line segments, perhaps in order to locate the boundary of the arbitrary form shown. The output is another image of the same dimension as $I(i, j)$ in which each pixel value gives an indication of the correctness of the window model in its neighborhood.

Let the image $I(i, j)$ be of dimension $M \times N$, where $1 \leq i \leq M$, $1 \leq j \leq N$, and let the window $W(p, q)$ be of dimension $(2m+1) \times (2n+1)$, where generally $m \ll M$ and $n \ll N$. Most often both I and W are square arrays. One method of comparing a model or reference pattern $W(p, q)$ with $I(i, j)$ at every pixel location (i, j) is by cross-correlation matching techniques. Thus the discrete cross-correlation $\rho(i, j)$ is given by

$$\rho(i, j) = \sum_{p=-m}^{+m} \sum_{q=-n}^{+n} W(p, q) I(i+p, j+q) \qquad \begin{array}{l} m \leq i \leq M - m \\ n \leq j \leq N - n \end{array} \tag{2.31}$$

which may be written in the conventional notation as

$$\rho(i, j) = W(i, j) \times I(i, j) \tag{2.32}$$

This is equivalent to sliding the window over the image, at every location multiplying the overlaid pixels together, and adding them all up. It can be shown that the Cauchy-Schwarz inequality (for $W > 0$, $I > 0$) applied at each pixel (i, j) yields

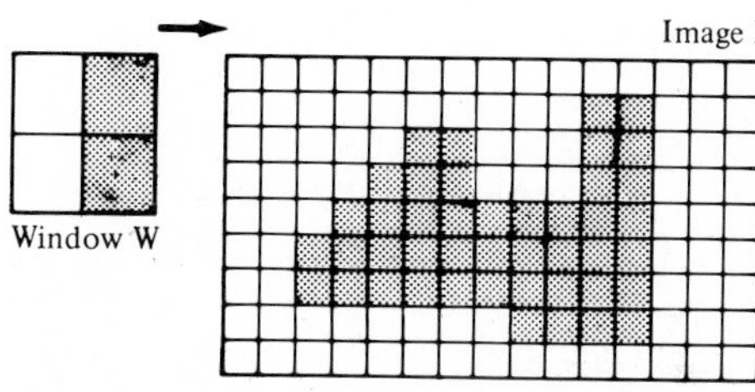

Figure 2.13 An edge template is passed over an arbitrary pattern in search of vertical edge segments.

$$\rho(i, j) \leq \left[\sum_{p=-m}^{+m} \sum_{q=-n}^{+n} W^2(p, q)\right]^{1/2} \left[\sum_{p=-m}^{+m} \sum_{q=-n}^{+n} I^2(i+p, j+q)\right]^{1/2} \qquad (2.33)$$

The left-hand side is a maximum (at which point equality holds) when

$$I(i, j) = kW(i, j) \qquad (2.34)$$

where k is a constant. In other words, the cross-correlation is maximized when the model matches the picture at pixel location (i, j). However, we observe that $\rho(i, j)$ is not an appropriate measure of this match since the right-hand side of Equation (2.33) varies with (i, j) in that the second factor is not constant. The first factor, of course, is a constant once a template model has been selected. In order to be able to make comparisons of matches at different points in the image, we define the normalized correlation function $\rho'(i, j)$ such that

$$\rho'(i, j) = \frac{\rho(i, j)}{[\sum_{p=-m}^{+m} \sum_{q=-n}^{+n} W^2(p, q)]^{1/2} [\sum_{p=-m}^{+m} \sum_{q=-n}^{+n} I^2(i+p, j+q)]^{1/2}} \qquad (2.35)$$

which is independent of $I(i, j)$. Note that an alternative definition of $\rho'(i, j)$ may have been suggested by dividing $\rho(i, j)$ by the second factor alone. Now the normalized cross-correlation $\rho'(i, j)$ takes on a maximum value of 1 when Equation (2.34) holds. A simple example is shown in Figure 2.14, in which a model of a short horizontal line segment is matched with four sample images. Only one image gives a maximum value of $\rho'(i, j) = 1$, even though at least three of the four shown contain a horizontal segment as a subimage. This is indicated by maxima in locations where the template matches best. Examination of the results shows that the values of $\rho'(i, j)$ are indeed rank-ordered according to their similarity to the original model.

The process of cross-correlation of a template with an image can also be justified on the basis of other factors. In an analogy to signal detection in communication systems (see [66]), it is possible to derive a so-called two-dimensional matched filter. This is an optimum filter which is chosen to maximize certain criteria such as signal-to-noise ratio, likelihood ratio, or inverse probability (see [44, pp. 296–306] and [2, chap. 4]). It turns out that the optimum filter is given by $W(i, j)$ correlated with $I(i, j)$. Furthermore, this operation is equivalent in some sense to a two-dimensional discrete convolution:

$$g(i, j) = \sum_{p=-m}^{+m} \sum_{q=-n}^{+n} W(i-p, j-q) I(p, q) \qquad (2.36)$$

that is, cross-correlating W with I is equivalent to convolving I with W rotated by 180°. Obviously, for vertically symmetric templates the two operations are exactly equivalent. In the Fourier domain convolution becomes a multiplicative operation in that

$$F\{g\} = F\{W\} F\{I\} \qquad (2.37)$$

Cross-correlation in the Fourier domain is given by

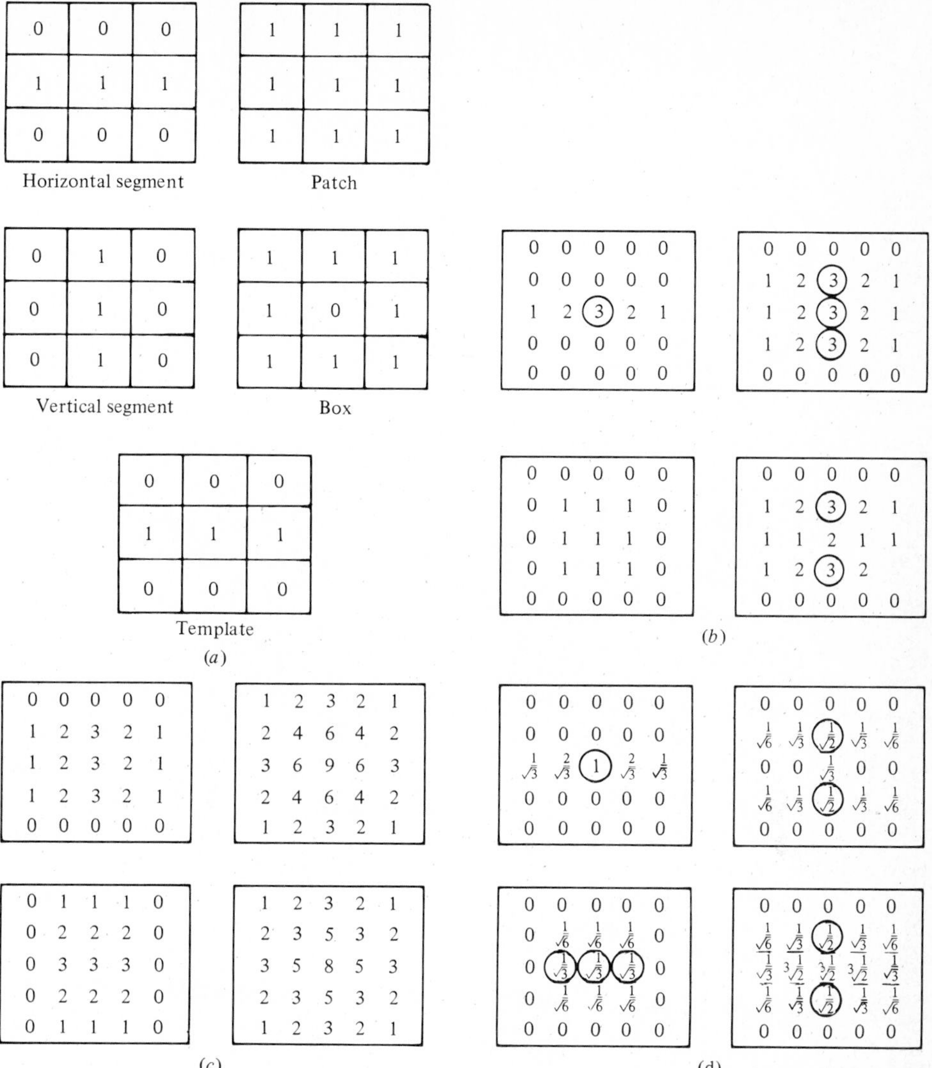

Figure 2.14 An example of template matching. (*a*) Picture fragments. (*b*) $p(i, j)$. (*c*) $\Sigma\Sigma I^2$ (note $\Sigma\Sigma W^2 = 3$). (*Adapted from A. Rosenfeld and A. C. Kak, "Digital Picture Processing," Academic, New York, 1976, p. 299.*)

$$F\{\rho\} = F\{W^*\}F\{I\} \tag{2.38}$$

so that it is sometimes called a "conjugate filter." These two equations also suggest that windowing in the two-dimensional spatial domain is equivalent to conventional two-dimensional frequency-domain filtering. Each mask is a dual to a filter in the frequency domain. We shall pursue this subject in greater detail in Chapter 6.

From the definition of template matching and also from the example in Figure 2.14 it is clear that in order for the transformed output image to be of the same dimension (that is, $M \times N$) as the original image, special considerations must be taken into account along the border when $1 \leq i \leq m$ or $M - m \leq i \leq M$ and $1 \leq j \leq n$ or $N - n \leq j \leq N$. This is because there are not sufficient data to compute the result within this border frame. No solution is completely satisfactory and several algorithms are in use. One involves the linear extrapolation of the output result to obtain values within the frame. Another is to extend the input image on all four sides by invoking a mirror image along the two horizontal and vertical axes. This has the advantage of being simple and requiring little extra computation. In what follows we shall always assume that this border problem has been considered and solved in a

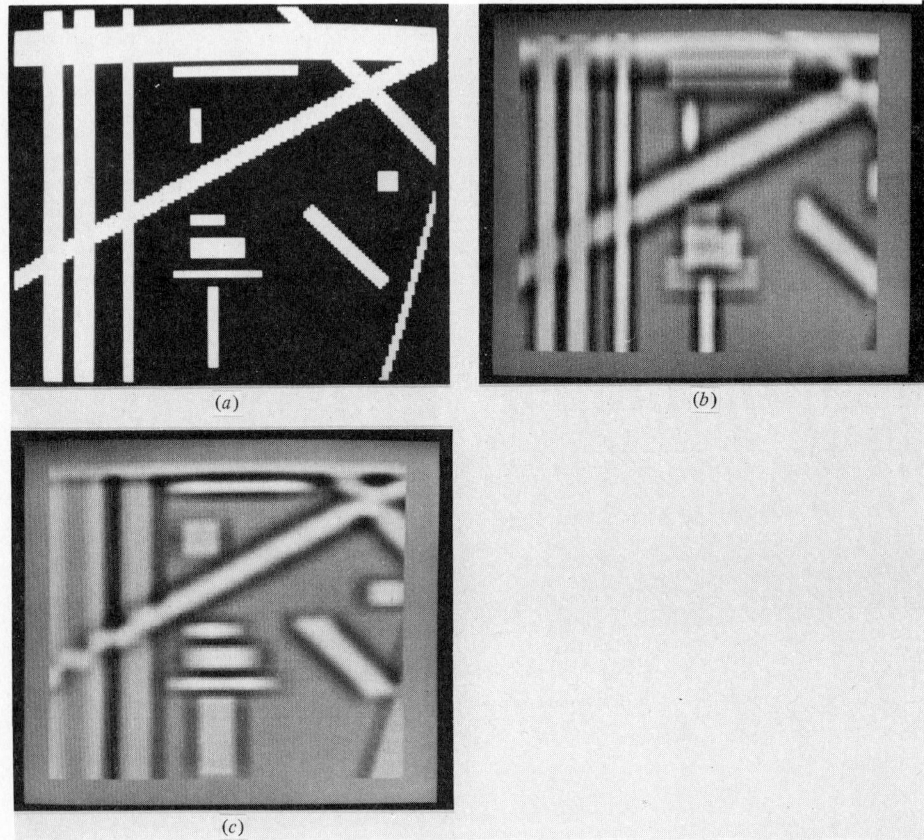

Figure 2.15 Example of template matching in search for line segments. (*a*) A pattern of lines. (*b*) The response of template matching using the short vertical bar at the top of the image in (*a*) as a model. Here, and in (*c*), the template consists of the model represented by +'s, surrounded by a frame of −'s. The degree of match is represented by the brightness of the output image. (*c*) The response of template matching using the short horizontal bar below the vertical one as a model.

satisfactory way. Thus, output images are always of the same dimension as input images.

An example of a window having been passed over an image in search of line segments is shown in Figure 2.15. An arbitrary pattern of lines is illustrated in (*a*). A template, which is identical to the short vertical bar within the top third of the picture, is passed over the image. The maximum response of 63 occurs only at one point, as shown in (*b*). However, there exist many subsidiary extrema. Similarly, in (*c*) the short horizontal segment just below the vertical one is used as a model. Again, only one point of maximum template response is evident. Readers should note that this is an ideal situation in which there is no artifact or noise in the image.

What kind of difficulties can one expect in the application of such a methodology? Most of these are directly related to the fact that a specific and fixed geometric model is selected for the template. Thus geometric distortions and artifacts which appear in the data input will definitely result in erroneous matches. Even as simple a concept as a line detector will suffer from this. For example, Figure 2.16 shows the effect of varying the width and length of a mask which is passed over an image of a rectangular bar (dimension 3 rows by 7 columns). The response ρ of the correlation process is given by the height of the vertical axis. Clearly, when the mask is identical to (or greater than) the image, we obtain a maximum response. Dissimilarities in the model and the image result in a noticeable decrease in the value of ρ. Note also the importance of template orientation. To be able to detect line segments at any orientation requires that at each pixel location (i, j) we perform a correlation at

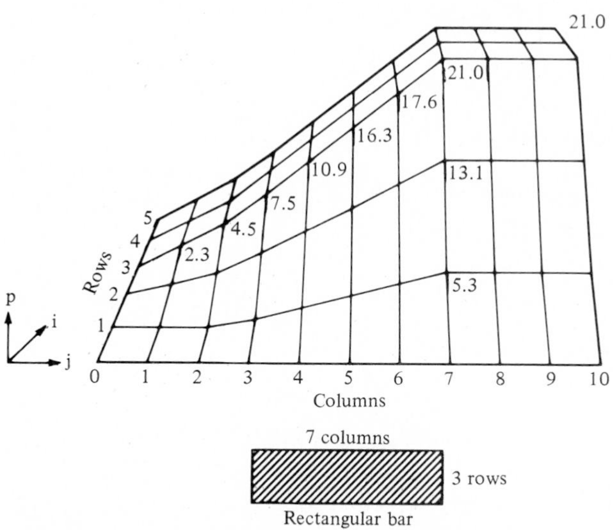

Figure 2.16 The effect of geometric distortions in a rectangular bar mask when matched with an image of a rectangular bar of fixed size (3 rows by 7 columns). The vertical axis represents the response of the correlation process.

a set of orientations. If this is not done, the results are difficult to interpret indeed. Figure 2.17 shows the effect of passing an "infinite" rectangular window of width 7 in one direction when the image contains edges with varying curvatures and therefore different orientations. The figure is a plot of template response ρ on the vertical axis versus the width and curvature of the line in the image of interest. In the limit, as the curvature becomes larger and approaches the orientation of the straight line, the maximum occurs at the appropriate width. However, the response is obviously quite sensitive to the two parameters.

In the examples so far, we have exhibited binary templates when in fact the data are a gray level image characterized by a whole set of gray levels. No satisfactory theoretical approach for designing nonbinary templates has emerged. However, we shall come across many different windowing operations in the following chapters, which have been designed on the basis of numerous criteria, in order to analyze various pictorial patterns.

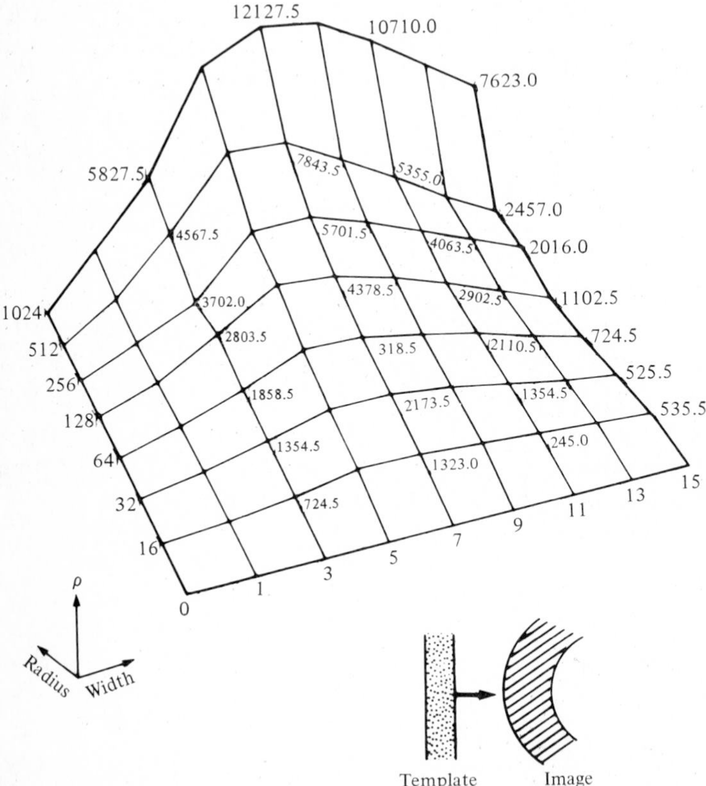

Figure 2.17 The result of passing an "infinite" rectangular window of width 7 in a horizontal direction over an image containing curved bars of varying width and radius. The template response is plotted on the vertical axis.

Finally, an aspect which is most important is the computational time needed for template matching. For an $N \times N$ picture and $n \times n$ window with $N \gg n$, we require n^2 multiplications for each of the N^2 correlation points. Thus, this means that n^2N^2 multiplications are needed for one image at each orientation. Typically, n is taken as being equal to 3, but larger values would probably yield better results, since the data model could be made more complex. To overcome the excessive time requirements for correlation on a conventional sequential-processing computer, special-purpose computer architectures have been developed [73]. An interesting, fast template matching algorithm for a conventional sequential processor is presented in [26]. Other approaches are discussed in [4, 52, 5, 3, 64, 46, 72, 55, 71, 63].

Computer hardware for performing image processing computations efficiently are generally based on cellular logic (see [53] for a tutorial article). Given an input array $I(i, j)$, a neighborhood mapping function is used to create a new array $I'(i, j)$. In the correlation process discussed above, obviously

$$I'(i, j) = \rho(i, j) \tag{2.39}$$

Each pixel (i, j) in the new array has a value which depends solely on its cell or neighborhood in the original array $I(i, j)$. The computation may be speeded up by either special-purpose sequential or parallel-type hardware. An example is a supercomputer, capable of processing images at the rate of 10^{11} operations per second, presently being developed by the National Aeronautics and Space Administration in the United States [58]. Readers interested in this subject of computer architectures for image processing are referred to the review papers [68] by Ullman on sequential processing, [19] by Danielsson and Levialdi on parallel processing, and [53] on both sequential and parallel processing. An example of the use of hardware correlation techniques for real-time compensation of an image digitizer in order to correct for scanner imperfections and noise is discussed in [41].

Finally, we mention the pictorial output, for example as shown in Figures 2.15, 2.16, and 2.17. These are generally obtained from either a gray tone or color display in conjunction with some type of terminal for symbolic and character output. Special-purpose picture memories and graphics techniques are also employed in this context [48]. Specially designed hard-copy units are also in use [23].

REFERENCES

1. Aggarwal, J. K., and Badler, N. I. (eds.), *Abstracts of the Workshop on Computer Analysis of Time-Varying Imagery, IEEE Computer Society*, Philadelphia, Apr. 5–6, 1979.
2. Andrews, H. C., "Computer Techniques in Image Processing," Academic, New York, 1970.
3. Andrus, J. F., Campbell, C. W., and Jayroe, R. R., "Digital Image Registration Method Using Boundary Maps," *IEEE Transactions on Computers*, vol. C-24, no. 9, September 1975, pp. 935–940.

4. Anuta, P. E., "Spatial Registration of Multispectral and Multitemporal Digital Imagery Using Fast Fourier Transform Techniques," *IEEE Transactions on Geoscience Electronics*, vol. GE-8, no. 4, October 1970, pp. 353–368.
5. Barnea, D. I., and Silverman, H. F., "Class of Algorithms for Fast Digital Image Registration," *IEEE Transactions on Computers*, vol. C-21, no. 2, February 1972, pp. 179–186.
6. Barrow, H. G., and Tenenbaum, J. M., "Recovering Intrinsic Scene Characteristics from Images," in Hanson, A. R., and Riseman, E. M. (eds.), "Computer Vision Systems," Academic, New York, 1978, pp. 3–26.
7. Bashe, R., "CCD Imaging, A Revolution for Electro Optical Systems," *Military Electronics Defense Expo '77*, Rhein-Main-Halle, Wiesbaden, Germany, 28 Sept. 1977. Obtainable as Report P-39, Fairchild Camera and Instrument Corp., 300 Robbins Lane, Syosset, New York, 11791.
8. Bauer, M., "Technological Basis and Applications of Remote Sensing of the Earth's Resources," *IEEE Transactions on Geoscience and Remote Sensing*, vol. Ge-14, no. 1, January 1976, pp. 3–9.
9. Billingsley, F. C., "Noise Considerations in Digital Image Processing Hardware," in Huang, T. S. (ed.), "Picture Processing and Digital Filtering," Springer-Verlag, New York, 1975, pp. 249–281.
10. Booth, J. M., and Schroeder, J. B., "Design Considerations for Digital Image Processing Systems," *Computer*, vol. 10, no. 8, August 1977, pp. 15–20.
11. Chien, R. T., and Snyder, W. E., "Hardware for Visual Image Processing," *IEEE Transactions on Circuits and Systems*, vol. CAS-22, no. 6, June 1975, pp. 541–551.
12. Compton, R. D., "The Solid State Imaging Revolution," *Electro-Optical Systems Design*, April 1974, pp. 22–29.
13. Cook, R. L., "A Reflectance Model for Computer Graphics," *SIGGRAPH-81, Conference Proceedings*, Dallas, Aug. 3–7, 1981 (Computer Graphics, SIGGRAPH-ACM, vol. 15, no. 3, August 1981), pp. 307–315.
14. Cordella, L. P., and Nagy, G., "Quantitative Functional Characterization of an Image Digitization System," *Proceedings of the Sixth International Conference on Pattern Recognition*, Munich, Oct. 19–22, 1982, pp. 535–537.
15. Cutrona, L. J., Leith, E. N., Palermo, C. J., and Porcelli, L. J., "Optical Data Processing and Filtering Systems," *IRE Transactions on Information Theory*, vol. IT-6, no. 3, June 1960, pp. 386–400.
16. Daele, J. V., Oosterlinck, A., and Van den Berghe, H., "Television Scanners, *Society of Photo-Optical Instrumentation Engineers, Proceedings International Seminar on Automation and Inspection Applications of Image Processing Techniques, SPIE* vol. 130, Sira, London, Sept. 12–13, 1977, pp. 75–82.
17. Dahlberg, R., "Digital Image Processor Links TV Signal Sources to Computer," *Computer Design*, vol. 16, no. 10, October 1977, pp. 115–120.
18. Dainty, J. C., and Shaw, R., "Image Science," Academic, London, 1974.
19. Danielsson, P.-E., and Levialdi, S., "Computer Architectures for Pictorial Information Systems," *Computer*, vol. 14, no. 11, November 1981, pp. 53–67.
20. Dillon, P. L. P., Lewis, D. M., and Kaspar, F. G., "Color Imaging System Using a Single CCD Area Array," *IEEE Transactions on Electron Devices*, vol. ED-25, no. 2, February 1978, pp. 102–107.
21. Duda, R. O., and Hart, P. E., "Pattern Classification and Scene Analysis," Wiley, New York, 1973, pp. 405–424.
22. Elkind, D., "Perceptual Development in Children," *American Scientist*, vol. 63, no. 5, September/October 1975, pp. 533–541.
23. Eriksen, J., "Making a Hard Copy from a Raster Scan Monitor," *Electro-Optical Systems Design*, vol. 12, no. 7, July 1980, pp. 37–44.
24. Fairchild Camera and Instrument Corp., "Single-CCD-Sensor Demonstration Color Camera," *Journal of Semiconductor Progress*, vol. 9, no. 2, 2d Quarter 1981, pp. 17–23.

25. Feather, A. E., Siegel, L. J., and Siegel, H. J., "Image Correlation Using Parallel Processing," *Proceedings 5th International Conference on Pattern Recognition*, Miami Beach, Dec. 1–4, 1980, pp. 503–507.
26. Frei, W., Shibata, T., and Chen, C. C., "Fast Matching of Known-Stationary Images with False Fix Protection," *5th International Conference on Pattern Recognition*, Miami Beach, Dec. 1–4, 1980, pp. 208–212.
27. Golab, T., Ledley, R. S., and Rotolo, L. S., "FIDAC-Film Input to Digital Automatic Computer," *Pattern Recognition*, vol. 3, no. 2, July 1971, pp. 123–156.
28. Haralick, R. M., "Using Perspective Transformations in Scene Analysis," *Computer Graphics and Image Processing*, vol. 13 no. 3, July 1980, pp. 191–221.
29. Horn, B. K. P., "Obtaining Shape From Shading Information," in Winston, P. H. (ed.), "The Psychology of Computer Vision," McGraw-Hill, New York, 1975, pp. 115–155.
30. Horn, B. K. P., "Understanding Image Intensities," *Artificial Intelligence*, vol. 8, no. 2, 1977, pp. 201–231.
31. Horn, B. K. P., "Hill Shading and the Reflectance Map," *Proceedings IEEE*, vol. 69, no. 1, January 1981, pp. 14–47.
32. Horn, B. K. P., Woodham, R. J., and Silver, W. M., "Determining Shape and Reflectors Using Multiple Images," MIT A. I. Memo 490, Massachusetts Institute of Technology, Cambridge, Mass., August 1978.
33. Jarvis, R. A., "A Colour Television Image Acquisition, Manipulation and Display System for Computer Vision Research," *Proceedings Workshop on Picture Data Description and Management*, Asilomar, Calif., Aug. 27–28, 1980, pp. 187–197.
34. Koike, N., Takemoto, I., Sato, K., Matsumaru, H., Ashikawa, M., and Kubo, M., "An NPN Structure 484×384 MOS Imager for a Single-Chip Color Camera," *1979 IEEE International Solid State Circuits Conference, Digest of Technical Papers*, 1979, pp. 192–193.
35. Kosonocky, W. F., and Sauer, D. J., "The ABCs of CCDs," *Electronic Design*, Apr. 12, 1975, pp. 58–63.
36. Kosonocky, W. F., and Sauer, D. J., "Consider CCDs for a Wide Range of Uses," *Electronic Design*, vol. 24, no. 6, Mar. 15, 1976, pp. 70–78.
37. Kovasznay, L. S., and Joseph, H. M., "Processing of Two-Dimensional Patterns by Scanning Techniques," *Science*, vol. 118, no. 3069, Oct. 25, 1953, pp. 475–477.
38. Kruger, R. P., and Thompson, W. B., "A Technical and Economic Assessment of Computer Vision for Industrial Inspection and Robotic Assembly," *Proceedings IEEE*, vol. 69, no. 12, December 1981, pp. 1524–1538.
39. Le Grand, Y., "Light, Colour and Vision," Chapman and Hall, London, 1957.
40. Le Grand, Y., "Measurement of the Visual Stimulus," chap. 2 in Carterette, E. C., and Friedman, M. P. (eds.), "Handbook of Perception, Seeing," Academic, New York, 1975, pp. 25–55.
41. Mayeda, T., "Using the Digital Video Scanner System," Image Processing Application Note, Comtal Corp., P.O. Box 5087, Pasadena, Calif., 91107, 1979.
42. Mercer, H. D., and Younse, J. M., "Miniature TV Compatible CCD Camera," *1978 IEEE International Solid State Circuits Conference, Digest of Technical Papers*, 1978, pp. 38–39.
43. Mohwinkel, C., and Kurz, L., "Computer Picture Processing and Enhancement by Localized Operations," *Computer Graphics and Image Processing*, vol. 5, no. 4, 1976, pp. 401–424.
44. Moore, G. A., "Design of a Practical Scanner Unit for Precision Analyses of Micrographs," *Pattern Recognition*, vol. 3, no. 2, July 1971, pp. 91–122.
45. Nagel, H. H., "Analysis Techniques for Image Sequence," *Proceedings Fourth International Joint Conference on Pattern Recognition*, Kyoto, Japan, Nov. 7–10, 1978, pp. 186–211.
46. Nagel, R. N., and Rosenfeld, A., "Ordered Search Techniques in Template Matching," *Proceedings IEEE*, vol. 60, no. 2, February 1972, pp. 242–244.
47. Nagy, G., "Digital Image Processing Activities in Remote Sensing For Earth Resources," *Proceedings IEEE*, vol. 60, no. 10, October 1972, pp. 1177–1200.

48. Newman, W. M., and Sproull, R. F., "Principles of Interactive Computer Graphics," 2d ed., McGraw-Hill, 1979.
49. Parks, J. R., "Industrial Sensory Devices," in Batchelor, B. G. (ed.), "Pattern Recognition," Plenum, New York, 1978, pp. 253–286.
50. Parrish, E. A. Jr., and Goksel, A. K., "A Camera Model for Natural Scene Processing," *Pattern Recognition*, vol. 9, no. 3, October 1977, pp. 131–136.
51. Phong, B. T., "Illumination for Computer Generated Pictures," *CACM*, vol. 18, no. 6, 1975, pp. 311–317.
52. Pratt, W. K., "Correlation Techniques of Image Registration," *IEEE Transactions on Aerospace Electronics and Systems*, vol. AES-10, no. 3, May 1974, pp. 353–357.
53. Preston, K. Jr., Duff, M. J. B., Levialdi, S., Norgren, P. E., and Toriwaki, J. I., "Basics of Cellular Logic with Some Applications of Medical Image Processing," *Proceedings IEEE*, vol. 67, no. 5, May 1979, pp. 826–856.
54. Rogers, R. L., "Charge-Coupled Imager for 525–Live Television," *IEEE Intercon*, New York, March 1974.
55. Rosenfeld, A., and VanderBrug, G. J., "Coarse-Fine Template Matching," Technical Report TR-398, Computer Science, TR Series, University of Maryland, August 1975.
56. Rosenfeld, A., and Kak, A. C., "Digital Image Processing," Academic, New York, 1976.
57. Sandini, G., and Tagliasco, V., "An Anthropomorphic Retina-like Structure for Scene Analysis," *Computer Graphics and Image Processing*, vol. 14, 1980, pp. 365–372.
58. Schaefer, D. H., and Fischer, J. R., "Beyond the Supercomputer," *IEEE Spectrum*, vol. 19, no. 3, March 1982, pp. 32–37.
59. Schreiber, W. F., "Image Processing for Quality Improvements," *Proceedings IEEE*, vol. 66, no. 12, December 1978, pp. 1640–1651.
60. Snow, E. H., and Weckler, G. P., "Self-Scanned Charge Coupled Photodiode (CCPD) Sensor Arrays," *Proceedings Society Photo-Optical Instrumentation Engineers*, San Diego, Aug. 23–24, 1977, pp. 2–9.
61. Sternberg, S. R., "Architectures for Neighborhood Processing," *PRIP-81, IEEE Computer Society Conference on Pattern Recognition and Image Processing*, Dallas, Aug. 3–5, 1981, pp. 374–380.
62. Stockham, T., "Image Processing in the Context of a Visual Model," *Proceedings IEEE*, vol. 60, no. 7, July 1972, pp. 828–842.
63. Stockman, G., Kopstein, S., and Benett, S., "Matching Images to Models for Registration and Object Detection Via Clustering," *IEEE Transactions on Pattern Analysis and Machine Intelligence*, vol. PAMI-4, no. 3, May 1982, pp. 229–241.
64. Tasto, M., and Block, U., "Locating Objects in Complex Scenes Using a Spatial Distance Measure," *Proceedings 2d International Joint Conference on Pattern Recognition*, Copenhagen, Aug. 13–15, 1974, pp. 336–340.
65. Tenenbaum, J. M., Barrow, H. G., and Bolles, R. C., "Prospects for Industrial Vision," *SRI Technical Note 175*, Menlo Park, Calif., November 1978.
66. Turin, G. L., "An Introduction to Matched Filters," *IRE Transactions Information Theory*, vol. IT-6, no. 3, June 1960, pp. 311–329.
67. Ullman, J. R., "A Review of Optical Pattern Recognition Techniques," *Opto-Electronics*, vol. 6, no. 4, 1974, pp. 319–332.
68. Ullman, J. R., "Hardware Versus Software for Image Processing," *British Pattern Recognition Association 1980 Conference on Pattern Recognition*, Oxford University, 9–11 Jan. 1980, p. 107.
69. Ullman, J. R., "Video-Rate Digital Image Analysis Equipment," *Pattern Recognition*, vol. 14, nos. 1–6, 1981, pp. 305–318.
70. Ullman, S., "Interfacing the One-Dimensional Scanning of an Image With the Application of Two-Dimensional Operators," *Computer Graphics and Image Processing*, vol. 16, no. 2, June 1981, pp. 150–157.
71. VanderBrug, G. J., and Rosenfeld, A., "Two-Stage Template Matching," Technical Report TR-364, Computer Science TR Series, University of Maryland, March 1975.

72. VanderBrug, G. J., "Two-Stage Template Matching: The Grayscale Case," Technical Report TR-398, Computer Science TR Series, University of Maryland, August 1975.
73. Wambacq, L., Van Eycken, L., De Roo, J., Oosterlinck, A., and Van den Berghe, H., Description of Two Hardware Convolvers as a Part of a General Image Computer, *PRIP-81, IEEE Computer Society Conference on Pattern Recognition and Image Processing*, Dallas, Aug. 3–5, 1981, pp. 294–296.
74. Wang, R. T., "Sensor Transformations," *IEEE Transactions on Systems, Man, and Cybernetics*, vol. SMC-7, no. 12, December 1977, pp. 836–841.
75. Whitted, T., "An Improved Illumination Model for Shaded Display," *Communications of the ACM*, vol. 23, no. 6, June 1980, pp. 343–349.
76. Woodham, R., "Analyzed Curved Surfaces Using Reflectance Map Techniques," in Winston, P. H., and Brown, R. H. (eds.), "Artificial Intelligence: An MIT Perspective," vol. 2, MIT Press, Cambridge, Mass., 1979, pp. 161–182.
77. Wyszecki, G., and Stiles, W. S., "Color Science," Wiley, New York, 1967.

BIBLIOGRAPHY

A glossary of terms and definitions for image processing can be found in [8]. Readers who wish to quickly familiarize themselves with the terminology of image pattern recognition are advised to read this paper.

Chien and Snyder [5] provide a good summary describing image digitizers used in research laboratories and industry, while Bauer [2] and Nagy [13] should be consulted for remote sensing applications. Both these sources contain excellent descriptions, with the latter emphasizing methods for data correction due to various important error sources. A solid-state automated microscope for digitizing images is discussed in [21]. Additional papers on digitizing systems may be found in [16]. The actual photoelectric transduction devices are described in [3, 15].

A significant proportion of the research related to the material in Section 2.1.2 is being carried out in the Artificial Intelligence Laboratory at the Massachusetts Institute of Technology. This work, under the direction of Berthold Horn, is concerned with the study of the underlying physical principles of image formation. Readers are referred to [4, 9, 10, 11, 12, 17] for further material. A comprehensive review of the literature has been written by Barrow and Tenenbaum [1]. Reference [12] deals briefly with the issue of man's ability to extract shape and intrinsic features from views of his environment. To what extent are these learned or "computed"?

General-purpose cellular processors suitable for image processing, both sequential and parallel, are increasing in importance. An introductory survey paper on this topic is presented by Danielsson and Levialdi [7]. An excellent introduction to the integrated circuits which make these architectures practically feasible may be found in [6]. The design of software as it relates to picture processing is discussed in [18].

Readers interested in learning more about matched filtering might consult the special June 1960 issue of the *IEEE Transactions on Information Theory* and [19]. Applications to medical image processing of windowing techniques can be found in [14], while Van der Lugt [20] discusses these issues in the context of optical data processing.

1. Barrow, H. G., and Tenenbaum, J. M., "Computational Vision," *Proceedings IEEE*, vol. 69, no. 5, May 1981, pp. 572–595.
2. Bauer, M. E., "Technological Basis and Applications of Remote Sensing of the Earth's Resources," *IEEE Transactions on Geoscience Electronics*, vol. GE-14, no. 1, January 1976, pp. 3–9.
3. Biberman, L. M., and Nudelman, S. (eds.), "Photoelectric Imaging Devices," Plenum, New York, 1971.
4. Bruss, A. R., "Some Properties of Discontinuities in the Image Irradiance Equation," Massachusetts Institute of Technology, Artificial Intelligence Laboratory, A.I. Memo no. 517, April 1979.
5. Chien, R. T., and Snyder, W. E., "Hardware for Visual Image Processing," *IEEE Transactions on Circuits and Systems*, vol. CAS-22, no. 6, June 1975, pp. 541–551.
6. Clark, W. A., "From Electron Mobility to Logical Structure: A View of Integrated Circuits," *Computing Surveys*, vol. 12, no. 3, September 1980, pp. 325–356.
7. Danielsson, P.-E., and Levialdi, S., "Computer Architectures for Pictorial Information Systems," *Computer*, vol. 14, no. 11, November 1981, pp. 53–67.
8. Haralick, R. M., "Glossary and Index to Remotely Sensed Images Pattern Recognition Concepts," *Pattern Recognition*, vol. 5, no. 4, 1973, pp. 391–403.
9. Horn, B. K. P., "SEQUINS and QUILLS—Representations for Surface Topography," Massachusetts Institute of Technology, Artificial Intelligence Laboratory, A.I. Memo no. 536, May 1979.
10. Ikeuchi, K., and Horn, B. K. P., An Application of the Photometric Stereo Method, Massachusetts Institute of Technology, Artificial Intelligence Laboratory, A.I. Memo no. 539, August 1979.
11. Ikeuchi, K., "Numerical Shape from Shading and Occluding Contours in a Single View," Massachusetts Institute of Technology, Artificial Intelligence Laboratory, A.I. Memo no. 566, February 1980.
12. Ikeuchi, K., "Shape from Regular Patterns (An Example of Constraint Propagation in Vision)," Massachusetts Institute of Technology, Artificial Intelligence Laboratory, A.I. Memo no. 567, March 1980.
13. Nagy, G., "Digital Image Processing Activities in Remote Sensing for Earth Resources," *Proceedings IEEE*, vol. 60, no. 10, October 1972, pp. 1177–1200.
14. Nawrath, R., and Serra, J., "Quantitative Image Analysis: Applications Using Sequential Transformations," *Microscopica Acta*, vol. 82, no. 2, September 1979, pp. 113–128.
15. Palmieri, G., "Image Devices for Pattern Recognition," *Pattern Recognition*, vol. 3, no. 2, July 1971, pp. 157–168.
16. Proceedings Society of Photo-Optical Instrumentation Engineers, vol. 48, "Acquisition and Analysis of Pictorial Data," *The Modern Science of Imagery Conference*, San Diego, Aug. 19–20, 1974.
17. Smith, D. A., "Using Enhanced Spherical Images for Object Representation," Massachusetts Institute of Technology, Artificial Intelligence Laboratory, A.I. Memo no. 530, May 1979.
18. Tanimoto, S. L., "Advances in Software Engineering and Their Relations to Pattern Recognition and Image Processing," *Proceedings 5th International Conference Pattern Recognition*, Miami Beach, Dec. 1–4, 1980, pp. 734–741.
19. Turin, G. L., "An Introduction to Digital Matched Filters," *Proceedings IEEE*, vol. 64, no. 7, July 1976, pp. 1092–1112.
20. Van der Lugt, A., "A Review of Optical Data Processing Techniques," *Optica Acta*, vol. 15, no. 1, 1968, pp. 1–33.
21. Young, I. T., Balasubramanian, Dunbar, D. L., Peverini, R. L., and Bishop, R. P., "SSAM: Solid-State Automated Microscope," *IEEE Transactions on Biomedical Engineering*, vol. BME-29, no. 2, February 1982, pp. 70–82.

CHAPTER

THREE

BIOLOGICAL VISION SYSTEMS

3.1 INTRODUCTION

Humans and animals are capable of accomplishing a wide range of perceptual tasks, most of which we understand very little about from the point of view of how the brain functions. We have noted that the visual system may be considered as a mechanism that converts input light patterns into perceptions, which are usually reported verbally or by a motor action. Most of our basic knowledge about this activity relates to the early stages of the processing, as will become apparent from the descriptions in this chapter and those following. Moreover, even the early stages are not fully understood.

If we model the visual system as a living optical transduction device followed by a computer, we must appreciate that even though the transducer is physically in the eye, some portion of the image processing may also take place there. In fact, the less advanced the living form, the greater the fraction of its computational power that is located in the eye. Physically it is convenient to distinguish three stages, as shown in Figure 3.1. None of these is simple in design, although the first stage of optical processing is the least complex, mostly because the smallest amount of neural activity is associated with it. The second, retinal stage, providing the sensory transduction as well as some cellular processing, is also located in the eye. The last stage in this sequence is essentially a rubric for the myriad of connections and many complex levels of processing. These begin at the retinal level and continue in an analysis hierarchy (see Figure 1.10) toward and within the brain, the so-called meat machine or wetware.

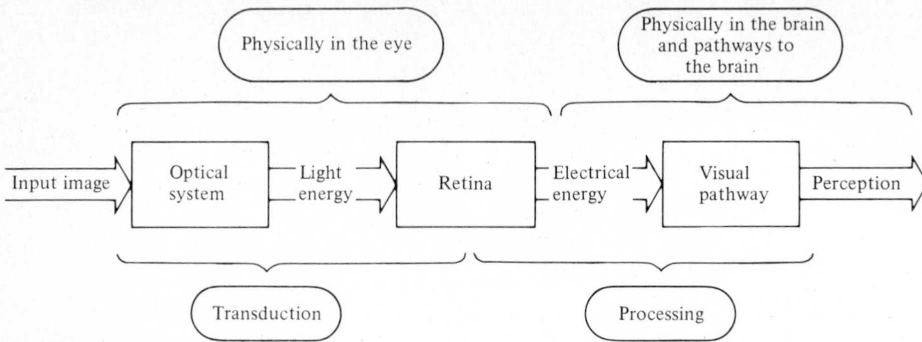

Figure 3.1 The human visual system viewed as consisting of a camera and a computer, providing for transduction and processing, respectively.

Section 3.2 will describe the optical system, the "front-end" or "camera" aspects of the human visual system. At this point light energy is input and is controlled somewhat, but the major function of the system is to provide a focused image at the retina. Therefore, we see that energy conversion takes place at this interface. The retina, described in Section 3.3, serves the twofold roles of transduction and processing. First the signal is converted to a frequency-coded format by a photochemical process and then the resulting electrical signals are further analyzed. The amount of high-level retinal processing is inversely related to the intelligence and evolutionary complexity of the animal. This is true only in general terms, since the phylogeny of the vertebrate eye is unknown.

Since the eyes of the various vertebrates are not greatly different, it has been convenient for experimental purposes to examine and study such animals as cats and monkeys rather than humans. This, of course, can only be carried out to a certain point, because the visual pathway, which will be described in Section 3.4, finally outputs as a human action. However, animals have a limited facility for explaining their behavior. This serves at present as a real stumbling block to achieving further knowledge about the higher processes of the human visual apparatus. A new experimental technique must be found before any great strides can be taken to increase our comprehension of the brain.

Notwithstanding the above arguments, we do know how the neurons in the brain function as individual computational units, even if we are at a loss to explain how they cooperate and compete to provide a given perceptual experience. Section 3.5 will explain in very simplified terms a general model of cellular behavior which seems to be consistent with our present knowledge.

3.2 THE OPTICAL SYSTEM

In Figure 3.1, the ocular optical system of a human is seen to produce a transformation of the light energy of the visual input stimulus impinging on the eye to an output which is similarly a high-energy signal. A horizontal cross section of the human eye is shown in Figure 3.2. The input light pattern enters the cornea and then passes in sequence through the anterior chamber, the pupil opening of the iris, the lens, and the vitreous humor before impinging on the layer of photoreceptors which constitutes the retina at the rear. The latter is responsible for the actual transduction from light energy into electrical energy in the form of a train of frequency-modulated pulses and will be discussed in detail in Section 3.4. A system block diagram showing the main stages of the optical system is shown in Figure 3.3.

The human eyeball, which is about 25 mm in diameter, is flexible, so that even this first step of optical processing results in image distortion. The stages

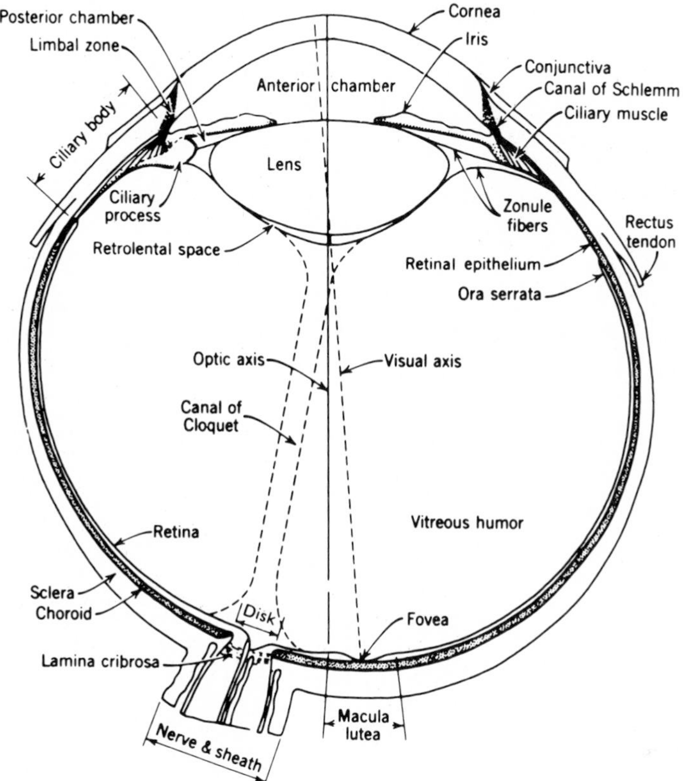

Figure 3.2 A horizontal cross section of the human eye viewed from above and showing the different stages of the optical system. The retina appears at the rear and is well protected from environmental disturbances. [*From W. R. Uttal, "The Psychobiology of Sensory Coding," Harper & Row, New York, 1973, p. 102, in J. L. Brown, "The Structure of the Visual System," in C. H. Graham (ed.), "Vision and Visual Perception," Wiley, New York, 1965, pp. 39–59; after G. L. Walls, "The Vertebrate Eye," Cranbrook Institute of Science, Bloomfield Hills, Mich., 1942, as modified from M. Salzmann, "The Anatomy and Physiology of the Human Eyeball in the Normal State," University of Chicago Press, Chicago, 1912.*]

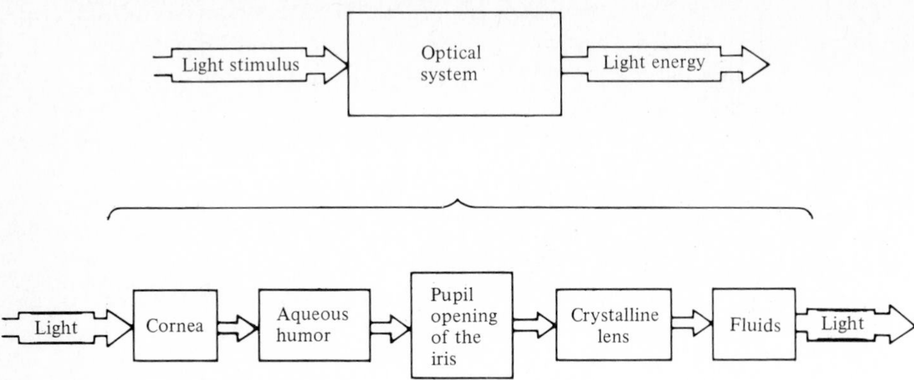

Figure 3.3 A block diagram of the light pathway of the human eye as sketched in Figure 3.2.

shown in Figure 3.3 which the light path must traverse contain many impurities which obstruct and nonlinearly transform the signal. Evidently no correction is made for the ensuing chromatic or spherical aberrations. Remarkably, only about 50 percent of the light energy entering the cornea in fact even arrives at the retina. The optical system therefore projects a recognizable but definitely imperfect image on the receptor cells.

This method of image formation in the vertebrate eye has not necessarily been replicated by the evolutionary process in other animals. Figure 3.4 shows several interesting cases of invertebrate photoreceptor organs. For example, the limpet (Figure 3.4*a*) and the nautilus (Figure 3.4*b*) do not even possess focusing lenses and the images falling on their retinas are controlled in a very rudimentary fashion. The photoreceptors of the limpet are protected by a secretion and are located within a so-called visual pit. The latter has the effect of reducing the amount of input ambient light, thereby increasing the contrast and enhancing the effectiveness of the eye in detecting enemy shadows. Image formation in the nautilus, a spiral-shelled mollusk related to the octopus and the squid, resembles that in the simple pinhole camera, except that the eye is continuously being washed by seawater. This type of arrangement has the advantage of always keeping the image in focus, with the concomitant disadvantage of seriously reducing the amount of light falling on the retina. Other invertebrates possess more sophisticated optical systems containing lenses. In the case of the scorpion (Figure 3.4*c*), an aggressive, nocturnal, eight-legged animal, the optical system is relatively large and located externally, while in the slow-moving snail (Figure 3.4*d*) the light must first pass through retinal ephithelium, the retina, and a liquid secretion before reaching the internal lens. On the other hand, the squid (Figure 3.4*e*) has highly developed eyes which contain a lens capable of forming an image. If two eyes are necessary for the survival of the normal vertebrate (Figure 3.4*f*), then four eyes must be twice as useful. Figure 3.5 shows such a fish, the *Anableps microlepis*, which is capable of simultaneously monitoring both aquatic and aerial activity. When it is

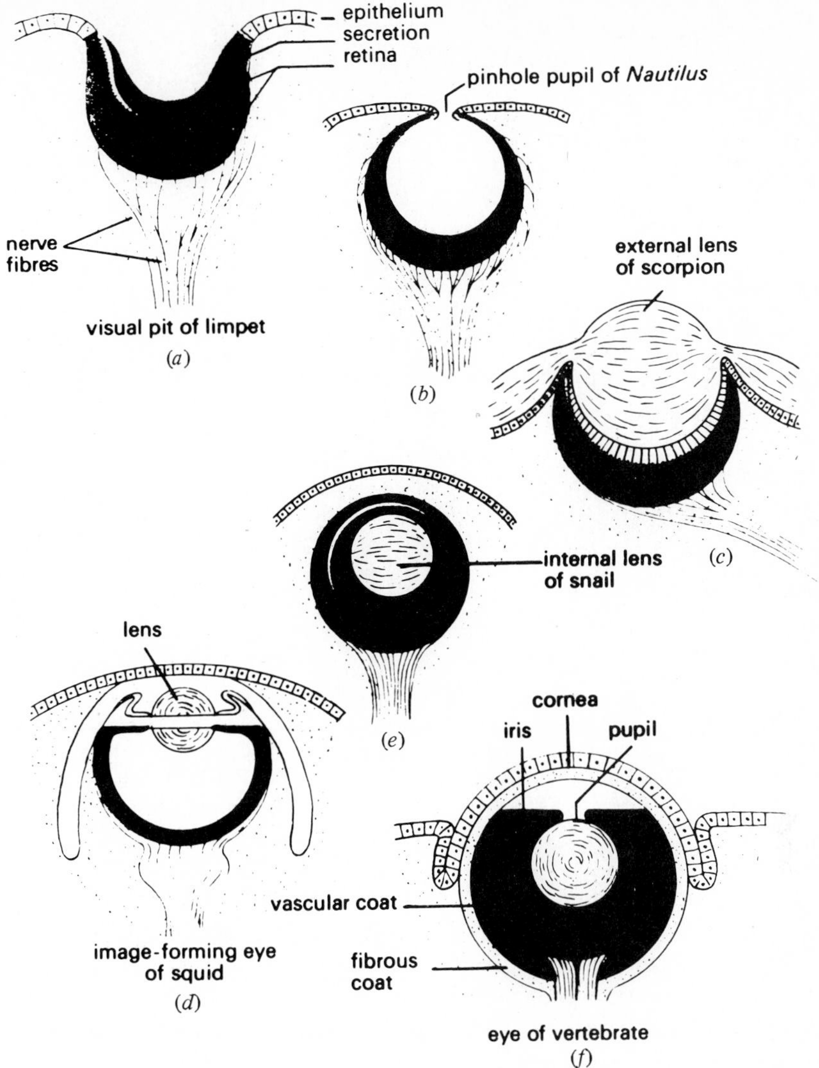

Figure 3.4 A comparison of several interesting eyes of invertebrates (a–e) with those of a vertebrate (f). How and why these eyes developed as they did is not known. (*From R. L. Gregory, "Eye and Brain, the Psychology of Seeing," World University Library, McGraw-Hill, New York, 1966, p. 24.*)

submerged, a horizontal flap is retracted to effectively provide only two eyes. It possesses a strong muscle capable of moving its lens to the proper position for maximum visual acuity depending on whether it is attacking an insect on the water surface or other prey underwater.

Another interesting eye is the compound eye of the invertebrate arthropod, which possesses thousands of lens facets. Each lens facet contains one

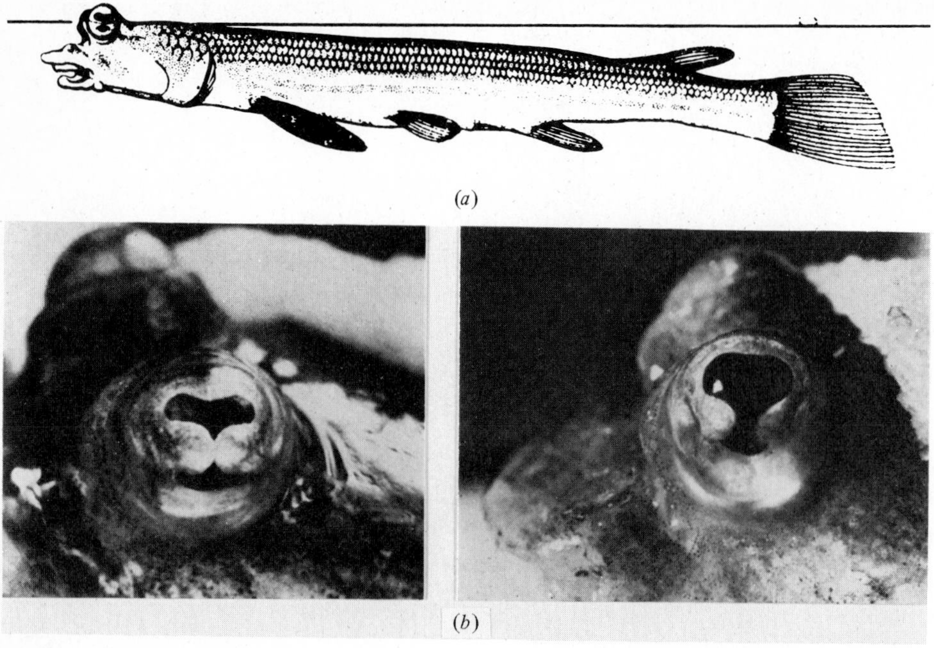

Figure 3.5 The *Anableps microlepis* can control its visual system so that it effectively has four eyes. The light-adapted condition shown in (*a*) allows it to simultaneously view prey both above and below the waterline. In (*b*) the pupillary aperture is one complete unit, a situation which occurs when the fish is submerged and the pupil is dark-adapted. (*From H. O. Schwassman and L. Kruger, Experimental Analysis of the Visual System of the 4-Eyed Fish Anableps microlepis, Vision Research, vol. 5, 1975, pp. 269–281.*)

receptor element and is stimulated by the light directly impinging upon it. An example of an insect is shown in Figure 3.6. This mosaic arrangement would seem to yield a one-to-one mapping between the viewed light patterns and the retinal electrical signal. For the most part this is correct, except that there is some interaction at the electrical-signal-processing level. Later on we shall discuss some interesting experiments with the compound eye of the horseshoe crab, which demonstrate how this lateral interaction tends to accentuate borders between light and dark areas. Instead of a dense receptor mosaic, suppose that an animal has a lens system but only one photoreceptor capable of generating an electrical signal. This is the case for the arthropod *Copilia* (Figure 3.7), in which mechanical scanning of the receptor (recall that the *Anableps microlepis* moves the lens) is seemingly used to ensure that the anterior lens focuses on this transduction element. Finally, consider the rattlesnake, which has two sources of imagery, one in the visible and the other in the infrared range. There is evidence that these are integrated to give the snake a composite view of its environment [15].

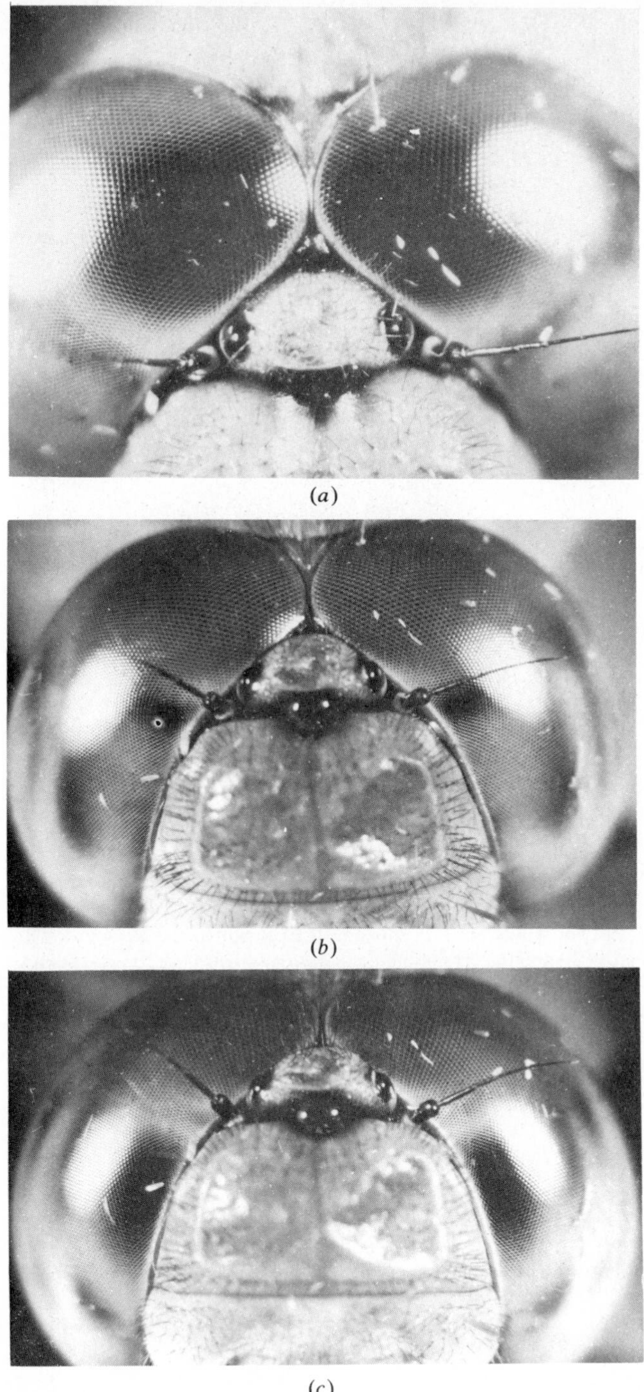
(a)
(b)
(c)

Figure 3.6 (Caption on page 66.)

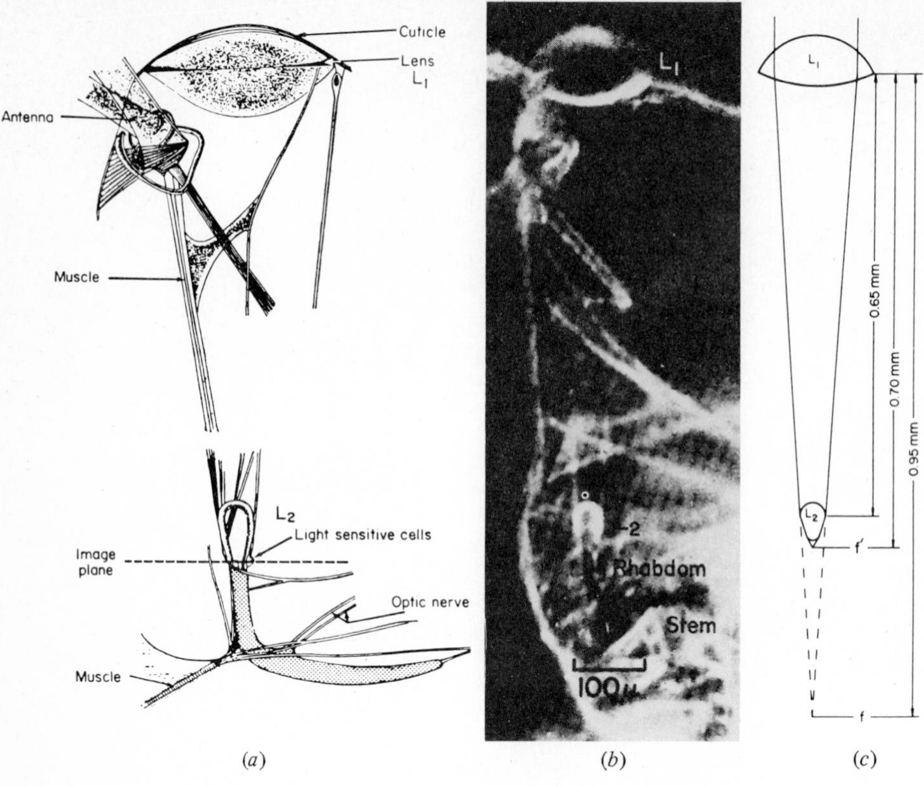

Figure 3.7 *Copilia quadrata.* (*a*) The scanning eye of the copepod, *Copilia quadrata*, which possesses a fixed anterior lens (L_1) as well as a smaller, movable posterior lens (L_2) attached to a single photoreceptor within its body. This interior lens and receptor assembly continuously moves across the image plane of the anterior lens, possibly in analogy to the mechanical scanning microdensitometer discussed in Chapter 2. (*b*) Dark-field photomicrograph of the eye. (*c*) The optical system showing the positions of the corneal anterior lens (L_1) and the crystalline-cone posterior lens (L_2); f : focal point of the corneal (anterior lens); f': focal point of the total optical system. [*From J. J. Wolken, "Comparative Structure of Invertebrate Photoreceptor," in H. Davson (ed.), "The Eye," vol. 6, "Comparative Physiology," Academic, New York, 1974, pp. 111–154, after H. Grenacher, "Untersuchungen über das Sehorgan der Arthropoden, insbesondere der Spinnen, Insekten and Crustaceen," p. 145, Vanderhoeck and Ruprecht, Göttingen, Germany, 1879.*]

Figure 3.6 Photographs of the head of the dragonfly *Orthetrum*, showing two foveas, one pointing directly ahead and the other forward and upward, for catching prey in flight. (*a*) Camera at 35° to the longitudinal axis of the animal, forward and upward. (*b*) Camera at 15° to the longitudinal axis, forward and upward, with minimum size of pseudopupil between the two foveas. (*c*) Camera on the horizontal axis, looking straight forward. The black area of facets is the pseudopupil. The larger the pseudopupil, the greater the density of the visual units (ommatidia) looking in that direction. The white dirt on the eye serves to mark the facets. (*Photographs provided by G. A. Horridge, Australian National University, Canberra.*)

Let us now consider each of the different stages in Figure 3.3. The "cornea" (which is covered with a film of tears) is the front surface of the eye which bends the light to form the image. It is transparent and supported by an opaque layer of fibrous membrane called the "sclera" (see Figure 3.2), part of which is seen as the white of the eye. Although the air-cornea-aqueous humor (contained in the anterior chamber) pathway is responsible for approximately two-thirds of the optical power of the eye (42 diopters compared with 57 to 62 total), it is not a very good optical instrument.

After the light emerges from the aqueous humor, it passes through the pupil, which is a diaphragm or opening in the center of the iris [11]. The characteristic pigmentation of the iris is what gives us the color of our eyes. Curiously, women usually possess larger pupils than men and blue-eyed persons have larger pupils than those with brown eyes. This circular hole is similar to an aperture stop for a lens in a photographic camera [18]. Thus the iris behaves in a certain sense just like a servomechanism by contracting and expanding the size of the pupil. In this fashion it controls the amount of light which passes on to the next stage, which is the crystalline lens. Figure 3.8*a* is a schematic frontal view of the human eye. Variations in the diameter of the diaphragm are achieved by the contraction of two kinds of smooth muscle fibers, the sphincter and the dilator pupillae. The sphincter is responsible for constriction and runs parallel to the circular iris; the dilator activates expansion and functions radially. In cooperation these muscles can achieve a 16-fold

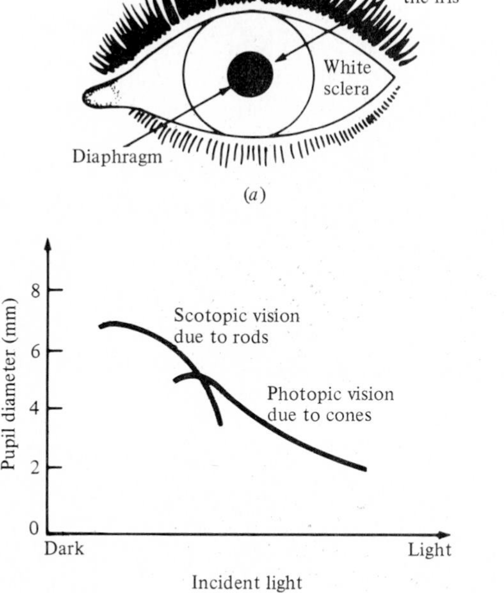

Figure 3.8 The two modes of operation of the pupil. Note that the incident light is only one of many factors that control the diameter of the pupil at any time. (*a*) Schematic frontal view of the human eye. (*b*) Sketch of the variation of pupil size as a function of incident light.

change in aperture area by varying the diameter from about 2 mm to a maximum of 8 mm. Control of the size of this area is such that it is normally kept as small as possible in order to maximize the focus. The time constant associated with this action is about 10 s for the full diameter range. The activation of the control is extremely complex and is due to numerous factors but mainly to the amount of incident light and the emotional state of the viewer. Indeed, a recent survey has listed 23 different sources of variation, including sexual preference, political attitude, fatigue, semantic stimuli, and signal wavelength [32]. The dynamic characteristics of this pupillary light reflex system also appear to be related to certain neurological disorders. Readers who are interested in models of this dynamic control system should consult [21, 22, 24, 25, 33]. Pupil size as a function of the amount of incident light is sketched in Figure 3.8*b*.

Varying the size of the pupil of the eye serves three objectives [8]. The first effect is the light reflex function discussed above, which controls the amount of light that enters the eye and therefore impinges on the retina. The second, known as the near response, constricts the size of the pupil in order to control the depth of focus of near objects. The third, which is particularly important under bright light conditions, is reduction of the pupil size in order to reduce image aberrations. It appears that only the first two factors can be quantitatively controlled by external inputs.

After the pupil, the incident light passes through the crystalline lens, which is responsible for about one-third of the total optical power of the eye. It provides accommodation to near and far vision by changing its geometry, a function which is achieved in a camera by moving the lens. This second lens in the light pathway is made up of nonrigid laminae, much like an onion, and control is achieved by the action of the ciliary muscles, which vary the laminar thickness and shape. The control response time is approximately 0.4 s. Thus this lens guarantees that the image is in focus at the retinal plane, where an inverted image is provided.

Finally, we have the fluid, or vitreous humor as it is called, which is gelatinous and is essentially the means by which the shape of the eye is maintained. Light passes through the fluid to the retina, which is responsible for the electrooptical conversion between the incident light patterns and the resulting first stage of electrical activity in the nerve cells.

We may view the optical system in Figure 3.3 as an input/output transformation of a three-dimensional space whose range is restricted by the physical capacity of the human eye. We observe this space through a two-dimensional "window." The input light patterns result in an output falling on the retina which originates from the three-dimensional scene viewed by the eye and which contains objects to be recognized. The height of the resulting inverted image in this retinal plane is related to the size of the object subtended (see Figure 3.9). Let S be the size of the object at a distance d from the eye and P the size of the projection on the retina. Then if we assume that the focal length of the eye is about 17 mm,

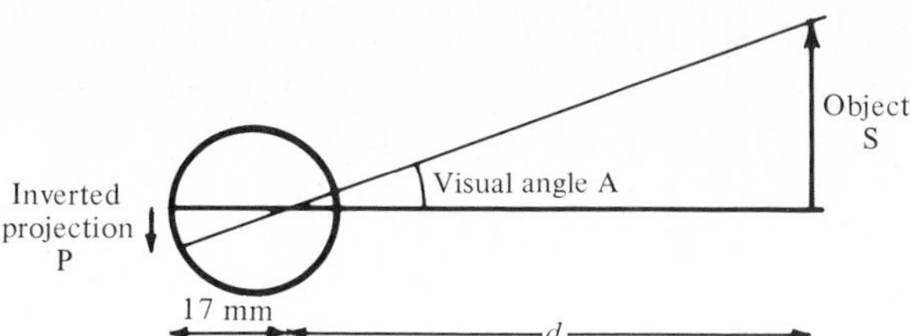

Figure 3.9 The retinal projection of an object viewed by the human eye.

$$P = \frac{17S}{d} \quad \text{mm} \tag{3.1}$$

and the visual angle A is given by

$$A = \tan^{-1}\left(\frac{S}{d}\right) \quad \text{degrees} \tag{3.2}$$

For example we can compute that a thumbnail (= 1.5 cm) at arm's length (= 60 cm) will subtend a visual angle of about 1.5°. The most sensitive part of the retina, the "fovea," subtends an angle of only about 2°.

The breadth of the scene is governed by the limit of the eyes' peripheral vision. Experiments have shown that retinal stimulation occurs for bright point

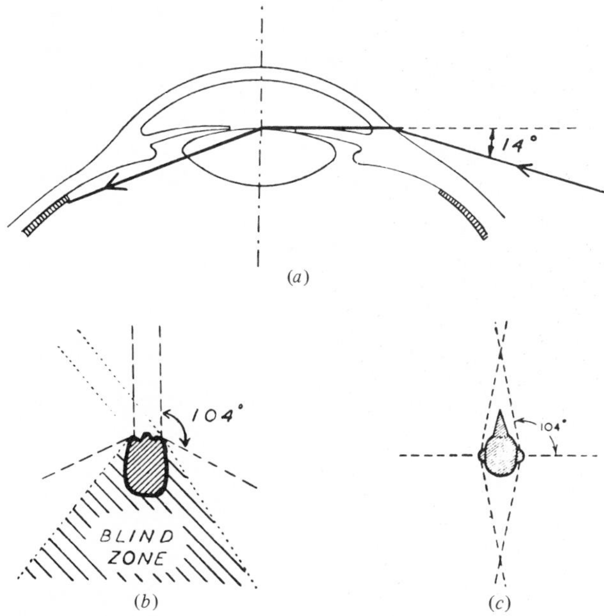

Figure 3.10 Peripheral vision. (*a*) A schematic showing the limits of the peripheral vision of man. Light originating from behind the head will project onto the retina. (*b*) The blind zone of man when physical movement of the eye is taken into account. (*c*) The peripheral vision of a bird is much more extensive than that of man because of the placement of its two eyes. (*From M. H. Pirenne, "Vision and the Eye," 2d ed., Associated Book Publishers, London, 1967, p. 20.*)

sources of light that extend to about 104° from the optical axis, as shown in Figure 3.10*a*. We note that even objects lying behind the viewer are able to affect the retinal projection. Taking into account the ability of the eyeball to move horizontally as well, Figure 3.10*b* shows what portion of the circle centered at the human is a blind zone. Although this small angle is indeed impressive, it does not compare with the peripheral vision of birds, which have their eyes mounted on the side of the head, as shown in Figure 3.10*c*. No doubt this developed as a result of the distinctive requirements of life in the bird's habitat.

We see, therefore, that the geometry of the ocular optic system limits to a certain extent the ability of the eye to view the three-dimensional world around it. There are two additional important limitations which arise in the dioptric system. First, optical aberrations due to diffraction tend to limit the spatial frequency response, acting as a low-pass filter to image patterns at the input. We shall consider this concept in greater detail in later chapters but for the moment it is simplest to visualize spatial frequency as the number of alternating black and white bars of equal width per unit length of a given visual stimulus. The higher the frequency, the greater the number of oscillations; above a certain frequency the ocular system attenuates the signal reaching the

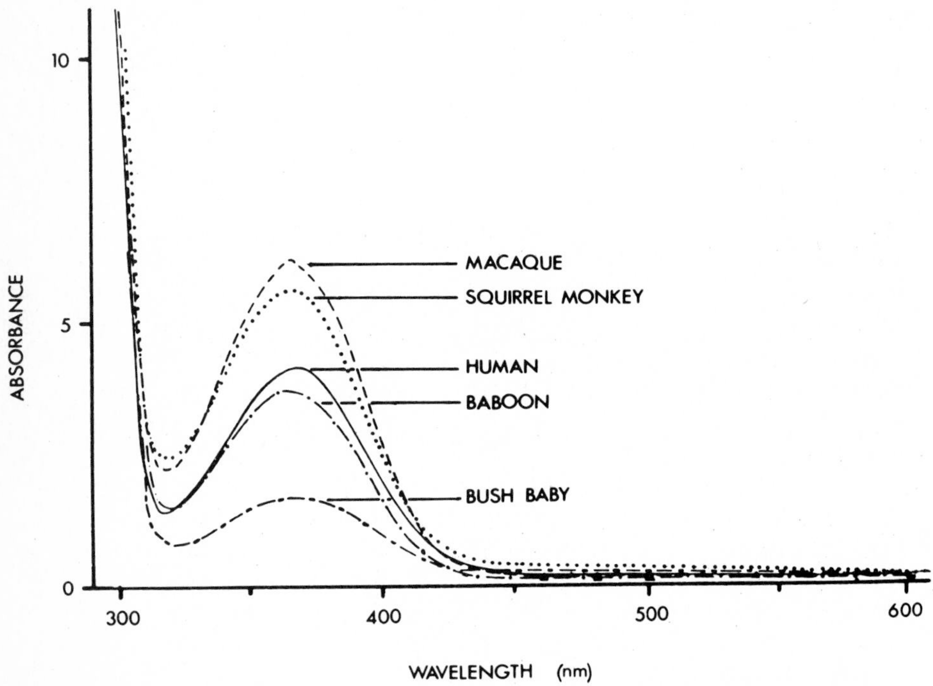

Figure 3.11 The absorbance spectra of various primate lenses. (*Adapted from G. F. Cooper and J. G. Robson, "The Yellow Colour of the Lens of Man and Other Primates," Journal of Physiology, vol. 203, 1969, pp. 411–417.*)

retina much in the same way as does any optical instrument. A mathematical treatment of this phenomenon is given in [17, pp. 265–272] where the characteristics of the retinal image with respect to these optical factors is detailed. The second aberration is chromatic in nature in that the refractive indices of the various ocular media are dependent on the wavelengths constituting the input signal. For example, Figure 3.11 shows the absorbance spectra of the lenses of various primates. It is interesting that these spectra also change considerably with age (see [17, p. 246]).

In this section we have considered as a black-box transformation the optical preprocessing that takes place in the human eye. The input is the three-dimensional visual space and the output a corresponding inverted two-dimensional retinal projection. We note that even this potentially simple operation is quite complicated when it occurs in nature, as opposed to being man-made, as was the case for the computer vision systems discussed in Chapter 2. Generally the farther we are in the human vision system from the stimulus input, the more involved and unknown are the operations.

3.3 ELECTROOPTICAL RECEPTORS

A striking feature of the primate retina is that it consists of essentially five distinct elements. These are situated at the rear of the eyeball and are structured in vertical layers, the whole assembly having approximately the thickness of a sheet of paper. These processing elements, shown schematically in Figure 3.12, are: (1) rod and cone photoreceptors; (2) horizontal cells; (3) bipolar cells; (4) amacrine cells; and (5) ganglion cells. An actual cross section of a human retina is shown in Figure 3.13. The input light must first pass through the relatively transparent optic nerve fibers, the blood vessels, and the different layers of cells before reaching the only existing visual transducers, which are situated at the outermost extent of the outer plexiform layer. This obviously attenuates the arriving signal, a curious inversion by nature! Furthermore the rod-and-cone transducers are so arranged that their light-sensitive surfaces actually point away from the incoming image. The output electrical signals from the retina (see Figure 3.1) are transmitted by the axons of the ganglion cells, which together form the optic nerve. Electrooptical transduction is accomplished by the rods and cones and these will be discussed in this section. The next four layers of cells are actually involved in image signal processing and their anatomical arrangement will be covered in the next section. We note that these would normally be considered as a functional extension of the brain, or the "human vision computer."

Since about the early 1960s and especially during the 1970s, the electron microscope has contributed a significant amount of knowledge regarding the ultramicroanatomy of the rods and cones as well as the specific synaptic interconnections in the retina. These are extremely complex, and considerable uncertainty still remains regarding many facets of the retinal structure. Around

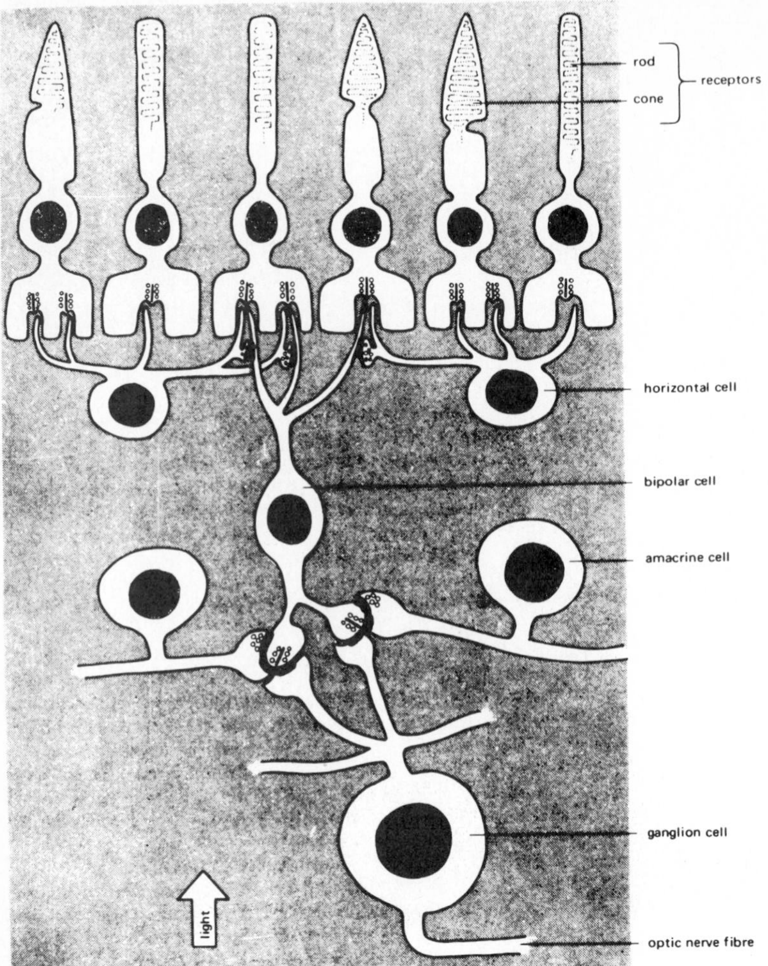

Figure 3.12 A highly schematic diagram of the human retina. [*From C. Blakemore, The Baffled Brain, in R. L. Gregory and E. H. Gombrich (eds.), "Illusions in Nature and Art," Duckworth, London, 1973, pp. 9–48.*]

the turn of this century important contributions to our knowledge of the vertebrate retina were made by Cajal [5, 6] (see [17] pp. 770–904 for a translation of [5]), who suggested that a commonalty of structure existed for all vertebrates. More recent discussions can be found in [3, 4, 7, 10, 14].

We can see from Figure 3.2 that the retina upon which our visual world is projected is concave and surrounds nearly 200° of the eye. One small portion, where the optic nerve leaves the eye, is a blind spot at which no photoreceptors exist at all and which is therefore insensitive to light. In the human eye any light which fails to be absorbed by the receptors is then absorbed by the retinal epithelium and choroid layer, which tend to minimize the effect of stray light.

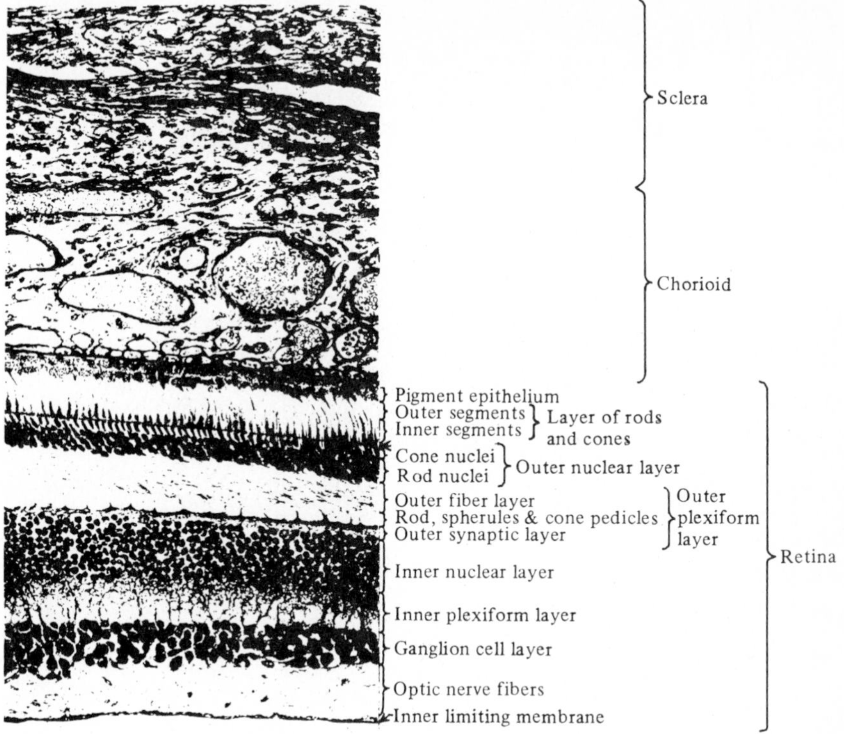

Figure 3.13 Cross section through the human retina in the region of the central area at a medium magnification. The light entering the eye from the outside through the pupillary aperture—from below in the figure—passes through all retinal layers until it reaches the bacillary layer of the rods and cones, where it elicits coded electrical signals. These, in turn, pass in the opposite direction, from the rods and cones to the ganglion cells, along whose fibers they are transmitted to the brain. (*From S. L. Polyak, "The Retina," University of Chicago Press, Chicago, 1941.*)

There are also large differences between the sensitivity of the retina at its center and periphery because the distribution of the transducing elements, the rods and cones, is not uniform.

The "fovea" of the retina (see Figure 3.2) defines the visual axis of the eye and is responsible for highly detailed and exact vision. There are no blood vessels covering this area to interfere with the impinging image, and the correspondence of the cones with the next levels of cells is one-to-one. Nevertheless, the fovea is quite small, consisting of about a 1.5-mm-diameter depression (corresponding to 5.2° of the visual angle) in the retina situated near the optic axis. Figure 3.14 shows a cross section of the human retina at the fovea. Its center contains only cone receptors and no rods, and the cones here are much longer and thinner than those on the periphery. This rod free area, responsible for central vision, is about 0.3 mm in diameter, corresponding to only 1° of visual angle and only 0.5 percent of the total extent of photoreceptor coverage. This turns out to be twice the visual angle subtended by the sun or

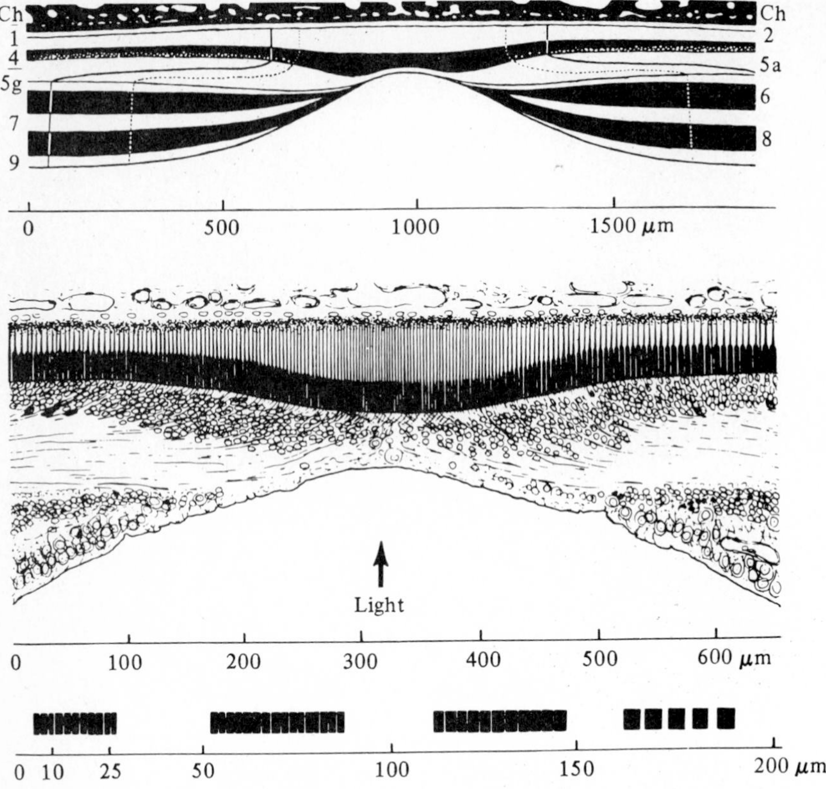

Figure 3.14 The central fovea of the adult human eye, whose diameter is approximately 1.5 mm (5.2°). The upper sketch shows, semidiagrammatically, changes in the relative thickness and position of the retinal layers. It also shows the relationships of the photoreceptor layer (2) and the deeper layers (4 to 9) caused by the latters' displacement owing to the formation of the fovea. The three black layers indicate the outer nuclear (4), inner nuclear (6), and ganglion cell (8) bodies. White dots in layer (4) represent the rod nuclei; Ch refers to the choroid membrane. The broken lines encompass the rodless territory and the portion of the foveal pit functionally related to it. The solid lines mark the region (2) within which the inner and outer segments of the cones are observed to be very thin and long. The middle drawing represents the foveal center filled with its thin, elongated cones. The most centrally located rods correspond with the most central rod nuclei in the outer nuclear layer (4). Note the practical disappearance of the remaining inner layers in the foveal center. The lower sketch represents samples from four localities showing relative size and number of cones (inner segments), beginning from the left: center of the fovea, slope of the same, edge of the same, and periphery of the central area. Upper sketch reproduced at 80×, middle at 250×, lower at 700× magnification. (*Adapted from S. L. Polyak, "The Retina," University of Chicago Press, Chicago, 1941.*)

the moon. Lateral vision is governed by the loosely defined concentric regions surrounding the fovea centralis, which depend on the density of the cones in the region. The "parafovea" is defined as being 2.5 mm in diameter (8.6° of the visual angle) and this area already contains more rods than cones. Figure 3.15*a* shows the density of rods and cones in the parafovea. The next concentric region, the "perifovea," is defined by the annulus having an inner diameter of

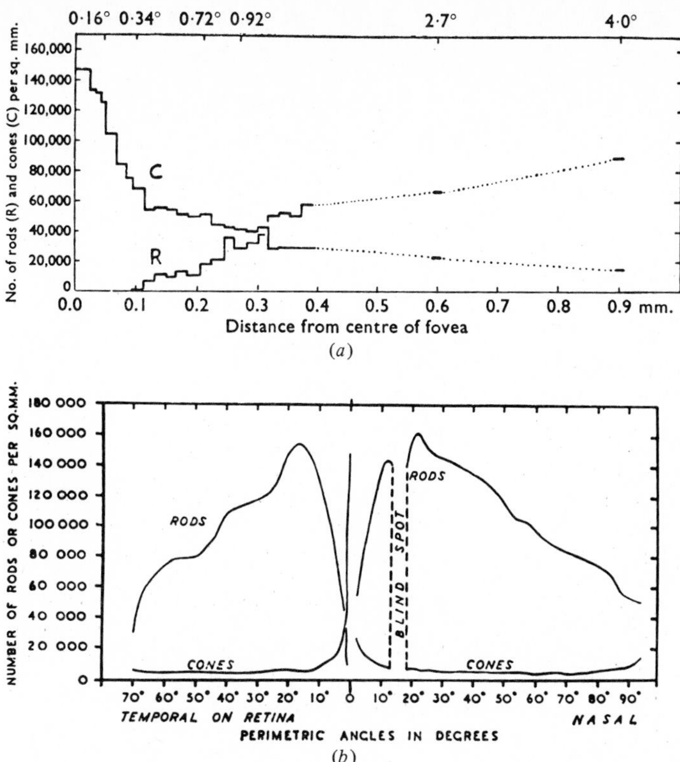

Figure 3.15 The spatial distribution of rods and cones. (*a*) The distribution of rods and cones centered around the visual axis, which is at the center of the fovea. (*b*) The complete density distribution for rods and cones in the human retina. (*From M. H. Pirenne, "Vision and the Eye," 2d ed., Associated Book Publishers, London, 1967.*)

2.5 mm and an outer diameter of about 5.5 mm (19° of the visual angle). Then, beyond this region is the "peripheral retina," constituting about 97.25 percent of the retinal concave surface and consisting largely of rods. Figure 3.15*b* is an overview of the spatial distribution of rods and cones for the complete human retina. We note that there are about an order of magnitude more rods than cones in the human retina: about 120×10^6 rods compared with 6.5×10^6 cones in each eye. We are not really aware of this distribution of photoreceptors and the ensuing loss of acuity away from the fovea because the latter is usually centered on the image we are observing.

As we observed in Chapter 1, it is most common in picture processing by machine to specify a rectangular tesselation of the image plane. Thus, each pixel is taken to have a square shape, although triangular and hexagonal pixel shapes have also been suggested. The idea is based on the observation that retinal receptors are distributed in a hexagonal array of cones with the intermediate space filled by the smaller rods. This tesselation is optimal in the sense that each element has a maximum number of equidistant neighbors. Such a scheme turns out to be impractical for implementation on a general-purpose computer. Another observation is that the sampling frequency in the retina is greater near the fovea and falls off towards the periphery. Such a so-called foveated array has been represented mathematically by using logarithmic spiral grids [34]. A short review of data structures for computer images is presented in [31].

This unique distribution of photoreceptors is responsible for the "duplicity theory" of the retina, in which two kinds of vision are distinguished in man. Of course their underlying processes constantly interact; for example, we are aware of their functioning when we initially enter a darkened cinema. First consider photopic vision, which describes the activity of the cones. These are responsible for day vision and the exacting discriminative power of the retina, providing a high degree of acuity. Color processing is also an important function of these transducing units. The second aspect, scotopic vision, is provided by the rods. It is concerned with night viewing and therefore tends to integrate the input light in order to allow for increased sensitivity under these generally more trying conditions. The rods are thought to be achromatic. Thus, the fine mosaic of the cones in the fovea adapts quickly to bright light and color, while the rods are relatively slow in response, are coarsely distributed, and only adapt to the shades of gray of dim light. For both rods and cones, the coded output signal associated with a particular input light pattern is a sequence of frequency-modulated pulses. The actual process of transduction is still not completely understood.

Figure 3.16 is a drawing of a rod and cone from a human eye. Although vertebrate receptors vary in size and shape, their basic organization is quite similar. The outer part contains a photosensitive material, while the inner part forms the contact with other cells. For the retina to be capable of detecting the incoming light patterns, it must contain a photosensitive light-absorbing material. This so-called visual pigment is different for rods and cones.

The outer segment of the rod contains a substance referred to as "rhodopsin" or "visual purple," which has been known for over a century and has been studied extensively. It appears pink in color and is bleached or made white by light. There also exists a close correspondence between the spectral response curves of human rhodopsin, which can be readily extracted and studied in vitro, and human rods. It is therefore quite reasonable to attribute the behavior of the latter largely to the properties of the former. Figure 3.17 shows an example of the spectral sensitivity curve for human rhodopsin. Essentially, therefore, the rods behave like bandpass filters, basically operating within the visible spectrum between approximately 400 and 700 nm, as shown in Figure 2.2.

In distinction to the rods, the cones possess three different kinds of photopigments, each of which responds differently to a stimulus wavelength, as shown in Figure 3.17. Cone pigments are difficult to extract, and have been studied mainly in situ by reflection densitometry [19]. From these experiments we know that the spectral absorption functions for different species are similar in general shape. We shall see in Chapter 7 that these three different kinds of

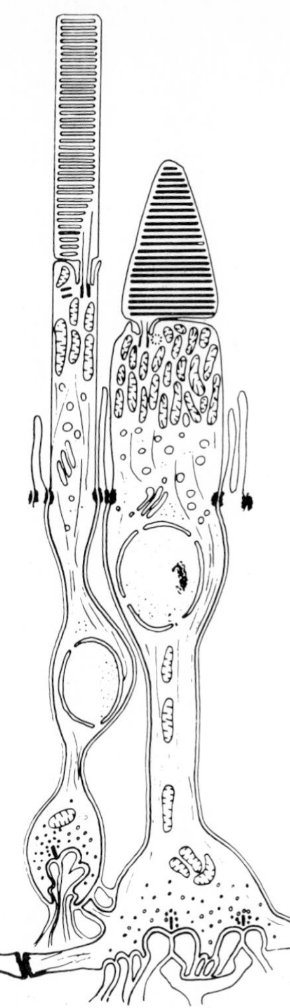

Figure 3.16 Human rod (left) and cone (right). (*From L. Missotten, "The Ultrastructure of the Human Retina," Editions Arscia Uitgaven, N.V., Brussels, 1965.*)

cones with their different bandpass characteristics are responsible for three independent information channels, which then characterize color vision. It is not clear whether the cones in primates interact, although it is possible that they do at the ganglion cell level and most probably in the lateral geniculate nucleus (see Figure 3.18). There is evidence that neighboring cones in the retina of the turtle do interact [2], so that some questioning of the premise of independence for humans may be warranted. In the case of vertebrates, it appears that this electrical coupling tends to reduce photoreceptor noise in the presence of low light levels. It is also interesting that spatial visual acuity is not necessarily degraded and photoreceptor communication might even enhance image processing at high light levels [12].

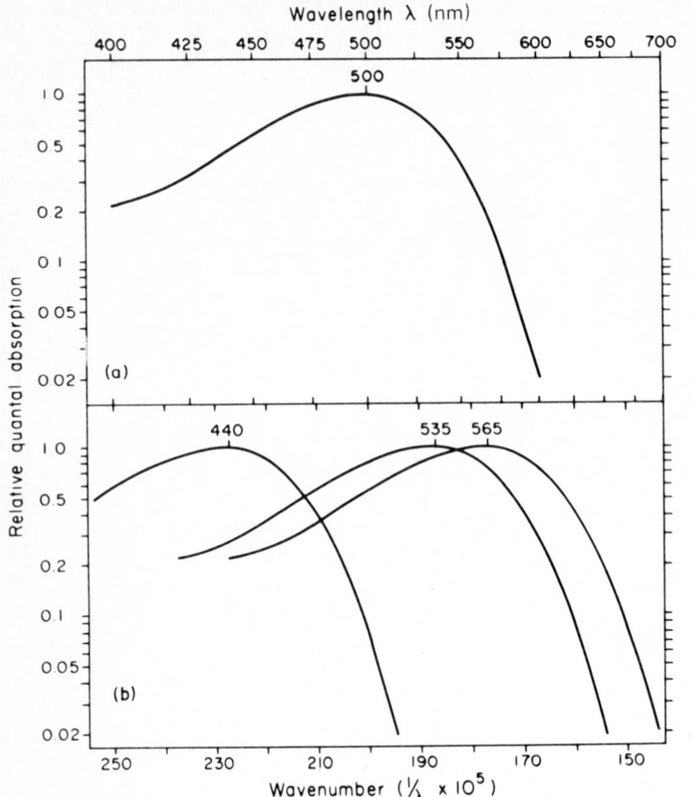

Figure 3.17 A representative set of absorption spectra for rhodopsin, the rod photopigment (a), and the cone photopigments (b). [*From I. Abramov and J. Gordon, "Vision," in E. C. Carterette and M. P. Friedman (eds.), "Handbook of Perception: Biology of Perceptual Systems," vol. 3, Academic, New York, 1974, pp. 327–406.*]

In one particular location of the retina there is some additional spectral processing. Observe in Figure 3.2 that a region of about 6° to 10° centered on the fovea has been labeled "macula lutea." This is a yellow screening pigment, which has only been found in primates and which tends to filter out light in the blue-violet portion of the spectrum. This filtering effect, in addition to the filtering action at short wavelengths of the lens in the optical system (see Figure 3.11) and the absence in the central ($\frac{1}{2}°$) region of the fovea of cones with pigments sensitive to blue, significantly attenuates the contribution to human vision at these high frequencies.

Summarizing this section, we may say that the rod and cone photoreceptors in the retina are the transducing elements of the human visual system. They transform the focused image on the retina into an electrical energy signal according to the principles to be described in Section 3.4.

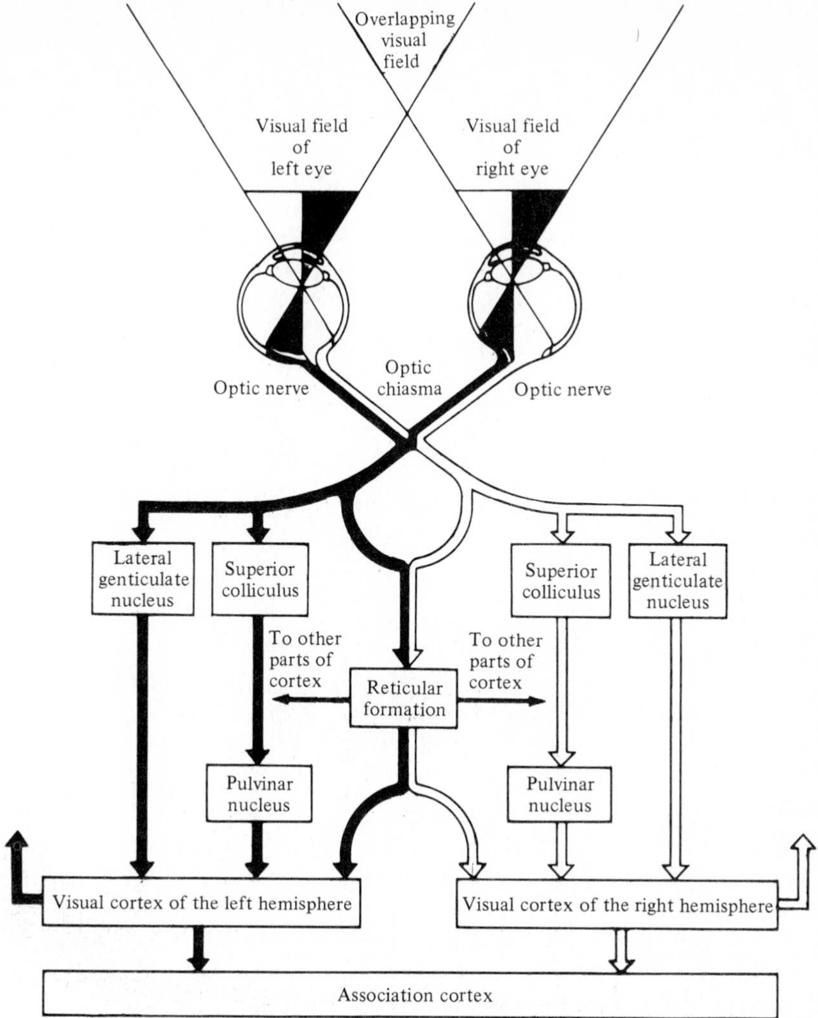

Figure 3.18 Block diagram showing the major known interconnections in the visual pathway.

3.4 THE VISUAL PATHWAY

In Section 3.3 we referred to a stack of five layers of cells in the retina: the photoreceptors responsible for image transduction and the bipolar, horizontal, amacrine, and ganglion cells, which are already involved in some low-level processing. This section will attempt to delineate the major visual pathways involving these cells, as well as their connections. In doing so it will become clear that visual processing in living organisms is constituted as a hierarchy of analyses. It goes without saying that this will be a necessarily incomplete presentation, first, because the topic is very complex and would require a comprehensive treatment to do it justice and second, because our knowledge at this point of many of the details of even the major interconnections in the brain is severely limited. The literature is often conflicting in nature and is based on a relatively small sample of cells.

Figure 3.18 is a simplified diagram of the visual pathways of the primate visual system. We note that the axons of the retinal ganglion cells form the optic nerve, and that these fibers of each eye are divided into two groups according to which part of the retina they project from. The axons meet just before they reach the brain at the optic chiasma, after which a large proportion of them pass on to the lateral geniculate nucleus. The latter is arranged in distinct horizontal layers and its function is not well understood. We see in the diagram that a number of fibers also project to the superior colliculus and the reticular formation. From the lateral geniculate nucleus, where some processing of the image information does occur, the fibers project to one or the other of the two hemispheres of the occipital cortex. Signals from the reticular formation go to other parts of the cortex and are thought to be responsible for sensory-motor control [30]. Not much is known about the detailed functional organization of the brain, which contains many distinct horizontal layers of cells of various sizes and shapes. However in Chapter 8 we shall discuss some very interesting experiments which suggest the existence of a data organization which could support form recognition. Nevertheless the organization of the brain, or even of the sections of the brain responsible for vision, is nearly a complete unknown from the point of view of information processing. In the following chapters we shall present what evidence exists for image processing in the different stages of the visual pathway.

Let us now examine in more detail, enough to comprehend the complexity of the organization, the elements of the anatomy of the visual pathway. Figure 3.19 shows in a more or less realistic fashion the layers of cells in the retina just before they exit from the eye. This figure should be compared with the more schematic version shown in Figure 3.12, which is greatly simplified and represents our knowledge until about the early 1960s. Indeed the situation is even more complicated than in Figure 3.19, since many subcategories of cells have since been discovered, although their exact nature and function are often not clear. Basically two kinds of connections exist, those that are vertical and carry information from the photoreceptor to the brain and those that are horizontal and provide for lateral interaction among cells. The following observations about these connections are pertinent to experiments made on human and monkey retinas.

After the light striking the eye passes through the different strata of cells and membranes and is transduced by the layer of rods and cones, all subsequent stages of processing are electrical in nature. At the first level are the horizontal cells, probably of two kinds, one large and the other small. These cells interconnect and mediate between the rods and cones by means of the outer synaptic layer of the nuclei of these receptors. The connections are simpler

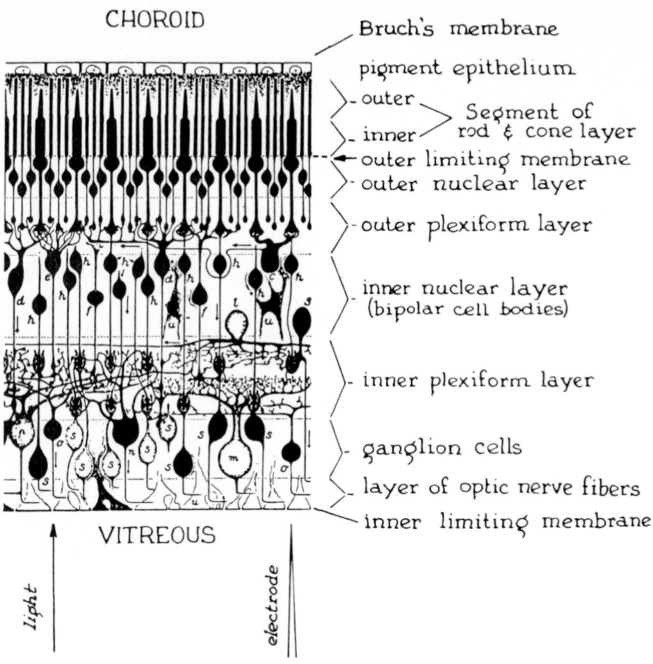

Figure 3.19 A sketched representation of an actual retinal cross section. Figure 3.12 is an abstract version of this diagram and Figure 3.13 is a view at a lower magnification. Here it is about 400. [*From T. C. Ruch, "Vision and the Retina," in T. C. Ruch and H. D. Patton (eds.), "Physiology and Biophysics," vol. 1, "The Brain and Neural Function," 20th ed., 1979, Saunders, Philadelphia, pp. 461–513, from S. L. Polyak, "The Retina," University of Chicago Press, Chicago, 1941.*]

than those that appear at the input to the next level of cells, the bipolars, thereby implying a lesser degree of sophistication in the processing. There are four kinds of bipolars: rod bipolar, invaginating midget bipolar, flat midget bipolar, and flat bipolar. The rods synapse (connect) with the rod bipolars, while the cones synapse with the others. Each receptor projects to at least one bipolar cell. In the fovea, usually one cone is connected to one bipolar, which is then, in turn, usually linked to only one ganglion cell. Outside the central region of the fovea, many rods or cones communicate with a single bipolar, to the point, for example, that beyond 20° from the visual axis hundreds of cones converge on an individual bipolar. Obviously some process of spatial integration related to visual resolution is occurring, with inputs being provided by both photoreceptors and horizontal cells. It has been hypothesized on the basis of experiments with catfish that the horizontal cells produce an integrated signal, which is used to filter out the low spatial frequency components in the image [23]. The bipolar output signal paths or, equivalently, the axons of these cells synapse with amacrine and ganglion cells. The role of the amacrine cells is to horizontally interconnect and modify the signals at the junction of bipolar and ganglion cells. They may be involved in such visual processes as inhibition, a phenomenon dealing with contrast enhancement that will be discussed in Chapter 6.

The ganglion cells are connected to bipolar and amacrine cells and also synapse with each other. Although the fine details of this anatomy are not well known, in later chapters we shall describe some very interesting experimental results dealing with image processing by ganglion cells in animals. Apparently, there are three kinds of ganglion cells, referred to as W-, X-, and Y-type cells [26]. They are thought to serve different functional roles. At the output from the retina the axons of these cells form the optic nerve, a bundle about the thickness of a pencil, which contains only about 1 million fibers. This is an extremely small number considering the tens of millions of rods and cones in the retina and the fact that this represents the entirety of the visual input to the brain. As noted previously (see Figures 3.2 and 3.15*b*), in the location where this optic nerve leaves the visual field, about 16° nasally from the optic axis, there is a blind spot (scotoma) with horizontal and vertical dimensions of about 5° to 6° and 7° to 8°, respectively. As can be seen from Figure 3.18, the input from a particular optic tract to a particular brain hemisphere contains only half of the visual field. Because of the action of the visual optical system, the left half of each visual field projects onto the right half of the retina; for the left eye this is on the so-called nasal retina and for the right eye on the temporal retina. These come together at the optical chiasma, where they collect, to proceed to the right hemisphere of the brain. Similarly, the right part of the visual field projects to the left hemisphere. Since the visual fields of the two hemispheres overlap in front of the viewer, each hemisphere possesses data about this common projection. These binocular views are combined by the brain to provide us with the ability of stereoscopic depth perception [9, 30]. At the periphery, however, there is no overlap and only monocular vision is possible.

In man about 20 to 30 percent of the fibers in the optic nerve connect to the superior colliculus, while in lower vertebrates and birds most nerve fibers actually terminate here. Figure 3.20 shows a comparison of the visual pathway for two different species. For example, the frog does not have any cortex and its visual pathway ceases in the so-called optic tectum. Nevertheless the frog is capable of some elementary but interesting image processing operations, which we shall discuss in later chapters. Some animals, such as squirrels, are somewhat intermediate in that they do possess a small visual cortex. Thus we may generalize by pointing out the two categories, one having a relatively large visual cortex such as man, monkey, or cat; the other a rudimentary or nonexistent cortex such as frog, rabbit, and squirrel. In the first case it appears that most processes of vision are carried out in the brain, while in the second case the retinal ganglion cells are capable of some rather important vision computations.

In man it appears that the superior colliculus is responsible for controlling eye movements [20, 35]. Upon leaving this area, most of the fibers then connect to the pulvinar nuclei of the thalamus, after which they pass on to the occipital cortex, as shown in Figure 3.18. The pulvinar nuclei mediate the pupillary

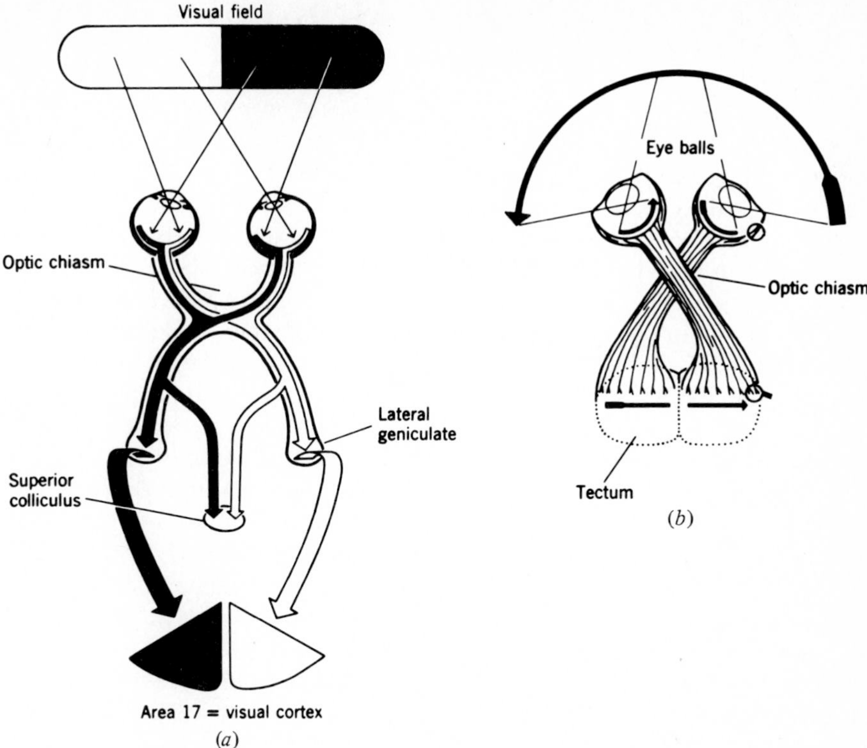

Figure 3.20 A comparative view of the visual systems of a human and a frog. In the human visual system (*a*) we see the predominance of messages going via the lateral geniculate nucleus of the thalamus up to the cortex with relatively little going to the superior colliculus, while in the frog (*b*) it is the connections to the tectum (which is the amphibian analog of the mammalian superior colliculus) that predominate. Note also the splitting of the two halves of the visual field, so noticeable at the human optic chiasma yet absent in the frog. (*Adapted from M. A. Arbib, "The Metaphorical Brain," Wiley, New York, 1972.*)

reflexes discussed in Section 3.3, thereby providing some feedback from the higher to the lower vision processes. The thalamus, which also contains the lateral geniculate body, is a portion of the brain where all the sensory signals except those for olfaction congregate before passing on. We could imagine some degree of low-level interaction at this point which would integrate the various environmental data that the body senses.

The lateral geniculate body of the thalamus is a major pathway for man in that a significant fraction of the optic fibers connect here, as do fibers from other parts of the central nervous system. It is a laminated structure containing six distinct layers of cells. At present no evidence exists to imply that any major visual analysis occurs at this point, although there is strong evidence that the cells here are implicated in color vision (see Chapter 7). Signals from more than one layer of the lateral geniculate body project primarily to the visual cortex. Another area whose function is unclear and which receives input from the optic tract is the reticular formation. Signals from here pass on to other parts of the cortex.

In 1893 Ramon y Cajal was responsible for publishing the first comprehensive study of the anatomy of the human brain [6]. About 30 years earlier Golgi had established its organization, using a technique which allowed for the selective staining of small groups of neurons. By late in the nineteenth century it was known that the cortex is divided into different areas, each one responsible for a different function. The occipital area of the brain, where the sensory paths terminate, is called the "cerebral cortex." It contains about 70 percent of all the neurons in the human central nervous system, which attests to its importance. For example, the so-called area 17 of this occipital cortical lobe is referred to as the "primary visual" or "striate" cortex, the former term describing its function and the latter its appearance. As might be expected, the fovea of each retina occupies a disproportionately large projection on the visual cortex. It is probably also the case that inputs from both retinas first converge here on a single neuron cell. It is generally assumed that this physical location is concerned with the perception of light, color, and form, although the complexity of the analysis is completely uncertain. Surprisingly, the partial destruction of this area does leave man with some pattern recognition abilities intact. Experiments to relate visual stimuli with cortical events in vertebrates are difficult to perform and probably limited in maximum scope. After all, a monkey is quite incapable of accurately verbalizing its perceptions, a major link for man between the neurophysiology and psychology of vision.

The visual cortex projects back to the lateral geniculate body, whence, as we saw, it receives input, thereby providing top-down feedback in the hierarchy. Also, it is only the first stage of visual processing and thus is involved in further interconnections to the important association areas nearby, which in man represent the major part of the cortex. It is interesting to note that the visual, auditory and somatic areas of the cortex are together responsible for about one-quarter of its total size.

What physical characteristics does this important part of the human body, the cerebral cortex, have? It is a folded plate about 2 mm thick, which fits just inside the skull. The total area in man if unfolded would only be about $\frac{1}{7}\,\mathrm{m}^2$. It is densely packed with neurons, containing about 10^5 neurons per square millimeter of surface, whereas the cortex as a whole consists of a network of about 10^{10} neurons. These cells are not randomly located but are arranged in layers, which alternate regions densely packed with cells with those that are sparsely populated. Within a plane in a particular region, a large degree of apparent uniformity may be observed. Processing in the cortex appears to be very local in the lateral direction, providing for the effect of a columnar structure radiating from the surface. This aspect will be discussed in Chapter 8, where the consequences for image processing will also be given.

Information from area 17, the primary visual cortex, projects to the adjacent prestriate cortex, areas 18 and 19, together referred to as the "association cortex." From here, the visual pathway projects to the "inferotemporal cortex," largely corresponding to areas 20 and 21. Areas 17, 18, and 19 are generally considered as the "visual cortex" and are sometimes referred to as visual areas I, II, and III, respectively. They seem to be mainly concerned with relatively low-level processing roles. However, lesions in the association areas definitely affect visual pattern discrimination capabilities. Thus, these areas serve the important function of associating memory with visual input patterns. In contrast, the inferotemporal cortex is significant to visual discrimination learning and is probably involved in higher-level visual processing. Perception obviously requires that all these centers function in concert.

The visual pathway is a massively interconnected and complex "vision computer" about which there is obviously much to discover. In this section we have briefly discussed from a macroscopic point of view the various sub-processes and their connections. Taking the computer analogy one step further, we might say that vision in the human is achieved by the interaction of many processors. The low level of processing is the one we know the most about, largely because of experimentation with animals. But what about the microscopic units, the individual "integrated circuit" computational elements which make up these processors? These are the neuron cells, which are discussed in the next section.

3.5 SIGNAL CODING AND PROCESSING

It has been mentioned previously that the stimulus signals are coded into sequences of frequency-modulated pulses. In fact the neuron, which is the elemental anatomic unit of the nervous system, operates by processing these pulse trains. It is well-known that frequency modulation offers a higher degree of noise rejection and stability than amplitude modulation, and it is interesting that the basic human computational circuit functions according to this design [27]. This section will describe in an introductory fashion the mechanisms involved.

Figure 3.21 is a schematic diagram of a single nerve cell, showing the "soma" or cell body surrounded by a thin plasma membrane, which is filled with cytoplasm and contains a nucleus. Such cells are usually roughly about 30 μm in diameter. Neural networks are configured by means of the "dendrites," which are the inputs to the cell, and the "axons," which constitute the single output. There are many inputs, typically perhaps 2000 for small cells to 16,000 for large cells, and this collection of dendrites for a particular cell is called a "dendritic tree." Note that some of the inputs are excitatory in that they promote the cell firing while others are inhibitory and retard it. The dendrites are perhaps 200 to 300 μm long and thus a cell may receive input from locations a considerable distance from it. On output, information flows from the cell via its axon termination to another by chemical means. This is achieved by the so-called chemical transmitter substance, which diffuses across a synaptic gap, as shown in Figure 3.21.

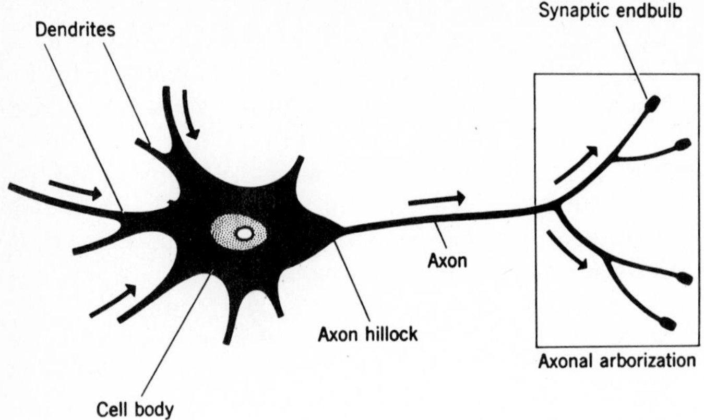

Figure 3.21 Schematic view of a neuron. Activity from receptors and other neurons modifies membrane potentials on the dendrites and cell body. The effects of these changes converge upon the axon hillock whence—for appropriate spatiotemporal patterns of incoming activity—a pulse of membrane potential will be propagated along the axon, branching out into the axonal arborization to activate the synaptic end bulbs, which modify the membrane potential of other neurons or of muscle fibers in turn. In this way, axons from many cells serve as input connections to the dendrites of a particular cell. The output from the above cell appears on its axon. (*From M. A. Arbib, "The Metaphorical Brain," Wiley, New York, 1972.*)

In this section, we will describe how this chemical process results in a coded pulse train. The range of lengths for axons can be even larger than for dendrites, from about 50 μm to possibly even several meters. A single axon may be involved with perhaps hundreds of synaptic contacts. As we have seen in the previous sections, many cells are usually packed together in layers and the connections must be rather intricate. These nerve cells are embedded in a supporting protective network of glial cells, whose function is not yet completely understood. Figure 3.22 is a schematic diagram of the basic computational unit, while Figure 3.23 shows in a more or less realistic fashion how three neurons might be interconnected via their dendritic trees.

In addition to these basic elements, the human body contains specialized cells which are dedicated to sensing the environment and therefore act as energy transformation units. The rods and cones discussed previously are one such set of sensing elements, which convert light energy at the input to membrane potential changes at their output. Other sensory transduction systems are auditory (hearing), somesthetic (touch), olfactory (smell), and gustatory (taste). The

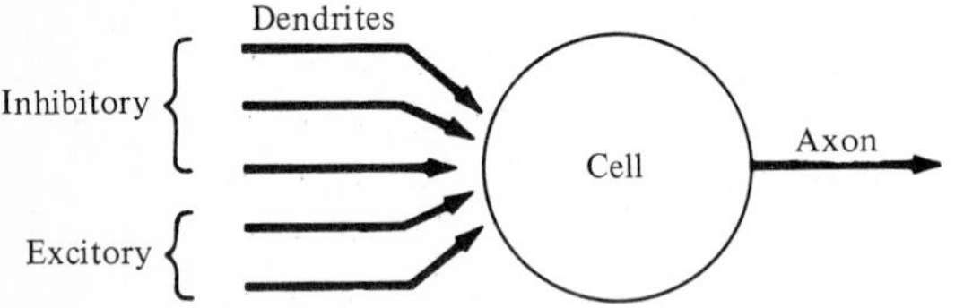

Figure 3.22 An input/output representation for a typical neuron.

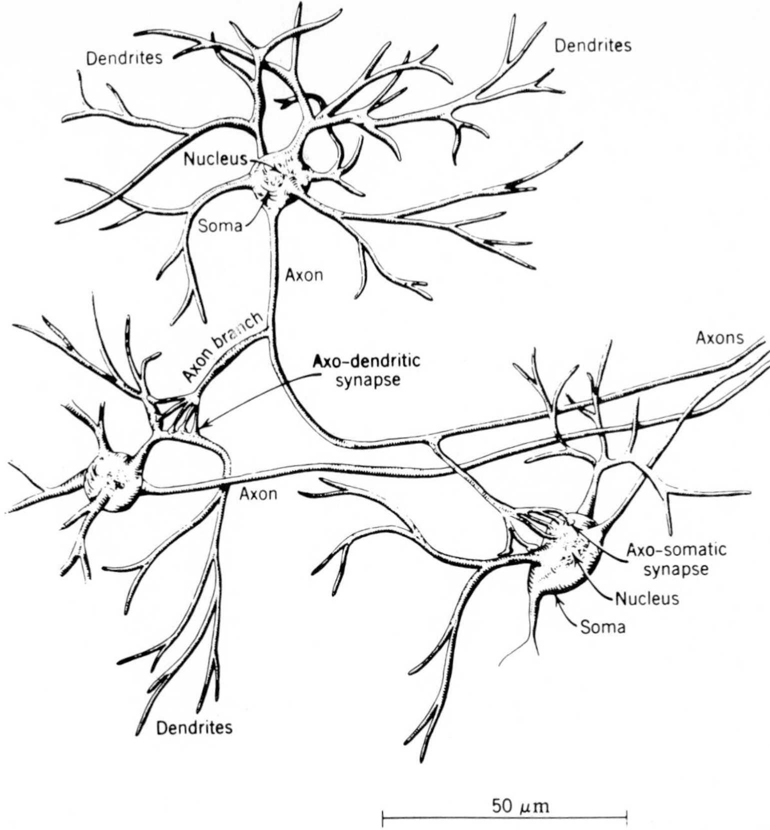

Figure 3.23 A semischematic rendition of the interaction of three neurons. (*From C. F. Stevens, "Neurophysiology: A Primer," Wiley, New York, 1966, p. 2.*)

transducer units of the visual system are extremely sensitive and require only very small amounts of light to be activated; perhaps one photon is sufficient for the receptors of the human eye. Detailed knowledge of the photochemistry of the eye is available; however, the mechanism by which the transduced electrical signal is created is unfortunately not yet understood.

What follows is a simplification and generalization of how the process of frequency coding is achieved. The explanation is presented in stages, beginning with the neuron axon, which, as we have seen, is the output. Consider an electrophysiological experiment in which a microelectrode is inserted into the interior of an initial segment of axon near the cell body and a step voltage stimulus is applied. The resulting membrane potential or inside-outside voltage of the axon is then measured with a probe. It will be seen that a maintained voltage stimulus produces a frequency-coded pulse train whose frequency of oscillation is proportional to the stimulus voltage.

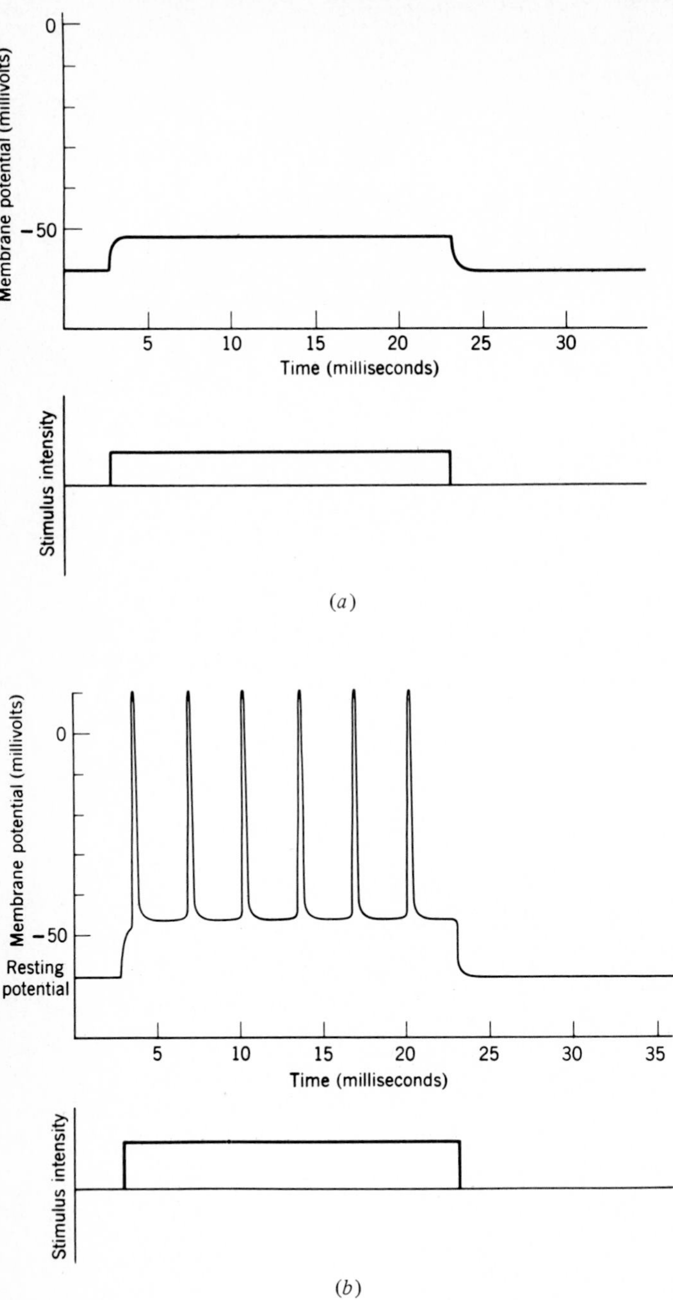

Figure 3.24 When the amplitude of the depolarizing rectangular pulse stimulus is below threshold, the axon response is passive (a). If it goes above threshold, a sequence of spike action potentials superimposed on the generator potential is communicated along the neuron's axon (b). (*From C. F. Stevens, "Neurophysiology: A Primer," Wiley, New York, 1966, pp. 21–22.*)

To explain how this comes about, let us define the two responses, "depolarization" and "hyperpolarization," as positive and negative excursions from the resting potential of the neuron, taken to be about −60 mV. If we apply a negative rectangular pulse to the axon, we observe a passive response consisting of a hyperpolarization; the resulting negative pulse is merely a slightly distorted version of the input. Similarly, for a positive pulse going below a certain threshold value we obtain a passive depolarization (see Figure 3.24*a*). On the other hand, if the amplitude exceeds the threshold, the probe records an active response, referred to as an "action potential" and shown in Figure 3.25. This voltage transient is initiated by the input going above the threshold and does not depend in any way on the pulse width. Therefore exceeding the stimulus threshold results in an action potential whose shape is substantially independent of the input and which travels along the axon at about 1 m/s, in a range of 0.1 to 10 m/s, the higher values attributed to the larger fibers. Of course distortions do occur over the length of this transmission line, but we will neglect these here.

Two aspects of the action potential are directly related to the frequency-coding property of the input: the "latency" and the "refractory period." The latency, or effective rise time, of the action potential is defined as the time between the application of the stimulus and the peak of the resulting output. This response time decreases exponentially as the stimulus intensity increases. The shape of the curve is similar for different axons but the time scale would tend to vary from cell to cell. The second aspect, the refractory period, is the minimum time between two successive stimuli which will evoke two consecutive action potential responses. This period might be measured in milliseconds. It turns out that the threshold for the second stimulus to fire the

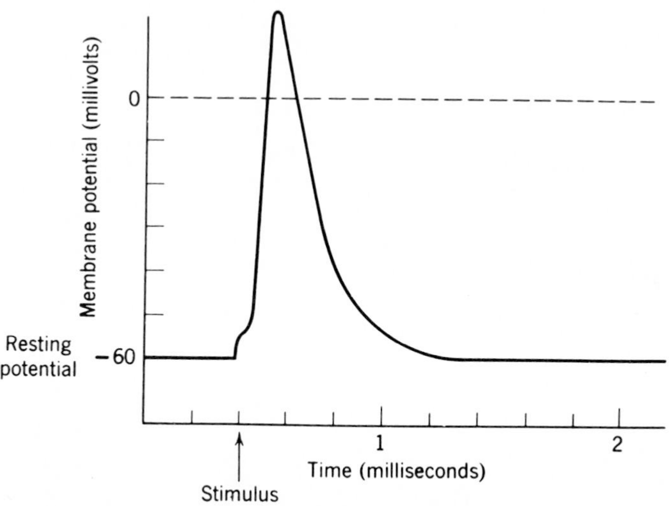

Figure 3.25 An idealized version of an action potential. (*From C. F. Stevens, "Neurophysiology: A Primer," Wiley, New York, 1966, p. 14.*)

neuron is dependent on the refractory period. There is a dead-zone period, the so-called absolute refractory period, before which it is impossible to have another output pulse. After the dead zone has expired, the input amplitude threshold for the second pulse decreases exponentially as the refractory period increases. Thus, depending on the amplitude of the stimulus input, the threshold will decrease to a point where the neuron will be able to fire again. It again goes without saying that the characteristic of this relative refractory period is similar in shape for different axons and differs only in scale. From the above discussions, we see that if a constant voltage above threshold is applied, the latency and refractory period will both control the frequency of the output pulses. For example, a strong stimulus will yield a smaller refractory period and a faster rise time, thereby resulting in a higher frequency. An example of such an axonal response is shown in Figure 3.24*b*. By experimenting with a particular neuron, we may obtain a curve similar to that shown in Figure 3.26, a representative relationship between stimulus intensity and nerve impulse frequency. The time scales will differ for different axons. A typical output might have a 10 mV depolarization above threshold, resulting in 10 to 500 pulses per second.

It is interesting that some neurons do not behave in the manner described when subjected to a maintained input. In fact the axons of these cells accommodate to the unchanging input and the threshold remains high, so that no further impulses can occur. In order for this threshold to change and thereby fire the neurons, the input must either be increased or decreased. Thus we observe that this axon responds only to differential changes in the input. This type of cell is referred to as a "phasic neuron," in distinction to the previously described so-called tonic neuron.

Having described the existence of a process which converts axonal voltage potentials to a frequency-modulated pulse train, we shall examine the next stages in the process, all of which together permit cellular signal processing to

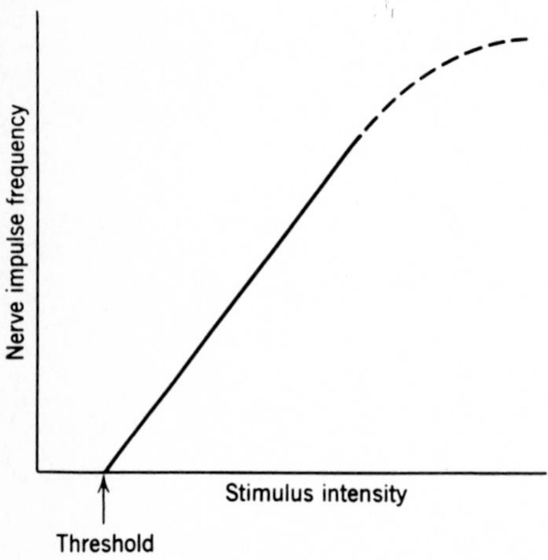

Figure 3.26 The relationship between the nerve impulse frequency and the stimulus intensity. (*From C. F. Stevens, "Neurophysiology: A Primer," Wiley, New York, 1966, p. 24.*)

occur. The axon of one cell is connected to the dendritic inputs of other cells via a synaptic termination. This synapse is a chemical connection which employs a transmitter substance to convey information across its boundary. The action potential pulses conducted along the axon are converted by the synapse to a voltage in the dendrite, referred to as the "postsynaptic potential" (PSP). The PSP is proportional to the amount of transmitter released but becomes saturated for large amounts of transmitter substance. Because the junction has a much larger time constant than the spacing between pulses, a temporal summation occurs. Hence new potentials are simply added to what remains of the previous, now partially decayed PSP, thereby yielding the so-called slow potential. The resulting magnitude of this dendritic depolarization is proportional to the average frequency at which pulses arrive at the synapse, a form of frequency-voltage coding. This slow potential is shown in Figure 3.27; a typical neuron may have 10^3 to 10^5 synapses of the type shown.

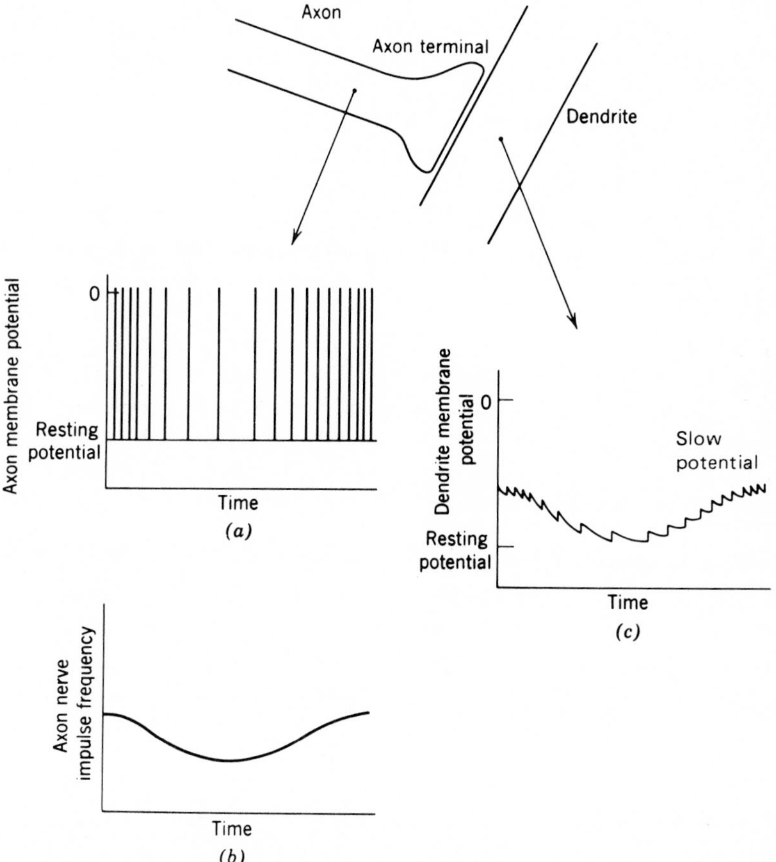

Figure 3.27 The process of frequency-voltage coding at the synaptic junction of an axon and a dendrite. The input frequency-modulated pulse train (*a*) represents an average frequency versus time relationship (*b*), which is converted by the synapse into a slow potential on the dendrite (*c*). (*Adapted from C. F. Stevens, "Neurophysiology: A Primer," Wiley, New York, 1966, p. 33.*)

However, these originate from perhaps only about 10 other neurons [28]. Thus it would appear that each neuron must project a large number of synapses to each of the neurons to which it is connected. Because of this large set of input paths, an average of 10^4 to 10^5 PSPs per second will be conducted over all the synapses. Synaptic junctions usually occur between axons and dendrites but can also appear between axon and axon, dendrite and dendrite, and axon and cell body.

An interesting aspect from the point of view of computation is that there can exist two types of synapses at the junction, excitory and inhibitory, and these are not necessarily synonomous with positive and negative increments, respectively. Furthermore the amount of depolarization or hyperpolarization is weighted by each particular synapse, thereby providing multiplication by a parameter. The magnitude of the parameter may depend on such fixed anatomical features as the physical size of the synapse and the distance of the synapse from the soma, that is, the length of the dendrite. It turns out that adaptation is also possible at the synaptic input if it possesses an additional connection just prior to the same junction, thereby exhibiting an axo-axonal synapse. This less frequently observed synapse is used to transmit a slow potential (with respect to the frequency of the arriving pulses at the junction), which controls the incremental amount of transmitter substance secreted by the terminal. Therefore the presynaptic potential magnitude, which depends on this axon terminal membrane potential, is slowly altered, and in this way it controls the increments contributing to the amplitude of the slow potentials at the junction. In other words, incremental additions are multiplicatively modulated by the input from this axon. Since only depolarizing axo-axonal synapses have been found to date, this mechanism is referred to as "presynaptic inhibition."

So far we have discussed the mechanism by which frequency-coded information originating on the axon is transmitted via a synapse to a dendrite of a cell. We observed that the dendrite conveys a slow potential to the soma or cell body of the neuron. We note another interesting computational aspect that occurs at this point. The cell output projected along its axon only appears if the input slow potential is above a certain threshold. Under these circumstances, as we might expect, this output is none other than the stream of nerve impulses which we have previously called action potentials. In that experiment we had artificially stimulated the axon to respond. Here we observe that the dendritic inputs cause the pulses to form at the axon hillock, which is the junction between the soma and the cell axon. The action potential frequency is proportional to the input slow potential, as shown in Figure 3.28, where only one input to neuron N is shown.

What happens with the multitude of dendritic inputs to a cell? A process of weighted spatial summation in the cell body yields a weighted average of all the input signals, which is then linearly converted to the appropriate output frequency. Figure 3.29 demonstrates this process for the situation where one neuron input is inhibitory and the other excitory, resulting in a weighted

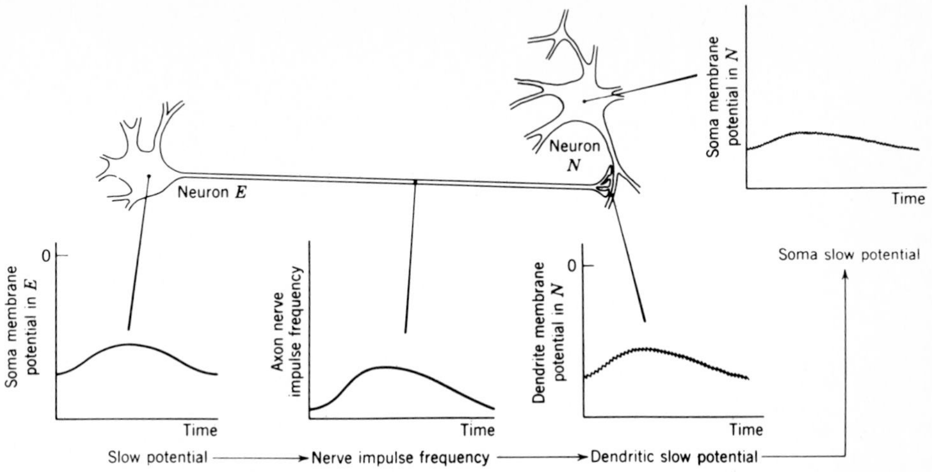

Figure 3.28 The steps involved in communicating a signal from a neuron E to a neuron N. (*From C. F. Stevens, "Neurophysiology: A Primer," Wiley, New York, 1966, p. 50.*)

difference between the two slow potentials. We remind the reader that this is a simplification and that the significance of deviations from this model is not yet entirely clear. Additionally, in the retina only the ganglion cells generate pulse trains in the fashion described above; the other cells generate slow potentials.

Having described elemental cellular processing, we now consider how the nervous system communicates with the external visual environment. This process of photoreception is in fact quite similar to that of the other receptors in the body which are responsible for detecting other physical properties. The light intensity is photochemically transformed by such a specialized cell into a graded or slow potential. This is in distinction to the ganglion cells we have already discussed, which generate nerve impulses along their axons. The magnitude of the slow potential at any instant in time is proportional to the logarithm of the input light intensity. This mechanism for enhancing the dynamic range will be discussed in detail in Chapter 4. We have already mentioned how the amount of light that impinges upon the retina is quite rapidly controlled by the pupillary reflex over a range of about 100 to 1. Another, slower mechanism for modulating the input is the process of adaptation to a constant signal. The resulting slow potential decreases with time for constant input, thereby allowing the photoreceptor to operate in a range where it is more sensitive to the incoming light.

There is evidence that vertebrate receptors are hyperpolarized by a light stimulus. The rods and cones of the carp, frog, gekko, and mud puppy possess this property. On the other hand, receptors in invertebrate eyes are depolarized by the incoming light. In most cases the visual receptors are specialized in their function; however, in certain primitive living things the same cell may be responsible for the dual action of sensing the environment

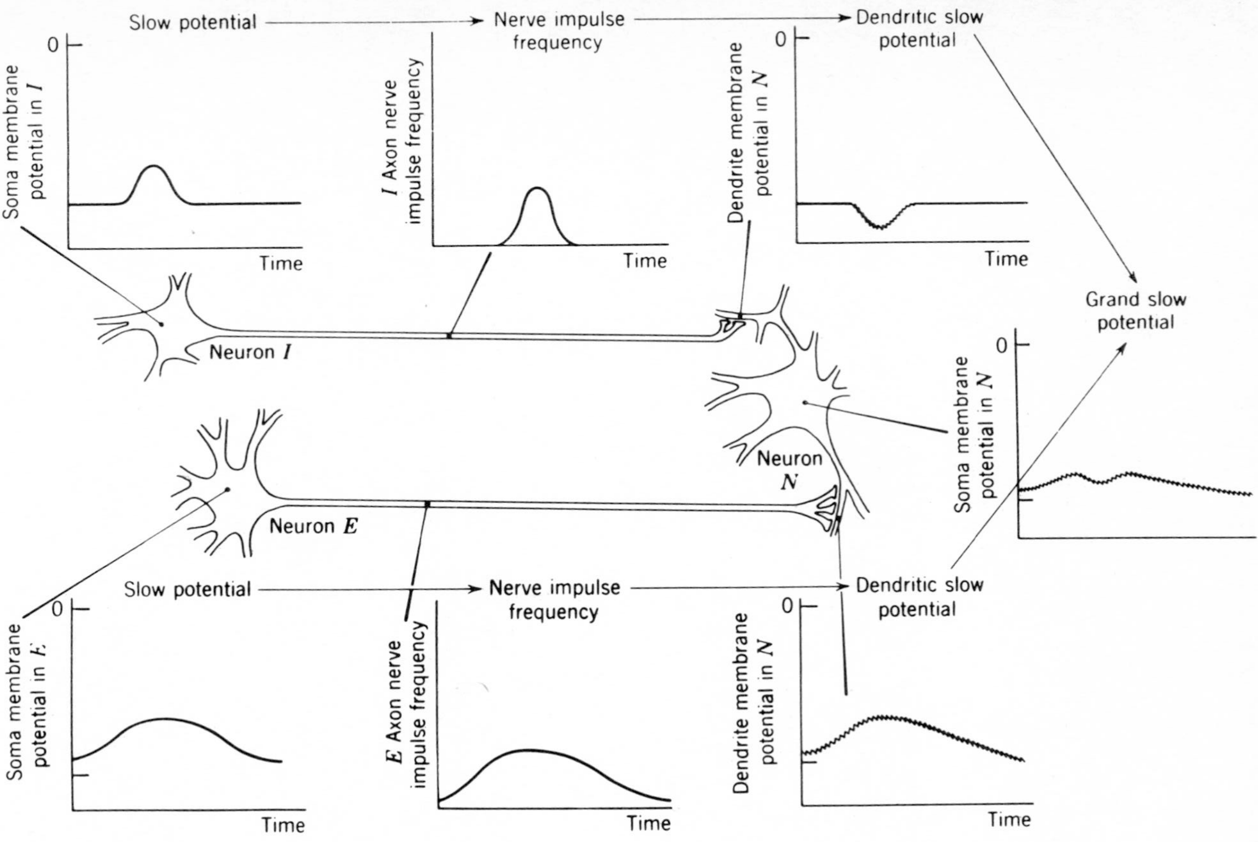

Figure 3.29 A small neuronal network in which the weighted difference between two input signals is computed. (*From C. F. Stevens, "Neurophysiology: A Primer," Wiley, New York, 1966, p. 54.*)

and responding to it by controlling an affector. The higher organisms tend to possess cells which are more focused in their roles, thereby providing enhanced sensitivity for each independent function. We see therefore, that the sensory input to the "vision computer," the receptor mosaic, is capable of providing information about the light input with regard to both its intensity and spatial location.

Based on the above discussion, McCulloch and Pitts [13] postulated a simple mathematical model of a neuron, shown in Figure 3.30. The dendritic inputs to the neuron are given by $y_1, y_2, \ldots, y_n$ and the corresponding synaptic weights, either positive or negative, by $w_1, w_2, \ldots, w_n$. The axonal output x is given by

$$x = \operatorname{sign}\left[\sum_{i=1}^{n} (w_i y_i - \theta)\right] \tag{3.3}$$

where θ is a threshold value and obviously only takes on values of either -1 or $+1$. A more realistic model, in which the input and output signals represent actual firing rates, can also be derived [1]:

$$\tau \frac{du(t)}{dt} = -u(t) + \sum_{i=1}^{n} w_i y_i(t) \tag{3.4}$$

$$x(t) = f[u(t) - \theta] \tag{3.5}$$

Here the function f may be considered to be monotonic with saturation at both negative and positive values, a slight relaxation of the stringent condition imposed by the sign function above. It turns out that as far as the macroscopic behavior of neural nets is concerned, these two models are equivalent. Thus the simpler McCulloch–Pitts representation is more convenient computation-

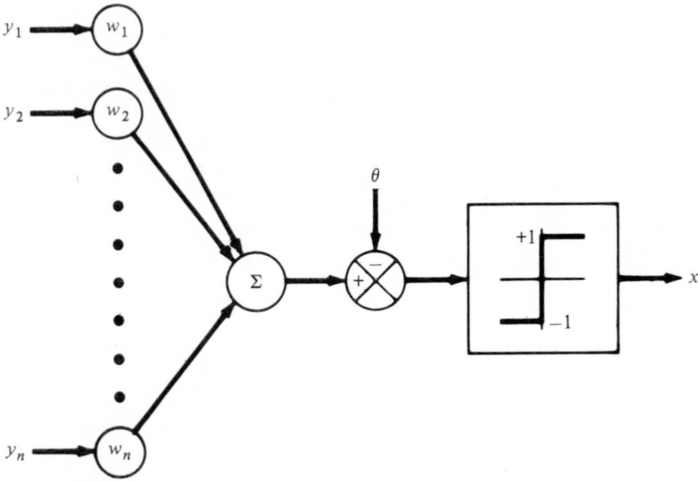

Figure 3.30 The classical McCulloch-Pitts model of the neuron.

ally. Readers are referred to [1] for a discussion of the analysis of neuron networks using these models. Some interesting mathematical idealizations of these models, suitable for pattern analysis and recognition, are given in [16]. Adaptive neural networks are discussed in [29].

It is the connectivity of these neurons in the cortex which, of course, defines the particular functions being computed. The degree of complexity of this network in the mammalian brain turns out to be related to intelligence [28].

REFERENCES

1. Amari, S. I., "A Mathematical Approach to Neural Systems," in Metzler, J. (ed.), "Systems Neuroscience," Academic, New York, 1977, pp. 67–117.
2. Baylor, D. A., Fuortes, M. G. F., and O'Bryan, P. M., "Receptive Fields of Cones in the Retina of the Turtle," *Journal of Physiology* (*London*), vol. 173, no. 3, 1964, pp. 377–407.
3. Borwein, B., Borwein, D., Medeiros, J., and McGowan, J. W., "The Ultrastructure of Monkey Foveal Photoreceptors, with Special Reference to the Structure, Shape, Size, and Spacing of the Foveal Cones," *American Journal of Anatomy*, vol. 159, 1980, pp. 125–146.
4. Boycott, B. B., and Dowling, J. E., "Organization of the Primate Retina; Light Microscopy," *Philosophical Transactions of the Royal Society* (*London*), ser. B, vol. 255, 1969, pp. 109–176.
5. Cajal, S. R., "La Rétine des Vertebres," *La Cellule*, vol. 9, 1893, pp. 17–257.
6. Cajal, S. R., "Histologie des Systèmes Nerveux de l'Homme et des Vertebres," vol. 2, Maloine, Paris, 1911.
7. Dowling, J. E., and Boycott, B. B., "Organization of the Primate Retina: Electron Microscopy," *Proceedings of the Royal Society* (*London*), ser. B, vol. 166, no. 1002, 1966, pp. 80–111.
8. Graham, C. H., "Vision and Visual Perception," Wiley, New York, 1965.
9. Julesz, B., "Foundations of Cyclopean Perception," University of Chicago Press, Chicago, 1971.
10. Kolb, H., "Organization of the Outer Plexiform Layer of the Primate Retina: Electron Microscopy of Golgi-Impregnated Cells," *Philosophical Transactions of the Royal Society* (*London*), ser. B, vol. 258, 1970, pp. 261–283.
11. Lowenstein, O., and Loewenfeld, I. E., "The Pupil," in Davson, H. (ed.), "The Eye," vol. 3, Academic, New York, 1962, pp. 231–267.
12. Marcelja, S., "Electrical Coupling of Photoreceptors in Retinal Network Models," *Biological Cybernetics*, vol. 39, no. 1, 1980, pp. 15–20.
13. McCulloch, W. S., and Pitts, W. H., "A Logical Calculus of the Ideas Imminent in Neural Nets," *Bulletin of Mathematical Biophysics*, vol. 5, 1943, pp. 115–133.
14. Missothen, L., "The Ultrastructure of the Human Retina," Arscia Uitgaven, N.V., Brussels, 1965.
15. Newman, E. A., and Hartline, P. H., "The Infrared 'Vision' of Snakes," *Scientific American*, vol. 246, no. 3, March 1982, pp. 116–127.
16. Nilsson, N. J., "Learning Machines, Foundations of Trainable Pattern Classifying Systems," McGraw-Hill, New York, 1965.
17. Rodieck, R. W., "The Vertebrate Retina," Freeman, San Francisco, 1973.
18. Rolls, P., "Photographic Optics," in Engels, C. E. (ed.), "Photography for the Scientist," Academic, New York, 1968, pp. 67–174.
19. Rushton, W. A. H., "Visual Pigments in Man," *Scientific American*, vol. 207, no. 5, November 1962, pp. 120–132.
20. Schiller, P. H., and Stryker, M., "Single-Unit Recording and Stimulation in Superior Colliculus of the Alert Rhesus Monkey," *Journal of Neurophysiology*, vol. 35, no. 6, 1972, pp. 915–924.

21. Semmlow, J., and Stark, L., "Simulation of a Biomechanical Model of the Human Pupil," *Mathematical Biosciences*, vol. 11, 1971, pp. 109–128.
22. Semmlow, J., and Chen, D. C., "A Simulation Model of the Human Pupil Light Reflex," *Mathematical Biosciences*, vol. 33, 1977, pp. 5–24.
23. Shantz, M., and Naka, K. I., "The Bipolar Cell," *Vision Research*, vol. 16, 1976, pp. 1517–1518.
24. Stark, L., "Stability, Oscillations, and Noise in the Human Pupil Servomechanism," *Proceeding of the IRE*, vol. 47, 1959, pp. 1925–1939.
25. Stark, L., "Pupillary Control System; Its Nonlinear Adaptive and Stochastic Engineering Design Characteristics," *Automatica*, vol. 5, 1969, pp. 655–676.
26. Stone, J., Dreher, B., and Leventhal, A., "Hierarchical and Parallel Mechanisms in the Organization of Visual Cortex," *Brain Research Reviews*, vol. 1, 1979, pp. 345–394.
27. Stubbs, D. F., "Frequency and the Brain," *Life Sciences*, vol. 18, 1976, pp. 1–14.
28. Stubbs, D. F., "Connectivity and the Brain," *Kybernetes*, vol. 7, no. 2, 1978, pp. 93–98.
29. Sutton, R. S., and Barto, A. G., "Toward a Modern Theory of Adaptive Networks: Expectation and Prediction," *Psychological Review*, vol. 88, no. 2, 1981, pp. 135–170.
30. Szentagothai, J., and Arbib, M. A., "Conceptual Models of Neural Organization," *Neurosciences Research Progress Bulletin*, vol. 12, no. 1, 1975, pp. 90–93.
31. Tanimoto, S. L., "Image Data Structures," in Tanimoto, S., and Klinger, A. (eds.), "Structured Computer Vision, Machine Perception Through Hierarchical Computation Structures," Academic, New York, 1980, pp. 31–55.
32. Tryon, W. T., "Pupillometry: A Survey of Sources of Variation," *Psychophysiology*, vol. 12, no. 1, 1975, pp. 90–93.
33. Webster, J. G., "Pupillary Light Reflex: Development of Teaching Models," *IEEE Transactions on Biomedical Engineering*, vol. BME-18, no. 3, 1971, pp. 25–33.
34. Weiman, C. F. R., and Chaikin, G. M., "Logarithmic Spiral Grids for Image Processing," *Proceedings 1979 IEEE Computer Society Conference on Pattern Recognition and Image Processing*, Chicago, 1979, pp. 25–31.
35. Wurtz, R. H., and Goldberg, M. E., "Activity of Superior Colliculus in Behaving Monkey, IV. Effects of Lesions on Eye Movements," *Journal of Neurophysiology*, vol. 35, no. 4, 1972, pp. 587–596.

BIBLIOGRAPHY

A good introduction to the neurophysiology and neuroanatomy discussed in this chapter is provided by the many very well written articles which have appeared in *Scientific American* over the years. In particular, we recommend the collection of offprints on the mechanisms and models of perception [7] and the September 1979 issue which deals specifically with the brain. A very complete early history of the development of man's knowledge of the eye is given in [20].

Two more advanced and often cited books which will still be understandable to the lay reader are by Brindley [3] and Pirenne [19], both distinguished workers in the field. Absolutely everything you would ever want to know about the vertebrate retina can be found in the book by Rodieck [22], a scholarly tome but one containing much accessible material. The "Handbook of Sensory Physiology," published by Springer-Verlag, and the "Handbook of Perception," published by Academic Press, have both issued many volumes over the years which contain articles of a survey nature by active researchers. These are particularly useful for obtaining a detailed knowledge about the history and development of a specific research problem.

For the reader with no particular background in the biological sciences, Kuffler and Nicholls [10] explain how the nervous system functions. State-of-the-art papers including discussions on the neurosciences can be found in the *Neuroscience Research Progress Bulletins* published by the MIT Press in Cambridge, Massachusetts. These are edited and written by various scholars and are concerned with how the central nervous system controls the behavior and thought processes of man. An excellent and succinct introductory book on neural physiology is that by Stevens [25]. Most of the material in Section 3.5 is adapted from this source. A more advanced treatment can be found in [16] and [17]. A recent review of the literature on the visual pathway appears in [11].

In contrast to the conventional approach to the subject in the above sources, the reader may also wish to consult two other books which view the brain from completely different standpoints. The first, by Michael Arbib, is concerned with the brain as a cybernetic system and is aimed at the intelligent layman [1]. The second, by Uttal, is a unique and detailed exposition of the relationship between the psychology and the biology of the human mind [26].

The study of the simpler visual system of insects is also intriguing and was originated in modern times by Muller in 1829. The existence of a compound eye in insects led him to propose a theory of mosaic vision involving an array sensor and a processor. Readers interested in the subject of insect vision may consult [5, 8, 9, 13, 21, 23, 24, 27].

Research into the visual systems of simpler and smaller animals has provided significant clues to the properties of the more complex human visual system. Section 3.5 deals with certain elementary aspects of the neural networks which necessarily constitute the biological vision "computer." Further discussions may be found in [2, 4, 6, 12, 14, 15, 18].

1. Arbib, M. A., "The Metaphorical Brain, An Introduction to Cybernetics as Artificial Intelligence and Brain Theory," Wiley, New York, 1972.
2. Arbib, M. A., Kilmer, W. L., and Spinelli, D. N., "Neural Models and Memory," in Rosenzweig, M. R., and Bennet, E. L. (eds.), "Neural Mechanisms of Learning and Memory," MIT Press, Cambridge, Mass., 1976, pp. 109–132.
3. Brindley, G. S., "Physiology of the Retina and Visual Pathway," Physiological Society. Monograph No. 6, Edward Arnold Ltd., London, 1970.
4. Caianiello, E. R. (ed.), "Neural Networks," Springer-Verlag, New York, 1968.
5. Dethier, V. G., "The Physiology of Insect Senses," Wiley, New York, 1963.
6. Harmon, L. D., and Lewis, E. R., "Neural Modelling," *Physiological Review*, vol. 46, no. 5, July 1966, pp. 513–591.
7. Held, R., and Richards, W., (eds.), "Perception: Mechanisms and Models," Freeman, San Francisco, 1971.
8. Horridge, E. A. (ed.), "The Compound Eye and Vision of Insects," Clarendon Press, Oxford, 1975.
9. Horridge, E. A., "The Compound Eye of Insects," *Scientific American*, July 1977, pp. 108–120.
10. Kuffler, S. W., and Nicholls, J. G., "From Neuron to Brain," Sinauer Associates, Sunderland, Mass., 1976.
11. Lennie, P., "Parallel Visual Pathways: A Review," *Vision Research*, vol. 20, 1980, pp. 561–594.

12. MacGregor, R. J., and Lewis, E. R., "Neural Modelling," Plenum, New York, 1977.
13. Mazokhin-Porshnyakov, G. A., "Insect Vision," Masiromi, R., and Masiromi, L. (trans.), Goldsmith, T. H., trans. ed., Plenum, New York, 1969.
14. Morishita, I., and Yajima, A., "Analysis and Simulation of Networks of Mutually Inhibiting Neurons," *Kybernetik*, vol. 11, no. 3, 1972, pp. 154–156.
15. Mountcastle, V. B., "The Problem of Sensing and the Neural Coding of Sensory Events," in Quarton, G. C., Melnechnuk, T., and Schmidt, F. O. (eds.), "The Neuro Sciences," Rockefeller University Press, New York, 1967, pp. 393–408.
16. Mountcastle, V. B., "Medical Physiology," vol. II, Mosby, St. Louis, 1968.
17. Ochs, S., "Elements of Neurophysiology," Wiley, New York, 1965.
18. Perkel, D. H., and Bullock, T. H., "Neural Coding," *Neurosciences Research Progress Bulletin*, vol. 6, no. 3, 1968, pp. 221–348.
19. Pirenne, M. H., "Vision and the Eye," 2d ed., Associated Book Publishers, London, 1967.
20. Polyak, S. L., "The Retina," University of Chicago Press, Chicago, 1941.
21. Rockstein, M. (ed.), "The Physiology of Insects," 2d ed., vol. 1, Academic, New York, 1973.
22. Rodieck, R. W., "The Vertebrate Retina, Principles of Structure and Function," Freeman, San Francisco, 1973, p. 366.
23. Smith, D. S., "Insect Cells, Their Structure and Function," Oliver and Boyd, Edinburgh, 1968.
24. Smythe, R. H., "Vision in the Animal World," Macmillan, New York, 1975.
25. Stevens, C. F., "Neurophysiology: A Primer," Wiley, New York, 1966.
26. Uttal, W. R., "The Psychobiology of the Mind," Lawrence Erlbaum Associates, Hillsdale, N.J., 1978.
27. Wiggleworth, V. B., "The Principles of Insect Physiology," Halsted, New York, 1972.

CHAPTER

FOUR

BIOLOGICAL SIGNAL PROCESSING

4.1 INTRODUCTION

The basic anatomy of the human visual system has been presented in the previous chapter. As far as it goes, this anatomy is the underlying "wiring diagram" which results in the processing of images. In the following chapters we shall examine some of the details of this biological picture processing from the point of view of computation. Here we focus on the visual system as a black-box processor in which the image presented is the input and the psychophysical response is the output.

A most important variable, one would expect, is how the signal magnitude is processed by the human visual system. As with the computer vision system, initially it is sampled, quantized, coded (as described in Section 3.4) and then "manipulated" by the next stages. This chapter is concerned with these aspects of vision, both from a psychophysical and neurophysiological point of view. At first glance it might appear that this should not be a very complex consideration, but this is far from being the case. With human experimentation, one of the primary methods for recording an output variable is by verbal response or physical action. An attempt is made when studying a particular phenomenon to assume that all other known variables are held constant or at least are negligible in effect. But is it realistically possible to isolate a single phenomenon when one is not completely aware of the intricate system processes and interactions? In essence, this is a chicken and egg problem. Even strictly neurophysiological experiments may suffer from this state of affairs. Over 100 years ago it was found that when a frog's eye was removed in a dark chamber and then brought out into the daylight, the original pinkish rose color gradually whitened until it almost became transparent. This chemical, or bleaching, effect appears to be obviously behind the ability of the rods in our eyes to adapt to varying environmental lighting conditions. But is it really? More recently it has become evident that there is a strong and important neural control component as well, and that its contribution is not so easily isolated from all the others. We know that the higher we are in the visual pathway, the more complicated the processing, and one would expect that the signal would definitely also be altered in this hierarchy in a nontrivial fashion. Yet the psychophysical experiments to be described in this chapter seem to ignore the many intermediate stages at the highest cognitive levels.

In the discussion on electronic and mechanical digitizers in Chapter 2, it was seen that signal digitization is essentially a mapping from a continuous analog domain to a sampled and quantized digital array. This step necessarily involves a compression of information although, of course, the sampling theorem in digitization provides a theoretical basis for minimizing the loss. The human "digitizer," that is, the retinal array, is similarly a mechanism for spatial and temporal sampling of the picture input. Section 4.2 discusses how this is accomplished by the photoreceptors and what the implications are for the following stages in the processing chain. What is truly remarkable is the relatively simple and effective way nature has chosen to sample the incoming data and reduce it in size by two orders of magnitude.

The immediate physical effect of sampling on the black box is to characterize and limit the so-called resolving power of human vision. For example, how far apart do two parallel black bars have to be before we can distinguish them? We shall examine this in two ways: one is in the spatial domain as represented by the above question, and the other is in the frequency domain as in classical electronic system analysis. Thus, Sections 4.3.1 and 4.3.2 deal with visual acuity and spatial frequency response, respectively.

What is really significant about the measurement of resolving power is that it allows us to link the two domains of interest and thereby create a conventional Fourier domain model of signal-magnitude processing by man. Earlier attempts were restricted to the spatial domain, and Section 4.4 on photometric methods defines a paradigm developed in order to be capable of proceeding with very practical problems, such as the design of television. The more recent input/output frequency domain models, discussed in Section 4.5, seem to be more realistic and are grounded in current experimental findings. In fact, these models lead to some very interesting hypotheses about human image processing, which will be considered in Chapter 6.

4.2 RECEPTIVE FIELDS

The first significant level of cellular signal processing in the eye about which we have some relatively detailed knowledge involves the ganglion cells. In this section we shall relate these to the basic spatial organization of the photoreceptors by introducing the concept of a "receptive field." The latter is a pattern of receptor cells in the retina which results in a specific firing behavior for a particular single cell anywhere in the visual pathway. Moreover, here we shall focus on the signals appearing on the ganglion cells' axons, which form the optic nerve, in order to first study the spatial sampling of the image input. It has been hypothesized that the spatial organization of these receptive fields occurs at a level in the hierarchy shown in Figure 3.12 which is associated with the bipolar cells [51].

Perhaps the prototypical shape of the receptive field is that found in the cat, which is roughly circular or elliptical and consists of two concentric fields with antagonistic responses. It is important to note that the receptive field is not a fixed anatomical unit but varies according to many factors; for example, the background illumination of the scene, the scene itself, the state of adaptation, or the distance from the fovea. Very close to the fovea the receptive field is small, growing in size more or less linearly with distance from the visual axis and saturating at a maximum size. This allows for variable spatial sampling of the input light pattern and is obviously in concert with the existing cone distribution (see Figure 3.15). To achieve such a configuration with an electronic sensor would be a difficult task indeed. The functional organization of the sampling pattern has not been found to be the same for all animals and this is probably due to structural differences ("wiring"). For example, we shall consider in some detail in Chapter 5 the organizational distinctions between the frog and cat. The two concentric areas of the receptive field are found to interact, generally by exhibiting a spatial summation of excitory and inhibitory responses. This simple spatial contrast computation is known to be responsible for some very important visual phenomena. From the point of view of a "biological digitizer," we observe that the receptive field is equivalent to input sampling in the spatial domain.

Adrian [1] was the first to present a formal description of the concept of receptive fields based on his research with skin receptors. He was also the first to record action potentials from the optic nerve, using a conger eel [2]. In this way he showed that if the eye is illuminated, the nerve responds with a burst of pulses whose frequency decreases if the illumination persists. This work was later followed by the seminal experiments of Hartline [33] on the receptive fields of frogs. Having solved the problem of dissecting a bundle of fibers to excise a single one, he was for the first time able to map a receptive field of a retinal ganglion cell as a function of the stimulus signal. In 1967 he was awarded a Nobel prize for these studies. Hartline had suggested by his results that there exists a spatial interaction between the retinal cells that constitute a given receptive field. In the early fifties, Barlow working with frogs [3] and Kuffler with cats [43] clearly demonstrated the existence of these concentric circularly shaped fields, and since that time many more experiments have been performed on many different animals.

We shall see in the coming chapters how certain receptive fields possess complex geometric shapes in order to be able to recognize specific light patterns and features at the input. This was demonstrated by the work of Hartline on the frog. He showed that single ganglion cells in the retina did not necessarily respond in the same way to all light patterns. Cells seemed to be specialized to sensing specific inputs falling on the retina. Working with individual fibers to map a large number of receptive fields, he was able to postulate the existence of three types of ganglion cells. About 20 percent of the cells responded to a rectangular pulse (with regard to the time variable) of light by the continuous production of output pulses, ceasing to fire only when the light was turned off. These were termed "ON units." About 30 percent responded to the cessation of light, did not maintain an output in darkness, and were termed "OFF units." The ON-OFF units, characterizing about 50 percent of the cells, seemed to be sensitive to changes in light input, whether transitions from dark to light or the reverse. We therefore see that the ON units are responsible for detecting a light pattern falling on a region of the retina, while both the OFF and ON-OFF units are only sensitive to changes. These three kinds of receptive fields are distributed throughout the frog's retina.

The first study of the visual receptive field in a mammal was carried out by Kuffler [43], who used an intraocular microelectrode to record the action potentials of the ganglion cells of a cat subjected to a stabilized retinal image. He found that a spot of light on the retina produced a response from a particular ganglion cell, even when the light was moved within a roughly circular area. The shape of this receptive field is not simple and depends on several factors, including probably the stimulus. An additional important geometric property exists, since the field is made up of two concentric regions, the outer one being referred to as the "receptive field surround." For a specific ganglion cell, excitation of the surround produces the opposite effect to excitation within the smaller inner region.

Kuffler [43] found that essentially two kinds of ganglion cells existed in about equal number, the ON-center and OFF-center units. One responded with an increase in the pulse frequency at the ganglion axon when the light came on, and the other when it went off. Figure 4.1 shows these two characteristic receptive fields schematically. More recent studies have been made by Rodieck [52], who employed a small flashing spot of light (2 to 4′ in diameter) as an input and cumulative averaging techniques to measure the output. Although there was considerable variation from cell to cell, Figure 4.2 shows a schematic of a typical averaged response for an ON-type cell. We observe that the transient response to this rectangular pulse input is characteristic of a first-order linear system. Note that the OFF type would exhibit exactly the same type of histogram, except in response to an extinction of light (a negative-going rectangular pulse). In fact one cannot distinguish the two types solely by observing their response.

Figure 4.3 shows some receptive fields which were obtained from actual experiments. Some indication is given of the amplitude or strength of response by the ganglion cell to a step change in light at different positions in the

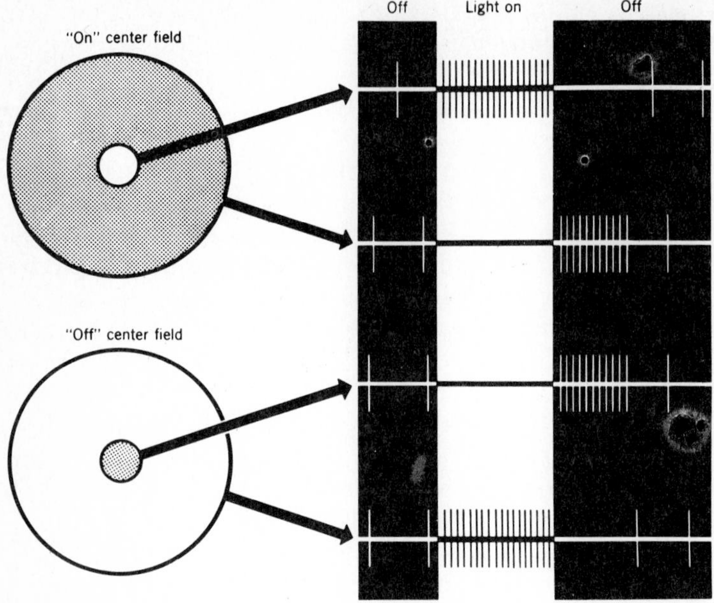

Figure 4.1 Response characteristics of two types of ganglion cells in the cat. The top half represents a cell with an ON-center field and an inhibitory surround; the bottom shows a cell with an OFF-center field and an excitatory surround. On the right-hand side of the figure we see a record of the impulses that a typical experiment might show traversing the axon of a cell of each type. The left-hand column shows the low level of spontaneous firing one might see from such a cell when it has been sitting in the dark for a while. The middle column indicates the level of firing that we get when a small spot of light is switched on in the indicated area. For instance, turning on a spot of light in an ON-center field will greatly increase the rate of firing, while turning on a spot of light in an OFF-center field will greatly reduce the rate of firing. The third column indicates the transient change in the firing level that occurs when the light is first turned off before the return to normal. Note the complementary actions of the two types of receptive fields. (*From M. A. Arbib, "The Metaphorical Brain," Wiley, New York, 1972.*)

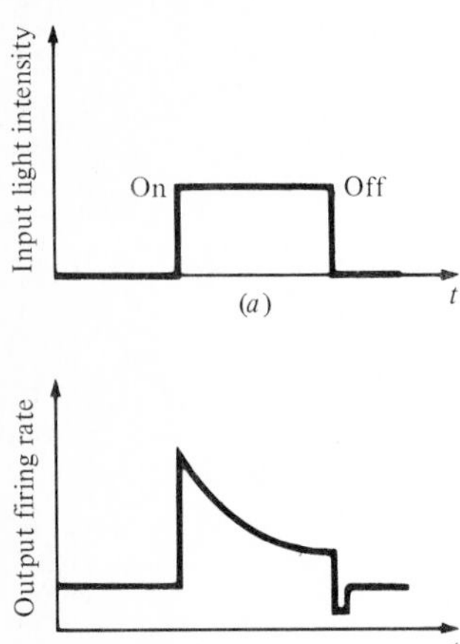

Figure 4.2 The input stimulus pulse of light in (a) results in the output firing rate shown in (b) for an ON-center unit. The response is seen to exhibit a first-order behavior pattern.

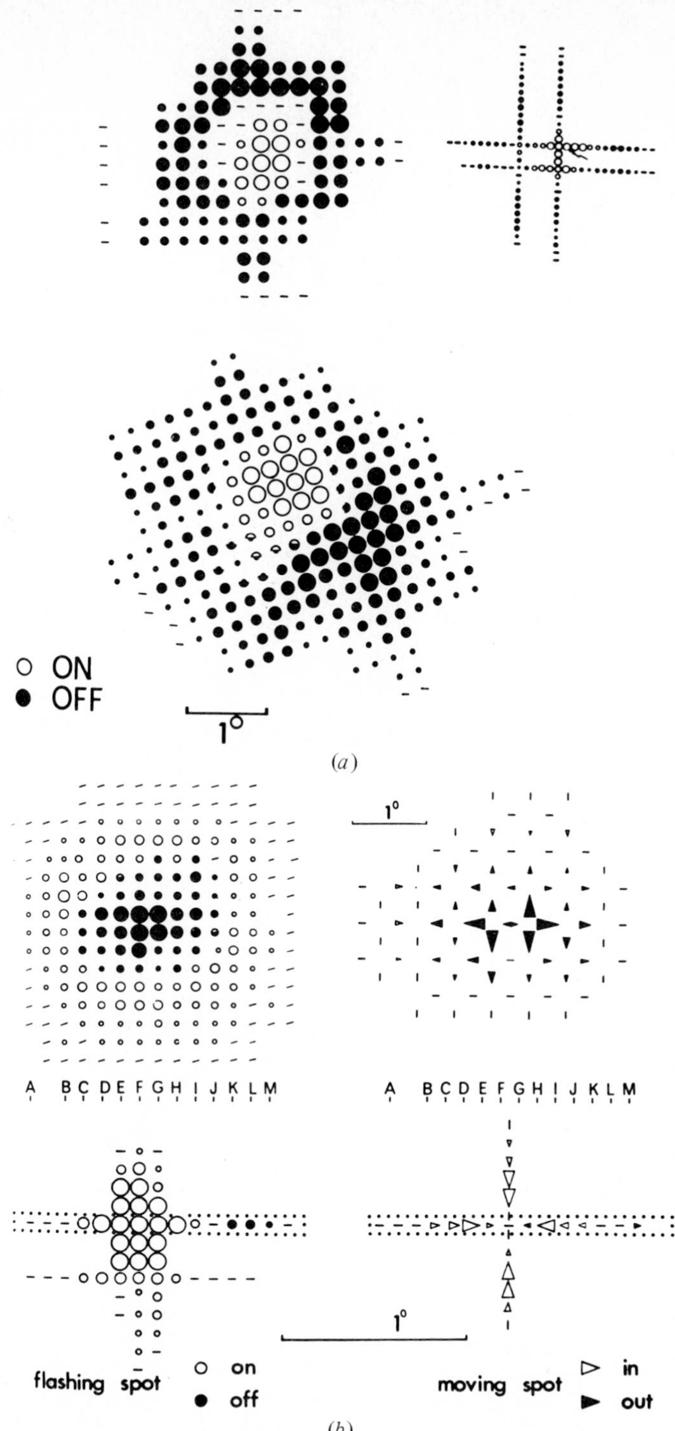

Figure 4.3 (*Caption on page 106.*)

receptive field. Using threshold techniques it is possible to map out a sensitivity profile across a given diameter of the field. Stimulation in the central area elicits the strongest response, with the firing rate increasing from the normal, background frequency. The maximum response occurs at the middle point of the region. Shining a light on the surround results in a decrease in the firing rate. At the interface of these two areas there is either no response or a weak ON-OFF response. This behavior is normally confined to a very narrow annulus and is more often observed for larger receptive fields. The profile containing two concentric antagonistic fields can therefore be described as approximating a section of the shape of a Mexican sombrero (see Figure 4.4).

What happens when the input light pattern is more complex and covers a larger portion of the receptive field? As early as 1928 as a result of their experiments with the conger eel, Adrian and Matthews [2] proposed physiological evidence for the existence of spatial summation at the input, resulting in response signals in the axons of retinal ganglion cells. More recent studies using patterns moving across the receptive field have indicated that the ganglion cell output is a computed spatial and temporal summation of the input light signals [55]. Simultaneous stimulation of both the center and surround regions results in a reduced response of the ganglion cell, which depends on the relative stimulus intensity and area of the two regions. Therefore, we observe that the photoreceptor arrays can act as contrast detectors, implying a stage of low-level image processing even at this very early point in the visual pathway of the cat and other mammals. We shall return to this concept in Chapter 6. Although to a first-order approximation the response is linear, there are indications of nonlinear effects [66]. There is also, as one might expect, a reciprocal relationship between the intensity level and the area of stimulation

---

Figure 4.3 Experimentation with receptive fields of cat retinal ganglion cells. (*a*) Receptive fields of three cat ON-center units. Open circles represent ON responses, while closed circles represent OFF responses. The size of a circle is a measure of the strength of the response at that point. All responses were judged to be "weak," "moderate," or "strong" with occasional judgments of "weak to moderate" and "moderate to strong." A short line indicates no detectable response. Positions without symbols were not judged. The light spot was 2 to 4′ in diameter and flashed 1 s on, 1 s off. The receptive field in the upper right was only partially plotted. It possessed a maximum center ON response displaced to the right of the center of the receptive field. The small black dot indicated by the arrow is the center of the receptive field as determined by a small moving spot of light. In contrast, the receptive field plotted in the lower half of the figure has an asymmetric OFF surround. (*b*) Receptive field of a cat OFF-center unit to flashing (left) and moving (right) spots of light. The symbols for the flashing spots are the same as in (*a*). In the diagram on the right, the light spot, 2 to 4′ in diameter, moved back and forth over a distance of 6′. The spot moved horizontally at the indicated points along the vertical line of symbols. The symbols point in the direction in which the movement of the spot produced an increase in the unit's firing rate. Movement in the opposite direction caused a decrease in firing rate. The response was judged to be "weak," "moderate," or "strong." The size of the symbol is a measure of the strength of the response. A short line indicates no detectable response. Positions or directions without symbols were not judged. Symbols which point toward the center are open, those pointing away from the center are filled. (*From R. W. Rodieck and J. Stone, "Analysis of Receptive Fields of Cat Retinal Ganglion Cells," Journal of Neurophysiology, vol. 28, no. 5, 1965, pp. 833–849.*)

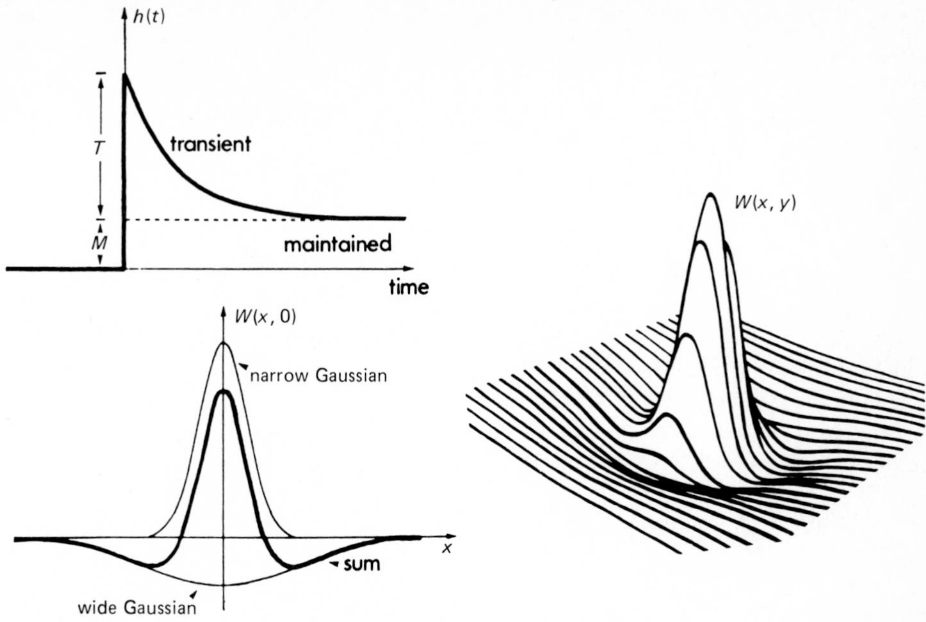

Figure 4.4 The functions $h(t)$ and $W(x, 0)$ which characterize the receptive-field model of the cat. As indicated, this leads to a sombrero shape in three dimensions. (*From R. W. Rodieck, "Quantitative Analysis of Cat Retinal Ganglion Cell Response to Visual Stimuli," Vision Research, vol. 5, no. 11/12, 1965, pp. 583–601.*)

and this can be used to determine the dimensions of the center and surround of the receptive field. In the area-threshold mapping experiments with cats, a flashing spot of light is first focused on the middle of the inner region of the receptive field. Within this region, the intensity that is needed to provoke a threshold response decreases as the spot diameter increases. When the spot covers the surround as well, the threshold begins to rise because of the inhibitory effect of the surround. The diameter at the minimum threshold corresponds to the diameter of the center region. Increasing the spot diameter, of course, increases the threshold required, but a saturation level is reached which signifies the border of the surround. This has been summarized as Ricco's law [54], as follows: The product of the spot intensity and the threshold value is constant. This relationship has been generally confirmed by psychophysical experiments as well.

Rodieck [52] has derived an analytical relationship for the receptive field–ganglion cell mapping. Naturally it is only approximate in nature, but it does adequately describe the general trends of experimental results. We must first assume that the ganglion-cell response function $f(x, y, t)$ is separable such that

$$f(x, y, t) = W(x, y)h(t) \tag{4.1}$$

where $W(x, y)$ is the window or template describing the spatial pattern of the receptive field and $h(t)$ is the impulse response of the ganglion cell. In the discussion that follows, it should be appreciated that the exact expressions for $W(x, y)$ and $h(t)$ are not too important and similar functions do lead to more or less equivalent results.

Since the transient behavior of the cell has been likened to a first-order linear system, let

$$h(t) = [M + Te^{-\alpha t}]\mu_{-1}(t) \tag{4.2}$$

where M is the magnitude of the maintained response component, T is the magnitude of the transient component, α is inversely related to the time constant of the cell, and $\mu_{-1}(t)$ is the step function singularity. Figure 4.4 shows a graph of the function $h(t)$. Assume that the template $W(x, y)$ is radially symmetric and that each profile can be described by the sum of a positive and negative Gaussian. Then

$$W(x, y) = \left(\frac{k_1}{\sigma_1^2\pi}\right)\exp[-(x^2 + y^2)/\sigma_1^2] - \left(\frac{k_2}{\sigma_2^2\pi}\right)\exp[-(x^2 + y^2)/\sigma_2^2] \tag{4.3}$$

where k_1 and $k_2 > 0$, and σ_1 and σ_2 are measures of the width of the central and surround regions, respectively. Note that the two terms in the above expression for $W(x, y)$ have no physical significance of their own. Figure 4.4 contains a plot of a typical receptive-field profile as well as a projective three-dimensional view, very similar to the sombrero mentioned previously.

We assume now that the stimulus input is a two-dimensional moving binary closed form with an amplitude of unity and velocity v. Also let

$$x = g_1(y) \tag{4.4}$$

and

$$x = g_2(y) \tag{4.5}$$

describe the leading and trailing edges, respectively, of the stimulus shape. We shall assume that these functions are single-valued and completely describe the input. Then the response $\psi(t)$, given as a firing rate, is a spatial convolution of the geometric shape of the receptive field with the impulse response of the unit. Thus

$$\psi(t) = \int_{-\infty}^{+\infty}\int_{-\infty}^{+\infty} W(x, y)\left\{h\left(t - \frac{1}{v}[x + g_1(y)]\right) - h\left(t - \frac{1}{v}[x + g_2(y)]\right)\right\} dx\, dy \tag{4.6}$$

with $h(t)$ and $W(x, y)$ given by Equations (4.2) and (4.3) respectively. To express ψ as a function of position as the input moves across the field, substitute $t = x/v$ into Equation (4.6). Although $\psi(t)$ or $\psi(x/v)$ compares well with experimental results [55], there are limitations to this approach. Among these are the requirements that the stimulus duration be short enough so that adaptation does not occur and long enough so that it does not become comparable with $1/\alpha$. Also the model does not make allowance for very bright inputs. Other simulation studies of the two-dimensional processing in the retina are discussed in [49, 23].

Experiments have shown that σ_1 ranges in value between 0.1° and 2° of visual angle in the cat, with σ_2 being a little larger. It is interesting that the extent of the dendritic trees of retinal ganglion cells matches quite closely with this size of the receptive fields [8, 9]. The receptive fields of ganglion cells of monkeys seem to be similar to those of the cat [29, 30]. However, they are smaller, varying in size from 4′ to 2° of visual angle. Therefore we observe that even different mammals possess different kinds of sampling configurations.

The situation as described above existed until the middle sixties [40]. Since then three different kinds of ganglion cells have been found in the cat's retina, rather noncommittally named as *W* [53, 68], *X*, and *Y* [21]. The distinctive features and functional roles are still not very clear, and present conclusions are based on an inadequate number of experiments. One simple way of grouping these cells is in increasing order of pulse-train conduction velocities along the axons, with their alphabetic order representing increasing velocity. Does perhaps the detection of certain spatial properties by ganglion cells require a faster response? It also appears that the X cell predominates in the central retina and the Y cell in the periphery. The former project to the lateral geniculate nucleus (LGN), the latter there and to the superior colliculus, and the W type to the superior colliculus. Other more complex properties are summarized in [48] and detailed in [54, 67]. An interesting mathematical model describing the spatiotemporal organization of the X- and Y-type ganglion cells of the primate retina has recently been suggested [51]. By and large, a comprehensive picture of the details is not possible at present, and it appears that some very basic information about these categories is still missing.

Receptive fields do not only map into ganglion cell outputs, but also project onto cells in the LGN and the visual cortex. For example, a cell in the cat's LGN receives its primary excitory input from one or a small number of retinal ganglion cells whose receptive fields are physically close together. A simplified hierarchic model describing this retinogeniculate convergence has been suggested by Hammond [32]. The topographic organization of the receptive fields of cortical cells is less rigid than at the lower levels of processing and can exhibit rather complex detection capabilities. These may serve the role of feature detectors, which we shall examine in detail in Chapter 5.

We have observed that neither ON units nor OFF units provide a good relationship between the axonal frequency output and the general level of retinal illumination. They do however, indicate small signal differences between the center and surround. It is in this way that a pattern of input light is spatially sampled and its existence is transmitted via the ganglion cell to the appropriate location in the central nervous system. We have also noted previously that the number of photoreceptors exceeds by two orders of magnitude the number of axonal nerve fibers in the optic nerve. Obviously a sampling of the input by the receptive field provides for a spatial convergence in which many input fibers map onto a single output fiber. This sampling process will obviously affect the spatial resolving power, as we shall see in the next section.

4.3 VISUAL RESOLVING POWER

4.3.1 Visual Acuity

The measure by which two spatially or temporally separated visual signals can just be distinguished from each other is referred to as the resolving power of the system. One aspect which influences this property is the size of the elements in the retinal mosaic, as demonstrated in Figure 4.5. In Figure 4.5*a* a geometric pattern of black and white objects is shown, while Figure 4.5*b*, *c*, and *d* gives the sampled output for progressively larger sampling elements. We note that as the number of elements per unit area decreases, so does the ability to resolve small gaps in the image. Observe that the single vertical line remains resolvable even after the response to the grating containing lines of similar width has been considerably degraded. Why is this?

Resolving power can be considered in terms of either visual acuity or contrast sensitivity. The former is a measure of the smallest spatial pattern that can be distinguished. The latter is the minimum signal contrast required to just perceive a bar pattern such as a grating of alternating black and white bars. We shall discuss these in turn. Both are properties of the human visual system treated as a black-box processor. The inputs are the patterns of light stimuli presented to the viewer, and the outputs the perceptual response. The two measures are complementary in nature, the first one defined in the spatial domain and the other in the corresponding frequency domain. It is the experiments in the latter domain, to be discussed in Section 4.3.2, that lead to a conventional linear system model of the visual system.

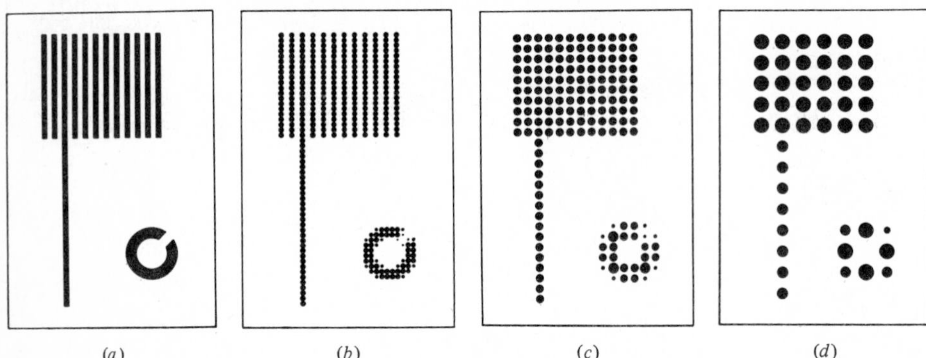

Figure 4.5 The pattern in (*a*) is assumed to be the input to three different systems with progressively coarser retinal mosaics. The resulting sensed signal is shown in (*b*), (*c*), and (*d*), where it is observed that the resolving power decreases as the size of the sensing element increases. (*From M. H. Pirenne, "Vision and the Eye," 2d ed., Chapman and Hall, London, 1967, p. 129.*)

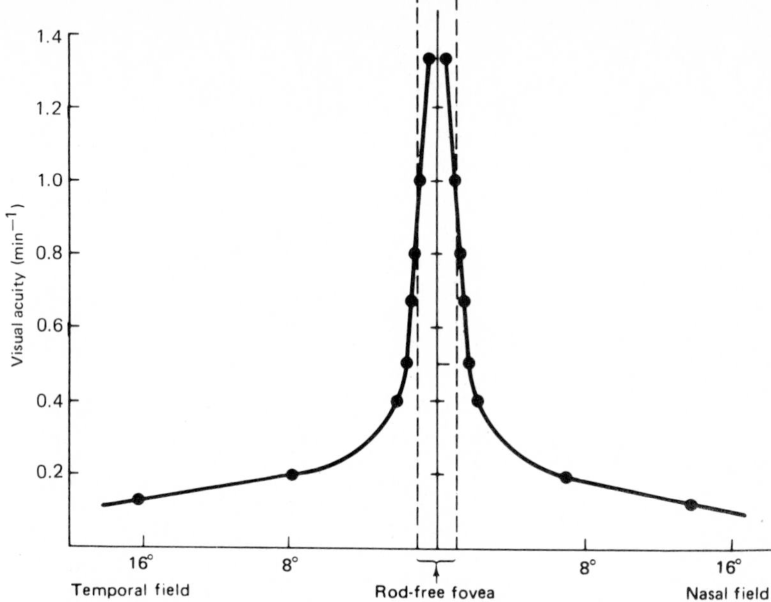

Figure 4.6 The visual acuity of man plotted as a function of visual angle. [*From W. R. Uttal, "The Psychobiology of Sensory Coding," Harper & Row, New York, 1973, after M. Alpern, "Movements of the Eyes," in "The Eye," H. Davson (ed.), vol. 3, 2d ed., Academic, New York, 1969, pp. 1–252.*]

Pirenne [50] has offered the following definition of visual acuity: "For any particular test object, the numerical value of visual acuity is by definition the reciprocal $1/\alpha$ of the visual angle α, in minutes of arc, subtended at the eye by the smallest detail in the test object." Visual acuity for the human eye as a function of visual angle is shown in Figure 4.6. The eye is most sensitive in the 4° region of the fovea centralis, where the density of cones is the greatest. The sensitivity decreases monotonically but rapidly within this region and decreases more slowly outside it. Such nonuniform resolving power leads to poor visual acuity in the peripheral regions of the retina, probably a result of the high convergence of rods onto ganglion cells. Although, obviously, the neural receptive field we discussed in the previous section is the neurophysiological correlate of visual acuity, the exact relationship between the two is unknown.

Psychophysical measurements of visual acuity are normally made for the whole eye, so that in fact it is an integrative function of the retinal elements. Typical test patterns are shown in Figure 4.7; these are usually black and white, with the contrast as high as possible. From the figure we observe that four different types of visual tasks may be involved. A visit to the ophthalmologist usually entails the recognition of letters, as shown in Figure 4.7*f*. Second, we have the resolution of separate entities as given in Figure 4.7*b* and the Landolt ring in Figure 4.7*d*. Detection of the presence or absence of a pattern is represented by Figure 4.7*a*, while localization in terms of the displacement of

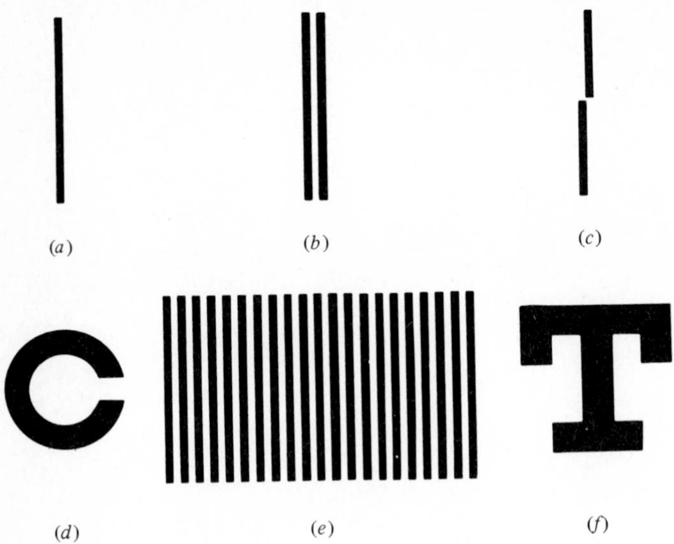

Figure 4.7 Classical patterns used to measure visual acuity. (*a*) A single thin, dark line. (*b*) Minimum separation. (*c*) Vernier. (*d*) Landolt ring. (*e*) Bar pattern or grating. (*f*) Snellen letter. [*From J. P. Thomas, "Spatial Resolution and Spatial Interaction," in E. C. Carterette and M. P. Friedman (eds.), "Handbook of Perception," vol. V. "Seeing," Academic, New York, 1975, p. 234.*]

one element with respect to another is shown in Figure 4.7*c*. An important question arises about the equivalence of these measures. Generally a subject is tested by reducing the size of the pattern or the appropriate pattern feature until it is just barely resolvable. This threshold conforms to the definition given above and is nominally equal to unity for a normal viewer, although higher values are obtained under laboratory conditions. Thus visual acuity will vary with the stimulus and the particular experimental conditions. For example, given a grating of alternating black and white bars (Figure 4.7*e*), the human under optimal conditions can reach a value of $\alpha = 2.1$; that is, the angular distance between the bars is 28″ of arc.

Three different types of visual discrimination modes appear to exist [73]. The first measures our ability to judge the minimum separation between two features and is generally accepted as characterizing the underlying behavior of the human visual system. Visual acuity tests are carried out with such forms as those shown in Figure 4.7*b*, *d*, and *f* and yield spatial thresholds of about 1′ of visual arc.

The second type of discrimination task is called "hyperacuity" and may be measured by using the vernier shown in Figure 4.7*c*. In this case, visual discrimination is an order of magnitude better than one would normally expect from a physical point of view. Westheimer [72] discusses this phenomenon from the standpoint of the diffraction theory of light and one would expect this theory to provide a lower limit on the visual acuity of the human optical system. It is possible to achieve a threshold of a few seconds of visual arc! Apparently, even target motion does not affect this threshold value [75, 76]. Barlow [4] has suggested that the phenomenon may be due to a process of data interpolation and has indicated a possible neurophysiological mechanism. He has also speculated that this may produce a much larger effective array size in the visual cortex than is estimated by the actual number of afferent optic nerve fibers. A comprehensive explanation of this hyperacuity phenomenon awaits discovery.

The third type of visual discrimination is referred to as "minimum visible acuity." Amazingly, in this case a long single opaque line subtending a visual arc of just 0.5″ (see Figure 4.5*d*) can be detected against an evenly and brightly lit background [36]. This equals a visual acuity of 120, making this task apparently very different from the others. It is equivalent to viewing in a vacuum a bar of width about 8 mm at a distance of 3 km. The image of such a thin line on the retina is not the same as the geometrical pattern, since the width of the bar is only about one-sixtieth the diameter of a single cone! This phenomenon has been explained by diffraction effects in the optical ocular system. These result in image blurring, so that the projected retinal image is considerably expanded in range, even though the signal is weak. Nevertheless the latter is adequate to activate the photoreceptors [37]. On the other hand, for white lines on a black background it does not seem to matter how thin the line is as long as enough light is received by the receptors [37]. Westheimer [72], however, has argued against this. It is also interesting that the amount of light involved in the visual experiments, which lead to these high values of resolving power, is only in the order of magnitude of the absolute sensing threshold for the projected retinal area.

In addition to the neurophysiological experiments with receptive fields discussed in Section 4.2, psychophysical experiments have been directed towards isolating those factors which affect the resolving power [69]. Let us first consider the nature of the illuminating pattern of light. Figure 4.8 shows the relationship between the visual acuity of man and the stimulus illumination. It is also interesting that insects such as bees, for example, show a curve of similar shape. For high intensities the acuity is independent of the input, although there is an effect for weak illuminants. The latter probably results from the action of the rods, and the saturated part of the curve from that of the cones. The curve has this form because as the intensity increases, the subject tends to use the more central portions of the retina. However acuity can vary by wide limits within one region of the retina. There is even some evidence that the actual number of light detectors which function at any one time increases with input light intensity.

With regard to the optical ocular system, for high intensities and pupils of moderate diameter (>3 mm) visual acuity is also more or less independent of the color content of the input. However, such is not the case for the weaker signals. This is particularly a problem for white light, which we shall see is a mixture of all wavelengths; in this case the image is more blurred, and

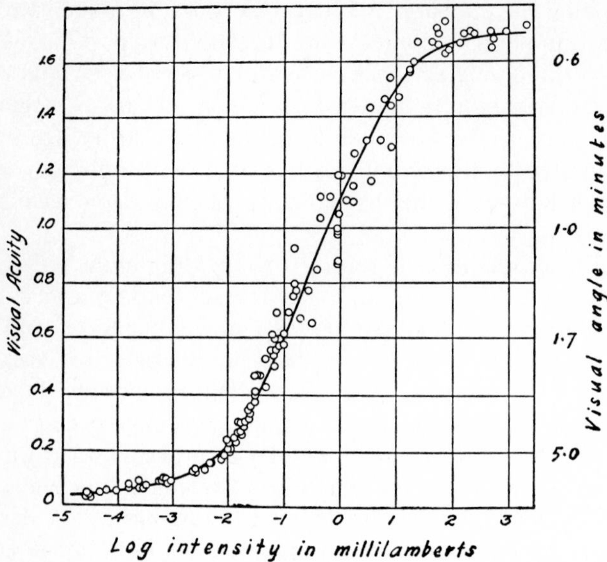

Figure 4.8 The relationship between human visual acuity and background illumination. The results were obtained in the nineteenth century using Snellen letters. (*From M. H. Pirenne, "Vision and the Eye," 2d ed., Chapman and Hall, London, 1967, p. 132.*)

therefore the acuity poorer, because the cornea and the lens are not able to focus all the wavelength components in the same plane.

The variation with intensity is not related to the contraction of the pupil, and this is a factor which is responsible for maintaining the accuracy of the focal system. We know this from experiments made with humans fitted with artificial pupils, since the results are unchanged. However, the pupil size is a factor in another context. For small pupils, diffraction effects in the optical ocular system predominate. The pupil acts as a low-pass filter whose cutoff frequency is proportional to its diameter, so that the visual acuity increases with pupil diameter. As the pupil becomes larger, the stimulus wavelength begins to limit acuity at a diameter of 2.35 mm for red and 2 mm for shorter wavelengths. Thus for large pupils, acuity is nearly independent of diameter. However as the pupil diameter increases beyond 5.6 mm, the image quality begins to deteriorate again. This is largely due to spherical and chromatic aberrations, which lead to errors of focus. The amount of degradation is proportional to pupil size. We observe that the optimal pupil size lies somewhere between 2 and 4 mm, possibly at 2.4 mm [13]. A recent paper [62] determines that from a theoretical point of view this pupil diameter would yield an optimal photoreceptor spacing of 27.4″, a result consistent with the anatomy. We have noted how the sharpness of the image formed by the optical system is a major factor limiting visual acuity. Accommodation by the lens system to viewing distance does not seem to be too important except that there is a degradation in resolving power if the position of the viewed object is either closer than the near point or more distant than the far point (shortsightedness).

Having considered the optical system, let us now turn to the transducing elements discussed in the previous section. The retinal locus of the image plays an important role since it governs the fineness of the activated retinal mosaic. Anatomical measurements yield a 2.0 to 2.3 μm intercenter distance for cones in the fovea centralis. This is equivalent to a subtended angle of 25 to 29″ (equivalent to 120 cones per degree) or approximately 60 Hz/degree. For a black-and-white grating pattern the highest visual acuity achieved under the best viewing conditions is 2.3 μm. We therefore conclude that the mosaic of cones must be the constraint on the visual acuity. The periphery is considerably poorer in performance, most likely because of the high convergence of rods, possibly several thousand to one. Nevertheless it is interesting that this cannot be the complete story, since the resolving power is much worse than might be expected as a result of both the quality of the retinal image and the fineness of the distribution of rods and cones. Even more curious is the fact that the resolution of bars oriented vertically or horizontally is superior to that for oblique lines. Thus the interconnectivity of the ganglion cells and others higher in the visual pathway, which, as we saw, form receptive fields, appears to have a great influence on the characteristic of visual acuity. For more complex input patterns than the bars that have typically constituted the experimental input stimulus, we would expect that the receptive field would constitute the primary limitation to visual acuity.

4.3.2 Contrast Sensitivity

Having considered spatial visual acuity as one aspect of resolving power, we shall now examine the sensitivity of the human visual system to the spacing of a set of contrasting areas. To do this, it is necessary to assume that the three stages in the block diagram of Figure 3.1 are contained within a black box, the input being a bar pattern and the output a particular psychophysical measurement. If we further make the major assumption that this black box is a linear system, we may examine its behavior in the spatial frequency domain. This may be related to the resolving power and is characterized by a plot of perceptual measure versus spatial frequency. The implication of the linearity assumption will be discussed later, but for the moment the reader is asked to accept it with reservations.

The inputs used to date tend to be bar gratings in which the intensity along a horizontal profile varies in a sinusoidal manner, as shown in Figure 4.9. Although the two-dimensional spatial frequency response is ostensibly being sought, these patterns are obviously one-dimensional. The units of frequency can be expressed as cycles per centimeter of test pattern or cycles per millimeter on the retina, but most often are given as cycles per degree of visual angle subtended. The contrast of the output pattern is measured by computing the contrast C in terms of the ratio of the maximum to the average difference

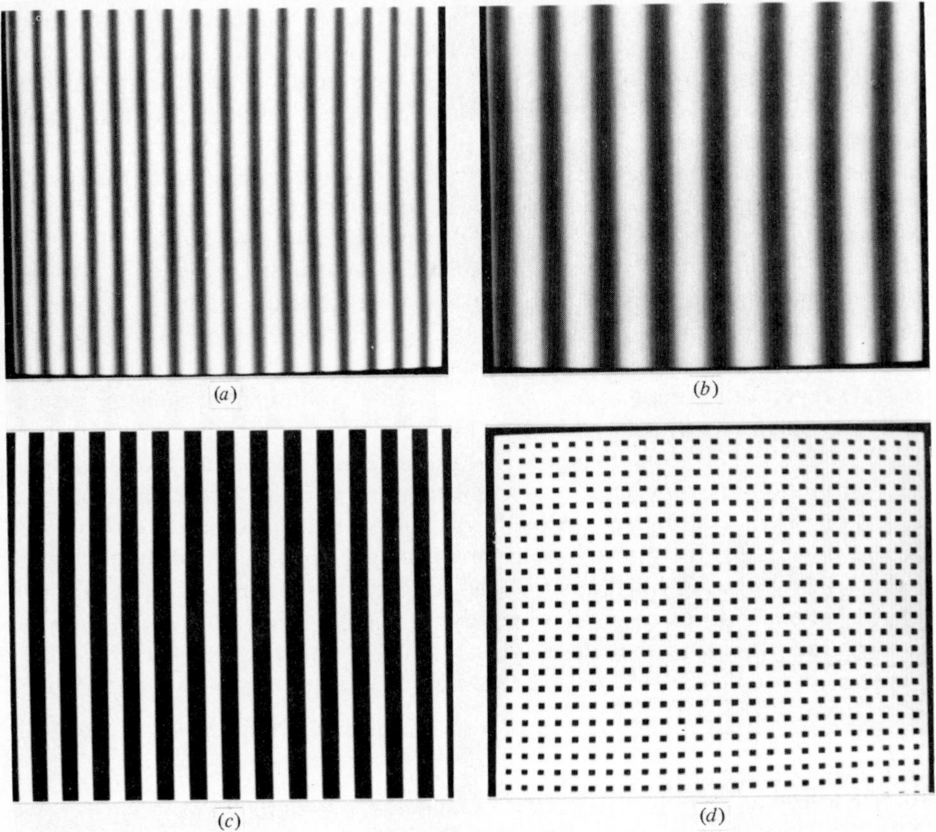

Figure 4.9 Examples of two-dimensional periodic patterns. (*a*) Sine-wave grating of moderate contrast. (*b*) Sine wave of half the frequency in (*a*). (*c*) A square wave (bar pattern) of very high contrast (nearly 1.0). (*d*) The patterns in (*a*), (*b*), and (*c*) are essentially one-dimensional because they can be described by a single horizontal profile and a one-dimensional Fourier spectrum. On the other hand, the dot pattern in (*d*) is completely described only by a two-dimensional spectrum. In fact, the spectrum has strong horizontal and vertical components. [*Adapted from M. Georgeson, "Spatial Fourier Analysis and Human Vision," chapter II in "Tutorial Essays in Psychology, A Guide to Recent Advances," vol. 2, N.S. Sutherland* (ed.), *Lawrence Erlbaum Associates, Hillsdale, N.J., 1979, p. 45.*]

in intensity. This is the degree of modulation of intensity above a mean level and is given by

$$C = \frac{I_{max} - I_{min}}{I_{max} + I_{min}} \tag{4.7}$$

where I_{max} and I_{min} are the maximum and minimum intensities in a pattern, respectively. For an absolutely uniformly shaded field, $I_{max} = I_{min}$ and $C = 0$; when the bars are as black as possible, $I_{min} = 0$ and $C = 1$. Thus, the contrast can vary in magnitude between 0 and 1. We are now able to define the so-called spatial modulation transfer function of the black box in an exactly analogous fashion to the one-dimensional transfer function of an electronic circuit (where the independent variable is time rather than distance) or the two-dimensional transfer function of a lens in an optical system. The reader is referred to [16, chap. XII] and [17, chap. 6] for an elaboration of this concept.

We define the transfer function $H(u)$ of the system as†

$$H(u) = \frac{\text{output contrast}}{\text{input contrast}} \tag{4.8}$$

where u is the spatial frequency variable. Since we are dealing with an essentially one-dimensional bar pattern, we may use an analogy to the more familiar impulse response of the electrical network. That is, we assume that a very thin line is equivalent to an impulse in the spatial domain rather than the time domain. The response to this ideal input is referred to as the "line-spread function." Just as the Fourier transform of the impulse response is equivalent to the transfer function, so is the transform of the line-spread function equivalent to the transfer function. Thus, if we were able to perform the appropriate experiments and measure the input and output contrast values, it would be possible to characterize the human visual system in the Fourier domain, an attractive proposition indeed. However, it is not always feasible to measure the output for humans in a completely controlled fashion. Necessarily, psychological variables are used, requiring many assumptions about the system behavior.

In order to obtain $H(u)$ it has become the practice to measure the contrast sensitivity instead and then to equate the two. The experimental procedure involves presenting each of a set of stationary sinusoidal patterns of the type shown in Figure 4.9 on a visual display to a viewer who can vary the contrast control while maintaining a constant average luminance. For a given pattern coarseness, the viewer is asked to adjust the contrast until the grating is just barely distinguishable. As with similar standard techniques, the threshold of contrast perception $C_\theta(u)$ is obtained at difference spatial frequencies u and the contrast sensitivity function (CSF) is then taken as the inverse [12]:

$$H(u) \equiv \text{CSF}(u) = \frac{1}{\text{threshold }(u)} = \frac{1}{C_\theta(u)} \tag{4.9}$$

Thus the sensitivity increases as the contrast required to perceive the pattern decreases, as would be expected. Many experiments have been made, and with some minor variations they all more or less agree with the result shown in Figure 4.10. (The shape of the function for humans is similar to that for the cat, as illustrated in the figure.) This function is a bandpass filter with a peak or optimal spatial frequency in the range of 2 to 5 cycles/degree. It is asymmetrical in that the high-frequency asymptote is steeper than the low-frequency

† The reader is cautioned that this relationship holds only for a sinusoidal input.

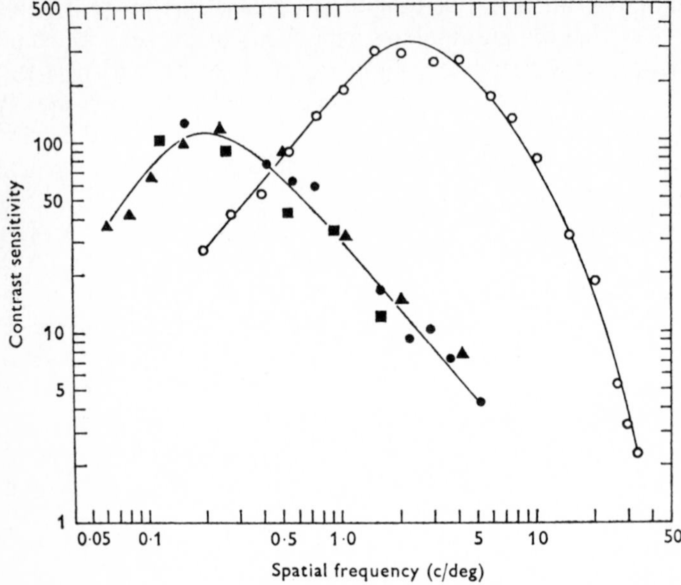

Figure 4.10 Contrast sensitivity functions for man and cat. The black symbols were obtained from evoked-potential experiments with three cats. The open circles represent the results of a monocular experiment with a human. (*From F. W. Campbell, L. Maffei, and M. Piccolino, "The Contrast Sensitivity of the Cat," Journal of Physiology, vol. 229, no. 3, March 1973, pp. 719–731.*)

one. The system may be described as a differentiator which exhibits midrange emphasis and can be modeled by a combination of two low-pass filters [27].

We note that less than 1 percent contrast is needed to resolve the most visible pattern, an impressive performance characteristic. The classical acuity measure for measuring the resolving power is now recognized as the highest spatial frequency on the curve that can be resolved at 100 percent contrast. Viewing Figure 4.11 demonstrates quantitatively the effect of contrast sensitivity on the human visual system. Dooley [19] has provided the following equation to fit the experimental data:

$$H(u) = 5.05(e^{-0.138u})(1 - e^{0.1u}) \tag{4.10}$$

where u is in cycles per degree and the curve has been normalized so that the peak corresponds to a just visible modulation of 0.005. An alternative expression may be found in [60].

To evaluate what the CSF as given by Equation 4.9 actually determines and how it relates to the desired modulation transfer function $H(u)$ as given by Equation (4.8), Campbell and Green [12] considered Figure 3.1 as a cascaded system comprised of an optical subsystem followed by a receptor-neuron processor. The output of the latter is, of course, the psychophysical variable in the experiment. The approach was to measure the two stages independently in order to delineate their separate contributions. First the CSF was obtained as

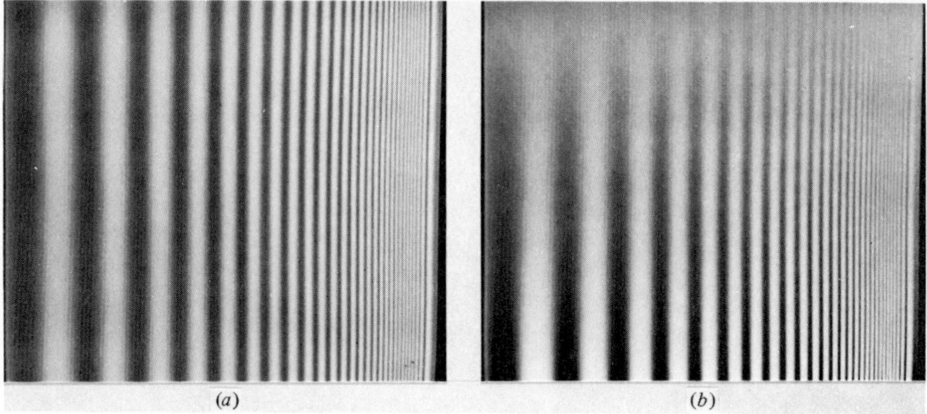

Figure 4.11 Composite sinusoidal grating. By comparing (*b*) with (*a*), we observe the effect of the response function in Figure 4.10. The intermediate frequencies are visible at lower contrast than either the low or high spatial frequencies. (*a*) A sinusoidal grating in which the spatial frequency changes logarithmically. The frequency increases from left to right. (*b*) A sinusoidal grating in which both the spatial frequency and the contrast vary logarithmically. The contrast decreases from bottom to top.

described above. Then the CSF of the receptor-neuron stage alone was determined by focusing a sinusoidal interference pattern directly on the retina using two coherent light sources originating from a single laser. By controlling the separation between the two beams, the spatial frequency could be altered, while the contrast was varied by superimposing a uniform field of light. Assuming linearity and ignoring scattering effects, the ratio of these two functions yields the optical CSF. The results are shown in Figure 4.12. Surprisingly, the optical subsystem contributes only one-third of the attenuation at high frequencies when compared with the receptor-neuron subsystem. At low frequencies the latter is largely responsible for the degradation. Thus it appears that the contrast sensitivity degradation is primarily a function of the processing by the nervous system and is hardly limited by the ocular optical system. Using ophthalmoscopic techniques, Campbell and Gubisch [13] were able to duplicate these results when scattering properties were also taken into account. Similarly, an alternative confirmation has been made by Campbell and Maffei [14] using evoked potential techniques. The latter involves a localized response in the visual cortex of the brain to an input light pattern in which a group of neurons respond simultaneously and synchronously, thereby providing an associated voltage signal which can be easily measured.

Evoked potential experiments can also be performed with cats to determine their CSF, as shown in Figure 4.10. What is really intriguing is that Bisti and Maffei [6] have actually managed to confirm these data using behavioral methods in which cats were painstakingly trained to respond to a grating pattern by employing food rewards. Food was offered only if the cat responded when a grating was visible. The cat's curve can be seen to be similar in shape to

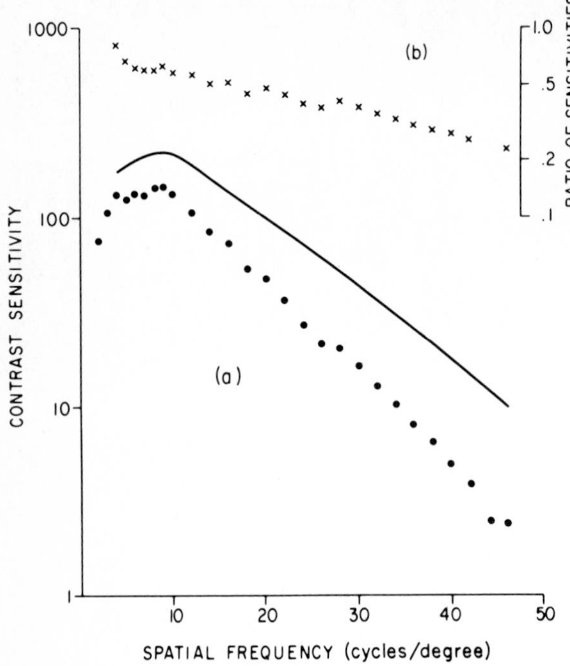

Figure 4.12 Experimental determination of the contrast sensitivity function (CSF). (*a*) The black dots indicate the CSF for the entire human visual system, the black curve that of the receptor-neural component. (*b*) The ratio of the two functions in (*a*) yields the CSF of the ocular optical system. [*After J. P. Thomas, "Spatial Resolution and Spatial Interaction," in E. C. Carterette and M. P. Friedman (eds.), "Handbook of Perception," vol. V, "Seeing," Academic, New York, 1976.*]

that of man, except shifted by about 1 log unit towards the lower frequencies. Thus a cat is able to perceive low-contrast detail at low frequencies, which man cannot. This superior closeup vision does not depend on the size of the image projected on the cat's retina, which is only about 1.3 times smaller than that for humans.

Having described how the CSF measures the resolving power of both man and cat, it is legitimate to query the obvious underlying assumption of a linear model. Is the CSF the modulation transfer function of the system? The answer is that to a first approximation it can be represented as such, although we shall later examine some very important nonlinearities such as logarithmic stretching, brightness constancy, and simultaneous contrast. For the moment we shall assume that Figure 4.10 is the transfer function of a linear, isotropic, time- and space-invariant system, with the implied subsidiary conditions that it is also monocular, monochromatic, and photopic. These assumptions are detailed in [16, pp. 335–342], [26, pp. 49–51], and [31, pp. 161–163]. Further support for a linear human visual system is provided by recent contrast perception experiments which indicate that suprathreshold processing can also be represented by a linear model [28].

Several interesting properties arise out of considering the CSF as a black-box description of the behavior of the human visual system. We have already noted in the previous section that visual acuity degrades in the periphery; analogously, the CSF is found to be reduced and the peak shifted to lower frequencies in this region [39]. The CSF is also a function of the orientation of the grating; that is, for a rotated grating it is found that the response at high frequencies is degraded while that at lower frequencies remains unchanged [15]. Also, a practical result applicable to digital picture processing has been obtained by Roetling [56], who was concerned with the number of bits needed to accurately represent the information in a digitized picture. Conventionally, it is common to treat the image sampling rate and number of quantization levels as independent entities. Thus the sample spacing should be made equal to 20 pixels per millimeter digitization on the basis of the high-frequency cutoff of the visual system. Also, the signal should be quantized, to, perhaps, 8 bits per pixel to conform with the human's ability to perceive low-contrast differentials at low spatial frequencies. This yields an overestimation of the total number of bits required. Using the complete CSF curve and not just these two points, Roetling [56] has derived the following equation:

$$\text{Number of bits per pixel} = 2\pi\Delta^{-2}(177.5) \tag{4.11}$$

where Δ is the number of samples per millimeter of the picture. Thus for $\Delta = 20$ samples per millimeter this relationship now gives a maximum quantization of 2.8 bits per pixel. In other words, only about eight gray levels are needed to represent a digital picture if the spatial sampling rate is chosen to be equal to the limit of the visual system. This is in harmony with other indications that the human brain does not code variables into a very great many levels even though it is obviously capable of performing some very powerful processing [57].

It is also surprising that the classical one-bit-per-pixel code that is used in the graphic arts industry provides such acceptable images to the human viewer [42, 41]. For example, these so-called halftone pictures are commonly used in newspapers. In this approach, gray levels are represented by an appropriate texture pattern of black and white dots. It turns out that the distribution of number of perceived gray levels versus spatial frequency for such halftone images matches the human visual system quite well [56].

In this section we have examined the quantitative representation of human visual resolving power. This has been done in both the spatial and spatial frequency domains by using different experimental paradigms but has essentially produced consistent results. The CSF has been found to be a measure which is compatible with being the frequency-response function of the system treated as a black box. In the next section we shall consider an early model of the visual system and shall follow this in Section 4.5 by a discussion which takes into account the more recent experiments with the CSF.

4.4 PHOTOMETRY

In the previous section we suggested that the contrast sensitivity function might be considered as the black-box transfer function of the human visual system.

The data from these relatively recent experiments have indeed been used to derive mathematical models and these will be considered in the next section. Prior to these experiments, however, there was still a practical need to describe in a methodological fashion the result of the biological processing of input light sources. After all, we are speaking of the period during which cinema, photography, and television had all been developed. This requirement was filled by what is essentially a set of definitions, loosely based on the then current knowledge and referred to as "photometry." The paradigm was as follows. Suppose we present a certain light pattern to the viewer and measure in some way the magnitude of the response, taking into account the existence of photopic (cone) and scotopic (rod) vision. Photometry is an attempt to model an average human observer so that the output for the given experiments matches the appropriate input.

In Section 2.2.2 we defined the radiometric measurements used to describe source inputs. At the output, the normal visual system can respond over a range of 10^{13} millilamberts (mL), the scotopic range being from 10^{-6} to 1 mL and the photopic range from 1 to 10^{7} mL.† Both radiometric and photometric units are a measure of the amount of light emitted by a light source, the former in terms of physical energy and the latter in terms of the perceptual effects. The photometric units defined below are obviously equivalent to their radiometric counterparts:

Luminous flux	(lumen)
Luminous intensity, I	(lumen/sr) (lumens per steradian)
Luminous emittance, M	(lumen/m)
Illuminance, E	(lumen/m = lux)
Luminance, L	(lumen/sr/m = 3.14 mL)

Often the above units and terms are used interchangeably (and incorrectly) with those defined in Chapter 2. In order to examine the basic tenets of photometry we must take into account such biological constraints as the range $380\ \text{nm} < \lambda < 780\ \text{nm}$, which defines the sensitivity of the human eye to input wavelengths, and the different spectral sensitivities of the processing stages.

Suppose the input is an extended monochromatic source of radiance $L_e(\lambda)$. We assume central vision and negligible atmospheric absorption effects. The irradiance $E_e(\lambda)$ falling on the retina is given by Le Grand [44, chap. 5] as

$$E_e(\lambda) = \frac{L_e(\lambda)}{f^2} S H_1(\lambda) \tag{4.12}$$

where f is the focal length of the eye, S is the cross-sectional area of the entrance pupil (here assumed to be independent of λ), and $H_1(\lambda)$ is the spectral

† The reader is referred to another footnote in [16, p. 7] for a humorous description of photometric units. The exact definition is of little concern to us, although interested readers may consult [77] for more details.

sensitivity function of the ocular optics†. $H_1(\lambda)$ does not take into account all the filtering action at this stage; for example, we noted the spatially variant effect of the macula lutea in Section 3.2. We may now ask how many photons per unit time will fall on each rod or cone as a result of this retinal spectral flux? The quantum catch rate $N_e(\lambda)$ is given by Equation (2.15) in Section 2.2.1. If $\tau(\lambda)$ is the spectral absorption curve for a single rod or cone, then the number of photons per unit time which are active for each photoreceptor, $N_a(\lambda)$, is given by:

$$N_a(\lambda) = QN_e(\lambda)\tau(\lambda) \tag{4.13}$$

where Q is the quantum efficiency, here assumed to be independent of λ. The variable Q accounts for the fraction of photons that actually contributes to visual excitation. It is therefore less than unity (but probably not much less) since not all the absorbed photons affect vision. Substituting in Equation (4.13) for $N_e(\lambda)$ and noting the relationship between $E_e(\lambda)$ and $\phi_e(\lambda)$ in Equation (2.10) of Section 2.2.1, we obtain

$$N_a(\lambda) = Q\left[\frac{\lambda E_e(\lambda)A_r}{hc}\right]\tau(\lambda)$$

Using Equation (4.12) yields

$$N_a(\lambda) = kQS\lambda L_e(\lambda)H_1(\lambda)\tau(\lambda) \tag{4.14}$$

where k is a constant of the system. This is the effect on one photoreceptor.

The next question is how does one aggregate the effect of all the receptors to provide a global response? Here we come to the primary experimental paradigm of photometry, the visual comparison of the subjective brightness of two different radiant sources. Given two such adjacent patches of light, the subject is asked to adjust the luminance (or is it the radiance?) $L_{e_1}(\lambda_1)$ and $L_{e_2}(\lambda_2)$ of the two sources. A brightness match occurs, that is, the observer sees the two patches as identical if $\lambda_1 = \lambda_2$ and $L_{e_1} = L_{e_2}$. This turns out to be true even if the distances to each patch differ. Note also that if L_{e_1} and L_{e_2} are indistinguishable on the basis of subjective brightness, it does not necessarily mean that they cannot be distinguished on the basis of other criteria, such as color, for example. If $\lambda_1 = \lambda_2$ but $L_{e_1} \neq L_{e_2}$, the source for which L_e is greater will appear to be brighter and the other darker. That is, there exists a strictly monotonic relationship between source radiance and perceived brightness. If both $\lambda_1 \neq \lambda_2$ and $L_{e_1} \neq L_{e_2}$ and we obtain a match, we can state that this visual subjective effect depends on processes that are being activated by distinctly different wavelengths. Any system of definitions must be consistent with these observations of human behavior.

With the above in mind, let us rewrite Equation (4.14) as

$$N_a(\lambda) = [kQS]L_e(\lambda)[\lambda\tau(\lambda)H_1(\lambda)] \tag{4.15}$$

† Note that λ is the wavelength and u the spatial frequency variable. Since $\lambda u = c$, the functions $H_1(\lambda)$ and $H_1(u)$ are related.

By grouping all the wavelength-dependent processing into one variable, we define by analogy the photometric luminance $L_v(\lambda)$:

$$L_v(\lambda) = K_m L_e(\lambda) V(\lambda) \tag{4.16}$$

where K_m is a constant and $L_e(\lambda)$ is the source luminance. In fact it is necessary to distinguish two processes and define $V(\lambda)$ in the above equation as the photopic (cones) relative luminous efficiency function and $V'(\lambda)$ as the scotopic (rods) relative luminous efficiency function. Both $V(\lambda)$ and $V'(\lambda)$ lie between 0 and 1, are defined between $\lambda = 400$ nm and 700 nm, and attempt to represent a so-called standard observer. The curves are shown in Figure 4.13, where the scotopic curve $V'(\lambda)$ peaks at about 505 nm as compared with 555 nm for the photopic curve. This so-called Purkinje effect was discovered in 1925 by the Czech physician of that name, who observed that a red and a blue signpost each had the same luminance in daylight while the blue one was much brighter than the red at early dawn (see [46, p. 216c]). The defined photometric quantities are thus the photopic luminance given by

$$\mathscr{L}_v = K_v \int L_e(\lambda) V(\lambda)\, d\lambda \tag{4.17}$$

and the scotopic luminance given by

$$\mathscr{L}'_v = K'_v \int L'_e(\lambda) V'(\lambda)\, d\lambda \tag{4.18}$$

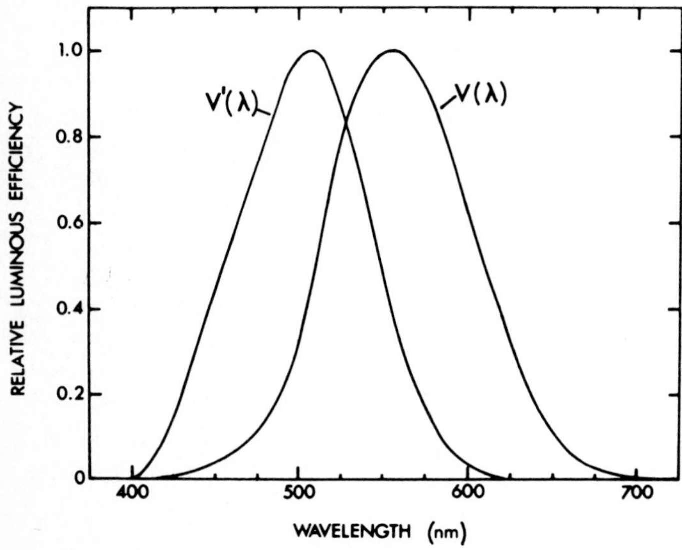

Figure 4.13 The functions $V(\lambda)$ and $V'(\lambda)$ are the normalized photopic and scotopic relative spectral luminosity efficiency curves for a standard observer. (*From R. W. Rodieck, "The Vertebrate Retina, Principles of Structure and Function," Freeman, San Francisco, 1973, p. 274.*)

Note that in Figure 4.13 $V(\lambda)$ and $V'(\lambda)$ have been normalized. However since $K'_v > K_v$, $\mathcal{L}'_v$ is in fact greater than $\mathcal{L}_v$ for equal $L_e(\lambda)$. In addition to the particular observer, the actual photometric functions are also dependent on certain other factors such as the size of the photometric field, the retinal region employed, the luminance of the retinal stimulus, the surrounding field, the adaptation of the retina, and, surprisingly, seasonal variations [45].

Let us briefly in turn consider scotopic and photopic vision. The former is associated with viewing conditions of dim illumination under which only the rods are operative and therefore there is no color vision. A relatively large peripheral test area is involved in order to include many rods. The function $V'(\lambda)$ is derived through matching experiments using many observers, the data being averaged to yield the standard observer. It has been found that the subjective brightness (output) is a monotonic function of the source radiance (input). We note from Equations (4.15) and (4.16) that

$$V'(\lambda) \sim \lambda \tau(\lambda) H_1(\lambda) \tag{4.19}$$

Since $\tau(\lambda)$ is the photosensitivity of the visual pigment rhodopsin of the rods and its absorption curve has been determined independently, it is possible to compare both sides of the above equation. It turns out that $V'(\lambda)$ measured from perceptual response data is quite similar in shape to $\lambda\tau(\lambda)H_1(\lambda)$, with $\tau(\lambda)$ obtained by physical techniques. Examples include fundus reflectometry (see [54, pp. 125–132] and [59]) and extraction methods. This confirms in a general way the usefulness of the standard observer. Thus $\mathcal{L}'_v$ becomes a physical quantity in a certain sense, measuring the "psychophysical magnitude" or brightness of a particular light stimulus.

Photopic photometry is more complex since it involves the process of color vision associated with the three types of cones, each with a different pigment. We assume central vision and relatively high light levels, again determining the standard observer by averaging over many experiments. We now make the major assumption that if Equation (4.16) holds for each of the cones (and as we saw for the rods as well) independently, then the multichromatic source responds in the aggregate is given by Equation (4.17), sometimes referred to as Abney's law of additivity. The source may be defined by three variables; one, as we have already seen, is the luminance while the other two, dominant wavelength and purity, characterize the colorimetric properties. Similarly, there are three equivalent perceptual quantities: the brightness, which is a correlate of the luminance, plus the two color measures of hue and saturation. Our only concern here is the brightness and we shall study color processing in great detail in Chapter 7.

Let us examine the basic assumption underlying this aggregation. There exist three types of cones, different for each animal, which we shall refer to as red, green, and blue. The spectral radiance of a source $L_A(\lambda)$ is in fact mapped into three spectral luminances according to the equations [adapted from Equation (4.17)]

$$A_L = k_R \int L_A(\lambda)L(\lambda)\, d\lambda \tag{4.20}$$

$$A_M = k_G \int L_A(\lambda)M(\lambda)\, d\lambda \tag{4.21}$$

$$A_S = k_B \int L_A(\lambda)S(\lambda)\, d\lambda \tag{4.22}$$

where $L(\lambda)$, $M(\lambda)$, and $S(\lambda)$ are the spectral sensitivity curves for the red, green, and blue cones, respectively. The symbols stand for long, medium, and short. One may expect therefore that the photochemical measurements physically exist somewhere at the retinal stage, resulting in the neuron firing rates represented by A_L, A_M, and A_S.

Suppose it were feasible to perform some color matching experiments similar to those done with brightness in scotopic vision. If we were able to measure the actual cone responses for two adjacent color patches A and B, we would expect that if $A_L = B_L$, $A_M = B_M$, and $A_S = B_S$, then logically the two sources would be indistinguishable to a viewer observing the two lights in the pure cone region of the fovea. This is therefore a sufficient condition for psychophysical response invariance and is in concert with our knowledge of how the cones actually function. Each source may thus be represented as a point in a three-dimensional color space, called the "trivariance space." Let $\mathbf{A}^T = [A_L \; A_M \; A_S]$ be a source point in this space which we may also represent as a vector. If a neutral density filter with transmittance T is placed over the original color patch having spectral radiance $L_A(\lambda)$, what happens to the vector $\mathbf{A}$? From Equations (4.20), (4.21), and (4.22) we note that if

$$L'_A(\lambda) = TL_A(\lambda)$$

then

$$\mathbf{A}' = T\mathbf{A} \tag{4.23}$$

that is, the filter reduces the magnitude of the vector $\mathbf{A}$ but does not change its direction in trivariance space.

Now reconsider the original achromatic matching experiment in which two color sources $L_A(\lambda)$ and $L_B(\lambda)$ are to be matched for brightness equality only. This may be done so that $\mathbf{A} \equiv \mathbf{B}$. Note that the symbol $\equiv$ refers strictly to equal brightness in that only the lengths of the vectors in trivariance space are equal. Their directions are in general not the same so that the two sources could be distinguished by means of other criteria, presumably their color attributes. It turns out that the property of transitivity holds for these brightness matches. Thus if $\mathbf{A} \equiv \mathbf{B}$ and $\mathbf{A} \equiv \mathbf{C}$; then $\mathbf{B} \equiv \mathbf{C}$, indicating that the points of equal brightness constitute a surface in trivariance space. Furthermore, just as in the case of scotopic vision, there is a monotonic relationship between the luminance of the input and the photopic brightness. The implication is that the surfaces of constant brightness are convex, do not intersect, and therefore may be ranked.

Again examining the photometric Equation (4.17), it is emphasized that the assumption has so far been made that the photopic spectral sensitivity curve is a scalar summation of the individual cone responses [see Figure 4.13 for $V(\lambda)$]. That is

$$V(\lambda) \propto \alpha_L L(\lambda) + \alpha_M M(\lambda) + \alpha_S S(\lambda) \tag{4.24}$$

where α_L, α_M, and α_S are proportionality constants. But we have just observed that a source is defined as a vector in trivariance space, so that vector addition is in fact called for. The hypothesis underlying Equation (4.24) is therefore not supported by experimental evidence. Photopic photometry allows us to match or rank the brightness of two color patches just as does scotopic photometry, but the former seems to be based on a faulty assumption. An elaboration of the models of color vision, which take into account the phenomena described here, is found in Chapter 7.

So far we have discussed scotopic and photopic vision as if they were completely independent phenomena, and this is the manner in which they have usually been studied. However, there is an interaction at some level between the rod and cone signals such that the overall human visual system exhibits a spatially variable gain related to the characteristics of the input stimulus. This process is referred to as "adaptation" in that there is an adjustment of the processing capabilities according to changing inputs in order to optimize performance.

Over the years a large number of psychophysical experiments have been performed to study control of sensitivity in the retina. However, the physiological basis of many of the results is still ambiguous. Some of the latter confirm the perceptual theories, others present data which are difficult to explain. Also, since most of the electrophysiological experimentation is rather recent, it obviously still remains to explain the intricacies of the mechanism. The considerable complexity of the problem can be easily appreciated by even a cursory examination of [20].

Two kinds of perceptual adaptation have been distinguished. "Dark adaptation" has a long time constant and tends to increase visual sensitivity if no input stimulus is present for a long time. This is responsible for the change in our ability to see detail in a darkened room upon entering it from the outside. "Light adaptation" has a short time constant and attempts to decrease the sensitivity as the strength of the input increases. We observe therefore that adaptation works in a very logical way to maintain a constant signal sensitivity independent of the input magnitude. Recently these mechanisms have been studied in vertebrate eyes [50], and it appears that in addition to photochemical adaptation, a relatively fast neural control also intervenes. When a cloud covers the moon for a short time, apparently the response of the observer's eyes is much faster than would be expected for rhodopsin alone. Furthermore, there seems to be a strong interaction between the two controlling forces.

Light, or so-called background adaptation, has classically been studied by superimposing a transient test flash of light of intensity I_t upon a steady-state background illuminance I_b. It emerges that our ability to just perceive a given magnitude of I_t is strengthened as I_b is raised. This type of threshold activity is shown for human rods in Figure (4.14) and is apparently completely independent of any cone behavior. For very dim background intensities the threshold is more or less independent of I_b. There exists an absolute minimum threshold I_{t0} for this rod mechanism, such that $I_t = I_{t0}$ in the dark adapted state when $I_b = 0$. As the background increases in brightness, the retinal sensitivity is linearly related to the fraction of pigment already bleached. If the duration and/or the area of the spot is made small, the slope decreases, ultimately to $\frac{1}{2}$. Interestingly enough, this value is predicted on the basis of optimal threshold detection [54, chap. XXII]. A further point of interest is that after a certain maximum background intensity the rod mechanism saturates at the point where $I_t = I_T$. Above this background saturation value no threshold exists which will allow us to see the flash. This saturation can apparently not be explained by the amount of rhodopsin bleached by the background since at this point only about 5 percent of the total has been bleached. Most likely it is the neural component that is mainly responsible.

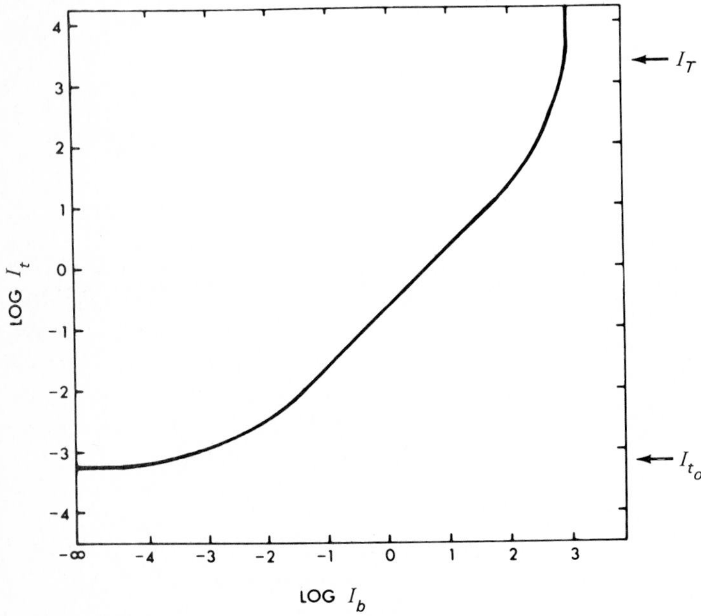

Figure 4.14 Background adaptation experiment showing the rod increment threshold I_t as a function of the background illumination I_b for a normal human observer. (*From R. W. Rodieck, "The Vertebrate Retina, Principles of Structure and Function," W. H. Freeman, San Francisco, 1973, p. 274, after M. Aguilar and W. S. Stiles, "Saturation of the Rod Mechanism of the Retina at High Levels of Stimulation," Optica Acta, vol. 1, 1954, pp. 59–65.*)

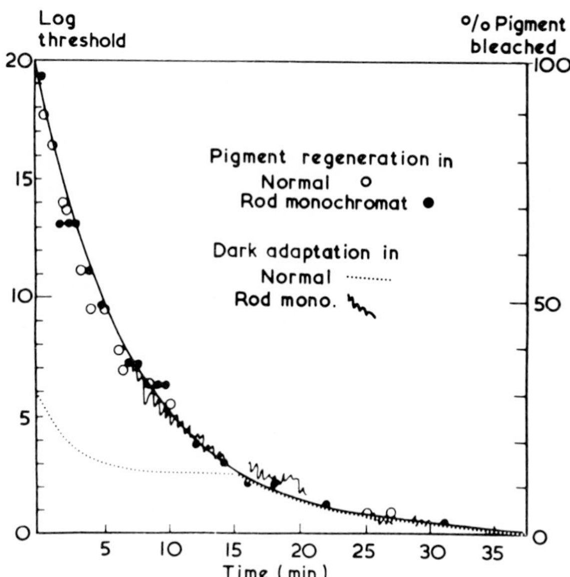

Figure 4.15 Dark adaptation curves (scale on left) obtained using threshold experiments show the light sensitivity for the human retina. The normal dark adaptation curve (shown dotted) consists of two parts: the initial one due to the faster-acting cones and the latter one due to rod adaptation. Persons lacking cones are called rod monochromats and the irregular tracing shows their response, obviously compatible with the normal curve. Rhodopsin measurements, done independently for rod monochromats (black circles) and the normal eyes (white circles), are also compatible with the adaptation curve. [*From W. A. H. Rushton, "Dark Adaptation of the Retina," in B. R. Straatsma, M. O. Hall, R. A. Allen, and F. Crescitelli (eds.), "The Retina: Morphology, Function and Clinical Characteristics," UCLA Forum on Medical Science no. 8, University of California Press, Los Angeles, 1969, pp. 257–280.*]

The second adaptive characteristic, bleaching or dark adaptation, may be observed in the dark ($I_b = 0$) after a bleaching exposure. As regeneration reduces the fraction of visual pigment in the bleached state, the threshold I_t to a test flash falls. Thus I_t is raised by the presence of bleached visual pigment in the receptors so that a brighter flash is required for perception. Figure 4.15 shows an example of a dark adaptation curve. The initial part of the response is thought to be due to the faster reaction of the cones, while the second slower recovery is thought to be a result of the rods. The physiological basis for this activity is not well understood and no consistent theory of the interaction of the rod and cone signals has been accepted. The effect cannot be explained simply on the basis of light absorption although this is obviously an important aspect.

An interesting model, based on research with the mud puppy, involves the cells in the retina [71]. The details are presented in Figure 4.16. We observe that the model is an attempt to integrate several of the known adaptive phenomena. Although the exact mechanism is unclear at the moment, adaptation might in future serve to unify the processes of scotopic and photopic vision, as described in this section.

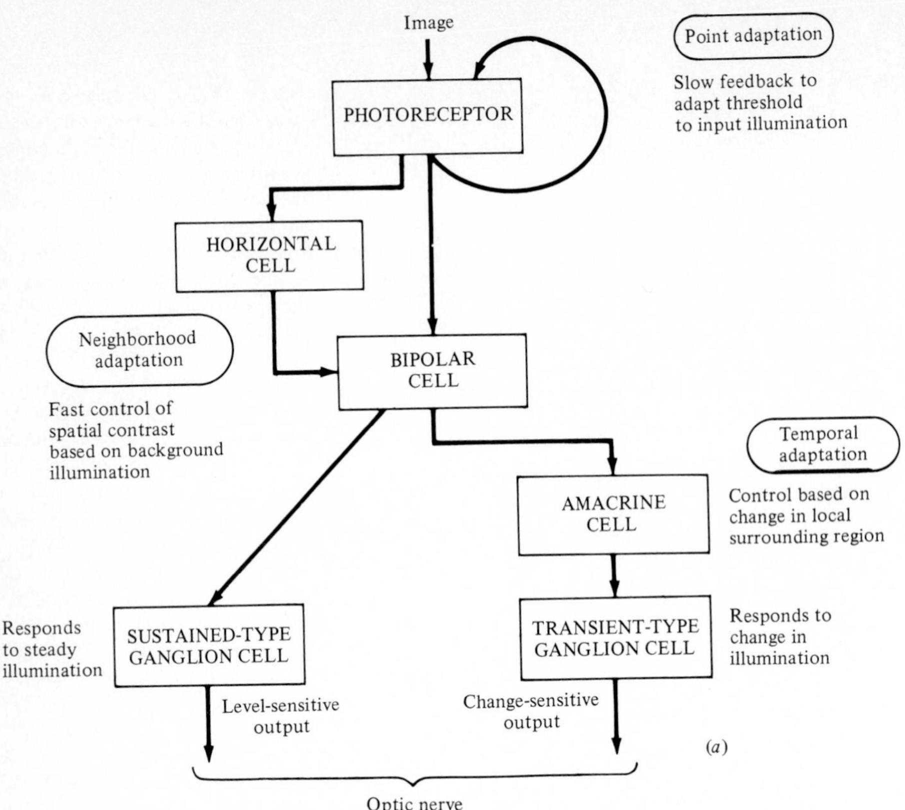

Figure 4.16 A simple adaptation model. (*a*) A model of the control mechanisms in the retina of the mud puppy, based on the discussion of [71]. At the level of the photoreceptor, the degree of independence between rods and cones has not yet been established. Therefore, this aspect is ignored in the figure. The horizontal cells control the response curves of the bipolar cells by translating the curve according to neighborhood illumination characteristics. Since this is done throughout the sampled image array, the adaptation provides for very fine local area tuning. The amacrine cells mediate the response of the so-called transient-type ganglion cells by adapting to spatiotemporal variations in the surrounding regions of the receptor cell. This is achieved by compressing the operating curve. The sustained-type ganglion cells respond to a steady illumination. Outputs from both of these cells constitute the optic nerve. (*b*) Receptor-cell response range is shown at six background illumination levels. This is referred to as point adaptation in *a*. The rods (broken curves) are more sensitive than the cones in that they begin to respond at lower intensity levels, but they saturate quickly with increasing background illumination. Cones, however, appear not to saturate; their operating curves (unbroken curves) shift along the intensity axis with increasing background illumination, so that they are optimally responsive over a narrow intensity range near each background level. (*c*) A first transformation of operating curves comes between receptor cells and bipolar cells and is termed neighborhood adaptation in (*a*). The response range of the bipolar cells follows that of the receptor cells with increasing background illumination, but the narrower bipolar-cell curve is further fine-tuned within the receptor-cell range by input from the surround: an increase in the ring brightness shifts the curve to the right. (*d*) A second transformation comes between bipolar and ganglion cells. Bipolar-cell curves are shifted by increasing surround illumination (brighter windmill vanes). The curves for both sustained and transient ganglion cells driven by bipolar cells follow these shifts. When the windmill is spun in order to test for temporal adaptation (broken curves), the amacrine system suppresses the activity of the change-detecting transient ganglion cells: their operating curves are compressed. [(*b*), (*c*), *and* (*d*) *from F. S. Werblin, "The Control of Sensitivity in the Retina," Scientific American, vol. 228, no. 1, January 1973, pp. 71–79.*]

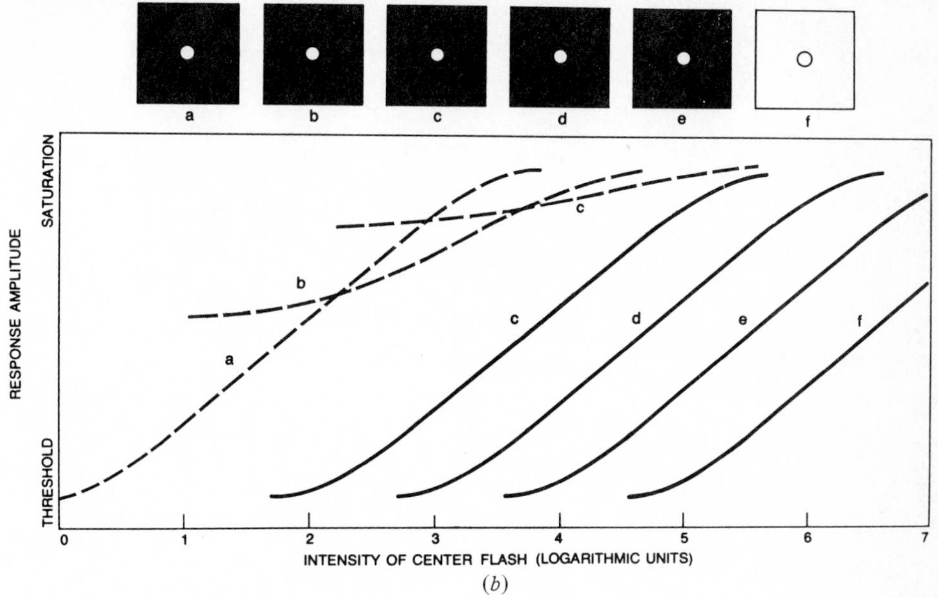
a
b
c
d
e
f
SATURATION
RESPONSE AMPLITUDE
THRESHOLD
a
b
c
c
d
e
f
0
1
2
3
4
5
6
7
INTENSITY OF CENTER FLASH (LOGARITHMIC UNITS)

(*b*)

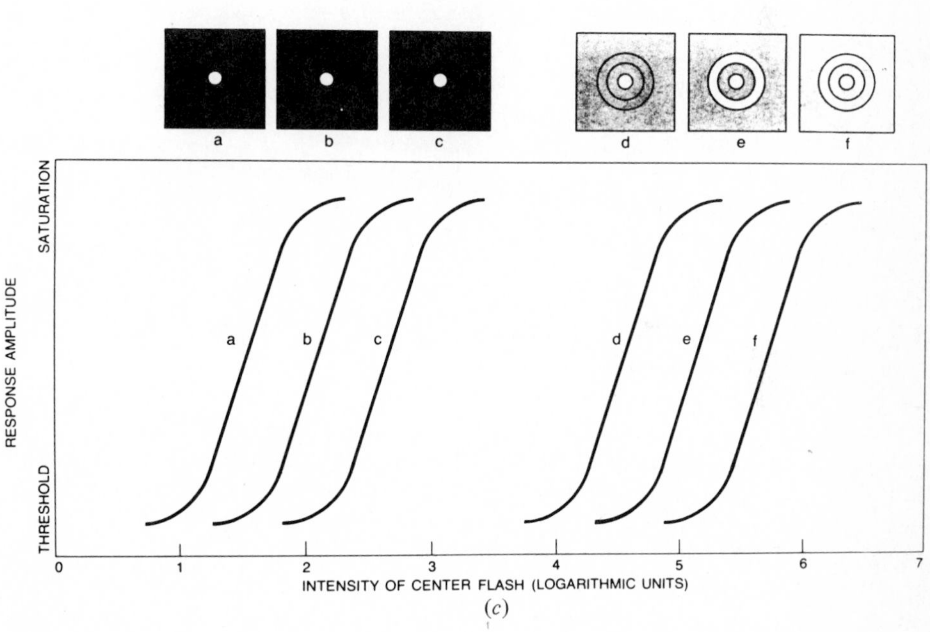
a
b
c
d
e
f
SATURATION
RESPONSE AMPLITUDE
THRESHOLD
a
b
c
d
e
f
0
1
2
3
4
5
6
7
INTENSITY OF CENTER FLASH (LOGARITHMIC UNITS)

(*c*)

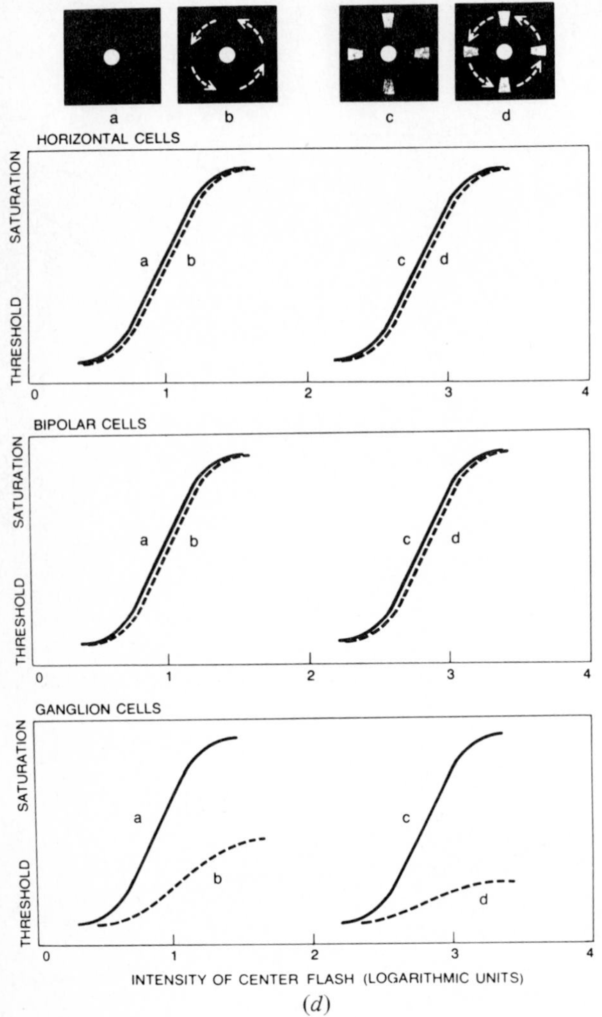

(*d*)

4.5 A MODEL OF THE HUMAN VISUAL SYSTEM

In Figure 3.1 the human visual system was crudely broken down into three stages: (1) the ocular optical system; (2) the phototransducers; and (3) all the rest of the cellular image processing. The experiments described in Section 4.2 led to the definition of the optics as essentially a low-pass filter. In Section 4.5.1 we consider an important aspect related to the coding of the projected optical image into pulse trains. This will be followed in the next section by a model for the third stage, thereby completing the presentation of the overall model. We stress that the latter is primarily concerned with a black-box approach and therefore is mainly intended to account for experimental results associated with magnitude processing as a function of input wavelength.

4.5.1 Nonlinear Coding of Input Signals

In this section we shall focus on threshold and logarithmic nonlinearities in the analysis path. As indicated in the visual acuity experiments, the eye is extremely sensitive to even the smallest amount of light. For example, experiments with human observation of flashes of light in a dark room have shown that only one quantum of light is sufficient to stimulate a single rod. This is quite remarkable when one observes that a home flashlight might radiate about 2×10^{15} quanta/ms. A detailed discussion of the implications of such small quantities of light is provided by Cornsweet [16, chap. IV] who concluded that quantal fluctuations defining an absolute threshold may only be of significance at very low input intensities. Notwithstanding these observations, the existence of visual thresholds below which signal perception is not possible has been a consistent factor in psychological models of vision. The adaptation phenomena in the previous section were obviously couched in these terms. Uttal [70, pp. 232–258] discusses such psychophysical experiments in terms of signal detection theory as conventionally applied to communication systems, using the notion of probabilistic rather than deterministic signals. He concludes that perhaps these thresholds are not significant. From a neurophysiological point of view there does exist a continuous spontaneous neural activity which might lead to the necessity of treating these signals as defining a threshold. But is it really spontaneous, or perhaps the result of inputs or activities of which we are as yet not aware? We shall assume that the image impinging on the photoreceptors via the ocular optical system always remains above threshold, thereby eliminating it from further consideration. This leads to another nonlinearity for which there is considerable evidence.

The question arises as to how the photoreceptors are capable of maintaining a more or less consistent response to a very large range of input stimulus intensities. It is known that the range of inputs that can activate the system is of the order of 10^{13} to 1 even though the pupil area can only be varied by a factor of 16 to 1. We observed in Section 3.4 that the magnitude of the intensity impinging on the photoreceptors is ultimately coded into a frequency of spike action potentials at the output of the ganglion cells. But these frequencies are indeed quite limited in their range, not exceeding a maximum of perhaps 1000 Hz; 40 to 50 pulses per second would be considered as the result of spontaneous and therefore undetermined activity. Thus the coded frequency range is at most 100 to 1, from which we observe that there is a significant compression from the input to the output. Since linearity prevails between the receptor potential output and the resulting coded frequency, it appears that this data compression is a result of the photochemical action of the transducing elements.

There has been comparatively little neurophysiological experimentation to link neural response to the magnitude of the stimulus input. Much of the research has been performed with submammalian creatures such as the horseshoe crab, turtle, and frog. It is quite difficult to experiment with higher animals, particularly humans, because of the difficulty of isolating this single factor to make the observations independent of other variables. The *Limulus* (king or horseshoe crab) has been involved in many of these experiments because of its relatively simple anatomy. It has two primitive lateral eyes, which are faceted in the same way as those of insects. Each eye is made up of elements called "ommatidia," which are coarsely arranged in a mosaic of about 1000 units. Each ommatidium (see Figure 4.17) contains about 12 retinular cells, which are sensitive to light and project onto the same dendrite of a single eccentric cell. The ommatidia are large (about the diameter of a pencil lead) and the neural organization is simple, which facilitates recordings from a single axon in the optic nerve. These were first reported by Hartline and Graham [35] (see also [34]).

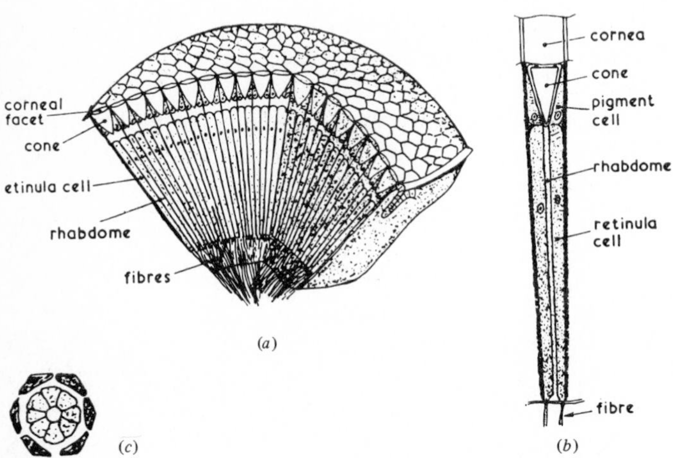

Figure 4.17 The faceted eye. Essentially, the compound eye of insects and crustaceans is an aggregation of many unit eyes or ommatidia, each of these units having its own dioptric apparatus that concentrates light onto its individual light-sensitive surface, made up of specialized retinula cells. The faceted appearance of the compound eye is thus due to the regular arrangement of the transparent surfaces of these unit eyes (*a*). The longitudinal section of an ommatidium is illustrated schematically in (*b*); light is focused by the crystalline cone onto the highly refractile rhabdom, which constitutes an aggregation of specialized regions of the retinula cells. These retinula cells are wedge-shaped and are symmetrically arranged around the axial canal like the segments of an orange (*c*); the rhabdom is made up of the apical portions of these wedge-shaped cells, the separate portions being called "rhabdomeres." In the *Limulus* (horseshoe crab) ommatidium, the cross section (approximately the size of a pencil lead) appears like the spokes of a wheel, the axle being the central canal. This canal contains the process of the eccentric cell; this is apparently a neuron with its cell body squeezed between the retinula cells at the base of the ommatidium; its long, spearlike process fills the central canal and may be regarded as a dendrite; the central end of the cell consists of a long process that passes out of the ommatidium in the optic nerve. (*From H. Davson, "Physiology of the Eye," 4th ed., Academic, New York, 1980.*)

Measurements with the optic nerve fiber of the *Limulus* showed that a steady-state firing of pulses is evoked when a single ommatidium is illuminated. Figure 4.18*a* shows that there is a monotonic relationship between the stimulus intensity and the action potential response. Further, it can be demonstrated that equal amounts of energy elicit equal pulse frequencies, in that the product of the intensity and the duration of the rectangular pulse of light remains constant. This is shown in Figure 4.18*b* for the *Limulus* and is known to be a property of human vision as well. There is a maximum limit to the frequency, as mentioned above. If the experiment with the *Limulus* is repeated with a

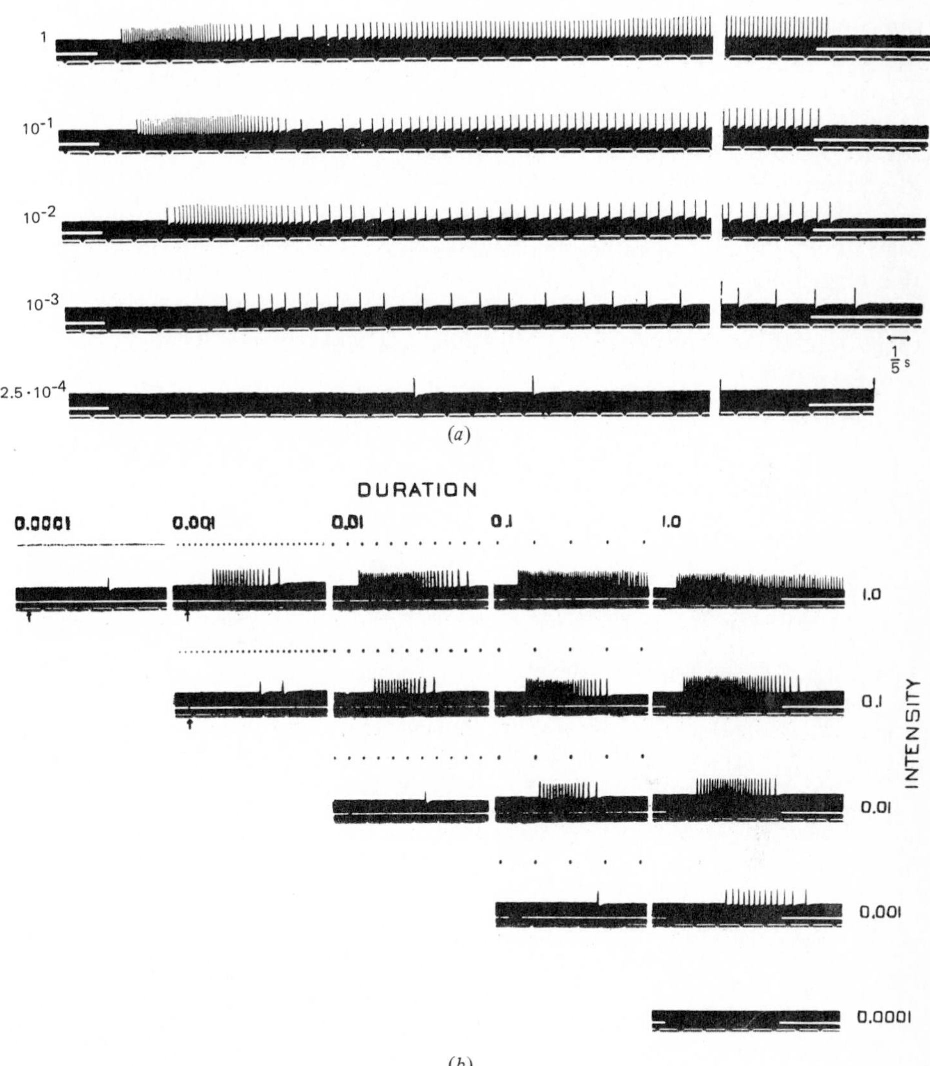

Figure 4.18 (*Caption on page 136.*)

square pulse train, that is, a flickering light, we would expect each pulse to result in an appropriate burst of frequency-coded output on the axon. As noted in Figure 4.19, this is indeed true, except that above a certain input flicker rate a maximum frequency is obtained which is equal to that elicited by a constant step of illumination. This so-called flicker fusion is responsible for a phenomenon recognized by the early makers of motion pictures, namely, that above a certain input frame rate, the perceived image appears to be fixed and not flickering.

Using measurements on a single cell body, Fuortes [24, 25] later studied the electrical properties of the *Limulus* eye. He showed that the membrane potential change that occurred in response to light stimulation was exactly the same nonlinear function of input intensity. Also, this was exactly the same function that related the input to the frequency of the spike action potentials. Therefore, it would appear that the functional relationship between these sequential processes is a linear one, and that the nonlinearity occurs earlier as a result of the preceding photochemical transduction stage. But what exactly is this function? We can see from Figure 4.20 that it is definitely not linear, and Fuortes suggested that the physiological evidence supported the hypothesis of a logarithmic function. That is, the magnitude of the neural firing rate is equal to the logarithm of the input light intensity, a phenomenon that is curiously compatible with our earlier observations in Chapter 2 regarding the digitization of photographic transparencies. Rushton [58] pointed out that it is the trans-

---

Figure 4.18 Experiments with the *Limulus* involving a spot of light projected on a single ommatidium. (*a*) Recording of frequency-coded spike trains (action potentials) appearing on the optic nerve fiber of a *Limulus* when a spot of light is projected on a single ommatidium. Relative intensities are given at the left of each record. The time marker beats $\frac{1}{5}$ s; above its record is the signal marking the period of illumination (the white line disappears while the light is shining). After the initial burst of impulses, there is, at high intensities, a relatively "silent" period in which fewer impulses are discharged than before or after. The silent period is not observed in light-adapted preparations. The frequency is obviously not a linear function of the input light intensity and has been shown to be logarithmically related. Thus, the maximum frequency observed may be about 130 impulses per second, while the input light intensity varies over a range of 1,000,000 to 1. (*b*) The product of the intensity of the spot of light and its duration is constant with respect to determining the firing rate. The oscillograph records show action potentials from single optic nerve fibers of *Limulus* in response to illumination of the eye by flashes of light of various intensities and durations. Horizontal rows contain responses to flashes of constant intensity and varying duration. Vertical columns contain responses to flashes of constant duration and varying intensity. Values of intensity of flash (in arbitrary units) on the surface of the eye are given at the right, opposite the respective rows. Values of duration of flash (in seconds) are given at the top, above the respective columns. In any given record the lower white line marks fifths of seconds; above this is a white line containing the light signal recording the interval (gap in the white line) during which the eye is illuminated. For very short flashes this signal does not reproduce clearly; its position is shown by the arrows. The black edge records electrical potential between two points on the nerve fiber. [(*a*) *From H. K. Hartline, "The Discharge of Nerve Impulses from the Single Visual Sense Cell," Cold Spring Harbor Symposia on Quantitative Biology, vol. 3, 1935, pp. 245–250.* (*b*) *Adapted from H. K. Hartline, "Intensity and Duration in the Excitation of Single Photoreceptor Units," Journal of Cellular and Comparative Physiology, vol. 5, no. 2, October 1934, pp. 229–247.*]

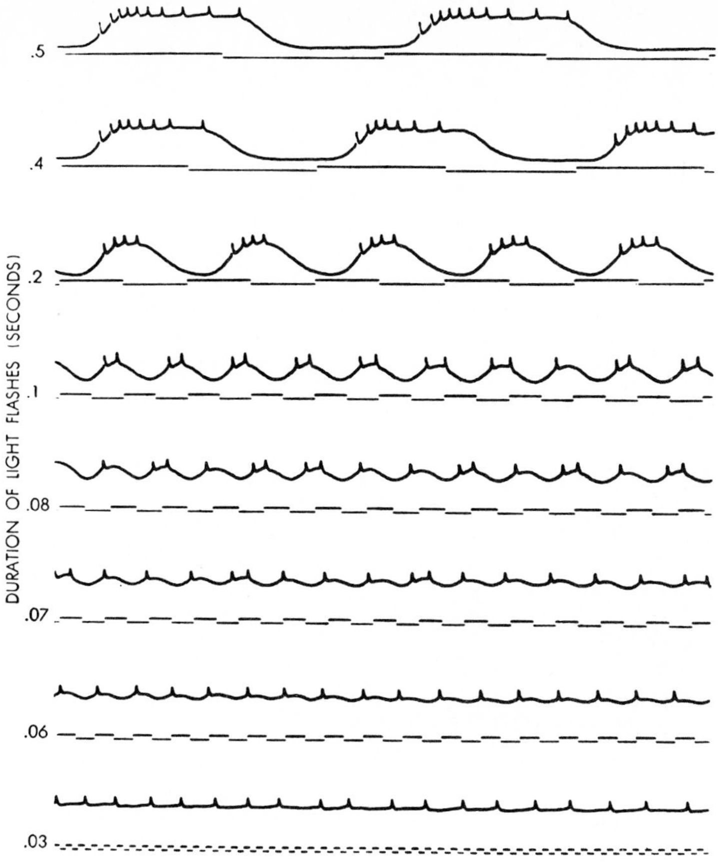

Figure 4.19 These graphs show what happens when the ommatidium of the *Limulus* is presented with a flickering light (the square pulse train below each recording) of different frequency. A maximum firing rate response, called the flicker fusion rate, is reached. (*From W. H. Miller, F. Ratliff, and H. K. Hartline, "How Cells Receive Stimuli," Scientific American, vol. 205, no. 3, September 1961, pp. 222–238.*)

membrane resistance of the receptor cell which decreased logarithmically with an increase in light input. This resistance drop is responsible for the decrease in voltage (hyperpolarization) between the outside and inside of the cell.

It is really of no great consequence what mathematical expression is used to model this input-output relationship, although it has been a subject of great controversy over the years, mainly with regard to the psychophysical correlates we shall be discussing soon [70, chap. VI]. Another alternative is the power law proposed by Stevens [64], whereby the response ψ is related to the input intensity I by the equation

$$\psi = K(I - I_0)^n \tag{4.25}$$

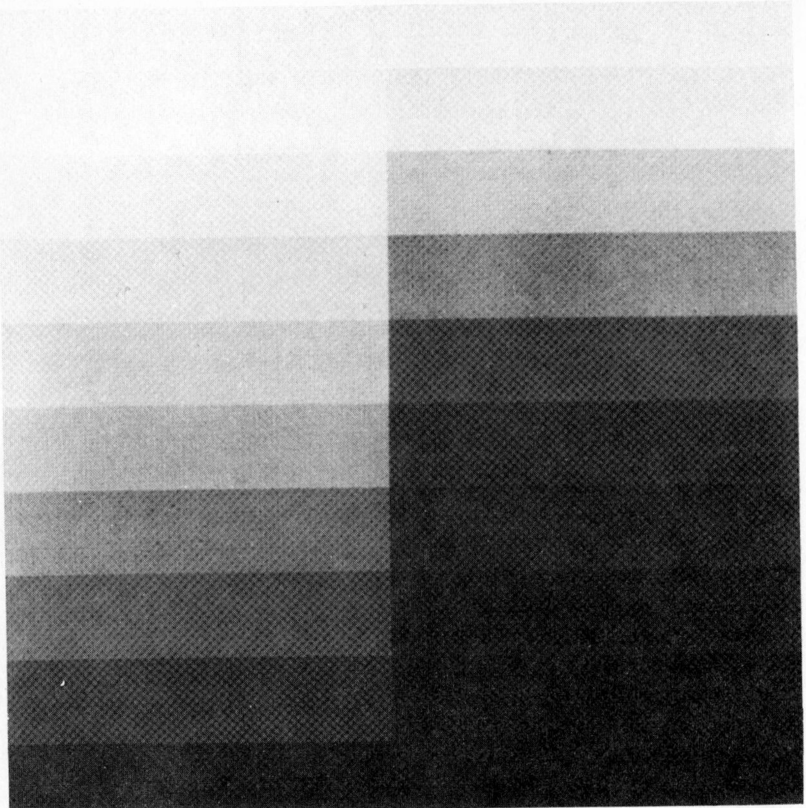

Figure 4.20 The gray scale on the left is ordered linearly according to intensity. The one on the right is ordered logarithmically in intensity or, what is equivalent, linearly in density. As support for the hypothesis that man possesses a logarithmic nonlinearity in his magnitude processing, observe that the scale on the right appears to be linear, rather than the one on the left. This phenomenon has actually been confirmed for humans by means of intensity matching experiments. (*From T. G. Stockham, Jr., "Image Processing in the Context of a Visual Model," Proceedings of the IEEE, vol. 60, no. 7, 1972, pp. 828–842.*)

where K and I_0 (the absolute threshold intensity) are constants and n is an appropriate exponent. If $n = 1$, this is a linear relationship; $n < 1$ implies compression and $n > 1$ expansion of the response. It is therefore possible to compare different plots of experimental data by examining the values of n needed for the fit. For example, the data of Fuortes shown in Figure 4.21 may also be represented by a power law with $n = 0.28$, approximately the cube root.

Intracellular recordings from the receptor units of vertebrates, such as carp cones, gekko rods, turtle cones, rat rods, and frog cones, have yielded similar results. For example, by presenting a brief flash of light in a darkened environment, Baylor and Fuortes [5] were able to measure the behavior of a turtle cone. We have already noted in Section 3.4 that this results in a

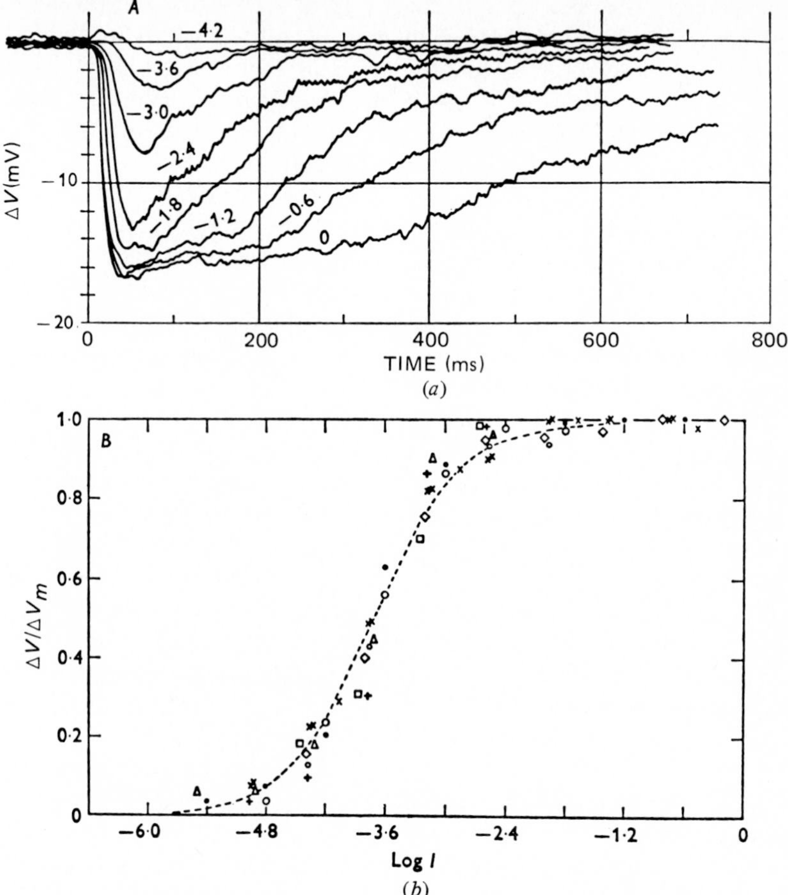

Figure 4.21 Intracellular recordings from turtle cones in response to light flashes of different intensities. (*a*) Superimposed tracings of responses to 10-ms flashes of increasing intensity, as indicated (log units), applied at time zero. The brightest flash delivered about 8.5×10^6 absorbable photons to the cone. Potential drop on penetration of cell was 22 mV. Downward deflection represents hyperpolarization. (*b*) Peak height of response plotted as a function of light intensity. The symbols plot normalized voltages obtained from 10 different cells. As different cells had different sensitivities to light, some shift along the abscissa was necessary to superimpose all points. The largest shift was about 0.6 log units. The broken curve plots Equation (4.25) in the text. [*From D. A. Baylor and M. G. F. Fuortes, "Electrical Responses of Single Cones in the Retina of the Turtle," Journal of Physiology (London), vol. 207, no. 1, March 1970, pp. 77–92.*]

hyperpolarization, which they expressed as:

$$\frac{\Delta V}{\Delta V_m} = \frac{I}{I + I_0} \tag{4.26}$$

where ΔV is the change in membrane voltage, ΔV_m is the maximum voltage difference observed, I is the intensity of the light flash, and I_0 is a constant defined as being equal to I when $\Delta V = \frac{1}{2}\Delta V_m$. Figure 4.21 shows the results of some of their experiments. The curve in b may be fitted by a two-segment, piecewise continuous power law given by $n = 0.58$ followed by $n = 0.04$ at higher intensities. Buchsbaum [10] has considered curves compiled from various other experiments, carried out over a period of 30 years, with different animals. Although, obviously, the experimental conditions differed in each case, the results show a striking similarity in shape to Figure 4.21*b*.

We observe that the photoreceptor dynamic range of the turtle is somewhere between 2 and 3 log units. It has been found to be about 4.2 log units for human rods [54, pp. 323–328]. Surprisingly, however, the psychophysical range for human rods is equal to about 6.9 log units, with the difference occurring at lower intensities. This implies a pooling of rods to achieve the perceptual response measured.

Having considered the frequency-coded signal as it emerges from a single photoreceptor of an animal, we now examine the aggregated response of networks of neurons in the human retina and the cortex. Psychophysical perceptual experiments purport to deal with outputs at the cortical level, so that we may in this way consider the response of the overall system to a stimulus input. We seek to understand why we do not turn on the lights during the day even though they contribute exactly the same amount of light as during the night. The experimental paradigm, which is equivalent to the neurophysiological experiments discussed above, attempts to determine the incremental change in light intensity that must be added to the input signal so that a difference is just noticeable. The experiment consists of presenting to the subject two neighboring illuminated areas, one with a luminance of I and the other with $I + \Delta I$. The incremental difference ΔI is increased until the brightness of the adjacent areas can be just distinguished. The procedure is then repeated for a whole range of luminance values I. The resulting curve for the human visual system is similar in shape to Figure 4.21*b* plotted as $\log \Delta I$ versus $\log I$, without the saturation at high values of $\log I$ [10]. Traditionally, human behavior in this context has been described by the linear equation, known as Weber's law [7]:

$$\frac{\Delta I}{I} = \text{constant} \tag{4.27}$$

This conforms to the high-intensity portion of the curve in Figure 4.21*b*. An alternative relationship was suggested by Fechner over 100 years ago [22]:

$$\frac{\Delta I}{\log I} = \text{constant} \tag{4.28}$$

Obviously, both laws do not deal with the same range of intensities; Fechner's law relates to the lower values in Figure 4.21*b*. Hence, this fundamental relationship between visual stimulus and perceived sensation is often referred to as the Weber-Fechner law. Recently, Buchsbaum [10] has modeled the human visual system as an optimum statistical detector. He has shown mathematically that the nonlinear compressive transformation under discussion here can be represented by a logarithmic squared function. The latter is also shown to be similar in shape to the physiological curves in Figure 4.21*b*.

For a long time the logarithmic relationship between subjective sensory magnitude and input intensity [Equation (4.28)] was considered to be an intrinsic and fundamental property rather than simply a model. It is now recognized to be, in fact, just that, and Stevens' power law, mentioned previously [Equation (4.24)], might indeed be more appropriate. For small values of n the two approximations yield more or less similar results. In additional experiments, Stevens [63] has shown that the brightness of a 5° target observed in darkness is given by a power law relationship to the input with $n = 0.33$ and that the brightness of a brief flash of light is modeled by $n = 0.5$. In general, although the experiments to date are far from conclusive, it seems that the power n found at the pooled perceptual output is quite similar in value to n at the single cell or receptor levels. Indeed, the receptor potential or optic nerve frequency seems to be equally or more compressed than the psychophysical correlate. Again the implication is that most of the compression occurs at the transduction stage, which appears to serve the dual functions of energy transformation and dynamic range compression.

There does not seem to be any clear relationship between the neurophysiological and psychophysical results, and this is to be expected. Apart from the fact that one is often comparing data from different animals at different stages in the analysis chain, it is known that the visual pathway processes inputs in very complex ways. It is extremely difficult to separate the magnitude phenomenon from others when performing the perceptual experiments. Therefore the output at the transduction stage should not be expected to be simply related to the output at the perceptual stage. For the moment, therefore, we shall limit our assumptions to the fact that the second block in Figure 3.1 exhibits a logarithmic nonlinearity.

4.5.2 A System Model

As discussed in Section 4.4, photometry is really just a set of arbitrary definitions reflecting inadequate information about the human visual system. Thus, such an approach is not really meaningful as a test of basic scientific ideas, although the definitions have proved to be useful for certain practical applications. This has been the case in the area of television design, for example, where specific answers were required for particular design problems. Now we are more aware of the mechanisms underlying human vision, although obviously there is much to be learned, particularly about the visual pathway. In this section we shall consider a simple model of monochromatic human vision which is made up of the three sequential stages shown in Figure 3.1. The objective is to match the black box results described in Section 4.3.2, which were obtained in experiments aimed at measuring human contrast sensitivity.

It may be recalled from the discussion in Section 4.3.2 that the black box was decomposed into a low-pass system, modeling the optics of the eye, followed by a high-pass system. Westheimer and Campbell [74] have described the optical subsystem as an isotropic two-dimensional low-pass filter with a line-spread function of the form

$$h_1(x) = \exp(-\alpha|x|) \tag{4.29}$$

so that

$$H_1(\omega) = \frac{2\alpha}{\alpha^2 + \omega^2} \tag{4.30}$$

where $\alpha = 2\pi u$ is the spatial angular frequency; $\alpha = 0.7$ for a pupil diameter of 3 mm (recall that the optimal size lies between 2 and 4 mm) and a white light input stimulus. This function corresponds to a -3 db point of 6.6 cycles/degree. We shall not be concerned here with the exact details of the frequency response curve except to stress that it is similar in shape to that of typical optical lens systems. An excellent discussion of the physical basis for these models can be found in [44, chap. 5] and [77, pp. 202–227].

Let us ignore the first subsystem for the moment and concentrate on the last two processes. We saw in the previous section, that contrary to the linearity assumptions made in Section 4.3.2, a logarithmic process is actually involved. Thus the CSF results are only valid at a fixed amplitude or for small excursions. Secondly, we also know that $H_1(\omega)$ must be followed by an $H_2(\omega)$ which is a high-pass filter, so that the overall response will more or less approximate Figure 4.10. The question of the order in which these processes should appear was essentially settled in the last section by neurophysiological arguments. These are reinforced by the requirements imposed on human perception by the phenomenon of brightness constancy.

It can easily be observed that the brightness of an object remains fairly constant despite very large changes in illumination. Thus we are able to maintain the appropriate brightness ranking for a piece of coal and a sheet of white paper when observed in direct sunlight and under normal indoor illumination. Indeed, notwithstanding the very different radiant intensities of the sources, the white paper will seem to be more or less equally bright under the two conditions; in fact the paper indoors will be perceived as brighter than the coal outdoors even though the latter reflects more light to the viewer! It is as if the observer were responding to the intrinsic ability of the object to reflect light, independent of the source illumination or the amount of light actually conveyed to and presumably entering the visual system. This phenomenon can also be easily verified by brightness matching experiments in which the two patches to be compared are illuminated by light sources of different strength. We observe, therefore, that lightness and darkness are attributes of a surface. This physical property is related to the perception of monochromatic light intensities and is called its reflectivity, as discussed in Section 2.1. Reflectivity takes on values between 0 and 1; for example, black would be considered as less than 0.04 or 0.05, white as greater than 0.80, and shades of gray as intervening values.

One way of modeling this brightness constancy phenomenon is to place the logarithmic process before the high-pass filter. To see this, consider Figure 4.22*a*, which shows the intensity profiles of two images, one six times brighter than the other. A human observer would not be able to distinguish images with the two profiles! If however, the inputs were first processed nonlinearly by a logarithmic function, Figure 4.22*b* would result; the size of the rectangular pulse is identical in both cases, and this is all that would remain after the ensuing high-pass filtering operation. Therefore, both objects would be perceived to exhibit brightness constancy, which we observe is a result of reducing the input dynamic range to the cellular processing stage. We saw, of course, that the human visual system is capable of maintaining a constant contrast sensitivity over a very large input dynamic range. In addition, Stockham [65] has attempted to use these arguments to explain human sensitivity to the reflectivity of an object. The illumination component generally dominates the low spatial frequencies of the spectrum while the reflective component is largely mapped into the higher frequencies. Thus the spatial high-pass linear filtering reduces the effect of the illumination component so that our perceptual response is focused on the reflectance. Stockham [65] has used these arguments to propose an objective criterion for image quality which is based on such a

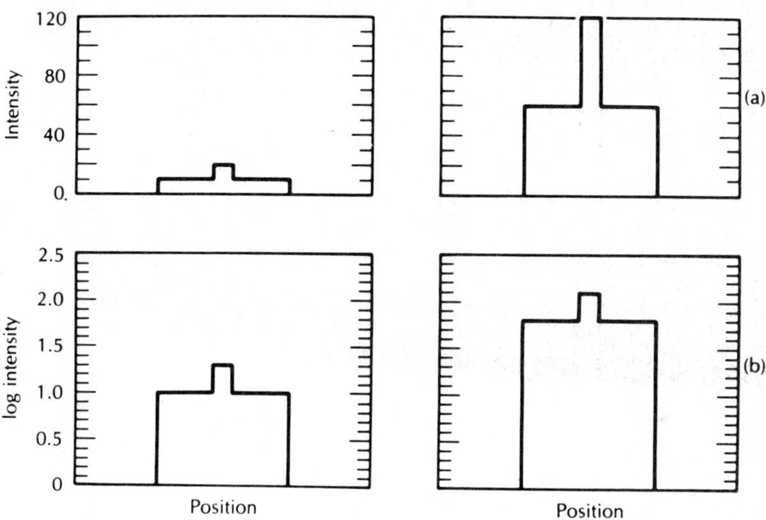

Figure 4.22 A demonstration of the phenomenon of brightness constancy. The profile of an input light pattern on the right-hand side of (*a*) is six times that of the one on the left. A human observer would nevertheless not be able to perceive any difference in the resulting light patterns. If both of these are processed logarithmically, the result is (*b*), in which it is observed that the two patterns are identical except for the (reference-level) zero-frequency component, which is then filtered out by the following high-pass filter. (*From T. Cornsweet, "Visual Perception," Academic, New York, 1970, p. 355.*)

model (see also [47] for an application to image coding). He suggests the model, referred to as "homomorphic filtering," as a means of processing images in order to improve the picture sharpness while simultaneously increasing the contrast between its light and dark areas. Schreiber [61] has shown that this model can be represented by a power law followed by the linear filter, and Mannos and Sakrison [47] suggest that the power should be $n = 0.33$. A general discussion of visual fidelity criteria based on human vision modeling can be found in [11]. Readers interested in further details of the psychophysical experiments with brightness constancy should consult [16, pp. 365–380].

Having established the order of the three stages in the model representation, we shall now briefly turn to the most complex process, the multicellular system of the visual pathway. Clearly it must take the form of a high-pass filter in the frequency domain if the global characteristic shown in Figure 4.10 is to be maintained. Other evidence to support this as a hypothesis will be considered in Chapter 6. Hall and Hall [31] use a pool of neurons configured in a particular way (the so-called backward inhibitor model) to derive the following second-order expression for $H_2(\omega)$

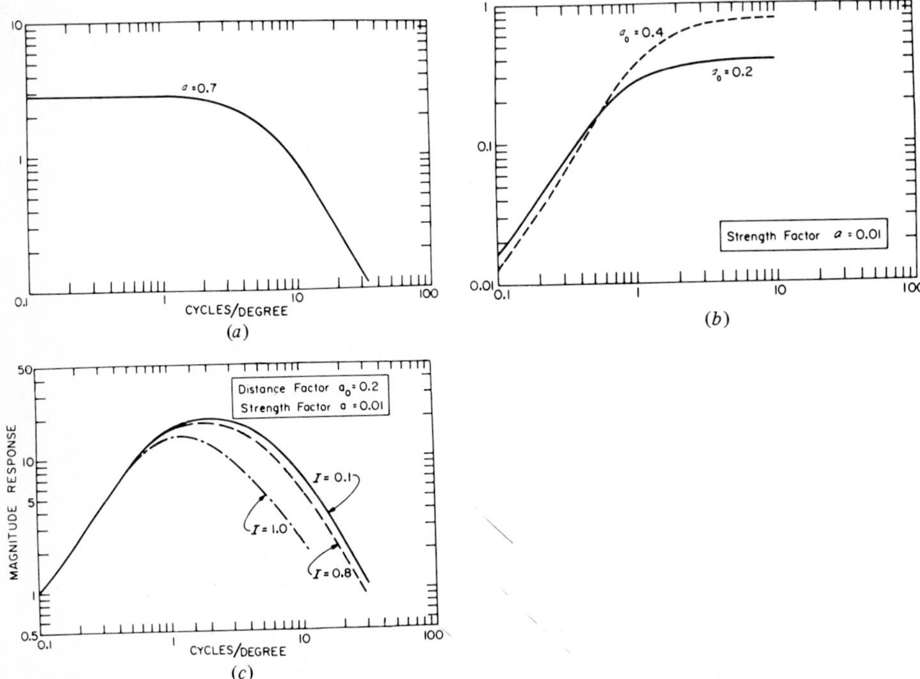

Figure 4.23 Spatial frequency responses. (*a*) Low-pass filter characteristic $H_1(u)$ of the optical ocular system. (*b*) High-pass filter characteristic $H_2(u)$ of the cellular processing system. (*c*) Overall response of human visual system including logarithmic nonlinearity. The transfer function is shown parameterized by the amplitude I of the input sine wave. (*From C. F. Hall and E. L. Hall, "A Nonlinear Model for the Spatial Characteristics of the Human Visual System," IEEE Transactions on Systems, Man, and Cybernetics, vol. SMC-7, no. 3, March 1977, pp. 161–170.*)

$$H_2(\omega) = \frac{a^2 + \omega^2}{2a_0a + (1 - a_0)(a^2 + \omega^2)} \tag{4.31}$$

where a_0 (the distance factor) and a (the strength factor) are two constants which relate to the neuron model. Values of $a_0 = 0.01$ and $a = 0.2$ yield

$$H_2(\omega) = \frac{10^{-4} + \omega^2}{4 \times 10^{-3} + 0.8\omega^2} \tag{4.32}$$

These were selected by Hall and Hall [31] to match the experimental data of Davidson [18], who took particular account of the system nonlinearity by finding the response to several inputs. In this way he was able to determine the classical system-describing function. The resulting $H_1(\omega)$, $H_2(\omega)$, and overall spatial frequency response function are shown in Figure 4.23. The last of these is actually given as a function of the input amplitude I, as would be expected for a nonlinear system. This confirms Davidson's experiments, which indicated that the human visual system behaves like a variable bandwidth filter with its bandwidth inversely related to the contrast within the input image. The results of Davidson, shown in Figure 4.23, and later confirmed by Henning et al. [38], do not differ much from those of Campbell in Figure 4.10. However, sufficient data are not available to make an intelligent comparison.

The nonlinear model discussed in this section assumes, among other things, that the system is strictly photopic. However, we have already seen that human vision can accommodate itself to both dim and bright light conditions by means of adaptation. A more comprehensive model combining scotopic with photopic vision is still awaited.

REFERENCES

1. Adrian, E. D., "The Basis of Sensation," Norton, New York, 1928.
2. Adrian, E. D., and Matthews, R., "The Action of Light on the Eye. III. The Interaction of Retinal Neurons," *Journal of Physiology* (*London*), vol. 65, no. 3, July 24, 1928, pp. 273–298.
3. Barlow, H. B., "Summation and Inhibition in the Frog's Retina," *Journal of Physiology* (*London*), vol. 119, no. 1, 1953, pp. 69–88.
4. Barlow, H. B., "Reconstructing the Visual Image in Space and Time," *Nature*, vol. 279, 17 May 1979, pp. 189–190.
5. Baylor, D. A., and Fuortes, M. G. F., "Electrical Responses of Single Cones in the Retina of the Turtle," *Journal of Physiology* (*London*), vol. 207, no. 1, 1970, pp. 77–92.
6. Bisti, S., and Maffei, L., "Behavioral Contrast Sensitivity of the Cat in Various Visual Meridians," *Journal of Physiology* (*London*), vol. 241, no. 1, 1974, pp. 201–210.
7. Blackwell, H. R., "Luminance Difference Thresholds," in Jameson, D., and Hurvich, L.M. (eds.), "Handbook of Sensory Physiology," Springer-Verlag, New York, 1972, pp. 78–101.
8. Boycott, B. B., and Dowling, J. E., "Organization of the Primate Retina: Light Microscopy," *Philosophical Transactions of the Royal Society* ser. B, vol. 255, 1969, pp. 109–184.
9. Brown, J. E., and Major, D., "Cat Retinal Ganglion Cell Dentritic Fields," *Experimental Neurology*, vol. 15, no. 1, 1966, pp. 70–78.
10. Buchsbaum, G., "An Analytical Derivation of Visual Nonlinearity," *IEEE Transactions on Biomedical Engineering*, vol. BME-27, no. 5, May 1980, pp. 237–242.

11. Budrikis, Z., "*Visual Fidelity Criterion and Modelling*," *Proceedings of the IEEE*, vol. 60, no. 7, July 1972, pp. 771–779.
12. Campbell, F. W., and Green, D. G., "Optical and Retinal Factors Affecting Visual Resolution," *Journal of Physiology* (*London*), vol. 181, no. 3, December 1965, pp. 576–593.
13. Campbell, F. W., and Gubisch, R. W., "Optical Quality of the Human Eye," *Journal of Physiology* (*London*), vol. 186, no. 3, October 1966, pp. 558–578.
14. Campbell, F. W., and Maffei, L., "Contrast and Spatial Frequency," *Scientific American*, vol. 231, no. 5, November 1974, pp. 106–114.
15. Campbell, F. W., Kulikowski, J. J., and Levinson, J., "The Effect of Orientation on the Visual Resolution of Gratings," *Journal of Physiology* (*London*), vol. 187, no. 2, 1966, pp. 427–436.
16. Cornsweet, T., "Visual Perception," Academic, New York, 1970.
17. Dainty, J. C., and Shaw, R., "Image Science," Academic, London, 1974.
18. Davidson, M., "Perturbation Approach to Spatial Brightness Interaction in Human Vision," *Journal of the Optical Society of America*, vol. 58, no. 9, 1968, pp. 1300–1309.
19. Dooley, R. P., "Predicting Brightness Appearance at Edges Using Linear and Non-Linear Visual Describing Functions," *SPIE Annual Meeting*, Denver, May 14, 1975.
20. Dowling, J. E., "Receptoral and Network Mechanisms of Visual Adaptation," *Neurosciences Research Program Bulletin*, vol. 15, no. 3, October, 1977, pp. 397–405.
21. Enroth-Cugell, C., and Robson, J. G., "The Contrast Sensitivity of Retinal Ganglion Cells of the Cat," *Journal of Physiology* (*London*), vol. 187, no. 3, 1966, pp. 517–552.
22. Fechner, G. T., "Elemente der Psychophysik," Breitkopf u. Hartel, Leipzig, 1860.
23. Fukushima, K., "Visual Feature Extraction by a Multilayered Network of Analog Threshold Elements," *IEEE Transactions on Systems Science Cybernetics*, vol. SSC-5, no. 4, October 1969, pp. 322–333.
24. Fuortes, M. G. F., "Electric Activity of Cells in the Eye of the *Limulus*," *American Journal of Ophthalmology*, vol. 46, 1958, pp. 210–223.
25. Fuortes, M. G. F., "Initiation of Impulses in the Visual Cells of *Limulus*," *Journal of Physiology* (*London*), vol. 148, no. 1, 1959, pp. 14–28.
26. Georgeson, M., "Spatial Fourier Analysis and Human Vision," chap. 2 in Sutherland, N. S. (ed.), "Tutorial Essays in Psychology, A Guide to Recent Advances," vol. 2, Lawrence Erlbaum Associates, Hillsdale, N.J., 1979.
27. Geuen, W., and Widzgowski, E., "A Simple Edge Detection Algorithm on the Basis of Visual Contour Perception," *Proceedings 6th International Conference on Pattern Recognition*, Munich, Oct. 19–22, 1982.
28. Ginsburg, A. P., Cannon, M. W., and Nelson, M. A., "Suprathreshold Processing of Complex Visual Stimuli: Evidence for Linearity in Contrast Perception," *Science*, vol. 208, 9 May 1980, pp. 619–621.
29. Gouras, P., "Identification of Cone Mechanisms in Monkey Ganglion Cells," *Journal of Physiology* (*London*), vol. 199, no. 3, 1968, pp. 533–547.
30. Gouras, P., "Antidromic Responses of Orthodromically Identified Ganglion Cells in Monkey Retina," *Journal of Physiology*, vol. 204, no. 2, 1969, pp. 407–419.
31. Hall, C. F., and Hall, E. L., "A Nonlinear Model for the Spatial Characteristics of the Human Visual System," *IEEE Transactions on Systems, Man, and Cybernetics*, vol. SMC-7, no. 3, March 1977, pp. 161–170.
32. Hammond, P., "Contrasts in Spatial Organization of Receptive Fields at Geniculate and Retinal Levels: Centre, Surround, and Outer Surround," *Journal of Physiology* (*London*), vol. 228, no. 1, 1973, pp. 115–137.
33. Hartline, H. K., "The Receptive Fields of Optic Nerve Fibers," *American Journal of Physiology*, vol. 130, no. 4, 1940, pp. 690–699.
34. Hartline, H. K., "The Neural Mechanisms of Vision," The Harvey Lectures, 1941–1942, ser. 37, 1942, pp. 39–68.
35. Hartline, H. K., and Graham, C. H., "Nerve Impulses from Single Receptors in the Eye," *Journal of Cellular and Comparative Physiology*, vol. 1, no. 2, 1932, pp. 277–295.

36. Hecht, S., and Mintz, E. U., "The Visibility of Single Lines of Various Illuminations and the Retinal Basis of Visual Resolution," *Journal of General Physiology*, vol. 22, no. 5, 1939, pp. 593–612.
37. Hecht, S., Schlaer, S., and Pirenne, M. H., "Energy, Quanta, and Vision," *Journal of General Physiology*, vol. 25, 1942, pp. 819–840.
38. Henning, G. D., Hertz, D. G., and Broadbent, D. E., "Some Experiments Bearing on the Hypothesis That the Visual System Analyses Spatial Patterns in Independent Bands of Spatial Frequency," *Vision Research*, vol. 15, 1975, pp. 887–897.
39. Hilz, R., and Cavonius, C. R., "Functional Organization of the Peripheral Retina: Sensitivity to Periodic Stimuli," *Vision Research*, vol. 14, no. 12, 1974, pp. 1333–1337.
40. Jacobs, G., "Receptive Fields in Visual Systems," *Brain Research*, vol. 14, 1969, pp. 553–573.
41. Kermisch, D., and Roetling, P. G., "Fourier Spectrum of Halftone Images," *Journal of the Optical Society of America*, vol. 65, 1975, pp. 716–723.
42. Klensch, R. J., "Electrically Generated Halftone Pictures," *RCA Review*, September 1970, pp. 517–533.
43. Kuffler, S. W., "Discharge Patterns and Functional Organization of Mammalian Retina," *Journal of Neurophysiology*, vol. 16, no. 1, 1953, pp. 37–68.
44. Le Grand, Y., "Colour and Vision," Wiley, New York, 1957.
45. Le Grand, Y., "Light, Colour, and Vision," 2d ed., Chapman and Hall, London, 1968.
46. Lindsay, P. H., and Norman, D. A., "Human Information Processing, An Introduction to Psychology," Academic, New York, 1972.
47. Mannos, J. L., and Sakrison, D., "The Effects of a Visual Fidelity Criterion on the Encoding of Images," *IEEE Transactions Information Theory*, vol. IT-20, 1974, pp. 525–536.
48. Marr, D., "An Essay on the Primate Retina," A.I. Memo 296, Massachusetts Institute of Technology, Artificial Intelligence Laboratory, Cambridge, Mass., January 1974.
49. Ochs, A. L., "Two-Dimensional Analysis of Retinal Information Transfer," *Journal of the Optical Society of America*, vol. 65, no. 7, July 1975, pp. 842–846.
50. Pirenne, M. H., "Vision and the Eye," 2d ed., Chapman and Hall, London, 1967.
51. Richter, J., and Ullman, S., "A Model for the Spatio-Temporal Organization of X- and Y-Type Ganglion Cells in the Primate Retina," A.I. Memo no. 573, Massachusetts Institute of Technology, Artificial Intelligence Laboratory, Cambridge, Mass., April 1980.
52. Rodieck, R. W., "Quantitative Analysis of Cat Retinal Ganglion Cell Response to Visual Stimuli," *Vision Research*, vol. 5, nos. 11/12, 1965, pp. 583–601.
53. Rodieck, R. W., "Receptive Fields in the Cat Retina: A New Type," *Science*, vol. 157, no. 3784, 1967, pp. 90–92.
54. Rodieck, R. W., "The Vertebrate Retina," Freeman, San Francisco, 1973.
55. Rodieck, R. W., and Stone, J., "Analysis of Receptive Fields of Cat Retinal Ganglion Cells," *Journal of Neurophysiology*, vol. 28, no. 5, 1965, pp. 833–849.
56. Roetling, P. G., "Visual Performance and Image Coding," *Proceedings of the Society of Photo-Optical Instrumentation Engineers*, vol. 74, "Image Processing," Pacific Grove, Calif., Feb. 24–26 1976, pp. 195–199.
57. Rosch, E., "Human Categorization," in Warren, N. (ed.), "Studies in Cross-Culture Psychology," vol. 1, Academic, New York, 1977.
58. Rushton, W. A. H., "Peripheral Coding in the Nervous System," in Rosenblith, W. A. (ed.), "Sensory Communication," MIT Press, Cambridge, Mass., 1961, pp. 169–181.
59. Rushton, W. A. H., "Visual Pigments in Man," *Scientific American*, vol. 207, no. 5, 1961, pp. 120–132.
60. Sakrison, D. J., and Algazi, V. R., "Comparison of Line-by-Line and Two-Dimensional Encoding of Random Images," *IEEE Transactions Information Theory*, vol. IT-17, no. 4, July 1971, pp. 386–398.
61. Schreiber, W. F., "Image Processing for Quality Improvement," *Proceedings of the IEEE*, vol. 66, no. 12, December 1978, pp. 1640–1651.
62. Snyder, A. W., and Miller W. H., "The Tiered Vertebrate Retina," *Vision Research*, vol. 17, no. 2, 1977, pp. 239–255.

63. Stevens, S. S., "The Psychophysics of Sensory Function," in Rosenblith, W. A. (ed.), "Sensory Communication," MIT Press, Cambridge, Mass., 1961, pp. 1–34.
64. Stevens, S. S., "Sensory Power Functions and Neural Events," in Lowenstein, W. E. (ed.), "Principles of Receptor Physiology," Springer-Verlag, New York, 1971, pp. 226–242.
65. Stockham, T. G., Jr., "Image Processing in the Context of a Visual Model," *Proceedings of the IEEE*, vol. 60, no. 7, 1972, pp. 828–842.
66. Stone, J., and Fabian, M., "Summing Properties of the Cat's Retinal Ganglion Cell," *Vision Research*, vol. 18, no. 8, 1968, pp. 1023–1040.
67. Stone, J., Dreher, D., and Leventhal, A., "Hierarchical and Parallel Mechanisms in the Organization of Visual Cortex," *Brain Research Reviews*, vol. 1, 1979, pp. 345–394.
68. Stone, J., and Hoffman, K. P., "Very Slow Conduction Ganglion Cells in the Cat's Retina: A Major New Functional Type?," *Brain Research*, vol. 43, 1972, pp. 610–616.
69. Thomas, J. P., "Spatial Resolution and Spatial Interaction," in Carterette, E. C., and Friedman, M. P. (eds.), "Handbook of Perception," vol. V, "Seeing," Academic, New York, 1975.
70. Uttal, W. R., "The Psychobiology of Sensory Coding," Harper & Row, New York, 1973.
71. Werblin, F. S., "The Control of Sensitivity in the Retina," *Scientific American*, vol. 228, no. 1, January 1973, pp. 71–79.
72. Westheimer, G., "Diffraction Theory and Visual Hyperacuity," *American Journal of Optometry and Physiological Optics*, vol. 53, no. 7, July 1976, pp. 362–364.
73. Westheimer, G., "Spatial Frequency and Light-Spread Descriptions of Visual Acuity and Hyperacuity," *Journal of the Optical Society of America*, vol. 67, no. 2, February 1977, pp. 207–212.
74. Westheimer, G., and Campbell, F. W., "Light Distribution in the Image Formed by the Living Human Eye," *Journal of the Optical Society of America*, vol. 52, no. 9, 1962, pp. 1040–1045.
75. Westheimer, G., and McKee, S. P., "Visual Acuity in the Presence of Retinal-Image Motion," *Journal of the Optical Society of America*, vol. 65, no. 7, July 1975, pp. 847–850.
76. Westheimer, G., and McKee, S. P., "Spatial Configurations for Visual Hyperacuity," *Vision Research*, vol. 17, 1977, pp. 89–93.
77. Wyszecki, G., and Stiles, W. S., "Color Science, Concepts and Methods, Quantitative Data and Formulas," Wiley, New York, 1967.

BIBILIOGRAPHY

Most of the topics in this chapter, except perhaps those in Section 4.5, are treated to some degree in conventional books on the psychology or neurophysiology of vision. However, they are usually not presented in the same context or with the same objective in mind.

An excellent review article on receptive fields is the one by Jacobs [8]. It is complete and clearly written and contains 90 references to the literature. A more advanced and current review has been written by Robson [10]. A good discussion on the psychophysical aspects of visual acuity can be found in [9]. Readers who are interested in the details of the patterns used in testing acuity, especially for clinical purposes, should consult [15].

A very complete book, which contains a lot of material on photometry and other practical aspects of vision, is the one by Wyszecki and Stiles [17]. This has by now become a classic reference book. Adaptation is a complex subject and readers wishing to learn more about the psychophysical aspects are directed to two papers by Rushton [13, 14]. More recently, Rodieck [11] has also discussed the neurophysiology of adaptation, including simple mathematical models of the experimental data.

Contrast sensitivity and its supposed correlate, the modulation transfer function of the human visual system, are still controversial subjects, which we shall return to in Chapter 6. A good, but probably biased, review of the research in this area is given by Campbell [3]. Readers are referred to a recent chapter written by Georgeson which attempts to discuss the pros and cons of the black-box approach to magnitude processing by humans [6]. It includes a short, elementary introduction to frequency-response methods which might be of interest to those unfamiliar with this topic. Over 100 references are listed. Algazi [1] also discusses these aspects in addition to their application to quantitative measurement of picture quality and distortion and how they constrain the coding process.

An interesting discussion of mathematical modeling of the human visual system can be found in [16] and the several University of Utah Ph.D. theses which followed its publication (see [2, 4, 5, 12]). A recent paper by Hall and Hall [7] is also worth reading, and it forms the basis for the material in Section 4.5.

1. Algazi, V. R., "The Psycho-Physics of Vision and Their Relation to Picture Quality and Coding Limitations," *Acta Electronica*, vol. 19, no. 3, 1976, pp. 225–232.
2. Baxter, B. S., "Image Processing in the Human Visual System," Ph.D. thesis, Computer Science Department, University of Utah, Salt Lake City, UTEC-CSs-75-168, December 1975.
3. Campbell, F. W., "The Transmission of Spatial Information Through the Visual System," in Worden, F., and Schmitt, F. O. (eds.), "The Neurosciences Third Study Program," MIT Press, Cambridge, Mass., 1973, pp. 95–103.
4. Colas-Baudelaire, P., "Digital Picture Processing and Psychophysics: A Study of Brightness Perception," Computer Science Department, University of Utah, Salt Lake City, UTEC-CSc-74-025, March 1973.
5. Faugeras, O., "Digital Color Image Processing and Psychophysics Within the Framework of a Human Visual Model," Ph.D. thesis, University of Utah, Salt Lake City, June 1976.
6. Georgeson, M., "Spatial Fourier Analysis and Human Vision," chap. II in Sutherland, N. S., (ed.), "Tutorial Essays in Psychology, A Guide to Recent Advances," vol. 2, Lawrence Erlbaum Associates, Hillsdale, 1979.
7. Hall, C. F., and Hall, E. L., "A Nonlinear Model for the Spatial Characteristics of the Human Visual System," *IEEE Transactions on Systems, Man, and Cybernetics*, vol. SMC-7, no. 3, March 1977, pp. 161–170.
8. Jacobs, G. H., "Receptive Fields in Visual Systems," *Brain Research*, vol. 14, 1969, pp. 553–573.
9. Riggs, L. A., "Visual Acuity," in Graham, C. H. (ed.), "Vision and Visual Perception," Wiley, New York, 1965.
10. Robson, J. G., "Receptive Fields: Neural Representation of the Spatial and Intensive Attributes of the Visual Image," in Carterette, E. C., and Friedman, M. D. (eds.), "Handbook of Perception," vol. V, "Seeing," Academic, New York, 1975.
11. Rodieck, R. W., "The Vertebrate Retina," Freeman, San Francisco, 1973.
12. Rom, R., "Image Transmission and Coding Based on Human Vision," Ph.D. thesis, Computer Science Department, University of Utah, Salt Lake City, UTEC-CSc-75-115, August 1975.
13. Rushton, W. A. H., "Visual Adaptation," The Ferrier Lecture, *Proceedings of the Royal Society*, ser. B, vol. 162, 1965, pp. 20–46.

14. Rushton, W. A. H., "Light and Dark Adaptation of the Retina," in Straatsma, B. R. Hall, M. O., Allen, R. A., and Crescitelli, F. (eds.), "The Retina: Morphology, Function and Clinical Characteristics," Forum in Medical Sciences, no. 8, University of California Press, Berkeley, 1969, pp. 257–280.
15. Sloan, L. L., "Measurement of Visual Acuity," *Archives of Ophthalmology*, vol. 45, no. 6, 1951, pp. 704–725.
16. Stockham, T. G., Jr., "Image Processing in the Context of a Visual Model," *Proceedings of the IEEE*, vol. 60, no. 7, 1972, pp. 828–842.
17. Wyszecki, G., and Stiles, W. S., "Color Science Concepts and Methods, Quantitative Data and Formulas," Wiley, New York, 1967.

CHAPTER

FIVE

EDGE DETECTION

5.1 THE SEX LIFE OF A JUMPING SPIDER

It appears that the sexual behavior of the jumping spider involves perception of its mate as a shaded circle with short lines (the legs) protruding from the bottom on both sides [66]. This image is differentiated from others, since the presentation of different kinds of small objects tends to elicit a prey capture response. The spider's pattern recognition system seems to be scanning for edges or short lines at the appropriate orientation. It does this by moving its retina in a scanning locus which allows for both horizontal and rotational movement. This is just the right "equipment" it would require in order to match a simple mask edge detector to a stored model at a particular location and orientation.

We shall see in this chapter that it is not only the jumping spider that performs edge detection. Some very interesting experiments have also been done with frogs, cats, and monkeys which illustrate the "computational" nature of groups of neurons acting together in concert. These neuron networks are apparently capable of extracting various edge-dependent features from the input image. What is even more exciting is that these feature detectors seem to be organized in a hierarchical fashion, much as might be done in writing a structured computer program. Section 5.2 examines this process of edge and feature detection in animals; we know little about this topic as it relates to humans. In Chapters 8, 9, and 10 we shall return to this subject when we consider how the results of those "biological algorithms" are organized and perhaps utilized to characterize the texture and shape of objects.

Edge detection by digital computer has been of interest to scientists from the outset [64]. Perhaps this is because of a stubborn belief that there exists somewhere a "perfect" edge detector which could isolate the exact boundaries of objects in pictures without involving any significant intermediate computational processes. We saw in Figure 1.3 that this is not possible even for simple objects in a scene. The reason seems to be that there are discrepancies between the physical edge, its image, and our mental abstraction of it. Although we are able to make this mental leap with ease, it has proved to be more of an intractable problem for computer analysis systems. Obviously, the high-level abstract model is achieved by means of relatively complex processes. However, edges do exist as discontinuities in the image, and therefore conventional mathematical techniques seem to be applicable. Also, there is neurophysiological evidence for the existence of relatively simple biological edge detectors. Thus, the perverse search for better and better edge detectors goes on, and some of the main trends are discussed in this chapter. From the point of view of this book we note that the results of these computations are later employed at other levels in the picture interpretation hierarchy.

In Section 5.3 we shall examine some of the characteristics of edges and see why their detection is difficult. A useful research objective at present would be to attempt to categorize various edge profiles according to the perceived lighting conditions that existed in the original three-dimensional scene. If this could be done, then perhaps it would then be possible to obtain for arbitrary images some of the intrinsic features shown in Figure 2.5.

Sections 5.4 and 5.5 deal with two different families of edge detection techniques. The most popular, discussed first, are essentially parallel-processing template-matching methods. A particular set of windows is swept over the input in an attempt to isolate specific edge features, very similar to those sought by the neuron networks mentioned above. The second category includes sequential scanning techniques in which some ordered heuristic search is made to locate particular features. These methods were originally developed for game playing programs such as chess, and are now finding renewed embodiment in many commercial microprocessor-based electronic games. In order to find edges, we shall see that this approach usually requires a data model, albeit a crude one.

Edge detection has had the single greatest influence on computational algorithms for picture processing to date. It is a simple, yet powerful concept and very intimately involved with vision in both man and machine. An interesting symbiosis of these is a prosthesis for the blind being developed at the Smith-Kettlewell Institute of Visual Sciences in San Francisco [18]. With the aid of a miniature camera and a microprocessor, objects are located and analyzed by edge detection methods. A voice synthesizer and a tactile stimulator belt provide suitable collision avoidance data to the blind person. This appears to be the first step towards enhancing human vision by a machine equivalent.

5.2 FEATURE DETECTION IN ANIMALS

"What the Frog's Eye Tells the Frog's Brain" was the slightly provocative title of a now classic paper by Lettvin and his associates at MIT, who proposed that the frog's retina actually contains feature detectors that are sensitive to patterns in an image [68]. This seminal publication has been responsible for encouraging the novel consideration of the visual system of man and animal as a computational processor with hard-wired algorithms. In this case, the "biological computation" is the detection of edges and patterns of edges called features in the input visual image. The implication is that it is the output of these feature computations that gets analyzed at higher levels and not just the raw input data. This should not surprise us, since we have already seen in Section 4.2 that there exist receptive fields which compute contrast.

Two broad classes of visual systems have been suggested so far. The first, of which the systems of the frog, rabbit, and squirrel are representative (see Figure 3.20), possesses ganglion cells in the retina which perform low-level feature detection. We shall see that these animals have detectors which are sensitive to edges, orientation, and directional movement, in addition to their expected response to color and contrast. The second category consists of the visual systems of the so-called higher animals, such as cats, monkeys, and humans. In this case it is thought that the ganglion cells are restricted to measuring color and contrast only. Remarkably however, there is ample neurophysiological evidence at the cortical levels of cats and monkeys that geometrical edge features are computed there. Furthermore, it seems that this computation is hierarchical in nature so that more complex feature detectors are constructed out of the simpler ones. Essentially then, the categorization is based on the existence, or nonexistence of a developed visual cortex, which in turn must be highly dependent on the environment in which the animal lives.

In this section we shall examine feature detection in the frog as representative of the first class and then in the cat and monkey for the second class. However, there is some behavioral evidence that feature analysis in the two classes is related [57]. Ideally we would be interested in knowing what happens in man's visual cortex, but it is not possible with the techniques available to ethically perform on humans the electrophysiological experiments made on animals. However, it is assumed that the properties of the monkey's visual system are strongly indicative of our own. Perceptual experiments alone are definitely inadequate for delineating the cellular mechanisms involved. For example, in 1957 Sutherland suggested that the octopus discriminated orientation and shape on the basis of feature detectors which computed the one-dimensional horizontal and vertical signatures of the two-dimensional input pattern [111]. A heated controversy ensued (see [19, 20, 22, 112, 113]) and Sutherland was later forced to revise his theory (essentially drop the original hypothesis) on the basis of new neurophysiological evidence [114].

The edge and feature detectors are defined as two-dimensional patterns in the spatial domain. Thus they are exactly the same as the windows or templates defined in Section 2.4 and which will be used in the following sections to define

Table 5.1 Anatomical locations and specific triggers of feature-sensitive neurons in the nervous systems of various species*

Anatomical location	Trigger feature	Anatomical location	Trigger feature
Goldfish		*Cat (main types)*	
Retina	Local redness or greenness; Direct movement	Retina	Local brightening and dimming
		Lateral geniculate	Local brightening and dimming
Frog		Visual cortex Area 17	
Retina	Convex edge; Sustained edge; Changing contrast; Dimming; Dark	Simple cells	Moving, slits, bars, edges with specific orientation
Optic tectum	Newness; Sameness; Binocularity	Complex cells	Combinations of simple cell outputs of same orientation
Pigeon		Visual cortex Area 18	
Retina	Directed movement; Oriented edges	Hypercomplex I cells	Ends of lines
		Hypercomplex II cells	Line segments and corners
Ground squirrel		*Cat (infrequent types)*	
Retina	Local brightening or dimming; Local blueness or greenness	Retina	Directed movement; Uniformity detectors
Binocular	Directed movement		
Lateral geniculate	Color-coded units	Lateral geniculate	Local blueness or greenness, directional and orientational units
Optic tectum	Directional units; Oriented slits or bars; Complex units	Optic tectum	Directed movement; Complex units
Rabbit		*Monkey*	
Retina	Local brightening or dimming; Directed movement; Fast or slow movement; Edge detectors; Oriented slits or bars; Uniformity detectors	Retina	Local brightening or dimming; Local redness, greenness, or blueness
		Lateral geniculate	Various forms of color coding
		Cortex	Similar to cat; some color-coded
Lateral geniculate	Greater directional selectivity	Infero-temperal cortex	Very complex; possible hand detector
Tectum	Habituating units		

* Adapted from Barlow, H. B., Narasimhan, R., and Rosenfeld, A., "Visual Pattern Recognition in Machines and Animals," *Science*, vol. 177, no. 4049, Aug. 18, 1972, pp. 567–575 *in* Uttal, W. R., "The Psychobiology of Mind," Lawrence Erlbaum Associates, Hillsdale, N.J., 1978, pp. 468–469.

computational edge detectors for digital image processing. Table 5.1 is a summary of detected features at different anatomical levels of several animals for which experiments have been carried out. Of course, this is not the end of the story; in order to "perceive" arrangements of these edges as shapes or forms, some higher level of processing in the central nervous system is required to organize the data into a global perspective. Both neurophysiological and psychophysical experiments indicating the probable nature of these aggregative procedures are discussed in Chapters 8, 9, and 10.

The experiments of Hartline in the late thirties had established the hypothesis that different units in the frog's retina respond to different patterns of light [47]. Twenty years later, Lettvin, Maturana, McCulloch, and Pitts showed that certain ganglion cells of the frog each measure a particular feature of the light pattern in an area of receptive field [68, 79]. Figure 5.1 shows an experimental setup used at that time [79], which resulted in the identification of four major types of feature detectors to be described below.

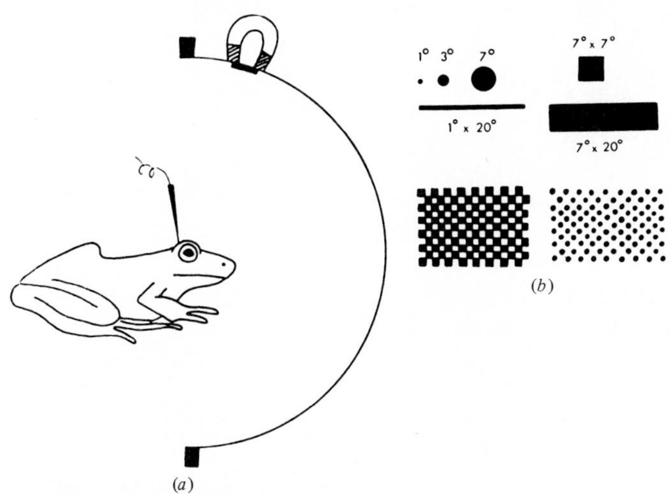

Figure 5.1 Experiments described in [68] with the visual system of the frog. (*a*) A schematic drawing of the relationship between the frog and the aluminum hemisphere that constituted the experimental visual field. The frog was placed so that one eye was situated at the center of the hemisphere. This provided a view of about two-thirds of the visual field of a single frog's eye. The stimuli were moved on the inner surface of the hemisphere by a magnet on its outer surface. (*b*) Scale drawings of some of the objects used as stimuli. The degrees indicate their diameter if placed inside a hemisphere of the same radius as that represented in (*a*). The actual hemisphere used was larger (36 cm) than that shown. Numerous kinds and shapes of objects were used: (i) dark disks 1°, 3°, and 7° in diameter; (*b*) dark strips 1° and 7° in width and 20° in length; (iii) a square 7° on a side. Various kinds of backgrounds were used: (i) uniform gray; (ii) checkerboard pattern; (iii) dotted pattern; (iv) striped pattern; (v) color photograph of grass and flowers from a frog's point of view. In the various experiments the backgrounds could be kept stationary or moved at will. [*From H. R. Maturana, J. Y. Lettvin, and W. S. McCulloch, "Anatomy and Physiology of Vision in the Frog (Rana pipiens)," J. General Physiology, vol. 43, suppl. 2 (Mechanisms of Vision), 1960, pp. 129–171.*]

Inhibitory receptive field

(*a*)

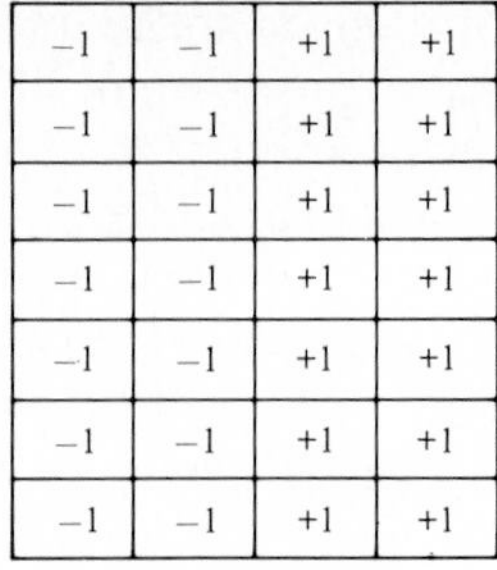

−1	−1	+1	+1
−1	−1	+1	+1
−1	−1	+1	+1
−1	−1	+1	+1
−1	−1	+1	+1
−1	−1	+1	+1
−1	−1	+1	+1

Excitory receptive field

(*b*)

Figure 5.2 A sustained-edge detector of the frog is shown in (*a*) with a possible idealized equivalent computational window in (*b*). The output of the ganglion cell with this receptive field responds strongly to edges that conform to the template pattern.

One of the most important visual cues in our environment, which is probably more important for the frog, is the existence of sharp dark or light edges. Thus the first type of unit is the "sustained-edge detector" shown in Figure 5.2. This template or window consists of a single inhibitory and excitory receptive field whose sum yields a response sensitive to edges occurring against a contrasting background. The resulting maintained firing rate of the ganglion cell is initially 30 to 40 spikes per second, reducing to 10 to 15 spikes per second if the edge is left in place. Such a receptive field is different from the one discussed in Section 4.2 in that it responds to the particular shape of the input and not just to the existence of contrast. The receptive field has been shown to have a diameter of 1° to 3° (44 to 130 μm on the retina). The size of the object exhibiting the edge does not seem to be a factor, although objects subtending a diameter greater than 20° do tend to result in a smaller response. Therefore the implication is that the edge detector is capable of sensing an edge feature of part of the boundary of an object; it is an elemental computation.

An experiment is described in [68] in which a color photograph of flowers and grass normally found in the frog's habitat is moved in front of its eyes. No reaction. However, when a small magnet simulating a fly was superimposed on and moved over this scene, it did elicit a response. Not all edges are linear as required by the sustained edge detector, and indeed frogs are quite interested in roundish-looking flies moving across their field of view. Thus the second class of detector is the "convex-edge detector." This unit responds to the movement of a small object that exhibits a sharp edge and is darker than its background. The diameter of the receptive field is generally between 2° and 5°. As can be observed from Figure 5.3*a*, *b*, and *c*, it is the curvature of the input pattern and not its actual size that is significant to the response. Thus the pattern that excited the sustained-edge detector is ignored (Figure 5.3*c*). Another interesting property is that the ganglion cell firing rate has been shown to be proportional to the velocity of the convex object raised to the power 0.7. This movement into the field is quite important, as is evident from Figure 5.3*d*, *e*, *f*, and *g*. Extinction of the ambient light results in the cessation of firing,

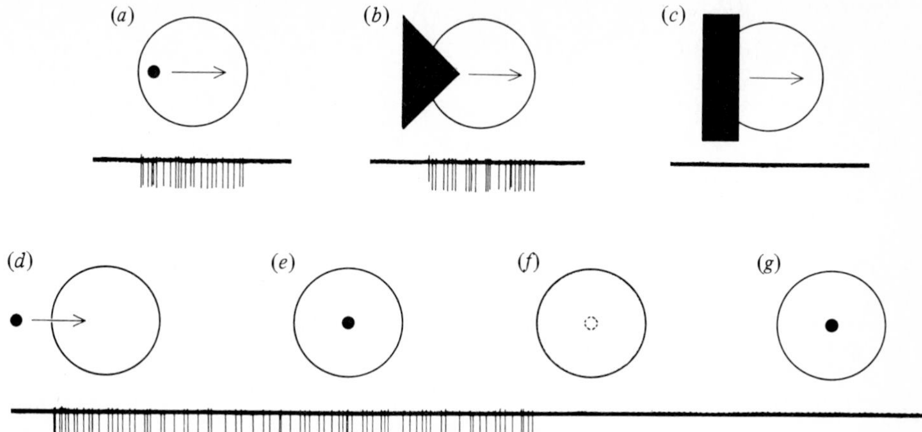

Figure 5.3 Convex-edge detectors in the frog's retina respond to a moving stimulus that has a positive curvature (*a*) or contains an angle (*b*) but not to a moving straightedge (*c*). The response to an object entering the field (*d*) continues when the object stops within the field (*e*). The response ceases when the background light goes off (*f*) and does not occur if the light goes on again (*g*). (*From C. R. Michael, "Retinal Processing of Visual Images," Scientific American, vol. 220, no. 5, May 1969, pp. 104–114.*)

which does not resume even if the light is turned on again. This so-called property of erasability is evidence of the adaptation ability of the frog's retina. If the spot were brought into the field during darkness, there would also be no response. Thus, perceived movement is a prerequisite for response. An ideal bug detector!

The third type is referred to as a "moving-edge" or "changing-contrast detector" and is equivalent to the ON-OFF units found earlier by Hartline. The template is identical to that shown in Figure 5.2 except that this edge must now be moving through the field in order for the cell to respond by firing. The receptive field is larger, having a diameter range of 7° to 12°. The response is related to the velocity of movement but does not depend on the direction. Similarly the fourth type, the "net-dimming detector," is the same as Hartline's OFF detector. It responds to the cessation of illumination; the lower the resulting level, the higher the discharge. The receptive field is usually larger and ranges in diameter from 10° to 15°. The axons of this unit are the fastest of the four categories, and in conjunction with such a large receptive field it was perhaps meant to signal an escape response, possibly in the presence of an attacking bird.

In addition to these types, a fifth class was reported by the MIT group, but has not been subsequently found by others [68]. This simply consists of dark detectors which are characterized by continuous activity, responding with a firing rate which is inversely proportional to the amount of impinging light and is a maximum in the dark. In any event, it is most likely that experiments to date have not yet revealed the complete story regarding the number and type of feature detectors.

Each of the first four classes of feature detectors has been found to project onto a different anatomical layer in the optic tectum of the frog, the analog to the superior colliculus in man. Thus, each layer contains independent information resulting from a transformation of the input image impinging on the complete retinal field to a different attribute of this input. Hence the data are available in a four-dimensional space to be used essentially without further processing by the frog's motor control and response system. Furthermore, it is just these data that would be best suited to the life and death issues appropriate to a frog. Arbib [4] discusses a mechanism by which such decisions might be made.

We may observe in Table 5.1 that the frog, squirrel, and rabbit, listed on the left as being in our first class because their retinal receptive fields perform complex feature computations, possess different sets of feature detectors. Presumably as more animals of this class are studied, the same situation will prevail for them. As yet no consistent pattern or theory has developed, although environmental conditions are thought to be important.

We next turn to the second major class of visual system, which is characterized by complex feature analysis at the cortical levels. The results of these experiments are shown on the right-hand side of Table 5.1. They are largely motivated by the pioneering work of Hubel and Wiesel on cats and monkeys [50, 51, 52, 53], research for which they recently received the Nobel prize for physiology and medicine [67]. It is assumed that a similar kind of image processing to that which takes place in animals is carried out in the human brain.

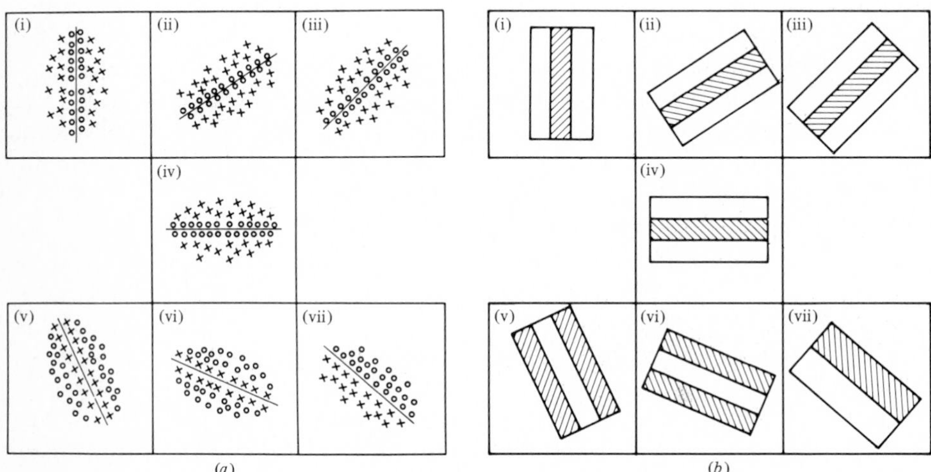

Figure 5.4 Typical receptive fields and their associated templates. (*a*) Hubel and Wiesel found in cat cortex a population of cells, which they called "simple" cells, whose receptive fields comprise ON and OFF areas separated by straight boundaries. The orientations vary from cell to cell and in the cat the total size of the receptive field is about 4° of visual angle. Circles mark ON areas while crosses mark OFF areas. (*b*) Equivalent templates for the receptive fields shown in (*a*). Note that some respond to bars and others to edges. [(*a*) *From M. A. Arbib, "The Metaphorical Brain," Wiley, New York, 1972.*]

At the retinal and lateral geniculate levels of the cat, contrast-sensitive ON-center and OFF-center units of the type shown in Figure 4.1 are found. These concentric templates have been referred to as "local brightening and dimming detectors" and have actually also been recorded in human retinas [116]. It is thought that no significant reorganization of the data occurs at these levels.

This leads us to processing in the cat's visual cortex, which has been hypothesized as being structured in a hierarchy of computational complexity.

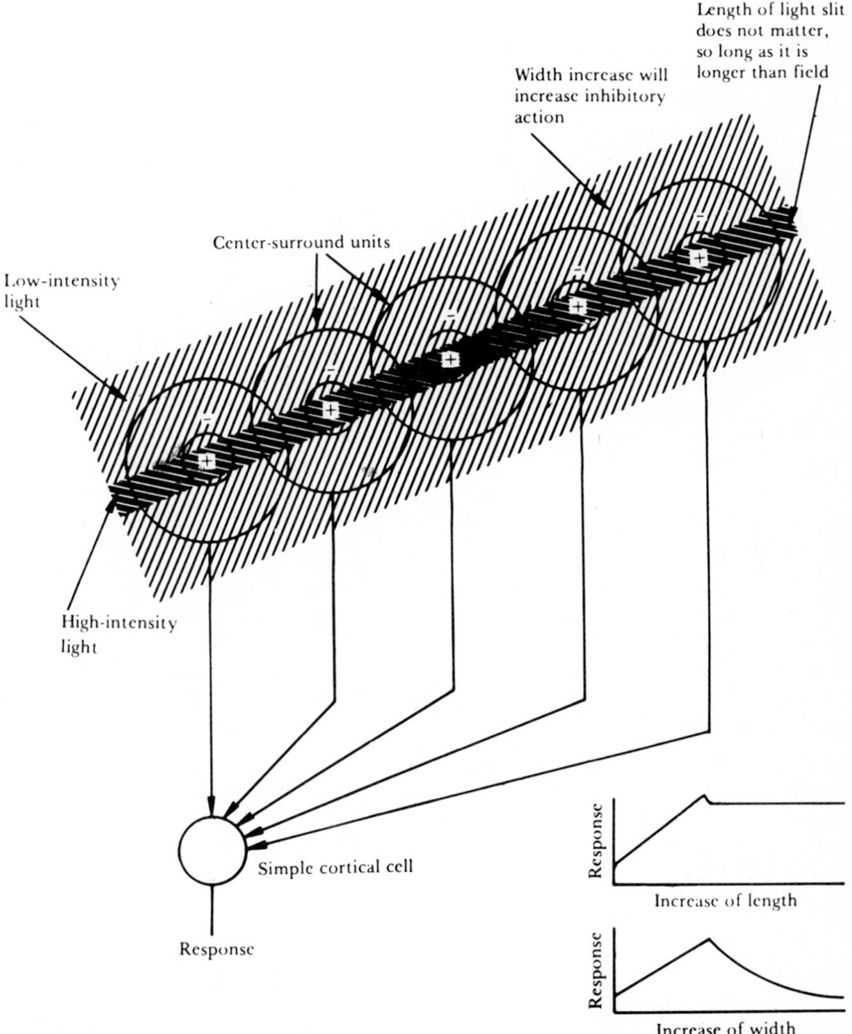

Figure 5.5 A model of a simple cortical cell sensitive to thin bright lines. The receptive field is made up of a spatial sequence of retinal receptive fields. The effect of varying the length and width of the stimulus on the neuron response is also shown. (*From T. H. Lindsay and D. A. Norman, "Human Information Processing, an Introduction to Psychology," Academic, New York, 1972.*)

The simple neurons in area 17 of the cortex have receptive fields which are sensitive to slits, bars, or edges which are position- and orientation-selective. The response is similar if the pattern sweeps across the receptive field. Figure 5.4 shows a selection of different receptive fields exhibited by such simple cortical cells. One hypothesis regarding how such templates might arise in the cortex is shown in Figure 5.5. A line detector could be constructed from a set of ON-center units in the retina or the lateral geniculate nucleus (LGN), all of whose axonal outputs synapse with the dendritic tree of a single cortical cell

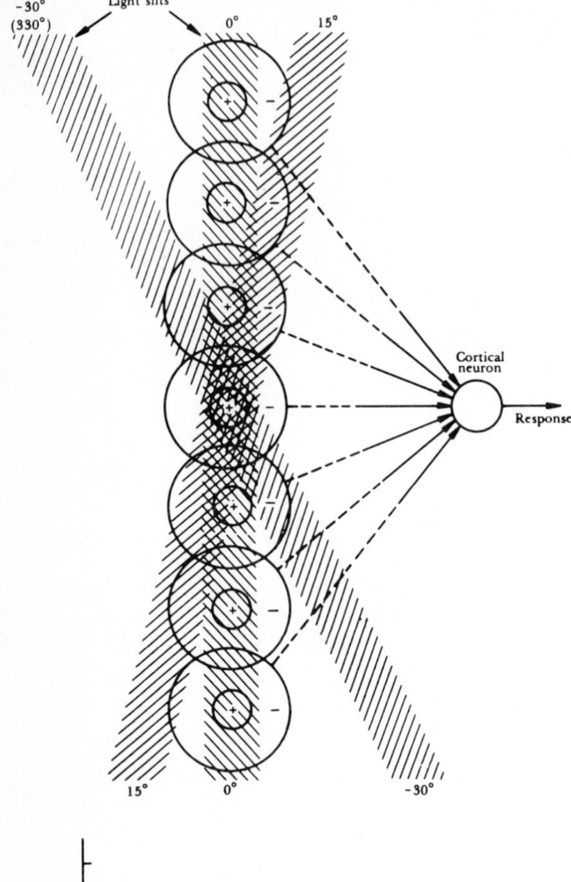

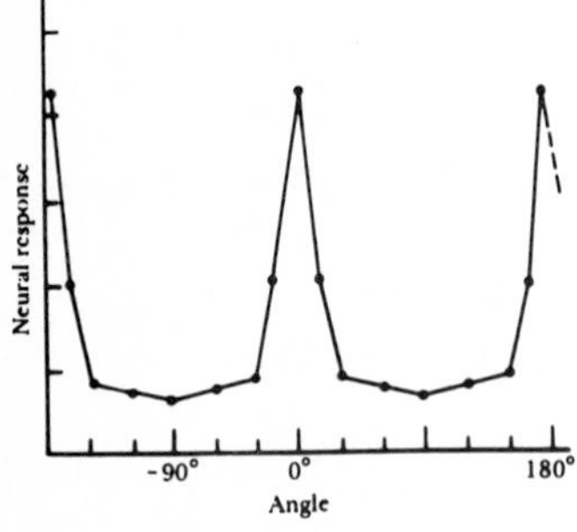

Figure 5.6 The response of the simple cortical cell in Figure 5.5 to lines at different orientations exhibits a sharp tuning curve. (*From T. H. Lindsay and D. A. Norman, "Human Information Processing, an Introduction to Psychology," Academic, New York, 1972, pp. 99–100.*)

which sums their contributions. It is interesting that such an arrangement would actually be sampling along the length of the line and therefore would be insensitive to small breaks in it. A decrease in the line length would reduce the firing rate of the cortical neuron, while an increase would have no effect. Increasing the width of the line would tend to decrease the response.

The property of sensitivity to the orientation of the input signal, depicted in Figure 5.6 for a neuron possessing a vertical line template, is particularly important for shape recognition. Again, as can be seen from the figure, the set of concentric receptive fields, perhaps oriented to detect vertical lines, would exhibit a maximal response at this specific orientation. Lines falling on this feature detector at other angles would obviously result in greater contributions by the surroundings and thus the cortical cell response would be reduced. We shall return in Chapter 8 to this aspect of signal tuning and the method by which the data from such detectors are actually aggregated.

The next type of feature detector in the computational hierarchy, also found in area 17 of the cortex, is referred to as a "complex receptive field." Units of this type appear to be combinations of the simple feature detectors. They also respond maximally to spatially oriented slits, bars, and edges and are directionally sensitive. However, the difference between these and the simple detectors is that the exact position of the input pattern within the receptive field is of no consequence. This is true even when the pattern is moving through the receptive field, as can be seen from Figure 5.7. As long as the

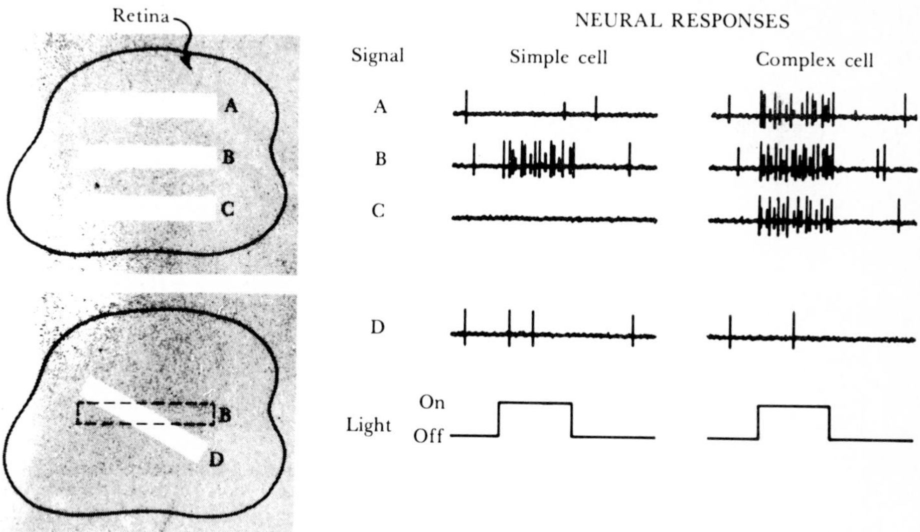

Figure 5.7 The response of a cortical complex cell to a bar moving vertically through the receptive field at the appropriate orientation. At positions *A*, *B*, and *C* the neuron responds vigorously while at *D*, in the wrong orientation, there is no response. Note that if this were the receptive field of a simple cell, it would only fire at a single location *B*. However, location is not important for a complex cell. (*After T. H. Lindsay and D. A. Norman, "Human Information Processing, an Introduction to Psychology," Academic, New York, 1972, p. 103.*)

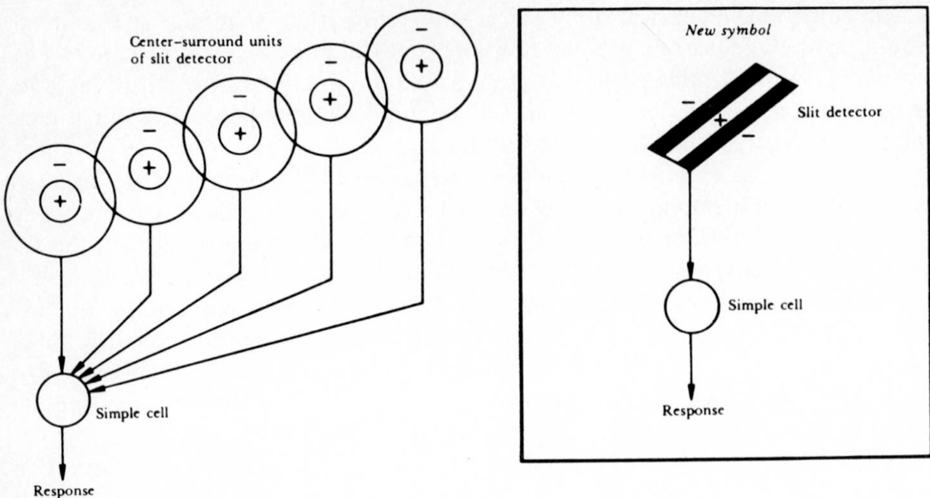

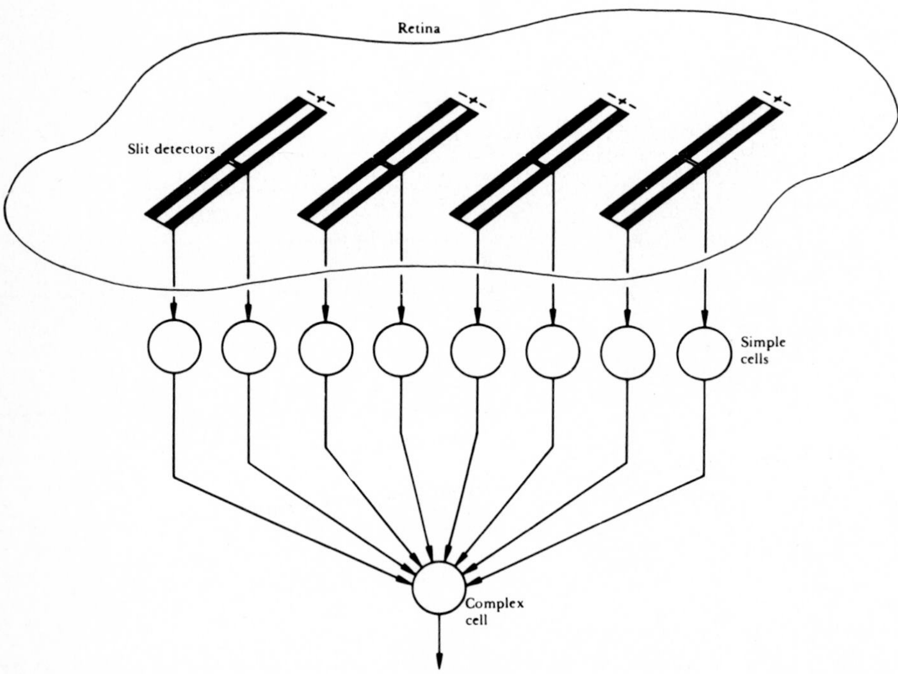

Figure 5.8 A possible three-level hierarchical structure for a complex cell performing bar detection. (*From T. H. Lindsay and D. A. Norman, "Human Information Processing, an Introduction to Psychology," Academic, New York, 1972, p. 104.*)

stimulus matches the template in shape, orientation, and direction of movement, a response is elicited by such a cortical neuron within the neighborhood of its receptive field. We observe that the latter cannot be simply mapped into just ON and OFF regions, as was the case for simple cells. Figure 5.8 shows how a complex cortical cell might be constructed from simple cortical and retinal ganglion cell receptive fields, and an alternative model is given in [84].

The highest points in the hierarchy discovered so far are neurons in area 17 of the cortex, and are referred to as hypercomplexes I and II. The former respond to moving, oriented, and directionally selective lines with either one or two definitive ends, while the latter actually respond to corners. Thus the distinctive attribute of these detectors in comparison with the simple and complex ones is the importance of the physical termination of the input pattern. Figure 5.9 is an example of a lower-order hypercomplex cell which

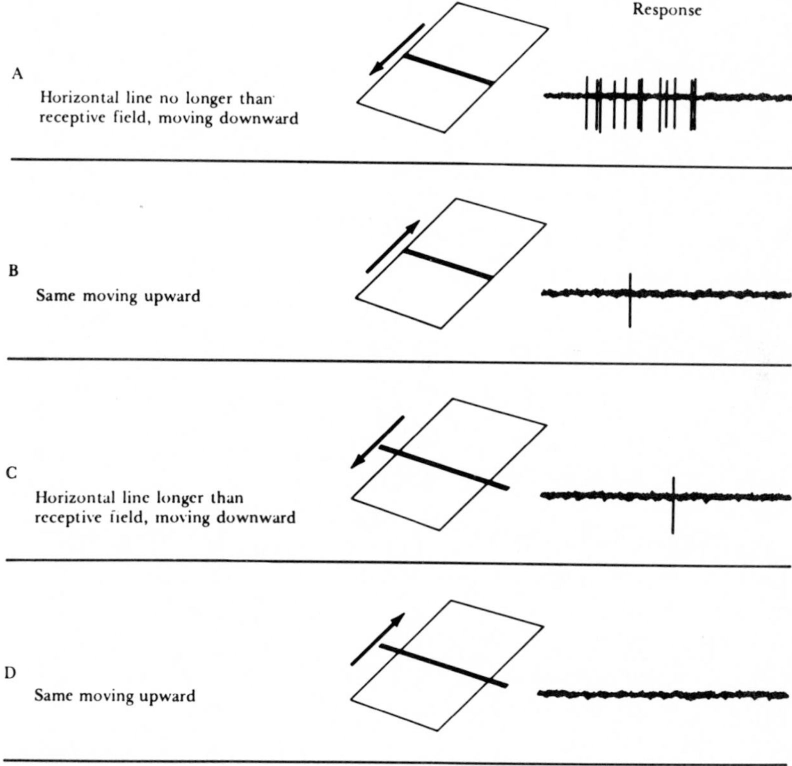

Figure 5.9 The effect of employing a line whose length does not match that of the hypercomplex-cell bar detector. Line length is obviously of great importance, as is direction of movement. [*From T. H. Lindsay and D. A. Norman, "Human Information Processing, an Introduction to Psychology," Academic, New York, 1972; p. 106, in D. G. Hubel and T. N. Wiesel, "Receptive Fields and Functional Architecture in Two Nonstriate Visual Areas (18 and 19) of the Cat," Journal of Neurophysiology, 1965, vol. 28, pp. 229–289.*]

responds maximally to a line segment moving in the appropriate direction. Elongating the line results in a suppression of the response. Figure 5.10 further demonstrates how such a line-segment detector responds "gracefully" as a function of deviation from optimal line segment length, a property we also observed for the detector in Figure 5.6. There definitely seems to be a tuning curve associated with the unit's response. Figure 5.11 indicates that it does not matter where in the receptive field the line segment passes through in order that it respond positively. Figure 5.12 shows the effect of having a line width which is not tuned to the characteristic of the particular hypercomplex neuron.

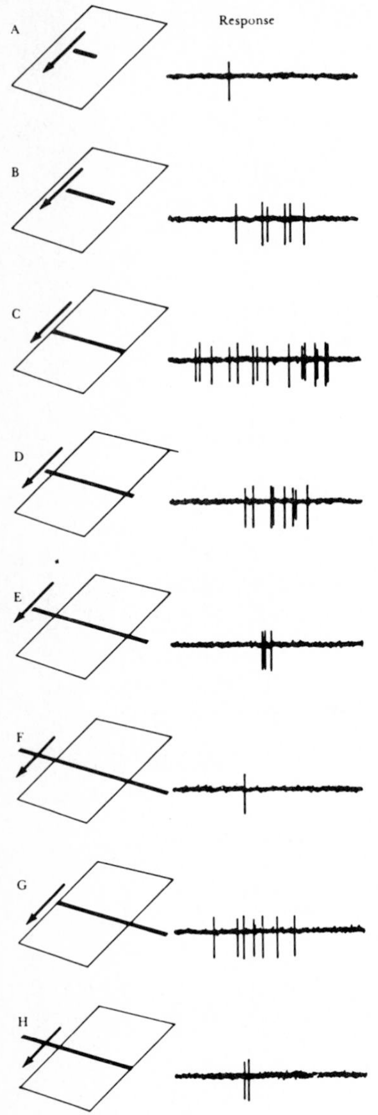

Figure 5.10 A hypercomplex receptive field showing that the dependence on line length is "graceful" in that some response is also evoked for improperly tuned line lengths. Nevertheless, as shown in (g) and (h), proper segment termination is important. [*From T. H. Lindsay and D. A. Norman, "Human Information Processing, an Introduction to Psychology," Academic, New York, 1972, p. 107, after D. G. Hubel and T. N. Wiesel, "Receptive Fields and Functional Architecture in Two Nonstriate Visual Areas* (*18 and 19*) *of the Cat," Journal of Neurophysiology, vol. 28, 1965, pp. 229–289.*]

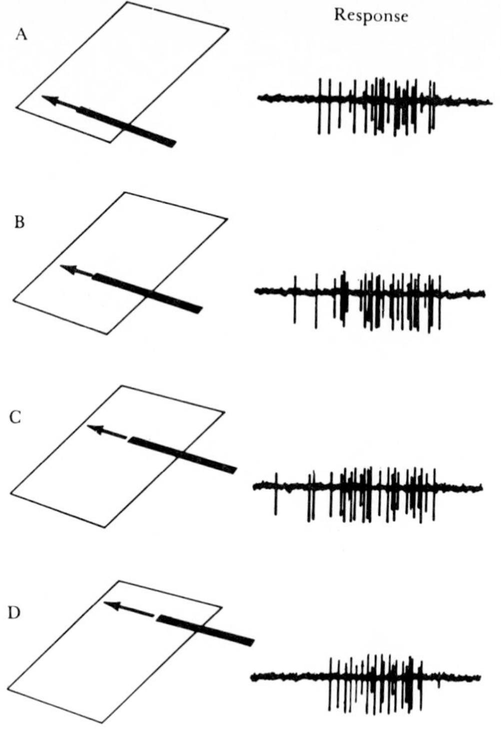

Figure 5.11 Movement through the field of a line segment of the correct length and width elicits the identical response at any point in the field. [*From T. H. Lindsay and D. A. Norman, "Human Information Processing, an Introduction to Psychology," Academic, New York, 1972, p. 107, after D. G. Hubel and T. N. Wiesel, "Receptive Fields and Functional Architecture in Two Nonstriate Visual Areas (18 and 19) of the Cat," Journal of Neurophysiology, 1965, vol. 28, pp. 229–289.*]

A higher-order, or hypercomplex II, cell behavior is shown in Figure 5.13. It is seen that a 90° corner moving from right to left elicits the maximum response. Just as for the lower levels in the hierarchy, it was once thought that the hypercomplex detectors could be constructed by configuring a set of complex cells. This model has now been rejected on the basis of new experimental evidence.

At present we obviously are not fully aware of the specific details of the discussed feature detectors and their interconnections. Nevertheless they seem to exist in some form and play an important role in the cat's, and presumably the human's, visual apparatus. These results are summarized in Figure 5.14, showing a sequence of six distinct levels in the hierarchy of analysis. Most likely, in actuality there is a continuum from simple to complex feature detectors. The hierarchy is also probably not rigid, so that not all the lower-order cells necessarily project to the higher levels. A simulation of a feature extractor based on the properties of the mammalian visual system is discussed by Fukushima [35].

Notwithstanding the attractiveness of the above theory from the point of view of simplicity and information processing, a challenge to its validity has recently been made by Stone et al. [110]. This new model is based on the classification of the retinal ganglion cells as being W, X, and Y types. It appears

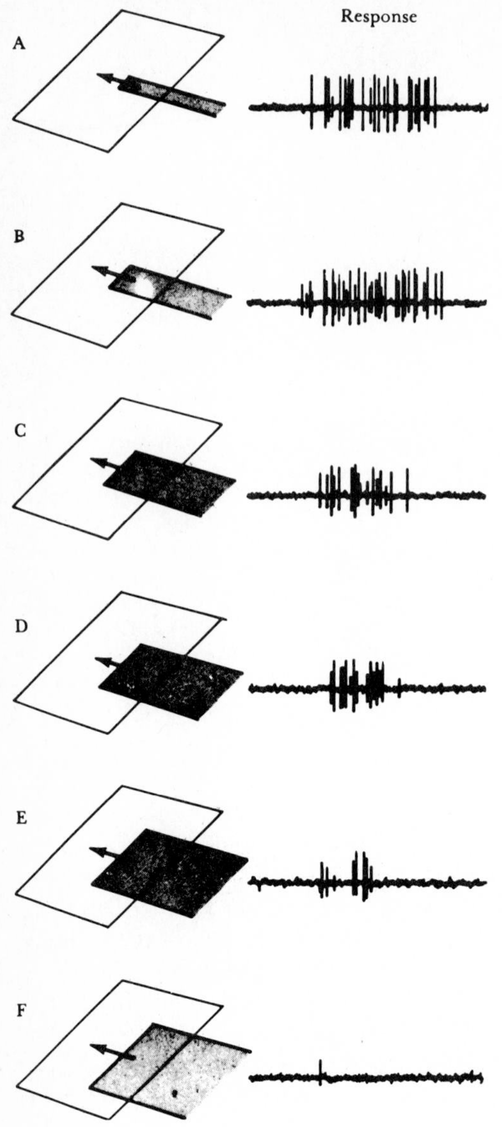

Figure 5.12 The hypercomplex cell is sensitive to the width of the line segment. When compared with Figure 5.10, the response decreases, albeit again "gracefully," as the width increases. [*From T. H. Lindsay and D. A. Norman, "Human Information Processing, an Introduction to Psychology," Academic, New York, 1972, p. 108, after D. G. Hubel and T. N. Wiesel, "Receptive Fields and Functional Architecture in Two Nonstriate Visual Areas (18 and 19) of the Cat," Journal of Neurophysiology, vol. 28, 1965, pp.* 229–289.]

to be more compatible with the body of research results published subsequent to the introduction of the Hubel-Wiesel hierarchical theory. However, it is less comprehensive.

Retinal ganglion cells of the X type seem to be concerned with static features such as light contrast, while dynamic visual discriminations are attributed to the Y cells. Both have a conventional center-surround receptive field; the X-cell center is very small compared with the large center of the Y cell. A

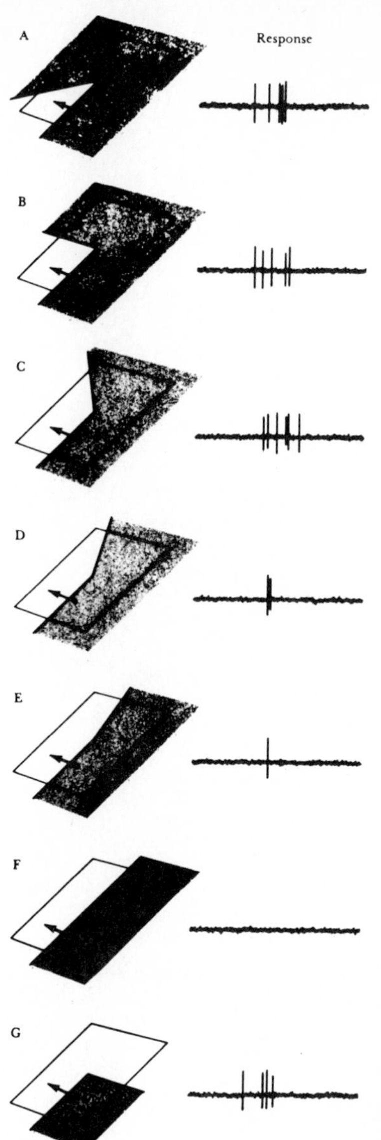

Figure 5.13 A hypercomplex cell which detects right angles moving in a particular direction. [*From T. H. Lindsay and D. A. Norman, "Human Information Processing, an Introduction to Psychology," Academic, New York, 1972, p. 103, after D. G. Hubel and T. N. Wiesel, "Receptive Fields and Functional Architecture in Two Nonstriate Visual Areas (18 and 19) of the Cat," Journal of Neurophysiology, 1965, vol. 28, pp. 229–289.*]

similar comparison can be made of their actual cell body size and dendritic fields. As might be expected of cells sensitive to movement, Y cells have thick, fast-conducting axons (30 to 40 m/s). The X cells possess much more slowly conducting axons (15 to 23 m/s). Also, the X cells are concentrated in the area centralis of the retina and appear to be responsible for high-resolution vision. The Y cells are more numerous in the periphery. The receptive field configurations of W cells seem to be more uncertain. Their center size and dendritic

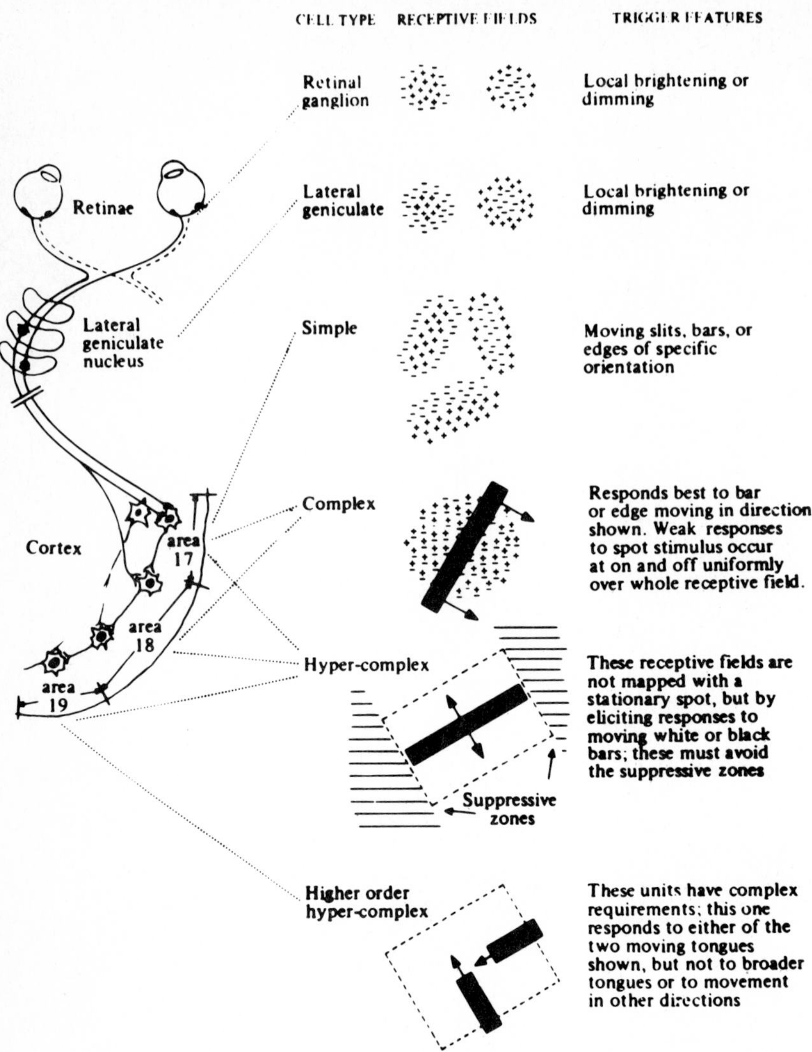
CELL TYPE
RECEPTIVE FIELDS
TRIGGER FEATURES
Retinal ganglion
Local brightening or dimming
Lateral geniculate
Local brightening or dimming
Simple
Moving slits, bars, or edges of specific orientation
Complex
Responds best to bar or edge moving in direction shown. Weak responses to spot stimulus occur at on and off uniformly over whole receptive field.
Hyper-complex
These receptive fields are not mapped with a stationary spot, but by eliciting responses to moving white or black bars; these must avoid the suppressive zones
Suppressive zones
Higher order hyper-complex
These units have complex requirements; this one responds to either of the two moving tongues shown, but not to broader tongues or to movement in other directions
Retinae
Lateral geniculate nucleus
Cortex
area 17
area 18
area 19

Figure 5.14 Cell types and trigger features at different positions in the visual pathway of the cat, shown diagrammatically. Monkey cortex is mainly similar. The elongated receptive fields in area 17 are sensitive to bars and edges of the appropriate orientation and size. This pattern selectivity results from the excitatory and inhibitory connections to cortical neurons made by LGN neurons with concentric receptive fields. The more complex properties of cells in areas 18 and 19 result from connections made to these areas from cells in area 17, though there is also a direct input of area 18 from the LGN. [*From H. B. Barlow, "General Principles: the Senses Considered as Physical Instruments," chap. 1 in H. B. Barlow and J. D. Mollen (eds.), "The Senses," Cambridge University Press, Cambridge, 1982.*]

fields are relatively large, and they respond to either static or dynamic stimuli. A distinction from the X- and Y-type cells is that they have thin axons, exhibiting very low conducting velocities (2 to 18 m/s). A summary of W, X, and Y cells is found in [110].

The theory also differs with regard to the system structure. It suggests that these cells project to both the LGN and the cortex in parallel, with minor interconnections. Parallelism is also maintained in the cortex. For example, in the visual cortex of the cat, the W-, X-, and Y-type cells largely connect to areas 19, 17, and 18, respectively. Area 17 does have inputs from W- and Y-type cells as well, but these are not as numerous as inputs from the X type. Similarly, the association area 18 does receive secondary projections from W-type cells. It has also been observed that the different parallel projections to area 17 terminate in different and distinct laminae. Therefore, Stone et al. state that a parallel computational structure exists, but that the latter may indeed also be hierarchical. However, they present detailed arguments contradicting the existence of the simple-complex-hypercomplex model [110]. Which, or to what degree each, is the correct view remains to be established.

We have described, albeit with a certain degree of vagueness and a large degree of verbal association, some aspects of low-level feature detection in the mammal. One reason for the uncertainty relates to the experimental paradigm adopted by neurophysiologists. Typically, the scientist will record the activity of a single neuron in response to a particular light pattern. A more useful approach from the point of view of modeling would be to examine the behavior of groups of interconnected cells as a function of different input images. Various test patterns and sequences could then be designed in order to extract information regarding cell output and network connectivity. From this it would then be possible to learn a lot more about the structure of receptive fields.

It is also unclear whether or not these "biological algorithms" are prewired at birth or are learned in the early stages of contact with the environment. Evidence based on experiments with kittens and adult cats seems to point to the latter as the most plausible hypothesis. In any case, low-level vision apparently can be characterized in terms of line segments and edges moving in specified directions and orientations. It is highly unlikely that this information is stored as absolute measurements in memory and more probable that a coding into symbolic descriptors occurs at an early stage. It is well known that humans are quite poor at distinguishing absolute values of physical stimuli and can generally only cope with four to seven categories at a time regardless of the range of choice. For example, this is evident in the judgment of the size of objects [30]. Transfers occur which also imply symbolic representations of patterns; when animals are trained to discriminate two patterns projected on one portion of the retina, they can transfer the concept by responding in a similar fashion to similar patterns on another part of the retina. We obviously possess a large degree of insensitivity to variations in learned shaped and it would appear that symbolic coding of patterns, even at the lowest level of lines and edges, is a major factor [73].

How these low-level visual data are organized so that we are able to perceive different shapes is not yet evident. A possible neurophysiological theory is presented in Chapter 8. Low-level edge detectors usually form the basis for complex digital image-processing analysis as well, and these detectors will now be discussed. The similarity to their biological counterparts is intriguing.

5.3 CHARACTERISTICS OF EDGES

An edge in a picture may be defined as a discontinuity or abrupt change in the gray level or color [107]. In general, pictures may contain a variety of edge sizes, some short and others long. What is more significant, however, is that these contrasting segments may occur at any orientation. Therefore, given the common rectangular raster scanning pattern, an efficient edge-detection procedure would necessarily have to be able to distinguish contrast at different angles. Also in terms of the spatial frequency, if we consider input bar patterns such as were used in Section 4.3.2, it is apparent that groups of such edges will appear in a picture and will occupy different portions of the frequency scale. This perhaps suggests the further necessity of analyzing edge content at a particular point in a picture by observing the local data at a set of frequency bandwidths. Some of the techniques in the following sections will be seen to take this aspect into consideration.

It is clear from the previous section that animals use edge content as a means of understanding their environment. In this regard it is necessary for us to distinguish between two concepts. The first is our abstract understanding of what edges and collections of edges are. The second involves the same idealizations corrupted by various forms of noise. Most of these are quite significant, making it generally very difficult for us to design edge detectors which manifest good performance characteristics.

Idealized edge models can be represented by the conventional singularity functions in mathematics. For example, an abrupt change in intensity can be defined by an ideal step, as shown in Figure 5.15*a*. Most likely this is what we conjure up in our minds when we think of an edge profile. Scenes with solid objects made up of planar surfaces may exhibit sharp angles in their intensity versus distance characterizations. For example, Figure 5.15*b* shows an ideal roof edge, which can be seen to be made up of two ramp singularities. We may also combine the unit step with the unit ramp to obtain a quite common profile, modeled as shown in Figure 5.15*c*. Pictures containing lines which are highly contrasted might exhibit a profile as shown in Figure 5.15*d*, a pulse made up of two unit steps. This is sometimes referred to as a "spike edge."

The origin of these one-dimensional profiles clearly relates to the particular geometry of the three-dimensional scene. For opaque, rigid polyhedra, edges in the picture occur at the intersection of surfaces in the scene. Different types of edges may be observed by examining a depth map, shown in Figure 5.16. These edges are the graphs below each object and plot the distance from the observer to the closest point on the object surface at a given angle α. Note in Figure 5.16*a* and *b* that the scan does not include a discontinuity in range, and the graph is therefore smooth. The concave edge (α_1) in Figure 5.16*c* and convex edge (α_2) in Figure 5.16*d* result in discontinuities in *r*, with the sign of the tangent defining the type. Eclipsing edges occur when there is a discontinuity in the depth, as seen in Figure 5.16*d*, where the two object surfaces involved are not touching (α_3). This type of edge is said to be "occluding" or "disoccluding,"

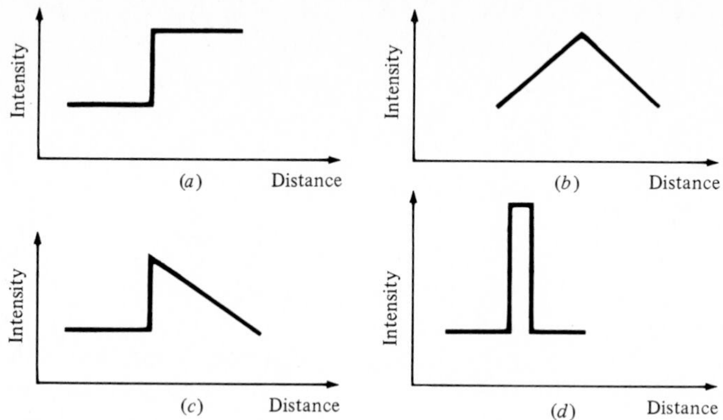

Figure 5.15 Ideal edge functions which result from abstract images containing opaque polyhedra. As such, they can only be considered as representing "perfect" models of real objects appearing in actual images. (*a*) Ideal step. (*b*) Ideal roof edge. (*c*) Combination of ideal step and ideal roof. (*d*) Spike edge.

depending on whether or not a background surface is being covered. A fifth category is the "contour edge," which delineates the border between an object and its background. This would have occurred in Figure 5.16*a*, *b*, *c*, or *d* if the scan had been continued to the extreme left or right of the polyhedron. In general, how to transform edge profiles into depth maps has not as yet been determined.

It has been suggested that certain specific profiles in the image may sometimes be linked to particular kinds of object surfaces in scenes [49, 26]. For example, a peak or a step with superimposed peak is probably the result of a convex edge. On the other hand, a roof or a step with a superimposed roof

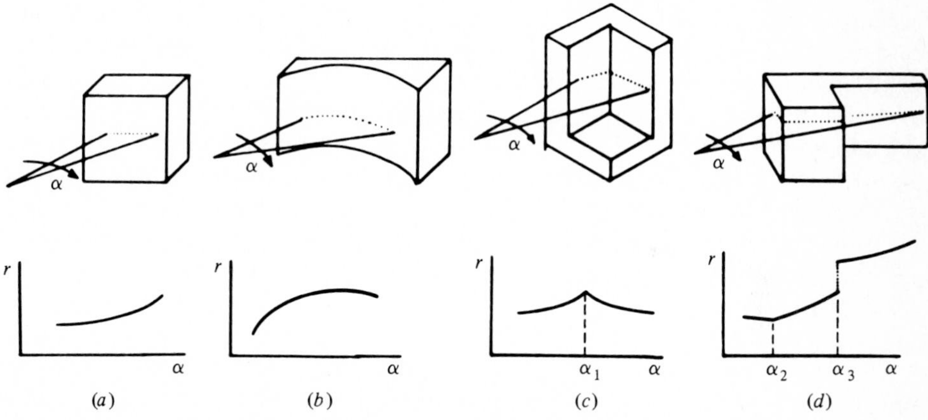

Figure 5.16 How depth maps inform about surface and edge structure. (Note that the viewing point is actually directly in front of the object but for convenience has been placed over to the left.) (*Adapted from W. F. Clocksin, "Perception of Surface Slant and Edge Labels from Optical Flow: A Computational Approach," Perception, vol. 9, 1980, pp. 253–269.*)

would most likely correspond to a concave edge. Finally a step, a negative peak, or a step with a superimposed negative peak occurs for both convex and concave edges in the original scene. It turns out that this situation is most frequent when one opaque polyhedron occludes another. It is quite evident that if we were able to characterize a whole series of profiles by a set of such inverse mappings, the problem of making the transformation from the input image back to the three-dimensional world from which it was obtained would be greatly simplified.

So much for the ideal cases; these are actually never found in real data. The latter exhibit variations from these models due to a combination of influences. One important aspect relates to the source of illumination. So-called illumination edges are attributed to the illumination of surfaces and are characterized by the position and orientation in three-dimensional space of the light source with respect to an object's surfaces [36, 37]. An example is a shadow. The edges in an image also depend on the spectral reflectivity of the surfaces in the three-dimensional scene, and these are referred to as "reflectivity edges" [10, 12, 37]. It is interesting that humans distinguish these two cases on the basis of the perceived spatial relationship between adjacent surfaces and not just the luminance pattern sensed by the retina [36, 37]. Another source of artifact depends on the type of input digitization mechanism employed. Thus, the digitizer may introduce a sufficient amount of noise to degrade our ability to classify the type of edge. The sampling process is another source of error because a fixed raster is used to observe the data, which most likely will contain edges and lines which are not parallel to the scanning axes. This may result in distortions. Finally, we mention an important source of variation which is particularly significant when dealing with natural scenes such as might be obtained outdoors. That is, most objects that we observe are not polyhedra but are characterized by surfaces which, when viewed, are seen to contain a whole range of gray-level variations superimposed upon them. We refer to this surface structure as "texture," and will discuss this in more detail in Chapter 9. The viewed texture will, of course, also be influenced by the type and orientation of the source of illumination, as well as by the arrangement of the objects in a scene. Figure 5.17 shows two examples of profiles taken on actual image data. The distinction between the idealizations we first spoke about and the actual data should be obvious to the reader.

Edges are important to animals and man and are also useful to computer vision systems. This is because they provide an excellent indication of the shape of the objects in a picture. Nevertheless they are often incomplete and degraded when compared with the abstract model. The question arises as to how man or machine should process this edge data. Marr [73] has suggested that this should be done by using a symbolic data representation rather than the original numerical output from an edge detector. To this end he associates a vector description with each edge element in the two-dimensional image. This vector contains information about the type of edge, the degree of contrast as given by the gradient, the position of the edge, its orientation, and its fuzziness.

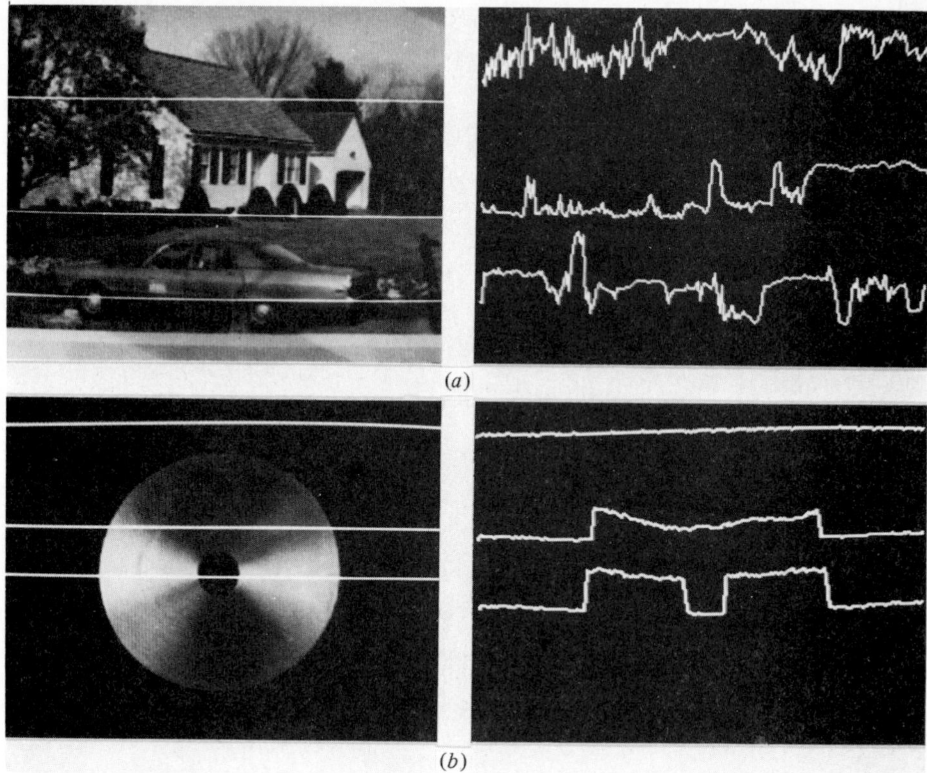

Figure 5.17 Examples of profiles taken from actual images. (*a*) Natural scene. (*b*) Man-made object.

The latter is meant to provide some information about the frequency content of the edge pattern under consideration. After applying an elementary edge detector, not too different from the one shown in Figure 5.2, Marr uses a set of simple rules for aggregating the edges into line segments. These rules are based on an examination of the compatibility of the symbolic edge descriptions in a local region. This new data array is termed the "primal sketch," an example of which is shown in Figure 5.18.

In the following sections we shall describe several of the more popular and useful edge detection techniques. We note from Figure 5.19*a* that these result in an image array $A(i, j)$ which is a measure of the discontinuities in the picture. We may refer to this output as the edge-enhanced array of the original input image. A second operation follows in the sequence, in which $A(i, j)$ is thresholded in order to obtain $E(i, j)$, the binary edge map (see Section 5.4.4). A primal sketch may simply be considered as a labeled edge map in which each edge element is described by a feature vector. Generally the two operations shown in the figure are treated independently. It is difficult, if not impossible, to characterize the quality of these computations as a means of obtaining

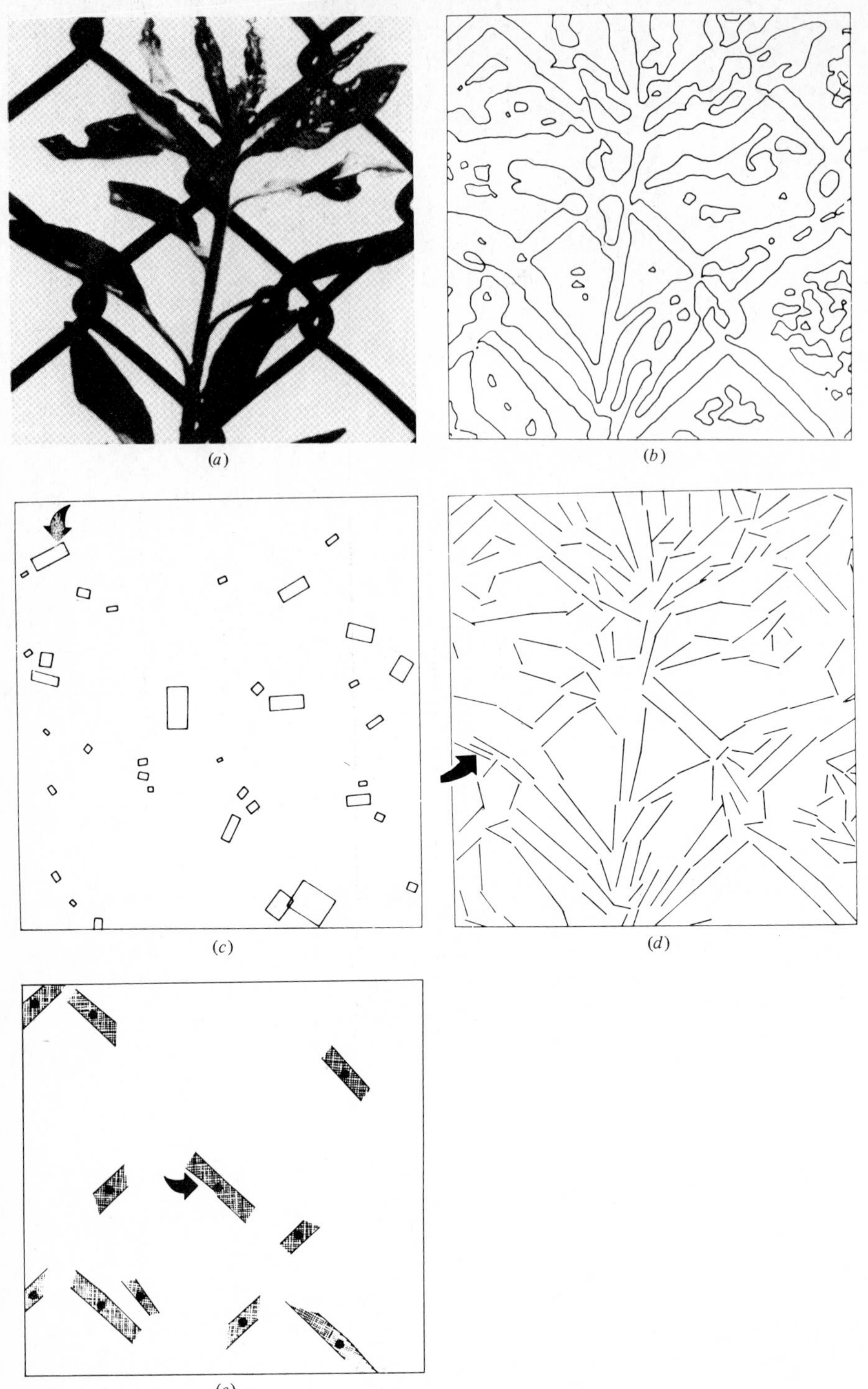
(a)
(b)
(c)
(d)
(e)

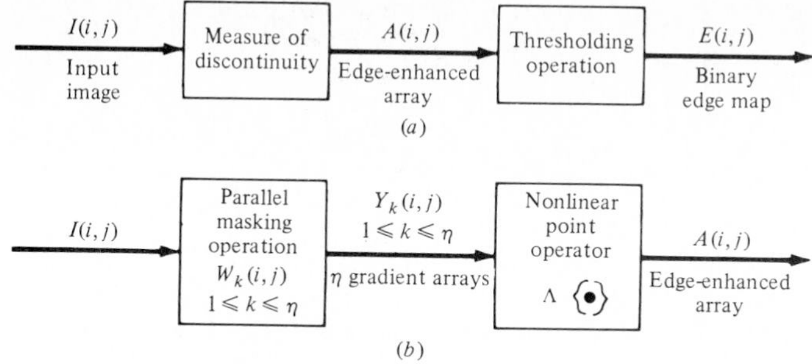

Figure 5.19 (*a*) A block diagram showing the two major processing steps needed to obtain the binary edge map from an input gray level image. Note that the primal sketch is equivalent to a labeled edge map. (*b*) For one class of edge-detection operators, the first block in (*a*) may be represented as a parallel masking operation in which η masks are applied to $I(i, j)$, resulting in η arrays $Y_k(i, j)$, $1 \leq k \leq \eta$. The nonlinear function $\Lambda\{\cdot\}$ of these η arrays yields the edge-enhanced array $A(i, j)$.

edges. In most cases the objective is not very clearly defined. Figures of merit for comparing different edge detectors can be found in [2, 14, 32, 34, 61, 93, 108].

Two types of discontinuity measurements will be considered. One is a parallel masking operation in which conceptually we can consider that a mask is simultaneously applied to the original image at each location (i, j). The second is a sequential process in which the edges are obtained by means of a graph search. Figure 5.19*b* shows the two elements of the parallel masking operation. Each edge detector in this category will be described by a set of templates $W_k(i, j)$ whose application results in a set of gradient arrays $Y_k(i, j)$, where $1 \leq k \leq \eta$. As shown in the figure, $A(i, j)$ is sometimes obtained by the

---

Figure 5.18 The primal sketch. Descriptors can be associated with patterns of lines, as indicated in (*c*), (*d*), and (*e*). The diagrams show only the spatial information contained in the descriptors. Typical examples of the full descriptors are:

BLOB	EDGE	BAR
(POSITION 146, 21) (ORIENTATION 105) (CONTRAST 76) (LENGTH 16) (WIDTH 6)	(POSITION 184, 23) (ORIENTATION 128) (CONTRAST −25) (LENGTH 25) (WIDTH 4)	(POSITION 118, 134) (ORIENTATION 128) (CONTRAST −25) (LENGTH 25) (WIDTH 4)

The descriptors to which these correspond are marked with arrows. The resolution of this analysis roughly corresponds to what a human would see when viewing it from a distance of about 6 ft. (*a*) Image. (*b*) Raw primal sketch. (*c*) Blobs. (*d*) Local orientations assigned to the edge segments. (*e*) Bars. [(*a*) *From D. Marr, "Vision," Freeman, San Francisco, 1982*; (*b through e*) *from D. Marr and E. Hildreth, "Theory of Edge Detection," Proceedings of the Royal Society* (*London*), *ser. B, vol. 207, 1980, pp. 187–217.*]

further application of a nonlinear point operator $\Lambda\{\cdot\}$. From the discussions in Chapter 2 we recall that the parallel masking operation is obtained by means of a cross-correlation operation:

$$Y_k(i, j) = W_k(i, j) * I(i, j) \tag{5.1}$$

The nonlinear point operation is given by

$$A(i, j) = \Lambda[Y_1(i, j), Y_2(i, j), \ldots, Y_\eta(i, j)] \tag{5.2}$$

The sequential masking techniques are not as easily described. In this case the templates are not applied uniformly but according to some prescribed search procedure.

Obviously edge detectors discussed in this section are local in nature and are usually obtained by using windows of size 3×3. However, once we have computed the edges, we may wish to collect them into longer edge segments or lines. Readers are referred to [58] for a survey of these techniques. We shall discuss this concept of aggregation in Chapters 8, 9, and 10.

5.4 PARALLEL SCANNING METHODS

5.4.1 Directional Differentiation

Edge detection in a discrete picture array may be conceptually linked to the process of differentiation of an analog signal. It is therefore not surprising that both one-dimensional and two-dimensional difference masks have been proposed for performing directional differentiation. For example, Figure 5.20*a* shows the simplest possible one-dimensional horizontal edge detector. In this case only one mask ($\eta = 1$) is applied at each (i, j), so that

$$\Lambda(i, j) = |Y_1(i, j)| \tag{5.3}$$

If the value of $\Lambda(i, j)$ is high, the implication is that a vertical edge exists, while low values indicate uniform areas. The obvious advantage of this method is that it is simple and quick. Figure 5.20*b* demonstrates the effect of applying the operator in the case of an ideal step profile, while Figure 5.20*c* shows its application to real pictures. In the ideal case the response is an impulse function which yields an unambiguous indication of the edge being modeled. Clearly, the real picture does not consist primarily of these models.

In order to reduce some of the effects of noise and perhaps pick out more of the global edges, we may use the mask shown in Figure 5.21*a*, which tends to spread out the response. This is demonstrated in Figure 5.21*b* for the ideal case and Figure 5.21*c* for real data. The amount of spreading is governed by the parameter Δ. Perhaps it would also make more sense to include both a W_1 (shown in Figures 5.20*a* and 5.21*a*) to detect vertical edges and a W_2 (W_1 rotated by 90°) to detect horizontal edges. The question then arises as to how the two responses should be combined.

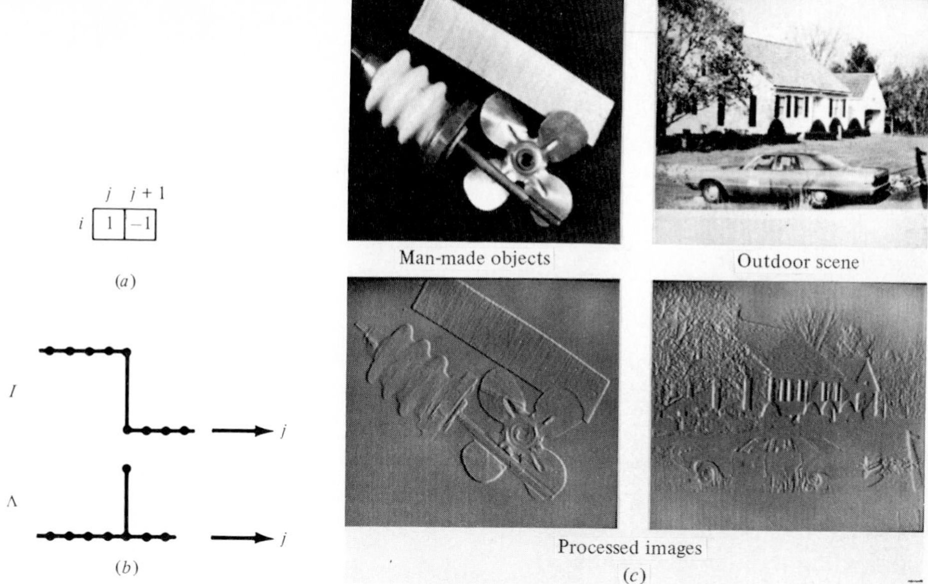

Figure 5.20 A one-dimensional horizontal edge detector. Note that positive and negative gradients are denoted by white and black gray levels, respectively. Zero response is associated with gray level 31. (*a*) Mask W_1. (*b*) Ideal profile. (*c*) Application of the operator to complex images.

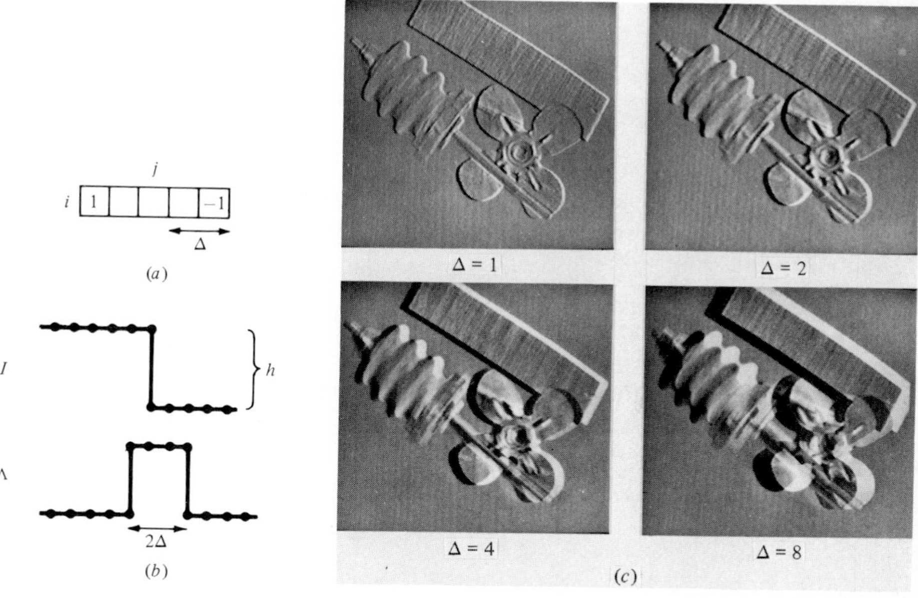

Figure 5.21 A variation of the one-dimensional filter shown in Figure 5.20. Positive and negative gradients are denoted by white and black gray levels, respectively. (*a*) Mask W_1. (*b*) Ideal profile. (*c*) Application of the operator.

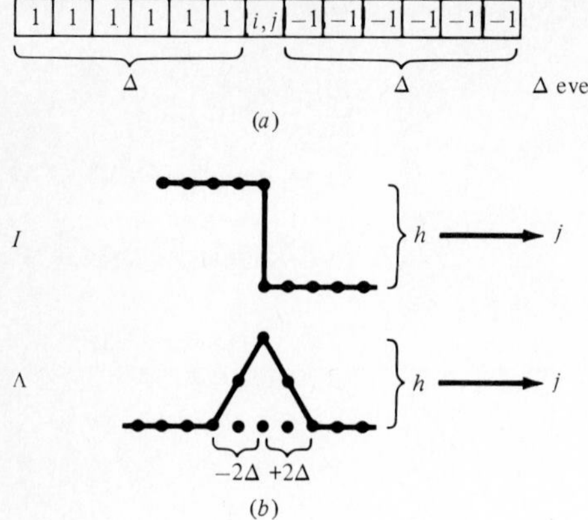

Figure 5.22 A one-dimensional horizontal averaging operator. (*a*) Mask W_1. (*b*) Ideal profile.

An extension of these ideas is shown in Figure 5.22, in which the noise is filtered out by averaging over Δ horizontal pixels (or vertical pixels in the case of the other kind of detector) on each side of the pixel of interest, and computing a difference. Then

$$\Lambda(i, j) = \frac{1}{\Delta} |Y_1| \tag{5.4}$$

Instead of an impulse function in the ideal case (see Figure 5.20) we now obtain a triangular pulse, still a good indicator of an edge. Noise effects are generally quite pervasive so that the two-dimensional $m \times n$ mask shown in Figure 5.23 might be more useful. In this case

$$\Lambda(i, j) = \frac{1}{mn} |Y_1| \tag{5.5}$$

There is a contradiction however. We would like to have small neighborhoods to detect the microedges in the picture and simultaneously large neighborhoods to filter out noise and surface irregularities. Thus we must find a size which is a compromise between these two opposing requirements. On the other hand, an alternative implication is that it would also be quite appropriate to

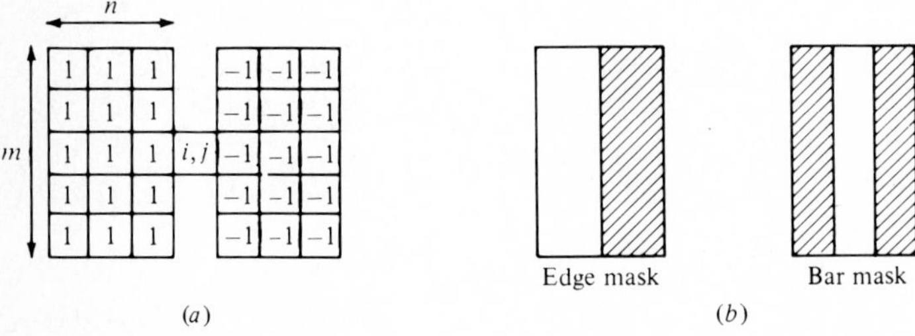

Figure 5.23 Two-dimensional edge operators which compute differences of the average response over a local neighborhood. (*a*) An $m \times n$ averaging mask. (*b*) Two masks for detecting linelike features.

determine the edge content using different window sizes. We shall observe in Sections 5.4.3 and 6.3 that there is some indication that the biological edge-detecting mechanism, discussed in the previous section, is constructed in this way. In any event, such a mask does evoke the edge and bar templates found in the visual cortex of the cat, for example. These are shown in Figure 5.23*b* and only require some "bookkeeping" to be made equivalent to the mask in Figure 5.23*a*. Marr [73] followed such operators by a process that searches for peaks of $\Lambda(i, j)$, which are then used to describe and group the edge segments in the picture. The resulting edge map with associated edge features is a primal sketch, an example of which has already been given in Figure 5.18.

The detection of peaks in $\Lambda(i, j)$ is equivalent to using a second-difference cutoff filter [48]. For the one-dimensional case, Figure 5.24*b* shows the result of computing the second difference, from which a function $F(x)$ may be determined. This function is the difference of means of points on each side of (i, j) which are Δ pixels apart. Thus if the second difference $D^2(x)$ is given by

$$D^2I(x) = -2I(x) + I(x+\Delta) + I(x-\Delta) \tag{5.6}$$

then $F(x)$ is defined by

$$F(x) = \frac{1}{\Delta}\left[\sum_{i=1}^{\Delta} D^2I(x+i) - \sum_{i=1}^{\Delta} D^2I(x-i)\right] \tag{5.7}$$

As shown in Figure 5.24*c*, $F(x)$ exhibits a strong peak in the neighborhood of a vertical edge.

In order to make this edge detector more sensitive, we select a two-dimensional neighborhood on the left (L) and the right (R) of the pixel of interest in which the function $F(x)$ is computed over every profile. If we then apply a threshold or cutoff to $F(x)$, we obtain the second-difference cutoff filter. The detector is based on the difference between the number of pixels with $F(x)$ above the cutoff minus the number of pixels with $F(x)$ below cutoff for each region. This number is then used to form a difference between L and R. Using the template in Figure 5.24*d* and a neighborhood size of $\eta \times \Delta$, the windows in R are given by

$$W_{i,j+1}(i,j), \ldots\ldots\ldots, W_{i,j+\Delta}(i,j) \qquad i = 1, \ldots, \eta$$

and in L by

$$W_{i,j-1}(i,j), \ldots\ldots\ldots, W_{i,j-\Delta}(i,j) \qquad i = 1, \ldots, \eta$$

Then

$$\Lambda(i,j) = \underbrace{\sum_{q=1}^{\eta}\sum_{p=1}^{\Delta} \operatorname{sign}[Y_{q,j+p}(i,j)]}_{R} - \underbrace{\sum_{q=1}^{\eta}\sum_{p=1}^{\Delta} \operatorname{sign}[Y_{q,j-p}(i,j)]}_{L}\,. \tag{5.8}$$

An example of the application of this detector is given in Figure 5.24*e*.

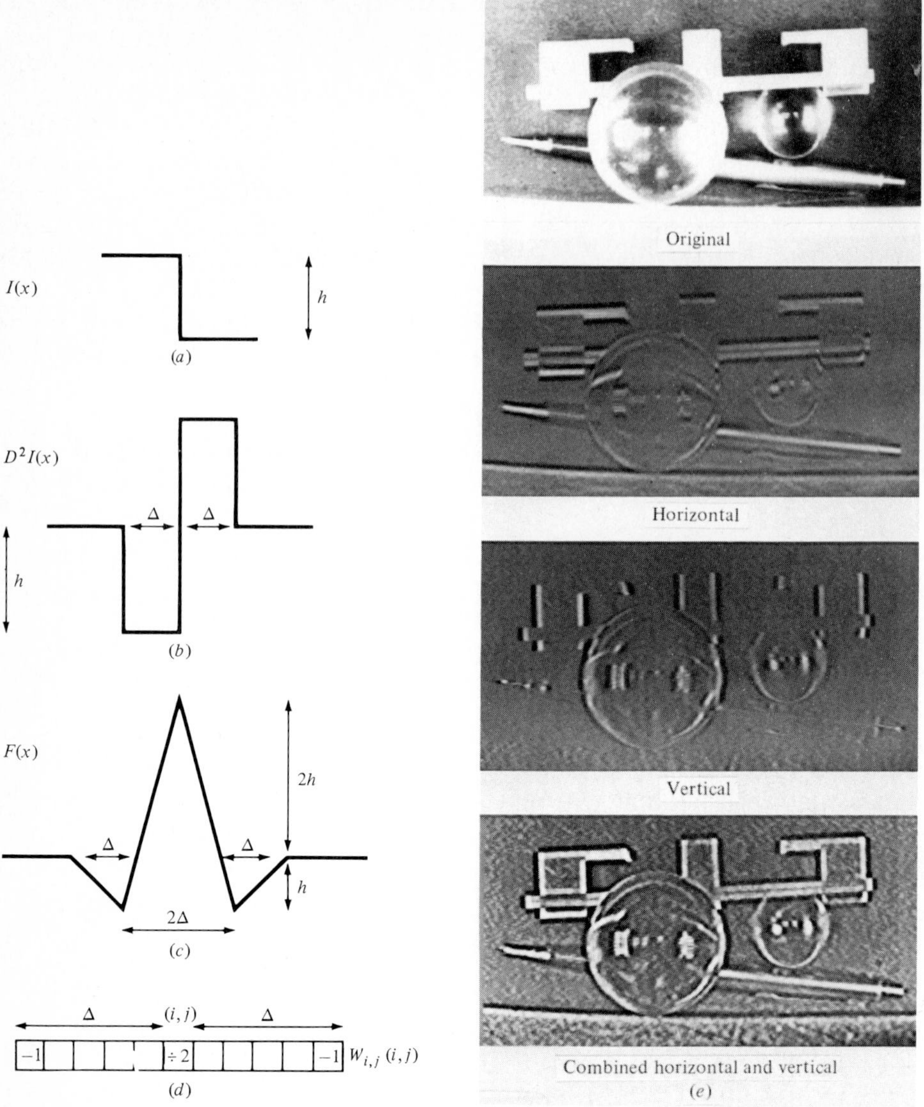

Figure 5.24 The second difference cutoff filter. (*a*) An ideal edge profile. (*b*) Second difference. (*c*) The output of the function $F(x)$ for the ideal step profile. (*d*) The equivalent template window for implementing the function $F(x)$ in (*c*). This mask is slid horizontally and vertically within both L and R. (*e*) An example of the application of the second-difference cutoff filter. Extrema are denoted by white gray levels.

Directional differentiation of the type discussed in this section is only an example of a general class of edge operators defined by masks. In the next section we shall examine certain of the more useful and popular mask operators.

5.4.2 Mask Operators

Many of the edge operators which have been suggested have originated in research dealing with the analysis of opaque polyhedra. The first significant paper on this topic was due to Roberts [97], who employed a simple 2×2 operator to enhance the edges of solids.

> Three main criteria can be used to judge such an operation. The edges produced should be as sharp as possible, the background should produce as little noise as possible, and the intensity of the lines produced should correspond closely to a human's ability to perceive the edge in the original picture (p. 168).

Figure 5.25*a* shows the two masks of the so-called Roberts cross operator, which are responsible for the output of a horizontal and vertical component. The nonlinear point operator $\Lambda(i, j)$ may be computed using either

$$\Lambda(i, j) = \{[Y_1(i, j)^2] + [Y_2(i, j)^2]\}^{1/2} \tag{5.9}$$

$$\Lambda(i, j) = \max\{|Y_1(i, j)|, |Y_2(i, j)|\} \tag{5.10}$$

or

$$\Lambda(i, j) = \{|Y_1(i, j)| + |Y_2(i, j)|\} \tag{5.11}$$

the latter two equations being more efficient. The angle $\theta(i, j)$, with respect to the horizontal, of output array $A(i, j)$ may be obtained from

$$\theta(i, j) = \frac{\pi}{4} + \tan^{-1}\frac{Y_2(i, j)}{Y_1(i, j)} \tag{5.12}$$

An example of its application is given in Figure 5.25*a*. The local angle measurement is seen to be a weak indicator of edge orientation.

Note that the one-dimensional operators in the previous section also yield both horizontal and vertical components, so that the same relationship for $\theta(i, j)$ could have been involved. The Roberts cross operator detects both horizontal and vertical edges but is sensitive to noise and object surface irregularities. It has been used in computerized tomography to detect edges in three-dimensional object space [72] and for color edge detection in the three-dimensional color space [106]. Other references which discuss three-dimensional edge detection are [5, 56, 86, 96, 98, 118].

The Sobel operator [23] was designed to approximate the discrete gradient function by computation of the appropriate horizontal and vertical components. Figure 5.25*b* shows the two masks, where it should be noted, in this case as in all others, that the sum of the weights is always zero. Also the weights reflect the proximity of a particular pixel to (i, j). The function $\Lambda(i, j)$ is the same as for the Roberts operator [Equation (5.9)] and the angle is given by

$$\theta(i, j) = \tan^{-1}\left[\frac{Y_2(i, j)}{Y_1(i, j)}\right] \tag{5.13}$$

An example of the application of this window operator is given in Figure 5.25*b*. It has been used in the automatic visual inspection of valve spring assemblies on engine heads [92].

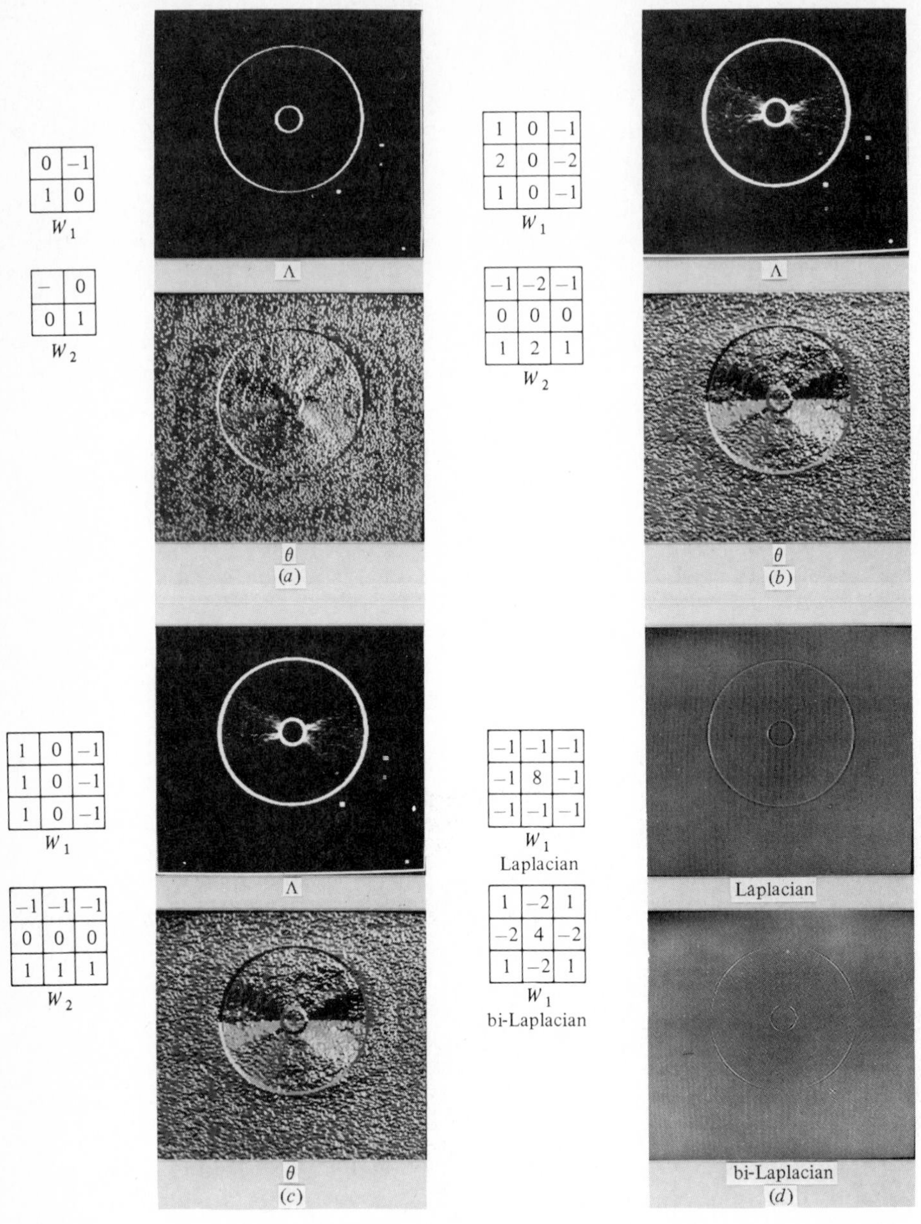

Figure 5.25 A selection of mask operators. The original input image is shown in Figure 5.17*b*. High gradient is represented by white gray levels. The scale for θ is such that the angle varies from 0° to 360° as the gray level changes from black to white. (*a*) The 2D masks for the Roberts cross operator. (*b*) The two Sobel masks, which compute the vertical and horizontal components of the gradient. (*c*) The two masks for the Prewitt operator. (*d*) Laplacian operators suggested in [94].

The Sobel operator estimates the partial derivative in the two directions and is slightly more complex than the Roberts operator. A variation of this detector is the Prewitt operator (see Figure 5.25*c*), in which the 2s are all replaced by 1s [94]. It was derived by fitting a quadratic surface over an arbitrary 3×3 neighborhood by a least-squares approximation. The gradient of the resulting surface is then embodied by the masks shown.

Instead of taking a set of directional masks as done by Roberts and Sobel, it is also possible to employ a scalar, isotropic (omnidirectional) edge detector. Prewitt [94] suggests the use of the Laplacian operator

$$\nabla^2 = \frac{\partial^2}{\partial x^2} + \frac{\partial^2}{\partial y^2} \tag{5.14}$$

or bi-Laplacian operator

$$\nabla^4 = \frac{\partial^4}{\partial x^2 \partial y^2} \tag{5.15}$$

Both these sharpening filters are shown in Figure 5.25*d*. It is interesting that one of the earliest projects in digital image processing employed a Laplacian operator in sequence with a simple contour follower to find the outlines in a picture [64, 65].

The directionally selective operators discussed above compute $\theta(i, j)$ by means of mask contributions in two directions. An alternative approach is to employ compass gradient masks in order to directly find the best orientation [99]. This requires the application of eight parallel masks ($\eta = 8$) at each location (i, j), where each mask is just the rotated version of a standard operator. The orientations are shown in Figure 5.26*a*, where the compass names indicate the direction of maximum response; this eight-direction 3-bit chain code for defining the orientation of an edge element was originally suggested in [33]. Although the sketch indicates a 3×3 window, the mask could be of any dimension but is usually not much greater. Figure 5.26*b* illustrates four different types of masks of this genre. The first and third (see Figure 5.25*c*) columns are due to Prewitt [94], and the second is due to Kirsch [60], who proposed this as a homogeneity operator. It is quite sensitive to small changes in gradient and generally tends to be superior to other methods in comparison trials. The last column is just the Sobel operator, where W_1 and W_3 approximate the partial derivatives in the horizontal and vertical directions, respectively. The use of zero weights along the edge for this operator tends to suppress jitter. Also, in comparison to the first two operators, the last two actually require only four masks as a result of their symmetry. Thus, for example, if $W_1 > 0$, the edge direction is E; if $W_1 < 0$, the edge direction is W. These operators are defined by

$$\Lambda(i, j) = \max\{|Y_1(i, j)|, \ldots, |Y_8(i, j)|\} \tag{5.16}$$

and

$$\theta(i, j) = \text{compass direction of largest } Y_k \tag{5.17}$$

An example of the application of compass masks is shown in Figure 5.26*c*.

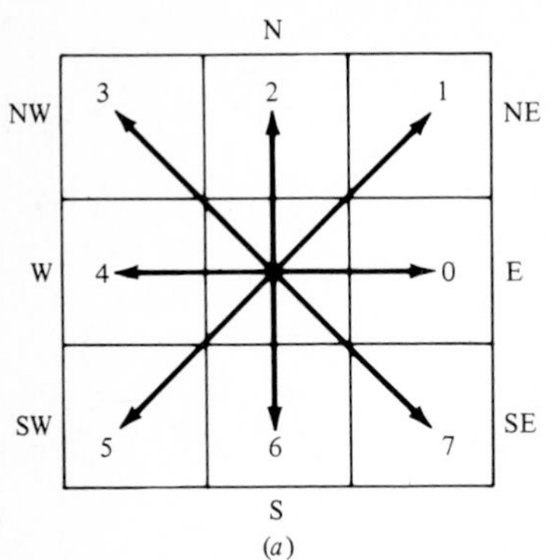

(a)

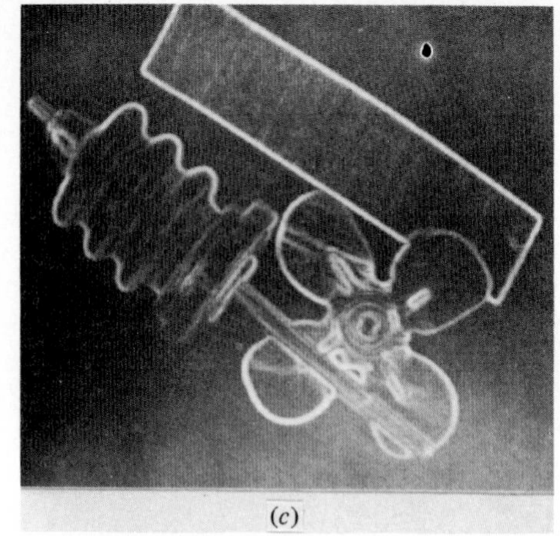
(c)

Direction of edge	Direction of gradient	Prewitt operator	Kirsch operator	Prewitt operator	Sobel operator	
0	N	$\begin{bmatrix} 1 & 1 & 1 \\ 1 & -2 & 1 \\ -1 & -1 & -1 \end{bmatrix}$	$\begin{bmatrix} 5 & 5 & 5 \\ -3 & 0 & -3 \\ -3 & -3 & -3 \end{bmatrix}$	$\begin{bmatrix} 1 & 1 & 1 \\ 0 & 0 & 0 \\ -1 & -1 & -1 \end{bmatrix}$	$\begin{bmatrix} 1 & 2 & 1 \\ 0 & 0 & 0 \\ -1 & -2 & -1 \end{bmatrix}$	W_1
1	NW	$\begin{bmatrix} 1 & 1 & 1 \\ 1 & -2 & -1 \\ 1 & -1 & -1 \end{bmatrix}$	$\begin{bmatrix} 5 & 5 & -3 \\ 5 & 0 & -3 \\ -3 & -3 & -3 \end{bmatrix}$	$\begin{bmatrix} 1 & 1 & 0 \\ 1 & 0 & -1 \\ 0 & -1 & -1 \end{bmatrix}$	$\begin{bmatrix} 2 & 1 & 0 \\ 1 & 0 & -1 \\ 0 & -1 & -2 \end{bmatrix}$	W_2
2	W	$\begin{bmatrix} 1 & 1 & -1 \\ 1 & -2 & -1 \\ 1 & 1 & -1 \end{bmatrix}$	$\begin{bmatrix} 5 & -3 & -3 \\ 5 & 0 & -3 \\ 5 & -3 & -3 \end{bmatrix}$	$\begin{bmatrix} 1 & 0 & -1 \\ 1 & 0 & -1 \\ 1 & 0 & -1 \end{bmatrix}$	$\begin{bmatrix} 1 & 0 & -1 \\ 2 & 0 & -2 \\ 1 & 0 & -1 \end{bmatrix}$	W_3
3	SW	$\begin{bmatrix} 1 & -1 & -1 \\ 1 & -2 & -1 \\ 1 & 1 & 1 \end{bmatrix}$	$\begin{bmatrix} -3 & -3 & -3 \\ 5 & 0 & -3 \\ 5 & 5 & -3 \end{bmatrix}$	$\begin{bmatrix} 0 & -1 & -1 \\ 1 & 0 & -1 \\ 1 & 1 & 0 \end{bmatrix}$	$\begin{bmatrix} 0 & -1 & -2 \\ 1 & 0 & -1 \\ 2 & 1 & 0 \end{bmatrix}$	W_4
4	S	$\begin{bmatrix} -1 & -1 & -1 \\ 1 & -2 & 1 \\ 1 & 1 & 1 \end{bmatrix}$	$\begin{bmatrix} -3 & -3 & -3 \\ -3 & 0 & -3 \\ 5 & 5 & 5 \end{bmatrix}$	$\begin{bmatrix} -1 & -1 & -1 \\ 0 & 0 & 0 \\ 1 & 1 & 1 \end{bmatrix}$	$\begin{bmatrix} -1 & -2 & -1 \\ 0 & 0 & 0 \\ 1 & 2 & 1 \end{bmatrix}$	W_5
5	SE	$\begin{bmatrix} -1 & -1 & 1 \\ -1 & -2 & 1 \\ 1 & 1 & 1 \end{bmatrix}$	$\begin{bmatrix} -3 & -3 & -3 \\ -3 & 0 & 5 \\ -3 & 5 & 5 \end{bmatrix}$	$\begin{bmatrix} -1 & -1 & 0 \\ -1 & 0 & 1 \\ 0 & 1 & 1 \end{bmatrix}$	$\begin{bmatrix} -2 & -1 & 0 \\ -1 & 0 & 1 \\ 0 & 1 & 2 \end{bmatrix}$	W_6
6	E	$\begin{bmatrix} -1 & 1 & 1 \\ -1 & -2 & 1 \\ -1 & 1 & 1 \end{bmatrix}$	$\begin{bmatrix} -3 & -3 & 5 \\ -3 & 0 & 5 \\ -3 & -3 & 5 \end{bmatrix}$	$\begin{bmatrix} -1 & 0 & 1 \\ -1 & 0 & 1 \\ -1 & 0 & 1 \end{bmatrix}$	$\begin{bmatrix} -1 & 0 & 1 \\ -2 & 0 & 2 \\ -1 & 0 & 1 \end{bmatrix}$	W_7
7	NE	$\begin{bmatrix} 1 & 1 & 1 \\ -1 & -2 & 1 \\ -1 & -1 & 1 \end{bmatrix}$	$\begin{bmatrix} -3 & 5 & 5 \\ -3 & 0 & 5 \\ -3 & -3 & -3 \end{bmatrix}$	$\begin{bmatrix} 0 & 1 & 1 \\ -1 & 0 & 1 \\ -1 & -1 & 0 \end{bmatrix}$	$\begin{bmatrix} 0 & 1 & 2 \\ -1 & 0 & 1 \\ -2 & -1 & 0 \end{bmatrix}$	W_8

(b)

Figure 5.26 Edge detection using compass gradient operators. (*a*) The compass directions. (*b*) Four sets of masks for computing the compass gradient. (*c*) Applying each of the four operators shown in (*b*) results in four very similar output arrays. An example is shown above. [(*a*) *From H. Freeman, "Boundary Encoding and Processing," in B. S. Lipkin and A. Rosenfeld (eds.), "Picture Processing and Psychopictorics," Academic, New York, 1970, pp. 241–266*; (*b*) *From G. S. Robinson, "Edge Detection by Compass Gradient Masks, Computer Graphics and Image Processing, vol. 6, no. 5, October 1977, pp. 492–501.*]

The compass-gradient edge operators require a considerable amount of time on a sequential computer. Parallel-processing hardware of the type referred to in Chapter 2 makes this approach practical.

An interesting variation of the application of a set of orientation-selective templates at each pixel in the picture is the Hueckel operator [13, 54, 55]. The latter uses an explicit ideal edge model defined within a circular region, which is then fitted to the pictorial data. Of course it should be understood that all mask operators assume some underlying data model for the edges in the image [42].

Rather than applying the model directly, both it and the data can be approximated by an orthogonal expansion in terms of a set of basis functions. A mean-square-error fit then results in an "edge goodness" variable computed from the model parameters, and this factor can be employed to decide whether or not an edge segment actually exists in the selected neighborhood. The

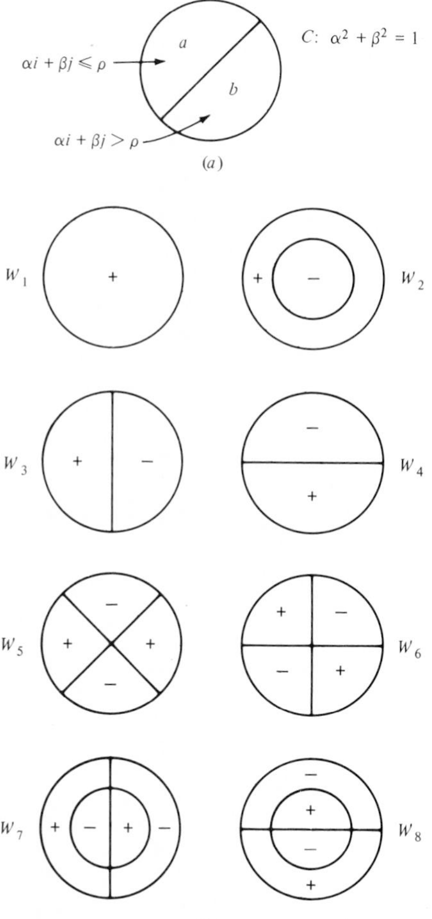

Figure 5.27 [(*c*) *and caption on page 186.*]

Hueckel approach is an order of magnitude slower computationally than a simple 3×3 gradient operator.

The model $M(i, j)$ shown in Figure 5.27*a* is a step function (see Figure 5.15*a*) oriented arbitrarily within a circular region C. In order to maintain the circularity assumption, C must be relatively large, so the smallest number of elements used by Hueckel was 32 [54]. Define a model parameter vector $\mathbf{p} = [\alpha, \beta, \rho, a, b]^T$, where α, β, and ρ delineate the two regions constituting the step and a and b are their respective gray levels. Given an image $I(i, j)$, we then wish to select $\mathbf{p}$ to minimize the error criterion

$$E = \sum_{i,j \in C} \sum [I(i, j) - M(i, j)]^2 \tag{5.18}$$

An edge with the model defined by $\mathbf{p} = \mathbf{p}^*$ is accepted if the error E is less than some threshold.

The minimization is not performed directly. Both $I(i, j)$ and $M(i, j)$ are first represented in terms of a set of orthogonal basis functions $W_k(i, j)$. These templates, shown in Figure 5.27*b*, essentially yield a Fourier series expansion in

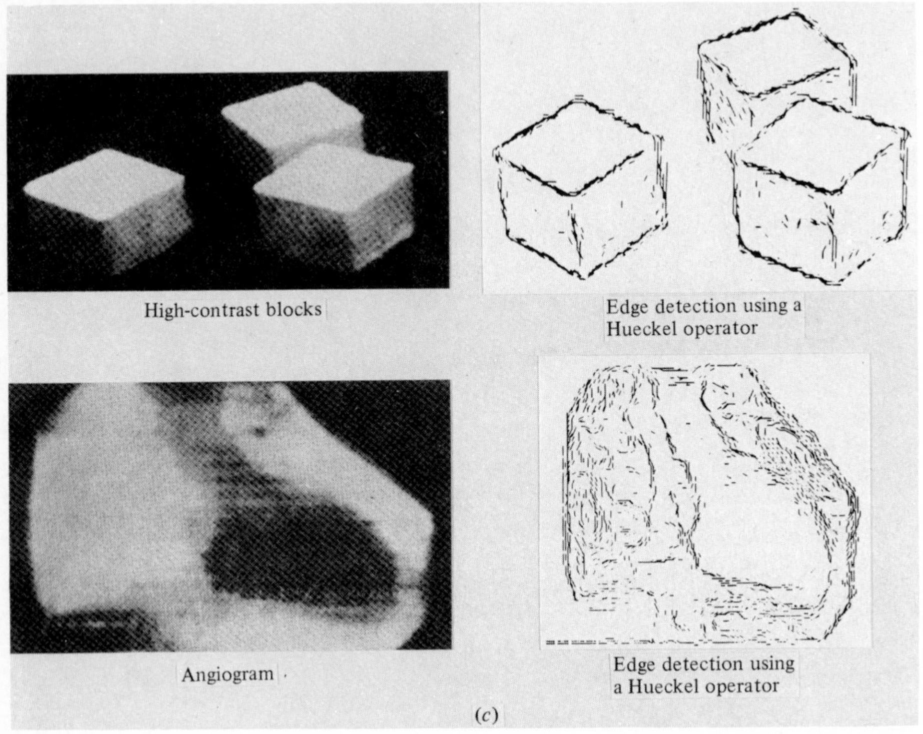

Figure 5.27 Examples of the application of the Hueckel operator. (*a*) The model $M(i, j)$ of the edge data, consisting of a step function within a circular disk. (*b*) The eight templates obtained by Hueckel. (*c*) Edge detection. (*From B. Bullock, "The Performance of Edge Operators on Images with Texture," Technical Report, Hughes Research Laboratories, Malibu, Calif., October 1974.*)

polar coordinates, truncated to eight terms. Thus this algorithm can also be considered in terms of the basic formalism shown in Figure 5.19*b*, where

$$Y_k(i,j) = I(i,j) * W_k(i,j), \ k = 1, \dots, 8 \tag{5.19}$$

The approximated image $\bar{I}(i,j)$ is then given by the function

$$\bar{I}(i,j) = \sum_{k=1}^{8} Y_k(i,j) W_k(i,j) \tag{5.20}$$

The model $M(i,j)$ may also be approximated in the same way by use of the same eight basis functions; thus

$$M_k(i,j) = M(i,j) * W_k(i,j) \tag{5.21}$$

so that

$$\bar{M}(i,j) = \sum_{k=1}^{8} M_k(i,j) W_k(i,j) \tag{5.22}$$

Having represented both the model and the data by an eight-vector of coefficients, the minimization problem now becomes one of selecting $\mathbf{p}$ such that

$$E = \sum_{k=1}^{8} (Y_k - M_k)^2 \tag{5.23}$$

is minimized at each pixel location. The number of terms in the expansion governs the accuracy of the approximation and, equivalently, how close to $E = 0$ we can get for a given $\mathbf{p} = \mathbf{p}^*$. The measure of goodness of the match is obtained by calculating the cosine of the angle between $Y_k(i,j)$ and $M_k(i,j)$. A perfect match exists when this parameter equals unity, and the edge is rejected as being too noisy for values less than 0.9.

This process of computing $\mathbf{p}^*$ embodies the second stage shown in Figure 5.19*b*, that is, the computation of $\Lambda\{\cdot\}$. Hueckel [54, 55] showed that E can be minimized by considering an equivalent problem. This involves first finding the extremum of another function $e(\alpha, \beta)$, which is solely dependent on the two variables α and β. Also, since C is defined by $\alpha^2 + \beta^2 = 1$, one of these variables is therefore fixed and $e(\alpha, \beta)$ may be minimized by one-dimensional numerical optimization techniques to yield α and β. Then a, b, and ρ can be computed by using a set of simple algebraic equations, finally yielding $\mathbf{p}^*$. An example of the application of the Hueckel operator is shown in Figure 5.27*c*.

Hueckel argued that truncation of the series expansion to eight terms is justified because the higher frequency components may be neglected as noise. However, Abdou [1] has shown that the error incurred is indeed significant for the orthogonal functions in Figure 5.27*b*. Perhaps another set would be superior. In addition he has claimed that the computational procedure involving $e(\alpha, \beta)$ resulted in a suboptimal solution. Shaw [108] has also discussed this problem.

O'Gorman [88] has employed Walsh functions as his set of orthogonal basis functions with the hope that these would better fit the model M. He concluded that all except the first Walsh function (a simple edge template similar to W_4 in Figure 5.27*b*, except placed within a square window) could be neglected since the regions of the model were uniform. Hummel [56] used a Karhunen-Loève expansion for his approximation. Other variations may be found in [24, 80, 83, 85]. In general it is feasible to select an arbitrary set of orthogonal basis functions which attempt to model certain distinctive edge characteristics [34]. Ramer [95] has used the Hueckel edge-element operator as the basis for detecting short line segments. It is also interesting that Rosenfeld [100, 101] has shown that the simplest Hueckel operator within a square 2×2 window is in fact the Roberts operator. The converse is discussed in [3].

In this section we have considered edge detectors whose design was based on spatial domain considerations. Next we shall examine an alternative approach, one in which the set of masks is related to the spatial frequency content of the image.

5.4.3 Multichannel Methods

In this section we shall discuss methods of edge detection which presuppose that the image contains gray-level variations occurring at different spatial frequencies. This assumption is usually borne out by any realistic imagery and is consistent with linear signal theory. An early reference to this possibility is the paper by Graham [38]. While dealing with an image communication system, he suggested that the picture be separated into low- and high-frequency channels; the data for the latter were obtained by using a Laplacian operator. Efficiencies could be achieved by transmitting these signals independently. Generally it seems that some of the edges are small and local in nature; others are large and coarser. One solution to this implied problem is to use different size masks at each pixel location in the image in order to detect a range of edge elements.

The method of expanding masks, which is due to Rosenfeld and his colleagues [102, 104, 105], is such an approach. It is simply an extension of the techniques described in the previous sections, essentially measuring a set of first differences of average responses. A set of masks of dimension $2^n \times 2^n$, $n = 0, 1, \ldots,$ is selected, although experiments have indicated that the size of these masks is not crucial to the results. Since the masks have sizes that are powers of 2, the pair of differencing neighborhoods required for each differential mask cannot be symmetrical with respect to (i, j).

Instead of the conventional masking process we have suggested here, it is also feasible to employ a data-shifting process to compute the averages. For masks of sizes $1, 2, 4, 8, \ldots, 2^{N-1}$, we require $2N$ shifts and additions to compute the N local averages; then the differences can be computed by a shift of 2^{N-1} and pointwise subtraction. Parallel processing could obviously greatly enhance the speed of this computation.

Edges can occur at different orientations so that each size mask at each (i, j) must also be rotated in order to take this into account. Only four different masks are required because of symmetry: H horizontal; V vertical; $D1$, $D2$ diagonal. The equations for the set of expanding masks in the horizontal direction are given by $W_{k,H}(i, j)$:

$$
\begin{aligned}
W_{k,H}(i,j) = \{W(p,q) | W(p,q) &= -1, p = i, q = j+1\,; \\
W(p,q) &= +1, p = i, q = j\} \qquad n = 0 \\
W_{k,H}(i,j) = \{W(p,q) | W(p,q) &= -1, i - 2^{n-1} \leq p \leq i + 2^{n-1} - 1\,, \\
& j + 1 \leq q \leq j + 2^n\,; \\
W(p,q) &= +1, i - 2^{n-1} \leq p \leq i + 2^{n-1} - 1\,, \\
& j \leq q \leq j - 2^n + 1\} \qquad n \geq 1
\end{aligned}
\tag{5.24}
$$

The response to the other masks, $W_{k,V}(i, j)$, $W_{k,D_1}(i, j)$, and $W_{k,D_2}(i, j)$, is obtained by rotating the picture by $-90°$, $45°$, and $-45°$, respectively, and then using Equation (5.24) in each case.

Two different approaches to edge detection may be pursued at this point. One is referred to as edge sharpening since it tends to enhance changes in gray level. For example, considering the horizontal direction, let

$$\{W_k(i,j)\} = \{W_{n,H}, n = 0, 1, \ldots, N\} \tag{5.25}$$

be the set of masks. Then, using a multiplicative detector, we obtain as the output of the first stage of processing (see Figure 5.19*b*):

$$\Lambda_H(i,j) = |Y_{0,H}(i,j)|\,|Y_{1,H}(i,j)| \cdots |Y_{N,H}(i,j)| \tag{5.26}$$

Thus $A_H(i, j)$ will be large only in the situation in which where all the outputs of the masks are large. The inclusion of large neighborhoods ensures the detection of the major edges and has the effect of rejecting noise. Small neighborhoods will make $A_H(i, j)$ large only near an edge. Figure 5.28 shows an example of the application of this type of product operator.

The second approach involves the detection of edges in all four directions and is therefore more useful. Let the output from each application of a template of size n at orientation θ be $Y_{n,\theta}(i, j)$. Then the nonlinear function $\Lambda(i, j)$ is given by the following [104, 105]:

1. For each $n = 0, 1, \ldots, N$, select the best orientation θ_n^* from the set

   $$\theta = \{H, V, D_1, D_2\}$$

   such that
   $$Y_{n,\theta_n^*} = \max_\theta \{|Y_{n,\theta}|\} \tag{5.27}$$

2. Select the best $n = n^*$; that is, the largest n for which

   $$|Y_{n,\theta_n^*} - Y_{n-1,\theta_n^*}| \leq \epsilon (\epsilon \text{ small}) \tag{5.28}$$

   thereby yielding

   $$Y_{n^*,\theta_{n^*}^*}.$$

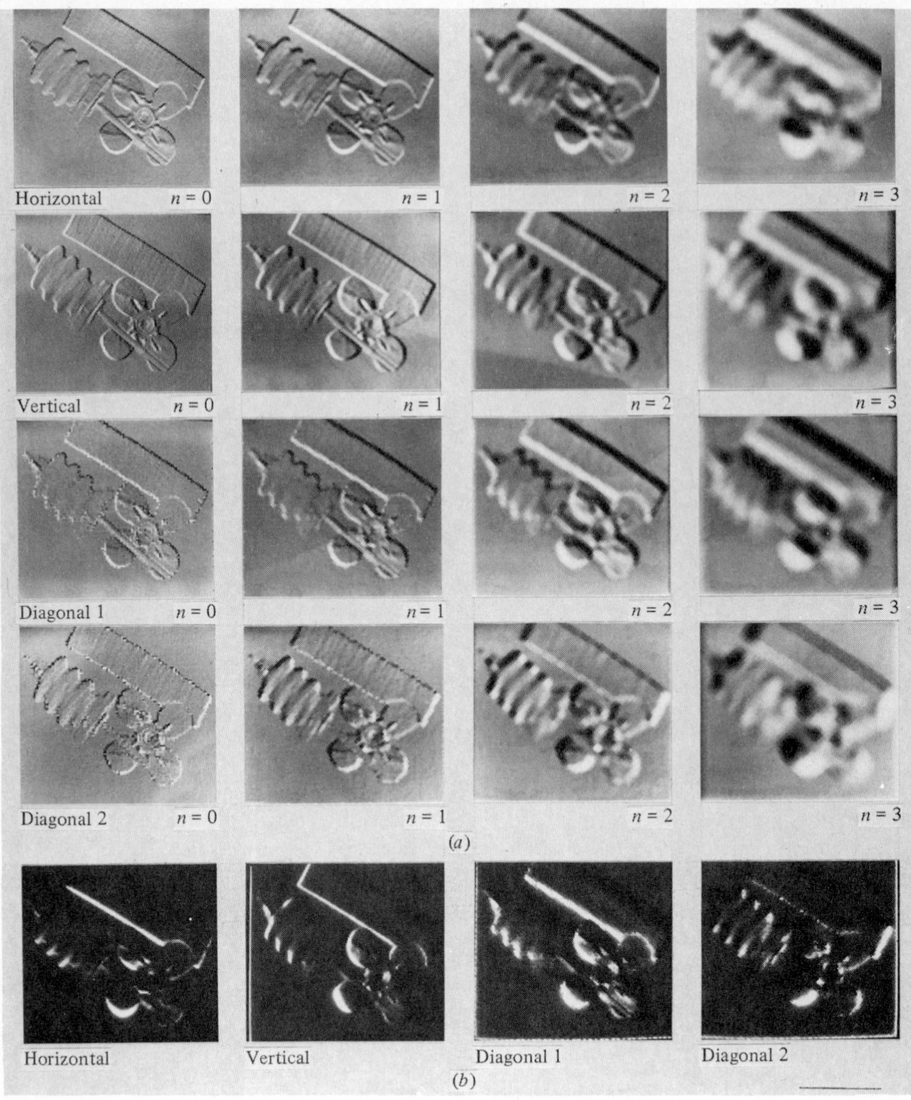

Figure 5.28 Examples of the application of the product operator version of the method of expanding masks. (*a*) Individual mask outputs. (*b*) Result of computing the product of each set of four outputs shown in (*a*).

A third step in which nonmaxima are suppressed may also be included [104, 105].

For edges existing between textured areas it is quite possible for a particular template $W(i, j)$ to yield zero output even though a conspicuous edge is visible. This may be overcome by first applying the method of expanding masks not to $I(i, j)$ but to a transformed image array $I'(i, j)$. The latter would have to represent the value of the texture in the image at a given pixel location (i, j). As we shall see later in Chapter 9, a given texture measure outputs a value at each point (i, j) which is related to the gray-level texture in a local neighborhood. A simple example might be the number of edge elements per unit area where the edges could be obtained by application of the Roberts cross operator. Rosenfeld and Thurston [104] demonstrate how this approach is able to extract global edges embedded in a picture array containing many small edge elements.

A generalization of this theory, which is sympathetic to certain biological considerations, has been presented by Marr and Hildreth [74]. They propose as an optimal smoothing filter a Gaussian operator (see [62] for a different filter function). In one dimension the Fourier transform pair is given by:

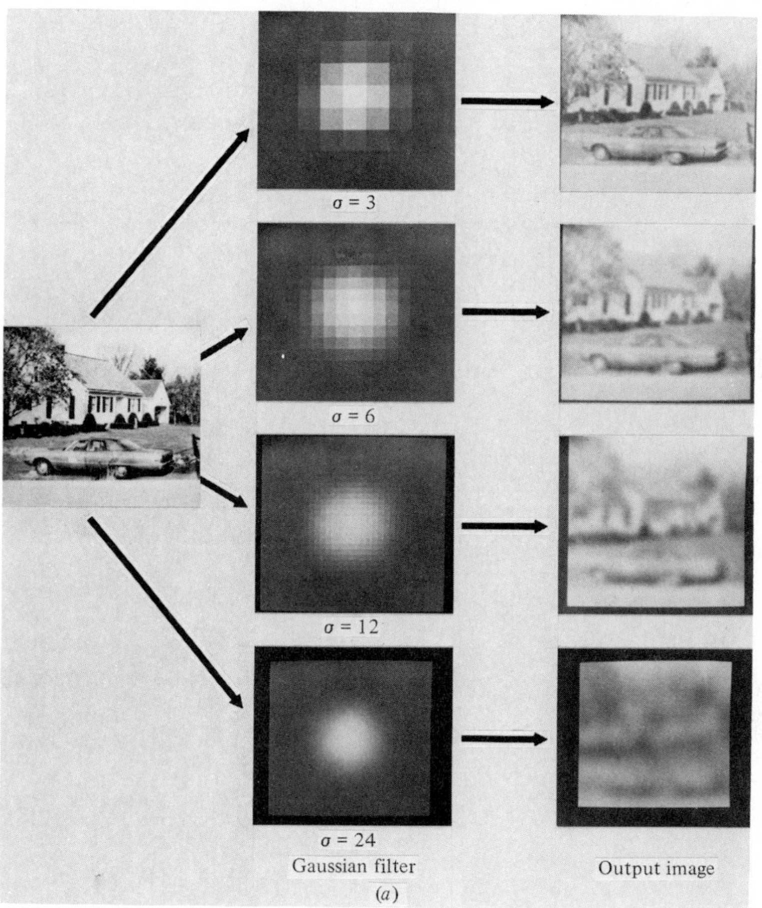

Figure 5.29 [(*b*) *and caption on page 192.*]

$$W'(i) = \frac{1}{2\pi\sigma^2} \exp\left[-\frac{i^2}{2\sigma^2}\right]$$

$$\mathscr{F}[W'(\omega)] = \exp[-\sigma^2\omega^2] \tag{5.29}$$

The two-dimensional version, given as a function of the radius r, can be computed by:

$$W'(r) = -\frac{1}{2\pi\sigma^2} \exp\left[-\frac{r^2}{2\sigma^2}\right] \tag{5.30}$$

Figure 5.29a shows the result of smoothing an image by using Gaussian filters with different values of σ. We note that the level of detail in each of the

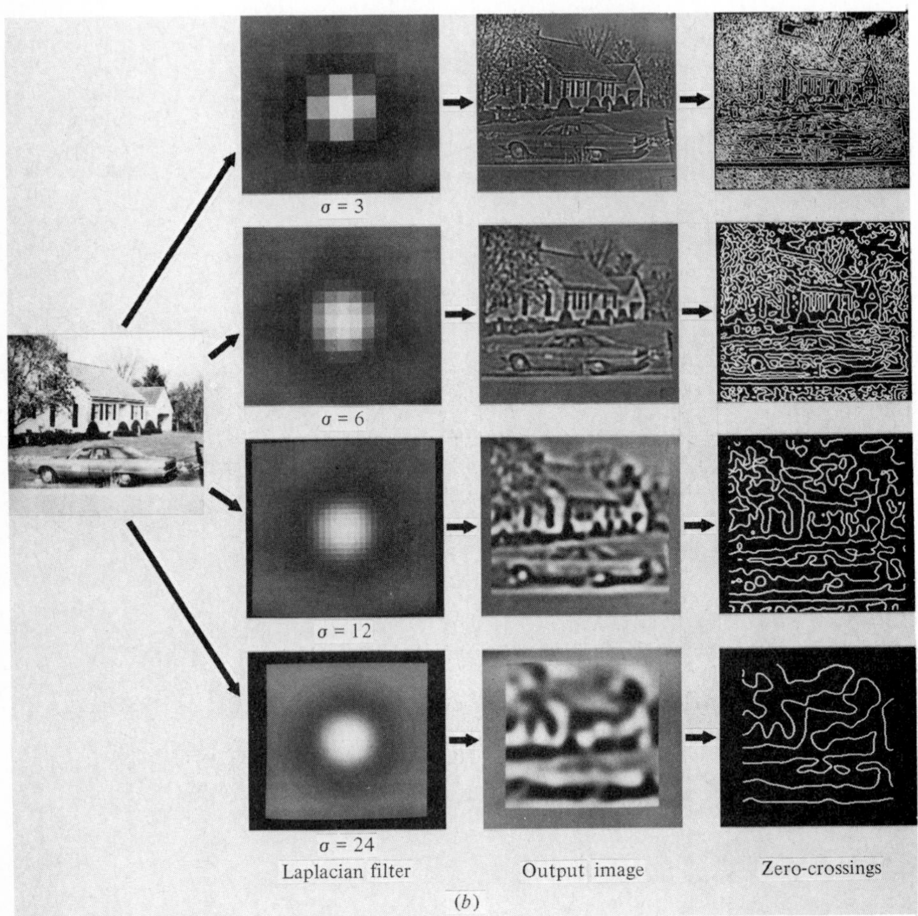

Figure 5.29 Examples of the application of the multichannel operators. (a) Multidimensional Gaussian smoothing. The output is a set of images, each of which characterizes a different level of detail in the original image. (b) An example of Laplacian filtering and the detection of zero-crossings.

output representations varies with σ. A stack of such outputs has been termed a "cone" or "pyramid" and will be discussed in the next section. Thus, to take into account the variation in the data occurring at different spatial frequencies, we define a set of templates $\{W'_k(i,j)\} = \{W'_n | n = 1, 2, \ldots, N\}$. The intensity changes in $I(i,j)$ will manifest themselves in the outputs $I(i,j) * W'_k(i,j)$ as peaks in the first derivative $D(I * W'_k)$, or as zero-crossings in the second derivative $D^2(I * W'_k)$ in the appropriate direction. In other words, the original edge-detection problem may be replaced by an equivalent one in which the zero-crossings of $D^2(I * W'_k)$ or, what is equivalent, $D^2 W'_k * I$, are sought. Thus for each k the template becomes:

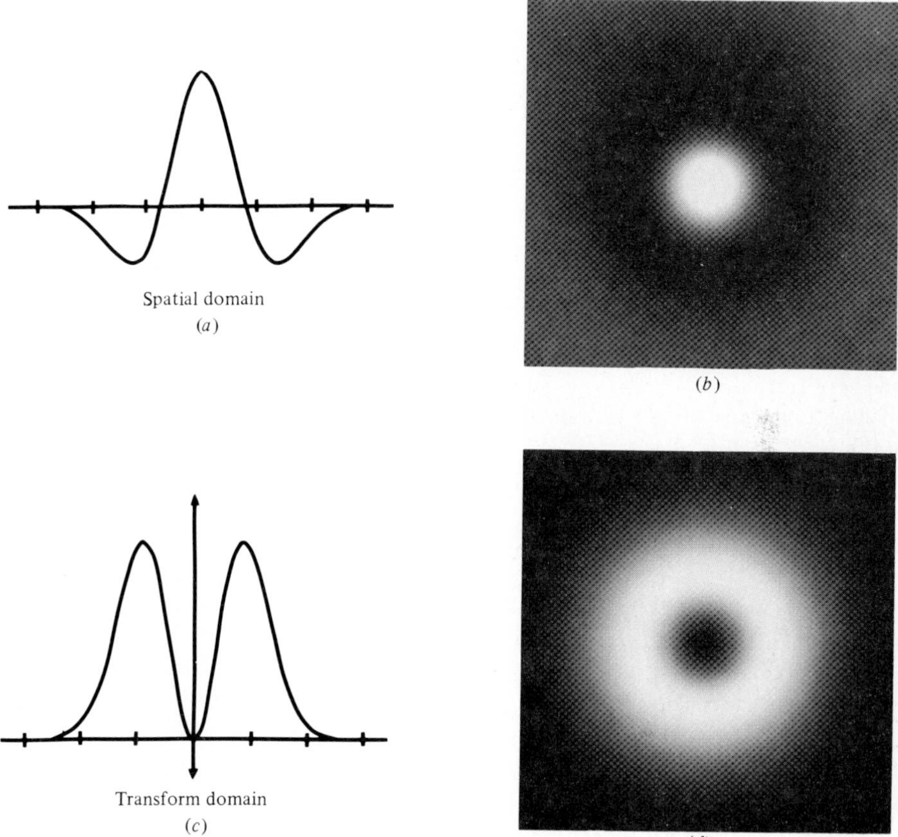

Figure 5.30 The operators $D^2 W_k$ and $\nabla^2 W'_k$. (a) $D^2 W'_k$, the second derivative of the one-dimensional Gaussian distribution. (c) Its Fourier transform. (b) $\nabla^2 W'_k$, its rotationally symmetric two-dimensional counterpart. (d) The Fourier transform of (b). [*Adapted from D. Marr and E. Hildreth, "Theory of Edge Detection," Proceedings of the Royal Society (London), ser. B, vol. 207, 1980, pp. 187–217.*]

$$W_k(i) = D^2 W'_k$$

or
$$W_k(i) = \frac{1}{2\pi\sigma_k^3}\left[0.1 - \frac{i^2}{\sigma_k^2}\right]\exp\left[\frac{-i^2}{2\sigma_k^2}\right] \tag{5.31}$$

which is shown in Figure 5.30*a* and *c* in the spatial and frequency domains, respectively. We observe that its cross section in the spatial domain is just the same Mexican hat operator we have already noted as a model of simple cells in the retina and LGN of mammals. In the spatial frequency domain, this operator behaves as a bandpass filter with a half-power bandwidth of approximately 1.2 octaves.

To obtain the edges in the picture, it is necessary to find the zero-crossings of W_k, and in the correct direction. Marr and Hildreth [74] show that if the local intensity variations near a zero-crossing can be assumed to be linear, then we may employ the Laplacian operator in place of Equation (5.31). Thus the template is chosen to be $\nabla^2 W'_k$, an orientation-independent second-order differential operator:

$$W_k(i, j) = \nabla^2 W'_k = -\frac{1}{\pi\sigma_k^4}\left[1 - \frac{(i^2 + j^2)}{2\sigma_k^2}\right]\exp\left[-\frac{(i^2 + j^2)}{2\sigma_k^2}\right]$$

or, normalizing to unity

$$W_k(i, j) = \frac{1}{2}\left[2 - \frac{(i^2 + j^2)}{\sigma_k^2}\right]\exp\left[-\frac{(i^2 + j^2)}{2\sigma_k^2}\right] \tag{5.32}$$

The diameter of the central region of the mask is given by $d = 2\sqrt{2}\sigma$; the total extent in one dimension is about $4d$. Grimson [40] has indicated that in order to make the diameters of the filters compatible with experimental evidence, σ should be selected in the range of 3 to 23 pixels. This corresponds to a range for the width of the central excitory region of 3.1′ to 21′ of visual arc. Four different-sized masks have been indicated, but there is some suggestion of a fifth mask with excitory width of 1.5′ of visual arc [75]. Typical filters $W_k(i, j)$ are shown in Figure 5.29*b*, again a Mexican hat operator. The figure illustrates the result of applying this edge detector with different values of σ_k. The zero-crossings are also shown. It turns out that this gradient filter can also be approximated by a difference of two Gaussians (see Section 6.3). Using this property, a fast hierarchical discrete correlation algorithm for implementing the operator has been defined [15, 16].

Mask operators of the type discussed in the previous section can be used to actually detect the zero-crossings of W_k. We observed in Section 5.2 that simple cells similar to these can be found in area 17 of the cortex.

According to Marr and Hildreth [74], the information from the different bandwidth channels may be combined by referring to the so-called spatial coincidence assumption:

If a zero-crossing segment is present in a set of independent $[W_k(i,j)]$ channels over a continuous range of sizes, and the segment has the same position and orientation in each channel, then the set of such zero-crossing segments may be taken to indicate the presence of an intensity change in the image that is due to a single physical phenomenon (a change in reflectance, illumination, depth or surface orientation).

The authors propose a set of parsing rules for summarizing the data into isolated edges, bars, and blobs characterized by the following attributes: position, orientation, contrast, length, width. By using the spatial coincidence assumption, the so-called raw primal sketch of the input picture is obtained. In fact, however, it is really not very clear how to interpret the information from the different channels, and research on this problem continues [27].

From the point of view of human vision, Marr and Hildreth [74] suggest that perhaps it is the X cells in the LGN which compute the Laplacian operator $W_k(i,j)$ and that they are combined to construct a simple cell in the manner shown in Figure 5.5. We also note that at a minimum at least two such channels would be required to implement this edge detector. Interestingly enough, we shall examine just such a multichannel model of the human visual system in Section 6.3.

5.4.4 Thresholding the Gradient Picture

So far in Section 5.4 we have discussed the transformation from the input image $I(i,j)$ to the gradient picture $A(i,j)$, as shown in Figure 5.19*b*. The next step in the determination of the edge map $E(i,j)$ is the thresholding operation (see Figure 5.19*a*). Obviously it is simple to select a threshold θ which will label none of the pixels as an edge or all of them as edges. However, what we are seeking is an intelligent means by which an intermediate value can be selected to determine the edges. This is a circular argument, since we shall define as edge elements in the array $E(i,j)$ only those pixels in $A(i,j)$ that are above threshold. That is,

$$E(i,j) = 1 \qquad \text{if } A(i,j) \geq \theta$$

and

$$E(i,j) = 0 \qquad \text{if } A(i,j) < \theta \tag{5.33}$$

Thus the array $E(i,j)$, while intended to isolate the strong edges in array $A(i,j)$, is in a certain sense arbitrary.

The threshold θ may be fixed a priori or determined adaptively according to the data prevailing in $A(i,j)$ [99]. In the case of the fixed threshold, a simple method is to use the mean of $A(i,j)$ as the value of θ. Alternatively, the histogram of $A(i,j)$ could be computed and θ chosen to yield a fixed number of edge pixels. Thus we may select θ so that the values of $A(i,j)$ that are above the pth percentile in the histogram are labeled as edges. This only makes sense when a priori knowledge of the size and number of the objects in the picture is available. Figure 5.31 demonstrates the effect of using a fixed threshold. There

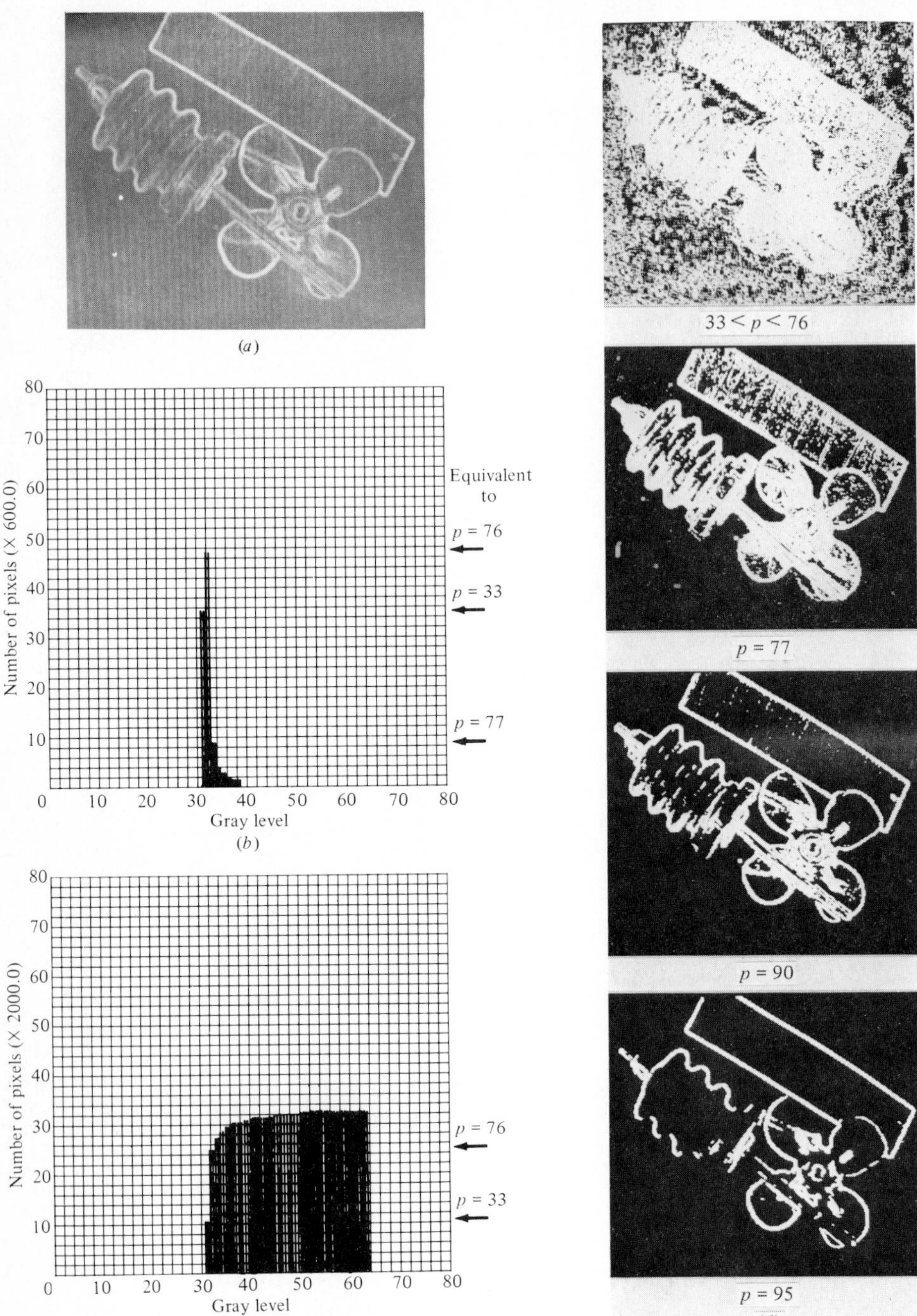
(a)
80
70
60
50
40
30
20
10
0
10
20
30
40
50
60
70
80
Number of pixels (× 600.0)
Gray level
Equivalent to
p = 76
p = 33
p = 77
(b)
Number of pixels (× 2000.0)
Gray level
p = 76
p = 33
(c)
33 < p < 76
p = 77
p = 90
p = 95
(d)

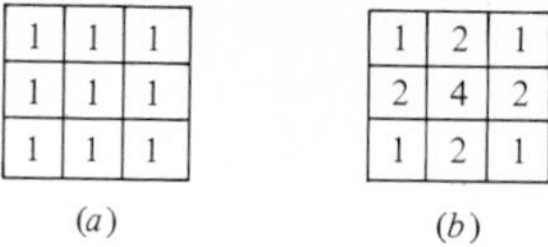

Figure 5.32 Masks for obtaining the locally average image $A'(i, j)$ from the gradient image $A(i, j)$. (a) An averaging mask. (b) A low-pass mask.

are many variations of the fixed threshold method, and readers are referred to [63] for a summary of the algorithms studied to date.

The second approach is to use adaptive selection, and again different strategies are possible. Essentially the basic idea is to attempt to eliminate the influence of local effects. Examples of this, discussed in Chapter 2, are camera input characteristics and illumination conditions. One possibility is to compute the average value of the gradient in an $n \times n$ window centered at pixel (i, j). Thus we obtain $A_{\text{avg}}(i, j)$

$$A_{\text{avg}}(i, j) = \frac{\sum_{\text{window}} A(i, j)}{n \times n} \tag{5.34}$$

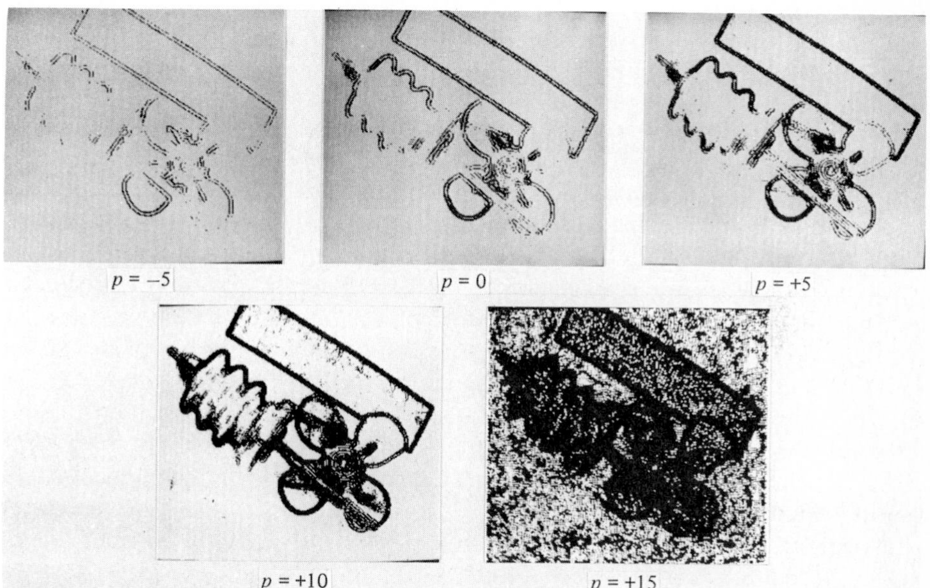

Figure 5.33 Adaptive thresholding.

Figure 5.31 The effect of using a fixed threshold for transforming the gradient image $A(i, j)$ into the edge map $E(i, j)$. As observed in (b) and (c), thresholds selected below gray level 31 (equivalent to $p = 33$) will result in a completely white image. Thus, the complete image has a high gradient and every point is an edge! Between $p = 33$ and $p = 76$ the resulting thresholded picture remains unchanged. When the peak of the histogram is excluded by selecting the threshold at gray level 33 (equivalent to $p = 77$), a reasonable edge map is produced. Selecting higher values of p limits the number of points considered as edges. (a) Gradient image. (b) Histogram of gradient image. (c) Cumulative distribution function of gradient image. (d) Edge map for different values of p.

this being equivalent to transforming $A(i, j)$ into $A'(i, j)$ using the averaging mask shown in Figure 5.32*a*. An alternative is shown in Figure 5.32*b* where the low-pass mask has a better side-lobe response structure. We then choose [43, 44]:

$$\theta = A'\left[1 + \frac{p}{100}\right] \tag{5.35}$$

where p is the percentage above or below the local average.

We observe that larger windows will in general produce more connected edges, but the use of small windows will significantly speed up the computation. It is difficult to select p on the basis of an intelligent argument since the results seem to be picture-dependent. Figure 5.33 demonstrates the use of the adaptive strategy, where we note that the number of edge pixels in $E(i, j)$ is directly controlled by the parameter p.

5.5 SEQUENTIAL SCANNING METHODS

In the previous section, the computational window was applied to each pixel in the array $I(i, j)$ in a manner which could be described conceptually as in parallel. An alternative approach is to scan the picture sequentially with a local edge detector, selecting only those paths in $I(i, j)$ that are most likely to follow contours of gray-level discontinuity. The question arises, of course, as to what specific paths should be chosen. The method of heuristic programming is useful in this context [87, 91, 109]; it was originally developed to solve problems in artificial intelligence, such as game playing. An example is computer chess, in which a large number of different alternatives must be evaluated before a decision can be made. We shall show that the edge-detection problem can be regarded in an equivalent formulation.

The state-space approach [87] to heuristic programming is based on the search of an appropriately defined state space for a minimal cost path to a specified terminal constraint. To define this representation mathematically, we require several elements. First and foremost is the actual form of the state, which in our case is taken as the pixel location (i, j). Then an operator is needed which maps states into other states and has an associated cost of application. An edge operator defined by $W(i, j)$ is used to transform states into states; its direction defines the location of the next state and its magnitude may be related to the cost. Either four or eight next directions are possible, as shown in Figure 5.26*a*. If we associate the states with the nodes of a graph and the edge operators with the edges of the graph, we may then observe that the state-space search is equivalent to a graph search [46, 87].

To complete the formulation of this problem statement we need to specify a beginning and an end for the path. The set of initial states may be arbitrary or could be determined by a separate algorithm which makes use of some knowledge about the picture. Another choice is the top of the image. The set of goal or termination states may include the initial state, which would then result in a closed contour. The bottom of the picture could also be used in this context. Having specified the initial and final constraints, we then seek a path from a root node to a goal node. The order in which the nodes of the graph are generated or traversed is defined by a so-called merit ordering or evaluation function [6, 8, 9, 17, 39, 117]. Examples of graph search applied to edge detection are discussed in [28, 29, 39, 81, 82].

An example of a search graph that might arise from an edge-detection problem is shown in Figure 5.34 [76, 77, 78]. Suppose we wish to find an edge contour that starts at the top of the picture and ends at the bottom. We define an edge element by the two horizontally adjacent pixels, shown in Figure 5.34*a*. We observe in this case that the edge exists as the boundary between two pixels. Let the cost $c(n)$ associated with each node n (really the edge attached

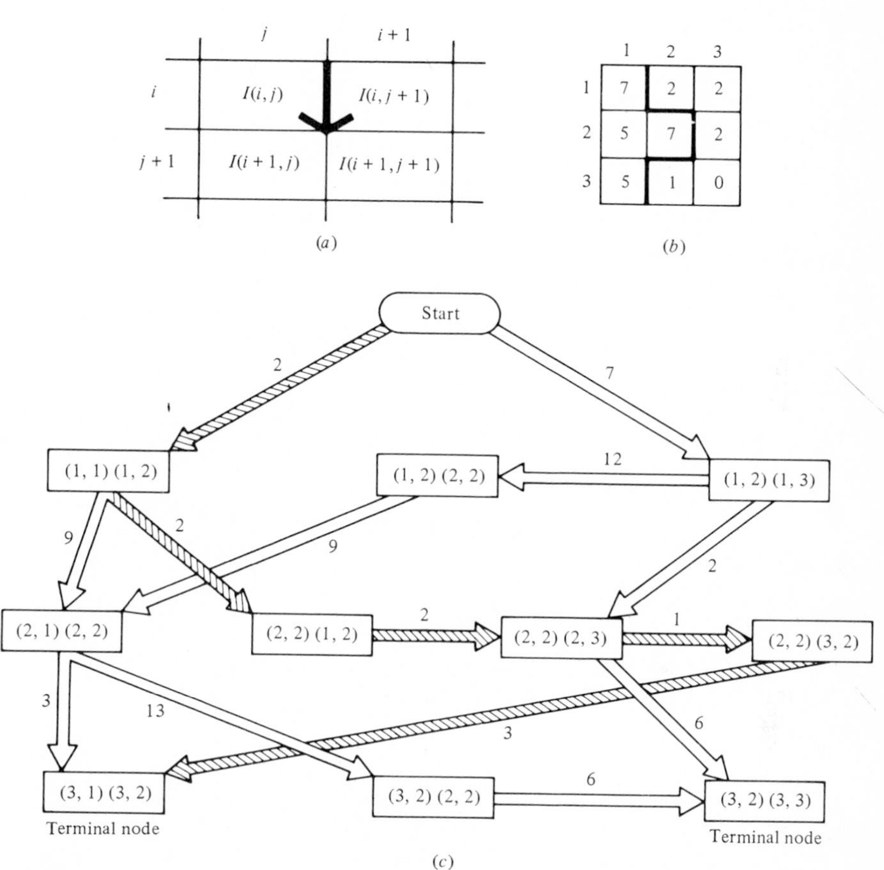

Figure 5.34 An example of edge detection using heuristic search. (*a*) An edge element. (*b*) A small subimage with the optimal edge boundary shown in heavy print. (*c*) The search graph with the associated cost shown for each edge. The optimal path is crosshatched.

to n) be given by

$$c(n) = I_{max} - [I(i, j) - I(i, j + 1)] \tag{5.36}$$

where $I_{max} = 7$ is the maximum intensity in the picture. Thus $c(n)$ is low for large step changes and we therefore seek to minimize the accumulated cost. If $I(i, j) = I_{max}$ and $I(i, j + 1) = 0$, $c(n) = 0$ and we have a perfect match. The reader may wish to apply the A^* algorithm [87] on paper in order to verify that it will yield the correct path shown in Figure 5.34*b*. A slightly more complex function $c(n)$ is provided by Ramer [95]. Given two edge elements, perhaps separated by a gap, he suggests three components: one related to the strength of the successor edge element, a second measuring their relative orientation, and a third computing the distance between the beginning of one and the end of another. This search problem is characterized as organizing stroke arrays into streaks (that is, lines), which tend to indicate the partial outline of objects.

It would appear that the incorporation of specific knowledge about the domain of interest would enhance the search for edges in a picture. The use of a model for this purpose has been referred to as "planning" [59]. The approach that is sometimes taken is to employ the plan as a default decision when the heuristic search is unable to proceed on the basis of its usual criteria. Such a plan follower is illustrated in Figure 5.35. In general, the plan is used to constrain the search within bounds set by an a priori model of the image.

An interesting type of plan is that of a pyramid, which is created by dividing the image into four pixel square neighborhoods and mapping each such neighborhood into one pixel at the next highest level in the pyramid [115]. The mapping process is recursively applied at each level until the top of the

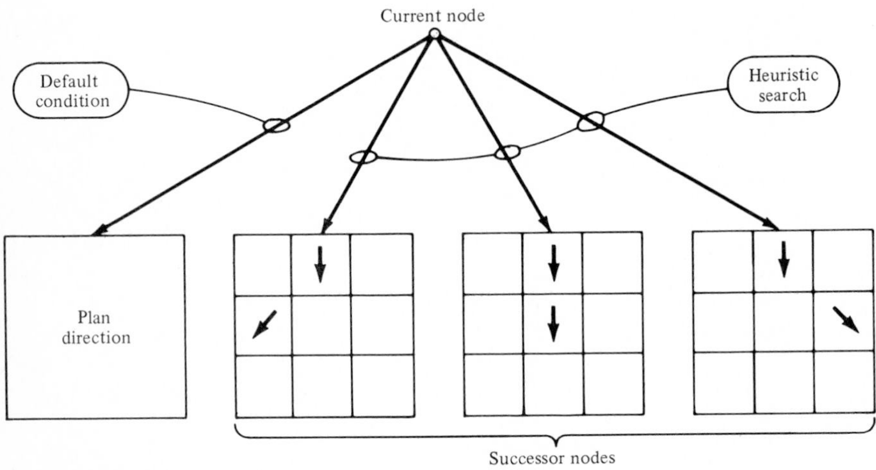

Figure 5.35 A plan follower. (*After D. H. Ballard and J. Sklansky, "A Ladder-Structured Decision Tree for Recognizing Tumors in Chest Radiographs," IEEE Transactions on Computers, vol. C-25, no. 5, May 1976, pp. 503–513.*)

pyramid is reached. A pyramid therefore is a data structure containing $N+1$ planes, each of dimension $2^n \times 2^n$, with $n = 0, 1, \ldots, N$. A plane of dimension $2^N \times 2^N$ $(L = 0)$ is placed at the base of the pyramid and the $2^0 \times 2^0$ single-pixel image tops it off at the apex. Let $L = N - n$ be defined as the level in the structure; then each plane in the pyramid is represented by $I_L(i, j)$, as shown in Figure 5.36.

For an arbitrary level k, array $I_{k+1}(i, j)$ is obtained from $I_k(i, j)$ by using one of a set of possible mapping functions. This is illustrated in Figure 5.37, where an arbitrary set of 2×2 pixels at level k is projected to one pixel labeled p_0 at level $k+1$. The projection is defined by the function π, where

$$I_{k+1}(p_0) = \pi[I_k(p_1), I_k(p_2), I_k(p_3), I_k(p_4)] \tag{5.37}$$

An example is

$$\pi_{\text{avg}} = \frac{1}{4}\sum_{i=1}^{4} I_k(p_i) \tag{5.38}$$

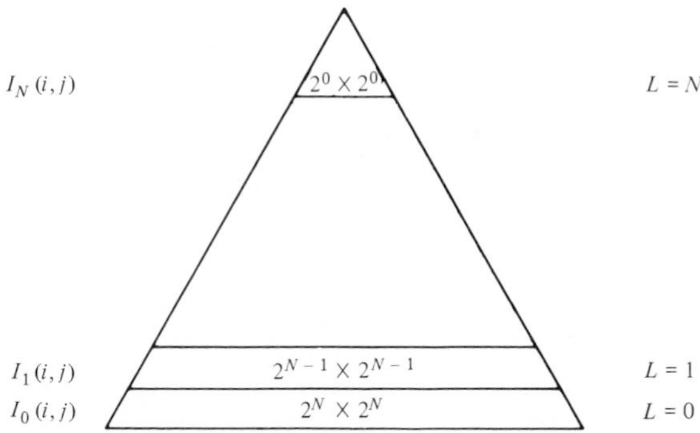

Figure 5.36 A pyramid data structure. [*Adapted from M. D. Levine, "Region Analysis Using a Pyramid Data Structure," in S. Tanimoto and A. Klinger (eds.), "Structured Computer Vision, Machine Perception Through Hierarchical Computation Structures," Academic, New York, 1980, pp. 57–100.*]

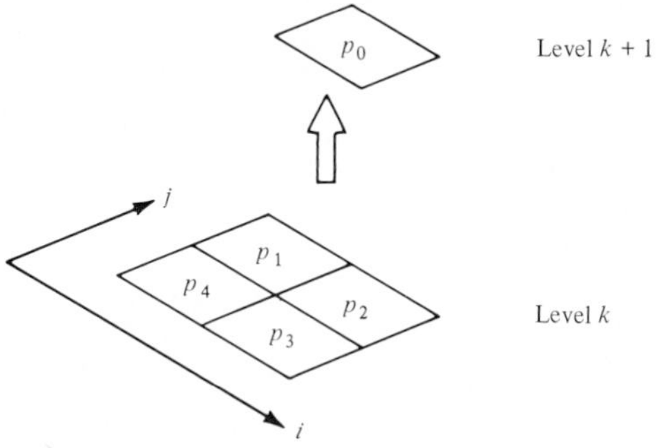

Figure 5.37 A fragment of the mapping from $I_k(i, j)$ at level k to $I_{k+1}(i, j)$ at level $k+1$. Many possible mapping functions may be employed.

which replaces $I_{k+1}(p_0)$ by the average of its four predecessors at level k. Thus each successive picture in the hierarchy is a smoothed version of the previous one, so that the finer details (high spatial frequency components) tend to disappear as one ascends the pyramid. The properties of this operator have been discussed in detail by Tanimoto and Pavlidis [115]. An example of such an image pyramid is shown in Figure 5.38, where we observe that the effect is to successively defocus the image. Other possible transformations are π_{min}, which selects the minimum of the four pixels $I_k(p_1)$, $I_k(p_2)$, $I_k(p_3)$, and $I_k(p_4)$; π_{max}, which selects the maximum; π_{rand}, which selects a value at random. As a sequential operation on a conventional computer this computation is relatively slow. Therefore Dyer [25] has outlined a parallel computer architecture for constructing a pyramid machine, implemented in VLSI (Very Large Scale Integration). Readers should also take note that the information stored in the pyramid governed by Equation (5.38) is similar in content to that of the output of the biological multichannel edge detector discussed in Section 5.4.3.

For binary pictures, logical AND and OR mappings can also be computed. For example, consider the image at level $L = 0$ in Figure 5.17b. The Roberts

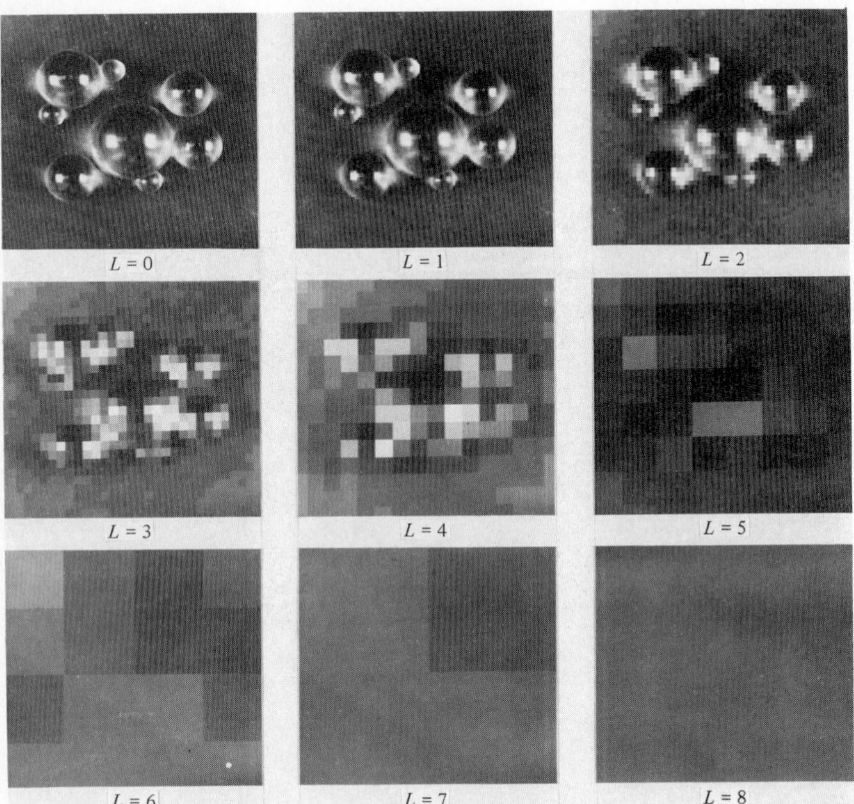

Figure 5.38 A pyramid data structure based on Equation (5.38).

cross operator yields an image which may then be adaptively thresholded to give an edge map $E(i, j)$. With the latter as the base of the pyramid, we may create an edge pyramid by mapping with the logical OR operation. The effect is to progressively thicken the edges at each successive level in the pyramid, as shown in Figure 5.39. We observe that as we progress up the pyramid, the edges behave in the manner of a contracting wavefront until at some arbitrary level k all the edges are completely extinguished. The pixels in the regions existing at the next lowest level $k-1$ are most likely to be found in the smoothest and most unchanging areas of the picture, as remote from any edges as possible.

We note that both types of pyramids provide a means of compressing the data in the original picture [21]. Thus this structure lends itself to being used as a plan for edge detection. This was originally done by Kelly [59], who was concerned with the problem of visual identification of human faces by computer. He employs one of the planes at the higher levels of the intensity pyramid in order to characterize the global edges. Discovering these in the smaller array pictures is obviously simpler because of the general suppression of detail. A very simple geometrical model of the face outline at this same scale is used as part of a heuristic search process to sift out the relevant edges. The plan follower then employs this boundary as a plan in the original larger image to control the overall search. The program only investigates edge directions in a narrow band (16 pixels wide in a 226×325 array) surrounding the plan path, thereby reducing the search combinatorics. More or less the same heuristics are then used to eliminate spurious edges. Other references to the use of this

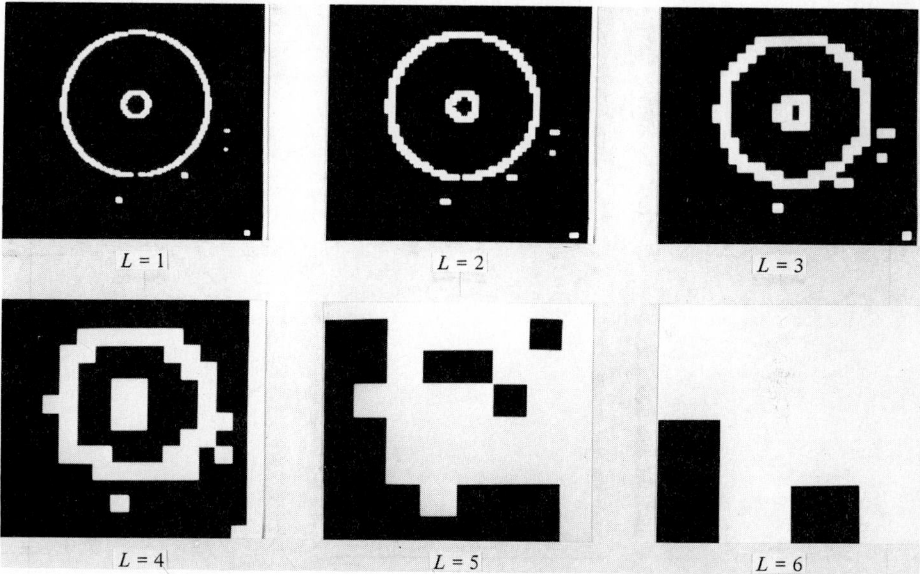

Figure 5.39 The binary pyramid for a thresholded version of the gradient image in Figure 5.25*a*.

approach can be found in [69, 88]. Levine [69] has, in fact, employed both the image and edge pyramids to find the uniform regions in a picture, a subject we shall discuss in detail in Chapter 8. Obviously the boundaries of these regions may be taken as the edges in the picture.

Another type of plan is one that is obtained from horizontal and vertical signatures, as previously defined in Section 1.4 [11, 41, 90]. An example is the analysis of radiographs [7, 70]. More detailed generic models for guiding the edge-detection process are discussed in [45].

A good model describes where in the picture we should search for the objects, what they should look like, and what their spatial relationship to the neighboring objects should be. Obviously this type of plan would provide considerably more knowledge than the plans described in this section and should lead to a more accurate edge boundary. An interesting application of this philosophy can be found in [31, 71].

REFERENCES

1. Abdou, I. E., "Quantitative Methods of Edge Detection," Technical Report USCIPI 830, Image Processing Institute, University of Southern California, Los Angeles, July 1978.
2. Abdou, I. E., and Pratt, W. K., "Quantitative Design and Evaluation of Enhancement/Thresholding Edge Detectors," *Proceedings IEEE*, vol. 67, no. 5, May 1979, pp. 753–763.
3. Abramatic, J. F., "Why the Simplest 'Hueckel' Edge Detector is a Roberts Operator," *Computer Graphics and Image Processing*, vol. 17, no. 1, September 1981, pp. 79–83.
4. Arbib, M. A., "Artificial Intelligence and Brain Theory: Unities and Diversities," *Annals of Biomedical Engineering*, vol. 3, no. 3, 1975, pp. 238–274.
5. Artzy, E., Frieder, G., and Herman, G. T., "The Theory, Design, Implementation and Evaluation of a Three-Dimensional Surface Detection Algorithm," *Computer Graphics and Image Processing*, vol. 15, no. 1, January 1981, pp. 1–24.
6. Ashkar, G. P., and Modestino, J. W., "The Contour Extraction Problem With Biomedical Applications," in *Proceedings IEEE Computer Society Conference on Pattern Recognition and Image Processing*, PRIP 77, Rensselaer Polytechnic Institute, Troy, N.Y., June 6–8, 1977, pp. 216–221.
7. Ausherman, D. A., Dwyer, S. J., and Lodwick, G. S., "Extraction of Connected Edges From Knee Radiographs," *IEEE Transactions on Computers*, vol. C-21, no. 7, July 1972, pp. 753–758.
8. Ballard, D. H., and Sklansky, J., "Tumor Detection in Radiographs," *Computers in Biomedical Research*, vol. 6, 1973, pp. 299–322.
9. Ballard, D. H., and Sklansky, J., "A Ladder-Structured Decision Tree for Recognizing Tumors in Chest Radiographs," *IEEE Transactions on Computers*, vol. C-25, no. 2, May 1976, pp. 503–513.
10. Barrow, H. G., and Tenenbaum, J. M., "Interpreting Line Drawings as Three-Dimensional Surfaces," *Artificial Intelligence*, vol. 17, nos. 1–3, 1981, pp. 75–116.
11. Becker, H. E., Nettleton, W. J., and Meyers, P. H., "Digital Computer Determination of a Medical Diagnostic Index Directly From Chest X-ray Images," *IEEE Transactions on Biomedical Engineering*, vol. 11, no. 2, July 1964, pp. 67–76.
12. Boulter, J. F., "Recognition of Reflection and Illumination Edges by the Human Visual System," *Applied Optics*, vol. 19, no. 12, June 15, 1980, pp. 2077–2079.

13. Brooks, M. J., "Rationalizing Edge Detectors," *Computer Graphics and Image Processing*, vol. 8, no. 2, 1978, pp. 277–285.
14. Bryant, D. J., and Bouldin, D. W., "Evaluation of Edge Operators Using Relative and Absolute Graphing," *Proceedings of the IEEE Computer Society Conference on Pattern Recognition and Image Processing*, PRIP-79, Chicago, Aug. 6–8, 1979, pp. 138–145.
15. Burt, P. J., "Fast Hierarchical Correlations With Gaussian-Like Kernels," in *Proceedings of Fifth International Conference on Pattern Recognition*, Miami, Dec. 1–4, 1980, pp. 828–830.
16. Burt, P. J., "Fast Filter Transforms for Image Processing," *Computer Graphics and Image Processing*, vol. 16, no. 1, May 1981, pp. 20–51.
17. Chien, Y. P., and Fu, K. S., "A Decision Function Method For Boundary Detection," *Computer Graphics and Image Processing*, vol. 3, no. 2, 1974, pp. 125–140.
18. Deering, M. F., and Collins, C., "Real-Time Natural Scene Analysis for a Blind Prosthesis," *Proceedings 7th International Joint Conference on Artificial Intelligence*, IJCAI-81, 24–28 Aug. 1981, Vancouver, B.C., pp. 704–709.
19. Deutsch, J. A., "The Plexiform Zone and Shape Recognition in the Octopus," *Nature*, vol. 185, no. 4711, Feb. 13, 1960, pp. 443–446.
20. Deutsch, J. A., "Theories of Shape Discrimination in Octopus," *Nature*, vol. 188, no. 4756, Dec. 24, 1960, pp. 1090–1092.
21. Doctor, L. J., and Torborg, J. G., "Display Techniques for Octree-Encoded Objects," *IEEE Computer Graphics and Applications*, vol. 2, no. 3, July 1981, pp. 29–38.
22. Dodwell, P. C., "Facts and Theories of Shape Discrimination," *Nature*, vol. 191, no. 4788, Apr. 5, 1961, pp. 578–581.
23. Duda, R., and Hart, P., "Pattern Classification and Scene Analysis," Wiley, New York, 1973.
24. Dudani, S. A., and Luk, A. L., "Locating Straight-Line Edge Segments on Outdoor Scenes," *Pattern Recognition*, vol. 10, no. 3, 1978, pp. 145–157.
25. Dyer, C. R., "A VLSI Pyramid Machine for Hierarchical Parallel Image Processing," *IEEE Computer Society Conference on Pattern Recognition and Image Processing*, PRIP-81, Dallas, Aug. 3–5, 1981, pp. 381–386.
26. Ehrich, R. W., and Schroeder, F. H., "Contextual Boundary Formation by One-Dimensional Edge Detection and Scan Line Matching," *Computer Graphics and Image Processing*, vol. 16, no. 2, June 1981, pp. 116–149.
27. Eklundh, J.-O., Elfving, T., and Nyberg, S., "Edge Detection Using the Marr-Hildreth Operator With Different Sizes," *Proceedings 6th International Conference on Pattern Recognition*, Munich, Oct. 19–22, 1982, pp. 1109–1112.
28. Elliot, H., Cooper, D. B., Cohen, F. S., and Symosek, P. F., "Implementation, Interpretation, and Analysis of a Suboptimal Boundary Finding Algorithm," *IEEE Transactions on Pattern Analysis and Machine Intelligence*, vol. PAMI-4, no. 2, March 1982, pp. 167–182.
29. Elliot, H., and Srinivasan, L., "An Application of Dynamic Programming to Sequential Boundary Estimation," *Computer Graphics and Image Processing*, vol. 17, no. 4, December 1981, pp. 291–314.
30. Eriksen, C. W., and Hake, H. W., "Absolute Judgments as a Function of the Stimulus Range and the Number of Stimulus and Response Categories," *Journal of Experimental Psychology*, vol. 49, no. 5, 1955, pp. 323–332.
31. Fischler, M. A., and Elschlager, R. A., "The Representation and Matching of Pictorial Structures," *IEEE Transactions on Computers*, vol. C-22, no. 1, June 1973, pp. 67–92.
32. Fram, J. R., and Deutsch, E. S., "On the Quantitative Evaluation of Edge Detection Schemes and Their Comparison with Human Performance," *IEEE Transactions on Computers*, vol. C-24, no. 6, June 1975, pp. 616–628.
33. Freeman, H., "Boundary Encoding and Processing," in Lipkin, B. S., and Rosenfeld, A. (eds.), "Picture Processing and Psychopictorics," Academic, New York, 1970, pp. 241–266.
34. Frei, W., and Chen, C. C., "Fast Boundary Detection: A Generalization and a New Algorithm," *IEEE Transactions on Computers*, vol. C-26, no. 10, October 1977, pp. 988–998.
35. Fukushima, K., "A Feature Extractor for Curvilinear Patterns: A Design Suggested by the Mammalian Visual System," *Kybernetik*, vol. 7, no. 4, 1970, pp. 153–160.

36. Gilchrist, A. L., "Perceived Lightness Depends on Perceived Spatial Arrangement," *Science*, vol. 195, no. 4274, Jan. 14, 1977, pp. 185–187.
37. Gilchrist, A. L., "The Perception of Surface Black and Whites," *Scientific American*, vol. 240, no. 3, March 1979, pp. 112–124.
38. Graham, D. N., "Image Transmission by Two-Dimensional Contour Coding," *Proceedings of the IEEE*, vol. 55, no. 3, March 1967, pp. 336–346.
39. Greer, D. S., "Use of Heuristic Search to Find Lung Boundaries in Conventional Tomographs," *Proceedings of the IEEE Computer Society Conference on Pattern Recognition and Image Processing*, Chicago, May 31–June 2, 1978, pp. 62–65.
40. Grimson, W. E. L., "A Computer Implementation of a Theory of Human Stereo Vision," A.I. Memo 565, Artificial Intelligence Laboratory, Massachusetts Institute of Technology, Cambridge, Mass., January, 1980.
41. Hall, E. L., Kruger, R. P., Dwyer, S. J., Hall, D. L., McLaren, R. W., and Lodwick, G. S., "A Survey of Pre-processing and Feature Extraction Techniques for Radiographic Images," *IEEE Transactions on Computers*, vol. C-20, no. 9, September 1971, pp. 1032–1044.
42. Haralick, R. M., "The Digital Edge," *IEEE Computer Society Conference on Pattern Recognition and Image Processing*, PRIP-81 Dallas, Aug. 3–5, 1981, pp. 285–290.
43. Haralick, R. M., and Dinstein, I., "A Spatial Clustering Procedure for Multi-Image Data," *IEEE Transactions on Circuits and Systems*, vol. CAS-22, no. 5, May 1975, pp. 440–450.
44. Haralick, R. M., and Shanmugan, K., "Computer Classification of Reservoir Sandstones," *IEEE Transactions on Geoscience Electronics*, vol. GE-11, no. 4, October 1973, pp. 171–177.
45. Harlow, C. A., and Eisenbeis, S. A., "The Analysis of Radiographic Images," *IEEE Transactions on Computers*, vol. C-22, no. 7, July 1973, pp. 678–689.
46. Hart, P., Nilsson, N., and Raphael, B., "A Formal Basis For the Heuristic Determination of Minimum Cost Paths," *IEEE Transactions on Man, System and Cybernetics*, vol. MSC-4, no. 2, 1968, pp. 100–107.
47. Hartline, H. K., "The Receptive Fields of Optic Nerve Fibers," *American Journal of Physiology*, vol. 130, no. 4, 1940, pp. 690–699.
48. Herskovits, A., and Binford, T. O., "On Boundary Detection," Artificial Intelligence Memo 183, Massachusetts Institute of Technology, Cambridge, Mass., July 1970.
49. Horn, B. K. P., "Understanding Image Intensities," *Artificial Intelligence*, vol. 8, no. 2, 1977, pp. 201–231.
50. Hubel, D. H., and Wiesel, T. N., "Receptive Fields, Binocular Interaction and Functional Architecture in the Cat's Visual Cortex," *Journal of Physiology* (*London*), vol. 160, no. 1, 1962, pp. 106–154.
51. Hubel, D. H., and Wiesel, T. N., "Shape and Arrangement of Columns in Cat's Striate Cortex," *Journal of Physiology* (*London*), vol. 165, no. 3, 1963, pp. 559–568.
52. Hubel, D. H., and Wiesel, T. N., "Receptive Fields and Functional Architecture in Two Nonstriate Visual Areas (18 and 19) of the Cat," *Journal of Neurophysiology*, vol. 28, no. 2, 1965, pp. 229–289.
53. Hubel, D. H., and Wiesel, T. N., "Receptive Fields and Functional Architecture in Monkey Striate Cortex," *The Journal of Physiology* (*London*), vol. 195, no. 1, November 1968, pp. 215–244.
54. Hueckel, M. H., "An Operator Which Locates Edges in Digitized Pictures," *Journal of the Association of Computing Machines*, vol. 18, no. 1, January 1971, pp. 113–125.
55. Hueckel, M. H., "A Local Visual Operator Which Recognizes Edges and Lines," *Journal of the Association of Computing Machines*, vol. 20, no. 4, October 1973, pp. 634–647.
56. Hummel, R. A., "Feature Detection Using Basis Functions," *Computer Graphics and Image Processing*, vol. 9, no. 1, 1979, pp. 40–55.
57. Humphrey, N. K., "What the Frog's Eye Tells the Monkey's Brain," *Brain Behavior and Evolution* vol. 3, 1970, pp. 324–337.
58. Iannino, A., and Shapiro, S. D., "A Survey of the Hough Transform and its Extensions for Curve Detection," *IEEE Computer Society Conference on Pattern Recognition and Image Processing*, May 31–June 2, Chicago, 1979, pp. 32–38.

59. Kelly, M. D., "Edge Detection in Pictures by Computer Using Planning," in "Machine Intelligence," vol. 6, Elsevier, New York, 1971, pp. 397–409.
60. Kirsch, R. A., "Computer Determination of the Constituent Structure of Biological Images," *Computers and Biomedical Research*, vol. 4, no. 3, June 1971, pp. 315–328.
61. Kitchen, L., and Rosenfeld, A., "Edge Evaluation Using Local Edge Coherence," *IEEE Transactions on Systems, Man, and Cybernetics*, vol. SMC-11, no. 9, September 1981, pp. 597–605.
62. Knutsson, H., and Granlund, G. H., "Fourier Domain Design of Line and Edge Detectors," *Proceedings 5th International Conference on Pattern Recognition*, Miami Beach, Dec. 1–4, 1980, pp. 45–47.
63. Kohler, R., "A Segmentation System Based on Thresholding," *Computer Graphics and Image Processing*, vol. 15, no. 4, April 1981, pp. 319–338.
64. Kovasznay, L. S., and Joseph, H. M., "Processing of Two-Dimensional Patterns by Scanning Techniques," *Science*, vol. 118, no. 3069, Oct. 25, 1953, pp. 475–477.
65. Kovasznay, L. S., and Joseph, H. M., "Image Processing," *Proceedings of the IRE*, vol. 43, no. 5, May 1955, pp. 560–570.
66. Land, M. F., "A Comparison of the Visual Behavior of a Predatory Arthropod with That of a Mammal," in Schmitt, F. O., and Worden, F. G. (eds.), "The Neurosciences Third Study Program," MIT Press, Cambridge, Mass., 1974, pp. 411–418.
67. Lettvin, J. Y., "Filling Out the Forms, an Appreciation of Hubel and Wiesel," *Science*, vol. 214, Oct. 30, 1981, pp. 518–520.
68. Lettvin, J. Y., Maturana, H. R., McCulloch, W. S., and Pitts, W. H., "What the Frog's Eye Tells the Frog's Brain," *Proceedings of the IRE*, vol. 47, no. 11, 1959, pp. 1940–1951.
69. Levine, M. D., "Region Analysis Using a Pyramid Data Structure," In Tanimoto, S., and Klinger, A. (eds.): "Structured Computer Vision, Machine Perception through Hierarchical Computation Structures," Academic, New York, 1980, pp. 57–100.
70. Levine, M. D., and Leemet, J., "Computer Recognition of the Human Spinal Outline Using Radiographic Image Processing," *Pattern Recognition*, vol. 7, no. 4, 1975, pp. 177–185.
71. Levine, M. D., and Ting, D., "Intermediate Level Picture Interpretation Using Complete Two-Dimensional Models," *Computer Graphics and Image Processing*, vol. 16, no. 3, 1981, pp. 185–209.
72. Liu, H. K., "Two- and Three-Dimensional Boundary Detection," *Computer Graphics and Image Processing*, vol. 6, no. 2, 1977, pp. 123–134.
73. Marr, D., "Early Processing of Visual Information," *Philosophical Transactions of the Royal Society of London*, ser. B, vol. 275, no. 942, Oct. 19, 1976, pp. 483–524.
74. Marr, D., and Hildreth, E., "Theory of Edge Detection," *Proceedings of the Royal Society, (London)*, ser. B, vol. 207, 1980, pp. 187–217.
75. Marr, D., Hildreth, E., and Poggio, T., "Evidence for a Fifth, Smaller Channel in Early Human Vision," AI Memo 541, Artificial Intelligence Laboratory, Massachusetts Institute of Technology, Cambridge, Mass., 1979.
76. Martelli, A., "Edge Detection Using Heuristic Search Methods," *Computer Graphics and Image Processing*, vol. 1, no. 2, August 1972, pp. 169–182.
77. Martelli, A., "Contour Detection in Noisy Pictures Using Heuristic Search Methods," *Proceedings First International Joint Conference on Pattern Recognition*, Washington, Oct. 30–Nov. 1, 1973, pp. 375–388.
78. Martelli, A., "An Application of Heuristic Search Methods to Edge and Contour Detection," *Communications of the ACM*, vol. 19, no. 2, February 1976, pp. 73–83.
79. Maturana, H. R., Lettvin, J. Y., McCulloch, W. S., and Pitts, W. H., "Anatomy and Physiology of Vision in the Frog (*Rana pipiens*)," *Journal of General Physiology*, vol. 43, suppl. 2 (Mechanisms of Vision), 1960, pp. 129–171.
80. Mero, L., and Vassy, Z., "A Simplified and Fast Version of the Hueckel Operator For Finding Optimal Edges in Pictures," in *Proceedings Fourth International Joint Conference on Artificial Intelligence*, Tbilisi, Georgia (USSR), 1975, pp. 650–654.
81. Montanari, U., "On the Optimal Detection of Curves in Noisy Pictures," *Communications of the ACM*, vol. 14, no. 5, May 1971, pp. 335–345.

82. Montanari, U., "Optimization Methods in Image Processing," in Rosenfeld, J. L. (ed.), "Information Processing 74 (Proceedings of the IFIP Congress 1974)," North-Holland, Amsterdam, 1974, pp. 727–732.
83. Morgenthaler, D. G., "A New Hybrid Edge Detector," *Computer Graphics and Image Processing*, vol. 16, no. 2, June 1981, pp. 166–176.
84. Nagano, T., and Kurata, K., "A Self-Organizing Neural Network Model for the Development of Complex Cells," *Biological Cybernetics*, vol. 40, no. 3, 1981, pp. 195–200.
85. Nevatia, R., "Evaluation of a Simplified Hueckel Edge-Line Detector," *Computer Graphics and Image Processing*, vol. 6, no. 6, December 1977, pp. 582–588.
86. Nevatia, R., "A Color Edge Detector and Its Use in Scene Segmentation," *IEEE Transactions on Systems, Man, and Cybernetics*, vol. SMC-7, no. 11, 1977, pp. 820–826.
87. Nilsson, N. J., "Problem Solving Methods in Artificial Intelligence," McGraw-Hill, New York, 1971.
88. O'Gorman, F., "Edge Detection Using Walsh Functions," *Artificial Intelligence*, vol. 10, no. 2, 1978, pp. 215–223.
89. Ohlander, R., Price, K., and Reddy, D. R., "Picture Segmentation Using a Recursive Region Splitting Method," *Computer Graphics and Image Processing*, vol. 8, 1978, pp. 313–333.
90. Paul, J. L., Levine, M. D., Fraser, R., and Laszlo, C. A., "The Measurement of Total Lung Capacity Based on a Computer Analysis of an Anterior and Lateral Radiographic Chest Image," *IEEE Transactions Biomedical Engineering*, vol. 21, no. 6, 1974, pp. 444–451.
91. Pearl, J., "Heuristic Search Theory: Survey of Recent Results," *Proceedings of the Seventh International Joint Conference on Artificial Intelligence*, IJCAI-81, University of British Columbia, Vancouver, Aug. 24–28, 1981, pp. 554–562.
92. Perkins, W. A., "Using Circular Symmetry and Intensity Profiles for Computer Vision Inspection," *Computer Graphics and Image Processing*, vol. 17, no. 2, October 1981, pp. 161–172.
93. Pratt, W. K., "Digital Image Processing," Wiley, New York, 1978.
94. Prewitt, J. M. S., "Object Enhancement and Extraction," in Lipkin, B. S., and Rosenfeld, A. (eds.) "Picture Processing and Psychopictorics," Academic, New York, 1970, pp. 75–149.
95. Ramer, E. U., "The Transformation of Photographic Images into Stroke Arrays," *IEEE Transactions on Circuits and Systems*, vol. CAS-22, no. 4, April 1975, pp. 363–374.
96. Riseman, E. M., and Arbib, M. A., "Computational Techniques in the Visual Segmentation of Static Scenes," *Computer Graphics and Image Processing*, vol. 6, no. 3, 1977, pp. 221–276.
97. Roberts, L. G., "Machine Perception of Three-Dimensional Solids," in Tippett, J. T., et al. (eds.), "Optical and Electro-Optical Information Processing," MIT Press, Cambridge, Mass., 1965, pp. 159–197.
98. Robinson, G. S., "Color Edge Detection," *Optical Engineering*, vol. 16, no. 5, September/October, 1977, pp. 479–484.
99. Robinson, G. S., "Edge Detection by Compact Gradient Masks," *Computer Graphics and Image Processing*, vol. 6, no. 5, October 1977, pp. 492–501.
100. Rosenfeld, A., "The Simplest 'Hueckel' Edge Detector is a Roberts Operator," TR-747, Computer Science Center, University of Maryland, College Park, March 1979.
101. Rosenfeld, A., "The Max Roberts Operator is a Hueckel-Type Edge Detector," *IEEE Transactions on Pattern Analysis and Machine Intelligence*, vol. PAMI-3, no. 1, January 1981, pp. 101–103.
102. Rosenfeld, A., and Kak, A. C., "Digital Picture Processing," Academic, New York, 1976.
103. Rosenfeld, A., Lee, Y. H., and Thomas, R. B., "Edge and Curve Detection for Texture Discrimination," in Lipkin, B. S., and Rosenfeld, A. (eds.), "Picture Processing and Psychopictorics," Academic, New York, 1970, pp. 381–393.
104. Rosenfeld, A., and Thurston, M., "Edge and Curve Detection for Visual Scene Analysis," *IEEE Transactions on Computers*, vol. C-20, no. 5, May 1970, pp. 562–569.
105. Rosenfeld, A., Thurston, M., and Lee, Y. H., "Edge and Curve Detection: Further Experiments," *IEEE Transactions on Computers*, vol. C-21, no. 7, July 1972, pp. 677–715.
106. Sankar, P. V., "Color Edge Detection: A Comparative Study," Technical Report TR-666, Computer Science, University of Maryland, College Park, June 1978.

107. Schumann, F., "Einige Beobachtungen über die Zusammenfassung von Gesichtseindrucken zu Einheiten," *Psychologische Studien*, vol. 1, 1904, pp. 1–32.
108. Shaw, G. B., "Local and Regional Edge Detectors: Some Comparisons," *Computer Graphics and Image Processing*, vol. 9, no. 2, February 1979, pp. 135–149.
109. Slagle, J. R., "Artificial Intelligence: The Heuristic Programming Approach," McGraw-Hill, New York, 1971.
110. Stone, J., Dreher, B., and Leventhal, A., "Hierarchical and Parallel Mechanisms in the Organization of Visual Cortex," *Brain Research Reviews*, vol. 1, 1979, pp. 345–394.
111. Sutherland, N. S., "Visual Discrimination of Orientation and Shape by Octopus," *Nature*, 1957, vol. 179, no. 4549, pp. 11–13.
112. Sutherland, N. S., "Theories of Shape Discrimination in Octopus," *Nature*, vol. 188, no. 4756, December 24, 1960, pp. 1092–1094.
113. Sutherland, N. S., "Facts and Theories of Shape Discrimination," *Nature*, vol. 191, no. 4788, April 5, 1961, pp. 580–583.
114. Sutherland, N. S., "Shape Discrimination and Receptive Fields," *Nature*, vol. 197, no. 4863, 1963, pp. 118–122.
115. Tanimoto, S., and Pavlidis, T., "A Hierarchical Data Structure for Picture Processing," *Computer Graphics and Image Processing*, vol. 4, no. 2, 1975, pp. 104–119.
116. Weinstein, G. W., Hobson, R. R., and Baker, F. H., "Extracellular Recordings from Human Retinal Ganglion Cells," *Science*, vol. 171, no. 12, March 1971, pp. 1021–1022.
117. Yashida, M., Ikeda, M., and Tsuji, S., "A Plan-Guided Analysis of Cineangiograms for Measurement of Dynamic Behavior of Heart Wall," *IEEE Transactions on Pattern Analysis and Machine Intelligence*, vol. PAMI-2, no. 6, November 1980, pp. 537–543.
118. Zucker, S. W., and Hummel, R. A., "An Optimal Three-Dimensional Edge Operator," Report No. 79-10, Department of Electrical Engineering, McGill University, Montreal, April 1979.

BIBLIOGRAPHY

Although many papers discuss some of the aspects considered in this chapter, good surveys are hardly bountiful. Perhaps the only comprehensive study of the common principles underlying edge-feature detection by man and machine is that by Barlow, Narasimhan, and Rosenfeld [1].

With regard to the material in Section 5.2, readers are counseled to consult the original articles by Hubel and Wiesel. These papers are quite readable, even for the nonspecialist. For example, a complete description of simple cells can be found in Hubel and Wiesel [4]. Jacobs [5] and Levick [6] review the receptive field research up to about 10 years ago. For a more current view, which relates to the multichannel model in Section 5.4.3, see [2, 7]. An excellent up-to-date discussion of the organizational mechanisms that exist in the visual cortex is found in [11].

Probably the best references for the material in the rest of this chapter are the books by Rosenfeld [8] and Rosenfeld and Kak [9]. A recent survey can be found in Davis [3], while Shaw [10] compares some of the most popular edge detectors on a set of test images. Thresholding methods are surveyed by Weszka [13]. The nature and design of plans for edge detection comprise a still active area of research. The book by Tanimoto and Klinger [12] provides some insight into the pyramid data structure.

1. Barlow, H. B., Narasimhan, R., and Rosenfeld, A., "Visual Pattern Recognition in Machines and Animals," *Science*, vol. 177, no. 4049, Aug. 18, 1972, pp. 567–575.
2. Crick, F. H. C., Marr, D. C., and Poggio, T., "An Information Processing Approach to Understanding the Visual Cortex," A.I. Memo No. 557, Artificial Intelligence Laboratory, Massachusetts Institute of Technology, Cambridge, Mass., April 1980.
3. Davis, L. S., "A Survey of Edge Detection Techniques," *Computer Graphics and Image Processing*, vol. 4, no. 3, September 1975, pp. 270–284.
4. Hubel, D. H., and Wiesel, T. N., "Receptive Fields and Functional Architecture in Two Non-Striate Visual Areas (18-19) of the Cat," *Journal of Neurophysiology*, vol. 28, 1965, pp. 228–289.
5. Jacobs, G., "Receptive Fields in Visual Systems," *Brain Research*, vol. 14, 1969, pp. 553–573.
6. Levick, W. R., "Maintained Discharge in the Visual System and Its Role for Information Processing," chap. 8, in Jung, R. (ed.), "Handbook of Sensory Physiology," vol. VII/3, "Central Processing of Visual Information," Part A, Springer-Verlag, Berlin, 1973, pp. 575–598.
7. Marr, D., "Visual Information Processing: The Structure and Creation of Visual Representations," *Proceedings 6th International Joint Conference on Artificial Intelligence*, Tokyo, Aug. 20–23, 1979, pp. 1108–1126.
8. Rosenfeld, A., "Picture Processing by Computer," Academic, New York, 1969.
9. Rosenfeld, A., and Kak, A. C., "Digital Picture Processing," Academic, New York, 1976.
10. Shaw, G. B., "Local and Regional Edge Detectors: Some Comparisons," *Computer Graphics and Image Processing*, vol. 9, no. 2, February 1979, pp. 135–149.
11. Stone, J., Dreher, B., and Leventhal, A., "Hierarchical and Parallel Mechanisms in the Organization of Visual Cortex," *Brain Research Reviews*, vol. 1, 1979, pp. 345–394.
12. Tanimoto, S., and Klinger, A. (eds.), "Structured Computer Vision, Machine Perception Through Hierarchical Computation Structures," Academic, New York, 1980.
13. Weszka, J. S., "A Survey of Threshold Selection Techniques," *Computer Graphics and Image Processing*, vol. 7, no. 2, April 1978, pp. 259–265.

CHAPTER

SIX

SPATIAL- AND FREQUENCY-DOMAIN PROCESSING

6.1 INTRODUCTION

Linear systems analysis has played a strong role in facilitating our basic understanding of physical processes. Although it often provides just an approximate representation, the ease by which the mathematics can be analyzed makes the theory very convenient indeed. Thus, for example, the rapid development of electronics technology in the latter half of this century has been accompanied by a parallel effort to expand our knowledge of linear theory. Naturally each field has fed on the other, to the point where today it is possible to purchase special processors for computing linear transformations. (Ironically, these are composed largely of nonlinear elements.) Electronics is usually concerned with the representation of one-dimensional signals in the time and frequency domains. In this chapter we shall discuss the two-dimensional spatial pictorial domain with its equivalent spatial frequency domain.

The major reason this subject is of interest is that linear techniques have been extremely useful in the study of image communications and analysis. In general, the two-dimensional approaches have not been different from their one-dimensional counterparts. A major preoccupation is to process or filter the frequency-domain representation in order to obtain more useful data. For example, in image communications it is of interest to eliminate those frequency components which do not contribute significantly to the signal in order to reduce the bandwidth required for the channel. Many of the applications in digital picture processing are concerned with enhancing detail to emphasize certain specific properties. One would expect that both these aspects should also be of prime concern to the human visual system. We are constantly observing images which contain a lot of information, and one method of reducing the throughput might be to utilize some bandwidth compression. Similarly, couldn't our view of the environment be improved by using image enhancement? Some degree of compression is achieved as a result of the bandpass characteristic exhibited by the model described in Chapter 4. However, it would seem that any further economies are obtained by a symbolic coding process, even at this low level of analysis. The feature detectors discussed in Chapter 5 evidently serve this role.

The subject of contrast enhancement in the human visual system is surrounded by some degree of controversy. This concerns the interaction between the so-called neuronal receptive field and the perceptive field. Figure 6.1 shows the relationship between the two concepts in terms of a simple model of the visual system. The neuronal receptive field is determined by means of electrophysiological recordings from physical cells. The perceptive field, which some might consider to be the result of less objective experimentation, is a psychophysical equivalent. The difficulty arises over the question of what connection exists, if any, between very similar phenomena observed in the behavior of both types of fields.

In Section 6.2 we shall discuss some experiments with a horseshoe crab. These studies indicate that there is a lateral interaction between the retinal ganglion cells in the peripheral visual system. It turns out that the coded signals in the optic nerve of the crab are enhanced by this phenomenon. Edge patterns have their boundaries accentuated. Of course, these measurements take place at the level of the neuronal receptive field and there is obviously no way we can ask this creature what it sees. But we can ask humans. Astoundingly, similar patterns presented as stimuli to the human retina also result in image enhancement, but now at the perceptive field level. The patterns which we actually perceive are not in a one-to-one relationship to the intensities in the image but are seen to be increased in contrast. Can we therefore assume that the measurements made at the single-cell level of the crab are related to those made at the perceptual level of man? The answer, discussed in Section 6.2,

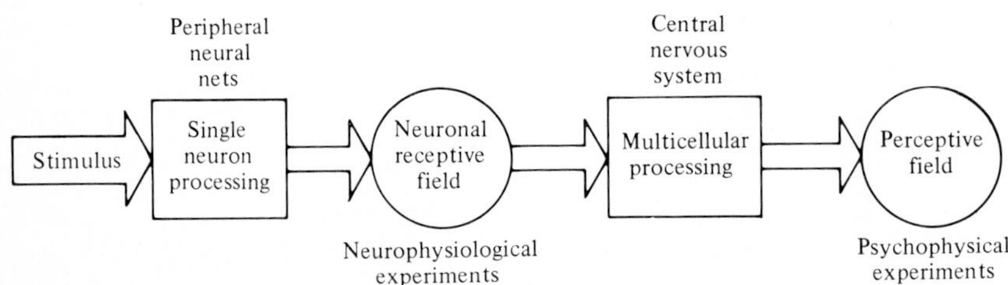

Figure 6.1 Two types of "receptive field," one in the domain of neurophysiology and the other in that of psychophysics.

seems to be in the affirmative, although some doubts do exist. There we distinguish between local processing, of which this type of enhancement is an example, and global processing, which most likely involves complex interaction by the cells in the central nervous system (CNS). Such perceptions as simultaneous contrast, optical illusions, and subjective contours, are also discussed in this context. There seems to be no doubt, although evidence to the contrary is constantly being sought and proposed, that these are indicative of complex global cellular interactions which relate to the overall geometry of the scene.

Having discussed simple enhancement processes in biological systems, we next entertain, in Section 6.3, the possibility of the existence of a complete multichannel biological spectrum analyzer. Evidence pro and con has been found. The implications, if such a configuration were in fact available to the CNS even as an approximation, are enormous. We could then begin to consider the possibility that many of the digital image-processing techniques to be described in the rest of this chapter also exist in some form as a tool for the human brain's analysis of pictures.

The usefulness of spatial frequency techniques in certain types of image-processing problems has been demonstrated, although perhaps the number of applications is exaggerated. Just as some life scientists are keen to see Fourier analysis as an actual mechanism in the brain, engineers and exact scientists very often tend to apply the theory without due consideration to what is being modeled. The temptation of the linear mathematics is just too great! Sections 6.4, 6.5, and 6.6 discuss the general trends of contrast enhancement and restoration of digital pictures in both the spatial and frequency domains. Section 6.4 deals with image coding in both representations, while Sections 6.5 and 6.6 present digital frequency- and spatial-domain processing, respectively. For the most part, these techniques are equivalent, but it is important to understand the nature of the correspondence when analyzing pictures employing computer methods. Both approaches have spawned successful applications, in particular, in the fields of space technology and medicine.

6.2 DATA INTERACTION IN BIOLOGICAL SYSTEMS

6.2.1 Local Spatial Interaction

In 1865 the brilliant scientist Ernst Mach began writing about a phenomenon, to be discussed in this section, that was later to be termed "Mach bands" in his honor. This refers to a physical phenomenon in which what we actually perceive is not present in the viewed stimulus. In addition, the subjective perception is enhanced or accentuated, as if the human visual system finds it necessary to improve the contrast in the original image. In fact, it is often difficult to actually convince people that what they see is not actually physically there.

Another interesting aspect of this discovery is its influence on psychophysical explanation, particularly in recent years. As we shall see in this section, in 1949 Hartline used electrophysiological experiments with the horseshoe crab eye to convincingly demonstrate the existence of this same phenomenon at the level of the single cell. He was also able to show that this was due to spatial interaction of the neurons. Does this mean that the crab also perceives these Mach bands? If this were the case, images processed at the single-cell level and then analyzed at the pooled multicellular level in some unknown fashion, would result in an exactly equivalent phenomenon (see Figure 6.1). Of course, we don't know the answer to this question since the crab is not able to report what it sees. However, there is strong, although not totally convincing evidence, that the Mach bands we perceive are indeed functionally related to a similar retinal, and therefore low-level, neuronal interaction. The latter is strictly a local phenomenon and will be discussed in this section. We shall then present a set of global perceptual phenomena for which there is strong evidence that some degree of high-level processing is taking place in the visual cortex. Nevertheless, as we have previously seen in the introduction, there have been many attempts made to explain these complex perceptions in terms of simple, low-level neuronal interactions, completely ignoring the existence of the intermediate stages (see [166] for a thorough debunking of this practice).

First, let us consider the neurophysiological phenomenon. We have previously discussed how elements of the retina are combined to form a receptive field, a process which can easily be modeled by a summation of individual effects. We have also seen in Chapter 5 that in certain animals, such as frogs, these retinal neurons are spatially organized into specific feature detectors. The latter are primarily responsible for the observance and detection of edges in the image. Again, summation is the operative descriptive mechanism. For mammals such as cats, however, we suggested that these receptive fields can also be structured in a vertical hierarchy aimed at detecting patterns of lines, edges, and even corners. Here we consider spatial, or equivalently, horizontal interaction between the retinal elements. Essentially then, this is a modification of the receptive field theory we have already presented.

The first demonstrations of "lateral inhibition," the term commonly used to describe the interaction, were made by Hartline [71, 73, 74]. He showed conclusively that there were reciprocal antagonisms between the elements of the compound retina and that this produced an enhancement of edges and pattern contrast in the coded optic nerve signal. Consider the two-dimensional array of *Limulus* photoreceptors (see Figure 4.17), each with its own lens and its own optic nerve fiber. We have already noted that the visual field maps on a one-to-one basis from the stimulus to the optic nerve. That is, if we were to arrange for light to fall on a single ommatidium, the resulting generator potential would only be a function of this single input. However, if for example, an edge pattern were to fall on the retinal mosaic, we would expect that the overlapping of the receptive fields would cause a kind of blurring due to the averaging effect. This does not in fact happen! The *Limulus* is able to

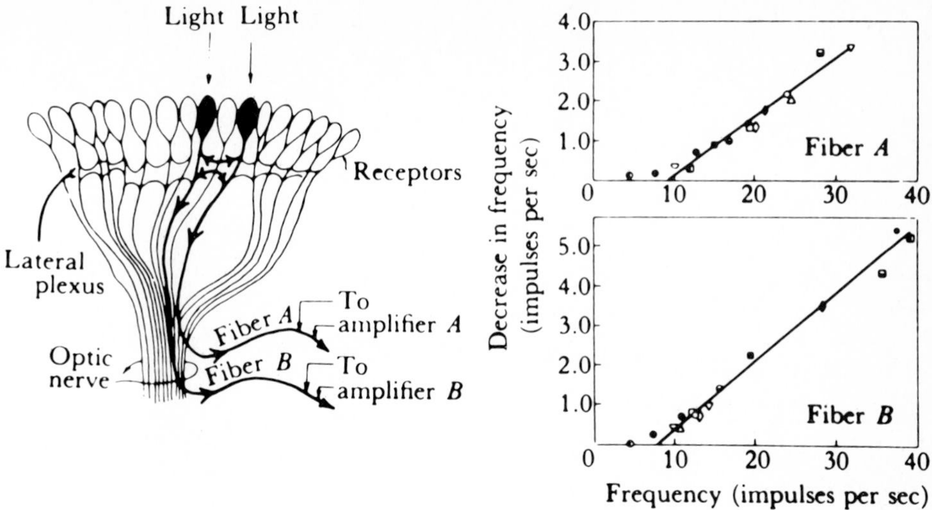

Figure 6.2 Lateral inhibition in the eye of *Limulus.* Spikes were recorded simultaneously from the optic nerve fibers of two receptors, as shown on the left. Each receptor was stimulated either alone or together with the other. The graphs on the right plot the inhibitory effect of one receptor unit on the other; the ordinate gives the decrease in a given fiber's response as a function of the rate of response in the other when both are stimulated together. For example, in the upper graph fiber A fires about 3 spikes per second fewer when fiber B is firing at a rate of about 30 spikes per second. (*From H. R. Hartline, and F. Ratliff, "Inhibitory Interaction of Receptor Units in the Eye of Limulus," Journal of General Physiology, vol. 40, no. 3, 1957, pp. 357–376.*)

compensate for the effect of overlapping receptive fields and surprisingly even enhance the frequency-coded edge response. This is achieved by using lateral inhibition, whereby each receptor inhibits its neighbor. The receptor generator potential is coded into pulses, transmitted, and then made into a slow potential at the input synapses of neighboring receptors. Here a group of weighted inputs is subtracted (and hence the term inhibition) from the receptor's own generator potential, resulting in the inhibitory effect shown in Figure 6.2. We observe that when both are stimulated simultaneously, the reduction in firing rate recorded on the optic nerve fiber of one receptor is linearly related to the firing rate of a neighboring receptor.

An interesting experiment can be performed with the eye of the *Limulus* to clearly demonstrate its ability to perform image enhancement [136, 137]. In Figure 6.3*a*, suppose we first cover the complete retinal mosaic, except for the single facet marked by the symbol of a circle containing a cross ($\otimes$). As the edge pattern is moved over the eye from left to right, there can be no lateral inhibition and hence the response of the appropriate nerve fiber would be as shown in the upper curve in Figure 6.3*b*. This is a replica of the input. When the eye is uncovered and the experiment repeated, the lower curve in Figure 6.3*b* results. This is equivalent to the spatial response that would have been recorded from a set of receptors in the neighborhood of $\otimes$ if the pattern had

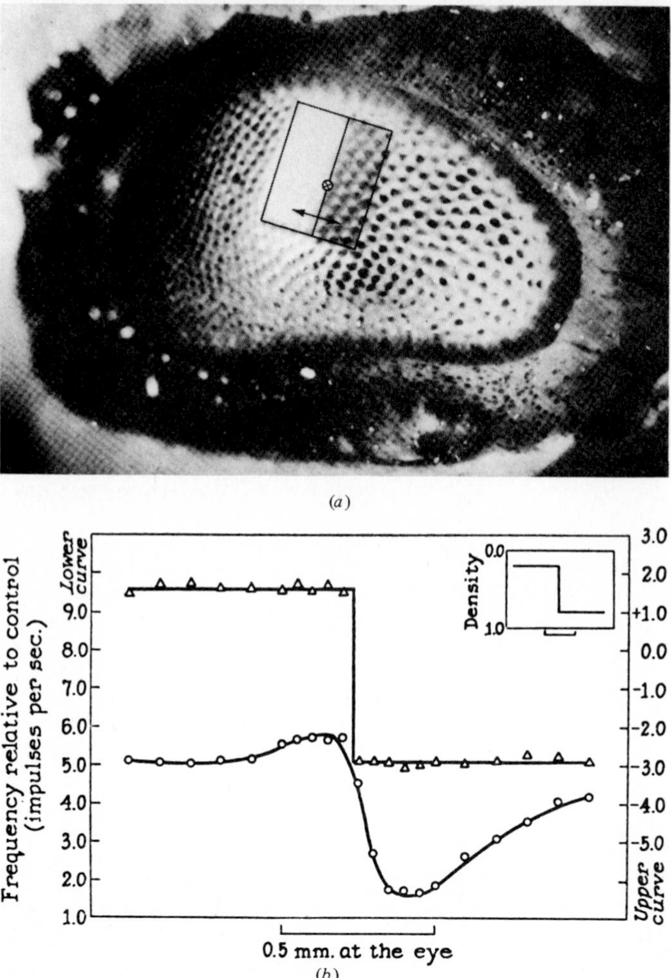

Figure 6.3 Lateral inhibition experiments with *Limulus*. (*a*) The projection of the input pattern onto the compound eye of *Limulus*. (*b*) The effect of lateral inhibition is to enhance the signal by differentiation. [(*a*) *From F. Ratliff, "Mach Bands: Quantitative Studies on Neural Networks in the Retina," Holden-Day, San Francisco, 1965*; (*b*) *from F. Ratliff and H. R. Hartline, "The Responses of Limulus Optic Nerve Fibers to Patterns of Illumination on the Receptor Mosaic," Journal of General Physiology, vol. 42, no. 6, 1959, pp. 1241–1255.*]

remained stationary. Thus the effect of the input edge pattern is actually enhanced! Let us see why. The receptors on the far left of the pattern will be surrounded by neighbors with bright light falling on them. Thus there will be a large degree of inhibition, resulting in the dip in the curve at the left. Similarly on the far right, because the ommatidia are in the dark, there will be a low firing rate, not much affected by its neighbors. Just to the left of the edge a receptor will receive a large degree of inhibition from the receptors on its left (in the bright part of the pattern), and relatively less from those receptors in the dark on its right. This effect increases as we get closer to ⊗, resulting in a higher rate of firing than that of the cells at the far left. To the right of the ⊗, receptors are in the dark and inhibited by those in bright areas to the left, yielding a very low firing rate. As we move from this edge, the inhibitory effect decreases and the rate therefore increases.

We note that the magnitude of the inhibitory effect depends on such factors as the intensity of illumination, the area of illumination, and the separation of the receptor cells. The spatial interaction is complex but simplifications have yielded several mathematical models, apparently all more or less equivalent [135, chap. 3]. Figure 6.4 shows one of these due to Hartline and Ratliff [72], called the "backward inhibitor" or the "nonrecurrent lateral reciprocal inhibitory" model. Suppose R_i is a receptor cell in a neural network. Let e_i define the signal output when it is illuminated alone, and ψ_i the firing rate at its output. Also b_{ij} is the strength of inhibition that R_i exerts on R_j, while θ_{ij} is the threshold of inhibition of i on j. For the two cells in Figure 6.4 we have

$$\psi_1 = \begin{cases} e_1 - b_{21}(\psi_2 - \theta_{21}) & \psi_2 \geq \theta_{21} \\ e_1 & \psi_2 < \theta_{21} \end{cases}$$

$$\psi_2 = \begin{cases} e_2 - b_{12}(\psi_1 - \theta_{12}) & \psi_1 \geq \theta_{12} \\ e_2 & \psi_1 < \theta_{12} \end{cases}$$

which can be generalized to

$$\psi_i = \begin{cases} e_i - \sum_{j=1}^{n} b_{ji}(\psi_j - \theta_{ji}) & \psi_j \geq \theta_{ji} \\ e_i & \psi_j < \theta_{ji} \end{cases} \tag{6.1}$$

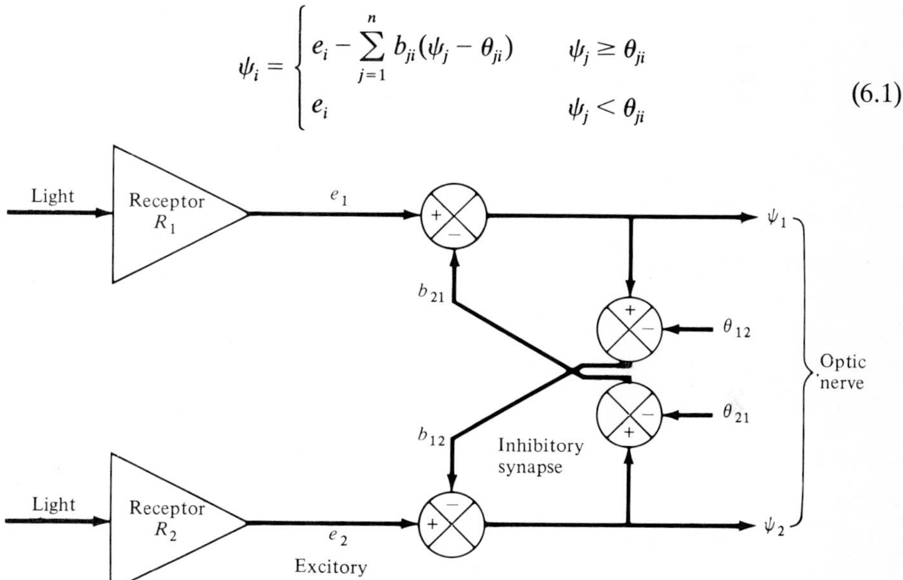

Figure 6.4 The Hartline-Ratliff backward inhibitor model. The thresholds θ_{12} and θ_{21} could be determined from experiments similar to those shown in Figure 6.2.

By assuming symmetry ($\theta_{ij} = \theta_{ji}$ and $b_{ij} = b_{ji}$), the model is simplified slightly and any variations that might exist are averaged out when a pooled computation is performed. It is reasonable to assume that b_{ij} is an exponentially decreasing function of the distance between the receptors:

$$b_{ij} = \begin{cases} 0 & i = j \\ a_0 e^{-a|i-j|} & i \neq j \end{cases} \tag{6.2}$$

where a is a distance factor and a_0 is the inhibition strength factor. Recall that these same parameters were previously defined in Equation (4.31) in conjunction with the definition of $H_2(u)$, the high-pass filter component of the visual system. Ratliff [135] offers five other possible forms for b_{ij} in his discussion on the equivalence of the different models. Finally, if we assume that the firing rate is always above threshold ($\psi_i \gg \theta_{ij}$), then $\theta_{ij} = 0$ and the model becomes

$$\psi_i = e_i - \sum_{j=1}^{n} b_{ij}\psi_j \tag{6.3}$$

It was this formulation that was used by Hall and Hall [65] to derive the expression for $H_2(u)$ given in Chapter 4, thereby providing a link between local neuron interaction and the global frequency-domain description. Of course, we should realize that the spatial-domain model is based on electrophysiological experiments with a *Limulus*, while $H_2(u)$ is a black-box model of the human visual system. Is this therefore a reasonable linkage?

If we do consider mammals such as cats or monkeys, it is no longer feasible to illuminate just a single receptor as was the case with the *Limulus*. It is even difficult to determine the extent of the illumination with respect to the receptors. We have already observed in Section 4.2 that these animals possess retinal ganglion cells characterized by circularly concentric receptive fields. We also saw that the experiments and resulting mathematical model indicated that one of these regions is responsible for inhibition, the other for excitation. The mammalian inhibitory action is shown in Figure 6.5*a*, and it obviously involves more than one photoreceptor. Examination of Figure 4.4, which might be considered as its corresponding spatial-domain response to small-spot mapping, shows that spatial differentiation or, equivalently, enhancement also occurs in this case. This is a high-pass filtering operation, which is also indicated in the human visual system [129]. Just as with the *Limulus*, if we pass an edge pattern over the retina, the ganglion cell of the cat will respond spatially in a manner such that the border between the edges is enhanced [43]. As seen in Figure 6.5*b*, such a response is also compatible with the cat's spatial modulation transfer function (MTF) (see Figure 4.10). It has been shown that the lateral geniculate cells of the cat enhance the contours in two-dimensional figures, for example, squares and triangles. This also occurs with projections of three-dimensional objects, such as a photograph of a cube [91]. Mathematical analyses of pools of neurons and their interconnections have been reported [4, 5]. However, it is not at present possible to link this type of analysis with the "actual perceptual output," the variable we shall consider next.

When a human observes an edge pattern consisting of a black and a white region, one would expect that the visually perceived field is related to the intensities at any given point. Wrong! By 1865 Mach had demonstrated and discussed the existence of light and dark bands in the perceived pattern which had no analog in the actual input [135]. He suggested that this could somehow be accounted for by a second-derivative operation in the early part of the visual

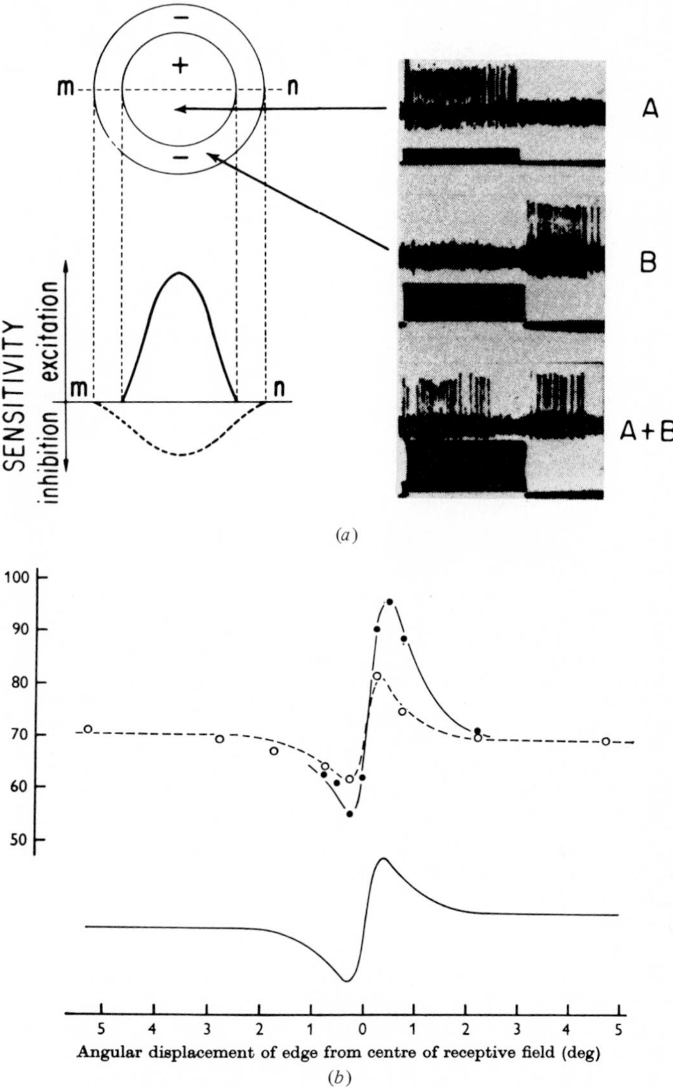

Figure 6.5 (Caption on page 220.)

pathway (recall the discussion in Section 5.4.3). Indeed, if we assume an intensity gradient input to the linear shift-invariant spatial high-pass filter $H_2(u)$, the response is similar to these Mach bands. Thus, it is necessary to make a clear distinction between light intensity, which can be measured by photometric techniques, and its perceptual correlate. The term "brightness" is often used for objects which are perceived to be self-luminous, for example, lights. On the other hand, "lightness" is used when the object is not seen to be self-luminous but reflects light. However, in general, these terms are used interchangeably.

Figure 6.6 demonstrates the existence of the Mach bands. It is important to realize that both the thin white and black lines in the center of the image do not exist as intensity levels in the original picture. They are only perceived as brightness, although many people have difficulty believing this. The profiles in the figure show the actual intensities and associated perceived values. It is clear that some form of second-derivative operation has taken place. Another startling example is shown in Figure 6.7, where the border between the steps is considerably enhanced, to the point where a slight three-dimensional effect may be observed. We stress that the phenomenon depends only on the input intensity profile, and the discrepancy between the objective and subjective appearance is sometimes referred to as "apparent brightness." A simple way readers might generate Mach bands is to stand with their backs to the sun, casting a shadow on a uniform surface such as a road. The Mach bands are

---

Figure 6.5 (*a*) Typical organization of the receptive field of a ganglion cell. The cell receives inputs from excitatory and inhibitory systems. Each of these systems varies in sensitivity across the receptive field; the graphs in the lower left show how the sensitivities of the opposed systems might be distributed across the field. A small spot on the center of the field stimulates the excitatory system more than the inhibitory, thereby eliciting an ON response; similarly, a spot near the edge of the field stimulates primarily the inhibitory system, eliciting an OFF response. Note that in each case the small spot covers a field containing a very large number of receptor cells. On the top left is shown a map of the areas giving rise to ON and OFF responses. On the right are shown records from a single ganglion cell in the cat. The light intensity of the small spot as a function of time is plotted below each response. Records A and B show the responses of the cell evoked by small spots imaged respectively on the field's center and periphery. When both spots are presented together, an ON-OFF response is produced which is less than the sum of the separate responses in A and B. This illustrates the phenomenon of mutual inhibition in the mammalian eye. (*b*) Response of a single ganglion cell in the cat to a step pattern of illumination; the border was presented at different positions on the cell's receptive field. Two different luminance steps were used; responses to the step with the larger difference are shown as filled circles while the responses to the smaller difference are the open circles; mean luminance was the same in both cases. If the step stimulus is appropriately scaled according to the spatial-modulation transfer function of this cell, the predicted output of the cell is shown as the lower curve. [(*a*) *From I. Abramov and J. Gordon, "Vision," Chapter 16 in E. C. Carterette and M. P. Friedman (eds.), "Handbook of Perception, Biology of Perceptual Systems," vol. III, Academic, New York, 1974, pp. 327–357, with records from S. W. Kuffler, "Discharge Patterns and Functional Organization of Mammalian Retina," Journal of Neurophysiology, vol. 16, 1953, pp. 37–68;* (*b*) *from C. Enroth-Cugell and J. G. Robson, "The Contrast Sensitivity of Retinal Ganglion Cells of the Cat," Journal of Physiology, vol. 187, no. 3, December 1966, pp. 517–542.*]

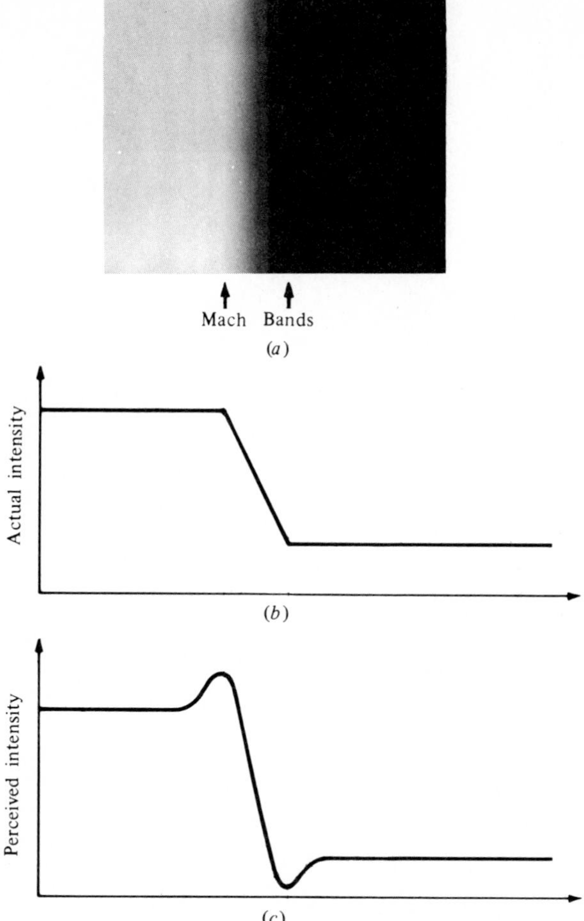

Figure 6.6 The formation of Mach bands, in which what you see is not what you get!

clearly visible in the border area between shadow and light. Ratliff [136] gives several examples of art in which this effect has been taken into account in order to enhance the realism.

The question now arises as to how we know whether the cellular processing is a result of a local or global computation. The answer is that we cannot really be sure that the spatial interaction is indeed local, although the evidence favors such an interpretation. Even if we accept this, it is not clear at all what happens with the data at the higher levels of analysis, which ultimately result in our perceptions. Support for the local hypothesis is offered by the Hermann grid illusion (see Figure 6.8), which is strongly dependent on local geometry; as the grid lines become smaller, the effect is enhanced. This has been tested by experiments in which the effect of an inducing field (I) on one's ability to visually match a test patch (T) to a reference (R) is measured. The arrange-

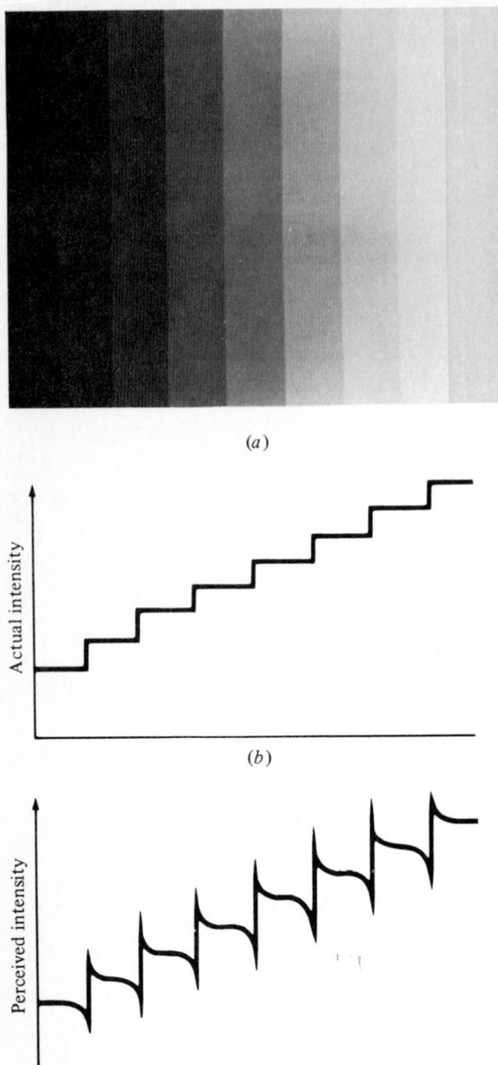

Figure 6.7 The striking effect of Mach band formation in a uniform gray-scale step wedge. The latter is often used to calibrate the gray scale of the image digitizers discussed in Chapter 2.

ment is shown in Figure 6.9*a*, where the distance between *I* and *T* is varied after each experiment in order to detect how the spatial interaction is affected. The results are graphed in Figure 6.9*b*, where the distance between *I* and *T* is shown in minutes at the right. For a given separation, it is obvious that the greater the illuminance of the inducing field *I*, the greater the illuminance of *T* must be made for its brightness to match that of *R*. Thus, the strength of the inducing field is an effective parameter in influencing the response. What is more interesting, however, is that for a given value of *I* the brightness of the

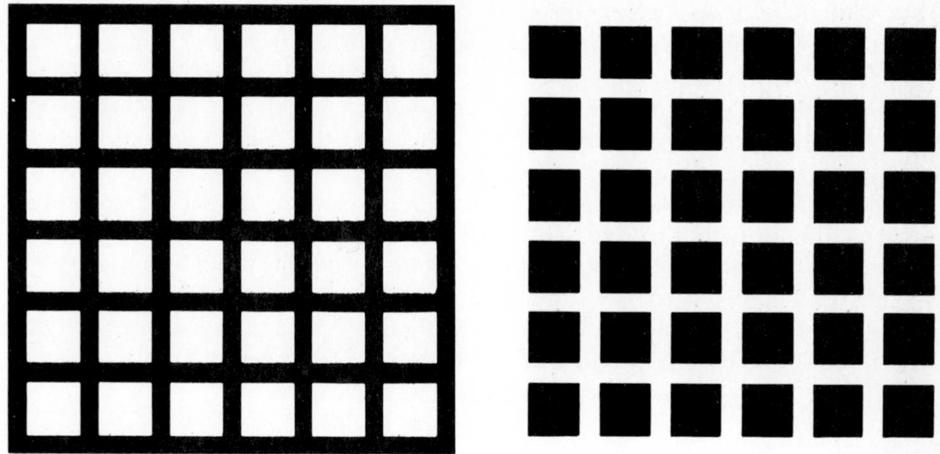

Figure 6.8 The Hermann grid illusion. After fixating on the pattern for a few seconds, you will begin to notice spots at the intersections of lines.

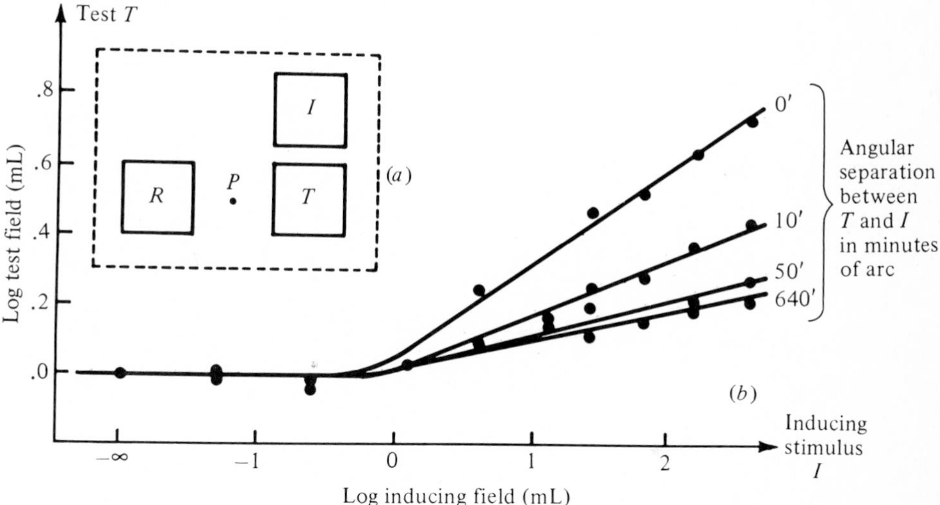

Figure 6.9 A graph showing the lateral inhibitory interaction (b), which can be observed in a human visual psychophysical experiment by using a stimulus as shown in (a), as a function of the spatial separation between the test (T) and inducing stimulus (I). The brightness of the inducing field I is measured with a reference (R) as a function of angular separation and brightness of the test T. P is a fixation point. (*Adapted from W. R. Uttal, "The Psychobiology of Sensory Coding," Harper & Row, New York, 1973, p. 371, and originating in H. Leibowitz, F. A. Mote, and W. R. Thurlow, "Simultaneous Contrast as a Function of Separation Between Test and Inducing Fields," Journal of Experimental Psychology, vol. 46, 1953, pp. 453–456.*)

test field T must be increased as the distance between them is decreased. Therefore, proximity is also a factor and the shape of the graphs implies local spatial interaction, as would be necessary for the Mach band phenomenon [167, pp. 369–400, 443–456]. If the Hermann grid pattern is prepared as a stereoscopic slide and presented to both eyes, it turns out that the illusion cannot be seen, even though the pattern can be fused into a single image. Since it is known that binocular fusion does not occur at a level below that of the lateral geniculate nucleus, this is further evidence of low-level and local processing.

Finally it is interesting to examine whether the black-box approach considered in Chapter 4 leads to the output of the Mach bands when presented with the appropriate input. As shown in Figure 6.10, this is indeed the case. The model predicts Mach bands which correspond in strength and location to

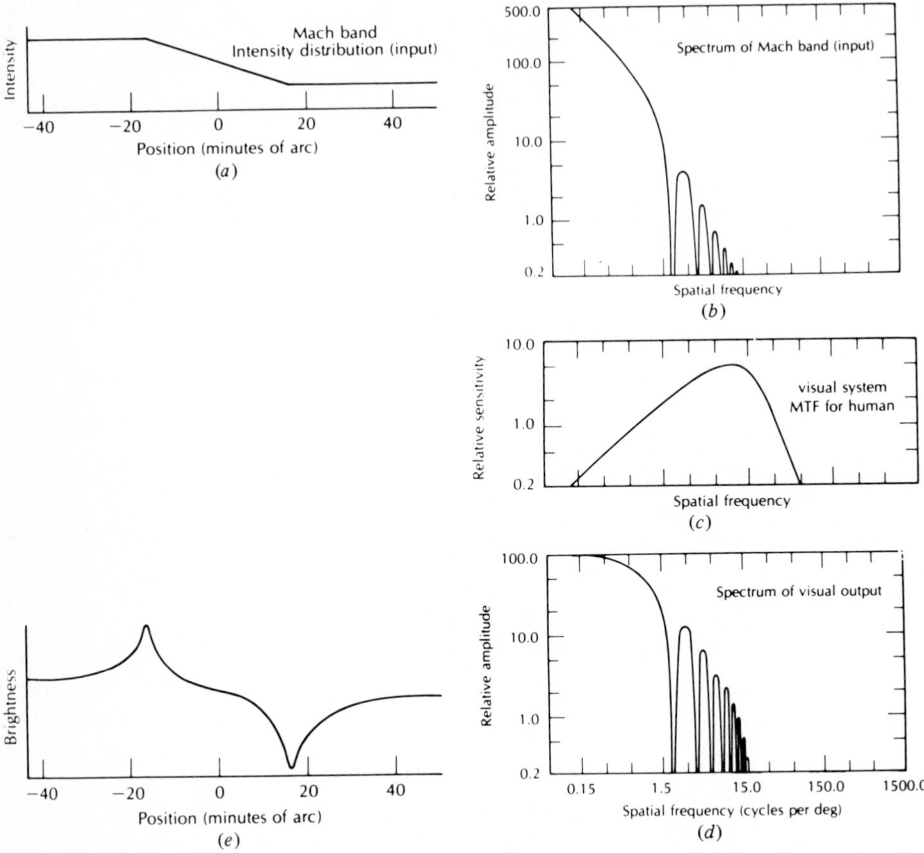

Figure 6.10 A demonstration of the existence of Mach bands using the single-channel black-box model for human vision discussed in Chapter 4. An input stimulus (*a*) having a Fourier spectrum (*b*) is filtered by the human modulation transfer function (MTF) shown in (*c*). The product of the two yields the output shown in (*d*). The inverse Fourier transform results in the supposed "perceived output" in (*e*). The Mach band phenomenon is evident in this response to (*a*). (*From T. N. Cornsweet, "Visual Perception," Academic, New York, 1970, p. 344.*)

(a)

(b)

Figure 6.11 The effect of suppressing the Mach band phenomenon in the model of human vision. The picture in (a) would be perceived as (b)! (*From T. G. Stockham, Jr., "Image Processing in the Context of a Visual Model," Proceedings of the IEEE, vol. 60, no. 7, July 1972, pp. 828–842.*)

exactly those that would be perceived by a human. The implication, of course, is that the MTF of the human visual system corresponds only to the low-level image processing activity, as would be expected, based on the type of edge pattern used as input in these experiments. What would the world look like if we inserted an inversion filter in the visual system to cancel out the effect of $H_2(u)$, the high-pass filter component of the model? Stockham [155, 156] has experimented with this idea as a means of computing $H_2(u)$, and Figure 6.11 is a striking demonstration of the effect. As might be expected, the elimination of the differentiation effect of $H_2(u)$ leads to a blurring of the image, making it difficult to perceive the fine detail. We shall examine this concept of frequency-domain filtering in greater detail later in this chapter.

This section may be summarized by stating that there is clear, but not absolutely certain, evidence that the perceptual Mach bands observed by humans are a result of the low-level spatial interaction of the neurons in the retina. The fact that such interaction has been demonstrated at the neuronal level for the *Limulus* does not necessarily imply that the same happens for humans. At present we are neither able to perform perceptual experiments with the *Limulus* nor electrophysiological experiments with humans in order to test the theory.

6.2.2. Global Interaction

Introduction Over the years several interesting phenomena have been studied by psychologists. Some of the important ones will be briefly discussed in this section. Many explanations have been offered for the processing mechanisms thought to be responsible for the effects observed. None of these have been substantiated by neurophysiological experimentation. However, there does seem to be general agreement that the processes involved are multicellular and therefore the result of a complex global interaction of the neurons [5] (see Figure 6.1). It is for this reason that they are presented together in this section and not because it is intended to imply that similar computations are involved. Most probably, a different biological "algorithm" is needed in each case.

Subjective contours "Subjective contours" are edges which are perceived, but in areas where no physical change in gray level actually exists [92]. The first report of this illusion was by F. Schumann in 1904. These contours are sometimes referred to as "anomalous" or "illusory contours," and it is highly unlikely that they are related to the functioning of low-level edge detectors of the type described in the previous chapter.

We find it necessary to distinguish three types of data models [16]. The first is an abstract model of the image, which is what most of us think of when drawing or looking at a picture. The second is a perceptual model, which embodies the attributes that are perceived. The third is concerned with the actual physical image, the measurements that can be made which characterize the shapes of objects and their topological placement. Subjective contours are thought to be the result of an interplay between all three of these models in which, apparently, the perceived image differs from the physical image because of a stored abstract model. A simple example of a subjective contour is the so-called sun illusion shown in Figure 6.12. The boundary of a disk is clearly perceived even though physically it does not exist. The edge appears to be there from a global perspective but not from the point of view of local data analysis. Therefore template edge detectors of the type discussed in Chapter 5 are ineffectual under these circumstances. This is clearly demonstrated in Figure 6.13.

An interesting set of experiments has been performed by Stevens [154] with patients suffering from visual agnosia, who are therefore unable to perceive subjective contours. He concludes that the contours are partially the result of detecting two-dimensional occlusion cues which relate to an apparently three-dimensional scene. A similar suggestion has been made by

Figure 6.12 A subjective contour, the so-called sun illusion.

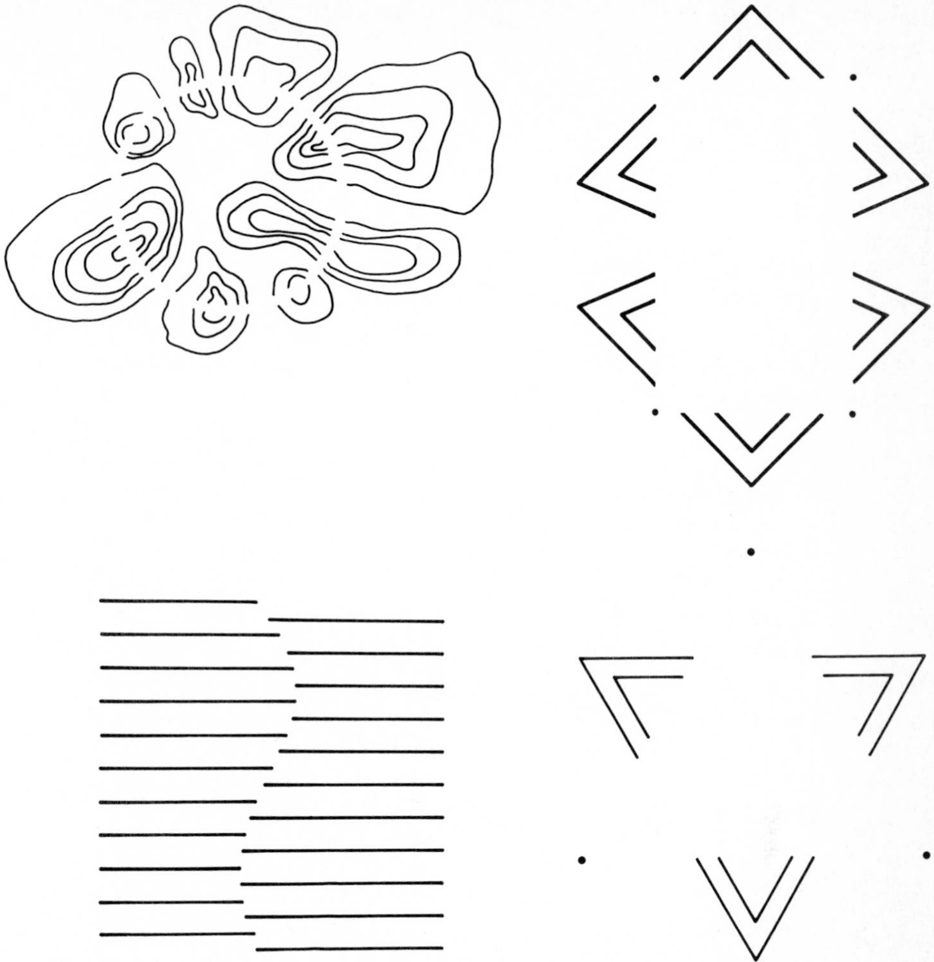

Figure 6.13 The hypothesis that the subjective contour is the result of the activation of edge detectors seems to be contradicted by the figures on the left. The subjective contours are actually orthogonal to the edge segments; nevertheless, the curved boundary is clearly visible. On the right, we note that absolutely no edges are present; yet the dots are ample cues for us to perceive the geometric figures. (*From G. Kanizsa, "Organization in Vision," Praeger, New York, 1979.*)

Coren [30]. It is known that two independent processes are used for the perception of occlusion. One is stereoscopic in nature and is solely based on the computation of disparity which results from a parallax phenomenon. This is similar to the one used by Levine [99] for the range finder of a *Mars Rover*. The other distinct process is monocular. It is generally thought to depend on the presence of local evidence that points to the existence of one opaque body occluding another. These clues have been successfully used to interpret complex pictures containing polyhedra [169]. Clearly, a global spatial interaction is responsible for this phenomenon.

Simultaneous contrast The preceding section dealt with edges which are perceived but which are not physically present at all. Here we discuss the existence of gray-level patches which are observed to have intensities different from those that might actually be measured by a densitometer [123]. This phenomenon is called "simultaneous contrast," a perceptual effect in which what we see is affected by neighboring areas. It is thought to be the result of global interactions and as such differs from both Mach bands and the Hermann grid illusion.

We may delineate both positive and negative simultaneous contrast effects. The first occurs when viewing a spot of light—the spot is easier to see if a dim light is placed nearby. The second happens when observing a small gray area surrounded by a white border—the area will actually appear to be darker if the border is made black. Figure 6.14 shows the striking effect of the simultaneous contrast phenomenon; the two bars are actually identical shades of gray, yet the one on the right is seen to be much darker. The classical stimulus for demonstrating simultaneous contrast is given in Figure 6.15. Again, the two squares are actually physically the same. The contrast is enhanced if the size of the stimulus is increased, and the phenomenon can also involve color. Other parameters which have been shown to influence the perceptual effect include the size and intensity of the background and the location of the stimulus with respect to the border of the background. There have been considerable speculation and analysis regarding this phenomenon. Attempts to explain the underlying mechanism have included low-level spatial interaction of the type we have discussed in conjunction with the Mach band phenomenon. However, as we have already implied, the interactions under discussion here are most likely global in nature.

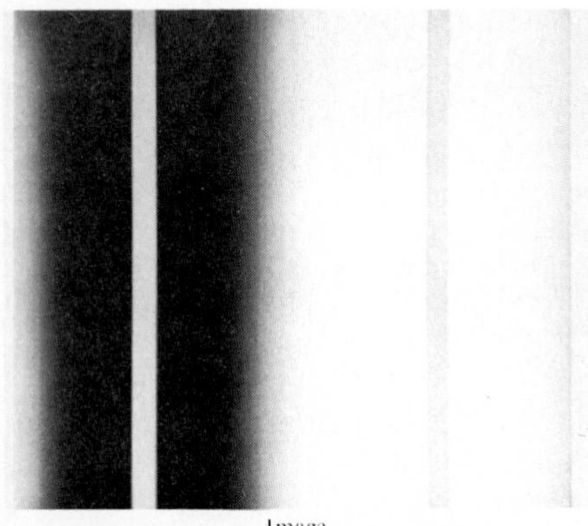

Image

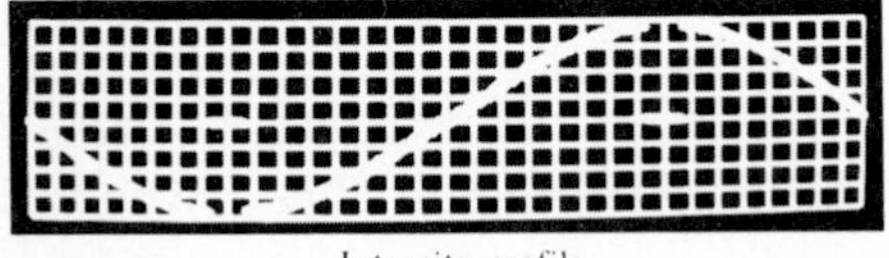

Intensity profile

Figure 6.14 The simultaneous contrast phenomenon is demonstrated here by two identical bars superimposed upon a sinusoidal background. They appear to be different but are actually the exact same shade of gray. This may be seen by covering up everything in the picture except for the bars.

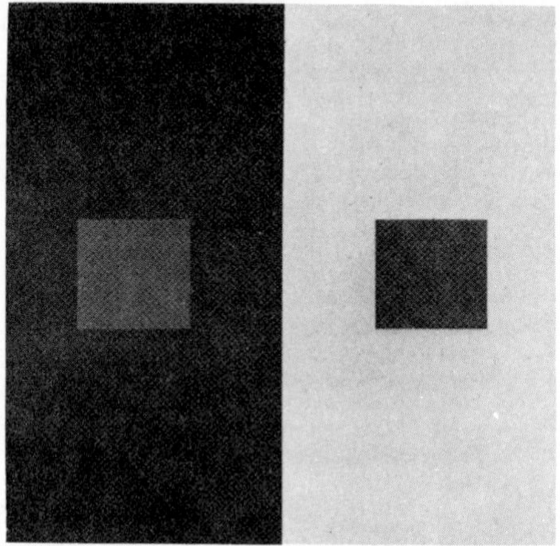

Figure 6.15 The classical version of the simultaneous contrast phenomenon. Needless to say, the two small patches are both the same shade of gray. (*From T. G. Stockham, Jr., "Image Processing in the Context of a Visual Model," Proceedings of the IEEE, vol. 60, no. 7, July 1972, pp. 828–842.*)

Consider the two experiments which were used to demonstrate the effect of local processing, shown in Figure 6.9. Here the brightness of the test field is a monotonic function of the distance to the inducing field. This correlates well with the lateral inhibition model suggested. On the other hand, simultaneous contrast is binary in the sense that it is either present or not. This holistic, or global, effect clearly implies more complex computations than are possible by the simple model. We have also seen that the latter is additive, providing a linear relationship between the response and the size of the receptive field. This has been demonstrated not to be the case for simultaneous contrast observed on the fovea [27]. The amount of surround is not important and does not seem to affect the perception; only the separation between the test and inducing fields is of consequence. The apparent brightness of the test patch increases significantly with separation. Various other experiments with stereoscopic presentations have established situations in which Mach bands cannot be produced but simultaneous contrast is possible. This implies that the latter is a result of more complex neuronal processes at a higher level.

Other examples of simultaneous contrast are given in [33, chap. 11]. Ratliff [135] shows some similar phenomena in art, where a suitably placed contour is actually able to reverse the perceived contrast when compared with the physical luminances.

Complex multicellular processes are involved, yes. But what they are, we do not know.

Spatial illusions Spatial illusions, sometimes called "visual" or "optical illusions," present clear indications that the global appearance and organization of the objects in a scene strongly affect our perception of them. What we see obviously does not depend strictly on the local intensities. In modern times, J. J. Opel published the first paper on this subject in 1854; he suggested that a space which is divided tends to look longer than a space of exactly equivalent length but undivided (see Figure 6.16*j*). However it appears that even the classical

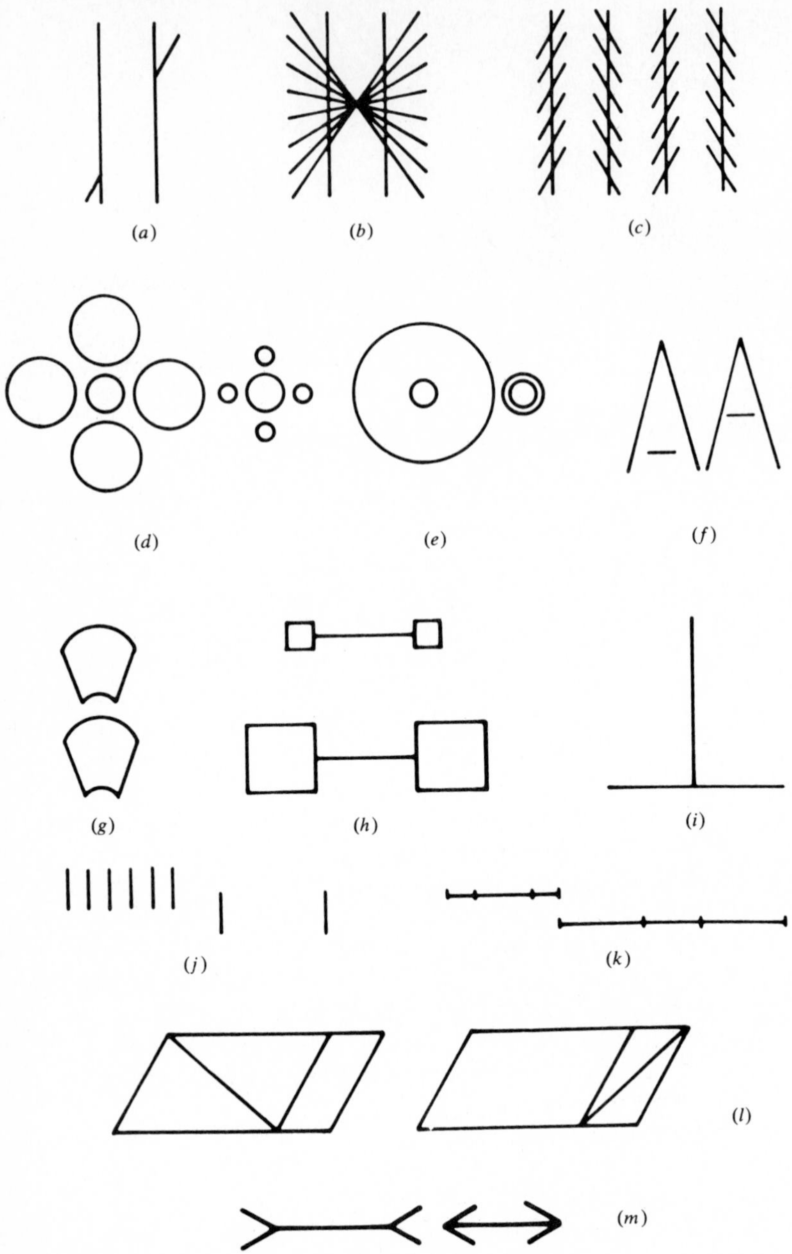

Figure 6.16 Thirteen common illusion forms used by [30]. (*a*) The Poggendorff illusion; (*b*) the Wundt illusion; (*c*) the Zoellner illusion; (*d*) the Ebbinghaus illusion; (*e*) the Delboeuf illusion; (*f*) the Ponzo illusion; (*g*) the Jastrow illusion; (*h*) the Baldwin illusion; (*i*) the horizontal-vertical illusion; (*j*) the Opel-Kundt illusion; (*k*) the divided-line illusion; (*l*) the Sander parallelogram; (*m*) the Mueller-Lyer illusion. (*After S. Coren and J. S. Girgus, "Seeing Is Deceiving: The Psychology of Visual Illusions," Lawrence Erlbaum Associates, Hillsdale, N.J., 1978.*)

Greek architects were aware of spatial illusions and introduced compensatory corrections in the design of buildings in order to preserve their perceived symmetry. Theories to explain the origins of these illusions are many, and over 1000 papers on this topic have appeared since Opel's time. Nevertheless, no satisfactory psychological or neurophysiological model has yet been accepted. This, it seems, must await a more comprehensive understanding on our part of the functioning of the brain. Readers who have a further interest in this often fascinating subject are referred to [25, 31, 140].

There is not even agreement on how to categorize the many manifestations of this phenomenon. Coren and his associates [32] used factor analysis in an attempt to determine a satisfactory taxonomy for visual illusions. They employed the 13 most popular illusions, which are shown in Figure 6.16. Two major categories were isolated: those based on size contrast and those based on shape and direction. Size contrast can depend on either length or area. The former is represented by seven illusions: (1) the Opel-Kundt illusion (see Figure 6.16*j*), in which the divided linear extent looks greater than the undivided one; (2) the horizontal-vertical illusion (see Figure 6.16*i*), in which it appears that the vertical segment is longer than the horizontal one, even though they are of equal length (this may depend on the fact that the lines fall on the retina at different orientations); (3) The Mueller-Lyer illusion (see Figure 6.16*m*), a very popular one, in which again all linear extents are equal but do not appear to be; (4) the Baldwin illusion (see Figure 6.16*h*), in which the effect of the larger squares is to make the associated joining line look shorter; (5) the Ponzo illusion (see Figure 6.16*f*), which has fascinated many, in which the horizontal line on the right appears to be longer and generally lines closer to the apex will have their length overestimated; (6) the divided-line illusion (see Figure 6.16*k*), in which the central portion of the upper line looks bigger, even though it isn't; and finally (7) the Sander illusion (see Figure 6.16*l*), in which the undivided figure on the right looks longer.

Size contrast based on area comparisons is represented by three examples: (1) the Ebbinghaus illusion (see Figure 6.16*d*), in which the central object surrounded by the larger objects appears to be smaller (this is similar to the Baldwin illusion); (2) the Delboeuf illusion (see Figure 6.16*e*), in which the apparent size of the inner of two concentric circles is a function of the diameter of the outer circle; and (3) the Jastrow illusion (see Figure 6.16*g*), in which the upper figure appears smaller although both are of exactly the same area.

The second category, based on shape and direction, consists of three illusions: (1) the Zoellner illusion (see Figure 6.16*c*), in which two parallel lines appear to be tilted when they are intersected by numerous short line segments forming acute angles with them; (2) the Poggendorff illusion (see Figure 6.16*a*), in which the two line segments do not appear to be collinear; and (3) the Wundt illusion (see Figure 6.16*b*), in which the lines appear to be curved although they are actually parallel. The first two are illusions of direction, and the Wundt illusion is one of shape. It also is interesting that some of these illusions can be observed by using subjective contours [18].

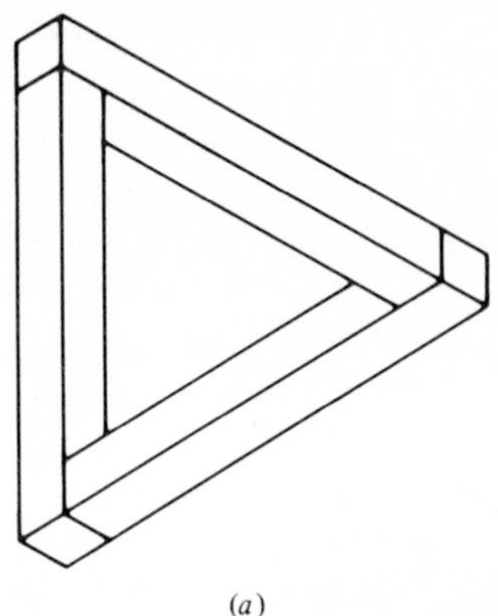

(*a*)

(*b*)

Figure 6.17 (*a*) The impossible (?) Penrose triangle. This figure is consistent locally but not from a global perspective. In fact, it is possible to construct this scene, as shown in (*b*), an untouched photograph of a wooden object which appears impossible to construct because the visual system accepts a false assumption, from which the "perceptual hypothesis" is developed. The perception is paradoxical. Perceptual hypotheses are not always corrected by intellectual knowledge. [*From R. L. Gregory, "Illusions and Hallucinations," chap. 9 in E. C. Carterette and M. P. Friedman (eds.), "Handbook of Perception," vol. IX, "Perceptual Processing," Academic, New York, 1978, pp. 337–357.*]

The two major categories distinguished above have been suggested to be the result of certain unspecified underlying mechanisms [32]. However, the other categories that were found must also be related to neuronal and perceptual mechanisms. The best we can say is that illusions are controversial and as yet unexplained. No doubt they depend on complex global analysis, which seems to be related to how the cortex employs perspective to judge distance and depth, that is, how the two-dimensional image is perceived with respect to our ability to use certain local contextual clues to isolate the organization of the original three-dimensional scene [51]. The elements of perspective, contrast, orientation, and past experience are all involved. A good example of this is the Penrose triangle, shown in Figure 6.17*a*. Here the local perspective geometry is always correct; however when it is put together, an apparently impossible figure results [62]! But is this really the case? Readers are referred to Figure 6.17*b* for a solution to this particular puzzle.

6.3 A BIOLOGICAL SPECTRUM ANALYZER?

During the last decade a very successful application of digital image processing has been the use of computational techniques to reconstruct pictures from a sequence of projections. This has led to the development of computerized tomography in medicine, whereby with a relatively small amount of radiation a medical practitioner is able to observe the three-dimensional structure within an organ, for example the brain. Whole body scanners of this type are also available. One approach to the mathematical analysis of this method necessitates the computation of the Fourier transform, from which the desired reconstruction is then determined. Thus, a discrete sequence of one-dimensional Fourier transforms can be converted into a three-dimensional spatial image representation in the computer. But can this also occur within the human brain? Much as this seems improbable, a suggestion has been made that complex cells might physically exist in the cortex which actually compute the Fourier transform [131]. This appears highly unlikely, and the hypothesis is perhaps based mainly on an enthusiastic confusion between the model and an actual mechanism. But not completely! In this section we shall examine some of the experiments and theories which led to this still unresolved issue.

The beginning of the story is Figure 4.10, which shows the spatial frequency response of the human and cat visual systems, respectively. We have described these graphs in Chapter 4 as black-box models, thereby implying that they provided a good description of the input/output behavior. The advantage of such a paradigm is the obvious mathematical tractability of linear systems, that is, the ease and simplicity of the representation. A large body of knowledge and experiments has grown up over the years attesting to the generality of this formalism. For example, Granlund has recently shown how the linearity property can even be used to define a general-purpose picture-processing operator [60]. However, opposed to this essentially descriptive mechanism, which is referred to in the literature as the "single-channel theory," there has emerged since the late sixties a so-called multichannel theory [102]. The main hypothesis underlying this model is that there exist several independent frequency-selective channels which combine to give the responses shown in Figure 4.10. This implies the existence of actual physical elements which are sensitive to a band of frequencies, much like bandpass filters. We can now see how the acceptance of the multichannel theory led to the suggestion of the biological spectrum analyzer being incorporated in a cortical system for image reconstruction. In any event, a considerable amount of experimentation in both psychophysics and neurophysiology has developed around this interesting hypothesis.

Does the evidence support the concept of a spectrum analyzer in the human cortex? Arguments for and against have been presented. As an example, readers are referred to [166; 167, pp. 474–480], and the excellent review article of Georgeson [50], who tries to present both sides of the issue. There does seem to be direct physiological evidence of neuronal elements sensitive to frequency, analogous to the feature detectors in the spatial domain that we discussed in Chapter 5. The assumption of its existence can even be used to explain perceptual phenomena, for example the pincushion illusion [124]. However, perhaps there is a philosophical question about our ability ever to be able to resolve this question satisfactorily. The generality of the spatial-frequency-domain description hinders us from being able to isolate the physical phenomenon from the model. Nevertheless, the concept has led to some very interesting experiments and in addition is presently the focus of a considerable amount of research.

Although the first experiments were done by DePalma and Lowry [40], the seminal investigations were performed by Campbell and Robson in 1968 using grating patterns of different kinds [22]. We have already noted in the discussions in Section 4.3.2 that these periodic waveforms are essentially one-dimensional. By employing gratings made up of a sum of components of different frequencies, Campbell and Robson concluded that above about 1 cycle/degree the contrast sensitivity was only dependent on the fundamental spectral component in the signal input. The authors then initiated an essentially new area of investigation by proposing the existence of multiply tuned independent channels. Thus, a given frequency component was assumed to be detected only when its particular channel exceeded a threshold. Further, they suggested that the channels were noninteracting and narrowly tuned. A convincing aspect of their argument is given in Figure 6.18, where the human contrast sensitivity function (CSF) is shown for both a sine-wave and square-wave stimulus input. We know, of course, that the latter consists of a fundamental plus the odd harmonics. Above 1 cycle/degree, the CSFs are quite similar in shape. This lends support to the multichannel theory, since the harmonics can be assumed to be below threshold. What turned out to be even more exciting was that the ratio of the CSF of the square wave to that of the sine wave was plotted and proved to be more or less equal to $4/\pi$, independent of frequency (see Figure 6.18). This is exactly the ratio of the

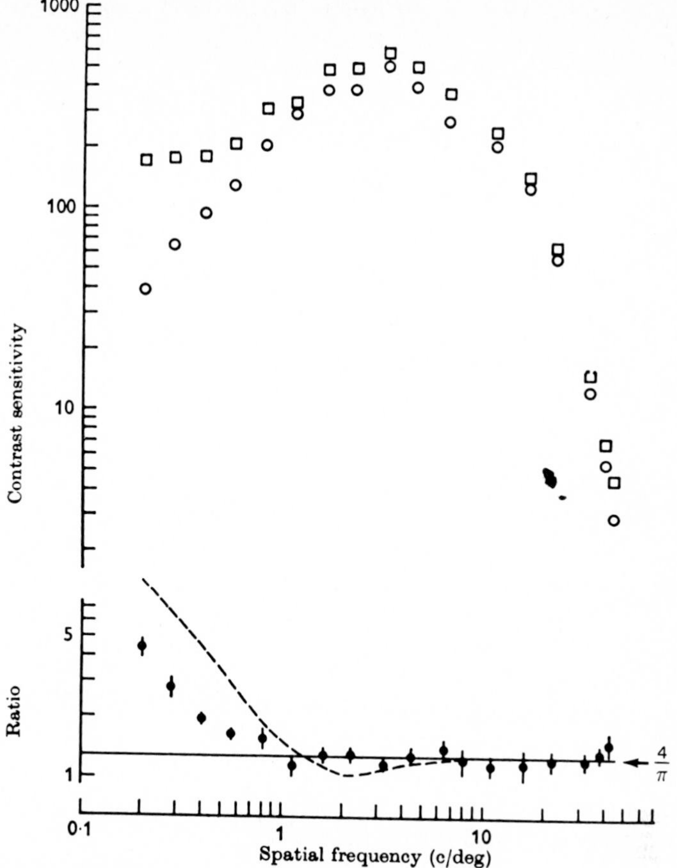

Figure 6.18 At the top is shown the contrast sensitivity function for a subject with sine-wave (○) and square-wave (□) grating stimulus. The ratio of the two is shown below. (*From F. W. Campbell and J. G. Robson, "Application of Fourier Analysis to the Visibility of Gratings," Journal of Physiology, vol. 197, no. 3, 1978, pp. 551–566.*)

square-wave fundamental frequency to the sine-wave fundamental frequency. The two image patterns were not distinguishable by observers until the amplitude of the square wave was increased to the point where the third harmonic went above the specific threshold required for that frequency. These experiments were also repeated with other signal stimuli which had large second harmonic content with similarly good results. However, and this has by now become a very common occurrence, Georgeson [49] and Nachmias and Weber [118] have used a different experimental psychophysical technique to contradict the original conclusions. Both have shown that, in fact, the signals can be distinguished even though the harmonics may still be below threshold. Their postulated explanation was that the channels were not narrowly tuned as originally suggested. Nevertheless the multichannel theory was still upheld but with the proviso that the channels seem to have wider bandwidths.

There seems to be general agreement for the existence of a multichannel model with independent bandpass filters which are relatively broad, perhaps one octave in width. This is true even for suprathreshold experiments, but it appears that the perceived contrast characteristic is different [23]. Recent experiments suggest that in this case the contrast perception is a linear function of stimulus contrast [54]. Although the multichannel model does not allow us to speak about spectral analysis in the classical sense, it still remains an interesting formulation, one which could benefit by the use of Fourier transform analysis techniques. It also implies some degree of separation of the data according to spatial frequency.

Let us briefly examine some other experiments and evidence for the correctness of this model. One of these relates to the psychophysical adaptation to grating patterns; in classical adaptation the system becomes accommodated to an input stimulus so that the response to such a signal eventually declines. It is as if the system were inclined to respond to changes in conditions rather than to ongoing situations. Blakemore and Campbell [15] have performed some experiments with stationary sinusoidal gratings. They showed that the contrast increased, or equivalently the contrast sensitivity decreased, when the input spatial frequency was similar to the frequency of the adapting signal. Furthermore, the adaptation turns out to be orientation-selective. This conforms to the results of experiments by Campbell and Kulikowski [21], in which maximum contrast sensitivity was demonstrated for orientations around 0 or 90°. The sensitivity decreased in a monotonic manner, reaching a minimum at 45°. These findings for humans are of interest because the cells in the visual cortex of cats and monkeys are also both orientation- and frequency-selective. Could there be a relationship between this two-dimensional neuronal parameterization and the perceptual experiments? Orientation sensitivity in these animals has been reported in [20, 80, 81]. Spatial-frequency sensitivity of cat cortical neurons has been suggested in [88, 104], and similar conclusions have been reached for the monkey [41]. These experiments purport to find cortical neurons which are tuned to certain frequencies, the bandwidth of the filter being about one octave wide.

Figure 6.19 shows how the detectability of a pattern is affected by grating adaptation [12]. View the square wave in Figure 6.19*a* at arm's length for 30 to 60 s. We see the edges clearly because the contrast is above the threshold of detection. However, adaptation alters our sensitivity to images containing similar spatial-frequency components. Thus, because the bars in Figure 6.19*b* are three times wider than those in *a*, our sensitivity is reduced to the third harmonic, ninth harmonic, and so on. When we view the third harmonic bar pattern in *b*, it temporarily appears blurred because of this lowered sensitivity. In fact, if *b* were a low-contrast version of *a* with the same bar size, the image would disappear. Angular sensitivity may be tested by repeating the experiment with the image in *a* rotated by 90°. Now there is no blurring effect!

If we are not prepared to accept these results as evidence of the existence of frequency-selective neurons, an alternative but equivalent formulation might

(a) (b)

Figure 6.19 Visual adaptation. The reader should view the horizontal bars in (*a*) for about 1 min in order to adapt to the spatial frequency. The sensitivity to the third harmonic of the latter is then reduced, so that the grating in (*b*) appears to be blurred.

be proposed. This is based on the duality of the frequency and spatial domains. One argument rests on the hypothesis that the neurons are actually organized into computational networks which model multiple bar detectors. This is just a slight extension of the concept of line detectors shown in Figure 5.4, with the exception that instead of three zones we add on, for example, an extra excitory zone at each end. To conform with experimental evidence, the zones are weighted, so that the outer ones are taken to be weaker than the inner ones. Such a neuron is in a certain sense a local grating detector. Macleod and Rosenfeld [103] have used this spatial-domain model to show that it can account for all the experimental data of Campbell and Robson, even below 1 cycle/degree. An interesting discussion of the properties of these localized "spectral analyzers" can be found in [107].

Kulikowski and King-Smith [94, 95] have added some support to this idea by proposing that the phenomenon is in fact due to the existence of line detectors. They have performed experiments involving the threshold detection of such a pattern superimposed on a background pattern which was just below threshold. The latter was made to be an invisible grating, and a dark test line was superimposed and lined up with the dark zone of the grating. They then plotted the threshold of detection of a specific line for different grating frequencies. The result is claimed to be the tuning curve of the line detector, and indeed the resulting line-spread function (LSF) is compatible with the Macleod-Rosenfeld hypothesis. The tuning curve was found to be narrower than the CSF in Figure 4.10, thereby implying that perhaps other channels exist for various line widths. Employing different line widths, Kulikowski and King-Smith found tuning curves centered at 3, 5, and 9 cycles/degree; not surprisingly, the envelope of these curves is very similar in shape to the human

CSF shown in Figure 4.10. Further support for grating detectors is provided by Glezer and Cooperman [58], albeit as part of a generalized piecewise Fourier transform computation in the cortex.

Of the available models in the literature, the multichannel model with pooling has the most scientific support at present, and we shall therefore examine it in more detail. It must be emphasized that the experimental situation under consideration is low-contrast detection using matching experiments to obtain the threshold data, as discussed in Chapter 4. The assumption is that there exist n independent channels with bandwidths about one octave wide [34]. These are pooled to give the same overall modulation transfer function as that of the single-channel hypothesis (see Figure 6.18). However, there is also a pooling phenomenon within each individual channel. Each so-called channel actually consists of a collection of cells which are distributed over the retinal field. Together they combine to exhibit the behavior of a single channel.

Figure 6.20a illustrates the probability summation model [59, 142]. In the matching experiments, the presented input stimulus is a sine-wave pattern superimposed on a constant gray value. Thus, a grating of spatial frequency u oriented at an arbitrary angle β is given by

$$I(x, y) = i_0[1 + C \cdot i(x, y)] \tag{6.4}$$

where

$$i(x, y) = \cos[2\pi u(x \cos \beta - y \sin \beta)] , \tag{6.5}$$

i_0 is a fixed gray tone, and C is the contrast for a selected frequency of oscillations [see Equation (4.7)]. We note that as a first approximation the model in Figure 6.20 does not include the function $H_1(u)$ due to the ocular optical system. Thus, the first stage of processing has been taken as the logarithmic nonlinearity, so that

$$\begin{aligned}\psi(x, y) &= \ln I(x, y)\\ &= \ln\{i_0[1 + C \cdot i(x, y)]\}\\ &= \ln i_0 + \ln[1 + C \cdot i(x, y)]\end{aligned}$$

Since i_0 is constant, we may assume that the bandpass nature of each channel filter will eliminate $\ln i_0$. However, realistically it must, of course, affect the channel characteristics. With this in mind, we can let

$$\begin{aligned}\psi(x, y) &= \ln[1 + C \cdot i(x, y)]\\ &\approx C \cdot i(x, y)\end{aligned} \tag{6.6}$$

be the input to the individual channels.

Each of the n parallel channels in Figure 6.20a is independent and sensitive to a different range of spatial frequencies according to the characteristic $F_i(u)$. The output r_i from each channel is corrupted by additive random noise, taken to be uncorrelated to that of the other channels and introduced to characterize differences among subjects. The detection process is then modeled by a threshold detector, which outputs a 1 or 0 depending upon whether its

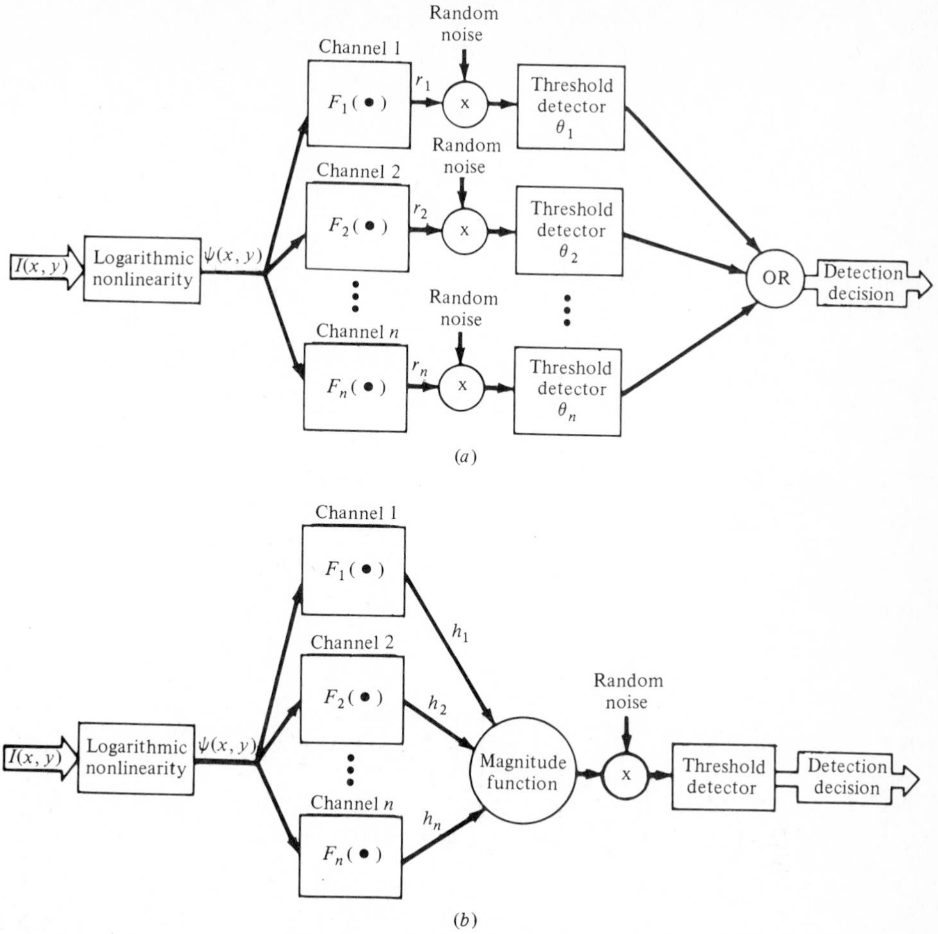

(*a*)

(*b*)

Figure 6.20 Two equivalent multichannel models. (*a*) The probability summation model. (*b*) The vector magnitude model. (*Adapted from J. D. Cowan, "Some Remarks on Channel Bandwidths for Visual Contrast Detection," in "Neural Mechanisms in Visual Perception," Neurosciences Research Program Bulletin, vol. 15, no. 3, October, 1977, pp. 492–517.*)

input is above or below threshold. These binary variables are combined by a logical OR operation to yield the model output. The latter is a 1 if the signal is detected by any of the channels and a 0 otherwise. This model is obviously meant to characterize a specific psychophysical experiment. However, the underlying expectation of all this work is that Figure 6.20*a* may be decomposed into two parts. The first maps the input $I(x, y)$ into the filter outputs r_i; the second deals only with the particular decision process associated with the experiment. We shall see that the first part can be satisfactorily accounted for by what seems to be an appropriate neurophysiological model. This is not the case for the second part!

It appears that the channel detection mechanism is spatially incoherent [34, 143]. This was demonstrated by decomposing the input image into a center patch flanked by two adjoining patches out of phase with it by different multiples of 90°. The phasing had no significant effect on the detectability of the image. With this assumption, we may let $P_i[r_i]$ define the probability that the ith channel will detect the ith frequency component in the stimulus input, given that the channel output is r_i. It is assumed that, most likely, all the channels have the same form for P_i [140]. The probability P that the multichannel model of Figure 6.20a will detect any input stimulus is given by

$$P = 1 - \prod_{i=1}^{n} (1 - P_i) \tag{6.7}$$

Now $P_i[r_i] = P_i[F_i(\psi)]$, where ψ is given by Equation (6.6). However, for the low-contrast condition that we are considering, the channels seem to be approximately linear [1]. Therefore

$$\begin{aligned} P_i[F_i(\psi)] &= P_i[F_i(C_i \cdot i(x, y))] \\ &= P_i[CF_i(i(x, y))] \end{aligned} \tag{6.8}$$

and the psychometric function P becomes

$$P = 1 - \prod_{i=1}^{n} \{1 - P_i[CF_i(i(x, y))]\} \tag{6.9}$$

If we now assume a Gaussian noise process in Figure 6.20a, the variable P may be determined, but it is a difficult computation.

Quick [134] has proposed an alternative, the vector magnitude model outlined in Figure 6.20b. The magnitude function shown there is taken as the so-called α-norm†

$$\|\mathbf{F}\| = \left| \sum_i [F_i(\psi)]^\alpha \right|^{1/\alpha} \tag{6.10}$$

where $\mathbf{F} = [F_1, F_2, \ldots, F_n]$. The probability that an input stimulus will be detected is given by Quick [134] as

$$P = [1 - 2^{-\|\mathbf{F}\|^\alpha}] \tag{6.11}$$

This expression for P can easily be shown to be equivalent to

$$P = 1 - \prod_{i=1}^{n} \{1 - [1 - 2^{-[F_i(\psi)]^\alpha}]\} \tag{6.12}$$

Comparing the two models for P given by Equations (6.9) and (6.12), we observe that they are equivalent if

† Yet another formulation, consistent with Equation (6.10), has been suggested by Wilson [174]. In this model, probability summation is replaced by a nonlinear transducer function, and the result is shown to be compatible with both threshold and suprathreshold vision.

$$P_i = 1 - 2^{-[F_i(\psi)]^\alpha} \tag{6.13}$$

Equation (6.13) can be made to satisfy the experimental data for a value of $\alpha = 7.8$. Wilson and Bergen [175] use a log normal distribution for the noise and show that Equation (6.13) holds (so that the two models are equivalent) when $\alpha = 4$ (the best integer value). Obviously the experimental procedure is not sensitive enough to precisely model the decision process. However, the predictions are adequate for the purpose of characterizing the general nature of the multichannel model.

The vector magnitude model is preferable to the equivalent probability summation model because of its simplicity. It is also convenient for defining the pooling of the different channels. To see this, substitute

$$F_i(\psi) = C \cdot F_i(u)$$

[see Equation (6.8)] into Equation (6.11) to obtain

$$P = 1 - 2^{-\|C\mathbf{F}(u)\|^\alpha} = 1 - 2^{-C^\alpha \|\mathbf{F}(u)\|^\alpha} \tag{6.14}$$

Now detection in a particular channel will take place when C is adjusted to be above the threshold θ for that channel. In Chapter 4 we referred to this variable as the contrast threshold C_θ [see Equation (4.9)] and noted that it was a function of frequency. For a particular input spatial frequency, if the probability of threshold detection P is set equal to $\frac{1}{2}$, the contrast $C_\theta(u)$ at threshold θ, given by the above equation is

$$C_\theta(u) = \frac{1}{\|\mathbf{F}\|} \tag{6.15}$$

Thus, since the system transfer function is assumed to be the CSF [Equation (4.8)] and inversely proportional to $C_\theta(u)$ [Equation (4.9)], we conclude that

$$H(u) = \|\mathbf{F}\| \tag{6.16}$$

We have therefore shown that vector magnitude pooling (or the equivalent, probability summation pooling) in Figure 6.20 leads to an overall transfer function which is related to each of the individual channel characteristics. These equations have been found to be consistent with experimental data obtained so far.

We now turn to the properties of the individual channels themselves. Although it is quite possible that other channels exist outside the spatial frequency range of 0.25 to 16.0 cycles/degree that they examined [106], Wilson and Bergen [175] present evidence for four mechanisms. These are presumed to be found at every location in the visual field, each possessing a different-size receptive field. The study of the monkey anatomy has indicated that relatively few types of center-surround receptive fields exist in any retinal neighborhood. Furthermore, the linear variation of receptive field dimension with eccentricity enforces a spatial inhomogeneity on the visual field.

A possible model for this mechanism, described as a difference of two

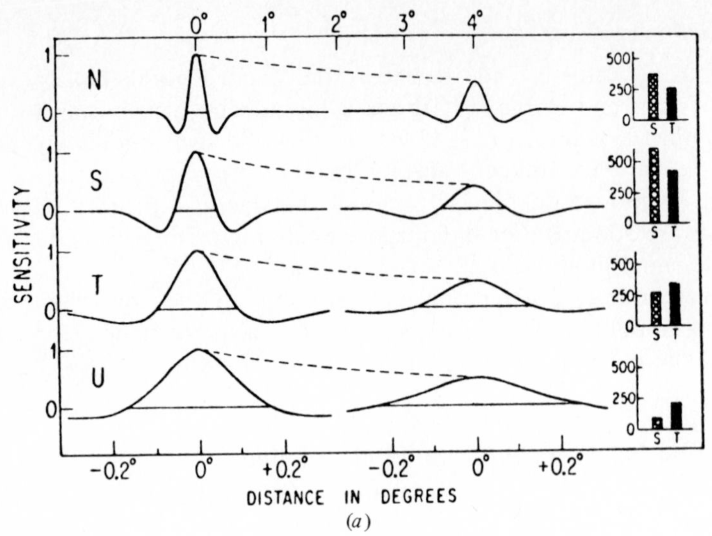

0°
1°
2°
3°
4°
N
S
T
U
SENSITIVITY
1
0
500
250
S
T
-0.2°
0°
+0.2°
DISTANCE IN DEGREES

(a)

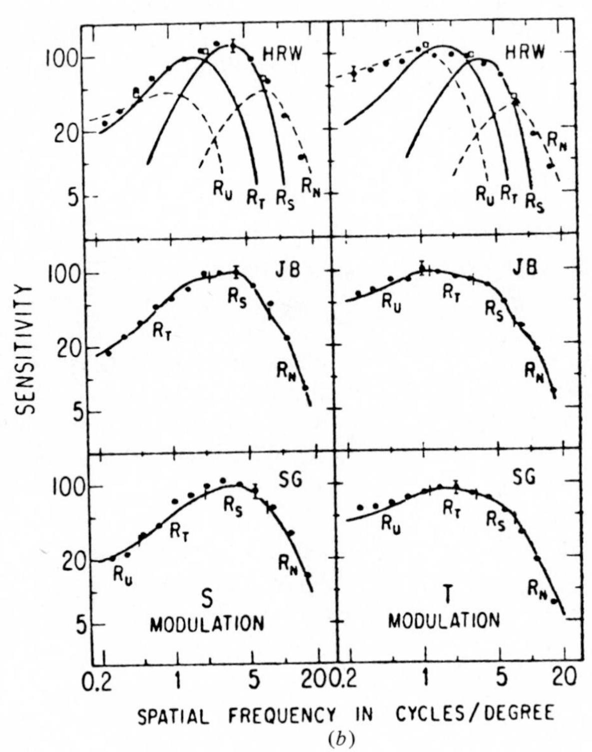

HRW
JB
SG
SENSITIVITY
100
20
5
R_U
R_T
R_S
R_N
S
MODULATION
T
MODULATION
0.2
1
5
20
SPATIAL FREQUENCY IN CYCLES/DEGREE

(b)

Gaussians, is given in [175]:

$$f_i(x, x_0) = A_i(x_0)\left\{\exp\left[-\frac{(x - x_0)^2}{\sigma_i^2(x_0)}\right] - c_i \exp\left[-\frac{(x - x_0)^2}{(b_i\sigma_i(x_0))^2}\right]\right\} \qquad i = 1, 2, 3, 4 \tag{6.17}$$

where $f_i(x, x_0)$ is the LSF, x_0 is the location, in degrees, of the LSF, and x is the eccentricity in degrees. It is assumed that the LSF is rotationally symmetric in the two-dimensional visual field. The index i is a label for the different channels, referred to as $N(i = 1)$, $S(i = 2)$, $T(i = 3)$, and $U(i = 4)$ in [175], where the first two are the building blocks for sustained channels and the latter two are for transient channels [174]. $A_i(x_0)$ and $\sigma_i(x_0)$ are given by

$$A_i(x_0) = \frac{A_i}{1 + a_i|x_0|} \tag{6.18}$$

and

$$\sigma_i(x_0) = \sigma_i(1 + k|x_0|) \tag{6.19}$$

where A_i and σ_i are values defined at the fovea and a_i and k govern the rate of spatial variation. Equation (6.19) indicates that the size of the receptive fields in any channel increases linearly with eccentricity. It turns out that there is a factor of 1.5 increase when comparing a cell at an eccentricity of 4.0° with one at fixation. Note that $c_i(= 0.57, 0.57, 0.30, 0.20$ for $i = 1, 2, 3, 4$, respectively) and b_i ($= 1, 1.75, 3, 3$ for $i = 1, 2, 3, 4$, respectively) are constants. There is some speculation that the LSFs for $i = 1, 2$ and $i = 3, 4$ are models for X-type and Y-type cells, respectively (see Chapter 4 and [108]). Figure 6.21*a* is a

---

Figure 6.21 Experimental and model data related to the multichannel representation of the human visual system. (*a*) Summary diagram of the four-mechanism model. The sensitivity profile $f_i(x, x_0)$, is plotted for each of the mechanisms at 0° (left) and at an eccentricity of 4° (right). Distance relative to the center of each mechanism appears on the lower scale, and the horizontal line shows the extent of the excitatory center. Each of the sensitivity plots on the left has been normalized to unity sensitivity to facilitate a comparison of shapes. The mechanisms at 4°, however, are shown with the correct sensitivities relative to those at 0°. The dashed lines indicate the variation of relative sensitivity as a function of eccentricity, as indicated by the distance scale at the top of the diagram (note that this scale differs from the lower one). Thus, reading the diagram vertically provides a view of the model at a given eccentricity, while reading it horizontally indicates the variation in sensitivity and field size as a function of eccentricity. The bar graphs to the right plot the true peak sensitivity of each mechanism (i.e., its sensitivity to a single line) under S (hatched) and T (gray) modulation. The N and S mechanisms are more sensitive under S than under T modulation, while the reverse is true for the T and U mechanisms. By this criterion, therefore, N and S are relatively sustained in their temporal characteristics, while T and U are relatively transient. (*b*) Measured and predicted spatial-modulation transfer functions (cosine grating sensitivities) for three subjects under each of two temporal conditions. The gratings were 1.5° high by 8.0° wide and were centrally fixated. The individual mechanism response curves are shown for HRW, while for JB and SG only the overall model response is plotted. The overall response for HRW would be obtained through probability summation among the curves shown. Open squares show the effect of this operation where mechanism responses cross. For JB and SG, regions where the response of each individual mechanism predominates have been indicated. R_U and R_N are dashed for HRW to emphasize that the properties of these mechanisms were estimated.

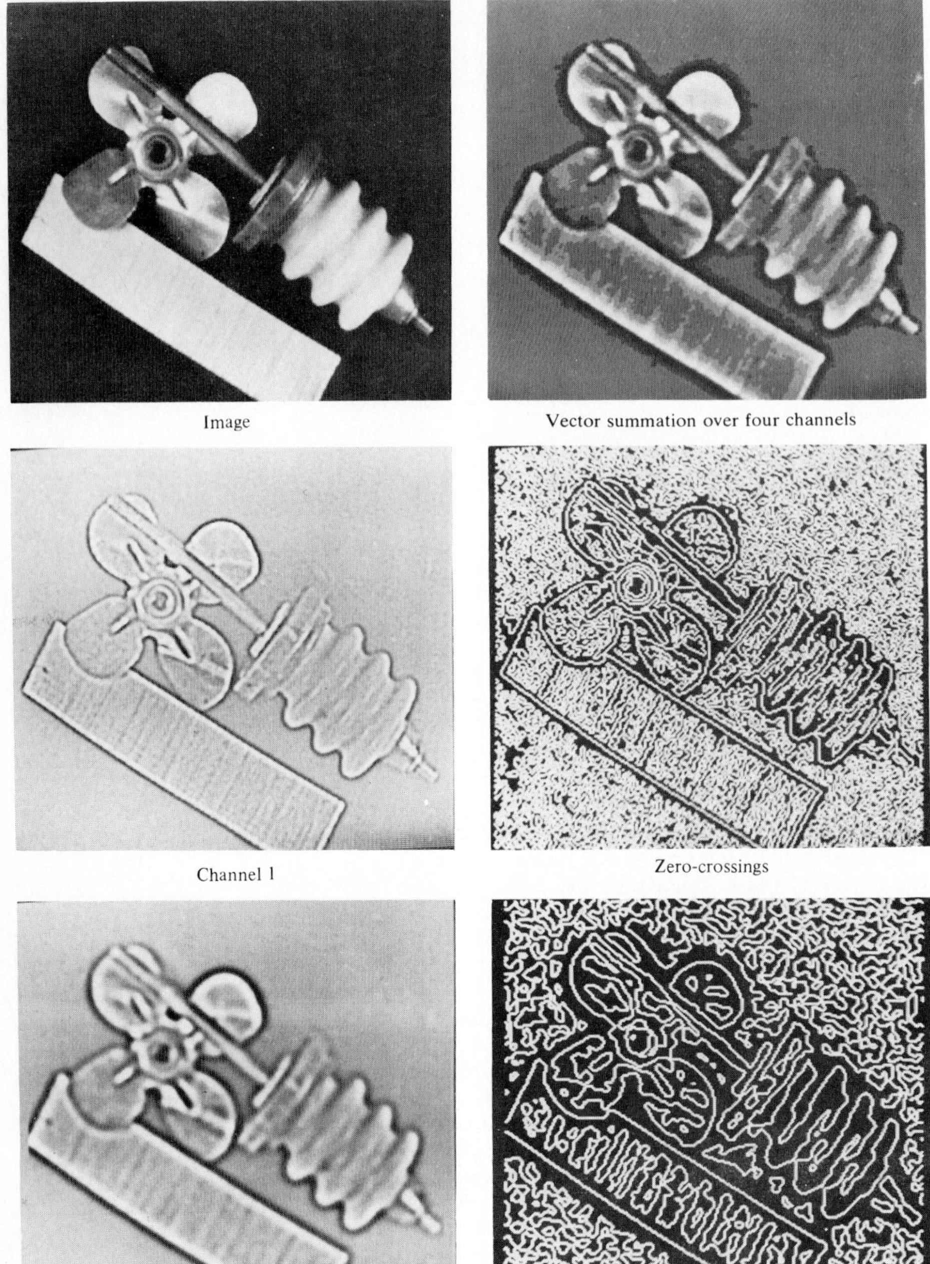
Image

Vector summation over four channels

Channel 1

Zero-crossings

Channel 2

Zero-crossings

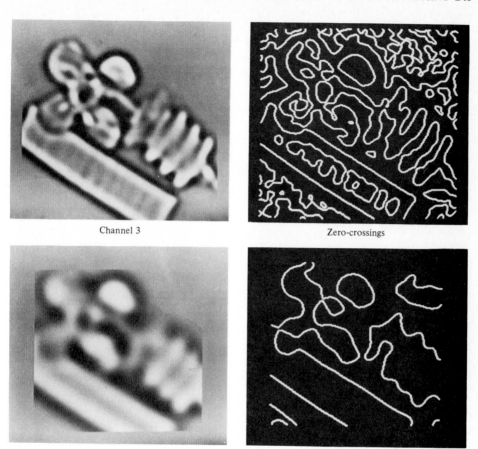

Channel 3

Zero-crossings

Channel 4

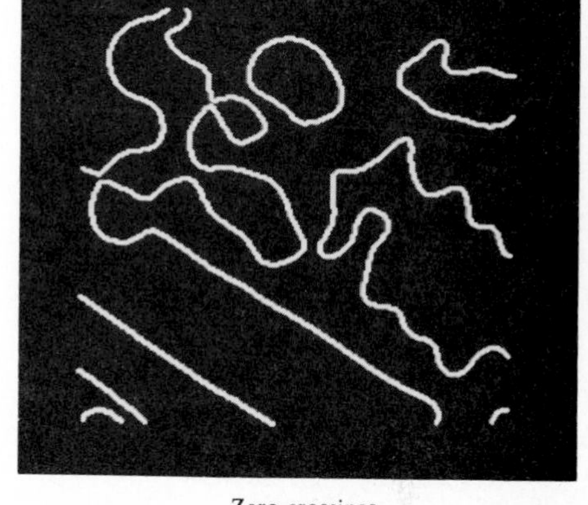

Zero-crossings

Figure 6.22 Picture processing using the multichannel model.

sketch of $f_i(x, x_0)$ showing the effect of eccentricity variation. Readers will note that the model for $f_i(x, x_0)$ is similar to the edge detector described in Section 5.4.3, although orientation sensitivity has not been included above [105]. However, there is clearly a relationship between these two paradigms. Furthermore, it has been demonstrated that this model results in optimal edge detection, yielding maximum energy output at the site of an edge [89].

Each cell of a given size contributes to the overall response characteristic of one of the four channels in the multichannel model. Thus, r_i in Figure 6.20 is a summed response of a collection of such differences of two Gaussians. The response r_i of each channel to an input pattern $\psi(x)$, is obtained by spatial probability summation [159]:

$$r_i = F_i(\psi) = \left[\sum_{x=-4}^{+4} \left| \int_{-x}^{x} f_i(x, x_0)\psi(x)dx \right|^{\alpha} \right]^{1/\alpha}, \alpha = 4 \tag{6.20}$$

Wilson and Bergen [175] justify the choice of $\alpha = 4$ and an increment of $\Delta x = 2.0'$ when the integral is replaced by a summation in order to evaluate the equation numerically. The latter assumption is made compatible with the neurophysiological condition that an $8° \times 8°$ area centered at the fovea is sampled by an array of approximately 1000×1000 ganglion cells. Using this formulation it is possible to derive the frequency characteristic of each individual channel and compare it with experimental data, as shown in Figure 6.21*b*. These four filter response curves have peaks at about 1.0, 2.0, 4.0, and 8.0 cycles/degree.

In order to now combine all the channels, vector summation is assumed [see Equation (6.10)]:

$$\|\mathbf{F}\| = (r_1^4 + r_2^4 + r_3^4 + r_4^4)^{1/4} \tag{6.21}$$

According to Equation (6.16) this gives $H(u)$, the overall transfer function of the early visual system, as shown in Figure 6.18. The individual F_i's and $H(u)$ were obtained, experimentally and computationally, by using cosine gratings and are shown in Figure 6.21*b*. An example of the output of each of the four channels is illustrated in Figure 6.22. The combined output of these channels is also shown.

Mostafavi and Sakrison [115] have conducted some interesting experiments to determine the properties of a single pooled channel, discussed above. Their work differs from that of others in that pseudorandom stimulus patterns were employed rather than sine waves. The use of such an input to compute $H(u)$ results in exactly the same function found by Campbell and Robson [22]. Experimentation was then carried out on the assumption that only one channel was active at any given time. This restricts the overlap between the individual filters, so that the channel bandwidths may have been overestimated as a result. The authors claim to have found strong support for a model similar to that shown in Figure 6.20. In addition, they modeled the orientation sensitivity for the channel $i = 2$, although presumably all the channels depend on the orientation of the input grating. The angular half-amplitude bandwidth was found to be approximately equal to 10°, while other investigators have suggested that it lies between 10 and 20° [161]. This implies that the phenomenon is related to activity occurring at higher levels, perhaps the result of the aggregative effect of simple cortical cells [107, 106]. If this is indeed the case, then the multichannel edge detector in Section 5.4.3 is compatible with the model presented in this section. In addition, the radial bandwidth was determined to be ± 2.5 cycles/degree.

We conclude this section by emphasizing that there exists strong evidence for the formulation presented here. It appears that a "biological spectrum analyzer" does exist in the form of a specific set of medium bandwidth filters. Tests indicate that this formulation can also account for such perceptual phenomena as gestalt grouping (see Chapters 8 and 9), contrast, and size judgments [53]. There has even been a suggestion that the illusory geometric shapes in Figure 6.13 are actually physically recreated by the spatial filtering

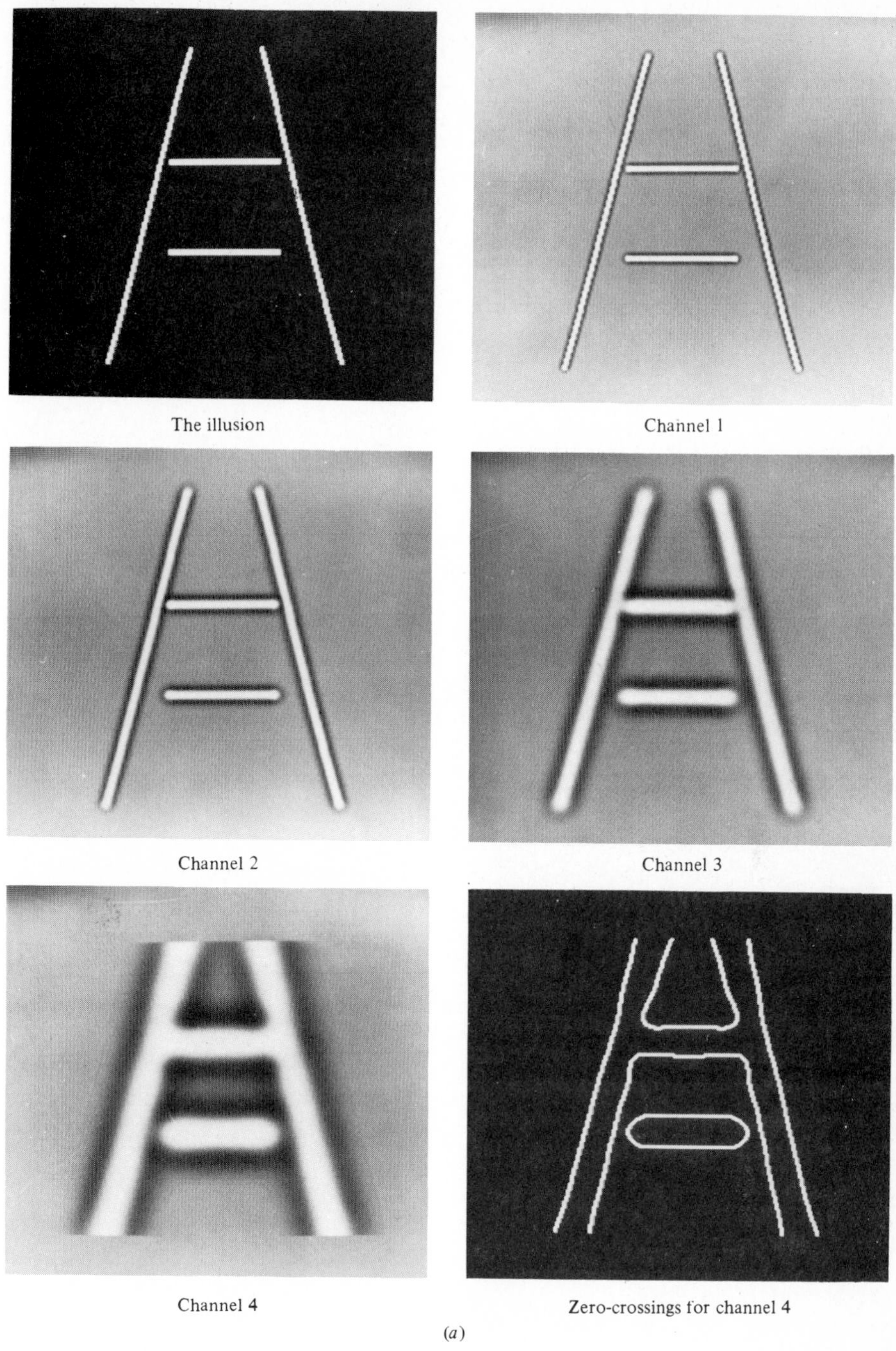

Figure 6.23(*a*) (Caption on page 251.)

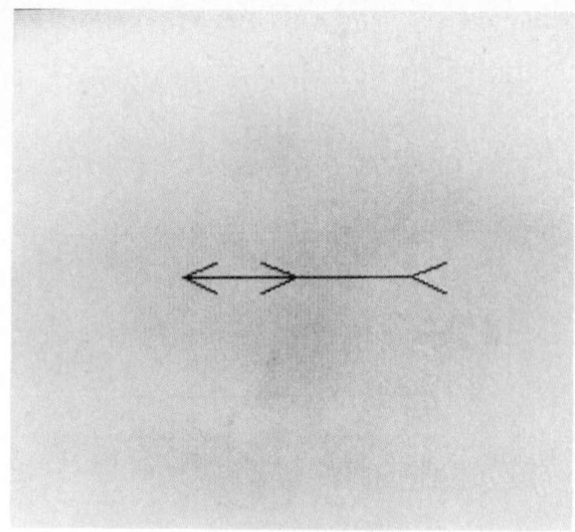

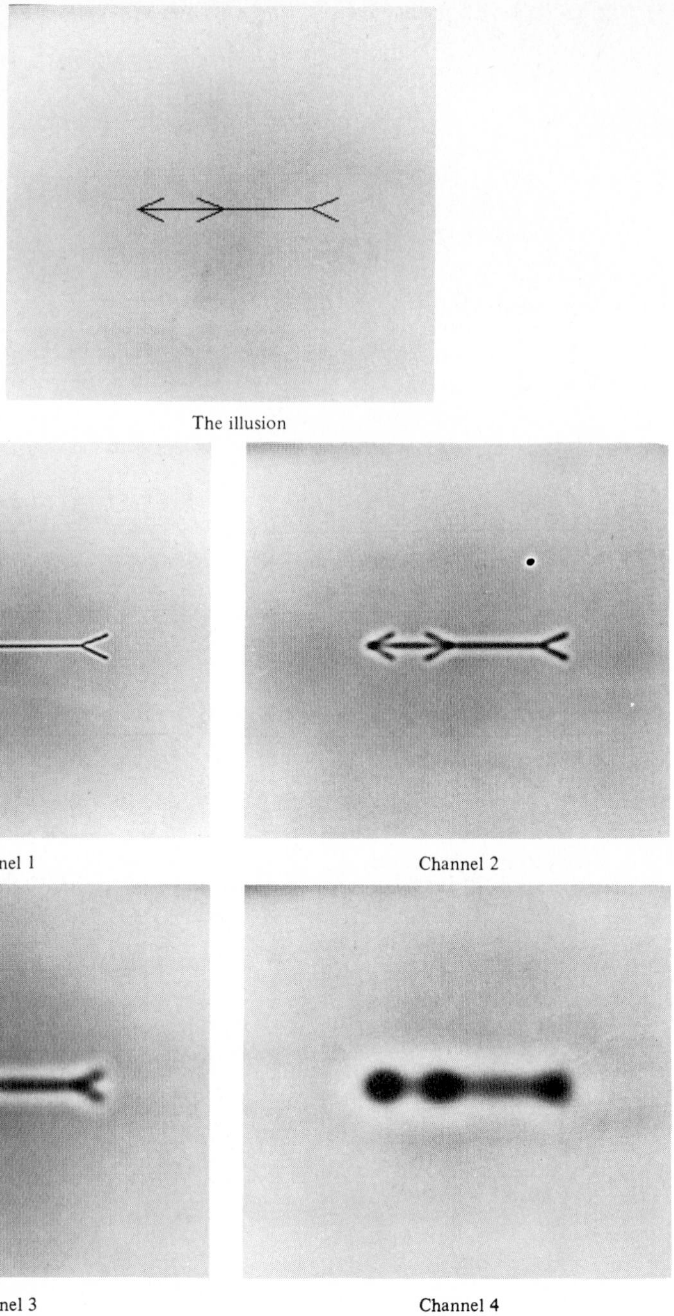

The illusion

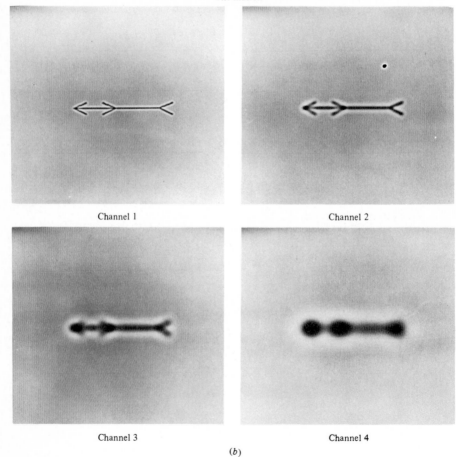

Channel 1

Channel 2

Channel 3

Channel 4

(*b*)

Figure 6.23(*b*) (Caption on page 251.)

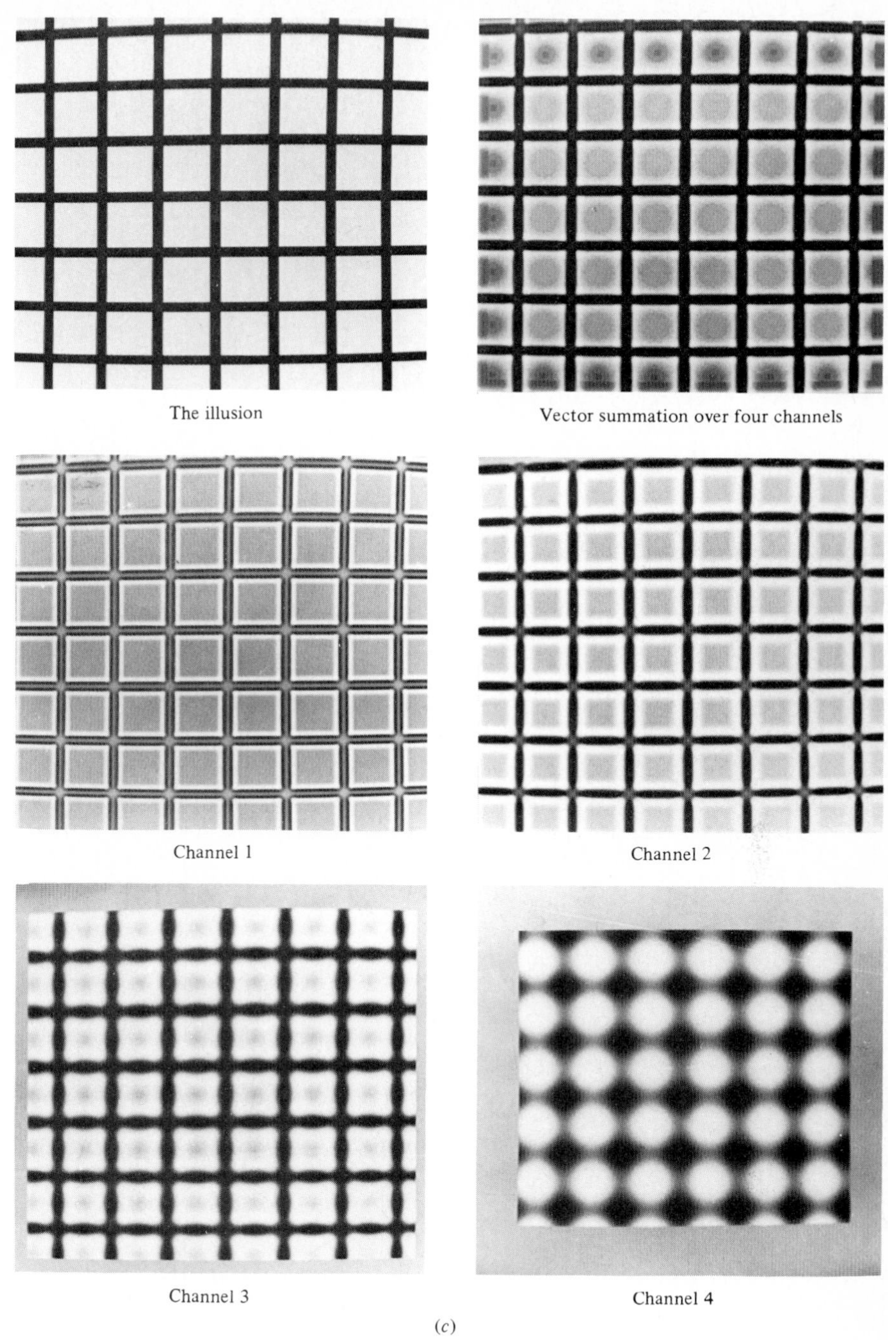

Figure 6.23(*c*) (Caption on page 251.)

Figure 6.23(*d*) (Caption on page 251.)

model [52]. Similarly, the perceived spatial distortions in the Mueller-Lyer illusion (see Figure 6.16*m*) may be accounted for by the multichannel model [55, 56, 57]. Examples of the outputs from the four-channel model for some of the visual illusions discussed in Section 6.2.2 are presented in Figure 6.23. However, we should note that this particular model is based on the assumption of center-surround receptive fields and therefore is not orientation-selective. Thus, it likely corresponds to activity originating at the ganglion and lateral geniculate nucleus (LGN) cell levels. In addition, at the cortical level, most neurophysiologists believe that simple cells, which are directionally selective, implement local two-dimensional spatial-frequency analysis.

Whether the multichannel paradigm will survive further experimentation, especially in the field of neurophysiology, remains to be seen. Nevertheless, such a formulation is indeed very useful in the domain of computer picture processing, and the rest of this chapter will be concerned with its elaboration.

6.4 IMAGE CODING

6.4.1 From Mars to Earth

In the previous sections of this chapter we examined some of the spatial- and frequency-domain characteristics of the biological visual system. The remaining discussions in the chapter address themselves to similar issues, but now with respect to machine vision. The image transformations under consideration are those that transform an image array into another array. These mappings are of particular importance in the design of image communication systems. These systems are concerned with both pictorial and nonpictorial data represented by binary, monochrome, color, or multispectral images.

Two aspects predominate. If we are to transmit pictures from one place to another, for example from Mars to earth, then their communication and storage is one issue. The second deals with the reality that during this process the data will often be degraded by unwanted noise. It may therefore be necessary to restore and enhance the images for the purposes of either viewing or measurement. Sections 6.4, 6.5, and 6.6 present an introduction to these

---

Figure 6.23 Various illusions as processed by the multichannel model. Do the outputs from the four channels explain the existence of the illusions? (*a*) Application of the multichannel model to the Ponzo illusion. Note that in channel 4 the upper horizontal segment is about 30 percent longer than the lower one. (*b*) Application of the multichannel model to the Mueller-Lyer illusion. As we examine the channel outputs in sequence, we note that the segment on the right actually increases in length with respect to one on the left. (*c*) Application of the multichannel model to the Hermann grid illusion. The two higher-frequency channels (channels 1 and 2) contain white spots at the intersections of the bars, as observed in the original illusion. Note how the reconstructed image also exhibits spots at the intersections. (*d*) Application of the multichannel model to the sun illusion.

topics in order to acquaint the reader with the issues and techniques currently under consideration. The subject is vast, and no attempt has been made to provide a comprehensive presentation. However, we may also study this topic to acquire an appreciation of the general complexity of images. It is not known exactly how or even if the human visual system performs these transformations from array to array. Nevertheless, perhaps studying computer methods will also provide some new insights into these processes.

The amount of data that must be processed in any practical picture transmission system is usually overwhelming. For example, let us consider a digital television system with an array size of 525×525, about 2^{18} pixels. Suppose that the gray-level intensity were to be coded into 64 levels, that is, 2^6 bits per pixel. Then a monochrome picture array would require 2^{24} bits. A flicker-free presentation at 30 frames per second indicates a throughput of 2^{29}, or about 5×10^8 bits per second! Color imagery would require in excess of 10^9 bits per second. A medical image-communication system for x-rays presents even greater difficulties [97]. Because of the demands these specifications put on both the transmission channel capacity and the computer memory, it would appear that some means of bandwidth or data reduction would be desirable. This is one of the primary advantages of image coding.

Figure 6.24 is a block diagram of a typical picture transmission system. Here, an analog image source is digitized and then communicated to a picture display device, such as a television monitor. The latter's screen may be refreshed, pixel by pixel, in a digital fashion, but our viewing of it tends to be as an analog image. The source encoder transforms $I(i, j)$ into a sequence of bits. We saw in Chapter 3 how the human visual system captures and samples a given scene, and then how the retinal photoreceptor neurons encode the data. Ideally, this process should be optimal with respect to both the amount of data reduction and the fidelity. The channel is the medium by which the image is

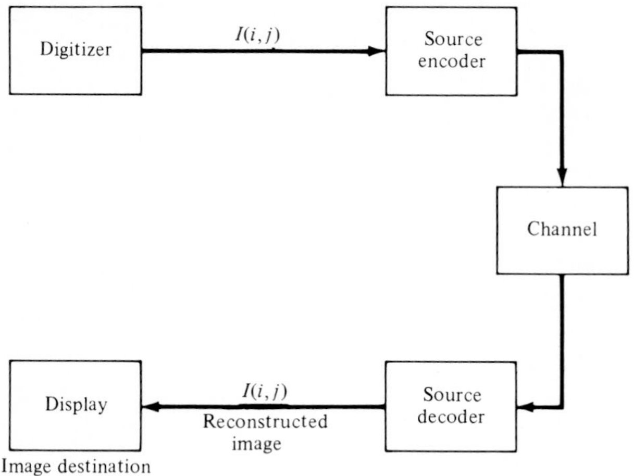

Figure 6.24 A block diagram of a typical picture transmission system.

communicated. It must also match any disparities in the properties of the source encoder and decoder. The main parameter of interest to us is the channel rate, measured in bits per pixel. Given the latter, the picture dimensions, and the dynamic specifications of the channel, we may then easily compute the channel capacity. The source decoder is usually very similar to the encoder; it performs an inverse operation to retrieve the original image.

We shall discuss two methods for picture coding and bandwidth compression, that is, reducing the channel rate. These occur in the spatial image domain (Section 6.4.2) and the spatial frequency domain (Section 6.4.3). Three other types of approaches have also appeared in the literature. One involves the use of psychovisual models in order to encode only those picture aspects that are visually meaningful [144, 176]. Another employs statistical coding which takes advantage of the fact that a high degree of correlation exists between adjacent pixels in an image [38, 138]. This method requires a knowledge of the picture statistics and is generally not practical to implement. The third type uses rate distortion theory, which attempts to mathematically specify the minimum channel capacity needed to transmit information from an input source to a receiver at a given average level [13, 39, 48].

Whether sending images from Mars to earth or from the retina to the cortex, one characteristic definitely stands out. There are a lot of data to be processed! The pictures from Mars may be slowed down for transmission purposes, but the "biological picture pathway" must function in real time.

6.4.2 Spatial-Domain Coding

The standard by which all picture coding methods are evaluated is "pulse code modulation" (PCM). This involves sampling the analog signal at a constant rate, quantizing it, and then using a binary code for its representation. It is the digital code that is transmitted, and we note that this is the very same approach described in Section 2.3 with respect to image digitization for computer vision. Therefore, with PCM, the digitizer and the source encoder are in fact both integrated into one unit. Each pixel is treated independently and assigned the same number of bits even though we realize that the image data in a given neighborhood are correlated. Although the method is simple and accurate, it is also very inefficient.

The only design issue associated with PCM is the question of how many bits are required for the binary code. Reducing the number of quantization levels allows for a direct reduction in the channel rate. However, the number of levels must be large enough so that gray-scale contouring does not occur. As can be seen from Figure 6.25, this type of noise is highly structured and quite objectionable. It is caused by a change in the quantization level in areas of the image which are quite uniform or untextured. About 5 to 7 bits per pixel are needed, depending on the signal-to-noise ratio, in order to create a picture for viewing purposes [79]. About 1 bit per pixel may be saved by preceding the coding step by a logarithmic operation, as suggested by considerations of

Figure 6.25 Examples of PCM coding with different numbers of gray levels. Note that image quality does not affect our ability to interpret the picture, for which even the binary version seems to be adequate.

human vision, discussed earlier in Chapter 4. The U.S. digital television standard is 525×525 lines, with 8-bit quantization.

The degradation caused by this quantization noise may be alleviated by superimposing a low-amplitude pseudorandom noise signal upon the video before quantization and then subtracting an identical signal at the receiver [139]. Other methods that have been suggested include the use of filters [18] and nonuniform quantization [109, 128]. These techniques tend to eliminate the false contours, so that fewer bits per pixel are needed to code the image. For example, with the addition of pseudorandom noise, 4 bits per pixel will yield a good picture; even 2 bits per pixel gives a usable, but poor, image which could be filtered to eliminate the noise.

A powerful method for reducing the channel rate can be achieved by a complementary increase in complexity. The approach involves coding differences, rather than absolute values, as in the case of PCM. It is referred to as "predictive coding," and "differential pulse code modulation" (DPCM) is probably its most popular embodiment. An excellent history of DPCM is provided by Musmann [117].

Predictive coding takes advantage of two points. First, the eye is more sensitive to intensity differences than to absolute intensity values [150]. Second, it is noted that neighboring pixels are related and do not just occur randomly. Changes take place relatively slowly. Figure 6.26 is a block diagram of an nth order DPCM system in which the n previous samples of the image are used to predict the present value of the input image [64]. The difference signal $D(i, j)$ is computed by subtracting the predicted estimate $\tilde{I}(i, j)$ from the image $I(i, j)$ at each pixel (i, j). Obviously the predictor must possess a memory in order to base the new estimate on the past history. We observe that it is $D(i, j)$ that is quantized to produce a "quantized difference signal" $\hat{D}(i, j)$. The latter is sometimes referred to as the "prediction error." Quantization may be based on minimizing the error due to this process or may perhaps be matched to the

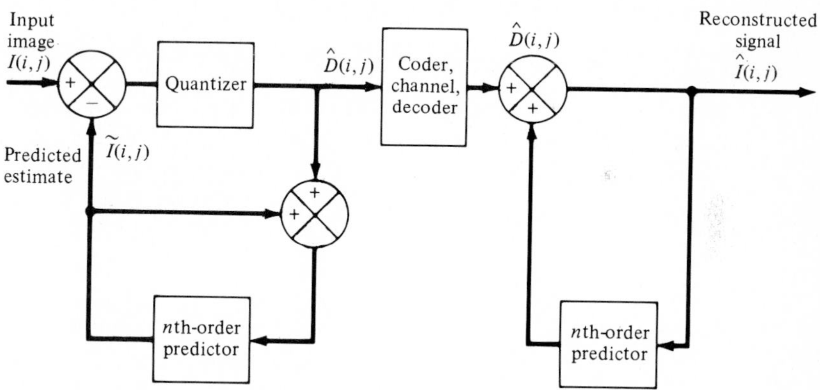

Figure 6.26 A block diagram of an nth order DPCM system. Note that the past history of the previous n values of $I(i, j)$ must be stored in the memory of both predictors.

characteristics of the human perceiver [122]. It is $\hat{D}(i, j)$ that is transmitted over the channel. The advantage of this approach may be best understood by considering the image and difference histograms of a typical image. The variance of the difference signal $\hat{D}(i, j)$ is smaller than that of $I(i, j)$, so that the former requires fewer bits for its transmission. At the receiving end, the signal is reconstructed on the basis of the predicted estimate $\tilde{I}(i, j)$. This yields $\hat{I}(i, j)$. The reconstruction is achieved by summing the successive differences, a simple form of numerical integration. Hence we may view the source encoder as a differentiator and the receiver as an integrator.

Mathematically, we may suppose that the input image $I(i, j)$ is sampled and quantized at regular time intervals to yield a set of picture samples $\{g_l\}$. The predicted estimate of the input at sample $(l + 1)$ is based on the previous n samples:

$$\tilde{g}_{l+1} = \sum_{k=1}^{n} a_k g_{l+1-k} \tag{6.22}$$

where the n parameters a_k of the system must be specified. Since it is $\{g_l\}$ that is transmitted, the receiver is also able to compute $\{\tilde{g}_l\}$ from Equation (6.22) if it stores the history of the previous n samples. The parameters a_k are computed by first defining the prediction error according to

$$D_{l+1} = g_{l+1} - \tilde{g}_{l+1} \tag{6.23}$$

They are then selected to minimize D_{l+1} in a least-mean-square error sense. It can easily be shown that this requires the solution of n linear algebraic equations [64]. It is important to recognize that the parameters obtained from this minimization are necessarily optimally matched to the statistics of the particular picture in question.

The simplest and most basic DPCM system is one in which only a single previous pixel is used to predict the signal (a first-order predictor) [2, 35, 36, 70, 101, 114, 125]. A block diagram is shown in Figure 6.27, where it should be noted that normally the delay would be one sampling interval. Thus, we are comparing the actual value of $I(i, j)$ at pixel (i, j) with the predicted value of $\tilde{I}(i, j)$, which is based only on the previous pixel in the raster, that is, the one at $(i, j - 1)$. However, the delay could be one line (intraframe coding) [28] or even one complete frame (interframe coding) [75]. In Figure 6.27, the implicit assumption is made that the image does not change very much from one pixel to the next.

The difference signal is quantized [122], not necessarily by means of a linear function, and the resulting binary stream of b bits per sample is transmitted. The question arises as to how many bits or levels are required. The most elementary version, with $b = 1$, is termed "delta modulation," and is shown in Figure 6.28*a*. The output signal, which is transmitted, is limited to taking on either of two levels. Thus the latter essentially codes whether the signal is increasing or decreasing. When the signal changes slowly in large uniform areas, there is a tendency for an oscillatory response. Similarly, sudden

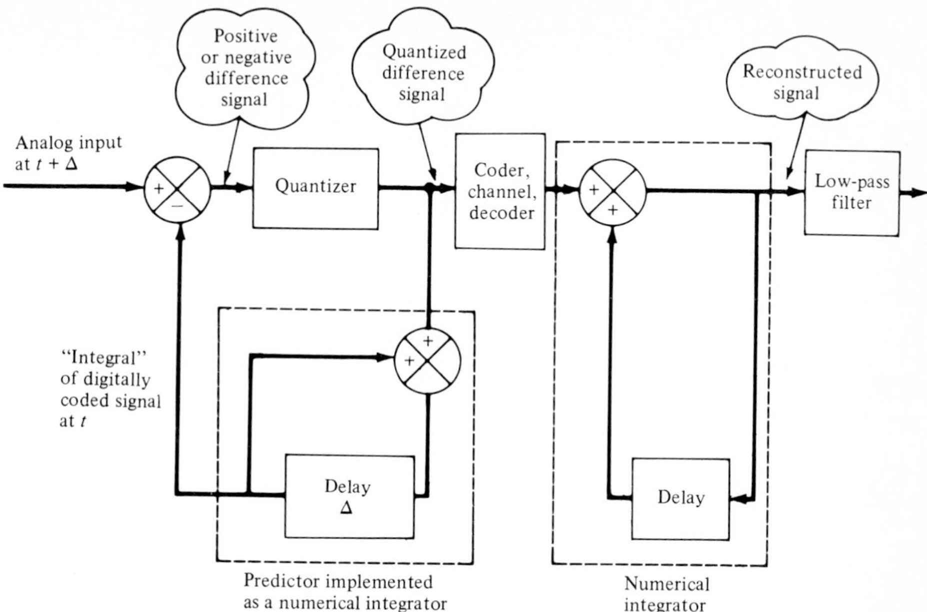

Figure 6.27 A block diagram of a basic DPCM system where the nth-order predictor in Figure 6.24 has $n = 1$. Note that the reconstructed signal $\hat{I}(i, j)$ is passed through a filter to eliminate quantization noise. We shall examine image enhancement of this type in Sections 6.5 and 6.6.

changes such as might occur at edges may not be trackable. The gain G of the integrator could obviously be used to correct for one of these phenomena but not both simultaneously. Therefore we introduce, in Figure 6.28*b*, an "adaptive delta modulation system" in which the gain is automatically adjusted according to the trends in the data. This is accomplished by storing and examining, let us say, the three previous outputs $\hat{D}(i, j)$, $\hat{D}(i, j-1)$, and $\hat{D}(i, j-2)$ in the array. If all three are of the same sign, it is assumed by the system that the signal is changing rapidly, and G is increased by the adaptive logic. If there is a mixture of polarities, it is assumed that the signal is varying slowly, and the gain in the feedback loop is reduced. Logic could also be employed to implement a variable sampling rate to match the data characteristics. A memory buffer at the output would then be required before transmission in order to regularize the data rate through the channel.

Notwithstanding these simplifications, a DPCM system will normally have $b = 2, 3$, or 4. Generally this will produce a better quality picture than PCM for the same channel rate. Or for the same quality, about half the rate is needed. The reconstructed images at the receiver are acceptable, even at 3 bits per pixel.

Figure 6.29 shows a comparison between PCM and the one-dimensional ($n = 1$) DPCM. In this case, there is only one parameter, $a_1 = 1$. Although we are comparing an 8-bit PCM with a 4-bit DPCM, the quality of the two images

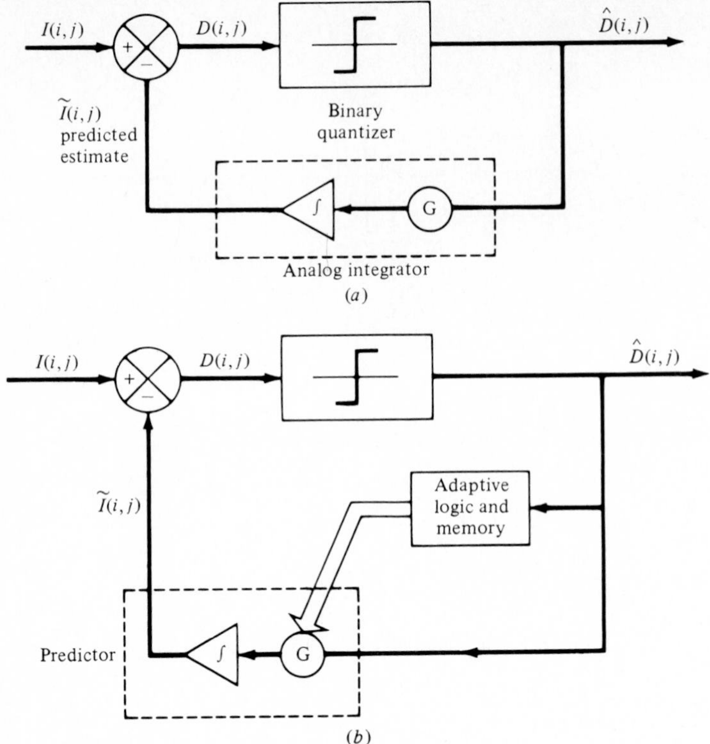

Figure 6.28 Simple predictive modulators. (*a*) With binary quantization, a delta modulation system is the simplest predictive coding system. The delta modulator both samples and quantizes the input signal, so that the latter could in fact even be an analog signal. The quantizer could be considered to sample the input at regular time intervals, thereby producing a digitally coded bit stream $\hat{D}(i, j)$. (*b*) If we insert some logic and memory in the feedback loop of the delta modulator, the result is the so-called adaptive delta modulation system. Adaptation to the data is achieved by automatically varying the gain of the integrator.

in Figure 6.29*a* and *b* is quite comparable. As would be expected, the prediction error (or difference signal) as shown in Figure 6.29*c* is large primarily at edges. It is this signal that is quantized and transmitted. The reconstructed signal $\hat{g}_{l+1}$ differs from the input g_{l+1} by the amount of the quantization error, defined as (refer to Figure 6.26)

$$\begin{aligned} e_{l+1} &= D_{l+1} - \hat{D}_{l+1} \\ &= (g_{l+1} - \tilde{g}_{l+1}) - (\hat{g}_{l+1} - \tilde{g}_{l+1}) \\ &= g_{l+1} - \hat{g}_{l+1} \end{aligned} \tag{6.24}$$

The quantization error e is shown in *d*, magnified by a factor of 8. As would be expected, this one-dimensional DPCM system is not as accurate as the two-dimensional version but is often favored because it is simpler in design.

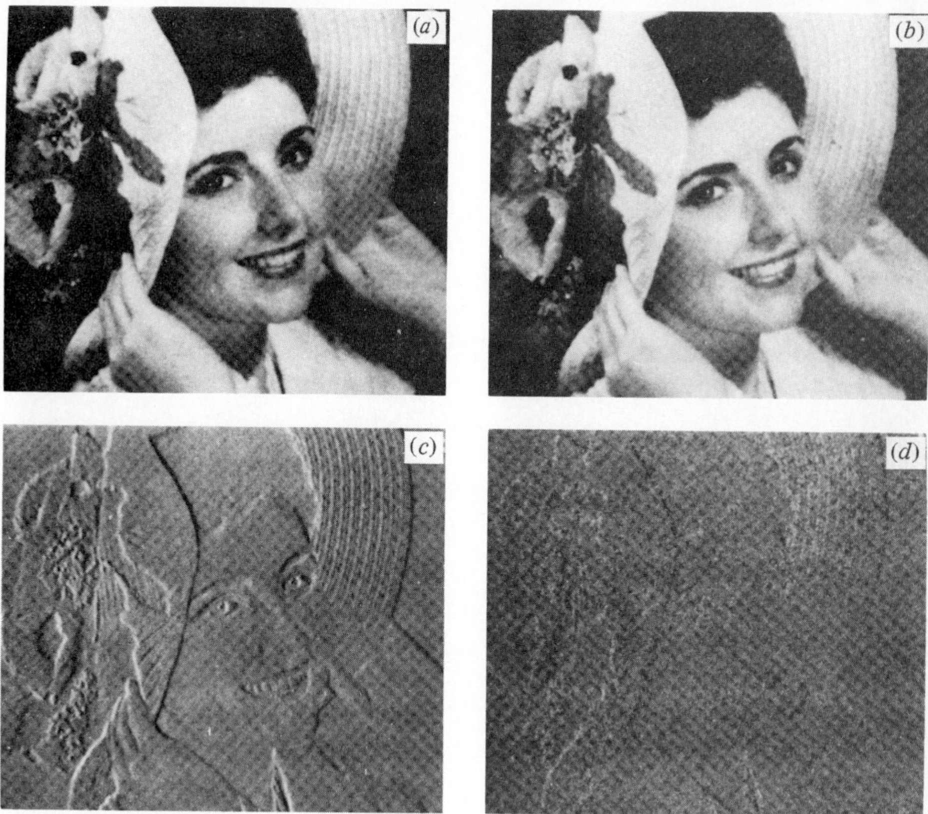

Figure 6.29 Television pictures processed with a PCM and DPCM system using 10-MHz sampling frequency. (*a*) Original 8-bit PCM picture. (*b*) Reconstructed 4-bit DPCM picture. (*c*) Prediction error. (*d*) Quantization error magnified by a factor of 8. [*From H. G. Musmann, "Predictive Image Coding," in W. K. Pratt (ed.), "Image Transmission Techniques," Academic, New York, 1979, pp. 73–112.*]

Figure 6.30*a* shows a set of picture elements that might be employed for a two-dimensional predictor. Extensive studies by Habibi [64] have suggested that an increase beyond three points in the predictor will not substantially improve the performance of the encoder. The elements of a typical third-order predictor are shown shaded in the figure. A comparison between the prediction errors obtained with a one-dimensional predictor ($a_1 = 1$) and a two-dimensional predictor ($a_1 = 0.75$, $a_4 = -0.5$, $a_5 = 0.75$) for an interlaced television picture is given in Figure 6.30*b*. Recall that these coefficients are computed from the particular picture's statistics.

If optimized for picture statistics, DPCM is considered to be superior to the transform coding methods to be discussed in the next section. This is particularly true if such design considerations as complexity and cost are included [64]. The coded signal does, however, have a tendency to oscillate in large,

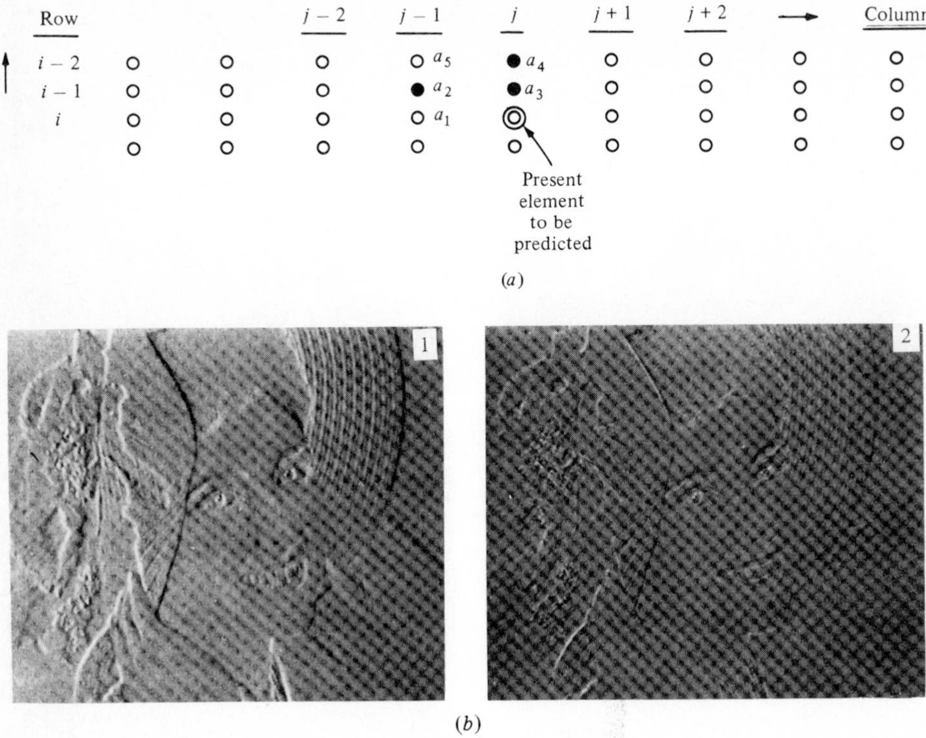

Figure 6.30 Third-order two-dimensional predictive coding. (*a*) The pixels (shown as ○) in a two-dimensional array which can be used to predict $\tilde{I}(i, j)$. It has been found that using only the three elements shown shaded to produce the prediction yields accurate results. (*b*) Prediction error of a television picture processed with a 4-bit DPCM system using (1) one-dimensional prediction ($a = 1.0$) and (2) two-dimensional prediction ($a_1 = 0.75$, $a_4 = -0.5$, $a_5 = 0.75$). [*From H. G. Musmann, "Predictive Image Coding," in W. K. Pratt (ed.), "Image Transmission Techniques," Academic, New York, 1979, pp. 73–112.*]

uniform gray areas and is sensitive to noise. Errors are cumulative as a result of the very nature of the coding. Also, the performance depends on how well the assumed picture statistics actually do match the image being coded. DPCM could be improved by the use of variable length coding, but a data buffer would be required, thereby introducing a delay in transmission.

6.4.3 Transform Coding

In Section 6.4.3 the transmission of images was considered as a problem of representation in the actual picture domain. Here we examine it in the so-called transform domain [7, 9, 141]. Figure 6.31 shows a sketch of an image-transform communications system, the major components being forward and inverse transformation. Recall from our discussion of the multichannel

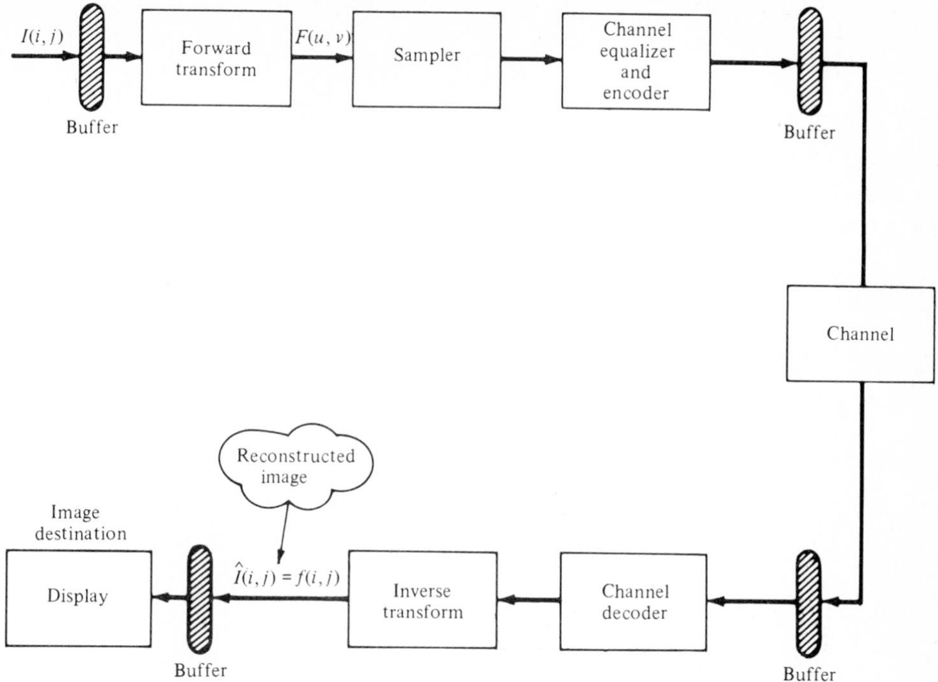

Figure 6.31 A general block diagram from an image-transform coding system. Data buffers may be required at certain points in the transmission process in order to match varying processing rates.

model of human vision in Section 6.3 that the bank of filters in the model (see Figure 6.20) were considered by some to be computing the Fourier transform, one particular type of transform.

In the latter part of the 1960s and the beginning of the following decade, great interest developed in transform coding as a mechanism for image transmission. This was a direct outgrowth of the generally pervasive interest in linear systems theory in both communications and control. Its relative simplicity and ease of mathematical manipulation make it an attractive approach to the problem even to this day. Many different transform types have been studied. These include Fourier [9], Walsh-Hadamard [9, 133], Karhunen-Loève [63, 177], cosine [3], slant [132], and Haar [9]. An excellent tutorial article on this subject can be found in [177]. Perhaps one of the most thoroughly investigated of these transforms is the Karhunen-Loève. It has been shown to be optimal in the sense of minimizing the mean-square error of the approximation between $I(i, j)$ and $\hat{I}(i, j)$ for a given number of parameters in the approximation [177]. From the point of view of error in or subjective quality of the reconstructed image, the performance of all these transforms is not very different. It is difficult to choose among them, and Tescher [159] has recently summarized this research as follows:

(1) No deterministic transform has equalled the performance of the cosine transform.
(2) No theoretical justification ... [has been] offered ... as to why the "other" transforms should be beneficial.

The cosine transform is a simple outgrowth of the Fourier transform, and we shall therefore limit ourselves in this book to the latter.

The Fourier integral transform for the two-dimensional continuous function $I(x, y)$ is given by

$$F(u, v) = \int_{-\infty}^{\infty} \int_{-\infty}^{\infty} I(x, y) e^{-2\pi i(ux+vy)}\, dx\, dy \tag{6.25}$$

and its associated inverse transform by

$$I(x, y) = \int_{-\infty}^{\infty} \int_{-\infty}^{\infty} F(u, v) e^{2\pi i(ux+vy)}\, du\, dv \tag{6.26}$$

This is the two-dimensional extension of the well-known one-dimensional Fourier transform pair. As it deals with a continuous function $I(x, y)$, it is defined over the entire real axis. The sampled version of $I(x, y)$, that is $I(i, j)$, must, however, be coded by the discrete Fourier series as given by

$$F(u, v) = \frac{1}{N} \sum_{i=0}^{N-1} \sum_{j=0}^{N-1} I(i, j) \exp\left[-\frac{2\pi i}{N}(iu + jv)\right] \tag{6.27}$$

and

$$I(i, j) = \frac{1}{N} \sum_{u=0}^{N-1} \sum_{v=0}^{N-1} F(u, v) \exp\left[\frac{2\pi i}{N}(iu + jv)\right] \tag{6.28}$$

where $u = 0, 1, \ldots, N-1$ and $v = 0, 1, \ldots, N-1$

This series is defined over a finite interval, and in order for it to be valid it is also necessary to assume that the picture is periodic. This is shown in Figure 6.32*a*, where both vertical and horizontal periodicity have been artificially introduced. Obviously, discontinuities arise which create undesirable spatial frequency components [159, p. 116–117].

The cosine transform [3] ameliorates this problem by the creation of an artificial symmetric version of the image $I(i, j)$, as shown in Figure 6.32*b*. It turns out that the cosine transform is just the Fourier transform applied to this larger image of dimension $2N \times 2N$. There are now no discontinuities and, what is even more interesting, the performance is very close to that of the optimal Karhunen-Loève transform. However, the latter must utilize picture statistics for its implementation, while the former is strictly deterministic. Another distinction is that the cosine transform can be computed by using so-called fast algorithms [17].

Figure 6.33 is an example of the two-dimensional transform and shows only the magnitude component. We note a very basic property of images, namely, they can generally be modeled as low-pass systems. Their energy is concentrated in the low-spatial-frequency components. Thus, for a typical set of

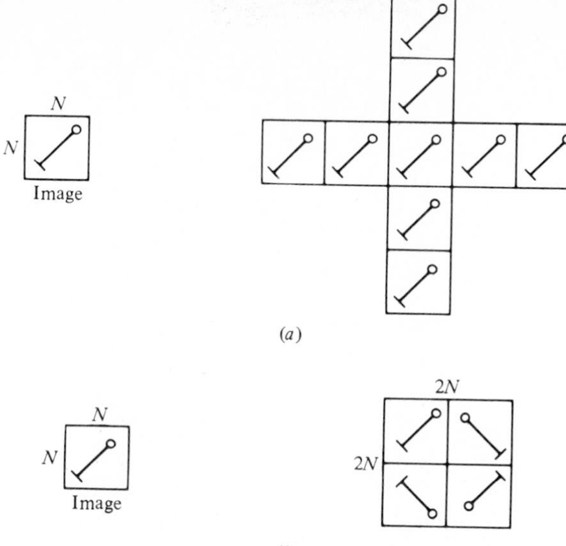

Figure 6.32 Required assumptions for Fourier and cosine transforms. (*a*) Forced periodicity assumed for Fourier series approximation. (*b*) Forced symmetry assumed for cosine transform.

pictures less than 1 percent of the coefficients are required to achieve 95 percent of the energy content in the signal [9]!

Why is it so attractive to consider the image $I(i, j)$ in the transform domain? The major reason is that in this domain the components of the image representation may be treated as independent entities. We note the familiar property that convolution in the spatial domain becomes pointwise multiplication in the transform domain. Also, when random noise corrupts the image signal, the pixels in $I(i, j)$ are highly correlated but the elements of $F(u, v)$ are decorrelated [78]. This is achieved without any structural or statistical model of the data. Thus, the sampler in Figure 6.31 is able to independently process the coefficients of $F(u, v)$, a concept more commonly referred to as "filtering." Readers should note the similarity of these arguments to those that were offered in conjunction with the multichannel model of human vision in Figure 6.20. The second attraction is the evidence of energy clustering.

The objective of the sampling process in Figure 6.31 is to reduce the amount of information to be transmitted across the data channel. This may be achieved by the use of zonal sampling or filtering. The latter is a technique for retaining only those coefficients of the transform which contain the major portion of the energy in the image. As observed in Figure 6.33 it would appear that these could be masked out by an appropriate two-dimensional filter. Figure 6.34*a* shows an example of a binary circular low-pass mask, which would capture the majority of the low-energy components. Examples of its use are given in Figure 6.35. We observe that although only a small porportion of the high-frequency components are not being transmitted, these do have a decidedly pivotal effect on our appreciation of the edge detail in the picture.

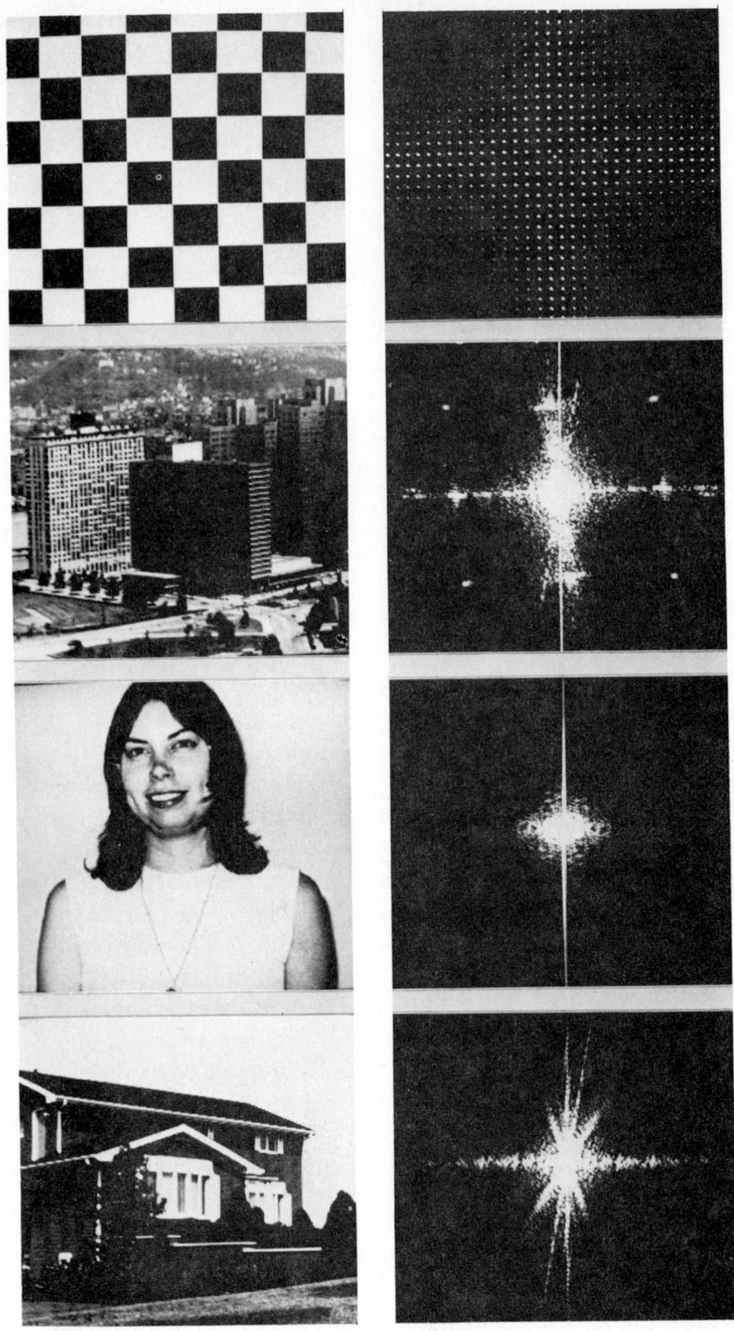

Figure 6.33 Four examples of the Fourier transform. (Note that zero frequency occurs at the center of the transform domain [11].)

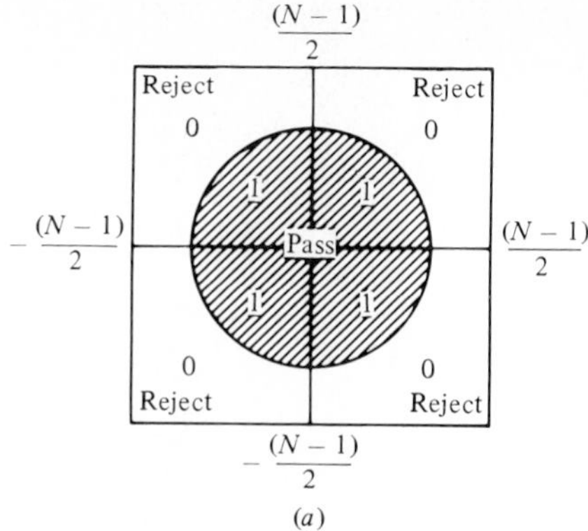

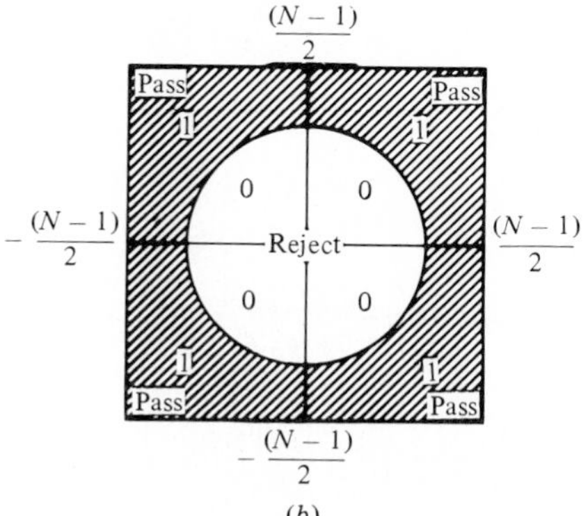

Figure 6.34 Two types of zonal filters. (*a*) A binary low-pass template. (*b*) A binary high-pass template.

The low spatial frequencies provide the gray levels in the picture, while the high spatial frequencies are related to the sharp brightness transitions. The latter could be isolated by the binary circular zonal rejection filter shown in Figure 6.34*b*. Generally, 50 percent of the coefficients of the Fourier transform are needed for good reconstructions, and perhaps 7 bits per coefficient must be employed to code them.

An alternative to this approach is "threshold sampling," in which only those coefficients with magnitudes above a certain fixed threshold are transmitted [6, 7]. This technique has several disadvantages, the most important being the necessity for coding and transmitting the coordinates (u, v) of the retained coefficients in addition to the coefficients themselves [159].

After sampling the transform array in Figure 6.31 must be quantized [9, chap. 7; 177]. A good discussion of this process as it relates to the human visual system can be found in [122]. By suitably choosing an appropriate sampler and quantizer, the data requirements for transform image coding may be reduced to between 1 and 2 bits per pixel.

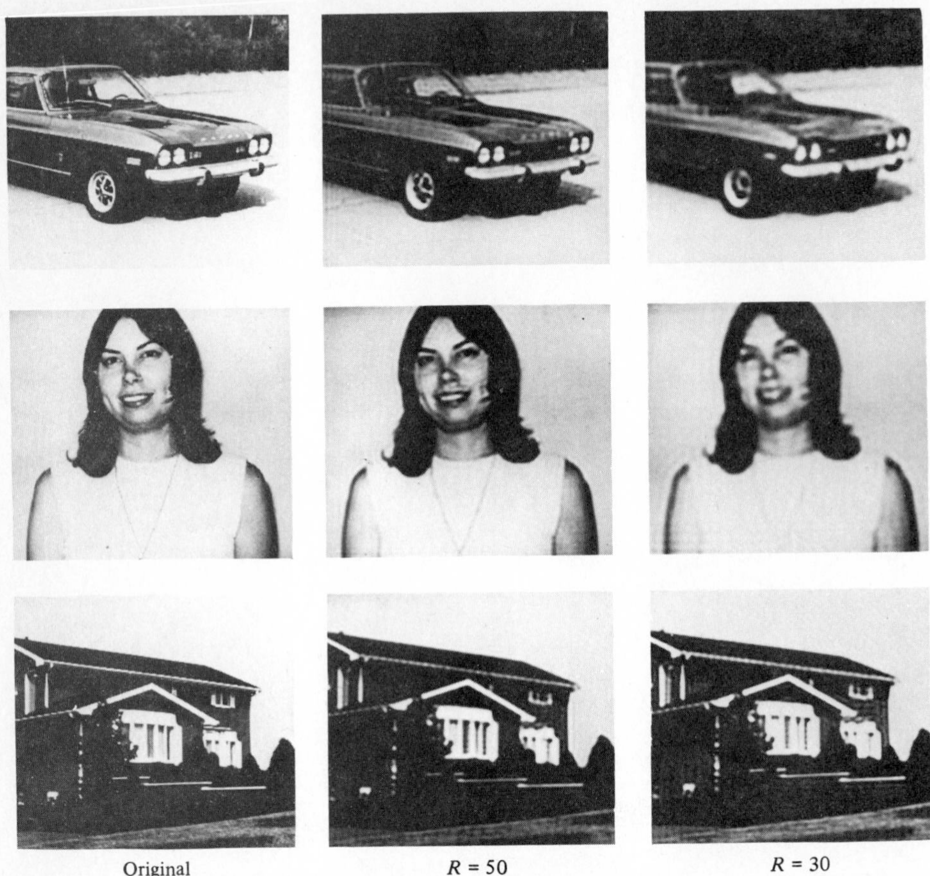

Original $R = 50$ $R = 30$

Figure 6.35 The application of a binary circular low-pass zonal filter to the two-dimensional Fourier transform of a 256 × 256 image. The images shown above were reconstructed by using the inverse Fourier transform. The values of R refer to the radius of the circular zonal filter shown in Figure 6.34. The maximum radius is 128. Note that the larger the value of R, the more spatial frequencies are passed by the filter, and therefore the sharper the picture.

The hardware needs for this type of coding are relatively complex [159]. A discussion of the trade-offs made in some initial attempts at hardware implementation can be found in [19]. The ultimate objective is to place a complete transform processor on a single integrated-circuit chip.

6.5 FREQUENCY-DOMAIN FILTERING

6.5.1 Introduction

In Section 6.3 we hypothesized the existence in the visual pathway of a set of transformations of the input stimulus image. Each of the members of this set is a bandpass-filtered version of the input. Each is characterized by a more or less different frequency range. We noted in Chapter 5 that edge detection is applied to each of these filtered arrays and shall discuss in Chapters 8, 9, and 10 how these edge data are organized. However, the question still remains as to whether the visual system also utilizes the frequency-domain data in another context. Are the channels processed further by frequency-domain filters [130]? It has been suggested that various other important "biological computations" are actually performed [56]. For the computer image-transmission systems discussed in Section 6.4, the answer is definitely in the affirmative, and this will constitute the subject matter for the last two sections of this chapter. Here, however, we will concentrate on a view of the problem in the spatial-frequency domain [42].

Figure 6.36*a* shows the context in which this type of image processing will be studied. As discussed in Chapter 2, a two-dimensional image $I(x, y)$ is formed from a three-dimensional object source $L(x, y)$. The image is recorded, a process which can easily introduce noise and distortion. However, it is usual in the literature to ignore this stage (or equivalently to assume that an intensity image is available) and deal with the ideal model in Figure 6.36*b*. The process of image formation does alter the image in some ways. We wish to process $I(x, y)$ to reconstruct an image of $L(x, y)$ to achieve either of two aims, image restoration or image enhancement. Image restoration is concerned with the computation of $\hat{L}$ to make it appear as much as possible like the original scene $L(x, y)$. This is accomplished by taking into account models of the degradation phenomena. For example, the images that were first transmitted from the moon to earth were characterized by many distortions. The resulting pictures shown to the public after digital image restoration were meant to appear to us just as if we were viewing the scene standing on the surface of the moon. The list of scene models available is quite extensive and includes such fields as

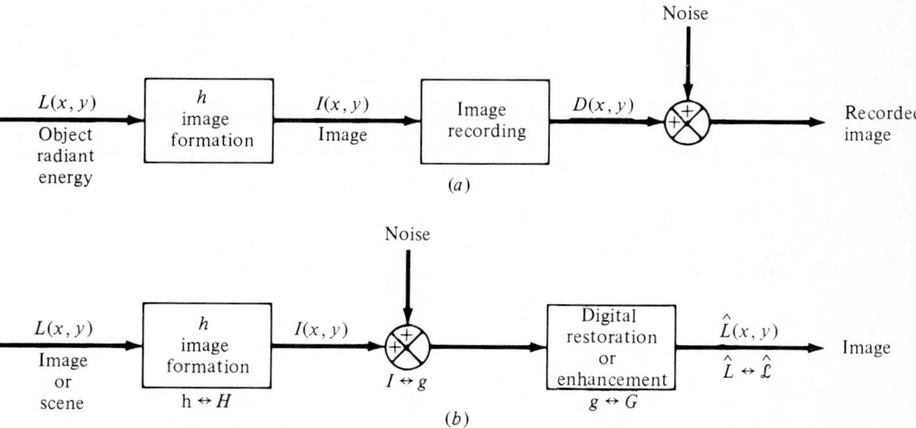

Figure 6.36 A block diagram representing the digital image restoration and enhancement problem. (*a*) Obtaining an image for analysis. (*b*) Processing the image to improve its quality.

atmospheric physics, spectroscopy, geophysics, medical image reconstruction, and radio astronomy [46].

But what happens if no appropriate model is available? We may then use image enhancement to improve the appearance of the image for the purpose of human viewing or further picture processing. No theoretical or experimental model is used—only techniques which have been developed over the years and which are known to enhance desirable picture features.

As we shall observe, the primary assumption upon which most useful restoration and enhancement techniques are based is linearity. The image formation process is assumed to be linear and usually spatially invariant as well. A further constraint imposed by the definition of the image itself is that I, L, and $\hat{L}$ are all positive semidefinite functions. Notwithstanding these generalizations, it will be seen that some very striking results have been obtained by practitioners in this field. Can we expect that the human visual system performs similarly?

Section 6.5.2 will discuss image restoration and Section 6.5.3 image enhancement. It is only possible to present an introduction to these subjects as there is a vast amount of material available. References to the literature will be provided for the interested reader. However, forays into this publication jungle may often prove unsatisfactory to the ambitious: there is very little of a critical nature in press, so that it is extremely difficult to judge the numerous trends and fancies. In any event, this study is only recommended to those who are quite proficient in linear systems theory and probabilistic systems.

6.5.2 Restoration

The power of the restoration techniques to be discussed in this section is illustrated in Figure 6.37. A typical lunar scene is shown in *a*, with a highly distorted version due to motion degradation in *b*. The restored image $\hat{L}$ in *c* is an excellent reconstitution of the original data, bordering on the truly amazing.

In order to understand the process of restoration, it is first necessary to consider the sources of image degradation, that is, the process of image formation in Figure 6.36. The most general model for the impulse response function h is a nonlinear one, in which this point-spread function (PSF) depends on the properties of the objects in the scene. Examples of this are phenomena in which a source of energy is transmitted through the object of interest. Such is the case in biomedical and industrial imaging, where x-rays are passed through objects to obtain a three-dimensional model. The image $I(x, y)$ is then given by

$$I(x, y) = \int_{-\infty}^{\infty} \int_{-\infty}^{\infty} h(x, y, \xi, \eta, L) L(\xi, \eta)\, d\xi\, d\eta \qquad (6.29)$$

Although the representation here is in the more familiar continuous form, the discrete versions of this equation and of those that follow present no particular

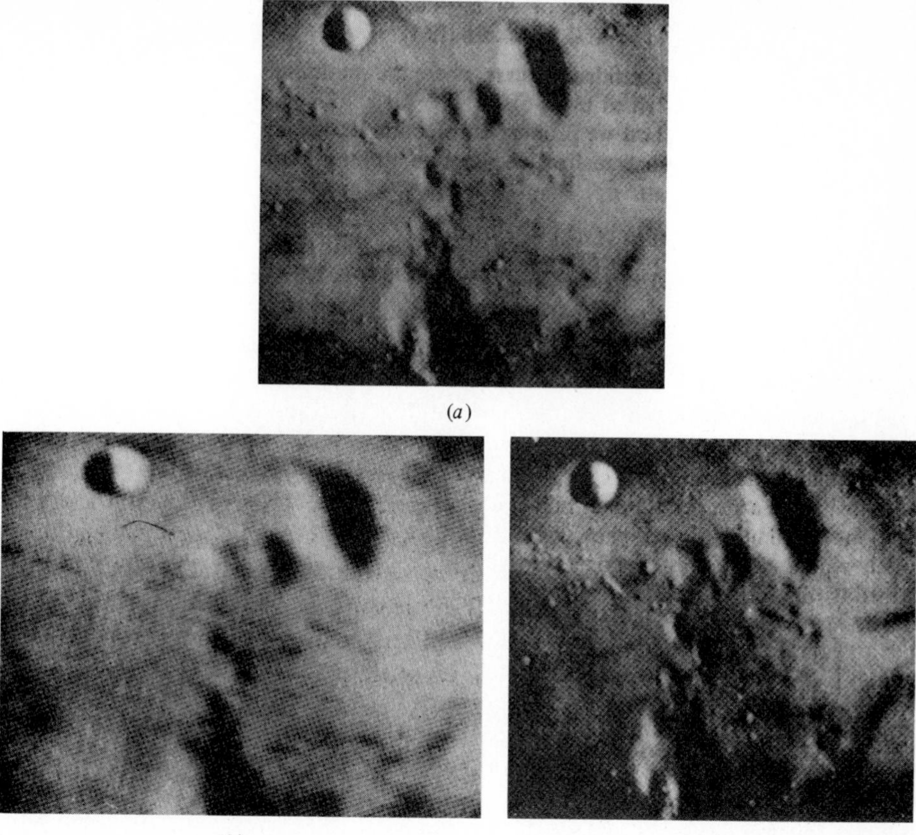

(a)

(b) (c)

Figure 6.37 The use of inverse filtering to restore degraded images. (a) Lunar object. (b) Motion-degraded lunar object (10 pixels). (c) Restored image of (b). (*From A. O. Aboutalib and L. M. Silverman, "Restoration of Motion Degraded Images," IEEE Transactions on Circuits and Systems, vol. CAS-22, no. 3, March 1975, pp. 178–286.*)

conceptual difficulties. The general formulation represented by Equation (6.29) has by and large been ignored in the literature.

Even restricting ourselves to linear models does not trivialize the solution. In this section we shall consider only point and spatial degradations, ignoring temporal and chromatic effects or combinations of these as being too complex. For the general linear case, h may involve a PSF that is either spatially varying (SVPSF) or spatially invariant (SIPSF). Thus

$$I(x, y) = \int_{-\infty}^{\infty} \int_{-\infty}^{\infty} h(x, y, \xi, \eta) L(\xi, \eta)\, d\xi\, d\eta + n(x, y) \tag{6.30}$$

for the SVPSF and

$$I(x, y) = \int_{-\infty}^{\infty} \int_{-\infty}^{\infty} h(x - \xi, y - \eta) L(\xi, \eta) \, d\xi \, d\eta + n(x, y) \tag{6.31}$$

for the SIPSF if we include additive noise. For the latter in the transform domain we have

$$I(u, v) = H(u, v) L(u, v) + N(u, v) \tag{6.32}$$

The problem of image restoration can then be stated as follows. Given $I(x, y)$, the available information about $n(x, y)$, $h(x, y)$, and $L(x, y)$ is used to estimate $\hat{L}(x, y)$ as it would be seen by a human observer of $L(x, y)$. The solutions differ according to what models are assumed as well as the particular error judgment criterion used for evaluating the quality of $\hat{L}(x, y)$ as an estimate of $L(x, y)$.

Let us examine some specific cases of degradation. We first observe that an ideal system is obtained from Equation (6.31) if we eliminate the noise component $[n(x, y) = 0]$ and select the system impulse response so that no image smearing takes places $[h(x, y) = \delta(x, y)]$. Thus Equation (6.31) becomes

$$I(x, y) = \int_{-\infty}^{\infty} \int_{-\infty}^{\infty} \delta(x - \xi, y - \eta) L(\xi, \eta) \, d\xi \, d\eta \tag{6.33}$$

which reduces to

$$I(x, y) = L(x, y) \tag{6.34}$$

This is therefore the situation with perfect image formation.

Now suppose that a geometric point distortion occurs, defined by the transformation

$$\begin{aligned} x &= p_1(x, y) \\ y &= p_2(x, y) \end{aligned} \tag{6.35}$$

Then Equation (6.31) becomes

$$\begin{aligned} I(x, y) &= \int_{-\infty}^{\infty} \int_{-\infty}^{\infty} h(x, y) \delta[p_1(x, y) - \xi, p_2(x, y) - \eta] L(\xi, \eta) \, d\xi \, d\eta \\ &= h(x, y) L(p_1, p_2) \end{aligned} \tag{6.36}$$

There is still no spatial blurring in that $h(x, y)$ provides for multiplicative degradation only. However, the geometrical coordinate transformation causes distortion.

Elimination of the geometric point degradation manifested by Equation (6.35) alters Equation (6.36) to

$$\begin{aligned} I(x, y) &= \int_{-\infty}^{\infty} \int_{-\infty}^{\infty} h(x, y) \delta(x - \xi, y - \eta) L(\xi, \eta) \, d\xi \, d\eta \\ &= h(x, y) L(x, y) \end{aligned} \tag{6.37}$$

This equation still yields a point degradation. It obviously allows for multiplicative degradations and if noise is added [as in Equation (6.31)], additive point degradation as well. Multiplicative distortion in the image formation process may be attributed to the film grain, lens, or camera tube shading or perhaps other sensor defects (see Chapter 2). Additive distortion may be due to scanner noise or perhaps to interference of scattered light with the illumation source.

Finally, we may generalize Equation (6.31) to include the common situation of spatial degradation. If the impulse response of the system becomes a function of the relative (SIPSF) or absolute (SVPSF) object coordinates, there is a smearing effect leading to a loss of image resolution. Thus, for the SVPSF we have

$$I(x, y) = \int_{-\infty}^{\infty} \int_{-\infty}^{\infty} h(x, y, \xi, \eta) L(\xi, \eta)\, d\xi\, d\eta \tag{6.38}$$

and for the SIPSF

$$I(x, y) = \int_{-\infty}^{\infty} \int_{-\infty}^{\infty} h(x - \xi, y - \eta) L(\xi, \eta)\, d\xi\, d\eta \tag{6.39}$$

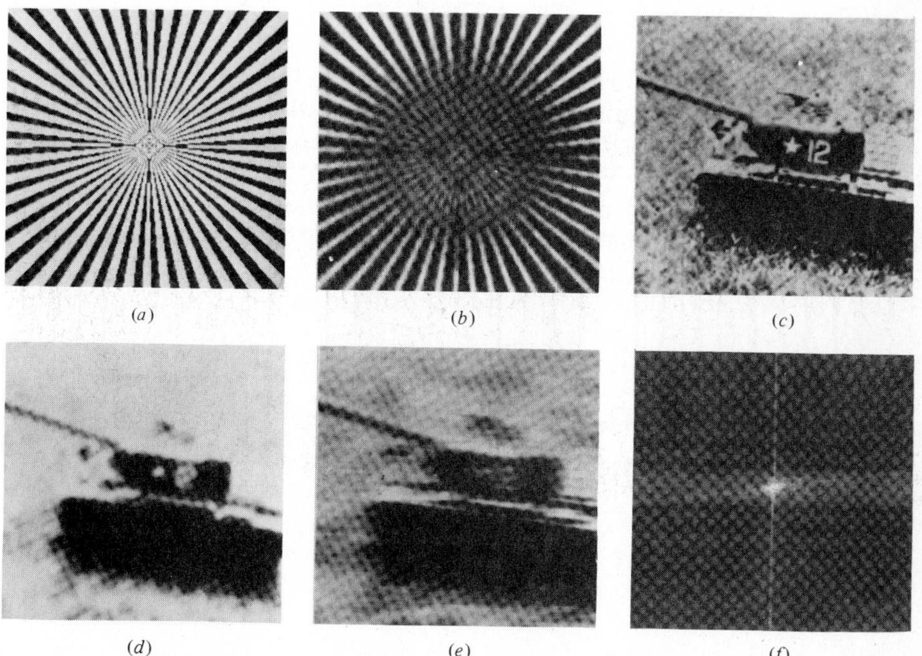

Figure 6.38 Space-invariant point-spread-function simulation examples. (*a*) Resolution chart. (*b*) Defocused resolution chart. (*c*) Toy tank. (*d*) Long-exposure atmospheric blur (Gaussian PSF). (*e*) Uniform motion blur. (*f*) Fourier transform modulus displaying uniform motion blur. (*From H. C. Andrews and B. R. Hunt, "Digital Image Restoration," Prentice-Hall, Englewood Cliffs, N.J., 1977, p. 82.*)

Examples of the SIPSF which cause spatial degradation are defocused images, atmospheric blur, and uniform motion blur [153]. These are illustrated in Figure 6.38. Sawchuck [145, 146, 147] discusses the problem of motion blur in a two-dimensional incoherent optical system using an SVPSF. The degradation in this case was caused by photographing planets from moving spacecraft.

In all these situations, given that $L(x, y)$ has been degraded as discussed, what kind of information can be employed to make the restored image $\hat{L}(x, y)$ as accurate as possible? Both a priori and a posteriori information may be useful. An example of "a priori" information is a knowledge of the geometrical equations of relative motion or position that exist between an object and the image film plane during exposure. Camera actions such as pan, pitch, linear motion, and tilt may be accounted for. Another example is the assumption of a particular two-dimensional probability density function for the image. By "a posteriori information" is meant the employment of the image $I(x, y)$ itself as an aid in computing the parameters associated with the degradation. Thus, controlled experiments could be performed to evaluate the PSF. These might also be used to obtain estimates of the noise variance and power spectrum. The uniform areas in a picture tend to make the noise explicit, so that it is possible to separate out signal from noise by means of filtering. Analysis of the Fourier domain representation of the image may point to certain types of scanner noise, such as jitter and hum. It may also indicate badly defocused imaging systems or images blurred by linear motion. Both of these affect the PSF in a similar manner. An interesting and informative discussion of the "art" of image restoration using a posteriori evaluation of degradation parameters may be found in [10, chap. 5].

The actual techniques of restoration are often quite complex and very numerous. In the short space allotted to this subject, the reader will only be given a "snapshot," with the emphasis on certain simple methodologies. The bibliography at the end of this chapter points to many sources for further reading.

In a certain sense restoration is like magic, enabling us to reconstitute pictures of objects from distorted images, albeit using certain additional information. How well this may be accomplished is influenced by many issues. These include the character of the PSF, the signal-to-noise ratio, the correlation properties of the image and the noise, and, of course, the information available. Perhaps the most obvious approach is to use inverse filtering.

Consider Figure 6.36*b* in which the restoration filter $G(u, v)$ is being sought. The idea of choosing $G(u, v)$ to be an inversion filter, one which attempts to somehow compensate exactly for the image formation process, was proposed in the early 1960s [68, 82, 112, 116, 165]. The output $\hat{\mathscr{L}}$ is given by

$$\hat{\mathscr{L}}(u, v) = \mathscr{L}(u, v)H(u, v)G(u, v) + G(u, v)N(u, v) \tag{6.40}$$

Now suppose that the filter is selected to be the inverse of the known image formation process. Then

$$G(u, v) = H^{-1}(u, v) \tag{6.41}$$

and Equation (6.40) becomes

$$\hat{\mathscr{L}}(u, v) = \mathscr{L}(u, v) + H^{-1}(u, v)N(u, v) \tag{6.42}$$

If we assume that $H^{-1}(u, v)$ is finite and the noise component is small, then

$$\hat{\mathscr{L}}(u, v) \approx \mathscr{L}(u, v) \tag{6.43}$$

and the output scene $\hat{\mathscr{L}}(u, v)$ is a restored version of the input.

Because generally $H(u, v)$ is a low-pass system, its inverse would approach infinity in the limit, which would make this theoretical analysis impractical. Therefore, we assume that the filter is band-limited, giving a zonal filter

$$G(u, v) = \operatorname{sign}\left(\frac{u}{\Omega}, \frac{v}{\Omega}\right) H^{-1}(u, v) \tag{6.44}$$

where

$$\operatorname{sign}\left(\frac{u}{\Omega}, \frac{v}{\Omega}\right) = \begin{cases} 1 & \left|\frac{u}{\Omega}\right|, \left|\frac{v}{\Omega}\right| \leq 1 \\ 0 & \left|\frac{u}{\Omega}\right|, \left|\frac{v}{\Omega}\right| > 1 \end{cases} \tag{6.45}$$

and Ω is the filter cutoff frequency. We would like the latter to be as large as possible for the purpose of restoration but note that it must be designed to restrain $H^{-1}(u, v)$ from "blowing up." We observe that the second term in Equation (6.42) grows with frequency and thus introduces error to the restoration. This interjects a not very welcome high-frequency noise enhancement. These are contradictory requirements, and therefore Ω should be chosen very carefully. An alternative to Equation (6.44) is a truncated correction filter such that

$$G(u, v) = \min[H^{-1}(u, v), SH^{-1}(0, 0)] \tag{6.46}$$

where S is a selected truncated (or saturation) parameter. In either case, the restored image may be computed from the inverse transformation

$$\hat{L}(x, y) = \int_{-\Omega}^{\Omega} \int_{-\Omega}^{\Omega} \hat{\mathscr{L}}(u, v) e^{2\pi i(ux+vy)}\, du\, dv \tag{6.47}$$

Figure 6.37 is an example of the restoration of an image distorted by motion degradation. Details which are hardly visible in the original $I(x, y)$ shown in Figure 6.37*a*, or which are blurred in Figure 6.37*b*, can be brought out in $\hat{L}(x, y)$ shown in Figure 6.37*c*. The effect of noise is demonstrated in Figure 6.39. It is observed that a large degree of noise negates the action of the restoration filter by introducing unwanted artifact. The truncated restoration filter, given by Equation (6.46), has been used to correct for the MTF of the *Apollo 10* vidicon camera system which was used on the moon [148]. On the assumption that the camera was linear and isotropic over the field of view, a sine wave target was used to compute $H(u, v)$. A least-squares approach was

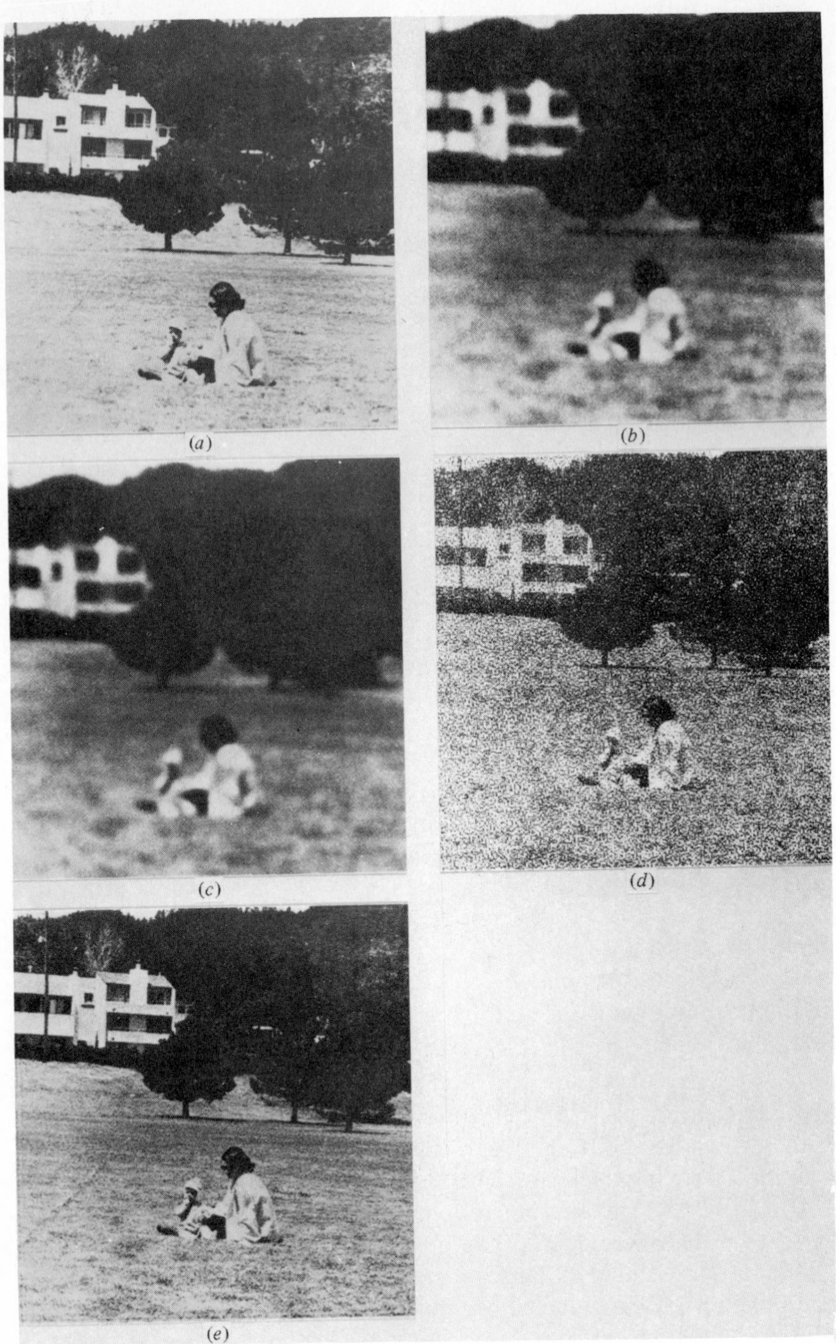

Figure 6.39

then employed to obtain the response on a statistical basis and thereby make allowance for noise and spatial variations.

Readers should consult [160] for a discussion of the specific methodology and difficulties associated with the experimental determination of $H(u, v)$. Other examples can be found in [11], where $H(u, v)$ is modeled by a Gaussian, and in [43, pp. 196–206], where some ad hoc linear methods are discussed. Frieden [47] discusses image models for restoration which reduce the effects of the filter instability. The models essentially consist of a priori knowledge about the image, formulated as constraints.

Several other approaches to image restoration have been developed [10, 46]. Prominent among these are statistically based methods. Instead of requiring "perfect" restoration as given by Equation (6.43), these techniques seek to minimize the mean square error (MSE) [76, 77]:

$$\text{MSE} = \int_{-\Omega}^{\Omega} \int_{-\Omega}^{\Omega} [\mathscr{L}(u, v) - \hat{\mathscr{L}}(u, v)]^2 \, du \, dv \tag{6.48}$$

It should be noted that the eye demands accurate representation in those areas of a picture where the intensity values change abruptly, that is, at edges. It is also the case that the sensitivity to errors in intensity is related to the actual magnitude of the intensity. However, the MSE performs a kind of averaging, weighting all errors between $\mathscr{L}(u, v)$ and $\hat{\mathscr{L}}(u, v)$ equally, independently of both intensity and intensity gradient. The advantage is its mathematical tractability and ease of inclusion of noise characteristics.

Assume that the image and the noise are stationary and Gaussian, have zero mean, and are statistically independent. The best Wiener linear spatial filter can be shown to be (see Figure 6.36*b*)

$$G(u, v) = H^*(u, v) \Big/ \left[|H(u, v)|^2 + \frac{\phi_n(u, v)}{\phi_h(u, v)} \right] \tag{6.49}$$

where $H^*(u, v)$ is the complex conjugate of $H(u, v)$, ϕ_n is the noise power spectrum, and ϕ_h is the system power spectrum. The spectra are usually not known, and a method for computing them from the actual data is given in [10, p. 144]. One possibility is to assume that (ϕ_n/ϕ_h) is constant over the frequency range of interest. The function $H(u, v)$ may be computed from the original image by using blind deconvolution [24, 110, 157]. In any event, it is assumed that the a priori information includes ϕ_n, ϕ_h, and $H(u, v)$. Note that as $\phi_n \to 0$, $G(u, v)$ becomes the inverse filter [see Equation (6.41)]. The application of the

---

Figure 6.39 The effect of noise on the restoration of images by inverse filtering. (*a*) Original image, 500 × 500 pixels. (*b*) The original, blurred by using a low-pass filter, with noise added at the output. The signal-to-noise ratio (SNR) is 2000 : 1, as measured by the variance. (*c*) The original, blurred by the same process as in (*b*) but without noise, now yields a low SNR of 200 : 1. (*d*) Restoration of the image in (*b*) by an inverse filter. (*e*) Restoration of the image in (c) by an inverse filter. (*From H. C. Andrews and B. R. Hunt, "Digital Image Restoration," Prentice-Hall, Englewood Cliffs, N.J., 1977, pp. 129–130.*)

Wiener filter to the restoration of a *Voyager 1* image of Jupiter's moon Io is discussed in [110]. Generally speaking, Wiener filtering is superior to inverse filtering, when applied to an image which has been degraded by uniform motion blur and additive noise.

A variation of the Wiener filter eliminates the need for the knowledge of ϕ_n and ϕ_h. This is the so-called constrained least-square filter [84]

$$G(u, v) = \frac{H^*(u, v)}{|H(u, v)| + \gamma |C(u, v)|^2} \tag{6.50}$$

where γ is a parameter and $C(u, v)$ defines an appropriate constraint. For example, the latter might be selected to relate to the spatial frequency response of the human visual system [81, pp. 702–705].

An interesting technique is that of homomorphic filtering, which will be detailed in the next section on enhancement [26]. As will be seen, it is actually a nonlinear filter, consisting of a logarithmic operator, a linear filter $G(u, v)$, and an exponential function. The linear filter is given by

$$G(u, v) = \left\{ 1 \Big/ \left[|H(u, v)|^2 + \frac{\phi_n}{\phi_h} \right] \right\}^{1/2} \tag{6.51}$$

Apparently, the visual quality of this restoration is superior to that obtained by the other techniques discussed above [85].

A special situation arises when the degradation is not additive as in Equation (6.40) but multiplicative as in Equation (6.37). It turns out that it is still feasible to cancel out a noise pattern by using notch filters. Thus, suppose that we are able to isolate rectangular regions M_i, which contain the noise in the image transform. Then let the mask filter $G(u, v)$ be defined by

$$G(u, v) = \begin{cases} 0 & \text{for all } (u, v) \in M_i \text{ if } |N(u, v)| > \text{threshold} \\ 1 & \text{elsewhere} \end{cases} \tag{6.52}$$

A curious example of the application of this filter is discussed by Blackwell and Crisci [14] in the "case of the bloody palm print." The evidence left at the scene of the crime was a bloody palm print image superimposed on a cotton fiber bed sheet, as shown in Figure 6.40*a*. The processing objective was to abstract the original hand print from the weave pattern of the bed sheet, thereby producing the more conventional ridge pattern employed by police for identification purposes. The weave pattern is assumed to be the noise. It is coherent and therefore, as we shall see, easily distinguished from the other signals on the basis of its structure.

First consider the simple test example in Figure 6.41. A pattern $H(x, y)$ in (*a*) is overlain by the pattern $N(x, y)$ in (*b*), which is assumed to play the role of the unwanted noise. Equation (6.47) then provides that

$$I(x, y) = H(x, y)N(x, y)L(x, y) \tag{6.53}$$

Here $L(x, y)$ is assumed to be an illumination signal which passes through the

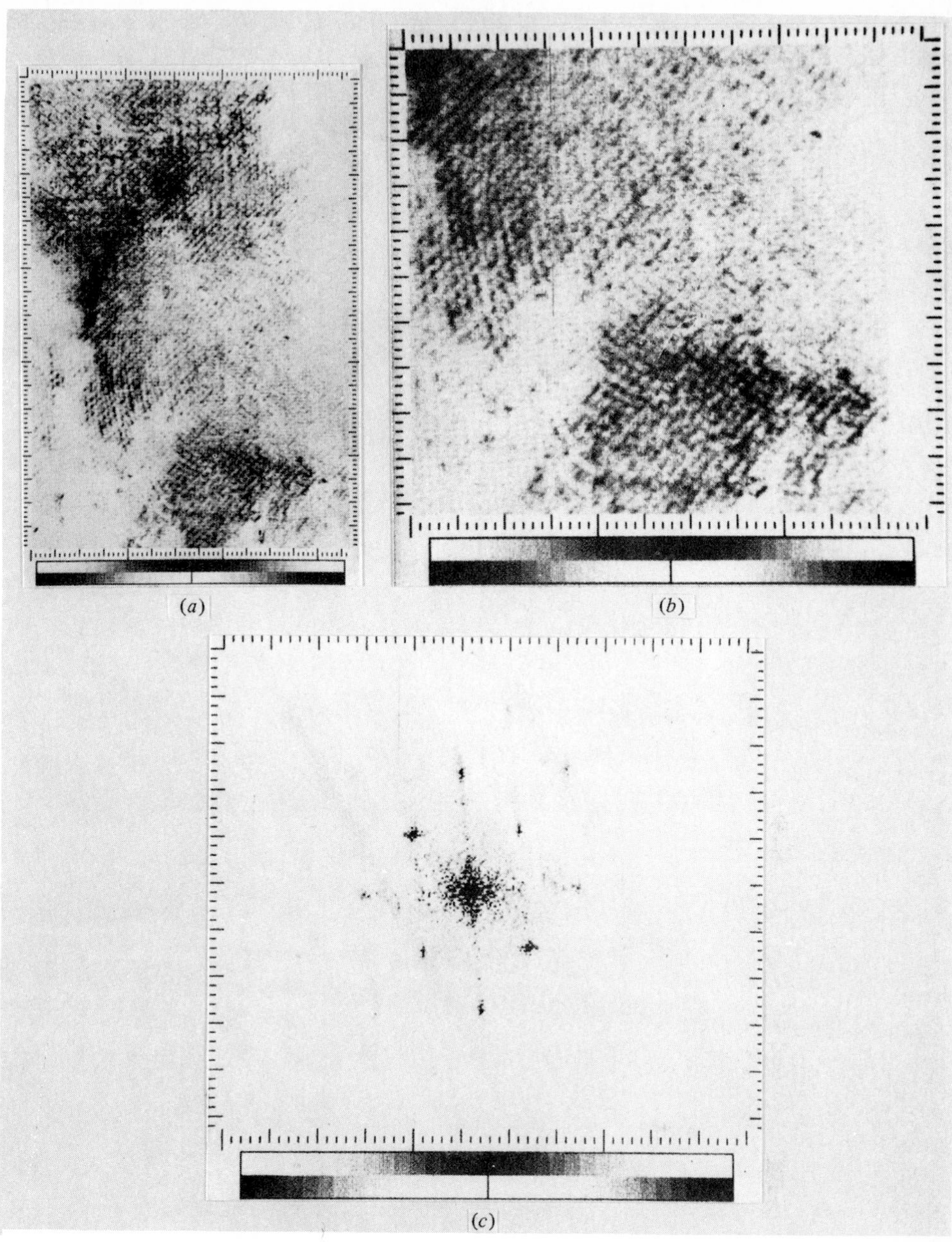

Figure 6.40 Fourier transform of a palm print corrupted by bed sheet "noise." (*a*) Palm print picture before processing. (*b*) Area of palm print picture selected for noise removal processing. (*c*) Fourier transform of picture's area selected for noise removal processing. (*From R. J. Blackwell and W. A. Crisci, "Digital Image Processing Technology and Its Application to Forensic Sciences," Journal of Forensic Sciences, vol. 20, no. 2, 1975, pp. 288–304.*)

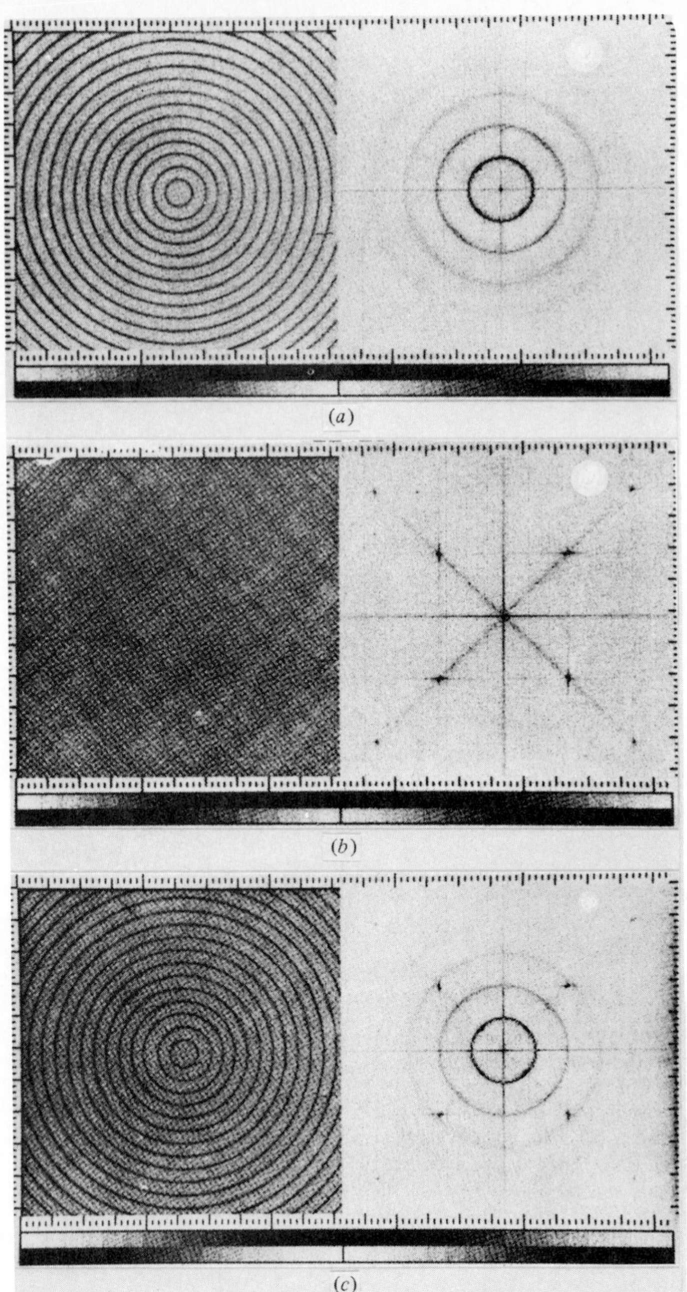

Figure 6.41(a)–(c).

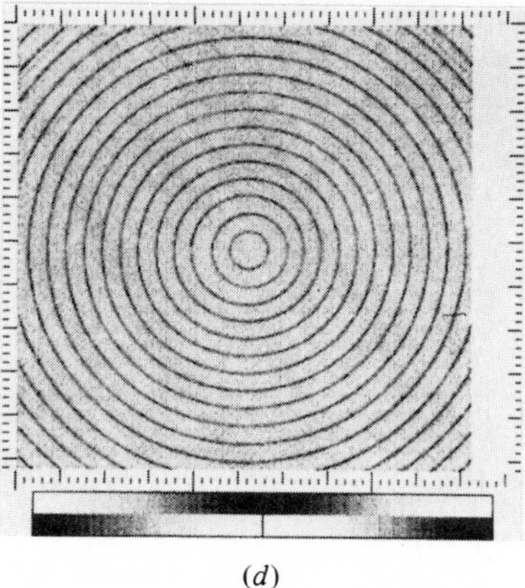

(*d*)

Figure 6.41 Restoration of artificially generated patterns corrupted by noise, using Fourier domain techniques. (*a*) The desired data: $\log H(x, y)$ and $\mathscr{F}[\log H]$. (*b*) The noise pattern: $\log N(x, y)$ and $\mathscr{F}[\log N]$. (*c*) The composite pattern: $\log H + \log N$ and $\mathscr{F}[\log H] + \mathscr{F}[\log N]$. (*d*) The restoration of the original pattern: $\mathscr{F}^{-1}\{\mathscr{F}[\log H] + \mathscr{F}[\log N] - \mathscr{F}[\log N]\}$.

overlay pattern $H(x, y)N(x, y)$. If we now assume that the composite is photographed by using top lighting (see Figure 2.4), the resultant density image $D(x, y)$ becomes

$$D(x, y) = \log H(x, y) + \log N(x, y) + \log L(x, y) \tag{6.54}$$

In other words, the resulting photographic image is an additive combination of the densities (see Chapter 2).† We shall ignore the effect of the last term, due to illumination by assuming it to be constant. It is easily seen from the figure that the coherent noise results in the Fourier transform exhibiting four spikes, which can easily be isolated in the combined transform. The filter $G(u, v)$ is thus selected to consist of four rectangular masks, just large enough to remove the noise spikes. Because it is being assumed that $H(u, v)$ and $N(u, v)$ in Figure 6.41*c* are separable, the filter of Equation (6.52) is equivalent to subtracting the Fourier transform of $\log N(x, y)$ from the right-hand side of Equation (6.54). The transform of the desired image remains, and its inverse is shown in Figure 6.41*d*.

A portion of the photographic transparency of the bed sheet shown in Figure 6.40*a* was digitized into an array of dimension 256×256, as shown in Figure 6.40*b*. Figure 6.40*c* is the Fourier transform of this image. Again, we observe the essentially low-pass characteristic of the signal and the separable localized spikes of the noise. Processing this transform with the notch filter yields the sheet-weave noise pattern in Figure 6.42*a* and the palm print in Figure 6.42*b*. The ridge pattern is now visible without the disturbing interference of the bed sheet, which presumably facilitates its characterization and

† In the next section, we shall discuss a similar nonlinear filtering process which performs an equivalent type of linearization in order to allow for subsequent linear analysis.

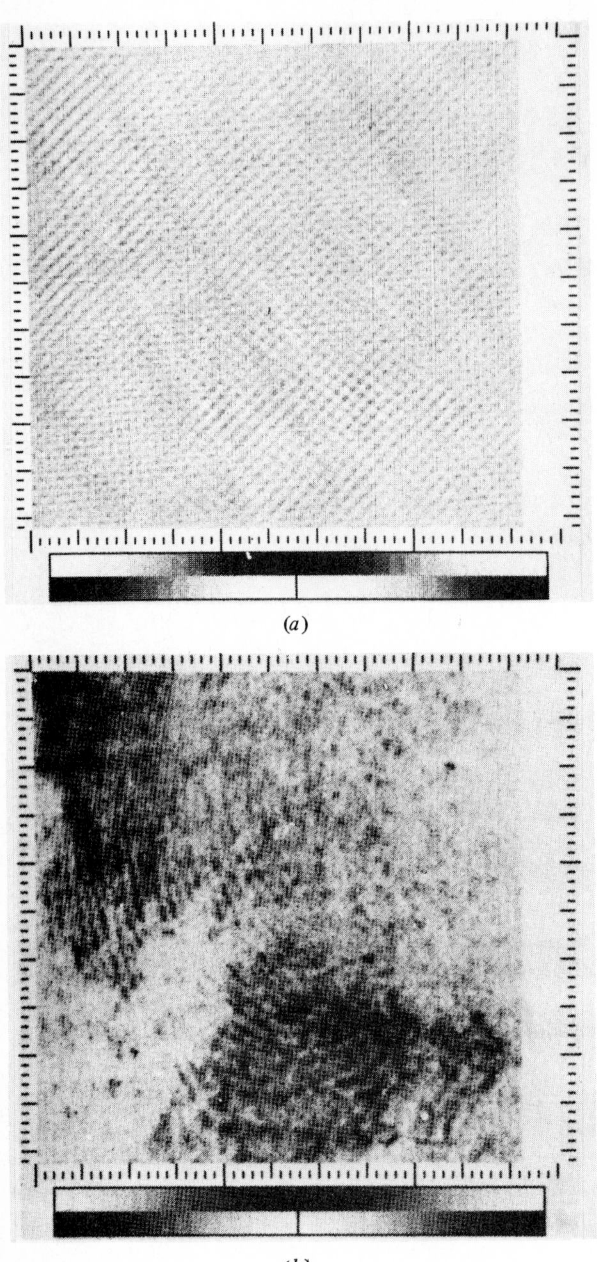

(*a*)

(*b*)

Figure 6.42 Restoration of a palm print pattern after elimination of noise effects. (*a*) Sheet-weave noise pattern removed from Figure 6.40*b*. (*b*) Ridge pattern remaining after sheet-weave pattern removal. (*From R. J. Blackwell and W. A. Crisci, "Digital Image Processing Technology and Its Application to Forensic Sciences," Journal of Forensic Sciences, vol. 20, no. 2, 1975, pp. 288–304.*)

identification with the ridge pattern of the suspect. However, the court held this evidence to be inadmissible, although the accused was convicted on the basis of other evidence. One of the major reasons for setting aside the results obtained by Fourier analysis was the uncertainty as to whether Figure 6.40*b* was the summation of two signals or their product.

In this section, we have dealt with the restoration of an image so that it may appear to the viewer to be as similar to the original scene as possible. The approach is a form of compensation based on some knowledge of the degradation processes.

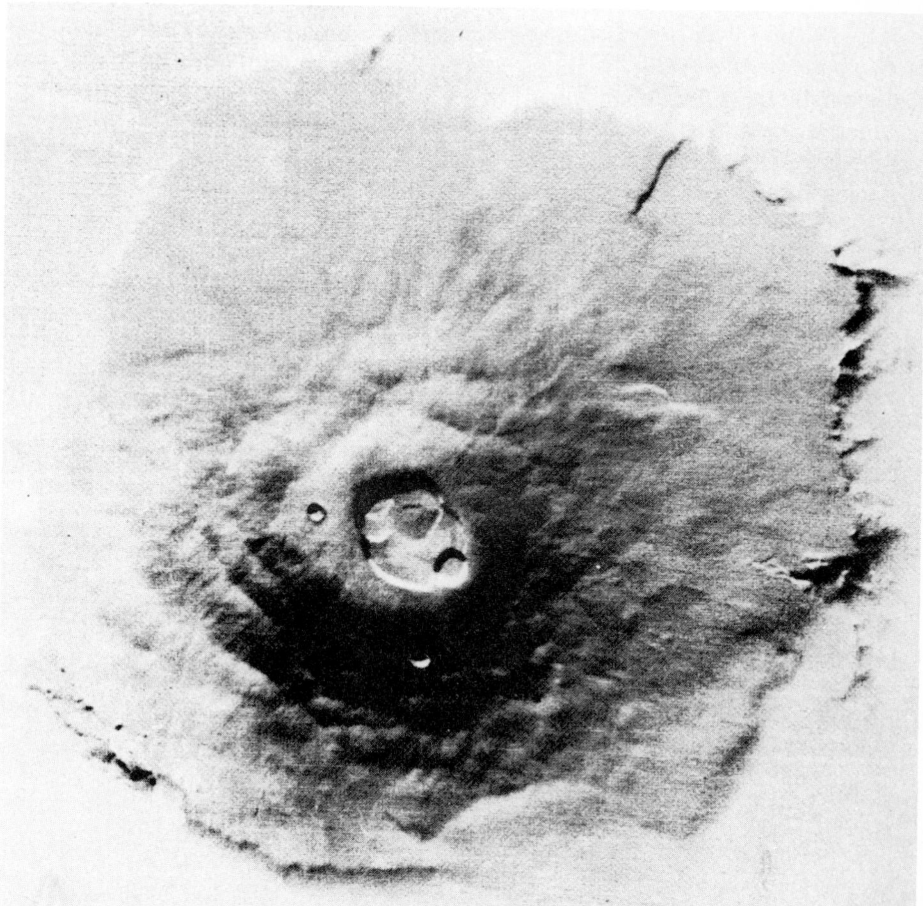

Figure 6.43 This figure shows the first photographic view of the entire south polar cap of Mars (*Mariner 6* and *Mariner 7*) in a standard mapping projection. This orthographic photomap, simulating a view of the polar cap from directly over the south pole, was constructed from 14 television pictures of Mars obtained in 1969 by the *Mariner 6* and *Mariner 7* spacecraft. (*From D. A. O'Handley, "Recent Developments in Digital Image Processing at the Image Processing Laboratory of JPL," First National Conference on Remotely Manned Systems (RMS), California Institute of Technology, Pasadena, Sept. 13–15, 1972.*)

6.5.3 Enhancement

Essentially, enhancement is "making a picture look nice," or attempting to represent an original scene as it actually looked by producing a processed image. Sometimes this is a prerequisite to analysis, sometimes it is done just to improve the appearance of the picture. Perhaps the best examples of this methodology pertain to the pictures obtained from the various American space missions. For example, Figure 6.43 shows an image produced by *Mariner 9* of the crater Nix Olympica on the surface of Mars. It was actually obtained from a set of individual frames, each taken from a different perspective and each distorted by the imaging and data communication process. The flyby occurred in late January after a dust storm and revealed a mountain of 500-km diameter at the base of the crater. In this section we shall consider simple linear and nonlinear filtering for enhancement.

In the linear case, a filter such as one of those shown in Figure 6.44 is sought [11]. However, binary or 0–1 zonal filters, as illustrated in Figure 6.34, are often employed. Bandpass and bandstop filters are also easily defined in

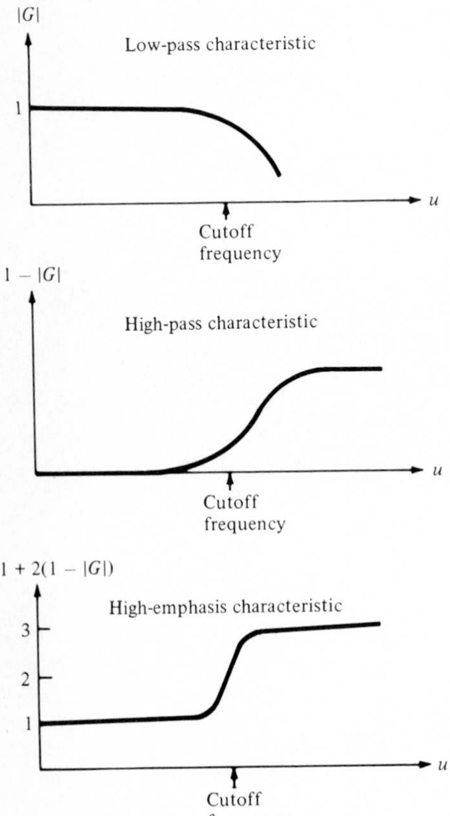

Figure 6.44 Typical filter characteristics employed for image enhancement. Two-dimensional filters can be constructed from these curves by assuming rotational symmetry.

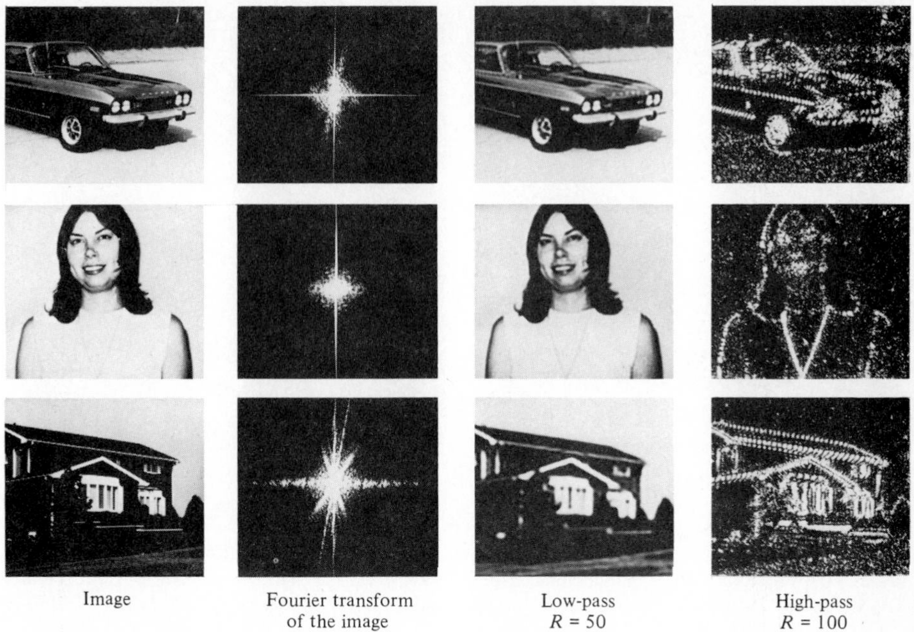

Figure 6.45 Filtering of 256×256 images using first-order circular filters. The cutoff frequencies for the low-pass and high-pass filters are 50 and 100, respectively. The maximum value of R is 128.

this way. Figure 6.45 shows an image which has been filtered by using both a low-pass and a high-pass characteristic for $G(u, v)$. The former contains spatial frequency elements clustered around the vicinity of $(u, v) = (0, 0)$. It tends to isolate the broad constant-gray level areas. On the other hand, the high-pass filter accentuates the edge data and enhances the image texture (see Chapter 9). At this point, it is interesting to compare these pictures with the pyramid in Figure 5.38 and the multichannel output data in Figure 6.22.

An alternative to high-pass filtering is high-frequency emphasis, in which the low frequencies are retained. However, the higher frequencies are amplified with respect to the lower ones, as sketched in Figure 6.44. An example of this is the industrial betatron radiograph of a hollow metal shell, shown in Figure 6.46*a* [86, 87]. The inner border is not well defined, a situation caused by the radiographic imaging process. With high-emphasis filtering, the shell in Figure 6.46*b* is now quite visible and delineated. In addition, features not apparent in (*a*) have become quite obvious in (*b*). Another example is shown in Figure 6.47 [87]. Figure 6.47*a* is a radiograph of a reactor fuel element consisting of an outer and inner tube. The latter is loaded with cylindrical fuel pellets and the whole assembly is placed into a nuclear reactor, where it is subjected to high temperature and neutron flux. Again, emphasizing the higher frequencies brings out the desired detail. Figure 6.47*b* shows that the horizon-

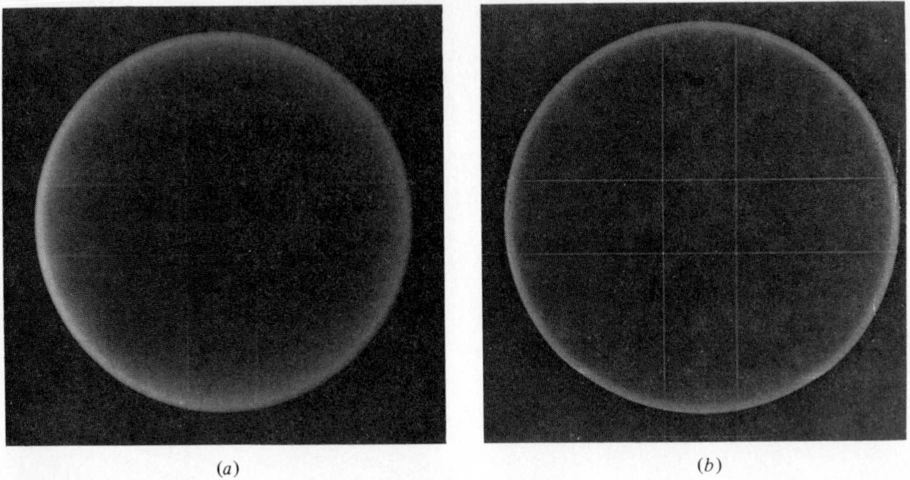

(*a*) (*b*)

Figure 6.46 An example of high-emphasis filtering for image enhancement. Information is extracted which is not readily visible in the original. (*a*) A radiograph of a hollow metal shell. (*b*) The same shell after computer enhancement. The boundary of the inner wall is now more clearly defined. (*From B. R. Hunt, D. H. Janney, and R. K. Zeigler, "A Survey of Radiographic Image Enhancement Experience," Report LA-DC-72-69, Los Alamos Scientific Laboratory, 1972.*)

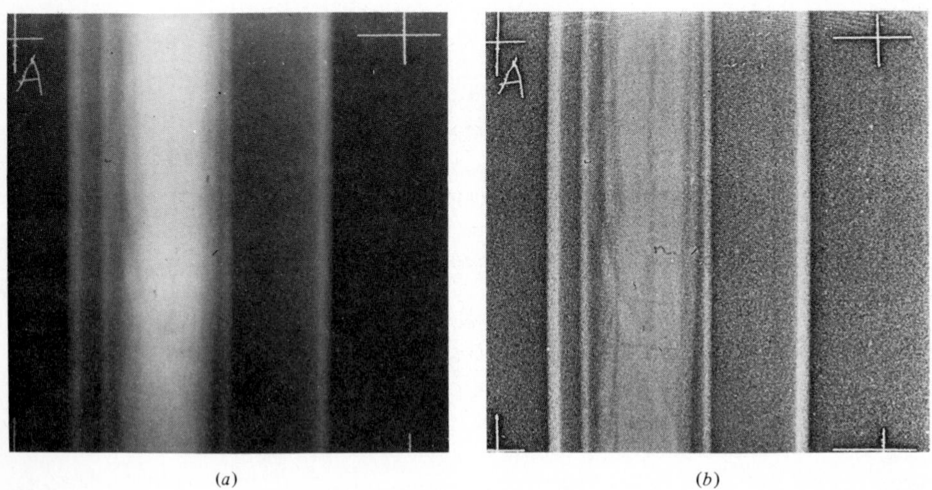

(*a*) (*b*)

Figure 6.47 An example of linear filtering for image enhancement. (*a*) A radiograph of a reactor fuel element. (*b*) The result of high-emphasis filtering. (*From B. R. Hunt, D. H. Janney, and R. K. Zeigler, "A Survey of Radiographic Image Enhancement Experience," Report LA-DC-72-69, Los Alamos Scientific Laboratory, Los Alamos, 1972.*)

tally stacked pellets have been deformed, and a rupture of the inner tube is visible at the bottom left. Other examples of linear filtering may be found in [40, pp. 308–318], where the "blocks" world of Shakey the robot is enhanced in a similar fashion.

Nonlinear filtering is also an effective means of enhancing and restoring an image [168]. One approach to this problem is so-called homomorphic filtering [126]. When applied to image enhancement, it will be seen that this technique takes into account certain aspects related to the psychophysical model discussed in Chapter 4. Further, it may be used to separate signals which are multiplicatively combined. A fascinating application of this same method is the restoration of old acoustic recordings to eliminate the annoying resonant characteristic due to the original recording horn [157].

Figure 6.48 is a block diagram of a homomorphic filter. It is assumed that the picture formation process is ideal, so that $I(x, y) = L_1(x, y)$ or $L_2(x, y)$. Also, we note that whether we are observing a scene [Equation (2.18)] or transmitting light through a photographic transparency [Equation (2.19)], the intensity array can be represented as the product of an input light source and a modulated data source. Thus we have either Equation (2.18) (with $\theta_r = 0$ degrees)

$$L_1(x, y) = r(x, y)E_e(x, y) \tag{6.55}$$

or Equation (2.19)

$$L_2(x, y) = t(x, y)E_e(x, y) \tag{6.56}$$

No generality is lost by restricting the discussion to Equation (6.55). Then, from the figure it is obvious that

$$D(x, y) = \log r(x, y) + \log E_e(x, y) \tag{6.57}$$

an additive combination. The linear filter computes $[\hat{D}(u, v)]$:

$$\hat{D}(u, v) = G(u, v)D(u, v) \tag{6.58}$$

from which $\hat{D}(x, y)$ is easily obtained by transform inversion. Since the two

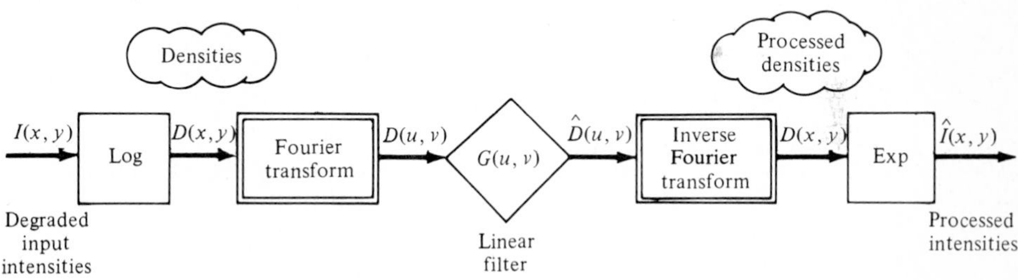

Figure 6.48 A homomorphic filter for image enhancement. A nonlinear relationship exists between $\hat{I}(x, y)$ and $I(x, y)$ although the system is governed by multiplicative superposition.

components in Equation (6.57) are processed independently by the filter $G(u, v)$, we may write

$$[\hat{D}(x, y)] = [\widehat{\log r(x, y)}] + [\widehat{\log E_e(x, y)}] \tag{6.59}$$

where the symbol ^ is meant to apply to the function within the square brackets after linear filtering. From the figure, the last stage is given by

$$[\hat{I}(x, y)] = \exp[\hat{D}(x, y)] = \exp[\widehat{\log I(x, y)}] > 0 \tag{6.60}$$

(Frei [45] has proposed an alternative to this function in which $[\hat{I}(x, y)]$ is obtained by ensuring that all perceived brightness levels are equiprobable.) By substituting Equation (6.59) we obtain

$$\begin{aligned}[\hat{I}(x, y)] &= \exp\{[\widehat{\log r(x, y)}] + [\widehat{\log E_e(x, y)}]\} \\ &= \exp[\widehat{\log r(x, y)}] \exp[\widehat{\log E(x_e, y)}]\end{aligned}$$

By analogy to Equation (6.60)

$$[\hat{r}(x, y)] = \exp[\log \hat{r}(x, y)]$$

and

$$[\hat{E}_e(x, y)] = \exp[\widehat{\log E_e(x, y)}]$$

so that

$$[\hat{I}(x, y)] = [\hat{r}(x, y)][\hat{E}_e(x, y)] \tag{6.61}$$

In terms of the convolution operator $*$, $[\hat{I}(x, y)]$ can also be written as

$$[\hat{I}(x, y)] = \exp\{g(x, y) * \log r(x, y) + g(x, y) * \log E_e(x, y)\} \tag{6.62}$$

Equation (6.61) has been described as multiplicative superposition [126]. This is because each element of the input product [Equation (6.55)] is processed independently and so represented in the output Equation (6.61).

Suppose that the filter in Figure 6.48 was made an attenuator or amplifier having constant gain γ. With

$$G(u, v) = \gamma \tag{6.63}$$

it is easily shown that Equation (6.61) [or equivalently Equation (6.62)] reduces to

$$\hat{I}(x, y) = I(x, y)^{\gamma} \tag{6.64}$$

This "power-law" relationship between input and output intensities is equivalent to the process of photography, in which γ may be controlled by selecting appropriate photographic materials and adjusting the development time (see Chapter 2). However, it is evident that the homomorphic filter creates the possibility of controlling this type of enhancement digitally. In fact, it is much more flexible. Thus if we selected

$$G(u, v) = \gamma(u, v) \tag{6.65}$$

this would now be equivalent to a frequency-sensitive γ in the sense that it exhibits a different power-law behavior for each spatial frequency of the density of the input-image intensity.

In order to design an appropriate enhancement filter, Stockham [156] has claimed certain properties for the two factors $r(x, y)$ and E_e in Equation (6.61). It is suggested that there is a certain degree of independence between the two

(*a*)

(*b*)

(*c*)

Figure 6.49 Homomorphic filtering. (*a*) A test image. (*b*) The image in (*a*) processed using $\gamma = \frac{1}{2}$. (*c*) The image in (*a*) processed using $\gamma = 2$. (*From A. V. Oppenheim, R. W. Schafer, and T. G. Stockham, Jr., "Nonlinear Filtering of Multiplied and Convolved Signals," Proceedings of the IEEE, vol. 56, no. 8, August 1968, p. 1265.*)

effects. The illumination component $E_e(x, y)$ can be approximately associated with the low frequencies. These tend to control the dynamic range and are largely related to the diffuse and smooth areas in the picture $I(x, y)$. Similarly, the reflectance component can be approximately associated with the high frequencies, which provide the edge content. However, this interpretation has been shown to be incorrect for specular scenes [127].

To reduce the dynamic range in an image, we may select $\gamma = \frac{1}{2}$ [Equation (6.63)], as shown in Figure 6.49*b*. Although the photographic medium is now no longer the limit on the dynamic range, as is the case in Figure 6.49*a*, the image appears to be "washed out." On the other hand, Figure 6.49*c* shows that with $\gamma = 2$ the edges may be enhanced, but now the dynamic range is excessive, and saturation occurs at both limits of the gray scale. Because of the approximate independence of $r(x, y)$ and $E_e(x, y)$, the high-frequency-enhancement filter $G(u, v)$ in Figure 6.50*b* can be thought of as "simultaneously" reducing the dynamic range and enhancing the edges. Thus we might claim that

$$\hat{I}(x, y) \approx E_e(x, y)^{1/2} r(x, y)^2 \tag{6.66}$$

The effect of this sharpening filter is strikingly demonstrated in Figure 6.50*a*. The results are truly impressive, although some artifact has been introduced.

(*a*)

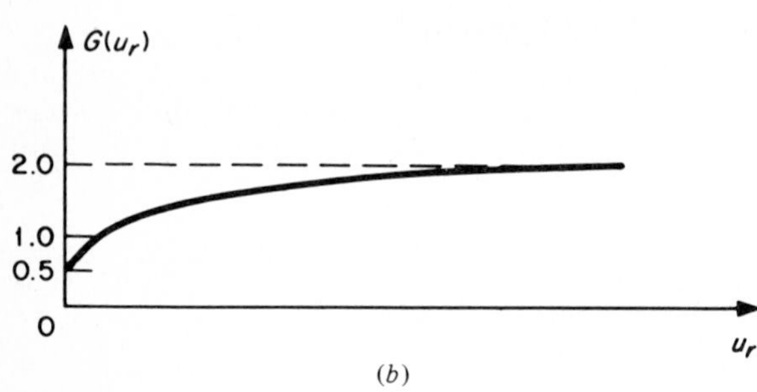

(*b*)

Figure 6.50 An example of homomorphic filtering. (*a*) The image of Figure 6.49*a* processed by using a frequency-dependent γ with low-frequency attenuation and high-frequency amplification. (*b*) The radial cross section of the multiplicative frequency response used to produce (*a*). (*From A. V. Oppenheim, R. W. Schafer, and T. G. Stockham, Jr., "Nonlinear Filtering of Multiplied and Convolved Signals," Proceedings of the IEEE, vol. 56, no. 8, August 1968, p. 1265.*)

Details within the dark room, as well as outside in the background, are now well defined.

Schreiber [151] has challenged the above interpretation of the reason for the success of homomorphic filtering. His claim is that a cascade of a power-law and a linear filter (or vice versa) would give equivalent results. It is indeed curious that this is the very same argument that has raged within the psychological community, a topic we discussed in Section 4.5.1.

6.6 SPATIAL-DOMAIN PROCESSING

6.6.1 Point Operations

In Section 6.5 picture processing was discussed from the point of view of the spatial frequency domain. Here we shall briefly examine some equivalent filtering techniques in the spatial domain. Of course, examples of this approach have already been considered in Chapter 5 with the definition of the edge detectors as templates. An interesting practical application of spatial-domain processing is the editing and enhancement of news photographs [163].

"Point operations" may be defined as transformations of an input image $I(i, j)$ into an output image $A(i, j)$ (see Figure 5.19*b*, where we now assume that the parallel masking operation is nonexistent) by means of a nonlinear operator $\Lambda\{\cdot\}$, which maps the input gray levels into different gray levels according to certain criteria dedicated to achieving enhancement or restoration of the original picture. It may also be thought of as a process of transforming the histogram of the input image into a new histogram for the output image array. Hummel [83] has discussed a general technique for determining $\Lambda\{\cdot\}$, given the two distributions.

One of the simplest of such point operators is the reduction of the gray scale of the input image. As discussed in Section 2.2, the image has been quantized into the integer set $I = \{I_1, I_2, \ldots, I_n\}$, where n is the total number of gray levels. Data compression may be achieved by altering the number of output quantization levels. The transformation Λ is a staircase graph in which $\theta_1, \theta_2, \ldots, \theta_{K-1}$ are the thresholds which define the output picture quantization. Figure 6.25 presents the effect of this type of linear thresholding for an input array $I(i, j)$ of 64 gray levels and output with $K = 32, 16, 8, 4$, and 2. Clearly, a certain amount of detail is lost with fewer gray levels.

Instead of a linear scale, the thresholds may also be selected by specific reference to the original histogram in order to enhance the information in the picture. For example, binary (one-threshold) pictures are meaningful for basically black-and-white data such as handwritten characters. Sometimes one end of the gray scale is mapped into a single gray level, for example, the background, while the complete original scale is maintained for the rest. This is referred to as "semithresholding." Either

$$A(i, j) = \begin{cases} I(i, j) & \text{if } I(i, j) \geq \theta \\ \text{lowest gray level} & \text{if } I(i, j) < \theta \end{cases} \tag{6.67}$$

or

$$A(i, j) = \begin{cases} \text{highest gray level} & \text{if } I(i, j) \geq \theta \\ I(i, j) & \text{if } I(i, j) < \theta \end{cases} \tag{6.68}$$

holds, depending on whether it is the upper or the lower part of the gray scale that is being reproduced. One application of this approach is data compression. It is particularly advantageous when the area covered by the objects is but a small fraction of the total image array. An example is the analysis of cervical smears or chromosome spreads. We shall see in Chapter 8 that for more complex images a particular set of thresholds may be selected to isolate or segment the different regions in the image. This may be achieved interactively by an experimenter or automatically by a computer program. A survey of such techniques is given in [170]. Figure 6.51 illustrates two examples in which the image histogram is a mixture of three Gaussians. Two thresholds have been selected, but clearly the modes do not conform to objects in the scene. In the case of the industrial parts, the largest peak is associated with the background while the other two are interpreted as the objects. Note that the illumination has produced these two object peaks. The situation for the car is much more complicated.

Another form of enhancement is achieved by translating and/or scaling the gray scale of the image. A familiar example of this is the contrast adjustment knob on a television set; it alters the gain applied to the input image. By increasing the amplification the saturation point of the display tube is exceeded. This results in fewer input gray levels being required to cover the complete output range of the tube, thereby improving the image contrast. Suppose, as shown in Figure 6.52*a*, the histogram only covered a fraction of the available gray scale. Then the so-called stretch operation produces a picture with gray levels spread over the maximum range. The result tends to display detail more clearly than in the original (see Figure 6.52*b* and *c*). Arbitrary degrees of contrast enhancement may also be achieved by selectively stretching the dark areas, the bright areas, or the midrange of gray levels, as shown in Figure 6.53 [8]. Compensation for various point nonlinearities that arise in image digitization is also usefully achieved by a suitable selection of $\Lambda(i, j)$ [10].

Pictures are sometimes enhanced not just to correct for known degradations but to make them more meaningful. One example is the so-called sawtooth enhancement procedure. In this method the input gray scale is arbitrarily divided into cycles, each of which is linearly stretched to the maximum. Figure 6.54*a* and *b* gives two examples in which it is seen that the effect is to remove the most significant bit and the most significant 2 bits, respectively. This multiple-cycle enhancement tends to accentuate the edge contours, as shown in the photographs of the eye in Figure 6.54*c*. It also introduces a great deal of artifact.

It is often useful to determine Λ by imposing specific constraints on the histogram of the resulting enhanced picture [83, 152]. One common example of

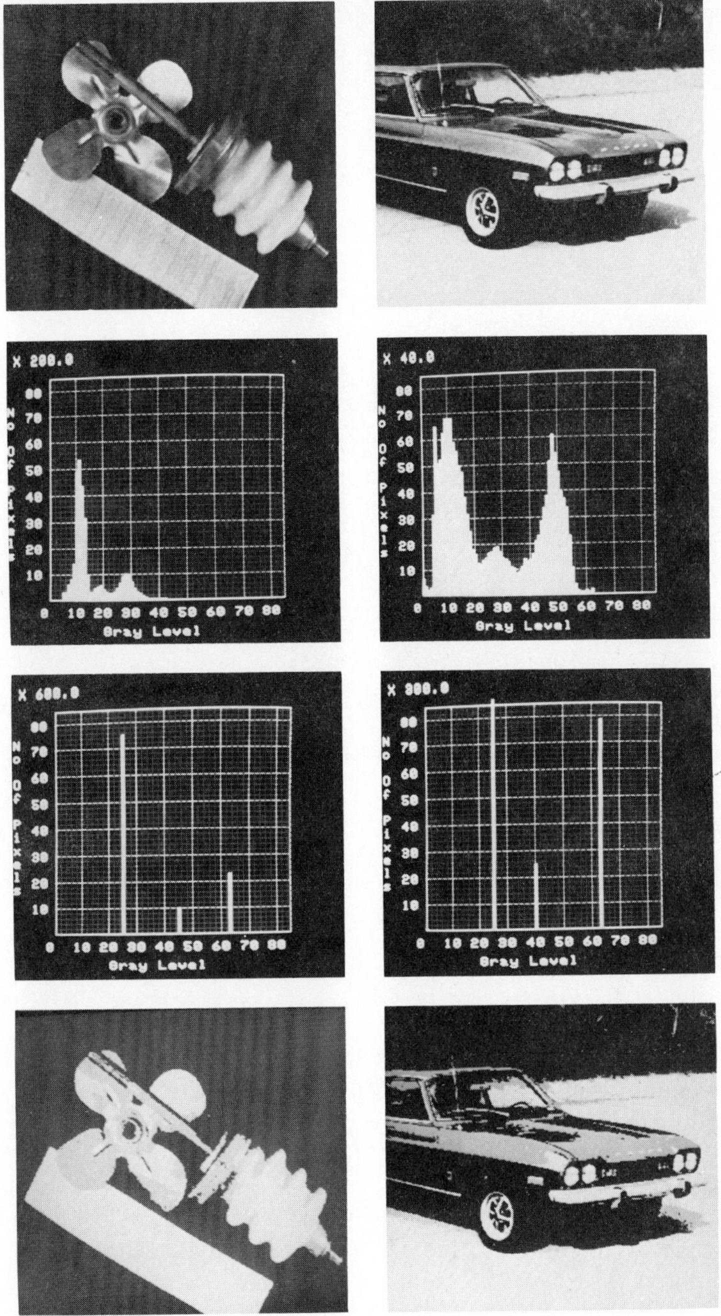

Figure 6.51 Interactive thresholding of histograms. In both cases the two thresholds were chosen as the gray levels in the valleys at the left and right of the central peak of the histogram. The resulting three modes were then arbitrarily shaded as shown.

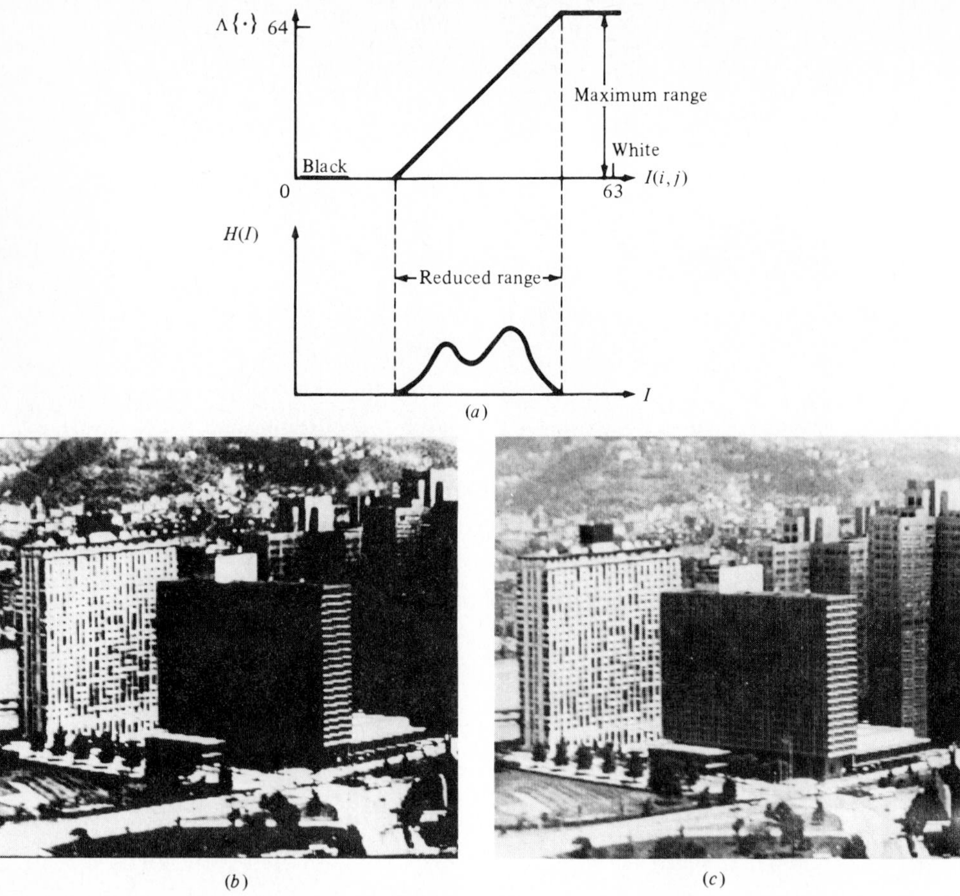

Figure 6.52 Contrast enhancement by stretching. (*a*) The transformation from input to output. (*b*) Original. (*c*) Stretched version.

this is "histogram equalization" [66]. In this procedure the histogram of the input image is mapped into another in which each gray level has a uniform probability, as shown in Figure 6.55*a*. Algorithms for computing Λ are given in [66; 67; 141, p. 173] and are based on the selection of thresholds for $H_1(I)$ which map into equal areas ("vertical slices") of $H_2(I)$. This rescaling may easily be done by reference to the cumulative density function of $H_1(I)$. Note that the number of gray levels defining $H_2(I)$ must be less than the number defining $H_1(I)$ and that because of the discrete nature of the histograms, $H_2(I)$ can only be made approximately uniform. Figure 6.55*b* is an example of histogram equalization in which contrast enhancement is easily observed in two cases. However, the contrast in the picture of the girl seems already to have been appropriate, so that equalization actually destroys the quality. As noted in

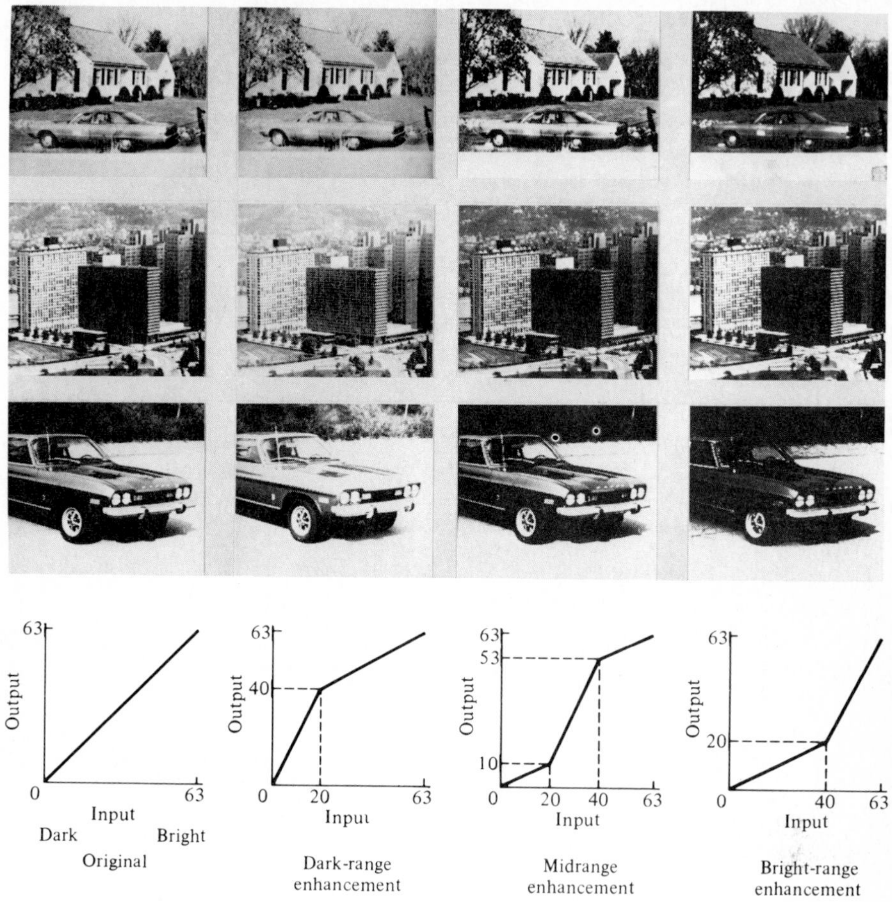

Figure 6.53 Contrast enhancement in different gray-level domains.

Chapter 9, this approach has been extensively used in texture analysis to eliminate the dependence of computer methods on various input data degradations [29]. Moreover, the effect is also of theoretical interest since it can be shown that this transformation is optimal in the sense that it maximizes the expected information content in the picture [83]. We may contemplate whether the human visual system would also possibly perform the same normalization operation.

Histogram modification has proved to be a very useful means for enhancing picture quality. Moreover, recent advances in computer technology now make it feasible to perform this image-processing computation at video rates [178].

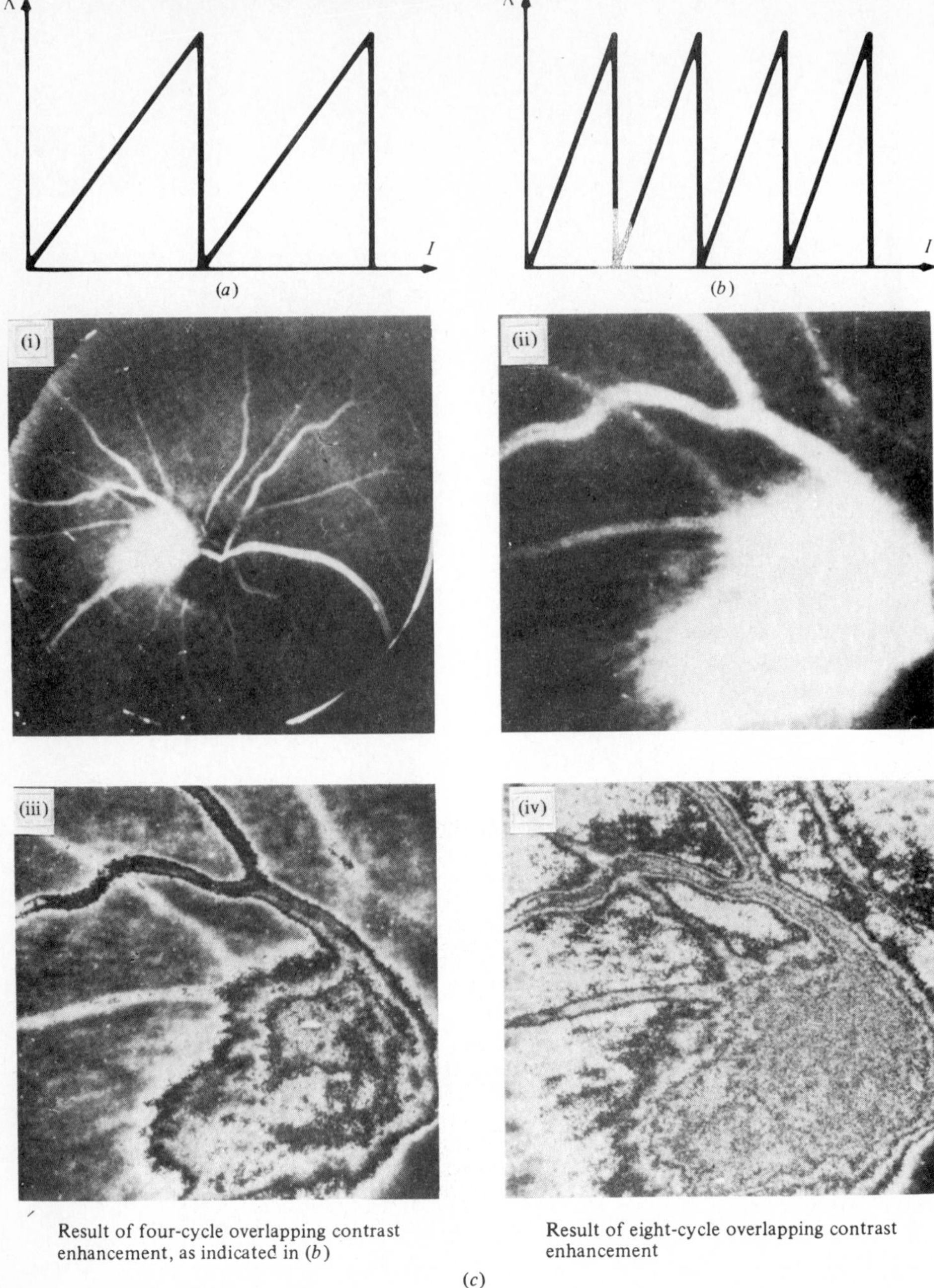

Result of four-cycle overlapping contrast enhancement, as indicated in (*b*)

Result of eight-cycle overlapping contrast enhancement

(*c*)

Figure 6.54 Retina photograph showing multiple-cycle contrast enhancement. (*a*) Two-cycle enhancement curve in which the most significant bit is removed. (*b*) Four-cycle enhancement curve in which the two most significant bits are removed. (*c*) The results of the enhancement specified in (*a*) and (*b*). Considerably more detail is now visible. (*From R. Selzer, "The Use of Computers to Improve Biomedical Image Quality," AFIPS-1968, Proceedings of the Fall Joint Computer Conference, vol. 33, pt. 1, 1968, pp. 817–834.*)

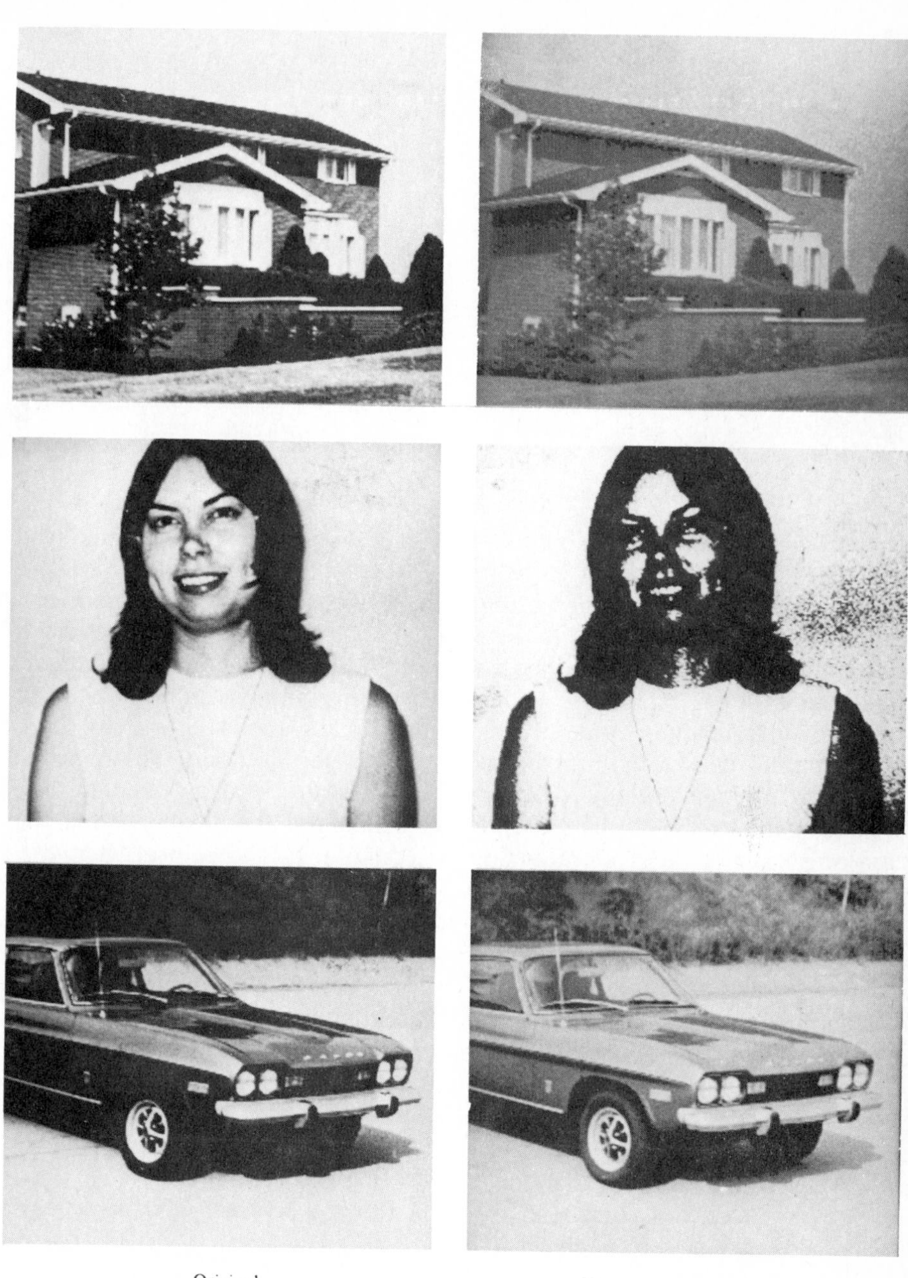

(a)

Figure 6.55(*a*) (Caption on page 296.)

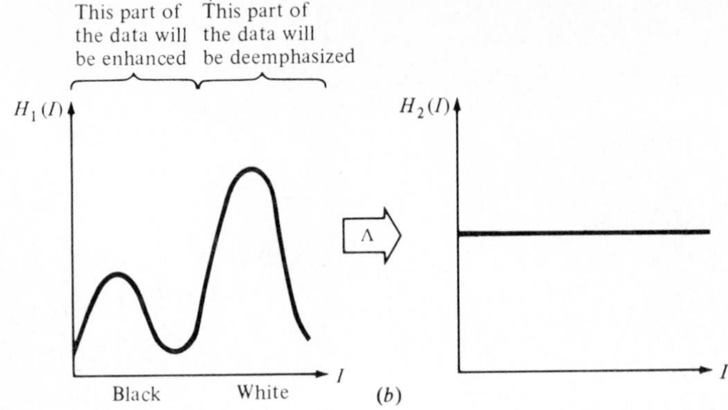

Figure 6.55 Histogram equalization, a transformation often used for the purpose of normalizing images prior to texture analysis (see Chapter 9). (*a*) Examples of using the transformation in (*b*). (*b*) The transformation of the input histogram into an output histogram with a specific property.

6.6.2 Neighborhood Operations

Numerous examples of neighborhood operations defined by templates or windows have already been given. In this section attention will be drawn to a set of spatial-domain computations which are analogous to those in the frequency domain discussed in Section 6.5. These are often characterized as being filters since they tend to pass only certain components of the two-dimensional input image. In distinction to the point operations discussed in Section 6.6.1, here the value of the output-image array $A(i, j)$ at any location (i, j) depends on a group of pixels in $I(i, j)$, centered around (i, j)†. As we have seen, it is the conventional practice to select a square array template of size 3×3, sometimes slightly larger. A simple example is the neighborhood operation which mimics the zoom function of a camera. It is often used in computer graphics to magnify an image for display purposes. Typically, simple replication of $I(i, j)$ in a 2×2 window of $A(i, j)$ is used. An example is shown in Figure 6.56. Although replication is simpler, linear interpolation would provide a more accurate representation.

As indicated in Figure 6.44 for the spatial frequency domain, the techniques to be discussed in this section can also be conveniently divided into low-pass and high-pass operators. We shall begin with the former, which is often achieved by averaging, for example, within a 3×3 window, as follows:

$$A(i, j) = \frac{1}{9}\left[\sum_{k=i-1}^{i+1} \sum_{l=j-1}^{j+1} I(k, l)\right] \tag{6.69}$$

Examination of the effect of the equal-weight filters in Figure 6.57 shows that the image is blurred or defocused and that the effect is increased with larger templates. An interesting extension of the averaging filter approach is the so-called box filtering technique [111]. Other examples of the enhancement and restoration of biomedical imagery are found in [149].

† See Figure 5.19*b*, in which we have assumed $\Lambda(i, j) = 1$ so that $A(i, j) = I(i, j) * W(i, j)$.

Figure 6.56 The zoom function.

Original

3 X 3 template

5 X 5 template

7 X 7 template

9 X 9 template

Figure 6.57 Low-pass filtering by averaging in the image domain.

One useful application of low-pass filtering is noise cleaning [37]. The median filter, in which $I(i, j)$ is replaced in $A(i, j)$ by the median gray level in the local neighborhood of $I(i, j)$, is an alternative to simple averaging [90, 119]. Compared with the latter, it tends to better preserve the edges in the picture but also manages to filter out small spiky artifacts and sharp edges. For example, it has been used to process an image of the holy shroud of Turin [158]. A special-purpose hardware device for median filtering, using very large-scale integration (VLSI) technology, is discussed in [44]. Many other methods have also been suggested in the literature: gradient smoothing [139, pp. 192–200], maximum homogeneity smoothing [162], neighbor weighting [98], and weighted averaging [164]. However, a study by Davenport [37] has found that the median filter produces the best results.

Another application of low-pass neighborhood operations is for adaptive contrast enhancement [69, 93]. This is useful when the image has a high dynamic range with considerable low-contrast local detail. Under these circumstances a global approach, such as adjustment of overall gain and bias control, is inadequate. However, it is possible to slide a template over the image, computing local area statistics, and to control the bias level and gain adaptively. In this fashion, local contrast can be enhanced without exceeding the available dynamic range. The bias level, $\mu(i, j)$, is a measure of the local average brightness. The adaptive gain $G(i, j)$ is given by

$$G(i, j) = \alpha \frac{\mu(i, j)}{\sigma(i, j)} \qquad 0 < \alpha < 1 \tag{6.70}$$

where μ and σ are the mean and standard deviation within the template. The enhanced local intensity $A(i, j)$ is then taken as

$$A(i, j) = G(i, j)[I(i, j) - \mu(i, j)] + \mu(i, j) \tag{6.71}$$

This is consistent with Weber's law (see Section 4.5.1), in that to maintain a constant contrast sensitivity, the gain must be increased if the average intensity increases. Also, small uniform areas will tend to produce larger gains, according to Equation (6.70). A real-time hardware implementation of this algorithm is discussed in [120].

High-pass filters are often used for enhancing image data, as shown in Figure 6.58. The edge operators discussed in Chapter 5 are examples of this computational process. An interesting application is to real-time autofocus algorithms for microscope zoom control [100].

As indicated in this section, most computations in computer vision are performed locally. An exception is geometric restoration [121]. This is the problem of restoring an image when it has been distorted by a nonlinear position-dependent process. Examples are discussed in [61, 145, 147, 171, 172].

The formal equivalence of the image and spatial frequency domains allows for the design of filters from either point of view. Conceptually, it was seen in Section 6.5 to be quite straightforward to use the frequency domain. The actual

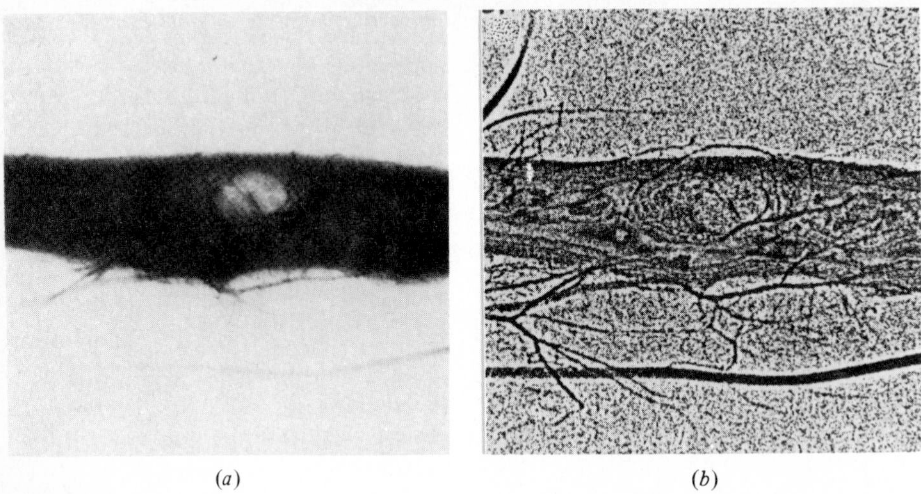

(a) (b)

Figure 6.58 Angiogram of bone showing background removal. (*a*) Unprocessed. (*b*) After high-pass filter and contrast enhancement by a factor of 4. (*From R. Selzer, "The Use of Computers to Improve Biomedical Image Quality," AFIPS-1968, Proceedings of the Fall Joint Computer Conference, vol. 33, pt. 1, 1968, pp. 817–834.*)

choice is usually based on technological considerations rather than theoretical ones. The theory of the synthesis of digital filters is beyond the scope of this book. Readers may refer to [113] for a review of this subject.

References

1. Abadi, R. V., and Kulikowski, J. J., "Linear Summation of Spatial Harmonics in Human Vision," *Vision Research*, vol. 13, no. 9, 1973, pp. 1625–1628.
2. Abbott, R. P., "DPCM Codes for Video Telephony Using 4 Bits per Sample," *IEEE Transactions on Communications Technology*, vol. COM-19, no. 12, December 1971, pp. 907–913.
3. Ahmed, N., Natarajan, T., and Rao, K. R., "Discrete Cosine Transform," *IEEE Transactions on Computers*, vol. C-23, no. 1, January 1974, pp. 90–93.
4. Amari, S. I., "A Mathematical Approach to Neural Systems," in Metzler, J. (ed.), "Systems Neuroscience," Academic, New York, 1977, pp. 67–117.
5. Amari, S. I., Lieblich, I., and Karshmer, A. I., "A Neural Model for the Handling of Phenomena Associated with Trains of Light Stimuli: An Updated Version to Fit Fusion Data," in Metzler, J. (ed.), "Systems Neuroscience," Academic, New York, 1977, pp. 55–56.
6. Anderson, G. B., and Huang, T. S., "Piecework Fourier Transformation for Picture Bandwidth Compression," *IEEE Transactions on Communications*, vol. COM-20, 3, June 1972, pp. 488–491.
7. Andrews, H. C., "Computer Techniques in Image Processing," Academic, New York, 1970.
8. Andrews, H. C., "Digital Image Restoration: A Survey," *Computer*, vol. 7, no. 5, May 1974, pp. 36–45.
9. Andrews, H. C., "Computer Techniques in Image Processing," Academic, New York, 1976.
10. Andrews, H. C., and Hunt, B. R., "Digital Image Restoration," Prentice-Hall, Englewood Cliffs, N.J., 1977.

11. Andrews, H. C., Tescher, A. G., and Kruger, R. P., "Image Processing by Digital Computer," *IEEE Spectrum*, vol. 9, no. 7, July 1972, pp. 20–22.
12. Baxter, B. S., "Image Processing in the Human Visual System," Ph.D. thesis, Department of Electrical Engineering, University of Utah, Salt Lake City, 1975.
13. Berger, T., "Rate Distortion Theory, A Mathematical Basis for Data Compression," Prentice-Hall, Englewood Cliffs, N.J., 1971.
14. Blackwell, R. J., and Crisci, W. A., "Digital Image Processing Technology and Its Application to Forensic Sciences," *Journal of Forensic Sciences*, vol. 20, no. 2, 1975, pp. 288–304.
15. Blakemore, C., and Campbell, F. W., "On the Existence of Neurons in the Human Visual System Selectively Sensitive to the Orientation and Size of Retinal Images," *Journal of Physiology*, vol. 203, no. 1, 1969, pp. 237–260.
16. Blesser, B., Shillman, R., Kuklinski, T., Cox, C., Eden, M., and Venture, J., "A Theoretical Approach for Character Recognition Based on Phenomenological Attributes," *Proceedings of the First International Joint Conference on Pattern Recognition*, Washington, Oct. 30–Nov. 1, 1973, IEEE, New York, 1973, pp. 33–40.
17. Brigham, E. O., "The Fast Fourier Transform," Prentice-Hall, Englewood Cliffs, N.J., 1974.
18. Bruce, R. A., "Optimum Pre-emphasis Networks for Transmission of Television by PCM," *IEEE Transactions on Communication Systems and Communication Technology*, vol. COM-12, September 1964, pp. 91–96.
19. Camana, P., "Video-Bandwidth Compression: A Study in Tradeoffs," *IEEE Spectrum*, vol. 16, no. 6, June 1979, pp. 24–29.
20. Campbell, F. W., Cleland, B. G., Cooper, G. F., and Enroth-Cugell, C., "The Angular Selectivity of Visual Cortical Cells to Moving Gratings," *Journal of Physiology*, vol. 198, no. 1, 1968, pp. 237–250.
21. Campbell, F. W., and Kulikowski, J. J., "Orientational Selectivity of the Human Visual System," *Journal of Physiology*, vol. 187, no. 2, 1966, pp. 437–441.
22. Campbell, F. W., and Robson, J. G., "Application of Fourier Analysis to the Visibility of Gratings," *Journal of Physiology*, vol. 197, no. 3, 1968, pp. 511–566.
23. Cannon, M. W., "Suprathreshold Transfer Characteristics of the Human Visual System," *Proceedings International Conference on Cybernetics and Society*, Cambridge, Mass., Oct. 8–10, 1980, pp. 410–414.
24. Cannon, T. M., "Digital Image Deblurring by Nonlinear Homomorphic Filtering," Ph.D. thesis, Computer Science Department, University of Utah, Salt Lake City, 1974.
25. Carrahar, R. G., and Thurston, J. B., "Optical Illusions and the Visual Arts," Reinhold, New York, 1966.
26. Cole, E. R., "The Removal of Unknown Image Blurs by Homomorphic Filtering," Ph.D. thesis, Department of Electrical Engineering, University of Utah, Salt Lake City, 1973.
27. Cole, E. R., and Diamond, A. L., "Amount of Surround and Test-Inducing Separation in Simultaneous Brightness Contrast," *Perception and Psychophysics*, vol. 9, no. 1–8, 1971, pp. 125–128.
28. Connor, D. J., Brainard, R. C., and Limb, J. O., "Intra-frame Coding for Picture Transmission," *Proceedings of the IEEE*, vol. 60, no. 7, July 1972, pp. 779–791.
29. Connors, R. W., and Harlow, C. A., "Equal Probability Quantizing and Texture Analysis of Radiographic Images," *Computer Graphics and Image Processing*, vol. 8, 1978, pp. 447–463.
30. Coren, S., "Subjective Contours and Apparent Depth," *Psychological Review*, vol. 79, no. 4, July 1972, pp. 359–367.
31. Coren, S., and Girgus, J. S., "Seeing is Deceiving: The Psychology of Visual Illusions," Lawrence Erlbaum Associates, Hillsdale, N.J., 1978.
32. Coren, S., Girgus, J. S., Ehrlichman, H., and Hakstian, A. R., "An Empirical Taxonomy of Visual Illusions," *Perception and Psychophysics*, vol. 20, no. 2, 1976, pp. 129–137.
33. Cornsweet, T., "Visual Perception," Academic, New York, 1970.
34. Cowan, J. D., "Some Remarks on Channel Bandwidths for Visual Contrast Detection," in "Neural Mechanisms in Visual Perception," Neurosciences Research Progress Bulletin, vol. 15, no. 3, October 1977, pp. 492–517.

35. Cutler, C. C., Differential Quantization of Communication Signals, U.S. Patent 2,605,361, July 1952.
36. Cutler, C. C., and Graham, R. E., "Predictive Quantizing of Television Signals," *IRE Wescon Convention Record*, vol. 2, part 4, 1958, pp. 147–157.
37. Davenport, J. P., "A Comparison of Noise Cleaning Techniques," Technical Report TR-689, Computer Science, University of Maryland, College Park, September 1978.
38. Davisson, L. D., and Kutz, R. L., "A Real Time Programmable Data Compression System," *National Telemetering Conference*, December 1971, pp. 34A-1 to 34A-4.
39. Davisson, L. D., "Rate-Distortion Theory and Application," *Proceedings IEEE*, vol. 60, no. 7, July 1972, pp. 800–808.
40. DePalma, J. J., and Lowry, E. M., "Sine-Wave Response of the Visual System," *Journal of the Optical Society of America*, vol. 52, no. 3, March 1962, pp. 328–335.
41. De Valois, R. L., "Spatial Tuning of LGN and Cortical Cells in Monkey Visual Systems," in Spekreijse, H., and Van den Tweel, L. H. (eds.), "Spatial Contrast," North-Holland, Amsterdam, 1977.
42. Duda, R. O., and Hart, P. E., "Pattern Classification and Scene Analysis," Wiley, New York, 1973.
43. Enroth-Cugell, C., and Robson, J. G., "The Contrast Sensitivity of Retinal Ganglion Cells of the Cat," *Journal of Physiology*, vol. 187, no. 3, December 1966, pp. 517–552.
44. Fisher, A. L., "Systolic Algorithms for Running Order Statistics in Signal and Image Processing," Technical Report no. CMU-CS-81-130, Department of Computer Science, Carnegie-Mellon University, Pittsburgh, July 1981.
45. Frei, W., "Image Enhancement by Histogram Hyperbolization," *Computer Graphics and Image Processing*, vol. 6, no. 3, 1977, pp. 286–294.
46. Frieden, B. R., "Image Enhancement and Restoration," in Huang, T. S. (ed.), "Picture Processing and Digital Filtering," "Topics in Applied Physics," vol. 6, Springer-Verlag, New York, 1975, pp. 177–248.
47. Frieden, B. R., "Statistical Models for the Image Restoration Problem," in Rosenfeld, A. (ed.), "Image Modeling," Academic, New York, 1981, pp. 133–152.
48. Gallager, R. G., "Information Theory and Reliable Communication," Wiley, New York, 1968, chap. 9, pp. 442–502.
49. Georgeson, M. A., "Mechanisms of Visual Image Processing: Studies on Pattern Interaction and Selective Channels in Human Vision," doctoral dissertation, University of Sussex, Brighton, England, 1975.
50. Georgeson, M. A., "Spatial Fourier Analysis and Human Vision," Chapter 2, in Sutherland, N. S. (ed.), "Tutorial Essays in Psychology, A Guide to Recent Advances," vol. 2, Lawrence Erlbaum Associates, Hillsdale, N.J., 1979.
51. Gillam, B., "Geometrical Illusions," *Scientific American*, vol. 242, no. 1, January 1980, pp. 102–111.
52. Ginsburg, A. P., "Is the Illusory Triangle Physical or Imaginary?," *Nature*, vol. 257, no. 5523, Sept. 18, 1975, pp. 219–220.
53. Ginsburg, A. P., "Visual Perception Based on Biological Filtering of Spatial Information," *Proceedings of the International Conference on Cybernetics and Society*, Cambridge, Mass., Oct. 8–10, 1980, pp. 424–428.
54. Ginsburg, A. P., Cannon, M. W., and Nelson, M. A., "Suprathreshold Processing of Complex Visual Stimuli: Evidence for Linearity in Contrast Perception," *Science*, vol. 208, 9 May 1980, pp. 619–621.
55. Ginsburg, A. P., and Evans, D. W., "Predicting Visual Illusions From Filtered Images Based Upon Biological Data," Optical Society of America, Annual Meeting Program, Rochester, New York, Oct. 9–12, 1979, (Abstract) *Journal of the Optical Society of America*, p. 1443.
56. Ginsburg, A. P., "Visual Information Processing Based on Spatial Filters Constrained by Biological Data," Report no. AMRL-TR-78-129, vols. I and II, Aerospace Medical Research Laboratory, Wright-Patterson Air Force Base, Ohio, December 1978.

57. Ginsburg, A. P., "Predicting Visual Illusions From Filtered Images Based Upon Biological Data," Optical Society of America, Annual Meeting Program, Rochester, New York, Oct. 9-12, 1979, (Abstract) *Journal of the Optical Society of America*, p. 1443.
58. Glezer, V. D., and Cooperman, A. M., "Local Spectral Analysis in the Visual Cortex," *Biological Cybernetics*, vol. 28, no. 2, 1977, pp. 101–108.
59. Graham, N., "Visual Detection of Aperiodic Spatial Stimuli by Probability Summation Among Narrowband Channels," *Vision Research*, vol. 17, no. 5, 1977, pp. 637–652.
60. Granlund, G. H., "In Search of a General Picture Processing Operator," *Computer Graphics and Image Processing*, vol. 8, no. 2, October, 1978, pp. 1956–172.
61. Green, W. B., "Computer Image Processing—The Viking Experience," *IEEE Transactions on Consumer Electronics*, vol. CE-23, no. 3, August 1977, pp. 281–299.
62. Gregory, R. L., "Visual Illusions," *Scientific American*, vol. 219, no. 5, 1968, pp. 66–76.
63. Habibi, A., and Wintz, P. A., "Image Coding by Linear Transformations and Block Quantization," *IEEE Transactions on Communication Technology*, vol. COM-19, no. 1, February 1971, pp. 50–63.
64. Habibi, A., "Comparison of n-th Order DPCM Encoder with Linear Transformations and Block Quantization Techniques," *IEEE Transactions on Communication Technology*, vol. COM-19, no. 6, December 1971, pp. 948–956.
65. Hall, C. F., and Hall, E. L., "A Nonlinear Model of the Spatial Characteristics of the Human Visual System," *IEEE Transactions on Systems, Man, and Cybernetics*, vol. SMC-7, no. 3, 1977, pp. 161–170.
66. Hall, E. L., Kruger, R. P., Dwyer, S. J., Hall, D. L., McLaren, R. W., and Lodevick, G. S., "A Survey of Preprocessing and Feature Extraction Techniques for Radiographic Images," *IEEE Transactions on Computers*, vol. C-20, September 1971, pp. 1032–1044.
67. Haralick, R. M., Shanmugam, K., and Dinstein, I., "On Some Quickly Computable Features for Texture," *Proceedings of the Symposium on Computer Image Processing and Recognition*, vol. 2, Department of Electrical Engineering, University of Missouri, Columbia, Aug. 24–26, 1972, pp. 12-2-1 to 12-2-10.
68. Harris, J. L., Sr., "Image Evaluation and Restoration," *Journal of the Optical Society of America*, vol. 56, no. 5, May 1966, pp. 569–574.
69. Harris, J. L., Sr., "Constant Variance Enhancement—A Digital Processing Technique," *Applied Optics*, vol. 16, May 1977, pp. 1268–1271.
70. Harrison, C. W., "Experiments with Linear Prediction in Television," *Bell System Technical Journal*, vol. 31, July 1952, pp. 764–783.
71. Hartline, H. R., "Inhibition of Activity of Visual Receptors by Illuminating Nearby Retinal Elements in the *Limulus* Eye," *Federation Proceedings*, vol. 8, no. 1, 1949, p. 69.
72. Hartline, H. R., and Ratliff, F., "Spatial Summation of Inhibitory Influences in the Eye of the *Limulus*," *Science*, vol. 120, no. 3124, 1954, p. 781.
73. Hartline, H. R., and Ratliff, F., "Inhibitory Interaction of Receptor Units in the Eye of *Limulus*," *Journal of General Physiology*, vol. 40, no. 3, 1957, pp. 357–376.
74. Hartline, H. R., Wagner, H. G., and Ratliff, F., "Inhibition in the Eye of *Limulus*," *Journal of General Physiology*, vol. 39, no. 5, 1956, pp. 651–673.
75. Haskell, B. G., Mounts, F. W., and Candy, J. C., "Interframe Coding of Videotelephone Pictures," *Proceedings of the IEEE*, vol. 60, no. 7, July 1972, pp. 792–800.
76. Horner, J. L., "Optical Spatial Filtering With the Least-Mean-Square-Error Filter," *Journal of the Optical Society of America*, vol. 51, no. 5, May 1969, pp. 553–558.
77. Horner, J. L., "Optical Restoration of Images Blurred by Atmospheric Turbulence Using Optimum Filter Theory," *Applied Optics*, vol. 9, no. 1, January 1970, pp. 167–171.
78. Huang, T. T. Y., and Schultheiss, P. M., "Block Quantization of Correlated Gaussian Random Variables," *IRE Transactions on Communication Systems*, vol. CS-11, no. 3, September 1963, pp. 289–296.
79. Huang, T. S., Tretiak, O. J., Prasada, B., and Yamaguchi, Y., "Design Considerations in PCM Transmission of Low-Resolution Monochrome Still Pictures," *Proceedings of the IEEE*, vol. 5, no. 3, March 1967, pp. 331–335.

80. Hubel, D. H., and Wiesel, T. N., "Receptive Fields, Binocular Interaction and Functional Architecture in the Cat's Visual Cortex," *Journal of Physiology*, vol. 160, no. 1, 1962, pp. 106–154.
81. Hubel, D. H., and Wiesel, T. N., Receptive Fields and Functional Architecture of Monkey Striate Cortex, *Journal of Physiology* (*London*), vol. 195, no. 1, 1968, pp. 215–243.
82. Hufnagel, R. E., and Stanley, N. R., "Modulation Transfer Function Associated with Image Transmission Through Turbulent Media," *Journal of the Optical Society of America*, vol. 54, no. 1, January 1964, pp. 52–61.
83. Hummel, R. A., "Histogram Modification Techniques," *Computer Graphics and Image Processing*, vol. 4, no. 3, 1975, pp. 209–224.
84. Hunt, B. R., "The Application of Constrained Least Squares Estimation to Image Restoration by Digital Computer," *IEEE Transactions on Computers*, vol. C-22, no. 9, September 1973, pp. 805–812.
85. Hunt, B. R., "Digital Image Processing," *Proceedings of the IEEE*, vol. 63, no. 4, April 1975, pp. 693–708.
86. Hunt, B. R., Janney, D. H., and Zeigler, R. K., "A Survey of Radiographic Image Enhancement Experience," Report LA-DC-72-69, Los Alamos Scientific Laboratory, 1972.
87. Hunt, B. R., Janney, D. H., and Zeigler, R. K., "Radiographic Image Enhancement by Digital Computers," *Materials Evaluation*, vol. 31, January 1973, pp. 1–5.
88. Ikeda, H., and Wright, M. J., "Spatial and Temporal Properties of 'Sustained' and 'Transient' Neurons in Area 17 of the Cat's Visual Cortex," *Experimental Brain Research*, vol. 22, no. 4, 1975, pp. 363–383.
89. Jarnigan, M. E., and Wardell, R. W., "Does the Eye Contain Optimal Edge Detection Mechanisms?" *IEEE Transactions on Systems, Man, and Cybernetics*, vol. SMC-11, no. 6, June 1981, pp. 441–444.
90. Justusson, B., "Noise Reduction by Median Filtering," *4th International Conference on Pattern Recognition*, Kyoto, Japan, Nov. 7–10, 1978, pp. 502–504.
91. Kaji, S., Yamane, S., Yoshimura, M., and Sugie, N., "Contour Enhancement of Two-Dimensional Figures Observed in the Lateral Geniculate Cells of Cats," *Vision Research*, vol. 14, no. 1, January 1974, pp. 113–117.
92. Kanizsa, G., "Subjective Contours," *Scientific American*, vol. 234, no. 4, 1976, pp. 48–52.
93. Ketcham, D. J., "Real-Time Image Enhancement Techniques," *Proceedings of the Society for Photo-Optical Instrumentation Engineers*, vol. 74 ("Image Processing"), February 1976, pp. 120–125.
94. King-Smith, P. E., and Kulikowski, J. J., "The Detection of Gratings by Independent Activation of Line Detectors," *Journal of Physiology*, vol. 247, no. 2, 1975, pp. 237–271.
95. Kulikowski, J. J., and King-Smith, P. E., "Spatial Arrangement of Line, Edge and Grating Detectors Revealed by Subthreshold Summation," *Vision Research*, vol. 13, no. 8, August 1975, pp. 1455–1478.
96. Kulikowski, J. J., Marcelja, S., and Bishop, P. O., "Theory of Spatial Position and Spatial Frequency Relations in the Receptive Fields of Simple Cells in the Visual Cortex," *Biological Cybernetics*, vol. 43, no. 3, 1982, pp. 187–198.
97. Kunt, M., "Source Coding of X-Ray Pictures," *IEEE Transactions on Biomedical Engineering*, vol. BME-25, no. 2, March 1978, pp. 121–138.
98. Lev, A., Zucker, S. W., and Rosenfeld, A., "Iterative Enhancement of Noisy Images," *IEEE Transactions on Systems, Man, and Cybernetics*, vol. SMC-7, no. 6, June, 1977, pp. 435–442.
99. Levine, M. D., O'Handley, D. A., and Yagi, G. M., "Computer Determination of Depth Maps," *Computer Graphics and Image Processing*, vol. 2, no. 2, October 1973, pp. 131–151.
100. Ligthart, G., and Groen, F. C. A., "A Comparison of Different Autofocus Algorithms," *Proceedings of the 6th International Conference on Pattern Recognition*, Munich, Oct. 19–22, 1982, pp. 597–600.
101. Limb, J. O., and Mounts, F. W., "Digital Differential Quantizer for Television," *Bell System Technical Journal*, vol. 48, no. 9, September 1969, pp. 2583–2599.

102. Limb, J. O., and Rubenstein, C. B., "A Model of Threshold Vision Incorporating Inhomogeneity of the Visual Fields," *Vision Research*, vol. 17, no. 4, 1977, pp. 571–584.
103. Macleod, I. D. G., and Rosenfeld, A., "The Visibility of Gratings: Spatial Frequency Channels or Bar-Detecting Units?" *Vision Research*, vol. 14, no. 10, 1974, pp. 909–915.
104. Maffei, M., and Fiorentini, A., "The Visual Cortex as a Spatial Frequency Analyzer," *Vision Research*, vol. 13, no. 7, 1973, pp. 1255–1267.
105. Marr, D., and Hildreth, E., "Theory of Edge Detection," A.I. Memo No. 518, Massachusetts Institute of Technology, Artificial Intelligence Laboratory, Cambridge, Mass., April 1979.
106. Marr, D., Poggio, T., and Hildreth, E., "Smallest Channel in Early Human Vision," *Journal of the Optical Society of America*, vol. 70, no. 7, July 1980, pp. 868–870.
107. Marr, D., Poggio, T., and Ullman, S., "Bandpass Channels, Zero-Crossings, and Early Visual Information Processing," A.I. Memo no. 491, Massachusetts Institute of Technology, Artificial Intelligence Laboratory, Cambridge, Mass., 1978.
108. Marr, D., and Ullman, S., "Directional Selectivity and Its Use in Early Visual Processing," A.I. Memo no. 524, Massachusetts Institute of Technology, Artificial Intelligence Laboratory, Cambridge, Mass., June 1979.
109. Max, T., "Quantizing for Minimum Distortion," *IRE Transactions on Information Theory*, vol. IT-6, no. 1, March 1960, pp. 7–12.
110. McDonnell, M. J., "Restoration of *Voyager 1* Images of Io," *Computer Graphics and Image Processing*, vol. 15, no. 1, January 1981, pp. 79–86.
111. McDonnell, M. J., "Box Filtering Techniques," *Computer Graphics and Image Processing*, vol. 17, no. 1, September 1981, pp. 65–70.
112. McGlamery, B. L., "Restoration of Turbulence-Degraded Images," *Journal of the Optical Society of America*, vol. 57, no. 3, March 1967, pp. 293–297.
113. Mersereau, R. M., Dudgeon, D. E., "Two-Dimensional Digital Filtering," *Proceedings of the IEEE*, vol. 63, no. 4, April 1975, pp. 610–623.
114. Millard, J. B., and Maunsell, H. I., "Digital Encoding of the Video Signal," *Bell System Technical Journal*, vol. 50, no. 2, February 1971, pp. 459–480.
115. Mostafavi, H., and Sakrison, D. J., "Structure and Properties of a Single Channel in the Human Visual System," *Vision Research*, vol. 16, no. 9, 1976, pp. 957–968.
116. Mueller, P. F., and Reynolds, G. O., "Image Restoration by Removal of Random Media Degradations," *Journal of the Optical Society of America*, vol. 57, no. 11, November 1967, pp. 1338–1344.
117. Musmann, H. G., "Predictive Image Coding," in Pratt, W. K. (ed.), "Image Transmission Techniques," Academic, New York, 1979, pp. 73–112.
118. Nachmias, J., and Weber, A., "Discrimination of Simple and Complex Gratings," *Vision Research*, vol. 15, no. 2, 1975, pp. 217–223.
119. Narendra, P. M., "A Separable Median Filter for Image Noise Smoothing," *IEEE Transactions on Pattern Analysis and Machine Intelligence*, vol. PAMI-3, no. 2, January 1981, pp. 20–29.
120. Narendra, P. M., and Fitch, R. C., "Real-Time Adaptive Contrast Enhancement," *IEEE Transactions on Pattern Analysis and Machine Intelligence*, vol. PAMI-3, no. 6, November 1981, pp. 655–661.
121. Nathan, R., "Picture Enhancement for the Moon, Mars and Man," in Cheng, G. C., Ledley, R. S., Pollack, D. K., and Rosenfeld, A. (eds.), "Pictorial Pattern Recognition," Thompson, Washington, 1968, pp. 239–266.
122. Netravali, A. N., and Prasada, B., "Adaptive Quantization of Picture Signals Using Spatial Masking," *Proceedings of the IEEE*, vol. 65, no. 4, April 1977, pp. 536–548.
123. O'Brien, V., "Contour Perception, Illusion and Reality," *Journal of Optical Society of America*, vol. 48, no. 2, 1958, pp. 112–119.
124. Ochs, A. L., "Is Fourier Analysis Performed by the Visual System or by the Visual Investigator?" *Journal of the Optical Society of America*, vol. 69, no. 1, January 1979, pp. 95–98.

125. Oliver, B. N., "Efficient Coding," *Bell System Technical Journal*, vol. 31, no. 4, July 1952, pp. 724–750.
126. Oppenheim, A. V., Schafer, R. W., and Stockham, T. G. Jr., "Nonlinear Filtering of Multiplied and Convolved Signals," *Proceedings of the IEEE*, vol. 56, no. 8, August 1968, pp. 1264–1291.
127. Ostrem, J. S., "Homomorphic Filtering of Specular Scenes," *IEEE Transactions on Systems, Man, and Cybernetics*, vol. SMC-11, no. 5, May 1981, pp. 385–387.
128. Panter, P. F., and Dite, W., "Quantization Distortion in Pulse Count Modulation with Nonuniform Spacing of Levels," *Proceedings of the IRE*, vol. 39, no. 1, January 1951, pp. 44–48.
129. Patel, A. S., "Spatial Resolution by the Human Visual System. The Effect of Mean Retinal Illuminance," *Journal of the Optical Society of America*, vol. 56, no. 5, 1966, pp. 689–694.
130. Pollen, D. A., Lee, J. R., and Taylor, J. H., "How Does the Striate Cortex Begin the Reconstruction of the Visual World?" *Science*, vol. 173, no. 3991, July 1971, pp. 74–77.
131. Pollen, D. A., and Taylor, J. H., "The Striate Cortex and the Spatial Analysis of Visual Space," in Schmitt, F. O., and Worden, F. G. (eds.), "The neurosciences Third Study Program," MIT Press, Cambridge, Mass., 1974.
132. Pratt, W. K., Chen, W., and Welch, L., "Slant Transform Image Coding," *IEEE Transactions on Communication Technology*, vol. COM-22, no. 8, August 1974, pp. 1075–1093.
133. Pratt, W. K., Kane, J., and Andrews, H. C., "Hadamard Transform Image Coding," *Proceedings of the IEEE*, vol. 57, no. 1, Jan. 1969, pp. 58–68.
134. Quick, R. F., "A Vector Magnitude Model of Contrast Detection," *Kybernetik*, vol. 16, no. 2, 1974, pp. 65–67.
135. Ratliff, F., "Mach Bands: Quantitative Studies on Neural Networks in the Retina," Holden-Day, San Francisco, 1965.
136. Ratliff, F., "Contour and Contrast," *Scientific American*, vol. 226, no. 6, June 1972, pp. 90–101.
137. Ratliff, F., and Hartline, H. R., "The Responses of Limulus Optic Nerve Fibers to Patterns of Illumination on the Receptor Mosaic," *Journal of General Physiology*, vol. 42, no. 6, 1959, pp. 1241–1255.
138. Rice, R. F., and Plaunt, F. R., "Adaptive Variable-Length Coding for Efficient Compression of Spacecraft Television Data," *IEEE Transactions on Communication Technology*, vol. COM-19, no. 6, December 1971, pp. 889–897.
139. Roberts, L. G., "Picture Coding Using Pseudo-Random Noise," *IRE Transactions on Information Theory*, vol. IT-8, no. 2, February 1962, pp. 145–154.
140. Robinson, J. O., "The Psychology of Visual Illusions," Hutchinson University Library, London, 1973.
141. Rosenfeld, A., and Kak, A. C., "Digital Picture Processing," Academic, New York, 1976.
142. Sachs, M. B., Nachmias, J., and Robson, J. G., "Spatial Frequency Channels in Human Vision," *Journal of the Optical Society of America*, vol. 61, no. 9, 1971, pp. 1176–1186.
143. Sakrison, D. J., "On the Role of the Observer and a Distortion Measure in Image Transmission," *IEEE Transactions* on *Communication Technology*, vol. COM-25, no. 11, November 1977, pp. 1251–1267.
144. Sakrison, D. J., "Image Coding Applications of Vision Models," in Pratt, W. K. (ed.), "Image Transmission Techniques," Academic, New York, 1979, pp. 21–71.
145. Sawchuck, A. A., "Space-Variant Image Motion Degradation and Restoration," *Proceedings of the IEEE*, vol. 60, no. 7, July 1972, pp. 854–861.
146. Sawchuck, A. A., "Space-Variant System Analysis of Image Motion," *Journal of the Optical Society of America*, vol. 63, no. 9, September 1973, pp. 1052–1063.
147. Sawchuck, A. A., "Space-Variant Image Restoration by Coordinate Transformations," *Journal of the Optical Society of America*, vol. 64, no. 2, February 1974, pp. 138–144.
148. Seidman, J., "Some Practical Applications of Digital Filtering in Image Processing," *Proceedings of the Symposium on Computer Image Processing and Recognition*, Department of Electrical Engineering, University of Missouri, Columbia, Aug. 24–26, 1972, pp. 9-1-1 to 9-1-16.

149. Selzer, R. H., "The Use of Computers to Improve Biomedical Image Quality," AFIPS-1968, *Proceedings of the Fall Joint Computer Conference*, vol. 33, part 1, 1968, pp. 817–834.
150. Schreiber, W. F., "Picture Coding," *Proceedings of the IEEE*, vol. 55, no. 3, March 1967, pp. 320–330.
151. Schreiber, W. F., "Image Processing for Quality Improvements," *Proceedings of the IEEE*, vol. 66, no. 12, December 1978, pp. 1640–1651.
152. Sklansky, J., "Image Segmentation and Feature Extraction," *IEEE Transactions on Systems, Man, and Cybernetics*, vol. SMC-8, no. 4, April 1978, pp. 237–247.
153. Sondhi, M. M., "Image Restoration: The Removal of Spatially Invariant Degradations," *Proceedings of the IEEE*, vol. 60, no. 7, July 1972, pp. 842–852.
154. Stevens, K., "Occlusion Clues and Subjective Contours," A.I. Memo No. 363, Massachusetts Institute of Technology, Artificial Intelligence Laboratory, Cambridge, Mass., June 1976.
155. Stockham, T. G., Jr., "Intra-Frame Encoding for Monochrome Images by Means of a Psychophysical Model Based on Nonlinear Filtering of Multiplied Signals," *Symposium on Picture Bandwidth Compression*, Massachusetts Institute of Technology, Cambridge, Mass., Apr. 2–4, 1969. Appeared in Huang, T. S., and Tretiak, O. J. (eds.), "Picture Bandwidth Compression," Gordon and Breach, New York, 1972, pp. 415–442.
156. Stockham, T. G., Jr., "Image Processing in the Context of a Visual Model," *Proceedings of the IEEE*, vol. 60, no. 7, July 1972, pp. 828–842.
157. Stockham, T. G., Jr., Cannon, T. M., and Ingebretsen, R. B., "Blind Deconvolution Through Digital Signal Processing," *Proceedings of the IEEE*, vol. 63, no. 4, April 1975, pp. 678–692.
158. Tamburelli, G., "Some Results in the Processing of the Holy Shroud of Turin," *IEEE Transactions on Pattern Analysis and Machine Intelligence*, vol. PAMI-3, no. 6, November 1981, pp. 670–676.
159. Tescher, A. G., "Transform Image Coding," in Pratt, W. K. (ed.), "Image Transmission Techniques," Academic, New York, 1979, pp. 113–155.
160. Tescher, A. G., and Andrew, H. C., "Data Compression and Enhancement of Sampled Images," *Applied Optics*, vol. 11, no. 4, April 1972, pp. 919–925.
161. Thomas, J. P., and Gille, J., "Bandwidths of Orientation Channels in Human Vision," *Journal of the Optical Society of America*, vol. 69, no. 5, May 1979, pp. 652–660.
162. Tomita, F., and Tsumi, S., "Extraction of Multiple Regions by Smoothing," *IEEE Transactions on Pattern Analysis and Machine Intelligence*, vol. PAMI-3, no. 1, January 1981, pp. 20–29.
163. Troxel, D. E., and Lynn, C. Jr., "Enhancement of News Photos," *Computer Graphics and Image Processing*, vol. 7, no. 2, 1978, pp. 266–281.
164. Trussell, H. J., "A Fast Algorithm for Noise Smoothing Based on a Subjective Criterion," *IEEE Transactions on Systems, Man and Cybernetics*, vol. SMC-7, 1977, pp. 677–678.
165. Tsujiuchi, J., "Correction of Optical Images by Compensation of Aberrations and by Spatial Frequency Filtering" in "Progress in Optics," vol. 2, Wiley, New York, 1963, pp. 131–180.
166. Uttal, W. R., "The Psychobiological Silly Season, or What Happens When Neurophysiological Data Becomes Psychological Theories," *Journal of General Psychology*, vol. 84, 1971, pp. 151–166.
167. Uttal, W. R., "The Psychobiology of Sensory Coding," Harper & Row, New York, 1973.
168. Varoutas, P. P., Nardizzi, L. R., and Stokely, E. M., "Digital Image Processing Applied to Scintillation Images from Biomedical Systems," *IEEE Transactions on Biomedical Engineering*, vol. BME-24, no. 4, July 1977, pp. 337–347.
169. Waltz, D., "Understanding Line Drawings of Scenes with Shadows," in Winston, P. H. (ed.), "The Psychology of Computer Vision," McGraw-Hill, New York, 1975, pp. 19–91.
170. Weszka, J. S., "A Survey of Threshold Selection Techniques," *Computer Graphics and Image Processing*, vol. 7, no. 2, 1978, pp. 259–265.
171. Widrow, B., "The 'Rubber-Mask' Technique—I. Pattern Measurement and Analysis," *Pattern Recognition*, vol. 5, no. 3, September 1973, pp. 175–197.
172. Widrow, B., "The 'Rubber-Mask' Technique-II. Pattern Storage and Recognition," *Pattern Recognition*, vol. 5, no. 3, September 1973, pp. 199–211.

173. Wilson, H. R., "Spatiotemporal Characterization of a Transient Mechanism in the Human Visual System," *Vision Research*, vol. 20, 1980, pp. 443–452.
174. Wilson, H. R., "A Transducer Function for Threshold and Suprathreshold Human Vision," *Biological Cybernetics*, vol. 38, 1980, pp. 171–178.
175. Wilson, H. R., and Bergen, J. R., "A Four Mechanism Model for Threshold Spatial Vision," *Vision Research*, vol. 19, no. 1, 1979, pp. 19–32.
176. Winston, P. H. (ed.), "The Psychology of Computer Vision," McGraw-Hill, New York, 1975.
177. Wintz, P. A., "Transform Picture Coding," *Proceedings of the IEEE*, vol. 60, no. 7, July 1972, pp. 809–820.
178. Woods, R. E., and Gonzalez, R. C., "Real-Time Digital Image Enhancement," *Proceedings of the IEEE*, vol. 69, no. 5, May 1981, pp. 643–654.

BIBLIOGRAPHY

The experiments with the *Limulus* (horseshoe crab) investigating lateral interaction are detailed in [30, 44]. The book by Ratliff [44] is a particularly good source of material on the Mach band phenomenon and includes a considerable amount of interesting historical material on the subject. The psychophysical Mach bands are also reviewed by Fiorentini [19] and a good expository paper has been written by Von Bekesy [52]. Two other references on the related subject of luminance difference thresholds are [7, 10]. An excellent review paper containing 468 references is the one by Jung [33], in which clear distinctions and correlations are made between neurophysiology and psychophysics and many of the issues related to postulating suitable analogies are discussed.

There are many articles and books on the subject of visual illusions, for example, [12, 18, 35, 36]. The series of offprints by *Scientific American* entitled "Image, Object and Illusion" is recommended as an introduction [31]. This volume contains an excellent summary article by Gregory, who also presents his interpretation of the origin of some of these illusions. A more recent review article is that by Gillam [23].

Temporal aspects of visual processing have not been discussed in this book. Readers wishing to explore this subject are directed to the excellent discussion by Kahneman [34] on visual masking and to Weisstein [53] for the controversial subject of metacontrast, in which a stimulus presented after a given event seems to still affect the preceding stimulus response.

A good introduction to the important early experiments related to contrast and spatial frequency is the paper by Campbell and Maffei [16]. Most of the issues and studies associated with the possibility of a biological spectrum analyzer are concisely discussed by Georgeson [21]. However readers are cautioned that they may still remain confused about this subject after having studied it or, indeed, the literature in general. A review of the evidence supporting the multichannel model discussed in Section 6.3 can be found in [13, 14, 15, 24, 46, 49].

There are numerous papers and books dealing with the subject matter of the last three sections in the chapter. Three books with good coverage are by

Andrews [4], Pratt [41], and Rosenfeld and Kak [47]. Andrews [4] also presents a collection of important papers on digital image processing which might serve as supplementary material to Sections 6.4, 6.5, and 6.6. A concise review of the literature to 1972 is given in [50]. The application of human visual models to image coding, enhancement, and quality assessment is reviewed by Granrath [25].

A good discussion of the history of picture coding to 1967 is [48]. This article attempts to relate the different coding schemes to psychophysical experiments and properties of human vision. A bibliography on data compression, picture properties, and picture coding is given in [54]. The period covered terminates at about 1970. Two surveys of the literature to the mid-1970s are by Habibi and Robinson [27] and Pratt [40]. A guide for the designer of image communication systems and an excellent summary of the research in the field is Pratt's book [42].

The classic paper on pulse code modulation PCM is by Goodall [23]. Image quantization has not been discussed in this chapter, and readers may consult [39] for a summary. An early paper on Fourier-transform image coding is by Andrews and Pratt [6]. Cosine transforms were first discussed by Ahmed, Natarajan, and Rao [1]. Other transforms of interest include the Karhunen-Loève [28] and the Hadamard [43].

An introductory article on digital image restoration and enhancement may be found in [17]. A bibliography to 1972 is given in [3], and the same issue of the *Proceedings of the IEEE* contains many other pertinent articles. Both these topics involve the use of digital filtering, and a good introduction to this subject is that by Hamming [29]. The design and implementation of shift-invariant filters for two-dimensional filtering is reviewed by Mersereau and Dudgeon [37]. The associated mathematics and available techniques are introduced and 50 references to the literature provided. Both topics also involve computational and theoretical models for image data and these are reviewed in [32].

A comprehensive book on image restoration is that by Andrews and Hunt [5]. Radiometric decalibration of cameras is discussed in [26, 45, 51], and some interesting applications are considered in [8, 9, 11, 37]. Readers who would like to examine the tremendous potential of the restoration and enhancement techniques available through the vehicle of digital image processing should consult [20]. Space pictures taken in conjunction with the Viking mission to Mars are quite extraordinary!

1. Ahmed, N., Natarajan, T., and Rao, K., "Discrete Cosine Transform," *IEEE Transactions on Computers*, vol. C-23, no. 1, January, 1974, pp. 90–93.
2. Andrews, H. C., "Computer Techniques in Image Processing," Academic, New York, 1970.
3. Andrews, H. C., "N Topics in Search of an Editorial: Heuristics, Superresolution, and Bibliography," *Proceedings of the IEEE*, vol. 60, no. 7, July 1972, pp. 891–894.
4. Andrews, H. C. (ed.), "Tutorial and Selected Papers in Digital Image Processing," IEEE, New York, 1978.
5. Andrews, H. C., and Hunt, B. R., "Digital Image Restoration," Prentice-Hall, Englewood Cliffs, N.J., 1977.

6. Andrews, H. C., and Pratt, W. K., "Fourier Transform Coding of Images," *Hawaii International Conference on Systems Science,* Western Periodicals Co., North Hollywood, Calif., January 1968, pp. 677–679.
7. Aulhorn, E., and Harms, H., "Visual Perimetry," in Jameson, D., and Hurvich, L. M. (eds.), "Handbook of Sensory Physiology," vol. VII/4, "Visual Psychophysics," Springer-Verlag, New York, 1972, pp. 102–145.
8. Billingsley, F. C., "Computer-Generated Color Image Display of Lunar Spectral Reflectance Ratios," *Photographic Science and Engineering,* vol. 16, 1972, p. 51.
9. Billingsley, F. C., Goetz, A. F. H., and Lindsley, J. N., "Color Differentiation by Computer Image Processing," Society for Photographic Science and Engineering, Annual Conference on Photographic Science and Engineering, Los Angeles, *Photographic Science and Engineering,* vol. 14, January-February 1970, p. 28.
10. Blackwell, H. R., "Luminance Difference Thresholds," in Jameson, D., and Hurvich, L. M. (eds.), "Handbook of Sensory Physiology," vol. VII/4, "Psychophysics," Springer-Verlag, New York, 1972, pp. 78–101.
11. Blackwell, R. J., "Fingerprint Image Enhancement by Computer Methods," 1970 Carnahan Conference on Electronic Crime Countermeasures, Lexington, Ky., Apr. 17, 1970.
12. Blakemore, C., "The Baffled Brain, Illusions in Nature and Art," Scribner and Sons, New York, 1973, pp. 9–48.
13. Braddick, O., Campbell, F. W., and Atkinson, J., "Channels in Vision: Basic Aspects," in Held, R., Leibowitz, H., and Teuber, H. L. (eds.), "Handbook of Sensory Physiology," vol. VIII, "Perception," Springer-Verlag, Heidelberg, 1978, pp. 3–38.
14. Breitmeyer, B. G., and Ganz, L., "Implications of Sustained and Transient Channels for Theories of Visual Pattern Masking, Saccadic Suppression, and Information Processing," *Psychological Review,* vol. 83, no. 1, 1976, pp. 1–36.
15. Campbell, F. W., "The Transmission of Spatial Information Through the Visual System," in Schmitt, F. O., and Worden, F. G. (eds.), "The Neurosciences Third Study Program," MIT Press, Cambridge, Mass., 1973, pp. 95–103.
16. Campbell, F. W., and Maffei, L., "Contrast and Spatial Frequency," *Scientific American,* vol. 231, November 1974, pp. 106–114. Reprinted in Held, R. and Richards, W. (eds.), "Recent Progress in Perception," Freeman, San Francisco, 1976.
17. Cannon, T. M., and Hunt, B. R., "Image Processing by Computer," *Scientific American,* vol. 245, no. 4, October 1981, pp. 213–225.
18. Coren, S., and Girgus, J. S., "Seeing is Deceiving: The Psychology of Visual Illusions," Lawrence Erlbaum Associates, Hillsdale, N.J., 1978.
19. Fiorentini, A., "Mach Band Phenomena," Chapter 8 in Jameson, D., and Hurvich, L. M. (eds.), "Visual Psychophysics Handbook of Sensory Physiology," vol. VII/4, Springer-Verlag, Berlin, 1972, pp. 188–201.
20. Flinn, E. A. (ed.), "Scientific Results of the Viking Project," *Journal of Geophysical Research,* vol. 82, no. 28, Sept. 30, 1977, pp. 3955–4683.
21. Georgeson, M., "Spatial Fourier Analysis and Human Vision," chap. II in Sutherland, N. S. (ed.), "Tutorial Essays in Psychology, A Guide to Recent Advances," vol. 2, Lawrence Erlbaum Associates, Hillsdale, N.J., 1979.
22. Gillam, B., "Geometrical Illusions," *Scientific American,* vol. 242, no. 1, January 1980, pp. 102–110.
23. Goodall, W. M., "Television by Pulse Code Modulation," *Bell Systems Technical Journal,* vol. 30, no. 1, January 1951, pp. 33–49.
24. Graham, N., "Visual Detection of Aperiodic Spatial Stimuli by Probability Summation Among Narrowband Channels," *Vision Research,* vol. 17, 1977, pp. 637–652.
25. Granrath, D. J., "The Role of Human Visual Models in Image Processing," *Proceedings of the IEEE,* vol. 69, no. 5, May 1981, pp. 552–561.
26. Green, W. B., Jepsen, P. L., Kreznar, J. E., Ruiz, R. M., Schwartz, A. A., and Seidman, J. B., "Removal of Instrument Signature from *Mariner 9* Television Images of Mars," *Applied Optics,* vol. 14, no. 1, 1975, pp. 105–114.

27. Habibi, A., and Robinson, G. S., "A Survey of Digital Picture Coding," *Computer*, vol. 7, no. 5, May 1974, pp. 22–34.
28. Habibi, A., and Wintz, P., "Image Coding by Linear Transformation and Block Quantization," *IEEE Transactions on Communication Technology*, vol. COM-19, no. 1, 1971, pp. 957–972.
29. Hamming, R. W., "Digital Filters," Prentice-Hall, Englewood Cliffs, N.J., 1977.
30. Hartline, H. R., and Ratliff, F., "Inhibitory Interaction in the Retina of *Limulus*," in Fuortes, M. G. F. (ed.), "Physiology of Photoreceptor Organs," "Handbook of Sensory Physiology," vol. 7/2, Springer-Verlag, Berlin, 1972, pp. 381–447.
31. Held, R. (ed.), "Image Object and Illusion," Readings from *Scientific American*," Freeman, San Francisco, 1974.
32. Jain, A. K., "Advances in Mathematical Models for Image Processing," *Proceedings of the IEEE*, vol. 69, no. 5, May 1981, pp. 502–528.
33. Jung, R., "Visual Perception and Neurophysiology," Chapter I in Jung, R. (ed.), "Handbook of Sensory Physiology," vol. VII/3, Springer-Verlag, Berlin, 1973.
34. Kahneman, D., "Method, Findings, and Theory in Studies of Visual Masking," *Psychological Bulletin*, vol. 70, no. 6, 1968, pp. 404–425.
35. Kanizsa, G., "Organization in Vision, Essays on Gestalt Perception," Praeger, New York, 1979.
36. Luckiesh, M., "Visual Illusions," Dover, New York, 1965.
37. Mersereau, R. M., and Dudgeon, D. E., "Two-dimensional Digital Filtering," *Proceedings of the IEEE*, vol. 63, April 1975, pp. 610–623.
38. Nathan, R., "Image Processing for Electron Microscopy. I. Enhancement Procedures," vol. 4 in "Advances in Optical and Electron Microscopy," Academic, New York, 1971, pp. 85–125.
39. Netravali, A. N., "On Quantizers for DPCM Coding of Picture Signals," *IEEE Transactions on Information Theory*, vol. IT-23, no. 3, May 1977, pp. 360–370.
40. Pratt, W. K., "Survey and Analysis of Image Coding Techniques," *Proceedings of the Society of Photo-Optical Instrumentation Engineers*, vol. 74, "Image Processing," Pacific Grove, Calif., Feb. 24–26, 1976, pp. 178–184.
41. Pratt, W. K., "Digital Image Processing," Wiley, New York, 1978.
42. Pratt, W. K. (ed.), "Image Transmission Techniques," Academic, New York, 1979.
43. Pratt, W. K., and Andrews, H. C., "Application of Fourier-Hadamard Transformation to Bandwidth Compression," in Huang, T. S., and Tretiak, O. J. (eds.), "Picture Bandwidth Compression," Gordon and Breach, New York, 1972, pp. 515–554 (*Proceedings of the 1969 Symposium on Picture Bandwidth Compression*, Massachusetts Institute of Technology, Cambridge, Mass.)
44. Ratliff, F., "Mach Bands: Quantitative Studies on Neural Networks in the Retina," Holden-Day, San Francisco, 1965.
45. Reindfleisch, T. C., Dunne, J. A., Frieden, H. J., Stromberg, W. D., and Ruiz, R. M., "Digital Processing of the *Mariner 6* and *7* Pictures," *Journal of Geophysical Research*, vol. 76, no. 2, 1971, pp. 394–417.
46. Robson, J. G., "Receptive Fields: Neural Representation of the Spatial and Intensive Attributes of the Visual Image," in Carterette, E. C., and Friedman, M. P. (eds.), "Handbook of Perception," vol. V, "Seeing," Academic Press, New York, 1975, pp. 81–116.
47. Rosenfeld, A., and Kak, A. C., "Digital Picture Processing," Academic, New York, 1976.
48. Schreiber, W. F., "Picture Coding," *Proceedings of the IEEE*, vol. 55, no. 3, March 1967, pp. 320–330.
49. Sekuler, R., "Spatial Vision," *Annual Review of Psychology*, vol. 25, 1974, pp. 195–232.
50. Shiva, S. G. S., Dion, J.-P., and Chau, V. C., "Review of Digital Image Processing Techniques for Bandwidth Reduction," Report, Electrical Engineering Department, University of Ottawa, Dec. 15, 1972.
51. Soha, J. M., Lynn, D. J., Lorre, J. J., Mosher, J. A., Thayer, N. N., Elliot, D. A., Benton, W. D., and Dewar, R. E., "IPL Processing of the *Mariner 10* Images of Mercury," *Journal of Geophysical Research*, vol. 80, no. 17, June 10, 1975, pp. 2394–2414.

52. Von Bekesy, G., "Mach-and Hering-Type Lateral Inhibition in Vision," *Vision Research*, vol. 8, no. 12, December 1968, pp. 1483–1499.
53. Weisstein, N. A., "Metacontrast," in Jameson, D., and Hurvich, L. M. (eds.), "Handbook of Sensory Physiology," vol. VII/4, "Visual Psychophysics," Springer-Verlag, New York, 1972, pp. 233–272.
54. Wilkens, L. C., and Wintz, P. A., "Bibliography on Data Compression, Picture Properties, and Picture Coding," *IEEE Transactions on Information Theory*, vol. IT-17, no. 2, 1971, pp. 180–197.

CHAPTER

SEVEN

COLOR

7.1 WHY DO FROGS PREFER BLUE?

Color is a phenomenon in which we visually perceive some function of the spectral content of the radiant energy emanating from an object. As such, it is essentially a filtering of the input signal which results in a coded version characterized by a color name. This involves a considerable degree of data compression, with the resulting coded representation obviously being adequate for the purpose of human visual understanding. Some colors are monochromatic in that they can be completely described by a single wavelength (λ), an impulse at a given λ value. We refer to these as "spectral colors." However, in general, the perceived radiant energy consists of a mixture of these. When we say that the sky is blue, we do not mean that its spectral response is a single impulse; on the contrary, it obviously consists of a response made up of contributions at many wavelengths. A mixture of wavelengths, but what kind? There is overwhelming evidence that each sampled point in the input image is coded into three distinct signals, each corresponding to the output firing rates of the three types of cones (see Section 3.3). Since the same kind of code is used in all three cases, the next stage of processing can be directly involved in computing an appropriate function of three normalized inputs.

The history of the development of this trichromatic theory can be found in [13]. Sir Isaac Newton is credited with discovering the nature of color in 1704, employing an experimental technique centered on the use of a glass prism.

Selecting as a light source the sunlight entering through the shutter of the window in his study, he produced a spectrum of colors on a white background. It was then found that these colors could be recombined into the white light with a lens. Newton also demonstrated that the set of perceived colors is but a small subset of all the possible colors obtainable by mixing different combinations of colors. He performed experiments using the technique of color matching of lights. First he mixed monochromatic (single-wavelength) red with monochromatic green and created yellow. Then he took a monochromatic yellow light and mixed it with white; it was found that an appropriate amount of white could be chosen so that the resulting two yellow mixtures are indistinguishable. Newton employed a prism to decompose the two yellows into their constituents and showed convincingly that they were made up of different components. Figure 7.1 is a sketch of his proposed color diagram, in which the monochromatic spectral colors are placed around the periphery of a circle in the order that they appear in the spectrum. The figure also shows how linear combinations could account for the nonuniqueness of color mixtures.

It was not until about 100 years later in 1801 that the English physician Thomas Young, in a lecture to the Royal Society, casually suggested that physiological color processing in man must be restricted to the involvement of three independent variables [56]:

> Now, as it is almost impossible to conceive each sensitive point of the retina to contain an infinite number of particles, each capable of vibrating in perfect unison with every possible undulation, it becomes necessary to suppose the number limited; for instance, to the three principal colors, red, yellow and blue.

Although primarily recognized for his work on the theory of light, Young was also an accomplished Egyptologist and concerned himself with the deciphering of Egyptian hieroglyphics.

In 1852 and 1866 H. L. F. Helmholtz published the hypothesis that there

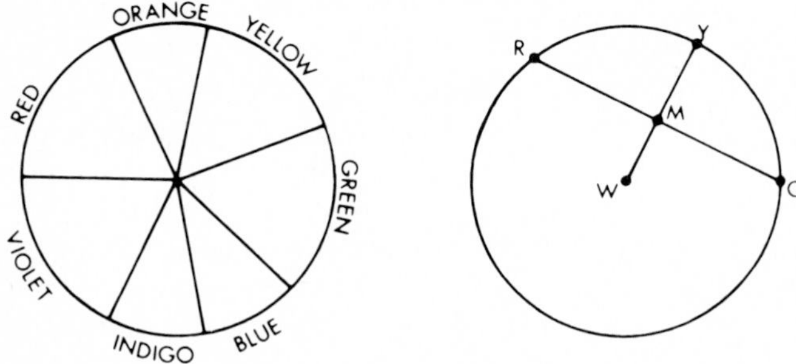

Figure 7.1 Isaac Newton's color circle, which he proposed in the early part of the eighteenth century. The order of the colors on the left is obviously based on the spectrum. On the right is shown how he demonstrated that an appropriate mixture of R (red) and G (green) which yielded the color mixture M could be matched to a mixture of Y (yellow) and W (white light). To the viewer, both mixtures look identical, although their constituents are different. (*From R. W. Rodieck, "The Vertebrate Retina, Principles of Structure and Function," Freeman, San Francisco, 1973.*)

exist three different channels with three different filters and even proposed the spectral response curves. We now know that these responses are due to three cone types, which are loosely referred to as red, green, and blue cones. The first quantitative confirmation of the Young-Helmholtz theory was published by Maxwell in 1855 and 1860. Probably the other significant contribution to color theory was due to Grassmann, who in 1854 suggested that color matches are in effect based on linear operations. His law of additivity of color matches forms much of the conceptual support for discussions in color, even today.

There are limited studies available pertaining to psychophysical evidence for color vision in animals. It appears that most mammals are monochromatic. Squirrels, frogs, and salamanders are dichromatic and cats possess only a limited amount of color vision. Primates have trichromatic visual systems, so that monkeys and humans possess complete color vision. Goldfish also have three cone types. No animal has been confirmed to have tetrachromatic or higher polychromatic vision although the retina of the turtle is characterized by six independent coded signals. We should also note that man actually has four different types of receptors. Is it possible that the rods also contribute to color vision in some way?

From a physiological point of view we know that the pigments responsible for color vision are contained in the cones. It also follows that we require at least two separate signals in order to define a color space. However, we should caution the reader that even though an animal may have two- or three-dimensional retinal coding, it may still have monochromatic vision. Perhaps the brain does not use all the signals. Obviously perceptual experiments are paramount for the establishment of any assumptions regarding color vision, and these are difficult to perform with animals, to say the least.

Some rudimentary perceptual experiments are possible. The behavioral response of frogs can be measured by placing them at one end of a box with two large color patches at the other end. The color preference is determined by counting the number of times the frog jumps in the direction of a particular color [54]. It turns out that frogs really hop for blue, even preferring it to blue-green mixtures that have an equal amount of blue but are four times brighter. The implication is that this could not be due solely to the transduced energy signals but results from some sort of signal processing. It is also fascinating that these nerve fibers, related to the onset of illumination and color, project to the dorsal thalamus. However, the feature detectors which pertain to object shape project only to the optic tectum. Furthermore, although this shape and color information initially remains anatomically separated, there are many interconnecting nerve fibers between the optic tectum and the dorsal thalamus of the frog. We shall see that there is evidence that man also seems to process shape and color information separately, providing seemingly independent feature measurements. We may postulate a theory regarding the frog's "psychological" preference and sensitivity to blue: after all, it spends a lot of time in the water. But why does man seem to prefer red?

In this chapter we attempt to explain the phenomenon of color, first by the introduction of a neurophysiological model and then by a corresponding psychophysical model. Color is a complex feature, and readers may often be confused when consulting the literature as to which of these two aspects is under discussion at any given time. We have tried to make a clear distinction and have carried this to the definition of the model of computer color vision discussed in Section 7.5. Ultimately the three signals from the retinal cones are output as a perceptual color name. The goal of this chapter is to explain what is known about how this is accomplished.

7.2 COLOR CODING AT THE CELLULAR LEVEL

The sensation of color is experienced by man when his eye views energy signals containing wavelengths in approximately the range between 380 and 780 nm. Outside this band of frequencies (see Figure 2.2), the transducers in the retina are unable to detect a stimulus. Generally speaking, man is superior to animals in his ability to discriminate color. For example, while a cat may experience difficulty with the 150 nm difference between green and red, man can easily distinguish between the two wavelengths 590 and 595 nm. Why color vision in man is so different from that of animals is unknown, but perhaps it is because of his superior intelligence, which led to an artistic appreciation of color combinations. Thus he may have developed his sense of color independently of his day-to-day existential needs. Only the macaque monkey, which is close to man on the phylogenetic scale, bears any similarity to him in this regard. Hence the study of these monkeys is quite important, although it is interesting to note that the pigments in their cone transducers are different from those of humans.

In Chapters 3 and 4 we elaborated a duplex theory of the retina involving rods and cones. The former is monochromatic and the latter trichromatic. The trichromatic theory of color vision implies three independent color processes in the retina and was originally suggested by Young in 1801 in a seemingly extemporaneous remark during a lecture. This theory was developed by Helmholtz in 1862 and all subsequent experimentation has lent support to such a model. What is more, the three processes are thought to be due to three different types of pigments, each residing in different cones. Figure 7.2 is a block diagram outlining the concept of trichromacy. There exist three photochemicals or photopigments, called "erythrolabe," "chlorolabe," and "cyanolabe," resulting in what are commonly called the red, green, and blue channels. These names are misleading since they neither exactly characterize the color associated with the sensitivity curve nor describe the color of the pigment. The three sensitivity curves are quite broadly tuned and will be referred to as the long [$L(\lambda)$], medium [$M(\lambda)$], and short [$S(\lambda)$] responses. The three types of cones are distributed throughout the retinal mosaic in the foveal region, yielding three types of spatially coded signals. As shown in Figure 7.1, these are somehow processed to provide a perceptual sensation or, in the case of man, a color name. In 1872 Hering proposed an opponent theory of color which seemed to contradict this established trivariance theory. He suggested

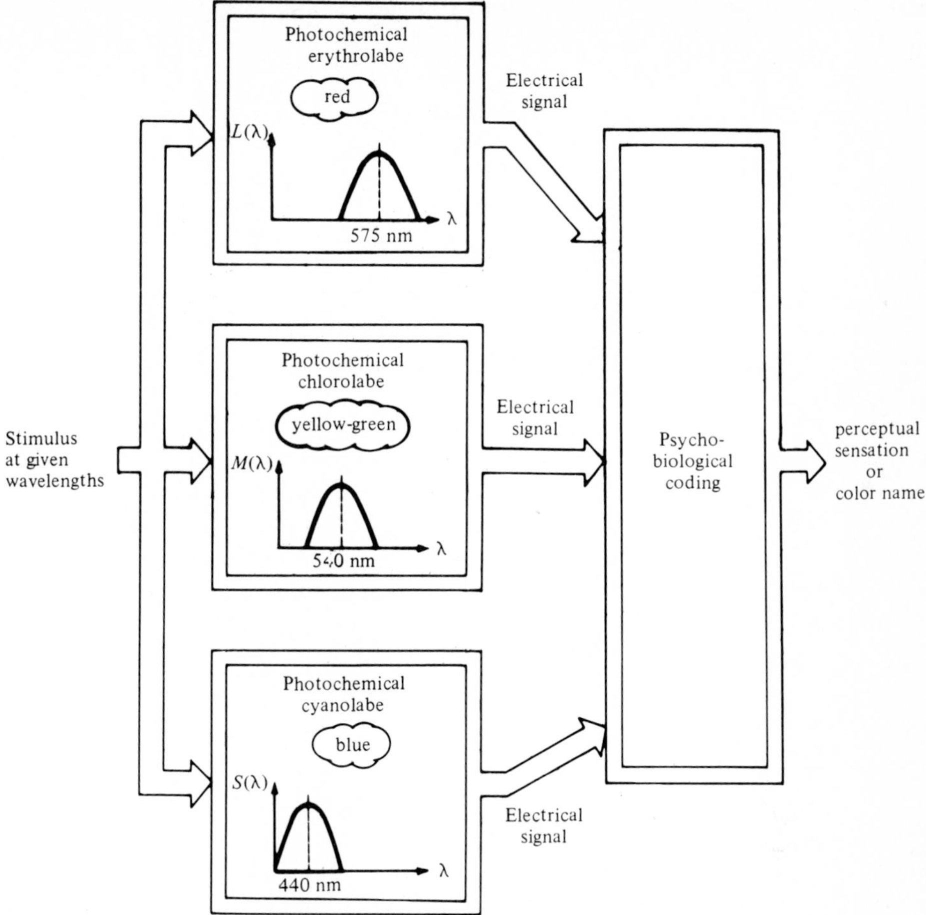

Figure 7.2 Three types of cones with different filtering actions result in three independent signals, which are used to code the color.

that there exist mechanisms at the retinal level which operate on the basis of color differences. Considerable argument about the appropriateness of such a model ensued, continuing even until recent times. However, it now appears that both models are correct but as we shall see, they function at different anatomical levels.

The photopigments in the cones obey the law of invariance. This is, each type of pigment provides an output coded in exactly the same fashion, and each pigment always responds identically to a similar spectral distribution of the input. Although this need not necessarily have been the case, it obviously makes a lot of sense from an information-processing point of view. The coding mechanism has been elaborated in Sections 3.5 and 4.4. The response of a particular photopigment to an appropriate stimulus produces a graded or slow

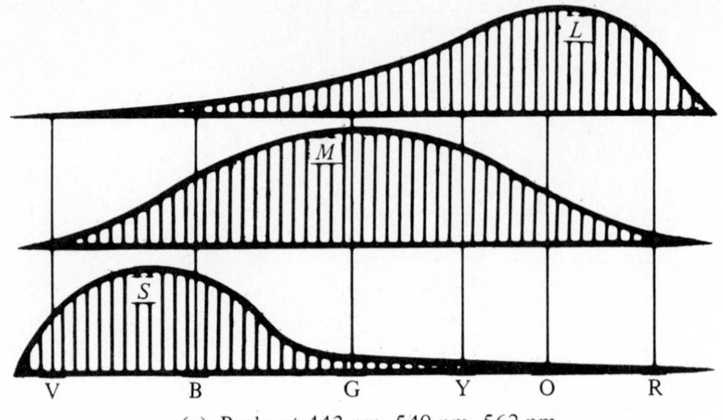

(*a*) Peaks at 443 nm, 540 nm, 562 nm

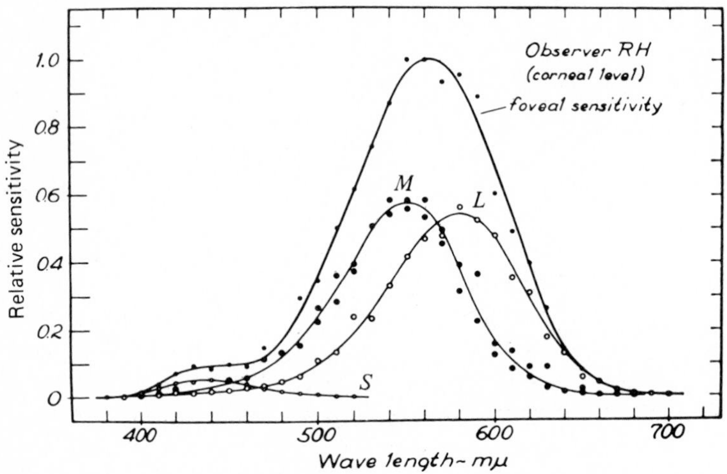

(*b*) Peaks at 445 nm, 540 nm, 570 nm

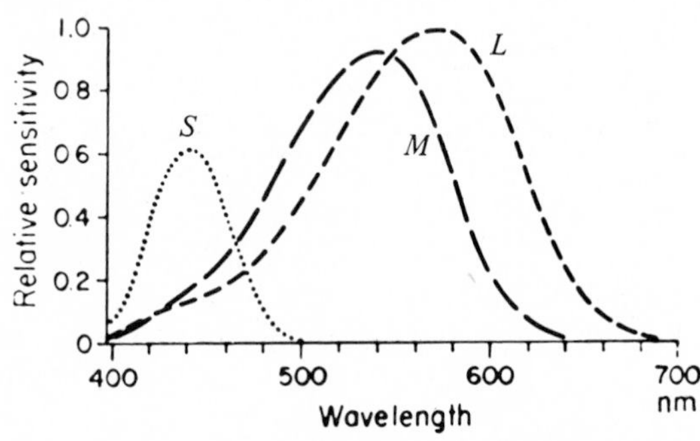

(*c*) Peaks at 430 nm, 530 nm, 560 nm

potential. The magnitude of the latter, as given by Equation (4.14), depends on the photon catch rate $N_a(\lambda)$ [see Equation (4.13)], which itself is dependent on the magnitude and wavelength of the stimulus input as well as on the photosensitivity characteristic curve. This latter function, which is the relationship between the response and the input for human cones, has not been directly ascertained. Nevertheless, Equations (4.20) to (4.22) are considered to be a good representation of the linear component of the actual physical situation.

The three cone spectral characteristics for humans have been measured by many people using different methods, and the results differ slightly. Figure 7.3*a* shows the estimate of Helmholtz, which was based on psychophysical data. Comparison of this result with the more recent physiological results shown in Figure 7.3*b* and *c* indicates, surprisingly, that the peaks of the three sets of curves do not differ by much. The responses are only relative in that the three constants k_R, k_G, and k_B in Equations (4.20) to (4.22) are unknown. One might expect an equal spatial distribution in the retina of the three cone types but this is apparently not the case; the green and blue cones are more numerous than the red. We have also assumed that only one pigment exists per cone, but experiments have been made which contradict this hypothesis. There are some other problems with the model and data in Figures 7.2 and 7.3. Observe that above 600 nm the blue cones are ineffective. Therefore we would expect that stimulation above this wavelength would result in a greenish red perception, but what we actually see is yellowish red or orange. Also, at 580 nm the red and green curves cross, implying equality of response—actually yellow is seen! Finally, we note that the model does not take into account white or black. The implication of all these observations is that (at least) one additional level of processing follows the cones, a level which maps the signal resulting from a transformation by the data shown in Figure 7.2 into a new space. It seems likely that this space is characterized by the opponents-color system of Hering, and this will be discussed later on in this section.

Suppose we first accept the hypothesis of trivariance. Then an arbitrary input stimulus $I(\lambda)$ will be mapped by the cones into the so-called tricone space, as shown in the block diagram of Figure 7.4. Each of the three paths in the model is meant to include all linear and nonlinear effects. Each block may be represented by two sequential stages of processing. The first is a linear one-to-one mapping of $I(\lambda)$ into trivariance space. This linear transformation is defined by Equations (4.20) to (4.22) and is characterized by the number of absorbed photons. The second is a one-to-many nonlinear transformation which accounts for phenomena which are still considered to operate in-

---

Figure 7.3 Three different estimates of the cone spectral characteristics: (*a*) based on psychophysical data; (*b*) and (*c*) based on physiological data. [(*a*) *After H. Helmholtz, "Handbook of Physiological Optics," Dover reprint 1962*; (*b*) *from G. Wald, "The Receptors of Human Color Vision," Science, vol. 145, no. 3626, Sept. 4, 1964, pp. 1007–1017*; (*c*) *after F. Ratliff, "On the Psychophysical Basis of Universal Color Terms," Proceedings of the American Philosophical Society, vol. 120, no. 5, 1976.*]

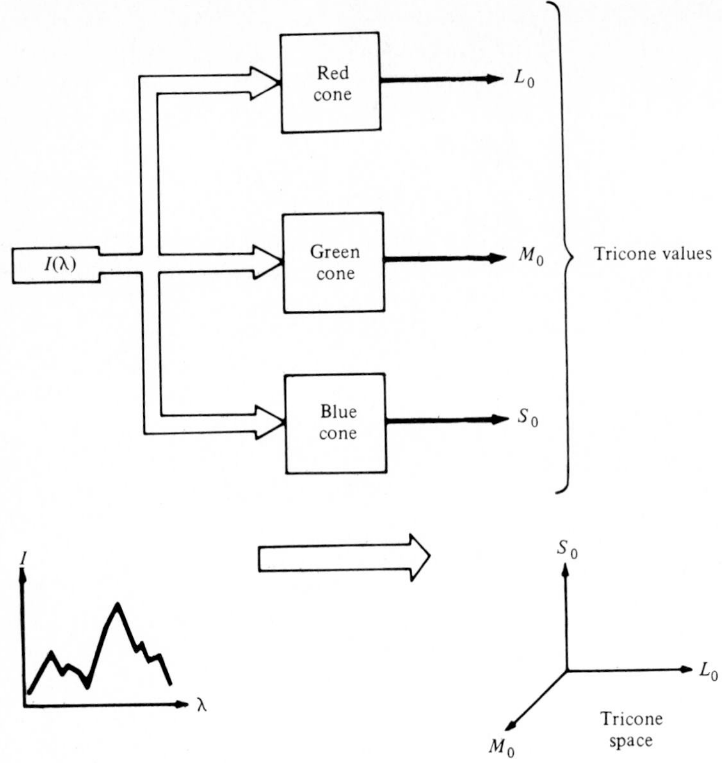

Figure 7.4 A neurophysiological model of the first stage of color processing. The input spectrum is transformed into the three-dimensional tricone space by the three types of cones. (*Adapted from R. W. Rodieck, "The Vertebrate Retina, Principles of Structure and Function," Freeman, San Francisco, 1973.*)

dependently on the three channels. These are not very well understood and might include chromatic adaptation and other intensity and temporal effects. Thus we may write

$$L_0(t) = f_l[A_L(t), t)] \tag{7.1}$$

$$M_0(t) = f_m[A_M(t), t)] \tag{7.2}$$

$$S_0(t) = f_s[A_S(t), t)] \tag{7.3}$$

where probably the functions f_l, f_m, and f_s (which are presently undetermined) are identical. Figure 7.5 is an elaboration of Figure 7.4 to include these ideas.

There are still some important stages missing! The tricone values L_0, M_0, and S_0 are processed further at other levels in the cellular hierarchy elaborated in Chapter 3. The output is the human color perception as determined by psychophysical experimentation, usually based on the matching of two patches of color. As we shall see in the next section, such experiments usually implicitly ignore all phenomena following the coding into trivariance space.

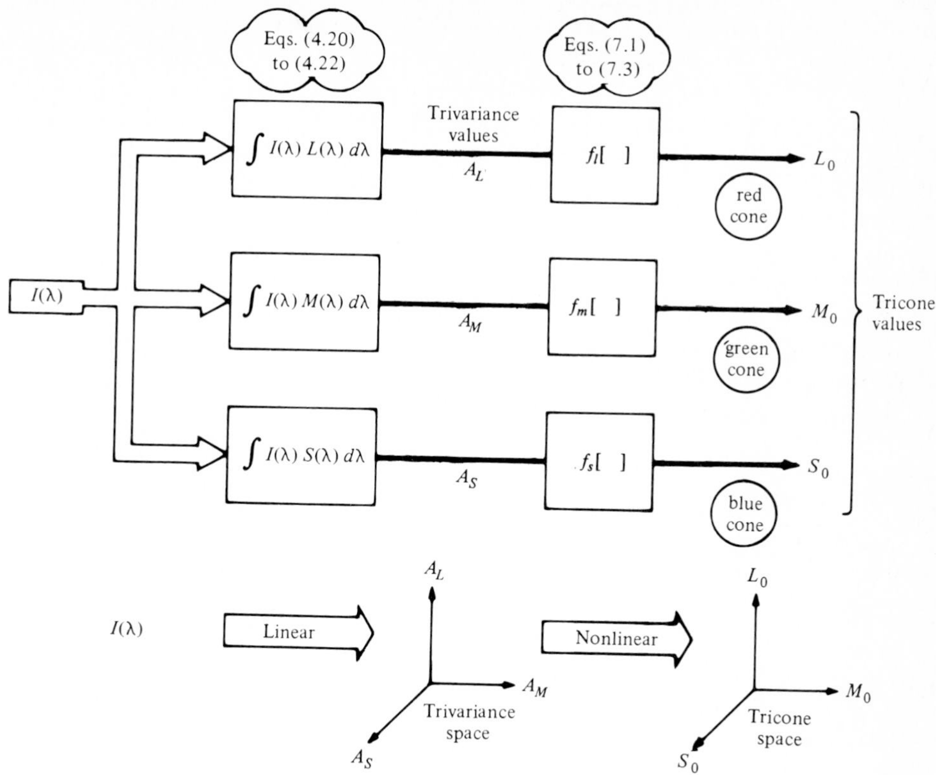

Figure 7.5 An elaboration of the model in Figure 7.4 in which the linear effects have been separated.

As implied above, there is ample physiological evidence that in addition to the initial trivariant coding process, there exists a further stage of processing in which color differences play an operative role. For example, spectrally opponent cells apparently exist at different cellular levels in the retina of the goldfish [67]. Although this does not seem to be the case for primates, we cannot as yet rule out the possibility [24]. Nevertheless, at the higher levels of the lateral geniculate body and the cortex of primates, an opponent-color system is indeed indicated. Considerable experimentation on this has been done with the macaque monkey [20, 23, 29, 75].

What do we mean by a spectral opponent system? Figures 4.1, 4.3, and 4.4 are elucidations of a spatial opponent system in which the two concentric regions of the receptive field demonstrate antagonistic behavior. We may superimpose on this spatial inhibition and excitation the considerations of color. Thus each region may either be excited, be inhibited, or possibly not even contribute when activated by any of the three cone color channels. For example, the ground squirrel possesses cells whose center is sensitive to green light and whose surround is sensitive to blue light [52]. However, this is an idealization. In many cases, the center and the surround regions receive inputs from a mixed population of cones. Twenty types of idealized spatial opponent cells are described by Rodieck as having been found [56]. Such cells are very numerous among ganglion and LGN cells of the cat and macaque monkey. Spectrally nonopponent cells are also found; these are not sensitive at all to the wavelength of the input and behave as described in Section 4.2, responding only to luminance. A most likely explanation is that in this case all the cone signals feed both their center and surround regions, thereby in some way cancelling out the chromatic sensitivity. We make the observation that at present it is very difficult to obtain intelligent comparisons of color processing in the visual systems of different animals on the basis of receptive field mapping.

In most descriptions of the spectral opponent system, the spatial cone distributions of the receptive field of the LGN neuron which were discussed above are ignored. A particular LGN cell is described as responding only to the spectral attributes of the input, although Wiesel and Hubel [75] have clearly demonstrated that the organization is such that both the color and spatial properties are simultaneously operative. Indeed, they found four distinct types of cells which differentiated these two features according to different con-

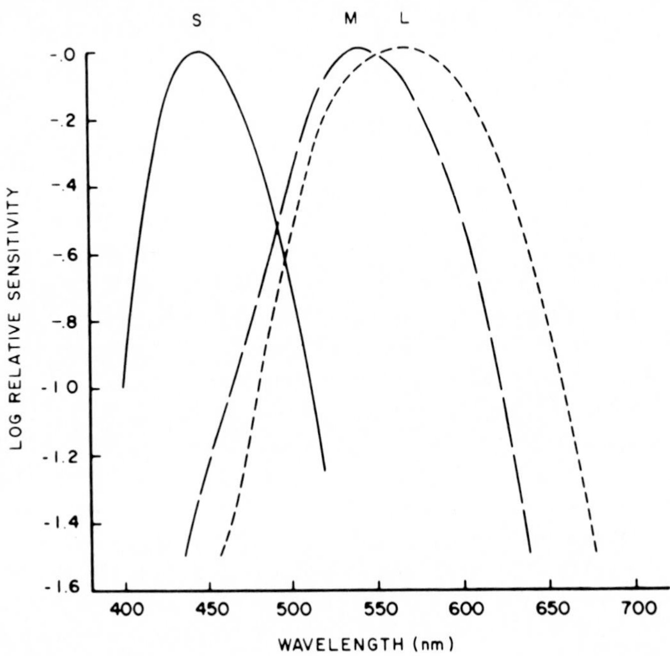

Figure 7.6 A set of normalized spectral sensitivity curves for the macaque monkey cones. These data are based on a comparison of spectrophotometric, physiological, and psychophysical experiments. [*From R. L. De Valois and K. K. De Valois, "Neural Coding of Color," chap. 5, in E. C. Carterette and M. P. Friedman (eds.), "Handbook of Perception," vol. V, "Seeing," Academic, New York, 1975, pp. 117–166.*]

straints. As would be expected for efficient coding of the information, there is a considerable overlap of the receptive fields and their sizes also vary. Each LGN cell most probably receives inputs from at least two different types of cones, but explicit confirmation of which ones and what their response functions are is still awaited. In fact it is not even clear yet that the ganglion retinal cells do not behave in a similar fashion to the LGN cells.

De Valois and his associates have conducted numerous experiments in recent years with the LGN cells of the macaque monkey [23]. About 70 percent of these cells turn out to be spectrally opponent and the other 30 percent nonopponent, both having equal numbers of ON- and OFF-center units. Four major types of cells have been described [1, 22]. One type is excited by a red signal and inhibited by a green. Another type, found in equal number, exhibits just the opposite behavior. This pair is sometimes referred to as "+ R − G" and "− R + G," or the "RG" system. The other two types are responsive to yellow and blue and are labeled "+ Y − B" and "− Y + B," or the "YB" system. The two nonopponent types, which are only sensitive to intensity variations, are called the "Wh − Bl" system. Figure 7.6 shows the normalized spectral response curves for the three cone types of a macaque monkey. Some experimental results showing the response of the six LGN cell types discussed are given in Figure 7.7. These data are normally obtained by sweeping the input across the whole visual spectrum and measuring the average spontaneous firing rate. We note, for example, in the + R − G curves that this cell responds strongly to the wavelengths at the red end of the spectrum while it is inhibited by the wavelengths in the green region. Note also that the strengths of these responses have not been analytically related to the input stimulus signals. The +R − G (and −R + G) cell is most likely receiving inputs from the red and green cones (see Figure 7.8) and therefore it seems to be sensitive to their difference spectrum. Thus the peak at around 640 nm occurs where the difference between $L(\lambda)$ and $M(\lambda)$ is maximized. As far as the YB system is concerned, there seems to be support for it receiving inputs from the blue cones but some uncertainty about the other component: All three, the $S(\lambda)$ and $M(\lambda)$, or the $S(\lambda)$ and $L(\lambda)$ cones? Similarly disagreement exists about the origin of the inputs to the Wh − Bl system. We observe that there is yet much to learn about the neurophysiology of color vision, although evidence has accumulated to provide support for some sort of opponent activity.

As a consequence of the uncertainties alluded to above, many different models exist, depending on the hypothesized interactions among the cells. An example due to De Valois [21] is given in Figure 7.8. Note that the actual signals that should be shown entering the LGN cells are the logarithms of the input stimulus signals, in conformity with our previous discussions in Chapter 4. In addition it is obvious that many intermediate levels of cells have been omitted from the diagram, since we know from Chapter 3 that the cones are not directly connected to the LGN cells. In monkeys there is also some evidence of differential spectral sensitivity occurring after the LGN cells, in the cortex, but this is not conclusive.

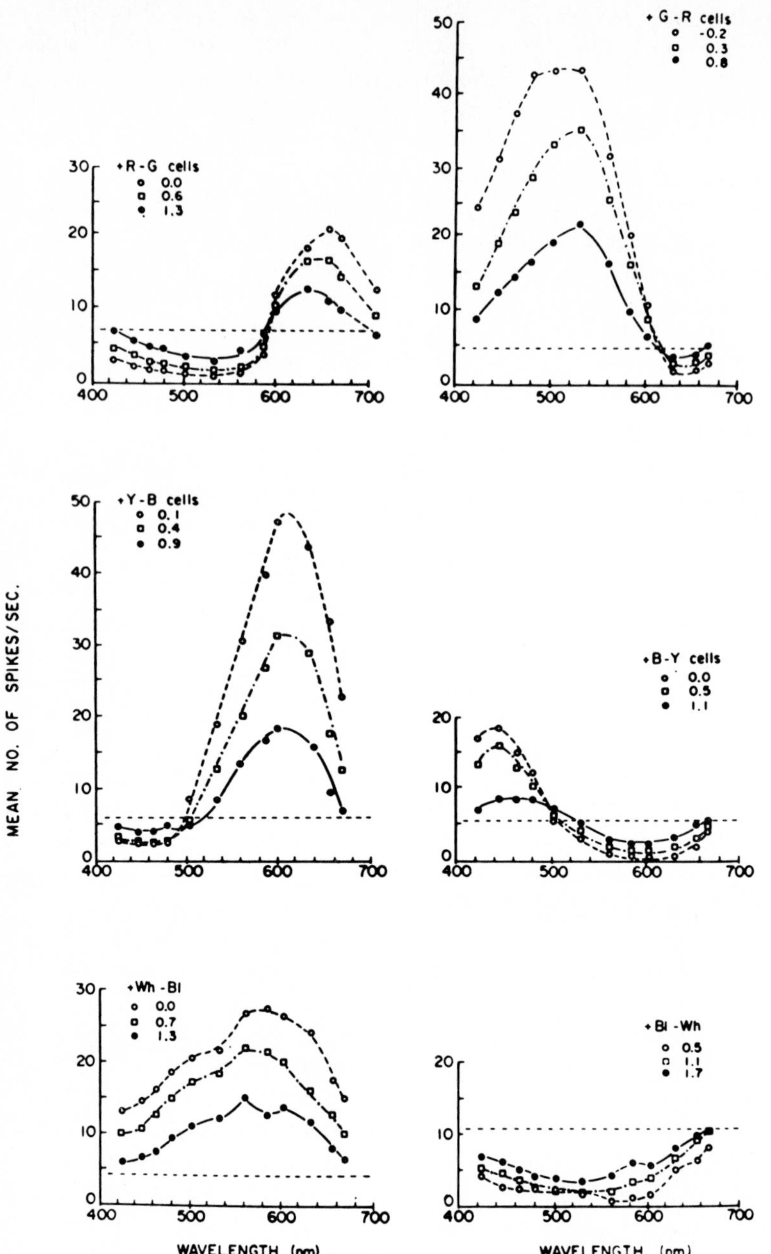

Figure 7.7 Different LGN cell responses in the macaque monkey. (*From R. L. De Valois, "Central Mechanisms of Color Vision," in "Handbook of Sensory Physiology," vol. VIII, "Central Processing of Visual Information," part A, Springer-Verlag, New York, 1973, pp. 209–253.*)

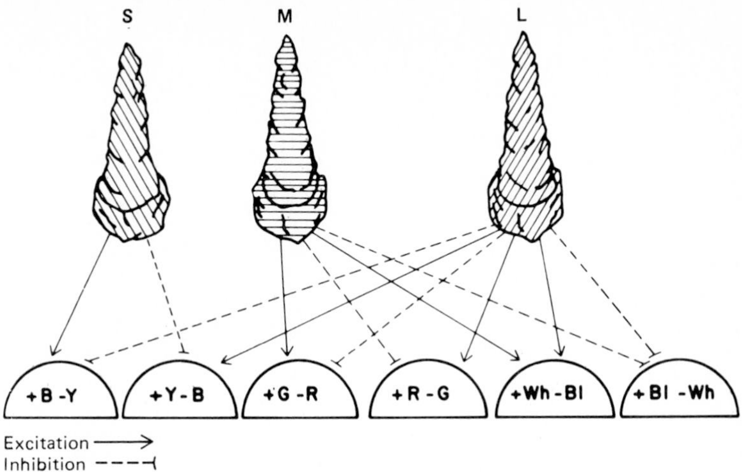

Figure 7.8 A possible simplified model showing how the three cone types provide inputs to the six LGN cell types. [*From R. L. De Valois and K. K. De Valois, "Neural Coding of Color," in E. C. Carterette and M. P. Friedman (eds.), "Handbook of Perception," vol. V, "Seeing," Academic, New York, 1975, pp. 117–166.*]

The coding by the LGN cells suggests the three-dimensional arrangement shown in Figure 7.9, which should be compared with the Newton circle in Figure 7.1. The horizontal section in the middle of the solid double cones provides for the two color variables, hue and saturation, and these will be discussed in Section 7.4. The third variable, luminance, is determined by the position along the vertical axis, running from black through gray to white at the top. We shall see later that this system provides an alternative three-dimensional representation of color to the RGB system we have discussed so far.

Cells responsive to color have also been found in the striate cortex, an area which is associated with vision processing. These cells have been shown to be organized retinotopically [78]. From here the signals are transmitted to the prestriate cortex, often assumed to be involved in associational processes. Zeki [79] has indicated that different areas in the prestriate cortex seem to be specialized to particular "functions" such as color, orientation, motion, and luminance. What is more, he has demonstrated that the mapping from the visual to the associational cortex results in cells which are no longer retinotopically organized. The color-sensitive cells are relatively large, relate to the central 20 to 30° portion of the retina, and are narrowly tuned (10 to 50 nm at half-maximum response). The responses cover the complete visual spectrum but have peak sensitivities that cluster around blue (480 nm), green (500 nm), orange-red (620 nm), and extra-spectral purple. Within this area of the cortex the cells are organized into regions based on different colors and not on retinal topography [79]. It is as if a particular feature of the input image has been computed and represented in an alternative format, perhaps for further processing.

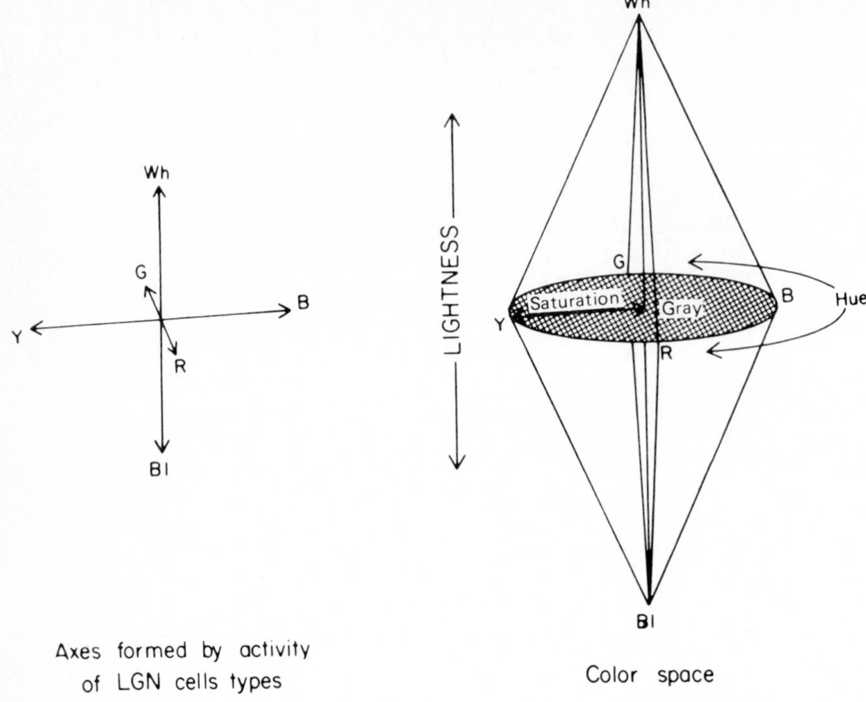

Figure 7.9 A suggestion of how the location of a stimulus in color space (right) might be determined by the relative activity rates of each of the six LGN cell types (left). The hue would be determined by the activity rates among the four opponent cell types, i.e., which were most active, the lightness by the two activity rates of the two nonopponent cells, and the saturation by the relative activity rates of the opponent and nonopponent cells. [*From R. L. De Valois and K. K. De Valois, "Neural Coding of Color," chap. 5, in E. C. Carterette and M. P. Friedman (eds.), "Handbook of Perception," vol. V, "Seeing," Academic, New York, 1975, pp. 117–166.*]

This evidence also lends credibility to the concept of independent analysis of color and luminance information. Perhaps the latter channels are uniquely concerned with form or shape recognition, which is most likely achieved independently of color considerations.

7.3 A PRACTICAL PSYCHOPHYSICAL MODEL

7.3.1 A Color-Matching Model

In the previous section the human color processing system was divided into two conceptual stages, as indicated in Figure 7.2. The first stage, about which we know a lot but by no means the complete story, is represented by the action of the three cone types. The second, about which we know very little, is the transformation of these tricone data into what we actually physically perceive as color. This section will concern itself with the practical measurement of the color sensation and briefly describe some of the competing theories. An excellent summary of the available experimental data is presented by Buchsbaum [16, fig. 4]. In Section 7.4 we will take this coding one step further by considering the mapping from the perceptual into the linguistic domain, where colors are coded by the names we use to describe them.

Notwithstanding the basic fact that color processing in the human visual system is not completely understood, there is still a practical need to deal with color in fields such as television, movies, photography, and the manufacture of paints. Some method of color standardization is imperative. Therefore in 1931 the CIE (Commission Internationale de L'Eclairage) adopted a standard based on the assumption of color trichromacy as provided by matching experiments similar to those discussed briefly in Section 4.3 and the photopic visual model given by Equation (4.17). Trichromacy has been taken to imply two basic assumptions:

1. Any color can be matched by a vectorially additive combination of three primaries.
2. The color processing is linear, indicating the properties of proportionality and additivity.

These are based on the Grassmann laws of additive color mixture, expounded in 1853 [30, p. 372; 77]. The model, shown in Figure 7.10, is an analog of the neurophysiological model in Figure 7.5 but characterizes only the first stage of processing at the left of this figure. Thus, whereas in the latter the input is mapped into trivariance space by Equations (4.20) to (4.22), the psychophysical mapping results in a representation in the three-dimensional tristimulus space.

The equations governing this transformation are:

$$R = \int_{\lambda} I(\lambda) S_R(\lambda)\, d\lambda \tag{7.4}$$

$$G = \int_{\lambda} I(\lambda) S_G(\lambda)\, d\lambda \tag{7.5}$$

$$B = \int_{\lambda} I(\lambda) S_B(\lambda)\, d\lambda \tag{7.6}$$

where the scalars R, G, and B are the tristimulus values and $S_R(\lambda)$, $S_G(\lambda)$, and $S_B(\lambda)$ are three hypothetical color filters which obviously play a role similar to that of the color absorption curves of the cone pigments.

Is there any way to determine the $S_R(\lambda)$, $S_G(\lambda)$, and $S_B(\lambda)$ by experimentation with humans? The answer is yes, by using color-matching experiments. Suppose we select any three monochromatic primaries given by the three unit vectors $\mathbf{R}(\lambda_1)$, $\mathbf{G}(\lambda_2)$, and $\mathbf{B}(\lambda_3)$, but impose the condition that they be linearly independent. Having selected these, the psychophysical measurements are

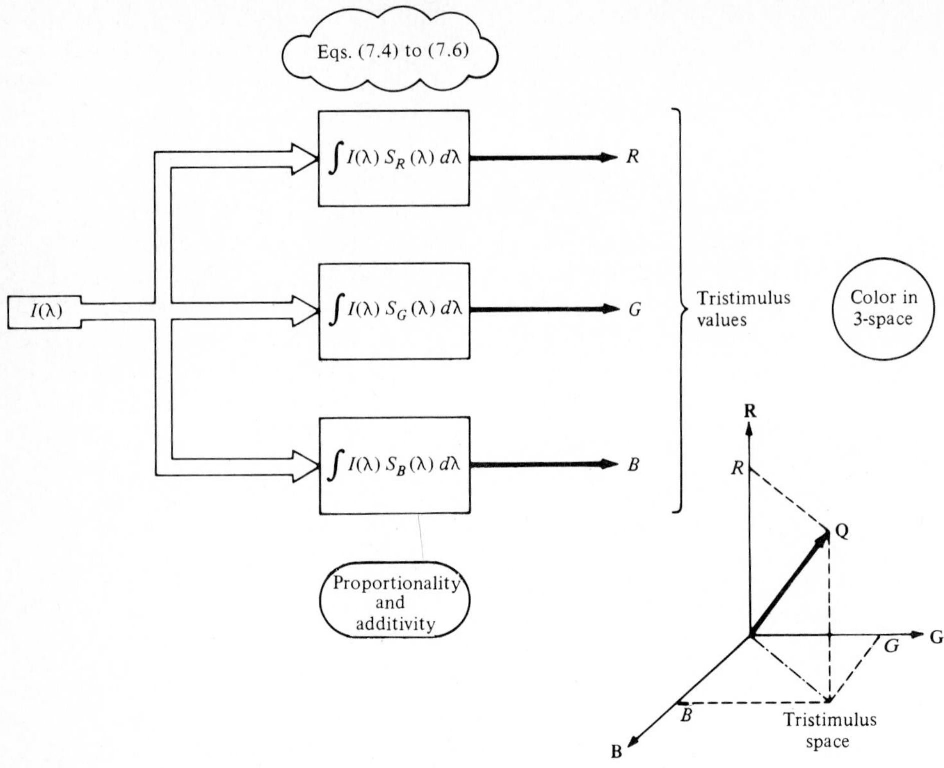

Figure 7.10 A psychophysical model based on the filtering action of three hypothetical filters $S_R(\lambda)$, $S_G(\lambda)$, and $S_B(\lambda)$. The input $I(\lambda)$ is mapped into the three-dimensional tristimulus space. An arbitrary vector **Q** in this space can be specified by the three tristimulus coordinates.

usually made with a trichrometer, which requires the matching of colors in a bipartite field, as shown schematically in Figure 7.11*a* [63]. Trichromatic theory implies that only three coordinates are required to specify any color. Therefore given the four lights **R**, **G**, **B**, and **Q**, each with a different wavelength λ, it is only necessary to adjust the intensities S_R, S_G, and S_B of the three monochromatic colors in the left-hand field in order to visually match the color of the chosen fourth light **Q**. We note that these experiments imply that the rods are inoperative; we assume either that the rod-free area of the fovea is stimulated or perhaps that the rods are saturated. In any event, there is some evidence that the rods do in fact affect color matches, but the mechanism is not understood.

From Figures 7.10 and 7.11*a* we observe that when a match occurs, we have the following relationship in three-space:

$$\mathbf{Q}(\lambda) = R\mathbf{R} + G\mathbf{G} + B\mathbf{B} \tag{7.7}$$

But since the input $I(\lambda)$ is the sum of three unit impulses (see Figure 7.11*b*),

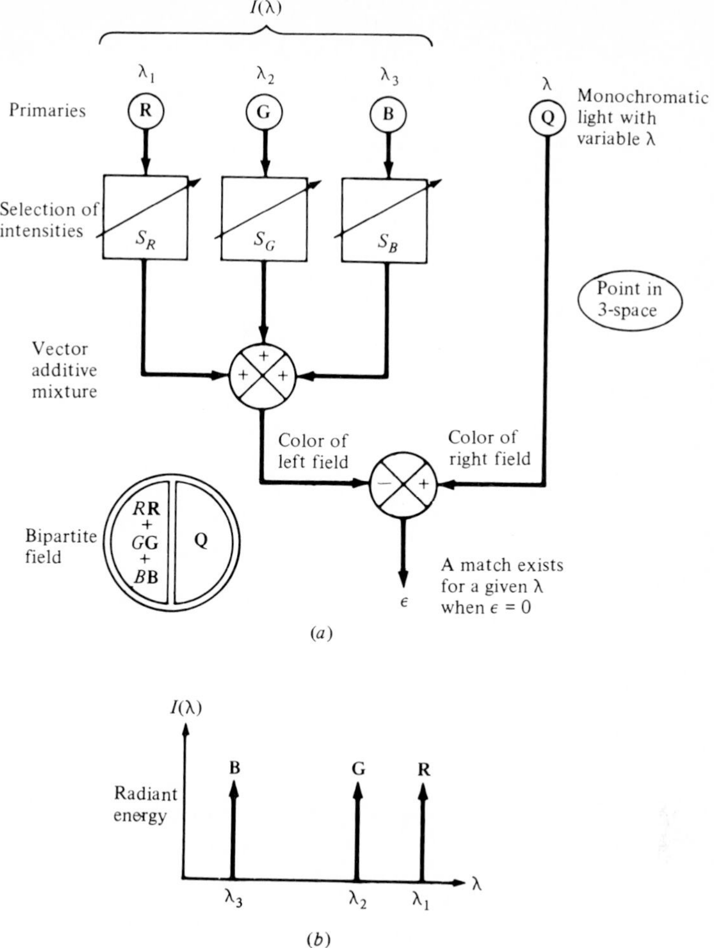

Figure 7.11 Color matching using a trichrometer. (*a*) A block diagram of a trichrometer, explaining the basis of its operation. (*b*) The input $I(\lambda)$ to the trichrometer. $I(\lambda)$ consists of three impulse functions which constitute the three chosen primaries.

the contributions by *R*, *G*, and *B* as given by Equations (7.4) to (7.6) result in the following:

$$\mathbf{Q}(\lambda) = S_R(\lambda_1)\mathbf{R} + S_G(\lambda_2)\mathbf{G} + S_B(\lambda_3)\mathbf{B} \tag{7.8}$$

where λ_1, λ_2, and λ_3 are the wavelengths of the three color primaries. Now let $\mathbf{Q}(\lambda)$ be the set of monochromatic and equal energy signals which define the spectrum colors†. Then this range of wavelengths λ will yield the so-called

† Conceptually it is useful here to consider this set as consisting of a large number of unit impulses of the type shown in Figure 7.11*b*.

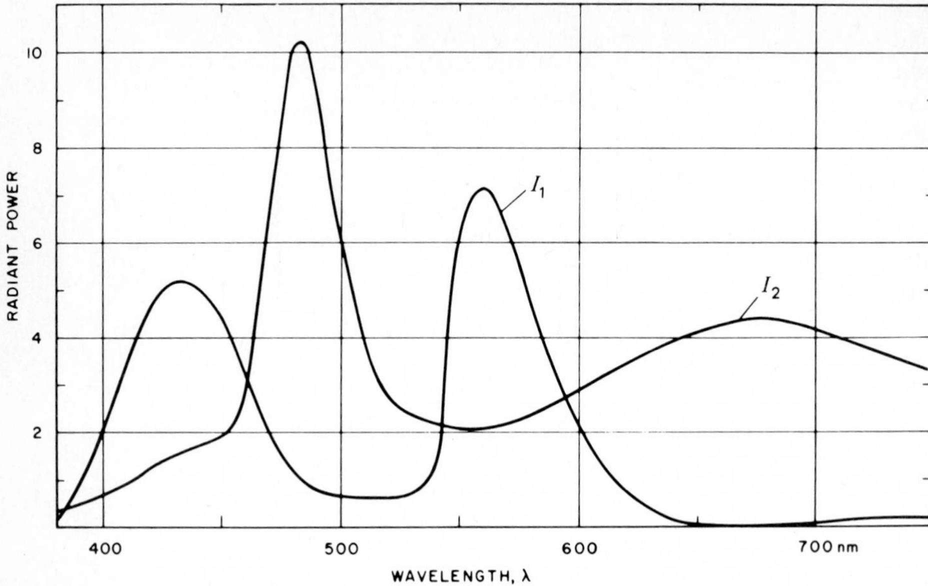

Figure 7.12 I_1 and I_2 are two spectral energy distributions which are metameric with respect to a given set of color-matching functions. These two inputs could be matched by using the trichrometer shown in Figure 7.11 so that they would appear identical to the normal viewer. (*From G. Wyszecki and W. S. Stiles, "Color Science," Wiley, New York, 1967.*)

color-matching functions $S_R(\lambda)$, $S_G(\lambda)$, and $S_B(\lambda)$ for this particular primary color system. Essentially these functions define the amount of each wavelength needed to match an arbitrary color in the spectrum. In addition, we note that the functions themselves are also tristimulus values. Because of the linearity assumption, we may now use the model with these color matching functions to predict tristimulus values for any arbitrary input $I(\lambda)$.

Two colors represented by two spectral distributions $I_1(\lambda)$ and $I_2(\lambda)$ are matched when their three tristimulus values are equal according to Equations (7.4) to (7.6). If $I_1(\lambda) = I_2(\lambda)$, then we say we have an isomeric match. However it is also possible to achieve match conditions when the two spectral distributions are not equal. In this case the colors are referred to as "metameric." Figure 7.12 shows an example of two such inputs. We therefore note that man is actually incapable of discriminating wavelengths and functions in the color domain by making equivalences between metamers.

So far we have spoken in terms of a particular set of primaries, **R**, **G**, and **B**. In fact any set of primaries which is a linear combination of the original will also suffice. We may define a linear transformation $[A]$ of the coordinate system given by **R**, **G**, and **B** as follows:

$$\begin{bmatrix} \mathbf{R}' \\ \mathbf{G}' \\ \mathbf{B}' \end{bmatrix} = \begin{bmatrix} a_{11} & a_{12} & a_{13} \\ a_{21} & a_{22} & a_{23} \\ a_{31} & a_{32} & a_{33} \end{bmatrix} \begin{bmatrix} \mathbf{R} \\ \mathbf{G} \\ \mathbf{B} \end{bmatrix} \tag{7.9}$$

where $\mathbf{R}'$, $\mathbf{G}'$, and $\mathbf{B}'$ constitute a new set of primaries and $[A^*] \neq 0$ for linear independence. The color-matching functions in one of these coordinate systems will also be a linear combination of the others. Of course, each set of primaries leads to another set of matching functions which may be used in the model in Figure 7.10. The model is therefore not unique.

The above equations refer to the situation in which a set of three colored lights is combined additively using a tristimulus colormeter of the type shown in Figure 7.11. To produce an actual colored image in this way, we require three "color separation negatives." The latter could be obtained by using black and white film to photograph a scene three times, each time using one of three primary color filters. These yield the red, green, and blue separation negatives, which can then be combined additively, by using three projectors, for example. We shall return to this approach in Section 7.5. A more common alternative is to use color film. This consists of three separate layers of photographic emulsion, with each layer sensitive to a different color. Thus, only a single exposure is required to produce either a color transparency or a color print.

How do we arrange for this multilayer film to represent the color in the original scene? A little thought on the part of the reader should make it obvious that if the light is to pass through the layers sequentially, they cannot be independently sensitive to the red, green, and blue additive primaries. Instead, the dyes associated with each of the three emulsion layers in the film are selected to be the "subtractive primaries." Each of these subtracts or filters out one of the additive primaries from white light. There are three such primaries: yellow (white minus blue), magenta (white minus green), and cyan (white minus red). The two colors involved in each relationship are referred to as complementary colors (see Figure 7.1). Also, note that because of the property of additivity and the fact that white is a mixture of red, green, and blue, we have yellow as the sum of red and green, cyan the sum of green and blue, and magenta the sum of red and blue.

Photographic film is composed of three layers of the subtractive primaries. Each layer filters out one of the primary colors. Upon exposure of the film, the amount of dye density in each layer is proportional to the amount of additive primary that impinges upon it. For example, in a positive transparency the density of the magenta dye decreases with the amount of exposure to green light, while the cyan and yellow dyes are unaffected. In a print negative the opposite holds true, with the density increasing with greater exposure. Suppose that the positive and negative films were now exposed to pure green. The reader might consider what color the deposited dye would appear to be if white light were transmitted through it (green and magenta, respectively). It is interesting that paint mixtures are also produced by using the principle of subtractive primaries. In the case of either primary or secondary mixtures, all the actual colors are not given by a single wavelength. Whether we are referring to lights or dyes, the spectral components involved cover a band of wavelengths.

We have mentioned previously that a practical means for defining color was needed and this was achieved by the CIE by defining $S_R(\lambda)$, $S_G(\lambda)$, and

$S_B(\lambda)$ for a standard observer. The 1931 CIE Standard Observer was determined by using color matches within a 4° area centered on the fovea and averaged over 20 observers. More recently the 1964 CIE Large-Field Standard Observer has been specified by using stimulation within a 10° region. The methodology of the latter is superior to the former in that the earlier results were based on the assumption that Equation (4.24) was valid, which we now know is not the case. However, although the magnitude of the error incurred because of this faulty assumption is not clear, it does not seem to be of great significance.

The 1931 CIE RGB and 1931 CIE XYZ systems are mathematically equivalent. The former was defined by the primaries $\mathbf{R} = 700$ nm, $\mathbf{G} =$

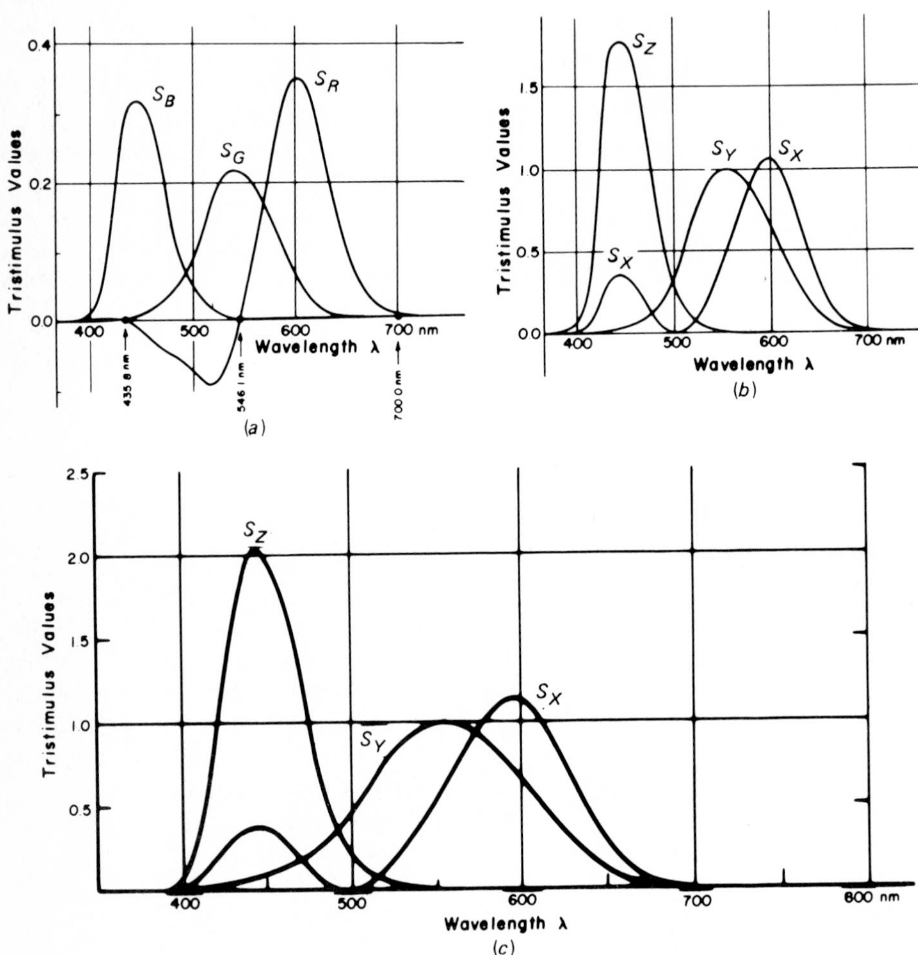

Figure 7.13 Three sets of CIE color-matching functions. (*a*) 1931 CIE RGB system. (*b*) 1931 CIE XYZ system. (*c*) 1964 CIE XYZ system. (*From G. Wyszecki and W. S. Stiles, "Color Science," Wiley, New York, 1967.*)

546.1 nm, and **B** = 435.8 nm and results in the color-matching curves shown in Figure 7.13*a*. We observe that $S(\lambda)$ takes on negative values for certain values of λ; the implication is that under these circumstances its contribution must be added to the right side of the bipartite field in order to achieve a match. The XYZ system is based on the use of three unreal or imaginary primaries, so that the resulting color-matching functions will be positive for all λ. These curves are shown in Figure 7.13*b*. The 1964 CIE system is based on the data of Stiles and Burch [64] and Speranskaya [61], using the primaries **R** = 645.2 nm, **G** = 526.3 nm, and **B** = 444.4 nm, and is shown in Figure 7.13*c*. Readers interested in a further elaboration of the derivation of these functions should consult [77, pp. 263–274].

Cornsweet claims that "with a lot of brain work, and luck, the logic of the CIE system may reveal itself," although he bravely attempts a rather concise explanation in a rather lengthy footnote [19, pp. 230, 231]. He also includes a three-dimensional representation of three color-matching curves derived by using equal-quanta spectra rather than equal-energy spectra, as was done for the CIE system. The results are shown in Figure 7.14, where it is noted that the

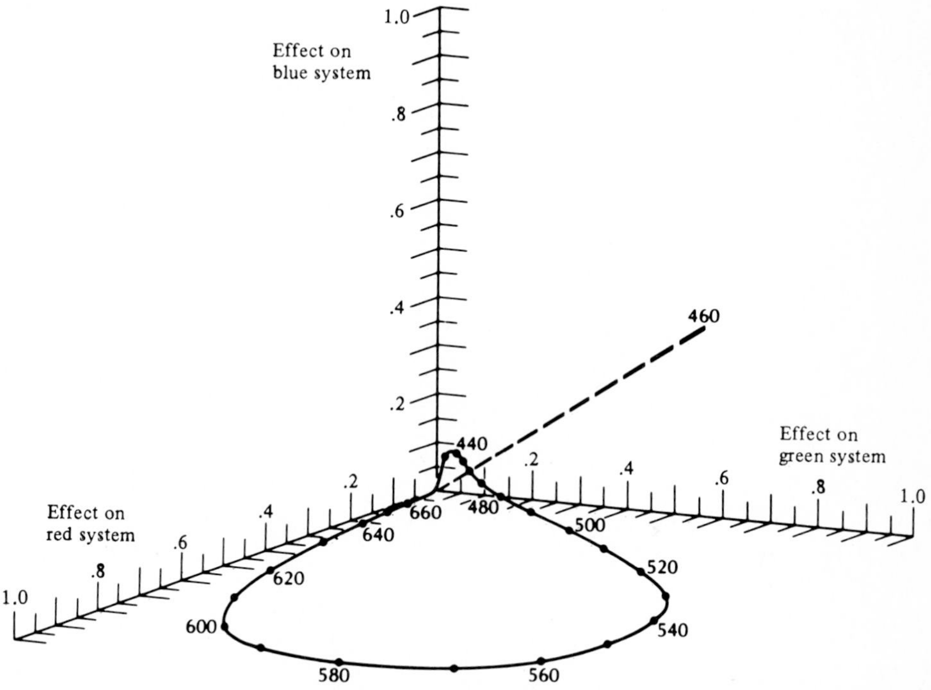

Figure 7.14 In addition to the color-matching functions in Figure 7.13, we also have the equivalent cone responses shown in Figure 7.3. Using the curves of Figure 7.3*b*, we may plot the equivalent spectral locus in the three-dimensional space, as shown above. (*Adapted from T. Cornsweet, "Visual Perception," Academic, New York, 1970.*)

segment related to the blue curve is more or less orthogonal to the part due to the other two. This curve was actually obtained by using $L(\lambda)$, $M(\lambda)$, and $S(\lambda)$ as shown in Figure 7.3*b*, which are based on neurophysiological data, but is equivalent to the psychophysical curves, since only the first linear stage of processing is being modeled in both cases.

The important issue here is that the CIE methodology does provide a practical psychophysical model for defining colors as viewed by humans. As we have seen, the model is definitely not unique and does not really attempt to explain the underlying physical phenomena. Readers may be interested in examining a mathematical model based on optical probabilistic processing, which attempts to deal with such phenomena as color discrimination and color constancy [15, 16, 17, 18]. On the other hand, the neurophysiological model discussed in Section 7.2 is perhaps more ambitious in its intent. However, it is observed that the two models are actually equivalent. The major distinction is that in one case we use the actual pigment absorption curves $L(\lambda)$, $M(\lambda)$, and $S(\lambda)$ to compute a three-dimensional signal vector and thereby ignore any normalization with regard to the perceptual output. On the other hand, the psychophysical model does accept this as a constraint, so that clearly the CIE color-matching functions cannot be said to model any specific physical aspect of the system. There does exist a linear relationship between these two models, essentially a mapping from trivariance to tristimulus space. How this mapping is obtained is discussed in the next section.

7.3.2 Color Blindness

How do we relate the neurophysiological "filters" in Figure 7.3*b* and *c* to the psychophysical filters in Figure 7.13? The answer turns out to be related to the phenomenon of color blindness.

Let $S_X(\lambda)$, $S_Y(\lambda)$, and $S_Z(\lambda)$ be the color-matching functions for the 1931 CIE XYZ system (see Figure 7.13*b*). Then define the matrix (B) as a transformation from one system to the other according to the equations [56, 77]

$$\lambda L(\lambda) = b_{11}S_X(\lambda) + b_{12}S_Y(\lambda) + b_{13}S_Z(\lambda) \tag{7.10}$$

$$\lambda M(\lambda) = b_{21}S_X(\lambda) + b_{22}S_Y(\lambda) + b_{23}S_Z(\lambda) \tag{7.11}$$

$$\lambda S(\lambda) = b_{31}S_X(\lambda) + b_{32}S_Y(\lambda) + b_{33}S_Z(\lambda) \tag{7.12}$$

The parameter λ is needed on the left side of these equations because the matching experiments are based on energy units (see Sections 2.2.1 and 4.4). The relationship cannot be exactly correct because of the arguments set forth above; however, the error turns out to be of little consequence. We would like to determine the coefficients of the matrix $[B]$ so that given $S_X(\lambda)$, $S_Y(\lambda)$, and $S_Z(\lambda)$, we may estimate the spectral sensitivities of the foveal cones and compare the results with those of more direct physiological methods.

The approach generally taken to this problem is based on the existence of individuals who suffer from color blindness and we shall digress for a moment to explain this phenomenon in terms of our previous discussions. This will also perhaps serve the purpose of again clarifying the principles of trivariance. We observed in Section 4.4 that only the directions of the vectors in three-dimensional color space are important. That is, only the ratios of the trivariance or tristimulus parameters are significant. The implication for Equations (7.10) to (7.12) is that we need only determine six of the b_{ij} coefficients instead of nine, which greatly simplifies matters. Using data obtained from color-blind people, we are able to reduce the problem to the solution of three pairs of simultaneous equations.

Color-blind people can usually see some colors but have difficulty in discriminating others, the most common problem being red-green discrimination. There seems to be a genetic linkage involved, since about 8 percent of men have abnormal vision, while the corresponding statistic for women is only $\frac{1}{2}$ percent. There are essentially three basic types of anomalous behavior. The monochromats, accounting for only 0.003 percent of the abnormals, cannot distinguish any colors and are unfortunately able to match any given color to another if the gray-level intensities are similar. Rod monochromats probably possess inoperative cones, while the rare cone monochromats most likely have cones filled with rhodopsin. The second type, dichromats, who account for 2.6 percent of the abnormals, are able to match any color to a suitable mixture of two colors. The rest of the abnormals are anomalous trichromats, who do indeed perform matches using three color components, as is the case with normals. However, they tend to employ incorrect proportions of red and green.

To see how these anomalies arise, let us examine hypothetical matching experiments performed with each of the three categories. The monochromat possesses only one visual pigment, resulting in a bell-shaped sensitivity curve, which is probably that of rhodopsin. For any two wavelengths λ_1 and λ_2, it is only necessary to adjust the amplitude of one of the inputs $I_1(\lambda)$ or $I_2(\lambda)$ to achieve a match (see Figure 7.15). Because of the principle of invariance (see Section 7.2) the two wavelengths cannot be distinguished, and this is the source of the color blindness. This phenomenon seems to be similar to what normal people experience in twilight or moonlight.

There are three categories of dichromats, each possessing another pair of cone types, according to the Helmholtz-König hypothesis of the nineteenth century. Densitometric confirmation has established that the protanope lacks red cones, the deuteranope lacks green cones, and the rarer tritanope lacks blue cones. For example, protanopes have $L(\lambda) = 0$ and are therefore blind to red. They have difficulty telling red and green apart, as well as anything in between. However we note in Figure 7.3 that the red and green sensitivity curves manifest considerable overlap. Therefore when such persons are made to match a red with a green, they will require 10 times the intensity of deuteranopes.

Consider the hypothetical dichromat in Figure 7.16*a*, in which there is no overlap between the two channels. With $I_1(\lambda_1)$ on the left side of the bipartite

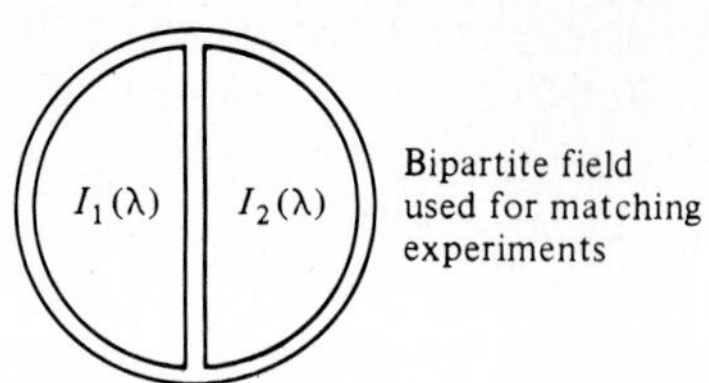

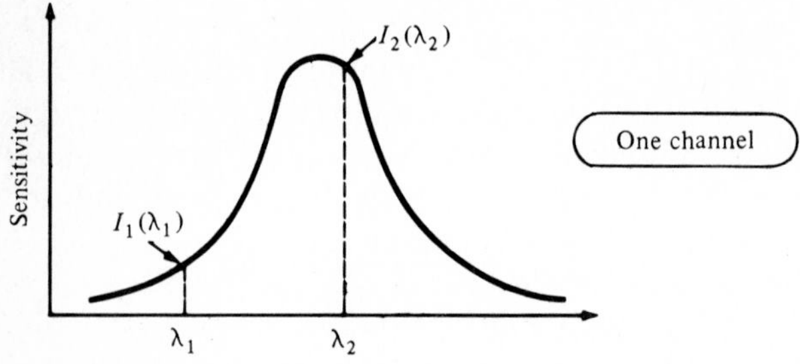

Figure 7.15. Visual matching by monochromats. A match can be easily made by a monochromat when the amplitudes are adjusted to be equal by increasing the amplitude of $I_1(\lambda_1)$.

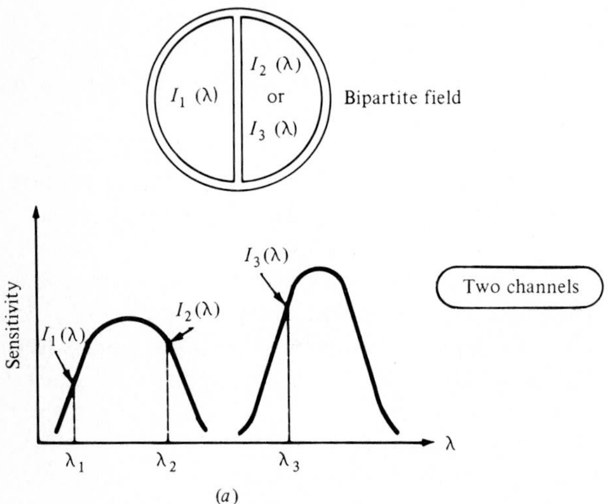

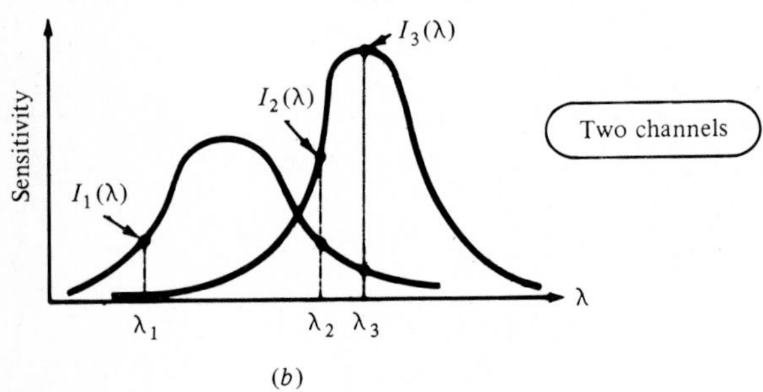

Figure 7.16 Two examples of dichromats: (*a*) shows a hypothetical case and (*b*) a more realistic situation in which the two curves overlap. (*Adapted from T. Cornsweet, "Visual Perception," Academic, New York, 1970.*)

field and $I_2(\lambda_2)$ on the right, no discrimination would be possible and we have the exact same situation as with the monochromat. If however, $I_2(\lambda_2)$ is replaced by $I_3(\lambda_3)$, both channels respond and discrimination can be achieved. We therefore observe that two channels are necessary but not sufficient to account for the dichromat. A more realistic dichromat is shown in Figure 7.16*b* (see also Figure 7.3). Now $I_1(\lambda_1)$ and $I_2(\lambda_2)$ can be distinguished because they result in different responses in the two color channels. There is no way to adjust the amplitude of $I_2(\lambda_2)$ on the right side so that the response from both channels would be identical. There is an exception to this: if we can find two wavelengths λ_1 and λ_2 so that the ratio of the two respective sensitivities is identical, such an adjustment could be made. Under these restrictions the person would indeed be color-blind. This situation occurs when the sensitivities are very low, as is the case at both extremities of the visual spectrum.

What happens when the dichromat is asked to match a mixture of two wavelengths? Suppose the left side is $I_1(\lambda_1)$ and the right side contains the vector sum of $I_2(\lambda_2)$ plus $I_3(\lambda_3)$, as shown in Figure 7.16*b*. With the two parameters, the dichromat would now be able to adjust the amplitudes of $I_2(\lambda_2)$ and $I_3(\lambda_3)$ independently so that the two sides looked identical. Therefore, given three colors, the dichromat is always able to match two of them to the third. Of course, the two fields would still look different to the average person.

As we saw previously, trichromacy implies that a normal observer given four colors would be able to match any three of them to the fourth. There do exist anomalous trichromats, who although they are able to make these distinctions, require proportions of the three colors which differ from the normal. This may be due to their having different $L(\lambda)$, $M(\lambda)$, and $S(\lambda)$ or perhaps to a different weighting in the vector summation of Equation (7.8). The protanomalous trichromat needs more red than normal and the deuteranomalous trichromat more green than normal. They are often confused by autumn colors such as brown or olive green. Notwithstanding these comments, we should note that the perfectly normal trichromat is also color-blind in a certain sense. The three filters in Figure 7.2 only pass certain signals so that our vision is, so to speak, colored by this fact.

Returning to the problem of computing the six components of the matrix $[B]$, it can be shown that if we know the color-matching functions of the three different types of dichromats, the problem reduces to the solution of three pairs of equations. Readers interested in the details should consult [77, pp. 400–418]. Rodieck [56] gives the following data for $[B]$ (λ in nanometers):

$$[B] = \begin{bmatrix} 1.43947 & 4.15546 & -0.29692 \\ -2.35030 & 6.93934 & 0.48480 \\ 0 & 0 & 4.23788 \end{bmatrix} \tag{7.13}$$

The spectral sensitivities $L(\lambda)$, $M(\lambda)$, and $S(\lambda)$ of the three foveal cones obtained in this way and then normalized to unit area are shown in Figure 7.17. We observe that the results are quite consistent with previous curves. These are

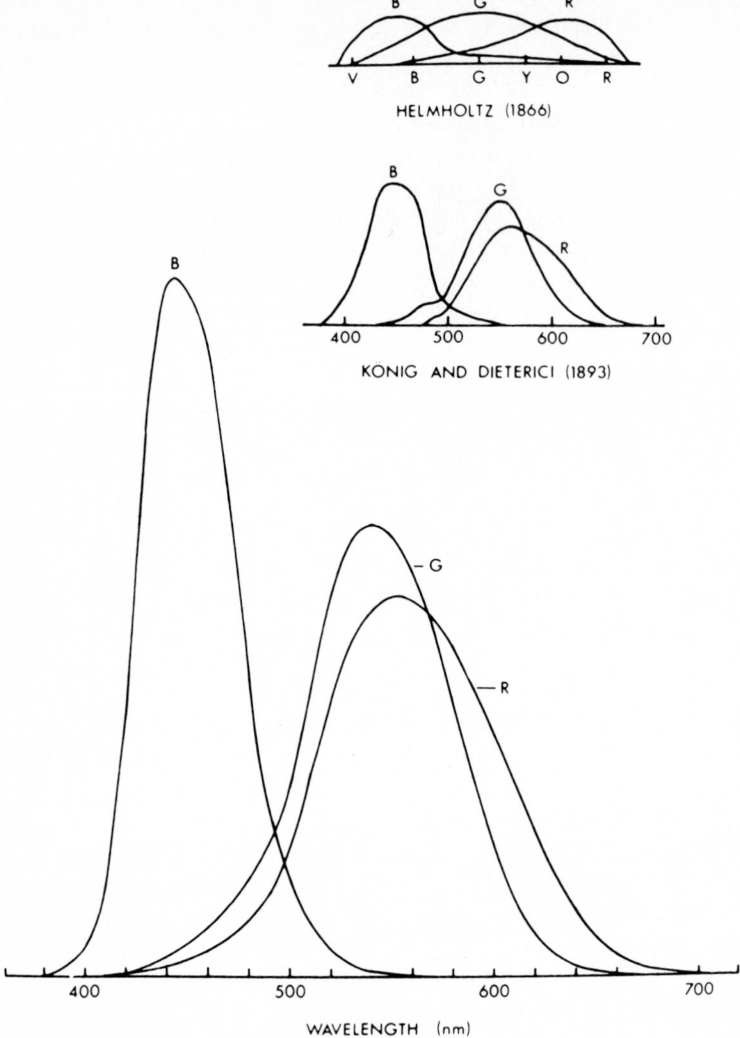

Figure 7.17 The spectral responses of the three cone types found in the human fovea. The curves are normalized to unit area. Compare these more recent results with those obtained in the last century. (*From R. W. Rodieck, "The Vertebrate Retina, Principles of Structure and Function," Freeman, San Francisco, 1973.*)

only relative functions because the proportionality constants relating them are unknown.

7.3.3 An Opponent Theory Model

So far in this section we have restricted our considerations to the classical trichromatic Young-Helmholtz theory. However we did observe in Section 7.2

that although the first stage of transduction by the cones could be modeled in this way, there developed in the 1960s considerable neurophysiological evidence of an opponent action in the LGN. Thus the simple psychophysical model in Figure 7.10 is apparently inadequate to account for all the experimental evidence available at the cellular level. There are difficulties at the perceptual level as well. Color constancy (see the discussion on brightness constancy in Section 4.5.2), a phenomenon in which colors are perceived independent of the incident illumination, is also ignored. As discussed in the case of brightness, it seems that here also it is the surface properties that are important [46]. A second problem is color contrast [31, 36]. Just as in the case of the simultaneous contrast phenomenon [72] (Section 6.2.2), perceived color is not just a point property but depends on the color attributes of the surrounding field. It is interesting that an alternative to the Young-Helmholtz theory was proposed by Hering as far back as 1875 on the basis of psychophysical evidence. This opponent theory was not widely accepted, although more recently Hurvich and Jameson [35] have revived interest in it. The trichromatic and opponent theories turn out to be complementary [50], the first dealing with retinal processing and the second with modeling phenomena that occur at the LGN cellular level. The opponent theory, it should be noted, is still essentially a point theory, so that color constancy and contrast must be treated as special cases.

We observed in Section 7.2 that the theory rests on the assumption that the output signals from the cones are organized in such a way that the next stage of color processing deals with pairs of colors which function in opposition to each other. Thus we have the three systems, red-green, yellow-blue, and black-white. This theory readily accounts for the observation that no reddish green or yellowish blue colors are perceived. What we do not know are the exact connections between the first stage and the next. Figure 7.8 presents one hypothesis, while another, due to Hurvich and Jameson [35], is shown in Figure 7.18. We note in the latter model that each of the cone receptors has an output connected to each of the postulated cells at the LGN level. Some of these outputs are excitory and others inhibitory. The result after this stage is two chromatic variables and one intensity variable.

Faugeras [26, 27] has extended the model shown in Figure 7.10, or, equivalently, on the left side of Figure 7.5, to include the opponent theory. Note that from here on we make no distinction between the psychophysical and neurophysiological models because the phenomena we are attempting to represent are identical in both cases. Figure 7.19 is a block diagram of the model, which we shall briefly discuss. The first stage embodies the linear transformation of the cones and is followed by the nonlinear, logarithmic operation, which we have so far ignored in this chapter but emphasized in Section 4.5.1. These processed tristimulus values R^*, G^*, and B^* are then followed by the opponent model, in which a separation of the chromatic and achromatic components occur. Note that the "wiring" of Figure 7.18 is used, but this need not always be the case. The outputs are the luminosity variable L

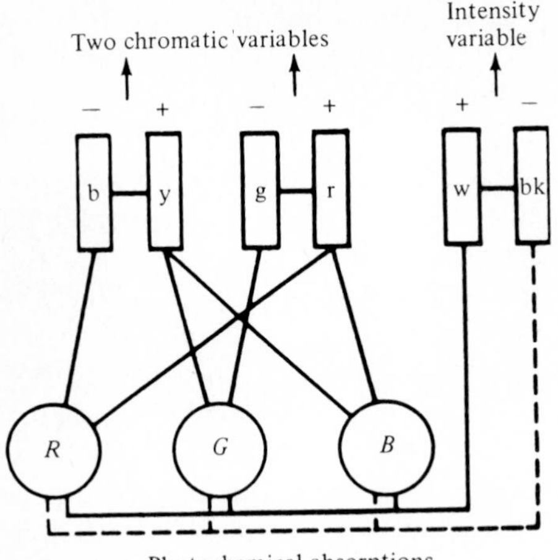

Figure 7.18 A schematic sketch of a plausible neural mechanism, which could convert a trichromatic (R, G, and B) photoreceptor coding scheme to an opponent mechanism (b-y, g-r, and bk-w). (*From L. M. Hurvich and D. Jameson, "Color Theory and Abnormal Red-Green Vision," Documenta Ophthalmologica, vol. 16, 1962, pp. 409–442.*)

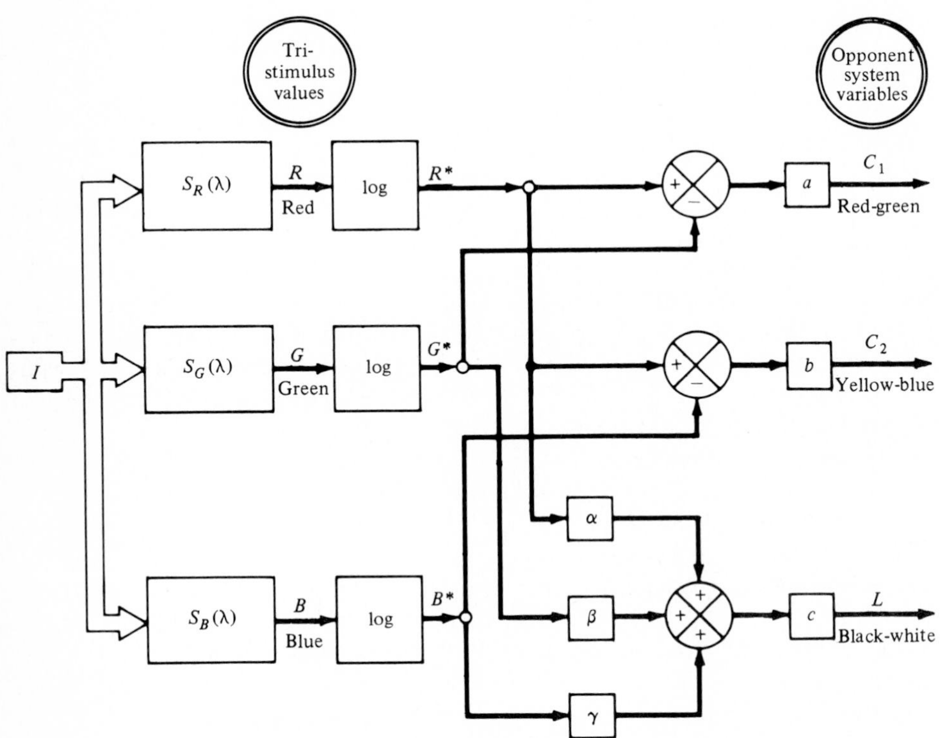

Figure 7.19 A model of the opponent color system. (*Adapted from O. D. Faugeras, "Digital Color Image Processing Within the Framework of a Human Visual System," IEEE Transactions on Acoustics, Speech and Signal Processing, vol. ASSP-27, no. 4, August 1979, pp. 380–393.*)

(black-white) and the two chromatic variables C_1 (red-green) and C_2 (yellow-blue) (see Figure 7.9):

$$L = c[R^* + G^* + B^*]$$
$$= c[\alpha \log R + \beta \log G + \gamma \log B] \tag{7.14}$$

$$C_1 = a[R^* - G^*] = a \log\left(\frac{R}{G}\right) \tag{7.15}$$

$$C_2 = b[R^* - B^*] = b \log\left(\frac{R}{B}\right) \tag{7.16}$$

Faugeras [27] takes this model one step further by including the effects of spatial frequency filtering that we know exists. The sampling due to the retinal mosaic results in high-frequency attenuation, which, as we saw, limits the visual acuity. The sharpening effect in the spatial domain which is due to lateral inhibition creates a low-frequency cutoff. Bandpass filters $H(u)$, $H_a(u)$, and $H_b(u)$ have hence been placed so as to follow the three outputs L, C_1, and C_2, respectively. For an achromatic input stimulus pattern, it is seen that $C_1 = C_2 = 0$ and the only output L is filtered through $H(u)$. The latter is just the overall transfer function $H_a(u)H_b(u)$ of the human visual system discussed in Section 4.5; that is, Stockham's homomorphic model of achromatic vision [65]. However, the reader should note that if the neurophysiology is taken into account, it is not at all clear that these filtering stages should be placed at this particular point in the sequence [76].

Using the spectral responses of the cones (see Figure 7.17) for $S_R(\lambda)$, $S_G(\lambda)$, and $S_B(\lambda)$, Faugeras [27] has employed the CIE Standard Observer relative luminosity efficiency function $V(\lambda)$ to compute α, β, and γ under achromatic conditions ($\alpha = 0.612$, $\beta = 0.369$, $\gamma = 0.019$; $\alpha + \beta + \gamma = 1$). In addition $H_a(u)$ and $H_b(u)$ were determined by a methodology, similar to that of Stockham [65], which required observers to make color matches [25]. The transfer functions and associated point-spread functions are shown in Figure 7.20. The complete model of human color vision was then applied to image processing and coding.

We have already noted that the theories discussed so far are basically point theories. They do not naturally and easily account for such important but poorly understood phenomena as spatial and temporal chromatic adaptation. For example, what mechanism is involved when the surrounding neighborhood of a patch of color influences our perception of it? Many theories about this have been proposed but no generally accepted one has been adopted. Wyszecki and Stiles [77, pp. 435–446] describe seven different ones, among which is found Land's [45] retinex (from "retina" and "cortex") theory, which is perhaps the best known.

The retinex theory has been the subject of much controversy [38, 42, 73, 74] and is based on the observation that the stimulus wavelength and its actual color perception are independent in some way. The sensation of color is a

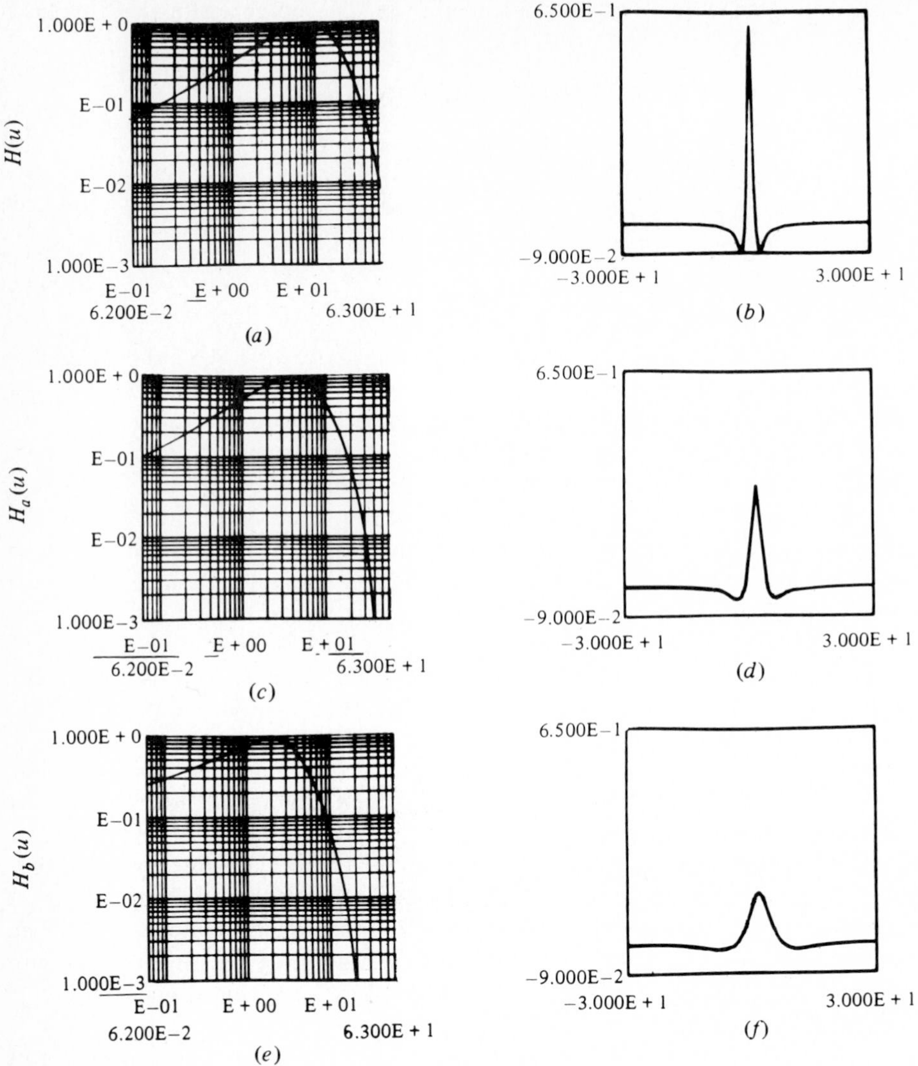

Figure 7.20 The frequency responses $H(u)$, $H_a(u)$ and $H_b(u)$ of the filters operating on the L, C_1, and C_2 channels in Figure 7.19, respectively. The corresponding point-spread functions (for a span of 1° of visual angle) to these filters are shown on the right. (*From O. Faugeras, "Digital Color Image Processing within the Framework of a Human Visual Model," IEEE Transactions on Acoustics, Speech, and Signal Processing, vol. ASSP-27, no. 4, August 1979, pp. 380–393.*)

property of the reflectivity from the surface of an object [3], a signal which is then processed by the three cone types of the retina. In the nineteenth century Helmholtz had already noted that it is independent of the illumination component. To account for this, Land has proposed that the three-dimensional retinal signal is further processed in three independent channels. The role of these channels is to eliminate the effects of illumination so that the perceived color will be based exclusively on the surface properties of the object, that is, on the "lightness." Further, it seems that the visual system only requires two of the channels to perceive color in a picture. This is demonstrated by first producing two registered positive photographic transparencies of a natural scene, one through a red filter and the other through a green filter. Two projectors are then used to merge the two images on a screen. If the red-filtered slide is illuminated by red light and the green-filtered slide by white incandescent light, a complete range of colors is observed. This seems to contradict the trivariance theories, which would indicate that only red, white, and pink should be visible. Indeed, if we view only a small area of the projected image through a cylindrical tube, it is just these colors that appear [73]. It seems that the neighboring pictorial context might influence our perception of color.

Marr [49] supports the retinex theory, using arguments based on anatomy, physiology, and psychophysics. Computational models exist based on the assumptions that the stimulus illumination varies smoothly over the object and that the reflectance from the surface of the object is constant within its boundaries [35, 46]. In other words, the picture must be restricted to patches of uniform matte color with distinct delineations between them, as in a style adopted by the Dutch painter Mondrian. Readers who are interested in an elaboration of the retinex theory are referred to [40, 41, 43, 44, 51].

It is clear from these discussions that the major reason for the proliferation of color theories is our basic lack of understanding of the processing mechanisms beyond the LGN. Nevertheless, we accept that the subsequent three-dimensional signal, containing two chromatic components and one that is achromatic, is somehow mapped into perceived colors for which we have names. In the next section we examine how this is accomplished.

7.4 COLOR DESCRIPTION

So far we have considered two essentially equivalent models of human color vision. Both result in a transformation of the input signal into a three-dimensional color space: the neurophysiological model into trivariance space and the variables $\mathbf{A}_L$, $\mathbf{A}_M$, and $\mathbf{A}_S$; the psychophysical model into tristimulus space and such variables as $\mathbf{X}$, $\mathbf{Y}$, and $\mathbf{Z}$ in the CIE XYZ color system. However, it has also been intimated in the discussion on the opponent color system that there exist only two chromatic variables, the third being achromatic and providing for the luminance. Thus it appears that it is the ratio of the tristimulus (or trivariance) values that is important and that given any two of these parameters, the third is fixed. Readers may again wish to peruse Section 4.4, where the equivalent argument is made to the effect that only the direction of the vectors in three-dimensional space is of significance.

We define the property of a color field which describes the two now independent color variables as the chromaticity. In the color-matching experiments, all metameric matches result in tristimulus values which are in the same ratio; that is, the fields I_1 and I_2 have the same chromaticity but at different luminances. We would therefore expect that lines in the tristimulus or trivariance space would represent the same color. In fact, the two fields would actually not look quite the same along one of these lines in color space. First, one would be darker than the other. Second, the curves are slightly nonlinear, exhibiting a degree of curvature; this is known as the Bezold-Brücke effect [14].

Neglecting these nonlinearities, however, we could imagine a completely filled three-dimensional color space of color lines. A section taken symmetrically with respect to the three axes would result in the two-dimensional representation shown in Figure 7.21. If all the lines were indeed straight, then all such sections would appear identical. An arbitrary plane which intersects all

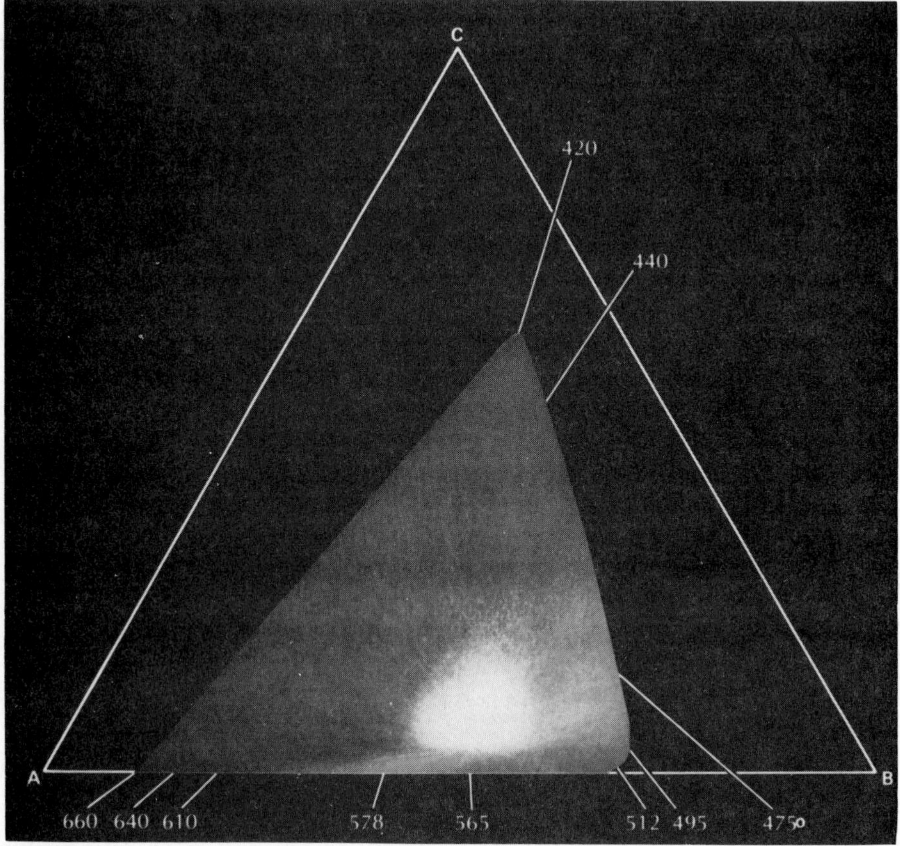

Figure 7.21 A color triangle obtained by taking a symmetrical section in color space. The actual colors are shown, with a large whitish area in the middle. (*From T. Cornsweet, "Visual Perception," Academic, New York, 1970.*) (See back endpapers for the color figure.)

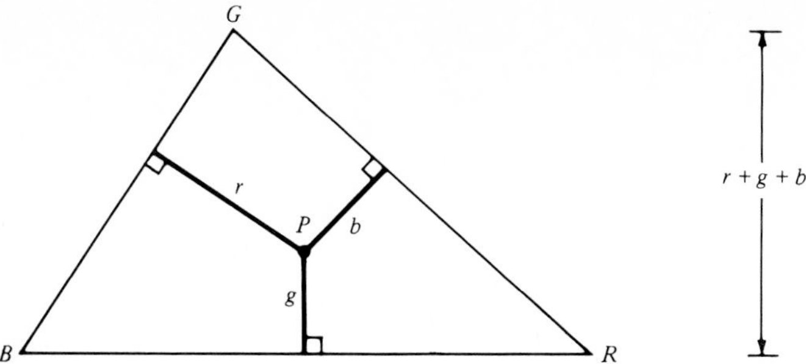

Figure 7.22 The symmetrical chromaticity section showing the geometrical relationship among the chromaticity coefficients for an arbitrary color point *P*. The height of the triangle $(r + g + b)$ is always constant.

the vectors, called a "chromaticity diagram," yields the equilateral triangle shown in the figure. We note that the chromaticity diagram may be defined in terms of $\mathbf{A}_L$, $\mathbf{A}_M$, $\mathbf{A}_S$, or **X**, **Y**, **Z**, or **R**, **G**, **B**. For simplicity we shall only use the latter symbols, but note that they are all equivalent in the sense discussed previously. The chromaticity coordinates *r*, *g*, and *b* may be computed as follows:

$$r = \frac{R}{R + G + B} \tag{7.17}$$

$$g = \frac{G}{R + G + B} \tag{7.18}$$

$$b = \frac{B}{R + G + B} \tag{7.19}$$

where $r + g + b = 1$. This is shown schematically in Figure 7.22. By use of the spectral sensitivity curves of Figure 7.17 the two-dimensional spectral loci of Figure 7.23 may be generated. We shall discuss below some interesting properties of this diagram. The equivalent 1931 CIE chromaticity diagram (shown in an orthogonal coordinate system with chromaticity coordinates *x* and *y*) is given in Figure 7.24.

All the visible colors map into the U-shaped region shown. We observe a large white area in Figure 7.21 at the center of the equilateral triangle. This is considered to be achromatic and is also delineated in the CIE curve in Figure 7.24. The U-shaped curve is referred to as the "spectral locus." It is the path in tristimulus (or trivariance) space of all the visible colors that are monochromatic, that is, the colors that require only a single vector at one wavelength for their definition. This wavelength is called the "dominant wavelength." The horizontal line at the bottom of the U is termed the "nonspectral purple line" (see Figure 7.21).

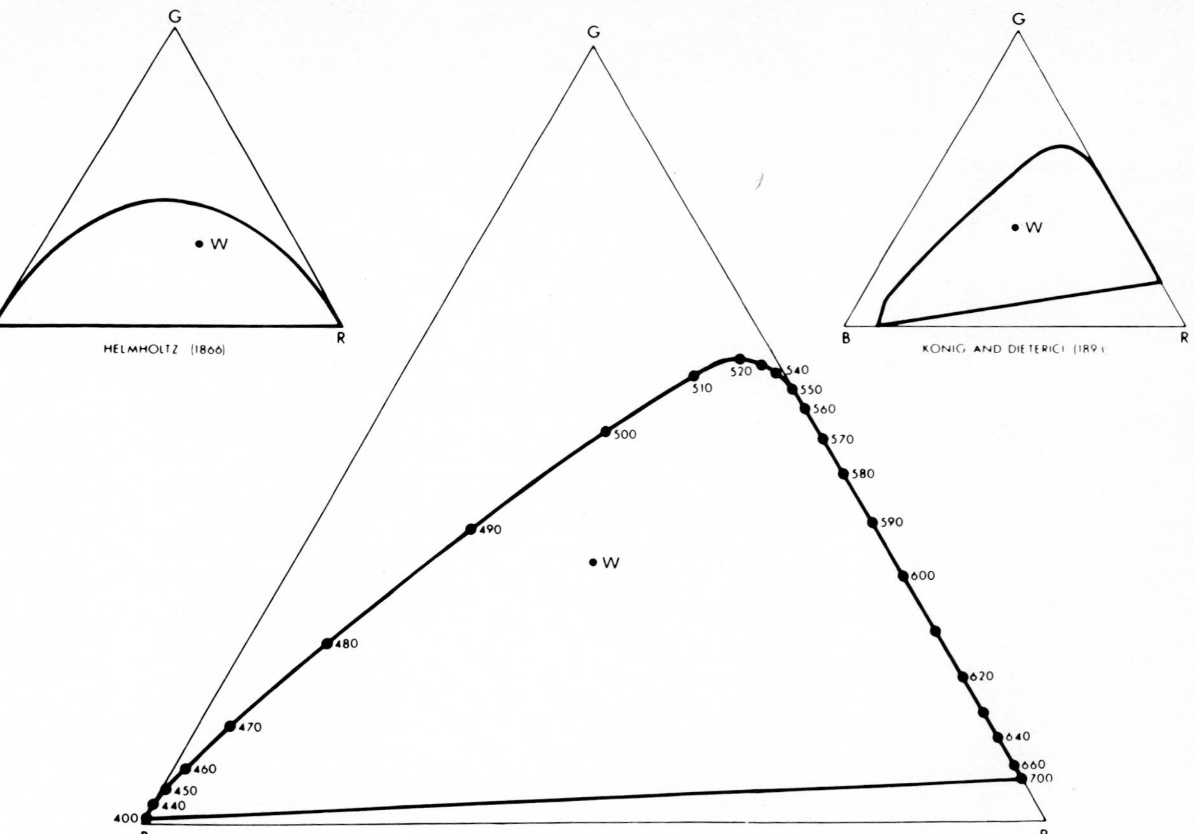

Figure 7.23 The two-dimensional spectral loci associated with the cone response curves in Figure 7.17. These are sometimes referred to as "cone triangles." (*From R. W. Rodieck, "The Vertebrate Retina, Principles of Structure and Function," Freeman, San Francisco, 1973.*)

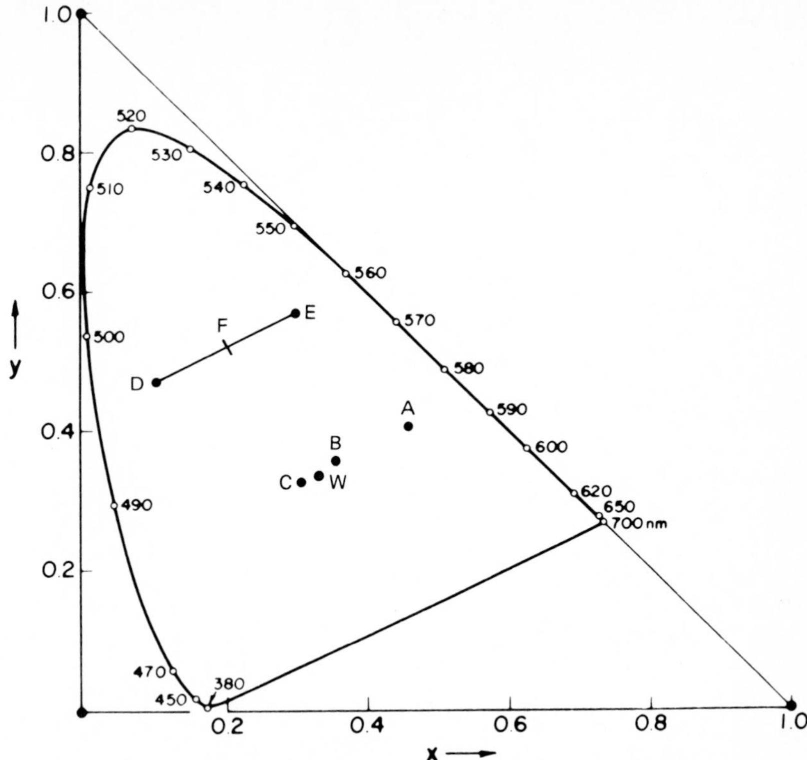

Figure 7.24 The 1931 CIE XYZ chromaticity diagram. Points *A*, *B*, and *C* are standard CIE sources meant to represent white, the point *W* in the diagram. *D* and *E* are two arbitrary colors which have been mixed to produce a color *F*. The amounts of *D* and *E* required are proportional to the lengths *DF* and *EF*, respectively. (*From G. Wyszecki and W. S. Stiles, "Color Science," Wiley, New York, 1967.*)

Color mixtures, of course, are obtained by vector addition in three-dimensional color space. This is based on Grassmann's laws and neglects any of the nonlinearities mentioned. Suppose we add any two vectors **D** and **E** linearly and project them onto the chromaticity diagram. Then their sum **F** will lie on a line joining the endpoints of the two vectors at a location proportional to their respective magnitudes (see Figure 7.24). It is in this way that we are able to specify the color of any mixture of two arbitrary colors.

The CIE curve may be used to examine the gamut of colors available by mixing a particular choice of three primaries. Selecting a set for the purposes of reproduction, for example in television or paint mixtures, is equivalent to choosing three points in the chromaticity diagram. These define a triangle which may not necessarily include all the visible colors! Figure 7.25 shows the National Television System Committee (NTSC) standard in the United States; only the colors within the triangle are reproducible on the television monitor. One method of selecting three primaries is by ensuring that given a mixture of

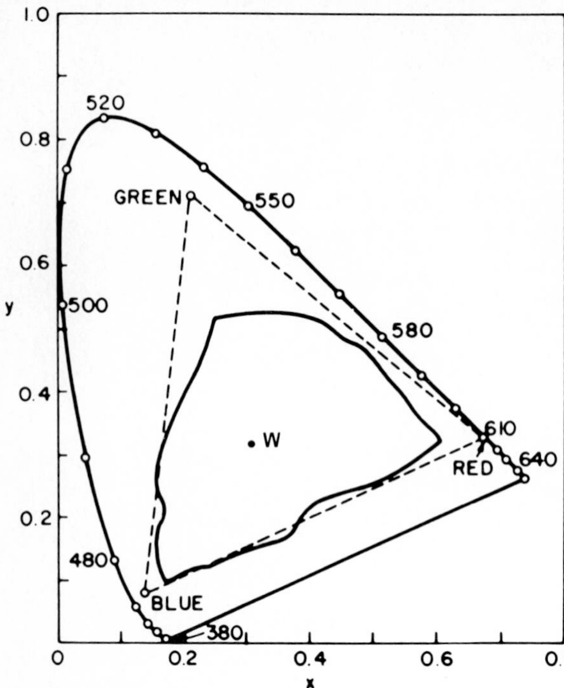

Figure 7.25 The CIE chromaticity diagram. The dashed triangle shows the NTSC color television gamut, and the solid curve shows the paint, pigment, and dye gamut. The point W is the theoretical white point at which $x = y = \frac{1}{3}$. [*Adapted from D. G. Fink (ed.), "Color Television Standards," McGraw-Hill, New York, 1955.*]

equal amounts of each component, the result is a "good white." Theoretically the point W in Figure 7.24, given by $x = y = 0.33$, is the hypothetical equal-energy source which yields white. However, we have already seen that there exists a larger region which is white and in which we may place standard reference illuminants such as A, B, and C in Figure 7.24. The first is an incandescent lamp, the second noon sunlight, and the third average daylight. We refer to two colors whose mixture passes through this white region as complementary colors (see Figure 7.26).

All the evidence we have discussed so far has pointed to the existence of two chromatic variables. Instead of using the rectangular (x, y) coordinate system to define these variables, it is of interest to consider a cylindrical coordinate system centered at the point W. Take, for example, the line in Figure 7.26 emanating from W and terminating on the locus. The point on the locus, here defined by $\lambda = 520$ nm, is what we have termed the dominant wavelength. Points along the line are seen to be defined in terms of the percentage of the total distance, that is, the "excitation purity" ratio. The perceptual correlates of the two physical variables dominant wavelength and excitation purity are referred to as "hue" and "saturation," respectively. The term hue is associated with the actual color name we would give such a color patch, as red or green or blue. It seems to be independent of illumination characteristics. But we should emphasize that there is no one-to-one correlation between hue and any parameter of either the tristimulus or trivariance spaces. Saturation, the second

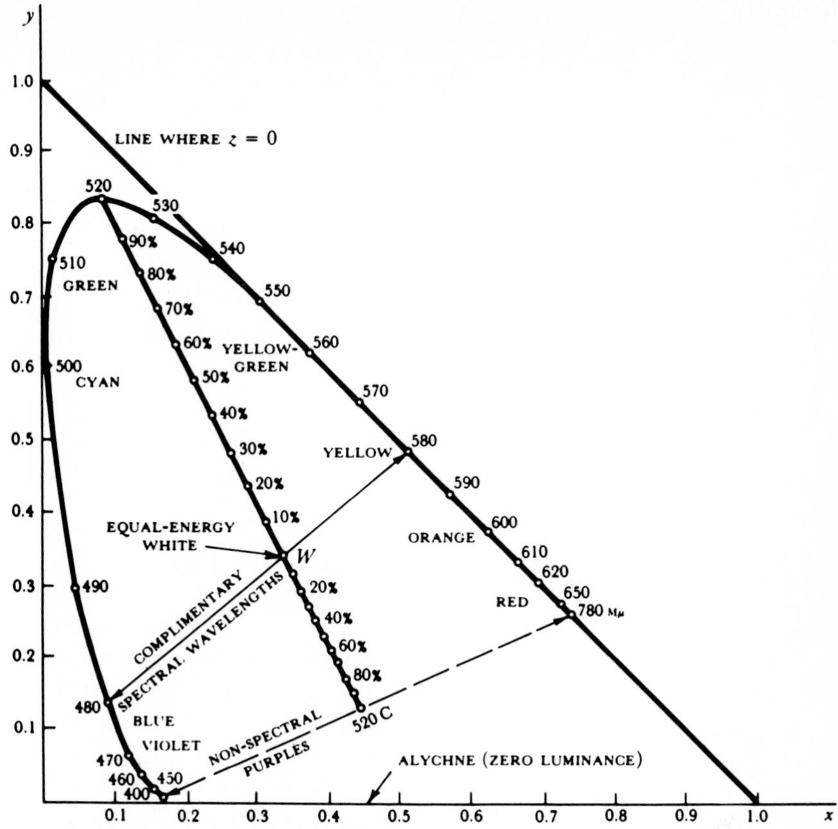

Figure 7.26 The CIE chromaticity diagram used to explicate the relationship between dominant wavelength and hue and between excitation purity and saturation. [*From R. M. Boynton, "Vision," in "Experimental Methods and Instrumentation in Psychology," J. Sidowski (ed.), McGraw-Hill, New York, 1966, pp. 273–330.*]

chromatic variable, refers to the degree of whiteness in the color. For example, red is just a saturated version of pink. The 1920 Schrödinger hypothesis stated that along a ray of constant hue the saturation changes monotonically. Of course, by now we appreciate that there must be other considerations which affect these variables, such as the luminosity, retinal locus, stimulus, and size and temporal factors.

The method by which our visual system actually codes hue and saturation is unknown. Uttal [71] has suggested that a hierarchy of color coding schemes exists, so that after the opponent color stage "there is some evidence in the cortex that the opponent mechanisms are encoded by a different peak spectral sensitivity for the ON and OFF responses of single cells . . . ." [71, p. 521]. Table 7.1 (from [71]) shows a hypothetical code in which the number of pluses or minuses indicates the strength of the response in a very rough manner. Whether or not this is accurate, it is obvious that the single achromatic and two

Table 7.1 A suggested hypothetical color coding scheme following the opponent color system

The number of pluses or minuses represents a coarse indication of the strength of the signal from an arbitrary base. They are then coded into the description shown in the first column

	B − Y	G − R	Wh − Bl
Unsaturated red	+ +	+ +	+ +
Saturated red	+	+ +	+
Unsaturated green	+ +	− −	+ +
Saturated green	+	− −	+
Unsaturated blue	− −	+ +	+ +
Saturated blue	− −	+	+

From W. R. Uttal, "The Psychobiology of Sensory Coding," Harper & Row, New York, 1973.

chromatic variables are somehow mapped into perceptual labels or color names.

Boynton [10] and Rosch [57] have suggested that yellow, green, blue, and red are the four psychologically unique hues, a theory which obviously conforms with our knowledge of the opponent color system. However, this fails to take cognizance of the other known chromatic colors. Nevertheless, the theory does seem to account for color mixtures which exist and even some which seem not to exist. Comparisons between human color-naming experiments involving these four basic primaries [12] and experiments with LGN cells of monkey are quite favorable [22], at least at longer wavelengths (above 500 nm). Further, the wavelength discrimination threshold for humans and monkeys is optimal at 490 and 590 nm, respectively. These are approximately the zero crossover points for the yellow-blue and red-green cells, respectively (see Figure 7.7), and we would therefore expect the highest sensitivities at these wavelengths.

A popular descriptive system, often employed for the purpose of color television calibration, is the Munsell color specification system. This psychological ordering of colors is based on a 100-division hue scale and a 10-division saturation and intensity scale, as shown in Figure 7.27. The "Munsell Book of Color" contains patches of color appropriate to positions in this scale, and these are meant to be used for comparison purposes [53]. They have also been calibrated with respect to the CIE data, with allowance for the transformation from one system into the other [77, pp. 479–487]. Figure 7.28*a* is the chromaticity diagram with 10 Munsell colors shown. Other naming boundaries are also possible, as shown in Figure 7.28*b*. We note that a linear relationship between the psychophysical data and their perceptual designations definitely does not exist. The question as to how close in the two-dimensional color space two colors may be and still be discriminated is, of course, pertinent here. The probability measure of color discrimination has been shown

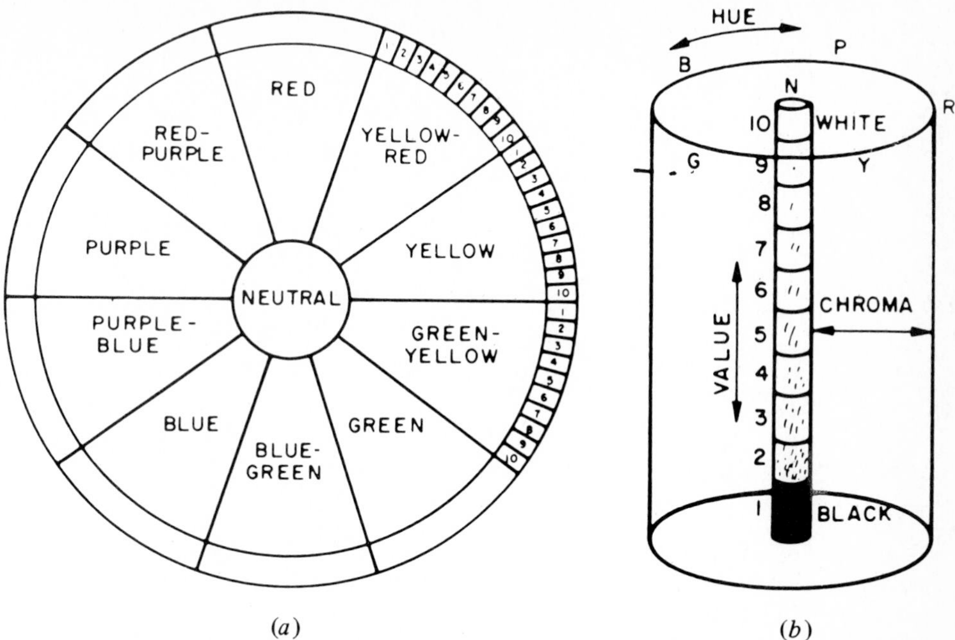

(*a*) (*b*)

Figure 7.27 Munsell color specification system. In the cylindrical Munsell color solid, various spectral hues are arranged in an equally divided circle. Saturation in this system is indicated by radial distance from the center. Brightness is denoted by the height of the cylindrical solid, with black at the bottom and unit, or normalized, white at the top of a 10-level cylinder. (*a*) Munsell hue circle. (*b*) Munsell color solid. (*From D. H. Pritchard, "U.S. Color Television Fundamentals—A Review," IEEE Transactions on Consumer Electronics, vol. CE-23, no. 4, November 1977, pp. 467–478, after J. W. Wentworth, "Color Television Engineering," McGraw-Hill, New York, 1955.*)

theoretically and experimentally to be described by ellipses [47]. Such a probability distribution function is most likely the result of the aggregate behavior of the threshold probability functions of individual and independent retinal cones. Attempts have been made to map these so-called MacAdam ellipses into a coordinate system in which they would become circular. This would then correspond to the situation in which equal distances are related to equal perceptual differences. An example is the CIE-UCS (Uniform Chromaticity Scale) system, but the results are not too interesting [77, Fig. 6.48].

Man is able to visually discriminate over 100,000 colors in psychophysical matching experiments. Naturally, common language does not support such a fine categorization. For example, over 3000 English color names are listed in an early study [48], while the more recent National Bureau of Standards compilation presents about 7500 descriptors [70]. A new color naming system based on commonly used English terms is suggested in [5, 6]. Five adjectives are employed for describing lightness or intensity: very dark, dark, medium, light, and very light. Saturation is qualified by four terms: grayish, moderate, strong, and vivid. The generic hues are chosen as red, orange, yellow, green, blue, and

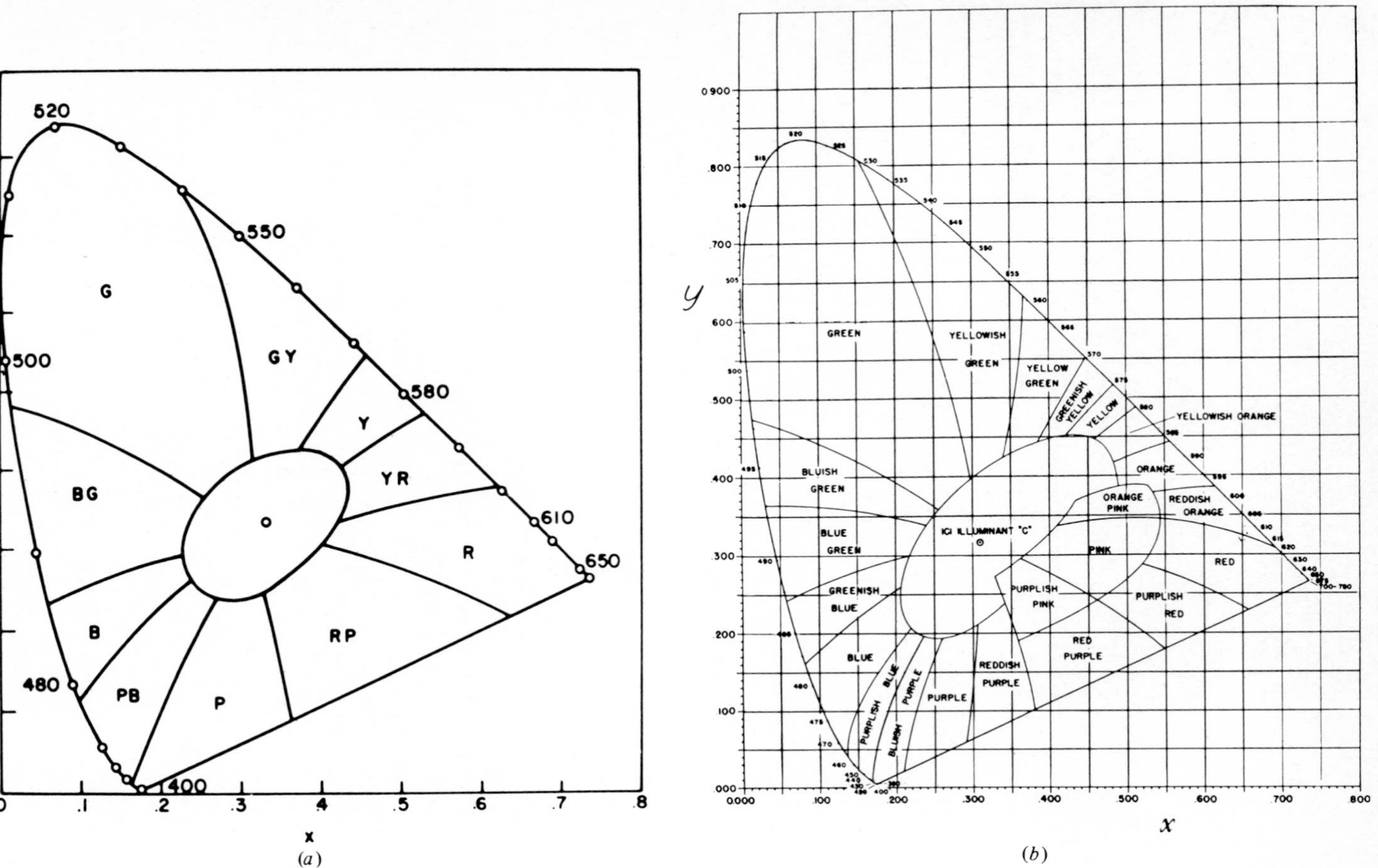
520
550
580
610
650
500
480
400
G
GY
Y
YR
R
RP
P
PB
B
BG
x
GREEN
YELLOWISH GREEN
YELLOW GREEN
GREENISH YELLOW
YELLOW
YELLOWISH ORANGE
ORANGE
ORANGE PINK
REDDISH ORANGE
RED
PINK
PURPLISH PINK
PURPLISH RED
RED PURPLE
REDDISH PURPLE
PURPLE
BLUISH PURPLE
PURPLISH BLUE
BLUE
GREENISH BLUE
BLUE GREEN
BLUISH GREEN
ICI ILLUMINANT "C"
y
x

(a)

(b)

purple, plus the achromatic shades black, white, and gray. A formal descriptive syntax based on these color names has been specified and produces a total of 627 different symbolic combinations. Not all these descriptors are synonymous with the Munsell colors. In addition, neither of these systems provides a computational mechanism for color processing, and therefore shading or highlighting cannot be accomplished. Quantitative color analysis must still be done by the techniques to be discussed in Section 7.5.

Notwithstanding the above considerations, ethnological studies suggest a maximum of only 11 basic categories, which oddly enough seem to exhibit a high degree of semantic universality across varying cultures [57]. Berlin and Kay [7] have suggested the following basic list of color names: black, white, red, yellow, green, blue, brown, purple, pink, orange, and gray. Of course there are many secondary terms; for example, it is known that the Eskimos of Canada have a multitude of designations for the color of snow. We would expect that the first two names on the list would be available in every language, and surprisingly there are nine examples of languages restricted to just these two gray shades. In addition to the three achromatic and eight chromatic colors included, a specific name for a ninth color, light blue, exists in Russian and Hungarian. It has been hypothesized that each culture maintains color categories selected from the set of 11 universals. Of course, not all the 2048 possible combinations have been found to occur (see [7, pp. 134–151] for a review of the literature on color vocabularies). Berlin and Kay [7] also suggest that there exists a particular evolutionary order in which children learn their colors, and that these "focal colors" are easier to remember and are learned faster and with fewer errors. There are seven stages in this evolution of the lexicon: (1) black and white; (2) red; (3) green or yellow; (4) yellow or green, depending on which one appears in step 3; (5) blue; (6) brown; (7) purple, pink, orange, and gray. Also note that even though they appear on the list, brown, purple, pink and orange are actually obtained as mixtures. Indeed, brown is not even recorded in the naming schemes of Figure 7.28. Apparently it is only perceived if a surface has a relatively low reflectance, which again implies the importance of this object property. Thus Boynton [10] contends that it occurs by induction, "the darkening of a yellow or orange color by a brighter surround field." If we view a brightly lit chocolate bar through a hole in a dark screen, it will appear to be orange in color. Thus a chocolate bar and an orange may have the same chromaticity but different surface reflectance properties [4]. Many experiments have been made in an attempt to associate spectral colors with color names and to provide a proper ordering. The spectral colors are, as we have seen, ordered

---

Figure 7.28 Two similar color naming systems. (*a*) The Munsell colors. (*b*) The standard ICI colorimetry system. [(*a*) *From D. A. Pritchard, "U.S. Color Television Fundamentals—A Review," IEEE Transactions on Consumer Electronics, vol. CE-23, no. 4, November 1977, pp. 467–478, after J. W. Wentworth, "Color Television Engineering," McGraw-Hill, New York, 1955*; (*b*) *from K. L. Kelly, "Color Designations for Lights," Journal of the Optical Society of America, vol. 33, no. 11, November 1943, pp. 627–632.*]

by the locus on the chromaticity diagram. Techniques such as color naming, hue discrimination, chromatic cancellation, and analysis of proximities have been employed to create a psychological ordering. There does not appear to be a simple relation between the two. Readers may consult a recent summary of this research by Boynton [10].

The naming of colors is further complicated by the knowledge that it is also important to take into account the surface properties of the object being viewed. We have seen that color perception is indicative of a relationship between the observer, the light source, and the objects themselves [4, 25]. How the physical and perceived color of objects are specifically defined is as yet unknown. However, there is obviously a high degree of color constancy notwithstanding these imperfections in our knowledge. Readers are referred to [11] for an interesting discussion of this complex subject.

We use color in our everyday lives for the purposes of identification and discrimination. It does not seem to be necessary for shape or contour perception, which is apparently accomplished in the achromatic plane. The visual system processes color in a very nonlinear fashion. This is, as we have seen, hierarchical in nature, leading to the use of the achromatic and two chromatic variables as the basis for some kind of sensory analysis. What the latter is we do not know exactly. That it results in our ability both to isolate objects and to provide them with an appropriate color description is universally accepted.

7.5 COLOR PROCESSING BY COMPUTER

The trivariance values $\mathbf{A}_L$, $\mathbf{A}_M$, and $\mathbf{A}_S$ are the result of a spectral filtering action by the cone responses $L(\lambda)$, $M(\lambda)$, and $S(\lambda)$ (see Figure 7.5). The tristimulus values depend on whether we are referring to the CIE RGB or XYZ system. The model of the former is specified by **R**, **G**, and **B**, whose filtering is a result of the color-matching functions $S_R(\lambda)$, $S_G(\lambda)$, and $S_B(\lambda)$ (see Figures 7.10 and 7.13*a*). Similarly, the latter yields tristimulus variables **X**, **Y**, and **Z** due to the color-matching functions $S_X(\lambda)$, $S_Y(\lambda)$, and $S_Z(\lambda)$ (see Figure 7.13*b*). Color processing by computer is usually performed by using a color wheel interposed between the transparency and the sensor [8, 9, 69] and sometimes by employing a color television camera. In either case the effect is to use three spectral filters $F_{\mathrm{P}}(\lambda)$, $F_{\Gamma}(\lambda)$, and $F_{\mathrm{B}}(\lambda)$ to obtain three color variables, which we shall here refer to as the trifilter variables Ρ, Γ, and Β for the red, green, and blue, respectively. The problem we shall address in this section is how to map from these actual computer measurements Ρ, Γ, and Β to the CIE chromaticity diagram and hence to a symbolic color name. We may also be interested in the reverse transformation for the purpose of color specification in computer graphics.

Figure 7.29 represents the two methods of color input to a computer. It is assumed that the trifilter values are digitized by an analog-to-digital converter to a maximum of, let us say, 6 bits (64 levels). In both cases the equivalent of

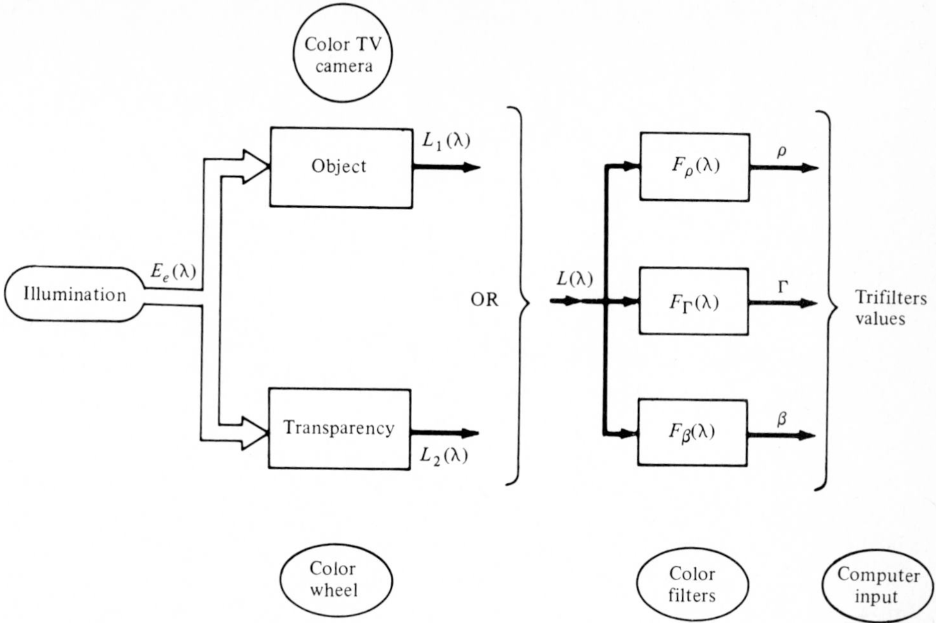

Figure 7.29 The derivation of the trifilter values which are input to the computer. The latter process is achieved by using an analog-to-digital converter, which we have arbitrarily assumed to yield 6 bits (64 levels).

three separate scans is required; the mechanically operated color wheel will obviously be a much slower proposition, although considerably less costly. The three filters are assumed to be ideal bandpass in a direct analogy to the processing of the three cone types. This is therefore equivalent to using yet another set of color primaries all of which are linearly related to each other [see Equation (7.9)]. In order to concentrate on the chromatic nature of the stimulus, we shall again introduce associated chromaticity coefficients ρ, γ, and β, defined as usual:

$$\rho = \frac{\mathrm{P}}{\mathrm{P}+\Gamma+\mathrm{B}} \tag{7.20}$$

$$\gamma = \frac{\Gamma}{\mathrm{P}+\Gamma+\mathrm{B}} \tag{7.21}$$

$$\beta = \frac{\mathrm{B}}{\mathrm{P}+\Gamma+\mathrm{B}} \tag{7.22}$$

where $\rho+\gamma+\beta=1$ and the total luminosity or intensity is given by the sum $\mathrm{P}+\Gamma+\mathrm{B}$. After digitization, the trifilter values define a color cube of dimension $64\times 64\times 64$, as shown in Figure 7.30. Colors are defined within the cube by the triplet $(\mathrm{P}, \Gamma, \mathrm{B})$, which specifies a vector in this three-space. If the

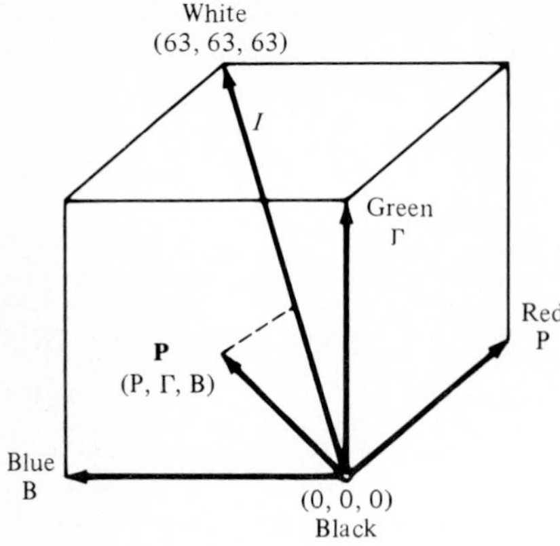

Figure 7.30 The color cube of dimension 64 × 64. The point **P** in three-space defines an arbitrary color given by the trifilter values (P, Γ, B). The intensity I of point **P** is determined by simple projection to the line joining white to black.

digitizer is assumed to work on the basis of transmittance, the point (0, 0, 0) is black and (63, 63, 63) is white, each an equal mixture of the three primaries. The line joining black and white defines a gray scale of intensity. The intensity I of an arbitrary color is determined by simple projection, as shown in the figure.

Our main objective is to use these trifilter values in conjunction with the known CIE chromaticity data to provide correct color names. The first step then, is the relationship between the XYZ tristimulus values and PΓB [77]:

$$\begin{bmatrix} X \\ Y \\ Z \end{bmatrix} = \begin{bmatrix} x_r/y_r & x_g/y_g & x_b/y_b \\ 1 & 1 & 1 \\ z_r/y_r & z_g/y_g & z_b/y_b \end{bmatrix} \begin{bmatrix} \mathrm{P} \\ \Gamma \\ \mathrm{B} \end{bmatrix} \tag{7.23}$$

where (x_r, y_r), (x_g, y_g), and (x_b, y_b) are the chromaticity coefficients for the red, green, and blue filters, respectively. A set of typical Kodak-Wratten separation filters is defined by the transmittance functions shown in Figure 7.31. The filter coordinates are easily obtained [77]. For example, the tristimulus values for the red filter are given by:

$$X = \int_\lambda E_e(\lambda) F_\Gamma(\lambda) S_X(\lambda)\, d\lambda \tag{7.24}$$

$$Y = \int_\lambda E_e(\lambda) F_\Gamma(\lambda) S_Y(\lambda)\, d\lambda \tag{7.25}$$

$$Z = \int_\lambda E_e(\lambda) F_\Gamma(\lambda) S_Z(\lambda)\, d\lambda \tag{7.26}$$

so that

$$x_r = X/Z \tag{7.27}$$

and

$$y_r = Y/Z \tag{7.28}$$

Similar equations are used for the blue and green filters. Note that these

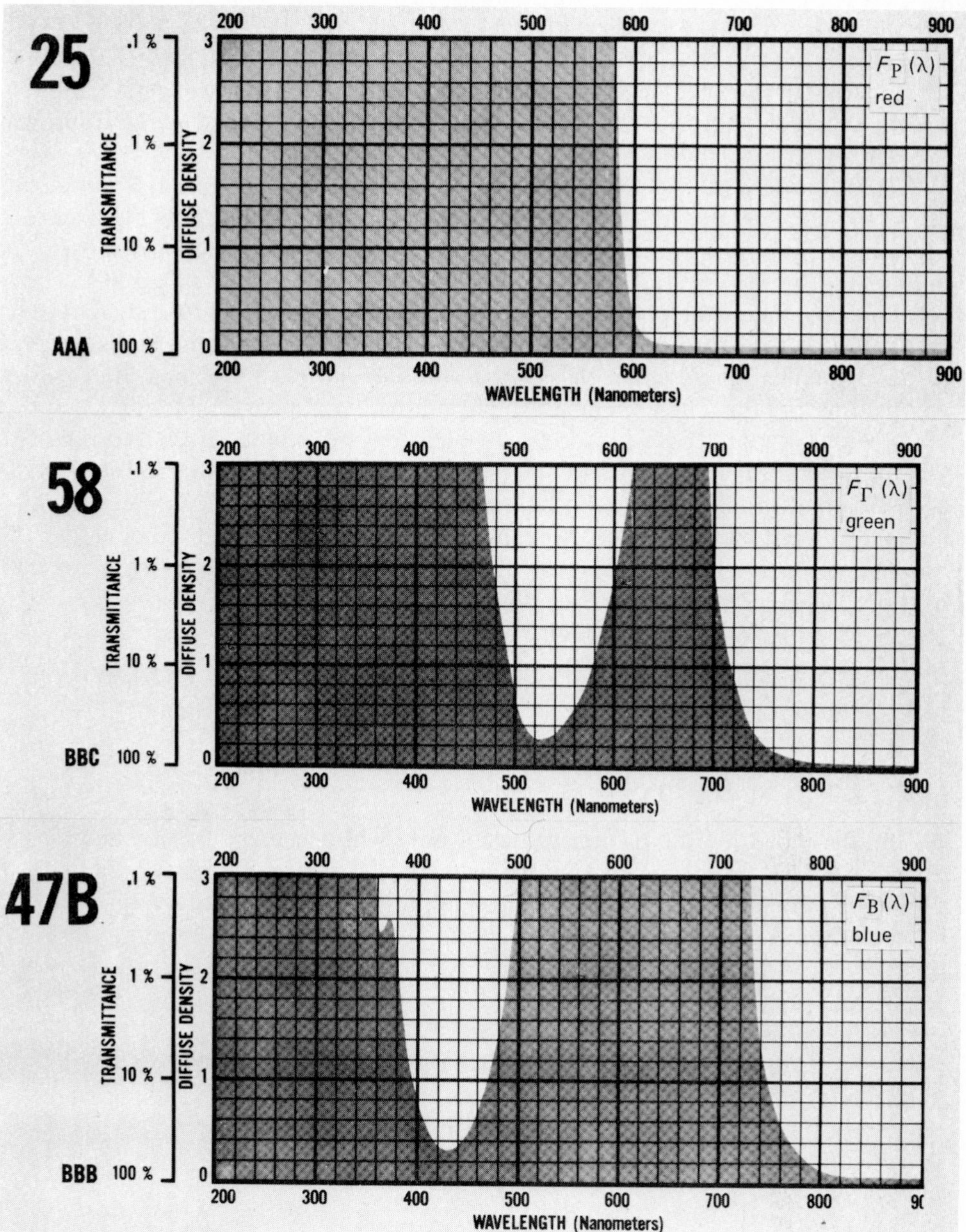

Figure 7.31 Response of three Kodak color separation filters. Note that the actual responses $F_P(\lambda)$, $F_\Gamma(\lambda)$, and $F_B(\lambda)$ must be determined in conjunction with an infrared blocking filter in order to yield the desired bandpass characteristics. (*From "Kodak Filters for Scientific and Technical Uses," Kodak Publication no. B-3, Eastman Kodak Co., Rochester, N.Y., 1981.*)

equations essentially determine the chromaticity coefficients of the filters by assuming them to be scanned objects. The coefficients are here assumed to be dependent on the specific spectral characteristics of the source illumination, which would usually be a fixed apparatus associated with the digitization mechanism.

There are several practical problems with this formulation. First, Equations (7.24) to (7.26) assume that the spectral response of the camera or digitizer is uniform over the bandwidth of interest. This can easily be compensated for by multiplying by the spectral response $S(\lambda)$ of the sensor (see Figure 2.10). The second issue is that the color separation filters are obviously not bandpass (see Figure 7.31); they do not block the infrared light which the sensor $S(\lambda)$ may respond to. The employment of a fourth filter, an infrared blocking filter, will compensate for this phenomenon. An alternative is to match $F_{\mathrm{P}}(\lambda)$, $F_{\Gamma}(\lambda)$, and $F_{\mathrm{B}}(\lambda)$ with an appropriate sensor $S(\lambda)$ which falls off rapidly in the red region of the spectral scale. Finally, the spectral responses and thus the chromaticity coefficients of the filters may not be precisely known. A compensation method directed toward correcting for these inaccuracies will be presented below.

The method is based on the use of a known color, most conveniently taken as pure white. In this case the chromaticity coefficients $x = y = z = \frac{1}{3}$ and $\mathrm{P} = \Gamma = \mathrm{B} = 63$. We wish to determine compensation factors C_ρ, C_γ, and C_β such that Equation (7.23) becomes:

$$\begin{bmatrix} X \\ Y \\ Z \end{bmatrix} = \begin{bmatrix} (x_r/y_r)C_\rho & (x_g/y_g)C_\gamma & (x_b/y_b)C_\beta \\ C_\rho & C_\gamma & C_\beta \\ (z_r/y_r)C_\rho & (z_g/y_g)C_\gamma & (z_b/y_b)C_\beta \end{bmatrix} \begin{bmatrix} \mathrm{P} \\ \Gamma \\ \mathrm{B} \end{bmatrix} \tag{7.29}$$

Let P_1, Γ_1, and B_1 be the trifilter value for pure white as computed by inverting Equation (7.23) and using reasonable values for the filter coordinates. Let P_2, Γ_2, and B_2 be the values observed experimentally by scanning a pure white light source. Then define

$$\mu = \max\left(\frac{\mathrm{P}_1}{\mathrm{P}_2}, \frac{\Gamma_1}{\Gamma_2}, \frac{\mathrm{B}_1}{\mathrm{B}_2}\right) \tag{7.30}$$

and the normalization factors are given by

$$C_\rho = \frac{\mathrm{P}_1}{\mu \mathrm{P}_2} \tag{7.31}$$

$$C_\gamma = \frac{\Gamma_1}{\mu \Gamma_2} \tag{7.32}$$

$$C_\beta = \frac{\mathrm{B}_1}{\mu \mathrm{B}_2} \tag{7.33}$$

This approach compensates for the nonlinearities in the spectral response of the sensor and for slight variations in the filter coordinates. What we are really accomplishing by using Equation (7.29) is to ensure that the values of P, Γ, and B are correctly mapped into the point W in the CIE plane (see Figure 7.24). Obviously the correction becomes less effective for trifilter values away from this white point in the chromaticity diagram.

Let us assume that we are able to obtain appropriate trifilter values from which X, Y, and Z can be computed according to Equation (7.29). Since P, Γ, and B are restricted in range, as shown in the color cube of Figure 7.30, then the scanned X, Y, and Z must also be restricted, as depicted in Figure 7.32. Note that if we are not interested in calibrated color variables, the raw trifilter variables or their values normalized by P_2, Γ_2, and B_2 may be substituted for the tristimulus values in the discussion that follows. As before (see Figure 7.21), the color cube contains within it a whole gamut of colors. We shall again arbitrarily select an equilateral triangle, shown in Figure 7.32, thereby yielding Figure 7.22. An arbitrary color vector **P** in the color cube is projected onto the point **P′** in the color triangle. We saw that the coordinates of **P′** are given by the chromaticity coefficients x, y, and z. The point W is at the triangle centroid, where $x = y = z = \frac{1}{3}$. Thus we have now succeeded in correlating the CIE XYZ color system with the trifilter variables.

Earlier it was noted that the color response may be described by the two chromatic variables hue and saturation plus a single achromatic variable. Referring to Figure 7.33, the hue of point **P′** is defined by the angle θ, where we have arbitrarily chosen the reference line WX to represent "zero hue." Saturation is given by the ratio of WP' to WC (see Figure 7.26). Hue (H) and saturation (S) may be defined as follows [68]:

$$H = \begin{cases} \theta & \text{if } z < y \\ 360 - \theta & \quad\;\, z > y \end{cases}$$

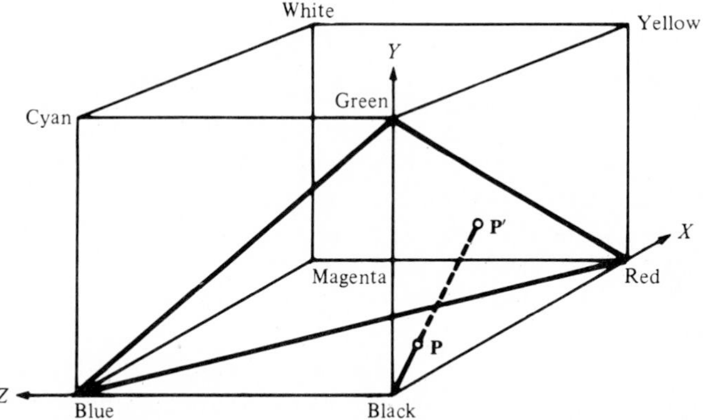

Figure 7.32 The resulting XYZ color cube from a given set of color separation filters. The colors are given at the extremities of the cube, but of course each point **P** within the cube has a particular color. The point **P** is projected onto the arbitrary color triangle at **P′**. This color triangle is so chosen as to form an equilateral triangle.

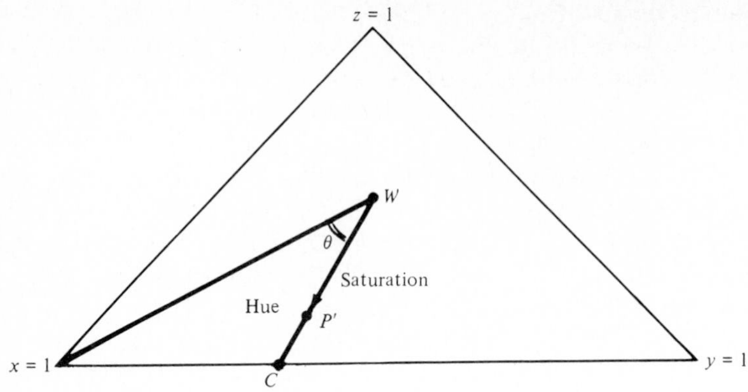

Figure 7.33 The unit plane or color triangle based on the *xyz* chromaticity coefficients. *W* defines the achromatic point at which $x = y = z - \frac{1}{3}$; *xW* is the hue reference line, chosen arbitrarily.

where
$$\theta = \arccos \frac{2x - y - z}{\sqrt{6}[(x - \frac{1}{3})^2 + (y - \frac{1}{3})^2 + (z - \frac{1}{3})^2]^{1/2}} \tag{7.34}$$

and
$$S = 1 - 3 \min(x, y, z) \tag{7.35}$$

An alternative formulation in terms of the tristimulus values is provided by Kender [39]:

$$H = \begin{cases} \theta & \text{if } Z < Y \\ 2\pi - \theta & \quad\; Z > Y \end{cases}$$

where
$$\theta = \arccos \frac{\frac{1}{2}[(X - Y) + (X - Z)]}{[(X - Y)^2 + (X - Z)(Y - Z)]^{1/2}} \tag{7.36}$$

and
$$S = 1 - 3\left[\frac{\min(X, Y, Z)}{X + Y + Z}\right] \tag{7.37}$$

A disadvantage of this color representation is that both H and S possess nonremovable singularities which result in undesirable instabilities [39]. These would definitely present problems to the region analysis algorithms to be discussed in Chapter 8. The reason is that the histograms of hue or saturation for a particular picture will be characterized by discontinuities such as gaps and impulses.

An alternative to the nonlinear hue and saturation transformation is to use a linear transformation of the trifilter values, such as the *YIQ* coordinates which constitute the NTSC transmission system. These were introduced for color television as a means of minimizing the signal bandwidth while simultaneously assuring good color perception. The information content is by no means evenly distributed among the intensity, hue, and saturation variables.

For example, we observe that the Munsell color system assigns 100 levels to hue and only 10 to saturation. Typically for a color television display, 64 levels are adequate for intensity while only 32 levels are sufficient for hue and 8 for saturation [14]. This is perhaps related to the fact that most colors in scenes of interest have chromaticity coefficients lying near the white point. The *YIQ* system also takes advantage of this property. The *Y* luminance signal, which can be used to display a monochrome picture, is transmitted over a bandwidth of 4 MHz; the *I* (in-phase) signal codes the orange-cyan color difference axis within a bandwidth of 1.5 MHz; and the *Q* (quadrature) signal codes the green-magenta color difference axis information within a bandwidth of 0.5 MHz, to make a total of 6 MHz. The relationship between the trifilter values and the *YIQ* system is given by:

$$\begin{bmatrix} Y \\ I \\ Q \end{bmatrix} = \begin{bmatrix} 0.299 & 0.587 & 0.144 \\ 0.596 & -0.274 & -0.322 \\ 0.211 & -0.523 & 0.312 \end{bmatrix} \begin{bmatrix} \mathrm{P} \\ \Gamma \\ \mathrm{B} \end{bmatrix} \tag{7.38}$$

Another alternative is to use a specifically chosen linear transformation based on a thorough study of the requirements for region segmentation [55]. Using a conventional Karhunen-Loève analysis formalism on a restricted set of natural images yields the following color variables in order of significance: $\frac{1}{3}(\mathrm{P} + \Gamma + \mathrm{B})$, $(\mathrm{P} - \mathrm{B})$, and $\frac{1}{2}(2\Gamma - \mathrm{P} - \mathrm{B})$.

Having discussed the mapping from the input filter space to the CIE system, let us now consider the actual naming of colors. There are two points of view. One is concerned with picture description by computer, where it is of interest to symbolically code a given region with a color name. The second involves picture generation, in which it is desirable for the user to interact with the computer by specifying colors verbally for the purpose of display. Since we have seen that color is generally given by two variables, in this case it would also be necessary to supply the third intensity variable. Readers are referred to [2, 28, 37, 60] for a discussion of these issues as they pertain to computer graphics in color.

One approach to color naming by computer is to employ the (x, y) chromaticity coefficients to cue into the psychophysical encoding of Figure 7.28*b*, which provides 22 colors, or Figure 7.28*a*, with the 10 primary Munsell colors. Of course, a complete implementation of the latter would allow for a much finer set of designations. The approach is identical in both cases in that a table is created to represent the boundaries in the chromaticity diagram. Given an (x, y) coordinate from Equation (7.29), the specific color name for the particular trifilter value may be looked up in the table.

There are some difficulties with such a technique. Man-made colors, such as might be found in advertising copy or cartoons, are usually highly saturated. This would place them far from the central white area and generally yield an unambiguous name. However, natural scenes, which might contain areas of green foliage, or skin tones possess very low saturation values [33]. Therefore they tend to map into a small region circumscribed around the white point, where it is very difficult to make a proper differentiation. It is interesting to note the distinction made between the actual color of natural objects, their memorized color, and the preferred color for reproduction [62]. The latter is always a more saturated version of the original. This suggests one solution to the problem: before encoding the colors, some form of color enhancement should be performed.

Color enhancement could be done by use of pseudocolor, a methodology developed for computer graphics [58, 59]. Pseudocolor images are created by assigning a color to a gray level in a black-and-white picture according to an arbitrary transformation. A quite common color ordering is one based on the colors of the rainbow. One reason for employing color is that the human visual system is very sensitive to color differences. In addition, we have seen in Chapter 6 that intensity may be optimally encoded by 3 bits or adequately encoded by 6, 7, or 8 bits. On the other hand, we are able to discriminate many thousands of distinct colors [66]. Figure 7.34 is an example of a black-and-white radiographic image which has been pseudocolored by assigning different parts of the intensity range to a single hue value (see Figure 7.35*a* for the specific assignment). In this case, highly saturated colors have been chosen to enhance the visual presentation. An alternative mapping, shown in Figure 7.35*b*, yields the striking results of Figure 7.36. We note that the effect of histogram equalization is also enhanced by the introduction of color. This type of color enhancement seems to be appropriate to medical imaging for diagnosis. An example is computer angiography, in which the blood dynamics of body organs are studied [32]. Another application of pseudocolor is the presentation of

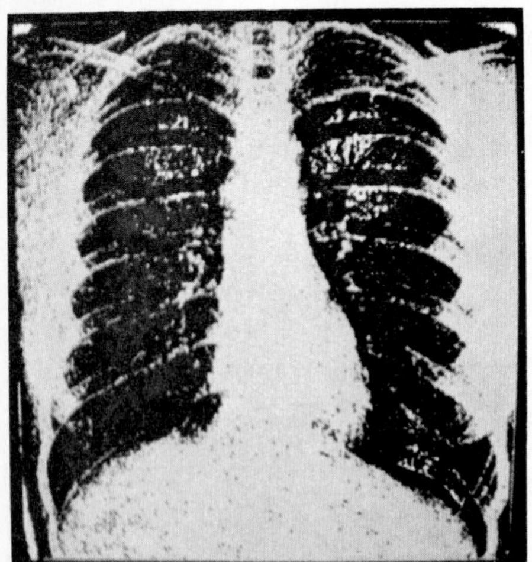

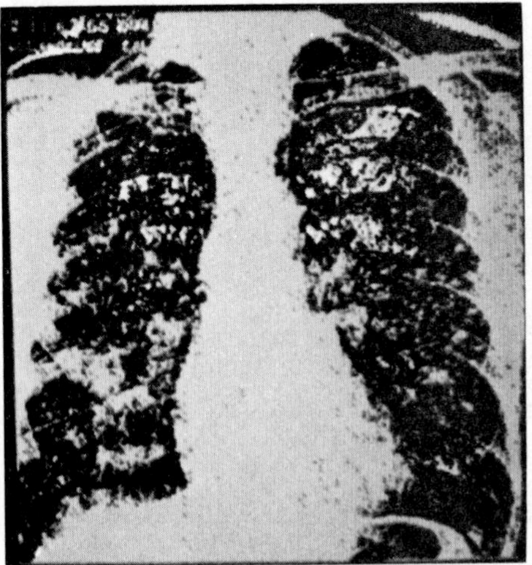

Figure 7.34 Lung x-rays enhanced by using the pseudocolor scheme of Figure 7.35*a*. The lung on the left is normal, while the one on the right is from a patient with pneumoconiosis. (*From H. C. Andrews, A. G. Tescher, and R. P. Kruger, "Image Processing by Digital Computer," IEEE Spectrum, vol. 9, no. 7, July 1972, pp. 20–32.*) (See back endpapers for the color figures.)

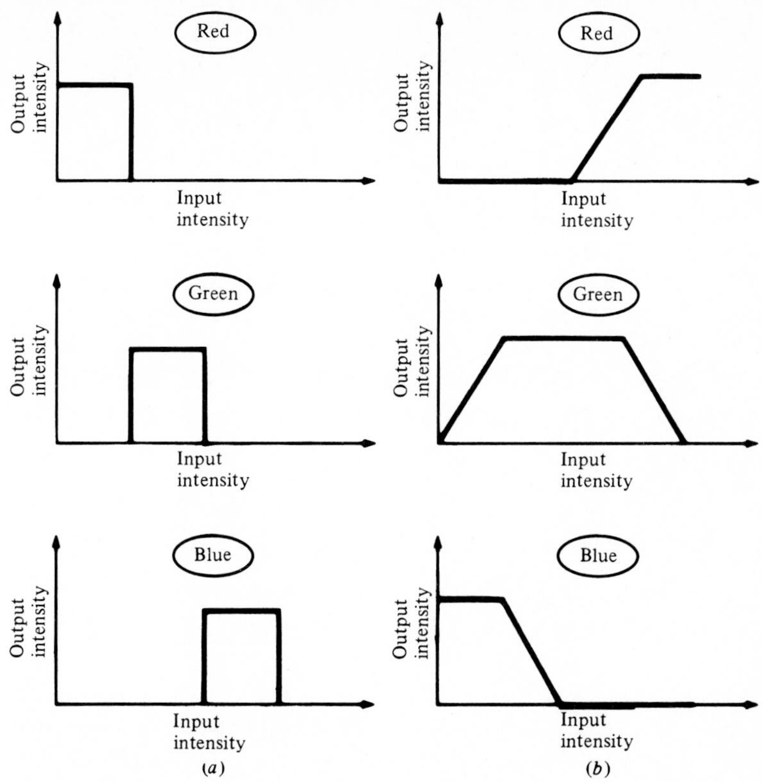

Figure 7.35 Two different pseudocolor assignment schemes. (*Adapted from H. C. Andrews, A. G. Tescher, and R. P. Kruger, "Image Processing by Digital Computer," IEEE Spectrum, vol. 9, no. 7, July 1972, pp. 20–32.*)

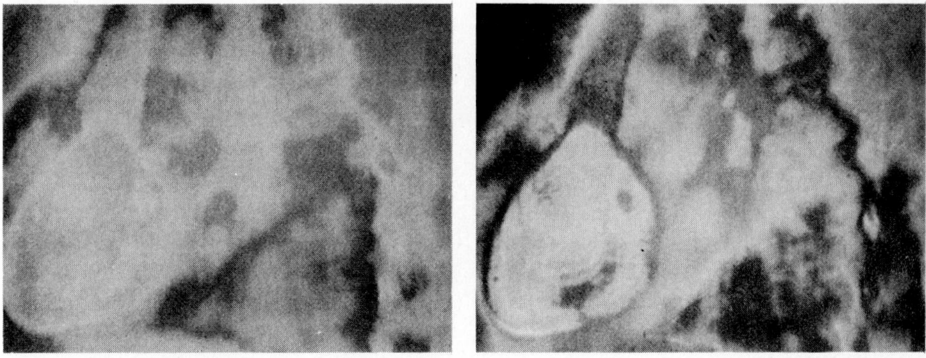

Figure 7.36 The pseudocolor process applied to a photograph of a dog's heart on the basis of Figure 7.35*b*. On the left is the original image; on the right is the pseudocolored version of the histogram equalized version. (*From H. C. Andrews, A. G. Tescher, and R. P. Kruger, "Image Processing by Digital Computer," IEEE Spectrum, vol. 9, no. 7, July 1972, pp. 20–32.*) (See back endpapers for the color figure.)

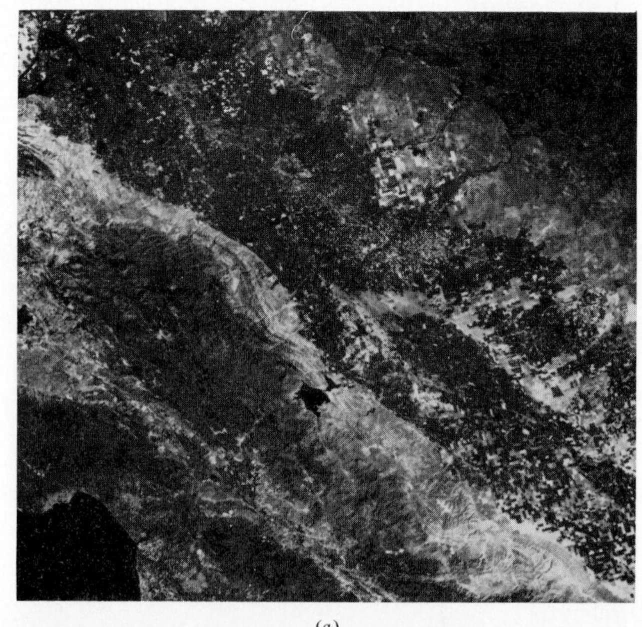

(*a*)

(*b*)

remote sensing data [69]. In this case the multispectral scanner data are arbitrarily mapped into colors, as shown in Figure 7.37.

As an extension of these techniques, it is obviously also possible to map one set of colors into another set of colors. A transformation of this kind might yield more suitable chromaticity values, which would then define more appropriate color names. Such a technique remains to be developed. However, this section does demonstrate that it is feasible to use the trifilter values and correlate them with accepted psychophysical experimental results to output a color name or symbol.

REFERENCES

1. Abramov, I., "Further Analysis of the Responses of LGN Cells," *Journal of the Optical Society of America*, vol. 58, 1968, pp. 574–579.
2. Allison, G. (ed.), *Tekscope*, Tektronix, Inc., Beaverton, Ore., vol. 10, no. 4, 1978.
3. Beck, J., "Surface Color Perception," Cornell University Press, Ithaca, N.Y., 1972.
4. Beck, J., "The Perception of Surface Color," *Scientific American*, vol. 233, no. 2, August 1975, pp. 62–75.
5. Berk, T., Brownston, L., and Kaufman, A., "A New Color-Naming System for Graphics Languages," *IEEE Computer Graphics and Applications*, vol. 2, no. 3, May 1982, pp. 37–44.
6. Berk, T., Brownston, L., and Kaufman, A., "A Human Factors Study of Color Notation Systems for Computer Graphics," *Communications of the ACM*, vol. 25, no. 8, August 1982, pp. 547–550.
7. Berlin, B., and Kay, P., "Basic Color Terms: Their Universality and Evolution," University of California Press, Berkeley, 1969.
8. Billingsley, F. C., "Computer-Generated Color Image Display of Lunar Spectral Reflectance Ratios," *Photographic Science and Engineering*, vol. 16, no. 1, January-February 1972, pp. 51–57.

Figure 7.37 An example of pseudocoloring applied to multispectral scanning data. (*a*) Color composite [Landsat spectral bands 4 (0.5 to 0.6 μm), 5 (0.6 to 0.7 μm), and 7 (0.8 to 1.1 μm)] of central California. Each digitally processed band is represented by a gray-level image which is arbitrarily assigned to a different color primary. The three registered color images are then combined to produce an "artificial" color picture by using each as one of the three inputs to a color monitor. Various agricultural, geological, hydrologic, and urban features can be observed in the color composite. For example, Monterey Bay is at the left. Near it, the San Andreas fault is seen running in a northwest-southeast direction. The Diablo Mountain range is indicated by a brownish color. The dark blue region in the center is the San Luis reservoir. Irrigation canals and aqueducts served by it are readily visible. Various urbanized areas can also be spotted on the basis of both color (generally light blue) and pattern, for example, San Jose (along the left border, near the middle) and Salinas (just west of Monterey Bay, at the bottom). Other urban areas are observed in the San Joaquin Valley. (*b*) Representational-color composite subimage [bottom right corner of image in (*a*)] of the San Joaquin valley showing agricultural features: red—alfalfa and other healthy green crops; orange—safflower; light yellow—barley; blue-green—fallow fields; blue—water; and black—barley fields recently harvested (and burned over). Clearly, spectral classification can be employed to identify crops and map the associated areas. (*From R. Bernstein, "Digital Image Processing of Earth Observation Sensor Data," IBM Journal of Research and Development, vol. 20, no. 1, January 1976, pp. 40–57.*) (See back endpapers for the color figures.)

9. Billingsley, F. C., Goetz, A. F. H., and Lindsley, J. N., "Color Differentiation by Computer Image Processing, *Photographic Science and Engineering*, vol. 14, no. 1, January-February 1970, pp. 28–35.
10. Boynton, R. M., "Color, Hue, and Wavelength," in Carterette, E. C., and Friedman, M. P. (eds.), "Handbook of Perception," vol. V, Academic, New York, 1975, pp. 301–347.
11. Boynton, R. M., "Color in Contour and Object Perception," in Carterette, E. C., and Friedman, M. P. (eds.), "Handbook of Perception," vol. VIII, "Perceptual Coding," Academic, New York, 1978, pp. 173–199.
12. Boynton, R. M., and Gordon, J., "Bezold-Brücke Hue Shift Measured by Color-Naming Technique," *Journal of the Optical Society of America*, vol. 55, no. 1, 1965, pp. 78–86.
13. Brindley, G. S., "Physiology of the Retina and the Visual Pathway," Arnold, London, 1969.
14. Buchanan, M. D., and Prendergrass, R., "Digital Image Processing: Can Intensity, Hue, and Saturation Replace Red, Green, and Blue?" *Electro-Optical Systems Design*, vol. 12, no. 3, March 1980, pp. 29–36.
15. Buchsbaum, G., "A Spatial Processor Model for Object Color Perception," *Journal of the Franklin Institute*, vol. 310, no. 1, July 1980, pp. 1–26.
16. Buchsbaum, G., "The Retina as a Two-Dimensional Detector Array in the Context of Color Vision Theories and Signal Detection Theory," *Proceedings of the IEEE*, vol. 69, no. 7, July 1981, pp. 772–786.
17. Buchsbaum, G., and Goldstein, J. L., "Optimum Probabilistic Processing in Colour Perception I. Colour, Discrimination," *Proceedings of the Royal Society, London*, ser. B., 1979, pp. 229–247.
18. Buchsbaum, G., and Goldstein, J. L., "Optimum Probabilistic Processing in Colour Perception II. Colour Vision as Template Matching," *Proceedings of the Royal Society, London*, ser. B, 1979, pp. 249–266.
19. Cornsweet, T., "Visual Perception," Academic, New York, 1970.
20. De Valois, R. L., "Behavioral and Electrophysiological Studies of Primate Vision," in Neff, W. D. (ed.), "Contributions to Sensory Physiology," vol. 1, Academic Press, New York, 1965, pp. 137–178.
21. De Valois, R. L., "Central Mechanisms of Color Vision," in "Handbook of Sensory Physiology," vol. VIII, "Central Processing of Visual Information," part A, Springer-Verlag, New York, 1973, pp. 209–253.
22. De Valois, R. L., Abramov, I., and Jacobs, G. H., "Analysis of Response Patterns of LGN Cells," *Journal of the Optical Society of America*, vol. 56, no. 7, 1966, pp. 966–977.
23. De Valois, R. L., Smith, C. J., Kitai, S. T., and Kardy, A. J., "Response of Single Cells in Monkey Lateral Geniculate Nucleus to Monochromatic Light," *Science*, vol. 127, no. 3292, 1958, pp. 238–239.
24. Ebenhoh, A., and Hemminger, H., "Scaling of Color Sensation by Magnitude Estimation: A Contribution to Opponent-Colors Theory," *Biological Cybernetics*, vol. 39, no. 3, 1981, pp. 227–237.
25. Evans, R. M., "The Perception of Color," Wiley, New York, 1974.
26. Faugeras, O. D., "Digital Color Image Processing and Psychophysics Within the Framework of a Human Visual Model," Ph.D. dissertation, University of Utah, Salt Lake City, June 1976.
27. Faugeras, O.D., "Digital Color Image Processing Within the Framework of a Human Visual System," *IEEE Transactions on Acoustics, Speech and Signal Processing*, vol. ASSP-27, no. 4, August 1979, pp. 380–393.
28. Field, H. P., "Color Measurement of Displays," *Electro-Optical Systems Design*, October 1978, pp. 34–41.
29. Gouras, P., "Identification of Cone Mechanisms in Monkey Ganglion Cells," *Journal of Physiology, London*, vol. 199, no. 3, 1968, pp. 533–548.
30. Graham, C. H. (ed.), "Vision and Visual Perception," Wiley, New York, 1965.
31. Green, D. G., and Fast, M. B., "On the Appearance of Mach Bands in Gradients of Varying Colors," *Vision Research*, vol. 11, no. 10, 1971, pp. 1147–1155.

32. Höhne, K. H., Böhm, M., Erbe, W., Nicolae, G. C., Pfeiffer, G., and Sonne, B., "Computer Angiography: A New Tool for X-Ray Functional Diagnostics," *Medical Progress Through Technology*, vol. 6, 1978, pp. 23–28.
33. Honjyo, K., and Shimada, T., "Evaluation of Color Discrimination in the White Region," *Journal of the Optical Society of America*, vol. 69, no. 10, October 1979, pp. 1355–1358.
34. Horn, B. K., "On Lightness," AI Memo 295, Artificial Intelligence Laboratory, Massachusetts Institute of Technology, Cambridge, Mass., October 1973.
35. Hurvich, L. M., and Jameson, D., "An Opponent-Process Theory of Color Vision," *Psychological Review*, vol. 64, no. 6, 1957, pp. 384–404.
36. Jacobson, J. Z., and McKinnon, G. E., "Colored Mach Bands," *Canadian Journal of Psychology*, vol. 23, no. 1, 1969, pp. 56–65.
37. Joblove, G. H., and Greenberg, D., "Color Spaces for Computer Graphics," SIGRAPH 1978, Proceedings Aug. 23–25, 1978; *Computer Graphics, SIGGRAPH-ACM*, vol. 13, no. 3, August 1978, pp. 20–25.
38. Judd, D. B., "Appraisal of Land's Work on Two-Primary Color Projections," *Journal of the Optical Society of America*, vol. 50, no. 3, 1960, pp. 254–268.
39. Kender, R. R., "Saturation, Hue, and Normalized Color; Calculation, Digitization Effects, and Use," Technical Report, Department of Computer Science, Carnegie-Mellon University, Pittsburgh, November 1976.
40. Land, E. H., "Color Vision and the Natural Image: part I, "*Proceedings of the National Academy of Sciences*, vol. 45, no. 1, January 1959, pp. 115–129.
41. Land, E. H., "Color Vision and the Natural Image: part II," *Proceedings of the National Academy of Sciences*, vol. 45, no. 1, April 1959, pp. 636–644.
42. Land, E. H., "Experiments in Color Vision," in Teevan, R. C., and Birney, R. C. (eds.), "Color Vision," Van Nostrand, Princeton, N.J., 1961, chap. 16, pp. 162–183.
43. Land, E. H., "The Retinex," *American Scientist*, vol. 52, 1964, pp. 247–264.
44. Land, E. H., "The Retinex Theory of Color Vision," *Proceedings of the IEEE*, vol. 47, no. 1, 1974, pp. 23–58.
45. Land, E. H., "The Retinex Theory of Color Vision," *Scientific American*, vol. 237, no. 6, December 1977, pp. 108–128.
46. Land, E. H., and McCann, J. J., "Lightness and Retinex Theory," *Journal of the Optical Society of America*, vol. 61, no. 1, January, 1971, pp. 1–11.
47. MacAdam, D. L., "Visual Sensitivities to Color Differences in Daylight," *Journal of the Optical Society of America*, vol. 32, no. 5, 1942, pp. 247–274.
48. Maerz, A., and Paul, M., "Dictionary of Color," McGraw-Hill, New York, 1930, 1950.
49. Marr, D., "An Essay on the Primate Retina," A.I. Memo 296, Massachusetts Institute of Technology, Artificial Intelligence Laboratory, Cambridge, Mass., January 1974.
50. Massof, R. W., and Bird, J. F., "A General Zone Theory of Color and Brightness Vision. I. Basic Formulation," *Journal of the Optical Society of America*, vol. 68, no. 11, November 1978, pp. 1465–1471.
51. McCann, J. J., McKee, S., and Taylor, T. H., "Quantitative Studies in Retinex Theory—A Comparison Between Theoretical Predictions and Observer Responses to the Color Mondrian Experiments," *Vision Research*, vol. 16, May 1976, pp. 445–458.
52. Michael, C. R., "Receptive Fields of Single Optic Nerve Fibers in a Mammal with an All-Cone Retina," *Journal of Neurophysiology*, vol. 31, no. 2, March 1968, pp. 249–282.
53. Munsell, A. H., "Munsell Book of Color," Munsell Color Co., Inc., 1929.
54. Muntz, W. R. A., "Vision in Frogs," *Scientific American*, March 1964, pp. 111–119.
55. Ohta, Y.-I., Kanade, T., and Sakai, T., "Color Information for Region Segmentation," *Computer Graphics and Image Processing*, vol. 13, 1980, pp. 222–241.
56. Rodieck, R. W., "The Vertebrate Retina, Principles of Structure and Function," Freeman, San Francisco, 1973.
57. Rosch, E., "Human Categorization," in Warren, N. (ed.), "Advances in Cross-Culture Psychology," vol. 1, Academic, London, 1977.
58. Sheppard, J. J., Stratton, R. H., and Gazley, C. G., "Pseudocolor as a Means of Image Enhancement," *American Journal of Optometry*, vol. 46, 1969, pp. 735–754.

59. Sloan, K. R., Jr., and Brown, C. M., "Color Map Techniques," *Computer Graphics and Image Processing*, vol. 10, no. 4, August 1979, pp. 297–317.
60. Smith, A. R., "Color Gamut Transform Pairs," SIGRAPH '78, Proceedings, Aug. 23–25, 1978; *Computer Graphics, SIGGRAPH-ACM*, vol. 13, no. 3, August 1978, pp. 12–19.
61. Speranskaya, N. O., "Determination of Spectrum Color Co-ordinates for Twenty-Seven Normal Observers," *Optics and Spectroscopy*, vol. 7, no. 5, 1959, pp. 424–428.
62. Staes, K., "The CIE Color Rendering Index and Its Application To Color Photography," *Journal of Applied Photographic Engineering*, vol. 3, 1977, pp. 209–215.
63. Stiles, W. S., "The Basic Data of Color Matching," The Physical Society Yearbook, London, 1955, pp. 44–65.
64. Stiles, W. S., and Burch, J. M., "N.P.L. Colour-Matching Investigation: Final Report (1958)," *Optica Acta*, vol. 6, no. 1, January 1959, pp. 1–26.
65. Stockham, T. G. Jr., "Image Processing in the Context of a Visual Model," *Proceedings of the IEEE*, vol. 60, no. 7, July 1972, pp. 828–842.
66. Stratton, R. H., and Sheppard, J. J. Jr., "A Photographic Technique for Image Enhancement: Pseudocolor Three-Separation Process," Rand Report, R-596-PR, Santa Monica, October 1970.
67. Svaetichin, G., and MacNichol, E. F. Jr., "Retinal Mechanisms for Chromatic and Achromatic Vision," *Annals of the New York Academy of Sciences*, vol. 74, 1958, pp. 385–404.
68. Tenenbaum, J. M., Garvey, T. D., Weyl, S., and Wolf, H. C., "An Interactive Facility for Scene Analysis Research," Stanford Research Institute, Artificial Intelligence Center, Technical Note 87, January 1974.
69. Underwood, S. A., and Aggarwal, J. K., "Interactive Computer Analysis of Aerial Color Infrared Photographs," *Computer Graphics and Image Processing*, vol. 6, no. 1, 1977, pp. 1–24.
70. U.S. National Bureau of Standards, "Color: Universal Language and Dictionary of Names," NBS Special Publication 440, U.S. Government Printing Office, Washington, S.D. catalog no. C13.10:440, 1976.
71. Uttal, W. R., "The Psychobiology of Sensory Coding," Harper & Row, New York, 1973.
72. Wallach, H., "The Perception of Neutral Colors," *Scientific American*, vol. 208, no. 1, January, 1963, pp. 107–116.
73. Walls, G. L., "Land! Land!," *Psychological Bulletin*, vol. 57, no. 1, 1960, pp. 29–48.
74. Wheeler, L., "Color Matching Responses to Red Light of Varying Luminance and Purity in Complex and Simple Images," *Journal of the Optical Society of America*, vol. 53, 1963, pp. 978–993.
75. Wiesel, T. N., and Hubel, D. H., "Spatial and Chromatic Interactions in the Lateral Geniculate Body of the Rhesus Monkey," *Journal of Neurophysiology*, vol. 29, no. 6, 1966, pp. 1115–1156.
76. Woolfson, M. M., "Some New Aspects of Color Perception," *IBM Journal for Research and Development*, vol. 3, no. 4, 1959, pp. 312–325.
77. Wyszecki, G., and Stiles, W. S., "Color Sciences," Wiley, New York, 1967.
78. Zeki, S. M., "Functional Specialization in the Visual Cortex of the Rhesus Monkey," *Nature*, vol. 274, no. 5670, Aug. 3, 1978, pp. 423–428.
79. Zeki, S. M., "The Representation of Colours in the Cerebral Cortex," *Nature*, vol. 284, no. 5755, Apr. 3, 1980, pp. 412–418.

BIBLIOGRAPHY

The most complete book on the subject of color is by Wyszecki and Stiles [24], while an excellent up-to-date review can be found in Buchsbaum [4]. Readers may also be interested in examining some of the early and important references on color by Hering [10], Helmholtz [9], Grassmann [8], König and Dietrici [18], Young [25], Schrödinger [22], and Newton [21]. Two collections of papers on the subject are by MacAdam [19] and Teevan and Birney [22]. Additional material for Section 7.2 can be found in [2] and [6]. Color blindness is discussed in [1] and [5].

The modeling of opponent-color processing is an interesting example of a psychophysical theory preceding neurophysiological verification by about 100 years. Maybe this is a justification for the large number of hypothetical psychological models which have been suggested over the years. Some additional references are found in [7, 11, 12, 17, 20].

Not much emphasis has been placed in this chapter on the effect of the properties of a surface on the perception of color. Although this is an extremely pertinent aspect of the whole phenomenon, it has so far not been possible to specify a complete and unequivocal model. Perhaps the reason for this, analogous to the discussion in Section 6.2, is that global processes are involved which await a better understanding. The book by Beck [3] provides the most complete coverage of this subject at this time. An earlier reference is by Judd [16].

Color processing by computer as discussed in this chapter is a relatively new subject. Consequently, there exist few articles and no books. In addition to the references cited, readers may wish to consult the papers by Ito [13, 14, 15].

1. Alpern, M., "What Is It That Confines in a World Without Color?" *Investigative Ophthalmology*, vol. 13, no. 9, 1974, pp. 648–674.
2. Autrum, H., and Thomas, I., "Comparative Physiology of Color Vision in Animals," in "Handbook of Sensory Physiology," vol. III/3, part A, Springer-Verlag, New York, 1973, pp. 661–692.
3. Beck, J., "Surface Color Perception," Cornell University Press, Ithaca, N.Y., 1972.
4. Buchsbaum, G., "The Retina as a Two-Dimensional Detector Array in the Context of Color Vision Theories and Signal Detection Theory," *Proceedings of the IEEE*, vol. 69, no. 7, July 1981, pp. 772–786.
5. Cruz-Coke, R., "Color Blindness," Thomas, Springfield, Ill., 1970.
6. De Valois, R. L., "Central Mechanisms of Color Vision," in "Handbook of Sensory Physiology," vol. III/3, part A, Springer-Verlag, New York, 1973, pp. 209–253.
7. Frei, W., "A New Model of Color Vision and Some Practical Implications," University of Southern California Image Processing Institute, Semiannual Technical Report, USCIPI Report 530, March 31, 1974, pp. 128–143.
8. Grassmann, H., "On the Theory of Compound Colors," *Philosophy Magazine*, vol. 7, 1854, pp. 254–264.
9. Helmholtz, H. L. F., "Treatise on Physiological Optics," Southall, J. P. C. (trans.), *Journal of the Optical Society of America*, 1924.
10. Hering, E., "Outlines of a Theory of the Light Sense," Hurvich, L. M., and Jameson, D. (trans.), Harvard University Press, Cambridge, Mass. 1964.
11. Hurvich, L. M., and Jameson, D., "Some Quantitative Aspects of an Opponents Colours Theory, II. Brightness Saturation and Hue in Normal and Dichromatic Vision," *Journal of the Optical Society of America*, vol. 45, 1955, pp. 602–616.
12. Hurvich, L. M., and Jameson, D., "An Opponent Process Theory of Color Vision," *Psychological Review*, vol. 64, no. 6, 1957, pp. 384–404.
13. Ito, T., "Toward Color Picture Processing," *Computer Graphics and Image Processing*, vol. 2, 1973, pp. 347–354.
14. Ito, T., "Color Picture Processing by Computer," *Proceedings of the 4th International Joint Conference on Artificial Intelligence*, Tbilisi, Georgia, USSR, 3–8 Sept. 1975, pp. 635–642.

15. Ito, T., and Fukushima, M., "Computer Analysis of Color Information with Applications to Picture Processing," *Proceedings of the 3rd International Joint Conference on Pattern Recognition*, Nov. 8–11, 1976, Kyoto, Japan, pp. 833–837.
16. Judd, D. B., "Hue, Saturation and Lightness of Surface Colors with Chromatic Illumination," *Journal of the Optical Society of America*, vol. 30, no. 1, 1940, pp. 2–32.
17. Koenderik, J. J., van de Grind, W. A., and Bouman, M. A., "Opponent Color Coding: A Mechanistic Model and a New Metric for Color Space," *Kybernetik*, vol. 10, February 1972, pp. 78–98.
18. König, A., and Dietrici, C., "Die Grundempfindungen im Normalen und Anomalen Farben Systemen und Ihre Intensitätsverteilung im Spectrum," *Zeitschrift für Psychologie und Physiologie der Sinnesorgane*, vol. 4, 1893, pp. 241–347.
19. MacAdam, D. L. (ed.), "Sources of Color Science," MIT Press, Cambridge, Mass., 1970.
20. Meessen, A., "A Simple Non-Linear Theory of Color Perception and Contrast Effect," *Kybernetik*, vol. 4, no. 1, 1967, pp. 48–54.
21. Newton, I., "A Treatise on the Reflections, Refractions and Colours of Light," Dover Publications, New York, 1952.
22. Schrödinger, E., "Outline of a Theory of Colour Measurements for Daylight Vision," in MacAdam, D. L. (ed.), "Sources of Colour Science," MIT Press, Cambridge, Mass., 1970.
23. Teevan, R. C., and Birney, R. C. (eds.), "Color Vision," Van Nostrand, Princeton, N.J. 1961.
24. Wyszecki, G., and Stiles, W. S., "Color Science Concepts and Methods, Quantitative Data and Formulae," Wiley, New York, 1967.
25. Young, T., "On the Theory of Light and Colours," *Philosophical Transactions of the Royal Society of London*, vol. 92, 1802, pp. 20–71.

CHAPTER

EIGHT

ORGANIZATION AND AGGREGATION

8.1 INTRODUCTION

In the previous chapters we were concerned with the analysis of certain visual patterns in a picture. These are the so-called low-level attributes, shown in Figure 1.4. The basic assumption has been that these features are first computed and then organized, aggregated, and described at a secondary level. Such a hierarchy may also exist in living things. For example, it is interesting that there exist projections from the primary visual cortex of such mammals as cats and monkeys onto separate, distinct areas of the secondary visual cortex [2]. Furthermore, Zeki [102] has experimented with rhesus monkeys and claims that they have parallel projections onto such cortical areas. These are identified as responsible for such attributes as shape, color, orientation, motion, and depth. Uhr [90] presents cogent arguments for assuming the existence of parallel computation in both man and machine.

This chapter deals mainly with the first stage of the organization of data and examines it from the points of view of biological and computer processing. Unfortunately, because of our limited knowledge of the subject these domains cannot be considered at the same conceptual level.

Section 8.2 discusses some interesting experiments with monkeys performed by Hubel and Wiesel. They have determined that the edge-element data that are sensed by the simple cortical cells are organized and aggregated into a tabular format. Even though this only gives us a hint about low-level processing at the cellular level, similar tabular methods, which are useful for obtaining global shape characteristics, will be discussed in Chapter 10.

From the point of view of pictorial data organization and aggregation, most computer vision models lie somewhere between those in psychology and those in neurophysiology. Thus, Sections 8.3 and 8.4 are concerned with computer region analysis, that is, the aggregation of the pixels into relatively uniform regions. Usually this is referred to as the "picture segmentation" problem. In Section 8.3 the concepts of similarity and proximity are employed to devise simple methods for region analysis. It will be seen that this model is motivated by the psychological literature. On the other hand, in Section 8.4 a method for data organization is presented which is based on the competition and cooperation of a set of processing units. This, it would appear, is consistent with the neurophysiological literature.

The existing models in psychology usually deal with the broader issues affecting the overall input/output perceptual behavior. Little is known about how features in an arbitrary two-dimensional picture are mapped into an acceptable interpretation. The research in this area generally addresses such important high-level processing issues as search, detection, and selection strategies. A model for this level of analysis which seems to be consistent with a large body of experimental evidence is presented in [80, 81]. It is also consistent with current machine models for vision. In [34, 35, 37, 83] a computer vision system which is quite similar to this perceptual model is presented.

At present it is not quite clear how all three approaches will be unified. An interesting discussion of the implications of computer vision for human visual perception may be found in [100]. In this book we have made the assumption that organization and aggregation of the feature data takes place at the initial stages of analysis, so that this might rightly be attributable to low-level processing. The major characteristic distinguishing low-level processing from the higher levels is that no knowledge specific to the scene in view is employed. Once the organizing process yields some entities, it is feasible to measure their texture and shape features. Chapters 9 and 10 deal with these issues.

8.2 DATA ORGANIZATION AT THE CELLULAR LEVEL

The detection of the elementary features that are most likely the basis for pattern description and recognition has been described in the previous chapters. Often a correlation can be established between an essentially low-level neurophysiological process and a given perceptual experience taking place at a higher level—not that we really know the specifics of the interconnections of the cells. However, it has been reasonably well established that features such as edges are available as data at both levels. This, of course, must be self-evident, since perception is simply the result of the collective behavior of networks of cells. We are unable to study psychology in this way because we presently lack both the experimental and mathematical techniques. A most important question, then, is: How are the elemental data at the cellular level organized? The fascinating research of Hubel, Wiesel, and others has at least provided us with some clues about the organization of the data in the cortex of the monkey and cat. Just as we refer to the "architecture" of a digital computer in order to describe its structure, we may possibly also speak of the architecture of the visual cortex. Whether or not the aggregative principles that have been discovered so far underlie the mechanism by which shape is perceived by man or, for that matter, animal, is still an open question. We cannot state definitely that these data constitute the information employed for shape analysis. Nevertheless, in this section we shall focus our attention on the important experiments done with the monkey [42]. It will be shown that the elementary edge information is actually organized in a tabular format in the visual cortex. In Chapter 10 we shall also observe that this data structure leads to a powerful computational technique for describing shape.

Section 5.2 dealt with feature detectors of varying complexity which were constructed by imposing a combined horizontal and vertical organization on the cells. The lowest level (retina, ganglion, and LGN) cells, organized in a center-surround configuration, were seen to be sensitive to the existence of contrast in the input image (see Figure 8.1). These projected to the cortex,

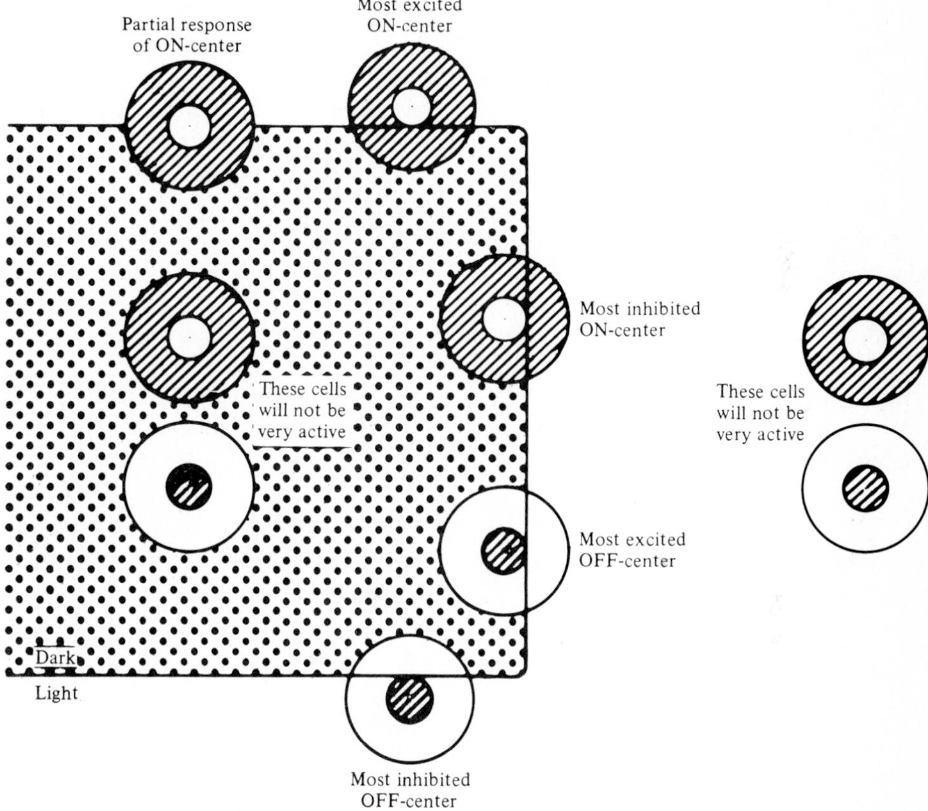

Figure 8.1 The detection of the edge of contour of a shape using ON-center contrast detectors.

where they were grouped to provide the input to individual cortical cells. The latter behaved like pattern templates, which were activated by edges or bar patterns (see Figure 5.4). These might be simple cells, sensitive to stationary inputs, or complex cells, sensitive to moving patterns. The bar detectors are orientation- and width-dependent, which is consistent with their usefulness as the elemental units for shape detection. What is more, it appears that the encoding of these parameters is quite coarse, to perhaps within 10 or 20° [25, 26], which implies the possibility of a certain amount of filtering action and insensitivity to imperfections in the contour of the form. There are many such template units which must be integrated, much as a jigsaw puzzle can be put together. It will be seen that the proposed architecture neatly solves this problem of feature-data aggregation.

We shall discuss in turn the input signals originating in the LGN, the organization in the cortex, and, briefly, the output destinations. In this way we can focus on the visual cortex as a black-box data processor.

The LGN itself receives signals from both eyes, but each individual LGN cell is restricted to processing inputs from only one eye. Thus, while each of these cells remains dedicated to either the left or right eye, there does exist a degree of image organization based on the origin of the field of view. The approximately 1 million input fibers on the left LGN are inputs which project from the right side of the visual field of view. A similar number on the right LGN originate in the left side of the field of view (see Figure 3.18). Figure 8.2 is a sketch showing the six monocular layers of the cells in the LGN with their point of origin labeled. The organization is curious in that layers 1, 4, and 6 receive input from the eye on the same side as the particular half of the LGN, and layers 2, 3, and 5 receive input from the eye on the opposite side. However, apart from this anomaly, there is a high degree of order in the spatial relationship between the cells. Along any vertical section of the six monocular layers of cells, it is found that the receptive fields originate in the same spatial neighborhood of the visual field. In addition, the relative position of the receptive fields is maintained, so that in any given horizontal layer spatial contiguity is preserved. The organization is said to be "retinotopic" [6].

Figure 8.2 also indicates the six layers of the visual cortex. The signals emanating from the LGN project to layer IV of the visual cortex, and mostly to the bottom of this layer, the layer IVc. It has been hypothesized by Crick et al. [14] that these signals constitute a high-resolution version of the original image filtered by the Laplacian operator discussed in Section 5.4.3. It is interesting that these cells in the visual cortex are similar to the originating LGN cells, having circularly symmetric receptive fields. Thus, there appears to be a kind of "impedance matching" process, in which the characteristics of the sender are compatible with those of the receiver. Based on an analysis of anatomical and physiological data, Schwartz [82] has suggested a specific mathematical relationship between the receptor surface of the retina, and layer IVc, where the afferent connections to the cortex from the LGN appear. It turns out that this transformation may be characterized by "a complex logarithmic (conformal)

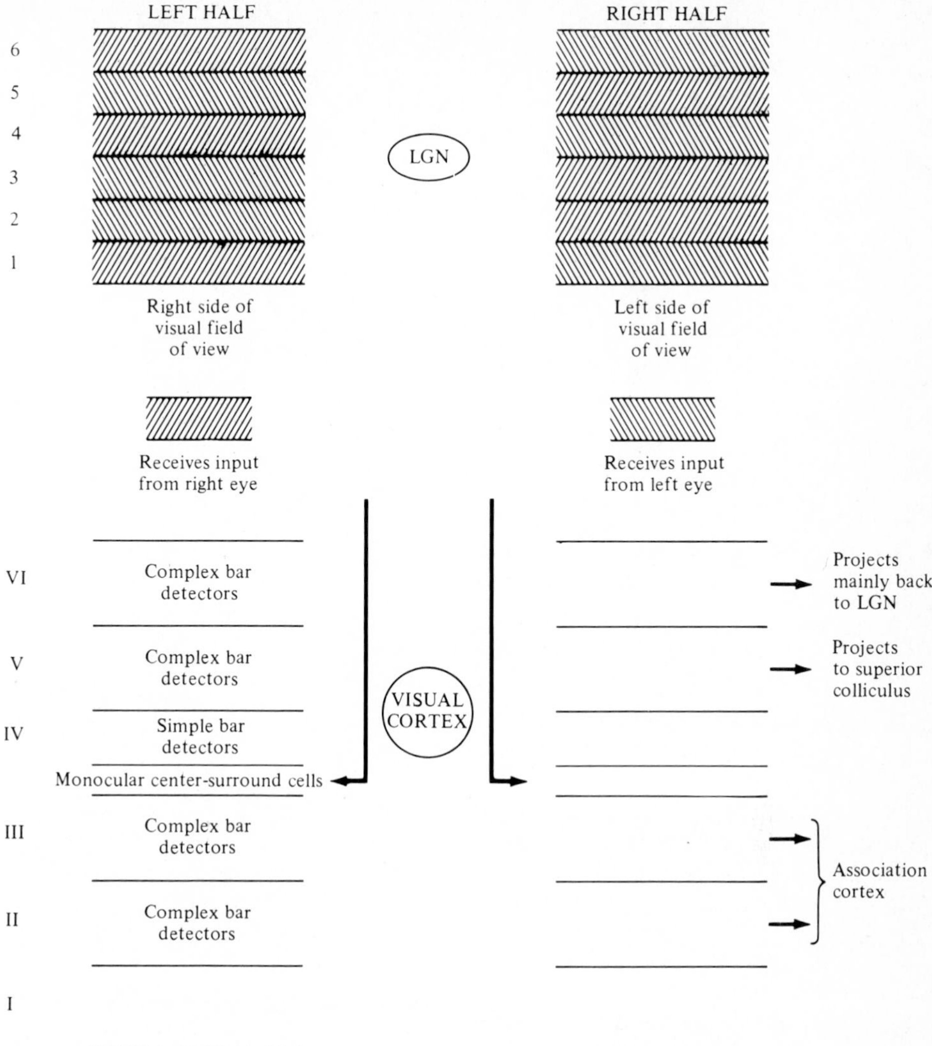

Figure 8.2 A crude block diagram of the monkey LGN and visual cortex.

mapping of the visual field onto the cortical surface" [82]. Thus, data compression, this time related to the spatial domain, is again described by a logarithmic function. Schwartz [82] also presents an interesting hypothesis, in which he indicates that perhaps the compound structure of the cortex is physically developed logarithmically!

From the bottom of layer IV the cell axons are connected to other cells in the upper part, where, it has been determined, simple bar detectors exist. All the simple cells in layer IV are still monocular with regard to input origin. Figure 8.3 shows an actual cross section of the visual cortex. It consists of two

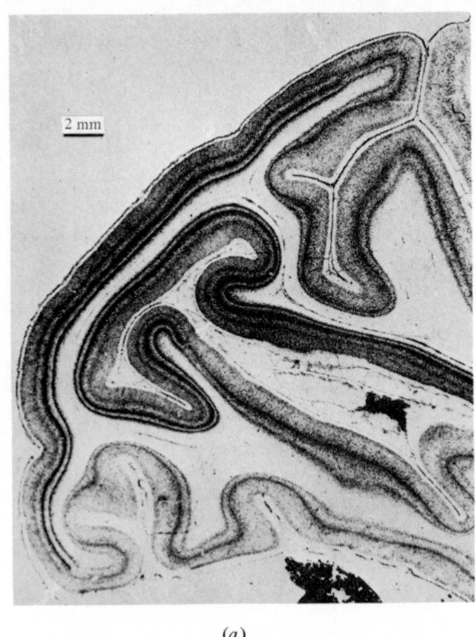

(*a*)

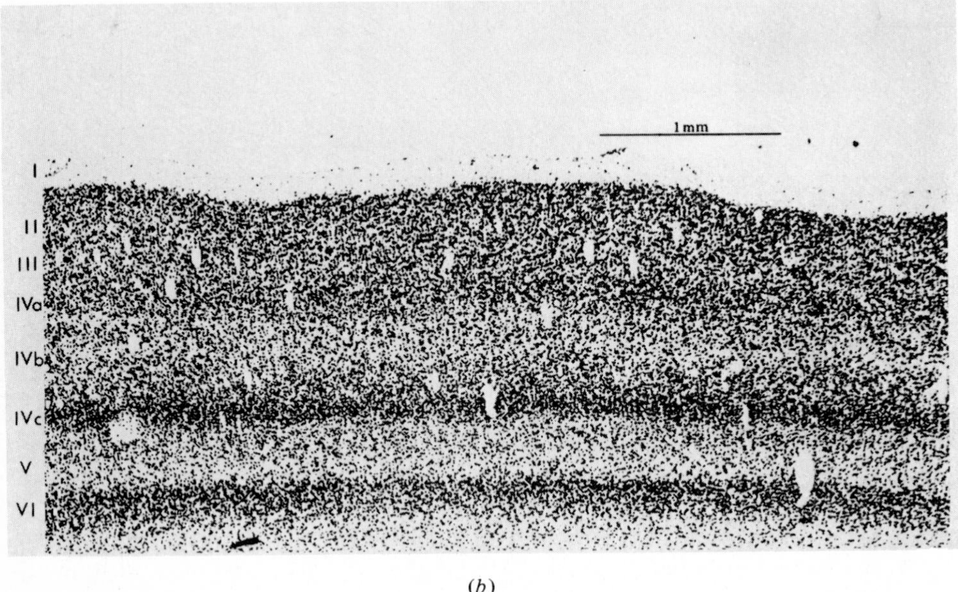

(*b*)

Figure 8.3 (*a*) Low-power Nissl-stained section from the visual cortex of a macaque monkey. This is the so-called striate cortex, which consists of a single bent plate of neurons about 2 mm thick. In the macaque monkey the total surface area of this layered sheet is about 13 cm^2. (*b*) Enlarged cross section through the monkey striate cortex in (*a*) showing the conventional layering designations. (*From D. H. Hubel and T. N. Wiesel, "Functional Architecture of Macaque Monkey Visual Cortex," Ferrier Lecture, Proceedings of the Royal Society, London, ser. B, vol. 198, 1977, pp. 1–59.*)

apparently similarly organized halves, which also seem to process the visual information in identical fashion. Perhaps one provides the hardware "backup" for the other. Although some controversy still exists, it seems likely that these "biological computers" are largely formed at birth and therefore genetically preordained.

What are some of the general properties of the visual cortex? Layers II, III, V, and VI contain complex cells which differ in certain respects but are significantly sensitive to bars oriented at a particular angle. We observed in Section 5.2 that these feature detectors, although tuned to a particular input pattern, are also relatively insensitive to imperfect data. This property would be quite important if the sensed oriented-bar segments are employed to describe form. A mathematical model for these complex cells is given in [49].

In order for the two halves of the visual cortex to function with similar "operating systems" and "programs," some interrelationship between the left and right eyes must exist. It is at the level of the visual cortex that data from the two eyes finally converge as input signals to single binocular cells, although not completely. About half the complex cells are monocular and half binocular. The latter will respond to visual patterns impinging on either eye. Nature has preserved the sense of order we have already alluded to by arranging for the receptive fields of the left and right eye inputs to originate at the same position in the retinal field. The optimal stimulus of the two types of input is generally similar with respect to pattern, orientation, and direction of movement. However the magnitude of the response, as manifested in the frequency of firing of the cell, is not usually the same for stimuli presented to the left and right eyes. There exists a so-called ocular dominance for the inputs to the binocular cell. The degree of dominance is different for each of these cells, and its significance is unclear.

The wiring of the visual cortex is extremely complex and remains largely unmapped. However, even though there are many connections between the layers, the spatial ordering which prevails in the LGN is still maintained in the visual cortex. Receptive fields spatially close to each other in the LGN are similarly close to each other in the visual cortex. Thus, structural relationships are maintained, from the photoreceptors in the retina to the cells in the visual cortex. Again, we have the property of retinotopy [6]. It would seem reasonable that the existing neuroarchitecture would constitute a distributed computational network, in which the loss of isolated units would not affect its performance in any significant manner. Uttal [93] has listed a set of general principles governing the organization of the cortical cells, which, he suggests, are common to all centers of processing in the cortex. Figure 8.4*a* outlines the basic structural concepts, and Figure 8.4*b* demonstrates a possible configuration which embodies these ideas. It is apparent from the model that this three-dimensional lattice network of neurons is involved in both a cooperative and competitive "computation" [5]. We shall consider techniques to perform this type of analysis in Section 8.4.

We know even less about where the signals from the visual cortex project

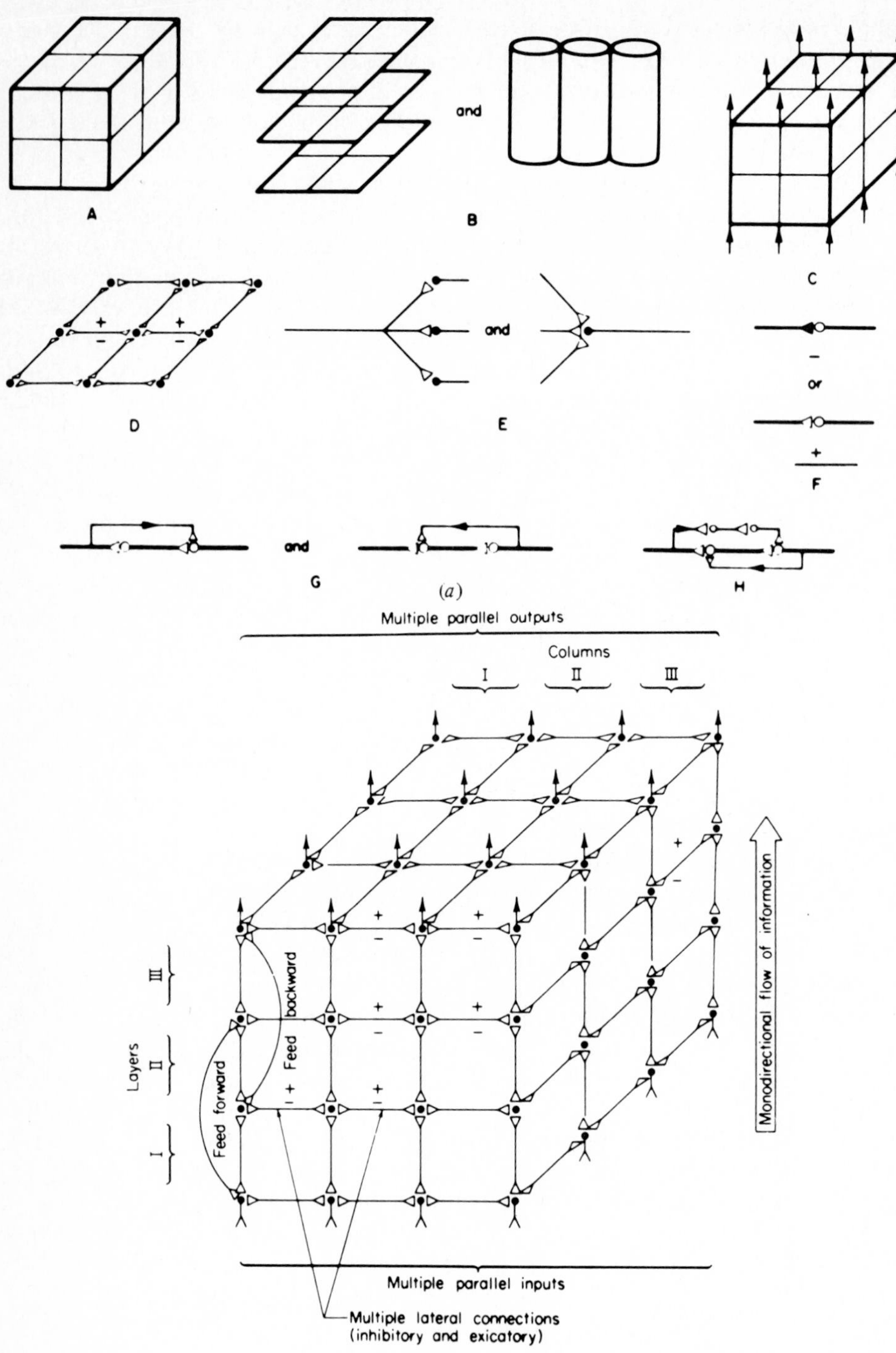

A
and
B
C
+
+
−
−
and
D
E
−
or
+
F
and
G
H
Multiple parallel outputs
Columns
I
II
III
Layers
III
II
I
Feed forward
Feed backward
Monodirectional flow of information
Multiple parallel inputs
Multiple lateral connections
(inhibitory and exicatory)

(a)

(b)

to. Figure 8.2 shows that the outputs from levels II and III are connected to the association cortex, where one might expect that the high-level visual analysis takes place, based on the available coded feature data (see Section 3.4). Zeki [102, 103, 104] has performed some interesting experiments in this regard and has postulated that different features are analyzed in different areas of the cerebral cortex. It has also been found that axons from layer V project to the superior colliculus; are these involved in the control of eye movements to focus our attention on certain objects in the scene? The function of the connections between the cells in level VI, which project mainly back to the LGN, is presently unknown. Perhaps some kind of adaptation of the contrast measurement is taking place. Basically the intricate wiring of the visual cortex remains a puzzle!

Let us now examine some of the details of the organization of the visual cortex of the monkey, an animal about which we have some knowledge. The results are exciting in that they conform to our expectations about how an efficient and error-insensitive system might be physically constructed. This, at least, provides some hope that in the future scientists will be able to unravel some further secrets of the cortical "wiring diagram."

The visual cortex seems to be constructed as a set of layers. Therefore, in order to study its properties it is necessary to investigate the cells along both a vertical axis and on a horizontal plane. Figure 8.5 shows what happens when we travel in a direction perpendicular to the horizontal layers. It turns out that the receptive fields which are encountered as we penetrate the layers overlap but vary in size. Hubel [27] refers to this "column" of receptive fields as an "aggregate field." What is more significant is the fact that each of the bar detectors in the column is tuned to the same angular orientation, so that we may refer to it as an "orientation column." The magnitude and scatter of the aggregate field, and therefore the size of the bars being detected, conform to our notions of visual acuity, as exemplified by Figure 4.6. The distance from the fovea is the significant parameter here, with the peripheral aggregate fields being larger than those nearer to the fovea.

An interesting property of this orientation column has been suggested by Maffei and Fiorentini [41] as a result of their experiments with cats. The column is similar to the edge detector proposed by Marr and shown in Section 5.4.3 to comprise a "stack" of bandpass filters, each tuned to a different passband. Maffei and Fiorentini have actually discovered that the optimal

---

Figure 8.4 (*a*) The basic modes of arrangement and interconnection in neural tissue: (A) the basic cubical arrangement; (B) lamina and columns; (C) the predominantly unidirectional flow of information; (D) reciprocal excitation and inhibition; (E) divergence and convergence; (F) excitation and inhibition; (G) feedforward and feedbackward; and (H) temporal dispersion due to multiple pathways of different lengths and reverberation. (*b*) A conceptual model of the arrangement of neurons in the nervous system embodying most of the basic modes of interconnection and organization described above. Although the nervous system never looks as neat and orderly as shown, there is a great deal of intrinsic order. (*From W. R. Uttal, "The Psychology of Mind," Lawrence Erlbaum Associates, Hillsdale, N.J., 1978, pp. 192, 194.*)

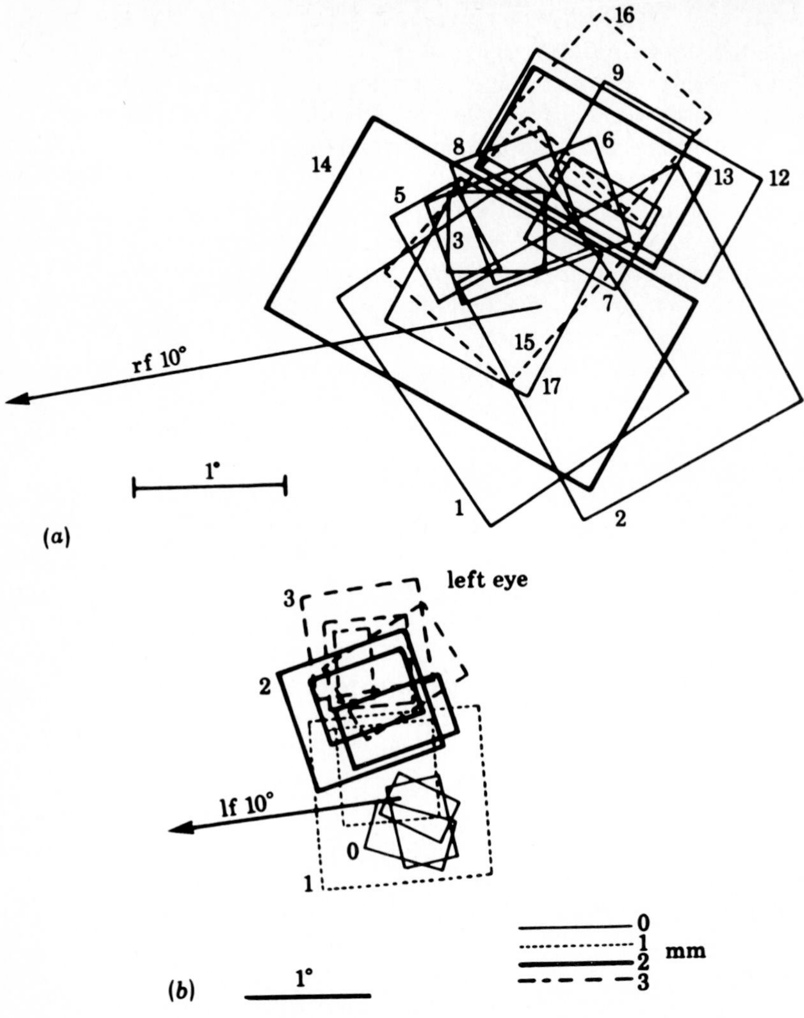

Figure 8.5 (*a*) Receptive-field scatter. Receptive-field boundaries of 17 cells were recorded in a penetration through monkey striate cortex in a direction perpendicular to the surface. Note the variation in size and the more or less random scatter in the precise positions of the fields. The penetration was made in a part of the cortex corresponding to a visual field location 10° from the center of gaze, just above the horizontal meridian. Fields are shown for one eye only. Numbers indicate the order in which the cells were recorded. (*b*) Receptive-field drift. Receptive fields were mapped during an oblique, almost tangential penetration through striate cortex, in roughly the same region as in (*a*). A few fields were mapped along each of four 100-μm segments, spaced at 1-mm intervals. These four groups of fields were labeled 0, 1, 2, and 3. Each new set of fields was slightly above the other, as predicted from the direction of movement of the electrode. Roughly a 2-mm movement through cortex was required to displace the fields from one region to an entirely new region. (*From D. H. Hubel and T. N. Wiesel, "Functional Architecture of Macaque Monkey Visual Cortex," Ferrier Lecture, Proceedings of the Royal Society, London, ser. B, vol. 198, 1977, pp. 1–59, after D. H. Hubel and T. N. Wiesel, "Uniformity of Monkey Striate Cortex: A Parallel Relationship Between Field Size, Scatter, and Magnification Factor," Journal of Comparative Neurology, vol. 158, no. 3, Dec. 1, 1974, pp. 295–306.*)

spatial frequency varies as one penetrates the column, and is constant in any horizontal layer. However, nothing is known about the ordering of the optimal frequencies. The idea of structuring a computation in an ordered sequence, based on spatial frequency, has recently gained some credence in the digital picture processing literature as well. The data structure is referred to as a pyramid, and was discussed in Section 5.5. It provides a comprehensive description of the image, which then lends itself to some very interesting computations [85].

It is, of course, not physically possible to traverse an exactly parallel path to the surface, so that a slightly oblique penetration must be employed. Figure 8.6 shows how the aggregate fields are displaced in a topologically consistent fashion; the consecutive penetrations of the cortex result in a similar sequence of slightly displaced groups of retinal receptive fields. What is more striking, however, is the fact that a movement of 1 or 2 mm along the path will always result in a different aggregate field, which is also sensitive to a different bar orientation. This perforce results in a spatial normalization of the data in that although the aggregate fields expand in size towards the visual periphery, the same amount of cortex area is allotted. A further complication should also be remembered: the receptive fields themselves possess varying distributions of the photosensing units (see Figure 3.15). The result of an oblique traverse is indicated in Figure 8.6*c* and supports the existence of the orientation column. There also exists anatomical evidence of the strikingly uniform nature of this region of the cortex [27].

We note from Figure 8.6 that the orientation columns are ordered sequentially according to the direction of their optimal response. Generally, a penetration of 25 or 50 μm results in about a 10° clockwise or counterclockwise change in direction. The total angular range without repetition is anywhere from 90 to 270°. Naturally, the ordering is not perfect, as is to be expected from a biological system. Sometimes there are sudden direction reversals, sometimes the orientation remains constant for a greater length of traverse. Nevertheless, the visual cortex may be conceptualized as being segmented into so-called hypercolumns approximately 1 mm $\times$ 1 mm in cross section. These volumetric sections correspond to one aggregate field and therefore originate from only one area of the visual field. Except for layer IV, each of these hypercolumns contains a complete set of orientation columns, as shown schematically in Figure 8.7. It is as if we sampled the visual field to determine local edge orientation and then collected the data for each of these samples in a "cortical table." We therefore have a transformation from angular strips to parallel strips as we map from the LGN afferents to the cortical simple cells. Again, this can be characterized mathematically by a complex logarithm [82].

A further degree of organization is imposed by the fact that each hypercolumn is divided into two equal columns, one sensitive to images falling on the left eye, the other sensitive to images falling on the right eye. The function of these ocular dominance columns is not known but perhaps it is related to the perception of the third dimension of depth of view. Scientists have determined

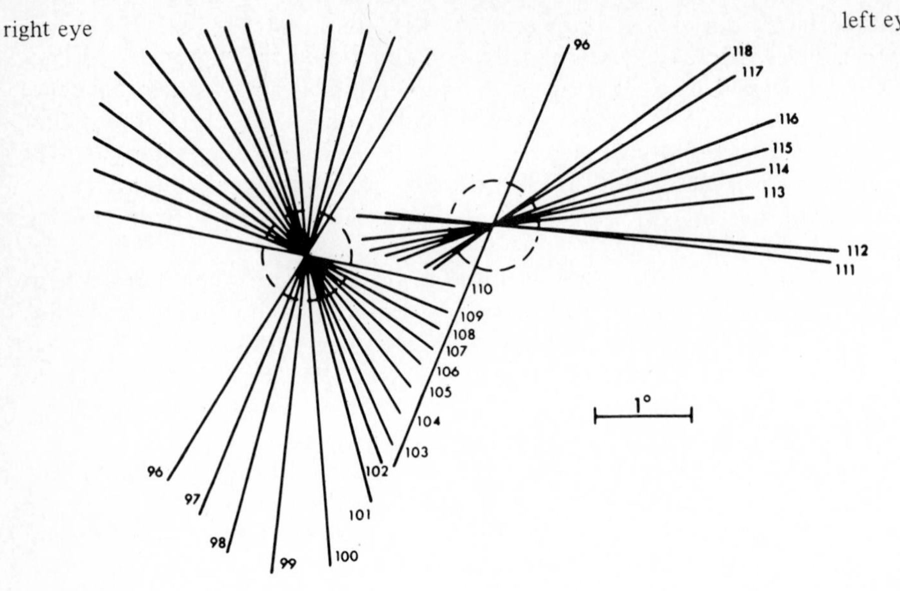
right eye
left eye
96
97
98
99
100
101
102
103
104
105
106
107
108
109
110
111
112
113
114
115
116
117
118
1°
(*a*)

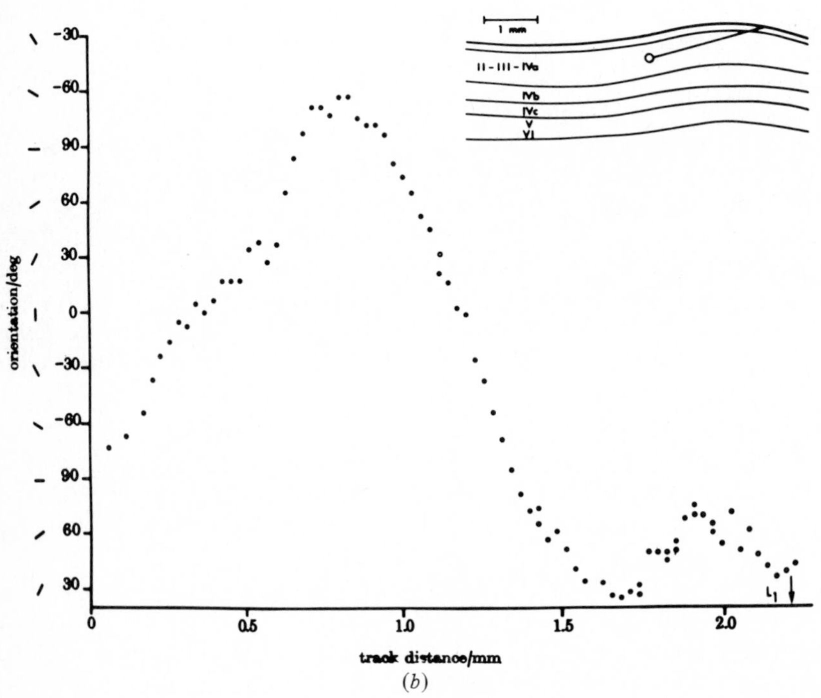
1 mm
II - III - IVa
IVb
IVc
V
VI
orientation/deg
-30
-60
90
60
30
0
-30
-60
90
60
30
0
0.5
1.0
1.5
2.0
track distance/mm
L_1
(*b*)

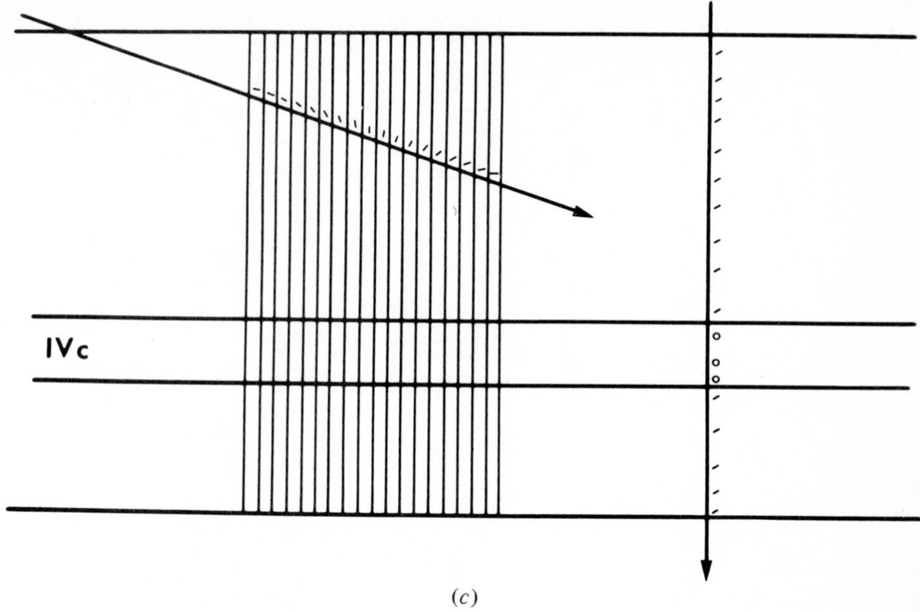

(*c*)

Figure 8.6 Orientation preferences in the visual cortex. (*a*) The receptive fields of 22 cells or clusters of cells observed during an oblique microelectrode penetration through the striate cortex of a normal 2- to 3-year-old monkey. The first cell in the sequence, cell 96 in the experiment, had an orientation 32° clockwise to the vertical and was influenced from both eyes but more strongly from the right (ipsilateral). Cells 97 to 110 were likewise strongly dominated by the right eye; at cell 111 there was an abrupt switch to the left (contralateral) eye, which dominated for the rest of the sequence. (*b*) Graph of orientation versus track distance for an experiment similar to that shown in (*a*). Again, the penetration was almost horizontal and was restricted to layers II and III (see inset). Several reversals in the direction of rotation occur, with two very long, almost linear, sequences followed by two short ones. The right eye was dominant until almost the end of the sequence [closed circles, ipsilateral (right) eye; open circles, contralateral (left) eye]. (*c*) Diagram to illustrate orientation columns in monkey striate cortex. Two penetrations are illustrated, one vertical, the other oblique. In the vertical penetration orientation is clearly defined and constant from cell to cell in layers above and below IVc. In layer IVc the cells have fields with circular symmetry, and there is no orientation preference. In an oblique penetration there is a systematic variation in orientation, clockwise or counterclockwise, in steps of about 10° or less that occur roughly every 50 μm. [(*a*) *From D. H. Hubel and T. N. Wiesel, "Sequence Regularity and Geometry of Orientation Columns in the Monkey Striate Cortex," Journal of Comparative Neurology, vol. 158, no. 3, Dec. 1, 1974, pp. 267–294*; *Ferrier Lecture, Proceedings of the Royal Society, London, ser. B, vol. 198, 1977, pp. 1–59*; (*b*) *and* (*c*) *from D. H. Hubel and T. N. Wiesel, "Functional Architecture of Macaque Monkey Visual Cortex," Ferrier Lecture, Proceedings of the Royal Society, London, ser. B, vol. 198, 1977, pp. 1–59.*]

that the slightly different images that fall on each of our eyes result in a parallax computation, which is one component of our depth perception. In addition to this binocular property, there exist monocular cues related to our knowledge about the occlusion relationships between objects in three-dimensional space.

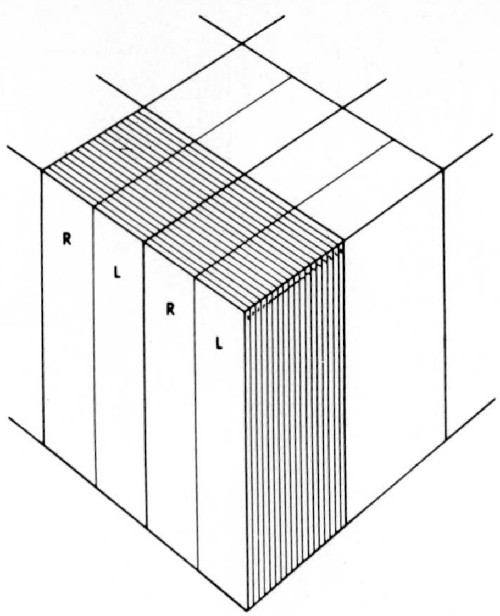

Figure 8.7 Model of the visual cortex to show roughly the dimensions of the ocular dominance slabs (L, R) in relation to the orientation slabs and the cortical thickness. Thinner lines separate individual columns; thicker lines demarcate hypercolumns, two pairs of ocular dominance columns and two sets of orientation columns. Each hypercolumn is a block approximately 1 mm by 1 mm square and 2 mm high. The orientation columns are about 50 μm in width and correspond to an angle of about 10°. The placing of the hypercolumn boundaries is of course arbitrary; one could as well begin at horizontal or any of the obliques. The decision to show the two sets of columns as intersecting at right angles is also arbitrary, since there is at present no evidence as to the relationship between the two sets. Finally, for convenience the slabs are shown as plane surfaces, but whereas the dominance columns are indeed more or less flat, the orientation columns are not known to be so and may when viewed from above have the form of swirls. (*From D. H. Hubel, "Functional Architecture of Macaque Monkey Visual Cortex," Ferrier Lecture, Proceedings of the Royal Society, London, ser. B, vol. 198, 1977, pp. 1–59.*)

The organization of area 17, the primary visual cortex, is summarized in Figure 8.8. Three variables are encoded in this table: the orientation, the relative location of the aggregate field, and the ocular dominance. Why the data is organized in this way is a mystery, but it is recognized to be a compact form of information storage and does provide for reinforcement by one eye of an edge sensed by the other. It could also lend itself very easily to the computation of the shape of an object. Because of the logarithmic transformation from the visual plane to the cortical table, size changes in a viewed object manifest themselves as simple translations in the table. Thus, this configuration does offer the hope of a size-invariance property, an important consideration indeed. Perhaps the table is used to obtain a histogram of edge response directions, from which a generalized Hough transform can be obtained. Ballard [8] has shown that this type of transform can be used to detect and recognize arbitrary shapes. This is all hypothetical, however, since there is no experimental evidence supporting these

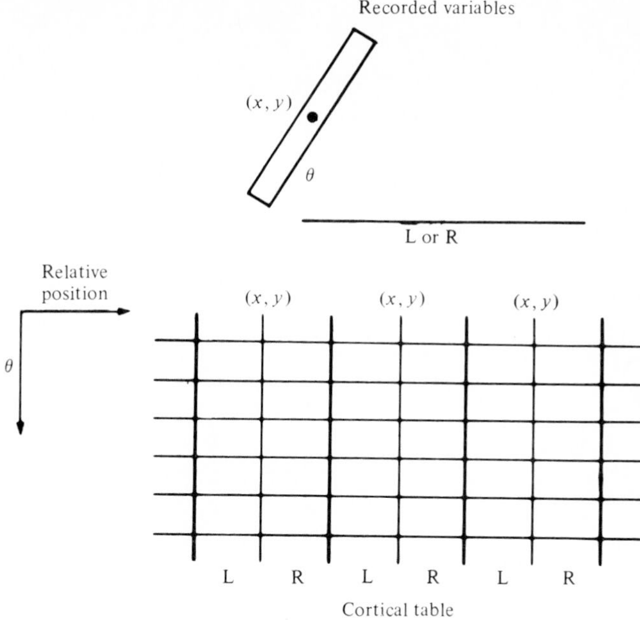

Figure 8.8 A section of the data in Figure 8.7 represented in tabular format, as it apparently is stored.

ideas. What we do know is that the edge data are tabulated in the visual cortex of the monkey and also of the cat, as confirmed by Maffei and Fiorentini [41].

This is only a small part of the story, since we have ignored other important attributes, such as color, texture, and depth. Where is this information aggregated, and how? The answers to these questions await discovery.

8.3 REGION ANALYSIS

8.3.1 Proximity and Similarity

In this section we shall examine some low-level picture processing operations which are concerned with the organization of pictorial data at a very elementary level. We shall seek methods for segmenting a picture array into regions which contain pixels with similar features [71].

It is again important to make a clear distinction between the different levels of analysis, so that the underlying complexity of the problem will become transparent to the reader. Figure 8.9 is a schematic which attempts to summarize the different conceptual stages associated with machine vision [29]. Beginning with the input image, the latter is first analyzed by techniques which

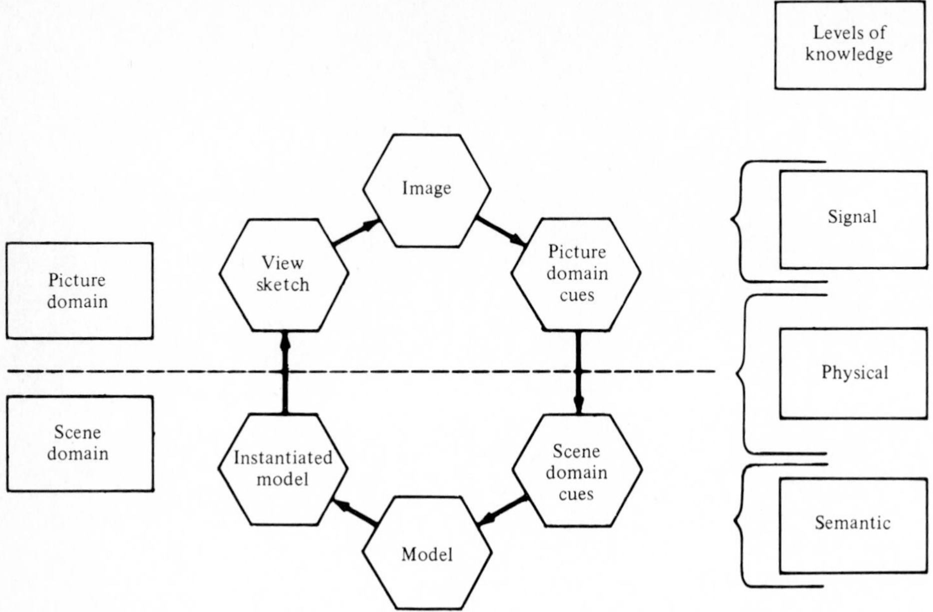

Figure 8.9 A computer model for machine vision. (*Adapted from T. Kanade, "Region Segmentation: Signal vs. Semantics," Proceedings of the Fourth International Conference on Pattern Recognition, Kyoto, Japan, Nov. 7–10, 1978, pp. 95–105.*)

do not in any way take into account the three-dimensional scene from which the picture originated. Each image is treated identically, strictly on the basis of the properties of the signal. Therefore this approach is said to use "general-purpose models" [109]:

> By definition, these are models which are applicable even when we have little or no a priori knowledge about the class of scenes that is to be analyzed. They include models for general classes of local features (edges, lines, angles, etc.) that occur in many different types of scenes, as well as models that describe how such features can be grouped into aggregates.

However, in Figure 8.9 objects are represented by models, so that it should be quite evident that general-purpose models do not as a rule or necessarily lead to entities which we can identify by name.

We make a distinction between two types of segmentation. The first has been called "partial segmentation" and is the subject of this section. It is based on very simple general-purpose models which result in the image being partitioned into regions, whose outlines do not necessarily correspond to the objects in the picture. When applied to a normal complex image, for example, a typical suburban scene (see Figure 1.13), the result is a set of regions which are uniform in the sense of their features. Any correspondence between a single uniform region and an object model is fortuitous.

However, there does exist a class of problems for which this type of low-level segmentation is completely effective, that is, the regions obtained do correspond to objects. Usually this is the case when the picture can be modeled by two-dimensional objects superimposed on a uniform background, for example, nonoverlapping chromosomes or blood cells [38]. Histogram thresholding (see Section 1.4), applied independently to each pixel, will generally result in a segmentation into objects and background. This is a context-independent segmentation process, as no descriptive information is utilized.

The second type, which has been termed "complete segmentation," also achieves a final result which consists of outlined regions in the two-dimensional image. However, in this case the regions correspond exactly to the object models in the three-dimensional scene. Obviously, this is the ideal outcome for both man and machine. We observe in Figure 8.9 that in general it will be necessary to invoke both physical and semantic knowledge to achieve such a complete segmentation. The physical models are also general-purpose models but ones which deal with scene domain cues which are evident in the picture. When the picture is formed (see Chapter 2), various shadings, shadows, and highlights will occur as a result of the lighting and observation conditions and the physical and geometrical nature of the objects, as well as their arrangement. Thus, these general physical models relate two-dimensional picture cues to three-dimensional scene domain occurrences. The semantic information, on the other hand, is specific to a generic class of objects. Scene domain cues are used to recognize the appropriate object model. The latter implies a knowledge data base governing the particular world model under consideration.

Kasvand [31] has commented on a significant paradox regarding partial and complete segmentation. In order to determine the correspondence between a group of regions with a specific object model, the latter must correspond to this group of regions so that their properties can be compared with a previously stored description in the knowledge representation data base. However, until we know what the object is, how do we extract the pertinent information from the data base in order to make the original comparisons? Perhaps an intermediate level of processing based on a two-dimensional analysis is the answer [34].

An implied by the loop in Figure 8.9, the process of image understanding involves an interactive computation, beginning with an image, which is then associated with a particular generic model. The specific features of the specific object in view yield an instantiated model but one that is nevertheless still symbolic in nature. It is a symbolic three-dimensional description of the scene in terms of the generic model, but with associated specific values for parameters. From this the view sketch may be obtained, and it is again seen to be an abstract model but now in the two-dimensional picture domain. The last stage, which is in the domain of computer graphics, is the synthesis of an actual image using this abstraction. From a conceptual point of view, we may hypothesize an error function which compares this image with the original input. The next iteration would employ the error information to alter some aspect or aspects in the analysis chain in order to achieve a null error.

Section 8.3 deals with region analysis, which can be viewed as signal-level processing and therefore involves only the first stage of the loop in Figure 8.9. The image is partitioned into homogeneous regions strictly on the basis of picture-domain cues. Two basic approaches are available, region merging, discussed in Section 8.3.2, and region splitting, discussed in Section 8.3.3. The first achieves its goal by placing the emphasis on the spatial properties of the pixels in the image array. The second emphasizes the gray-level, color, or perhaps texture properties.

Mathematically the problem has been defined as follows [24]. Let $I(i, j)$ be a picture function defined on the sampling lattice X, the domain of the picture. A logical predicate P is defined on the subsets $\{S_k\}$ of X, such that $P(S_k)$ evaluates a property of the pixels in X which belong to $\{S_k\}$. A segmentation of X is a partition of X into subsets or regions $\{S_k\}$, $k = 1, \ldots, m$ for some m such that†

1. $X = \cup_{k=1}^{m} S_k$	every pixel (i, j) must be in a region
2. $S_k \cap S_l = 0$	for all $k \neq 1$ (regions must not overlap)
3. $P(S_k) = \text{TRUE}$	for all k (P is the property that defines the segmentation)
4. $P(S_k \cup S_l) = \text{FALSE}$	for all $k \neq l$ provided that S_k and S_l are adjacent in X (adjacent regions must be different)

Note that adjacency may be based on either four- or eight-connectivity [72]. Also observe that segmentation is a simultaneous search in both picture and feature space.

What are the laws of organization embodied by the predicate P? Although we shall examine these in detail in the next two sections pertaining to computer algorithms, it is also of interest to mention briefly the perceptual theories. In this connection, during the first half of this century it was thought that gestalt theory was an appropriate model for human form perception [30, 32, 97]. This theory was based on a set of organizational principles which pertained to the whole visual field at once and were claimed to somehow function in a spontaneous manner. The underlying mechanisms were not precisely defined. This was in distinction to the previous classical atomistic theory, which assumed that some type of "unconscious conclusion" was reached on the basis of similarly "unconscious inferences" involving the smallest uniform subset (a pixel?) in the image [22]. Probably there is an element of truth in both theories, although to date there is no generally accepted paradigm (see [92] for a discussion of the constructive approach to human vision, which is the most commonly held view today and was first conceived by Hebb [21]).

The organizational principles proposed by gestalt psychologists embodied

† A discussion of data representations for image segmentation may be found in [29] and [74].

such concepts as grouping by similarity; grouping by proximity; principles of good continuation, symmetry, and simplicity; and the law of closure. Figure 8.10 illustrates the first two principles. In Figure 8.10*a* the greater proximity of the disks in the vertical direction imposes a vertical aggregation and we see five columns. The elements are equally spaced in Figure 8.10*b* but now similarity causes us to see six horizontal groups. In Figure 8.10*c* both principles operate independently so that we may observe both horizontal and vertical groupings. The laws would seem to make a lot of sense: physical objects tend to be compact, homogeneous, and bounded. Thus, one would expect a machine computation to embody similar concepts. Some interesting experiments with image organization, albeit binary dot patterns, are discussed in [1, 28, 48, 54, 55, 56, 57, 58, 76, 87, 89, 94, 101].

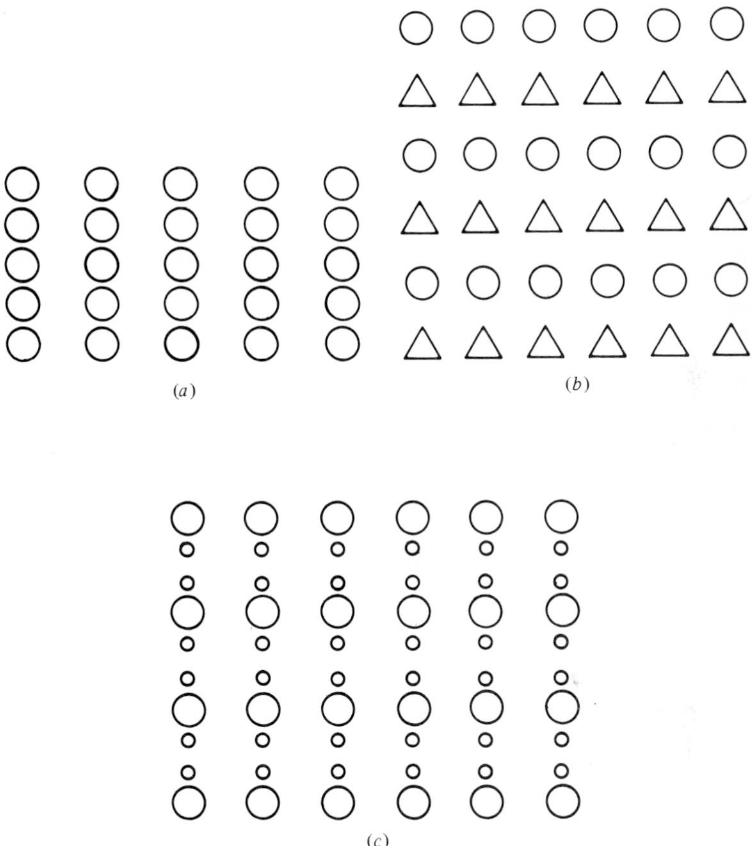

Figure 8.10 The gestalt principles of proximity and similarity. (*a*) Owing to the principle of proximity, the objects are perceived to be organized as columns. (*b*) Owing to the principle of similarity, in this case the objects are organized into rows. (*c*) As a result of both proximity and similarity, we perceive both columns and rows.

8.3.2 Merging Regions

Region merging is a process in which one begins with an image array $I(i, j)$ containing $N \times N$ elements and ends with a set of m regions S_k, m being less than N^2. It may therefore be viewed as a means of data compression in which the original image is approximated by uniform and arbitrarily colored patches. In this section we shall examine how these patches or regions are computed on the basis of proximity and similarity criteria.

Perhaps the first reference to region merging was by Meurle and Allen [44]. They suggested that a region is an area of an image in which the statistical distribution of the gray levels is reasonably uniform. Regions are merged, or pixels are merged to regions if they seem to come from the same distribution. The approach considers each pixel (or region†) in $I(i, j)$ as a candidate for merging by scanning the array in raster fashion row by row from the upper left-hand corner until the bottom right-hand corner is reached. Only one pass is required. The predicate P is based on a comparison of the statistics (really the parameters of the distribution) of the test pixel with each of its neighboring (proximity) regions to determine whether they are similar (similarity). If so, the pixel is merged to form a region. Otherwise it is given a different label and considered to be another region. The estimate of the probability density function of a region is updated after each merge, which makes it more accurate as a region description. In fact, this approach is essentially the basis for most region merging methods.

Let us consider in more detail the case in which the three color planes $\mathrm{P}(i, j)$, $\Gamma(i, j)$, and $\mathrm{B}(i, j)$ have been obtained (see Section 7.5). Levine and Shaheen [37] "grow" the regions by attempting to merge as many adjacent pixels as possible, provided that the difference between each color feature is less than some threshold value. Also the latter is adaptively adjusted to depend on region uniformity, so that as a region becomes less uniform, its growth is limited.

For every region S_k in the color picture specified by the three color planes, $C_q = \{\mathrm{P}, \Gamma, \mathrm{B}\}$, where $q = 1, 2, 3$, we define the mean $\mu_k(q)$ and standard deviation $\sigma_k(q)$ of the three color features as follows:

$$\mu_k(q) = \frac{1}{n} \sum_{(i,j)\in S_k} C_q(i, j)$$

$$\sigma_k(q) = \left\{\frac{1}{n} \sum_{(i,j)\in S_k} [C_q(i, j) - \mu_k(q)]^2\right\}^{1/2} \tag{8.1}$$

where it is assumed that the region S_k contains n pixels. Note that instead of, or in addition to, the three color planes, we may also perform region merging on the basis of other features. A prominent example is texture, which is discussed in Chapter 9.

† In their original formulation, Meurle and Allen [44] commenced by segmenting the picture into small square regions of size 2×2, 4×4, or 8×8.

Initially all pixels in X are assumed to have the null label; that is, they do not belong to any region. Again a raster scan is used; starting with the top left-hand corner, each pixel (i^*, j^*) is examined in order as follows:

1. Calculate the updated means $\{\mu_k'(q)\}$ and standard deviations $\{\sigma_k'(q)\}$ for every adjacent region S_k to pixel (i^*, j^*) as if it were merged†

$$\mu_k'(q) = \frac{1}{n+1}[C_q(i^*, j^*) + n\mu_k(q)]$$

$$\sigma_k'(q) = \left(\frac{1}{n+1}\left\{n\sigma_k^2 + \left(\frac{n}{n+1}\right)[C_q(i^*, j^*) - \mu_k(q)]^2\right\}\right)^{1/2} \tag{8.2}$$

   for each of the color planes in the set C_q.
2. Calculate three separate threshold values $\theta_k(q)$ for each of the possible mergings:

$$\theta_k(q) = \left\{\left[1 - \frac{\sigma_k'(q)}{\mu_k'(q)}\right]\theta\right\}_+ \tag{8.3}$$

   where θ is a constant threshold value selected by the user and $\theta_k(q)$ represents a set of adaptive threshold values.
3. For each of the adjacent regions S_k, we calculate

$$\Delta\mu_k(q) = |C_q(i^*, j^*) - \mu_k(q)| \tag{8.4}$$

   for each C_q. If

$$\Delta\mu_k(q) \le \theta_k(q) \tag{8.5}$$

   for each of the three planes, then S_k is merged with pixel (i^*, j^*). If more than one candidate presents itself, merging takes place with the region having the minimum value of $\Sigma_q [\Delta\mu_k(q)]^2$.
4. If none of the adjacent regions satisfies Equation (8.5) or if a pixel has no adjacent region,‡ pixel (i^*, j^*) is labeled as a new region.

We have noted that merging depends on the three adaptive threshold values [see Equation (8.5)], which are related to the average and standard deviation of the three color features of the adjacent regions. We observe from Equation (8.3) that the threshold depends on the uniformity of the merged regions. As the standard deviation $\sigma_k'(q)$ of the merged regions approaches zero, the threshold $\theta_k(q)$ tends towards the constant θ. Thus, the latter may be viewed as the minimum value for which a region S_k with all identical pixels would be merged with an (i^*, j^*) having a different value. As the region becomes less uniform, the ratio $[\sigma_k'(q)/\mu_k'(q)]$ grows, thereby causing the

† If four-connectedness is used to determine adjacency, only the regions containing the pixels $(i^* - 1, j^*)$ and $(i^*, j^* - 1)$ need be considered as a consequence of the raster scan.

‡ For example, the pixel at the top left-hand corner does not have any adjacent regions.

threshold to be smaller. This in turn makes it more difficult to satisfy Equation (8.5), and the growth of nonuniform regions is thus restricted.

Figure 8.11 shows typical segmentations of an outdoor scene based on the merging principles discussed here. Values $\theta = 7$, 10, and 15 were used in Equation (8.3). We would normally expect that both the sky and fence, being relatively uniform, would be merged into large regions. This occurs for $\theta = 10$ and $\theta = 15$ but not for $\theta = 7$. On the other hand, the highly textured tree resulted in a segmentation containing many small regions in all three cases. An intermediate situation is the house, which is best segmented with $\theta = 15$.

The reader should note that as θ tends to zero, we will obtain more and more regions. A limit will be reached in which each pixel could possibly form its own region, as would be the case with a checkerboard pattern containing four different colors or shades of gray. Under these circumstances, if the

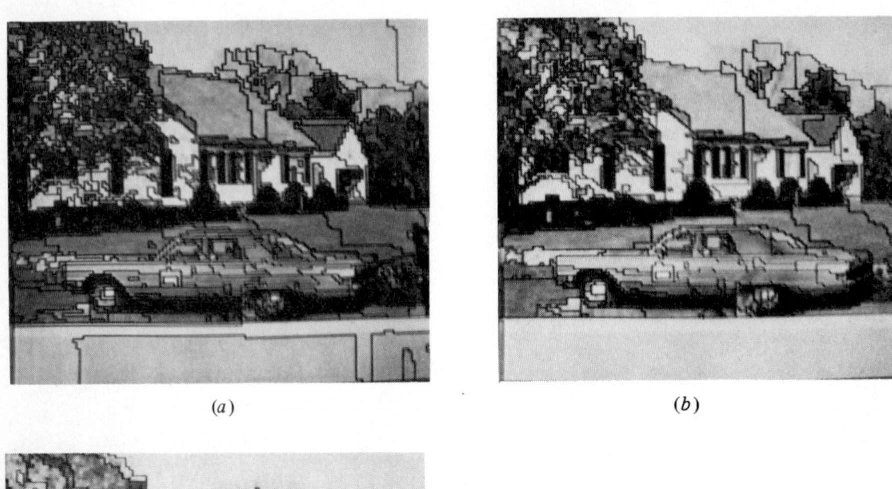

(*a*) (*b*)

(*c*)

Figure 8.11 Region boundaries obtained with different values of the threshold parameter θ. In each case, regions of size equal to eight pixels or less have been merged with their most similar adjacent region. (*a*) $\theta = 7$. (*b*) $\theta = 10$. (*c*) $\theta = 15$. (*From S. I. Shaheen, "Image Segmentation and Interpretation Using a Knowledge Database," Ph.D.* thesis, University of Montreal, *1979.*) (See back endpapers for color figures.)

pattern were to be less restricted, merging would take place only on the basis of exact color equality. At the other extreme, as θ becomes larger, merging is easier. In the limit, every pixel in $I(i, j)$ would belong to the same region. Figure 8.11 shows segmentations for different values of θ. Thus, we observe that picture segmentation based on a general-purpose model embodying the principles of proximity and similarity can (by selecting θ) be made to arbitrarily contain as many regions m $(1 \leq m \leq N^2)$ as desirable. If this partial segmentation does conform to the complete segmentation, it is only because it has been possible to select a specific θ to achieve this goal. In general, this cannot be done.

An alternative distance measure in color space to that given in Equation (8.5) may be found in [99]. A slightly more elaborate method, which employs hypothesis testing to decide on when to merge two regions, is given in [20].

Merging may also be based on the properties of the edge boundary between regions by using the two heuristics suggested by Brice and Fennema [10]. These have the rather colorful names of "phagocyte" and "weakness heuristics." A phagocyte is a leukocyte (white blood cell) capable of guarding against infection by absorbing microbes. In the analysis under discussion certain regions engulf others, thereby providing a merge.

Considering only one feature plane, the phagocyte heuristic merges adjacent regions if the boundary between them is weak and the resulting region has a shorter boundary than the original two. A weak boundary is taken to imply that the regions are similar and should be united. This is obviously not necessarily the case in general.

Let P_k and P_l be the perimeters of two adjacent regions S_k and S_l. Also let W_{kl} measure the weakness of the boundary between them. Define it as the number of boundary segments with strength less than θ_1, where the strength of a segment is taken as its gradient. Then, merging occurs if

$$\frac{W_{kl}}{\min(P_k, P_l)} > \theta_2 \tag{8.6}$$

where $0 < \theta_2 \leq 1$. The parameter θ_2 is data-dependent, being related to the number of gray levels in the picture and the dynamic range. It controls the merging: if it is small, many regions satisfy the criterion of Equation (8.6). If it is large, few regions are merged; in this case one region would practically have to surround another for merging to happen.

The weakness heuristic is usually applied after segmentation has been carried out by using the phagocyte heuristic, because its effect tends to be very local in nature. Two regions, S_k and S_l, are merged if W_{kl} is above a fixed percentage of their total shared boundary B_{kl}. Thus, we merge if

$$\frac{W_{kl}}{B_{kl}} > \theta_3 \tag{8.7}$$

Note that this criterion should be applied very reservedly because the absolute length of B_{kl} is not being taken into account. Therefore, short and weak shared boundaries of two large adjacent regions might be wrongly merged because of the gray-level properties in a local neighborhood of the boundary. This kind of "leakage" makes it even difficult to apply simple merging criteria to eliminate very small "noise" regions by merging them with their most similar neighbors.

Instead of considering each local neighborhood at one time for the purpose of region merging, Pavlidis [60, 61, 62, 63] has proposed a method based on functional approximation. Segmentation is conceived as an optimization problem in which the best piecewise approximation to the one-dimensional curve representing one row of the $N \times N$ image array $I(i, j)$ is sought. The resulting N approximations are then characterized by a graph. A heuristic graph search, based on criteria similar to those presented in this section, is used to merge the data into two-dimensional regions.

A recent paper by Zucker [105] has surveyed and discussed methods of partial segmentation. He raises three important issues, which should be addressed by any new approach to the problem. The first deals with the existence and number of absolute thresholds associated with a particular method. How sensitive is the final segmentation to these thresholds? Region merging requires a minimum of one threshold, and the result is directly related to this parameter value. The second point is concerned with the order in which the pixels are examined. All the variations discussed in this section are order-dependent! Finally, the last issue concerns a method of global initialization for the segmentation process. What are the "seeds" that are used to grow the regions? In this section, a simple raster scan of the pixels is employed.

From these comments we observe that region merging on the basis of a general-purpose model suffers from many computational disadvantages. Nevertheless, it is a fast and efficient method for obtaining the "uniform patches" that constitute a picture.

8.3.3 Splitting Regions

When attempting to merge two regions, a decision must be made whether a sufficient degree of similarity exists between the two entities. On the other hand, splitting a region implies the actual creation of entities according to some criterion. Initially, we really do not know into how many subregions a given region should be broken down. Hence, this makes region splitting a much more difficult task.

Region merging is based on the assumption of uniformity, thereby implying that a histogram of a cohesive region should be unimodal. We are therefore able to model it as a Gaussian distribution and use the mean and standard deviations as the parameters for controlling the merging process. The implication of this argument is that if a region is described by a multimodal histogram, it should be split in such a manner as to result in regions with unimodal histograms. Indeed, this is the major philosophy behind region splitting and was first introduced by Prewitt and Mendelsohn [69] in their research on the analysis of white blood cells for the automation of cervical screening. They found that the histogram of the array obtained by placing a window around a single cell was trimodal. One peak existed for each of the objects in the picture, namely, the nucleus, cytoplasm, and background. The problem is then reduced to one of threshold selection in a histogram [98].

This so-called mode method is the one that is most often used [69]. Segmentation is achieved by selecting the thresholds in the valleys of the histogram, as discussed earlier in Section 1.4. Usually the histogram is first smoothed and then an exhaustive search is made for all the peaks (modes) and valleys (antimodes). The peaks correspond to the objects in the picture, while the valleys are assumed to result from the much less numerous edge pixels. An alternative is to derive more complex models of the curve or parts of the curve based on a priori knowledge of the data [95].

Suppose we were first to isolate only one peak in the histogram using the "two-sigma" method [33]. Assuming a Gaussian representation, the peak can be described by

$$H(I) = \frac{1}{2\pi\sqrt{\sigma}} \exp\left[-\tfrac{1}{2}\left(\frac{I-\mu}{\sigma}\right)^2\right] \tag{8.8}$$

where μ and σ are the mean and standard deviation, respectively. A fast method for calculating σ is to first compute h, the "half-width," which is defined as the full width at half-maximum. Then it can be shown that

$$h = 2.354\sigma \tag{8.9}$$

Given that the peak in the distribution has been obtained by means of a search, h and thence 2σ can easily be computed. Thresholds

$$\theta_l = -2\sigma \qquad \text{and} \qquad \theta_r = 2\sigma \tag{8.10}$$

can arbitrarily be set to isolate those points in the image that are part of the object modeled by this mode. This method was used by Levine [33] in research related to scene analysis for a "breadboard" robot, which was ultimately to traverse the surface of the planet Mars, carrying out various scientific experiments.

For this method to be useful, it is necessary to associate the peaks in the histogram (signal-level data) with a particular generic object model (semantic meaning). In most cases in which the image consists of objects on a clear background, this is quite possible. However, complex indoor or outdoor scenes present difficulties to this approach. It is important to realize that although the method is based on the assumption of the existence of a cohesive region, there is no guarantee that the pixels obtained with the thresholds θ_l and θ_r will form a connected set. Also note that h may not always be computable in an arbitrary multimodal histogram, and an alternative approach is then indicated.

The next increment in complexity is to assume that a region contains two objects which produce a bimodal histogram. The method was originally suggested by Chow and Kaneko [12] as a means of detecting the boundary of the left ventricle from cineangiograms. The threshold separating the two modes is selected by minimizing the probability of misclassification. The analysis below is based on [52], in which the method is applied to images of machine parts, shown in Figure 8.12.

Let the $N \times N$ image $I(i, j)$ be divided into square windows of dimension $n \times n$. An attempt is made to fit a mixture of two Gaussians to each window, from which a complete threshold array $\theta(i, j)$ can be computed by interpolation. Three steps are invoked for each $n \times n$ window as follows.

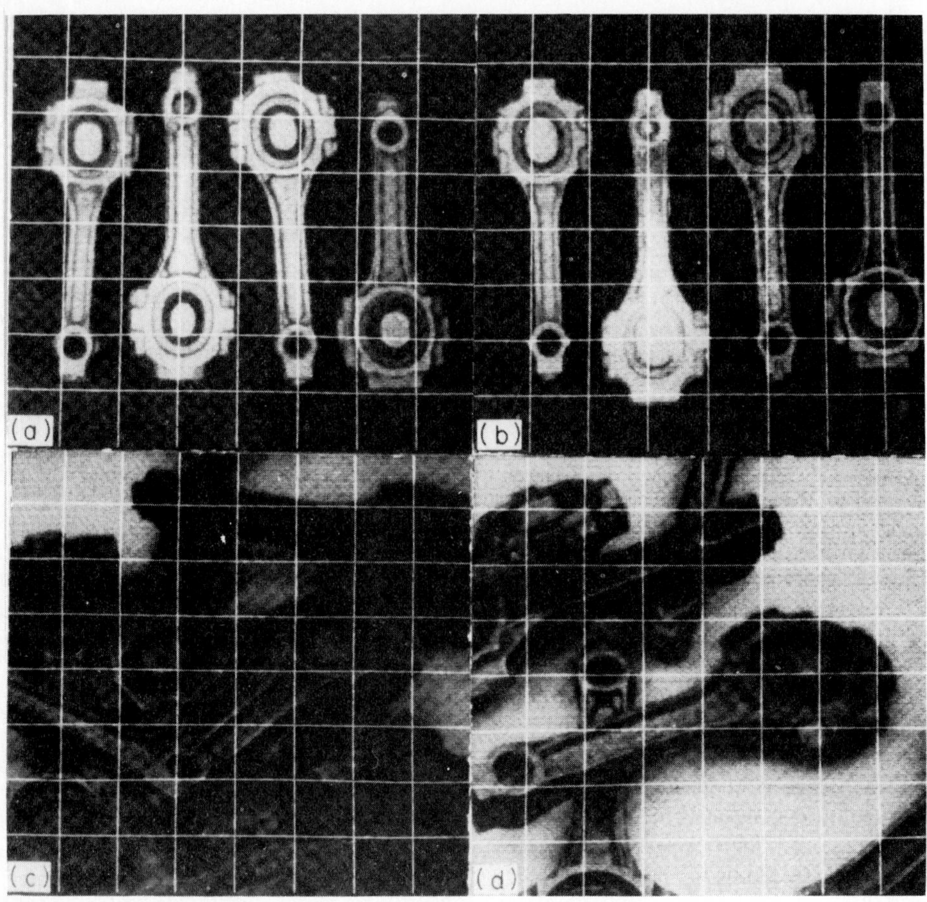

Figure 8.12 Four test pictures showing the windows over which the local histograms are computed. The connecting rods in pictures (*a*) and (*b*) are obviously prearranged and might be used for creating a model for a data base. The other pictures (*c*) and (*d*) present a scene which would be more appropriate for the bin-of-parts problem. The latter involves the selection of an object with a computer-controlled manipulator using visual feedback, that is, an intelligent robot. (*From Y. Nakagawa and A. Rosenfeld, "Some Experiments on Variable Thresholding," Pattern Recognition, vol. 11, no. 3, 1979, pp. 191–204.*)

The first step is a decision about whether or not bimodality exists. Define the mean μ and standard deviation σ of the histogram $H(I)$ (which runs from $I = 0$ to $I = I_m$) by

$$\mu = \frac{1}{n^2} \sum_I IH(I)$$

$$(8.11)$$

and

$$\sigma = \left[\frac{1}{n} \sum_I H(I)(I - \mu^2)\right]^{1/2}$$

respectively. We then decide that the histogram is bimodal if $\sigma > 3$. A threshold computation will be performed on all windows for which this condition holds.

The second step involves a least-squares fit to $H(I)$ of the mixture of two Gaussians $M(I)$, such that

$$M(I) = \frac{A_1}{\sigma_1} \exp\left[-\tfrac{1}{2}\left(\frac{I - \mu_1}{\sigma_1}\right)^2\right] + \frac{A_2}{\sigma_2} \exp\left[-\tfrac{1}{2}\left(\frac{I - \mu_2}{\sigma_2}\right)^2\right] \tag{8.12}$$

We wish to select the six parameters A_1, A_2, μ_1, μ_2, σ_1, and σ_2 to fit the model $M(I)$ to $H(I)$. By using a smoothed version of $H(I)$†, the deepest valley is obtained at $I = I_v$, which thereby permits us to divide the histogram into two unimodal curves. Estimates of the six parameters may then be obtained by treating the histogram as the sum of two independent curves as follows:

$$\mu_1 = \frac{1}{n_1} \sum_{I=0}^{I_v} IH(I) \qquad \mu_2 = \frac{1}{n_2} \sum_{I=I_v}^{I_m} IH(I)$$

$$\sigma_1 = \left[\frac{1}{n_1} \sum_{I=0}^{I_v} H(I)(I - \mu_1)^2\right]^{1/2} \qquad \sigma_2 = \left[\frac{1}{n_2} \sum_{I=I_v}^{I_m} H(I)(I - \mu_2)^2\right]^{1/2} \tag{8.13}$$

$$A_1 = \frac{n_1\sigma_1}{\sum_{I=0}^{I_v} \exp\left[-\tfrac{1}{2}\left(\frac{I - \mu_1}{\sigma_1}\right)^2\right]} \qquad A_2 = \frac{n_2\sigma_2}{\sum_{I=I_v}^{I_m} \exp\left[-\tfrac{1}{2}\left(\frac{I - \mu_2}{\sigma_2}\right)^2\right]}$$

where

$$n_1 = \sum_{I=0}^{I_v} H(I) \qquad \text{and} \qquad n_2 = \sum_{I=I_v}^{I_m} H(I)$$

With these values as good initial estimates, a standard optimization technique is used to minimize the quadratic function $\Sigma_I [M(I) - H(I)]^2$.

Finally, the third step again tests the bimodality of the approximation. A threshold is chosen for a particular $n \times n$ window if the following conditions

† The five-point filter $(\frac{1}{9}, \frac{2}{9}, \frac{3}{9}, \frac{2}{9}, \frac{1}{9})$ is used in [52].

are satisfied:

$$\mu_2 - \mu_1 > 4 \qquad 0.1 < \sigma_1/\sigma_2 < 1.00 \qquad \delta < 0.8 \tag{8.14}$$

where the valley-to-peak ratio δ is given by

$$\delta = \frac{\min M \text{ in } [\mu_1, \mu_2]}{\min[M(\mu_1), M(\mu_2)]} \tag{8.15}$$

The threshold θ, which minimizes the probability of misclassification, can be obtained by solving the quadratic equation.

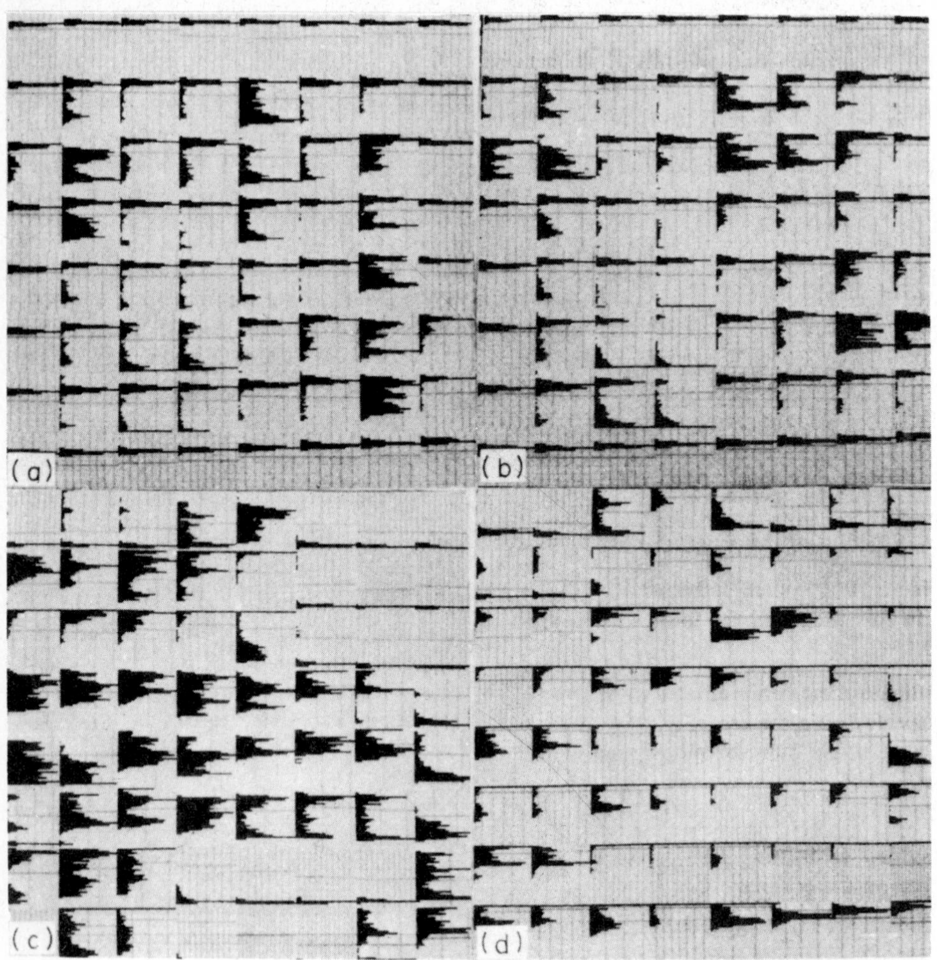

Figure 8.13 Window histograms for the pictures in Figure 8.12. (*From Y. Nakagawa and A. Rosenfeld, "Some Experiments on Variable Thresholding," Pattern Recognition, vol. 11, no. 3, 1979, pp. 191–204.*)

$$\left(\frac{1}{\sigma_1^2}-\frac{1}{\sigma_2^2}\right)\theta^2+2\left(\frac{\mu_2}{\sigma_2^2}-\frac{\mu_1}{\sigma_1^2}\right)\theta+\frac{\mu_1^2}{\sigma_1^2}-\frac{\mu_2^2}{\sigma_2^2}+2\ln\frac{A_2\sigma_1}{A_1\sigma_2}=0 \tag{8.16}$$

Given the thresholds θ for the windows of $I(i, j)$, $\theta(i, j)$ is then computed by straightforward interpolation methods [52]. Figure 8.13 gives $H(I)$ for each window in Figure 8.12, and Figure 8.14 shows the fitted $M(I)$ for those assumed to be bimodal. The variable $\theta(i, j)$ is presented in Figure 8.15, while the resulting thresholded images are given in Figure 8.16. The latter should be compared with Figure 8.17, which shows a single global threshold computed for each of the four pictures by fitting $M(I)$ in Equation (8.13) to the histogram of the complete picture array. The variable thresholding approach is superior in the first three pictures but seems to perform worse than the fixed threshold in

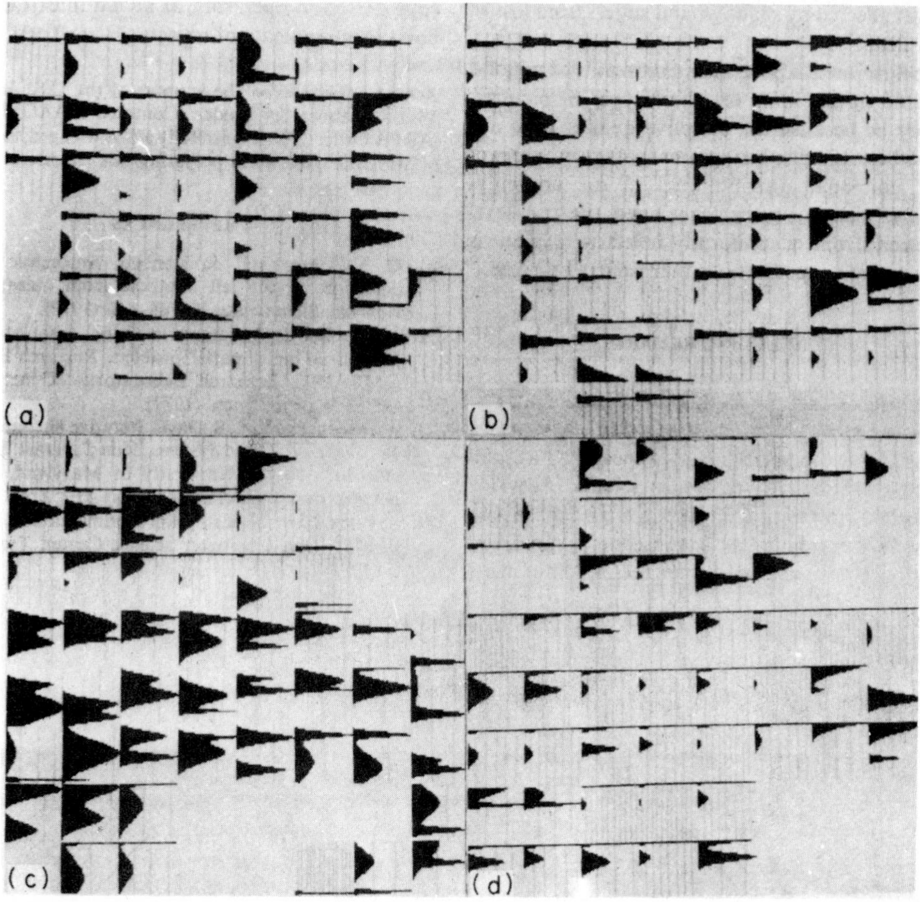

Figure 8.14 Two-Gaussian approximations to those window histograms in Figure 8.12 that were judged to be bimodal. (*From Y. Nakagawa and A. Rosenfeld, "Some Experiments on Variable Thresholding," Pattern Recognition, vol. 11, no. 3, 1979, pp. 191–204.*)

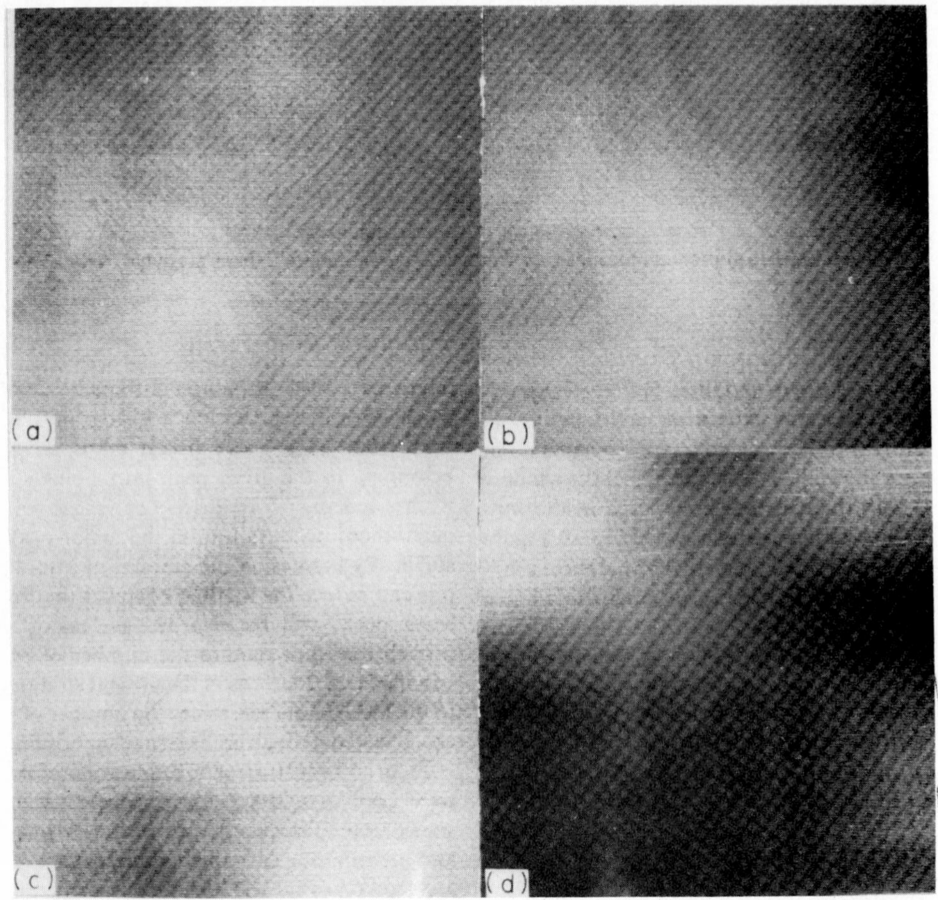

Figure 8.15 Point thresholds, obtained by interpolation on the window thresholds, for the four pictures. (*From Y. Nakagawa and A. Rosenfeld, "Some Experiments on Variable Thresholding," Pattern Recognition, vol. 11, no.* 3, *1979, pp. 191–204.*)

certain parts of the fourth picture. We note that the latter has a histogram which is probably the closest to a mixture of two Gaussians of approximately equal values of A_1 and A_2. The method has been extended to trimodal $M(I)$ in [52].

We have seen that threshold selection on the basis of the picture histogram can be used to split a region—not, of course, into two regions but into many. Tsuji and Tomita [86, 88] have used texture properties to compute a set of seven histograms, and Ohlander, Price and Reddy [59] have employed nine color attributes (P, Γ, B, I, H, S, Y, I, Q). These authors suggest a method in which region splitting is performed recursively, beginning with the complete image array $I(i, j)$, and subsequently, on the remaining portion of $I(i, j)$ at each

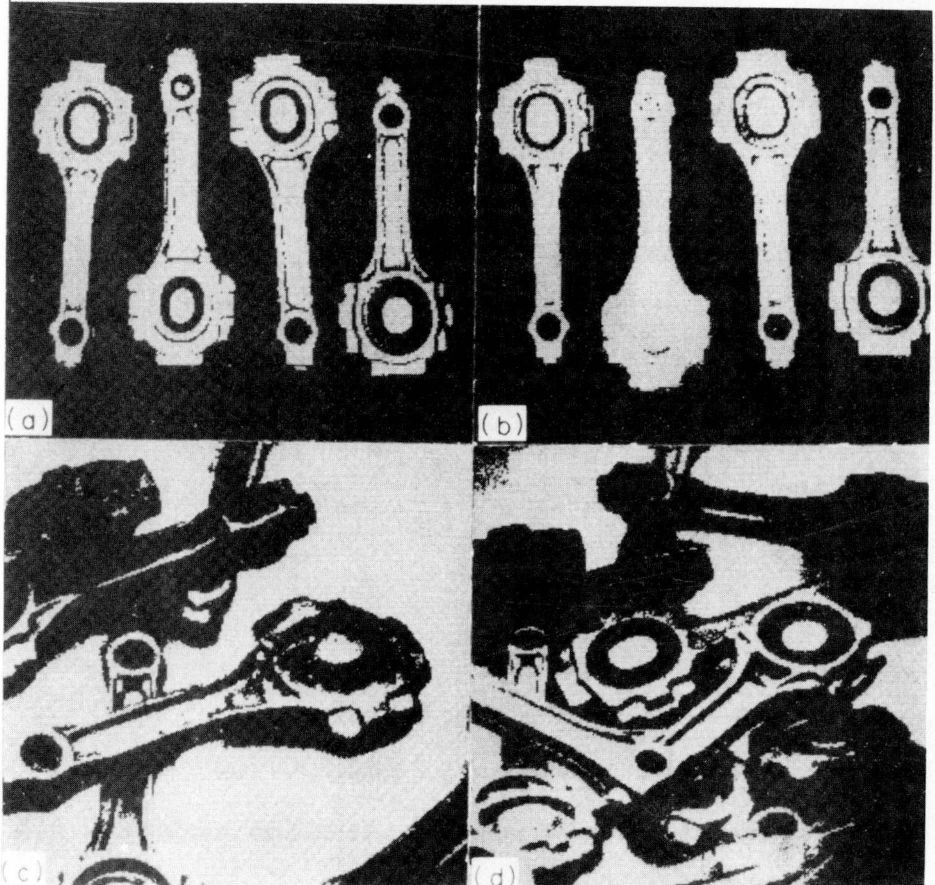

Figure 8.16 Results of applying the thresholds shown in Figure 8.15 to the pictures of Figure 8.12. (*From Y. Nakagawa and A. Rosenfeld, "Some Experiments on Variable Thresholding," Pattern Recognition, vol. 11, no. 3, 1979, pp. 191–204.*)

iteration. The "best" peak in the set of histograms is selected at each iteration and θ_l and θ_r are computed. The set of pixels having values of this particular feature (similarity) between these limits is labeled and a binary array mask describing the set is created. This process will generally result in a certain number of small regions, small holes in regions, or thin links between regions. Therefore, smoothing is applied to the binary mask as a means of reducing this "noise." Connected regions (proximity) are now extracted from the elements of the binary mask, and the regions covered are thus eliminated from further consideration. The process is reapplied to the remaining pixels. Figure 8.18 illustrates an example of this process of region splitting.

Instead of just analyzing a set of one-dimensional histograms, a multi-dimensional histogram may be computed and the boundaries between the

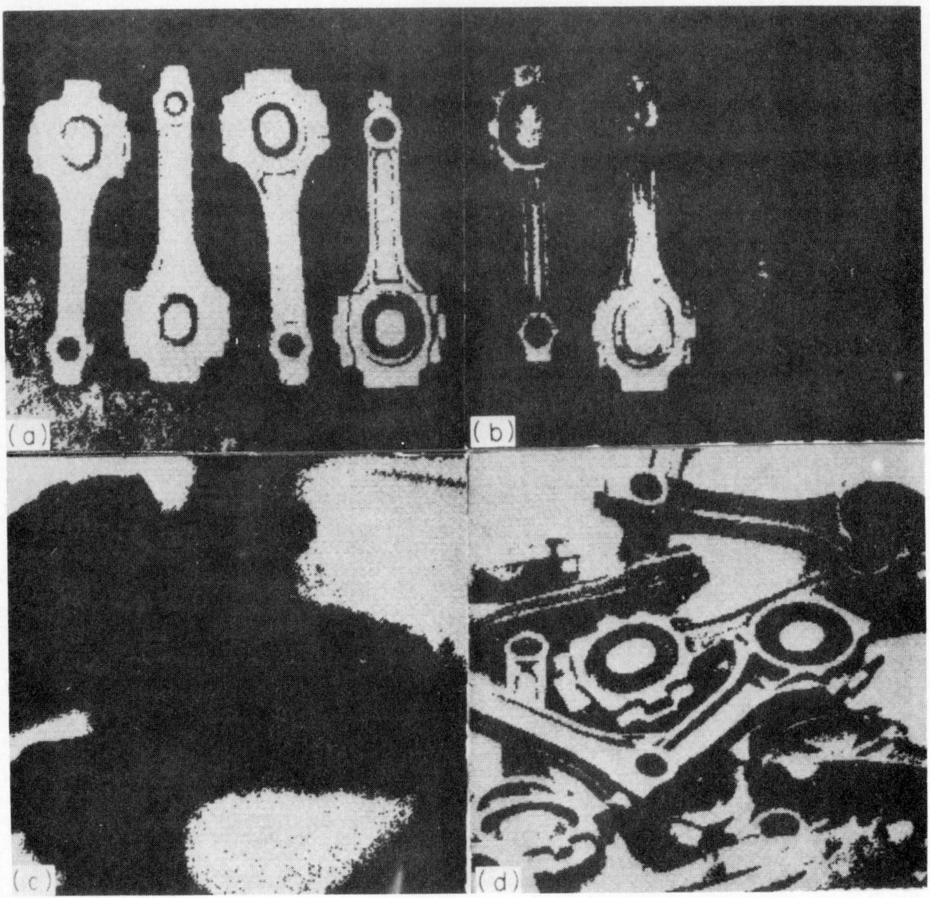

Figure 8.17 Results of applying fixed thresholds (obtained by fitting two Gaussians to the histograms of the entire pictures) to the pictures of Figure 8.12. (*From Y. Nakagawa and A. Rosenfeld, "Some Experiments on Variable Thresholding," Pattern Recognition, vol. 11, no. 3, 1979, pp. 191–204.*)

multidimensional clusters sought [11, 13, 19, 77, 78, 79]. This procedure is necessarily more complex but deals directly with the sought-after surfaces rather than looking at their projections. Other interesting applications of histogram analysis and thresholding for region segmentation can be found in [7, 50]. An alternative to splitting on the basis of the modes in a histogram, is the criterion

$$[\max I(i,j) - \min I(i,j)] \leq 2\epsilon \qquad \epsilon \text{ small} \tag{8.17}$$

used by Horowitz and Pavlidis [24] in the so-called split-and-merge procedure. This unique approach uses pyramids as the underlying data structure for region segmentation (see Chapter 5).

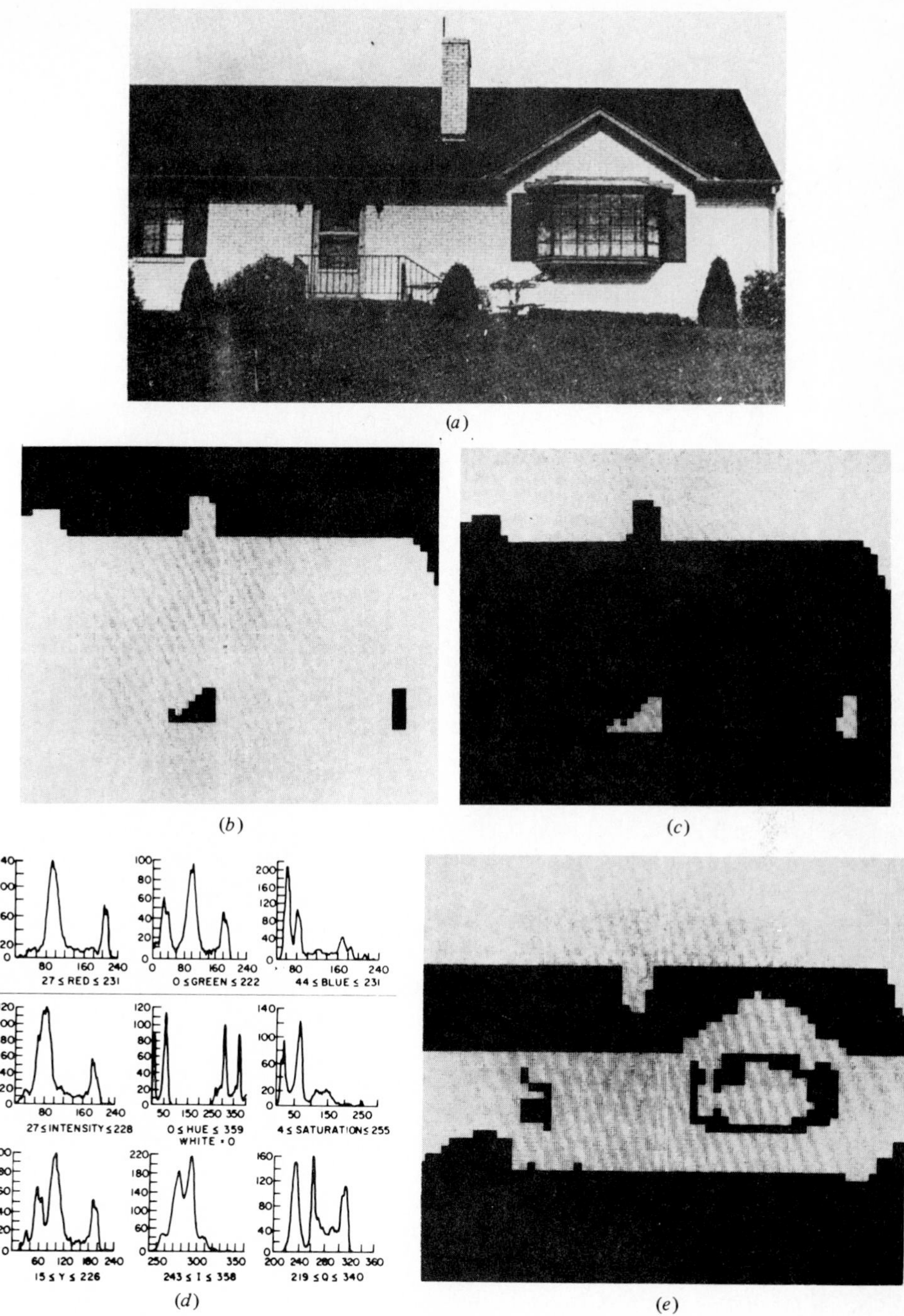

(*a*)

(*b*) (*c*)

(*d*) (*e*)

Figure 8.18(*a*)–(*e*) (Caption on page 404.)

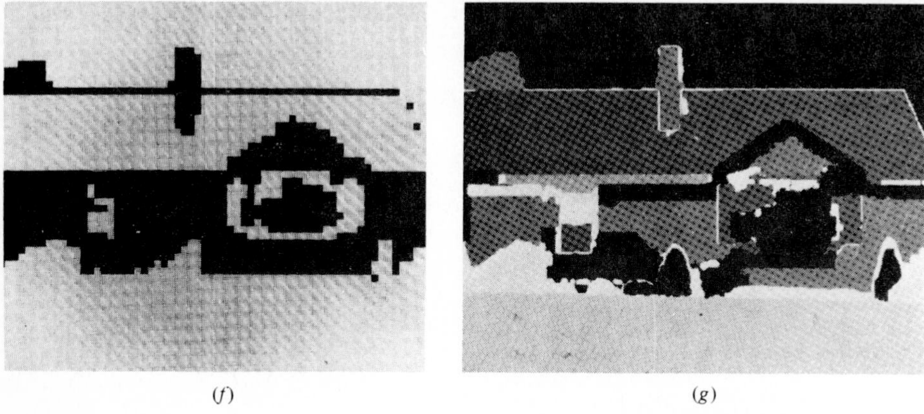

(f) (g)

Figure 8.18 Picture segmentation using recursive region splitting. (*a*) The house image. (*b*) At a certain stage in the processing of the house image, the three regions shown in black have already been segmented. (*c*) The area remaining to be segmented is the region shown in black. (*d*) Set of histograms for portions of house image shown in (*c*). (*e*) Using the histograms in (*d*), the best peak is selected. Four connected regions are then obtained by applying the upper and lower thresholds for this peak. (It may also be necessary to filter the result and eliminate "spurious" regions.) (*f*) These points remain to be segmented at the next step. New histograms are computed and the process is repeated until the complete image has been segmented. (*g*) Segmentation of the house image. (*From R. Ohlander, K. Price, and D. R. Reddy, "Picture Segmentation Using a Recursive Region Splitting Method," Computer Graphics and Image Processing, vol. 8, December 1978, pp. 313–333.*)

In this section we have discussed two segmentation processes, region merging and region splitting. Both are accomplished by using a general-purpose approach, which takes no account of the particular model of the scene under study. The next section deals with an approach which is capable of segmenting the picture and, in addition, assigning object names to the regions.

8.4 COMPETITION AND COOPERATION

The general problem of picture interpretation cannot be considered as a two-stage sequential process in which regions based on low-level features are first independently determined and then certain object names are associated with these regions. On the contrary, one would expect a cooperative computation, involving both region segmentation and object recognition [3, 4]. For example, Figure 8.19*a* shows a specific point in the image analysis at which the image segmentation has resulted in two regions. The top region is green and might assume the label of either pistachio ice cream or a crown of maple leaves; the bottom might perhaps be labeled an ice cream cone or a tree trunk. Note that the foliage and trunk combination cooperate (excitory interaction), as is also the case with the ice cream and cone combination. However, the two pairs of subgraphs compete (inhibitory interaction) with each other for supre-

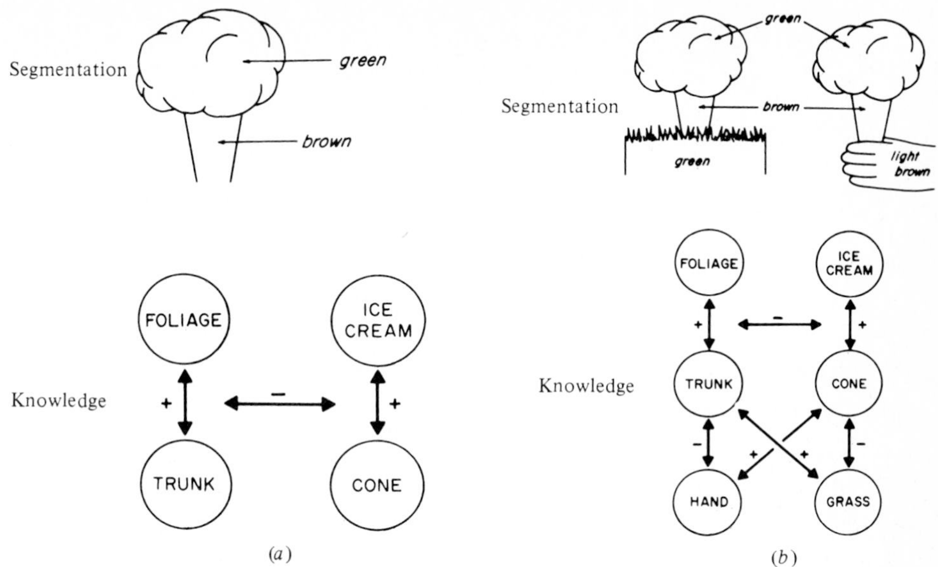

Figure 8.19 The use of context to resolve ambiguities. (*a*) The maple tree and ice cream cone hypotheses compete with each other as possible region labelings. (*b*) The addition of a third region could provide the contextual information to tip the balance to one of the interpretations. (*Adapted from M. A. Arbib, "Artificial Intelligence and Brain Theory: Unities and Diversities," Annals of Biomedical Engineering, vol. 3, 1975, pp. 238–274.*)

macy, since it is not evident which is the appropriate region labeling. This dilemma may be eliminated by introduction of local context, which depends on the interpretation of a neighboring third region, as shown in Figure 8.19*b*. If the latter seems to be grass, then the maple tree hypothesis would prevail; if the additional regions appeared to be a hand, we are probably looking at an ice cream cone. Ideally, the emergence of one of these interpretations should then have an influence on the basic low-level region partition as well (so-called top-down feedback). Such an interactive process of local competition and cooperation achieves a global result by means of propagation. The method to be discussed in this section is referred to as "relaxation labeling" [73].

"Relaxation" is an optimization technique in which a multivariable performance criterion is extremized, subject to the satisfaction of a set of constraints. It is characterized by the requirement that the problem be decomposed into many subproblems, the solution of which leads to a global result. This implies a distributed and parallel computation rather than the more usual sequential one. The constraints embody the knowledge about the problem and provide the underlying context which ultimately resolves the local ambiguities. The method was first employed in computer vision by Waltz [96], who applied it to line drawings of polyhedra subjected to complex lighting conditions. Mackworth [39] has described how attempts to understand the scene analysis of the so-called blocks world ultimately led to what is referred to as "discrete relaxation." This was then generalized and extended by Rosenfeld, Hummel and Zucker [75] to the case in which a probabilistic model of the data is more suitable.

The discrete algorithm can be described as follows. Suppose we have a set of nodes, for example, the regions in a picture. Also suppose that we have another list of possible class names (sometimes called "labels") which could be associated with each node. The nodes are locally related to each other by a neighborhood relationship governing which nodes are deemed to influence each other. This generally takes the form of a binary relationship defined over pairs of nodes, and it specifies which nodes can directly communicate with and influence each other. For example, in an image array, the four- or eight-connected pixels to (i, j) would constitute a neighborhood model. Adjacent regions in a picture segmentation are another good example. The knowledge about the scene is codified in a set of constraints among the class names.

With these four concepts defined (nodes, labels, neighborhood relationship, constraints), this iterative, parallel algorithm eliminates inconsistent names from the list associated with each node, according to the imposed constraints. Parallelism is implied, since the process may be independently carried out in each neighborhood. Probabilistic relaxation is an extension of this process in which we associate a confidence value with each of the possible labels for a node. It is as if, even with the constraints, we are not really sure which of the class names is the appropriate one for a particular node. The computation then updates the list of confidences for each node, ultimately iterating to a consistent situation in which one class label predominates for each node.

We note that the set of nodes and the associated neighborhood model (the arcs) define a graph in which a consistent label assignment for the nodes is sought. Thus, the relaxation process may also be viewed as a graph search in which a solution network is sought which is consistent with the given constraints. Mackworth [39, 40] has stated that this requires conditions of node consistency (unary predicates), arc consistency (binary predicates), and path consistency. Relaxation labeling is therefore seen as an example of an arc consistency algorithm. Montanari [47] has also proved that, although the minimal network satisfying these three consistency conditions cannot be solved efficiently, an equivalent but suboptimal path-consistent network can be found by ensuring that every path of length 2 is path-consistent. His algorithm for computing this network is a generalization of the relaxation-labeling algorithm [39, 40].

As an extension of this viewpoint, we observe that relaxation can also be viewed as a distributed network of processes operating in parallel while competing and cooperating in the search for a consistently labeled solution graph. The computation performed at each node processor is solely dependent on the information stored in the neighboring node processors. To relate this to biological systems it is interesting that Montalvo [45] has analyzed the underlying mechanisms of three different neural network models and shown that they function on a similar basis of local competition and consensus.

> [The] models provide a clear comparison between mutually facilitory units and mutually inhibitory units along two spatially distinct dimensions. The units along the consensus dimension tend to cluster themselves in state space while the units along the competition dimension tend to separate. Not only is this decomposition useful to dynamic characterization of the networks but it points up the decisionary nature of the networks. When populations of cells are clearly separated in state space decisive action is possible.

Thus relaxation labeling processes and conventional neural network models seem to be quite compatible!

We now turn to the mathematical details of the updating procedure, the so-called interaction model [75]. First, we shall present the discrete model, which has been referred to as a parallel version of the filtering algorithm of Waltz. Let $S = \{S_1, \ldots, S_k, \ldots, S_m\}$ be the set of nodes to be labeled and $\Lambda = \{\lambda_1, \ldots, \lambda_n\}$ be the set of allowable labels. Of course, not all the labels in Λ can be assigned to a particular $S_k \in S$. Therefore we define $\Lambda_k \subseteq \Lambda$, $1 \le k \le m$ as the set of possible labels for S_k (node consistency). Binary constraints for each pair of labels λ_k and λ_l are given in the form of a set of compatible labels defined as $\Lambda_{kl} \subseteq \Lambda_k \times \Lambda_l$, $k \neq l$. Thus, $(\lambda, \lambda') \in \Lambda_{kl}$ implies that node S_k with label λ is compatible, according to the world model, with node S_l having label λ'.

Let $\mathscr{L} = \{L_1, \ldots, L_m\}$ define a labeling of the nodes S in which a subset of m labels $L_k \subseteq \Lambda$ is assigned to each node $S_k \in S$. The set $\mathscr{L}$ is then said to be consistent if all the binary constraints implied by Λ_{kl} are satisfied. This means that

$$(\{\lambda\} \times L_l) \cap \Lambda_{kl} \neq 0 \tag{8.18}$$

for all $\lambda \in L_k$. A greatest consistent labeling $\mathscr{L}^{(\max)}$ can be shown to exist which contains as subsets all the other consistent labelings [75]. $\mathscr{L}^{(\max)}$ may be null and also does not necessarily associate only one label with each node. An interesting case is the Penrose triangle shown in Figure 6.17. Obviously, each vertex is locally consistent, but no global triangular interpretation is possible. Assume that $\Lambda = \{\lambda, \lambda'\}$ is the set of labels for the sides $S = \{S_1, S_2, S_3\}$ of the triangle. By staring at the figure it is observed that each side may be considered to be either projecting away from the viewer (into the plane of the paper) or towards the viewer (out of the paper). For a real triangle, it can be observed that all pairs of local combinations are consistent. That is

$$\Lambda_{kl}(\lambda, \lambda') = \{(\lambda, \lambda), (\lambda', \lambda'), (\lambda, \lambda'), (\lambda', \lambda)\} \tag{8.19}$$

Thus obviously, $L_1 = L_2 = L_3 = \Lambda = \mathscr{L}^{(\max)}$, and it is not possible to discard any of the labels from any of the nodes. There does not seem to be a labeling in which each side of the triangle assumes only one label. Locally, at each vertex four different combinations of assertions are possible, but no single, unambiguous global figure emerges. Clearly, this is an impossible object!

We observe that a labeling may be termed unambiguous if it is consistent and each node has assigned to it only one label. Since it is our objective to arrive at such a solution, the discrete relaxation algorithm must be defined as a two-stage process. First, a greatest consistent labeling is obtained, and then, an unambiguous one is derived from it.

The first step is the parallel label-discarding algorithm, Δ, as it is referred to in [75]. Suppose the initial labeling $\mathscr{L}^{(0)}$ is given by

$$\mathscr{L}^{(0)} = \{\Lambda_1, \ldots, \Lambda_m\} \tag{8.20}$$

and $\mathscr{L}^{(K)}$ is the labeling at the Kth iteration. To compute $\mathscr{L}^{(K+1)}$, we consider each set $L_k^{(K)}$ independently. We eliminate from the list any label λ which is inconsistent with the constraints associating node S_k and each neighboring node S_l. Therefore, the label λ for node S_k is retained if there exists a $\lambda' \in L_l^{(K)}$ for every node S_l for which compatibility can be established according to the binary constraints Λ_{kl}. This process converges, and it can be shown that after a finite number of iterations $\mathscr{L}^{(K)} = \mathscr{L}^{(\max)}$. That is, the algorithm Δ yields a maximally consistent labeling. However, this is only a locally consistent labeling, since in general each node will have associated with it more than one label.

The second step involves the determination of the unambiguous labeling and employs a tree search similar to that of Waltz [96]. Beginning with $\mathscr{L}^{(\max)}$, we consider each node S_k for which the set $L_k^{(\max)}$ contains two or more labels. We arbitrarily select the label $\lambda \in L_k^{(\max)}$ for this node and discard all the other labels in $L_k^{(\max)}$. Of course, one should initiate the search with each member $\lambda \in L_k^{(\max)}$, but generally a good initial label can be obtained from prior knowledge of the problem. If

$$\mathscr{L}' = \{L_1^{(\max)}, \ldots, L_{k-1}^{(\max)}, \{\lambda\}, L_{k+1}^{(\max)}, \ldots, L_m^{(\max)}\} \tag{8.21}$$

is consistent, consider another node S_l, and so on. However, if $\mathscr{L}'$ is not consistent, the algorithm Δ should be applied to it in order to converge to the new, but now reduced, maximally consistent labeling $\mathscr{L}'' \subseteq \mathscr{L}'$. If $\mathscr{L}''$ is the null set, there does not exist any unambiguous node labeling for which λ is the label for node S_k. Perhaps another $\lambda \in L^{(\max)}$ or another S_k should be used to initiate the search. If, on the other hand, $\mathscr{L}''$ is not null, a consistent and unambiguous labeling has been obtained for node S_k. The search is now repeated for another node S_l for which L_l'' contains more than one label, and so on. This procedure will eventually determine all the existing unambiguous labelings for this discrete model. Other algorithms are given in [43].

We now turn to the so-called stochastic or probabilistic model. Previously it was assumed that the assignment of possible labels to a node was done with perfect confidence. Either the node could or could not take on a given name based on the given constraint relationships. However, suppose that we are not that sure about this and would like to hedge our bets at each iteration. This can be accomplished by attaching to each label a parameter that measures the likelihood that it is indeed this label that is correct for this particular node. Define a probability or, more correctly, a confidence vector $\mathbf{p}_k$ for each node $S_k \subset S$; then, for each $\lambda \in \Lambda$, $p_k(\lambda)$ is the weight we attach to the node S_k when it is interpreted as the label λ. These weights are normalized by requiring that

$$0 \leq p_k(\lambda) \leq 1 \qquad \text{and} \qquad \sum_{l=1}^{m} p_k(\lambda_l) = 1 \tag{8.22}$$

With the discrete model labels were discarded at each iteration. In this case the vectors $\mathbf{p}_k$ for each node S_k will be updated based on an available constraint model.

Again, binary constraints are inadequate and we must define a compatibility function $r_{kl}(\lambda, \lambda')$ to characterize our knowledge of the scene or picture. The magnitude of this function measures the degree of compatibility of the label λ for node S_k with the label λ' for node S_l. Its determination may be as complex as desirable, perhaps even specified by a set of logical Boolean constraints. It is similar to a correlation function, being positive if the two labels λ and λ' occur quite frequently together, negative if they occur together rarely, and equal to zero if they are independent. Accordingly, let $r_{kl}\colon \Lambda_k \times \Lambda_l \rightarrow [-1, +1]$, and

1. $r_{kl}(\lambda, \lambda') > 0$ if λ and λ' are compatible labels for nodes S_k and S_l, respectively
2. $r_{kl}(\lambda, \lambda') < 0$ if λ and λ' are incompatible labels for nodes S_k and S_l, respectively
3. $r_{kl}(\lambda, \lambda') = 0$ if the label λ for node S_k is independent of the label λ' for node S_l

Generally compatibility functions are provided by users according to their perceived model of the image analysis problem. However, Peleg and Rosenfeld [66] have suggested a method for automatically computing $r_{kl}(\lambda, \lambda')$ in certain cases, and we shall return to this point later. A psychophysical method for determining compatibility functions is discussed in [46].

The change in confidence $\Delta p_k(\lambda)^{(K)}$ at iteration K may be given by [75]:

$$\Delta p_k(\lambda)^{(K)} = \sum_l d_{kl} \left[\sum_{\lambda'} r_{kl}(\lambda, \lambda') p_l(\lambda')^{(K)} \right] \tag{8.23}$$

where the variable d_{kl} may be selected to weight the contributions from the neighbors of S_k according to their importance and $\Sigma_l d_{kl} = 1$. Note that $\Delta p_k^{(K)}$ measures the degree of support in the neighborhood of S_k of the interpretation λ and is therefore locally determined. It is influenced by the compatibility of λ with the possible labelings for the neighboring nodes, all the while modified by how confident we are about the labels for these nodes. If $p_l(\lambda')^{(K)}$ is high and $r_{kl}(\lambda, \lambda')$ is positive, $\Delta p_k(\lambda)^{(K)}$ is positive, which indicates that the confidence in this interpretation should be increased. Similarly, if $p_l(\lambda')^{(K)}$ is high but $r_{kl}(\lambda, \lambda')$ is negative, the incremental contribution to the change in confidence can be seen to be negative. For low values of confidence $p_l(\lambda')^{(K)}$, the incremental changes would be small regardless of $r_{kl}(\lambda, \lambda')$. It is because of these positive and negative influences that we may speak of the algorithm as embodying both cooperation and competition [45].

The new values of the confidences of the node interpretations are given by the following nonlinear updating equation [75]:

$$p_k(\lambda)^{(K+1)} = \frac{p_k(\lambda)^{(K)}[1 + \Delta p_k(\lambda)^{(K)}]}{\sum_{\lambda} p_k(\lambda)^{(K)}[1 + \Delta p_k(\lambda)^{(K)}]} \tag{8.24}$$

The denominator ensures that Equation (8.22) is satisfied at each iteration. This is only one of the updating relationships given in the literature, but it is the one most often used. Other procedures may be found in [16, 17, 65, 91, 108]. Convergence of the algorithm to a fixed point is not guaranteed and readers are referred to [107, 111, 112] for more details on this subject. Because Equations (8.23) and (8.24) permit the evaluation of $p_k(\lambda)^{(K+1)}$ on the basis of neighborhood information, it can easily be computed in parallel by a set of m processors, one for each of the nodes S_k. At each iteration $(K+1)$, each processor must first read in each of the vectors $\mathbf{p}_l^{(K)}$ from the neighboring processors and then compute $\Delta\mathbf{p}_k$ according to Equation (8.23). All the processors must either have common access to the compatibility functions or have them stored in their own memories. After this step, each processor can update its own confidences independently on the basis of Equation (8.24). For m nodes and n labels, a sequential machine will require $O(Tmn)$ computations, where T is the number of iterations needed for convergence. A parallel configuration of the type discussed here will only need $O(Tm)$ computations.

Let us now examine how relaxation labeling can be adapted to the problem of region analysis. An interesting application of this approach is to the image analysis of the optic disk [51]. Feature measurements of the disk could be involved in the early diagnosis of certain ophthalmic disorders, such as glaucoma. Figure 8.20 shows the three objects of interest $\Lambda_k (k = 1, 2, 3)$, which can be distinguished on the basis of gray level. These are the choroidal or vascular layer (λ_1), the disk (λ_2), and the pallor (λ_3), which is the result of the atrophy of the optic nerve when subjected to excessive ocular pressure. It is the latter that indicates the onset of glaucoma, and the degree of pallor is sought as a quantification of this disease.

The pixels (i, j) constitute the elements of the set S to be labeled. For each pixel $(i, j) \in I(i, j)$, it is first necessary to compute an initial confidence $p_{(i,j)}(\lambda)^{(0)}$, $\lambda \in \Lambda$. This is our initial guess for the labeling of each pixel in the image. The method used in [51] is based on an analysis of the histogram, whereby a set of class means $\mu_\lambda = \{\mu_1, \mu_2, \mu_3\}$ is determined as being representative. Then $p_{(i,j)}(\lambda)^{(0)}$ is computed for each pixel (i, j) as the Euclidean distance between $I(i, j)$ and the closest mean in μ_λ:

$$p_{(i,j)}(\lambda)^{(0)} = \frac{1/|I(i,j) - \mu_\lambda|}{\sum_{\lambda} [1/|I(i,j) - \mu_\lambda|]} \tag{8.25}$$

Thus, the value of the initial confidence decreases monotonically as it moves

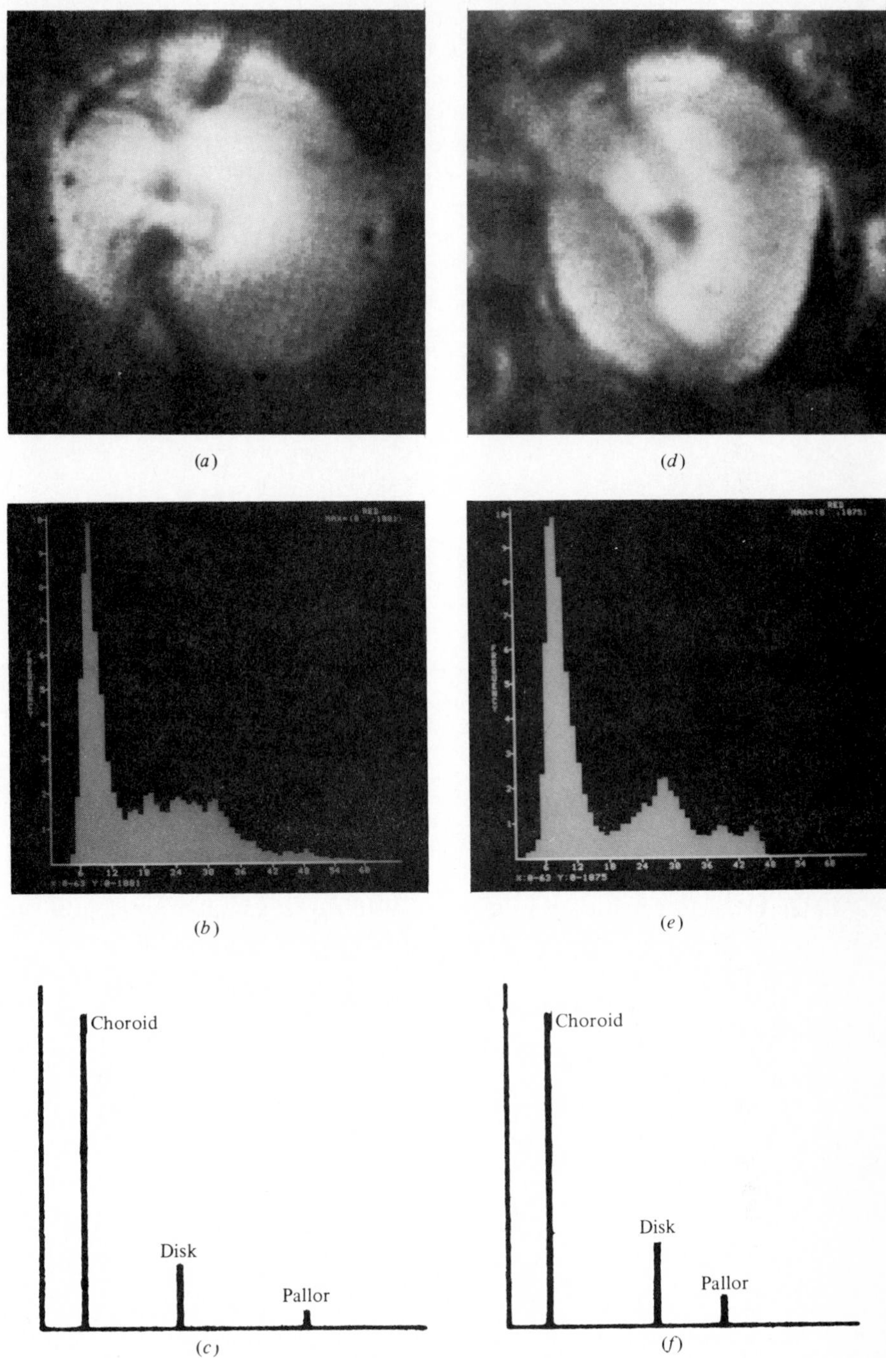

Figure 8.20 (Caption on page 412.)

away from the mean. The set of these three initial confidences, computed according to Equation (8.25), is shown in Figure 8.21. Here, the values from 0 to 1 are represented by the gray values from black to white, respectively. Alternative initial classification methods have also been used [15].

The next step is to define a neighborhood model which is assumed to influence the pixel (i, j). Using four-connectedness, we define this neighborhood as the set of pixels $(i^*, j^*) = \{(i, j+1), (i+1, j), (i, j-1), (i-1, j)\}$. The compatibility function $r_{(i,j)(i^*,j^*)}(\lambda, \lambda')$ is then precomputed on the basis of the initial labeling. Thus, it is a global estimate of the likelihood of a pair of neighboring pixel labels in a particular direction, given the initial image as the source of the statistics. The method involves an estimate based on the initial class probabilities and the joint probability of pairs of labels, as given by Peleg [66]. Using the concept of mutual information, he determined that

$$r_{(i,j)(i^*,j^*)}(\lambda, \lambda') = \ln \frac{N^2 \sum\limits_{\substack{\text{all}\\(i,j)}} p_{(i,j)}(\lambda)^{(0)} p_{(i^*,j^*)}(\lambda')^{(0)}}{\sum\limits_{\substack{\text{all}\\(i,j)}} p_{(i,j)}(\lambda)^{(0)} \sum\limits_{\substack{\text{all}\\(i,j)}} p_{(i^*,j^*)}(\lambda')^{(0)}} \tag{8.26}$$

To ensure that the updated probabilities do not become negative, it is necessary to truncate the expression in the brackets, for example, to keep it in the range e^{-3} to e^{+5}. Then r would fall in the range -5 to $+5$, and the right-hand side of Equation (8.26) would have to be divided by 5 to achieve $r \in [-1, +1]$. See [64] for a discussion of this and other approaches to the computation of compatibility functions from image data.

We now have all the information required, so that Equations (8.23) and (8.24) may be used for iteration to yield an image segmentation. The result is shown in Figure 8.21*b*. A similar approach has been used in multispectral pixel classification [15].

An interesting application of relaxation labeling to regions composed of dot clusters can be found in [110, 111]. Other instances of the use of this methodology in computer vision are line and curve enhancement [64, 68, 70, 106], the determination of depth relationships [36], and the disparity

---

Figure 8.20 The global analysis by histogram of the optic disk. Feature histograms can be used to measure the presence of pallor as skewness in the disk distribution or as areas under the curve components. (*a*) Normal disk, red images. (*b*) Histogram of normal image. Only two peaks are apparent, and there is a "tail" at the right end. (*c*) Schematic histogram of above showing mean brightness of target objects. (*d*) Glaucomatous disk, red image. (*e*) Histogram of the glaucomatous image. Three peaks are apparent owing to the increased pallor. (*f*) Schematic histogram of above. (*From P. A. Nagin and B. Schwartz, "Approaches to Image Analysis of the Optic Disc," Proceedings of the Fifth International Conference on Pattern Recognition, Miami Beach, Dec. 1–4, 1980, pp. 948–956.*)

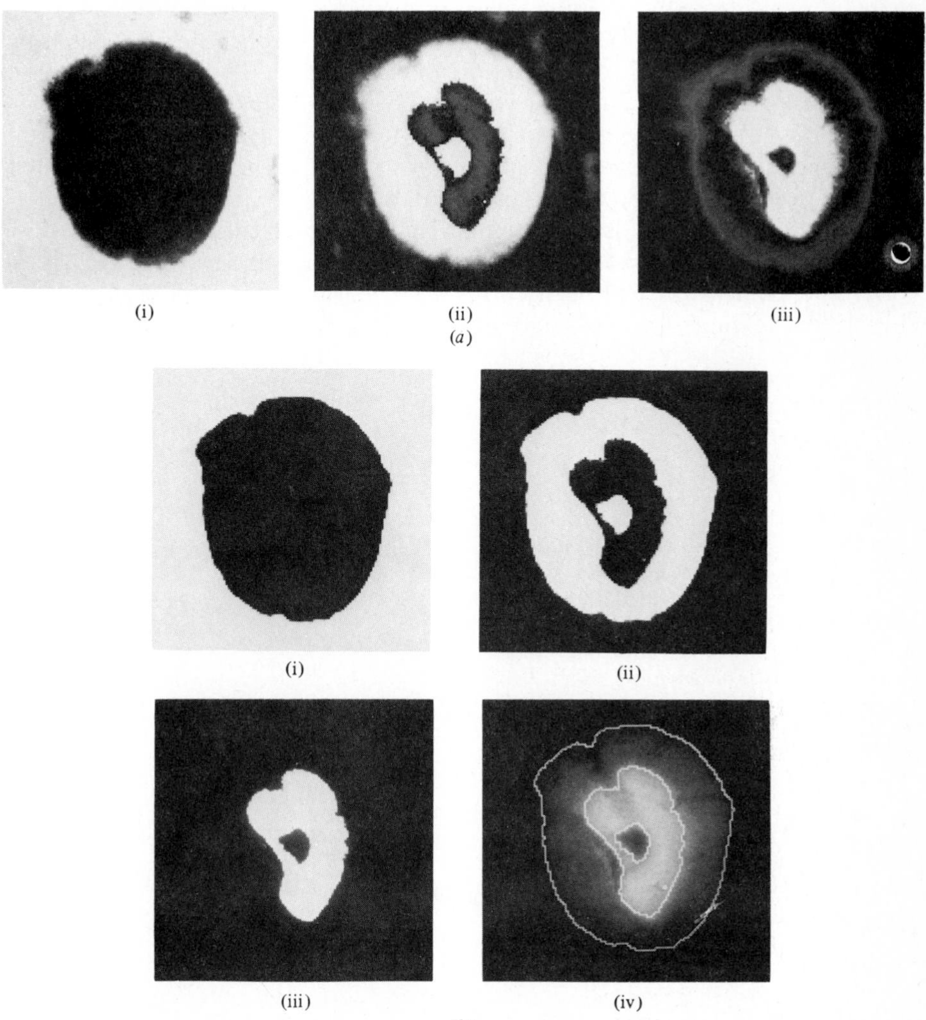

Figure 8.21 Spatial relaxation applied to images of the optic disk. (*a*) The initial confidences for probabilistic labeling. Each pixel is recoded by a brightness level which is proportional to the gray-level difference between its original value and the gray level of each cluster mean (black indicates low probability, white high probability). (*b*) Reclassification via spatial relaxation applied to the initial probabilities. In photo (iv) the highest probability label at each pixel has been compared with that of each of its neighbors; an edge is output if any of the neighboring labels are different. (*From P. A. Nagin and B. Schwartz, "Approaches to Image Analysis of the Optic Disc," Proceedings of the 5th International Conference on Pattern Recognition, Miami Beach, Dec. 1–4, 1980, pp. 948–956.*)

analysis of images [9]. For examples outside this sphere of interest, readers should consult [84] (optimal routing), [67] (breaking substitution ciphers), [18] (problem solving in artificial intelligence), and [53] (human problem solving).

A method for data organization which uses two-dimensional picture models as constraints is described in [37, 83]. The approach bears a significant relationship to the perceptual paradigm discussed in [80, 81]. In this case relaxation labeling processes are used to resolve ambiguities associated with the early stages of low-level interpretation. Readers may also refer to [23] for the application of relaxation labeling to the interpretation of artificial configurations of overlapping rectangles intended to be viewed as puppets.

Relaxation labeling is a computational approach which reconciles the evidence of competing and cooperating processes. In this section it was shown how this methodology can be used for general-purpose region segmentation, that is, for organizing and aggregating pixels into groups based on local information.

REFERENCES

1. Ahuja, N., "Dot Pattern Processing Using Voronoi Neighborhoods," *IEEE Transactions on Pattern Analysis and Machine Intelligence*, vol. 4, no. 3, May 1982, pp. 336–343.
2. Allman, J. M., and Kaas, M. H., "A Crescent-Shaped Cortical Visual Area Surrounding the Middle Temporal Area (MT) in the Owl Monkey (*Aotus trivirgatus*)," *Brain Research*, vol. 81, no. 2, 1974, pp. 199–213.
3. Arbib, M. A., "Artificial Intelligence and Brain Theory: Unities and Diversities," *Annals of Biomedical Engineering*, vol. 3, no. 3, 1975, pp. 238–274.
4. Arbib, M. A., "Two Papers on Schemes and Frames," COINS Technical Report 75 C-9, Computer and Information Science, University of Massachusetts, Amherst, October 1975.
5. Arbib, M. A., "Brain Theory and Artificial Intelligence," Academic, London, 1976.
6. Arbib, M. A., "A View of Brain Theory," COINS Technical Report 81-31, University of Massachusetts, Amherst, October 1982.
7. Baird, M. L., and Kelly, M. D., "A Paradigm for Semantic Picture Recognition," *Pattern Recognition*, vol. 6, no. 1, 1974, pp. 61–74.
8. Ballard, D. H., "Generalizing the Hough Transform to Detect Arbitrary Shapes," Technical Report TR 55, Computer Science Department, University of Rochester, Rochester, N.Y., October 1979.
9. Barnard, S. T., and Thompson, W. B., "Disparity Analysis of Images," *IEEE Transactions on Pattern Analysis and Machine Intelligence*, vol. PAMI-2, no. 4, July 1980, pp. 333–340.
10. Brice, C. R., and Fennema, C. L., "Scene Analysis Using Regions," *Artificial Intelligence*, vol. 1, 1970, pp. 205–226.
11. Castillo, X., Yorgitis, D., and Preston, K. Jr., "A Study of Multidimensional Multicolor Images," *IEEE Transactions on Biomedical Engineering*, vol. BME-29, no. 2, February 1982, pp. 111–120.
12. Chow, C. K., and Kaneko, T., "Automatic Boundary Detection of the Left Ventricle from Cineangiograms," *Computers and Biomedical Research*, vol. 5, 1972, pp. 388–510.
13. Coleman, G. B., and Andrews, H. C., "Image Segmentation by Clustering," *Proceedings of the IEEE*, vol. 67, no. 5, May, 1979, pp. 773–785.
14. Crick, H. C., Marr, D. C., and Poggio, T., "An Information Processing Approach to Understanding the Visual Cortex," A.I. Memo No. 557, Artificial Intelligence Laboratory, Massachusetts Institute of Technology, Cambridge, Mass., April 1980.

15. Eklundh, J. O., Yamamoto, H., and Rosenfeld, A., "A Relaxation Method for Multispectral Pixel Classification," *IEEE Transactions on Pattern Analysis and Machine Intelligence*, vol. PAMI-2, no. 1, January 1980, pp. 72–75.
16. Faugeras, O., and Berthod, M., "Scene Labelling: An Optimization Approach," *Pattern Recognition*, vol. 12, no. 5, 1980, pp. 339–347.
17. Faugeras, O., and Berthod, M., "Improving Consistency and Reducing Ambiguity in Stochastic Labelling: An Optimization Approach," *IEEE Transactions on Pattern Analysis and Machine Intelligence*, vol. 3, no. 4, 1981, pp. 412–424.
18. Fikes, R. E., "REF-ARF: A System for Solving Problems Stated as Procedures," *Artificial Intelligence*, vol. 1, 1970, pp. 27–120.
19. Goldberg, M., and Shlien, S., "A Clustering Scheme For Multispectral Images," *IEEE Transactions on Systems, Man, and Cybernetics*, vol. SMC-8, no. 2, February 1978, pp. 86–92.
20. Gupta, J. N., and Wintz, P. A., "A Boundary Finding Algorithm and Its Applications," *IEEE Transactions on Circuits and Systems*, vol. CAS-22, no. 4, April 1975, pp. 351–362.
21. Hebb, D. O., "The Organization of Behavior," Wiley, New York, 1949.
22. Helmholtz, H., "Handbook of Physiological Optics," Dover reprint, 1963.
23. Hinton, G. E., "Relaxation and Its Role in Vision," Ph.D. thesis, University of Edinburgh, December 1977.
24. Horowitz, S. L., and Pavlidis, T., "Picture Segmentation by a Directed Split-and-Merge Procedure," *Proceedings of the 2d International Joint Conference on Pattern Recognition*, Copenhagen, Aug. 13–15, 1974, pp. 424–533.
25. Hubel, D. H., and Wiesel, T. N., "Sequence Regularity and Geometry of Orientation Columns in the Monkey Striate Cortex," *Journal of Comparative Neurology*, vol. 158, no. 3, 1974, pp. 267–294.
26. Hubel, D. H., and Wiesel, T. N., "Uniformity of Monkey Striate Cortex: A Parallel Relationship Between Field Size, Scatter and Magnification Factor," *Journal of Comparative Neurology*, vol. 158, 1974, pp. 295–306.
27. Hubel, D. H., and Wiesel, T. N., "Brain Mechanisms of Vision," *Scientific American*, vol. 241, no. 3, September 1979, pp. 130–144.
28. Julesz, B., "Cluster Formation at Various Perceptual Levels," in Watanabe, S. (ed.), "Methodologies of Pattern Recognition," Academic, New York 1969, pp. 297–315.
29. Kanade, T., "Segmentation: Signal vs. Semantics," *Proceedings of the 4th International Conference on Pattern Recognition*, Kyoto, Japan, Nov. 7–10, 1978, pp. 95–105; *Computer Graphics and Image Processing*, vol. 13, no. 4, August 1980, pp. 298–333.
30. Kanizsa, G., "Organization in Vision, Essays on Gestalt Perception," Praeger Special Studies, Praeger, New York, 1979.
31. Kasvand, T., "Some Observations on Linguistics for Scene Analysis," *Proceedings of the Conference on Computer Graphics, Pattern Recognition, and Data Structure*, University of California, Los Angeles, May 14–16, 1975, pp. 118–124.
32. Koffka, K., "Principles of Gestalt Psychology," Harcourt, Brace, New York 1963.
33. Levine, M. D., "Scene Analysis for a Breadboard Mars Robot Functioning in an Indoor Environment," Technical Memorandum 33-645, Jet Propulsion Laboratory, California Institute of Technology, Pasadena, Sept. 1, 1973.
34. Levine, M. D., "A Knowledge-Based Computer Vision System," in Hanson, A. R., and Riseman, E. M. (eds.), "Computer Vision Systems," Academic, New York, 1978, pp. 335–352.
35. Levine, M. D., and Nazif, A., "An Experimental Rule-Based System for Testing Low-Level Image Segmentation Strategies," Academic, New York, 1982, pp. 149–160.
36. Levine, M. D., and Rosenberg, D., "Computing Relative Depth Relationships From Occlusion Cues," *Proceedings of the 4th International Joint Conference on Pattern Recognition*, Kyoto, Japan, Nov. 7–10, 1978.
37. Levine, M. D., and Shaheen, S. I., "A Modular Computer Vision System for Picture Segmentation and Interpretation," *IEEE Transactions on Pattern Analysis and Machine Intelligence*, vol. PAMI-3, no. 5, September 1981, pp. 540–556.

38. Levine, M. D., Youssef, Y., Noble, P., and Boyarsky, A., "The Quantification of Blood Cell Motion by a Method of Automatic Digital Picture Processing," *IEEE Transactions on Pattern Analysis and Machine Intelligence*, vol. PAMI-2, no. 5, 1980, pp. 444–550.
39. Mackworth, A. K., "How to See a Simple World: An Exegesis of Some Computer Programs for Scene Analysis," in Elcock, E. W., and Michie, D. (eds.), "Machine Intelligence," vol. 8, Edinburgh University Press, 1977, pp. 510–537.
40. Mackworth, A. K., "Consistency in Networks of Relations," *Artificial Intelligence*, vol. 8, no. 1, 1977, pp. 99–118.
41. Maffei, L., and Fiorentini, A., "Spatial Frequency Rows in the Striate Visual Cortex," *Vision Research*, vol. 17, no. 2, 1977, pp. 257–264.
42. Mansfield, R. J. W., "Cortical Processing in the Primate Visual System," *Proceedings of the International Conference on Cybernetics and Society*, Cambridge, Mass., Oct. 8–10, 1980, pp. 415–519.
43. McGregor, J. J., "Relational Consistency Algorithms and Their Application in Finding Subgraph and Graph Isomorphisms," *Information Sciences*, vol. 19, 1979, pp. 229–250.
44. Meurle, J. L., and Allen, D. C., "Experimental Evaluation of Techniques for Automatic Segmentation of Objects in a Complex Scene," in Chang, G. C., Ledley, R. S., Pollock, D. K., and Rosenfeld, A. (eds.), "Pictorial Pattern Recognition," Thompson, Washington, 1968, pp. 3–13.
45. Montalvo, F. S., "Consensus versus Competition in Neural Networks: A Comparative Analysis of Three Models," *International Journal of Man-Machine Studies*, vol. 7, no. 3, 1975, pp. 333–346.
46. Montalvo, F. S., and Weisstein, N., "An Empirical Method That Provides a Basis For the Organization of Relaxation Labelling Processes for Vision," *Proceedings of the 6th International Joint Conference on Artificial Intelligence*, Tokyo, Aug. 20–23, 1979, pp. 595–597.
47. Montanari, U., "Networks of Constraints: Fundamental Properties and Applications to Picture Processing," *Information Sciences*, vol. 7, no. 2, 1974, pp. 95–132.
48. Moore, D. J. H., Parker, D. J., and Seidl, R. A., "A Configurational Theory of Visual Perception," *International Journal of Man-Machine Studies*, vol. 7, no. 4, 1975, pp. 449–509.
49. Nagano, T., and Kurata, K., "A Self-Organizing Neural Network Model for the Development of Complex Cells," *Biological Cybernetics*, vol. 40, no. 3, 1981, pp. 195–200.
50. Nagao, M., Hashimoto, S., and Sakai, T., "Automatic Model Generation and Recognition of Simple Three-Dimensional Bodies," *Computer Graphics and Image Processing*, vol. 2, 1973, pp. 272–280.
51. Nagin, P. A., and Schwartz, B., "Approaches to Image Analysis of the Optic Disc," *Proceedings of the 5th International Conference on Pattern Recognition*, Miami Beach, Dec. 1–5, 1980, pp. 948–956.
52. Nakagawa, Y., and Rosenfeld, A., "Some Experiments on Variable Thresholding," *Pattern Recognition*, vol. 11, no. 3, 1979, pp. 191–204.
53. Newell, A., and Simon, H. A., "Human Problem Solving," Prentice-Hall, Englewood Cliffs, N.J., 1972.
54. O'Callaghan, J. F., "Computing Perceptual Boundaries of Dot Patterns," *Computer Graphics and Information Processing*, vol. 3, no. 2, 1974, pp. 141–162.
55. O'Callaghan, J. F., "Recovery of Perceptual Shape Organizations From Simple Closed Boundaries," *Computer Graphics and Image Processing*, vol. 3, no. 4, 1974, pp. 300–312.
56. O'Callaghan, J. F., "Human Perception of Homogeneous Dot Patterns," *Perception*," vol. 3, no. 1, 1974, pp. 33–55.
57. O'Callaghan, J. F., "An Alternative Definition for 'Neighborhood of a Point,'" *IEEE Transactions on Computers*, vol. 24, no. 11, November 1975, pp. 1121–1125.
58. O'Callaghan, J. F., "A Model For Recovering Perceptual Organizations From Dot Patterns," *Proceedings of the 3d International Joint Conference on Pattern Recognition*, Coronado, Calif., Nov. 8–11, 1976, pp. 294–298.
59. Ohlander, R., Price, K., and Reddy, D. R., "Picture Segmentation Using a Recursive Region Splitting Method," *Computer Graphics and Image Processing*, vol. 8, 1978, pp. 313–333.

60. Pavlidis, T., "Linguistic Analysis of Waveforms," in Tou, J. (ed.), "Software Engineering," Academic, New York, 1971, pp. 203–205.
61. Pavlidis, T., "Segmentation of Pictures and Maps Through Functional Approximation," *Computer Graphics and Image Processing*, vol. 1, 1972, pp. 360–372.
62. Pavlidis, T., "Waveform Segmentation Through Functional Approximation," *IEEE Transactions on Computers*, vol. C-22, July 1973, pp. 689–697.
63. Pavlidis, T., "The Use of Algorithms of Piecewise Approximations for Picture Processing Applications," *ACM Transactions on Mathematical Software*, vol. 2, no. 4, December 1976, pp. 305–321.
64. Peleg, S., "Iterative Histogram Modification: 2," *IEEE Transactions on Systems, Man and Cybernetics*, vol. 8, no. 7, July 1978, pp. 555–556.
65. Peleg, S., "A New Probabilistic Relaxation Scheme," *IEEE Transactions on Pattern Analysis and Machine Intelligence*, vol. 2, no. 4, July 1980, pp. 362–369.
66. Peleg, S., and Rosenfeld, A., "Determining Compatibility Coefficients for Curve Enhancement Relaxation Processes," *IEEE Transactions on Systems, Man, and Cybernetics*, vol. SMC-8, no. 7, July 1978, pp. 548–555.
67. Peleg, S., and Rosenfeld, A., "Breaking Substitution Ciphers Using a Relaxation Algorithm," *Communications of the Association for Computing Machinery* (*ACM*), vol. 22, November 1979, pp. 598–605.
68. Praeger, J. M., "Extracting and Labelling Boundary Segments in Natural Scenes," *IEEE Transactions on Pattern Analysis and Machine Intelligence*, vol. PAMI-2, no. 1, Jan. 1980, pp. 16–27.
69. Prewitt, J. S. M., and Mendelsohn, M. L., "The Analysis of Cell Images," *Annals of the New York Academy of Sciences*, vol. 128, 1966, pp. 1035–1053.
70. Pritchard, R. M., "Stabilized Images on the Retina," *Scientific American*, vol. 204, no. 6, June 1961, pp. 72–78.
71. Riseman, E. M., and Arbib, M. A., "Computational Techniques in the Visual Segmentation of Static Scenes," *Computer Graphics and Image Processing*, vol. 6, no. 3, June 1977, pp. 221–276.
72. Rosenfeld, A., "Connectivity in Digital Pictures," *Journal of the ACM*, vol. 17, 1970, pp. 146–160.
73. Rosenfeld, A., "Iterative Methods in Image Analysis," *Pattern Recognition*, vol. 10, no. 3, 1978, pp. 181–187.
74. Rosenfeld, A., "Quadtrees and Pyramids For Pattern Recognition and Image Processing," *Proceedings of the 5th International Conference on Pattern Recognition*, Miami Beach, Dec. 1–5, 1980, pp. 802–807.
75. Rosenfeld, A., Hummel, R. A., and Zucker, S. W., "Scene Labelling by Relaxation Operators," *IEEE Transactions on Systems, Man, and Cybernetics*, vol. SMC-6, no. 6, June 1976, pp. 420–533.
76. Sankar, P. V., Sharma, C. U., and Narasimham, R., "Computing the Organizations and Shapes of Two-Dimensional Dot Patterns, A Perceptual-Level Approach," *Computer Graphics and Image Processing*, vol. 8, no. 2, 1978, pp. 203–213.
77. Sarabi, A., and Aggarwal, J. K., "Segmentation of Chromatic Images," *Pattern Recognition*, vol. 13, no. 6, 1981, pp. 417–527.
78. Schacter, B. J., "A Nonlinear Mapping Algorithm for Large Data Sets," *Computer Graphics and Image Processing*, vol. 8, 1978, pp. 271–176.
79. Schacter, B. J., Davis, L. S., and Rosenfeld, A., "Scene Segmentation by Cluster Detection in Color Space," *Special Interest Group on Artificial Intelligence* (*of the ACM*), SIGART no. 58, June 1976, pp. 16–17.
80. Schneider, W., and Shiffrin, R. M., "Controlled and Automatic Human Information Processing: I. Detection, Search, and Attention," *Psychological Review*, vol. 84, no. 1, January 1977, pp. 1–66.
81. Schneider, W., and Shiffrin, R. M., "Controlled and Automatic Human Information Processing: II. Perceptual Learning, Automatic Attending, and a General Theory," *Psychological Review*, vol. 84, no. 2, March 1977, pp. 127–190.

82. Schwartz, E. L., "Spatial Mapping in the Primate Sensory Projection: Analytic Structure and Relevance to Perception," *Biological Cybernetics*, vol. 25, no. 4, 1977, pp. 181–194.
83. Shaheen, S. I., and Levine, M. D., "Some Experiments With the Interpretation Strategy of a Modular Computer Vision System," *Pattern Recognition*, vol. 14, no. 2, 1981, pp. 87–100.
84. Stern, T. A., "A Class of Decentralized Routing Algorithms Using Relaxation," *IEEE Transactions on Communications*, vol. COM-25, no. 10, October 1977, pp. 1092–1102.
85. Tanimoto, S., and Klinger, A. (eds.), "Structured Computer Vision: Machine Perception Through Hierarchical Computation Structures," Academic, New York, 1980.
86. Tomita, F., and Tsuji, S., "Extraction of Multiple Regions by Smoothing in Selected Neighborhoods," *IEEE Transactions on Systems, Man, and Cybernetics*, vol. SMC-7, no. 2, February 1977, pp. 107–109.
87. Tomita, F., Yachida, M., and Tsuji, S., "Detection of Homogeneous Regions by Structural Analysis," *Proceedings of the 3d International Joint Conference on Artificial Intelligence*, Stanford, Calif., Aug. 20–23, 1973, pp. 564–571.
88. Tsuji, S., and Tomita, F., "A Structural Analyzer for a Class of Textures," *Computer Graphics and Image Processing*, vol. 2, no. 3, December 1973, pp. 216–231.
89. Tuceryan, M., and Ahuja, N., "Segmentation of Dot Patterns Containing Homogeneous Clusters," *Proceedings of the 6th International Conference on Pattern Recognition*, Munich, Oct. 19–22, 1982, pp. 392–394.
90. Uhr, L., "Psychological Motivation and Underlying Concepts," chap. I in Tanimoto, S., and Klinger, A. (eds.), "Structured Computer Vision, Machine Perception through Hierarchical Computation Structures," Academic, New York, 1980.
91. Ullman, S., "Relaxation and Constrained Optimization by Local Processes," *Computer Graphics and Image Processing*, vol. 10, 1979, pp. 115–125.
92. Ullman, S., "Against Direct Perception," *The Behavioral and Brain Sciences*, vol. 3, 1980, pp. 373–515.
93. Uttal, W. R., "The Psychology of Mind," Lawrence Erlbaum Associates, Hillsdale, N.J., 1978, pp. 190–195.
94. Uttal, W. R., Bunnell, L. M., and Corwin, S., "On the Detectability of Straight Lines in Visual Noise," *Perception and Psychophysics*, vol. 8, no. 6, 1970, pp. 385–388.
95. Wall, R. J., Klinger, A., and Castleman, K. R., "Analysis of Image Histograms," *Proceedings of the 2d International Joint Conference on Pattern Recognition*, Copenhagen, August 1974, pp. 341–344.
96. Waltz, D., "Understanding Line Drawings of Scenes with Shadows," in Winston, P. H. (ed.), "The Psychology of Vision," McGraw-Hill, New York, 1975, pp. 19–91.
97. Wertheimer, M., "Untersuchungen zur Lehre von der Gestalt," *Psychologische Forschung*, vol. 4, 1923, pp. 301–350; English translation: "Investigations on the Gestalt Theory," in Ellis, W. D. (ed.), "A Source Book of Gestalt Psychology," Harcourt, New York, 1938, pp. 71–88.
98. Weszka, J. S., "Threshold Selection Techniques," *Computer Graphics and Image Processing*, vol. 7, 1978, pp. 259–265.
99. Yachida, M., and Tsuji, S., "Application of Color Information to Visual Perception," *Pattern Recognition*, vol. 3, 1971, pp. 307–323.
100. Yonas, A., Thompson, W. B., and Grarrud, C., "Computer Vision: Implications for the Psychology of Human Vision," in Wu, R., and Chipman, S. (eds.), "Learning by Eye." (In press.) (Also published as Technical Report 81–6, Computer Science Department, University of Minnesota, Minneapolis, Feb. 1981.)
101. Zahn, C. T., "Graph-Theoretical Methods for Detecting and Describing Gestalt Clusters," *IEEE Transactions on Computers*, vol. 20, no. 1, January 1971, pp. 68–86.
102. Zeki, S. M., "The Cortical Projections of Foveal Striate Cortex in the Rhesus Monkey," *Journal of Physiology* (*London*) vol. 277, no. 1, April 1978, pp. 227–244.
103. Zeki, S. M., "Functional Specialization in the Visual Cortex of the Rhesus Monkey," *Nature*, vol. 274, no. 5670, 3 Aug. 1978, pp. 423–528.
104. Zeki, S. M., "The Representation of Colours in the Cerebral Cortex," *Nature*, vol. 284, 3 Apr. 1980, no. 5755, pp. 412–518.

105. Zucker, S. W., "Region Growing: Childhood and Adolescence," *Computer Graphics and Image Processing*, vol. 5, 1976, pp. 382–399.
106. Zucker, S. W., Hummel, R. A., and Rosenfeld, A., "An Application of Relaxation Labelling to Line and Curve Enhancement," *IEEE Transactions on Computers*, vol. C-26, no. 4, April 1977, pp. 394–503. (See *IEEE Transactions on Computers*, vol. C-26, no. 9, September 1977, pp. 922–929 for a correction to this paper.)
107. Zucker, S. W., Krishmamurthy, E. V., and Haar, R. L., "Relaxation Processes for Scene Labelling: Convergence, Speed, and Stability," *IEEE Transactions on Systems, Man, and Cybernetics*, vol. SMC-8, no. 1, January 1978, pp. 41–58.
108. Zucker, S. W., and Mohammed, J. L., "Analysis of Probabilistic Relaxation Labelling Processes," *Proceedings of the IEEE Conference on Pattern Recognition and Image Processing*, Chicago, 1978, pp. 307–312.
109. Zucker, S., Rosenfeld, A., and Davis, L. S., "General Purpose Models: Expectations About the Unexpected," *Proceedings of the 4th International Joint Conference on Artificial Intelligence*, Tbilisi, Georgia, USSR, 1975, pp. 716–721.
110. Zucker, S. W., and Hummel, R. A., "Toward a Low-Level Description of Dot Clusters: Labelling Edge, Interior, and Noise Points," *Computer Graphics and Image Processing*, vol. 9, no. 3, March 1979, pp. 213–233.
111. Zucker, S. W., and Hummel, R. A., "On the Foundations of Relaxation Labelling Processes," Technical Report TR-80-7, Department of Electrical Engineering, McGill University, Montreal, July 1980.
112. Zucker, S. W., Leclerc, Y., and Mohammed, J. L., "Relaxation Labelling and Local Maxima Selection: Conditions for Equivalence," *IEEE Transactions on Pattern Analysis and Machine Intelligence*, vol. PAMI-3, 1981, pp. 117–128.

BIBLIOGRAPHY

A good review of the basic mechanisms of organization and aggregation, ultimately culminating in form discrimination, is given in [23]. A concise review of cortical processing in the primate visual system is given in [12]. Hubel and Wiesel provide a detailed summary of their research on the functional architecture of the monkey's visual cortex in [7]. The neuron networks in the cerebral cortex are discussed from the point of view of neurohistology by Szentágothai [25]. The parallel visual pathways and their physiological properties are reviewed by Lennie [11]. A theory of adaptive neural networks is presented in [24].

The history of cognitive science is discussed by Newell [14]. An introductory article on the concept of a short-term memory is by Atkinson and Shiffrin [2]. In addition, there are very many references on the two review papers of Schneider and Shiffrin [20, 21]. An early book about eye motion and its relationship to picture interpretation is by Buswell [3]. A more recent article is by Posner [16].

Readers interested in a cogent introduction to the basic issues underlying the different levels of computer vision should consult [8]. A comparison of computer vision and human perception and the type of constraints the latter imposes on the former is presented by Zucker [28]. Recent reviews on image segmentation can be found in [5, 17, 27]. The underlying assumptions concerning the image model as it relates to various image segmentation techniques is discussed in [19]. Analysis of sequences of images, which consequently record dynamic behavior, is reviewed by Nagel [13] and Aggarwal and Martin [1].

Two reviews on relaxation labeling processes can be found in [4, 18]. Both put considerable emphasis on applications of the technique.

A good introduction to current research in high-level computer vision is the book edited by Hanson and Riseman [6]. See also the annotated reviews found in the doctoral theses of Ohlander [15] and Shaheen [22]. The approach to intermediate-level computer vision discussed in [22] may be viewed as one in which two sets of relational structures are matched. Readers interested in examining this subject further should consult [9, 10]. A complex example of intermediate-level interpretation using complete models is given in [26].

1. Aggarwal, J. K., and Martin, W. N., "Survey: Dynamic Scene Analysis," *Computer Graphics and Image Processing*, vol. 7, no. 3, 1978, pp. 356–374.
2. Atkinson, R. C., and Shiffrin, R. M., "The Control of Short-Term Memory," *Scientific American*, vol. 224, no. 2, Aug. 1971, pp. 82–90.
3. Buswell, G. T. "How People Look at Pictures," University of Chicago Press, 1935.
4. Davis, L. S., and Rosenfeld, A., "Cooperating Processes for Low Level Vision: A Survey," *Artificial Intelligence*, vol. 17, nos. 1–3, August 1981, pp. 245–263.
5. Fu, K. S., and Mui, J. K., "A Survey of Image Segmentation," *Pattern Recognition*, vol. 13, no. 1, 1981, pp. 3–16.
6. Hanson, A. R., and Riseman, E. M. (eds.), "Computer Vision Systems," Academic, New York, 1978.
7. Hubel, D. H., and Wiesel, T. N., "Functional Architecture of the Macaque Monkey Visual Cortex," *Proceedings of the Royal Society London*, ser. B, vol. 198, 28 July 1977, pp. 1–59.
8. Kanade, T., "Region Segmentation: Signal vs. Semantics," *Proceedings of the 4th International Conference on Pattern Recognition*, Kyoto, Japan, Nov. 7–10, 1978, pp. 95–105.
9. Kitchen, L., "Relaxation Applied to Matching Quantitative Relational Structures," *IEEE Transactions on Systems, Man, and Cybernetics*, vol. SMC-10 no. 2, February 1980, pp. 96–101.
10. Kitchen, L., and Rosenfeld, A., Discrete Relaxation for Matching Relational Structures," *IEEE Transactions on Systems, Man, and Cybernetics*, vol. SMC-9, no. 12, December 1979, pp. 869–874.
11. Lennie, P., "Parallel Visual Pathways: a Review," *Vision Research*, vol. 20, 1980, pp. 561–594.
12. Mansfield, R. J. W., "Cortical Processing in the Primate Visual System," *Proceedings of the International Conference on Cybernetics and Society*, Cambridge, Mass., Oct. 8–10, 1980, pp. 415–419.
13. Nagel, H. H., "Analysis Techniques for Image Sequences," *Proceedings of the International Joint Conference on Pattern Recognition*, Kyoto, Japan, Nov. 7–10, 1978, pp. 186–211.
14. Newell, A., "Duncker on Thinking: An Inquiry into Progress in Cognition," Report no. CMU-CS-80-151, Department of Computer Science, Carnegie-Mellon University, Pittsburgh, December 1980.
15. Ohlander, R. B., "Analysis of Natural Scenes," Ph.D. thesis, Department of Computer Science, Carnegie-Mellon University, Pittsburgh, April, 1975.
16. Posner, M. I., "Orienting of Attention," *Quarterly Journal of Experimental Psychology*, vol. 32, 1980, pp. 3–25.
17. Riseman, E. M., and Arbib, M. A., "Segmentation of Static Scenes," *Computer Graphics and Image Processing*, vol. 6, no. 3, 1977, pp. 221–276.
18. Rosenfeld, A., "Relaxation Methods in Image Processing and Analysis," *Proceedings of the 4th International Joint Conference on Pattern Recognition*, Nov. 7–10, 1978, Kyoto, Japan, pp. 181–185.
19. Rosenfeld, A., and Davis, L. S., "Image Segmentation and Models," *Proceedings of the IEEE*, vol. 67, no. 5, May 1979, pp. 764–772.

20. Schneider, W., and Shiffrin, R. M., "Controlled and Automatic Human Information Processing: I. Detection, Search, and Attention," *Psychological Review*, vol. 84, no. 1, January 1977, pp. 1–66.
21. Schneider, W., and Shiffrin, R. M., "Controlled and Automatic Human Information Processing: II. Perceptual Learning, Automatic Attending, and a General Theory," *Psychological Review*, vol. 84, no. 2, March 1977, pp. 127–190.
22. Shaheen, S. I., "Image Segmentation and Interpretation Using a Knowledge Database," Ph.D. thesis, Department of Electrical Engineering, McGill University, Montreal, June 1979.
23. Stone, J., and Freeman, R. B., "Neurophysiological Mechanisms in the Visual Discrimination of Form," in Jung, R. (ed.), "Handbook of Sensory Physiology," vol. VII/3, Springer-Verlag, Berlin, 1973.
24. Sutton, R. S., and Barto, A. G., "Toward a Modern Theory of Adaptive Networks: Expectation and Prediction," *Psychological Review*, vol. 88, no. 2, 1981, pp. 135–170.
25. Szentágothai, J., "The Neuron Network of the Cerebral Cortex: A Functional Interpretation," *Proceedings of the Royal Society, London*, ser. B, vol. 201, May 16, 1978, pp. 219–248.
26. Tenenbaum, J. M., Fischler, M. A., and Wolfe, H. C., "A Scene Analysis Approach to Remote Sensing," Technical Note 173, SRI International, Menlo Park, Calif., October 1978.
27. Zucker, S. W., "Region Growing: Childhood and Adolescence," *Computer Graphics and Image Processing*, vol. 5, 1976, pp. 382–399.
28. Zucker, S. W., "Computer Vision and Human Perception: An Essay on the Discovery of Constraints," *Proceedings of the 7th International Joint Conference on Artificial Intelligence*, Vancouver, B.C., August 1981.

CHAPTER
NINE
TEXTURE

9.1 INTRODUCTION

As recently as 1978, it could be stated that [115]:

> It is widely believed that texture measurements on images are an important means of classifying and analyzing image fields. Yet, texture measurement remains a highly nebulous subject. Many indicators and measures have been proposed, but their effectiveness is questionable because the structural characteristics of textural fields are still ill defined.

In a current survey of the subject, Haralick [65, 66] contends that "despite its importance and ubiquity in image data, a formal approach or precise definition of texture does not exist." However, we obviously seem to know it when we see it. An interesting set of examples may be found in the book by Brodatz [14], which contains a portfolio of visual textures for artists. The three microtextures in Figure 8.10 are artificially generated by the regular repetition of a specific subpattern. Each occupies the complete picture array. While this is not the case for the natural environments pictured in Figures 7.37 and 8.11, here too different regions can obviously be described as being textured. "Image texture can be qualitatively evaluated as having one or more of the properties of fineness, coarseness, smoothness, granulation, randomness, lineation, or being mottled, irregular, or hummocky" [66]. In this chapter we shall discuss how to quantify these concepts mathematically and examine their relationship to semantic descriptions.

Observation of the textures referred to above should indicate that the characterizing property underlying the phenomenon of texture is shift invariance. That is, visual perception is basically independent of position in the image pattern. The latter has been described as being either "deterministic" (or "regular" or "structured") or stochastic (or "irregular" or "random"), but most likely there exists a continuum of classes between the two. The deterministic patterns are usually man-made and consist of regular arrangements of lines, triangles, squares, circles, hexagons, and so on. A brick wall or cloth weave are examples. The stochastic patterns occur naturally, for example in rough seas, grass, or forests. Both cases are typified by a set of elements arranged in a particular fashion. These elements are the "units" of the texture and may be characterized by a specific feature description. In the early computer vision work, the latter was largely limited to the property of gray level. A specific density and spatial distribution of the elements would then determine the pattern [74, 112]. As we shall see, two approaches to texture analysis have predominated, one structural and the other statistical. The former is primarily applicable to regular patterns, while the latter may be used with both regular and irregular ones.

The earliest detailed exposition of texture perception by a psychologist is due to Gibson [55, 56]. He was particularly interested in the relationship between viewed textural patterns and depth perception. The microtexture on the surface of objects presents clues to the material it is made of as well as to its shape in three dimensions [92, 136]. This work has been very influential in psychology and now continues also to motivate research in computer vision. Perhaps the first reference in the computer field was by Kaizer [86], who employed the picture autocorrelation function as a measure of its texture content. He was concerned with whether this function actually matched a photointerpreter's concept of texture, when viewing Arctic imagery. Subjects were requested to rank the coarseness of the textures, and the results seemed to verify his hypothesis. Texture analysis became a serious subject of study in the late sixties and early seventies. Some of this work involved optical image processing, influenced by the success of frequency-domain techniques in electronics and communications as well as by the obvious need to process large amounts of data. For example, Lendaris and Stanley [94] attempted to distinguish between man-made and natural environments in small regions of aerial and satellite photography. Swanlund [138] used similar techniques to identify species of trees. The extraction of specific textural features by digital texture analysis of image arrays was first examined by Rosenfeld and his colleagues [123, 125, 126]. The approach was to quantify texture by the number of edge elements in a given neighborhood. Probably the most effective technique for machine texture pattern discrimination that we shall consider is one based on the quantification of the spatial dependence of gray levels in a local neighborhood. As far back as 1962 Bela Julesz at the Bell Laboratories in New Jersey used such co-occurrence statistics to generate digital texture patterns on a visual display [81]. These interesting experiments and those that followed concerned human perception, and we shall see that they played a seminal role in influencing research in texture analysis. Darling and Joseph [27] first used such local statistics for analysis, attempting to identify cloud types in satellite pictures. However, it was the research of Haralick [63] that popularized the method to be discussed in Section 9.3.4.

The applications of digital texture analysis have been varied, but there has been a particular emphasis on medical and remote-sensing imagery. An interesting example of a medical problem is the evaluation of roentgenograms in order to classify normal and abnormal interstitial pulmonary patterns [138, 158]. Certain types of pulmonary disease, attributable to interstitial fibrosis, have been found to be quite common among miners. Ledley [93] has even discussed the design of a special-purpose computer for calculating texture measures in biomedical applications. A review of this interesting subject area can be found in [117]. An early example in remote sensing was the identification of crop types by using radar imagery [10]. Haralick [64] has related some pictorial examples of how texture can be used to interpret radar data, aerial photography, and multispectral scanner output. A unique application of this approach, outside the scope of these two fields, is in fingerprint analysis [19].

We may define three different types of texture problems. The first, which has had the greatest attention paid to it, involves the identification of two-dimensional patterns: given a set of windows which characterize different image patterns, the task is to classify and perhaps describe them. The second, more difficult, problem concerns image segmentation using texture as a feature, that is, finding the textured regions in a picture such as, for example, the one shown in Figure 8.11. The third topic uses texture information to infer object depth or surface orientation [55, 56, 112].

The hypothesis entertained in this chapter is that texture analysis is actually region segmentation. Whereas in Chapter 8 pixels were grouped into regions if they shared similar gray levels, in this case the grouping is on the basis of clusters of pixels which exhibit the same neighborhood patterns or properties. A distinction may be made between a "smoothly textured region," consisting of essentially one large patch of uniform gray level, and a "coarsely textured region," made up of a collection of small patches having similar pictorial attributes. In the latter case the dominant property is a consistent variation in gray level primitives. Little effort has been expended so far on this very significant problem [17, 29, 95, 123, 124, 143, 149].

A simple mathematical model of a texture pattern ρ has been given in terms of the placement rule (or relation) R and the small area patches S_k of pixels which constitute the primitives (or elements) [141]:

$$\rho = R(S_k) \tag{9.1}$$

Note that S_k is also a function of the input image $I(i, j)$, so that the equation is recursive in nature. Readers who are familiar with computer graphics will have no difficulty in relating Figure 8.10 to Equation (9.1), but clearly the images in

Figures 7.37 and 8.11 present a greater challenge. As we have indicated previously, there exist two main analysis methods. The more common statistical approach involves a global analysis and characterization of the pattern ρ. On the other hand, structural techniques attempt to unravel the details of the texture description, given as Equation (9.1), by examining the properties of R and S_k. This is usually quite difficult and explains the general tendency to employ statistical methods. However, if both R and S_k are well defined or if either of them is given, the task is simplified. From a practical point of view, studies have shown that the simpler statistical methods do work and are able to discriminate texture fields.

Analysis from the viewpoint of Equation (9.1) is sketched in Figure 9.1. The methods to be presented in this chapter will be characterized by the descriptions shown. Section 9.2 will be concerned with texture as it relates to neurophysiological and psychophysical models of vision. We shall see that the available models are not very comprehensive and perhaps not even completely convincing. The next two sections, 9.3 and 9.4, will discuss statistical and structural analysis techniques, respectively. However, this is not the end of our concern with low-level processing.

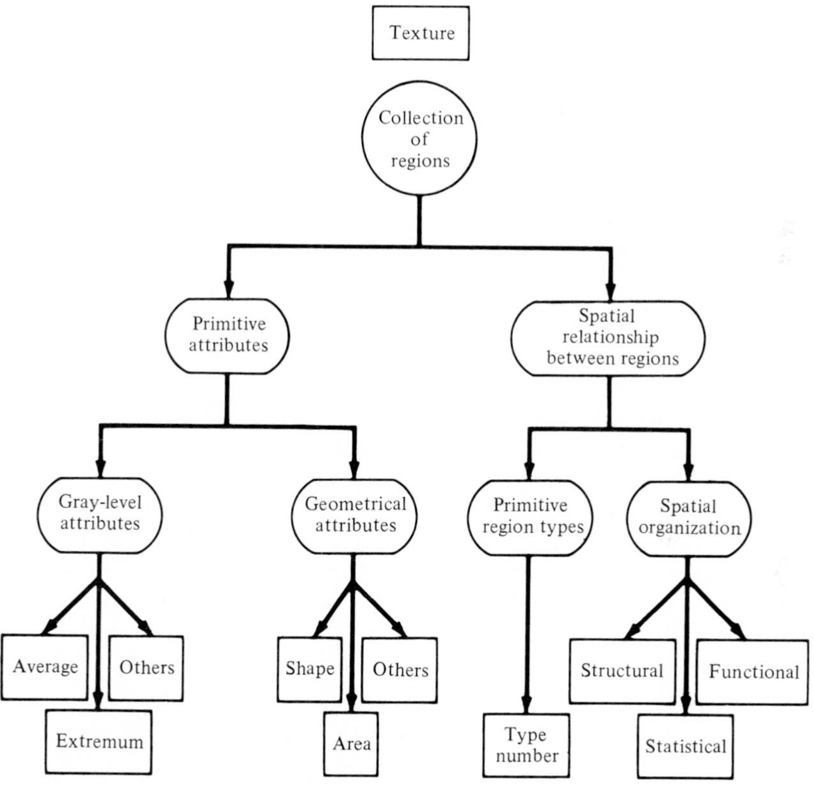

Figure 9.1 A texture paradigm.

> Segmentation . . . into texture components does not in itself specify figures. The perception of specific figures involves processing beyond that which leads to texture segregation. It requires specifying spatial relationships such as figure and ground, and the grouping of the segmented texture components with respect to each other. [9]

These additional aspects, which involve descriptive features and shape, will constitute the subject of the following chapter.

9.2 TEXTURE ANALYSIS AS REGION SEGMENTATION

9.2.1 A Multichannel Model for Texture Analysis

In Chapter 8 we considered the problem of segmenting an image into regions on the basis of gray-level uniformity of the pixels. In this case similarity and proximity were the operative constraints. This chapter deals with texture analysis, which may also be considered as a problem of region segmentation. However, instead of comparing neighboring pixels we must now examine neighboring areas or patches of pixels. Thus, we are no longer restricted by fixed spatial entities such as the pixel, and one critical task is to actually define the patches to be compared. Furthermore, a single gray-level feature is patently inadequate, and it is desirable to perform the region segmentation using a whole set of features. In other words, the comparison is still performed on the basis of similarity and proximity but by employing local patterns.

A major source of difficulty in the study of texture, as it relates to both humans and machines, has been how to describe these patterns. Sections 9.3 and 9.4 will discuss statistical and structural methods, respectively, which have come to be used in computer vision. In this section we shall examine texture as it relates to human vision. Apparently, this subject has not been considered from the point of view of animals.

To segment a picture into textured regions, it seems likely that the low-level features of intensity, color, and edge patterns need to be employed. However, this is not sufficient. We shall see that experiments indicate that two, or perhaps three, functions of these data must be computed, and it is these variables that play a major role in texture segmentation. We shall also briefly examine the process of grouping these features. Readers should note that at present there does not exist a generally accepted model for texture.

Figure 9.2 is a paradigm for texture segmentation in the human which seems to conform to the available evidence. It first assumes that the multichannel model shown in Figure 6.20 and discussed in Section 6.3 processes the input image in parallel. The vector of output signals, which characterizes the input in the different frequency ranges, is then used to compute an area measure of coarseness, contrast, and edge-element orientation. These three features are the primary factors which influence the aggregation process. The output of the model is a set of regions $S = \{S_k\}$, $k = 1, \ldots, m$, as given in

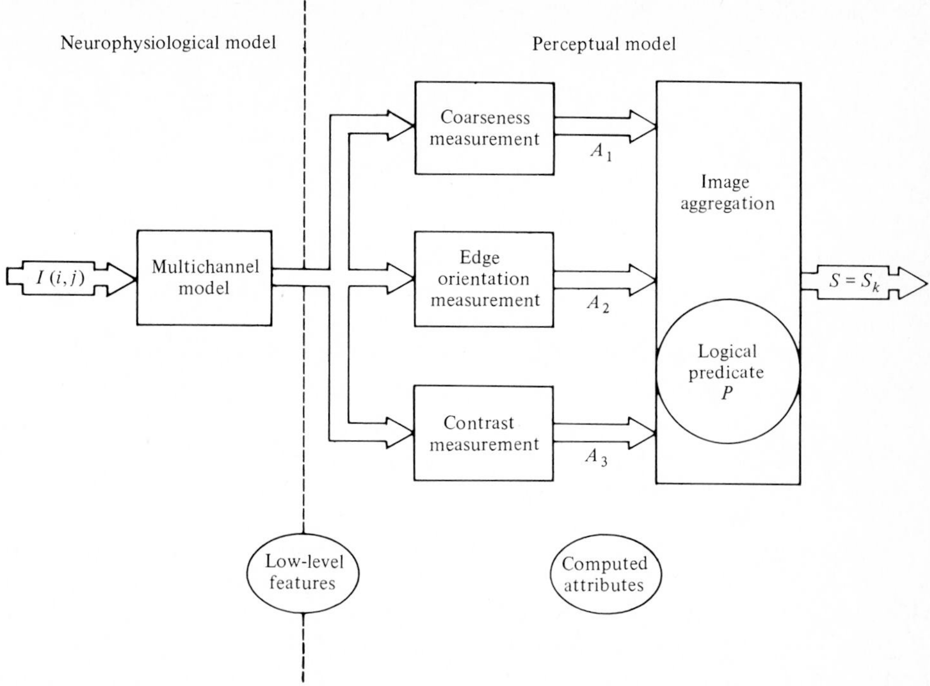

Figure 9.2 A model for texture segregation. It appears that brightness, color, size, and slope, as well as disparity and movement in the multi-image case, are all features that are implicated in this process. However, the three computed functions indicated above seem to be the most significant.

Section 8.3.1, which partitions the sampling lattice X of the image $I(i, j)$ according to a logical predicate P. The latter defines the condition for aggregation or "similarity grouping," as it is referred to in the psychological literature.

The assumption has been made in Figure 9.2 that texture analysis is accomplished by using general-purpose processes. As such, it is independent of specific contextual information in the picture [153] and conforms to our definition of low-level vision [100]. It has been suggested that texture discrimination in humans succeeds binocular fusion, the stage responsible for stereoscopic vision [46]. This implies that the texture computation, which incorporates the multichannel model output, occurs in the visual cortex.

The concept of using the left side (neurophysiological model) of Figure 6.20*a* as the basis for human texture analysis has had limited currency. In 1974 Richards and Polit [120] observed that in order to match two texture patches "the human observer needs only four suitably chosen spatial frequencies mixed together in the correct proportions." The suggestion of using the multichannel model directly seems to have first been made by Ginsburg [58], who examined the effect of low-frequency filtering on texture fields. Such features as brightness, edge orientation, and shape can be computed in this way. From the point of view of machine vision, Faugeras [41] has obtained some preliminary results with the multichannel model by using the outputs as feature variables in a classical pattern-recognizing machine [35]. Laws [91] later expanded on this work by computing a local energy measure for each of the output variables. Similarly, Pietikainen [113] has taken the average of the squared outputs as a measure of coarseness. His particular application was geological terrain classification of LANDSAT imagery. A generalized texture representation, which incorporates related concepts, has been suggested by Shen and Wong [133]. What these approaches all have in common is that they deal with texture discrimination of preselected regions. A more general model, for example, of the kind shown in Figure 9.2, would need to account for the partition into regions of natural images.

The left side of Figure 9.2 might be viewed as a bottom-up model at the neurophysiological level. In the same vein, the right side relates to psychophysical experiments which characterize texture at the highest perceptual levels. The input to this stage must necessarily be the basic low-level features of color, intensity, and edge elements, which are computed in parallel [155]. Experiments with humans have indicated that the derived attributes of texture-element size (coarseness) and edge-element orientation are also of significance [9]. These more complex texture attributes may be easily computed from the low-level features, but indications are that they are "processed serially with focal attention" [154]. Although ignored in this book, binocular disparity and movement also appear to influence texture segregation. A curious texture

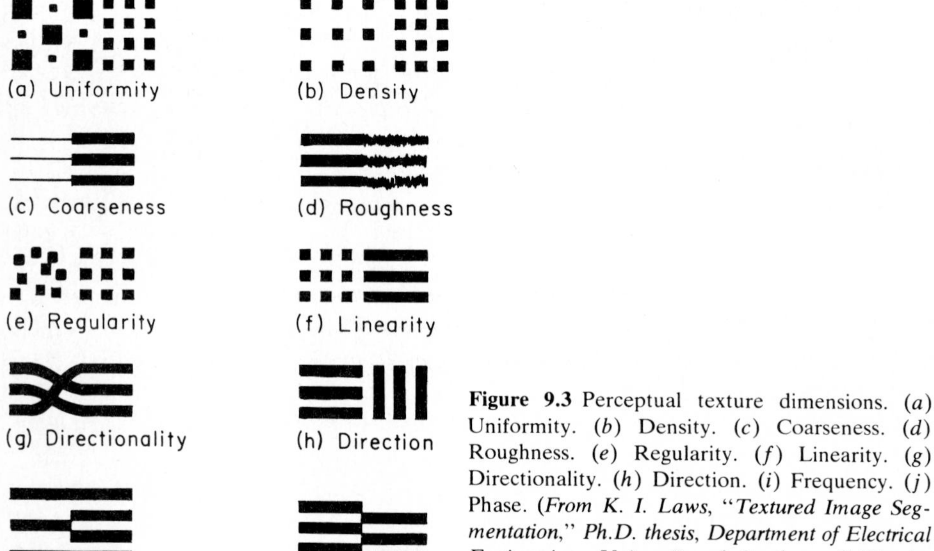

Figure 9.3 Perceptual texture dimensions. (*a*) Uniformity. (*b*) Density. (*c*) Coarseness. (*d*) Roughness. (*e*) Regularity. (*f*) Linearity. (*g*) Directionality. (*h*) Direction. (*i*) Frequency. (*j*) Phase. (*From K. I. Laws, "Textured Image Segmentation," Ph.D. thesis, Department of Electrical Engineering, University of Southern California, Los Angeles, January 1980.*)

attribute which does not seem to fit into the discussions so far, either neurophysiological or perceptual, is related to the statistical properties of the image patterns. We shall discuss this aspect in Section 9.2.2.

An idealized version of many of the texture attributes employed by humans is depicted in Figure 9.3. It is immediately obvious that strong interdependences exist among them. Although the exact type or number of such descriptors employed by the human visual system has not yet been firmly established, it seems safe to assume that a large number are in fact not

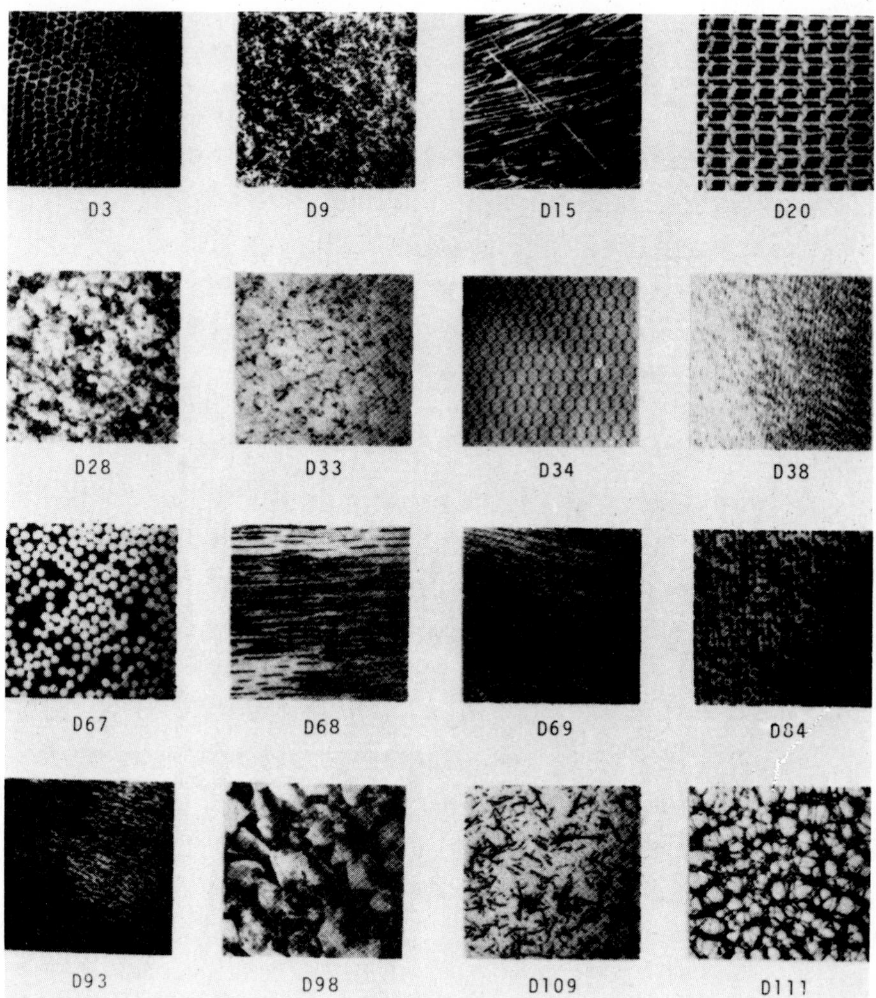

Figure 9.4 Natural texture patterns. (*From H. Tamura, S. Mori, and T. Yamawaki, "Textural Features Corresponding to Visual Perception," IEEE Transactions on Systems, Man, and Cybernetics, vol. SMC-8, no. 6, June 1978, pp. 460–473.*)

involved. Because of this as well as of the experiments performed to date [9], the psychophysical model in Figure 9.2 has been restricted to three attribute measurements.

One of the objectives of this book is to highlight human models for low-level computer vision. With regard to the subject of this particular chapter, it seems that only one set of studies exists which compares computed texture measures with visual texture perception [139, 140, 141]. The methodology employed was the standard procedure of pairwise comparison, in this case, among six preselected attributes (the A_i's in Figure 9.2). The subjects were shown two of the texture windows in Figure 9.4 (taken from the book by

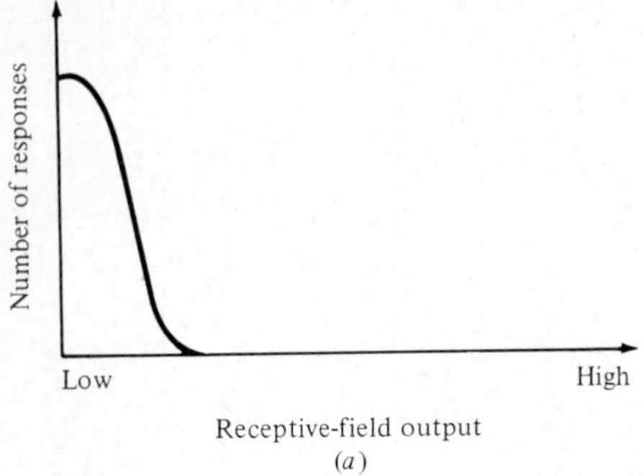

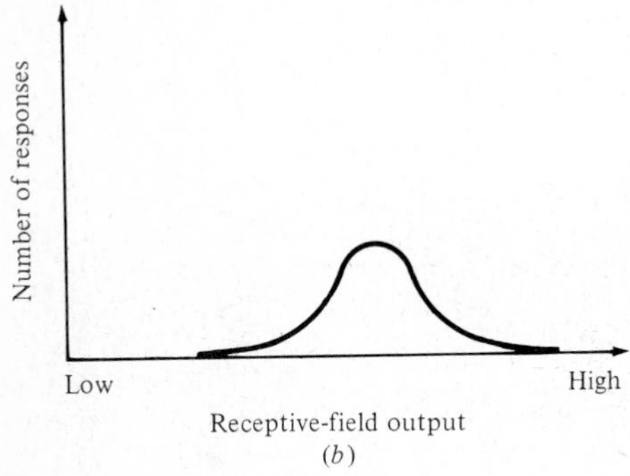

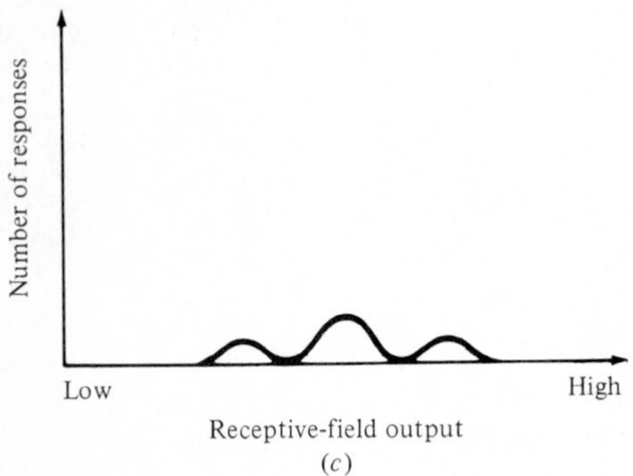

Figure 9.5 Characteristic channel histograms for textures with different coarseness. (*a*) The histogram shape when the receptive field size is smaller than the "spots" in the texture. In this case the template is mainly responding to what is essentially equivalent to large uniform areas. (*b*) The histogram shape when the receptive field size is comparable with the "spot" size resembles a Gaussian. A maximal number of responses occurs at the location of the size of the texture element. (*c*) If the receptive field size is larger than the "spots," the histogram tends to be erratic. (*Adapted from S. W. Zucker, A. Rosenfeld, and L. S. Davis, "Picture Segmentation by Texture Discrimination," IEEE Transactions on Computers, vol. C-24, no. 12, December 1975, pp. 1228–1233.*)

Brodatz [14]) and asked to rank them. The descriptors used were coarseness (Figure 9.3*c*), directionality (Figure 9.3*g* and *h*), contrast (Figure 9.3*a*), line-likeness (Figure 9.3*f*), regularity (Figure 9.3*e*), and roughness (Figure 9.3*d*).

The first three experimental descriptors listed above are indicated in Figure 9.2 as elements of the proposed texture model. Let us now consider these in turn. Probably the most common linguistic label we apply to a visual texture is coarse or fine. A precise definition of this attribute is not available, and perhaps it is overly optimistic to expect one. We observe the texture elements that make up the perceived pattern (for example, see D67 and D111 in Figure 9.4), and characterize the overall impression as coarse if the element size is large or if there are numerous repeated elements. Early references to this descriptor can be found in [75, 125, 126]. This work employed a version of the multichannel model discussed in Section 5.4.3. In each local neighborhood the set of channel outputs is examined to select the one with the strongest response. If two channels respond, suggesting both a micro- and macrotexture, the lowest spatial frequency is accepted as indicating a coarse texture. A high-spatial-frequency channel response indicates a fine texture. It turns out that the response of the channel that yields the maximum is governed by both the size of the texture element S_k and the placement rule R [141]. Therefore, an average taken over all local spatial neighborhoods corresponding to the optimum local channel would appear to be an excellent measure of A_1. Alternatively, suppose we plot a histogram of local responses for each channel, that is, each different-sized receptive field. As indicated in Figure 9.5, differently textured images will result in different characteristic channel curves [133, 170]. The properties of these histograms can be examined in order to compute the texture attribute of coarseness or element size.

The second texture descriptor used by Tamura et al. [141] was edge-element orientation, or "slope," as it is referred to in the psychological literature. Perceptual grouping experiments have indicated that this is a highly significant variable [7, 110]. Figure 9.6*a* shows the strong effect of element slope on texture discrimination. The upright and tilted Ts segregate very easily. The Ls and upright Ts, although seemingly more different in shape, appear to cluster into a single region. A similar effect is demonstrated in Figure 9.6*b*, consisting of (from right to left) cats, mirror-image cats, and rotated cats. Subjects who were asked to locate a boundary in the picture most often selected the one on the right [9]. This occurred even though on an individual basis the symmetric elements in the middle and on the right were judged to be more similar to each other than those in the middle and on the left. Some recent experiments with the Ehrenstein illusion have also given support to the importance of orientation in textural grouping [169].

Clearly we may view a texture as being either directional or nondirectional. Again, both elemental shape and structure (the placement rule) influence our perception of this attribute. As discussed in Chapter 5, the multichannel model output can be processed by simple edge-element templates to yield edge segments at a particular orientation θ. A histogram of directions can then be

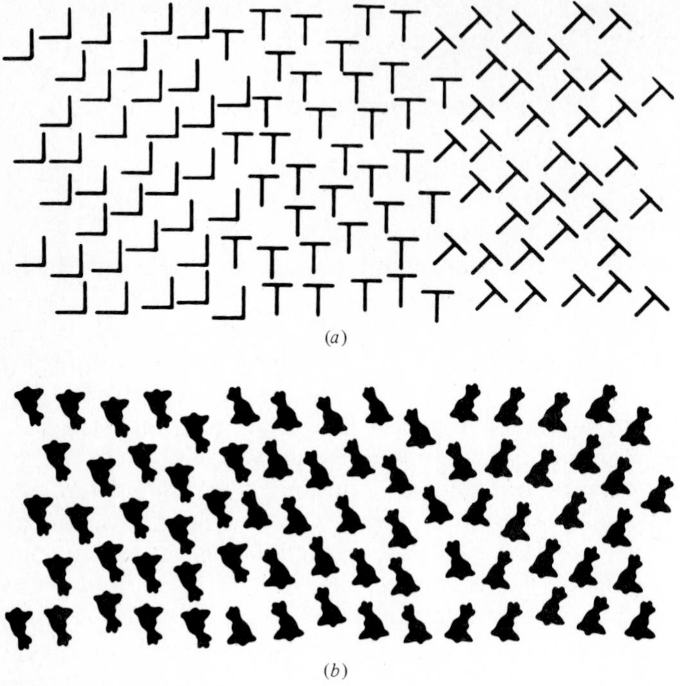

Figure 9.6 Factors affecting texture segregation. (a) Effect of element slope. (b) The mirror-image figures (a difference in overall figural slope) segregate themselves from the upright figures, while the inverted figures (no difference in overall slope) do not. [*From J. Beck, "Textural Segmentation," in J. Beck (ed.), "Organization and Representation in Perception," Lawrence Erlbaum Associates, Hillsdale, N.J., 1982, pp. 285–317.*]

employed to characterize the texture, as shown in Figure 9.7. We note that D15 has a very sharp and large peak, which implies a highly directional texture sloping at an angle of $\pi/16$ radians. Some directionality is observable in Figure 9.7b but it is relatively weak. The flat histogram in Figure 9.7c indicates a lack of directionality, while in Figure 9.7d we may discern the two observable angular orientations, one weak and one strong. Like other features, texture directionality is measured on a normalized scale but one admitting a relatively small number of quantization levels [100].

Tamura et al. [141] compute a measure of the sharpness of the peaks in the histogram $H(\theta)$ in order to quantify the directionality. This attribute A_2 determines the sum of the second moments [60] around each peak as follows:

$$A_2 = 1 - \alpha n_p \sum_{p}^{n_p} \sum_{\theta \in r_p} (\theta - \theta_p)^2 H(\theta) \tag{9.2}$$

where n_p is the number of peaks in $H(\theta)$, θ_p is the position of the pth peak, r_p is the range of the pth peak between the valleys, θ is the angular direction, and α is a normalizing factor. Recently, Davis [29] has suggested the use of a

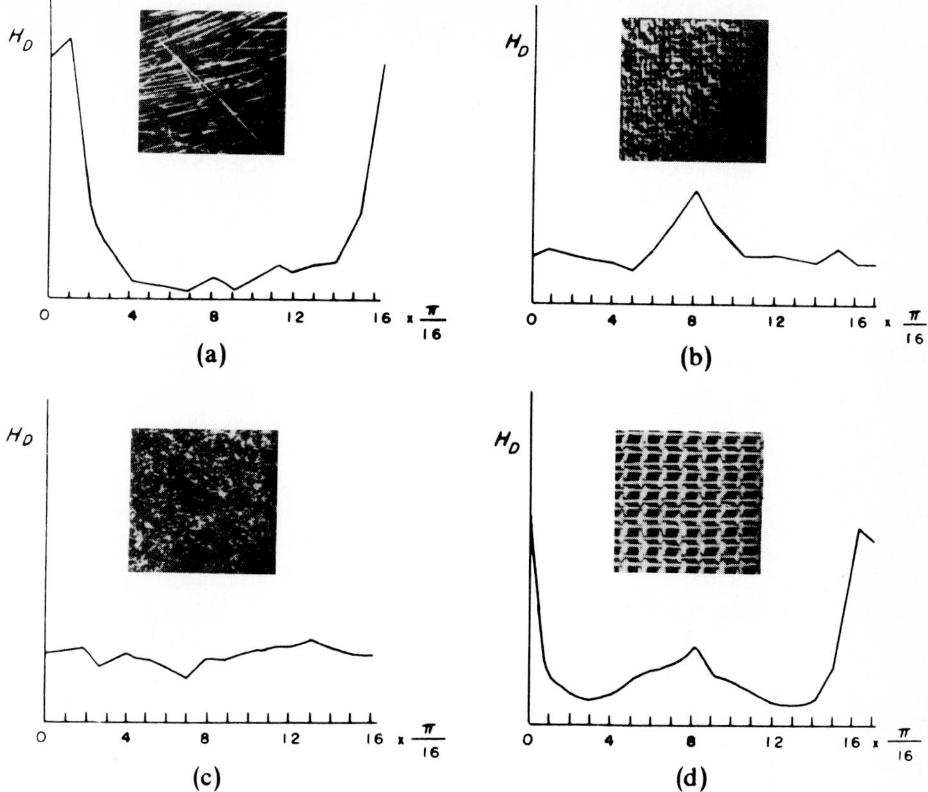

Figure 9.7 Examples of local direction histograms $H(\theta)$. (*a*) *D*15. (*b*) *D*84, (*c*) *D*9. (*d*) *D*20. (*Adapted from H. Tamura, S. Mori, and T. Yamawaki, "Textural Features Corresponding to Visual Perception," IEEE Transactions on Systems, Man, and Cybernetics, vol. SMC-8, no. 6, June 1978, pp. 460–473.*)

so-called polarogram to measure both texture coarseness and its directionality, the two attributes we have discussed so far.

The third important attribute which has been studied is picture contrast, a subject discussed in Section 6.6.1 in relation to histogram modification techniques. Clearly this variable may be obtained from the gray-level distribution. Let the contrast be expressed as

$$A_3 = \frac{\sigma}{(\mu_4)^n} \qquad n > 0 \tag{9.3}$$

where σ is the standard deviation, and μ_4, a normalized measure of polarization, is the kurtosis, given by

$$\mu_4 = \frac{M_4}{\sigma^4} \tag{9.4}$$

where M_4 is the fourth moment about the mean μ†. Experimentation with the parameter n yielded a value of $\frac{1}{4}$, which provided the best correlation between machine and human results. It is curious that contrast is employed in texture discrimination, since the opinion is often expressed that texture perception is independent of the actual shape of the image histogram. Indeed, we shall see later in this chapter that histogram-flattening techniques (see Section 6.6.1) are often applied prior to texture recognition by computer in order to achieve a certain degree of image normalization.

The other three features of line-likeness, regularity, and roughness (really a tactile measure) defined in [141] did not seem to achieve a high correlation between man and machine. The strongest cues for human perception seem to be coarseness and directionality, with some uncertainty regarding the role played by contrast. In general it has been found that those textures that stimulate the elementary feature detectors discussed in the previous chapters provide good texture segmentation.

We have restricted our considerations in this discussion to viewing two-dimensional images. However, it is known from the work of Gibson [55, 56], that texture gradients are involved in depth perception and thus assist in our perception of surface outline, range, and orientation [4, 87, 118, 135, 144, 163]. These processes are most likely attributable to the intermediate physical model indicated in Figure 8.9 and are concerned with the issues of three-dimensional object shape and surface microstructure.

9.2.2 A Conjecture

Perhaps all the above discussions would have been superfluous if the Julesz conjecture had held true. Julesz' innovative research into human texture perception since the early 1960s has been extremely influential. The early work is described in journal publications [81, 84] and a book [82]. Julesz hit upon the idea of using artificial textures generated by computer as the subject matter for human discrimination. Split-field displays, of the type we have already discussed in previous chapters but containing random dot patterns, were presented to the viewer. The significant aspect of this experimental procedure is that the probability density structure of the generated texture images can be precisely controlled. By restricting the amount of time a subject is allowed for viewing it is possible to study immediate or impressionistic (usually referred to as "preattentive") discrimination, as opposed to a more lengthy, deliberate (usually referred to as "attentive") analysis [112].

What is the essence of the Julesz conjecture? Before stating the basic premise, it is necessary to define first-, second-, and third-order statistics. This may be done in terms of "dropping" a point, a line, and a triangle, respectively, at random on an image pattern. In the first case we collect statistics on which pixel (monopole) gray level has been hit and represent the probability dis-

† See Section 10.4 for an elaboration of the concept of moments.

tribution in terms of a histogram. Second-order statistics are computed by randomly dropping a needle (dipole) of varying length and orientation and considering the gray levels at the two extremities. Similarly, the third-order distribution is obtained by examining the three vertices of triangles with arbitrary dimensions. Mathematically, these probability distributions are defined in terms of their normalized moments:

$$\mu = \xi\{I(i, j)\} \tag{9.5}$$

$$\sigma^2 = \xi\{[I(i, j) - \mu]^2\} \tag{9.6}$$

$$\mu_3 = \frac{\xi\{[I(i, j) - \mu][I(i', j') - \mu]\}}{\sigma^2} \tag{9.7}$$

$$\mu_4 = \frac{\xi\{[I(i, j) - \mu)[I(i', j') - \mu][I(i'', j'') - \mu]\}}{\sigma^3} \tag{9.8}$$

where (i, j), (i', j'), and (i'', j'') are three pixel locations in the picture array. The statistics of the texture synthesis are completely controlled by these moments [115] and are generated by a Markov process [121]. Examples of images with four gray levels are given in Figure 9.8. The total number of gray levels in the image does not affect the overall conclusions [115]. Numerous additional examples are provided in [83].

Figure 9.8*b* shows an example of fields which differ in their first-order statistics and for which visual discrimination is possible. Note that the means of the distributions *A* and *B* are identical, and only the standard deviations differ. In Figure 9.8*c*, the first-order probability distributions are identical but the second-order probability distributions are different; we still easily observe their characteristic visual fields. The last case, shown in Figure 9.8*d*, has both the first- and second-order statistics identical, a situation in which both *A* and *B* have the same power spectrum and autocorrelation functions. Even with attentive examination the texture fields are not discriminable! Thus the Julesz conjecture stated that humans are unable to visually distinguish between patterns with identical first- and second-order statistics. Presumably, differences in all distributions of third and higher order would yield the same effect. This would have been an attractive theory, since second-order statistics would then be sufficient for the human visual system. The idea stimulated great interest among researchers because of the inherent simplicity of the model and the possibility of a comprehensive biological theory. It appeared as if only an approximation to the pattern was needed even though, obviously, an arbitrary pattern requires nth-order statistics for its complete description.

Unfortunately, many counterexamples to the conjecture have been found [34, 50, 114, 115, 119], including some in the work of Julesz and his coworkers [15, 16, 83, 85]. Nevertheless, Pratt et al. [115] have restated the conjecture for the stochastic texture patterns that have been studied so far as follows: "... humans cannot effortlessly discriminate between pairs of spatially correlated texture fields with differing third-order probability densities when their

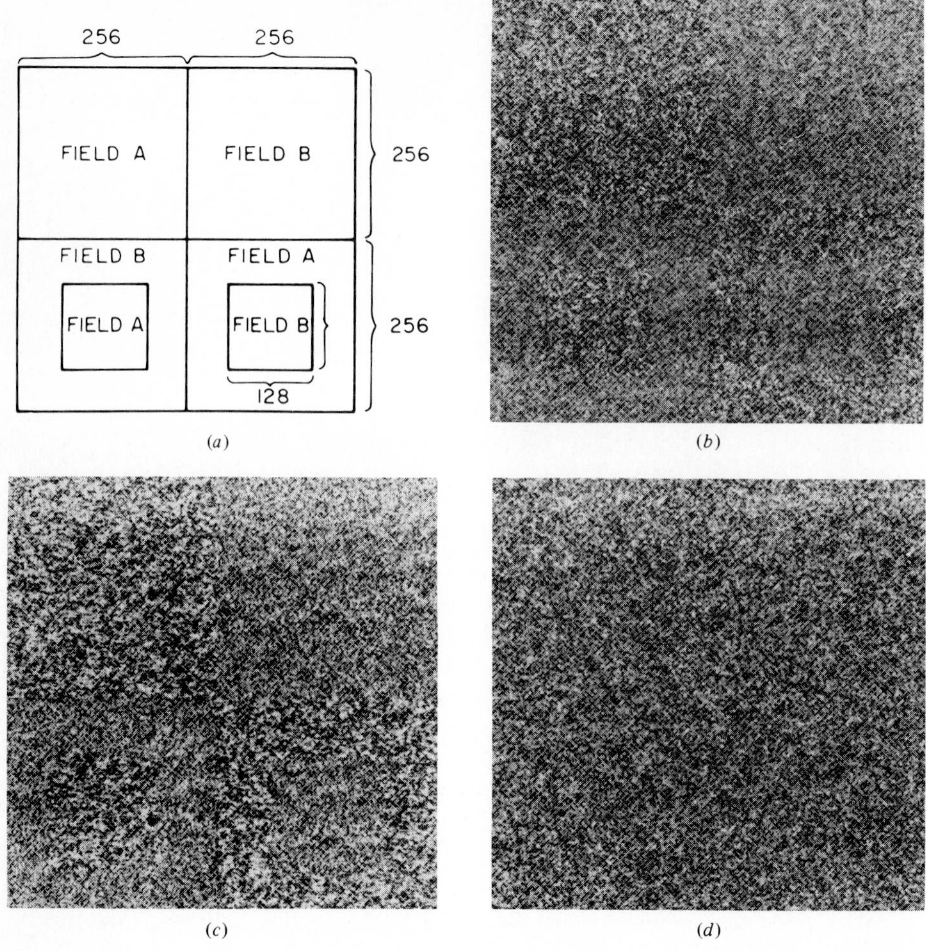

Figure 9.8 (*a*) Presentation format for visual discrimination experiments: (*b* through *d*) field comparison of Julesz stochastic fields with four gray levels; $\mu(A) = \mu(B) = 0.500$.

(*b*) Different first order:	$\sigma(A) = 0.280$, $\sigma\ (B) = 0.177$
(*c*) Different second order:	$\sigma(A) = 0.280$, $\alpha(B) = 0.280$ $\mu_3(A) = 0.333$, $\mu_3(B) = 0.067$
(*d*) Different third order:	$\sigma(A) = 0.280$, $\sigma(B) = 0.280$ $\mu_3(A) = 0.000$, $\mu_3(B) = 0.000$ $\mu_4(A) = 0.134$, $\mu_4(B) = 0.134$

(*From W. K. Pratt, O. D. Faugeras, and A. Gagalowicz, "Visual Discrimination of Stochastic Texture Fields," IEEE Transactions on Systems, Man, and Cybernetics, vol. SMC-8, no. 11, November 1978, pp. 976–804.*)

lower-order densities are pairwise equal." Indeed, from the point of view of machine vision, we shall see in Section 9.3 that techniques based on the use of second-order distributions have proved to be the most successful.

We should also take note that all these conjectures have dealt with patterns projecting onto a seemingly arbitrary region of the human retina. In addition, they have implied a kind of global processing, unaffected by the possible existence of structured micropatterns. This appears to contradict the prevailing neurophysiological knowledge we have discussed in previous chapters. As a result of the more recent research of Julesz [83] and others [51], it has become accepted that the characteristics of *local* neighborhood data are the primary determinators of visual discrimination. From his own experiments Gagalowicz [51] has even suggested that the property of locality is constrained by a circle of diameter equal to 8′ of visual arc. He has proposed yet another conjecture: "Visual discrimination of textures is achieved locally. (The) human eye cannot discriminate two texture fields which have locally the same second-order spatial averages" [52]. The operative words in this statement are the last two. The texture patterns originally used by Julesz [81] were both homogeneous and ergodic [49]. Because of this property, the second-order probability distributions, co-occurrence probabilities, and spatial averages are all identical. However, experiments with one of Julesz's counterexamples, in which the third-order probability distributions are equal [85], indicate that his texture synthesis methodology normally is not ergodic. Thus, the co-occurrence probabilities, which should be obtained from a class of representative pictures, are not equal to the statistics based on the second-order spatial averages obtained from a single picture. Gagalowicz [52] has proposed a texture synthesis method which is ergodic and has tested the resulting images in the context of human visual discrimination. On the basis of this, he makes the claim that

> ... all counterexamples [to the original Julesz conjecture] used [spatially] nonhomogeneous texture fields, and discrimination is precisely due to these inhomogeneities .... Most of the time second-order statistics in a local domain correspond to the global ones, but sometimes due to the nonhomogeneous synthesis procedure, local second-order statistics differ from the global ones. This difference is perceived by the eye and used for discrimination.

The most promising theory at present indicates that first-order statistics of local features is what governs texture discrimination by humans [83, 100]. Again, the evidence points to histogram analysis of low-level features, as with the texture attributes discussed previously (see Figure 9.2).

9.2.3 Attribute Aggregation

Let us now turn to the aggregation stage, which analyzes the texture attributes to yield the regions S in the two-dimensional image. The processing is achieved by using the logical predicate P, and we shall now briefly examine the underlying assumptions governing its operation. We note that in the psychology literature, most research characterizing P deals with binary or black-and-white patterns. Texture segregation is discussed in terms of the organization of texture elements [9] or place tokens [100]. Clearly, the computed attributes A_1, A_2, and A_3 in Figure 9.2 could be utilized to create these entities prior to aggregation. Marr [100] has suggested short lines, small blobs, ends of relatively long lines, and ends of elongated blobs as examples. Small collections of such blobs and lines are also assumed to be place tokens, thereby producing a logical transition from the local to global patterns. This recursive definition furnishes a convenient mechanism for defining a hierarchical data structure, which could also be employed by the logical predicate P. The final output, after grouping, was referred to by Marr [100] as the primal sketch, in distinction to the raw primal sketch which was the input (see Chapter 5). It should now be obvious that the strictly bottom-up procedure of Figure 9.2 is inadequate, since exactly the same features used to produce the raw primal sketch would most likely also be used to produce the primal sketch. What is more plausible as a hypothesis, given the above arguments, is that a cooperative computation of attribute measurement and aggregation may be applied at different levels of a data hierarchy (for example, Figure 9.1) to produce the set of regions S. Such a paradigm has not yet been extensively studied in the literature.

It is interesting that the underlying models used to specify the predicate P are largely based on gestalt psychology [89, 160], a theory long ago set aside as irrelevant to the information processing approach to human visual perception. The gestalt psychologists were concerned with the problem of distinguishing shapes (figure) from their background (ground), and developed a number of so-called grouping "laws" which governed human perception in this context. The major difficulty with the theory was related to the fact that although it appeared to be intuitively correct, there was no attempt at specifying or quantifying exactly (in mathematical form) the underlying mechanisms or how they functioned! A recent paper in the computer vision literature does address this subject from a mathematical point of view [166]. Frisch and Julesz [47] have summarized these rules, and they are listed in their order of importance to perceptual organization:

1. *Proximity and similarity*. Spatially adjacent units of similar brightness, color and shape form connected clusters. This cluster perception is not only fundamental in shape recognition, but is fundamental in texture discrimination as well.
2. *Area*. The smaller a closed region the more it tends to be seen as a figure. The complement holds as well; the larger the area of a region is the more it appears to be the ground.
3. *Closedness*. Areas with closed contours tend to be seen more likely as figure than do areas with open contours.
4. *Symmetry*. The more symmetrical a closed region is, the more it appears as figure. The greater the number of symmetries the region possesses, the greater will be this tendency.
5. *Smooth continuation*. From many possible perceptual organizations those tend to be perceived which will minimize changes or interruptions in the contours of the perceived constituents.

Readers will immediately recognize that rule 1 above was employed in the previous chapter to perform region analysis by machine (see Section 8.3).

The literature on human perception has also examined the concepts of proximity [44] and similarity [6, 8, 81, 100] for use in a model for aggregation of texture patterns. Ginsburg [58] has studied these perceptual organization laws in the context of the multichannel model shown in Figure 6.20. It appears that certain of the channels have the effect of highlighting organizational principles. The latter have been restated in the context of objects in the original three-dimensional scene as follows [76]:

1. *Existence of the surface*: The visible world can be regarded as being composed of smooth surfaces that have reflectance functions whose spatial structure may be elaborate.
2. *Hierarchical organization*: The spatial organization of a surface's reflectance function is often generated by a number of different processes operating at different scales.

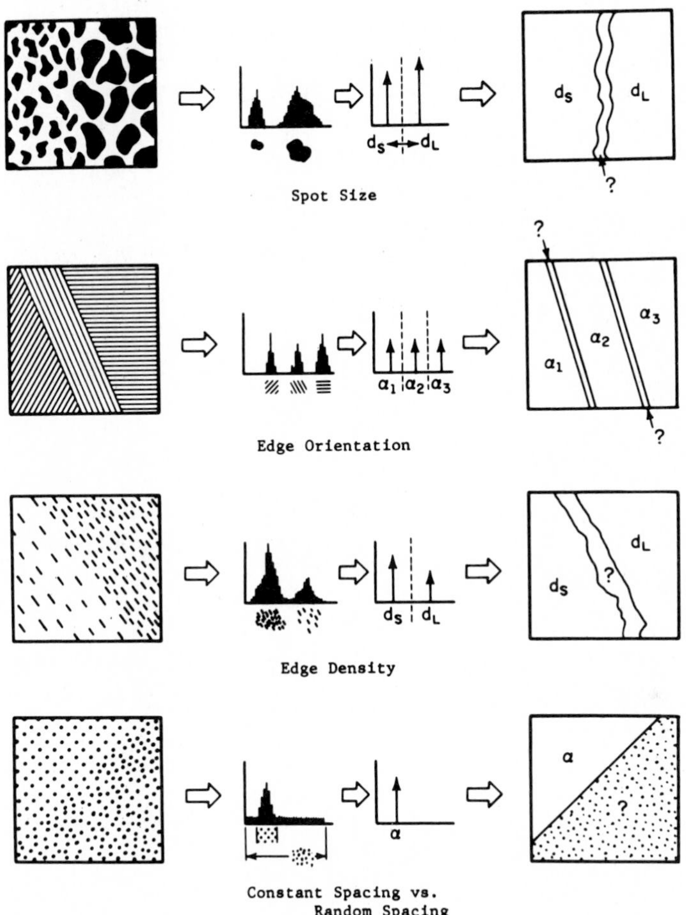

Figure 9.9 Examples of texture histograms. [*From C. Jacobus and R. T. Chien, "Intermediate-Level Vision Building—Building Vertex-String-Surface (V-S-S) Graphs," Computer Graphics and Image Processing, vol. 15, no. 4, April 1981, pp. 339–363.*]

3. *Similarity*: The items, generated on a given surface by a reflectance-generating process acting at a given scale, tend to be more similar to one another in their size, local contrast, color, and spatial organization, than to other items on that surface.
4. *Spatial continuity of spatial markings*: Tokens often form smooth contours on a surface.
5. *Continuity of discontinuities*: The loci of discontinuities in depth or in surface orientation are smooth almost everywhere.

At present, no model for human texture discrimination or, equivalently, region analysis of complex images has been adequately verified and accepted by the scientific community. From the discussions in this section and also Section 8.3, it would seem reasonable to assume that the aggregation function, the logical predicate P in Figure 9.2, is based on an analysis of the histograms of the texture attributes. This has been a recurring theme in our previous discussions and will again reappear in Chapter 10 with regard to shape analysis. Figure 9.9 is a schematic demonstration of the power of this simple first-order discrimination, which provides a good rough approximation to the data in the image. From the point of view of the human retina, Marr [100] has suggested that these distributions may be locally available "over moderately sized regions (0.5 to 1.0° at foveal resolution)."

The next two sections are concerned with processing textured images by machine. In most cases this has been restricted to pattern recognition, for example, identifying samples taken from a set generated by the same processes. The more difficult problem of region segmentation, considered as texture analysis, has been largely ignored.

9.3 STATISTICAL METHODS

9.3.1 Introduction

As we observed in Section 9.1, texture analysis techniques have traditionally been characterized as either statistical or structural [134]. In this section we shall address the former approach. At this point readers may again wish to consult Figure 9.1 in order to establish the specific role played by this technique.

The earliest reference to the texture analysis of imagery involved autocorrelation [86]. Other research followed in the sixties, with the consideration of power spectra [22], Markov processes [11], and co-occurrence statistics [81] as measures of texture content in an image. Except for Julesz, who worked with artificially generated texture patterns, the predominant application area seems to have been the study of aerial photographs. Of interest was the development of techniques which could automatically distinguish such natural categories as grass, water, forests, fields, and so on.

Figure 9.10 is a block diagram which characterizes the texture computations in this section. Note that although the input is shown to be an entire image array $I(i, j)$, we might just as well be referring to a single region. The

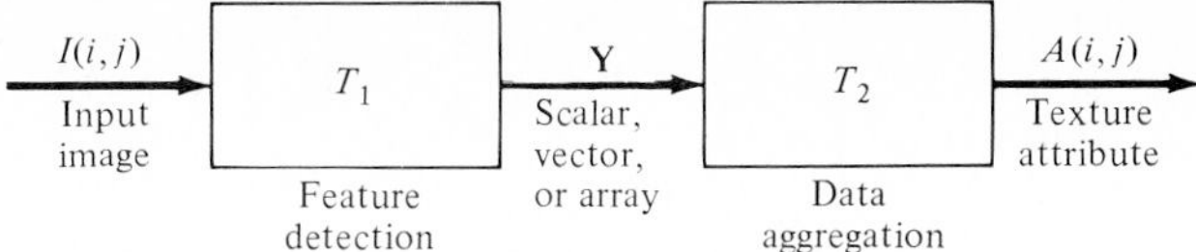

Figure 9.10 A block diagram depicting the process of statistical texture analysis.

transformation T_1 measures a statistical feature and provides as an output either a scalar, a vector, or an array **Y**, depending on the technique. In the latter two cases, the data must be aggregated to provide a unary measure. Thus, we require T_2 to compress the data, thereby computing a texture attribute $A(i, j)$. Most often A is a scalar which describes the texture in a given region of $I(i, j)$. The terms employed to describe texture are similar to those mentioned in Section 9.2.

It is often assumed by computer scientists that texture as viewed by humans is largely independent of illumination effects. To achieve a similar result with machines, it has been common practice to first preprocess the image using equal probability quantization (EPQ) [24, 62], a method we have discussed in Section 6.6.1. Based on the assumption that each of the stages of the camera-film-scanner input system can be modeled by a monotonic function, EPQ can be used to normalize image contrast in a set of images [69]. This is because two images that are monotonic transformations of each other and that have been normalized by EPQ will possess the same probability distribution functions [67]. It is these preprocessed images that are then used to compute the texture. The significance of this computational step is not clear, since we have observed in Section 9.2 that psychophysical experiments with humans indicate that contrast is, in fact, used by them to distinguish textures. Using EPQ, first-order discriminability is greatly reduced because first-order differences among the picture arrays have been removed. This leaves second-order statistics as the significant property.

The statistical methods to be discussed below have generally proved to be the most powerful and useful of the many suggested to date. Most probably, although they are convenient from machine vision, they are not directly relevant to human vision. This has not always been the prevailing opinion, as we saw in the previous section apropos the research of Julesz.

9.3.2 Texture as a Spatial Frequency

When we think of texture, we usually first conjure up a model of uniformly spaced elements of similar shape. The abstraction is one of regularity. Both the autocorrelation function of an image and its Fourier transform, the power spectral density function [165], are familiar measures of this property. Both are indicators of spatial frequency and will be discussed in this section.

The initial method to be presented is based on the autocorrelation function

[125, 126]. It provides an indication of how one pixel in an image array influences another. Suppose, for example, that we were to take two transparencies of the same image and overlay one with the other in registration. A uniform light is then projected through this "double transparency." Now one image is shifted with respect to the other in a particular direction and the transmitted light is recorded. This variable, plotted as a two-dimensional function of shift, is the autocorrelation function (see Section 2.4). Its peaks and troughs are assumed to be an indication of the size and separation of the basic texture elements constituting the pattern.

The first person to characterize texture in this way was Kaizer [86], who used aerial photographs of the Arctic as the patterns of interest. He undertook a comparison study of computed and perceived coarseness. The former was postulated to be a function of the autocorrelation, which was assumed to be circularly symmetric. It was taken to be equal to the number of pixels by which the image must be shifted in order that the autocorrelation function drop to $1/e$ of its maximum value. Twenty subjects were then asked to rank the same textures on the basis of perceived coarseness. There turned out to be a high correlation between the subjective measures and the computed ones. Later, however, Rosenfeld and Troy [125, 126] indicated that autocorrelation was not satisfactory as a measure of coarseness. To date, a conclusive study on its suitability for evaluating texture regularity and orientation has not been undertaken.

Mathematically, the two-dimensional autocorrelation function is given by

$$Y(\Delta_x, \Delta_y) = \frac{\sum_{i,j} I(i, j) I(i + \Delta_x, j + \Delta_y)}{\sum_{i,j} [I(i, j)]^2} \tag{9.9}$$

where i and j can be restricted to lie within a specific window, which is equivalent to assuming that the image is zero outside these limits. The incremental shifts are given by $\mathbf{d} = (\Delta_x, \Delta_y)$ and can obviously be negative. For a given image the autocorrelation will have a maximum value of 1 at $\mathbf{d} = 0$, with an exponential drop-off for both positive and negative shifts. Texture coarseness is indicated by the slope of the central peak. If the elements of the texture are large, this drop-off will be relatively slow. Conversely, small element size results in a fast drop-off of the curve. Another property, the periodicity or regularity in the texture pattern, manifests itself as a regularity of peaks in $Y(\Delta_x, \Delta_y)$. Circular symmetry in this variable indicates isotropy. For natural textures, however, it has been found that the autocorrelation function is not a very good discriminator. The curves are just not that distinct for different images [91].

Autocorrelation is a linear model. Similarly, autoregression models have also been studied, for both synthesis and analysis of texture patterns [32, 103, 104, 152]. The basic approach has been to use the time-series formalism [12]. The two-dimensional autoregressive process suffers from a general inability to describe replicated micropatterns [107].

The alternative to the autocorrelation function is examination of the frequency content in the image by means of the two-dimensional spatial Fourier transform (see Chapter 6). The latter has the ostensible advantage of being computable by either digital or optical means [140]. At just about the same time that texture analysis by computer began to attract attention, so did optical processing of satellite imagery to obtain texture features [37, 94, 138]. However, in order for this type of approach to be fruitful, a very tight coupling must exist between the computer and optical systems. This is because it is not enough to determine the features quickly. It is also, perhaps, necessary to preprocess the image and to classify the texture data according to specific categories. This is best done digitally. As a consequence, other researchers interested in classifying multispectral satellite or aerial imagery have approached the same problem by using fast Fourier transforms (FFT) and other so-called fast algorithms [59, 78, 88, 102]. Both digital and hybrid optical-digital systems for the diagnosis of coal miners' pneumoconiosis from posterior-anterior radiographs have been studied [90]. In each case the screening of normal and abnormal lung zones was comparable with that done by experienced radiologists.

We observed in Section 6.3 how the human visual system can be characterized by a set of bandpass filters. Section 9.2 discussed a model for texture analysis based on this approach. The reason that we are attracted to this method is that we are able to relate with relative ease the properties of the transform with those of the spatial-image domain [57], for example, the approximate size of the elements and their spatial organization. A disadvantage is that the transform is not invariant to linear transformations such as EPQ. The dynamic range of the gray scale matters. Also, transforms generally require large image arrays to capture the desirable textural properties. However, this may be difficult to achieve when attempting image region segmentation. Comparison studies have indicated that the performance of the spatial-frequency approach is poorer than that of other methods to be discussed in this section [137, 161].

The power spectral method is based on the Fourier transform of the image $I(i, j)$:

$$\mathscr{I}(u, v) = \frac{1}{N} \sum_{i=0}^{N-1} \sum_{j=0}^{N-1} I(i, j) \exp\left[-\frac{2\pi \mathrm{i}}{N}(\mathrm{i}u + jv)\right] \tag{9.10}$$

and

$$u = 0, 1, \ldots, N-1$$

$$v = 0, 1, \ldots, N-1$$

Then the power spectrum of $I(i, j)$ is given by the magnitude of $\mathscr{I}(u, v)$ such that

$$P(u, v) = (\{Re[\mathscr{I}(u, v)]\}^2 + \{Im[\mathscr{I}(u, v)]\}^2)^{1/2} \tag{9.11}$$

or equivalently

$$P(u, v) = [\mathscr{I}(u, v)\mathscr{I}^*(u, v)]^{1/2} \tag{9.12}$$

$P(u, v)$ is the Fourier transform of the autocorrelation function given in Equation (9.9). The phase spectrum, which has usually been ignored in texture computations as elsewhere, is given by

$$\psi(u, v) = \arctan\left\{\frac{Im[\mathscr{I}(u, v)]}{Re[\mathscr{I}(u, v)]}\right\} \tag{9.13}$$

It indicates position in the image [4]. Recall (from Chapter 6) that the determination of the transform $\mathscr{I}(u, v)$ depends on the assumption that the image $I(i, j)$ is periodic. Of course, it really is not. The resultant discontinuities at the border of the image produce spurious components in both the horizontal and vertical directions of the transform. The effect of this may be alleviated by placing an artificial border of zeros around the textural array of interest. Another approach is to employ the discrete cosine transform [36].

Texture coarseness is indicated by the character of the distribution $P(u, v)$ [4]. If high values of the latter are concentrated at the origin $(u, v) = (0, 0)$, then a rather coarse texture is implied. The low-frequency components are associated with large element size. On the other hand, a more spread-out distribution, with significant values at high frequencies, connotes a fine textural pattern. In this way the power spectrum appears to summarize the existence of periodic or almost periodic data. Texture directionality also seems to be described by $P(u, v)$. The latter turns out to be translation-invariant but does vary with rotation of the pattern. Consequently, directionality is preserved. Thus, if a texture pattern contains features which are largely oriented in one direction, then the high values of $P(u, v)$ will also tend to lie in a single direction. The orientation of the latter is perpendicular to its direction in the image $I(i, j)$. For example, horizontal streaks appearing in an image will result in vertical streaks in the power spectrum. However, if the texture is nondirectional or random, we would not expect to see any directional tendencies in $P(u, v)$. An example is the grass shown in Figure 6.39.

In order to simplify interpretation the two-dimensional power-spectral function has been condensed into a one-dimensional representation. To achieve this it is necessary to break up the spatial-frequency domain into either annular rings or wedges centered at the origin. Let us first consider the rings, which yield the function $P(r)$ in the polar coordinates (r, ϕ). For the continuous domain we can compute the average of $P(r, \phi)$ within a circle of radius r centered at the origin:

$$P(r) = \int_0^{2\pi} |\mathscr{I}(r, \phi)|^2 \, d\phi \tag{9.14}$$

Therefore, the rings are given by

$$P(r_1, r_2) = \int_{r_1}^{r_2} \int_0^{2\pi} |\mathscr{I}(r, \phi)|^2 \, d\phi \, dr \tag{9.15}$$

where r_1 and r_2 are the respective inner and outer radii of the annulus. The equivalent discrete version for an $N \times N$ image is given by

$$P(r_1, r_2) = \sum_{\substack{r_1^2 \le u^2 + v^2 \le r_2^2 \\ 0 \le u,\, v \le N-1}} |\mathcal{F}(u, v)|^2 \tag{9.16}$$

where r_1 and r_2 are defined in Equation (9.15).

The one-dimensional annular-ring signature is characteristic of the texture [2, 3]. Coarse textures result in high values at low spatial frequencies; fine textures will tend to exhibit predominant components at higher frequencies. A flat nonzero distribution implies a noisy texture. Peaks in the function indicate blobs of the appropriate sizes, given by the associated spatial frequency.

The second simplification, that of creating wedges, tends to measure the angular sensitivity $P(\phi)$. In the continuous domain we have

$$P(\phi_1, \phi_2) = \int_0^\infty \int_{\phi_1}^{\phi_2} |\mathcal{F}(r, \phi)|^2 \, d\phi \, dr \tag{9.17}$$

where the angles ϕ_1 and ϕ_2 delineate the wedge. The equivalent discrete equation is given by

$$P(\phi_1, \phi_2) = \sum_{\substack{\phi_1 \le \arctan\left(\frac{v}{u}\right) < \phi_2 \\ 0 < u,\, v \le N-1}} |\mathcal{F}(u, v)|^2 \tag{9.18}$$

In this case a flat distribution implies a nondirectional texture. On the other hand, peaks in the function suggest a specific orientation of the texture elements.

Studies of frequency domain textural features are discussed in [20, 25, 162]. A typical set of ring radii for a 256×256 image array is {[0, 1], [1, 2], [2, 4], [4, 8], [8, 16], [16, 32], [32, 64], [64, 128]}. Note that the frequencies 1, 2, 4, 8, 16, 32, 64, and 128 correspond to texture element sizes of 128, 64, 32, 16, 8, 4, 2, and 1, respectively. The wedges can be taken as 36° sectors. Figure 9.11 illustrates $P(r_1, r_2)$ and $P(\phi_1, \phi_2)$ for some of the textures shown in Figure 9.4. In addition to these functions, a different set of features can be generated on the basis of the intersection of the two variables radius and angle [161].

With respect to Figure 9.10 the process T_1 is given by Equation (9.16) or (9.18). The resulting vector output $\mathbf{Y}$ is, therefore, defined by either of the two distributions $P(r_1, r_2)$ and $P(\phi_1, \phi_2)$. Various texture attributes can then be computed. Some specific examples of the determination of the output A are given in [4], where the texture gradient information obtained is also used as a depth cue.

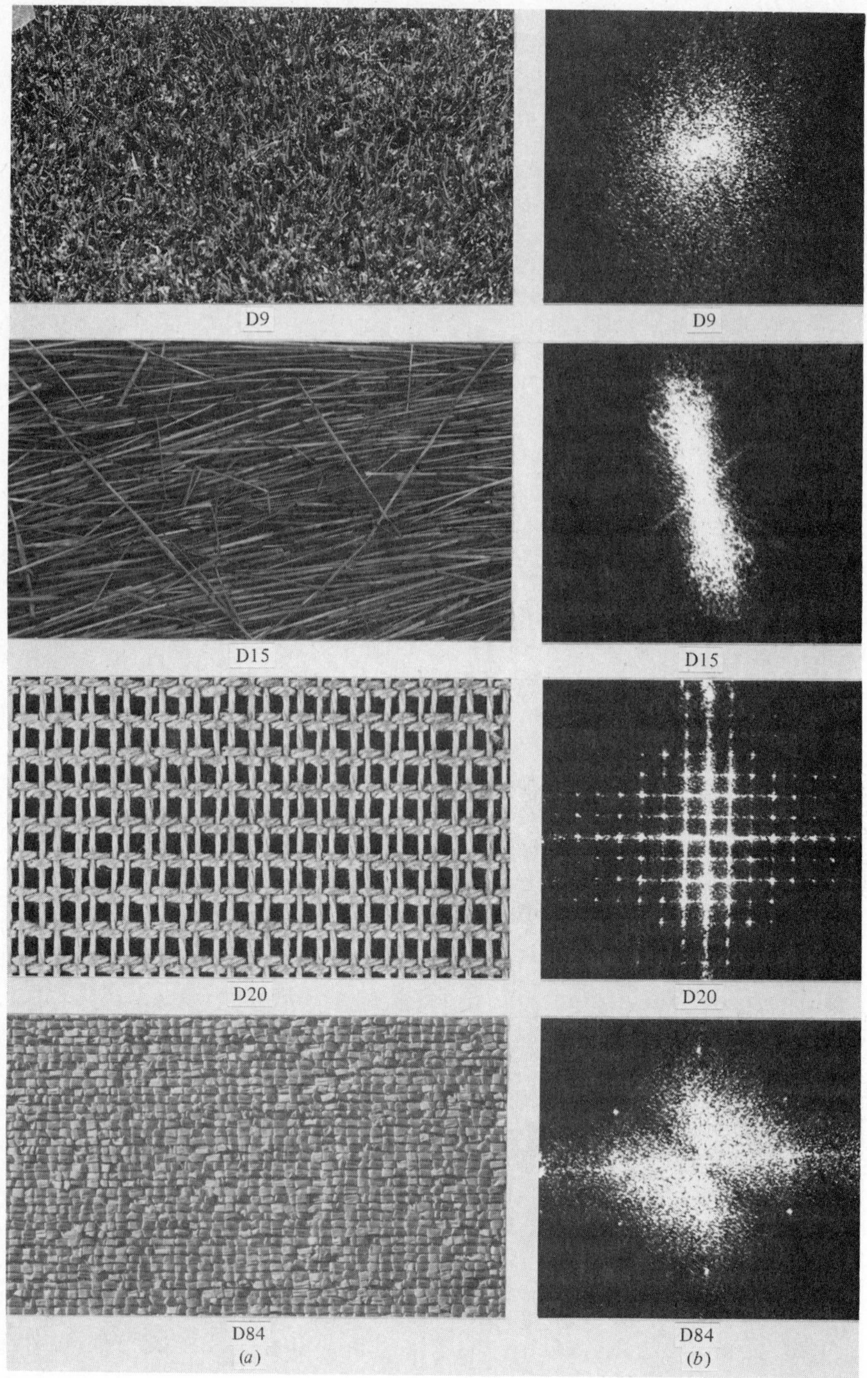

Figure 9.11(a) and (b) (Caption on page 448.)

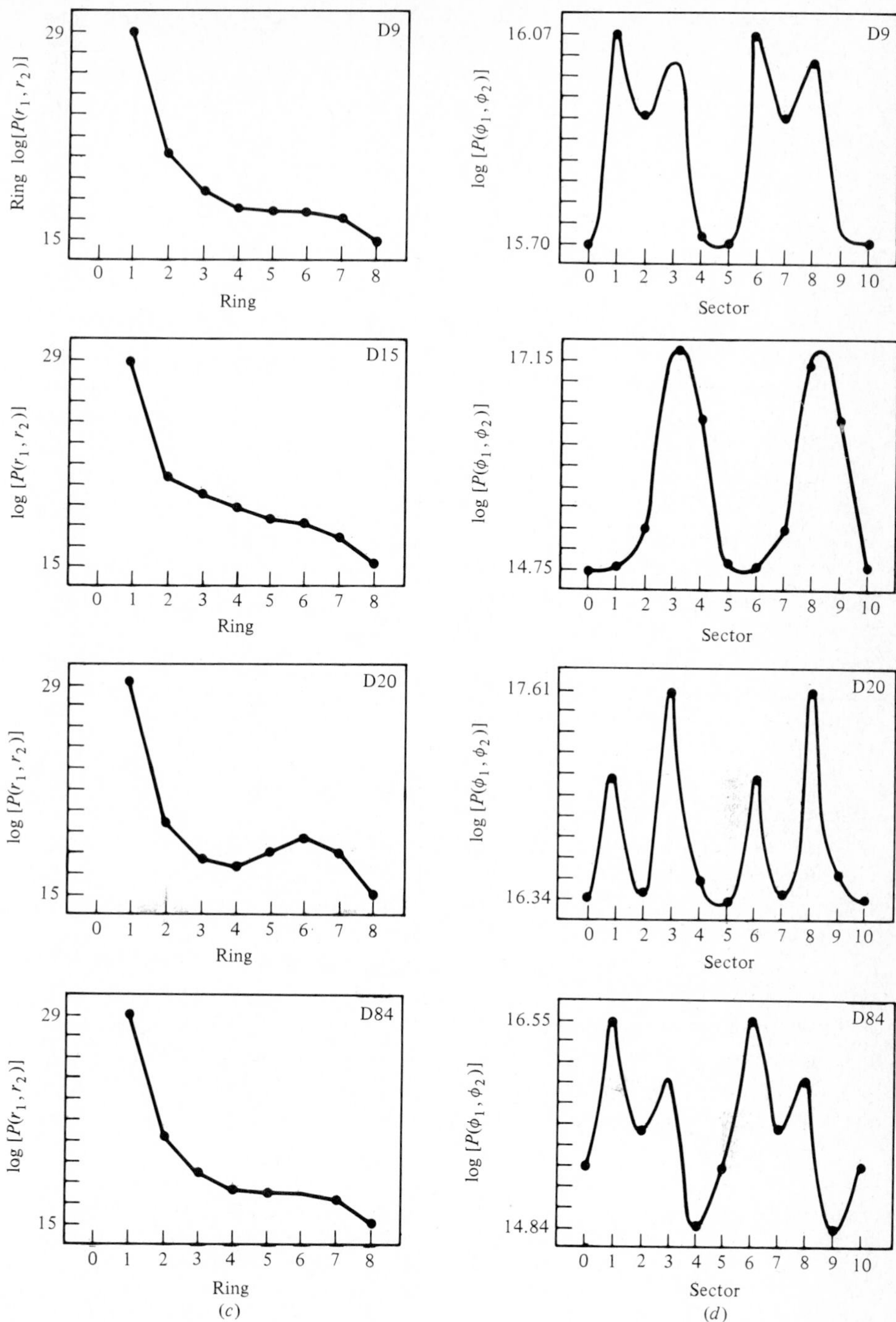

Figure 9.11(c) and (d) (Caption on page 448.)

In general, it has been found that Fourier descriptors are not quite as powerful texture descriptors as those methods based on difference and second-order statistics, to be discussed in Section 9.3.4. Perhaps the reason for this is related to the model or the computational algorithm [161]. However, readers should note that this frequency domain view tends to be sympathetic to the approach discussed in Section 9.2.

9.3.3 Simple Texture Measures

Simple statistical methods have always held an attraction as measures of texture. For example, in Section 8.3.2 we discussed similarity criteria for merging regions. One approach was to compare the statistical parameters of the cumulative distributions of two regions [105]. We would expect these parameters to be similar even if the regions were textured. Examination of a natural scene makes this quite evident. Whether the region is smooth or patterned, there does seem to be a certain "regularity" which can be captured by the local histogram of gray levels.

This idea has been used to advantage in automatically computing a depth map in order to determine the range for a proposed Mars Rover [96]. Disparity (or parallax) was calculated by examining the two images obtained from binocular vision, and range is inversely related to this variable. To measure disparity, correspondence between points in the stereoscopic pair had to be established. This was done by matching picture fragments. Care had to be taken that the window size was large enough to include a suitable amount of picture information to confirm a match but small enough not to include extraneous objects. Matching was therefore based on variable-sized windows, which were adjusted according to a simple statistical texture measure, the average gray level within the window. In the context of Figure 9.10 **Y** is the image array itself and T_2 involves the computation of a histogram, from which the mean is easily found. The latter represents the variable A.

The first-order probability distribution (or histogram) of the gray levels within a picture or picture fragment is obviously a concise and simple summary of the information contained in it. As we observed in Figure 9.9, other feature histograms are also of significance. In general we shall assume that $Y_k(i, j)$ is the kth feature computed in a local neighborhood $W(i, j)$ of (i, j). However, in order to simplify the notation the dependence on (i, j) will henceforth be

---

Figure 9.11 Radial and angular sensitivity of the Fourier transform. The radial sensitivity $\log[P(r_1, r_2)]$ is plotted as a function of the ring members $1, 2, \ldots, 8$, representing the following annuli, respectively: [0, 1], [1, 2], [4, 8], [8, 16], [16, 32], [32, 64], [64, 128]. The angular sensitivity is plotted as a function of sector numbers $1, 2, \ldots, 10$, representing the following wedges, respectively: [−108°, −144°], [−144°, −108°], [−108°, −72°], [−72°, −36°], [−36°, 0], [0°, 36°], [36°, 72°], [72°, 108°], [108°, 144°], [144°, 180°]. [(*a*) Textures. (*b*) Fourier transform. (*c*) $\log[P(r_1, r_2)]$. (*d*) $\log[P(\theta_1, \theta_2)]$. [(*a*) *from P. Brodatz, "Textures," Dover, New York, 1966.*]

ignored. Suppose that Y_k can only take on a set of discrete values $\{y_1, \ldots y_s \ldots y_t\}$. Then the probability density function or first-order histogram $H_k(y_s)$ can be easily computed according to Section 1.4. Four simple characteristics of $H_k(y_s)$ are the so-called central moments [115], and these are taken to be the texture attributes A in Figure 9.10:

Mean:
$$\mu = \sum_{y_s=y_1}^{y_t} y_s H_k(y_s) \tag{9.19}$$

Variance:
$$\sigma^2 = \sum_{y_s=y_1}^{y_t} (y_s - \mu)^2 H_k(y_s) \tag{9.20}$$

Skewness:
$$\mu_3 = \frac{1}{\sigma^3} \sum_{y_s=y_1}^{y_t} (y_s - \mu)^3 H_k(y_s) \tag{9.21}$$

Kurtosis:
$$\mu_4 = \frac{1}{4} \sum_{y_s=y_1}^{y_t} (y_s - \mu)^4 H_k(y_s) - 3 \tag{9.22}$$

Note that the value 3 is subtracted in Equation (9.22) in order to ensure that the kurtosis of a Gaussian histogram is normalized to zero. The fundamental variables, μ and σ^2, provide an indication of how uniform or regular a region is. Skewness is a measure of how much the outliers in the histogram favor one side or another of the mean. It is an indication of symmetry. Finally, kurtosis measures the effect of the outliers on the peak of the distribution, that is, the degree of peakedness. Other possible measures of $H_k(y_s)$ are the minimum, the maximum, the range, and the midrange value of y_s [91].

The major advantage of using the texture attributes discussed so far is obviously their simplicity. The most obvious property to select for Y_k is the gray level $I(i, j)$ of the image. In this way the image statistics are employed as measures of texture.

An alternative for Y_k is to characterize the histogram of some local property of the gray levels rather than relying on the gray levels themselves. A simple property is the gray-level difference between two pixels in the image [161]. We define a distance or displacement vector

$$\mathbf{d} = (\Delta_x, \Delta_y) \tag{9.23}$$

where both Δ_x and Δ_y are integers. Then the gray-level difference at a distance $\mathbf{d}$ is given by

$$Y(\mathbf{d}) = |I(i, j) - I(i + \Delta_x, j + \Delta_y)| \tag{9.24}$$

As before, the transformation T_1 in Figure 9.10 results in an array (for each value of $\mathbf{d}$). Let $H(y_s, \mathbf{d})$ be the probability that a given difference y_s [obtained from Equation (9.24)] occurs at a distance $\mathbf{d}$. An alternative is to compute the histogram based on differences between pairs of *average* gray levels at a specific distance apart. Again, the histograms embody certain clues regarding the image texture. For example, suppose that the image indicates a coarse texture and the distance **d** is relatively small with respect to the texture element size. Under these circumstances the histogram $H(y_s, \mathbf{d})$ would tend to cluster around $y_s = 0$. Now suppose that there is a fine texture and **d** is comparable in size with the elements. The effect is to spread out the histogram. These properties are demonstrated in the example of Figure 9.12.

Four transformations T_2 have been suggested for computing A [161]:

1. Contrast

$$A_1 = \sum_{y_s=y_1}^{y_t} y_s^2 H(y_s, \mathbf{d}) \tag{9.25}$$

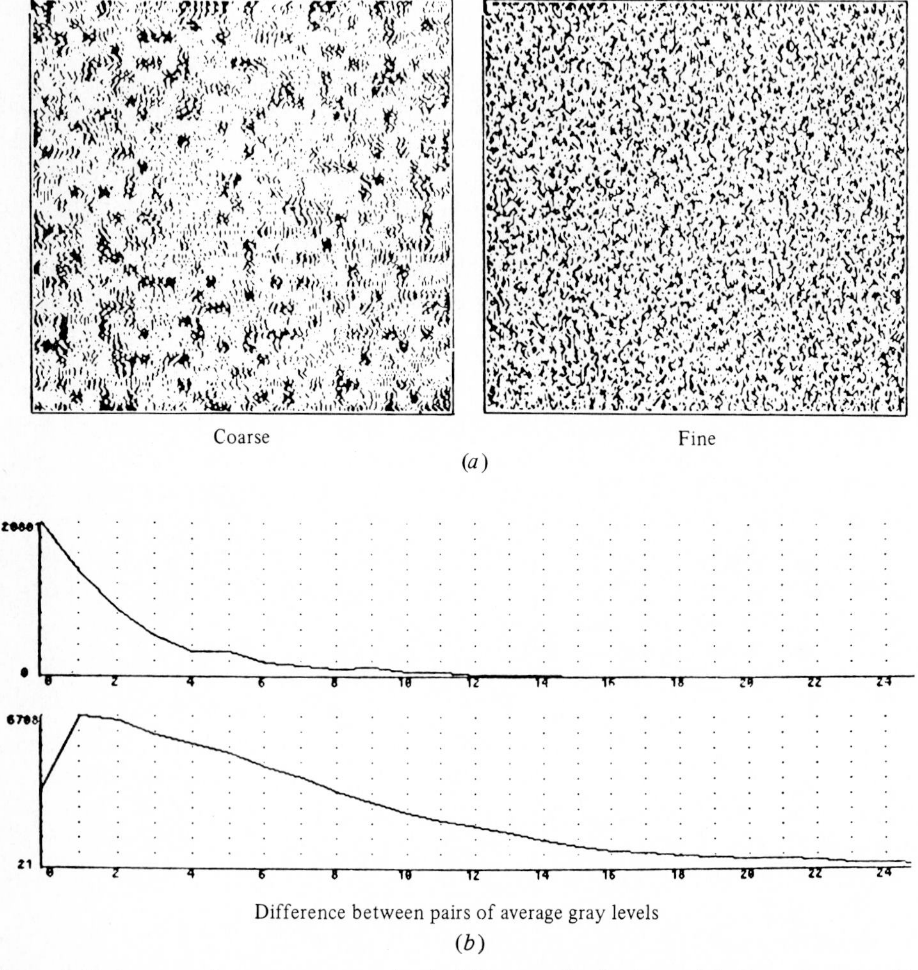

Figure 9.12 A comparison of two gray-level difference distributions. (*a*) Two textures. (*b*) Gray-level difference distributions $H(y_s, \mathbf{d})$ for the coarse texture (upper plot) and the fine texture (lower plot) in (*a*). In both cases $\mathbf{d} = [2, 0]$ was used. (*Courtesy of D. Terzopoulos.*)

This is the second moment of the histogram or, equivalently, the moment of inertia around the origin.

2. Angular second moment

$$A_2 = \sum_{y_s=y_1}^{y_t} [H(y_s^2, \mathbf{d})] \tag{9.26}$$

This attribute could possibly distinguish relatively flat histograms from those with values concentrated at the origin. A_2 tends to be small in the latter case and large in the former.

3. Entropy

$$A_3 = -\sum_{y_s=y_1}^{y_t} H(y_s, \mathbf{d}) \log H(y_s, \mathbf{d}) \tag{9.27}$$

This is a measure, taken from the field of communications, which is maximized for uniform $H(y_s, \mathbf{d})$.

4. Mean

$$A_4 = \left(\frac{1}{t}\right) \sum_{y_s=y_1}^{y_t} y_s H(y_s, \mathbf{d}) \tag{9.28}$$

Obviously, A_4 is small for histograms concentrated around $y_s = y_1$ and larger otherwise.

A major advantage of the gray-level difference approach is its computational simplicity. In addition, attribute A_4 [Equation (9.28)] has been demonstrated to perform nearly as well as other more complex measures [161]. This includes the second-order statistical approaches to be discussed in Section 9.3.4.

The feature histograms detailed above embody information regarding gray levels and gray-level differences. The latter also includes a concept of directionality. Another texture descriptor, gray-level run-length statistics, seems to measure the same properties [53]. In any given direction in a textured image there will exist runs of similar gray levels. For a coarse texture these runs will tend to be long and occur relatively often. A fine texture, on the other hand, will most likely exhibit short runs. Let $Y(l, I_m, \mathbf{d})$ be the number of times an $M \times N$ picture array contains a run length l for gray level I_m in direction $\mathbf{d}$. Figure 9.13 shows an example of four arrays computed for four different directions (0°, 45°, 90°, 135°) in a small picture array. Five texture features have been proposed [25, 53]:

1. Short-run emphasis

$$A_1 = \frac{1}{T_R} \sum_{m=1}^{n} \sum_{l=1}^{N_R} \frac{1}{m^2} Y(l, I_m, \mathbf{d}) \tag{9.29}$$

0	1	2	3
0	2	3	3
2	1	1	1
3	0	3	0

Picture array

Run length k

Gray level l	0°	1	2	3	4
	0	4	0	0	0
	1	1	0	1	0
	2	3	0	0	0
	3	3	1	0	0

Run length k

Gray level l	45°	1	2	3	4
	0	4	0	0	0
	1	4	0	0	0
	2	0	0	1	0
	3	3	1	0	0

Run length k

Gray level l	90°	1	2	3	4
	0	2	1	0	0
	1	4	0	0	0
	2	3	0	0	0
	3	3	1	0	0

Run length k

Gray level l	135°	1	2	3	4
		4	0	0	0
	1	4	0	0	0
	2	3	0	0	0
	3	5	0	0	0

Figure 9.13 The computation of run-length matrices for a small picture array.

2. Long-run emphasis

$$A_2 = \frac{1}{T_R} \sum_{m=1}^{n} \sum_{l=1}^{N_R} m^2 Y(l, I_m, \mathbf{d}) \tag{9.30}$$

3. Gray-level distribution

$$A_3 = \frac{1}{T_R} \sum_{m=1}^{n} \left[\sum_{l=1}^{N_R} Y(l, I_m, \mathbf{d}) \right]^2 \tag{9.31}$$

4. Run-length distribution

$$A_4 = \frac{1}{T_R} \sum_{l=1}^{N_R} \left[\sum_{m=1}^{n} Y(l, I_m, \mathbf{d}) \right]^2 \tag{9.32}$$

5. Run percentages

$$A_5 = \frac{1}{MN} \sum_{m=1}^{n} \sum_{l=1}^{N_R} Y(l, I_m, \mathbf{d}) \tag{9.33}$$

N_R is equal to the number of run lengths in the picture array and

$$T_R = \sum_{m=1}^{n} \sum_{l=1}^{N_R} Y(l, I_m, \mathbf{d}) \tag{9.34}$$

The computation of these texture attributes is relatively simple. Again, the property measured involves first-order statistics. However, experimental evidence indicates that this technique is not very powerful as a discriminator of texture patterns [25, 161].

In this section we have presented several first-order techniques for computing texture. A major advantage of using them is their inherent computational simplicity. The implication of the discussions in Section 9.2 was that first-order histograms were most probably instrumental in image segmentation. Therefore, one would expect that these approaches would gather more attention from scientists in the future.

9.3.4 Second-Order Statistics

The methods based on first-order statistics, which were discussed in the previous section, measure point properties. However, it would appear advantageous to also capture the spatial relationships in a texture pattern. Second-order statistics provide a simple approach for accomplishing this.

Recall from Section 9.2.2 the Julesz conjecture that the human visual system computes textural attributes on the basis of second-order statistics. He claimed that humans were unable to discriminate texture patterns that differed in their third-order statistics or higher. Although this postulate is no longer acceptable, the fact remains that Julesz was the first to introduce the concept of second-order statistics as a descriptor of texture [81]. Later, Darling and Joseph [27] were interested in classifying cloud types using texture features. They computed transition probability matrices for neighboring gray levels located in the horizontally adjacent pixel position. Thus, this co-occurrence matrix characterizes the probability that, given gray level I_k for pixel (i, j), then gray level I_l will be found in pixel location $(i, j + 1)$. Similar approaches have been employed in cell recognition [5, 162]. Arbitrary displacement in any direction leads to the concept of gray-level co-occurrence matrices (GLCM). Conceptually, we can think of obtaining the latter statistics by dropping a large number of independent "needles" on the image array. The gray levels occurring at the two endpoints are noted, and this joint occurrence (for a particular magnitude and argument of **d**) is accumulated in a probability matrix. Texture features are then computed from these matrices.

Co-occurrence matrices were first introduced by Rosenfeld and Troy [125, 126], Haralick et al. [63, 69], and Deutsch and Belknap [33]. Applications of this approach to biomedical image processing and remote sensing have clearly demonstrated its power [23, 54, 61, 67, 68, 70, 116, 142, 171]. Although mainly applied to texture discrimination of picture arrays, defined a priori, these co-occurrence matrices have also been used for region segmentation [21, 95].

Until recently, second-order statistics were computed using the pixel in the image array as the texture element (or primitive) [25]. The features recorded for these elements were pixel position and intensity. The spatial relationship between the elements was fixed by a displacement vector whose length and orientation could be specified. Figure 9.14*a* is a sketch of this situation, one that yields the GLCM. This viewpoint has now been generalized [30, 31]. Instead of the pixels being the texture elements, we may select such low-level entities as edge points, edge elements, or uniform regions. The first two could be computed by the windowing techniques discussed in Chapter 5. The third could be obtained by one of the methods in Chapter 8. The feature vector describing these texture primitives can possess an arbitrary number of components. For example, the edge element might be characterized by the following descriptors: position, contrast, orientation, fuzziness (see [100]). Similarly, the spatial relationship between the texture elements can be more general. Indeed, it may be defined by an arbitrarily complex spatial constraint predicate. Figure 9.14*b* shows an example of a group of edge points, one that yields the so-called generalized co-occurrence matrix (GCM) [30]. The GCM is obtained for each component of the feature vector of the texture primitive for a given spatial relationship.

Let us examine in more detail how the co-occurrence matrices are determined. As in Section 9.3.3, suppose that $Y_k(i, j)$ is the kth feature computed

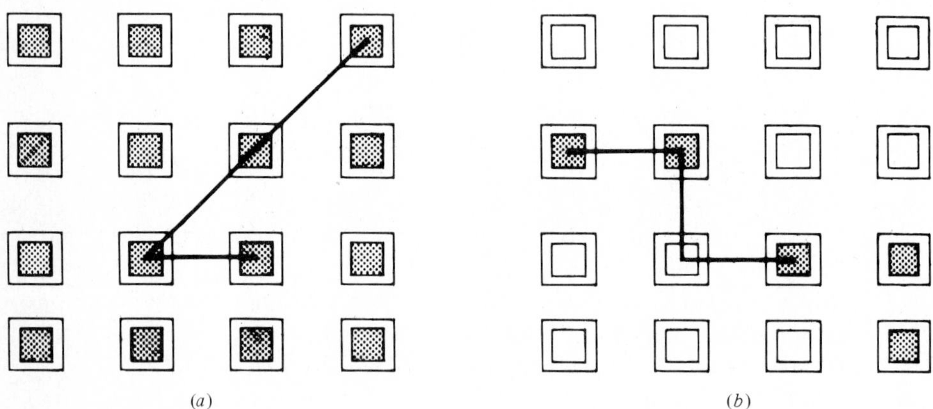

Figure 9.14 Defining the gray-level co-occurrence matrix (GLCM) and the generalized co-occurrence matrix (GCM). (*a*) A pixel array for which the texture is to be computed by using GLCMs. The primitives of the texture are constrained to be all of the pixel locations. Only pixel position and gray-level intensity are taken as components of the feature vector of the primitive (that is, each pixel). The spatial relationship between a pixel and its neighbors is given by a displacement vector, two possible examples of which are shown above. (*b*) A pixel array for which the texture is to be computed by using GCMs. The primitive texture elements in this case are the edge points shown, presumably computed by using a simple gradient operator. Associated with each edge point is a value of contrast as the feature. A typical spatial constraint predicate might be defined by two elements whose city-block distance is less than or equal to 2. The two edge elements which satisfy this constraint for one of the pixels are shown above.

for a given texture element. Again, we assume that it can only take on values in the integer set $\{y_1, \ldots, y_r, \ldots, y_s, \ldots, y_t\}$.† Second-order statistics are concerned with how frequently two values of $Y_k(i, j)$, y_r and y_s for example, occur in relation to a spatial constraint predicate. In general, for the GCM the predicate Ω is defined by

$$\Omega = \omega[(i, j), (i', j')] \tag{9.35}$$

where (i, j) and (i', j') are the pixel locations of the two texture elements and ω is a logical expression. For example, suppose that the spatial predicate ω_1 were true if the distance between the two pixel locations were less than or equal to ν, that is,

$$\begin{aligned}\omega_1[(i, j), (i', j'), \nu] &= [(i - i')^2 + (j - j')^2]^{1/2} \\ &= [(\Delta_x)^2 + (\Delta_y)^2]^{1/2} \leq \nu \end{aligned} \tag{9.36}$$

As another example, suppose that ω_2 were true if (i, j) and (i, j') were nearest neighbors. Then $\Omega = \omega_1 \wedge \omega_2$ specifies a constraint in which, for the texture elements to be considered as satisfying the condition, they must be nearest neighbors and within a distance ν of each other. For the GLCM all pixels (i, j) in the texture array are considered to be the texture elements. The spatial constraint predicate is given by:

$$\Omega\colon (i - i') = \Delta_x, \ (j - j') = \Delta_y \tag{9.37}$$

which is, therefore, defined by the displacement vector $\mathbf{d}$ [Equation (9.23)].

We may define the normalized histogram $H_k(y_r, y_s, \Omega)$ for the kth feature as the probability that two feature values y_r and y_s will occur given the spatial predicate Ω. The texture attribute A will then be characterized by a two-dimensional histogram, as against the one-dimensional version discussed for first-order statistics. These arrays will tend to be quite big. Perhaps a 16-level quantization for the feature values is the largest that is computationally practical. As a result, low contrast textures will often be masked out.

Most research to date has been restricted to GLCMs. This is because the obvious texture feature in an image is the gray level or average local gray level. In this case we estimate the probability that a pair of gray levels (I_1, I_2) will be found at a pair of pixels a displacement $\mathbf{d}$ apart. Consider the picture fragment shown in Figure 9.15*a*. The GLCM $\mathcal{H}(I_1, I_2, \Omega)$, with spatial constraint given by Equation (9.37) and $\mathbf{d} = (1, 0)$, is shown in Figure 9.15*b*. Probabilities can easily be obtained by dividing each entry by the total sum 20. It has also been the convention to ignore the distinction between positive and negative transitions. Thus, noting that

$$\mathcal{H}(I_1, I_2, \mathbf{d}) = \mathcal{H}^T(I_1, I_2, -\mathbf{d}) \tag{9.38}$$

† For convenience of notation, it has been assumed that all features have been normalized to the same range $y_1 \leq y_r < y_s \leq y_t$. This is actually often done in practice.

0	1	1	3	3
0	0	2	3	3
0	1	2	2	3
1	2	3	2	2
0	2	3	3	2

(*a*)

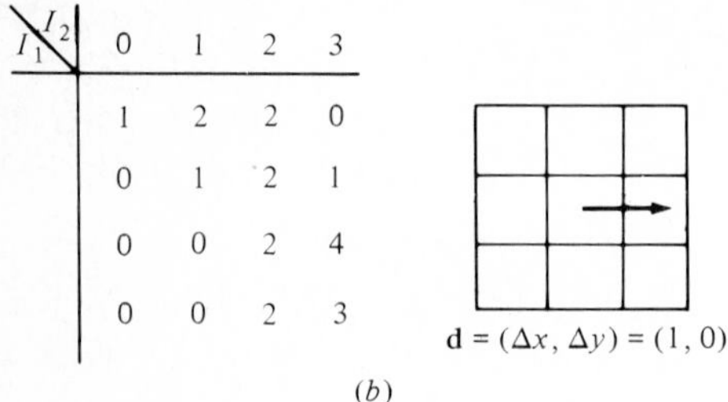

$I_1 \backslash I_2$	0	1	2	3
	1	2	2	0
	0	1	2	1
	0	0	2	4
	0	0	2	3

(*b*)

$I_1 \backslash I_2$	0	1	2	3
0	1	1	1	0
1	1	1	1	0.5
2	1	1	2	3
3	0	0.5	3	3

(*c*)

Figure 9.15 The computation of GLCMs. (*a*) The picture array. (*b*) The GLCM $H(I_1, I_2, \mathbf{d})$, $\mathbf{d} = [0, 1]$. (*c*) The symmetric GLCM $H(I_1, I_2, \mathbf{d})$. Probabilities can be obtained by dividing each entry by 20 (the sum of all the entries).

we may also compute a symmetric GLCM according to

$$H(I_1, I_2, \mathbf{d}) = \tfrac{1}{2}[\mathscr{H}(I_1, I_2, \mathbf{d}) + \mathscr{H}^T(I_1, I_2, \mathbf{d})] \tag{9.39}$$

The matrix H for the array in Figure 9.15*a* is shown in Figure 9.15*c*. It is often used instead of $\mathscr{H}$, thereby making no distinction between transitions in the direction $\mathbf{d}$ or $-\mathbf{d}$.

The matrix H can be used to distinguish texture patterns in an image. For example, consider a relatively coarse texture with large element size. If the magnitude of $\mathbf{d}$ is chosen to be small compared with the latter, pairs of neighboring pixels are most likely to exhibit similar gray levels. Under these circumstances the high values of $\mathscr{H}$ will tend to be clustered around the diagonal. For a fine texture, on the other hand, the magnitude of $\mathbf{d}$ will be of the same order as the texture element size. Consequently, in this case the values of H will now be more evenly distributed. These properties are evident in the example shown in Figure 9.16, which depicts the GLCMs for the two textures in Figure 9.12. Directionality can also be observed by comparing the spread of H for different orientations given by the vector $\mathbf{d}$.

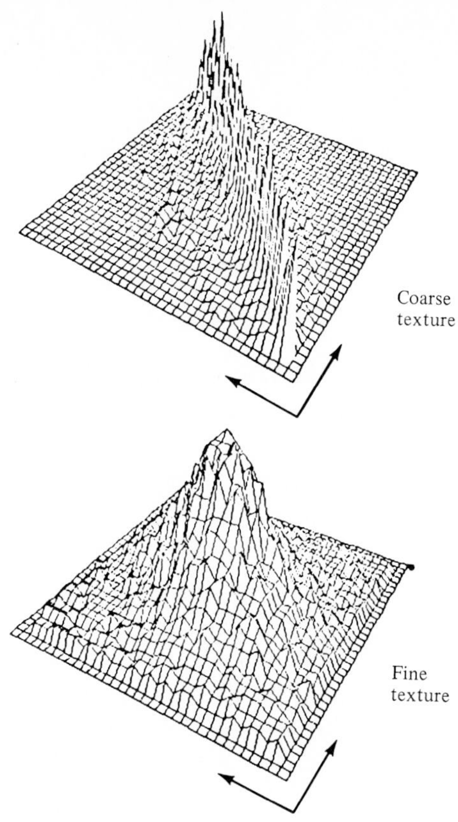

Figure 9.16 GLCMs $H(y_r, y_s, \mathbf{d})$ obtained from the coarse and fine textures (256×256, 32 gray-level images) shown in Figure 9.12. The displacement vector $\mathbf{d} = [2, 0]$ was used in generating both matrices. The matrices are displayed as 3D surfaces, where the height of the surface above the base plane is proportional to the matrix element. (*Courtesy of D. Terzopoulos.*)

It is also interesting that there exists a simple relationship between the first-order difference statistics (see Section 9.3.3) $H(y_s, \mathbf{d})$ and the second-order statistics $H(y_q, y_r, \mathbf{d})$. The former measures the frequency at which differences y_s of gray levels occur in the image at a distance given by $\mathbf{d}$. The latter indicates the frequency of occurrence of particular pairs y_r and y_s of gray levels that are separated by the vector $\mathbf{d}$. It can be shown that

$$H(y_s, \mathbf{d}) = \sum_{|y_q - y_r| = y_s} H(y_q, y_r, \mathbf{d}) \tag{9.40}$$

that is, adding the entries of $H(y_q, y_r, \mathbf{d})$ along an off-diagonal parallel to the main diagonal yields a number proportional to the first statistic for the difference $|y_q - y_r|$. Obviously, the GLCM is the more powerful measure. However, the texture attributes to be defined below [see Equations (9.41) through (9.45)] tend to blur this distinction as a result of the summation taken over all the elements of $H(y_q, y_r, \mathbf{d})$.

Let us also briefly consider an example of a GCM. Figure 9.17a illustrates a small pixel array, where the edge pixels have been labeled according to the orientation of the edge elements that they constitute. Blanks indicate that no

						H	*H*
	H	*H*	*H*		*R*		
L				*R*			
V				*V*			
V				*V*			
	H	*H*	*H*		*L*	*H*	*H*

(*a*)

	H	*V*	*L*	*R*
H	12	2	2	2
V	2	4	2	2
L	2	2	0	0
R	2	1	0	2

(*b*)

Figure 9.17 Computation of the GCM for a small picture array. (*a*) A texture array in which the edge elements are taken as the primitives of the texture. The feature of interest in this case is the edge orientation. (*b*) The elements of the array $H(y_r, y_s, \Omega)$, where Ω is given by Equation (9.36), with $\nu = 1$. Probabilities can easily be computed by dividing the elements by 37 (the sum of all the entries).

texture element is detected; *H*, *V*, *L*, and *R* indicate elements oriented horizontally, vertically, along a left diagonal, and along a right diagonal, respectively. Obviously, only these elements will participate in the computation of the GCM. This matrix $H(y_r, y_s, \Omega)$ is shown in Figure 9.17*b* for the spatial predicate Ω given by Equation (9.36) with $\nu = 1$.

We have seen that the matrix $H(y_r, y_s, \Omega)$ can be computed for different features. Accordingly, various measures for computing the texture attribute *A* have been suggested [69]. However, the reader should take note that these measures have not been shown to compute independent properties of the texture pattern. Some common attributes are given below:

1. Contrast

$$A_1 = \sum_{y_r=y_1}^{y_t} \sum_{y_s=y_1}^{y_t} \delta(y_r, y_s) H(y_r, y_s, \mathbf{d}) \tag{9.41}$$

where $\delta(y_r, y_s)$ is a dissimilarity measure which depends on the feature used. For example, in the case of the GLCMs the feature is intensity and $\delta = (y_r - y_s)^2$. If a GCM were computed on the basis of edge-point orientation as the feature, then we could use $\delta = |\sin(y_r - y_s)|$. Then A_1 would describe the variation in the orientation of the texture elements. Although it is claimed that A_1 characterizes the amount of spread in $\mathscr{H}$ and therefore the contrast [161], Tamura et al. [141] have found that no apparent correlation between A_1 and the actual human visual perception of contrast.

2. Angular second moment

$$A_2 = \sum_{y_r=y_1}^{y_t} \sum_{y_s=y_1}^{y_t} [H(y_r, y_s, \mathbf{d})]^2 \tag{9.42}$$

This is a measure of uniformity or homogeneity [70], and Connors and

Harlow [25] refer to A_2 as representing the energy in the image. It tends to be small when all entries in $\mathcal{H}$ are more or less similar. This situation occurs when the texture can be described as being fine. The matrix $\mathcal{H}$ is maximized as it becomes more and more diagonalized.

3. Inverse difference moment

$$A_3 = \sum_{\substack{y_r = y_1 \\ y_r \neq y_s}}^{y_t} \sum_{y_s = y_1}^{y_t} \left[\frac{H(y_r, y_s, \mathbf{d})}{1 + \delta(y_r, y_s)} \right] \tag{9.43}$$

where $\delta(y_r, y_s)$ is defined as above. This measure has also been referred to as "local homogeneity" [25].

4. Entropy

$$A_4 = -\sum_{y_r = y_1}^{y_t} \sum_{y_s = y_1}^{y_t} H(y_r, y_s, \mathbf{d}) \log H(y_r, y_s, \mathbf{d}) \tag{9.44}$$

A_4 is a measure of texture nonuniformity. It tends to be large when the elements of H are large and small when they are unequal. It appears that A_3 and A_4 seem to give the best separation of texture classes for remote sensing imagery [111].

5. Correlation

$$A_5 = \left[\frac{1}{\sigma_{y_r} \sigma_{y_s}} \right] \sum_{y_r = y_1}^{y_t} \sum_{y_s = y_1}^{y_t} (y_r - \mu_{y_r})(y_s - \mu_{y_s}) H(y_r, y_s, \mathbf{d}) \tag{9.45}$$

where μ_{y_r} and μ_{y_s} are the means and σ_{y_r} and σ_{y_s} the standard deviations of y_r and y_s, respectively. This measure tends to become larger as the elements of $H(y_r, y_s, \mathbf{d})$ become more similar in value. Alternative feature measures based on a maximum likelihood hypothesis test on $\mathcal{H}$ are discussed in [107].

For the coarse texture in Figure 9.12, three of the texture attributes defined above are found to give $A_1 = 1055.9$, $A_2 = 26.3$, and $A_4 = 109.8$. The fine texture yields $A_1 = 2027.3$, $A_2 = 107.4$, and $A_4 = 272.0$. Both theoretical [25] and experimental results [31, 161] indicate that the texture measures based on second-order statistics are more effective for pattern recognition than other methods. One major disadvantage is that the number of texture attributes that can be computed is very large. Fourteen are listed in [70]. Furthermore, these attributes can be computed as a function of the magnitude and direction of the displacement ($\mathbf{d}$).

One possible way of reducing the amount of data in certain cases is to assume rotational isotropy and average all the matrices in different directions for a fixed $|\mathbf{d}|$. The aggregate matrix is then used to compute the texture measure. This assumption may be valid, as has been demonstrated for textures generated by using a Markov model [25]. Another approach to aggregation is to average the matrices over the length $|\mathbf{d}|$ in a fixed direction. Again, it would appear that this assumption is counterproductive with respect to discriminating the microfeatures of the texture. Zucker and Terzopoulos [172] have suggested a statistical approach for determining the optimal magnitude and direction of **d**.

As has been pointed out earlier, these texture attributes have been mainly tested on their ability to discriminate different picture arrays. Thus, feature detection and texture classification are treated as a single problem. The more interesting problem of region analysis based on textural descriptions has received little attention in the literature.

9.4 STRUCTURAL METHODS

We have observed that texture can be described by means of a set of primitives and placement rules which govern the spatial relationships between them (see Figure 9.1). This point of view was first expounded by Rosenfeld and Lipkin [122]. Visual texture within such a framework seems to have a similarity to language. An analogy may be drawn between the symbols of the language and the texture primitives. The grammar may be associated with the spatial relationships in that it dictates how the symbols should be combined. Therefore, the symbols and the grammar together constitute a linguistic model of texture. Synthesis is achieved by creating allowed symbol strings in the language. Recognition is perhaps akin to syntax analysis or the parsing of symbol strings. More likely, it bears a closer similarity to human speech recognition.

Early formal texture models using grammars were detailed by Carlucci [18] and Jayaramamurthy [79]. The former used a tree representation to describe the regular arrangements of unit patterns, taken as either line segments or open or closed polygons. The latter employed a set of small picture-array templates as the primitives. Zucker [168] later proposed distorting the synthesized graphs describing the ideal texture patterns, in order to produce real textures, such as those shown in Figure 9.4. Fu and his students have developed the concept of a stochastic tree grammar to model texture images [48, 98] and have used it for pattern recognition. Applications have included bubble-chamber pictures, highways and rivers appearing in LANDSAT imagery, and fingerprints. One difficulty with this approach is how to specify the grammar. Ideally, this should be done by inference from the actual texture images [13, 99], but little work has been published on this subject to date. Jayaramamurthy [80] has recently introduced the concept of a multilevel array grammar, which facilitates the recursive description of complex texture patterns.

One advantage of the structural approach is that it provides a good symbolic description of the image. Texture synthesis then becomes a simple matter. As a model it is most useful for regular textures with well-defined primitives and patterns. It is less appropriate for the kinds of textures we studied in the previous section. Significantly, it has only been applied to pattern recognition and not to image segmentation. Nevertheless, there is a practical need to distinguish patterns, and Leitz, the optical microscope manufacturer, has developed a hardware structural analyzer just for texture [108]. This system is based on the unique research of Serra on mathematical morphology [130, 131, 132].

Structural approaches to texture have been classified by Haralick [66] into two groups, that is, weak and strong textures. These descriptions refer to the spatial interaction between the primitives. A weak interaction can most likely be characterized by local area statistics of the type discussed in Section 9.3. On the other hand, strong interaction requires the details of the actual topological relationships. In this case it is obvious why the grammars discussed above can serve as an appropriate model.

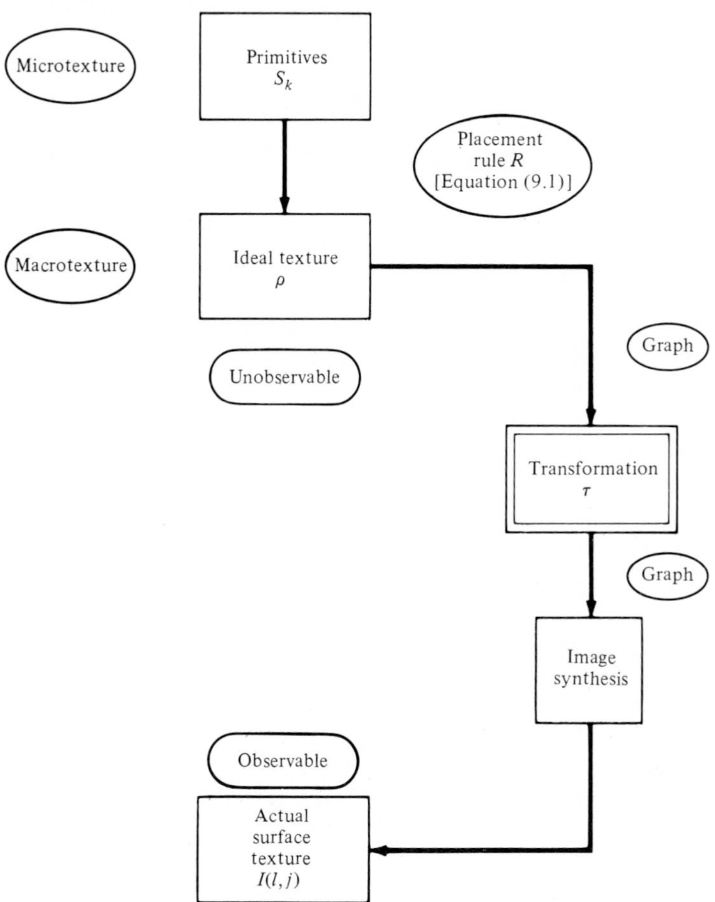

Figure 9.18 A transformational texture model, developed by Zucker [168]. As shown above, the arrows indicate a process of texture synthesis, in which τ distorts an ideal macrotexture to create a more realistic pattern $I(i, j)$. If the direction of the arrows were to be reversed, we would start with an actual surface texture $I(i, j)$. Then the two stages at the right would become a process of pattern recognition to determine p, R, and S_k.

A convenient model for texture synthesis and analysis, due to Zucker [167, 168], is indicated in Figure 9.18. Suppose we wished to generate a "real" texture image. Then according to the figure, it would be necessary to select a set of region primitives S_k and a placement rule R, thereby obtaining an ideal macrotexture ρ. The latter is unobservable in the sense that it is only an idealized version of the actual observable texture being sought. Formally, ρ may be represented by a graph [167]. Thus the transformation τ is a mapping from a graph description of an ideal texture pattern ρ into another (graph) description of a "real" texture. The image $I(i, j)$ is then created by computer graphics methods of image synthesis. In the case of a weak texture, τ is random; for strong textures, it tends to be systematic. Examples of these are shown in Figures 9.19 and 9.20, respectively.

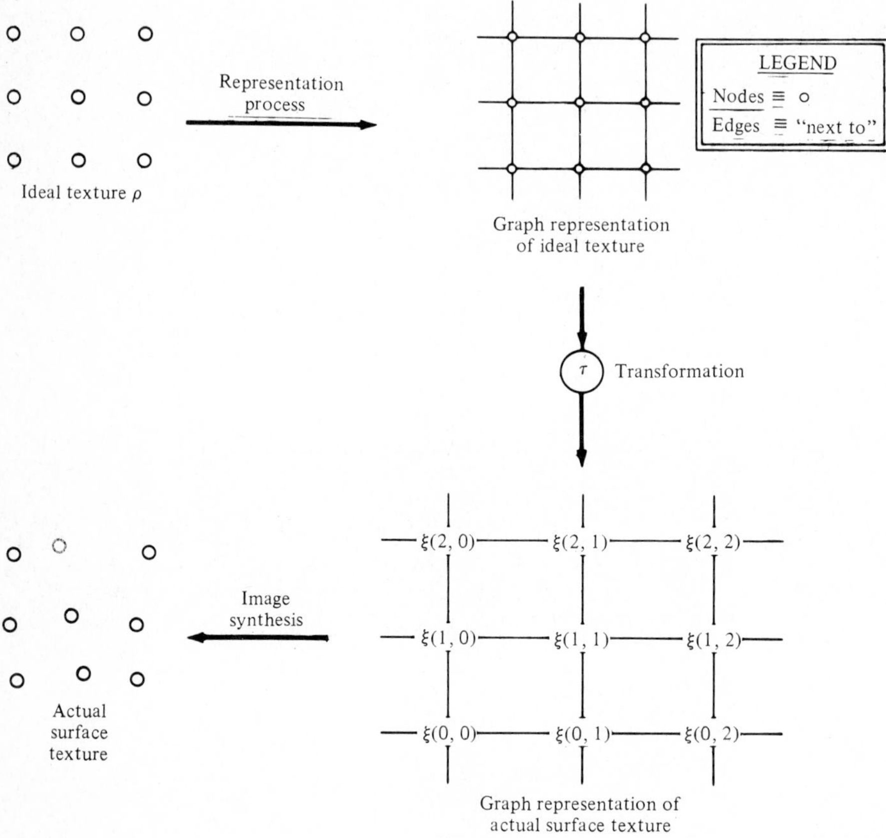

Figure 9.19 An example of texture generalization using a probabilistic transformation τ. The latter induces a set of node labels $\xi(i, j)$, which specifies the position of the primitive as a random variable according to a certain probability distribution. Image synthesis is then employed to create an actual surface texture. (*Adapted from S. W. Zucker, "On the Structure of Texture," Perception, vol. 5, 1976, pp. 419–436.*)

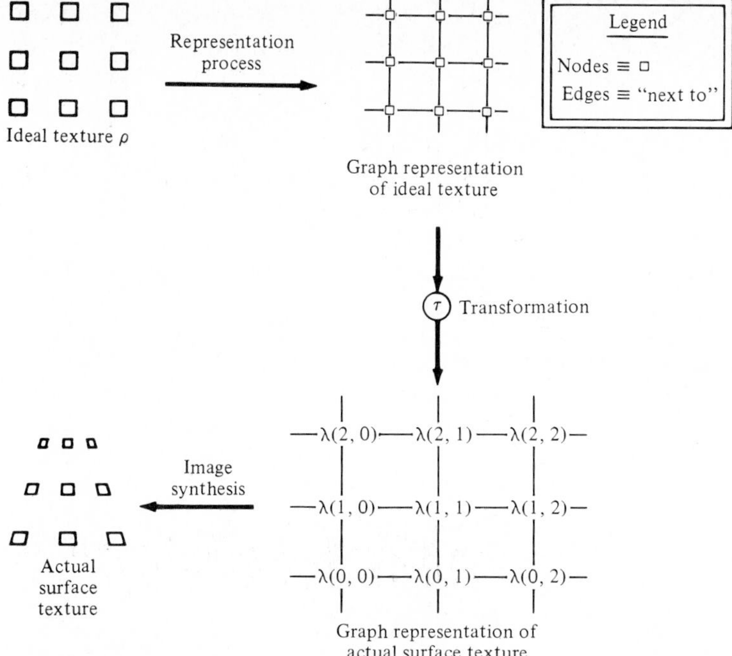

Figure 9.20 An example of texture generation using a projective transformation τ. The latter induces a set of node labels $\lambda(i, j)$, which specify the modification in primitive shape and size. Edge labels (not shown) indicate alterations in the relative position of the primitives. This information is used by a process of image synthesis to create an actual surface texture. (*Adapted from S. W. Zucker, "On the Structure of Texture," Perception, vol. 5, 1976, pp. 419–436.*)

The transformation τ is restricted by both physical and perceptual constraints, as follows [26, 167]:

1. The rules of projective geometry must be satisfied.
2. Limitations of and degradations due to the imaging process (see Sections 2.2 and 2.3) are operative.
3. Only certain distortions of the ideal texture, as well as certain noise processes, are physically realistic.
4. The black-box frequency-domain model of human vision (see Sections 4.3.2 and 6.3) applies.
5. Continuity of first- and second-order probabilities of the texture pattern must not in general be violated (see Section 9.2).
6. The principles of proximity and uniformity of texture attributes should be maintained (see Section 8.3.1).

Synthesis of observable textures, according to the methodology of Figure 9.18, is therefore governed by some relatively stringent conditions.

Texture analysis is concerned with unraveling the details of ideal texture generation and the transformation τ for a given observable $I(i, j)$. We seek $\rho(i, j)$, from which it is desirable to determine the primitive texture elements S_k and the underlying placement rule R. Obviously, given a set of primitives, many different textures can be generated according to the particular choice of R. Similarly, given either the surface texture $I(i, j)$ or the ideal texture $\rho(i, j)$, the primitives S_k are not unique. Many diverse elementary subpatterns can be utilized to generate the same texture [26].

Let us examine by what means the primitives S_k can be isolated. At first the emphasis will be on weak textures, in which the spatial interaction between the primitives is apparently random in nature. In this case two major issues predominate, namely, how to segment the individual elements and how to determine their density within a given area. The latter question is clearly related to the problem of region analysis in that before the density can be evaluated, the texture elements S_k must first be grouped into regions. This is accomplished by making use of the identical concepts considered in Chapter 8. Specifically, we observed there that the two paramount operative principles were those of similarity and proximity.

Segmentation of texture primitives usually involves the prior selection of shape. The most obvious choice is an edge element [53, 77, 123, 125, 126, 137, 156]. Therefore, most of the edge-detection methods discussed in Chapter 5 could be applied to advantage for this purpose. A second possible shape is the so-called spot, which can be detected by using the characteristic center-surround receptive field [170]. As a generalization of conventional edges and spots, it is perhaps more appropriate to describe a texture pattern as consisting of a set of "blobs" [17, 39, 106, 109, 147, 157, 164]. These may be isolated by thresholding the image [164], by region segmentation [157], or by extremum analysis [39]. Figure 9.21 illustrates the blobs obtained by segmenting an artificial or natural texture. An artificial pattern is sometimes intentionally superimposed on the surface of an object by means of structured light in order to facilitate the process of image segmentation. An interesting approach to defining the blobs in a texture, due to Ehrich and Foith [39, 40], makes use of the concept of parsing one-dimensional profiles into relational trees [38].

Having obtained the texture elements, the next step is to cluster them into groups. The basis for aggregation is a description which characterizes both the geometrical and gray-level attributes. Connors and Harlow [26] specify these mathematically in terms of a tiling model and a painting function, respectively. The latter can be portrayed by such intensity measurements as the average, minimum, maximum, and/or local contrast. In addition to the spatial arrangement of the elements, the former is concerned with size and shape [98, 99]. Size may be measured by area and perimeter. We note that in a textured pattern the size of S_k is an important indicator of the distance from the viewer of different locations on an object's surface [43]. Decreasing element size implies a surface slanting away from the observer. Note that although the S_ks

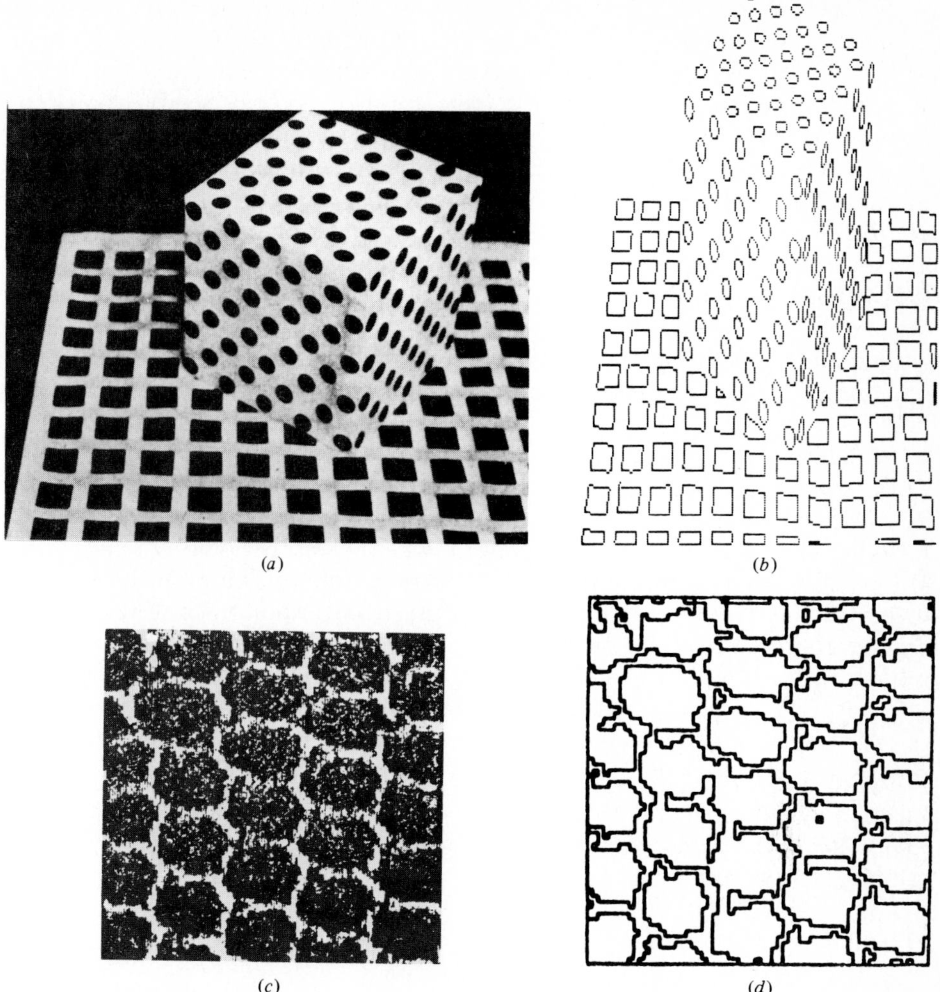

(*a*) (*b*) (*c*) (*d*)

Figure 9.21 Texture elements. (*a*) A robotic scene. (*b*) Detected atomic regions in 256×256 digitized picture of (*a*). (*c*) A textural image (reptilian skin). (*d*) Extracted elements. [(*a*) *and* (*b*) *from S. Tsuji and F. Tomita, "A Structural Analyzer for a Class of Textures," Computer Graphics and Image Processing, vol. 2, no. 3, December 1973, pp. 216–231;* (*c*) *and* (*d*) *from F. Tomita, "Hierarchical Description of Textures," Proceedings of the 7th International Joint Conference on Artificial Intelligence, IJCAI-81, University of British Columbia, Vancouver, B.C., Aug. 24–28, 1981, pp. 728–733.*]

may have similar shapes on the three-dimensional surface, their sizes in the two-dimensional image vary considerably (see Figure 9.20). Shape is a complex attribute to specify. There are many different shape attributes, and we shall discuss these in detail in Chapter 10. Examples of some simple ones are compactness, eccentricity, and orientation.

Clustering of the elements constituting these weak textures is most often done using a method of histogram analysis, as already discussed in Chapter 8 and in Section 9.2. This approach is illustrated in Figure 9.9.

Having discussed weak textures, let us now examine the case of strong textures. In this instance the structural properties of R define the details of the pattern, given the elements S_k. This topic has received little attention in the literature. As indicated in Figure 9.1, the spatial organization represented by R may be described as being either statistical or structural. We have already discussed the statistical descriptions in Section 9.3. For example, the GCM is clearly a good representation of the underlying statistical variations in the texture. Structural relationships among the primitives implies a syntactic (or grammatical) definition of R [98]. This can be achieved by using profile grammars [97] or by directly addressing the problem in two dimensions using descriptors such as LEFT-OF, RIGHT-OF, ABOVE, BELOW, ADJACENT, CONTAINS, ENCLOSED-BY, NEAR, FAR, TOUCHING, and BETWEEN. These spatial relations can easily be quantified [45, 145].

Suppose we were interested in obtaining the properties of R and S_k, knowing that the texture micropattern was almost periodic. Connors and Harlow [26] have suggested the use of a sixth texture attribute for this purpose to be included with the five already discussed in Section 9.3.4. They use the gray-level properties (GLCM) and define the inertia measure A_6 such that

$$A_6 = \sum_{y_r=y_1}^{y_t} \sum_{y_s=y_1}^{y_t} [y_r - y_s]^2 H(y_r, y_s, \mathbf{d}) \tag{9.46}$$

In the ideal case (unobservable texture ρ in Figure 9.18), A_6 will be a periodic function in those particular directions $\mathbf{d}$ in which the pattern ρ is also periodic [26]. The zeros of A_6 correspond to the period, thereby yielding the inter-sample spacing distance. In a sense this is similar to the autocorrelation

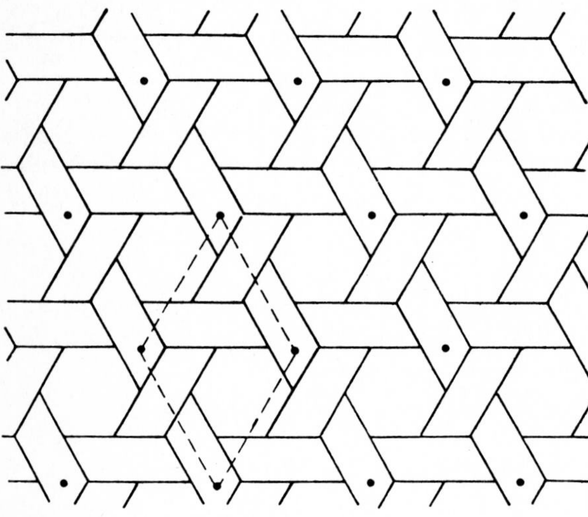

Figure 9.22 A period parallelogram of a periodic tiling. An ideal texture is illustrated as consisting of a set of tiles which would be "painted" with a certain gray level. The lattice points and the resulting period parallelogram define what is essentially a "pseudotile" (referred to as a "prototile" in [26]). This is the unit pattern S_k of the ideal texture p. [*From R. W. Conners and C. A. Harlow, "Toward a Structural Textural Analyzer Based on Statistical Methods," in A. Rosenfeld (ed.), "Image Modeling," Academic, New York, 1981, pp. 29–61.*]

function or the Fourier transform. The magnitude and directions specified by these extrema define a period parallelogram which constitutes the primitive of the ideal texture. This is comparable to placing a set of "painted tiles" end to end in order to create an image pattern [26]. An example is shown in Figure 9.22.

For real textures it is not possible to guarantee that all the minima of A_6 will correspond to a multiple of the texture period. Thus the local minima, which do not normally occur at $A_6 = 0$, are not sufficient to delineate the pattern. However, from this set of candidates it appears that the absolute minima may be selected for this purpose. As an example, consider the image of French canvas in Figure 9.23*a*. After equal probability quantization from 256 to 16 gray levels, both the horizontal $[\mathbf{d} = (\Delta_x, 0)]$ and vertical $[\mathbf{d} = (0, \Delta_y)]$ inertia measures A_6 can be plotted. This is shown in Figure 9.23*b*, where the absolute minima define the intersample spacing to be approximately $\Delta_x = 18$ and $\Delta_y = 20$. Note that A_6 computed in the other directions either yielded no periodicity or indicated a greater period than in the horizontal and vertical directions. Superimposing this parallelogram (rectangle) on the original image, it is clear from Figure 9.23*c* that the appropriate periodicity has been discovered. The two inertia measures for the raffia image in Figure 9.23*d* are plotted in Figure 9.23*e*. In this case the period parallelogram is of dimension 12 horizontally and 9 vertically. The relatively high values of A_6 compared with those in Figure 9.23*b* suggests that the replication process is not as uniformly distributed. This is quite evident from Figure 9.23*f*.

Thus by using Equation (9.46) it is possible to define the period parallelogram. This geometric shape serves the role of the unit pattern S_k in the case of an almost periodic texture. The placement rule R is defined by the two vectors associated with S_k. It is significant that the properties of S_k and R are obtainable as long as the image studied contains a sufficient number of repetitions of the basic pattern.

An analysis-by-synthesis approach has been employed by Tomita et al. [148] to analyze the structure of natural patterns. The primitive texture elements S_k are obtained by region analysis. In addition to brightness, such geometric attributes as area, size, directionality, and shape are used to describe S_k. Histogram analysis of these attributes then yields the distinct classes in the image under study. The texture pattern may be composed of elements, which constitute the "figure," superimposed on the background, referred to as the

Figure 9.23 (Overleaf.) The analysis of repetitive textures. (*a*) French canvas. (*b*) Plots of the horizontal and vertical inertia measures computed from French canvas given as a function of intersample spacing distance. (*c*) French canvas with the computed unit-cell rectangles overlaid. (*d*) Raffia. (*e*) Plots of the horizontal and vertical inertia measures computed from raffia given as a function of intersample spacing distance *d*. (*f*) Raffia with computed unit-cell rectangles overlaid. [*From R. W. Conners and C. A. Harlow, "Towards a Structural Textural Analyzer Based on Statistical Methods," in A. Rosenfeld (ed.), "Image Modeling," Academic, New York, 1981, pp. 29–61.*]

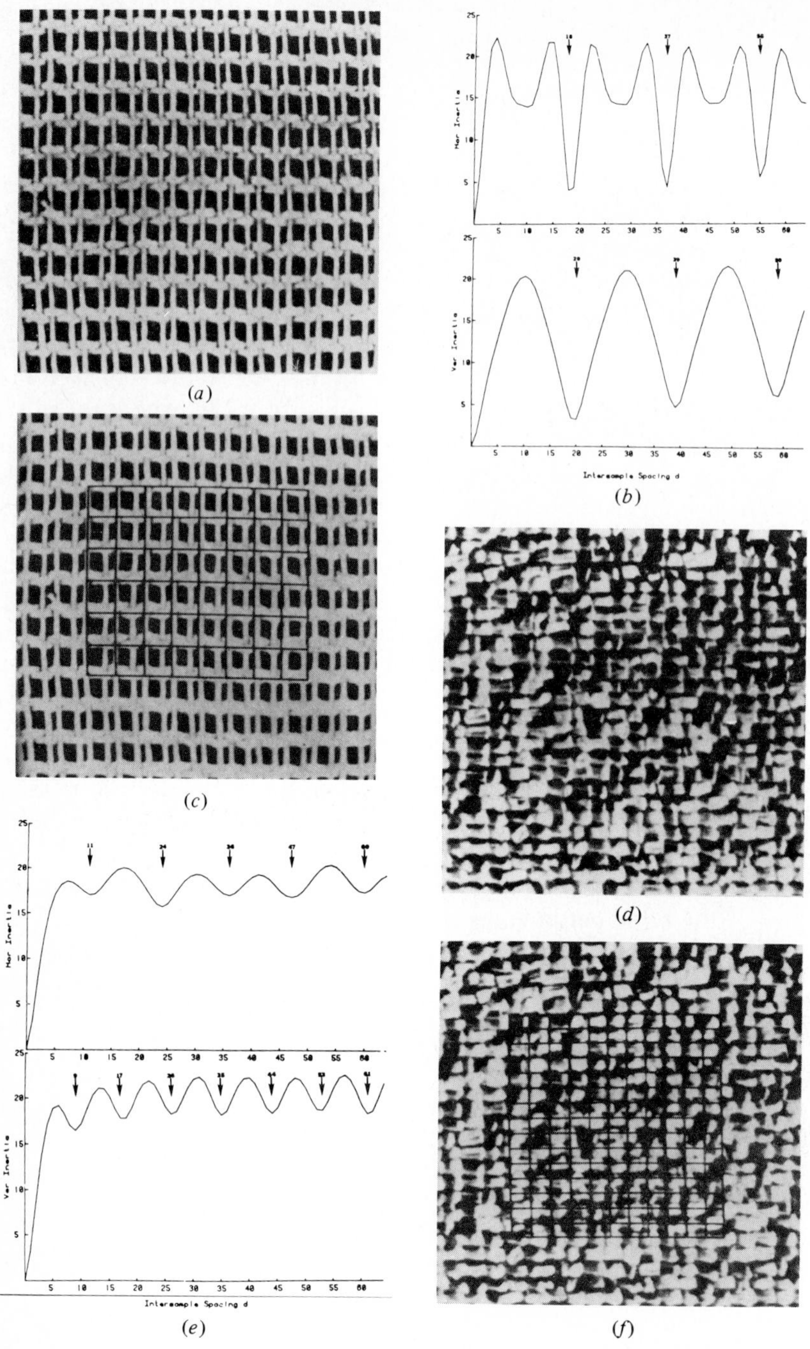

Figure 9.23 (Caption on page 467.)

"ground" in the psychology literature. Alternatively, the texture may be constituted of two or more different kinds of primitive elements. The mean and the standard deviation of each attribute in each such class are computed, and in addition the density of elements of each class and the adjacency probability

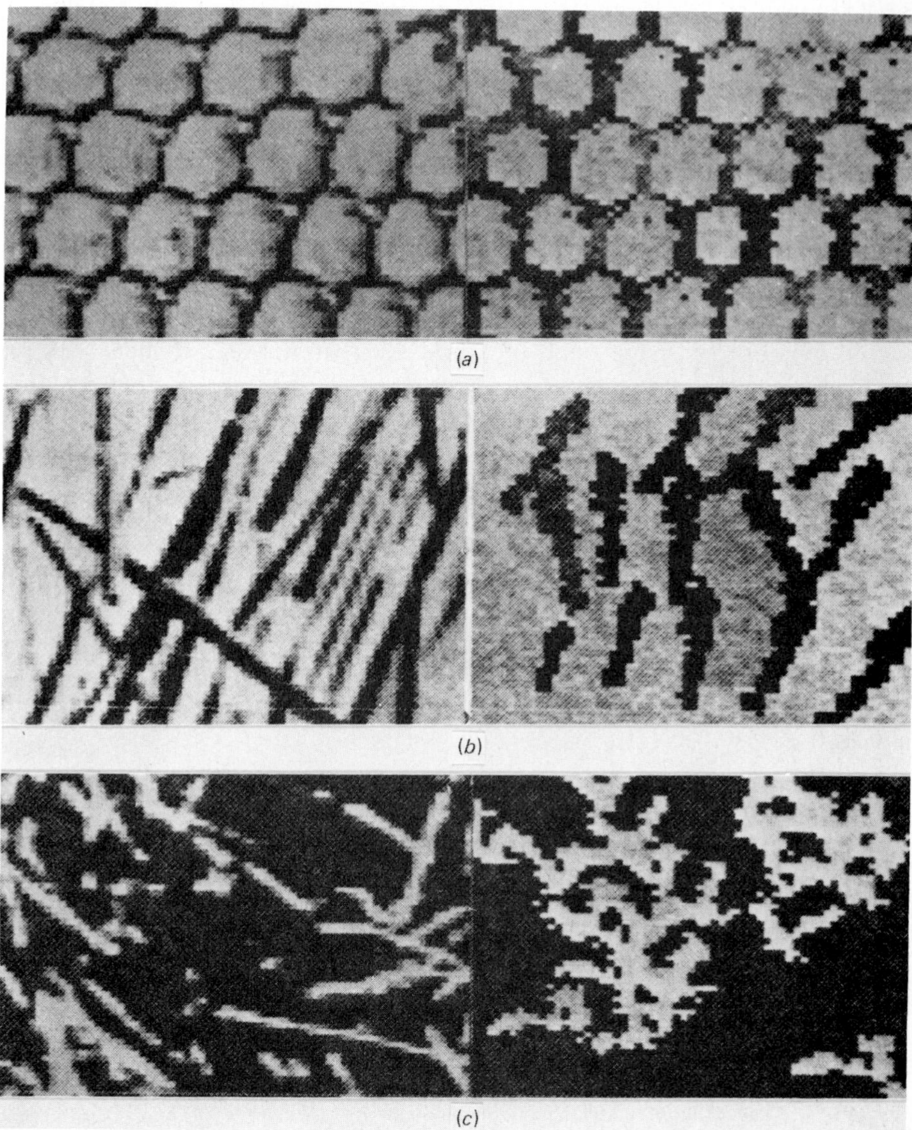

Figure 9.24 Original images (left) and reconstructed images (right). (*a*) Reptile skin. (*b*) Straw. (*c*) Handmade paper. (*From F. Tomita, Y. Shirai, and S. Tsuji, "Description of Textures by a Structural Analysis," Proceedings of the 6th International Joint Conference on Artificial Intelligence, Tokyo, Aug. 20–23, 1979, pp. 884–889.*)

between elements of any two classes are found. These then provide a description of typical elements S_k in the class.

The placement rule R may be determined by computing a two-dimensional histogram of the relative positions of every pair of texture elements S_k in the image. Each peak in the histogram defines a relative vector, which then characterizes the adjacency properties of the pattern. The textured image is assumed to be random if there are no clusters in the histogram. Thus, the spatial arrangement of the texture elements is governed by so-called regularity vectors [28, 101].

By taking into account the computed statistical variations in both S_k and R, it is possible to synthesize an artificial texture pattern similar to the original Examples are shown in Figure 9.24. The reconstructions are strongly influenced by the ability to segment appropriate elements S_k. Clearly, as the pattern becomes more complex, a simple region segmentation technique is inadequate for this purpose. A case in point is the difficulty of isolating the individual but overlapping straws in the figure. Under these circumstances it becomes necessary to employ the shape of the texture elements for region decomposition [146].

Other texture models have been suggested for describing Equation (9.1). These include random mosaic models [1, 128, 129], long-crested-wave models [127], stochastic field models [42, 71, 72, 73], random walk models [159], and time series models [103, 151].

There remains important research to be done on this problem of examining texture in pictures. Perhaps the most significant future task is the integration of the concepts relating region segmentation and texture analysis. After all, notwithstanding the existing literature they both refer to the same processes. Furthermore, as indicated in Section 9.2, this is most likely the case for both man and machine.

REFERENCES

1. Ahuja, N., and Rosenfeld, A., "Mosaic Models for Textures," *IEEE Transactions on Pattern Analysis and Machine Intelligence*, vol. PAMI-3, 1981, pp. 1–11.
2. Bajcsy, R., "Computer Identification of Textured Visual Scenes," Stanford Artificial Intelligence Laboratory, MEMO AIM-180, Stanford University, Stanford, Calif., October 1972.
3. Bajcsy, R., "Computer Description of Textured Surfaces," *Proceedings of the 3d International Joint Conference on Artificial Intelligence*, Stanford, Calif., Aug. 20–23, 1973, pp. 572–579.
4. Bajcsy, R., and Lieberman, L., "Texture Gradient as a Depth Cue," *Computer Graphics and Image Processing*, vol. 5, no. 1, March 1976, pp. 52–67.
5. Bartels, P., Bahr, G., and Wied, G., "Cell Recognition from Line Scan Transition Probability Profiles," *Acta Cytologica*, vol. 13, 1969, pp. 210–217.
6. Beck, J., "Effects of Orientation and of Shape Similarity on Perceptual Grouping," *Perception and Psychophysics*, vol. 1, 1966, pp. 300–302.
7. Beck, J., "Similarity Grouping and Peripheral Discriminability under Uncertainty," *American Journal of Psychology*, vol. 85, no. 1, June 1972, pp. 1–19.
8. Beck, J., "Similarity Grouping of Curves," *Perceptual and Motor Skills*, vol. 36, 1973, pp. 1331–1341.

9. Beck, J., "Texture Segmentation," in Beck, J. "Organization and Representation in Perception," Lawrence Erlbaum Associates, Hillsdale, N.J., 1982, pp. 285–317.
10. Berger, D. H., "Texture as a Discriminant of Crops on Radar Imagery," *IEEE Transactions on Geoscience Electronics*, vol. GE-8, no. 4, October 1970, pp. 344–348.
11. Bixby, R., Elderding, G., Fish, V., Hawkins, J., and Loewe, R., "Natural Image Computer," Aeronutronic Division, Philco-Ford Corp., Newport Beach, Calif., Final Technical Report, vol. 1, Publication C-4035, May 1967.
12. Box, J. E., and Jenkins, G. M., "Time Series Analysis," Holden-Day, San Francisco, 1970.
13. Brayer, J. M., and Fu, K. S., "A Note on the k-Tail Method of Grammar Influence," *IEEE Transactions on Systems, Man, and Cybernetics*, vol. SMC-7, no. 4, April 1977, pp. 293–300.
14. Brodatz, P., "Textures," Dover Publications, New York, 1966.
15. Caelli, T., and Julesz, B., "On Perceptual Analyzers Underlying Visual Texture Discrimination: Part I," *Biological Cybernetics*, vol. 28, 1978, pp. 167–175.
16. Caelli, T., and Julesz, B., "On Perceptual Analyzers Underlying Visual Texture Discrimination: Part II," *Biological Cybernetics*, vol. 29, 1978, pp. 201–214.
17. Carlton, S. G., and Mitchell, O. R., "Image Segmentation Using Texture and Gray Level," *Proceedings of the IEEE Conference on Pattern Recognition and Image Processing*, Troy, N.Y., June 6–8, 1977, pp. 387–391.
18. Carlucci, L., "A Formal System for Texture Languages," *Pattern Recognition*, vol. 4, no. 1, January 1972, pp. 53–72.
19. Chang, T. L., "Texture Analysis of Digitized Fingerprints for Singularity Detection," *Proceedings of the 5th International Conference on Pattern Recognition*, Miami Beach, Dec. 1–4, 1980, pp. 478–480.
20. Chen, C. H., "A Study of Texture Classification Using Spectral Features," *Proceedings of the 6th International Conference on Pattern Recognition*, Munich, Oct. 19–22, 1982, pp. 1074–1077.
21. Chen, P. C., and Pavlidis, T., "Segmentation by Texture Using a Co-occurrence Matrix and a Split-and-Merge Algorithm," *Computer Graphics and Image Processing*, vol. 10, no. 2, June 1979, pp. 172–182.
22. Chevallier, A., Fontanel, A., Gray, G., and Guy, M., "Application du Filtrage Optique à L'Etude des Photographies Aeriennes," 11th International Congress on Photogrammetry, July 1968.
23. Chien, Y. P., and Fu, K. S., "Recognition of X-Ray Picture Patterns," *IEEE Transactions on Systems, Man, and Cybernetics*," vol. SMC-4, no. 2, March 1974, pp. 145–156.
24. Connors, R. W., and Harlow, C. A., "Equal Probability Quantizing and Texture Analysis of Radiographic Images," *Computer Graphics and Image Processing*, vol. 8, no. 3, December 1978, pp. 447–463.
25. Connors, R. W., and Harlow, C. A., "A Theoretical Comparison of Texture Algorithms," *IEEE Transactions on Pattern Analysis and Machine Intelligence*, vol. PAMI-2, no. 3, May 1980, pp. 204–222.
26. Connors, R. W., and Harlow, C. A., "Toward a Structural Textural Analyzer Based on Statistical Methods," in Rosenfeld, A. (ed.), "Image Modelling," Academic, New York, 1981, pp. 29–61.
27. Darling, E. M., and Joseph, R. D., "Pattern Recognition from Satellite Attitudes," *IEEE Transactions on System, Man, and Cybernetics*, vol. SMC-4, March 1968, pp. 38–47.
28. Davis, L. S., "Computing the Spatial Structure of Cellular Textures," *Computer Graphics and Image Processing*, vol. 11, no. 2, October 1979, pp. 111–122.
29. Davis, L. S., "Polarograms: A New Tool for Image Texture Analysis," *Pattern Recognition*, vol. 13, no. 3, 1981, pp. 219–223.
30. Davis, L. S., Clearman, M., and Aggarwal, J. K., "An Empirical Evaluation of Generalized Co-occurrence Matrices," *IEEE Transactions on Pattern Analysis and Machine Intelligence*, vol. PAMI-3, no. 2, March 1981, pp. 214–221.
31. Davis, L. S., Johns, S., and Aggarwal, J. K., "Texture Analysis Using Generalized Co-occurrence Matrices," *IEEE Transactions on Pattern Analysis and Machine Intelligence*, vol. PAMI-1, no. 3, July 1979, pp. 251–258.

32. Deguchi, K., and Morishita, I., "Texture Characterization and Texture-Based Image Partitioning Using Two-Dimensional Linear Estimation Techniques," *IEEE Transactions on Computers*, vol. C-27, no. 8, August 1978, pp. 739–745.
33. Deutsch, E. S., and Belknap, J., "Texture Descriptors Using Neighborhood Information," *Computer Graphics and Image Processing*, vol. 1, no. 2, August 1972, pp. 145–168.
34. Diaconis, P., and Freedman, D., "The Statistics of the Julesz Conjecture in Visual Perception," Technical Report No. 161, Department of Statistics, Stanford University, Stanford, Calif. August 1980.
35. Duda, R. O., and Hart, P. E., "Pattern Classification and Scene Analysis," Wiley, New York, 1973.
36. Dyer, C. R., and Rosenfeld, A., "Fourier Texture Features: Suppression of Aperture Effects," *IEEE Transactions on Systems, Man, and Cybernetics*, vol. SMC-6, no. 10, October 1976, pp. 703–705.
37. Egbert, D., McCauley, J., and McNaughton, J., "Ground Pattern Analysis in the Great Plains," Semi-Annual ERTS A Investigation Report, Remote Sensing Laboratory, University of Kansas, Lawrence, August 1973.
38. Ehrich, R. W., and Foith, J. P., "Representation of Random Waveforms by Relational Trees," *IEEE Transactions on Computers*, vol. C-25, no. 7, July 1976, pp. 725–736.
39. Ehrich, R. W., and Foith, J. P., "A View of Texture Topology and Texture Description," *Computer Graphics and Image Processing*, vol. 8, no. 2, October 1978, pp. 174–202.
40. Ehrich, R. W., and Foith, J. P., "Topology and Semantics of Intensity Arrays," in Hanson, A. R., and Riseman, E. M. (eds.), "Computer Vision Systems," Academic, New York, 1978, pp. 111–127.
41. Faugeras, O. D., "Texture Analysis and Classification Using a Human Visual Model," *Proceedings of the 4th International Joint Conference on Pattern Recognition*, Kyoto, Japan, Nov. 7–10, 1978, pp. 549–552.
42. Faugeras, O. D., and Pratt, W. K., "Decorrelation Methods of Texture Feature Extraction," *IEEE Transactions on Pattern Analysis and Machine Intelligence*, vol. PAMI-2, no. 4, July 1980, pp. 323–332.
43. Flock, H. R., "Optical Texture and Linear Perspective as Stimuli for Slant Perception," *Psychological Review*, vol. 72, no. 6, 1965, pp. 505–514.
44. Fox, J., and Mayhew, J. E. W., "Texture Discrimination and the Analysis of Proximity," *Perception*, vol. 8, 1979, pp. 75–91.
45. Freeman, J., "The Modelling of Spatial Relations," *Computer Graphics and Image Processing*, vol. 4, no. 2, June 1975, pp. 156–171.
46. Frisby, J. P., and Mayhew, J. E. W., "Does Visual Texture Discrimination Precede Binocular Fusion?" *Perception*, vol. 8, 1979, pp. 153–156.
47. Frisch, H. L., and Julesz, B., "Figure-Ground Perception and Random Geometry," *Perception and Psychophysics*, vol. 1, 1966, pp. 389–398.
48. Fu, K. S., "Syntactic Image Modelling Using Stochastic Tree Grammars," in Rosenfeld, A. (ed.), "Image Modelling," Academic, New York, 1981, pp. 153–169.
49. Gagalowicz, A., "Analysis of Texture Using a Stochastic Model," *Proceedings of the 4th International Joint Conference on Pattern Recognition*, Kyoto, Japan, Nov. 3–13, 1978, pp. 541–544.
50. Gagalowicz, A., "Stochastic Texture Fields Synthesis from A Priori Given Second Order Statistics," *Proceedings of the IEEE Computer Society Conference on Pattern Recognition and Image Processing*, Chicago, Aug. 6–8, 1979, pp. 796–804.
51. Gagalowicz, A., "Visual Discrimination of Stochastic Texture Fields Based upon Their Second Order Statistics," *Proceedings of the 5th International Conference on Pattern Recognition*, Miami Beach, Dec. 1–4, 1980, pp. 786–788.
52. Gagalowicz, A., "A New Method for Texture Field Synthesis: Some Applications to the Study of Human Vision," *IEEE Transactions on Pattern Analysis and Machine Intelligence*, vol. PAMI-3, no. 5, September 1981, pp. 520–533.
53. Galloway, M. M., "Texture Classification Using Gray Level Run Lengths," *Computer Graphics and Image Processing*, vol. 4, no. 2, June 1975, pp. 172–179.

54. Gerson, D. J., "Computer Estimation of the Presence of Sea Ice in Satellite Pictures," Report TR-366, Computer Science Center, University of Maryland, College Park, April 1975.
55. Gibson, J. J., "The Perception of the Visual World," Houghton Mifflin, Boston, 1950.
56. Gibson, J. J., "The Perception of Visual Surfaces," *American Journal of Psychology*, vol. 63, 1950, pp. 367–384.
57. Ginsburg, A. P., "Pattern Recognition Techniques Suggested from Psychological Correlates of a Model of the Human Visual System," *IEEE Proceedings, 1973 NAECON*, Dayton, Ohio, May 1973, pp. 309–316.
58. Ginsburg, A. P., "Visual Information Processing Based on Spatial Filters Constrained by Biological Data," Tech. Report no. AMRL-TR-129, vols. I and II, Aerospace Medical Research Laboratory, Wright-Patterson Air Force Base, Ohio, December 1978.
59. Gramenopoulos, N., "Terrain Type Recognition Using ERTS-1 MSS Images," Symposium on Significant Results Obtained from the Earth Resources Technology Satellite, NASA SP-327, March 1973, pp. 1229–1241.
60. Hall, E. L., Crawford, W. O., Jr., Preston, K., Jr., and Roberts, F. E., "Classification of Profusion of Black Lung Disease from Chest X-rays," *Proceedings of the 1st International Joint Conference on Pattern Recognition*, Washington, Oct. 30–Nov. 1, 1973, pp. 73–87.
61. Hall, E. L., Crawford, W. O., Jr., and Roberts, F. E., "Computer Classification of Pneumoconiosis from Radiographs of Coal Workers," *IEEE Transactions on Biomedical Engineering*, vol. BME-22, November 1975, pp. 518–527.
62. Hall, E. L., Kruger, R. P., Dwyer, S. J. III, Hall, D. L., McLaren, R. W., and Lodwick, G. S., "A Survey of Preprocessing and Feature Extraction Techniques for Radiographic Images," *IEEE Transactions on Computers*, vol. C-20, no. 9, September 1971, pp. 1032–1044.
63. Haralick, R. M., "A Texture-Context Feature Extraction Algorithm for Remotely Sensed Imagery," *Proceedings of the 1971 IEEE Decision and Control Conference*, Gainesville, Fla., Dec. 15–17, 1971, pp. 650–657.
64. Haralick, R. M., "A Resolution Preserving Textural Transform for Images," *Proceedings of the Conference on Computer Graphics, Pattern Recognition, and Data Structure*, Los Angeles, May 14–16, 1975, pp. 51–61.
65. Haralick, R. M., "Statistical and Structural Approaches to Texture," *Proceedings of the 4th International Joint Conference on Pattern Recognition*, Kyoto, Japan, Nov. 7–10, 1978, pp. 45–69.
66. Haralick, R. M., "Statistical and Structural Approaches to Texture," *Proceedings of the IEEE*, vol. 67, no. 5, May 1979, pp. 786–804.
67. Haralick, R. M., and Shanmugam, K. S., "Computer Classification of Reservoir Sandstones," *IEEE Transactions on Geoscience Electronics*, vol. GE-11, October 1973, pp. 171–177.
68. Haralick, R. M., and Shanmugam, K. S., "Combined Spectral and Spatial Processing of ERTS Imagery Data," *Journal of Remote Sensing of the Environment*, vol. 3, 1974, pp. 3–13.
69. Haralick, R. M., Shanmugam, K. S., and Dinstein, I., "On Some Quickly Computable Features for Texture," *Proceedings of the 1972 Symposium on Computer Image Processing and Recognition*, University of Missouri, Columbia, vol. 2, August 1972, pp. 12-2-1 to 12-2-10.
70. Haralick, R. M., Shanmugam, K. S., and Dinstein, I., "Textural Features for Image Classification," *IEEE Transactions on Systems, Man, and Cybernetics*, vol. SMC-3, no. 6, November 1973, pp. 610–621.
71. Hassner, M., and Sklansky, J., "Markov Random Fields as Models of Digitized Image Texture," *PRIP-78, Proceedings of the IEEE Conference on Pattern Recognition and Image Processing*, Chicago, 1978, pp. 346–351.
72. Hassner, M., and Sklansky, J., "Markov Random Field Models of Digitized Image Texture," *Proceedings of the 4th International Joint Conference on Pattern Recognition*, Kyoto, Japan, November 1979, pp. 538–540.
73. Hassner, M., and Sklansky, J., "The Use of Markov Random Fields as Models of Texture," in Rosenfeld, A. (ed.), "Image Modelling," Academic, New York, 1981, pp. 185–198.
74. Hawkins, J. K., "Textural Properties for Pattern Recognition," in Lipkin, B. S., and Rosenfeld, A. (eds.), "Picture Processing and Psychopictorics," Academic Press, New York, 1970, pp. 347–371.

75. Hayes, K. C., Jr., Shah, A. N., and Rosenfeld, A., "Texture Coarseness: Further Experiments," *IEEE Transactions on Systems, Man, and Cybernetics*, vol. SMC-4, no. 5, September 1974, pp. 467–472.
76. Hildreth, E. C., "Implementation of a Theory of Edge Detection," Report No. AI-TR-579, Artificial Intelligence Laboratory, Massachusetts Institute of Technology, April 1980.
77. Hong, T. H., Dyer, C. R., and Rosenfeld, A., "Texture Primitive Extraction Using an Edge-Based Approach," *IEEE Transactions on Systems, Man, and Cybernetics*, vol. SMC-10, no. 10, October 1980, pp. 659–675.
78. Hornung, R. J., and Smith, J. A., "Application of Fourier Analysis to Multispectral/Spatial Recognition," Management and Utilization of Remote Sensing Data ASP Symposium, Sioux Falls, S.D., October 1973.
79. Jayaramamurthy, S. N., "Computer Methods for Analysis and Synthesis of Visual Texture," Technical Report no. UIUCDCS-R-73-601, Department of Computer Science, University of Illinois, Urbana, September 1973.
80. Jayaramamurthy, S. N., "Multilevel Array Grammars for Generating Texture Scenes," *PRIP-79, Proceedings of the IEEE Conference on Pattern Recognition and Image Processing*, Chicago, 1979, pp. 391–398.
81. Julesz, B., "Visual Pattern Discrimination," IRE *Transactions on Information Theory*, vol. IT-8, no. 2, February 1962, pp. 84–92.
82. Julesz, B., "Foundations of Cyclopean Perception," University of Chicago Press, 1971.
83. Julesz, B., "Textons, the Elements of Texture Perception and Their Interactions," *Nature*, vol. 290, Mar. 12, 1981, pp. 91–97.
84. Julesz, B., Gilbert, E. N., Shepp, L. A., and Frisch, H. L., "Inability of Humans to Discriminate Between Visual Textures That Agree in Second-Order Statistics—Revisited," *Perception*, vol. 2, 1973, pp. 391–405.
85. Julesz, B., Gilbert, E. N., and Victor J. D., "Visual Discrimination of Textures with Identical Third-Order Statistics," *Biological Cybernetics*, vol. 31, no. 3, 1978, pp. 137–140.
86. Kaizer, H., "A Quantification of Textures on Aerial Photographs," M. S. thesis, Boston University, 1955.
87. Kender, J. R., "Shape From Texture: An Aggregation Transform That Maps a Class of Textures into Surface Orientation," *IJCAI-79, Proceedings of the 6th International Joint Conference on Artificial Intelligence*, Tokyo, Aug. 20–23, 1979, pp. 475–480.
88. Kirvida, L., and Johnson, G., "Automatic Interpretation of Earth Resources Technology Satellite Data for Forest Management," Symposium on Significant Results Obtained from the Earth Resources Technology Satellite, NASA SP-327, March 1973, pp. 1076–1082.
89. Koffka, K., "Principles of Gestalt Psychology," Harcourt-Brace, New York, 1935.
90. Kruger, R. P., Thompson, W. B., and Twiner, A. F., "Computer Diagnosis of Pneumoconiosis," *IEEE Transactions on Systems, Man, and Cybernetics*, vol. SMC-4, no. 1, January 1974, pp. 40–49.
91. Laws, K. I., "Textured Image Segmentation," Ph.D. thesis, Department of Electrical Engineering, University of Southern California, Los Angeles, January 1980.
92. Lederman, S. J., and Taylor, M. M., "Fingertip Force, Surface Geometry, and the Perception of Roughness by Active Touch," *Perception and Psychophysics*, vol. 12, no. 5, 1972, pp. 401–408.
93. Ledley, R. S., Kulkarni, Y. G., Park, C. M., Shiu, M. R., and Rotolo, L. S., "TEXAC: A Powerful New Picture Pattern Recognition Computer," *Proceedings of the IEEE Computer Society Conference on Pattern Recognition and Image Processing, PRIP 78*, Chicago, May 31–June 2, 1978, pp. 396–401.
94. Lendaris, G., and Stanley, G., "Diffraction Pattern Sampling for Automatic Pattern Recognition," *Proceedings of the SPIE Pattern Recognition Studies Seminar*, June 9–10, 1969, pp. 127–154; *Proceedings of the IEEE*, vol. 58, no. 2, February 1970, pp. 198–216.
95. Levine, M. D., "Region Analysis Using a Pyramid Data Structure," in Tanimoto, S., and Klinger, A. (eds.), "Structured Computer Vision, Machine Perception Through Hierarchical Computation Structures," Academic Press, New York, 1980, pp. 57–100.

96. Levine, M. D., O'Handley, D., and Yagi, G., "Computer Determination of Depth Maps," *Computer Graphics and Image Processing*, vol. 2, no. 2, October 1973, pp. 131–151.
97. Lozano-Perez, T., "Parsing Intensity Profiles," *Computer Graphics and Image Processing*, vol. 6, no. 1, February 1977, pp. 43–60.
98. Lu, S. Y., and Fu, K. S., "A Syntactic Approach to Texture Analysis," *Computer Graphics and Image Processing*, vol. 7, 1978, pp. 303–330.
99. Lu, S. Y., and Fu, K. S., "Stochastic Tree Grammar Inference for Texture Synthesis and Discrimination," *Computer Graphics and Image Processing*, vol. 9, no. 3, March 1979, pp. 234–245.
100. Marr, D., "Early Processing of Visual Information," *Philosophical Transactions of the Royal Society, London*, ser. B, vol. 275, 1976. pp. 483–524.
101. Matsuyama, T., Saburi, K., and Nagao, M., "A Structural Analyzer for Regularly Arranged Textures," *Computer Graphics and Image Processing*, vol. 18, no. 3, March 1982, pp. 259–278.
102. Maurer, H., "Texture Analysis with Fourier Series," *Proceedings of the 9th International Symposium on Remote Sensing of Environment*, Environmental Research Institute of Michigan, Ann Arbor, April 1974, pp. 1411–1420.
103. McCormick, B. H., and Jayaramamurthy, S. N., "Time Series Model for Texture Synthesis," *International Journal of Computer and Information Sciences*, vol. 3, no. 4, December 1974, pp. 329–343.
104. McCormick, B. H., and Jayaramamurthy, S. N., "A Decision Theory Method for the Analysis of Texture," *International Journal of Computer and Information Sciences*, vol. 4, no. 1, March 1975, pp. 1–38.
105. Meurle, J. L., "Some Thoughts on Texture Discrimination by Computer," in Lipkin, B. S., and Rosenfeld, A. (eds.), "Picture Processing and Psychopictorics," Academic, New York, 1970, pp. 371–379.
106. Mitchell, O. R., Myers, C. R., and Boyne, W., "A Max-Min Measure for Image Texture Analysis," *IEEE Transactions on Computers*, vol. 26, no. 4, 1977, pp. 408–414.
107. Modestino, J. W., Fries, R. W., and Vickers, A. L., "Texture Discrimination Based upon an Assumed Stochastic Texture Model," IEEE *Transactions on Pattern Analysis and Machine Intelligence*, vol. PAMI-3, no. 5, September 1981, pp. 557–580.
108. Mueller, W., "The Leitz Texture Analyzer System," *Leitz Scientific and Technical Information*, Wetzlar, Germany, supplement I, vol. 4, April 1974, pp. 101–116.
109. Ohlander, R., "Analysis of Natural Scenes," Ph.D. thesis, Carnegie-Mellon University, Pittsburgh, 1975.
110. Olson, R., and Attneave, F., "What Variables Produce Similarity Grouping?" *American Journal of Psychology*, vol. 83, 1970, pp. 1–21.
111. Orsinger, R. J., "Texture Tone Study: Summary and Evaluation," Technical Report No. ETL-0006, U.S. Army Engineer Topographic Laboratories, Fort Belvoir, Va., March 1975.
112. Pickett, R. M., "Visual Analyses of Texture in the Detection and Recognition of Objects," in Lipkin, B. S., and Rosenfeld, A. (eds.), "Picture Processing and Psychopictorics," Academic, New York, 1970, pp. 289–308.
113. Pietikainen, M., "On the Use of Hierarchically Computed 'Mexican Hat' Features for Texture Discrimination," Technical Report no. TR-968, Computer Vision Laboratory, Computer Science Center, University of Maryland, College Park, November 1980.
114. Pollack, I., "Discrimination of Third-Order Markov Constraints within Visual Displays," *Perception and Psychophysics*, vol. 13, no. 2, April 1973, pp. 276–280.
115. Pratt, W. K., Faugeras, O. D., and Gagalowicz, A., "Visual Discrimination of Stochastic Texture Fields," *IEEE Transactions on Systems, Man, and Cybernetics*, vol. SMC-8, no. 11, November 1978, pp. 796–804.
116. Pressman, N. J., "Markovian Analysis of Cervical Cell Images," *Journal of Histochemistry and Cytochemistry*, vol. 24, no. 1, 1976, pp. 138–144.
117. Pressman, N. J., Haralick, R. M., Tyrer, H. W., and Frost, J. K., "Texture Analysis for Biomedical Imagery," in Fu, K. S., and Pavlidis, T. (eds.), "Biomedical Pattern Recognition

and Image Processing," Dahlem Konferenzen, Berlin, May 14–18, 1979, Verlag Chemie, Weinheim, pp. 153–178.

118. Purdy, W. C., "The Hypothesis of Psychophysical Correspondence in Space Perception," Ph.D. thesis, Cornell University, Ithaca, N.Y., February 1958.
119. Purks, S. R., and Richards, W., "Visual Texture Discrimination Using Random-Dot Patterns," *Journal of the Optical Society of America*, vol. 67, no. 6, June 1977, pp. 765–771.
120. Richards, W., and Polit, A., "Texture Matching," *Kybernetik*, vol. 16, 1974, pp. 155–162.
121. Rosenblatt, M., and Slepian, D., "Nth Order Markov Chains with Any Set of N Variables Independent," *Journal of the Society for Industrial and Applied Mathematics*, vol. 10, no. 3, September 1962, pp. 537–549.
122. Rosenfeld, A., and Lipkin, B. S., "Texture Synthesis," in Lipkin, B. S., and Rosenfeld, A. (eds.), "Picture Processing and Psychopictorics," Academic, New York, 1970, pp. 309–345.
123. Rosenfeld, A., and Thurston, M., "Edge and Curve Detection for Visual Scene Analysis," *IEEE Transactions on Computers*, vol. C-20, no. 5, May 1971, pp. 562–569.
124. Rosenfeld, A., Thurston, M., and Lee, Y. H., "Edge and Curve Detection: Further Experiments," *IEEE Transactions on Computers*, vol. C-21, July 1972, pp. 677–715.
125. Rosenfeld, A., and Troy, E. B., "Visual Texture Analysis," Computer Science Center, University of Maryland, College Park, Technical Report TR-116, June 1970.
126. Rosenfeld, A., and Troy, E. B., "Visual Texture Analysis," *Conference Record for Symposium on Feature Extraction and Selection in Pattern Recognition, IEEE Publication 70C-51C*, Argonne, Ill., October, 1970, pp. 115–124.
127. Schacter, B. J., "Model-Based Texture Measures," *IEEE Transactions on Pattern Analysis and Machine Intelligence*, vol. PAMI-2, no. 2, March 1980, pp. 169–171.
128. Schacter, B. J., "Long Crested Wave Models," in Rosenfeld, A. (ed.), "Image Modelling," Academic, New York, 1981, pp. 327–341.
129. Schacter, B. J., Rosenfeld, A., and Davis, L. S., "Random Mosaic Models for Textures," *IEEE Transactions on Systems, Man, and Cybernetics*, vol. SMC-8, no. 9, September 1978, pp. 694–702.
130. Serra, J., "Theoretical Bases of the Leitz Texture Analysis System," *Leitz Scientific and Technical Information*, Wetzlar, Germany, supplement I, vol. 4, April 1974, pp. 125–136.
131. Serra, J., "One, Two, Three, . . . , Infinity," in Chernant, J. L. (ed.), "Quantitative Analysis of Microstructures in Materials Science, Biology, and Medicine," Reiderer-Verlag, Stuttgart, Germany, 1978, pp. 9–24.
132. Serra, J., and Verchery, G., "Mathematical Morphology Applied to Fibre Composite Materials," *Film Science and Technology*, vol. 6, 1973, pp. 141–158.
133. Shen, H. C., and Wong, A. K. C., "Generalized Texture Representation and Metric," *Proceedings of the International Conference on Cybernetics and Society*, Cambridge, Mass., Oct. 8–10, 1980, pp. 695–703.
134. Sklansky, J., "Image Segmentation and Feature Extraction," *IEEE Transactions on Systems, Man, and Cybernetics*, vol. SMC-8, no. 4, April 1978, pp. 237–247.
135. Stevens, K. A., "Surface Perception from Local Analysis of Texture and Contour," Ph.D. thesis, Massachusetts Institute of Technology, Cambridge, Mass., February 1979.
136. Stevens, S. S., and Harris, J. R., "The Scaling of Subjective Roughness and Smoothness," *Journal of Experimental Psychology*, vol. 64, no. 5, 1962, pp. 489–494.
137. Sutton, R. N., and Hall, E. L., "Texture Measures for the Automatic Machine Recognition and Classification of Pulmonary Disease," *IEEE Transactions on Computers*, vol. C-21, no. 2, July 1972, pp. 667–676.
138. Swanlund, G., "Honeywell's Automatic Tree Species Classifier," Honeywell Systems and Research Division, Report 9D-G-24, Dec. 31, 1969.
139. Tamura, H., Mori, S., and Yamawaki, T., "Psychological and Computational Measurements of Basic Textural Features and Their Comparisons," *Proceedings of the 3d International Joint Conference on Pattern Recognition*, Coronado, Calif., Nov. 8–11, 1976, pp. 273–277.
140. Tamura, H., Mori, S., and Yamawaki, T., "Effectiveness of Textural Features for Classification of Aerial Multispectral Images," *PRIP-77, Proceedings of the IEEE Computer*

Society Conference on Pattern Recognition and Image Processing, Rensselaer Polytechnic Institute, Troy, N.Y., June 6–8, 1977, pp. 289–298.

141. Tamura, H., Mori, S., and Yamawaki, T., "Textural Features Corresponding to Visual Perception," *IEEE Transactions on Systems, Man, and Cybernetics*, vol. SMC-8, no. 6, June 1978, pp. 460–473.
142. Terzopoulos, D., and Zucker, S. W., "Detection of Osteogenesis Imperfecta by Automated Texture Analysis," Technical Report no. 80-8, Computer Vision and Graphics Laboratory, Department of Electrical Engineering, McGill University, Montreal, April 1980.
143. Thompson, W. B., "Textural Boundary Analysis," *IEEE Transactions on Computers*, vol. C-26, March 1977, pp. 272–276.
144. Thompson, W. B., and Lemche, C. L., "The Effects of Variability on Estimating Scale Change Using Texture," *Proceedings of the 5th International Conference on Pattern Recognition*, Miami Beach, Dec. 1–4, 1980, pp. 780–782.
145. Ting, D., "Intermediate Level Processing for a Computer Vision System," M. Eng. thesis, Department of Electrical Engineering, McGill University, Montreal, 1979.
146. Tomita, F., "Hierarchical Description of Textures," *Proceedings of the 7th International Joint Conference on Artificial Intelligence, IJCAI-81*, University of British Columbia, Vancouver, B.C., Aug. 24–28, 1981, pp. 728–733.
147. Tomita, F. Shirai, Y., and Tsuji, S., "Classification of Textures by a Structural Analysis," *Proceedings of the 4th International Joint Conference on Pattern Recognition*, Nov. 7–10, 1978, Kyoto, Japan, pp. 556–558.
148. Tomita, F., Shirai, Y., and Tsuji, S., "Description of Textures by a Structural Analysis," *Proceedings of the 6th International Joint Conference on Artificial Intelligence*, Tokyo, Aug. 20–23, 1979, pp. 884–889.
149. Tomita, F., and Tsuji, S., "Extraction of Multiple Regions by Smoothing in Selected Neighborhoods," *IEEE Transactions on Systems, Man, and Cybernetics*, vol. SMC-7, February 1977, pp. 107–109.
150. Tomita, F., Yachida, M., and Tsuji, S., "Detection of Homogeneous Regions by Structural Analysis," *Proceedings of the 3d International Joint Conference on Artificial Intelligence*, Stanford University, Stanford, Calif., Aug. 20–23, 1973, pp. 564–572.
151. Tou, J. T., and Chang, Y. S., "Picture Understanding by Machine via Textural Feature Extraction," *PRIP-77 Proceedings of the IEEE Conference on Pattern Recognition and Image Processing*, Troy, N.Y., 1977, pp. 392–399.
152. Tou, J. T., Kao, D. B., and Chang, Y. S., "Pictorial Picture Analysis and Synthesis," *Proceedings of the 3d International Joint Conference on Pattern Recognition*, Coronado, Calif., Nov. 8–11, 1976, pp. 590–590p.
153. Toussaint, G. T., "The Use of Context in Pattern Recognition," *Pattern Recognition*, vol. 10, no. 3, 1978, pp. 189–204.
154. Treisman, A. M., and Gelade, G., "A Feature-Integration Theory of Attention," *Cognitive Psychology*, vol. 12, 1980, pp. 97–136.
155. Treisman, A. M., Sykes, M., and Gelade, G., "Selective Attention and Stimulus Integration," in Dornic, S. (ed.), "Attention and Performance," vol. VI, Lawrence Erlbaum Associates, Hillsdale, N.J., 1977, pp. 333–361.
156. Triendl, E. E., "Automatic Terrain Mapping by Texture Recognition," *Proceedings of the 8th International Symposium on Remote Sensing of the Environment*, Environmental Research Institute of Michigan, Ann Arbor, October, 1972.
157. Tsuji, S., and Tomita, F., "A Structural Analyzer for a Class of Textures," *Computer Graphics and Image Processing*, vol. 2, no. 3, December 1973, pp. 216–231.
158. Tully, R. J., Connors, R. W., Harlow, C. A., Larsen, G. N., Dwyer, S. J., and Lodwick, G. S., "Interactive Analysis of Pulmonary Infiltration," *Proceedings of the 3d International Joint Conference on Pattern Recognition*, Coronado, Calif., Nov. 8–11, 1976, pp. 238–242.
159. Wechsler, H., and Kidode, M., "A Random Walk Procedure for Texture Discrimination," *IEEE Transactions on Pattern Analysis and Machine Intelligence*, vol. PAMI-1, no. 3, July 1979, pp. 272–280.

160. Werthheimer, M., "Laws of Organization in Perceptual Form," in Ellis, W. D. (ed.), "A Sourcebook of Gestalt Psychology," Routledge and Kegan Paul, London, England, 1938.
161. Weszka, J. S., Dyer, C. R., and Rosenfeld, A., "A Comparative Study of Texture Measure for Terrain Classification," *IEEE Transactions on Systems, Man, and Cybernetics*, vol. SMC-6, no. 4, April 1976, pp. 269–285.
162. Wied, G., Bahr, G., and Bartels, P., "Automatic Analysis of Cell Images," in Weid, G. and Bahr, G. (eds.), "Automated Cell Identification and Cell Sorting," Academic, New York, 1970, pp. 195–360.
163. Witkin, A. P., "Shape From Contour," Ph.D. thesis, Massachusetts Institute of Technology, Cambridge, Mass., 1980.
164. Wong, S., and Velasco, F. R. D., "A Comparison of Some Simple Methods for Extracting Texture Primitives and Their Effectiveness in Texture Discrimination," Technical Report no. TR-759, Computer Science Center, University of Maryland, College Park, April 1979.
165. Yaglom, A. M., "A Theory of Stationary Random Functions," Prentice-Hall, Englewood Cliffs, N.J., 1962.
166. Zobrist, A. L., and Thompson, W. B., "Building a Distance Function for Gestalt Grouping," *IEEE Transactions on Computers*, vol. C-4, no. 7, July 1975, pp. 718–728.
167. Zucker, S. W., "On the Structure of Texture," *Perception*, vol. 5, 1976, pp. 419–436.
168. Zucker, S. W., "Toward a Model of Texture," *Computer Graphics and Image Processing*, vol. 5, no. 2, 1976, pp. 190–202.
169. Zucker, S. W., and Cavanagh, P., "Constructive Texture Perception: Orientation Anisotropies in Discrimination," Technical Report no. 80-8, Department of Electrical Engineering, McGill University, Montreal, August 1980.
170. Zucker, S. W., Rosenfeld, A., and Davis, L. S., "Picture Segmentation by Texture Discrimination," *IEEE Transactions on Computers*, vol. C-24, no. 12, December 1975, pp. 1228–1233.
171. Zucker, S. W., and Terzopoulos, D., "Finding Structure in Co-occurrence Matrices for Texture Analysis," *Computer Graphics and Image Processing*, vol. 12, no. 3, March 1980, pp. 286–308.
172. Zucker, S. W., and Terzopoulos, D., "Finding Structure in Co-occurrence Matrices for Texture Analysis," in Rosenfeld, A. (ed.), "Image Modelling," Academic, New York, 1981, pp. 423–445.

BIBLIOGRAPHY

Early review papers on texture are by Hawkins [6] and Pickett [9]. The most current and complete discussion is by Haralick [4]. An interesting portfolio of photographs illustrating visual textures can be found in [1].

A general overview of the work of Julesz and his conjecture (Section 9.2.2), prior to the rejection of its basic tenets, can be found in [7]. A more recent update on this theory, incorporating the concept of the so-called texton, is given in a review article by Julesz [8].

The earliest attempts at texture analysis were in terms of a spatial-frequency representation. Optical processing methods were used to filter images and the output was classified into the different categories of objects visible in aerial photography. Readers interested in an introduction to these techniques should consult [2, 3, 10, 11]. Currently the most popular method is that of Haralick et al. [5].

1. Brodatz, P., "Texture: A Photographic Album for Artists and Designers," Dover, New York, 1956.
2. Cutrona, L. J., Leith, E. N., Palermo, C. J., and Porcello, L. J., "Optical Data Processing and Filtering Systems," *IRE Transactions on Information Theory*, vol. 15, no. 6, June 1969, pp. 386–400.
3. Goodman, J. W., "Introduction to Fourier Optics," McGraw-Hill, New York, 1968.
4. Haralick, R. M., "Statistical and Structural Approaches to Texture," *Proceedings of the IEEE*, vol. 67, no. 5, May 1979, pp. 786–804.
5. Haralick, R. M., Shanmugam, K., and Dinstein, I., "Textural Features for Image Classification," *IEEE Transactions on Systems, Man, and Cybernetics*, vol. SMC-3, no. 6, November 1973, pp. 610–621.
6. Hawkins, J. K., "Textural Properties for Pattern Recognition," in Lipkin, B. S., and Rosenfeld, A. (eds.), "Picture Processing and Psychopictorics," Academic, New York, 1970, pp. 347–371.
7. Julesz, B., "Experiments in the Visual Perception of Textures," *Scientific American*, vol. 232, no. 4, April 1975, pp. 34–43.
8. Julesz, B., "Textons, the Elements of Texture Perception, and their Interactions," *Nature*, vol. 290, Mar. 12, 1981, pp. 91–97.
9. Pickett, R. M., "Visual Analyses of Texture in the Detection and Recognition of Objects," in Lipkin, B. S., and Rosenfeld, A. (eds.), "Picture Processing and Psychopictorics," Academic, New York, 1970, pp. 289–308.
10. Preston, K., "Coherent Optical Computers," McGraw-Hill, New York, 1972.
11. Shulman, A. R., "Optical Data Processing," Wiley, New York, 1970.

CHAPTER
TEN
SHAPE

10.1 A MULTITUDE OF THEORIES

There exist many theories of shape description and recognition, each attempting to explain some specific aspect of the problem. This is so because it is possible to conceptualize shape as a high-level perceptual function. Since there is very little neurophysiological evidence about its nature and we are not really sure what the basic constituents are, the field has been open to freewheeling hypothesization. Readers are referred to three comprehensive books on this subject [57, 152, 255] but are warned that upon their completion they will still be largely in the dark regarding how form is biologically detected and computed.

Human analysis of shape is governed by the following principle of visual perception [92]:

> ....the human visual system is designed to produce organized perception. Information consisting of a variety of such spatial features as size, shape, distance, relative position, and texture is structured by the mind to represent visual scenes. These spatial features are perceived as properties of things, objects in the scene, and not merely as abstract lines or surfaces. We do not perceive lines or unattached extents; we perceive objects. All parts of each object are perceived together in one construction—not as separate, independent, and free-floating elements. And all the objects are perceived as related to each other near, far, behind, adjoining, and so forth.

However, the additional assumption made in this book is that form recognition is the result of both low-level and high-level stages of analysis, with our concern focused on the former. In a seminal essay on human vision, Marr declared the following [132]:

> If non-attentive vision may be implemented successfully by approximately the set of methods defined in this [book], it means that visual "forms" can usually be extracted from the image by using knowledge-free techniques. In other words, the extraction of a visual form can usually precede its description. From this it follows that it is usually easy to compute a coarse description of a form before having any idea about what the form is.

Therefore, we make a distinction between as yet unnamed shapes and objects which have linguistic connotations.

Low-level analysis involves the aggregation of imperfect edge data in the two-dimensional image projection, is imperfect, and probably takes place in area 17 (the primary visual cortex), as was indicated in Section 8.2 regarding research with the macaque monkey. Perhaps some shape attributes of this collection of edges are also computed. To this point edges and regions are important, and there has been no identification with a named object, as there ultimately must be for perception. Nevertheless, this information serves as input to a subsequent process of high-level organization and understanding, which deals primarily with the issues related to the three-dimensionality of the objects in the scene. It is interesting that although this is clearly true for humans, it may not be the case for all animals. For example, pigeons have been shown to be unable to perform three-dimensional projective transformations [44]. At this time there is a large gap in our knowledge which impedes our ability to bridge the low- and high-level processing stages.

The collection of edges at the low level constitutes or suggests a contour surrounding an area, but perhaps not completely. As we observed previously, these regions may have similar properties, for example color or texture. Psychologists generally do not seem to differentiate between the concepts of edges and contour, since the latter is most often considered to refer to a complete figure. Thus, Zusne [265] suggests the following definition: "A contour is a one-dimensional interface between figure and ground." This is only acceptable in the very restricted sense in which an object is superimposed on a background. We shall assume that a contour is made up of a set of edges connected to each other but not necessarily forming a closed curve.

Zusne [265] has characterized a hierarchy of definitions of increasing generality for "form," "figure," or "shape," terms which are synonomous. At the bottom of this hierarchy are the pixel and edge element, which represent the edge map or primal sketch defined in Chapter 5. The next level of complexity involves contours, which also circumscribe regions, as discussed in Chapters 8 and 9. At the following level, collections of contours, regions, and edges are used to model objects in two-dimensional space. As sketched in Figure 8.9, these are defined in the "picture domain." The next level in the hierarchy describes models of objects in three-dimensional space, which constitutes the "scene domain." Regions in the picture domain map into surfaces in the scene domain. The understanding of this transformation is sometimes clouded by the phenomenon of visual illusion (see Section 6.2.2). Contours in one domain appear to provide an explanation for the data which are in contradiction to their appearance in the other. Perhaps this is one reason why the first people interested in illusions were philosophers and artists.

Figure 10.1 illustrates how even a simple line drawing can be viewed in terms of a hierarchy of levels of complexity. Sets of concatenated edges produce the boundaries of regions in the picture. However, when the drawing is viewed as a whole, we observe a silhouette of a curved three-dimensional object, that is, a bowl of fruit. Further careful observation produces two facial profiles staring at each other. Then recognition! The silhouette is that of George Washington. Most likely this last level involves a complex picture and scene language. Support for this hypothesis emerges from an examination of brain damage in humans and how it affects their information processing abilities [107].

An early work in psychology which dealt with the perception of space was by James [103], who surveyed the subject up to the nineteenth century. Perhaps it was Ernst Mach, with his work on the enhancement of edges, who provided the impetus for the modern study of shape. He investigated the features which characterized our perception of form and suggested that the latter was an entity which somehow is processed independently of other low-level attributes [130]. During the first part of the twentieth century the gestalt school emerged. It proposed a set of laws of organization which were supposed to be implicated in form perception [111]. Such concepts as proximity, similarity, continuity, common fate, and closure were said to result in "good figures." Although the theory had a certain element of attractiveness to it, it was imprecise and not based on any supportive experimentation. It appears that [265, p. 12] "the first milestone in the *quantification* of form was

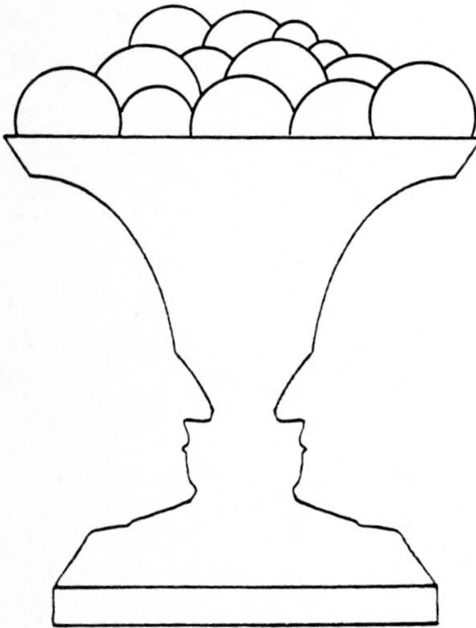

Figure 10.1 A simple line drawing which can be interpreted in a hierarchical manner in terms of progressively more complex pictorial concepts. (*From H. Freeman, "Lines, Curves, and the Characterization of Shape," Report no. IPL-TR-80-004, Image Processing Laboratory, Electrical and Systems Engineering Department, Rensselaer Polytechnic Institute, Troy, N.Y., March 1980.*)

the formulation of a theory of information by workers in nonbehavioral fields: communications and cybernetics" (see [211], [255]). This is an example of the interaction between seemingly disparate fields leading to quite a significant digression from the prevailing theories. Thus, the quantitative study of shape in terms of edges, angles, and contours had begun, spurred on by the information point of view taken by Attneave [12]. He suggested that a shape is segmented by means of dominant points which coincide with points of maximum inflection along its contour. The now classical cat picture shown in Figure 10.2 was used to further hypothesize that since the resulting piecewise linear approximation was obviously adequate for object recognition, this data structure was employed by the higher processing levels. It turns out that humans, when asked to segment curved shapes, usually indicate such an approximation [14, 28]. It seems that the simpler shapes are easier to process. The computation by machine of these dominant points is discussed [72, 202, 207].

Although there exist many approaches to shape, the problem of shape description and recognition as it pertains to both neurophysiology and perceptual psychology is far from solution. There are many theories, and Uttal [246] has categorized them as follows: sensory-motor, neurophysiological, computational network, and correlation. Which theory, if any, is correct? Are they all related? We do not know as yet. Perhaps psychologists will determine the basic categories of shapes that are discriminated, which will then encourage neurophysiologists to search for the underlying mechanisms. This will no doubt suggest further perceptual experiments and other studies.

The research on shape in computer vision has been heavily influenced by Attneave [12]. Mostly, it has been an outgrowth of interest in specific applications, the most common being the recognition of handwritten characters and chromosome types. However, many other interesting images have been analyzed for shape, for example, printed characters, Chinese characters, aircraft, machine parts, circuit boards, maps, and lung radiographs. Basically, two major problem tasks have been associated with shape processing [75]. The solution of both requires as a prerequisite the ability to obtain a concise description of the form. First, there is shape matching, in which it is desirable to establish the equivalence of two shapes. Second, there is shape classification or naming. Obviously, both of these are very sensitive to the orientation and

Figure 10.2 The outline of a sleeping cat. This drawing was obtained by detecting all points of maximum curvature on the original outline of the cat. The points of maximum curvature were then joined by straight lines. This simplified image representation, can, nevertheless, be easily interpreted. (*From F. Attneave, "Informational Aspects of Visual Perception," Psychological Review, vol. 61, 1954, pp. 183–193.*)

scale (size) of the objects under consideration. Clearly, a shape analysis technique should also be independent of the sampling grid, as illustrated in Figure 10.3.

A categorization of machine analysis techniques has been proposed by Pavlidis [166]. One dichotomy addresses the issue of external versus internal shape description algorithms. The former is based solely on the contour of the region under consideration; the latter deals with it as an enclosed area. Both approaches may also be described as information-preserving or non-information-preserving depending on whether or not the original shape can be reconstructed from the descriptor. Section 10.2 is concerned with some straightforward examples of non-information-preserving methods. A further distinction involves the type of method employed. On the one hand, there exist

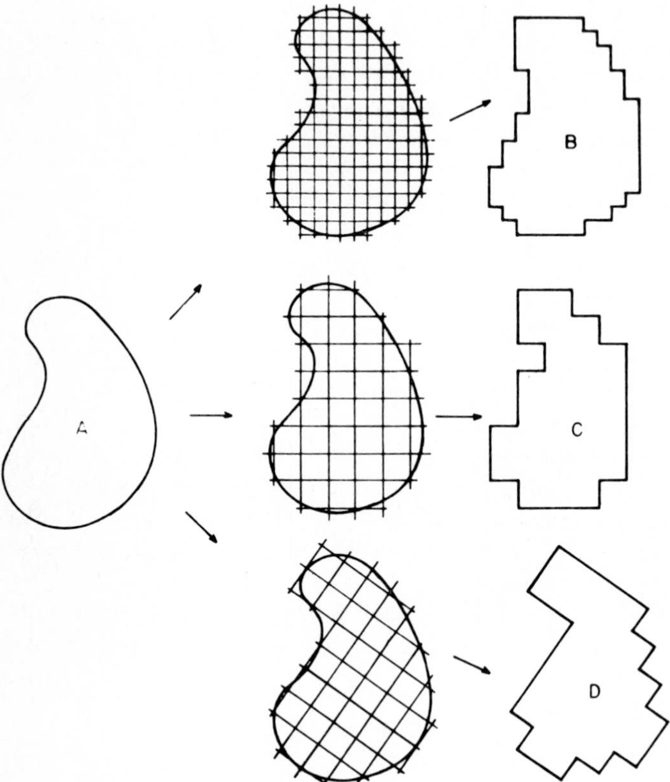

Figure 10.3 Continuous and discrete shapes. Continuous shape *A* gives rise to several discrete-shaped curves *B, C, D.* If it is desired to have a unique discrete shape derived from *A*, then it is necessary to specify the grid size as well as its orientation and position with respect to the continuous curve *A*. In this manner, for a given resolution the discrete shape corresponding to *A* will be unique. (*From E. Bribiesca and A. Guzman, "How to Describe Pure Form and How to Measure Differences in Shape Using Shape Numbers," Pattern Recognition, vol. 12, no. 2, 1980, pp. 101–112.*)

spatial domain approaches which transform the input image $I(i, j)$ into an alternative spatial domain representation. This subject is discussed in Section 10.3. Subsequent recognition of the shapes is most likely accomplished by means of syntactic or structural analysis [163, 165]. On the other hand scalar transform techniques map the image into an attribute vector description; they will be discussed in Section 10.4. Categorization of shapes with this approach is usually achieved by means of classical pattern recognition [242].

10.2 SIMPLE SHAPE FEATURES

10.2.1 Along the Border

An object in an image plane is defined by a border which segments it from the background. We may assume this border to be simple, bounded, and a closed curve which does not intersect with itself. We create a binary image by assigning a 1 to the set of pixels in the object set and a 0 to all the exterior pixels. Therefore, the elements of the border set must all touch at least one pixel in the exterior set, conceptually separating it from the interior.

In this chapter we shall ignore the process of segmentation which produces the binary object from the original gray-level image [240]. However, it is convenient to conceive of this object as being initially analog in nature. Two stages of approximation then follow to create the set of points $z_k(i, j)$ which delineate the object boundary (see Figure 10.4). The first is a quantization stage, which transforms the analog boundary into a digital representation by the superimposition of a uniform sampling grid (see Figure 10.3). The digital curve is then coded, often by using the "chain code," which we shall discuss below. The second stage of approximation is essentially one of data aggregation, in which curves are detected. Here the coded edge vectors are concatenated. Critical points, such as corners or points of maximum curvature, are employed to indicate the limits of the approximating curves. The resulting compressed polygonal data take the form of a line drawing, representing an abstraction of reality. Apart from the fact that shape variations exist in the members of any object class, other noise is also introduced. As indicated in Chapter 2, this may be due to the imaging process or to digitization. Consequently, filtering may be applied to the original image by using the methodologies described in Chapter 6 or may be applied directly to the line structure.

An alternative source of data is the result of the edge-detection process discussed in Chapter 5. The primal sketch is a two-dimensional line drawing of the projection of the original three-dimensional scene. However, the definition of the object presented above is now no longer completely valid. The situation is considerably more complex in that additional types of curves are possible. These are indicated in Figure 10.5 and referred to as "open," "closed," "intersecting," and "tangent" curves [75]. Note that the intersection of curves

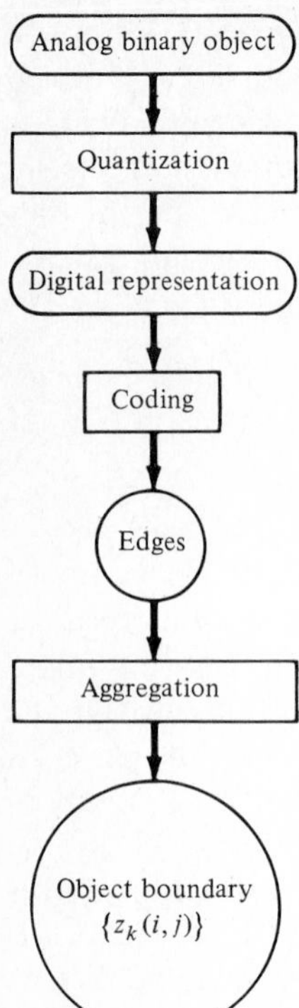

Figure 10.4 The stages of data approximation which transform any analog binary object into a digital and compressed representation of the object boundary. We have also seen in Chapter 5 that the edges are obtainable directly from the gray-level image. In this case, then, the coding stage would precede aggregation.

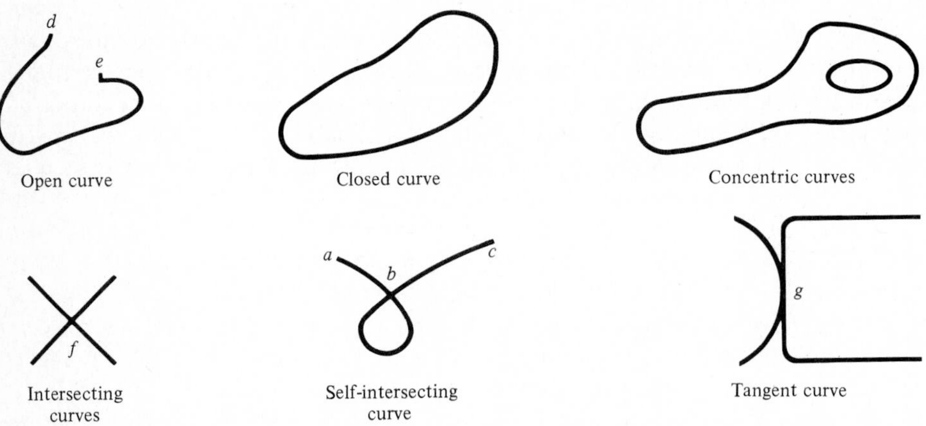

Figure 10.5 Line drawing abstractions of gray-tone images result in the different types of curves shown here.

is characterized by the property of radiality, that is, the number of lines emanating from the point of intersection. Natural processes rarely produce situations greater than triradiality. Indeed, a quadriradial junction is a good clue to the existence of man-made objects such as polyhedra. The reader should again note that the boundaries of objects or their parts are rarely well defined in the primal sketch. This is also the case for the aggregated data, as discussed in Chapters 8 and 9. In addition, the techniques described in this chapter are generally applicable to either inherently two-dimensional objects or clearly circumscribed projections. In both these cases it is assumed that a binary two-dimensional object is under consideration.

If we examine the analog representation of the object, it is observed from Figure 10.4 that quantization of this input is initially required [79]. In Chapter 2 we discussed the so-called computer eye, which effects this transformation into the digital domain. An alternative approach is to manually trace the picture by using a conventional graphics data tablet. In any case two issues predominate [77]. The first is the rule by which the analog input will be sampled. Usually a uniform square grid is used, although we have seen that this is not the case with the human retina. The second issue is addressed by the selection of the size of the resolution quanta. Both these decisions are governed by constraints imposed by the spatial frequency content of the input and the accuracy of the ensuing shape measurements.

The simplest quantization scheme is grid-intersect quantization [70, 71], although other approaches are possible [79]. This method involves the superimposition of a grid, usually square, on top of the line drawing or object. It is founded on the examination of the intersections of the mesh with the input image. For each individual point on a line which intersects the quantization mesh, a quantized curve point is selected to be the nearest point existing on the grid. This is illustrated in Figure 10.6. The approximating edge segments are of length 1 or $\sqrt{2}$, with the latter occurring about 41 percent of the time on average [71]. Note that two or more grid intersection points may yield the identical point on the approximating curve, for example, points b and c in the figure. Thus, given a particular quantized curve, it is clear that we cannot reconstruct a unique original analog curve. The domain of this quantized curve contains a set of curves, the smoothest one being the minimum-energy curve [79].

As indicated in Figure 10.4, the approximating curve in Figure 10.6 is then coded. A common approach is to use chain coding, first introduced by Freeman in 1961 [71]. Each directed edge element or link in the curve is coded by a number from the set $\{0, 1, \ldots, 7\}$ according to its direction, as designated in Figure 5.26a. Then an ordered sequence of links is denoted by $CC(k)$, $k = 1, \ldots, m$, and is called a "chain." Beginning at point a in Figure 10.6, the chain approximation is represented by the code 12010012244554445677. A more accurate approximation can be achieved with the generalized chain code [76, 77, 80, 205].

Many interesting applications of this coding scheme have been reported.

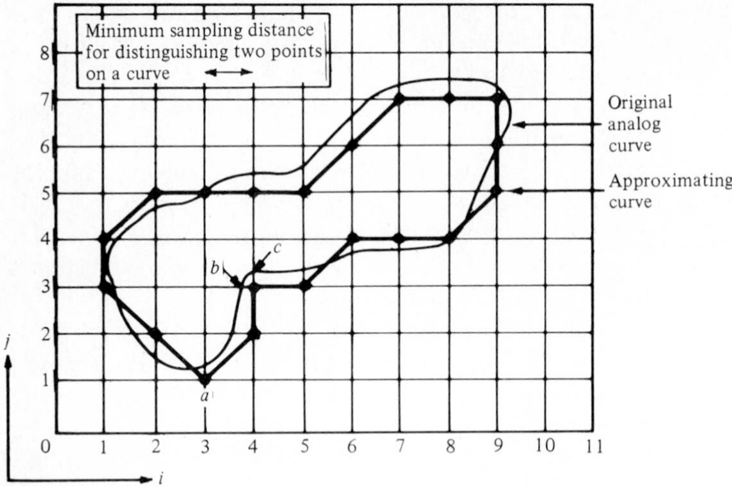

Figure 10.6 An example of grid-intersect quantization. The fineness of the sampling mesh is chosen to ensure that all the significant features of the original analog curve are retained (see Figure 10.3).

For example, Freeman [74] discusses the problem of pattern fitting such as is required by jigsaw puzzle assembly, map matching, and optimal two-dimensional layout (for example, of cloth for a dress). McKee and Aggarwal [134] have used chain coding in the process of recognizing such objects as tools and eyeglasses from the outlines of their two-dimensional projections.

Readers who are interested in the methods available for processing chains are referred to [74]. Various features may be computed directly from this representation. Examples are length, width, height, first- and second-order moments, and area. Such operations as object rotation, expansion, and contraction are also possible but are more convenient with the polygonal approximation to be discussed later. Contour smoothing and correlation for shape comparison are also relatively simple.

Other coding schemes are available, some related to the chain code [223]. Thus, parallel-scan codes can be used [137] instead of a sequential code. These require more memory storage than chain codes but are particularly advantageous for answering questions regarding closed contours circumscribing object areas. For example, is a particular point in the plane inside or outside the contour? Other such operations include region intersection, region union, containment, minimum distance between a point and the object contour, and the common boundary of two objects. However, issues related specifically to object shape are more conveniently addressed by chain codes.

As observed in Figure 10.4, it is desirable to aggregate the edge elements which constitute the boundary of an object. The objective is to compress the data while maintaining the approximation error within a defined bound.

Usually this aggregation results in a piecewise linear approximation, referred to as a "polygonal approximation." The rest of this section will deal with this topic.

Aggregation, in terms of polygonal approximations, is obtainable in two major ways. One of these methods relies on the determination of n critical points along the boundary, which then ipso facto define a polygon. The second relates to the use of successive approximations to iterate to a best-fit polygonal representation. We shall discuss these two approaches in the remaining portion of this section.

The mechanism for determining critical points must be based on the degree of bending exhibited by the object boundary. Thus, we note that curvature detectors in humans have been proposed at the neuronal level [188]. It has also been suggested that curved lines of less than 30′ curvature may be distinguished from straight-edge segments [6]. Of course, the hypercomplex cells we discussed in Section 5.2 are seen to respond proportionally to the curvature of a viewed fixed-length segment. Whatever the process, however, it seems likely that object boundaries are coded by a sequence of straight-line elements rather than curved ones [28].

Computer vision, as it relates to boundary representation, rests on the determination of these so-called critical points [75, 76]. From classical geometry we have maxima, minima, and points of inflection, which offer indications of curvature [175, 227, 259]. To these we may add the following [77]: discontinuities in curvature (point b on curve abc in Figure 10.5), endpoints (points d and e in Figure 10.5), intersections (point f in Figure 10.5), and tangent points (point g in Figure 10.5). The first three in this list delineate sharp discontinuities in curvature and therefore would be expected to be more significant as features when matching two shapes. Freeman [76] discusses algorithms for computing all these critical points. The advantage of using critical points is that they are unaffected by either scale or orientation. The disadvantage is that they are sensitive to the rotation of the object.

Let us examine the basic approach to extracting the critical points. What are being sought are the locations along the curve which exhibit discontinuities in curvature. These corners are usually not that well defined in terms of the tangential angle. Therefore, a decision process must be invoked which depends on the magnitude of the discontinuity, the sharpness of the angle, and the properties of the curve on either side of the corner. Based on the chain-code representation of the curve, the line-segment-scan method can be used to find the critical points [75, 78]. The technique is based on the computation of the discrete average slope at each point along the object boundary.

Suppose that we wish to measure the slope based on a moving average involving w nodes in the chain. The aperture size w will govern the amount of noise filtering and will normally lie in the range 4 to 9 [76]. We compute the angle θ_k with respect to the coordinate axes of a line segment having this length, as shown in Figure 10.7a. Thus

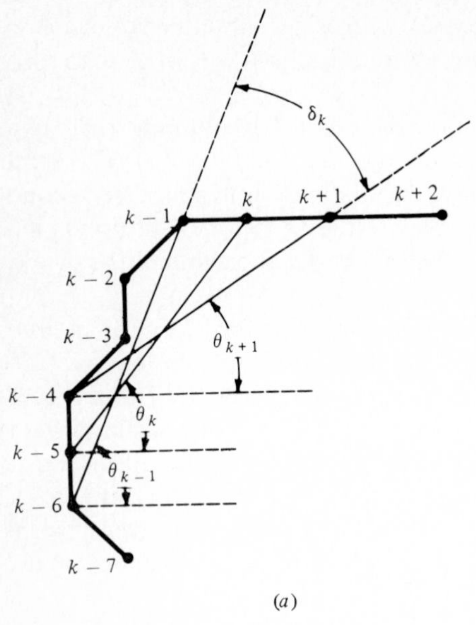

δ_k
$k-1$
k
$k+1$
$k+2$
$k-2$
$k-3$
θ_{k+1}
$k-4$
θ_k
$k-5$
θ_{k-1}
$k-6$
$k-7$

(*a*)

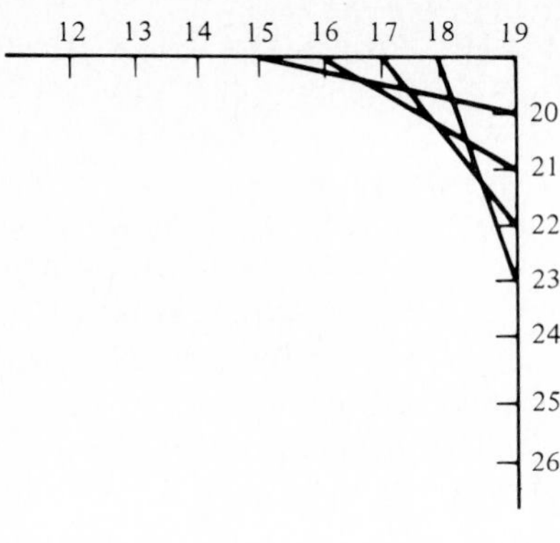

12 13 14 15 16 17 18 19
20
21
22
23
24
25
26

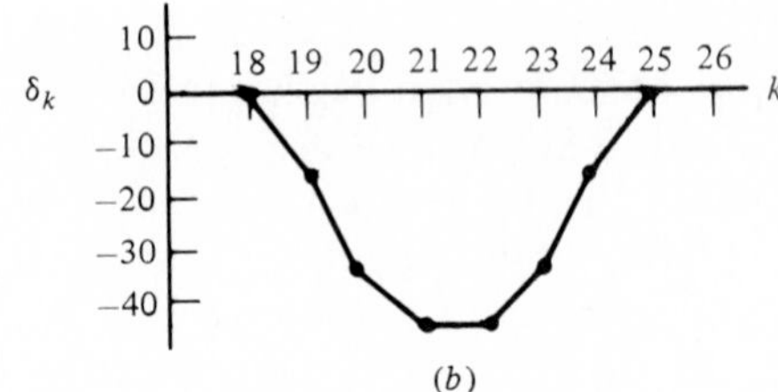

10
δ_k 0
−10
−20
−30
−40
18 19 20 21 22 23 24 25 26
k

(*b*)

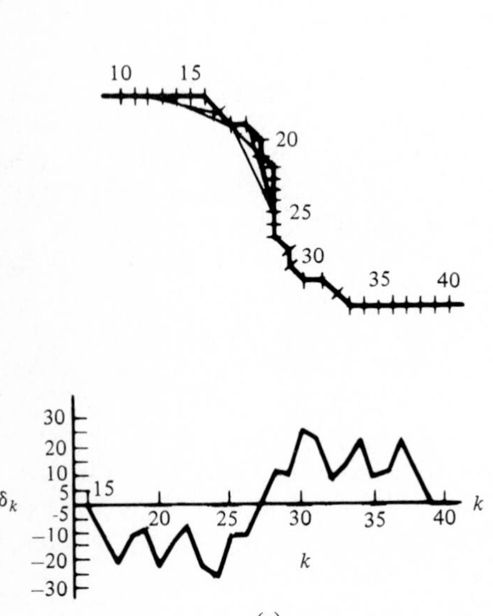

10 15
20
25
30
35 40
30
20
10
5
δ_k -5
−10
−20
−30
15
20 25 30 35 40
k
k

(*c*)

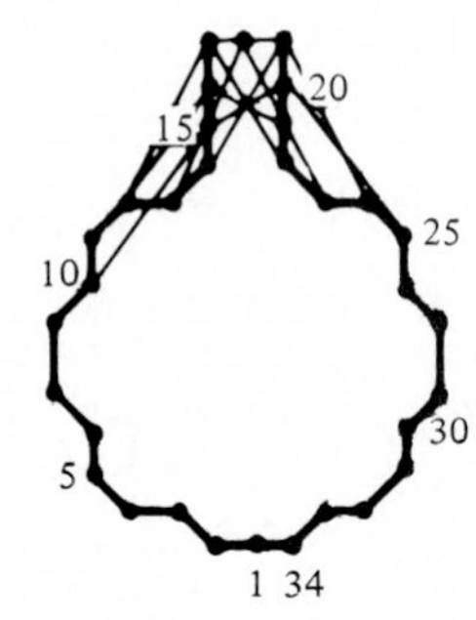

20
15
25
10
30
5
1 34

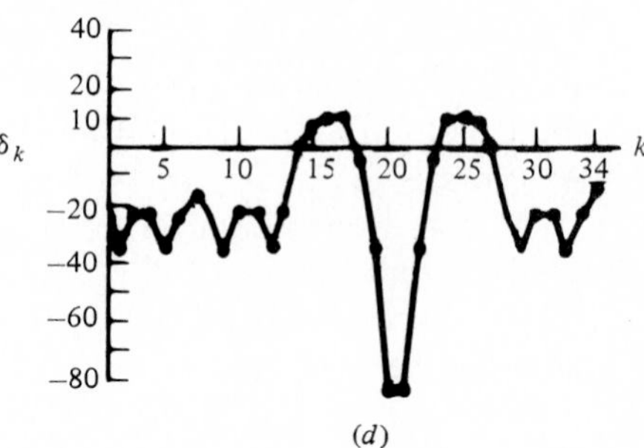

40
20
10
δ_k
−20
−40
−60
−80
5 10 15 20 25 30 34
k

(*d*)

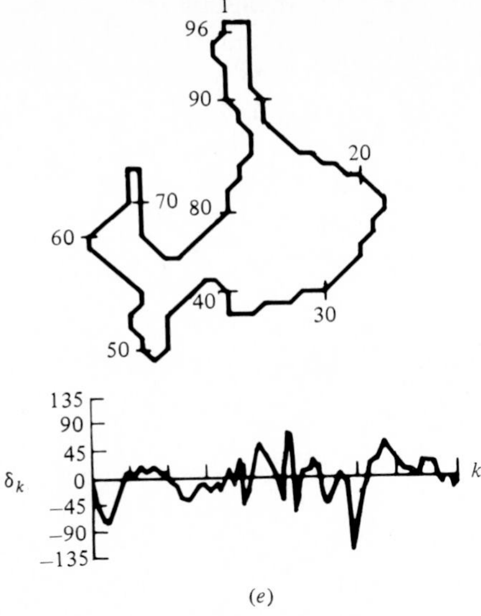

Figure 10.7 Incremental curvature. (*a*) The moving-line-segment-scan technique. The definition of θ_k and the incremental curvature δ_k at node k, given an aperture size $w = 5$. (*b*) The plot of incremental curvature δ_k ($w = 5$) for a chain-coded curve possessing a 90° turn. Note that the extrema in this curve and those following occur at $w/2$ units after the actual curve discontinuity. (*c*) The plot of incremental curvature δ_k ($w = 5$) for a chain-coded curve possessing a point of inflection. (*d*) Incremental curvature δ_k ($w = 5$) for a curve containing a curvature discontinuity. (*e*) A plot of the incremental curvature δ_k ($w = 5$) for the boundary of a white blood cell. [(*a*) *and* (*b*) *are adapted from H. Freeman, "Lines, Curves and the Characterization of Shape," Report no. IPL-TR-80-004, Image Processing Laboratory, Electrical and Systems Engineering Department, Rensselaer Polytechnic Institute, Troy, N.Y., March 1980.*]

$$\theta_k = \begin{cases} \arctan \dfrac{\bar{y}_k}{\bar{x}_k} & \text{for } |\bar{x}_k| \geq |\bar{y}_k| \\ \\ \operatorname{arccot} \dfrac{\bar{x}_k}{\bar{y}_k} & \text{for } |\bar{x}_k| < |\bar{y}_k| \end{cases} \tag{10.1}$$

where $\quad \bar{x}_k = \sum_{l=k-w}^{k-1} x_l \qquad \bar{y}_k = \sum_{l=k-w}^{k-1} y_l$

The variables x_l and y_l represent the x and y components of the chain-link vectors and can assume values of 1, 0, or -1 for a sampling grid of unit length. The incremental curvature δ_k at node k is given by

$$\delta_k = \theta_{k+1} - \theta_{k-1} \tag{10.2}$$

Figure 10.7*b* is a plot of $\delta_k (w = 5)$ as a function of curve node number. Clearly, δ_k equals zero along the straight-line segments and passes through an extremum at a sharp corner. The extremum occurs at $w/2$ units after the actual curve discontinuity. Figure 10.7*c* illustrates that points of inflection also result in characteristic δ_k curves. Figure 10.7*d* is a plot of δ_k for a curve containing a curvature discontinuity. Other feature interpretations which indicate shape properties of the object boundary are listed in Table 10.1. Figure 10.7*e* is a curvature plot for the boundary of a white blood cell. The important discontinuities are clearly evident and could be used to define the critical points for a polygonal approximation. The problem of determining these critical points has also been addressed by several other authors [43, 63, 66, 73, 105, 113, 136, 190, 202, 207].

We now turn to the second method for computing a polygonal representation, that of successive approximation. These algorithms tend to be easier to analyze theoretically but are more complex to program than the methods based on the detection of critical points. The basic problem formulation can be stated as follows: Find an approximating polygon to a digital curve, given an admissible error.

Typical of these iterative algorithms is the one due to Ramer [182]. This is basically a one-dimensional method in that the approximation is applied to a function of a single variable. Suppose it is desirable that these two curves not deviate by more than the Euclidean distance d. The algorithm is initiated by the selection of a starting and an ending point. For a closed curve these are chosen arbitrarily. However, a convenient choice is the pair of extreme points

Table 10.1 Some of the features that can be extracted from a plot of incremental curvature*

δ_k vs. k plot	Shape interpretation
Horizontal line	Constant curvature
Large-magnitude value	High curvature
Positive value	Curvature toward left (bay)
Negative value	Curvature toward right (peninsula)
Zero value	Straight line
Zero-crossing	Point of inflection
Peak or valley of width $w + 1$ and sum value D	Curvature discontinuity $w/2$ units toward right of peak (valley) center and of angular change of $D/2$ degrees
Pairs of opposite-sign peaks of width 2 and magnitude arctan $1/w$, separated by $w - 2$ points of constant value	Straight line or gentle curve
Increasing (decreasing) mean slope	Inward (outward) spiral

* Adapted from Freeman, H., "Lines, Curves and the Characterization of Shape," Report no. IPL-TR-80-004, Image Processing Laboratory, Electrical and Systems Engineering Department, Rensselaer Polytechnic Institute, Troy, N.Y., March, 1980.

delineating the maximum extent of the object in either the horizontal or vertical direction.

The method is as follows: The initial point is joined to the final point by a straight line. If this approximation is unsatisfactory because d is too large, then the curve is bisected. The splitting point is always chosen to be the point on the original curve farthest from the approximating curve. Both the initial and final points are joined to it, yielding a piecewise linear approximation with two segments. Each of these is then examined independently to determine whether the optimization criterion is satisfied. Splitting is performed if necessary and repeated until a satisfactory error is achieved for each line segment. Thus, the method provides a hierarchical decomposition in which the exact extrema are selected in order of their magnitude. The area between the actual curve and its approximation governs at what level in the hierarchy the process is terminated. Figure 10.8 is a sketch of the first few iterations for a closed object boundary.

In most cases the Euclidean distance can be approximated by the distance computed parallel to the coordinate axis [182]. Although the resulting approximation is not unique, convergence is fast. The method is quite robust, the result not being too sensitive to the tolerance d taken. The obtained polygonal approximation is a good approximation to the original boundary.

Related one-dimensional approaches are the split-and-merge method [173] and functional approximation [162]. Another one-dimensional approach is the fast method discussed by Tomek [239]. Conventional programming techniques such as Newton's method [164], nonlinear programming [144], and the minimax method [116] have also been employed. A fast two-dimensional method based on a minimum-perimeter polygonal approximation [225] is discussed in [226].

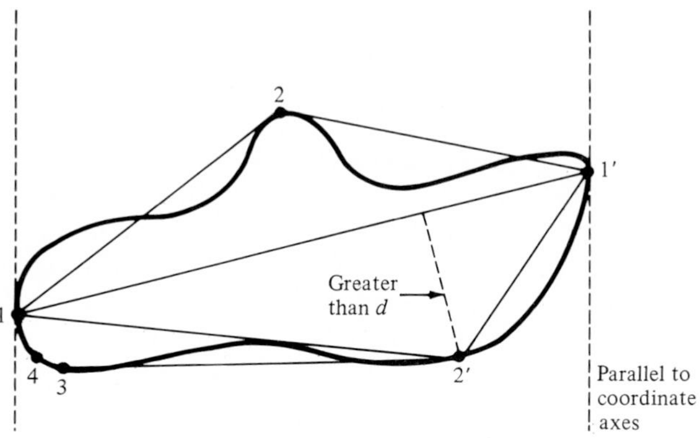

Figure 10.8 The first few iterations of an iterative technique for generating a polygonal approximation to a curve. The initial nodes 1 and 1′ are chosen arbitrarily. Nodes 2 and 2′ are generated, since neither satisfies the distance criterion. At this point the approximation is given by 1-2-1′-2′-1. Then each of the curve segments can be split independently. For example, segment 1-2′ is split into 1-3 and 3-2′; segment 1-3 into 1-4 and 4-3, and so on until the optimization criterion is satisfied.

So far, we have discussed methods for approximating the boundary curve of an object by short edge segments (chain code) or sides of a polygon. In this way the boundary is represented by an ordered set of curves. The next important stage, which involves the analysis of this set, is achieved by production rules or grammars which address the issue of computing global descriptions of the objects. This permits the classification of objects as well as shape matching. Numerous techniques have been suggested but their discussion is beyond the scope of this book. Readers are referred to [51, 84, 97, 104, 129, 134, 146, 168, 174, 233]. Hierarchical graph descriptions of approximating curves are discussed in [17, 18, 19, 20, 50, 172, 262].

10.2.2 Toads and Robots

There exists a physical barrier between a toad (*Bufo viridis*) and his next prey, some delicious mealworms! Should he circumvent this fence by hopping around it? Or should he pass through the gap in the fence? In planning his path to this meal, it appears that the toad measures both the distance to the barrier [127] and the size of the opening [128]. The latter is a good example of a simple shape feature, perhaps the simplest.

Robots that "see" are currently being developed to automate the inspection and manipulation of industrial parts in the manufacturing industries [112]. To accomplish this task, it is also necessary for the computer-controlled robot to visually distinguish the shapes of objects. Typically, such simple features as perimeter, area, and two-dimensional extent are employed.

What the toad and the robot have in common is that their actions are based on the use of non-information-preserving shape features. These are defined as measurements which do not permit the unique reconstruction of the original object. Nevertheless, they are very useful as approximate indicators of shape.

There is yet no agreement on a minimum set of shape descriptors to adequately quantify object form. Attneave [13] has described shape complexity in terms of the boundary curvedness, symmetry, compactness, and angular variability; the last seems to be a very significant indicator. An exhaustive study of the psychology literature is reported in [38]. Over 100 quantitative measures of shape had been discovered by 1967, but many of these are highly correlated with each other. Most of these measures are based on: (1) size of angles; (2) length of sides; (3) area; (4) perimeter; (5) radial lengths; and (6) actual boundary coordinates. Again certain properties seem to predominate. Compactness of shape, jaggedness of the border, and direction of the dominating axis emerge as being highly correlated with the other features. A more recent study [102] appearing in the computer literature focuses on four principal geometrical factors: complexity, uniformity of side lengths, shape elongation, and global roundness. Freeman [77] has suggested the following shape descriptors: round, straight, curved, narrow, convex, and smooth. We must therefore conclude that although there obviously are relationships between these different proposals and experimental results, a unique set of shape descriptors remains to be defined.

Before the shape of a two-dimensional object can be measured and described, it must first be isolated in the image. Chapters 8 and 9 have dealt with this issue. The next step is to trace a sequence of boundary points which define the object [121]. Methods based on both region analysis [88, 200] and line segments [3, 156, 189] are available. Section 10.2.1 addressed the issue of compressing and coding this boundary data. In this section, we shall discuss some representative simple feature descriptors, all of which are non-information-preserving.

Object Size The size of a region, often referred to as its diameter D, is clearly a very powerful shape indicator. It is perhaps the simplest and most preferred shape property. The diameter of a region is defined by those two extrema on the boundary that have the greatest distance between them. It has been shown that this chord is never greater in length than half the total perimeter of the region [193].

The computation of this feature may be treated as a heuristic search problem [231]. Given a set of m boundary points $Z = \{z_1, z_2, \ldots, z_k, \ldots, z_m\}$ in the two-dimensional plane, we seek the two points $z_1, z_2 \in Z$ such that

$$d(z_1, z_2) > d[(i_1, j_1), (i_2, j_2)] \tag{10.3}$$

for all $(i_1, j_1), (i_2, j_2) \in Z$, where d is a Euclidean distance measure. For a small number of boundary points, say 10 or 20, exhaustive search is practical. However, the number of comparisons grows as $\frac{1}{2}n(n-1)$ or $O(n^2)$.

An alternative, which is computationally fast but often inaccurate, is to construct a so-called Feret box [88]. As indicated in Figure 10.9*a*, this is simply the smallest circumscribing rectangle whose sides are (arbitrarily) chosen to be parallel to the coordinate axes. The intersection points associated with each of the pairs of parallel lines define two chords. The largest of these may be taken

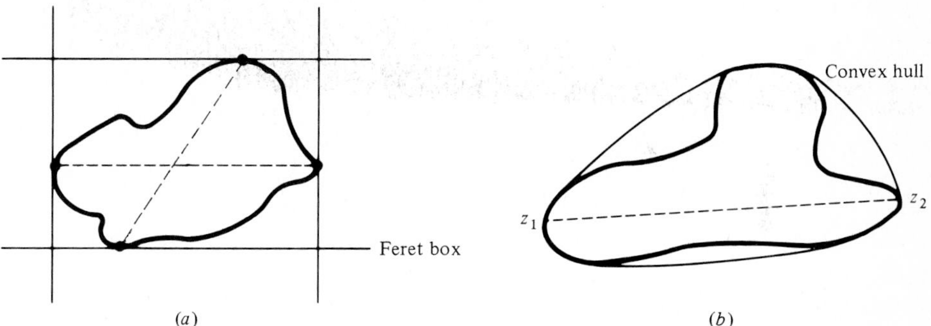

Figure 10.9 Two approximations of an object's shape which permit the simplification of the computation of size. (*a*) The intersection points of the Feret box define simple approximations to the spatial extent of the object. (*b*) The convex hull of an irregular object.

as the object diameter *D*. Although this might, for example, provide a good first approximation to the major caliper diameter for a grasping robot manipulator, the measure clearly depends on the orientation of the shape with respect to the axes. A second approach, sketched in Figure 10.9*b*, is to compute the convex hull of the irregular object. The search for the maximum of $d(z_1, z_2)$ in Equation (10.3) is then simplified, because now only a single global extremum exists [231]. The shape of the object concavities as delineated by the convex hull has been employed as a feature for the recognition of handprinted characters [258] and in industrial inspection [24]. Obviously, these so-called convex deficiencies are a good measure of boundary irregularity.

The next level of complexity of shape descriptor involves the perimeter *P* and area *A* of the object. The definitions are simple. To determine the perimeter, it is necessary to follow the boundary of the shape by distinguishing between its inside (binary 1) and outside (binary 0). Thus, a count of all pixels in the object having both 0 and 1 neighbors yields the perimeter. Similarly, adding up all the 1s within the object provides the area. Both these properties can be computed by using a local window operation [89], the computations being analogous to Perceptron devices [139], originally introduced as simulations of neuron behavior. At a minimum, area and perimeter require 1×1 and 2×2 windows, respectively. Gray [89] has indicated that windows of diameter 2 are probably sufficient for most useful shape measures. Both parallel [114, 141] and sequential [3] scanning of the image have been studied in the context of feature detection.

Certain inaccuracies in the values of *P* and *A* are introduced as a result of the original digitization process [95]. For example, the shape of the object will be mildly distorted and the feature measurements will be dependent on orientation. However, special care must also be taken with round objects [115]. Discretization of the analog shape may cause errors as great as 20 percent in the perimeter measurement [253]. The area measurements are more reliable as the errors tend to average out. Thus, the discrete area count approaches the actual analog area as the grid spacing is reduced; however, the perimeter count grows exponentially [199]. In many industrial vision tasks an accurate and fast determination of these two features is desired. A comparison of the different approaches is discussed by Wechsler [253], who introduces a new method based on detection and correction of explicit digitization errors.

The object size features discussed in this section are usually the first to be considered as shape descriptors. For example, in the field of robotics shape is often used to obtain a visual feedback signal for the manipulators. Many questions are of concern in this type of application: Which object is it? Is the object shape correct? Is it oriented properly? Is it upside down? Which stable state is it in? If the diameter, perimeter, and area can provide answers to these questions, then they are used instead of the more complex shape measures to be discussed below.

Goodness of Shape Gestalt psychologists have described "goodness of shape" in terms of the descriptors simplicity, regularity, and symmetry. However, an extensive set of recent experiments by Ishikawa [102] indicates that only the first two are really justified. What is being ultimately sought by researchers is a limited number of generic shapes or features to specify an arbitrary object. Such "good" shapes could then be used to analyze a two-dimensional contour in terms of well-defined primitives. This goal has not yet been achieved. Even the definitions of the shape terms commonly used in speech have not been standardized or associated with precise concepts.

Four principal factors in the description of a good object have been isolated by Ishikawa [102]. The first, referred to as "simplicity" (or its converse, "complexity"), is concerned with the extent of jaggedness of the boundary. That is, does the contour contain many undulations or is it smooth? One might refer to this as the "texture" of the object contour. The second factor measures the regularity of the "sides" of the shape. Are they uniformly distributed, or are there large variations in side lengths? This question is perhaps best addressed to the polygonal approximation of the boundary. We observe that the above two elements are concerned with the microproperties of the shape. The last two factors proposed by Ishikawa deal with global shape. They pertain to the overall impression of the object and measure elongation (referred to as "stability" in [102]) and roundness. These may be viewed as macrofeatures at either extreme of a hypothetical geometric shape scale. Thus, in the context of the above discussion, this section will examine the three properties of boundary complexity, regularity, and global geometric shape.

Perhaps the simplest measure of contour complexity is given by the number of vertices n in the polygonal approximation. Angle regularity, as originally studied by Attneave [13], also seems to be an appropriate feature. Let θ_k be the interior angle at the kth boundary point z_k. If three boundary points are colinear, then clearly the subtended angle will be 180°. If a corner exists, then z_k will constitute a vertex. Thus the angle regularity may be given by [261]

$$A_1 = \frac{1}{n}\left[(\theta_1 - \theta_m) + \sum_{k=1}^{m-1} (\theta_{k+1} - \theta_k)\right] \tag{10.4}$$

for a closed polygon with n vertices but m boundary points. For an open polygon it is necessary to define θ_k as the interior angle of the triangle formed by connecting z_{k-1} to z_{k+1}. Thus [261]

$$A_2 = \frac{1}{n}\sum_{k=2}^{m-2} (\theta_{k+1} - \theta_k) \tag{10.5}$$

Note that this attribute equals zero for a straight line. An alternative is to compare the boundary "texture" with that of a regular polygon having the same number of vertices. In this case, the internal angles at the corners of the regular polygon will be identical. Thus we have [264]

$$A_3 = \frac{1}{K}\sum_{l=1}^{n} \left|\theta_l - \frac{360}{n}\right| \tag{10.6}$$

$$\text{where} \qquad K = \begin{cases} \dfrac{360(n+2)}{n} & \text{for } n \text{ even} \\[2ex] \dfrac{360(n+1)}{n} & \text{for } n \text{ odd} \end{cases}$$

A_3 equals zero for the least complex contour and equals unity for the most complex. This formulation has been found to be useful in describing the shape of a moving white blood cell [123].

There exists another common feature which is often used to measure object complexity, namely [89, 197]

$$A_4 = \frac{P^2}{4\pi A} \tag{10.7}$$

where P and A are the perimeter and area, respectively, of the closed boundary. A_4 is often referred to as a measure of "compactness" or "circularity" and employed as a global shape measure. The reason for this is that A_4 takes on a minimum value of unity for a circle and larger values for distortions therefrom. For example, a square gives $A_4 = 4/\pi$, and values are derived for other generic shapes in [120]. An alternative normalization is provided by

$$A_5 = 1 - \frac{4\pi A}{P^2} \tag{10.8}$$

Now A_5 equals zero for circles and approaches unity for the least circular shapes.

It should be noted that the value of A_4 for a digital shape depends on how its perimeter is computed [179, 194]. In fact, under certain circumstances a diamond or octagonal shape might have a smaller value of A_4 than a digitized circle. Also, as the sampling resolution increases, A_4 approaches infinity. The abnormal nature of this feature is clearly demonstrated in Figure 10.10, in which the 20 seemingly different shapes possess the identical value of A_5 according to Equation (10.8). The major reason for this is that the summations (discrete integrals) defining P and A are not affected by the specific order of the shape discontinuities. However, visually their sequence will definitely affect the pattern we perceive. Recently a method has been suggested which circumvents the problem with circularity as given in Equation (10.7) by defining shape complexity in terms of its polygonal approximation [206].

Having discussed boundary complexity, let us now consider shape regularity. This concept is based on an examination of the uniformity of the side lengths of the figure. A simple example is the use of the variance of lengths of sides of the approximating polygon, or the ratio of the maximum to the minimum side length. An alternative is to compare the object shape with a regular polygon having exactly the same number of sides and total perimeter P. For a regular polygon with n sides of length L, let

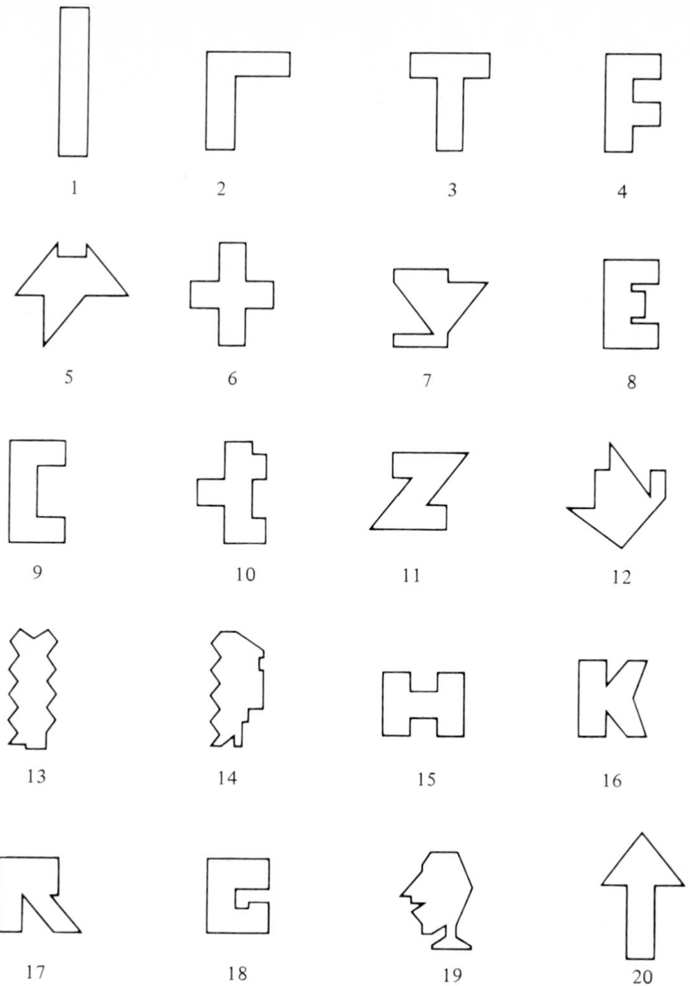

Figure 10.10 Different shapes having the same area and perimeter and hence the same circularity A_5. (*From Y. M. Youssef, "Quantification and Characterization of the Motion and Shape of a Moving Cell," Ph.D. thesis, Department of Electrical Engineering, McGill University, Montreal, 1982.*)

$$L = \frac{P}{n} \tag{10.9}$$

The side regularity is then given by [264]:

$$A_6 = \frac{\left[\sum_{k=1}^{n} (l_k - L)^2\right]^{1/2}}{2L(n-2)} \tag{10.10}$$

where l_k is the length of the kth side of the polygon. Note that A_6 equals zero for a regular polygon, and takes on a maximum value of unity for the most nonuniform shape.

Finally, we have the third category of shape descriptor, the global shape. This encompasses the macroconcepts of roundness and elongation, with a circle supposedly representing the most stable figure. Clearly, the objective is to be able to find an appropriate feature which can extract the essence of the shape while ignoring all irrelevant surface irregularities. One such shape factor, due to Danielsson [48], is based on the first-order moment of the binary 1s contained by the object. It is said to be an improvement over A_4 in Equation (10.7), but it is subject to some controversy [48, 167].

An interesting shape feature is derived from the minimum bending energy of the boundary curve [40, 263]. The average bending energy along the length of the boundary curve defined by the set Z is measured in terms of the curvature. Suppose that $z(i, j)$ is defined by a chain code CC of m links, with $CC(k)$ as the kth consecutive one. Then the curvature $R(k)$ at the point k is given by

$$R(k) = \frac{\Delta\theta(k)}{\Delta p(k)} \tag{10.11}$$

where

$$\Delta\theta(k) = CC(k) - CC(k-1) \tag{10.12}$$

and approximates the change in the tangent direction along the curve. Also, the associated path length surrounding the point k is given by

$$\Delta p(k) = L[CC(k)] + L[CC(k-1)] \tag{10.13}$$

where

$$L[l] = \begin{cases} \dfrac{1}{2} & \text{for } l \text{ even} \\[2ex] \dfrac{\sqrt{2}}{2} & \text{for } l \text{ odd} \end{cases}$$

Then, the total average bending energy A_7 is defined by [264]:

$$A_7 = \frac{1}{P} \sum_{k=0}^{m-1} |R(k)|^2 \tag{10.14}$$

where $R(k)$ is given as above and P is the perimeter of the chain. Note that the shape possessing the minimum value of A_7 for the equivalent value of P is the circle [263]. It yields

$$A_7 = \left(\frac{2\pi}{P}\right)^2$$

which, unfortunately, indicates that the average bending energy is dependent on the size. Normalization between 0 and 1 may be achieved by setting

$$A_8 = 1 - \frac{A_7 \text{ (circle)}}{A_7 \text{ (arbitrary shape)}}$$

thus

$$A_8 = 1 - \frac{4\pi^2}{P \sum_{k=0}^{m-1} |R(k)|^2} \tag{10.15}$$

where P is the perimeter of the arbitrary shape. Again A_8 equals zero for a circle and takes on the value unity for the most complex shape. This feature is particularly useful for the bloblike shapes that often occur in biomedical image processing.

In addition to circularity as discussed previously, elongation (or eccentricity) is an important global shape descriptor [201]. It is defined simply by

$$A_9 = \frac{|D - W|}{D} \tag{10.16}$$

where W is the object width (minor axis) and D is the diameter (major axis). With this expression, A_9 equals zero for a square and approaches a value of unity for very filamentary shapes. An interesting approach to computing the related feature of "parallelness," as well as "rectilinearity" and "hexagonal tendency," is discussed by Tanimoto [236]. It is based on the statistics associated with the polygonal approximation for the shape.

A different approach to global shape description is the "shape number" described in [37, 91]. The resulting characterization is independent of translation, rotation, and scaling. The major advantage of this shape measure is that shape decomposition and structural comparison are not required to establish the difference between two objects. It is only necessary to compare the associated shape numbers. The degree of similarity can be easily obtained by employing a binary search. Some minor disadvantages are discussed in [37].

We conclude this section by observing that no simple shape attribute is sufficient to describe an object [169, 264]. For example, Table 10.2 lists the shapes of Figure 10.10 sorted in terms of four different shape features. In the first column, the order is based on angle regularity according to Equation (10.6), in the second on side regularity according to Equation (10.10), and in the third on average bending energy according to Equation (10.15). Clearly, each of these features proposes a different ordering, depending on the unique characteristic it attempts to measure. None of these is adequate as a global shape measure and a combination is often useful. Thus, either a vector or composite description is required. For example, the geometric mean of the angle regularity (contour complexity), side regularity (shape uniformity), and global shape (average bending energy) is defined as

$$A_{10} = \sqrt[3]{A_3 \cdot A_6 \cdot A_8} \tag{10.17}$$

An ordering for the shapes in Figure 10.10, based on Equation (10.17), is presented in Table 10.2, fourth column. Another more realistic example relates

Table 10.2 Shapes ordered according to specific features*

Angle regularity A_3	Side regularity A_6	Average bending energy A_8	Geometric mean A_{10}
1†	13	1	1
2	6	20	13
19	10	9	6
9	14	2	2
3	16	7	9
7	15	3	10
13	17	17	16
14	19	11	20
4	4	16	17
16	9	5	7
17	20	4	14
8	5	6	15
6	12	12	3
15	2	15	4
10	7	10	19
18	11	8	11
20	8	13	12
12	3	19	8
11	18	14	5
5	1	18	18

* Data for first and third columns from Y. M. Youssef, "Quantification and Characterization of the Motion and Shape of a Moving Cell," Ph.D. thesis, Department of Electrical Engineering, McGill University, Montreal, May 1982; data for second and fourth columns provided by Y. M. Youssef.

† The numbers correspond to those in Fig. 10.10.

to the analysis of moving white blood cells [125]. We observe that the membrane (cell boundary) of the cell undergoes large changes in shape as it migrates in its environment [123]. The values of the composite shape descriptor A_{10}, shown in Figure 10.11*a*, may be used to symbolically describe the shape, as indicated in Figure 10.11*b*.

Alternatively, we would like to describe an arbitrary figure in terms of a set of generic shapes. For example, an unmanned underwater free-swimming robot would have to recognize objects in order to function autonomously. In most cases, the objects perceived by tactile or visual sensors will possess poorly defined edges and vertices. Thus the analysis problem may be stated as follows: Given a list of points in a plane, find the simplest shape which approximates it.† A tree search algorithm has been developed by Slagle and

† Realistically, the points should be approximated by a three-dimensional shape. However, the initial research has only addressed the analysis of the two-dimensional projection [228].

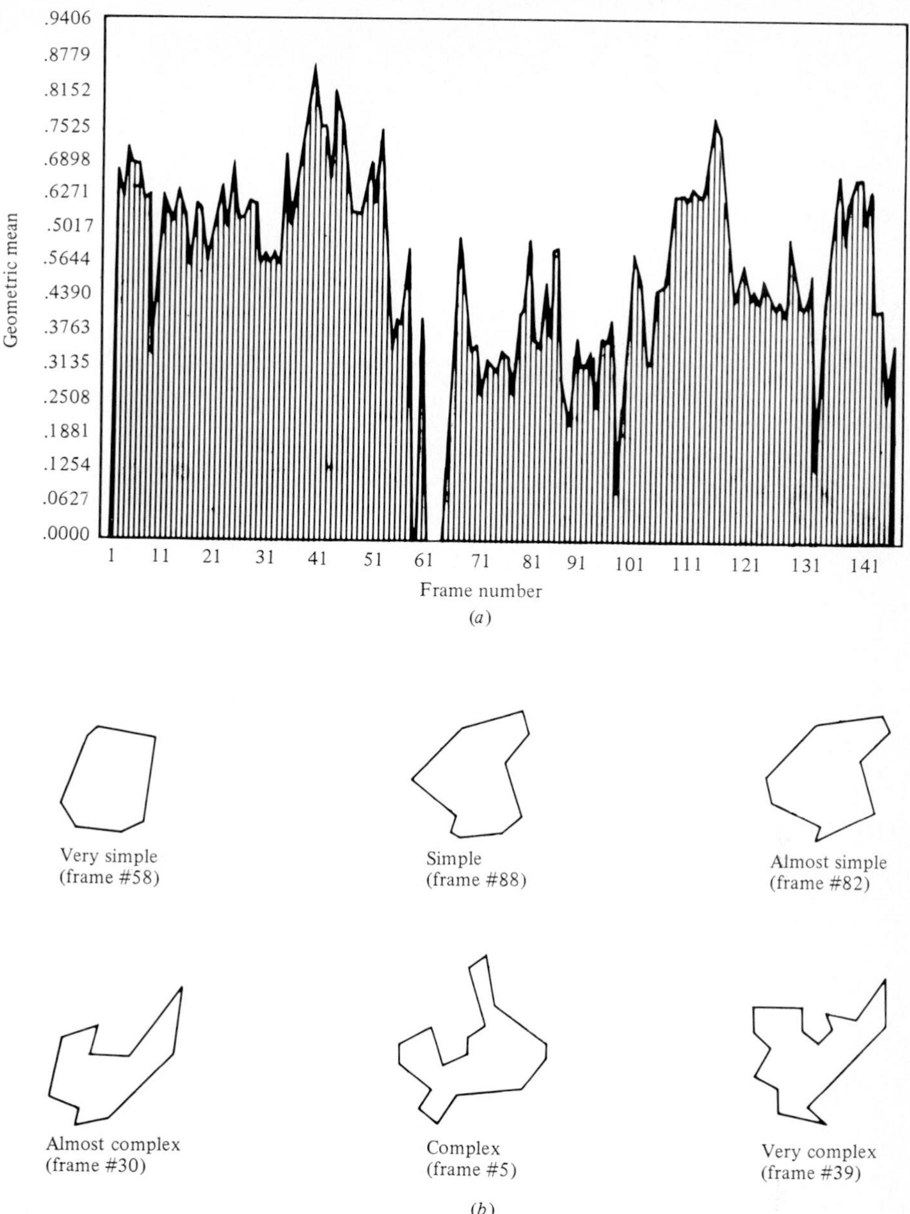

Figure 10.11 Characterization of the shape of a blood cell's surrounding membrane according to the geometric mean of three significant features. (*a*) Geometric mean of angle regularity, side regularity, and average bending energy, computed for cell shapes in a sequence of 150 frames. (*b*) Sample membrane shape descriptions. The categories are defined by the thresholds (0, 0.1, 0.3, 0.5, 0.7, 0.9, 1.0). (*Adapted from Y. M. Youssef, "Quantification and Characterization of the Motion and Shape of a Moving Cell," Ph.D. thesis, Department of Electrical Engineering, McGill University, Montreal, 1982.*)

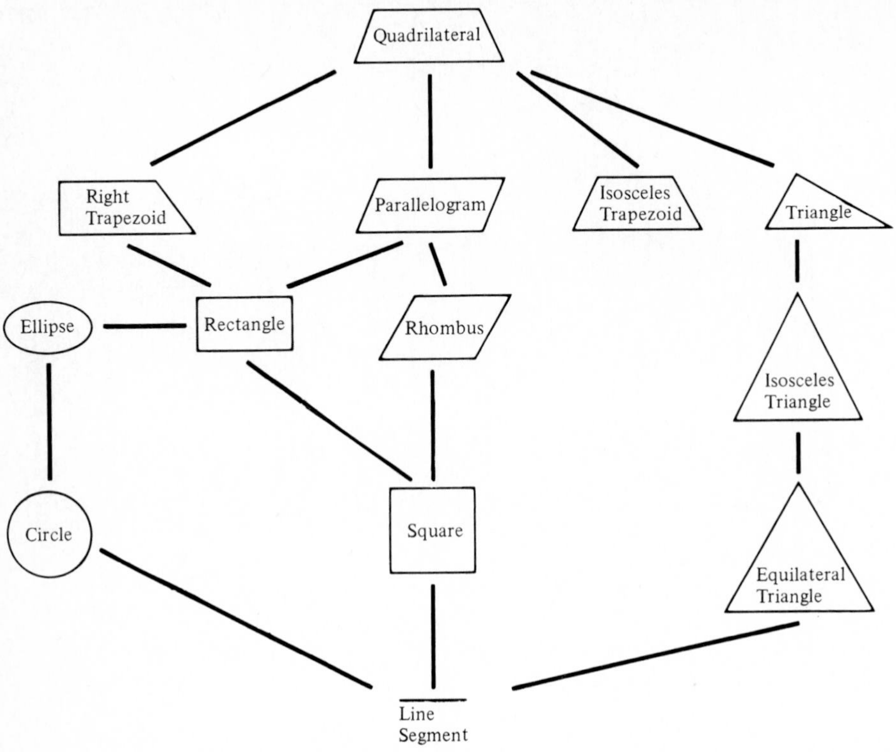

Figure 10.12 A figure network in which each node in the graph represents a generic shape. A link between two nodes indicates a degree of direct similarity between the two involved shapes. Shape complexity is indicated by the vertical position of the node. (*Adapted from J. R. Slagle and J. K. Dixon, "Using Descriptions to Find Figures That Approximate the Given Points," Proceedings of the 5th International Conference on Pattern Recognition, Miami Beach, Dec. 1–4, 1980, pp. 1049–1054.*)

Dixon [227, 228] to categorize the points into one of the following generic figures: line segment, circle, ellipse, rectangle, rhombus, square, right trapezoid, parallelogram, isosceles trapezoid, quadrilateral, triangle, isosceles triangle, and equilateral triangle. A figure network indicating the relationship between these shapes is presented in Figure 10.12. Fuzzy relations can also be employed to assign generic classifications to geometric shapes [119].

10.3 SPACE-DOMAIN TECHNIQUES

10.3.1 "Where is the Kidney Bean, the Tadpole?" [33]

The title of this section is not a reference to some new exotic theory of the frog's neurophysiology (see Section 5.2). Neither is it an expression of concern regarding its whereabouts. It is part of a plea by H. Blum to scientists studying the shape of objects [33]:

> Our concepts of space are deeply rooted in surveying. One need only look at the derivation of the word "geometry" to verify this. The first postulate of euclidean geometry is: "A straight line can be drawn from any point to any other point." One already sees the primitive act of surveying. With the line, the simplest "objects" do not yet appear. In 2-space, three lines are required; in 3-space, four triangles. The inclusion of the interior requires still other steps. Euclid goes from triangles to more complex rectilinear objects, polygons. The only seriously considered nonpolygon is the circle. Where are the objects of biology? Where is the kidney bean, the tadpole? Note that the latter wiggles and is not congruent with or similar to even itself.

Clearly, a more general and flexible mathematics for describing biological shape is desirable. Most effort to date has been addressed at specifying man-made objects which are primarily characterized by straight lines. In this regard, Blum poses three basic questions [33]:

> First there is the taxonomic or descriptive problem. How do we describe organisms in mathematical, yet natural, terms? Second, there is the psychological-neurophysiological problem. How do organisms, via their nervous system, categorize other organisms? Third, there is the developmental problem. How do organisms develop into the shapes that they do, in fact, achieve? (From an evolutionary point of view, these questions should be asked in the inverse order. Organisms appear first, nervous systems later, and scientists last.)

Needless to say, such a comprehensive theory of shape has not yet emerged.

In this section we shall examine two approaches to transforming the shape of an object into a representative graph. These methods have been referred to as "internal," since they are concerned with the area bounded by the shape contour [169]. The first to be discussed is called the "medial-axis transform." It is based on the outline of the shape and was originally suggested by Blum [29] as a reply to the three questions posed above. The second approach to be discussed in this section functions by decomposing a shape into a union of subsets. The simpler subsets, as well as their spatial relationships, provide the object description.

The result of the picture processing discussed in this section is a graph which portrays the two-dimensional shape. Such a formulation suggests three major advantages. First, it is independent of translation, rotation, registration, and size. Second, these descriptions are "anthropomorphic" in the sense that they seem to conform with a human's depiction of the object's shape. Finally, the resulting data structures are amenable to further analysis using syntactic [83] or structural [163] pattern recognition. The techniques examined in this section are generic since they are applied to arbitrary images and do not invoke any problem-dependent knowledge. However, interpreting and recognizing the graph as a symbolic representation is clearly the next stage in the analysis.

Skeletons Skeleton [94], medial-axis transform [30], distance transform [200], symmetric-axis transform [34], stick figure [133], and thinned shape [232]—these are the names given to the object descriptor discussed in this section. The method originated with Blum [29, 30, 31] who presents a detailed introduction and discussion of this topic in [32, 33]. In [33] Blum argues vehemently that neither the classical projective and coordinate geometries nor the more modern non-Euclidean and topological geometries are satisfactory as "a natural geometry for biological shape." Basically, the idea behind the skeleton is to provide a method which is capable of computing a description of a natural shape. These are generally amorphous and are sometimes simply referred to as "blobs." An appropriate description represents the intrinsic shape by a set of connected curves, which maintains the original topology. It should also preserve a correspondence with the spatial dimensions and orientation of the object and its subparts. The skeleton satisfies these criteria.

Blum has also proposed a geometry for biology which uses a point as the basic primitive and growth as the significant operation [32, 33]. The uniform growth of a point source yields a succession of ever larger disks [32]:

> Growth from a boundary generates a description of an object that is centered on the space it includes. Growth from this centered or core description generates the boundary by an inverse growth. This leads to new properties and descriptions which are particularly suitable for many biological objects.

The relationship of conventional geometry to this type of growth geometry is discussed in [32, pp. 277–279]. A classical reference on biological growth and shape is [238], first published in 1917.

In this section, we shall examine iterative growth processes which are based on the expansion or contraction of the pixels constituting the elements of a two-dimensional object. These computations are typically permitted to proceed until a one-pixel-wide stick figure results. Two types of algorithms will be discussed. The first is based on Blum's concept of the growth of simultaneous wavefronts. It tends to preserve the details of the object shape. However, the interpretation of the skeleton transform is sometimes difficult and the resulting set of curves is often disconnected. Each point of the transform has associated with it a value denoting its minimum distance to the contour. Therefore, this permits the reconstruction of the original object from the transform, and there is no loss of information. The second type of algorithm is referred to as "thinning" and differs because the shrinking of the figure is performed nonuniformly. The resulting representation indicates the broad global characteristics of the shape. Small, irrelevant indentations on the boundary are generally ignored, so that this approach is often invoked when comparison with a stored model is required. The underlying computational technique in this case is based on the concept of preserving connectivity of the pixels in the transform [195]. Thus, elements of the original shape are deleted, but only if they do not create a break. Reconstruction is not possible. Figure 10.13 indicates the two transforms obtained for the same object. We observe that the skeleton provides an indication of all the convex arcs in the boundary, while the thinned version denotes the "spine" of the shape.

The medial-axis transform, as initially defined by Blum, was specified for

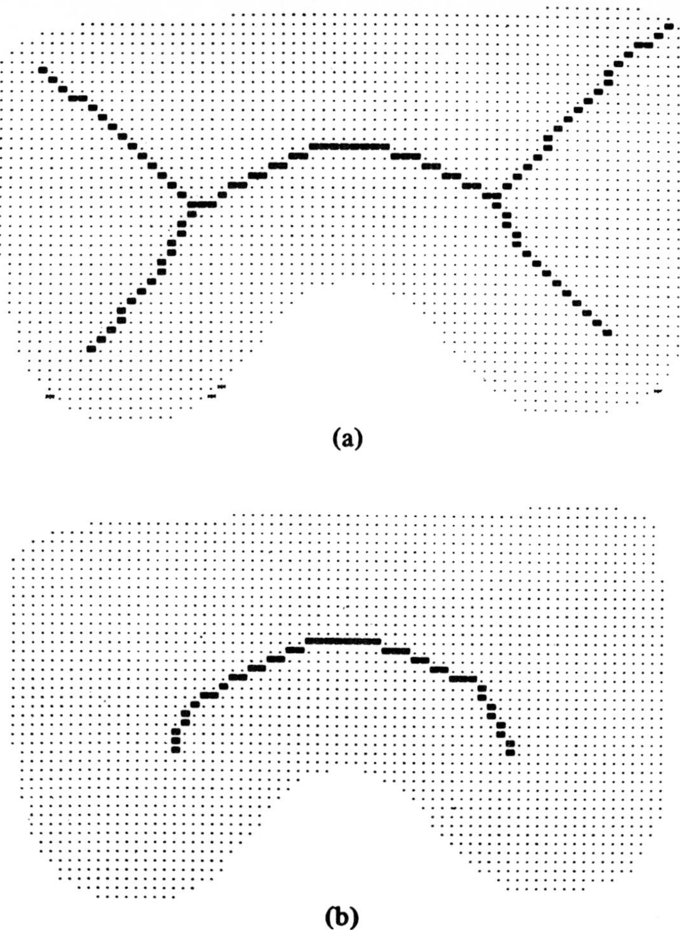

Figure 10.13 Differences between the skeletonized (*a*) and thinned (*b*) version of the same image. To obtain (*a*) the skeletonization algorithm in [10] was invoked. To obtain (*b*) the thinning algorithm described in [10] was used. (*From C. Arcelli, L. P. Cordella, and S. Levialdi, "From Local Maxima to Connected Skeletons," IEEE Transactions on Pattern Analysis and Machine Intelligence, vol. PAMI-3, no. 2, March 1981, pp. 134–143.*)

continuous shapes in the two-dimensional Euclidean space. This theory has since been investigated in considerable detail [34, 35, 36, 39]. Clearly, however, computer implementation requires that a discrete shape be defined and that the continuous theory be approximated in discrete space [147]. Rosenfeld and Pfaltz [178, 200, 201] were the first to explore the computation of the skeleton from this viewpoint. Perhaps an intermediate stage between the continuous and the discrete is the use of a polygonal approximation as the basis for determination of the skeleton [35, 143]. Under these circumstances an analytical solution to the problem is available.

Let us first consider the continuous, or propagation, theory. One method for generating the skeleton is by computing parallels to the boundary of the object. This approach utilizes the so-called grass fire analogy. Suppose we were to simultaneously light fires along the entire boundary of an object. Each point on the boundary is then considered to be a source which grows (by consuming the grass) uniformly in all directions, thereby producing a disk-shaped wavefront. When two disks intersect, the fire is extinguished at the point of contact. The extinction points delineate the skeleton. Figure 10.14 is an example of two point sources in which the fire is quenched when the wavefronts intersect. Note that this differs from the situation in which two pebbles are dropped into a lake. Under these circumstances the waves merely flow through each other and the result is just a superposition. The skeleton in the figure is given by the right bisector of the two points in the plane. Several simple examples of grass fire wavefronts are illustrated in Figure 10.15*a*. More complex nonconvex shapes are shown in Figure 10.15*b*. The transform itself consists of the skeleton plus a radius function, which is the minimum distance to the shape boundary from each point on the skeleton. Thus, the object may be reconstructed by a similar negative growth process [32, pp. 217–225].

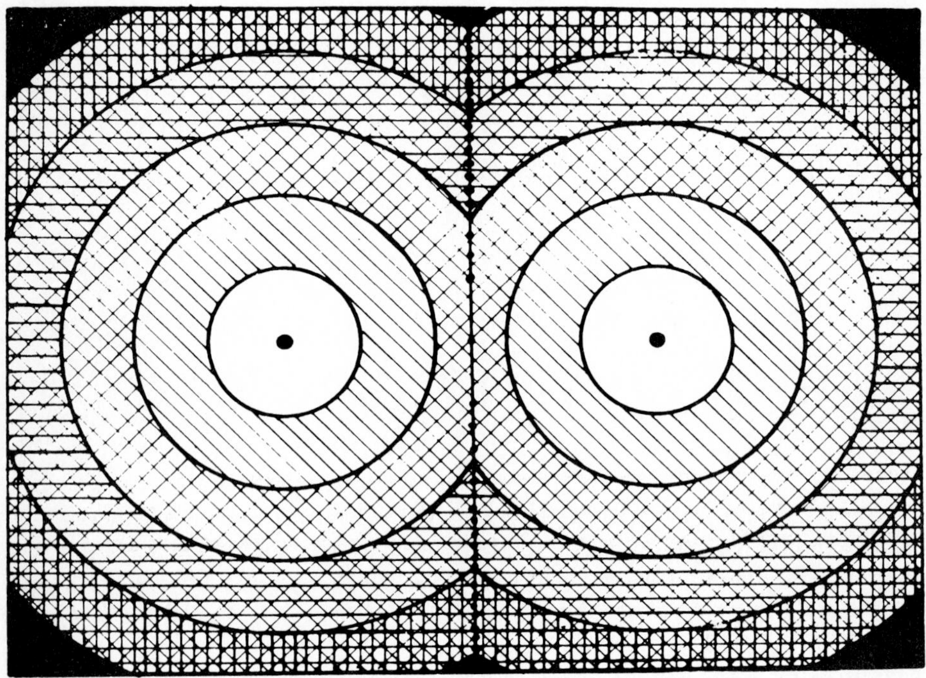

Figure 10.14 Intersection of two point-source wavefronts, resulting in extinction along their right bisector. (*From H. Blum, "A Geometry for Biology," in "Mathematical Analysis of Fundamental Biological Phenomena," Annals of the New York Academy of Sciences, vol. 231, 1974, pp. 19–30.*)

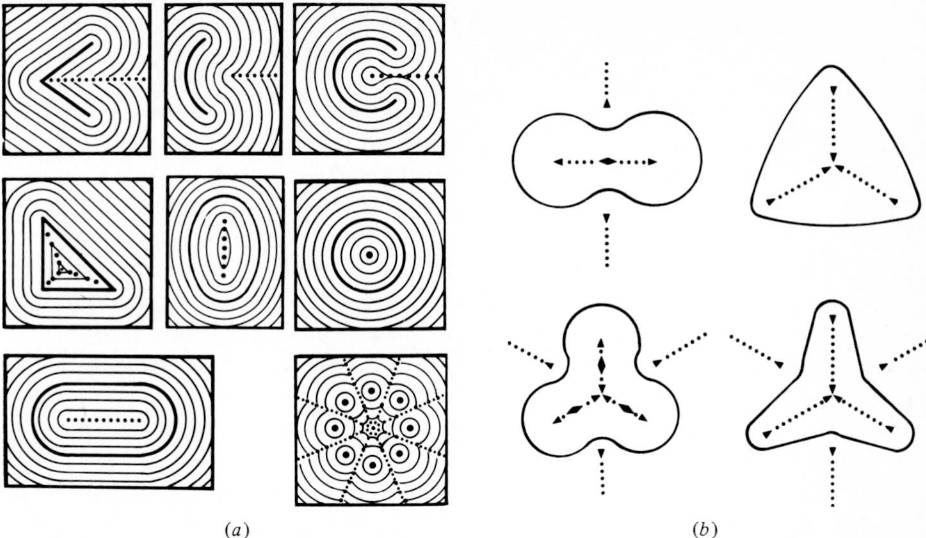

(*a*) (*b*)

Figure 10.15 Grass fire wavefronts and medial axis transforms. (*a*) A succession of grass fire wavefronts for some simple inputs. At the top the grass fire is started along open contours. The medial axis (shown dotted) occurs on the inside of the angle only, starting at the center of curvature and at a pinch at the center. The center panel shows some closed contours combining the above features. The medial axis disappears at the largest inscribed circle. Note the boundaries are convex and have no outside medial axis. The bottom panel shows the medial axis for a parallel boundary and for a set of points on a circle. In the parallel oval the grass fire disappears all at once. The points on a circle give an example whereby the object is in the ground and discrete points can be treated as equivalent to a contour in generating an object. (*b*) Medial axes of the boundaries of more complex objects. Arrows have been added to indicate direction of medial axis flow at places where it changes. Observe: (1) the appearance of double medial axes going in opposite directions at pinch in object; (2) the three-sided convergence of the medial axis that results from the three-sided objects; and (3) the existence of ground medical axes for the nonconvex objects. [*From H. Blum, "Biological Shape and Visual Science (Part I)," Journal of Theoretical Biology, vol. 38, 1972, pp. 205–287.*]

An alternative method of deriving the skeleton is by means of maximal disks. These are the largest disks that can just fit within the object at any point along its boundary. The locus of the centers of these disks comprises the skeleton, which is exactly equivalent to one obtained by using the grass fire analogy. Similarly, suppose the distance from each point in the object to its boundary is computed. Associated with each such point will be a minimum distance. The skeleton then consists of those points within the object which are simultaneously minimally distant to more than one boundary point. In fact, this last approach is the basis for most digital computations of the skeleton.

The continuous skeleton is defined in the Euclidean plane. However, the first proposed discrete skeleton used a non-Euclidean "city-block" distance metric [200, 201]. That is, the distance $d(1, 2)$ between two points was defined by

$$d(1, 2) = |x(1) - x(2)| + |y(1) - y(2)| \tag{10.18}$$

Because of this, the resulting skeleton is definitely not rotation-invariant. The algorithm suggested in [200] for computing the distance transform $D(i, j)$ requires two sequential passes. In the first, a top-down, raster scan, an integer is assigned to $D(i, j)$ which is equal to the minimum of $[1 + D(i-1, j)]$ and $[1 + D(i, j-1)]$. In the reverse right-to-left, bottom-up scan, the value at each location in the distance transform is relabeled according to the minimum of $[D(i, j)]$, $[1 + D(i+1, j)]$, and $[1 + D(i, j+1)]$. The ultimate integer array $D(i, j)$ assigns a value equal to the city-block distance from (i, j) to the boundary of the object. Local maxima of $D(i, j)$ are taken as the skeleton points [200]. An extension of this approach is the labeled distance transform presented in [69]. Here, semantic markers, which are assigned to certain subsets of pixels, are also propagated. The method is based on preserving the global outlines of the shape by incorporating and maintaining the influence of certain critical points such as corners (see Section 10.2.1) in the generation of the transform. This has the effect of filtering out various minor artifactual variations in the boundary. A striking application of this approach is for sketch completion when only subsets of the edges, regions, and objects in an image are unambiguously defined [69].

The computation of the skeleton in the Euclidean plane has also been studied [142]. A parallel algorithm which preserves both connectivity and reversibility is described in [9, 10, 241] and a sequential algorithm in [138, 150, 151]. The latter approach, which forms part of a theory of mathematical morphology [209], has been integrated into a commercial device by Leitz in West Germany [150]. Algorithms based on the computation of the maximal disk are presented in [212] and [260]. The computing time required is of order n, rather than n^2 as for methods based on the grass fire analogy. Skeletons of gray-tone pictures are examined in [174]. Three-dimensional skeletonization is presented in [1, 2, 11, 85, 126, 133, 158].

It is important that the reader understand that the above algorithms do not produce identical results. However, the computed skeleton generally does represent the global shape to a sufficient degree that simple shape features may be determined. The skeleton must first be segmented into simplified curve segments, as shown in Figure 10.16*d*. These are then analyzed and described [34]. A global feature analysis ultimately yields a labeled graph description, for example, as shown in Figure 10.16. A more complex example is discussed by Blum and Nagel [34], who present a detailed graph structure for the skeleton of a facial profile.

We now turn briefly to the second type of algorithm, thinning, mentioned at the beginning of this section. Thinning has been defined as [49]

> . . . the successive erosion of the outermost layers of a figure until only a connected unit width framework or "skeleton" remains. This skeleton runs, ideally, along the medial lines of the limbs of the figure.

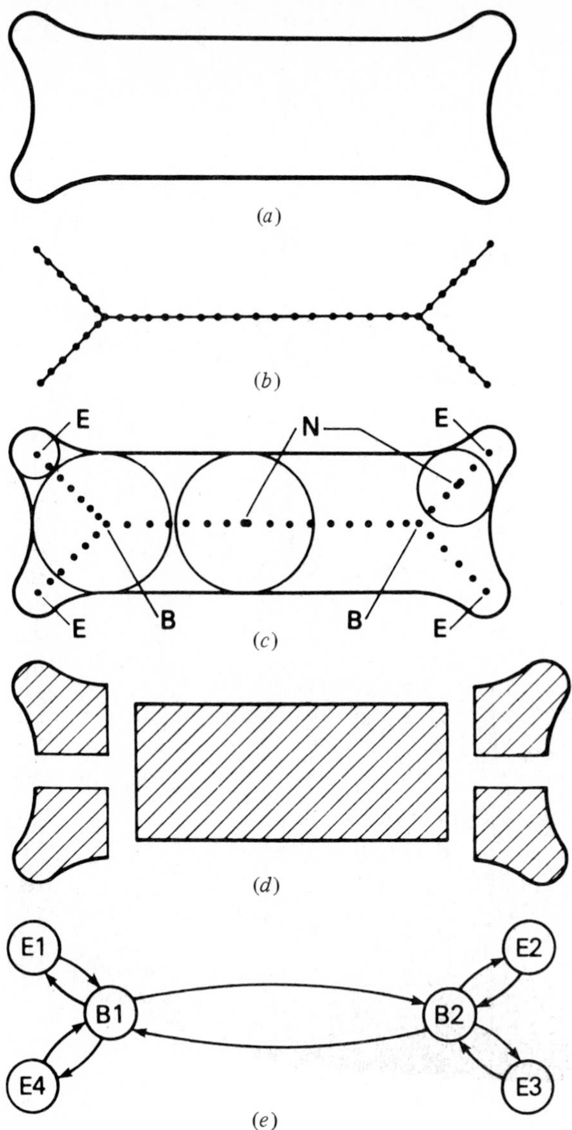

Figure 10.16 Using the shape skeleton to obtain a graph description of an object. (*a*) "Bone" shape and (*b*) its symmetric axis. (*c*) Symmetric axis POINT TYPES based on number of noncontiguous boundary touching arcs; "E" for END POINTS where only one such touching exists, "N" for normal points where two exist, and "B" for branch points where three or more exist. Normal points are the only kinds of points which can occur over an interval. (*d*) Object partitioned into SIMPLIFIED SEGMENTS at branch points. These are later given sequential descriptors. (*e*) GRAPH of the bone. (*Adapted from H. Blum and R. N. Nagel, "Shape Description Using Weighted Symmetric Axis Features," Pattern Recognition, vol. 10, no. 3, 1978, pp. 167–180.*)

Such a concept was first discussed by Sherman [221] and focuses primarily on the property of connectivity [8, 178, 192, 200]. Clearly, it is important that when pixels are deleted in the thinning process, the connectedness of the skeleton be maintained. This was not necessarily the case with the methods discussed earlier. Other requirements are that endpoints be retained and not eroded away and that the erosion process be symmetric with respect to the form. These properties are discussed in detail in [49, 170, 235].

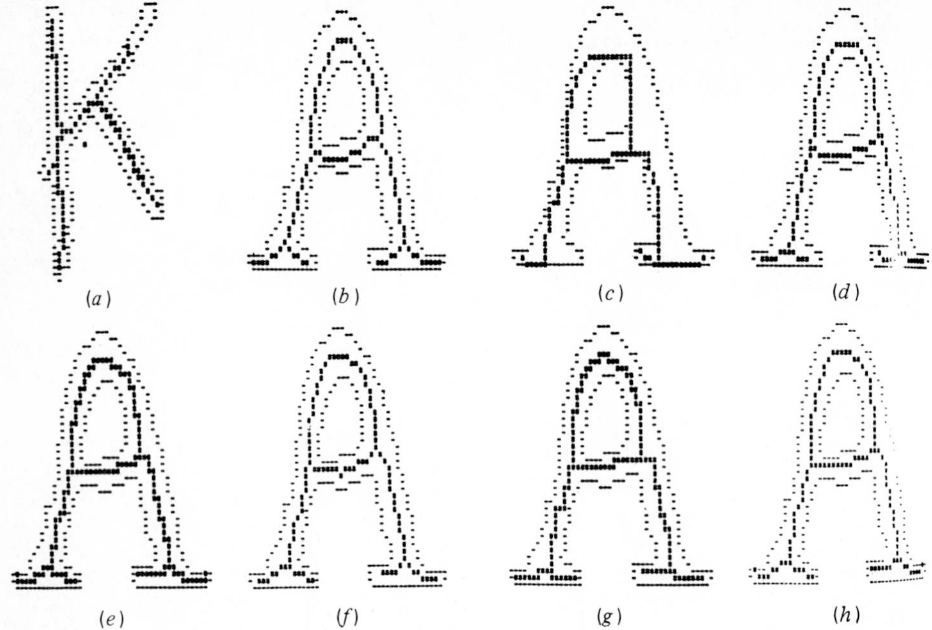

Figure 10.17 Examples of the result of shape thinning using different algorithms (see [236]). (*Adapted from H. Tamura, "A Comparison of Line Thinning Algorithms from Digital Geometry Viewpoint," Proceedings of the 4th International Joint Conference on Pattern Recognition, Kyoto, Japan, Nov. 7–10, 1978, pp. 715–719.*)

Numerous algorithms have appeared in the literature, each employing slightly different local templates for ensuring connectivity. A detailed analysis of these techniques can be found in [49, 232, 235]. Figure 10.17 illustrates some examples of these algorithms. In addition, thinning has been employed in many applications, including character recognition [26, 55, 243, 245], printed-circuit-board inspection [180], asbestos fiber counting [56], chromosome shape analysis [94], quantitative measurement of soil cracking patterns [154], fingerprint classification [140, 183], facsimile [106], and data reduction for map storage [54, 210].

Perhaps, as stated by Nagao in 1978 [148]: "There is still no definitely good method for thinning." Also, the distinction between the two approaches discussed in this section has not yet been clarified. Indeed, suggestions have been made to incorporate both propagation and thinning in a single analysis process [49, 198]. Finally, we conclude with a quotation by Blum [30], who has proposed the propagation process as a model of global brain function:

> My model consists of a volume of simple pulse receivers and transmitters in which waves propagate. It organizes the combinatorics of the primitive inputs geometrically by identification of points at which propagated waves impinge simultaneously. This leads to a system in which connection can be made independent of the distance of the exciting elements

and in which coding is precisely in location, all firing consisting of identical temporal signals. Since such a system quickly overloads with complexity, I have defined a quench process to reduce firings and to code acceptance of higher combinatorial entities. This leads to a "perceptual pot," where there is a conflict for the capture of the stimulus. Such a formulation proposes a primitive perceptual process in which the character of man as seen by the humanities and the clinical sciences is apparent. The process is built about the basic function of cognitive segmentation, which accesses a small set of the possible memory combinations to the stimulus to accept or interpret it. What results is a structure for a logic of relevance, which avoids the constraints of a hierarchical process. Mathematically, the process proposes a specific interlace in which the n-dimensional attribute space of mind can be mapped onto the three-dimensional constraints of brain.

Readers will note the similarity of this description to the relaxation labeling model discussed in Section 8.4.

Shape Decomposition Shapes are often quite complex, and it is therefore desirable to simplify their descriptions. One approach is to decompose the set of object pixels into a union of subsets. These will usually have simpler shapes and be more amenable to characterization in terms of the simple features discussed in Section 10.2. We have already seen how the skeleton can be used for decomposition. Perhaps the first literature citations dealt with the decomposition of cursive script into strokes [64, 82]. More recent attempts at segmenting what are essentially line drawings were referred to in Section 10.2.1. However, we are here concerned with the interior of an object.

The methods employed to date for this purpose are generally dependent on an a priori polygonal approximation (see Section 10.2.2) and the property of convexity. An interesting example occurs in the study of white blood cell motion [122, 123]. Figure 10.18*a* indicates a sequence of frames containing a single moving cell. The protrusions along the cell membrane are the pseudopods which are actually responsible for the cell's motion. The polygonal approximation is shown in Figure 10.18*b*. After decomposition into subsets (Figure 10.18*c*), each cell in the sequence is characterized by a star graph in which the body of the cell is represented by the central node and the pseudopods by the others. Characterization of the shape of the cell membrane is then based on an analysis of this sequence of graphs.

The problem of decomposing the set of object pixels R into a union of subsets $R_1, R_2, \ldots, R_n$ is governed by the following desirable properties [161]:

1. They must conform with our intuitive notions of "simpler" components of a "complex" picture. This is very important because our aim is shape recognition.
2. They must have a well defined mathematical characterization. This is necessary in order to be able to provide algorithms for determining them.
3. Their characterization must be subject independent, i.e., regardless of the nature of the picture from which R was derived.
4. The complexity of representing the set R through them should be comparable to the original description of R.
5. When a full set is reduced to a thin set by some type of limiting processes the "regularly" shaped components should be reduced to "regularly" shaped thin components.

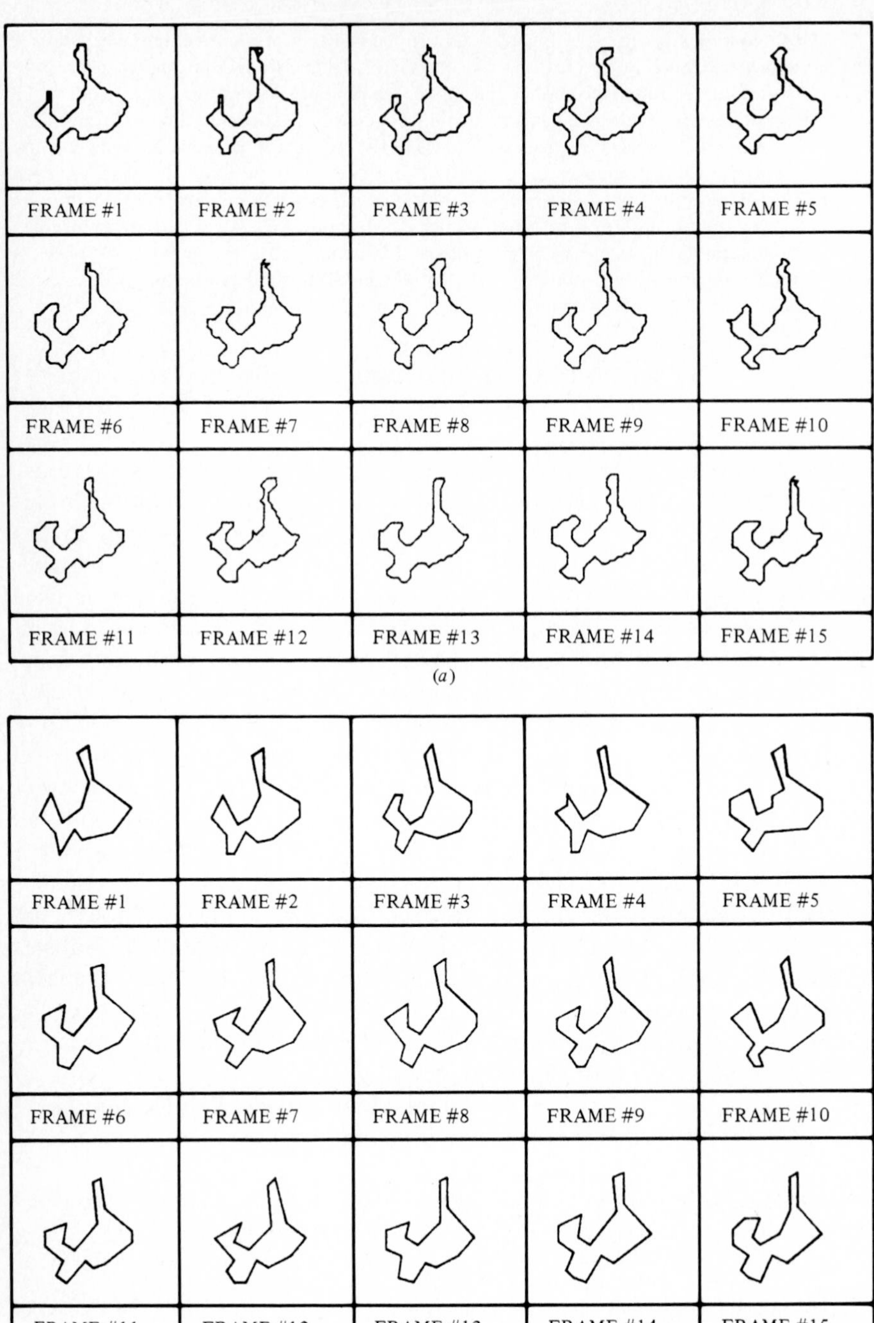

Figure 10.18(*a*) and (*b*) (Caption on page 516.)

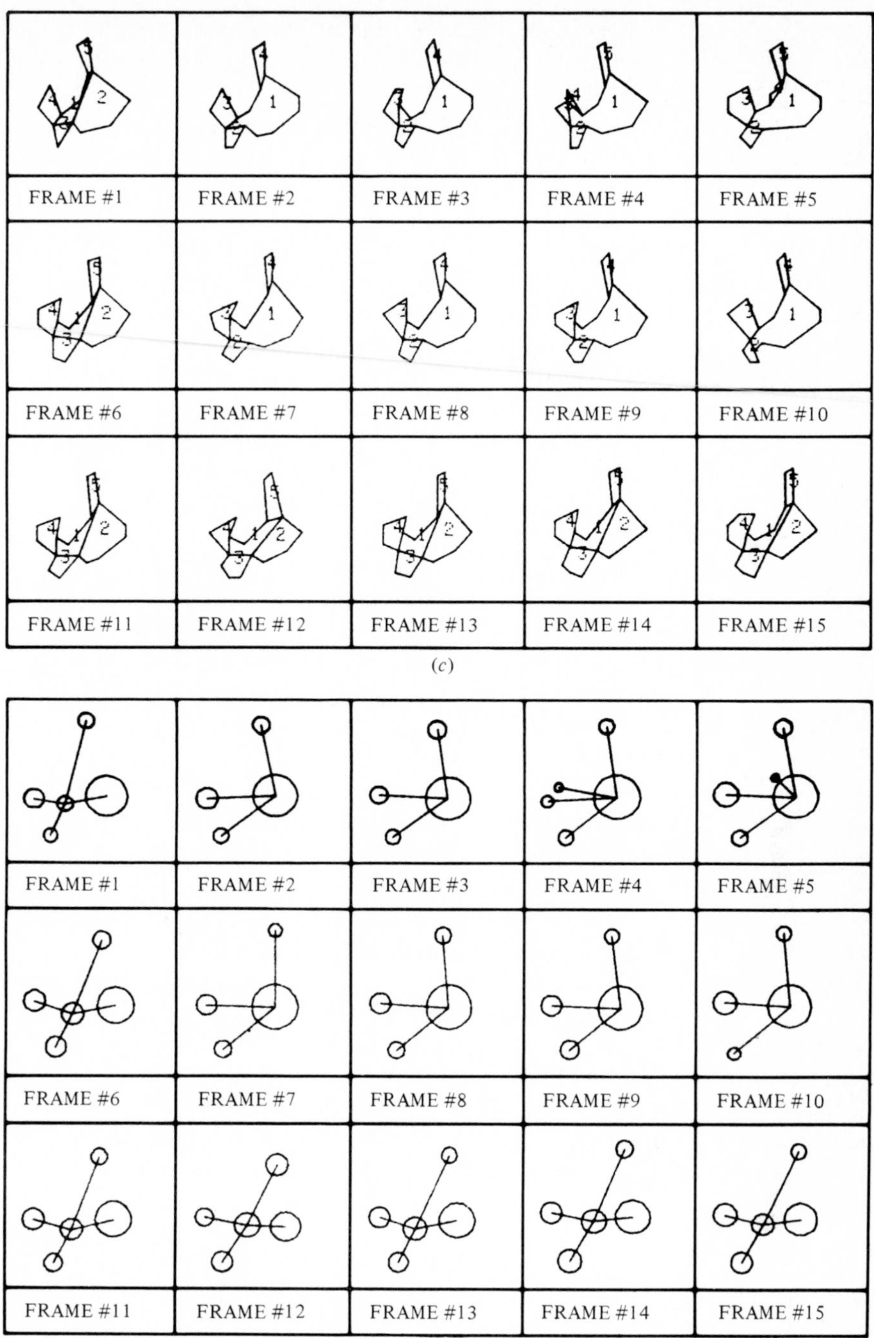

Figure 10.18(*c*) and (*d*) (Caption on page 516.)

Although the first point is perhaps the most significant, not all decomposition techniques will necessarily yield results which conform to our own intuitive graphical representation of shapes.

Even if we restrict the subsets R_i to being maximally convex, the resulting decomposition is not unique. Such a method, which requires a rather lengthy graph search for the analysis, has been proposed by Pavlidis [159, 160]. A simpler approach results if the convexity condition is relaxed somewhat [67]. In this case the decomposition is based on joining certain pairs of vertices occurring at concave corners. The resulting decomposition includes both convex sets and spirals. The method also allows for objects which contain holes.

An interesting and simple approach to decomposition, which is based on a growth process, has been described by Schachter [208]. The decomposition yields convex subsets R_i which arise out of a Delaunay tessellation of the polygon R. We shall first examine the definition of this tessellation, and then present the algorithm.

Delaunay tessellations are produced from Voronoi tessellations, which in turn are obtained by a growth mechanism. Each polygon vertex is assumed to be the nucleus of a uniform growth process propagating within the interior of R. As indicated in Figure 10.19*a*, local propagation ceases when two fronts intersect. The boundaries formed by these intersections define the Voronoi cells. Adjacent cells are termed Voronoi neighbors. The Delaunay tessellation is then obtained by joining the nuclei of each pair of Voronoi neighbors, as shown in Figure 10.19*b*. Note that Delaunay edges do not intersect each other.

The algorithm in [208] does not require a complete tessellation; only a Delaunay edge arising from a concave vertex V of polygon R need be examined, and of these, only a sufficient number to obtain a tessellation is required. The decomposition may be performed either iteratively or recursively, as follows. The nearest vertex V' to the concave vertex V is obtained such that it can be joined to it by a straight line falling within the boundaries of R. Vertex V' is said to be visible from V. Then two possibilities exist. Both depend on creating an "inner cone" of vertex V by extending towards the interior the edges of the polygon which form the angle. In the first case, V' falls within the inner cone, as shown in Figure 10.20*a*. Thus, the Delaunay edge is given by the line connecting V to V'. In the second case, shown in Figure 10.20*b*, the inner cone does not contain V'. Under these circumstances a pair of Delaunay edges on either side of the inner cone is determined. This is accomplished by a simple procedure described in [208]. The computational

---

Figure 10.18 Analysis of the structure of a moving blood cell. (*a*) Eight-connected boundaries of a sequence of cells. (*b*) Polygonal approximation of the cell shapes. (*c*) Polygonal decomposition of the cells in the sequence. (*d*) Graph representing the geometric structure of the cell as a function of time. (*Adapted from Y. M. Youssef, "Quantification and Characterization of the Motion and Shape of a Moving Cell," Ph.D. thesis, Department of Electrical Engineering, McGill University, Montreal, 1982.*)

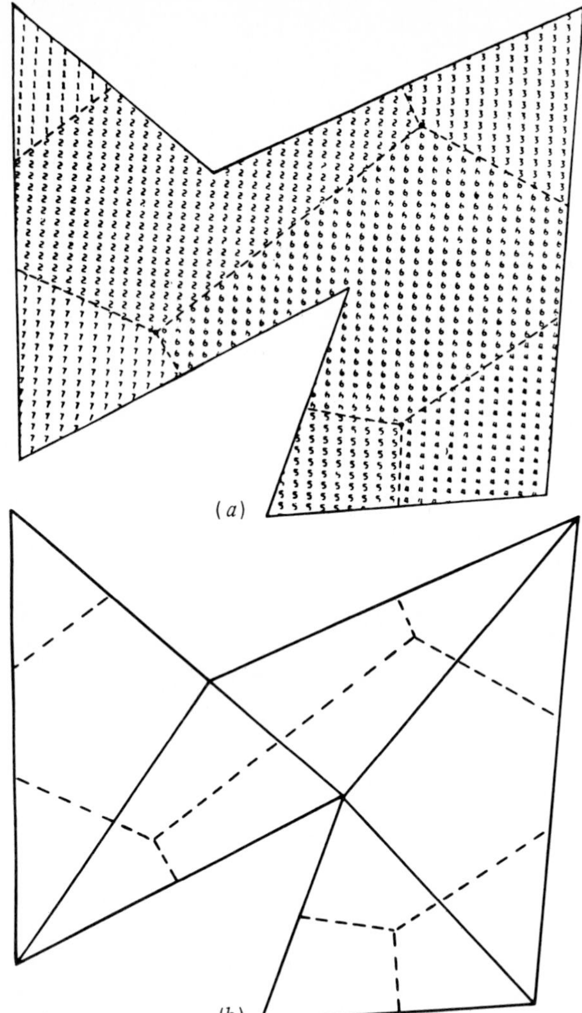

Figure 10.19 Two tessellations of a polygon. (a) Voronoi tesselation of a polygon (dashed lines). Points within the polygon are given the label of the nearest vertex. (b) Delaunay (triangle) tessellation. (*From B. Schachter, "Decomposition of Polygons into Convex Sets," IEEE Transactions on Computers, vol. C-27, no. 11, November 1978, pp. 1078–1082.*)

complexity of this approach is of order mN, where m and N are the number of polygon and concave vertices, respectively.

Another approach to object decomposition is related to the dot clustering methods of region analysis cited in Chapter 8. It is based on aggregating the lines joining all pairs of visible vertices into groups which delineate the simple parts of the shape. Graph-theoretic clustering is employed [90, 214, 247]. The computational complexity is of order N^2 [214].

Given the decomposition, a graphical representation can then be constructed to model the object shape [160]. Examples are found in the analysis of handwritten numerals [4, 171], the inspection of industrial parts [146], and the

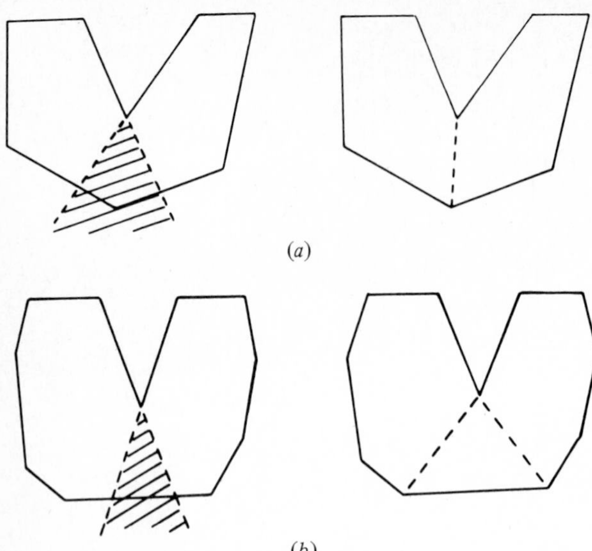

Figure 10.20 Finding the visible vertices. (*a*) Example showing a reflex vertex having a visible vertex within its inner cone. (*b*) Example showing a reflex vertex having no visible vertex within its inner cone. (*From B. Schachter, "Decomposition of Polygons into Convex Sets," IEEE Transactions on Computers, vol. C-27, no. 11, November 1978, pp. 1078–1082.*)

description of pottery found in archeological digs [96]. Various topological properties can also be extracted [196, 197] and shape symmetry examined [252]. Pattern recognition employing syntactic methods is usually the next stage of analysis [16, 83, 163, 213].

10.3.2 Shape from Projections

An interesting and powerful approach to space-domain analysis of shape is the use of the Hough transform. The basic concept is to project the elements of the boundary shape, which provide local evidence, into a different domain in which the global characteristics are more clearly manifested. Thus, two well-defined stages are indicated, first the projection into the transform space and then the analysis of shape information in that space.

The Hough transform had the unlikely origin of a patent, awarded to P. V. C. Hough in 1962, for a "method and means of recognizing complex patterns" [98]. His simple method for finding straight lines in images was first cited in the picture-processing literature by Rosenfeld [191]. However, it has recently been noted in [53] that the Hough transform is but a special case of the Radon transform published in 1917 [181]. The earliest computational improvements were due to Duda and Hart [58], and these were followed by an extensive literature appearing in the seventies. Furthermore, several interesting applications of the Hough transform approach have also been published. Biomedical examples are detection of the rib cage [254] and tumors [22, 110] in chest radiographs and finding human hemoglobin fingerprints. Scene analysis examples are line extraction in outdoor scenes [62], isolation of storage tanks in aerial photographs [118], image registration [257], and inspection of reed switches and metal surfaces [248]. Other examples include finding vanishing points in three-space [109, 149], binary image compression [219], and tracking moving targets [65, 157].

The Hough transform is a mapping from the primal sketch (see Chapter 5), which embodies the edge information, into a new space in which elementary shapes or shape components become more evident. For example, let us consider the four colinear points on edge element l', as shown in Figure 10.21*a*. Given any one of these points, say (x', y'), an infinite number of lines can be drawn to pass through it. Suppose that line l is typical. As illustrated, it may be characterized by two parameters. One is the angle θ of the normal to the line l passing through the origin (0, 0). The other is the length ρ of this normal. Thus, we observe that any arbitrary point (x, y) on line l is constrained by the following equation:

$$x \cos \theta + y \sin \theta = \rho \tag{10.19}$$

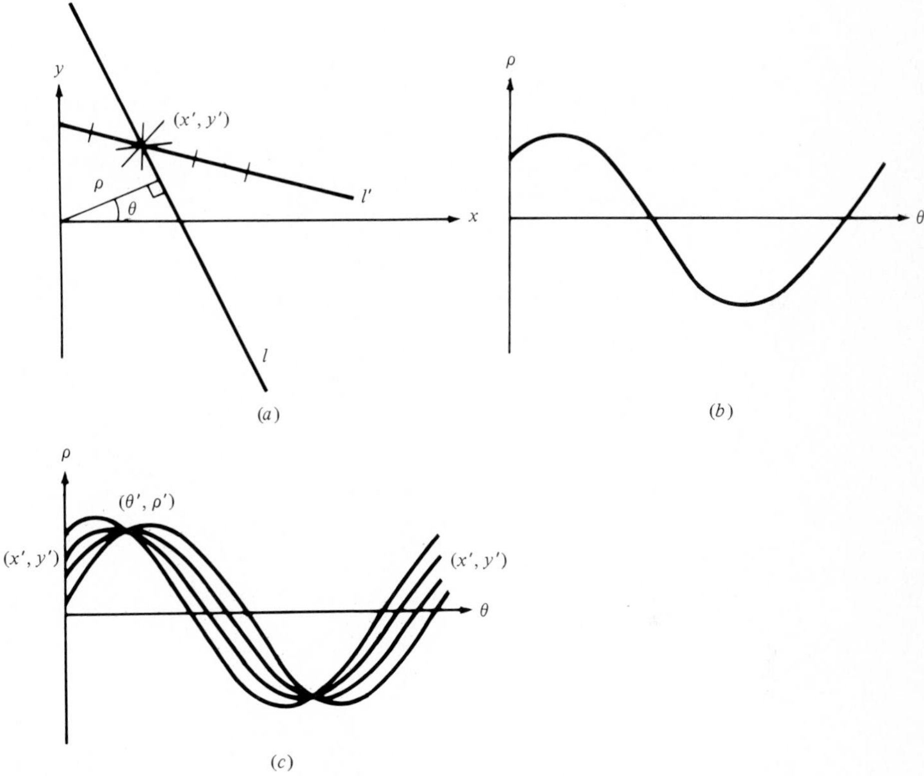

Figure 10.21 The Hough transform for points on a line. (*a*) The normal parametrization of the line l is given by $x \cos \theta + y \sin \theta = \rho$, where θ and ρ are fixed parameters. (*b*) ρ as a function of θ, where $\rho = x' \cos \theta + y' \sin \theta$ for fixed parameters x' and y'. (*c*) The Hough transform space representation of the points in (*a*). (θ', ρ') gives the parameters of the line through the points.

In this equation, treating θ and ρ as fixed parameters results in a linear relationship between the variables x and y. On the other hand, suppose we were to fix (x, y) in Equation (10.19) at (x', y'). Then, the equation will now define a relationship between θ and ρ. Moreover, this function is sinusoidal, as shown in Figure 10.21*b*. Each (θ, ρ) pair in the graph parameterizes one of an infinite number of straight lines passing through the point (x', y'). This is easily imagined by considering line l rotating around (x', y'); θ will change through 360° and ρ will vary between two limiting values. We therefore observe that the point (x', y') in the original X-Y image space has been projected into the (θ, ρ) Hough transform space as a sinusoidal curve. Indeed, we may perform the identical transformation for each of the four points in Figure 10.21*a*, as shown in Figure 10.21*c*. At this juncture we make an important observation. That is, each of the four image points lies on the same straight line l' parameterized by (θ', ρ'). Since Equation (10.19) must be satisfied for each of the four points, it follows that each of the transformed curves must pass through the point (θ', ρ'). The intersection is seen to characterize the value of (θ, ρ), which defines the line passing through all four image points. Thus the problem of detecting the colinear points in the X-Y image plane has been converted into a simpler one, in which intersections of curves are sought in the Hough transform plane.

A very simple implementation is available for discovering the point clusters produced by the intersecting lines. This is the so-called accumulator method. The approach is to quantize the variables θ and ρ into n and m levels, respectively, thereby converting the Hough transform space into an $n \times m$ array of accumulator cells. As the transform [Equation (10.19)] for a given value of (x', y') of each image point is plotted in the $\theta - \rho$ space, each accumulator cell (array element) is incremented whenever the sinusoidal curve passes through it. After all the points in the X-Y plane have been transformed, the array elements with high counts are determined, perhaps by thresholding. Obviously, these peaks in the array correspond to the intersections of many transform space curves, and the associated values of (θ, ρ) indicate the parameters of lines in the image space produced by colinear points. For example, in the case of Figure 10.21*a*, the array cell (θ', ρ') would register a count of 4; all other cells would either be equal to 1 or 0. Figure 10.22 illustrates the Hough transform accumulator array for a simple image containing four curves of colinear points.

The parameterization discussed above was proposed by Duda and Hart [58]. It has a distinct advantage over the slope-intercept formulation originally proposed by Hough. In the line representation

$$y = mx + c \tag{10.20}$$

where m and c are the slope and intercept, respectively, both these parameters are unbounded as the line in image space approaches vertical. On the other hand, θ and ρ are constrained within rigid limits:

$$0^\circ \leq \theta \leq 360^\circ$$

$$|\rho| \leq (M^2_{max} + N^2_{max})^{1/2} \tag{10.21}$$

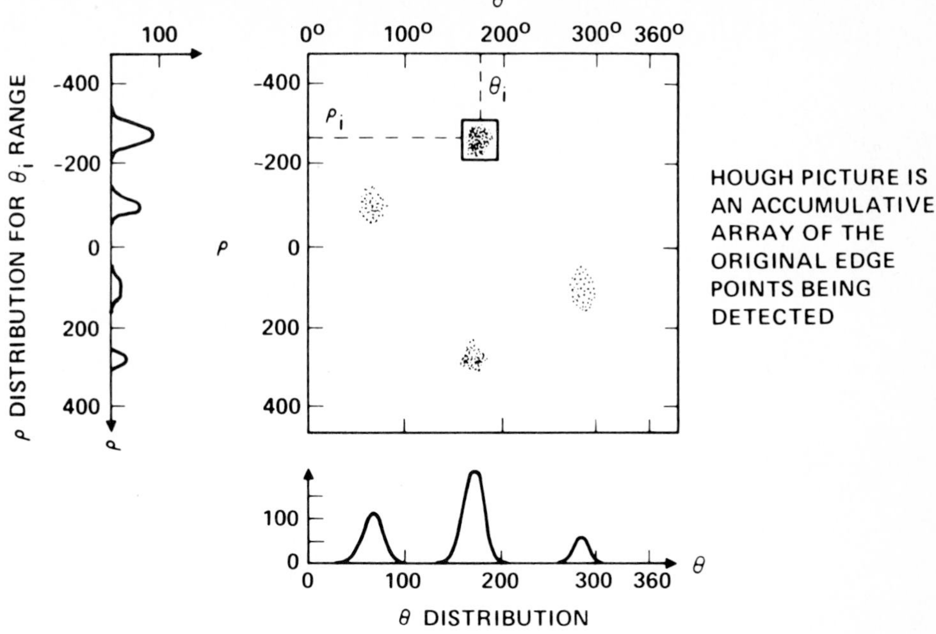

Figure 10.22 One-dimensional local minima search on the Hough picture. (*From S. A. Dudani and A. L. Luk, "Locating Straight-Line Edge Segments on Outdoor Scenes," Pattern Recognition, vol. 10, no. 3, 1978, pp. 145–157.*)

where M and N are the image dimensions. Discretization errors associated with the Hough transform are discussed in [249].

Let us study a simple example. Consider the scene containing blocks in Figure 10.23*a*, in which the Hueckel operator has been used to obtain a set of edge points Figure 10.23*b*. Dudani and Luk [62] have proposed a grouping technique for isolating the straight lines by an analysis of the Hough transform space. In the first step the two-dimensional Hough array is projected along the θ axis to give a θ distribution, as shown in Figure 10.23*c*. A moving average of this projection is employed to filter the noise, and nine clusters are obtained Figure 10.23*d*. For example, the edge elements for group 8, spanning the range 249° to 309°, are illustrated in Figure 10.23*e*. The next step involves finding the subgroups within each of the clusters already obtained. This is accomplished by examining the projection onto the ρ axis of each cluster found by ρ grouping; Figure 10.23*f* shows the ρ distribution for group 8. Figure 10.23*g* shows that after averaging, six clusters are detected. Figure 10.23*h* shows ρ group 5. The third step involves connecting two lines in the X-Y plane if they are colinear and very close together, thus signifying that they probably originated on the same line in the original image. Also, a straight-line fit is attempted for the edge elements in each (θ, ρ) subgroup, and the endpoints of the lines are determined [62]. Of course, the edge detection process was seen in Chapter 5

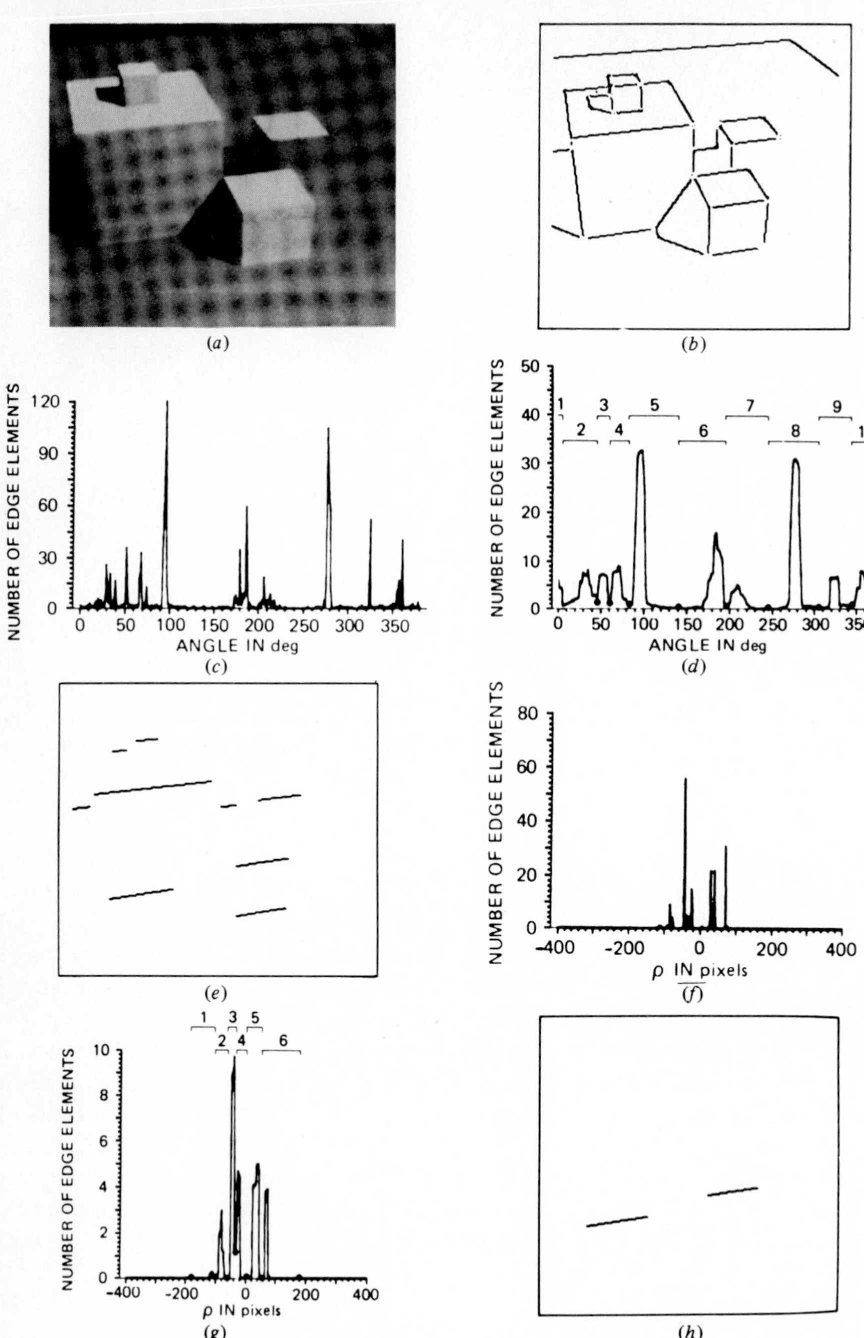
(a)
(b)
NUMBER OF EDGE ELEMENTS
ANGLE IN deg
(c)
1 3 5 7 9
2 4 6 8 1
NUMBER OF EDGE ELEMENTS
ANGLE IN deg
(d)
(e)
NUMBER OF EDGE ELEMENTS
ρ IN pixels
(f)
1 3 5
2 4 6
NUMBER OF EDGE ELEMENTS
ρ IN pixels
(g)
(h)

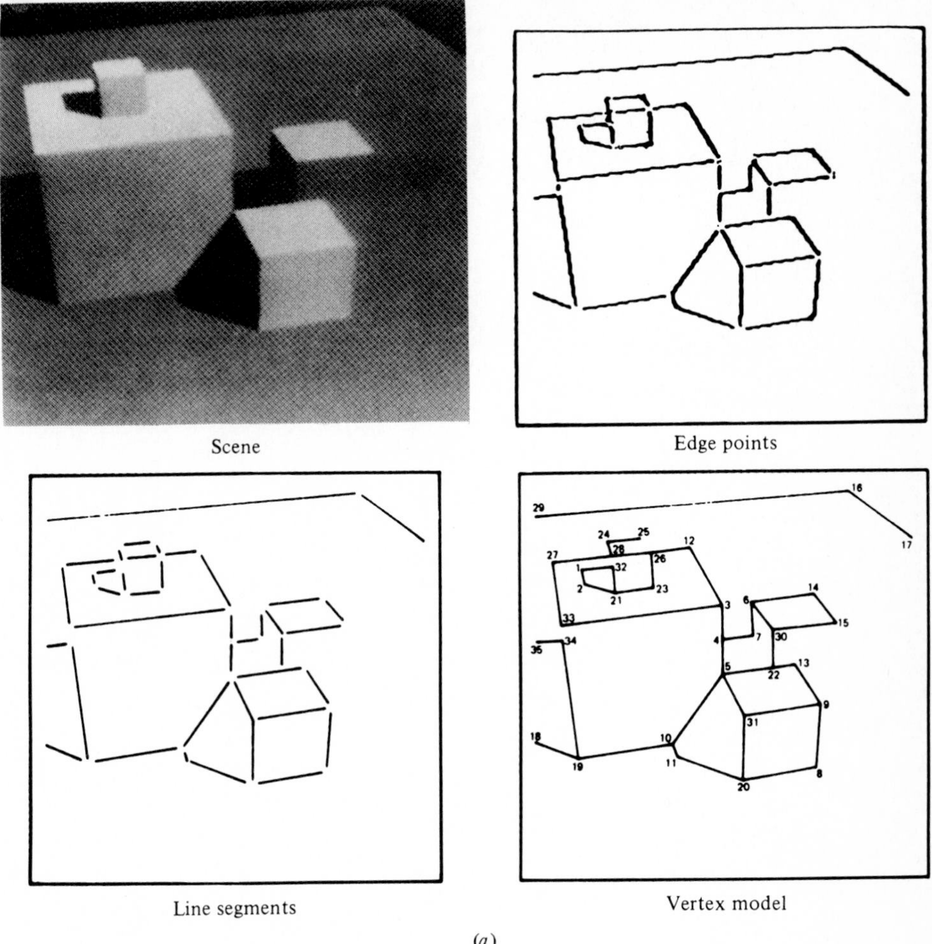

Figure 10.24(*a*) (Caption on page 524).

to be unable to perfectly obtain the outline of the objects in a scene, even a relatively simple one. Figure 10.24 shows two examples of the application of this clustering analysis.

The Hough transform can be extended to finding other analytical curves. However, the complexity increases exponentially with the number of curve parameters, which governs the dimension of the Hough transform space [58].

Figure 10.23 Locating straight-line edge segments using θ and ρ grouping. (*a*) Blocks scene. (*b*) Edge points. (*c*) θ distribution. (*d*) Grouping on averaged θ distribution. A local minimum point is given by (●). (*e*) Edge elements for θ group 8 (249° to 309°). (*f*) ρ distribution. (*g*) Grouping on averaged ρ distribution. A local minimum point is given by (●). (*h*) Edge elements for ρ group 5 (3 to 56). (*From S. A. Dudani and A. L. Luk, "Locating Straight-Line Edge Segments on Outdoor Scenes," Pattern Recognition, vol. 10, no. 3, 1978, pp. 145–157.*)

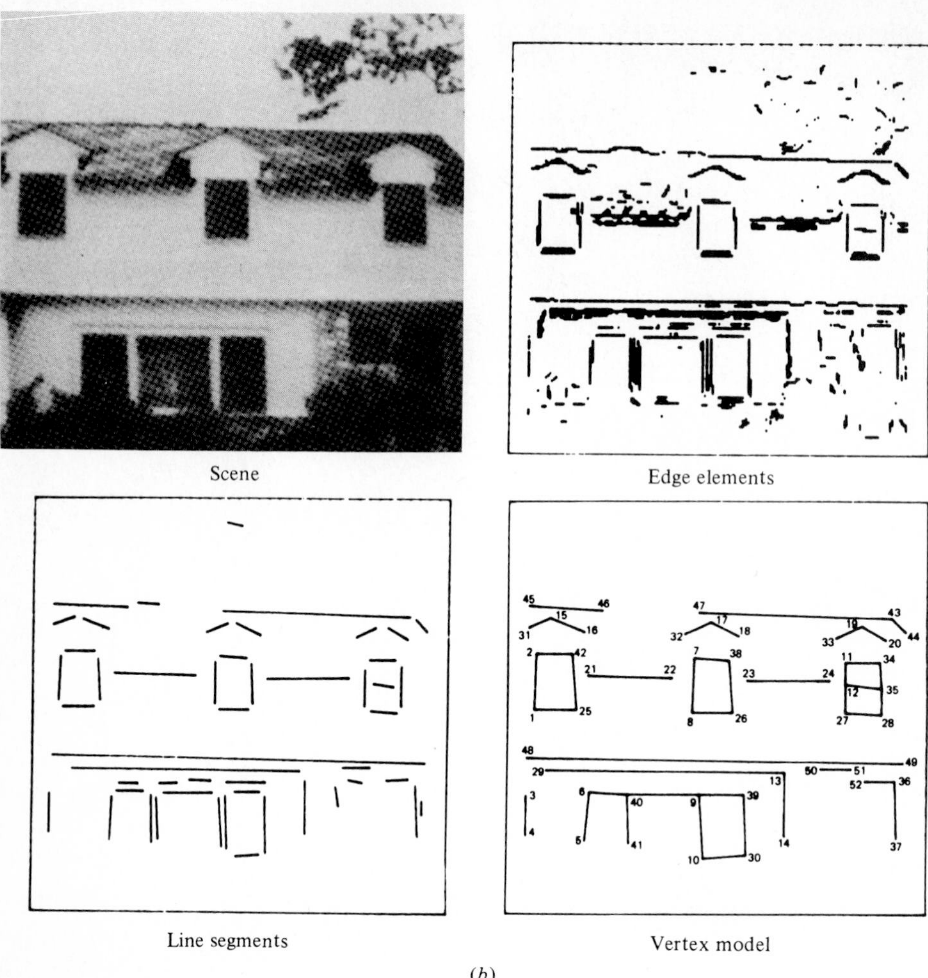

Figure 10.24 Using the Hough transform to detect geometric shapes in complex scenes. (*a*) Edge points, line segments, and vertex model for a scene containing some block structures. (*b*) Vertex model for a scene containing a house with a background of bushes and trees. (*From S. A. Dudani and A. L. Luk, "Locating Straight-Line Edge Segments on Outdoor Scenes," Pattern Recognition, vol. 10, no. 3, 1978, pp. 145–157.*)

For example, a circle in the X-Y plane

$$(x - x_0)^2 + (y - y_0)^2 = r^2 \tag{10.22}$$

is parameterized by triples (x_0, y_0, r). Here r is the radius of a circle located at $(x, y) = (x_0, y_0)$. Fixing x_0 and y_0 in this equation results in a right circular cone plotted in the three-dimensional parameter space (x_0, y_0, r). Similarly to the case with lines, the parameters of the detected circles are indicated by intersections of the cones.

Thus, object shapes other than straight lines are discussed in the literature, including corners [175], circles [22, 23, 25, 46, 110], ellipses [244], and parabolas [254]. The determination of planar surfaces in three-dimensional space is discussed in [60] and [21]. In fact, Merlin and Farber [135] and Ballard [20] present an extension to the Hough transform method which can be used to compute the best match for any arbitrary curve of specific size and orientation. It is interesting that these algorithms can be implemented by a parallel-processing machine [20]. A hierarchical generalized Hough transform is discussed in [52].

In addition to tracking lines in binary images, the Hough transform can also be employed to compute the gradient image [155, 145]. The angle θ in Equation (10.19) is assumed to be perpendicular to the direction of the gradient at each edge point. The gradient may be computed by any of the approaches discussed in Chapter 5. Thus, Equation (10.19) possesses only one unknown, ρ, which is easily found. Strong edges in the image domain can then be detected or enhanced, for example, by incrementing the appropriate accumulator cell (θ, ρ) by the magnitude of the gradient at that point [155].

As readers may have already inferred on their own, the Hough transform technique is equivalent to template matching [224, 234]. Suppose we reconsider the example illustrated in Figure 10.21. The problem of finding the four colinear points in image space was transformed into one which required the detection of a cluster of points in a parameter space. The identical result could have been achieved by scanning the image space with a line template. All values of (θ, ρ) would have to be examined. As seen in Figure 10.25*a*, at the correct orientation θ' the appropriate value $\rho = \rho'$ will yield a template response of 4. Thus, an alternative to use of the Hough transform is to rotate a template about each image point in the plane, as shown in Figure 10.25*b*. A strong response at orientation θ', as well as the coordinates (x', y'), can be used to compute ρ' from Equation (10.19). In this way the parameters of the colinear points can be determined. However, the major disadvantage from a practical

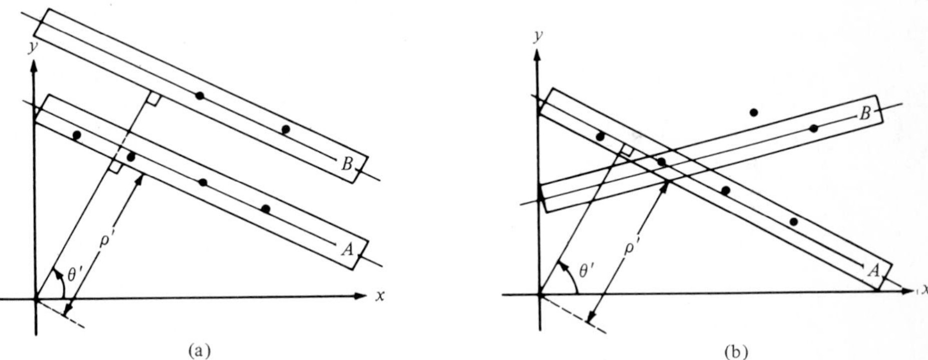

Figure 10.25 The Hough transform viewed as template matching. (*a*) The response of the line template *A* is 4, that of *B* is 2. (*b*) The response of the line template *A* is 4, that of *B* is 2.

point of view is that all values of (θ, ρ) at each (x, y) in the image must be examined. On the other hand, the Hough transform only indexes the points in the plane that are of immediate interest. The Hough transform can also be considered from the point of view of the dot-product space [68, 81, 229]. A number of applications of this approach have been reported [15, 17, 27, 59, 86, 231].

Note that in our discussion to this point we have largely ignored the issue of noise in the picture. Of course, the clustering technique mentioned previously will have some effect in excluding isolated noise points and connecting broken lines. What happens if the noise is random and uniformly distributed? It turns out that the accumulator counts in the Hough array are not as uniform as one might desire [46]. For a given θ the counts would be higher for small values of ρ than for larger ones. This bias in the projection histogram can mask the evidence of a straight line in the periphery. Other references dealing with curve detection in noisy and textured pictures are [153, 215, 216, 217, 218, 220].

We conclude this section by proposing a hypothesis to the reader. The resemblance of the Hough transform method to template matching has already been indicated, as has its reliance on histogram and accumulator array techniques. Recall the Hubel and Wiesel experiments discussed in Section 8.2, in which it appeared that the results of the template matching process in the cortex were accumulated in a tabular array. Is it possible that a Hough transform or equivalent is being computed? The required "hardware" would be relatively simple [234].

10.4 SCALAR TRANSFORM TECHNIQUES

One approach to shape description is to transform the boundary data into a new representation, one in which object translation, rotation, and size are no longer a factor. The method of moments offers such a possibility. It is simple to compute and requires only one pass over the image. However, it has two major disadvantages. The first relates to the fact that it is difficult to associate the moments with perceptual correlates. The second concerns the large dynamic range of the higher-order moments [186, 237]. This is particularly important because normally shape descriptions are restricted to the low-order moments. Also, the effect of sampling errors in digitizing the object boundary is greater for the higher-order moments. Nevertheless, there have been many applications of this methodology to pattern recognition problems. These have included printed characters and numerals [5, 117], hand-printed characters [42], chest x-rays [93], aircraft identification [61], and ship recognition [230]. A special-purpose parallel mesh moment computer has been proposed [185].

The two-dimensional $(p+q)$th order moments are defined as [100]

$$m_{pq} = \sum_i \sum_j i^p j^q I(i, j) \qquad p, q = 0, 1, 2, \ldots. \tag{10.23}$$

The image of the object $I(i, j)$ may be replaced by its binary representation $B(i, j)$. The center of gravity, or mean, of the pattern is then given by

$$\bar{x} = \frac{m_{10}}{m_{00}} \qquad \bar{y} = \frac{m_{01}}{m_{00}} \tag{10.24}$$

where we note that $m_{00} = A$, the area of the shape. This is a simple and robust measure for locating the approximate position of an object. An example is the tracking of white blood cells to determine the effect of external factors on the direction of cell motion [122].

The center of gravity $(\bar{x}, \bar{y})$ may be employed as a standard reference location. For example, consider an interesting approach to matching the shapes of two closed contours [75]. The shape representation used is referred to as the "centroidal profile" and consists of a plot of the distance from the centroid to each of the boundary points in sequence. The maximum such distance could be arbitrarily employed as the starting point. By normalizing the profile with respect to this parameter, a scale- and rotation-independent shape descriptor is achieved. An example is illustrated in Figure 10.26. Clearly, the essence of the major points of curvature along the boundary is represented by this one-dimensional profile.

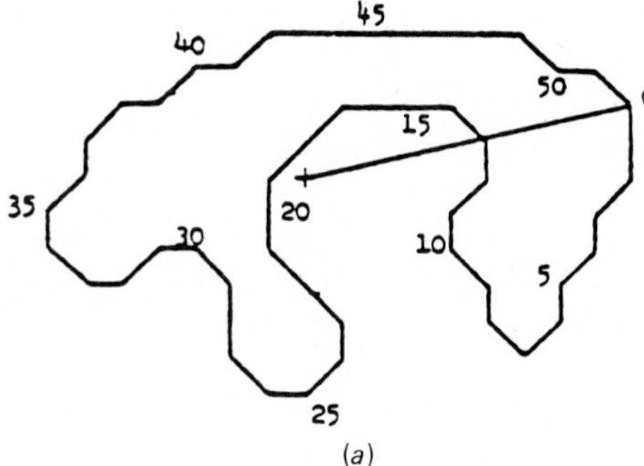

(a)

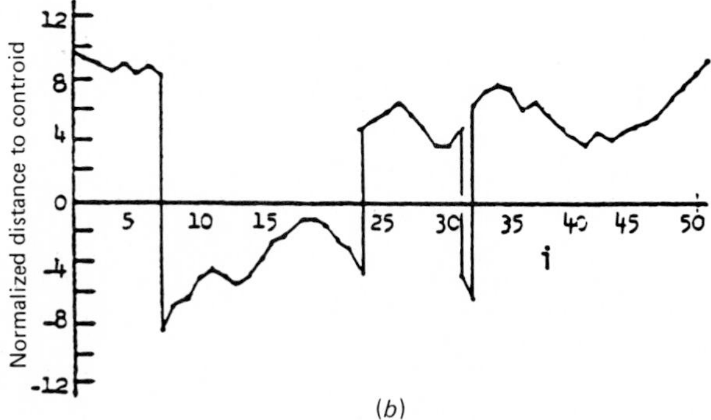

(b)

Figure 10.26 The centroidal profile indicates important aspects of the object shape. (*a*) A closed boundary chain. (*b*) The corresponding centroidal profile. (*From H. Freeman," Lines, Curves and the Characterization of Shape," Report no. IPL-TR-80-004, Image Processing Laboratory, Electrical and Systems Engineering Department, Rensselaer Polytechnic Institute, Troy, N.Y., March 1980.*)

A simplification of the moment description thus occurs if the coordinate system is shifted so that its origin coincides with $(\bar{x}, \bar{y})$. This translation normalization results in a set of central moments μ_{pq}, which are obviously invariant under translation. Thus [256]

$$\mu_{pq} = \sum_i \sum_j (i - \bar{x})^p (j - \bar{y})^q I(i, j) \tag{10.25}$$

The central moments μ_{pq} are defined in terms of the ordinary moments [100, 186, 256] by means of the following equation:

$$\mu_{pq} = \sum_{r=0}^{p} \sum_{s=0}^{q} C_r^p C_s^q (-\bar{x})^r (-\bar{y})^s m_{p-r,\, q-s} \tag{10.26}$$

where

$$C_r^p = \frac{p!}{r!(p-r)!} \tag{10.27}$$

Thus,

$$\mu_{00} = m_{00} = \mu \tag{10.28}$$

$$\mu_{10} = \mu_{01} = 0 \tag{10.29}$$

$$\mu_{20} = m_{20} - \mu\bar{x}^2 \tag{10.30}$$

$$\mu_{11} = m_{11} - \mu\bar{x}\bar{y} \tag{10.31}$$

$$\mu_{02} = m_{02} - \mu\bar{y}^2 \tag{10.32}$$

$$\mu_{30} = m_{30} - 3m_{20}\bar{x} + 2\mu\bar{x}^3 \tag{10.33}$$

$$\mu_{21} = m_{21} - m_{20}\bar{y} - 2m_{11}\bar{x} + 2\mu\bar{x}^2\bar{y} \tag{10.34}$$

$$\mu_{12} = m_{12} - m_{02}\bar{x} - 2m_{11}\bar{y} + 2\mu\bar{x}\bar{y}^2 \tag{10.35}$$

$$\mu_{03} = m_{03} - 3m_{02}\bar{y} + 2\mu\bar{y}^3 \tag{10.36}$$

Various shape attributes may be determined from these central moments.

In addition to the center of gravity given by $(\bar{x}, \bar{y})$, we may obtain the variances σ_x and σ_y in the two coordinate directions:

$$\sigma_x = \left[\frac{\mu_{20}}{m_{00}}\right]^{1/2} \qquad \sigma_y = \left[\frac{\mu_{02}}{m_{00}}\right]^{1/2} \tag{10.37}$$

On the basis of m_{00}, σ_x, and σ_y, Alt [5] has derived an additional set of normalized moments which are invariant to translation, magnification, and rubber-sheet stretching (or squeezing in the horizontal and vertical direction). Other features may also be computed. For example, the angle θ which the major axis of the shape makes with the horizontal direction is defined by

$$\theta = \tfrac{1}{2} \arctan\left[\frac{2\mu_{11}}{\mu_{20} - \mu_{02}}\right] \tag{10.38}$$

The eccentricity of the figure [see also the definition of A_9 in Equation (10.16)] is given by the following expression [251]:

$$\left[\frac{\mu_{02}\cos^2\theta + \mu_{20}\sin^2\theta - \mu_{11}\sin 2\theta}{\mu_{02}\sin^2\theta + \mu_{20}\cos^2\theta + \mu_{11}\cos 2\theta}\right]^{1/2} \tag{10.39}$$

An alternative formulation for the eccentricity is given in [237]. Spread or size may be measured by $(\mu_{20} + \mu_{02})$ [101]. These properties are non-information-preserving but are very useful as simple indicators of shape.

By using the central moments, a more elaborate set of moment-invariants can be derived [100, 203]. These are independent of size and orientation as well as of position. The seven low-order invariant moments $M_1, \ldots, M_7$, which are functions of the second- and third-order central moments, have been proposed by Hu [100, 101]:

$$M_1 = \mu_{20} + \mu_{02} \tag{10.40}$$

$$M_2 = (\mu_{20} - \mu_{02})^2 + 4\mu_{11}^2 \tag{10.41}$$

$$M_3 = (\mu_{30} - 3\mu_{12})^2 + (3\mu_{21} - \mu_{03})^2 \tag{10.42}$$

$$M_4 = (\mu_{30} + \mu_{12})^2 + (\mu_{21} + \mu_{03})^2 \tag{10.43}$$

$$\begin{aligned} M_5 = {} & (\mu_{30} - 3\mu_{12})(\mu_{30} + \mu_{12})[(\mu_{30} + \mu_{12})^2 - 3(\mu_{21} + \mu_{03})]^2 \\ & + (3\mu_{21} - \mu_{03})(\mu_{21} + \mu_{03})[3(\mu_{30} + \mu_{12})^2 - (\mu_{21} + \mu_{03})^2] \end{aligned} \tag{10.44}$$

$$\begin{aligned} M_6 = {} & (\mu_{20} - \mu_{02})[(\mu_{30} + \mu_{12})^2 - (\mu_{21} + \mu_{03})^2] \\ & + 4\mu_{11}(\mu_{30} + \mu_{12})(\mu_{21} + \mu_{03}) \end{aligned} \tag{10.45}$$

$$\begin{aligned} M_7 = {} & (3\mu_{21} - \mu_{03})(\mu_{30} + \mu_{12})[(\mu_{30} + \mu_{12})^2 - 3(\mu_{21} + \mu_{03})^2] \\ & - (\mu_{30} - 3\mu_{12})(\mu_{21} + \mu_{03})[3(\mu_{30} + \mu_{12})^2 - (\mu_{21} + \mu_{03})^2] \end{aligned} \tag{10.46}$$

The first six moments M_1 to M_6 are invariant under rotation and reflection. However, the last one, M_7, is sensitive to reflection; its value changes sign for a reflected image of the object, but its magnitude remains unaltered. Recently, a set of radial and angular moment invariants have been specified which are also invariant to reflection [185]. Often, perhaps 10 to 20 moments are required to adequately reconstruct the details of the object shape. In this case, it may be more useful to employ the simpler Zernike moments [238].

The moment invariants derived in [101] have also been used for the classification of two-dimensional projections of three-dimensional objects. An example is the case of determining the type of airplane approaching a viewing camera along a particular optical axis [61]. Three-dimensional moment invariants are derived in [205]. A discussion of the difficulties associated with the practical application of this approach appears in [99]. It has been pointed out that moment invariants are not independent of image contrast [131]. Also, they are extremely sensitive numerically when two shapes are compared. This leads to a certain sensitivity to rotational and scale changes [99, 204]. However, it has been shown experimentally that good results are obtainable for rotations up to 45° and changes of scale of about a factor of two [257]. This is illustrated in Figure 10.27, in which an optical image is scaled and rotated, and the invariant moments computed. The

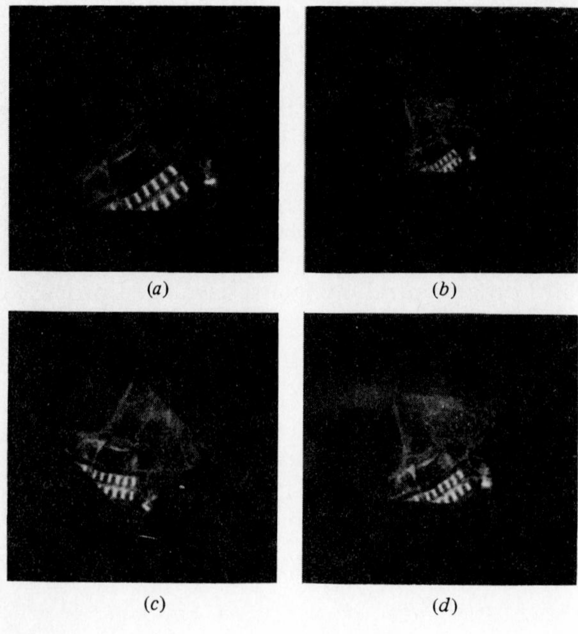

Log value			
Optical image (*a*)	Image size reduced by two (*b*)	Image rotated 45° (*c*)	Image rotated 2° (*d*)
6.24993	6.22637	6.31823	6.25346
17.18015	16.95439	16.80395	17.27091
22.65516	23.53142	19.72426	22.83652
22.91954	24.23687	20.43774	23.13025
45.74918	48.34990	40.52568	46.13627
31.82071	32.91619	29.31589	32.06803
45.58951	48.34356	40.47074	46.01707

(*e*)

Figure 10.27 Some experiments with invariant moments, indicating relative invariance to size and rotation. (*a*) Optical image. (*b*) Image size reduced by 2. (*c*) Image rotated 45°. (*d*) Image rotated 2°. (*e*) Seven invariant moments computed from the four images. (*From R. Y. Wong and E. L. Hall, "Scene Matching with Invariant Moments," Computer Graphics and Image Processing, vol. 8, no. 1, August 1978, pp. 16–24.*)

results indicate a high degree of invariance. This approach was used by Wong and Hall [256] to match fragments of radar imagery to a larger optical image. The matching process was hierarchical and employed a pyramid data structure similar to the one discussed in Chapter 5. Further experimentation and theoretical analysis with this technique are indicated.

An alternative to moment-invariants is provided by the standard moments defined in [186]. Translation normalization is achieved by means of the central moments [see Equation (10.26)]. Rotation normalization is achieved by rotating the coordinate axis θ degrees [see Equation (10.38)] to coincide with the major axis of the figure. The rotated moments ϕ_{pq} are given by

$$\phi_{pq} = \sum_{r=0}^{p} \sum_{s=0}^{q} (-1)^{q-s} C_r^p C_s^q (\cos\theta)^{p-r+s} (\sin\theta)^{q-s+r} \mu_{p-r+q-s,\, r+s} \tag{10.47}$$

where C_r^p is defined in Equation (10.27). Size normalization is achieved by using the area $A = m_{00}$. Thus, the standard moments are given by

$$N_{pq} = \frac{\phi_{pq}}{\phi_{00}^{\gamma}} \tag{10.48}$$

where $\gamma = \frac{1}{2}(p+q)+1$. We note that the standard moments for the normalized size, location, and orientation are given by $N_{00} = 1$, $N_{01} = N_{10} = 0$, and $N_{11} = 0$, respectively. In addition, six standard moments of second and third order can be determined. Standardized moments, which are also applicable to gray-level images, are given in [186]. These have been applied to the discrimination of buildings, a storage tank, and an airplane viewed in an aerial photograph.

The moments derived from a given shape constitute a feature vector which describes it. The moments can be computed for either the silhouette or the boundary of the object. The former is less affected by noise and is an indicator of gross shape. The latter is more sensitive to high-frequency detail. Both cases involve integrating information about the shape and consequently offer some degree of noise filtering. Readers interested in an examination of the problem of image reconstruction from these moments are referred to [237].

If we now consider an arbitrary curve, it may be described either by the tangent angle $\theta(p)$ or the coordinates $[x(p), y(p)]$ of the boundary. The parameter p indicates the distance along the boundary as the shape is traversed from an initium to the termination point. The latter will coincide with the initium for the generally closed shapes under consideration in this chapter. However, for any real situation in either computer or biological vision, the boundary will most likely be incomplete. In this situation, it is feasible to use the spatial-frequency transform to characterize the shape of the boundary. The reader will recall that this approach was invoked in Chapter 6 with respect to image restoration and enhancement. Typical applications of this approach have been to handwritten characters [7, 41], industrial parts [124, 177], blood cells [45], and aircraft [187, 250].

Frequency-domain descriptors of the object boundary are defined by computing the Fourier components [47]. These turn out to be good features in the sense that similar shapes yield similar descriptors. There are several advantages to this method. First, it has a solid theoretical base and is supported by experience. Second, the technique is simple to program, so-called fast algorithms exist, and special-purpose computer hardware to perform the analysis is widely available. Reconstruction of the original shape from a subset of the Fourier descriptors can be accomplished via the same methodology. Perhaps the major advantage relates to the descriptive power of the transform. The derived properties of a shape remain invariant if it is translated or rotated or its size is altered. In addition, as we observed in Chapter 6, spatial-frequency information is very suggestive of the shape properties of the object under study [108]. For example, it has been indicated that the human visual model discussed in Section 6.3 might also be employed for human shape perception [87]. Thus, the low-frequency channels provide information regarding the general shape. The higher frequencies indicate aspects of the boundary detail.

The disadvantages of frequency-domain analysis are few. One relates to the fact that only a small subset of the potentially infinite number of Fourier coefficients is normally employed. Since usually the higher-frequency components are neglected, local boundary variations tend to become obscured. Of course, this might also be cited as an advantage since when describing or comparing shapes, we are often only concerned about the global characteristics. A second point deals with the minor issue of distinguishing symmetric objects. This cannot be done solely on the basis of the magnitude of the Fourier components, and it is necessary to invoke their phase to perform the comparison.

Both moments and Fourier descriptors transform the object shape into a feature vector, which can then be used to recognize and distinguish different shapes.

REFERENCES

1. Agin, G. J., "Representation and Description of Curved Objects," Memo AIM-173, Stanford Artificial Intelligence Project, Stanford University, Stanford, Calif., 1972.
2. Agin, G. J., and Binford, T. O., "Computer Description of Curved Objects," *IEEE Transactions on Computers*, vol. C-25, no. 4, April 1976, pp. 439–449.
3. Agrawala, A. K., and Kulkarni, A. V., "A Sequential Approach to the Extraction of Shape Features," *Computer Graphics and Image Processing*, vol. 6, no. 6, December 1977, pp. 538–557.
4. Ali, F., and Pavlidis, T., "Syntactic Recognition of Handwritten Numerals," *IEEE Transactions on Systems, Man, and Cybernetics*, vol. SMC-7, no. 7, July 1977, pp. 537–541.
5. Alt, F., "Digital Pattern Recognition by Moments," *Journal of the ACM*, vol. 9, 1962, pp. 240–258.
6. Andrews, D. P., Butcher, A. K., and Buckley, B. R., "Acuities for Spatial Arrangement in Line Figures: Human and Ideal Observers Compared," *Vision Research*, vol. 13, 1973, pp. 599–620.
7. Arakawa, H., Odaka, K., and Masuda, I., "On-Line Recognition of Handwritten Characters—Alphanumerics, Hiragana, Katakana, Kanji," *Proceedings of the 4th International Joint Conference on Pattern Recognition*, Kyoto, Japan, Nov. 7–10, 1978, pp. 810–812.
8. Arcelli, C., "Pattern Thinning by Contour Tracing," *Computer Graphics and Image Processing*, vol. 17, no. 2, October 1981, pp. 130–144.
9. Arcelli, C., Cordella, L., and Levialdi, S., "Parallel Thinning of Binary Pictures," *Electronic Letters*, vol. 11, no. 7, 1975, pp. 148–149.
10. Arcelli, C., Cordella, L., and Levialdi, S., "From Local Maxima to Connected Skeletons," *IEEE Transactions on Pattern Analysis and Machine Intelligence*, vol. PAMI-3, no. 2, March 1981, pp. 134–143.
11. Arcelli, C., and Levialdi, S., "Parallel Shrinking in Three Dimensions," *Computer Graphics and Image Processing*, vol. 1, no. 1, April 1972, pp. 21–30.
12. Attneave, F., "Some Informational Aspects of Visual Perception," *Psychological Review*, vol. 61, no. 3, 1954, pp. 183–193.
13. Attneave, F., "Physical Determinants of the Judged Complexity of Shape," *Journal of Experimental Psychology*, vol. 53, 1957, pp. 221–227.
14. Attneave, F., and Arnoult, M. D., "The Quantitative Study of Shape and Pattern Recognition," *Psychological Bulletin*, vol. 53, 1956, pp. 452–471.

15. Baird, M. L., "An Application of Computer Vision to Automated IC Chip Manufacture," *Proceedings of the 3d International Joint Conference on Pattern Recognition*, Coronado, Calif., Nov. 8–11, 1976, pp. 3–7.
16. Baird, M. L., and Kelly, M., "A Paradigm for Semantic Pattern Recognition," *Pattern Recognition*, vol. 6, no. 1, June 1974, pp. 61–74.
17. Ballard, D. H., "Strip Trees: A Hierarchical Representation for Map Features," *PRIP-79, Proceedings of the IEEE Computer Society Conference on Pattern Recognition and Image Processing*, Chicago, Aug. 6–8, 1979, pp. 278–285.
18. Ballard, D. H., "Parameter Networks, Towards a Theory of Low-Level Vision," TR-75, Computer Science Department, University of Rochester, Rochester, N.Y., April 1981.
19. Ballard, D. H., "Strip Trees: A Hierarchical Representation of Curves," *Communications of the ACM*, vol. 24, no. 5, May 1981, pp. 320–321.
20. Ballard, D. H., "Generalizing the Hough Transform to Detect Arbitrary Shapes," *Pattern Recognition*, vol. 13, no. 2, 1981, pp. 111–122.
21. Ballard, D. H., and Sabbah, D., "On Shapes," *Proceedings of the 7th International Joint Conference on Artificial Intelligence, IJCAI-81*, Vancouver, B.C., 24–28 August 1981, pp. 607–612.
22. Ballard, D. H., and Sklansky, J., "A Ladder-Structured Decision Tree for Recognizing Tumors in Chest Radiographs," *IEEE Transactions on Computers*, vol. C-25, no. 5, May 1976, pp. 503–513.
23. Bastian, P., and Dunn, L., "Global Transformations in Pattern Recognition of Bubble Chamber Photographs," *IEEE Transactions on Computers*, vol. C-20, no. 9, September 1971, pp. 995–1001.
24. Batchelor, B. G., "Using Concavity Trees for Shape Description," *Computers and Digital Techniques*, vol. 2, no. 4, August 1979, pp. 157–165.
25. Bazin, M. J., and Benoit, J. W., "Off-Line Global Approach to Pattern Recognition for Bubble Chamber Pictures," *IEEE Transactions on Nuclear Science*, vol. NS-12, no. 4, August 1965, pp. 291–295.
26. Beun, M., "A Flexible Method for Automatic Reading of Handwritten Numerals," *Philips Technical Review*, vol. 33, 1973, pp. 89–101.
27. Birk, J., Kelley, N., Chen, N., and Wilson, L., "Image Feature Extraction Using Diameter-Limited Gradient Direction Histograms," *IEEE Transactions on Pattern Analysis and Machine Intelligence*, vol. PAMI-1, no. 2, April 1979, pp. 228–235.
28. Blakemore, C., and Owen, R., "Curvature Detectors in Human Vision?" *Perception*, vol. 3, 1974, pp. 3–7.
29. Blum, H., "An Associative Machine for Dealing with the Visual Field and Some of its Biological Implications," in Bernard, E. E., and Kare, M. R. (eds.) "Biological Prototypes and Synthetic Systems," Plenum, New York, 1962, pp. 244–260.
30. Blum, H., "A New Model of Global Brain Function," *Perspectives in Biology and Medicine*, vol. 10, 1967, pp. 381–408.
31. Blum, H., "A Transformation for Extracting New Descriptors of Shape," in Wathen-Dunn (ed.), "Models for the Perception of Speech and Visual Form," MIT Press, Cambridge, Mass., 1967, pp. 362–380.
32. Blum, H., "Biological Shape and Visual Science: Part I," *Journal of Theoretical Biology*, vol. 38, 1973, pp. 205–287.
33. Blum, H., "A Geometry for Biology," in "Mathematical Analysis of Fundamental Biological Phenomena," *Annals of the New York Academy of Sciences*, vol. 231, 1974, pp. 19–30.
34. Blum, H., and Nagel, R. N., "Shape Description Using Weighted Symmetric Axis Features," *Pattern Recognition*, vol. 10, no. 3, 1978, pp. 167–180.
35. Bookstein, F. L., "The Measurement of Biological Shape and Shape Change," Springer-Verlag, Berlin, 1978.
36. Bookstein, F. L., "The Line-Skeleton," *Computer Graphics and Image Processing*, vol. 11, no. 2, October 1979, pp. 123–137.

37. Bribiesca, E., and Guzman, A., "How to Describe Pure Form and How to Measure Differences in Shape Using Shape Numbers," *Pattern Recognition*," vol. 12, no. 2, 1980, pp. 101–112.
38. Brown, D. R., and Owen, D. H., The Metrics of Visual Form, *Psychological Bulletin*, vol. 68, 1967, pp. 243–249.
39. Calabi, L., and Hartnett, W. E., "Shape Recognition, Prairie Fires, Convex Deficiencies and Skeletons," *American Mathematics Monthly*, vol. 75, no. 4, April 1968, pp. 335–342.
40. Canham, P. B., "The Minimum Energy of Bending as a Possible Explanation of the Biconcave Shape of the Human Red Blood Cell," *Journal of Theoretical Biology*, vol. 26, 1970, pp. 61–81.
41. Carl, J. W., and Hall, C. F., "The Application of Filtered Transforms to the General Classification Problem," *IEEE Transactions on Computers*, vol. C-21, no. 7, July 1972, pp. 785–790.
42. Casey, R. G., "Moment Normalization of Handprinted Characters," *IBM Journal of Research and Development*, September 1970, pp. 548–557.
43. Cederberg, R. L. T., "An Iterative Algorithm for Angle Detection on Digital Curves," *Proceedings of the 4th International Joint Conference on Pattern Recognition*, Kyoto, Japan, Nov. 7–10, 1978, pp. 576–578.
44. Cerella, J., "Absence of Perspective Processing in the Pigeon," *Pattern Recognition*, vol. 9, no. 2, July 1977, pp. 65–68.
45. Chen, C.-J., and Shi, Q.-Y., "Shape Features for Cancer Cell Recognition," *Proceedings of the 5th International Conference on Pattern Recognition*, Miami Beach, Dec. 1–4, 1980, pp. 579–581.
46. Cohen, M., and Toussaint, G. T., "On the Detection of Structure in Noisy Pictures," *Pattern Recognition*, vol. 9, no. 2, July 1977, pp. 95–98.
47. Cosgriff, R. L., "Identification of Shape," Report 820-11, Ohio State University, Research Foundation, Columbus, Ohio, ASTIA AD 254 792, December 1960.
48. Danielsson, P.-E., "Reply to 'Comments on a New Shape Factor'," *Computer Graphics and Image Processing*, vol. 8, no. 2, October 1978, p. 312.
49. Davies, E. R., and Plummer, A. P. N., "Thinning Algorithms: A Critique and a New Methodology," *Pattern Recognition*, vol. 14, no. 1–6, 1981, pp. 53–63.
50. Davis, L. S., "Understanding Shape: Angles and Sides," *IEEE Transactions on Computers*, vol. C-26, no. 3, March 1977, pp. 236–242.
51. Davis, L. S., "Shape Matching Using Relaxation Techniques," *IEEE Transactions on Pattern Analysis and Machine Intelligence*, vol. PAMI-1, no. 1, January 1979, pp. 60–72.
52. Davis, L. S., "Hierarchical Generalized Hough Transforms and Line-Segment. Based Generalized Hough Transforms," *Pattern Recognition*, vol. 15, no. 4, 1982, pp. 277–285.
53. Deans, S. R., "Hough Transform from the Radon Transform," *IEEE Transactions on Pattern Analysis and Machine Intelligence*, vol. PAMI-3, no. 2, March 1981, pp. 185–188.
54. Deeker, G. F. P., and Penny, J. P., "On Interactive Map Storage and Retrieval," *Information*, vol. 10, 1972, pp. 62–74.
55. Deutsch, E. S., "Thinning Algorithms on Rectangular, Hexagonal, and Triangular Arrays," *Communications of the ACM*, vol. 15, no. 9, September 1972, pp. 827–837.
56. Dixon, R. N., and Taylor, C. J., "Automated Asbestos Fibre Counting," *Proceedings of the IOP Conference on Machine-Aided Image Analysis*, Institute of Physics, London, 1979, pp. 178–185.
57. Dodwell, P. C., "Visual Pattern Recognition," Holt, Rinehart, & Winston, New York, 1970.
58. Duda, R. O., and Hart, P. E., "Use of the Hough Transformation to Detect Lines and Curves in Pictures," *Communications of the ACM*, vol. 15, no. 1, January 1972, pp. 11–15.
59. Duda, R. O., and Hart, P. E., "Pattern Classification and Scene Analysis," Wiley, New York, 1973.
60. Duda, R. O., Nitzan, D., and Barrett, P., "Use of Range and Reflectance Data to Find Planar Surface Regions," *IEEE Transactions on Pattern Analysis and Machine Intelligence*, vol. PAMI-1, no. 3, July 1979, pp. 256–271.

61. Dudani, S. A., Breeding, K. J., and McGhee, R. B., "Aircraft Identification by Moment Invariants," *IEEE Transactions on Computers*, vol. C-26, no. 1, January 1977, pp. 39–46.
62. Dudani, S. A., and Luk, A. L., "Locating Straight-Line Edge Segments on Outdoor Scenes," *Pattern Recognition*, vol. 10, no. 3, 1978, pp. 145–157.
63. Eccles, M. J., McQueens, P. C., and Rosen, D., "Analysis of the Digitized Boundaries of Planar Objects," *Pattern Recognition*, vol. 9, no. 1, January 1977, pp. 31–41.
64. Eden, M., "Handwriting and Pattern Recognition," *IRE Transactions on Information Theory*, vol. IT-8, no. 2, February 1962, pp. 160–166.
65. Falconer, D. G., "Target Tracking With the Hough Transform and Fourier-Hough Transform," Technical Note 202, SRI International, Menlo Park, Calif., December 1979. Also presented at the 11th and 13th Annual Asilomar Conferences on Circuits, Systems, and Computers, Asilomar, Calif.
66. Feng, F. H.-Y., and Pavlidis, T., "Finding 'Vertices' in a Picture," *Computer Graphics and Image Processing*, vol. 2, no. 2, October 1973, pp. 103–117.
67. Feng, F. H.-Y., and Pavlidis, T., "Decomposition of Polygons into Simpler Components: Feature Generation for Syntactic Pattern Recognition," *IEEE Transactions on Computers*, vol. C-24, no. 6, June 1975, pp. 636–650.
68. Firschein, O., Eppler, W., and Fischler, M. A., "A Fast Defect Measurement Algorithm and Its Array Processor Mechanization," *Proceedings of the IEEE Conference on Pattern Recognition and Image Processing, PRIP-79*, Chicago, Aug. 6–8, 1979, pp. 109–113.
69. Fischler, P., and Barrett, P., "An Iconic Transform for Sketch Completion and Shape Abstraction," *Computer Graphics and Image Processing*, vol. 13, no. 4, August 1980, pp. 334–360.
70. Freeman, H., "A Technique for the Classification and Recognition of Geometric Patterns," *Proceedings of the 3d International Congress on Cybernetics*, Namur, Belgium, 1961, pp. 348–369.
71. Freeman, H., "On the Encoding of Arbitrary Geometric Configurations," *IRE Transactions on Electronic Computers*, vol. EC-10, no. 2, June 1961, pp. 260–268.
72. Freeman, H., "On the Classification of Line-Drawing Data," in Dunn, W. (ed.), "Models for the Perception of Speech and Visual Form," MIT Press, Cambridge, Mass., 1967, pp. 408–412.
73. Freeman, H., "Boundary Encoding and Processing," in Lipkin, B. S., and Rosenfeld, A. (eds.) "Picture Processing and Psychopictorics," Academic, New York, 1970, pp. 241–266.
74. Freeman, H., "Computer Processing of Line Drawing Images," *Computing Surveys*, vol. 5, no. 1, March 1974, pp. 57–97.
75. Freeman, H., "Shape Description Via the Use of Critical Points," *Proceedings of the IEEE Computer Society Conference on Pattern Recognition and Image Processing, PRIP-77*, Rensselaer Polytechnic Institute, Troy, N.Y., June 6–8, 1977, pp. 168–174.
76. Freeman, H., "Shape Description Via the Use of Critical Points," *Pattern Recognition*, vol. 10, no. 3, 1978, pp. 159–166.
77. Freeman, H., "Lines, Curves and the Characterization of Shape," Report no. IPL-TR-80-004, Image Processing Laboratory, Electrical and Systems Engineering Department, Rensselaer Polytechnic Institute, Troy, N.Y., March 1980.
78. Freeman, H., and Davis, L. S., "A Corner-Finding Algorithm for Chain-Coded Curves," *IEEE Transactions on Computers*, vol. C-26, no. 3, March 1977, pp. 297–303.
79. Freeman, H., and Glass, J. M., "On the Quantization of Line-Drawing Data," *IEEE Transactions on Systems, Science, and Cybernetics*, vol. SSC-5, no. 1, January 1969, pp. 70-79.
80. Freeman, H., and Saghri, A., "Generalized Chain Codes for Planar Curves," *Proceedings of the 4th International Joint Conference on Pattern Recognition*, Kyoto, Japan, Nov. 7–10, 1978, pp. 701–703.
81. Freeman, H., and Shapira, R., "Determining the Minimum-Area Enclosing Rectangle for an Arbitrary Enclosed Curve," *Communications of the ACM*, vol. 18, no. 18, July 1975, pp. 409–413.

82. Frischkopf, L. S., and Harmon, L. D., "Machine Reading of Cursive Script," in Cherry, C. (ed.), "Proceedings of the Symposium on Information Theory," Butterworths, London, 1961, pp. 306–316.
83. Fu, K. S., "Syntactic Methods in Pattern Recognition," Academic, New York, 1974.
84. Fu, K. S., and Lu, S. Y., "A Clustering Procedure for Syntactic Patterns," IEEE *Transactions Systems, Man, and Cybernetics*, vol. SMC-7, no. 10, October 1977, pp. 734–742.
85. Garibotto, G., and Tosini, R., "Description and Classification of 3-D Objects," *Proceedings of the 6th International Conference on Pattern Recognition*, Munich, Oct. 19–22, 1982, pp. 833–835.
86. Gilbert, A. L., Giles, M. K., Flachs, G. M., Rogers, R. B., and U, Y. H., "A Real-Time Video Tracking System," *IEEE Transactions on Pattern Analysis and Machine Intelligence*, vol. PAMI-2, no. 1, January 1980, pp. 47–56.
87. Ginsburg, A. P., Cannon, M. W., and Nelson, M. A., "Suprathreshold Processing of Complex Visual Stimuli: Evidence for Linearity in Contrast Perception," *Science*, vol. 208, May 9 1980, pp. 619–621.
88. Grant, G., and Reid, A. F., "An Efficient Algorithm for Boundary Tracing and Feature Extraction," *Computer Graphics and Image Processing*, vol. 17, no. 3, November 1981, pp. 225–237.
89. Gray, S. B., "Local Properties of Binary Images in Two Dimensions," *IEEE Transactions on Computers*, vol. C-20, no. 5, May 1971, pp. 551–561.
90. Guerra, C., and Pieroni, G. G., "A Graph-Theoretic Method for Decomposing Two-Dimensional Polygonal Shapes into Meaningful Parts," *IEEE Transactions on Pattern Analysis and Machine Intelligence*, vol. PAMI-4, no. 4, July 1982, pp. 405–408.
91. Guzman, A., and Bribiesca, E., "Shape Description and Shape Similarity Measurement for Two-Dimensional Regions," *Proceedings of the 4th International Joint Conference on Pattern Recognition*, Kyoto, Japan, Nov. 7–10, 1978, pp. 608–612.
92. Haber, R. N., and Wilkinson, L., "Perceptual Components of Computer Displays," *IEEE Computer Graphics and Applications*, vol. 2, no. 3, May 1982, pp. 23–34.
93. Hall, E. L., Crawford, W. O., and Roberts, F. E., "Computer Classification of Pneumoconiosis From Radiographs of Coal Workers," *IEEE Transactions on Biomedical Engineering*, vol. BME-22, no. 6, November 1975, pp. 518–527.
94. Hilditch, C. J., "Linear Skeletons from Square Cupboards," in Meltzar, B., and Michie, D. (eds.), "Machine Intelligence 4," Edinburgh University Press, 1969, pp. 403–420.
95. Ho, C.-S., "Precision of Vision System," *Conference Record, 1982 Workshop on Industrial Applications of Machine Vision*, Research Triangle Park, N.C., May 3–5, 1982, pp. 153–159.
96. Hollerbach, J. M., "Hierarchical Shape Description of Objects by Selection and Modification of Prototypes," Report no. AI-TR-346, Artificial Intelligence Laboratory, Massachusetts Institute of Technology, Cambridge, Mass., November 1975.
97. Horowitz, S. L., "Peak Recognition in Waveforms," in Fu, K. S. (ed.), "Syntactic Pattern Recognition, Applications," Springer-Verlag, New York, 1977, pp. 31–49.
98. Hough, P. V. C., Method and Means for Recognizing Complex Patterns, U.S. Patent 3,069,654, 1962.
99. Hsia, T. C., "A Note on Invariant Moments in Image Processing," *IEEE Transactions on Systems, Man, and Cybernetics*, vol. SMC-11, no. 12, December 1981, pp. 831–834.
100. Hu, M.-K., "Pattern Recognition by Moment Invariants," *Proceedings of the IEEE*, vol. 49, no. 9, September 1961, p. 1428.
101. Hu, M.-K., "Visual Pattern Recognition by Moment Invariants," *IRE Transactions on Information Theory*, vol. IT-8, no. 2, February 1962, pp. 179–187.
102. Ishikawa, S., "Geometrical Indices Characterizing Psychological Goodness of Random Shapes," *Proceedings of the 4th International Joint Conference on Pattern Recognition*, Kyoto Japan, Nov. 7–10, 1978, pp. 414–416.
103. James, W., "The Principles of Psychology," Holt, New York, 1890 (republished by Dover, New York, 1959).

104. Jarvis, J. F., "Regular Expressions as a Feature Selection Language for Pattern Recognition," *Proceedings of the 3d International Joint Conference on Pattern Recognition*, Coronado, Calif., Nov. 8–11, 1976, pp. 189–192.
105. Johnston, E., and Rosenfeld, A., "Angle Detection on Digital Curves," *IEEE Transactions on Computers*, vol. C-22, no. 9, September 1973, pp. 875–878.
106. Judd, I. D., "Compression of Binary Images by Stroke Encoding," *IEE Journal of Computer and Digital Techniques*, vol. 2, 1979, pp. 41–48.
107. Kasvand, T., "Some Observations on Linguistics for Scene Analysis," *Proceedings of the Conference on Computer Graphics, Pattern Recognition, and Data Structure*, Los Angeles, May 14–16, 1975, pp. 118–124.
108. Kaye, B. H., and Naylor, A. G., "An Optical Information Procedure for Characterizing the Shape of Fine Particle Images," *Pattern Recognition*, vol. 4, no. 2, May 1972, pp. 195–199.
109. Kender, J. R., "Shape from Texture: An Aggregation Transform That Maps a Class of Textures into Surface Orientation," *Proceedings of the 6th International Joint Conference on Artificial Intelligence, IJCAI-79*, Tokyo, 1979, pp. 475–480.
110. Kimme, D., Ballard, D., and Sklansky, J., "Finding Circles by an Array of Accumulators," *Communications of the ACM*, vol. 18, no. 2, February 1975, pp. 120–122.
111. Koffka, K., "Principles of Gestalt Psychology," Harcourt Brace, New York, 1935.
112. Kruger, R. P., and Thompson, W. B., "A Technical and Economic Assessment of Computer Vision for Industrial Inspection and Robotic Assembly," *Proceedings of the IEEE*, vol. 69, no. 12, December 1981, pp. 1524–1538.
113. Kruse, B., and Rao, C. V. K., "A Matched Filtering Technique for Corner Detection," *Proceedings of the 4th International Joint Conference on Pattern Recognition*, Kyoto, Japan, Nov. 7–10, 1978, pp. 642–644.
114. Kulpa, Z., "Area and Perimeter Measurement of Blobs in Discrete Binary Pictures," *Computer Graphics and Image Processing*, vol. 6, no. 5, 1977, pp. 434–451.
115. Kulpa, Z., "On the Properties of Discrete Circles, Rings, and Disks," *Computer Graphics and Image Processing*, vol. 10, no. 4, August 1979, pp. 348–365.
116. Kurozumi, Y., and Davis, W. A., "Polygonal Approximation by the Minimax Method," *Computer Graphics and Image Processing*, vol. 19, no. 3, July 1982, pp. 248–264.
117. Lambert, P. F., "Designing Pattern Categorizers With Extremal Paradigm Information," in Watanabe, S. (ed.), "Methodologies of Pattern Recognition," Academic, New York, 1969, pp. 359–381.
118. Lantz, K. A., Brown, C. M., and Ballard, D. H., "Model-Driven Vision Using Procedure Description: Motivation and Application to Photointerpretation and Medical Diagnosis," *Proceedings of the 22d International Symposium, Society of Photo-optical Instrumentation Engineers*, San Diego, August 1978.
119. Lee, E. T., "Proximity Measures for the Classification of Geometric Figures," *Journal of Cybernetics*, vol. 2, no. 4, 1972, pp. 43–59.
120. Lee, E. T., "Shape-Oriented Classification Storage and Retrieval of Leukocytes," *Proceedings of the 3d International Joint Conference on Pattern Recognition*, Coronado, Calif., Nov. 8–11, 1976, pp. 870–874.
121. Levine, M. D., "Feature Extraction: A Survey," *Proceedings of the IEEE*, vol. 57, no. 8, August 1969, pp. 1391–1407.
122. Levine, M. D., Noble, P. B., and Youssef, Y. M., "Understanding Blood Cell Motion," *Computer Graphics and Image Processing*, vol. 21, no. 1, January 1983, pp. 185–209.
123. Levine, M. D., Noble, P. B., and Youssef, Y. M., "A Rule-Based System for Characterizing Blood Cell Motion" in Huang, T. S. (ed.), "Image Sequence Processing and Dynamic Scene Analysis," NATO ASI series, vol. F2, Springer-Verlag, Berlin, 1983, pp. 663–709.
124. Levine, M. D., and Ting, D., "Intermediate Level Picture Interpretation Using Complete Two-Dimensional Models," *Computer Graphics and Image Processing*, vol. 16, 1981, pp. 185–209.
125. Levine, M. D., Youssef, Y. M., Noble, P. B., and Boyarsky, R., "The Quantification of Blood Cell Motion by a Method of Automatic Digital Picture Processing," *IEEE Transactions on Pattern Analysis and Machine Intelligence*, vol. PAMI-2, no. 5, 1980, pp. 444-450.

126. Lobregt, S., Verbeek, P. W., and Groen, F. C. A., "Three-Dimensional Skeletonization: Principle and Algorithm," *IEEE Transactions on Pattern Analysis and Machine Intelligence*, vol. PAMI-2, no. 1, January 1980, pp. 75–77.
127. Lock, A., and Collett, T., "A Toad's Devious Approach to Its Prey: a Study of Some Complex Uses of Depth Vision," *Journal of Comparative Physiology*, vol. 131, 1979, pp. 179–189.
128. Lock, A., and Collett, T., "The Three-Dimensional World of a Toad," *Proceedings of the Royal Society, London*, ser. B, vol. 206, 1980, pp. 481–487.
129. Lozano-Perez, T., "Parsing Intensity Profiles," *Computer Graphics and Image Processing*, vol. 6, no. 1, February 1977, pp. 43–60.
130. Mach, E., "The Analysis of Sensations" (translated from the 5th German ed.), Open Court, Chicago, 1914 (republished by Dover, New York, 1959).
131. Maitra, S., "Moment Invariants," *Proceedings of the IEEE*, vol. 67, no. 4, April 1979, pp. 697–699.
132. Marr, D., "Early Processing of Visual Information," *Philosophical Transactions of the Royal Society, London*, ser. B, vol. 275, 1976, pp. 483–524.
133. Marr, D., and Nishihara, K., "Representation and Recognition of the Spatial Organization of Three Dimensional Shapes," AI Memo 416, Massachusetts Institute of Technology, Cambridge, Mass., May 1977.
134. McKee, J. W., and Aggarwal, J. K., "Computer Recognition of Partial Views of Curved Objects," *IEEE Transactions on Computers*, vol. C-26, no. 8, August 1977, pp. 790–800.
135. Merlin, P. M., and Farber, D. J., "A Parallel Mechanism for Detecting Curves in Pictures," *IEEE Transactions on Computers*, vol. C-24, no. 1, January 1975, pp. 96–98.
136. Méró, L., "An Optimal Line Following Algorithm," *IEEE Transactions on Pattern Analysis and Machine Intelligence*, vol. PAMI-3, no. 5, September 1981, pp. 593–598.
137. Merrill, R. D., "Representation of Contours and Regions for Efficient Computer Search," *Communications of the ACM*, vol. 16, no. 2, February 1973, pp. 69–82.
138. Meyer, F., "Mathematical Morphology Used for Quantitative Cytology," in Rybak, B. (ed.), "Advanced Technobiology," Sijthoff and Noordhoff, Alphen aan den Rijn, Netherlands, 1979, pp. 65–95.
139. Minsky, M., and Papert, S., "Perceptrons," M.I.T. Press, Cambridge, Mass., 1968.
140. Moayer, B., and Fu, K. S., "A Tree System Approach of Fingerprint Pattern Recognition," *IEEE Transactions on Computers*, vol. C-25, no. 3, March 1976, pp. 262–274.
141. Mohwinkel, C., and Kurz, L., "Computer Picture Processing and Enhancement by Localized Operations," *Computer Graphics and Image Processing*, vol. 5, no. 4, December 1976, pp. 401–424.
142. Montanari, U., "A Method for Obtaining Skeletons Using a Quasi-Euclidean Distance," *Journal of the ACM*, vol. 15, no. 4, October 1968, pp. 600–625.
143. Montanari, U., "Continuous Skeletons from Digitized Images," *Journals of the ACM*, vol. 16, no. 4, October 1969, pp. 534–549.
144. Montanari, U., "A Note on Minimal Length Polygonal Approximation to a Digitized Contour," *Communications of the ACM*, vol. 13, no. 1, January 1970, pp. 41–46.
145. Mori, S., Monden, Y., and Mori, T., "Edge Representation in Gradient Space," *Computer Graphics and Image Processing*, vol. 2, nos. 3 and 4, December 1973, pp. 321–325.
146. Mundy, J. L., and Joynson, R. E., "Automatic Visual Inspection Using Syntactic Analysis," *PRIP-77, Proceedings of the IEEE Computer Society Conference on Pattern Recognition and Image Processing*, Rensselaer Polytechnic Institute, Troy, N.Y., June 6–8, 1977, pp. 144–147.
147. Mylopoulos, J. P., and Pavlidis, T., "On the Topological Properties of Quantized Spaces (Parts I and II)," *Journal of the ACM*, vol. 18, no. 2, April 1971, pp. 239–246.
148. Nagao, M., "A Survey of Pattern Recognition and Picture Processing," in Latombe, J. C. (ed.), "Artificial Intelligence and Pattern Recognition in Computer Aided Design," North Holland, Amsterdam, 1978, pp. 35–64.
149. Nakatani, H., Kimura, S., Saito, O., and Kitahashi, T., "Extraction of Vanishing Point and Its Application to Scene Analysis Based on Image Sequence," *Proceedings of the 5th International Conference on Pattern Recognition*, Miami Beach, Dec. 1–4 1980, pp. 370–372.

150. Nawrath, R., and Serra, J., "Quantitative Image Analysis: Theory and Instrumentation," *Microscopica Acta*, vol. 82, no. 2, September 1979, pp. 101–111.
151. Nawrath, R., and Serra, J., "Quantitative Image Analysis: Applications Using Sequential Transformations," *Microscopica Acta*, vol. 82, no. 2, September 1979, pp. 113–128.
152. Neisser, Y., "Cognitive Psychology," Appleton Century Crofts, New York, 1967.
153. Nevatia, R., "Locating Object Boundaries in Textured Environments," *IEEE Transactions on Computers*, vol. C-25, no. 11, November 1976, pp. 1170–1175.
154. O'Callaghan, J. F., and Loveday, J., "Quantitative Measurement of Soil Cracking Patterns," *Pattern Recognition*, vol. 5, no. 2, June 1973, pp. 83–98.
155. O'Gorman, F., and Clowes, M. B., "Finding Picture Edges, through Colinearity of Feature Points," *Proceedings of the 3d International Joint Conference on Artificial Intelligence*, Stanford University, Stanford, Calif., Aug. 20–23, 1973, pp. 543–555.
156. Onoe, M., Takagi, M., and Yukimatsu, K., "Chromosome Analysis by Minicomputer," *Computer Graphics and Image Processing*, vol. 2, nos. 3 and 4, December 1973, pp. 402–416.
157. O'Rourke, J., "Motion Detection Using Hough Techniques," *PRIP-81, IEEE Computer Society Conference on Pattern Recognition and Image Processing*, Dallas, Aug. 3–5, 1981, pp. 82–87.
158. O'Rourke, J., and Badler, N., "Decomposition of Three-Dimensional Objects into Spheres," *IEEE Transactions on Pattern Analysis and Machine Intelligence*, vol. PAMI-1, no. 3, July 1979, pp. 295–305.
159. Pavlidis, T., "Analysis of Set Patterns," *Pattern Recognition*, vol. 1, no. 2, November 1968, pp. 165–178.
160. Pavlidis, T., "Representation of Figures by Labeled Graphs," *Pattern Recognition*, vol. 4, no. 1, January 1972, pp. 5–17.
161. Pavlidis, T., "Structural Pattern Recognition: Primitives and Juxtaposition Relations," in Watanabe, S. (ed.), "Frontiers of Pattern Recognition," Academic, New York, 1972, pp. 421–451.
162. Pavlidis, T., "Waveform Segmentation Through Functional Approximation," *IEEE Transactions on Computers*, vol. C-22, no. 7, July 1973, pp. 689–697.
163. Pavlidis, T., "Syntactic Pattern Recognition of Shape," *PRIP-77, Proceedings of the IEEE Computer Society Conference on Pattern Recognition and Image Processing*, Rensselaer Polytechnic Institute, Troy, N.Y., June 6–8, 1977, pp. 98–107.
164. Pavlidis, T., "Polygonal Approximations by Newton's Method," *IEEE Transactions on Computers*, vol. C-26, no. 8, August 1977, pp. 800–807.
165. Pavlidis, T., "Structural Pattern Recognition," Springer-Verlag, New York, 1977.
166. Pavlidis, T., "A Review of Algorithms for Shape Analysis," *Computer Graphics and Image Processing*, vol. 7, no. 2, April 1978, pp. 243–258.
167. Pavlidis, T., "Comments on 'A New Shape Factor'," *Computer Graphics and Image Processing*, vol. 8, no. 2, October 1978, pp. 310–311.
168. Pavlidis, T., "The Use of a Syntactic Shape Analyzer for Contour Matching," *IEEE Transactions on Pattern Analysis and Machine Intelligence*, vol. PAMI-1, no. 3, July 1979, pp. 307–310.
169. Pavlidis, T., "Algorithms for Shape Analysis of Contours and Waveforms," *IEEE Transactions on Pattern Analysis and Machine Intelligence*, vol. PAMI-2, no. 4, July 1980, pp. 301–312.
170. Pavlidis, T., "A Flexible Parallel Thinning Algorithm," *PRIP-81, Proceedings of the IEEE Computer Society Conference on Pattern Recognition and Image Processing*, Dallas, Aug. 3–5, 1981, pp. 162–167.
171. Pavlidis, T., and Ali, F., "Computer Recognition of Handwritten Numerals by Polygonal Approximations," *IEEE Transactions on Systems, Man, and Cybernetics*, vol. SMC-5, no. 6, November 1975, pp. 610–614.
172. Pavlidis, T., and Ali, F., "A Hierarchical Syntactic Shape Analyzer," *IEEE Transactions on Pattern Analysis and Machine Intelligence*, vol. PAMI-1, no. 1, January, 1979, pp. 2–9.
173. Pavlidis, T., and Horowitz, S., "Segmentation of Plane Curves," *IEEE Transactions on Computers*, vol. C-23, no. 8, August, 1974, pp. 860–870.

174. Peleg, S., and Rosenfeld, A., "A Min-Max Medial Axis Transformation," *IEEE Transactions on Pattern Analysis and Machine Intelligence*, vol. PAMI-3, no. 2, March 1981, pp. 208–210.
175. Perkins, W. A., "A Model-Based Vision System for Industrial Parts," *IEEE Transactions on Computers*, vol. C-27, no. 2, February 1978, pp. 126–143.
176. Perkins, W. A., and Binford, T. O., "A Corner Finder for Visual Feedback," *Computer Graphics and Image Processing*, vol. 2, nos. 3 and 4, December 1973, pp. 355–376.
177. Persoon, E., and Fu, K. S., "Shape Discrimination Using Fourier Descriptors," *Proceedings of the 2d International Joint Conference on Pattern Recognition*, Copenhagen, August 13–15, 1974, pp. 126–130.
178. Pfaltz, J. L., and Rosenfeld, A., "Computer Representation of Planar Regions by Their Skeletons," *Communications of the ACM*, vol. 10, no. 2, February 1967, pp. 119–125.
179. Proffitt, D., "The Measurement of Circularity and Ellipticity on a Digital Grid," *Pattern Recognition*, vol. 15, no. 5, 1982, pp. 383–387.
180. Pullen, A. P., "Automatic Visual Inspection of Complex Industrial Components," British Pattern Recognition Association Meeting, University College, London, February 1977.
181. Radon, J., "Ueber die Bestimmung von Funktionen durche ihre Integralwerte laengs gewisser Mannigfaltigkeiten," *Berichte der Saechsischen Akademie Wissenschaften, Leipzig*, Math-Phys. Kl., vol. 62, April 1917, pp. 262–277.
182. Ramer, U., "An Iterative Procedure for the Polygonal Approximation of Plane Curves," *Computer Graphics and Image Processing*, vol. 1, no. 3, November 1972, pp. 244–256.
183. Rao, C. V. K., Prasada, B., and Sarma, K. R., "An Automatic Fingerprint Classification System," *Proceedings of the 2d International Joint Conference on Pattern Recognition*, Copenhagen, Aug. 13–15, 1974, pp. 180–184.
184. Reddi, S. S., "Radial and Angular Moment Invariants for Image Identification," *IEEE Transactions on Pattern Analysis and Machine Intelligence*, vol. PAMI-3, no. 2, March 1981, pp. 240–242.
185. Reeves, A. P., "A Parallel Mesh Moment Computer," *Proceedings of the 6th International Conference on Pattern Recognition*, Munich, Oct. 19–22, 1982, pp. 465–467.
186. Reeves, A. P., and Rostampour, A., "Shape Analysis of Segmented Objects Using Moments," *PRIP-81, Proceedings of the IEEE Computer Society Conference on Pattern Recognition and Image Processing*, Dallas, Aug. 3–5, 1981, pp. 171–174.
187. Richard, C. W., Jr., and Hemami, H., "Identification of Three-Dimensional Objects Using Fourier Descriptors of the Boundary Curve," *IEEE Transactions on Systems, Man, and Cybernetics*, vol. SMC-4, no. 4, July 1974, pp. 371–378.
188. Riggs, L. A., "Curvature as a Feature of Pattern Vision," *Science*, vol. 181, no. 4104, Sept. 14, 1973, pp. 1070–1072.
189. Rink, M., "A Computerized Quantitative Image Analysis Procedure for Investigating Features and an Adapted Image Process," *Journal of Microscopy*, vol. 107, 1976, pp. 267–286.
190. Rosenberg, B., "The Analysis of Convex Blobs," *Computer Graphics and Image Processing*, vol. 1, no. 2, August 1972, pp. 183–192.
191. Rosenfeld, A., "Picture Processing by Computer," Academic, New York, 1969.
192. Rosenfeld, A., "Connectivity in Digital Pictures," *Journal of the ACM*, vol. 17, no. 1, January 1970, pp. 146–160.
193. Rosenfeld, A., "Compact Figures in Digital Pictures," *IEEE Transactions on Systems, Man, and Cybernetics*, vol. SMC-4, no. 2, March 1974, pp. 221–223.
194. Rosenfeld, A., "A Note on Perimeter and Diameter in Digital Curves," *Information and Control*, vol. 24, no. 4, April 1974, pp. 384–388.
195. Rosenfeld, A., "A Characterization of Parallel Thinning Algorithms," *Information and Control*, vol. 29, 1975, pp. 286–291.
196. Rosenfeld, A., "Digital Topology," Technical Report no. TR-542, Computer Science Center, College Park, Md., May 1977.
197. Rosenfeld, A., "Extraction of Topological Information from Digital Images," Technical Report no. TR-547, Computer Science Center, University of Maryland, College Park, June 1977.

198. Rosenfeld, A., and Davis, L. S., "A Note on Thinning," *IEEE Transactions on Systems, Man, and Cybernetics*, vol. SMC-6, no. 3, March 1976, pp. 226–228.
199. Rosenfeld, A., and Kak, A. C., "Digital Picture Processing," Academic, New York, 1976.
200. Rosenfeld, A., and Pfaltz, J. L., "Sequential Operations in Digital Picture Processing," *Journal of the ACM*, vol. 13, no. 4, October 1966, pp. 471–494.
201. Rosenfeld, A., and Pfaltz, J. L., "Distance Functions on Digital Pictures," *Pattern Recognition*, vol. 1, no. 1, July 1968, pp. 33–61.
202. Rosenfeld, A., and Weszka, J. S., "An Improved Method of Angle Detection on Digital Curves," *IEEE Transactions on Computers*, vol. C-24, no. 9, September 1975, pp. 940–941.
203. Sadjadi, F. A., and Hall, E. L., "Numerical Computations of Moment Invariants for Scene Analysis," *Proceedings IEEE Computer Society Conference on Pattern Recognition and Image Processing, PRIP-78*, Chicago, May 31–June 2, 1978, pp. 181–187.
204. Sadjadi, F. A., and Hall, E. L., "Three-Dimensional Moment Invariants," *IEEE Transactions on Pattern Analysis and Machine Intelligence*, vol. PAMI-2, no. 2, March 1980, pp. 127–136.
205. Saghri, J. A., and Freeman, H., "Analysis of the Precision of Generalized Chain Codes for the Representation of Planar Curves," *IEEE Transactions on Pattern Analysis and Machine Intelligence*, vol. PAMI-3, no. 5, September 1981, pp. 533–539.
206. Sankar, P. V. and Krishnamurthy, E. V., "On the Compactness of Subsets of Digital Pictures," *Computer Graphics and Image Processing*, vol. 8, no. 1, August 1978, pp. 136–143.
207. Sankar, P. V., and Sharma, C. U., "A Parallel Procedure for the Detection of Dominant Points on a Digital Curve," *Computer Graphics and Image Processing*, vol. 7, 1978, pp. 403–412.
208. Schachter, B., "Decomposition of Polygons into Convex Sets," *IEEE Transactions on Computers*, vol. C-27, no. 11, November 1978, pp. 1078–1082.
209. Serra, J., "Image Analysis by Mathematical Morphology," Academic, London, 1982.
210. Seuffert, P., "An Application of Line and Character Recognition in Cartography," *Proceedings of the IEEE Conference on Pattern Recognition and Image Processing, PRIP-77*, Rensselaer Polytechnic Institute, Troy, N.Y., June 6–8, 1977, pp. 338–343.
211. Shannon, C. E., "A Mathematical Theory of Communication," *The Bell System Technical Journal*, vol. 27, no. 3, July 1948, pp. 379–423; vol. 27, no. 4, October 1948, pp. 623–656.
212. Shapiro, B., Pisa, J., and Sklansky, J., "Skeleton Generation from *x, y* Boundary Sequences," *Computer Graphics and Image Processing*, vol. 15, no. 2, February 1981, pp. 136–153.
213. Shapiro, L. G., "A Structural Model of Shape," *IEEE Transactions on Pattern Analysis and Machine Intelligence*, vol. PAMI-2, no. 2, March 1980, pp. 111–126.
214. Shapiro, L. G., and Haralick, R. M., "Decomposition of Two-Dimensional Shapes by Graph-Theoretic Clustering," *IEEE Transactions on Pattern Analysis and Machine Intelligence*, vol. PAMI-1, no. 1, January 1979, pp. 10–20.
215. Shapiro, S. D., "Transformations for the Computer Detection of Curves in Noisy Pictures," *Computer Graphics and Image Processing*, vol. 4, no. 4, December 1975, pp. 328–338.
216. Shapiro, S. D., "An Extension of the Transform Method to Curve Detection for Textured Image Data," *Proceedings of the 3d International Conference on Pattern Recognition*, Coronado, Calif., November 1976, pp. 205–207.
217. Shapiro, S. D., "Feature Space Transforms for Curve Detection," *Pattern Recognition*, vol. 10, no. 3, 1978, pp. 129–143.
218. Shapiro, S. D., "Properties of Transforms for the Detection of Curves in Noisy Pictures," *Computer Graphics and Image Processing*, vol. 8, no. 2, October 1978, pp. 219–236.
219. Shapiro, S. D., "Use of the Hough Transform for Image Data Compression," *Pattern Recognition*, vol. 12, no. 5, 1980, pp. 333–337.
220. Shapiro, S. D., and Iannino, A., "Geometric Constructions for Predicting Hough Transform Performance," *IEEE Transactions on Pattern Analysis and Machine Intelligence*, vol. PAMI-1, no. 3, July 1979, pp. 317–320.
221. Sherman, H., "A Quasi-Topological Method for the Recognition of Line Patterns," in "Proceedings of the UNESCO Conference on Information Processing," Butterworths, London, 1959, pp. 232–238.

222. Shirai, Y., "Edge Finding, Segmentation of Edges and Recognition of Complex Objects," *Proceedings of the 4th International Joint Conference on Artificial Intelligence*, Tbilisi, Georgia, USSR, Sept. 3–8, 1975, pp. 674–681.
223. Sidhu, G. S., and Boute, R. T., "Property Encoding: Applications in Binary Picture Encoding and Boundary Following," *IEEE Transactions on Computers*, vol. C-21, no. 11, November 1972, pp. 1206–1216.
224. Sklansky, J., "On the Hough Technique for Curve Detection," *IEEE Transactions on Computers*, vol. C-27, no. 10, 1978, pp. 923–926.
225. Sklansky, J., Chazin, R. L., and Hansen, B. J., "Minimum Perimeter Polygons of Digitized Silhouettes," *IEEE Transactions on Computers*, vol. C-21, no. 3, March 1972, pp. 260–268.
226. Sklansky, J., and Gonzalez, V., "Fast Polygonal Approximation of Digitized Curves," *Pattern Recognition*, vol. 12, no. 5, 1980, pp. 327–331.
227. Slagle, J. R., and Dixon, J. K., "Using Descriptions to Find Figures that Approximate the Given Points," *Proceedings of the 5th International Conference on Pattern Recognition*, Miami Beach, Dec. 1–4, 1980, pp. 1049–1054.
228. Slagle, J. R., and Dixon, J. K., "Finding a Good Figure That Approximately Passes through Given Points," *Pattern Recognition*, vol. 12, no. 5, 1980, pp. 319–326.
229. Sloan, K. R., Jr., "Analysis of 'Dot Product Space' Descriptions," *IEEE Transactions on Pattern Analysis and Machine Intelligence*, vol. PAMI-4, no. 1, January 1982, pp. 87–90.
230. Smith, F. W., and Wright, M. H., "Automatic Ship Photo Interpretation by the Method of Moments," *IEEE Transactions on Computers*, vol. C-20, no. 9, September 1971, pp. 1089–1095.
231. Snyder, W. E., and Tang, D. A., "Finding the Extrema of a Region," *IEEE Transactions on Pattern Analysis and Machine Intelligence*, vol. PAMI-2, no. 3, May 1980, pp. 266–269.
232. Stefanelli, R., and Rosenfeld, A., "Some Parallel Thinning Algorithms for Digital Pictures," *Journal of the ACM*, vol. 18, no. 2, April 1971, pp. 255–264.
233. Stockman, G., "Defining and Extracting Waveform Primitives for Linguistic Analysis," *Proceedings of the 4th International Joint Conference on Pattern Recognition*, Kyoto, Japan, Nov. 7–10, 1978, pp. 696–700.
234. Stockman, G., and Agrawala, A. K., "Equivalence of Hough Curve Detection to Template Matching," *Communications of the ACM*, vol. 20, no. 11, November 1977, pp. 820–822.
235. Tamura, H., "A Comparison of Line Thinning Algorithms from Digital Geometry Viewpoint, *Proceedings of the 4th International Conference on Pattern Recognition*, Kyoto, Japan, Nov. 7–10, 1978, pp. 715–719.
236. Tanimoto, S. L., "Measures for Shape Using Polygon Statistics," *Proceedings of the International Conference on Cybernetics and Society*, Cambridge, Mass., Oct. 8–10, 1980, pp. 43–46.
237. Teague, M. R., "Image Analysis via the General Theory of Moments," *Journal of the Optical Society of America*, vol. 70, no. 8, Aug. 1980, pp. 920–930.
238. Thompson, D'A. W., "On Growth and Form," Bonner, J. T. (ed.), abridged ed., Cambridge University Press, London, 1961.
239. Tomek, I., "Two Algorithms for Piecewise Linear Continuous Approximations of Functions of One Variable," *IEEE Transactions on Computers*, vol. C-23, no. 4, April 1974, pp. 445–448.
240. Toriwaki, J.-I., and Fukumura, T., "Extraction of Structural Information from Gray Pictures," *Computer Graphics and Image Processing*, vol. 7, no. 1, February 1978, pp. 30–51.
241. Toriwaki, J.-I., Kato, N., and Fukumura, T., "Parallel Local Operations for a New Distance Transformation of a Line Pattern and Their Applications," *IEEE Transactions on Systems, Man, and Cybernetics*, vol. SMC-9, no. 10, October 1979, pp. 628–643.
242. Tou, J. T., and Gonzalez, R. C., "Pattern Recognition Principles," Addison-Wesley, Reading, Mass., 1974.
243. Triendl, E. E., "Skeletonization of Noisy Handdrawn Symbols Using Parallel Operations," *Pattern Recognition*, vol. 2, no. 3, September 1970, pp. 215–226.
244. Tsuji, S., and Matsumoto, F., "Detection of Ellipses by a Modified Hough Transformation," *IEEE Transactions on Computers*, vol. C-27, no. 8, August 1978, pp. 777–781.

245. Udupa, K. J., and Murthy, I. S. N., "Some New Concepts for Encoding Line Patterns," *Pattern Recognition*, vol. 7, no. 4, December 1975, pp. 225–233.
246. Uttal, W. R., "An Autocorrelation Theory of Form Detection," Lawrence Erlbaum Associates, Hillsdale, N.J., 1975.
247. Vanderheydt, L., Dom, F., Oosterlinck, A., and Van Den Berghe, H., "Two-Dimensional Shape Decomposition Using Fuzzy Subset Theory Applied to Automated Chromosome Analysis," *Pattern Recognition*, vol. 13, no. 2, 1981, pp. 147–157.
248. Vanderheydt, L., Oosterlinck, A., and Van Den Berghe, H., "Experiments of Computer Vision Techniques for Industrial Applications," *Conference Record, 1982 Workshop on Industrial Applications of Machine Vision*, Research Triangle Park, N.C., 1982, pp. 21–25.
249. Van Veen, T. M., and Groen, F. C. A., "Discretization Errors in the Hough Transform," *Pattern Recognition*, vol. 14, no. 1–6, 1981, pp. 137–145.
250. Wallace, T. P., and Mitchell, O. R., "Analysis of Three-Dimensional Movement Using Fourier Descriptors," *IEEE Transactions on Pattern Analysis and Machine Intelligence*, vol. PAMI-2, no. 6, November 1980, pp. 583–588.
251. Wang, S., Dias Velasco, F. R., Wu, A.Y., and Rosenfeld, A., "Relative Effectiveness of Selected Texture Primitive Statistics for Texture Discrimination," *IEEE Transactions on Systems, Man, and Cybernetics*, vol. SMC-11, no. 5, May 1981, pp. 360–370.
252. Wechsler, H., "A Structural Approach to Shape Analysis Using Mirroring Axes," *Computer Graphics and Image Processing*, vol. 9, no. 3, March 1979, pp. 246–266.
253. Wechsler, H., "A New and Fast Algorithm for Estimating the Perimeter of Objects for Industrial Vision Tasks," *Computer Graphics and Image Processing*, vol. 17, no. 4, December 1981, pp. 375–381.
254. Wechsler, H., and Sklansky, J., "Finding the Rib Cage in Chest Radiographs," *Pattern Recognition*, vol. 9, no. 1, 1977, pp. 21–30.
255. Wiener, N., "Cybernetics," Wiley, New York, 1948.
256. Wong, R. Y., and Hall, E. L., "Scene Matching With Invariant Moments," *Computer Graphics and Image Processing*, vol. 8, no. 1, August 1978, pp. 16–24.
257. Yam, S., and Davis, L. S., "Image Registration Using Generalized Hough Transforms," *Proceedings of the IEEE Computer Society Conference on Pattern Recognition and Image Processing*, Dallas, August 1981, pp. 526–533.
258. Yamamoto, K., and Mori, S., "Recognition of Handprinted Characters by Outermost Point Method," *Proceedings of the 4th International Joint Conference on Pattern Recognition*, Kyoto, Japan, Nov. 7–10, 1978, pp. 794–796.
259. Yokoi, S., Toriwaki, J.-I., and Fukumura, T., "An Analysis of Topological Properties of Digitized Binary Pictures Using Local Features," *Computer Graphics and Image Processing*, vol. 4, no. 1, March 1975, pp. 63–73.
260. Yokoi, S., Toriwaki, J.-I., and Fukumura, T., "Generalized Distance Transformation of Digitized Binary Images," *Proceedings of the 5th International Conference on Pattern Recognition*, Miami Beach, Dec. 1–4, 1980, pp. 1201–1203.
261. York, B. W., "Shape Representation in Computer Vision," Ph.D. thesis, Department of Computer and Information Sciences, University of Massachusetts, Amherst, Mass., COINS Technical Report 82-13, May 1981.
262. You, K. C., and Fu, K. S., "A Syntactic Approach to Shape Recognition Using Attributed Grammars," *IEEE Transactions on Systems, Man, and Cybernetics*, vol. SMC-9, no. 6, June 1979, pp. 334–344.
263. Young, I. T., Walker, J. E., and Bowie, J. E., "An Analysis Technique for Biological Shape —I" *Information and Control*, vol. 25, no. 4, August 1974, pp. 357–370.
264. Youssef, Y. M., "Quantification and Characterization of the Motion and Shape of a Moving Cell," Ph.D. thesis, Department of Electrical Engineering, McGill University, Montreal, 1982.
265. Zusne, L., "Visual Perception of Form," Academic, New York, 1970.

BIBLIOGRAPHY

Pavlidis has prepared two excellent reviews on algorithms for shape analysis [10, 11]; an annotated literature survey can be found in [8]. The use of parallel processing logic for shape analysis is introduced in [12], which emphasizes applications in biomedical image processing.

As we observed in Section 10.2, the shape of an object is usually predicted on an analysis of its boundary. In general, line drawings are a good representation of real images, as observed by the popularity of cartoons. Freeman [1, 2] provides a general discussion and review of computer processing of line drawings. An early review of simple features based on these two-dimensional shapes is by Levine [7]; more recently, a review has appeared by Sklansky [14]. A comparison of polygonal approximation methods is presented in [6].

Two informative surveys on the Hough transform are found in [5] and [13].

Finally, the last stage of two-dimensional shape analysis involves the comparison of shapes and their structure. In this context the rubber-mask methods of Widrow [15, 16] are of interest. Both these papers contain many references to the literature on shape recognition. Syntactic methods are examined in [3, 4, 9].

1. Freeman, H., "Computer Processing of Line-Drawing Images," *Computing Surveys*, vol. 6, no. 1, March 1974, pp. 57–97.
2. Freeman, H., and Saghri, J. A., "Comparative Analysis of Line-Drawing Modelling Schemes," *Computer Graphics and Image Processing*, vol. 12, no. 3, March 1980, pp. 203–223.
3. Fu, K. S., "Syntactic Methods in Pattern Recognition," Academic, New York, 1974.
4. Fu, K. S. (ed.), "Syntactic Pattern Recognition, Applications," Springer-Verlag, Berlin, 1977.
5. Iannino, A., and Shapiro, S. D., "A Survey of the Hough Transform and its Extensions for Curve Detection," *Proceedings of the IEEE Computer Society Conference on Pattern Recognition and Image Processing, PRIP-78*, Chicago, May 31–June 2, 1978, pp. 32–38.
6. Kurozumi, Y., and Davis, W. A., "Polygonal Approximation by the Minimax Method," *Computer Graphics and Image Processing*, vol. 19, no. 3, July 1982, pp. 248–264.
7. Levine, M. D., "Feature Extraction: A Survey," *Proceedings of the IEEE*, vol. 57, no. 8, August 1969, pp. 1391–1407.
8. Meagher, D. J. R., "Computer Analysis of Shape: A Literature Survey," Report no. IPL-TR-79-001, Image Processing Laboratory, Rensselaer Polytechnic Institute, Troy, N. Y., May 1979.
9. Pavlidis, T., "Structural Pattern Recognition," Springer-Verlag, Berlin, 1977.
10. Pavlidis, T., "A Review of Algorithms for Shape Analysis," *Computer Graphics and Image Processing*, vol. 7, no. 2, April 1978, pp. 243–258.
11. Pavlidis, T., "Algorithms for Shape Analysis of Contours and Waveforms," *IEEE Transactions on Pattern Analysis and Machine Intelligence*, vol. PAMI-2, no. 4, July 1980, pp. 301–312.
12. Preston, K., Duff, M. J., Levialdi, S., Norgren, P., and Toriwaki, J.-I., "Basics of Cellular Logic With Some Applications in Biomedical Image Processing," *Proceedings of the IEEE*, vol. 67, no. 5, May 1979, pp. 826–856.
13. Shapiro, S. D., "Feature Space Transforms for Curve Detection," *Pattern Recognition*, vol. 10, no. 3, 1978, pp. 129–143.
14. Sklansky, J., "Image Segmentation and Feature Extraction," *IEEE Transactions on Systems, Man, and Cybernetics*, vol. SMC-8, no. 4, April 1978, pp. 237–247.
15. Widrow, B., "The 'Rubber-Mask' Technique—I. Pattern Measurement and Analysis," *Pattern Recognition*, vol. 5, no. 3, September 1973, pp. 175–197.
16. Widrow, B., "The 'Rubber-Mask' Technique—II. Pattern Storage and Recognition," *Pattern Recognition*, vol. 5, no. 3, September 1973, pp. 199–211.

APPENDIX

STUDENT PROJECTS

The research topics and programming exercises listed below are meant as a guideline to provide ideas for relevant and (hopefully!) interesting projects which can be performed by individuals studying this book. The suggestions are categorized roughly by chapter. Many of the problems require the use of a computer and in some cases additional equipment to input and display images. Under certain circumstances it may prove interesting to organize some problems into group projects, possibly interfacing the output of one project to the input of another. Some references are provided with the projects in order to give students a starting point for their work. Others appear at the end of the appropriate chapter.

Topics similar to these have been used by the author as term projects for a first-year graduate course in image processing. The level of difficulty varies and depends both on the topic and on the library and computer facilities available for doing the work.

CHAPTER 2 COMPUTER VISION SYSTEMS

2.1 Template matching provides a simple but useful method of detecting the presence or absence of spatial features in a scene. Write a computer program that takes arbitrary binary line images and applies a template matcher to them in order to find short straight-line segments. Generalize this template matcher to detect other configurations, such as circles, corners, or arcs. At each point, the output should reflect the closeness of the match between the primitive modeled by the template and the part of the image being examined. Note how the required computing time increases with the size of the template. [122]

2.2 As can be seen from the text as well as Project 2.1, image processing can require large amounts of computer time. This may cause serious problems when it is necessary to perform tasks in real time. To overcome this handicap many researchers look to the use of special-purpose hardware. Prepare a report on the types of equipment currently under development, the computations which will be enhanced by them, and the role of VLSI (very large scale integration) in implementing them. [57, 67, 86, 88]

2.3 Computer vision systems are not restricted to scenes illuminated with visible light. By the use of special cameras a large portion of the electromagnetic spectrum can be converted into images suitable for processing. This constitutes a significant portion of the field of remote sensing. Describe the various methods available for retrieving these "invisible" images and the ways in which they are processed to yield pertinent information. [71]

CHAPTER 3 BIOLOGICAL VISION SYSTEMS

3.1 Prepare a paper which describes the development of the eye in living organisms, starting with simple ones and tracing down the evolutionary tree [26, 42]. Try to direct attention to the following:

(*a*) What factors appear to have prompted the various evolutionary changes?

(*b*) What needs of the organism did (do) these primitive eyes satisfy?

(*c*) How have evolutionary constraints affected the structure of the eye in higher animals?

3.2 The fundamental unit of biological information processing appears to be the neuron [66, 116]. Present a paper which examines the following aspects of this structure from the standpoint of data processing:

(*a*) Its physiology and method of operation as an information processor.

(*b*) The different types of neurons that exist and the roles that have been postulated for them.

(*c*) Models of the computational action of neurons [48].

3.3 Neurons combine to form networks which are capable of performing various computations. Models have been presented that attempt to describe the activity of these neural nets [5, 19, 62, 66, 81, 119]. Prepare a paper which discusses the following:

(*a*) What limits on computational ability do these theories suggest?

(*b*) How does the computing power of a neural network compare with current serial and parallel computers?

3.4 Below are a few other topics pertaining to Chapter 3, which permit an interesting look at low-level biological image processing:

(*a*) The differences in anatomy and function of rods and cones in humans [102].

(*b*) The human pupil and its control system [110, 115].

(*c*) The operation of the optical system of the human eye as compared with that of the insect eye [53, 78, 93].

3.5 Simulate on a computer a small network of neurons. On the basis of the results of this simulation discuss such issues as timing, signal magnitude, frequency, connectivity, and so on [5, 19, 62, 66, 81, 119]. Can you draw any conclusions from this regarding the human brain as a "computer"?

CHAPTER 4 BIOLOGICAL SIGNAL PROCESSING

4.1 The nervous systems of small invertebrates are often easy to study because of their simplicity, as they usually possess comparatively small numbers of neurons and interconnections. It is hoped that by studying such systems insights can be gained into the operation of more complex ones. Report on one or more such studies, directing attention both to the functioning architectures that have been revealed and to how these may aid in understanding the nervous systems (and vision systems) of higher animals [62].

4.2 Consider a small animal as described in Project 4.1, but now concentrate on the interaction between the visual input and the motor control output. Interesting studies along these lines have been made with the frog and the housefly [69, 99].

4.3 The text refers to the contrast sensitivity function as a possible black-box model for the human visual system. Make a more detailed survey of the different black-box visual models that have been proposed, paying attention to their differences and what each has to offer in terms of the phenomena that it explains [11, 23, 46, 107].

4.4 Lateral inhibition in the *Limulus* (horseshoe crab) is discussed in the text as a primitive method of contrast enhancement. Program a simulation of lateral inhibition as it would apply to an $N \times N$ image and comment on the results observed. Relate your findings to the phenomenon of Mach bands [49, 96].

CHAPTER 5 EDGE DETECTION

5.1 A theory of low-level visual processing has been proposed by Marr. Outline his theory, discussing those elements of visual processing which it explains and those which it does not. [73, 74, 75]

5.2 Elementary feature detectors have been found in the visual pathway and observed as high as areas 18 and 19 of the visual cortex. Make a presentation of these findings to date in terms of apparent structure and the flow of information from one stage to the next. Include the work of neuroanatomists such as Hubel and Weisel. What feature detectors may be missing? Given the current experimental results, what might be some interesting things to look for next? [54, 121]

5.3 Develop a computer model of the simple, complex, and hypercomplex cells as described in this book and elsewhere. Have the model simulate the actions of a number of these cells over a small array of input elements. Test the program on a few image sequences and report on your success in detecting various features. Are there any additional feature detectors, perhaps not yet discovered, but which might be useful and appear possible to implement with this sort of scheme? Can you extend your program to cover them? [66]

5.4 Construct a computer program which can perform any of a number of filtering operations on an image, such as the Gaussian, Laplacian, and Marr filters. The program should also be capable of finding any zero-crossings in the output image. Use this program to experiment with processing an image by using different channels widths and comment on the results. What appears to be an optimum range of filter sizes? What sorts of edges seem to be difficult to find by the zero-crossing technique? [75]

5.5 Each of the edge operators described in Chapter 5 is responsive to particular image characteristics. Pick one or more edge operators and try to find ways of improving the response of that operator by varying parameters within the operator itself (such as mask size and individual mask values). Note the advantages and disadvantages of the different variations and also how the "quality" of an edge operator can depend on the image in question. Present theoretical justifications for your results. [2, 3, 104]

5.6 Chapter 5 has concentrated on edge detection. A related activity in vision systems is motion detection. Explore the current theories relating to dynamic scene analysis at the neurophysiological level. [70, 118]

5.7 Consider motion detection as mentioned in Project 5.6 but from the point of view of psychophysical models. [60, 70, 98]

5.8 There exist various algorithms to extract meaningful information from an image that has been preprocessed and reduced to a binary image. One such method is the Hough transform [27, sec. 10.3], which can be used to detect straight and parallel lines. Implement a program which takes a binary image as input and computes this transform. What conditions in the image would result in poor performance?

5.9 It has been possible to use image-processing techniques to determine the approximate volume of the human lung from two x-ray projections. One possible method [89] makes an estimate of the lung outline on the x-rays by using edge detection and heuristic search based on a presumed model of the lung shape. Then from the derived shape the lung volume may be calculated.

Construct a detailed flowchart for a system which is capable of computing lung volume from two x-rays. Obtain a pair of suitable radiographs and program the computer to determine the lung volume.

CHAPTER 6 SPATIAL- AND FREQUENCY-DOMAIN PROCESSING

6.1 Write a procedure that computes the fast Fourier transform of an $N \times N$ image. Compare the speed of this program with that of a "conventional" algorithm. Experiment with various digital filters in order to examine their effect on different types of images. [103]

6.2 Prepare a survey of the problem of correlating current neurophysiological understanding of the visual pathway with the more abstract model of multichannel processing. What is the evidence to support the latter and what are the difficulties? [15, 36, 101, 109, 124]

6.3 DPCM coding, as described in the text, involves predicing the next pixel value in a sequence of pixels taken by scanning across an image. The error between the predicted value and the actual value becomes the quantity transmitted. Sharp edges are likely to cause errors; hence a DPCM system acting with an appropriate prediction algorithm may make a good edge detector for edges parallel to the scan direction. Edges perpendicular to the scan direction may be found by applying the same process to the image rotated by 90°.

Develop an edge-detection program using this idea. Choose what you consider to be an appropriate prediction method and decide on how to combine the vertical and horizontal outputs. How do the computation time and accuracy compare with more conventional edge finders? [1]

6.4 Some of the visual illusions discussed in the text and elsewhere have had explanations postulated for them in terms of low-level visual processing operations. Prepare a brief survey of visual illusions and the role that some authors suggest they play in creating insights into biological vision systems. [12, 14, 50, 72]

6.5 If you have access to a computer graphics system, prepare a program which presents the user with one or two optical illusions such as the ones described in the text. The program should allow the user to vary certain relevant parameters in the illusion, such as line length, and contrast. Carry out some tests to determine how the strength of the illusion varies with these parameters. Can you relate your results to any model describing how the illusion may be formed? [12, 14, 50, 72]

6.6 Explore the phenomenon of subjective contours. What conditions must be met for subjective contours to be seen? How do these conditions fit in with the various explanations that have been proposed? [63, 117]

6.7 Examine simultaneous contrast in the same manner discussed in Project 6.6 [23, 97]

6.8 Some visual illusions relate to our ability to perceive three-dimensional images from two-dimensional figures. A popular example is the Necker cube. When observed, it may be perceived as a three-dimensional cube seen from either above or below. Other similar illusions abound in the literature. Consider further these "spatial illusions." How do they relate to our ability to infer three dimensions from two dimensions? [42, 43]

6.9 A recent application of image processing technology has been computed axial tomography (CAT). This allows the interior three-dimensional structure of an object to be inferred from images obtained by passing radiation through the object at different angles. Prepare a technical paper on this subject, presenting the theory, algorithms employed, uses, and problems of this new analytical technique. [18, 61]

6.10 Discuss in detail the image-processing technology currently being employed in space exploration as applied to, for example, satellite pictures of Earth and the remote pictures that were returned to Earth from Jupiter and Saturn by the *Voyager I* and *II* probes. How have the methods discussed in this book been put to use, and why were they necessary? [9, 83]

CHAPTER 7 COLOR

7.1 Project 10.5 discusses a method for recognizing specially coded labels by the differentiation of certain primitive shapes in the label. Prepare a program with the same objective as Project 10.5 but employ color as an additional aid in interpreting the label. Test this result on a colored image. [20]

7.2 If you have access to a computer-color-graphics-display monitor, write a "palette" program which allows a user to set different squares on the screen to arbitrary colors by adjusting the projected intensities of each of the three primary colors used by the monitor (red, green, and blue).

7.3 Develop a color-naming system which provides a transformation between the 11 basic colors as defined by Berlin and Kay [10] and the CIE color system. Program a "symbolic color palette" for a color display system.

7.4 Write a report on color television, paying attention to the ways in which color information is originally sensed in the camera, encoded, decoded, and displayed on the television set.

7.5 Mach bands were described in Chapter 6 in reference to gray-level images. Discuss the observed extension of this phenomenon to colored images. What bearing do these observations have on the way color information is processed in the visual system? [41, 59]

7.6 Different animals possess different color vision abilities. Compare these for an appropriate cross section of species. What theories have been proposed to relate the differences to the survival needs of the animals in question? [6]

7.7 Some models of color vision were referred to in the text. Select one listed below and elaborate on it. Discuss the reported experimental evidence and the aspects of the visual system the model deals with. If facilities are available to you, simulate the model on a computer and relate it to the CIE color system:

(*a*) The retinex color model [68]
(*b*) The opponent theory model [55, 56, 65]
(*c*) A neurophysiological model of color processing [23, 102]
(*d*) A psychophysical model of color processing [23, 125]

7.8 Some experimentation has been done to determine how color "symbols" are represented in the cerebral cortex. Describe the research reported to date. In what way has this work contributed to our overall understanding of color processing? What questions remain unanswered? [130]

7.9 Examine and describe mathematically the phenomenon of color blindness. What functional centers appear to fail, resulting in the disorder? What evidence do these characteristics provide in shaping theories of color? [4, 106]

CHAPTER 8 REGION ANALYSIS

8.1 Perceptual psychologists have long studied the role of "cues" in vision. These are characteristics of a scene which allow an observer to reach certain conclusions regarding the original physical situation. Consider the scene characteristics of shadow, highlight (or specularity), and occlusion. What information do these cues provide? [37, 50, 51, 123]

8.2 The ability of humans to perceive depth is assisted in part by the phenomenon of stereopsis [77, 100]. This refers to the disparity that occurs between the image of a scene observed by one eye and the image observed by the other. This disparity is related to the distance from the viewer of the objects being viewed. Explore this topic further, addressing the following:

(*a*) The actual information regarding depth that may be obtained by using this approach. Derive and present the mathematical relationships involved.

(*b*) Current theories of how the biological vision system may actually perform this computation.

8.3 Model, on a computer, one of the computational models of human stereopsis as described in Project 8.2. [44, 77]

8.4 A "random dot stereogram" is an array of alternately colored dots which, when seen through a stereogram viewer, gives an illusion of depth. The viewer is a pair of glasses with a different color filter over each eye. Consequently each eye sees dots of a different color. This configuration can be used to stimulate stereoscopic disparities, as described in Project 8.2. By appropriately specifying how the dots are positioned with respect to one another in the stereogram, the sensation of depth may be induced in the observer [43].

Write a program which generates a random-dot stereogram for a given "depth image." If possible, display the image on a color monitor and view it with a stereogram viewer.

8.5 A method is discussed in a paper by Zucker, Hummel, and Rosenfeld [131] which applies relaxation labeling to a noisy image in order to enhance lines present in the image. Write a program which is capable of accomplishing this, and test its effectiveness on some appropriate input images.

8.6 In his well-received book of 1950, Gibson [37] presented a comprehensive description of human visual perception. He concentrated on those aspects of the visual field that he considered to be "cues" to the recognition of real world properties, such as depth, object size, and orientation. Describe this system of cues as presented by Gibson and those who have followed him. Discuss what parts of this cue system have been put to use in present-day computer vision systems.

8.7 One of the more intractable problems confronting computer vision has been the so-called bin-of-parts problem. The problem concerns an image of a box of jumbled industrial parts. These are presented to a machine that is supposed to make some sense out of what it is looking at. Since industrial automation is frequently faced with the task of having to extract parts from such a box, it would be profitable to be able to do this automatically. This requires a system equipped with a robot arm which can "see" what is in the box and from this knowledge "know" how to pick an object out of the box. No general solution yet exists for this problem, although it is interesting to apply current image-processing techniques to this task. (The project requires some bin-of-parts images to work with [7].)

Develop a program which examines a picture and selects instances of features that are useful indicators of the parts being sought. For example, if one were looking for pieces which have holes in them, such as connecting rods for engines, it might be useful to look for ellipses or circles. It might also be useful in such instances to look for straight-line segments. (One useful tool in this situation is the Hough transform, described in Project 5.8 and Project 10.3.) Apply the procedure to some input images and consider the results.

8.8 Various algorithms have been proposed for segmenting an image into regions, with the objective of having these regions correspond to the relevant parts of the scene in question. Explain, implement, and test one of these algorithms. Some suggestions are given below. Apply them, if possible, to real world images, such as a natural scene, a bin-of-parts problem (Project 8.7), or a biomedical image.

(*a*) Segmentation using a split-and-merge algorithm [52]
(*b*) Statistical methods [45]
(*c*) Graph-theoretic methods [128]
(*d*) Variable thresholding [84]
(*e*) Histogram analysis [87]
(*f*) Methods based on similarity [17]
(*g*) Decision-theoretic approach [32]

CHAPTER 9 TEXTURE

9.1 Two general methods of texture analysis predominate, statistical and structural [47]. In both the aim is to specify an operator which can be applied to an image in order to yield a so-called texture array. The numbers in this array should represent the texture in the area of the corresponding point in the image. An edge detector or other process could then be applied to this array to locate edges indicated by texture differences.

Some of the better-known texture operators are listed below. Choose one and write a program which implements it, testing the program on a suitable set of input images. A survey of texture techniques is given in [47].

(*a*) The autocorrelation function and texture [47, 94]
(*b*) Digital transform methods [47]
(*c*) Textural edgeness [105]
(*d*) Spatial gray tone dependence and co-occurrence matrices [47]
(*e*) Generalized co-occurrence matrices [25, 132]
(*f*) Run lengths [35, 47]
(*g*) Autoregression models [47, 79]
(*h*) Gray-level difference method [22]
(*i*) Classification by histogram analysis [120]

9.2 One approach to texture analysis is based on the concept of multichannel processing in the spatial-frequency domain. Implement such a method and comment on how it relates to the multichannel models for the human visual system. [31, 124]

9.3 A method for region segmentation by textural differences has been suggested using co-occurrence matrices and the split-and-merge algorithms [21]. Write a program which performs this procedure and run it on some input images with varying texture patterns.

9.4 The qualitative description of image texture is often expressed with words such as "rough," "silky," "rippled," "checkered," and "mottled." See if you can establish some relationship between one of these subjective terms and one of the more precise structural models of texture. This might be done by generating different textures according to the model and then subjectively evaluating the results. These psychophysical results can be examined to see how they correspond to the model. [47]

9.5 In order to test texture-processing operators it is often convenient to have a program available which generates appropriate texture images. Such a method can often be used as a basis for analyzing these images as well. Various techniques exist for doing this [47, 105, 126]. Write a texture-generating program which is able to do the following:

(*a*) Produce an image split into several regions, each easily defined by differences in their texture

(*b*) Allow the user to specify whether the produced textures differ in their first-, second-, or third-order statistics

(*c*) Produce both structural and statistical textures

9.6 The Leitz texture analysis hardware is used for texture classification. It is based on the principle of filtering an image with a structural texture element and using the result as the basis of discrimination. Investigate the details of this technique and describe how it has been used in such applications as biomedical engineering and materials science. [47, 82, 111, 112]

9.7 Texture analysis has been applied successfully in remote sensing, particularly in examining data from satellite pictures. Explore this in greater detail, reporting on the different techniques used and their respective strong points and weaknesses. [9]

CHAPTER 10 SHAPE

10.1 Assume that a shape is defined by a simple closed binary region. Referring to the paper by Bribiesca and Guzman [16], develop a program that computes the shape number. Also calculate the degree of similarity between two arbitrary shapes of reasonable complexity.

10.2 Sometimes it is desirable to analyze objects with the objective of finding some defect in their shape. An example of this would be to examine the outlines of conductors on a printed circuit board to find the locations of rough or jagged sections. Some algorithms have been proposed which detect certain types of roughness in a given path. Make a presentation of these and program a simple version of one such algorithm. Test your program with some sample outlines and see what defects it picks out. [30]

10.3 The Hough transform mentioned in Problem 5.7 can be extended in principle to detect curves and other shapes in a binary picture [8, 113]. Develop a program which uses this idea to extract some simple shapes (such as rectangles, circles, and ellipses) from an input image. Preprocessed images of bins-of-parts (Project 8.7) can make interesting test cases for this method.

10.4 Assume you are given a shape defined by an eight-connected chain code of length N. Write a program subroutine which accepts as input such a chain code and outputs a polygonal approximation to the shape. The accuracy of the approximation should be governed by an input parameter to the module. A useful algorithm for producing such an approximation is described by Ramer [95]. Some interesting results can be obtained by running this on geographic maps.

10.5 Electronic parts handling can often be made more efficient by employing an automatic label reader. To keep the cost down and allow the system to operate in real time, the "label" that is read should be a coded set of elementary shapes. There should also be a "reference" shape which the system can easily find and which indicates the relative position of the other data to be read.

Design a labeling scheme for IC chips or electronic components, along with a program which is capable of reading the label when the object may appear at an arbitrary orientation (see also Project 7.1). [20]

10.6 An interesting method of shape description involves medial-axis transformation or skeletonization. A recent variation has been proposed by Blum and Nagel [13], where the skeleton is represented as a labeled graph structure. Write a program for obtaining the graph structure of a shape in this way and test it on some suitable inputs. Assume the shape is already available as a chain code.

10.7 The medial-axis transformation was mentioned in Problem 10.6 and yields the skeleton of a two-dimensional shape. Such a skeleton can also be obtained by thinning the shape appropriately. Implement the thinning algorithm of Pavlidis [90] and test its usefulness for some common shapes, such as the 10 numerals.

10.8 Write a shape analysis program for some variety of shapes such as handwritten numerals. It should be able to take a given shape described by a chain code or, at a higher level, by a polygonal approximation, and return a set of shape descriptors appropriate to the analysis technique chosen. A great many methods of classifying shape exist, with some of the more popular ones listed below. A general survey is given in [92].

(*a*) Representation of the shape curve by a Fourier series [129]
(*b*) The method of moments and other transform techniques [29]
(*c*) Decomposition into primary convex subsets [91]
(*d*) Decomposition at concave vertices [33, 127]
(*e*) Geometrical shape measures [24, 27, 34, 58, 91]

10.9 Use one of the shape analysis methods described in Project 10.8 to develop a simple system for character recognition which works with a simplified character set. Allow an input shape to be matched against a stored library of characters by means of an appropriate set of shape descriptors. Of course, this topic can be extended to the recognition of any class of two-dimensional shapes.

The methods of pattern matching employed for such work are usually either statistical [27] or syntactic [34], depending upon the particular shape descriptions employed. (This can be an interesting project but can also be rather lengthy. It may be best to perform it as a group project in conjunction with Project 10.8.)

10.10 Shape analysis has been useful in approaching a number of biomedical engineering tasks, such as the tracking of blood cell motion and the classification of chromosomes in cells. Report on the image-processing methods that have been used to perform such functions and the degree of success which has been obtained. Where is the field likely to go in the future? [64, 80]

10.11 Analysis of shape may be applied to signal waveforms as well as to closed curves. One application is in the monitoring of electrocardiogram (ECG) patterns, where it is possible to have a machine scan the pattern and report certain abnormalities.

Design a program which takes as input an ECG signal and recognizes if the pattern is normal or has some particular abnormality. Without getting too involved, use whatever techniques may be appropriate or in current use. Test the program on a few trial inputs and see what percentage of healthy individuals it accidentally assigns to the cardiac intensive care unit! (ECG waveforms are discussed in many physiology texts; much work on automated ECG analysis also appears in the *IEEE Transactions on Biomedical Engineering.*)

10.12 Suppose you were assigned the task of developing a computer program that recognizes faces. How would you approach the problem? What sort of program structure might you employ? What program modules would you use that are currently well defined? What modules might be necessary that are not currently well defined? Discuss the requirements of the latter and any suggestions you may have for implementing them. Various papers have dealt with this topic and a small survey of them may be useful. [38, 39, 40, 108]

10.13 More attention has been directed in recent years to the study of form and shape in three dimensions, in terms both of how to infer three-dimensional structure from a two-dimensional image [76, 114] and how to properly represent three-dimensional structures [76]. Prepare a short survey of some of the ideas which have currently gained attention in this field.

10.14 Consider the bin-of-parts problem from the point of view of a "bin of shapes." That is, assume that you are looking for a specific shape outline in a binary image. Now assume that the image contains many shapes, including the ones being sought, lying one on top of another. It is conceivable that for some applications it may only be necessary to locate the parts on top, as for example if a machine were to remove only these first.

Write a program which seeks instances of a particular shape in a line drawing such as the one shown. If it does not find the shape in question, it should indicate this. Do not worry particularly about instances in which the shape is occluded by other shapes. Can the techniques you have employed be applied at all to the more general bin-of-parts problem?

10.15 Carry out Project 10.14 but now concentrate solely on the partially occluded shapes. Discuss and program an algorithm for detecting these. [37, 117]

GENERAL

G.1 Various ways of making use of image-processing technology in prosthetic devices have been suggested, particularly in giving some form of sight to the blind. One method is briefly described below [85].

An array of electrodes is implanted in the visual cortex. When stimulated, each electrode in the array creates a small dot of light, called a "phosphene," at a unique point in the person's visual field. This array interfaces with an external image processor which the person wears. Depending on the scene in view, the processor induces a set of phosphenes, which hopefully gives the individual some idea of what the scene looks like. One of the significant features of this array is that the sampling resolution is very coarse indeed.

The next few projects consider some of the image-processing tasks that must be addressed by such a system. In designing these programs, make them simple in view of the fact that a real system would have to be implemented by VLSI circuitry (for example, use only fixed-point numbers). Design the task handlers as black boxes that can easily be used by the rest of the system.

(*a*) To decide what is important in the image being viewed, the processor should be able to enhance edges and contrast in the real world scene. Construct a module which performs such enhancement, write it as a computer subroutine, and test it.

(*b*) The relationship between the position of an electrode in the array and the position of the phosphene it produces in the visual field is most likely not direct. Moreover, the relationship between electrode current and perceived phosphene brightness is not linear. Report on the exact nature of these problems. Design a module which corrects for them and program it as a subroutine.

(*c*) Submit a technical paper on the subject, describing in greater detail the problem, proposed solutions, and current obstacles to implementation.

G.2 Consider the problem of designing a general-purpose image-processing system. Approaching the problem from the software level, decide what facilities such a system should have and how they should be interrelated. Provide separate modules for doing different types of computation. Base the functions of these modules on a comprehensive set of research and commercial requirements. Modules themselves will most likely have submodules. For example, a CREATE module which allows the user to create an arbitrary gray-level image would probably be useful. A submodule of this could be a LINE module, which allows for straight (or curved) lines to drawn at a given intensity. Another submodule could be called PAINT, which permits a given region to be colored with a given color/intensity. Computational modules could include an EDGE section, capable of applying different edge operators, a MATRIX section, which performs matrix operations such as can be applied to images in the frequency domain, etc.

Describe the system, indicating the utility of each of its parts and the usefulness of that part in performing or experimenting with the sort of image-processing tasks that have been described in this book.

REFERENCES

1. Abbott, R. P., "DPCM Codes for Video Telephony Using 4-bits Per Sample," *IEEE Transactions on Communication Technology*, vol. COM-19, no. 12, December 1971, pp. 907–913.
2. Abdou, I. E., "Quantitative Methods of Edge Detection," Technical Report USCIPI 830, Image Processing Institute, University of Southern California, Los Angeles, July 1978.
3. Abdou, I. E., and Pratt, W. K., "Quantitative Design and Evaluation of Enhancement/Thresholding Edge Detectors," *Proceedings of the IEEE*, vol. 67, no. 5, May 1979, pp. 753–763.
4. Alpern, M., "What Is It That Confines in a World without Color?," *Investigative Ophthalmology*, vol. 13, no. 9, 1974, pp. 648–674.
5. Amari, S. I., "A Mathematical Approach to Neural Systems," in Metzler, J. (ed.), "Systems Neuroscience," Academic, New York, 1977, pp. 67–117.
6. Autrum, H., and Thomas, I., "Comparative Physiology of Color Vision in Animals," in "Handbook of Sensory Physiology," vol. III/3, part A, Springer-Verlag, New York, 1973, pp. 661–692.
7. Baird, M. L., "A Computer Vision Data Base for the 'Industrial Bin of Parts Problem'," Research Publication GMR-2502, Computer Science Department, General Motors Research Laboratories, Warren, Mich., August 1977.
8. Ballard, D. H., "Generalizing the Hough Transform to Detect Arbitrary Shapes," *Pattern Recognition*, vol. 13, 1981, pp. 111–122.
9. Bauer, M., "Technological Basis and Applications of Remote Sensing of the Earth's Resources," *IEEE Transactions on Geoscience and Remote Sensing*, vol. GE-14, no. 1, January 1976, pp. 3–9.
10. Berlin, B., and Kay, P., "Basic Color Terms: Their Universality and Evolution," University of California Press, Berkeley, 1969.
11. Bisti, S., and Maffei, L., "Behavioral Contrast Sensitivity of the Cat in Various Visual Meridians," *Journal of Physiology* (*London*), vol. 241, no. 1, 1974, pp. 201–210.
12. Blakemore, C., "The Baffled Brain, Illusions in Nature and Art," Scribner, New York, 1973, pp. 9–48.
13. Blum, H., and Nagel, R. N., "Shape Description Using Weighted Symmetric Axis Features," *Pattern Recognition*, vol. 10, no. 3, 1978, pp. 167–180.

14. Braddick, O., Campbell, F. W., and Atkinson, J., "Channels in Vision: Basic Aspects," in Held, R., Leibowitz, H., and Teuber, H. L. (eds.) "Handbook of Sensory Physiology," vol. VIII: "Perception," Springer-Verlag, Heidelberg, 1977, pp. 3–38.
15. Breitmeyer, B. G., and Ganz, L., "Implications of Sustained and Transient Channels for Theories of Visual Pattern Masking, Saccadic Suppression, and Information Processing," *Psychological Review*, vol. 83, no. 1, January 1976, pp. 1–36.
16. Bribiesca, E., and Guzman, A., "How to Describe Pure Form and How to Measure Differences in Shapes Using Shape Numbers," *Pattern Recognition*, vol. 12, 1979, pp. 101–112.
17. Brice, C., and Fennema, C. L., "Scene Analysis Using Regions," *Artificial Intelligence*, vol. 1, 1970, pp. 205–226.
18. Brooks, R. A., and DiChiro, G., "Principles of Computer Assisted Tomography (CAT) in Radio-Graphic and Radio-Isotopic Imaging," *Physics in Medicine and Biology* (*London*), vol. 21, no. 5, 1976, pp. 689–732.
19. Caianiello, E. R. (ed.), "Neural Networks," Springer-Verlag, New York, 1968.
20. *Canadian Electronics Engineering*, "Scanner Speeds Parcel Handling, " vol. 19, no. 3, March 1975, MacLean-Hunter.
21. Chen, P. C., and Pavlidis, T., "Segmentation by Texture Using A Co-Occurrence Matrix and A Split-And-Merge Algorithm," *Proceedings of the 4th International Joint Conference on Pattern Recognition*, Kyoto, Japan, November 7–10, 1978, p. 565.
22. Conners, R. W., and Harlow, C. A., "A Theoretical Comparison of Texture Algorithms," *IEEE Transactions on Pattern Recognition and Machine Intelligence*, vol. PAMI-2, no. 3, May 1980, p. 206.
23. Cornsweet, T., "Visual Perception," Academic, New York, 1970.
24. Danielsson, P. E., "A New Shape Factor," *Computer Graphics and Image Processing*, vol. 7, 1978, pp. 292–299.
25. Davis, L. S., Johns, S., and Aggarwal, J. K., "Texture Analysis Using Generalized Co-occurrence Matrices," Pattern Recognition and Image Processing Conference, Chicago, May 31–June 2, 1978.
26. Davson, H., "Physiology of the Eye," 4th ed., Churchill Livingstone, Edinburgh, 1980.
27. Duda, R. O., and Hart, P. E., "Pattern Classification and Scene Analysis," Wiley, New York, 1973.
28. Duda, R. O., and Hart, P. E. "Use of the Hough Transform to Detect Lines and Curves in Pictures," *Communications of the Association for Computing Machinery*, 1975, no. 15, pp. 11–15.
29. Dudani, S. A., Breeding, K. J., and McGhee, R. B., "Aircraft Identification by Moment Invariants," *IEEE Transactions on Computers*, vol. C-26, 1977, pp. 39–46.
30. Ejiri, M., "A Process for Detecting Defects in Complicated Patterns," *Computer Graphics and Image Processing*, vol. 2, no. 3/4, December 1973, pp. 326–339.
31. Faugeras, O. D., "Texture Analysis and Classification Using a Human Vision Model," *Proceedings of the 4th International Joint Conference on Pattern Recognition*, Kyoto, Japan, Nov. 7–10, 1978, p. 549.
32. Feldman, J. A., and Yakimovsky, Y., "Decision Theory and Artificial Intelligence: I. A Semantics-Based Region Analyzer," *Artificial Intelligence*, vol. 5, no. 4, Winter 1974, pp. 349–371.
33. Feng, H. Y., and Pavlidis, T., "Decomposition of Polygons into Simpler Components: Feature Extraction for Syntactic Pattern Recognition," *IEEE Transactions on Computers*, vol. C-24, no. 6, June, 1975, pp. 636–650.
34. Fu, K. S., "Syntactic Methods in Pattern Recognition," Academic, New York, 1974.
35. Galloway, M., "Texture Analysis Using Gray Level Run Lengths," *Computer Graphics and Image Processing*, vol. 4, no. 2, June 1974, pp. 172–179.
36. Georgeson, M., "Spatial Fourier Analysis and Human Vision," chap. II in Sutherland, N. S. (ed.), "Tutorial Essays in Psychology, A Guide to Recent Advances," vol. 2, Lawrence Erlbaum Associates, Hillsdale, N.J., 1979.
37. Gibson, J. J., "The Perception of Visual World," Houghton-Mifflin, Boston, 1958.

38. Gillenson, M. L., and Chandrasekaran, B., "A Heuristic Strategy for Developing Human Facial Images on a CRT," *Pattern Recognition*, vol. 7, no. 4, December 1975, pp. 187–196.
39. Goldstein, A. J., Harmon, L. D., and Lesk, A. B., "Identification of Human Faces," *Proceedings of the IEEE*, vol. 59, no. 5, May 1971, pp. 748–760.
40. Goldstein, A. J., Harmon, L. D., and Lesk, A. B., "Man-Machine Interaction in Human-Face Identification," *Bell System Technical Journal*, vol. 51, no. 2, February 1972, pp. 399–427.
41. Green, D. G., and Fast, M. B., "On the Appearance of Mach Bands in Gradients of Varying Colors," *Vision Research*, vol. 11, no. 10, 1971, pp. 1147–1155.
42. Gregory, R. L., "Eye and Brain, The Psychology of Seeing," World University Library, McGraw-Hill, New York, 1966.
43. Gregory, R. L., "The Intelligent Eye," McGraw-Hill, New York, 1970.
44. Grimson, W. E. L., "A Computer Implementation of a Theory of Human Stereo Vision," A.I. Memo 565, M.I.T. Artificial Intelligence Laboratory, Cambridge, Mass., November 1977.
45. Gupta, J. N., and Wintz, P. A., "A Boundary Finding Algorithm and Its Applications," *IEEE Transactions on Circuits and Systems*, vol. CAS-22, no. 4, April 1975.
46. Hall, C. F., and Hall, E. L., "A Nonlinear Model of the Spatial Characteristics of the Human Visual System," *IEEE Transactions on Systems, Man, and Cybernetics*, vol. SMC-7, no. 3, 1977, pp. 161–170.
47. Haralick, R. M., "Statistical and Structural Approaches to Texture," *Proceedings of the 4th International Joint Conference on Pattern Recognition*, Kyoto, Japan, Nov. 7–10, 1978, pp. 45–69.
48. Harmon, L. D., "Neural Modelling," *Physiology Review*, vol. 46, no. 5, July 1966, pp. 513–591.
49. Hartline, H. K., and Ratliff, F., "Inhibitory Interaction in the Retina of the *Limulus*," in Fuortes, M. G. F. (ed.), "Physiology of Photoreceptor Organs, Handbook of Sensory Physiology," vol. 7/2, Springer-Verlag, Berlin, 1972, pp. 381–447.
50. Held, R. (ed.), "Image Object and Illusion," in "Readings from *Scientific American*," Freeman, San Francisco, 1974.
51. Horn, B., "Obtaining Shape from Shading Information," in Winston, P. H. (ed.), "The Psychology of Computer Vision," McGraw-Hill, New York, 1975, pp. 115–155.
52. Horowitz, S. L., and Pavlidis, T., "Picture Segmentation by a Directed Split-and-Merge Procedure," *Proceedings of the 2d International Joint Conference on Pattern Recognition*, Lynby-Copenhagen, Aug. 13–15, 1974, IEEE, New York, 1974, pp. 424–433.
53. Horridge, E. A., "The Compound Eye of Insects," *Scientific American*, July 1977, pp. 108–120.
54. Hubel, D. H., and Wiesel, T. N., "Brain Mechanisms of Vision," *Scientific American*, September 1979, pp. 150–163.
55. Hurvich, L. M., and Jameson, D., "Some Quantitative Aspects of an Opponents Colours Theory, II. Brightness Saturation and Hue in Normal and Dichromatic Vision," *Journal of the Optical Society of America*, vol. 45, 1955, pp. 602–616.
56. Hurvich, L. M., and Jameson, D., "An Opponent-Process Theory of Color Vision," *Psychological Review*, vol. 64, no. 6, 1957, pp. 384–404.
57. IEEE Computer Society, *Proceedings of the 1981 IEEE Computer Society Workshop on Computer Architecture for Pattern Analysis and Image Database Management*, November 1981.
58. Ishikawa, S., "Geometrical Indices Characterizing Psychological Goodness of Random Shapes," *Proceedings of the 4th International Joint Conference on Pattern Recognition*, Kyoto, Japan, Nov. 7–10, 1978, p. 414.
59. Jacobson, J. Z., and McKinnon, G. E., "Colored Mach Bands," *Canadian Journal of Psychology*, vol. 23, no. 1, 1969, pp. 56–65.
60. Johansson, G., "Visual Motion Perception," *Scientific American*, June 1975, vol. 232, no. 6, pp. 76–88.
61. Kak, A. C., "Computerized Tomography with X-Ray, Emission, and Ultrasound Sources," *Proceedings of the IEEE*, vol. 67, no. 9, September 1979, pp. 1245–1273.

62. Kandel, E. R., "Small Systems of Neurons," *Scientific American*, vol. 241, no. 3, September 1979, pp. 66–76.
63. Kanizsa, G., "Subjective Contours," *Scientific American*, vol. 234, no. 4, 1976, pp. 48–52.
64. Klinger, A., "Computer Analysis of Chromosome Patterns: Feature Encoding for Flexible Decision Making," *IEEE Transactions Computers*, vol. C-20, no. 9, September 1971, pp. 1014–1022.
65. Koenderik, J. J., van de Grind, W. A., and Bouman, M. A., "Opponent Color Coding: A Mechanistic Model and a New Metric for Color Space," *Kybernetik*, vol. 10, February 1972, pp. 78–98.
66. Kuffler, S. W., and Nicholls, J. G., "From Neuron to Brain," Sinauer Associates, Inc., Sunderland, Mass., 1976.
67. Kung, H. T., "Special-Purpose Devices for Signal and Image Processing: An Opportunity in VLSI," *Proceedings of the SPIE*, vol. 241, Real Time Signal Processing III, Society of Photo-Optical Instrumentation Engineers, July 1980.
68. Land, E. H., "The Retinex Theory of Color Vision," *Scientific American*, vol. 237, no. 6, December 1977, pp. 108–128.
69. Lettvin, J. Y., Maturana, H. R., McCulloch, W. S., and Pitts, W. H., "What the Frog's Eye Tells the Frog's Brain," *Proceedings of the Institute of Radio Engineers*, 1959, pp. 1940–1952.
70. Lindsay, T. H., and Norman, D. H., "Human Information Processing: An Introduction to Psychology," Academic, New York, 1967.
71. Lintz, J., "Remote Sensing of Environment," Addison-Wesley, Reading, Mass., 1976.
72. Luckiesh, M., "Visual Illusions," Dover, New York, 1965.
73. Marr, D., "Representing Visual Information," Massachusetts Institute of Technology, Artificial Intelligence Laboratory, Technical Report no. AIM-415, May 1977.
74. Marr, D., "Visual Information Processing: The Structure and Creation of Visual Representations," *Philosophical Transactions of the Royal Society, London*, ser. B, vol. 290, 1980.
75. Marr, D., and Hildreth, E., "Theory of Edge Detection," A.I. Memo no. 518, Massachusetts Institute of Technology, Artificial Intelligence Laboratory, April 1979.
76. Marr, D., and Nishihara, H. K., "Representation and Recognition of the Spatial Organization of Three Dimensional Shapes," Massachusetts Institute of Technology, Artificial Intelligence Laboratory, Technical Report AIM-416, May 1977.
77. Marr, D., and Poggio, T., "A Theory of Human Stereo Vision," Technical Report AIM-451, Massachusetts Institute of Technology, Artificial Intelligence Laboratory, November 1977.
78. Mazokhin-Porshnyakov, G. A., "Insect Vision," Masiromi, R., and Masiromi, L. (trans.), Goldsmith, T. H. (trans. ed.), Plenum, New York, 1969.
79. McCormick, B. H., and Jayaramamurthy, S. N., "Time Series Model for Texture Synthesis," *International Journal of Computer and Information Sciences*, vol. 3, no. 4, December 1974, pp. 329–343.
80. Montanari, U., "Heuristic Guided Search and Chromosome Matching," *Artificial Intelligence*, vol. 1, 1970, pp. 227–245.
81. Morishita, I., and Yajima, A., "Analysis and Simulation of Networks of Mutually Inhibiting Neurons," *Kybernetik*, vol. 11, no. 3, 1972, pp. 154–156.
82. Muller, W., and Herman, W., "Texture Analyses Systems," *Industrial Research*, November 1974.
83. Nagy, G., "Digital Image Processing Activities in Remote Sensing For Earth Resources," *Proceedings of the IEEE*, vol. 60, no. 10, October 1972, pp. 1177–1200.
84. Nakagowa, Y., and Rosenfeld, A., "Some Experiments in Variable Thresholding," *Pattern Recognition*, vol. 11, no. 3, 1979, pp. 191–204.
85. Neuroprostheses Program, Institute for Biomedical Engineering, University of Utah, "Data Processing, LSI Will Help to Bring Sight to the Blind," *Electronics*, Jan. 24, 1974, pp. 81–86.
86. Nudd, G. R., "Image Understanding Architectures," *AFIPS Conference Proceedings*, 1980, pp. 377–390.
87. Ohlander, R., Price, K., and Reddy, D. R., "Picture Segmentation Using a Recursive Region Splitting Method," *Computer Graphics and Image Processing*, vol. 8, no. 3, December 1978, pp. 313–333.

88. Onoe, M., Preston, K., and Rosenfeld, A., "Real-Time/Parallel Computing," "Proceedings of the Japan–United States Seminar on Research Towards Real-Time Parallel Image Analysis and Recognition," Plenum, New York, November 1978.
89. Paul, J. L., Levine, M. D., Fraser, R. G., and Laszlo, C. A., "The Measurement of Total Lung Capacity Based on a Computer Analysis of Anterior and Lateral Radiographic Chest Images," *IEEE Transactions on Biomedical Engineering*, vol. BME-21, no. 6, November 1974.
90. Pavlidis, T., "A Flexible Parallel Thinning Algorithm," *Proceedings of the IEEE Computer Society Conference on Pattern Recognition and Image Processing*, Dallas, Aug. 3–5, 1981, pp. 162–167.
91. Pavlidis, T., "Structural Pattern Recognition," Springer-Verlag, 1977.
92. Pavlidis, T., "The Algorithms for Shape Analysis of Contours and Waveforms," *Proceedings of the 4th International Joint Conference on Pattern Recognition*, Kyoto, Japan, Nov. 7–10, 1978, pp. 73–85.
93. Pirenne, M. H., "Vision and the Eye," 2d ed., Associated Book Publishers, London, 1967.
94. Pratt, W. K., and Faugeras, O. D., "Development and Evaluation of Stochastic-Based Visual Texture Features," *Proceedings of the 4th International Joint Conference on Pattern Recognition*, Kyoto, Japan, Nov. 7–10, 1978, pp. 545–548.
95. Ramer, U., "An Iterative Procedure for the Polygonal Approximation of Plane Closed Curves," *Computer Graphics and Image Processing*, vol. 1, no. 3, November 1972, pp. 244–256.
96. Ratliff, F., "Mach Bands: Quantitative Studies on Neural Networks in the Retina," Holden-Day, San Francisco, 1965.
97. Ratliff, F., "Contour and Contrast," *Scientific American*, vol. 226, no. 6, June 1972, pp. 90–101.
98. Regan, D., Beverley, K., and Cyander, M., "The Visual Perception of Motion in Depth," *Scientific American*, vol. 241, no. 1, July 1979, pp. 136–151.
99. Reichardt, W., and Poggio, T., "Visual Control of Flight in Flies," in Reichardt, W. E., Mountcastle, V. B., and Poggio, T. (eds.), "Recent Theoretical Developments in Neurobiology," MIT Press, Cambridge, Mass., 1979.
100. Richards, W., "Mechanisms For Stereopsis," in Cool, S. J., and Smith, E. L. (eds.), "Frontiers in Visual Science," Springer Series in Optical Science, vol. 8, Springer-Verlag, New York, 1977, pp. 387–395.
101. Robson, J. G., "Receptive Fields: Neural Representation of the Spatial and Intensive Attributes of the Visual Image," in Carterette, E. C., and Friedman, M. P. (eds.), "Handbook of Perception," vol. V, "Seeing," Academic, New York, 1975, pp. 81–116.
102. Rodieck, R. W., "The Vertebrate Retina," Freeman, San Francisco, 1973.
103. Rosenfeld, A., and Kak, A. C., "Digital Picture Processing," Academic, New York, 1976.
104. Rosenfeld, A., Thurston, M., and Lee, Y. H., "Edge and Curve Detection: Further Experiments," *IEEE Transactions on Computers*, vol. C-21, no. 7, July 1972, pp. 677–715.
105. Rosenfeld, A., and Troy, E., "Visual Texture Analysis," *Conference Record for Symposium on Feature Extraction and Selection in Pattern Recognition*, Argonne, Ill., October 1970, pp. 115–124.
106. Rushton, W. A. H., "Visual Pigments and Color Blindness," *Scientific American*, vol. 232, no. 3, 1975, pp. 64–75.
107. Sachs, M. B., Nachmias, J., and Robson, J. G., "Spatial Frequency Channels in Human Vision," *Journal of the Optical Society of America*, vol. 61, no. 9, 1971, pp. 1176–1186.
108. Sakai, T., Nagao, M., and Kanade, T., "Computer Analysis of Photographs of Human Faces," "1st USA-Japan Computer Conference Proceedings," October 1972, IEEE, New York, 1973, pp. 2-7-1 to 2-7-8.
109. Sekuler, R., "Spatial Vision," *Annual Review of Psychology*, vol. 25, 1974, pp. 195–232.
110. Semmlow, J., and Stark, L., "Simulation of a Biomechanical Model of the Human Pupil," *Mathematical Biosciences*, vol. 11, 1971, pp. 109–128.
111. Serra, J., "Mathematical Morphology Applied to Fibre Composite Materials," *Film Science and Technology*, vol. 6, 1973, pp. 141–158.

112. Serra, J., "'One, Two, Three, . . . Infinity,' Quantitative Analysis of Microstructures," in Chernant, J. L. (ed.), "Materials Science, Biology, and Medicine," Riederer-Verlag GmbH, Stuttgart, 1978, pp. 9–24.
113. Shapiro, S. D., "Use of the Hough Transform for Image Data Compression," *Pattern Recognition*, vol. 12, no. 5, 1980, pp. 333–337.
114. Shirai, Y., "Recent Advance in 3-D Scene Analysis," *Proceedings of the 4th International Joint Conference on Pattern Recognition*, Kyoto, Japan, Nov. 7–10, 1978, pp. 86–94.
115. Stark, L., "Pupillary Control System; Its Nonlinear Adaptive and Stochastic Engineering Design Characteristics," *Automatica*, vol. 5, 1969, pp. 655–676.
116. Stevens, C. F., "The Neuron," *Scientific American*, vol. 241, no. 3, September 1979, pp. 54–65.
117. Stevens, K., "Occlusion Clues and Subjective Contours," Memo No. 363, A.I. Laboratory, Memo no. 363, Massachusetts Institute of Technology, Cambridge, Mass., June 1976.
118. Stone, J., Dreher, B., and Leventhal, A., "Hierarchical and Parallel Mechanisms in Organization of Visual Cortex," *Brain Research Reviews*, vol. 1, 1979, pp. 345–394.
119. Szentagothai, J., and Arbib, M. A., "Conceptual Models of Neural Organization," *Neurosciences Research Progress Bulletin*, vol. 12, no. 3, October 1974, pp. 313–510.
120. Tomita, F., Shirai, Y., and Tsuji, S., "Classification of Textures by a Structural Analysis," *Proceedings of the 4th International Joint Conference on Pattern Recognition*, Kyoto, Japan, Nov. 7–10, 1978, p. 556.
121. Toyama, K., Kimura, M., and Tanaka, K., "Organization Of Cat Visual Cortex as Investigated by Cross-Correlation Techniques," *Journal of Neurophysiology*, vol. 46, pp. 202–214.
122. Ullman, J. R., "A Review of Optical Pattern Recognition Techniques," *Opto-Electronics*, vol. 6, no. 4, 1974, pp. 319–332.
123. Waltz, D., "Understanding Line Drawings of Scenes with Shadows," in Winston, P. H. (ed.), "The Psychology of Computer Vision," McGraw-Hill, New York, 1975, pp. 19–91.
124. Wilson, H. R., and Bergen, J. R., "A Four Mechanism Model for Threshold Spatial Vision," *Vision Research*, vol. 19, no. 1, 1979, pp. 19–32.
125. Wyszecki, G., and Stiles, W. S., "Color Science," Wiley, New York, 1967.
126. Yokoyama, R., and Haralick, R. N., "Texture Pattern Image Generation by Regular Markov Chain," *Pattern Recognition*, vol. 11, no. 4, 1979, pp. 225–234.
127. Young, I. T., Walker, J. E., and Bowie, J. E., "An Analysis Technique for Biological Shape," *Information and Control*, vol. 25, 1974, pp. 357–370.
128. Zahn, C. T., "Graph-Theoretical Methods for Detecting and Describing Gestalt Clusters," *IEEE Transactions on Computers*, vol. C-20, no. 1, 1971, pp. 68–86.
129. Zahn, C. T., and Roskies, R. Z., "Fourier Descriptors for Plane Closed Curves," *IEEE Transactions on Computers*, vol. C-21, no. 3, 1972, pp. 269–299.
130. Zeki, S. M., "The Representation of Colours in the Cerebral Cortex," *Nature*, vol. 284, no. 5755, Apr. 3 1980, pp. 412–418.
131. Zucker, S. W., Hummel, R. A., and Rosenfeld, A., "An Application of Relaxation Labeling to Line and Curve Enhancement," *IEEE Transactions on Computers*, vol. C-26, no. 4, April 1977, pp. 394–403.
132. Zucker, S. W., and Terzopoulos, D., "Finding Structure in Co-occurrence Matrices for Texture Analysis," *Computer Graphics and Image Processing*, vol. 12, no. 3, March 1980, pp. 286–308.

INDEX

INDEX

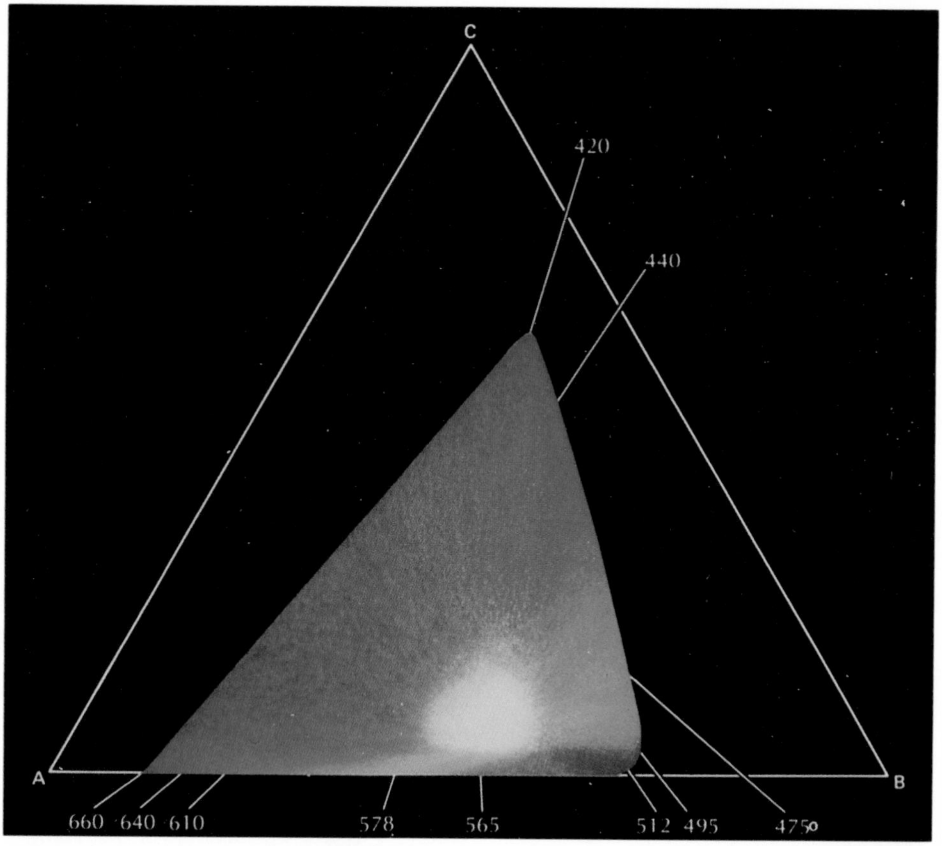

Figure 7.21

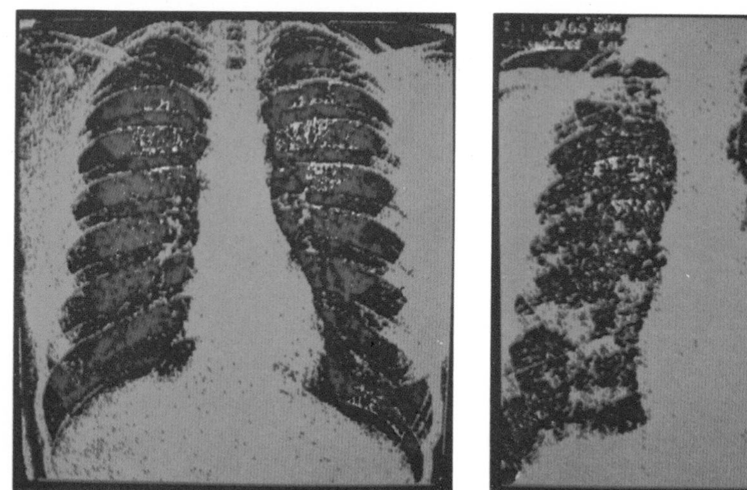

Figure 7.34

(*a*)

(*b*)

Figure 7.37

DEMCO, INC. 38-2971